The Tenmile Country
and
Its Pioneer Families

*A Genealogical History of
the Upper Monongahela Valley*
(With Surname Index)

By
HOWARD L. LECKEY
Historian

The Tenmile Country
And
Its Pioneer Families

Reprinted by:

Janaway Publishing, Inc.
732 Kelsey Ct.
Santa Maria, California 93454

www.janawaygenealogy.com

2021

Reprinted with permission from Closson Press - Index
in cooperation with
Cornerstone Genealogical Society
Greene County Historical Society
Rosemary Sullivan, Bookseller

Cover Photo: Neshaminy Episcopal Church, Bucks County

ISBN: 978-1-59641-461-7

Notice

In many older books, foxing (or discoloration) occurs and, in some instances, print lightens with wear and age. Reprinted books, such as this, often duplicate these flaws, notwithstanding efforts to reduce or eliminate them. The pages of this reprint have been digitally enhanced and, where possible, the flaws eliminated in order to provide clarity of content and a pleasant reading experience.

Made in the United States of America

TABLE OF ILLUSTRATIONS

Scull's Map 8

Original Discharge 19

Swan-Hughes Bible 166-167

The Alfree Log Cabin 182

Swan Family Tree 184

Map 185

Lucas Family Names 186

Kendall Bible Page 189

Henry Vanmeter Signature 192

Lindsey Bible Page 212

O'Neil Bible Page 217

Hughes Bible Page 222

Capt. William Harrod's Company 254

Map, Settlers near Fort Jackson & Fort Ankrom . . . . *opposite* 378

Letter of William Rhodes to Father 381

Samuel P. Flenniken 561

Neshaminy Episcopal Church 562

Henry Darrah's Commission 563

Darrah Sword 563

REPRINTING
DEDICATED TO
HOWARD L. LECKEY
Historian and Author

His work lives on... ... ...

HOWARD LOUIS LECKEY (1892-1951)

HOWARD LOUIS LECKEY, the Historian, and Author of this and other ensuing volumes, was born at Johnstown, Pennsylvania, on March 19, 1892. After graduating from High school, in 1910, at Johnstown, he worked for a time in the chemical laboratory of the Cambria Steel Company. In 1911 the mills shut down and he returned to the drug business, in which he had had some experience, and entered the Pittsburgh College of Pharmacy in the fall of that year. He graduated with fourth highest marks in his class in 1913. After spending the next few years in the drug business in Pittsburgh and Johnstown, he came to Waynesburg. In January, 1917, he entered Waynesburg College as an advanced student. When World War I broke out, these plans were abandoned, and Mr. Leckey became a member of Company K, Tenth Regiment, of the National Guard, which, after being mustered into Federal Service, became the 110th. Regiment of the 28th Division.

On January 22, 1919, he was discharged from the Army. In 1924 he went into business for himself in Waynesburg.

HOWARD L. LECKEY

Always a student, he took up genealogy and history as a hobby. In the years that followed many original works were prepared by him, including many family records.

Waynesburg College honored him by conferring the degree of Bachelor of Science, in 1936, and in 1943, he was elected to the Borough School Board, serving three years as its president.

Mr. Leckey is now a member of the local Health Board.

On February 18, 1919, in a ceremony at the home of the bride, Mr. Leckey was united in marriage with Helen Delilah Patton, daughter of Joseph and Ella (Webb) Patton, with Reverend F. D. Esenwein, now retired Methodist Minister, performing the ceremony. Mrs. Leckey, who was born in Waynesburg, is a graduate of Waynesburg College School of Music, and is a member of one of Greene County's pioneer families.

Mr. Leckey is nationally recognized as an outstanding genealogist and historian, and many substantiating original documents will be reproduced in this and ensuing volumes.

THE WAYNESBURG REPUBLICAN, 1950

Howard L. Leckey died Feb. 25, 1951, at his home, 664 E. Greene St., Waynesburg, Pa.

INTRODUCTION

THIS TITLE has been chosen for our series of books because it permits a wide latitude in the territory it purposes to cover, and it allows for the insertion of the great quantity of genealogical material the author has collected over a long period of years. The material printed will not refer to Tenmile Creek alone, but will include the Valleys of Muddy Creek, Big and Little Whiteley Creeks, Dunkard Creek, and Wheeling Creek. Little attention will be given to the geographical or political aspect of the subject as these items have been written up very completely in previous histories. An effort will be made to show that the Tenmile Country is years older in its settlements than previous historians have brought out. Names will be given, with dates and references taken from authentic sources, so that there can be no chance for controversy. Where family traditions are used in the subject matter, or where no proof is available for reasonable deductions, it will be so stated; since family traditions and deductions are frequently wide of the truth.

The genealogical data that will be printed will be taken from the usual sources, such as court records, family Bibles, printed genealogies, cemetery records, and the like. No effort will be made to carry these genealogies much beyond the first few generations, because many of our records are a book in themselves. Where dates are available in the genealogies, they will be given in good faith, but it is to be remembered that no such records as births, marriages, or deaths, were officially kept in this section of the Country until about seventy years ago. Even census records, now so complete, were taken on an estimate basis as to age, with names of members of the families omitted prior to 1850.

Where military records are given, they will include the service of the individuals, with references acceptable to national patriotic societies. Unfortunately several important records are missing or have been lost. This is especially regrettable for the pioneers that settled in what is now Jefferson Township and parts of Cumberland Township. The militia rolls for these sections have been the subject of a national search, but only scraps of records have been turned up. It is to be remembered that all men between 16 and 60 years were subject to military duty, incapacity and religious scruples alone exempting those called up for tours of duty, and it was not an infrequent occurrence for a boy of twelve or an old man to take the place of others in time of harvest.

Often Bible records and cemetery records have been found that conflict with each other, and in this case we have used the one first entered in our records, though Bible records have been favored where they have been entered in the period in question and not by later family historians. Tombstone records on the soft native sandstone are often hard to decipher, and at times practically illegible, and may be the source of some errors in this work. In many cases instances of longevity, where persons are credited with living years over the century mark, have been doubted, and efforts made to verify by other means. In almost every case determined the family tradition of old age proved erroneous.

Frequent reference is made in these pages to the earlier histories of Evans, Bates, Crumrine, Waychoff, Haddon, Veach, and other

INTRODUCTION

source material. These excellent histories, many of which were written when some of the pioneers' children still lived in the neighborhood, are an invaluable source of data. They were, however, histories first, and the genealogy they contain was secondary with the writers, and therefore, not always too accurate. We have tried to correct these wherever accurate material was available, and have been successful to a limited degree. At times, too, they have been off a few years in the placing of events in these valleys, because they depended on traditions that seemed authentic. But court records have uncovered some of these errors, setting new dates and furnishing different given names.

There is still much room for a more comprehensive history of this section. The Draper Manuscripts at Madison, Wisconsin, which deal a lot on these pioneers and events on the Tenmile, have barely been touched. An exhaustive search of pension records at the National Archives would also uncover many additional facts. Old ledgers and letters—forgotten in some obscure attic—could add features and facts not yet published.

In any work, such as this, much correspondence is involved. Thousands of letters have been written and received. Data has been turned up in most unexpected places. Contacts have been made that established life friendships. It has been pleasant work. It would be impossible to credit each and every person that helped make these records possible. The subject is one of unusual interest, as witness a fine, handwritten letter from a lady of 87 years, in which she put down in long hand, enough material to cover 35 typewritten sheets, eight generations of her family. I hope this lady, Mrs. Austa Heaton Daniels of Princeton, Illinois, may still be living to read some of her fine record of the Rees Heaton family. We are more than grateful to Mrs. Otis Swainson, now of Piedmont, California, and Mrs. John B. Mason, now of Oberlin, Ohio, who, when living in Washington, D. C., found time to look up so many pension and census records for these pages. We look forward to reading their own books on the Harrod family, who were original Tenmile settlers. Note is also taken of the many local people who were so kind as to share their own fine records. To list them all would take a book. Marie Perrine Lemley, a professional genealogist, of Los Angeles, has been of inestimable aid.

Someone has asked the reason for genealogy. This is a young nation, and for many years it seemed ashamed that it had ancestors. Outside of New England and among the Friends Families, few public records were kept. In the older countries of Europe one can get authentic data from the Church books or City registers, and our own experience has shown these records well kept as far back as the Fourteenth Century. Our answer is that genealogy is the history of people, and people make history. Lessons of inheritance, environment, psychology, etc., are to be learned from this study. Anything that teaches us something is worth while, and more so if it is fascinating to the individual. Most people find this study fascinating.

In every genealogy that has been written, there are errors, and this one will be no exception. The work was undertaken to correct a number of errors, and it is our hope we have corrected more than we have made. The writer will appreciate it if attention is called to any such errors and will try to correct them if possible. He also seeks any additional records of families not included in these volumes, where the families are identified with the Tenmile Country Pioneers.

HOWARD L. LECKEY

THE TENMILE COUNTRY

TENMILE CREEK is not one of the world's large streams, nor do its waters drain an imposing area of land as it meanders through Greene and Washington Counties in Southwestern Pennsylvania. Here and there it serves as a boundary line between the two counties, or between townships, but other than that it is insignificant geographically. Along its course one can still catch glimpses of what must at one time have been a beautiful stream, although coal developments and cinder dumps are now crowding the banks in many places. Living persons recall when it was still untouched by industrial enterprises other than the picturesque mill sites, and was as good as any for bass and other game fishing. Even today there are stretches where one can find exciting sport along the main stream or its tributaries.

From the beginning of its inhabited history the waters were sufficient to turn the many grist mills that grew up along its banks, but it is doubtful if any boat larger than a skiff or canoe ever navigate its waters any farther than a few miles from its mouth, and then only during high waters. To one who has seen the large wheatfields of the West, the land which it drains would not have much appeal as farming country, and while its hillsides were once covered by extensive stands of hard woods, its forests today are far from being commercially attractive. For many years now its value has been in the mineral resources of coal, gas, and oil that lie beneath its surface, prior to which the fecundity of its people supplied the hardy sons and daughters of the Westward migration.

Several theories have been advanced as to the origin of its name, but the one most likely and generally accepted is that it was so named because it was just ten miles from old Fort Redstone to the mouth of the stream at the present town of Millsboro. It is probable that the Indians had a name for it, because a map published by W. Scull, in 1770, has it fairly accurately placed and labeled "Cusuthas Creek," and it is regrettable that the Indian name was not retained, for the stream was a maker of history, though its commonplace name served to detract from its importance. It was one of the gateways to the West.

Just when Tenmile Creek was first seen by the White men may be lost in the maze of foreign archives, but there can be little doubt that the French Voyageurs camped along its banks long before the English or Colonial authorities took notice. Trappers and traders came here before claims were made by any Nation, probably before 1700. Well defined trails led across the Tenmile watershed joining the tidewater with the Ohio in the shortest way. They were old trails when Gist made his Western survey for the Ohio Company, and were followed to some extent by the surveyors who laid out the present roads. As early as 1728, the French began picking up lone trappers and conveying them to France by way of Canada. Even as early as 1714, the English forced the licensing of the traders at Chester County, Pennsylvania, in order to keep a rein on their activities, and to make them more responsible when conducting negotiations with the Indian tribes of the interior.

Indian speeches at treaty conventions give evidence that the country of the Tenmile was neutral territory when the White men began to visit it in any numbers, but the various burials disclosed by local archeologists, indicate that it was at one time well populated by the Indians. Remains of mounds of earth also suggest that it was at one time inhabited by those mysterious people—the mound builders. When the White men came they found it a neutral hunting ground, visited in season by many tribes who came to hunt and fish; a fact proved by the many arrow heads, tools, etc., that are still being found near and at the favorite camping sites. Deer skins were the main pelts taken in this section. The Greene County Museum contains as fine a collection of Indian artifacts as any museum of its size in the Country, and the major portion of its display has been gathered locally. There seems little doubt that a Trading Post was set up on the Tenmile, which became a favorite meeting place of the Indians and traders, for early deeds mention places named for members of Lowrey's Traders, and several families settled at the site of Fort Jackson, who were definitely connected with this early business venture. Not until the conflicting interests of the French and British disturbed the peace did the Indians resent the presence of the White men; in fact he pleaded for them to remain, when the authorities demanded they leave. Once the peace had been disturbed, history records many horrible massacres. Revolting as these were, the Indians were not always to blame. They exacted just punishment for cruel wrongs—and one wonders there were not more.

The Missionaries were here, too. French Jesuits always accompanied French attempts at colonization. And while no definite evidence exists that the French tried to locate at the Tenmile, they are known to have crossed trails here. There is, however, definite reference to the Moravians. The Euphrata Chronicles state that the Eckerlein Brothers were on Dunkard Creek in 1745, and, while they did not remain, they left their mark in the name of the Creek, since the Moravians were called Dunkards. Ministers of other denominations have also left journals that tell of their visits to the Tenmile Country.

The Indian Traders who covered this section have been typed, and all agree that they were a profligate lot. Usually raised on the frontier, they had picked up an Indian dialect or two, with smatterings of others, sufficient to carry on trade. Their stock of goods consisted in the main of rum, guns, powder and lead; knives, axes, awls, strouds, linen and other cloth; ribbons and stockings, which they carried on pack horses—and in this part of the country—exchanged for deer skins. The profits included a fair margin on the cost, plus a percentage for packing the goods over the mountains, usually from Philadelphia or Baltimore. Each trader seems to have had his own favorite stopping places and routes of travel. Frequently the stopping place was nothing more than a large fallen tree that gave some promise of shelter from the weather, or a sylvan spring that supplied water for his pack animals. These stopping places were respected by other traders, and names were given to them, associating the places with the trader. Rum was used freely to strike an advantageous bargain or violate a comely Indian Maiden, when peaceful persuasion failed. There were very few of these traders who did not have one or more Indian Women, whom they sometimes gave the status of wife, especially if she were a daughter of a Chief or influential tribesman. Indian morals were such that there seems to have been no resentment of this condition, and history records few instances of violence caused by it. Foreign travelers of that time, have reported that they frequently met unaccompanied Indian Women on the trails, with whom they camped at night, sharing the same blankets, for the sake of warmth, and other conveniences, and often traveled with them for days at a time. Hanna's "Wilderness Trail," and the "Journal of Nicholas Cresswell," give some interesting accounts of traders in general, and customs prevailing, while Kenneth Bailey's "Michael Cresap," and Volwiler's "George Croghan," tell of the two most prominent of the early Indian Traders, and Parkman's "Pontiac," has become a classic through his description of the period.

Of these Indian Traders, Croghan seems to have been primarily interested in land about the present site of Pittsburgh, although he had other posts scattered all through the Western country. Thomas Cresap and his son, Michael, seem to have been mainly interested in land about Redstone, although there may yet be found evidence to show that they knew the Tenmile Country and had a hand in its settlement. But it is most likely that less known traders were the first to set up trading posts on Tenmile.

One of the first Indian Traders, whose family is definitely connected with the section, is Isaac Mirandy, who was one of the Chester County, Pennsylvania, group, and who was licensed by the Colonial authorities in 1716. His son, George Mirandy, was reported on the Allegheny as early as 1736, when he was a member of the Lancaster County, Pennsylvania Group. A "James Mirandy" was the first patentee of land adjoining Fort Jackson, and, with his brother, Samuel Mirandy, were reported to Draper (Mss. 3 S. 256) by Mrs. Phoebe Mirandy, as being boys at Fort Jackson at the outbreak of the Revolution. There can be little doubt that Isaac, George, Jr., and N......... Mirandy, living here in 1789, (Rhodes Papers) were others of the same family, possibly sons of George Mirandy. Samuel, George, Jr., and James Mirandy left here to settle in Bracken County, Kentucky, where, on May 20, 1833, Samuel applied for a pension, stating in his application that most of his service was performed at Fort Jackson under Captain David Owens and Captain John Whetsel. James Mirandy died in Bracken County, Kentucky, and a George Mirandy married Sarah Wood on March 29, 1793, in Mason County, which adjoins Bracken County. A Polly Mirandy married in the same county, on May 5, 1803, David Owens, formerly of the Tenmile, a grandson of the Indian Trader. James Mirandy served in Captain James Archer's Company of Washington County, Pennsylvania, Militia, but there is no record of a pension granted him.

As mentioned in a previous article published by The Republican, John Owens, the Indian Trader, at Fort Pitt, and a militiaman under Boquet, was definitely connected with the Tenmile Country, for on December 12, 1757, he sold a tract of land "Situated on the Monongahela, between Enoch's Run (afterward John Swan's Run or Pumpkin Run) and near the mouth of Muddy Creek," to Abraham Teagarden of Frederick County, Maryland, with William Teagarden and John Owens, Jr., witnessing the deed. (See Washington County Deed Book—1-A—214.) At least two and possibly three sons of John Owens settled close to the site of Fort Jackson and are mentioned in early land transactions.

James and Henry Brenton (or Brinton), Indian Traders, also made improvements here prior to the erection of Fort Jackson, as shown by a deed from George Teagarden to Philomen (Felix) Askins, on March 16, 1770, the tract described as being "James Brenton's improvement on Tenmile Creek." (Washington County Deed Book—1-C—163.) This tract, later assigned to George Church, on October 26, 1772, seems to have taken in the land about a mile east of Fort Jackson, the site of the present "Colonial Place," which Church sold to the Rineharts, although the lines are indefinite at that date. James and Henry Brenton were named in the 1772 tax lists for Springhill

Township, Bedford County, Pennsylvania, which at that time included all of the Tenmile Country. They later are found in Washington County.

In any study of the Indian Traders one frequently comes across the name of John Kennedy. There can be little doubt that he is the same "John Kennedy" mentioned as a land jobber from the Conochacheague in the L. K. Evans Papers. With such frequent mention of his name in various histories it is hard to identify him as one person or more than one by the same name, yet he may well be the John Kennedy mentioned in all these records. He was one of Lowrey's Traders and later in business for himself, and is said to have been from Maytown, Lancaster County, Pennsylvania. (Hanna's "Wilderness Trail," pp. 179.) The same reference says he was taken prisoner at Gist's, in what is now Fayette County, in 1754. The French took him to Canada from whence he escaped and later raised and commanded a company of Rangers in the French and Indian War. A history of Lancaster County states he was taken prisoner July 29, 1754, after being shot in the leg, was sent to Fort Pitt and later to Canada. The "Boquet Papers" show a "John Kennedy" was acting as interpreter for the expedition at Fort Pitt on February 17, 1759. A man of the same name warranted a tract of land on Muddy Creek on January 17, 1778. Wither's "Border Warfare," claims a man of this name was able to escape at Harrodsburg, Kentucky, at the time of the killing of William Hudson. None of these writers give any hint as to the family of John Kennedy, but there is a circumstance which merits further investigation. The fact that a "John Kennedy" was taken prisoner at Gist's place, near Mount Braddock, Fayette County, Pennsylvania, in 1754, at which plantation Gist had settled members of his family some time before that date, and the fact that one "John Kennedy" married Sarah Gist, sister of Christopher Gist, suggests a kinship hitherto undisclosed. It would also be interesting to discover what relationship (if any) there might be with David Kennedy, a warrantee of land on Muddy Creek, whose widow, Rachel (Frazier) Kennedy, settled his estate in Greene County in 1797, and whose daughter, Katy, married David Bell, patentee of the Kennedy tract called "Sugar Camp." There must also be connection with Alice Kennedy, wife of Captain William Crawford, and Mary Kennedy, wife of John Armstrong.

It is reported that John Kennedy, the Indian Trader, died in Lancaster County, while on a journey to Philadelphia.

Some time before 1772, a man named Hendricks made an improvement on what is now Smith Creek, not far from the present town of Waynesburg, for the land which Ralph Smith bought for his father, Thomas Smith, of Baltimore, on December 10, 1772, is described as being "a tract of land joining Hendrick's place." Since most of the land about Waynesburg was settled by families from the head of Chesapeake Bay in Maryland, it is most likely that descendants of the early Maryland Trader, James Hendricks, were in the Tenmile Country, and had picked out a choice location for settlement. From Hanna we learn that James and John Hendricks, with Francis Worley, were traders at Conestoga in 1718, and that James Hendricks was 73 years of age in 1740. ("Wilderness Trails" (pp. 163-168). The knowledge of the age of this "James Hendricks" excludes him from this claim, but we find the name of John Hendricks in the Springhill Township, Bedford County, tax list for 1772. He could have been the man who made the improvement mentioned. (Greene County, Pennsylvania, Deed Book 1, pp. 25). Hendricks either sold out, of which there is no record, or he abandoned his claim, for we find no further mention of him, or any descendants living on Tenmile. The Worleys did, however, settle over the ridge from the tract, when Brice Worley became a poineer in the Blacksville Section.

In this same record of sale of land next Hendricks, the land is described as being on the south side of Williams' Run, indicating a man named Williams had also taken land here. We are inclined to identify him as William Williams, who is reported in the annals of Augusta County, Virginia, as having bought land on Tenmile on January 8, 1774, from John Jones, who had purchased it first from John Simpson, who made an improvement on what is now Bates Fork, before 1772. William Williams then sold it to Jacob Rees on July 31, 1775. Records show that Hannah, the wife of Jacob Rees, had accompanied him into the section, in 1773, as did Isaac Horner. There is no record to show that William Williams was one of the traders, but it is probable that he belonged to the Baltimore family of that name, and may have been related to Colonel John Minor, whose entry into the Tenmile is set at 1765, and whose first two wives were named Williams.

There were several "Daniel Stewarts" who settled in Greene County at an early date. It is most likely that all, or one of them, was a descendant of the "Daniel Stewart," who had a Chester County, Pennsylvania, trader's license, in 1742.

That these traders were on the Tenmile earlier than most historians have suspected, is proved by the deeds and facts concerning them. The exact dates must, however, be left to future discoveries, but it may be safely assumed that they were here shortly after 1750.

"Trans-Allegheny Pioneers" states that a Fort was raised on Tenmile Creek (at present Waynesburg) and at Prickett's Creek (five miles north of present Fairmont) in 1759. This fort must have been raised to protect these traders, whose post must have been near or at the place where Fort Jackson was later built. Trading Posts were usually established at convenient spots, on land acquired directly from the Indians, and rights to lands about the posts were respected by Whites and Indians alike, even though the authorities frowned on such practices. It is significant also that a trading post was still being kept on the site as late as 1792-93, when William Rhodes, a former sea captain, operated it within the confines of Fort Jackson. His old accounts are still in existence and are the property of the author. Fortunately, the Library of Congress has seen fit to photostat these accounts, and thereby preserve them for future historians.

The earliest post mentioned in the section is that of Christopher Gist on Redstone Creek, it having been established in 1752. After the defeat of the English, under Braddock, in 1755, Indian attacks on the posts became more frequent, culminating in the destruction of all of them during Pontiac's War. The loss of goods was enormous for the times, and the traders sought and received recompense in the treaty that followed. The Etting Collection, at the Pennsylvania Historical Society's Library, in Philadelphia, lists the names of the Traders who suffered and the amounts they received as damages. As the Indians had little in the way of Chattels, and depended on furs to pay for the things the White men had to offer, it was but natural that they were willing to turn over land in payment of these claims. It mattered little to them, since they did not have the same ideas of ownership of land as did the White men. Land to them was there for anyone to use for hunting, fishing and the like. Different tribes respected each others' rights to use it for such, more as a conservation measure than rights of ownership. Thus it was often necessary for the Colonial Authorities to buy the same land from several groups. So it was with little regret that they turned over land in what is now Greene County to the authorities at the Treaty of Fort Stanwix, and the Traders accepted it from the Colonies. Henceforth the Traders turned to land speculation, wherein we meet the settlers.

In passing, it is right that we know something of the families of the Traders, so far as the records disclose.

David Owens, son of John Owens, the Indian Trader, was a notorious character, as can be seen from the following quotations from reliable sources. We read in Hanna's "Wilderness Trail," (pp. 386): "Another of Boquet's guides and interpreters on the expedition, was a notorious villain, named 'David Owens,' son of 'John Owens,' a former Indian Trader. He appeared in Philadelphia the latter part of April, 1764, and Governor Penn gave him a pass to Lancaster and Carlisle, with a letter to Boquet. In reply to a letter from Sir William Johnson, in regard to Owens' character, the Baronet wrote to Governor Penn, June 16, 1764, 'David Owens was a corporal in Captain McClean's Company and lay once in garrison at my house. He deserted several times, as I am informed, and went to live among the Delawares and Shawnees, with whose language he was acquainted, his father having been a trader among them. The circumstances relating to his leaving the Indians have been told me by several Indians; that he went hunting with his Indian wife and several other relatives, most of whom, with his wife, he killed and scalped, while they were asleep. As he was always much attached to the Indians, I fancy he began to fear he was unsafe among them, and killed them, rather to make peace with the English, rather than from any dislike to them or their principles'." The other quotation is from "Narrative of Robert Robinson," published at Carlisle, in 1811, and says, "At this time Boquet went down the Ohio about 75 miles below Fort Pitt, and sent one David Owen, who had been married to an Indian Woman, and had by her three children, when taking a thought that he would advance himself, killed and scalped his wife and children and brought their scalps to Philadelphia. He received no reward, only he was made ambassador between Boquet and the Indians. When Owens was sent to let the Indians know they might have peace, they made a prisoner of him for the murder he had committed, two of his wife's brothers being there. Owens gave them to know, if they killed him, they never would have peace. The Indians held him for three days, then by decision of Council, they let him go, and came up themselves and agreed to give up the prisoners. So ended Boquet's campaign."

In spite of these unfavorable reports about David Owens, there are many records of his activites that seem to refute his general character. He is said to have made another marriage with a sister of Rev. David Jones, the chaplain of the Revolution. David Owens made an improvement on Grave Creek in 1770, and Rev. David Jones followed, to make one there in 1772. George Rogers Clark made the surveys for them and was with them in 1772 when they made a trip into the Indian Country. (Chalkley's "Augusta County"). When the Indians forced them out that winter, they returned to Tenmile, most likely to Owens' cabin there. David Owens lived on a tract of land, about one mile East of Fort Jackson, located on Owens' Run, (now

Lippencott's Run) a short distance from its mouth, opposite the Fair Grounds, rather than the site West of the Fort as reported by Evans. Owens' military experience was wide and varied, for in addition to his services with Boquet, he served as head of a party under Major Angus McDonald in the attack on the Shawnee Towns in Lord Dunmore's War. (Thwaite's "Dunmore's War") His experience and knowledge of the Indians well fitted him to become the first captain of the Frontier Rangers at Fort Jackson, a position he held until 1777. So great was his popularity among his men that when relieved of his command, a group of them petitioned Captain William Harrod, that they be permitted to serve under Owens in a proposed expedition into the Indian Country, and gave Barnet O'Neil as a reference to Owens' character and ability. (Draper Mss., 4NN30-31). A few years later on March 1, 1780, David Owens sold his tract to Captain James Hook, and removed to Kentucky. One of the witnesses to the deal was William English, who, with John Owens, brother of David, was killed by the Indians in the Spring of 1781.

In the Spring of 1781, John Owens, Jr., son of the Indian Trader, was living on his tract of land, about a mile West of the present Court House at Waynesburg. With his neighbors, William Brown, William English, another man not named, and some of their sons, John Owens, Jr., was out making maple sugar, as was the custom in those days, it being the only sweetening available to the pioneers. Having finished their work, they were on their way home when they were fired upon by some Indians. English, Brown, the unidentified man, and John Owens were killed in the first volley, but Vincent Brown and Mathew Brown escaped to reach home and spread the alarm.

John Owens was possessed of several pieces of land when he was killed, and one of these pieces must have been in Kentucky, where his will was filed (in Bracken County), and to which place some of his children soon after removed. His will, which was administered by his wife and a neighbor, Sebastian Shroffe, is on file in Washington, County, Pennsylvania, Will Book No. 1, pp. 51, and was probated April 6, 1781. In it he names his sons, David and John, but Orphans' Court records reveal that guardians were appointed for minor children whose names are listed as: David Owens, John Owens, Jr., Vincent Owens, George Owens, Mary Owens and James Owens. A daughter, Sarah, had married Richard Gragston, and shared in the estate. It was John Owens' son, David Owens, who served in James Archer's Company of Washington County Militia. Shortly after 1785, the family went to Kentucky and settled in Bracken County.

George Owens, half-brother of David and John Owens, also lived near Fort Jackson. He may have preceded Captain David Owens as captain of the Frontier Rangers at that place, for in 1776, he is reported to have been in charge of the detachment which killed two Indians, who had chased Cobus Linsecum into the Fort. He left here shortly afterward, and William H. English reports that he gave valiant service in the defense of Fort Jefferson, in Kentucky, in 1780.

Two of his sons, George and Thomas, later settled in Scott County, Indiana.

The elder George Owens was captured by the Indians some time after he went to Kentucky, and killed by them while in captivity, and English states the sons became bitter Indian haters, requiring restraining influence, even in the presence of friendly Indians.

A grandson of Captain George Owens, named Thomas Owens, settled in Texas.

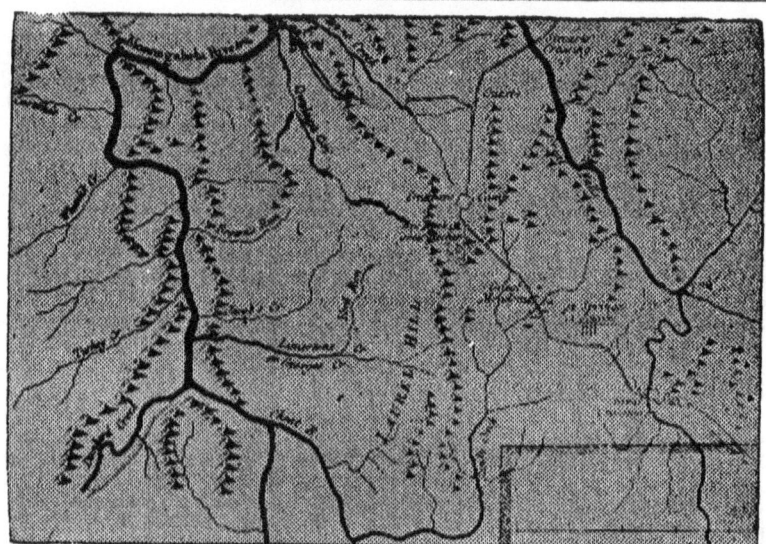

REPRODUCTION of a portion of William Scull's Map, printed in 1770, showing the Tenmile Country.

WESTWARD MIGRATION

In order to understand the reason for the settlement of the Tenmile Country it will be well to examine the forces that were in motion at that time. These forces had been the activating factor for several generations earlier and continued so until the entire land area of the United States was occupied. Since the Eastern Seaboard of the continent had been peopled by groups of persons seeking more opportunity and freedom, land and more land was the crying demand of the large families of the period. This led to successive waves of Westward migrations, all well defined.

Penn's Colony at Philadelphia, was perhaps the fastest growing of all the Colonies, due to the leniency of its charter and the character of its proprietors. Made up mostly of common folk from all parts of Western Europe, these immigrants knew the virtue of work. With their new freedom permitting them to retain the results of their industry, the way to independence was cleared for them if they could obtain land. From the settlement on the Delaware, in 1682, they spread across the river into New Jersey, into that part controlled by the Penns. Then reversing their direction, they came back to new lands purchased by the Penns from the Indians. Here they were joined by a flood of immigrants coming from the Palatinate and Rhine Valley. In 1730, Jost Hite, Thomas Shepherd, John and Isaac Vanmeter, and a number of others, who had moved to New Jersey, and from thence to the new Germantown section, explored the Shenandoah Valley of Virginia, which was still an unbroken wilderness. They received large grants of land from the Colonial Governor of Virginia, on the condition that they bring in a specified number of inhabitants to settle the country.

It is immaterial that they failed to meet the specifications, sufficient it is to know that this valley soon became filled. In fact, the influx of settlers so worried the authorities in Maryland that they sent emissaries to Europe to get inhabitants for the hinterlands of their Colony, and made the terms for land the equivalent of one cent per acre. But the Westward march had begun, and a generation later, we see it emerging in what is now Greene County, Pennsylvania, but considered at that time a part of Augusta County, Virginia.

Who were these prime movers of the migration? A glance at the tax lists for Monmouth County, New Jersey, for the year of 1714, discloses, among others, these names: Thomas Shepherd, John Vanmeter, John and Thomas Throckmorton, Richard Morris, Robert Barclay, John and William Montgomery, Samuel Leonard, William Estill, Henry and Rachel Bell, Remembrance Lippencott, David Harrod, Daniel Ketchum, John Morford, James Williamson, Mr. Liming, and others. A "John Harrod" was a sergeant of Militia there in 1715. Even today in this Greene County, Pennsylvania, the names are familiar. From other parts of New Jersey came the Waychoffs, Claytons, Hills, Van Vorhees, Pettits, Smiths, Gordons, Scotts, and other families, who joined the trek into the Shenandoah. At Germantown they were joined by William Hoge and a number of Welsh and Scottish families. The three original counties in Pennsylvania furnished many more Upper Shenandoah settlers and the names are later found among the Greene County pioneers. Augmenting this migration from the Eastern Colonies was a steady influx of European families by way of Baltimore, estimated by some authorities to be as many as ten thousand a year, mostly natives of the Rhine Valley. Still another group, composed of Scotch Irish and some Germans, filtered through Lancaster County, Pennsylvania, crossed the Susquehanna at Harris's Ferry, and then followed the Conochacheague into Maryland and the Shenandoah Valley.

As the Valley filled up and families increased, it was but natural that the sons of these settlers cast their eyes still Westward for new land and homes. Again the Hites, Vanmeters, Hogues, and Shepherds were ready to lead the way. The Traders saw to it that these people were informed of the favorable opportunities over the mountains, and in addition, informed the restless settlers of the more settled sections at the mouth of the Chesapeake Bay, the Valley of the Conochacheague, the Cumberland Valley in Central Pennsylvania, the crowded environs of Philadelphia and Baltimore, even those as far away as New England and the Carolinas. The Ohio Company, formed in 1748, was the first means by which organized settlement was attempted by the colony of Virginia. The Traders Company, Vandalia Company, Grand Ohio Company, and others, sought grants from the Crown, with the purpose of supplying the demand for land, and the colonies themselves assumed a dangerous rivalry to claim land from which they might obtain revenue. Even the two great nations, France and England, who had been watching the moves of each other for many years, now came out into the open with their claims, and war was the result.

Real settlement was delayed by Braddock's defeat, in 1755, and the French and Indian War, that followed; but even before and during these periods, there were a few permanent settlers.

The surveys made by the Ohio Company had started a land boom, and the many Colonials in Braddock's forces, who got a chance to view the country, advertised it, so that when peace was restored, a veritable stampede began. Land was sold, sight-unseen, to any and all who wanted it. Virginia's price was one shilling for ten acres, but the terms were so wide that almost anyone who wished land could obtain all he wished to improve. Pennsylvania asked a higher price and limited the number of acres to four hundred. This explains the reason why so many people were anxious to have Virginia claims, validated in the border controversy that followed, and were not settled until 1784. Tempers over this question, at one time, reached a height that caused armed forces, led by Henry Vanmeter and Jesse Pigman, camped on the North bank of Dunkard Creek, to dare the surveyors to run the line. Even in 1784, these same men were joined by others in refusing to turn in their land to Washington County, Pennsylvania, for tax purposes.

Historians have left the impression that this land could have been acquired by simply raising a field of corn or blazing a few trees to mark land boundaries. But it was not as simple as that. Most of those who came here brought deeds describing their lands, giving boundaries, and often naming the neighbors. It is true that often a claimant came and found another person squatting on the land he had bought. Rather than a fight or litigation, he would trade a rifle or great coat to the squatter, and take full possession.

But conveyances and sales were as much a matter of record in those days as they are today, and as important to ownership. Good deeds came only from the Colonial Authorities.

With this background to show why and how the settlement of the Tenmile Country came about, let us examine the conditions prevalent at the time of settlement, which came about the year of 1765. It is ever pointed out that the hardships endured by these pioneers were almost beyond comparison. It is pointed out that these people faced great dangers from ferocious beasts and more terrible Redmen. But there were no beasts in those days that do not exist some place in the United States today, and authorities agree that none of these, except perhaps the grizzly, will attack a man. And the Indians were at peace with the White Men from the close of Pontiac's War, in 1763, until the War of the Revolution. Even during the Revolution, there were probably no more persons killed by the Redmen in one year than are killed today by automobiles. Even these killings were often the result of individual grievances, and a few of them probably justified. The Quakers, who lived here—and there were quite a number—who practiced a life of non-violence, seem never to have been disturbed even in the worst years.

We must remember there was a large number of Tories here during the Revolution, and that they were known to have plotted violence against the leaders of the Patriots. Even the tragic Corbly massacre may have been instigated by enemies of Rev. John Corbly, since he was one of the most active in the suppression of the Tories.

Returning from the O'Felty massacre, the Indians stopped at the open door of the Edward Burson cabin, within sight of where the killing took place. The family was of the Quaker faith, and the protective door was only a blanket. Mrs. Burson had a pot of beans on the fire when the Indians appeared. They asked for something to eat, which, being given them, they departed without molesting the family.

What other hardships was the lot of these pioneers? They had to work long hours in the fields, after spending many longer ones clearing fields to plant. But they had left no worse a condition in the East. They had to live in log cabins with limited space and no conveniences, but they did not leave much better homes where they came from. They lacked for roads to travel, for a short time, but a land grant to John Willison, in 1792, shows a road running from Fort Jackson to Washington, Pennsylvania, at that date. Certainly not many of those who came here had carriages to ride in over the mountains, and, if they did, it is not likely the roads and streets were much better than the open country through which these people traveled on horse-back. The prisoners who were taken East after the Whiskey Rebellion were made to stand knee-deep in the mud on the Main Street of Carlisle. A picture of the loneliness of these pioneers has been the theme of the historian, but within five years after the first settlers came to the Tenmile, there were as many farms occupied in this section as there are today. One observer reports that in 1774 he watched a thousand families a day crossing the Monongahela River at Parkinson's Ferry in a single day, to escape the threats caused by Lord Dunsmore's War. And could a person be very lonely with a family of ten to fourteen children about him? On the other hand there were luxuries available even in those backwoods. I have an old ledger showing silk handkerchiefs, sugar plums, bombazine dresses, tea, coffee, sugar, silver buckles, and other items of the like, were for sale at the Mouth of Muddy Creek. One account even shows that a mattress was carried over the mountains from Philadelphia to John Minor. Having that kind of bed, it is no wonder he got the name of Father of the County.

It is perhaps true there were more poor people than there were wealthy ones, but that condition has always existed, and the degree of difference was probably no greater then than it is today. I have examined many wills of parents of those who left the East to settle here, and it is evident that much money came over the mountains in the settlements of estates. Money was also borrowed in the East by men living here, and men here loaned money in the East. One such case is found in the estate of John Douglass, who loaned four hundred pounds to General Daniel Morgan of Winchester, Virginia, and which was collected by his administrator. Full contact with the older settlements was kept up and there was a lot more travel than is generally supposed to have taken place. Within twenty years after the first permanent settlement was made, it was possible to travel from Winchester by carriage, as shown by a letter written by Rachel Colver, daughter of Isaac Heaton. She stated that her father left his home at Berkeley, on November 19, 1785, and arrived at their new home near Jefferson, on December 5, the same year, bringing his entire family and his slaves with him. A few years ago a part of the carriage that brought the Heatons to their new home, was owned by a man on Muddy Creek.

The first settlers came here by three main routes, the most prominent of which was approximately the present Route 40 or National Pike, which at that time went through Winchester. Most Eastern sections were joined to it by feeder roads, such as that from Carlisle to Winchester, and from Winchester to Cumberland, by way of Romney and Fort Ashby. Another route that was favored was much the same as that from the Shenandoah Valley to the head of the Cheat River, and from there to the Monongahela. The third main route approximated the present Lincoln Highway, but turned off at Ligonier, and came to the Monongahela by way of Jacob's Creek. In some known cases, soldiers quartered at Fort Pitt, made their way down the Monongahela to Fort at Redstone, and thence into the Tenmile Country. The journey of these pioneers was made by horseback or by oxen, or by both, and cattle were driven ahead by youths or slaves. Others walked, packing as much on their backs as they could carry. Usually they came in groups bound together by some mutual connections. Family groups, related or inter-married, groups held together by religious affiliation, or nationality, or neighborhood ties, would come together and usually settle close to each other. If the genealogist remembers this, his work is much easier, since there are excellent Quaker records throughout the East, and the Welsh Baptists also left fine records of their Chester County Churches.

Land being so cheap, it had little value for trading purposes. We note that Isaac Stewart, ancestor of the President of Waynesburg College, is reported to have sold land that he tomahawked for a rifle, while George Lemley, formerly a soldier at Fort Pitt, gave his army coat for a tract of land. A rifle had a value of about five pounds, with the exchange value at that time of about three dollars to the pound. Debts were not made thoughtlessly, unless there was some assurance that they could be met when the time came to pay, for the debtor, who could not meet his obligation when it became due, went to jail. The lot of the creditor was not always rosy, since he had to pay the board bill for the debtor.

Farms of the period were known as plantations, and, as in the South, most items needed for the family, were made or raised on the place. Thomas Mooney is said to have brought a loom all the way from Ireland to set up for his own use and for hire. Spinning and other tasks were done at home, but this does not mean that other industries did not develop nor that manufacturing was not done for profit. Tanneries were set up in several communities, flour and saw mills used all the available waterpower furnished by Tenmile and other creeks. One flour mill, at Carmichaels, operated by John Antill, would ship as many as a hundred and twenty barrels of flour to New Orleans each season. The account of one such expedition, with the mention of a previous one, prior to 1793, shows that even after building the flat boat to convey the flour, buying barrels from local cooperages, paying inspection fees and dues, as well as the employment of five or six men, the interested parties made more than eight hundred dollars on the venture.

Rifles and guns were manufactured across the river from the present town of Crucible, and were sold for five pounds each. Woolen mills were set up at Clarksville, and some iron was smelted there. Felt hats were made at Waynesburg before 1800. And cooperages were present in large numbers to supply the various still houses, numbering as high as seventy at one time, with barrels for their products. Salt, paper, powder, and indigo for dying cloth, were the principal items brought in from the outside. Besides farming for a living, each man had some trade by which he could earn a few pounds or dollars needed to supply his few wants at the trading post. There was some market for the surplus products he raised. During the Revolution, parties were sent here from Fort Pitt to buy stores for the troops quartered at that place, and after the war a Captain Craig made frequent trips here for the army.

Boat builders on several streams entering the Monongahela included John Minor at Whiteley, John Armstrong at Muddy Creek, another at the mouth of Tenmile, and one at Rices Landing. And coal was mined at Jefferson in an early day.

How long did it take to settle the Tenmile Country? Historians allow thirty years to a generation, and it took just about that length of time to settle the good lands in the section. It was the same picture in the other migrations. Just about a generation after the settlement of Philadelphia, we note the migration into Chester and Lancaster Counties in Pennsylvania, then in another generation or about 1730 we find the migration into the Shenandoah. About the same length of time later, or in 1763-5, the move was on again and this time into the Tenmile Country. Twenty years later the full force of the Kentucky migration was swinging down the Monongahela and Ohio in flat boats and all other means of travel. From the section about Fort Jackson alone more than two hundred persons departed for Bracken County in 1789. In 1808 the land office at Steubenville, Ohio, was being swamped by applicants from this section, who walked overland from Waynesburg to take up the vacant land being offered for sale in Ohio. Those who went to Kentucky were also filling up this new State from the South. The same pattern continued to operate until the entire United States had been settled. Examination of the lists of these emigrants finds the same family names as were in the migration to the Tenmile. The first migration out of the Tenmile is noted by William Rhodes in his journal. Rhodes, who came from New England about 1785, to operate the trading post at Fort Jackson, writes that "game had become scarce, and that the danger from Indians has made forting no longer necessary after the settlement by the New Englanders at the mouth of the Muskingum River (1782)". Indications are that the migration into this Tenmile Country had reached its peak about 1785, and from that time on, there were as many persons leaving as were arriving in the section. And then, in 1796, the people of the section decided they had reached maturity and the County of Greene was officially recognized by the State. It is fortunate that the quality of the migration was as high as the quantity, for they left a heritage of which their descendants may be justly proud.

THE REVOLUTION

In a previous article in The Republican, I touched on the military moves in the Tenmile, in Dunmore's War of 1774, and the Revolutionary War, that followed. Due to lack of space, muster rolls were omitted. The Militia arrangements for 1781-1782, are printed in Pennsylvania Archives, Series VI, Volume 2, and the names of the Rangers in Series III, Volume 23. But these lists are by no means complete for the services rendered during the struggle for independence. There are frequent references in pension applications to services performed under certain leaders, whose muster rolls are yet to be found. The Militia was, in theory, made up of all the men between the ages of sixteen and sixty, but it is not hard to see that many times, boys not yet in their teens, were sent out on duty, and less frequently, old men, in their dotage, performed tours of duty. On the whole, however, the services were performed by the younger males of the section, mostly boys from fourteen to twenty, with the more mature men serving as officers. Most of them served only in the districts in which they were drafted, although at times, calls for expeditions into the Indian Country were filled by volunteers. At such times it was a custom, of men in transit through the section, to go along, since it furnished a safe escort for their journeys.

Periods of service were short and the discipline was very loose. If men got tired, or were needed at home, they just left and went home. Sometimes they sent others in their place, thus the term "deserter", found in military records, does not have the meaning that it has in present military establishments.

During the first few years of the Revolution the border controversy with Virginia was almost as important to the settlers as the war with the British. It was also a convenient excuse for evading military service away from home. When Pennsylvania recruiting officers came down from Fort Pitt the inhabitants claimed Virginia allegiance, while if the Virginia officers came into the district, they would claim allegiance to Pennsylvania. The same held true in the furnishing of supplies. Not wishing to take depreciated currency, the settlers would evade the foraging officers with the same excuse. It was bitterly complained of by the officers of the Continental forces.

In spite of all this, patriotism was not lacking, and while it was of a selfish type, in that the men sought only to protect their homes and loved ones, at a time when the new nation was unable to help, it nevertheless made possible the complete utilization of Washington's small forces in the East. War had hardly been declared before companies were organized and men left to volunteer in the Eastern Armies. Recruiting officers were here as early as 1775. Captain Michael Cresap of Frederick County, Maryland, sent one of his lieutenants over the mountains to pick up as many frontiersman as they could get, and it is reliably reported that some twenty of more from this section marched to Cumberland to join him, and then went on to Boston to join Washington there. McSherry in his "History of Maryland" pp. 185) says of these men, that Cresap's Rifle Company numbered some one hundred and thirty men, who were armed with tomahawks and rifles, painted like Indians, and dressed in hunting shirts and moccasins. He and other historians recall that the settlers at Cumberland and Frederick turned out to watch their skill with the rifle, when the men would hold a target in their hand for another to shoot at. An eye witness watching them at Boston also reports their skill at this game. When their term was out at Boston, these men returned home, but were saddened by the death of the Captain while at New York. Cresap lies buried there in Trinity Church Yard, having died at that place in October 1775. When the men from the West of the mountains returned home they quickly took up the defense of the frontier, a number of them, because of their known experience, being elected captains of the militia.

Because of a number of false muster rolls of Captain Michael Cresap's Company, which have appeared, including the imaginary company listed by Horn, we think it well to give the full list of men who served under him, a list which was filed with the National Archives, October 7, 1775, and is reported by Burgess in his "Virginia Soldiers of 1776." (Vol. 3 pp. 1242.) From this list we can then select the men who came from the Tenmile Country. There are 155 names in this list, and the officers' names are not exactly the same as given in the Maryland Archives, (Vol. 18 pp. 28) but this can be explained by the fact that some only served for part time, and were replaced during the campaign. They were:

MICHAEL CRESAP, Captain

Michael Cresap, Jr., Lieutenant John Nicholas, Lieutenant
Thomas Wearing, Ensign William Ogle, Ensign
 (Maryland Archives gives Thomas Warren as First Lieutenant.)
Joseph Cresap, Sergeant Daniel Cresap, Jr., Sergeant
 (Listed as Lieutenant in Maryland Archives.)
Jacob Newland, Sergeant Daniel Greathouse, Sergeant
James Buchanan, Sergeant Joseph Ford, Sergeant
John Clendennin, Sergeant Cyrus McCracken, Sergeant
Brice Virgin, Sergeant

PRIVATES

Richard Adams
Isaac Adams
John Ahrson
 (Arrison?)
Andrew Anderson
Paul Armstrong
Jeremiah Arnold
Valentine Baker
Thomas Barnes
Frederick Barber
Freeman Battershell
Joseph Beckett
James Belford
Lewis Bennett
 (Bonnett?)
James Blackburn
Robert Blackburn
Samuel Blackburn
James Blair
Charles Bowman
William Bracken
David Brandy
Joseph Brashear
Richard Brashear
Thomas Brown

Alexander Byrnes
 (Burns?)
John Caine
James Campbell
James Campbell
James Cannady
 (Kennedy?)
Francis Chaine
 (Cheney?)
John Chenowith
Thomas Chenowith
Thomas Cisco
George Clay
John Cockran
Joseph Cockran
Joseph Cochrane
Henry Coffman
Isaac Collyer
Harmon Connolly
Strother Crawford
Michael Cresswell
Daniel Cristy
John Dean
Michael Delow
Henry Dennis

Paul Deskin
Peter Dewitt
Jacob Dick
Richard Dickman
Edward Dolling
James Downand
Andrew Fairley
Robert Farmer
Stephen Flarity
Thomas Forhee
Torrence Finnigan
John Fitzpatrick
Jacob Fry
John Glaze
Thomas Gilliland
Thomas Griffith
William Hall
John Hargus, guide
Phillip Hathaway
William Hawkins
George Hinch
Moses Hoffman
John Hughes
Joseph Hughes
Robert Hustead

Andrew Hynes
John Jacobs
James Johnson
Michael Johnson
Ignatius Jones
Osgood Jones
Benjamin Kelly
Elijah Kuykendall
Jacob Kuykendall
Mark Lee
Peter Lee
Richard Lee
Joseph Lock
John Lyon
Charles Magin
Nicholas Makin
Thomas Mason
Thomas Mathew
Peter McDaniel
Samuel McKenny
Richard Mercer
Conrad Mercerly
Charles Morgan
James Morton
Robert Moseley
Patrick Muckleroy
  Ensign (McElroy?)
Jacob Newland,
  later Sgt.
Samuel Noore
William Ogle,
  later Ensign
John O'Neal
Hugh Parker
John Pearsefall
  (Piersol?)
George Peck
George Peoples
John Phillips
Jesse Pigman
Charles Pogue
William Robinson
Tavenor Ross
  (Tychenor Rose?)
John M. Salliday
Phillip Saunders
Thomas Scott
Anthony Sells
Phillip Shover
  (Shaver?)
John Smith
David Solomon
Mathew Stephenson
Richard Stewart
William Stockwell
James Taylor
Abraham Teagarden
John Terrell
Edward Thomas
John Thomas
Edward Todd
Thomas Todd
Ninian Townshall
  (Tannehill?)
London Trotter
George Vest
John Virgin
Joseph Wade
John Waldrug
Moses Walker
Uriah Wegins
  (Wiggins?)
Michael Whitlock
  (Whitlatch?)
John Williams
David Williamson
James Wilson
John Winkfields
William Wiseman
William Workman

We can be reasonably certain that the men, whose names follow, were a part of the Western Pennsylvania contingent that joined Cresap. Going back a little, it is easily understood why Michael Cresap would send into this section for what he considered the finest material for his Company. He had lived near Fort Redstone with his father, who owned much land in Fayette County, Pennsylvania, and was well acquainted with these men. Some of them had come over the mountains from the vicinity of Cresap's Maryland home. He was not choosing strangers.

1. Jacob Newland, one of Cresap's sergeants, had come to the frontier from Maryland, and may have been a brother of George Newland, who took up the land on Stockton's lane, near Rices Landing. After returning from the campaign, he settled in the Western part of Washington County, in that section which was then claimed by Ohio County, Virginia, and where, on September 25, 1777, he took the Oath of Allegiance to the new government, before Daniel McClain. After the war he warranted a tract of land on Wheeling Creek, in what is now East Finley Township, but soon sold out and went to Bracken County, Kentucky. On June 18, 1782, he was a member of Captain John Wall's Company, Second Battalion, Washington County, Pennsylvania Militia.

2. Brice Virgin, sergeant under Cresap, was one of the four brothers, sons of Jeremiah Virgin. Rezin, John, Thomas, and Brice Virgin lived on the Fayette side of the Monongahela River, opposite the mouth of Tenmile Creek. All of them took an active part in the frontier defense. After Brice and John Virgin returned from the Boston journey, the brothers removed to Wheeling Creek, where John and Rezin took the Oath of Allegiance, as required, before Alfred Caldwell of Ohio County, Virginia, on September 4, 1777. Rezin and John Virgin, John Lyon, James Kelly, and others, made a survey trip

to Bracken County, Kentucky, in 1776, and it is likely that the other two brothers went along, although their names are missing from the Bracken County and Bourbon County account. Family records, however, say they were. Brice Virgin, on his return, took up land in the vicinity of Washington, Pennsylvania, and served as a Lieutenant under Captain William Leet, in the Fourth Battalion, Washington County Militia. In 1792, he settled at Cincinnati, Ohio.

3. John Virgin, who served with Cresap, after service similar to that of his brother, Brice Virgin, removed to Fayette County, where he was an inspector of troops under General Harrison, in 1790.

4. Andrew Fairley came back from Boston and was elected Captain of a Company of Washington County Militia in the First Battalion. His troops were recruited from the Castile Run section near Clarksville. He married Hannah Templeton, and records show he took up much land in what is now Richhill Township, Greene County, Pennsylvania, and the adjoining West Finley Township, in Washington County.

5. James Blackburn, of Cresap's Company, became First Lieutenant, under Captain Fairley, in the First Battalion, Washington County Militia.

6. John Lyon, brother of Samuel Lyon, with Brice Virgin and others in Kentucky, in 1776, came back to serve in Captain Andrew Fairley's Company.

7. Jeremiah Arnold, after returning from Boston, served in Captain Robert Sweeney's Company, Fifth Battalion, Washington County Militia. This company was recruited in the territory adjacent to Captain Fairley's. In 1777, he, with Joseph Arnold, was in Ohio County, Virginia, where they took the Oath of Allegiance before Thomas Waller.

8. Joseph Hughes, who married Sarah Swan, daughter of John Swan. He was a brother of Nathaniel Hughes. He went to Kentucky about 1781, and later to Estill County, Missouri.

9. Samuel Moore. There were three men of this name among the first settlers in Greene County. He may have been the man who married Mary Swan, sister of Sarah.

10. Jesse Pigman, Jr., son of Jesse Pigman and Sarah (Lucas) Pigman, and nephew of John Swan's wife. He came from the Boston Campaign and was chosen head of the Company of Militia and Frontier Rangers. He was perhaps the most active of the Militia Captains, being mentioned more frequently, in pension applications, as being in charge of the home troops. He is listed as Captain of a Company in the First Battalion of Washington County Militia in the arraignment for 1782, but refused his muster roll, claiming Virginia allegiance.

11. Abraham Teagarden, Jr., son of Abraham Teagarden, who operated the first ferry over the Monongahela at Fort Redstone. Abraham Teagarden, Jr., was a brother of George, of Clarksville. He returned from Boston to Fayette County, where, in 1778 and 1779, he served in Captain James Leech's Company of Westmoreland County Militia.

12. Thomas Scott. He patented a tract of land on "Wolfe's Point," near the present town of Crucible, Greene County, Pennsylvania, on a warrant issued December 21, 1769.

13. Alexander Burns. Before his return from Boston, he joined General Benedict Arnold in the expedition to Quebec, then served as a sergeant in Captain Benjamin Royce's Company. Most of these men were from Wheeling Creek, in Greene and Washington Counties.

On the Quebec Expedition he was taken prisoner while serving with Captain William Hendricks. No record is shown of his release.

14. John Hargus. In the Journal of the House of Representatives of the 24th Congress of the United States, during the First Session, John Hargus made application for a new pension, he having been allowed a pension previously—on July 30, 1818—for service as an officer, from the Fall of 1776 to July, 1778, under General Hand. He had served as an Ensign in the Thirteenth Virginia Regiment.

15. Tavenor Ross. We have seen the name of Tichicus Rose spelled incorrectly so often, and quite frequently it is spelled "Ross." The similarity with this copied name is so striking that we are inclined to include him in the list. He was one of the earliest settlers at Clarksville, along with Fairley, Teagarden, Arnold, Lyon, and Pigman. He died, leaving a will on file in Washington, Pennsylvania, in Will Book 1, pp. 202.

16. James Blair. A man so named was an original patentee of land at the mouth of Little Whiteley Creek. The name is so common we cannot be sure.

17. Thomas Brown, another common name. A young man so named was killed later while fleeing to Fort Jackson.

18. John Hughes was another common name with local connections.

19. Lewis Bennett. This is a frequent mis-spelling for Lewis Bonnett, and we feel sure that is the case here. He was an uncle of Lewis Wetsel, and brother-in-law of Conrad Sikes and Hezekiah Stewart. He was back on the Monongahela in July, 1778, serving under his brother-in-law, John Wetsel, and here again the name is spelled or copied from the original as Lewis "Bennett".

20. William Hawkins. Probably the man of that name who was the father of William G. Hawkins. He was an early settler in Fayette County, and his widow was the third wife of Colonel John Minor.

21. William Robinson.

22. Richard Brashear. A Thomas Brashear was an early officer at Fort Jackson.

23. Joseph Brashear.

24. Joseph Wade.

Quite a number of other names have a familiar ring to local historians, but they are not identified by any close association. The names that might be included are Jacob and Elijah Kuykendall; Hugh Parker, who may have owned "Parker's Scheme", north of Waynesburg, but who left to settle in Kentucky prior to the close of the Revolution, and William Hall. From these names we can be sure that we know the most likely recruits for Cresap's march to Boston.

In the early days of the Revolution (1775) Captain James Hook was elected a Captain in a Regiment raised by Colonel William Crawford of Fayette County. He was not commissioned until the following year (November, 1776). There can be little doubt that this was the first of the Companies raised at Fort Jackson. It was then joined to the Thirteenth Virginia Regiment at Pittsburgh. This Regiment was under the command of Colonel Gibson and was used in many of the campaigns into the Indian country. A part of the Company was sent East and took part in the Battles of Brandywine and Germantown.

We are indebted to the Honorable J. I. Hook, present Judge of Greene County, for the list of names, copied from the National Archives record at Washington, D. C. The pension application of Levi House (Va., R-5265) states he enlisted in May, 1777, in Captain James Hook's Calico Hunting Shirt Company, which assembled at old Fort Redstone, and marched down to Maryland to join Colonel Morgan's Rifle Company. When they had marched 80 miles, an express came to them and a part of the Company returned under orders from General Broadhead, to relieve the Garrison at Wheeling. House's name is not on the muster of those who were in the Eastern battles, so there were probably more men in the Company than those whose names are given.

*JAMES HOOK, Captain

*Uriah Springer, 1st Lieutenant Arthur Gordon, 2nd Lieutenant
*John Hargus, Ensign *James Brandon, Sgt.
*William Parkinson, Sgt.   (Brenton)
Thomas McClung, Sgt. Thomas Tannehill, Sgt.
William McNary, Corp. John Miller, Corp.
*James Gunner, Corp. *John Aldridge, Driver
William Coxon, Fifer

PRIVATES

*Cornelious Johnson Phillip Hawthorn
*John Johnson Cornelious Montgomery
Morgan Kelly Zachariah Ward
Mathew Morin John Barnes
Daniel Murray Francis Brannon
*John Duncan *Thomas Whine
*Thomas Hathaway   (Wier)
Henry Lawson *John Kirby
John Deforest *William Wood
Henry Charlton Samuel Haycraft
John Colbert *John Hook
Patrick Means James Williams
Abner Kendrick Thomas Burns
Benjamin Gerrard Thomas Hickenbottom
Elijah Veach James Dawson
*James Askins Thomas Conner
*James English James Conner
Thomas Walker Timothy Kline
John Thomas William Delanney
*James Hannah Alex Serge
Samuel Street *Benjamin White
William McClung   (Wright)

*Greene County names.

A goodly number of these names are those of Tenmile Country pioneers, and are found among the early taxpayers, and in the Rhodes Papers. A name missing from the list is that of Levi House, whose pension application claims to have served in this Company.

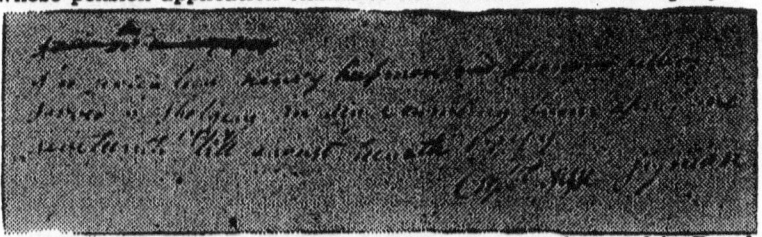

ORIGINAL DISCHARGE from Company Commander used in Revolution. Type frequently spoken of in pension applications. Property of and through the courtesy of Mrs. Mildred (Huffman) Russell of Waynesburg.

FRONTIER RANGERS

Frontier Rangers were the Minute Men of the Frontiers. They formed regular Militia Companies, under elected officers, and were subject to call at a minute's notice. Their service was not continuous like that of the Flying Camp or Continental Line, though they were often called out to assist these two regular services. But many of these men experienced more actual warfare than did their regular comrades. At each alarm a certain number or class would be called on to patrol the lines between the forts or penetrate deep into Indian territory to recover captives or punish a depredation. Always a certain number were held at Forts or strong points to make a show of strength and prevent incursions, with Scouts or Spies continuously moving from one Fort to another. During harvest time, and other busy days on the frontier farms, old men or boys often took up the job, to release their able-bodied fathers or sons for the heavy work. Examination of pension records show many boys of fourteen went out in place of the father and learned the soldier's job by experience. At times, in Western Pennsylvania, the Rangers were called on to make real campaigns, in considerable force, such as Williamson's Expedition, Lockry's Expedition, Crawford's ill-fated Expedition, and the George Rogers Clark Expedition. On the latter expedition at least two of the Companies were made up mostly of Greene County men, being under Captain Jesse Pigman, who was replaced by Captain William Harrod, and Captain John Swan, Jr., who later perished on his way down the Ohio to take up the land he received for this service. Many Greene County men missed the Crawford Expedition because, when they were assembled, an alarm sent them to Wheeling Creek to strengthen that threatened settlement. One gets an idea of the immense service rendered only when they read the thousands of names of those who received pay or were reported on the muster rolls of the different Company Commanders.

The type of service rendered can be understood better by reading a few of the records sent in by men applying for pensions. Here are a few examples:

Take the case of Eliel Long, who made application from Greene County, Pennsylvania, on September 17, 1833 (File Penna. S 2284), when he was seventy-seven years old. He states "that he entered the service in what is now Greene County as a drafted Militiaman under Captain John Guthrie in September, 1778, and was out for two months. He next went out in May, 1779, under Captain John Minor for two months, as a Militiaman, after which he served one month as a volunteer under Captain Volentine Nichols. In 1780, he served for one month under Captain Rail. He next served two months under Captain Samuel Swindler, guarding the frontier against hostile attacks of the Indians, pursuing them and driving them from the Western parts of Virginia and Pennsylvania. In the Fall of the same year he again went out with the same Captain under Crawford. In the Spring of 1781, he served under Captain John Holton in several tours of duty, including one in which they marched to Darroh's Station, where they were placed under command of Major Carmichaels. During the Revolutionary War he served more than a full year, his service consisting of scouting a few days or a few months at a time, so long as the emergency required, sometimes only on small parties without any organization or officers, but exposed to more danger and hardship than when in camp or field. His good character was attested by Reverend John Fordyce and Caleb Spragg. Stated he was born in Queene Anne's County, Maryland, on August 9, 1756."

Or take the application of Harrod Newland, from his statement made at Indianapolis, on July 7, 1833, when he was sixty-seven years of age.

"In March, 1779, (he was but thirteen years old at the time) he volunteered into a Company of Militia, in what is now Washington County, (later Greene) Pennsylvania, which Captain Jesse Pigman had raised for the purpose of pursuing a party of Indians that had made an attack upon and murdered a number of White persons engaged in sugar making on Tenmile Creek, about eight miles from his home. (He lived near present Dry Tavern). After about four or five days of ranging, he returned to his own neighborhood with his party, and finding all the inhabitants now forted at different stations and block-houses, he was at this time engaged in spying until the last of October, when his Company was dismissed and sent home, since their object was not to make long marches or carry on offensive warfare, but merely to guard and defend the frontier and warn the inhabitants of danger while they carried on their agricultural pursuits. In the month of April, 1780, the Indians having murdered a family by the name of McMillin, (or McClelland), the Whites found it necessary to fort and organize a party of spies and Militia. The declarant again volunteered and was again placed under command of Jesse Pigman. There was very little discipline established in the Company but they underwent many privations until October, when they were dismissed. The following year, in April, the Indians killed a man named Owen and one named William Brown as they were removing their sugar from a camp in kettles. Again he (Newland) volunteered and served under Captain Thomas Hughes and Lieutenant Joseph Vanmeter, until October of 1781. In 1782, when the Indians made another attack, he again went out, under Captain Thomas Hughes, after the Indians had killed a man at his home. This tour of duty lasted until Colonel William Crawford was about to march to Sandusky, when he volunteered to go on this expedition. However, an alarm in the vicinity of Wheeling Creek caused all the efficient men of the vicinity to be called off in that direction, and they took up the chase of the Indians who had killed the Davidson Family near Ryerson's Station. Harrod Newland states he was born in Berkeley County, Virginia, early in 1766, and had a Bible record of his age. He was a son of George Newland and Rachel (Harrod) Newland."

James Pribble (in File No. W-3595), applying for pension from Pendleton County, Kentucky, on April 1, 1833, gives a most enlightening account of his services while living in what is now Greene County, Pennsylvania, naming many officers under whom he served, and recalling forts not named in any histories. He states: "That in March, 1777, he volunteered, at the age of fifteen years, in place of his father, Stephen Pribble, under Colonel William Crawford and Major Thomas Hughes, his Company officers being Captain Jesse Pigman, Lieutenant Joseph Vanmeter, and Ensign Charles Swan. They marched to Ankrom's Fort on Tenmile Creek, in Washingtor County, Pennsylvania, where he was on duty for six months, their duties being to guard the Fort and range the line of settlements to prevent the Indians, who were in an alliance with the British, from raiding the frontier country. All men over sixteen and under forty-five years were held as Minutemen in the Militia of the State and held ready to march at a minute's notice until the close of the Revolution.

During this period a certain portion of these men were held to service regularly each year to go and guard the forts, blockhouses, and stations along the whole frontier, and prevent the Indians from entering the settlements or passing through to attack the American Army occupied against the British. The officers usually called for as many volunteers as would go and then make up the balance by drawing lots or draft. A large portion of the young men would volunteer, so that men of families, could remain at home and tend crops. But, if the alarm were of sufficient gravity, then all the Militia would be ordered to march. In 1778, in March, there were the usual calls for men, and he tendered his service, being then sixteen years of age, and reported again to the same officers and to the same fort. In the year 1779, he went as a Militiaman, under Captain Joseph Vanmeter, his former Lieutenant. Lieutenant this year was Jesse Vanmeter, brother of the Captain, and the Ensign was John Manning. During this year frequent detachments were sent out to range between the fort at Wheeling and the mouth of Dunkard's Creek on the Monongahela River. The detachments were often compelled to retreat because the enemy was too strong, at which time runners would be dispatched to other detachments, and when reinforced, they would cause the Indians to retreat. James Pribble was held as a Minute Man through 1780, but was not called on for duty as he recollects. In March, 1781, he, with Gabriel Eakins, with their consent, were ordered out by Colonel Crawford to serve as spies traversing the long wilderness trail, their duty being not to engage the Indians but to make haste back to warn the troops stationed at the forts and prevent any surprise attacks— always to use every effort to get back to Ankrom's, where Colonel Crawford was stationed. He was to be paid one dollar a day but, not knowing where to apply, he did not get paid for the duty he performed.

"In the year 1782, he was held as a Militiaman, under Captain Thomas Hughes, the same who had formerly been Major, he having resigned in the other Regiment to favor a division of the Regiment and the forming of two out of one, believing that by the division, the country would be placed in a better condition of defense, and accepting the appointment as Captain. His other officers were Jesse Pigman, Jr., and Ensign William Swan, with Colonel William McCleery and Major John (H)Eaton, as field officers, and the place of rendezvous was the same as in former years. Duty was between Dunkard Creek and Wheeling. He often met men from Jackson's Fort, which was four or five miles from Ankrom's, and when this took place they sometimes marched together for several days. This year, James Pribble was Second Sergeant, and Alex Monroe, who had served in the Regular Army below the mountains, was First Sergeant, the said Monroe having gotten a pension some years ago from the State of Indiana. He remembers Captain James Archer and Lieutenant Thomas Brashears, who were stationed at Jackson's Fort. His discharges from duty had all been consumed by fire, while living in Bracken County, Kentucky. He left Pennsylvania in 1789, and was in Bourbon and Fayette Counties before moving to Bracken County. He and his wife, Margaret Pribble, were married May 15, 1783, by Levi Harrod, a Justice of Peace."

The application of John Moore (File No. Va. S-11106), made at Mercer County, Kentucky, December 3, 1832, tells of the part played by this neighborhood in George Rogers Clark's Expedition, along with some experiences in Greene County, Pennsylvania. John Moore states: "He was born in Frederick County, Maryland, and was now seventy-five years of age but, as a boy, came with his father's family to Western Pennsylvania, near the Monongahela River, on Muddy

Creek, where he lived when the Revolution broke out. That in the year 1777, in June, he was drafted for three months' service in Captain Jesse Pigman's Company, and marched to Fort Pitt, where he was stationed as a guard under Colonel Gibson. While at this place it was frequently attacked by the Indians and some men were killed. In the Fall of the same year he was drafted into Captain Swan's Company to march in an expedition to the Shawnee towns. With Captain Cracraft, who was the Commander, he marched to Atkinson's Fort, at the head of Tenmile Creek. When, not being joined by other Companies that were called out, they returned to the mouth of Dunkard Creek, and served out the balance of their time here. Next Spring, in April of 1778, he enlisted in Captain William Harrod's Virginia Company, to join the Illinois Regiment, under George Rogers Clark. They rendezvoused near Fort Redstone, where they embarked in batteaux and sailed down the Monongahela and Ohio to the Falls, arriving there the last of May. After a month at that place they were joined by some men from Kentucky, and set sail again, landing at the Saline on the North bank at a place called Rocky Cave. From here they marched to Kaskaskia, arriving at midnight, capturing the place by surprise, before daylight. It was here that Captain Harrod resigned and returned home, as did many of his men (Clark sent Harrod to Falls to lay out town and a new fort), but Moore and his brother joined another Company to go with Clark to Vincennes. Shortly thereafter he was taken prisoner and remained in captivity until 1782, when he escaped and made his way back to Catfish Camp in Washington County, Pennsylvania, removing to Kentucky the following year. His brother, Thomas, was with him on the many expeditions."

In application No. W-7503, of Leonard Garrison for a pension for services in the Revolution, on September 17, 1833, when he was seventy-three years old, and living in Greene County, Pennsylvania. He states: "He was living in Greene County (then Washington) when he was drafted into the Militia at Garard's Fort, in July, 1777. He spent two months guarding the frontier, under Captain Samuel Swindler. He had just returned home when he was called up for another tour, under Captain Stephen Gapen, and later under other subordinate officers. In the Spring of 1778, he was called in May, to go with Colonel Alexander McClean to the Virginia line. In the Fall of 1778, he went out, in September, under (his brother) Captain George Garrison, because the Indians were continually committing robberies and murders on the settlement. Stated he was born in Frederick County, Maryland, on May 5, 1760. He died March 10, 1839, and his wife got a pension for herself and stated that she had been raised with John Gapen, which he confirmed in an appended paper. She named in her application, the following children, according to age: David, Jacob, Cassandra, Mary, John, Barbara, Margaret, William, Jeremiah, Hannah, Sarah, Elizabeth, and Adam, the latter 27 years of age. Her pension was increased in 1848-49."

Josiah Prickett's pension application No. W-5584, was made in Clarmont County, Ohio, on August 10, 1832. He stated "that he was born in Maryland, on Gunpowder Creek, near Baltimore, in 1764, but that on one occasion, when his father's family was compelled to hide out for several days when the Indians attacked their home in Western Pennsylvania, the family Bible and some other property had been taken. The Pricketts removed to Big Whiteley a year before the Revolution. He served for three months, beginning May 1, 1778, under Captain Samuel Swindler and Lieutenant Swearington, when he was fourteen years of age. His Sergeant was Henry Sykes, and the Company was billeted at Garard's Fort. He went out as a substitute for a man whose family was sick, and received five shillings per day for his services. On April 1, 1781, he was a member of Captain John Holton's Militia Company and was called out when some persons were killed near Garard's Fort. He was called out again in the Fall of that year, under Captain John Huston, for service on MacIntosh's Expedition, but after laying at the Ohio for ten or more days, was directed to go home, by Captain Brady, who had been sent out from Fort Pitt. He was hired as a spy the following year, along with John Guthery, John Knotts, Stephen Gapen, Jeremiah Williams, and two others. They worked Big Whiteley, while another Company was hired by William Minor to spy on Dunkard's Creek. William Hanna was killed, and Amos Morris wounded, while Richard Hall escaped, on one of the trips made during this tour of duty. Major James Carmichaels was their Commanding Officer. Was serving at Garrison's Fort when peace was declared. His brother, Richard Prickett, taken prisoner at Fort Hutson, during the last year of the War, and held for forty years. He was married to Sarah Van Camp, by the Reverend David Sutton, on July 4, 1783."

(Note there is mention of Fort Prickett in the Pennsylvania Archives.)

Henry Sykes entered the service as a volunteer, under Captain James Neal, in August, 1776, and marched from Dunkard Creek to a short distance below Yellow Creek, on the Ohio. The term of service was for three months, but, as no one showed up to supply their places, they served a half month longer. He next served at Garards Fort, under Captain Samuel Swindler, in 1777-8, after which he acted as Ensign at the same place, under Captain Minor. In 1782, he acted as a spy, under Colonel Crawford, during which time he took off the scalp of the Indian who killed a man named Hall. (Dick Hall?). Says he was in pursuit of the Indians who killed Enoch Enochs and a man named Robinson. Henry Sykes said he was born in the Shenandoah, February 12, 1757, and that his father had died in 1782.

The Thomas Smith (of Smith Creek) pension application is interesting because it shows the early service of Captain David Owens' Company, for he says that in the Fall of 1776, he was drafted into the Company commanded by Captain Owens. They were stationed on Fishing Creek, with a Lieutenant Boggs, and Ensign James Archer, as the other officers. In 1780, he was again employed under Captain Archer, in scouting on Fishing and Wheeling Creeks. From 1777 until 1781, he was listed at Fort Jackson, part of the time serving in the Fort and at other times scouting. (Affidavit filed September 10, 1832.)

David White was out with this same group in the Fall of 1776, but, after this service, he served at Fort Jackson with Sebastian Shroffe and Leonard Sellars. For three months they were spying on the waters of Tenmile Creek to the waters of Dunkard Creek. In 1780, he was employed at the mouth of Shining Run, on the Virginia side of Dunkard Creek, but had volunteered three times to go on missions to the Shawnee towns, twice getting as far as Wheeling and once to Mingo Bottom. (Affidavit filed May 13, 1833.)

Joseph Yard Province, while a resident of Fayette County, applied for a pension, saying that he volunteered on the First of May, 1780, when only sixteen years of age, in Captain John Patton's Virginia Militia Company, and went down the Monongahela to Kentucky. That in August, of the same year, he served under Captain John Atkins in the engagement at the Piqua Towns, where the Indians were commanded by the renegade, Simon Girty. Later he returned to Fayette County, and in 1782, was sent to a station on Whiteley Creek to protect the inhabitants. His widow, Rachel Province, got a pension on January 23, 1854, at the age of 71 years. Her pension was later paid to her from the Chicago office.

Andrew House, of Knox County, Ohio, in 1835, made application for services in May, 1776, under the command of Colonel McCleary, who commanded two Companies of Rangers, one under Captain William Harrod, the other under Captain Jesse Pigman. They served for some time between Fort Jackson and Wheeling, and then returned to Fort Jackson, where Captain Harrod resigned his command because of a wounded leg. Pigman then took over command at the time of the Statler Fort massacre, while Captain Phillip Catt took over Pigman's Company. They found Statler Fort had been burned, and followed the trail of the Indians as far as the Ohio, killing two of them. House reports he got five guns and some blankets. They then marched to Fort Pitt, and spent the rest of their service for the season at that place as spies. (Nat. Arch., 5261, Pa.)

William Harrod had been a soldier of the French and Indian War and had been a Captain under Lord Dunmore, so it was but natural that he should be chosen to lead an organization at the outbreak of the Revolution. The records show that he was out with a Company as soon as the frontiermen were organized, and that he served during the entire War, except for a brief period in which he was laid up with a leg wound. There are numerous muster rolls of the men who served under him. He led one Company in the George Rogers Clark Expedition to Kaskaskia in 1778, and was at Chillicothe with a Company in 1779. Between times he commanded at the Falls of the Ohio (Louisville). While the rolls of those serving under him differ slightly from year to year, the muster roll of his Company of 1780, is most likely comparable to the list of men who went on Clark's Expedition. This list, found in Collins' History of Kentucky, Vol. 1, pp. 12, contains some additions, and makes room for known casualties of previous campaigns. John Swan, Jr., is known to have been second in command at Kaskaskia, and is missing from the 1780 list, as are the names of John Moore, Simon Moore, James Francis Moore, Adam Wickersham, and others. We shall give the 1780 list, and also additions from the 1779 list. As muster rolls changed almost monthly, we think this a fair sample of the men who served under Harrod.

WILLIAM HARROD, Captain

James Patton, Lieutenant Edward Bulger, Ensign

(John Swan, Jr., known to have been on the Expedition as Lieutenant.)

PRIVATES

Peter Balance	Robert Dickey	Sam Goodwin
Alex. Barr	Dan Driscoll	James Guthrie
James Brand	Isaac Dye	Dan Hall
John Buckras	John Eastwood	William Hall
Angus Cameron	Samuel Forester	John Hatt
Amos Carpenter	(Foster)	Evan Henton
Benjamin Carter	Joseph Frakes	Thomas Henton
Thomas Carter	Sam Frazee	William Hickman
Reuben Case	John Galloway	A. Hill
Thomas Cochran	William Galloway	Andrew Hill
John Conway	James Garrison	Sam Hinch
John Corbly	Jos. Goins	Fred Honacker
John Crable	Isaac Goodwin	Joseph Hughes

Rowland Hughes	William Oldham	James Sullivan
Michael Humble	John Paul	William Swan
John Hunt	George Phelps	Joseph Swearingen
Abram James	James Phelps	Sam Swearingen
John Kenny	Sam Pottinger	Van Swearingen
Valentine Kinder	Jonas Potts	Robert Thorn
Moses Kuykendall	(written F. Potts)	John Tompton
John Lewis	Reuben Pribble	(Thompson?)
John Lincant	Urb Ranner	Beverly Trent
(Lincoln)	Benjamin Rice	Thomas Tribble
Samuel Lyon	Reed Robbins	Robert Tyler
Pat McGee	Thomas Settle	Abraham Vanmeter
Sam Major	William Smiley	Michael Valleto
Amos Mann	Jacob Speck	Joseph Warford
Edward Murdock	John Stapleton	James Welch
(Killed on the Ohio)	James Stewart	Abraham Whitacer
John Murdock	James Stewart (2)	Aquilla Whitacer
Richard Morris	Daniel Stull	Jacob Wickersham
William Morris	Minor Sturgis	Edward Wilson
	Peter Sturgis	

Men in the 1779 list, but not in 1780 muster:

Solomon Carpenter	Henry Hall	Adam Wickersham
Hardy Hill	Thomas Simpson	Peter Bello
	Thomas Suttles	

References: Draper Manuscripts, pension applications, etc.

We have seen where Jesse Pigman, Jr., was a member of Captain Michael Cresap's Company, which joined General Washington at Boston. When he returned to the frontier he was placed in command of a Company and was actively engaged with the Frontier Rangers for the balance of the Revolution. He was living in the vicinity of Jefferson, and most of his men were of the section roughly bounded by the present lines of Jefferson Township, Greene County. A nephew of the wife of John Swan, and related by marriage to Captain William Harrod, it is not surprising that the men who served with him were partly his relatives. His field officers, as shown by various pension applications, were at times Major Thomas Hughes and Major John Heaton. Colonel William Crawford and Colonel William McCleary commanded the Regiment of Rangers. No muster rolls of his Company are to be found, yet we have found the following men have served, at various times, in his Company:

Lieutenants—Joseph Vanmeter and Jesse Vanmeter.
Ensigns—Charles Swan, William Swan, and John Manning.
Sergeants—Alexander Monroe and James Pribble.
Orderly Sergeant—Thomas Wells. (Pension Appl. R-11318)

PRIVATES

Stephen Pribble—
  (See pension application W-3595, James Pribble, son of Stephen).
John Moore—
  (See pension application S-11106).
Thomas Moore—
  (See pension application W-564);
Andrew House—
  (See pension application R-5261).
Gabriel Eakins—
  (See pension application W-3595).

Harrod Newland—
   (See pension application 16-494).
Leonard Sellars—
Henry Huffman—
   (Mrs. Mildred (Huffman) Russell has the discharge papers of the last two named. They were written by Captain Jesse Pigman for service from April 17, 1777, to August 10, of the same year).

   It might be well to add, that for the good of the service, Major Thomas Hughes and Captain Jesse Pigman, Jr., accepted a reduction in rank, in 1782, and became Captain and Lieutenant, respectively.

   Since the remainder of the Company muster is not available, it will not be amiss to speculate as to the names of the men who could have served in this Company, since they were living in the precinct from which Pigman's Company was drafted. The following is a list of possible members, and in no way official, other than that they were eligible and in the precinct at the time:

PRIVATES

Thomas Adamson	William Hiller	John Rice
Charles Anderson	Solomon Hoge	Thomas Roach
James Anderson	John Hupp	Mathias Rofelty
Enoch Blackledge	Meredith Inghram	William Shephard
Edward Burson	Samuel Jackson	Richard Swan
Jacob Cline	Robert Kelly	George Teagarden
Thomas Crago	Benjamin Liming	Ellis Thomas
Oliver Crawford	Aquilla Martin	Edward Thomas
Silas Estle	Daniel Moredock	Samuel Thomas
Samuel Foster	James Moredock	William Thomas
Thomas Foster	Ezekiel Morris	William Thoroughman
Nathan Frakes	James Murato	Charles Thurman
James Gunner	Barnet O'Niel	Barnet Whitlatch
Adam Hartman	Charles Pigman	Thomas Wier
James Henderson	Samuel Pigman	
Peter Hiller	Samuel Poke	

   The following is a list of Captain Benjamin Royce's Company, which served nineteen days, beginning on April 10, 1781. They were of the North Branch of Tenmile but, as some of them lived in what became Greene County, the list must be included. (Found in Draper Mss., 4-SS—8-11-etc.)

BENJAMIN ROYCE, Captain

William Troup, Sgt.   John Miller, Lieutenant   Alexander Burns, Sgt.

PRIVATES

Joseph Bane	Abraham Hathaway	Daniel McFarland
Nathan Bane	Samuel Hardesty	Edward McVaugh
Richard Bilby	Jacob Husong	Isaac McVaugh
A. Burnett	Joseph Jennings	Cornelious Miller
Stephen Carter	James Johnson	William Morris
Gedion Dickeson	Elias Kelly	Ebeneezer Osburn
Nathan Evans	Caleb Lindley	Benjamin Ross
John Goodwin	Joseph Lindley	Jacob Rude
James Guffey	Zenas Lindley	John Whiting

   In the same group of papers there is listed as having served under Captain William Crawford, on April 2, 1781, a Company that differs somewhat from that found in the Pennsylvania Archives.

WILLIAM CRAWFORD, Captain
William Garritt, Sergeant (Garard?)

PRIVATES

M. (elchoir?) Baker	George Catt	Jacob Riffle
John Bradford	Michael Catt	Richard Seaton
Lewis Burnett	Lewis Grinstaff	Joseph Vanmeter
John Cain	Jacob Lawrence	Jeremiah Veach

In the Spring and early Summer of 1778, Captain John Wetsel had a Company of Rangers on duty in Monongalia and Ohio Counties, at the command of Colonel Daniel McFarland. The names of the members of his Company have been published in the Pennsylvania Archives (Series VI, Vol. 2, pp. 320-21), and appeared in other volumes, but has its place in this volume. Some corrections have been made in the spelling from the original list:

JOHN WETSEL, Captain
William Crawford, Lieutenant
John Madison, Ensign   Peter Miller, Sergeant

PRIVATES

John Andrew	Harvey Franks	John Nicholas
Phillip Baker	William Gardner	Phillip Nicholas
Lewis Bennet (Bonnett)	Harvey Goho (Geho?)	John Province, Jr. Jacob Riffle
Samuel Brown	Peter Goosey	Mathew Riffle
George Call	William Hall	John Six
Phillip Call	Conrad Hat (Haught?)	(Sykes)
Christian Caplayd		John Smith
Nicholas Chamber	Martin Hat, (Haught?)	Jacob Spangler
Daniel Cook		Jacob Tambaugh
Joseph Comb	Thomas Harges (Hargus)	Martin Whitsell (Wetsel)
John Duncan		
Abner Eakwood (Eastwood)	Jacob Lanebaugh Voluntine Lawrence	Benjamin Wright Joseph Yeager
Enoch Enochs	Joseph Morris	

List of twenty officers and men, under Lieutenant William Cross of Monongalia Militia, under command of Major James Chew, at Fort Pitt, in October, 1777.

John Mills, Lieutenant   Samuel Blackford, Sergeant
    (In command at Wheeling).

PRIVATES

Roger Barton	Stephen Gapen	James Purdie
Henry Franks	Peter Goosey	Henry Yoho
Aaron Flowers	Wm. Hall	John Yoho
James Flynn	Sebastian Keener	

(Frontier Defense on the Upper Ohio—pp. 302).

We are still seeking the muster rolls for a considerable number of early Companies, which are mentioned frequently in the early days of the Revolution. We shall publish a list of these, and some items that identify them, with the hope they can be found, to complete this history:

Captain Samuel Swindler's Company

This was one of the early Companies, and is mentioned frequently in pension applications. It seems to have been recruited in the Garards Fort area. Lieutenant Swearington was his officer in 1778, and Henry Sykes was his sergeant. Josiah Prickett was a member of the Company that year. Eliel Long and Leonard Garrison also served under this Captain.

Captain John Huston's Company

This Company was also from around Garards Fort, and was a part of the First Battalion, (Washington County) Pennsylvania Militia, in the arraignment, for February, 1782. Jacob Frazer was the Lieutenant, and Jonas Garard, the Ensign. The muster roll was not turned in to the Pennsylvania Commander.

Captain William Minor's Company

William Minor had a commission under Virginia command, but no list of his Company has been found. Pension claims show him in command.

Captain George Garrison's Company

George Garrison was the Captain of a Company from the Dunkard Creek section. He never made application for a pension, though he is known to have served for seven years. His brother, Leonard, reports having served under him.

Captain Stephen Gapen's Company

Stephen Gapen drew a pension for services while living in (West) Virginia. Several men claim service in his Company, which was recruited in the Dunkard Creek section.

Captain Voluntine Nichols' Company

Eliel Long reports having served under this officer, and Bates' History of Greene County mentions him as being a Captain. He was from the Jefferson district, and no doubt his Company would tally with that of Captain Jesse Pigman.

Captain Henry Enoch's Company

While this man was recorded as serving as Lieutenant-Colonel of the First Battalion of Washington County Militia in 1782, he is also known to have been a Captain of a Company earlier in the War. His Company would be expected to have been recruited in the vicinity of Clarksville, and it is of record that he also recruited at Fort Jackson.

Captain David Owens' Company

Captain David Owens was the first commander at Fort Jackson. James Seals, Thomas Smith, and others, report serving under him, but no list of his Company has been found. Some of his men asked to serve under him when his Company was taken over by Captain William Harrod, a move said to have been connected with his earlier reputation. This record is in the Draper Mss.—4-NN—30-31.

Captain John Minor's Company

While serving as a Captain in 1777, John Minor commanded a Company of men listed in Colonel Zack Morgan's Regiment of Monongalia County, Virginia. He later became a Colonel in his own right. (Draper Mss., 3-NN—128-30). Was active in the suppression of Tories.

Captain John Holton's Company

This Company was from the vicinity of Carmichaels, and the Colonel was Major James Carmichaels. List would compare with Captain William Crawford's Company.

Captain Abraham Scott's Company

After serving in the East at the Battle of Brandywine, etc., Captain Scott reports that he came to what is now Greene County, in 1778, and in 1779, was commissioned a Captain of Militia. In 1781, his Company was ordered to serve on Dunkard Creek, for which he got $40.00 from Pennsylvania.

COLONEL CRAWFORD'S EXPEDITION

June 6th. is the anniversary date of Colonel William Crawford's capture at Sandusky. Crawford's Expedition might well be known as Washington County's Expedition, and Washington County, at that time, included Greene County, Pennsylvania. Fully eighty per cent of those four hundred and eighty men who made the trip were from the section that now embraces these two counties, and many of the descendants of these men still live here. It is fortunate that a list of names of those who went on the Expedition has been preserved to us and can be found in the Pennsylvania Archives. Twenty-eight of them were killed in battle or at the hands of the Indians after capture.

The background of the Expedition suggests there may have been a plot on foot to kill Colonel Crawford, as there was a bitter fight going on regarding the allegiance to either Virginia or Pennsylvania, at that time. Hints are given in letters from the officers planning the Expedition which show that John Cannon and David Duncan were allegedly interfering with the recruiting, while Dorsey Pentecost, it seems, was carrying water on both shoulders. The controversy over the boundary line almost reached armed conflict, with both sides forgetting the common enemy. It does seem strange that Colonel Crawford, his son, son-in-law, and nephew, were among those killed, while John Canon, who accompanied the Expedition, and all other officers, escaped, except John McClelland, founder of McClellandtown, Fayette County, Pennsylvania. The renegade, Simon Girty, may have had financial reasons for not sparing the captives' lives, rather than the personal reasons that have been suggested.

The Sandusky Expedition seems to have been conceived by George Rogers Clark as a diversion to mask his own moves, for on June 3, 1781, he wrote the Westmoreland County Lieutenants, advising them to make the move. In due time the plan was sold to General Brodhead at Fort Pitt, and he wrote President Reed of the Supreme Council, that the Expedition was contemplated, the date of his letter being August 23, 1781. On September 24, 1781, General Irvine replaced Brodhead. On December 17, 1781, President Moore wrote General Irvine that, in spite of Colonel Loughry's defeat, the Expedition should be pushed in order to quiet the people, who were quarreling over the boundary question, and gave the opinion that it would be the best means of protection against the sporadic incursions. More treachery is disclosed in a letter of May 30, 1782, which shows that a British agent was working to get the inhabitants to move into the Indian Country and accept British protection at a time when they were clamoring for the formation of a new State. There can be little doubt that this agent, a Mr. Johnson, was also keeping the British informed of the preparations for the Expedition, so that when they were discovered at the mouth of the Muskingum River, it was not hard to guess the objective, and prepare the ambush.

Eyewitness accounts of the Expedition are given by Dr. Knight, an Army surgeon, from Fort Pitt, and by John Slover, one of the guides, both of whom were taken prisoner. Dr. Knight states that a rendezvous was fixed for May 20, 1782, and the place was the old Mingo town, some forty miles by land from Fort Pitt, on the Ohio River's West side. After all the volunteers had crossed the River they divided themselves into eighteen Companies and chose their

Captains by vote. Four hundred and sixty-five men cast their vote. On May 25, the march began, taking a due West course, and four days later, they were on the Muskingum River, about sixty miles from the Ohio River. Some of the men lost their horses the night before they reached the Muskingum, and returned home. On the evening of the 28th., Major Brinton and Captain Bane went on reconnoiter and, about a quarter of a mile from camp, they saw two Indians, and fired upon them. This was the first contact, and it was learned afterward that the Expedition was kept under surveillance from that time on. On the eleventh day of the march, the Fourth day of June, 1782, the Expedition reached the spot where Sandusky had formerly stood, but the Indians, having moved nearer Lower Sandusky, the leaders held a council to decide whether they should go further, as their supplies were getting low. Before calling the council, a small party of Light Horse was sent out to get information. They made contact with a large body of enemy about three miles from the main body. Battle was engaged that continued until dusk. Next day firing commenced at six o'clock in the morning and continued all day, with little damage on either side. The enemy being reinforced, and outnumbering the Expedition, it was finally decided to retreat as soon as night came. Four men had been killed and twenty-three wounded. The Indians discovered the plan as soon as it was put in effect, and began shooting, causing the retreat to be turned into a rout, with every man trying to get away as fast he could. About this time, Dr. Knight found Colonel Crawford, whose horse had about given out, and he could not keep up with his men. Dr. Knight then states that about this time they met an old man and a lad, showing that the ages of the men of the Expedition may have been anywhere from ten to seventy years. With few untoward experiences, they continued their march throughout the night, being joined by Captain John Biggs and Lieutenant Ashley, the latter seriously wounded and riding Biggs' horse.

(John Biggs' widow lived in Morgan Township, Greene County, Pennsylvania, for many years after the death of her husband.)

On the following day, June 6, 1781, Captain Crawford, Dr. Knight, and the rest of their party, were captured by a party of seventeen Delaware Indians. John Biggs and Lieutenant Ashley were killed and scalped the next day, and the rest were taken to the old town of Sandusky. In all, the Indians had four scalps and eleven prisoners, four of whom were tomahawked and scalped on the way to the town.

It is best to pass over the torture and death of Colonel Crawford, and the infamy of Simon Girty; nor is it necessary to go into the details of the escape and return of Dr. Knight to the frontier post at Wheeling. The tale told by John Slover adds to our knowledge of the fate of the others captured in the Crawford Expedition and who were killed or burned at the Shawnee towns, including Major Harrison, John Crawford, and Colonel McClelland.

Dorsey Pentecost wrote the Pennsylvania Authorities on June 17, 1782, regarding the Expedition, stating that there were 478 men on horses assembled at Mingo, under Colonel Crawford, and that they were discovered at the Muskingum River, and from that time on, were kept under surveillance, while the Indians and British Light Dragoons were gathering from as far North as Detroit. That, when Crawford ordered the retreat on the second day of the battle, some 200 men stayed together and returned safely, bringing all their wounded with them, except three. He further stated that there were scattered parties still coming in.

In his report on the battle, General Irvine wrote President Moore of the Supreme Council, on July 5, 1782, that Colonel Crawford and about eleven others, had been captured and burned, but that the people were eager and ready to try again, at their own expense, and proposed another expedition, to be undertaken in August of the same year. He hoped he might be allowed to command such an expedition. Nothing came of it, and the order was countermanded on January First, 1783.

The pension application of Harrod Newland (Nat. Arch., No. 16,494), discloses that Captain Thomas Hughes' Company, formerly Captain Jesse Pigman's, was scheduled to go on this Expedition, but, due to an Indian raid near Wheeling, was directed into that section. This Company was recruited in what is now Jefferson Township, Greene County, Pennsylvania.

THE PENNSYLVANIA MILITIA

From the beginning of the Revolution, Pennsylvania had set up an organization of Militia which was called on in times of need. It had done yeoman service in and around Philadelphia, and on the Northern frontiers of the State. The ranks had suffered terrible losses in the Battle of Long Island. As soon as the border controversy between Pennsylvania and Virginia had been settled, and Washington County (which at that time was still a part of Westmoreland, and included what is now Greene County) was established, five Battalions of Militia were ordered organized. Of these, which are reported for 1782, the First Battalion, under Lieutenant-Colonel Henry Enochs of Clarksville, and Major James Carmichaels of Muddy Creek, was almost wholly from what is now Greene County. The muster rolls of six of the eight Companies are available. Land grants and census records furnish the clue to which locality these men came from. Since its formation, in 1782, the Militia has continued down in an unbroken record to the present-day National Guard.

Pennsylvania Militia

Year: 1782—First Battalion, Washington County. Recruited on the Castile Run section (partly in Greene County):

ANDREW FERLEY, Captain

James Blackburn, Lieutenant
Jacob Stull, Ensign
Samuel Coll, Clerk

Andrew Cox, Sergeant
David Leonard, Sergeant
Joseph Line, Sergeant

PRIVATES

James Milligan
Michael Cox, Jr.
Joseph Roberts
Jacob Meek
Richard Hardesty
James Baily
Jacob Need
Frederick Arnold
John Roberts
Jesse Jackson
Peter Benham
Jesse Leonard
Joseph Linsecum
Solomon Grooms
John Stull
Thomas Kelsey
Andrew Kees
John Line
Jacob Jackson
John Messmore
William Jones
John Blackburn

Thomas Fowler
Michael Cox
John Hegle
Christopher Gayman
Henry Fix
John Miller
Elisha Morris
James Wright
Caleb Linsecum
John Wright
Thomas Ishmael
Edmaund Manning
(1781)
William Grooms
Isaac Meek
Phineas McCray
Daniel Arnold
Jeremiah Meek
Thomas Kelsey
Philip Fox
Thomas Humphreys
(1781)

John Lowrey
Samuel McCray
John Goodwin
Nathan Meek
Hugh Kees
John Bryant
William Line
Samuel Line
George Miles
John Moore
Tych Rose
Daniel Gayman
Benjamin Daniels
Thomas Hill
Tobias Moore
Daniel Arnold
(1781)
Miles Heaton
Alexander Jackson
Nathan Kelley
Henry Enoch

NOTE—These served also during this period:
Jeremiah Sargent
Adam Bowen

John Bradford
Michael Bowen

Daniel McFarland, Jr.

Reference: Penna. Archives, Series VI, Vol. 2, pp. 9, 10, 13, 14.

Pennsylvania Militia

Year: 1782—First Battalion, Washington County. Recruited in Morgan Township (now Greene County).

BENJAMIN STITES, Captain

Elijah Mills, Lieutenant
William Lee, Ensign
Mathew Gray, Sergeant
Joseph Mills, Sergeant
James Bell, Sergeant

PRIVATES

Philip Varvell
John Gray
Robert Timmons
Jacob Rush
Benjamin Jennings
Ebeneezer Brown
James Morris
William Hartley
Silas Crayne
Reuben Perkins
Samuel House
Amos Leonard
John Ross
John Martin
Eleven Timmons
William Wright
Nathaniel Bell
William Rush
Samuel Seals
Reuben Ross
Paul Brown
William Bonar
John Mills
Jacob Smitley
Elijah Stites
John Veach
Henry Jennings
Andrew Gray
John McKenna
Elisha Perkins
James Gunner
James Parker
Thomas Weekley
John Castile
Jacob Mills
Ziba Leonard
Abner Brown
Joseph Stewart
Isaiah Hoge
James Hook
Lewis Martin
Levi Harrod
Abel Bell
Robert Ross
William Ross
James Seals
Oldridge Chidester
John Oldridge
Job Walton
George Hoge
Davis Jennings
Cobus Linsecum
Ralph Smith
David Jennings
Amos Leonard
Andrew Gray

NOTE—Many other muster rolls are available to show that these men, located in Greene County borders, also served for varying periods of time:

Dennis Jones
Daniel Arnold
John Evans
John Hays
Edward McVay
George Morris
Edward Castile
Peter Hanks
Michael Cox
John Bills
Thomas Woolverton
Archibald Gray
James Milligan
James Blackburn
Andrew Cox
Jonah Garard
Jonathan Morris
Cyrennus Jennings
Joseph Eastwood
Jesse Rush
Alexander Jackson
James Steel

Others living across the present County lines also were in this Company.

Reference: Penna. Archives, Series VI, Vol. 2, pp. 20-21; pp. 253, etc.

Pennsylvania Militia

Years: 1781-82—First Battalion, Washington County. Recruited in the vicinity of Carmichaels, Greene County:

WILLIAM CRAWFORD, Captain

Richard Seaton, Lieutenant
Francis Seaton, Ensign
James Seaton, Clerk
John Garard, Sergeant
Abner Mundle, Sergeant
Alexander Finley, Sergeant

PRIVATES

Hugh Stephenson
Joseph Garard
Benjamin Hickson
Amos Gustin
William Smith
Zackariah Evans
John Brown
John Ivers
John Blair
John Armstrong
James Hazlett
Charles McDowell
John Broakin (?)
John Crawford
Richard Gregg
John Holton
Robert Lewis
John Gregg
William Gray
James Blair
Samuel McKee
Jeremiah Long
George Rankins
Thomas Askins
Charles Swan

William Hannah
Robert Cree
George Killgees
John McKee
John McClelland
Joseph Rankins
Peter Riley
Robert Kelso
Jacob Israel
Alexander Crawford
Thomas Trulock
James McClelland
Abraham Armstrong
John Davis
James Flenniken
John Provence
Joseph Garard
John Douglass
John Huston
Henry Franks
Robert McClelland
Francis Hannah
John Hill
Robert Ivers
John Jones

George Seaton
Thomas Garratt
Nicholas Shipman
George Gregg
Joseph Gwynne
James Winn
Bailey Johnson
William Hibbs
William McElroy
Jacob Blaney
Alexander Cowan
David Lewis
James Cummings
Hugh Johnston
David Casto
John Mundle
John Casto
Joseph Eastwood
William Diles (?)
Philip Neville
Samuel Barnhill
James Jones
Thomas Bowen
Clifton Bowen

NOTE—These men also served at times under Captain William Crawford:

Richard Gray
Aaron Luzada
John Askins
William Wright
Caleb Linsecum

Thomas Ishmael
Samuel McClelland
James McQuade
Levi Gregg
William Pyles
Joseph Gapen

Zebulon Lee
Edward Castile
Benjamin Hughes
James Jones
Samuel Shannon

It is to be noted that some of Captain William Crawford's men also served in other companies, even Officers of other Militia units served with him. This can be explained in the records that show he was one of the most active Patriots of the District and was often called out at a minute's notice. He would gather with him any members of the Militia who were handy and move rapidly to the points disturbed. One error that should be corrected in the Pennsylvania Archives is the placing of his Company in the Fifth Battalion. The Official Battalion reports show his Company was in the First Battalion, but the rosters of his Company are placed in the list of Fifth Battalion rolls. He was Captain of the Third Company of the First Battalion.

Reference: Penna. Archives, Series VI, Vol. 2; pp. 165-217, etc.

Pennsylvania Militia

Year: 1782—First Battalion, Washington County. Recruited in the vicinity of Garrard's Fort (Greene County).

JOHN HUSTON, Captain

Jacob Frazee, Lieutenant   Jonas Garrard, Ensign

Reference: Penna. Archives, Series VI, Vol. 2, pp. 217.

Pennsylvania Militia

Year: 1782—First Battalion, Washington County. Recruited in the vicinity of Fort Jackson (Waynesburg).

JAMES ARCHER, Captain

John Fee, Lieutenant   John Gray, Sergeant
David White, Ensign   John Bryan, Sergeant
     Stephen Styles, Sergeant

PRIVATES

Daniel Estill	James Stewart	Michael Archer
William Cathers	John Jones	Richard Stewart
Francis Feurt	William Inghram	John Reinhart
James Bradford	Alexander Moore	John Hathaway
Joseph Archer	Thomas Slater	George Sellars
Nathan Hughes	Daniel Stewart	William Carrol
Philip Newland	Arthur Inghram	George Fee
Ezekiel Morris	Israel White	Thomas Fee
Thomas Reinhart	Simeon Archer	Clifton Bowen
Hezekiah Stewart	Jacob Sellars	Samuel Miranda
Henry Huffman	Richard Morris	David Gray
Sebastian Sroufe	James Eagon	Leonard Sellars
(Crouse?)	Richard Jackson	George Lemley
William Wells	Robert Gorrel	Peter Dailey
Lot Leonard	David White	John Pursel (y?)
Barnet Reinhart	James Potter	William James
George Nott	David Owens	Samuel Hathaway
(Knotts?)	John Wiley	Elisha Wiley
John Thrasher	John Ankrom	John Burns
Joseph Reinhart	James Prickett	Barnet Eagon
	Rolin Hughes	

NOTE—All these men lived in what is now Franklin Township and Waynesburg, Greene County, Pennsylvania. Where it was possible to correct the spelling of the names, an effort has been made to do so.

Reference: Penna. Archives, Series VI, Vol. 2, pp. 17-18.

Pennsylvania Militia

Year: 1782—First Battalion, Washington County. Recruited in Whiteley and Greene Townships (now Greene County). A few from Dunkard.

JOHN GUTHREY, Captain

Eleazer Clegg, Lieutenant
Gideon Long, Ensign
Mathew Hanon, Sergeant

Richard Dotson, Sergeant
   (Dollison?)
John Roberts, Sergeant

PRIVATES

Baley Johnson
Ess Davis
John McMahon
Richard Pain
Nathaniel Kidd
John Clawson
David Flowers
Augustine Dillener
James Long
John Long
Zebidee Lee
John Six
  (Sykes?)
Nathan Curry
John Pettyjohn
William Notts
Charles McDowel
Solomon Hobbs

Thomas Flowers
Francis Hannah
Peter Yoho
John Evans, Jr.
Noah Long
Charles Scobey
Samuel Dutton
Jeremiah Long
Isaac Bozarth
Samuel Evans
William Masters
Michael Swope
Thomas Provence
William Hannah
William McCoy
John Brown
Benjamin Notts
Eliel Long

Henry Yoho
Aaron Jenkins
Elias Stone
David Long
John Douglass
William Robinson
Zachariah Evans
Henry Baker
Levi Hand
Benjamin Sutton
John Seryer
  (Sayer?)
Jeremiah Williams
Daniel Rinehart
George Evans
John Notts
Daniel Notts
Thomas Douglass

NOTE—These men also served tours with Captain John Guthery.

Samuel Swindler
Cecil Davis

John Minor
John Shipman

Reference: Penna. Archives, Series VI, Vol. 2, pp. 18-19, pp. 271.

Pennsylvania Militia

Year: 1782—First Battalion, Washington County. Recruited near Fort Lindley. Near present Greene County line.

JOHN MILLER, Captain

Cornelius Miller, Lieutenant
Henry Dickerson, Ensign
Gideon Dickerson, Sergeant
John Goble, Sergeant
John Lindley, Sergeant
Ephriam Bates, Sergeant
John Gwynne, Drummer

PRIVATES

Edward McVay
Zenas Lindley
Abraham Fordyce
Thomas Reynolds
George Atkinson, Ye first
James Tucker
Caleb Dille
Price Dille
Nathan Bane
Abram Hathaway
George Atkinson, 2d.
David Johnson
Benjamin McVay
John Carmichael
Daniel Axtell
James Hunter
Caleb Goble
Peter Hanks
Abram Lindley
Jacob Whosong
Timothy Ryan
Lawrence Craft
Ebeneezer Goble
Leonard Love
Patrick Allison
Francis Griffing
James Guffey
Dennis Carhill
Isaac McVay
Thomas Sargent
Stephen Carter
Stephen Sanders
Elihu Sanders
Thomas Axtell
Samuel Dille
Benjamin Goble
Daniel Parkhurst
James Johnson
Israel Dille
Noah Cook
Stephen Cook
John Whitten
Richard Hathaway
Samuel Craig
Ebeneezer Osborn
George Carter
Richard Lee
Isaac Dille
Joseph Bane
Caleb Lindley
Benjamin Rickey
Joseph Lindley
Jacob Whosong, Jr.
Abel Cook
David Dille
John Dille
Benjamin Royce
John Miller
Andrew Sheardine
John McVay
Thomas Craig
Nathan Hathaway
Joseph Pipes
Thomas Grim
William Craft
James Draper
Moses Williams
Jesse Bane
John Ryan
Jacob Rude
Daniel Veon
Joseph Col (Call?)
Conrad Whosong
Benjamin Frazee
Jabez Baldwin
Daniel Dodd
Mathew Golden
Ellis Bane
Daniel Crayne
Lewis Wright
Richard Sargent
Daniel Lindley
Isaac Bane

Reference: Penna. Archives, Series VI, Vol. 2, pp. 7, 8, 11-13, 217.

THE FORKS OF THE TENMILE

IN THE SEARCH for family records many unpublished facts of history have been uncovered, which add to the knowledge of this section, or correct previously written history which overlooked this source. These facts of history were too valuable to exclude them from the genealogical treatise being prepared. They formed the background for what was to follow. Whatever errors of genealogy that are found will be the same type as are usually found in works of this kind. Frequently when official data is missing, the genealogist has to depend upon family tradition or perfectly logical conclusions, which are sometimes wide of the mark.

The records most used are those taken from Bible records, Family Books, cemetery records, wills, estates, deeds, partition proceedings, quit claims, and all the usual sources of such material. Most diligent search has failed to locate the family records of some of the most prominent pioneers. At times two men of the same name are found living in the same neighborhood, so that it is impossible to say which is which. Where there is doubt, it shall be so noted.

In any such work, a plan must be selected which allows for systematic arrangement. Having chosen the title, "The Tenmile Country and Its Pioneer Families," it is our plan to take up first, those families that settled at the mouth of Tenmile and come up the South Branch of the stream to the head of the settlements. Now and then we shall enter allied families together rather than in the sections where they settled. After that we shall take up the pioneers on Ruffs Creek, Big and Little Whiteley Creeks, and Dunkard Creek. The few scattered families on Wheeling Creek within the boundaries of what is now Greene County will be written up if data and satisfactory material can be located. Some few families who settled on the North branch, but within the confines of the present County, shall be included. The families chosen will be those whose names appear in the earliest of records, such as those on deeds or land grants, those found in tax lists, military muster rolls, Church books, old ledgers, petitions, and the like. Not more than a few generations will be given in the history of each family, as it is most likely if these are shown, the later generations are known to the readers. Where family history gives records before coming to this section, some attention will be noted, in order to show the background of these pioneer families and the pattern of their migration.

As this part of the country has been settled for almost two hundred years, it is but natural that many names will be unfamiliar to the present generations. Some came here and left soon after; others sank roots into this fertile soil and left large family trees well known to the present day. This fact was forcibly recognized in the record-breaking charter enrollment of Fort Jackson Chapter, Sons of the American Revolution, which started out with more than 200 members.

The Tenmile enters the Monongahela River at the present town of Millsboro. To get an idea of what the Tenmile was like when the first hardy pioneers looked on the stream for the first time, one must look at it as it is today, for neither poet nor narrator has left any account of its pristine beauty. From people still living, we can get some idea of how it appeared before it was paralleled by railroads, and the scenery spoiled by mines and refuse dumps. It was deep enough at the mouth for towboats to tie up, and for a mile or more runs a straight course. Willows crowd the banks just as they must have done in the early days. Huge sycamores lean their broad trunks over the stream and from their tops one sees an occasional large crane fly from its nest high in the branches, while the lesser crane skims above the surface of the creek. Still greater trees of the same species lined the banks in the early days, for we learn from family traditions, that some of the pioneers spent their first hard winters securely holed up in the hollow trunks of some of these giants. The Tenmile is not wide at the mouth and the high hills on both sides of the creek attest to the big cutting job nature performed before the stream reached the mother river. We are told that in former days river steamers could occasionally make the trip up the Tenmile to Clarksville during high water.

It was to such surroundings that the Teagardens, Hupps, and Bumgarners came about the year of 1765. The history of the Teagardens in America begins with the arrival of Abraham Teagarden I, on the ship "Harle," in the year 1736. With him were the sons, Abraham Teagarden II, William and George Teagarden, the latter two not old enough to take the Oath of Allegiance, or to be listed among the ship's passengers. The family remained for a time in the vicinity of Philadelphia, but eventually, like so many of their Palatinate and German friends, drifted down into Maryland, where Abraham Teagarden II was living in Frederick County on December 12, 1757, when John Owens, the Indian trader at Fort Pitt, sold him land in the Tenmile Country, described as being between Enoch's Run and near the Mouth of Muddy Creek. (Washington County, Penna. Deed Book 1-A-214.) It is not certain just when this Abraham Teagarden first came into the Western Country, but it must have been shortly after this date, for General Boquet records that Teagarden passed Fort Littleton on his way to Fort Pitt, with four horses, on January 30, 1759, from which trip he returned from Fort Pitt, by way of Bedford, on February 28th of the same year. (Boquet Mss. 21644, Part 1, pp. 35 and 62). Abraham Teagarden II was one of the sutlers employed by Boquet at the time Boquet lists John Owens as one of the men living in the Lower Town at Fort Pitt. We may assume that Abraham Teagarden II's duties took him over both the new Forbes Road and the older Braddock Road through Fort Burd, where Boquet had a post under Sergeant Angus McDonald. In this way Teagarden became acquainted with the Redstone Country, where he finally settled at the present town of Brownsville. Here he built and operated a ferry over the Monongahela River, and lived for many years with other members of his family.

THE TEAGARDEN FAMILY

Abraham Teagarden II was born in Germany about 1718 and was married about 1744. It is a family tradition that after living to a good old age, at the site of his first settlement at Brownsville, he removed to the Tenmile and passed his last days in a cabin built for him by his son, George, on land long known as "Teagarden's Bottoms," situated where the present Pitt Gas Coal town now stands. His known children were:

1. William Teagarden, who was born January 17, 1746, at Philadelphia. He died in Richhill Township, Greene County, Pennsylvania about 1813. His wife, whom he married about 1774, was Bethia Craig.
2. Mary Teagarden, born April 15, 1747, in Frederick County, Maryland. She is said to have married John Shryock.
3. Abraham Teagarden III, born about 1748, died in Westmoreland County, Pennsylvania, about 1783. His wife was a widow, Mary Elizabeth (..........................) Parker. He was a member of Captain James Leech's Company, Westmoreland County Militia, and served in the Frontier Rangers. (Penna. Archives, Series III, Vol. 23, pp. 328).
4. George Teagarden, born June 29, 1750 (some say 1744), died in Greene County, Pennsylvania, about 1815. His wife was Rachel Pribble, born June 15, 1761, whose will gives the names of their children. Of whom later.
5. Aaron Teagarden, born 1754, died in Ohio in 1833. His wife was Margaret Debel or Debolt.
6. Moses Teagarden, born in 1762, died in Ohio in 1844. His wife was Mary Huston. He served in the Frontier Rangers with Abijah McClain and Thomas Hughes. Was probably in Lieutenant Richard Johnson's Company. (Penna. Archives, Series III, Vol. 23, pp. 325).
7. Thomas Teagarden. No record is available.
8. Elizabeth Teagarden (?) married George Debolt of Fayette County. He died there about 1828.

Family of William and Bethia (Craig) Teagarden

William Teagarden, eldest (?) son of Abraham Teagarden II, was born in Philadelphia on January 17, 1746. When but 11 years of age he appears to have accompanied his father on a sutler expedition during the General Henry Boquet Campaign, where he was the witness to the deed from John Owen at Fort Pitt on December 12, 1757. He later moved with his father to the Redstone settlement, where he lived until the time of his marriage. There is an interesting account of his marriage, as told by traditions among his descendants. In some way he seems to have legally acquired title to a tract of land on the Tenmile, although no official record shows him an owner in that section. It is most likely that he may have bought a part of the land owned officially by his brother, George Teagarden, near the town of Clarksville. At least the scene of the event of that day is placed in that locality, where it would seem, that following the custom of the times, his friends had gathered to build him a log cabin on the day he was married. At the site chosen the festivities had hardly begun when another claimant to the land appeared and disputed the ownership. The two claimants agreed to fight for the site; and in the battle that ensued, William Teagarden proved to be the better man, and the festivities proceeded without further hitch. The date of this event was just prior to the War of the Revolution in which William Teagarden took an active part.

Records indicate that he suffered wounds or was taken ill during one of his campaigns and was transferred to the Invalids Regiment where he was placed in Captain James McClean's Company. (Penna. Archives, Series V, Vol. 4, pp. 95). After returning from the War, the Continental currency, which he got for his services, proved worthless, and William Teagarden went with his neighbors, the Hupps, Stulls, Ferleys, Enochs, and others, to settle the unclaimed lands on Wheeling Creek, where he patented several tracts of land and spent the remainder of his life in the vicinity of Ryerson's Station in Richhill Township.

William Teagarden married, about 1774, Bethia Craig, who was born October 12, 1757, and died in Richhill Township, Greene County, in May, 1832. Her husband had died there in 1813. From Family records the names and birth dates of their children are taken.

Children of William and Bethia (Craig) Teagarden

1. Abraham Teagarden, born February 19, 1775, and died August 31, 1853. Married, about 1804, Anna McGuire. They were parents of 12 children, many of whom settled in Iowa.

    ### Children of Abraham and Anna (McGuire) Teagarden
    1. George Teagarden, born October 5, 1805.
    2. Elizabeth Teagarden, born.................... She married William Burt.
    3. Isaac Teagarden. Married Sarah Ann Parker.
    4. Mary Ann Teagarden, married Lewis Fields. Removed to Iowa.
    5. Bethia Teagarden. Married Joseph Seaman. Removed to Iowa.
    6. Eleanor Teagarden. Married Stephen Craft. Removed to Iowa.
    7. William Teagarden.
    8. Katherine Teagarden. Married William Booth.
    9. Charity Teagarden. Married George Frazier.
    10. John Teagarden. Died in infancy.
    11. Lydia Teagarden. Married William Trussell. Removed to Kansas.
    12. Jesse C. Teagarden. Died in Iowa.
2. Isaac Teagarden. Born May 3, 1776. Never married.
3. Jacob Teagarden. Born December 23, 1777. Married, in 1806, Elsie McGuire.
4. John B. Teagarden. Born October 21, 1779. Married, in 1805, Rosa McGuire.
5. George Teagarden. Born August 21, 1781. Married Abby................
6. William Teagarden, Jr. Born April 21, 1783. Died before 1829. He married, in 1819, Mary Holmes, who, after the death of her husband, married (2) Robert Cummins. They were parents of:
    1. Nancy Teagarden, who married John Chase.
    2. Nelson Teagarden, who wife's name was Elizabeth ....
    3. Hamilton Teagarden, whose wife was Sarah Ann ....
    4. Bethia Teagarden.
    5. Rachel Teagarden.
    6. William Teagarden. Died prior to 1845.
7. Elizabeth Teagarden. Born June 4, 1785. Married, in 1809, Daniel Clark.
8. Mary Teagarden. Born July 8, 1787.
9. Susan Teagarden. Born July 20, 1789. Married John P. Lindley.
10. Samuel Teagarden. Born August 17, 1791. Married Catherine McGuire

11. Artimissa Teagarden. Born March 31, 1793. Married .... Tucker.
12. Bethia Teagarden. Born October 31, 1794. Married Ezekiel Lyons.
13. Agnes (Nancy) Teagarden. Born December 18, 1796. Died December 21, 1880. Married John Cummins, who was born June 21, 1795, and died October 2, 1856.

GEORGE TEAGARDEN FAMILY

George Teagarden, son of Abraham Teagarden II, was born in Maryland on June 29, 1750. He came to the Tenmile Country with his father before 1768 for in that year he bought a tract of land from John Peters, described as being of Westmoreland County, Pennsylvania. (This is an error, for Westmoreland was not set up at that date, and the part wherein John Peters lived, became first a part of Westmoreland and later Fayette County). The land bought from Peters, is described as being "a tract of land situated one mile from the Monongahela River on Tenmile Creek, which had been improved by John Peters in 1765." This deed was filed in Washington County, Pennsylvania, on April 15, 1782, along with another given to George Teagarden on April 20, 1769, by Richard Ashcraft, which called for "uncertain lands" on the West side of the Monongahela River. (See Washington County Deed Book 1-A-pp. 62-63). The land at the south side of the mouth of the Tenmile, warranted to John Hupp in June, 1769, was also bought by George Teagarden and patented to him. On March 16, 1770, George Teagarden sold some of his land on the west side of the Monongahela to Philomen (Felix) Askins. (Washington County Deed Book 1-C, pp. 163). It was George Teagarden and not David as reported erroneously by Evans, and copied by Waychoff, who settled in the Clarksville section, and was the ancestor of that branch of the family, and there is no evidence to support the report that a David Teagarden existed at the early date. A William Teagarden, who witnessed one of the above deeds, and who witnessed the deeds of John Owens to Abraham Teagarden in 1757, was a brother of George, and became the ancestor of the Ryerson Station branch, although he lived for a time on the lower Tenmile. If George served in the Washington County, Pennsylvania, Militia, he must have been a member of Captain Jesse Pigman's Company, which was drafted from that part of the country wherein he lived. We are of the opinion that he was the George Tegard who served in Captain William Huston's Company of Cumberland County, Pennsylvania, Militia, under Colonel Samuel Culbertson in 1780. The Abraham Tegard who was in the same company would have been his brother. (Pennsylvania Archives, Series V, Vol. 6, pp. 269-283). After coming to the Tenmile Country, George Teagarden married Rachel Pribble, who was born June 15, 1761, and who was probably the daughter of Thomas Pribble, Sr. He was one of the witnesses to the aforementioned John Peters deed, and had settled on land bought from John Rice, founder of Rices Landing. George Teagarden died in Greene County about 1815 without leaving a will. His estate was administered by Thomas Fletcher and Thomas Teagarden. (Estate No. 245 probated August 9, 1815). His widow survived him by three years, and left a will in which she names her two daughters and son, Isaac Teagarden, as her heirs. (Estate 310, probated May 5, 1818). A partition proceedings in Orphans Court shows that the estate of George Teagarden was divided into eleven shares for distribution among his eleven children, all of whom are named, nine sons and two daughters. (O. C. Docket 1, pp. 132). The sons bought the shares of the two sisters after which a deed of record shows that the sons divided the land nine ways in accordance with a plan proposed by their father before death. The girls accepted $1200 for their shares. (Deed Book 4. pp. 667).

Children of George and Rachel (Pribble) Teagarden

1. William Teagarden, removed to Columbiana County, Ohio. His wife was Susannah Rofelty, whose family was massacred while the father was away, and she joined her husband in a deed of record. (Greene County Deed Book 6, pp. 401, dated April 14, 1828).
2. Abraham Teagarden, went to Ohio, dying in Montgomery County before 1838. His widow, Rebecca, married for her second husband Abraham Powers. (Greene County Deed Book 6. pp. 314).
3. Isaac Teagarden, died in Greene County a few years after his parents. (Estate No. 372, probated June 19, 1821, by his brother, Abraham Teagarden.
4. Jeremiah Teagarden, went to Bracken County, Kentucky, with his wife, Catherine Thomas. (Greene County Deed Book 8, pp. 337, dated December 16, 1819).
5. Thomas Teagarden, married Sarah Hiller, daughter of William and Margaret (Myers) Hiller. (Deed Book 7, pp. 75, dated September 5, 1829, Greene County).
6. George Teagarden, Jr., whose wife, Sarah ...., joined him in a deed dated March 14, 1826. (Greene County Deed Book 8, pp. 338).
7. Aaron Teagarden. No record.
8. Moses Teagarden married Margaret Hupp, daughter of Everhard and Margaret Hupp. They sold land to Michael Bowser on September 22, 1821. (Greene County Deed Book 4, pp. 673).
9. Job Teagarden, with his wife Seeley (Druscilla) while living in Mason County, Virginia, executed a deed on October 1, 1818. (Greene County Deed Book 4, pp. 159).
10. Polly Teagarden, married William Enochs.
11. Rachel Teagarden, married Kinsey Virgin, son of Captain Rezin Virgin, who lived across the Monongahela from the Teagardens. Rachel and her husband removed to Illinois.

Thomas Pribble, Sr., probable father-in-law of George Teagarden, who in 1768 was a witness in the John Peters to George Teagarden deed, was owner of a tract of land on Enoch's Run, (later Pumpkin Run) which had been surveyed to John Rice, and conveyed by Rice on April 24, 1787, to Thomas Pribble, Sr. Then in 1794 Thomas sold a portion of this land to Richard Swan, another portion to Job Priddle, and a third portion to Midian Garwood. (Washington County Deed Book 1-I-890, 1-K-94, 1-L-208.) From the list of signers of a petition for the formation of a new state to be called Westsylvania, sent the Continental Congress, we get the impression that Thomas Pribble, Sr., was the father of Thomas, Jr., Job, and Reuben Pribble, whose names are grouped together. A Stephen Pribble was in Jesse Pigman's Company and Stephen's son, James Pribble, got a pension from Pendleton County, Kentucky. The Pribbles seem to have migrated to that state about 1794.

THE HUPP FAMILY

Sometime before 1769, Crumrine says in 1766, Everhard Hupp came from Culpepper County, Virginia, to settle near the mouth of Tenmile. The location which he chose was at the place later known as Blackdog Hollow, about opposite where the first bridge spans the creek. Here he built a sizable cabin, which became a place of entertainment (perhaps for a price) for the immigrants, as well as a temporary stopping place. Famous personages are said to have stopped at Hupps, including George Washington on one of his western trips. We are told that one of the main attractions at Hupp's place was his wife, the former Margaret Thomas, who it is reliably claimed, was the first white woman to settle west of the Monongahela River. With Everhard Hupp were his brothers, John, Phillip, Frank, and probably George Hupp, since tradition states there were five bothers. Everhard Hupp was not long in seeing the possibilities of the section and bought land adjoining his original claim. Later he purchased two more tracts further up Tenmile Creek near the present village of Tenmile. He does not seem to have been disturbed by the Indians at any period, perhaps due to the fact that his hospitality was extended to white and redmen alike. He took an active part in the Revolutionary War, serving for a time as a lieutenant in Captain Robert Sweeney's Company, Fifth Battalion of Washington County Militia. Family traditions report that Everhard Hupp lived to the ripe age of 109 years and that his wife was 105 when she died. They were the ancestors of the Clarksville Hupps.

Children of Everhard and Margaret (Thomas) Hupp

1. Elizabeth Hupp. Born 1770.
2. George Hupp, born 1772, who remained on the home farm near Clarksville.
3. Annie Hupp. Born 1775.
4. Lewis (or Rezin) Hupp. Born 1776.
5. John Hupp, son of Everhard and Margaret (Thomas) Hupp, was born near Clarksville in 1778, according to the records of Mr. J. C. Hupp of Fairmont, West Virginia. Mr. Hupp notes, however, that he had seen the old sandstone marker, near the mining town of Besco, which stated that John Hupp died October 16, 1839, at the age of 66 years and 16 days, which would place his birth as 1773. His wife was Hannah Homer (Horner?)

Children of John Hupp

1. Uriah Hupp, married Marinda Cox, born December 21, 1831. Died November 19, 1899.

Children of Uriah Hupp

1. Elizabeth Hupp. Born August 2, 1852. Married William T. Arnold.
2. Abigail Hupp. Born February 23, 1854. Married Frank Miles.
3. Jane Hupp. Born March 4, 1856. Married Stiers Sharpnack.
4. Aaron Hupp. Born January 28, 1858. Died 1935. Married Emma Moore.
5. John Hupp. Born November 28, 1859. Married Caroline Miles. Lived near Amity, Pennsylvania.
6. Mina Hupp. Born September 16, 1861. Married William Teagarden.
7. Sarah Hupp. Born October 6, 1863. Married Henry Murray.
8. Harry Hupp. Born July 14, 1865. Married Jessie Craig.
9. David Hupp. Born August 2, 1866. Died in infancy.
10. William Hupp. Born February 17, 1870. Married Mary Rose Horner.
11. Alonzo Hupp. Born 1873. Married Anna Miller.

12. Frank Hupp. Born April 2, 1878. Married Clara Kelly.
6. Phillip Hupp, son of Everhard and Margaret (Thomas) Hupp, was born October 4, 1781. He married, November 9, 1815, Phoebe Johnson, born February 13, 1789. Phillip Hupp was a soldier in the War of 1812.

Children of Phillip Hupp

1. Imri Hupp. Born August 21, 1816.
2. Isaac Hupp. Born October 3, 1819. Kept a tavern at New Freeport.
3. Izra Bailey Hupp. Born December 19, 1820. He was a tailor by trade and a fox hunter by inclination. Moved first to Wetzel County, Virginia, and then to Fairmont.
4. Phoebe Ann Hupp. Born March 20, 1822.
5. Ellis Hadley Hupp. Born February 24, 1825.
6. Eli Lindley Hupp. Born October 6, 1826.

7. Francis Hupp, son of Everhard and Margaret (Thomas) Hupp, was born in 1784. He married Martha Debolt, daughter of George and Ann (Long) Debolt.

Children of Francis Hupp

1. George Hupp.
2. Margaret (Peggy) Hupp. Married .... Whitlatch.
3. Harriet Hupp. Married William Riggle.
4. Clarissa Hupp. Died young. Buried in Lazier Cemetery.
5. Everhard Hupp. Born November 18, 1824. Died September 10, 1895. Married Hannah Scherich. Born June 5, 1835; died September, 1921. Grandparents of J. C. Hupp, who supplied the records.

8. Michael Hupp. Born 1786. Served in the War of 1812. Died in Warren County, Ohio. He lived for a time in Columbiana County, Ohio.
9. David Hupp. Born 1789.
10. Henry Hupp. Born 1790.
11. Margaret Hupp. Born 1793. She married Moses Teagarden.

John Hupp, brother of Everhard Hupp, was born in 1747 and came to the Tenmile with his brother, settling at the mouth of Tenmile on the Greene County side. His application (No. 3319) obtained for him a warrant on June 3, 1769, for 131 acres, which he later sold to George Teagarden, who eventually patented the tract. After selling out on the Tenmile, John Hupp settled in Ohio County, Virginia, in that part which later became Donegal Township, Washington County, Pennsylvania. Here he patented two tracts of land and here, on October ...., 1777, he took the prescribed Oath of Allegiance to the Commonwealth of Virginia. Here also, on October 15, 1777, George Hupp took the same Oath, both being sworn by Thomas Waller, which leads us to the conclusion that George Hupp was living near or with his brother, John Hupp, at the time, and that he was the fifth member of the family to settle in the West. John Hupp was killed at Miller's Block House, near West Alexander, on Easter Sunday, 1782. His wife was Anne Rowe, a daughter of Adam Rowe. She was one of the children of Adam Rowe who escaped the Rowe massacre near Wheeling. This Rowe massacre appears in the West Virginia histories, and is noted by William Harrod, Jr., in his interview with Draper. The descendants of this pioneer John Hupp became very famous people in West Virginia Medical History and have left a good genealogy of the family.

Children of John and Anne (Rowe) Hupp

1. John Hupp, Jr. Born 1780. Married, 1813, Ann Cox. They were the parents of Dr. John Cox Hupp, Joseph Hupp, Isaac Hupp and Louisa Hupp, wife of John Clemmens.
2. Margaret Hupp. She married .... Titus.
3. Elizabeth Hupp. She married Francis Rogers.
4. Mary Hupp. She married .... Smith.

Clarksville is situated at the forks of the Tenmile, about three miles from where the stream joins the Monongahela River. Here the north fork of Tenmile, after draining a portion of northern Greene County and southern Washington County, joins with the south fork, which performs a like service to central Greene County. The broad bottom lands at the forks were a natural place to build a town, since the products of the many grist mills that grew up on both branches of Tenmile, had to pass this junction. The location was further enhanced by an early road that ran from Parkinson's Ferry (Monongahela City) to the mouth of the Cheat. The land on which the town was built may have been a part of the "uncertain" tract of land sold by Richard Ashcraft to George Teagarden, but the heirs of George Bumgarner made the first deed for the land, when they sold it to Henry Enochs, Jr., on February 23, 1787. In the recital of this deed the record states that Pennsylvania had made a grant of the land to George Bumgarner on June 3, 1769; however, Henry Enochs, Jr., took out the first patent. In 1787 the adjoining neighbors were Zachius (Tichnicus) Rose, John Miller, John Shidler, and Andrew Wise. (Washington County Deed Book 1-C, pp. 269). It is likely that the Fort George, erected at Clarksville, but which missed the notoriety of a massacre, was named for George Bumgarner or George Teagarden.

The town which sprang up at the forks, developed quite a number of industries, and became at one time, of first importance in the County. In addition to servicing the many grist mills on both branches of Tenmile, tanneries, woolen mills, and distilleries, did much business with lower river points. A vein of iron ore was opened up across the creek, from which iron was smelted for local consumption. A hundred years ago the town was one of the busiest in the county. Then it seems to have lapsed into a lethargy, which was broken by the coal operations that sprang up following World War I. Perhaps the busiest time in the whole existence of the town came during the Civil War days. When Morgan made his foray into the North and threatened Greene County, the entire county was jittery for a few days and nights. Farmers began to drive their cattle to safer places, and Clarksville was on the main route to safety. As the droves of cattle were passing through at all hours of the day and night, it is related that the night marches, with their torches, made a weird sight, and that the calls from the inhabitants, from one darkened home to another, made a never-to-be-forgotten bedlam. Scarcely had one drove passed through the town until another would be heard approaching. Cries of "Who's cattle goes now," would be shouted from one window, and from up the street would come back an answering cry, "Eli Long's Cattle," or, "Andy Lantz's Cattle," etc. Throughout the nights these cries would continue, and they made a lasting impression on the writer's father-in-law, a boy of ten, so vivid that seventy years later he could recall the scenes.

George Bumgarner was a native of Culpepper County, Virginia, when he joined the Hupps in their trek to the Tenmile, about 1768. He took title to the land at the mouth of Tenmile, where the town of Millsboro now stands. In a manner not known he got possession of the land, where Clarksville was later built, and received a title to warrant it on June 3, 1769, from the Pennsylvania authorities. George Bumgarner died about 1787, leaving but two "rightful" heirs, Jesse Bumgarner and Frederick Bumgarner. Jesse Bumgarner married Catherine Wise, only daughter of Frederick Wise, and retained the land at the mouth of Tenmile. Frederick Bumgarner, who seems to have remained in Culpepper County, Virginia, got the Clarksville land, which he sold, on February 23, 1787, to Henry Enochs, Sr. (Washington County Deed Book 1-Z-407, DB. 1-P-4, DB. 1-O-65—281-83).

THE BUMGARNER FAMILY

Jesse Bumgarner, son of George Bumgarner, of Culpepper County, Virginia, was the founder of Millsboro, at the mouth of Tenmile Creek, which town he laid out in 1809. His first wife was Catherine Wise, daughter of Frederick Wise, founder of Fredericktown. After her death he married Elizabeth .... He first made his will on February 21, 1839, but after successive deaths of sons named in the will, he added codicils on March 24, 1843, and on February 2, 1846. He died in the latter year and his will was probated in Washington on July 18, 1846. He was a very old man at the time of his death and it would appear his second wife had also preceded him, as she is not named. His children were:

Children Named by Jesse Bumgarner in Will

1. Joel Bumgarner, called the eldest son. Died before 1839. His wife was Lydia ....
    1. David Bumgarner.
    2. John Bumgarner.
    3. Elizabeth Bumgarner. Married .... Davis.
2. Jesse Bumgarner, Jr., named second son in will. Wife was Catherine .... He died between 1839 and 1843, leaving:
    1. Samuel Bumgarner.
    2. Frederick Bumgarner.
    3. Harriet Bumgarner.
    4. Malvina Bumgarner.
3. George W. Bumgarner, executor with Moses Phillips.
    1. Samuel Robert Bumgarner.
4. Abraham Bumgarner. Wife was Rebecca .... He died about 1843-46.
5. Elizabeth Bumgarner. Married Moses Phillips.
6. Rachel Bumgarner. Married .... Evans.
7. Hannah Bumgarner. Married .... Dille.
8. Susannah Bumgarner. Married .... McCoy.

THE ENOCH FAMILY

It is not surprising to find the Enoch Family among the first of those to settle on the West side of the Monongahela River in the Tenmile Country. Certainly these hardy sons of Henry Enoch, Sr., whom we shall designate as Henry Enoch I, had plenty of glowing accounts of "the land over the mountains," related to them by visitors to their father's home in Hampshire County, Virginia. Men like George Washington, Christopher Gist, and Thomas Cresap, made the home of Henry Enoch I a stopping place worthy of comment in their records. Since these men knew the back country since the early days of the Ohio Company, it is most likely that their stories of the land to be had for the asking, would have been a constant subject for conversation at Enoch's table and around his hospitable hearth. Perhaps Henry Enoch or some of his sons even accompanied one or all of these men on their survey tours, just as Henry Enoch acted as chain bearer for George Washington in the Fairfax Grant. Certainly they had been to the Tenmile Country before 1757 and gave their name to "Enoch's Run," (later known as Swan's Run and now Pumpkin Run, which empties into the Monongahela at Rices Landing) as shown by the deed of John Owens, in 1757, to Abraham Teagarden. This run is so called in other deeds and on some early maps. There is nothing to show that the Enochs built a cabin or planted crops on this land to claim it, and they may only have surveyed it and gave their name to the stream, nor is it quite clear where they made their first improvement in the Tenmile Country, but Henry Enoch II was among those in the Springhill Township Tax Lists for 1772, and one family was living on Dunkard Creek before the Revolution. It is also probable that they had selected land on Wheeling Creek at an early date. When the controversy over the boundary had been settled by Virginia and Pennsylvania, the Enochs began recording their land under Pennsylvania grants, and they are to be found owning tracts on North and South Tenmile, Dunkard Creek, and Wheeling Creek, and their methods of obtaining some of this land is shown in deeds of record.

A history of the family by Arthur L. Keith, Northfield, Minnesota, and published in Volume 4 of Tyler's Quarterly Magazine, has this to say of Henry Enoch I: "The first record of the Enochs is from the journal of George Washington, who, when a young man, made surveys in Hampshire County. The journal shows that on April 23, 1750, George Washington surveyed land for Henry Enoch in the forks of the Cacaphon to the extent of 388 acres, John Keith acting as chainman and John Constant as marker. On April 25, 1750, he surveyed another tract for John Newton, about a mile above said forks, beginning at Henry Enoch's Corner, with the same men as chainman and marker. The next day Washington surveyed a tract of 200 acres on the South branch of Little Cacaphon for John Parker, with Henry Enoch (probably Jr.) as chainman.

"In Hennings Statutes, Vol. VII, pp. 18, we find that in 1756 a line of forts were proposed, to start at Henry Enoch's place on the Great Cacaphon in Hampshire County, Virginia. (Maryland Archives, Vol. XXXI, pp. 247-253).

"Land records at Richmond give the following records: Henry Enoch of Frederick County (Hampshire County. originally a part of Frederick), received a grant of 388 acres on Cacaphon Creek on April 22, 1753, evidently the land surveyed by Washington. In 1761 he received a grant for 271½ acres and in 1762 a grant of 38 acres. In this last grant he is called Henry Enoch, Sr. In 1763 he got another grant of 100 acres, all of these being on the Cacaphon. In 1764 he got a grant of 57 acres in Enoch's Hollow. In 1765 Henry Enoch, Jr., got a grant of 308 acres of land situated between French's and Little Cacaphon. Enoch Enoch received a grant of 168 acres at the neck of the Potomac River in Frederick County on September 3, 1753.

"On August 10, 1762, in Hampshire County, Henry Enochs also spelled Enoch in deed, and wife, Elizabeth, sold land on Little Cacaphon to George Untis, said land granted to Enoch, February 20, 1761. Henry Enoch, Sr., and wife, Elizabeth, on February 14, 1765, sold land on South side of Great Cacaphon to William Bowells, witnesses to the deed being William Creacraft, Jeremiah York, and John Corbly, along with Henry Enoch, Jr. Then, on May 10, 1779, Henry Enoch and wife, Elizabeth, sold 134 acres of land at the forks of Great Cacaphon and North River, to Enoch Enoch. The last deed of Henry Enoch, Sr., is one dated August 1, 1782, selling land in

Enoch's Hollow, on both sides of Hollow Branch, which runs into North Rivers of Cacaphon, to John Chenoweth. Enoch Enoch was a witness of this deed.

"The Census of 1782 for Virginia shows Enoch Enoch head of a family of thirteen whites in Hampshire County, and Henry Enoch head of a family of two white persons. The Census for the same locality shows Enoch Enoch head of the same family, but Henry Enoch is not listed, instead we find Elizabeth Enoch the head of the family, indicating that Henry Enoch, Sr., died between the dates of the two censi. On July 26, 1788, Enoch Enoch and wife, Rebecca, indenture one James Sargent, who in 1790, bought land from Henry Enoch and wife, Sarah, of Washington County, Pennsylvania."

There can be little doubt about these records, which have to do with the Enoch Family through this period of years before they appear in Western Pennsylvania, nor with Mr. Keith's statement that the Enochs began to appear on the Tenmile about 1770. It is even probable that some of the family were on Dunkard Creek and possibly on Wheeling Creek, at least for survey of the land, before that date, although no actual settlement on the latter creek took place until after the Revolution. In respect to this settlement, Mrs. Myrtle Work Richey of Washington County, Pennsylvania, throws considerable light. She quotes a deed, the wording of which indicates that Henry Enoch II had made some sort of improvement at the place he was selling on Wheeling Creek, which, in his words, was "land which was taken up in Augusta County, Virginia, in 1777." As most authorities are in agreement that this part of Greene County was a sort of "no-man's land" during the Revolution, it is most certain that the land was not inhabited by him at that time. Further records show also that he was at the forks of the two branches of Tenmile at that time, for both he and son Henry Enoch III are found in militia lists from the Clarksville section at that period, and that Henry Enoch II was serving with his militia battalion, of which he was colonel, and had his headquarters at Fort Jackson as can be seen from several pension applications. The deed quoted by Mrs. Richey reads: "The said tract of four hundred acres of land, the same, more or less, including my actual settlement, and situated, lying, and being on the said forks of Dunkard and Wheeling Creeks, supposed at the time of granting the certificate, to be in the County of Ohio in the Commonwealth of Virginia, but by the extention of the line of the Western Boundaries of Pennsylvania, in the Commonwealth of Pennsylvania," etc. The deed was made February 12, 1788, to Thomas Ryerson and may be identified as the land on which the present Wind Ridge is built, and not Ryerson's Station as it is known today. It was probably here that William Enoch, son of Henry Enoch II, built the fort known as Fort Enoch about the close of the Revolution.

Mr. Keith surmises that since no will of the Henry Enoch I has been found, that he must have been the father of Henry Enoch II, and of Enoch Enoch, David Enoch, Mary Enoch, wife of Isaac Cox, Sarah Enoch, wife of Gabriel Cox, and possibly others. To this list might be added the names of John Enoch, who settled on Dunkard Creek, a Daniel Enoch, Sr., who patented a tract of land near Lone Pine, and possibly the wife of John Cox, whose warranted land on Dunkard Creek, fell to the heirs of an Enoch Enoch who was killed there by the Indians in 1775. Of these possibilities we shall write later.

Of the children of Henry Enoch I, Mr. Keith is of the opinion that Enoch Enoch was the only one who remained in Hampshire County, Virginia, where he was listed as the head of a family of thirteen whites in 1782, yet he could have been the man of that name who served in Captain John Wetsel's Company of Rangers in 1778.

From 1786 the record is less speculative, for on October 25, 1786, Henry Enoch II (called Henry Enoch, Sr.,) bought a tract of land of some three hundred acres, situated at the Forks of Tenmile Creek, from Frederick Bumgarner of Culpepper County, Virginia, son of George Bumgarner, who had obtained the land by a grant from Pennsylvania, dated June 3, 1769. (Washington County Deed Book 1-G—pp. 269). Here it was probably a part of a tract of uncertain description, sold by Richard Ashcraft to George Teagarden on April 20, 1769, and John Peters to George Teagarden in 1768, described as land on which Peters had made an improvement in 1765, a mile from the mouth of Tenmile. It is doubtful that Teagarden's deed held. (Washington County Deed Book 1-A—62-63). It was here that Henry Enoch II built his home and spent the remainder of his days. On June 13, 1786, he was issued a warrant for this tract as Henry Enoch, Jr., registering the title "Mount Pleasant," which was patented June 2, 1799, by Henry Enoch, Jr., (III) following the death of his father. Two hundred acres of it was deeded previously on January 18, 1794, to Henry Enoch III by Henry and Sarah Enoch, and a similar deed for 34 acres was deeded on January 18, 1796, to his son, William Enoch, by Henry Enoch alone, indicating that Sarah had died within this two-year period. (Washington County Deed Book 1-L—820 and 1-M—252). An article of agreement had been signed by Henry Enoch II and his son, Isaac Enoch, on October 23, 1790, by which Isaac was to take care of his father and mother until their death, for which Isaac was to get the home plantation and saw mill. Isaac Enoch got a warrant for this part under the title "Essex" on May 5, 1796, but it was sold to pay debts and William Bell got the patent to it. The balance of the land was sold by sheriff when Isaac Enoch got into financial difficulties in 1808 and Ellis Nichols bought the land.

For a list of the revolutionary services of Henry Enoch II we turn to Pennsylvania Archives, Series VI, Volume 2, pp. 3, 7, 75, 217, 249, and to pension applications of soldiers who served under him. He served on the Committee of Observation for that part of Augusta County that lies on the west side of Laurel Hill at Pittsburgh, chosen the 16th day of May, 1775. He was also Lieutenant-Colonel of the First Battalion, Washington County, Pennsylvania, Militia. Records also show that he went out on tours of duty at other times with his son, Henry Enoch III.

Henry Enoch II died about 1797, without a will. The record of his estate is in Greene County Will Book 1, pp. 7, Estate No. 6, which was probated September 12, 1797, letters being taken out at that time by Benjamin Bell, a son-in-law. In the papers of the estate are found the names of the heirs and children of Henry and Sarah Enoch II. The names of the children are given in Mrs. Richey's Manuscript, to which we have added items gleaned from official records.

Children of Henry and Sarah Enoch

1. Henry Enoch III. Born 1748. Wife's name was Elizabeth .... He served in the Continental Army for which he received depreciation pay. (Penna. Archives, Series V, Vol. 4, pp. 399). He also served in Captain Benjamin Stites' Company and other detachments of militia in his part of Washington County. On June 6, 1804, he was living in Wood County, (West) Virginia. He was given a part of the home plantation by his father.
2. Enoch Enoch. Born in 1750. Married Mary (Doughty?). He served in Captain Ezekiel Rose's Company of Washington County, Pennsylvania, Militia. (Penna. Archives, Series VI, Vol. 2, pp. 321). We are of the opinion that it was in his home near Lone

Pine, that the Baptist Meetings were held in 1773. While living in Ohio County, (West) Virginia, in 1798, he and wife, Mary, deeded land to Abijah McClain, who had married Permelia Doughty. (Greene County Deed Book 1, pp. 251). He and son, Enoch, were in William Crawford's Company in 1793.

3. Isaac Enoch. Born 1752. He patented land under the title "Essex." Got the house and mill on Henry Enoch's plantation. Served in the Washington County Militia. He sold land in 1798, and in 1808 was sold out by the sheriff of Greene County.
4. Sarah Enoch. Born in 1754. Married .... Bell. A Samuel Bell and a William Bell lived near the Enochs at Clarksville.
5. David Enoch. Born 1756, according to Mrs. Richey, who also states he married Elizabeth Peck, by whom he had a list of children, who in Crumrine's History of Washington County, are given to David Enoch, Jr. From the cemetery records of North Tenmile Baptist Church, we are sure that Crumrine was correct.
6. William Enoch. Born 1758. Served in Captain Benjamin Stites' Militia Company. Owned land near Clarksville, but appears to have moved to Wheeling Creek. William Harrod, Jr., told Draper that Captain William Enoch was a son of Colonel Henry Enoch, and was present when Abraham Enoch and others were killed on Captina Creek, following the Indians who had killed the Crow sisters in 1793.
7. Ann Enoch. Born 1760. Married Patrick Galloway, and had a son, Enoch Galloway, mentioned in the estate of Henry Enoch II. She probably died before her father.
8. Hannah Enoch. Born 1766. Married Thomas Pribble, son of Thomas Pribble, whose family lived near Rices Landing until after the Revolution, when they removed to Pendleton County, Kentucky.
9. Elizabeth Enoch. Born 1770. Married Benjamin Bell, son of Nathaniel and Hannah Bell. He was born in 1751 and married in 1788. Died in Boone County, Iowa, on February 10, 1853. His wife died in Indiana. Benjamin Bell was administrator of Henry Enoch's estate.

Children of Benjamin and Elizabeth (Enoch) Bell

1. Isaac Bell.
2. Elizabeth Bell. Married James Mitchell.
3. Henry Bell.
4. Amy Bell.
5. Nathaniel Bell. Born January 15, 1807. Married Celia Wright.
6. Nancy Bell.
7. Benjamin Bell.
8. Sarah Bell. Born 1790. Married (1) Joseph Williams, (2) Joseph Murray.
9. Jane Bell. Married Levi Mann.

From Crumrine we get the information that David Enoch, Sr., was a brother of Colonel Henry Enoch of Clarksville, although Crumrine says Colonel John Enoch an error by proven records. Quoting North Tenmile Baptist Church records, he says that the first meeting of that Church was held December 1, 1773, at the home of Enoch Enoch near the present village of Lone Pine. Then from the same records it is shown that on February 4, 1774, a meeting was held at the home of David Enoch in the Bane Settlement of North Tenmile. Again in this Church record it is found that David Enoch represented his Church at the Associated Meeting of all the Baptist Churches west of the Laurel Ridge, held at Great Bethel on October

7, 1776. This same David Enoch was in the first jury for the newly-formed Washington County, on June 17, 1781. He may have been the David Enoch who warranted a tract of land under the title of "Beautiful," in what is now Washington Township, Greene County, on November 17, 1787, a tract but one farm removed from that of his son, David Enoch, Jr., near the village of Tenmile. It is probable that both he and his son, David Enoch, Jr., served in the Frontier Rangers, where the name is found, and he may be the David Enoch who served in Captain George Myers' Company of Washington County Militia. In the Census of 1790 he is listed with a family of two grown adult males, two sons under 16 years, and three females. His son, David, lived nearby as shown in the list.

1. David Enoch, Jr., whose tombstone record in the North Tenmile Baptist Cemetery, says he died May 7, 1837, at the age of 70 years. If this record is correct, he was only 17 years of age when he had warranted to him on June 29, 1785, a tract of 300 acres of land, lying on the south bank of North Tenmile Creek, which was patented to Phillip Swart on November 29, 1787. Crumrine says he was twice married and tombstone records indicate this is correct, with his second wife being E(lizabeth) ...., for there are burials of three children of D. and E. Enoch, all in November, 1832, and aged 4, 6, and 8 years, they being George W., William, and Andrew J., respectively. By the two marriages, David Enoch, Jr., was father of fourteen children, and Crumrine gives this list as being:

Children of David and Elizabeth (Peck) Enoch

1. Elizabeth, wife of James Auton, who removed to Gallipolis, Ohio.
2. David Enoch, who married Susan Bigler and moved to Richhill Township, Greene County.
3. Sarah Enoch, wife of James Lowrey.
4. Eunice Enoch, wife of Henry Gardner.
5. Henry Enoch, who married Sarah Rees.
6. Cynthia Enoch, wife of Levi Sowers.
7. Margaret Enoch, married and moved to Greene County.
8. Abner Enoch, who married Elizabeth Davis.
9. Catherine Enoch, wife of Leonard Guthrie of Greene County.
10. Hiram Enoch.
11. George W. Enoch. Died November, 1832, aged 4 years, 7 months.
12. Andrew Enoch. Died November, 1832, aged 8 years, 10 months.
13. William Enoch. Died November, 1832, aged 6 years and 5 months.
14. ....

(The following is a record of the same family, but from another authority):

David Enoch. Born, 1756. Married Elizabeth Peck. Served in Captain George Myers' Company of Washington County, Pennsylvania, Militia.

1. Elizabeth Enoch, wife of James Auton, went to Marion County, Ohio.
2. Eunice Enoch, married George Gardner.
3. David Enoch, married Hannah ....
4. Hannah Enoch, married John Gardner.
5. Cynthia Enoch, married Levi Sowers.
6. Henry Enoch, married Sarah Rees.
7. Mary Ann Enoch.

8. Catherine Enoch.
9. Hiram Enoch, married Elizabeth Davis.
10. Abner Enoch.
11. Sally Enoch, married Robert Lowry.

As for the other branches of the Enoch Family who settled in the Tenmile Country, the records are a bit cloudy. All local histories speak of the massacre of Enoch Enoch (also spelled Enix) in the Dunkard Creek section of Greene County. Very good accounts of this killing are found in pension applications, including that of Henry Sykes, who, as a young man, was with Enoch Enoch when the murder took place. The account given in the Evans Papers gives no date, but states that Henry Sykes was a young man of 18 at the time. It was the same date that the same body of Indians took Christina Sykes prisoner. As Henry Sykes says he was born in 1757, it would place the date about 1775, a bit earlier than the evidence would confirm. For it was probably this Enoch Enoch who was in Captain John Wetzel's Company of Rangers on the Monongahela in the Spring of 1778. The men were all from the vicinity of Dunkard Creek. (Penna. Archives, Series VI, Vol. 2, pp. 321). Some light is thrown on the identity in the Census for 1790, when we find a Catherine Enoch at the head of a household of two females, while the very next name is that of John Enoch, Sr. The names in this column are of those living on Dunkard Creek, and this entry indicates that the "babe in arms" may be living with his grandparent, whom we take to be John Enoch, Sr. A deed of record dated November 21, 1826, further identifies the children of the slain man, when Enoch Enoch and wife, Mary, join with John Millburn and wife, Mary, to sell a tract that "descended from his father." (Deed Book 5, pp. 617, Greene County). Another deed in Deed Book 6, pp. 104, conveys land from Enoch Enoch and wife to David Stoneking. Examination of the patentee map shows this land to be part of a tract warranted to John Cox on December 31, 1773. Enoch Enoch, the younger, died in 1855, as shown by probate records in Greene County. His wife, Mary, administered his estate and in 1857 got a patent for a part of this tract that had been warranted to John Cox. This transaction recalls the close relationship between the Enoch and Cox families in Hampshire County, and seems to tie them definitely with that place. No records tell what happened to John Enoch, Sr., but Crumrine calls him a Colonel and says he lived at Clarksville. There is nothing to prove this and it is likely that Crumrine meant Colonel Henry Enoch, but from his knowledge of the family recalled a John Enoch, of whom no official account is given. He neither owned nor sold any property that is recorded here.

Crumrine also reports a business meeting of the Baptist Church was held in Enoch Enoch's home on December 1, 1773, saying he had a fort a mile-and-a-half below Lone Pine in Washington County. There are no land records to show he owned land in that section, and this could be the son of Henry Enoch II. However, there is a tract of land in that vicinity that was warranted in August, 1786, to John Hughes, and then patented to Daniel Enoch, Sr., on June 22, 1791. This tract was known as "Enoch's Delight."

When Henry Enoch II died, his sons, William and Isaac, were already in financial difficulties. Isaac Enoch had been deeded the home property for promising to take care of his parents during the remainder of their lives. But in 1799, owing money to Robert Clarke and Ezekiel Hoover, he found he was unable to pay. In April session of Court the sheriff of Greene County took over and proceeded to sell the assets available. These included the grist mill of his father, and the Iron Works Henry Enoch II had operated, as well as the land on which they stood, including the tracts of both Isaac and William

Enoch. The records of this sale were not entered in the Greene County Courts until late years, and are to be found in Deed Book 344, pp. 359.

The buyer at the sheriff's sale was Samuel Clarke, described as being of the town of Washington, Pennsylvania. This Samuel Clarke had begun to take an interest in Greene County land a few years before, when he purchased Lot No. 10 in the new Borough of Waynesburg, in 1796. In March, 1799, he had made a purchase of land on Tenmile from Abel Man, and situated near the Enochs. He added to this purchase on June 30, 1801, by purchasing the "Ashley" tract of Isaac Heaton and wife, Susannah. After adding still another tract, "Heaton's Cove," by a purchase from Isaac Heaton, he patented an unclaimed strip of land on the banks of Tenmile Creek at the forks. About 1811 he conceived the idea of laying out a town, and a long string of deeds shows the process of selling lots in the new town, which he named for himself. One of these deeds is of particular interest, when on April 15, 1813, Samuel Clarke and wife, Dorcas, sold to The Monongahela Manufacturing Society lots 92, 93 and 94, on which Clarke had built a fulling mill. These deeds attest to the importance of the village of Clarksville at the beginning of the 19th Century, and the varied types of industry that sprang up at that point.

It would appear that Samuel Clarke also got into financial difficulty, but his death, about 1834-36, spared him the inconveniences of foreclosure, so that his estate fell into the hands of the sheriff about 1836, and his remaining assets in the vicinity were disposed of by that officer.

THE STULL FAMILY

There are a number of adjoiner deeds that show the Stull family was at the Forks of the Tenmile with the first settlers. While living here in 1782, Jacob Stull served in Captain Andrew Fairley's Militia Company as the ensign, and John Stull was in the same company as a private. Here John Stull owned a tract of land called "Orleans," which was warranted to him on February 23, 1786. He was taxed in Morgan Township in both 1784 and 1785, along with a Henry Stull. Jacob Stull followed his captain and the Enochs, Teagardens, etc., to the Wheeling Creek section where, on May 1, 1789, he had recorded a deed for 205 acres of land that had been bought from Andrew and Susannah Fairley. (Washington County DB. 1, D 340).

There seems little doubt that these Stulls were descended from John Stull, a native of the part of Frederick County, Maryland, which later became Washington County, Maryland, and where on April 17, 1749, a John Stull made his will which was probated in Frederick County in the same year. His wife's name was Martha. (Frederick County WB. A-1, pp. 23).

Children of John and Martha Stull Named in Will of John Stull

1. Daniel Stull, whose will is recorded in both Frederick and Washington Counties in Maryland. He died in October or November of 1749, apparently a single man, for he left his estate to his mother, Martha Stull, and brothers, Jacob and Isaac Stull. (Washington County, Maryland, WB. 1—175). His will was made October 20, 1749, and probated the following November 22.
2. Isaac Stull made a will in Washington County, Maryland, on November 18, 1769, that was not probated until February 8, 1791. He, too, seems to have been a single man, as he left his estate to his brothers, Jacob and John, brother-in-law, Charles

Swearington, sister-in-law, Sarah Stull, wife of John; sisters, Mary and Susannah; nephew, John Stull, and nephew, Abijah Swearington. He, too, mentions his mother, Martha. (Frederick County Will Book 1, 261).

3. Jacob Stull, son of John and Martha Stull, died in Washington County, Maryland, in 1788, where his will, made January 7, 1788, was probated on September 13, 1788. No wife is named, and the three heirs named appear to have been children of his brother, John Stull, as his other brothers, Daniel Stull and Isaac Stull, both died unmarried. The wording of this will and property distributed definitely ties him in with the Tenmile Country. He gave to Jacob Stull, and Jacob Walling, relationship not mentioned, one-half of a tract of land called "Richhills," in Washington County, Pennsylvania. The other half went to Deleshmutt Walling. This is the same tract of land that Ensign Jacob Stull secured by a deed from Captain Andrew Fairley and wife, Susannah, by a deed dated May 1, 1789. (Washington County, Pennsylvania, Deed Book 1-D, pp. 340). Explanation of the transaction is that, due to uncertainty of lines and ownership of lands on Wheeling Creek, it was necessary to clear this property after succeeding to it by will. Certainly the five pounds mentioned in this deed from Andrew and Susan Fairley was but a nominal sum, and Jacob Stull and Jacob Wallin paid that sum for 205 acres. The land is described as being next the land of John Messmore, or Messer, Jacob Crow, and Peter Jolly.

4. John Stull, mentioned by his brother, Isaac Stull, in 1769. John Stull died in Frederick County, Maryland, where he too left a will, which was made May 20, 1786, and probated September 15, 1788. (Frederick County, Maryland Will Book 2, pp. 287). His will names a wife, Catherine Stull, while the will of his brother mentions a wife, Sarah, suggesting two marriages, partly confirmed by the number of his children. He was probably the father of the John Stull who settled at the Forks of the Tenmile, and Jacob Stull of Richhill.

Children of John Stull of Frederick County, Maryland
1. Jacob Stull.
2. Christopher Stull.
3. John Stull.
4. Lawrence Stull.
5. Catherine Stull, wife of .... Wier.
6. Margaret Stull.
7. Barbara Stull.
8. Mary Stull.
9. Caty Stull.
10. Magdeline Stull.
11. Christina Stull.
12. Susannah Stull. May have been the first wife of Captain Andrew Fairley.

5. Mary Stull, daughter of John and Martha Stull. Married .... Greathouse. They had a daughter, Rachel Greathouse.
6. Elizabeth Stull, daughter of John and Martha Stull, married .... Johnson.
7. Catherine Stull, daughter of John and Martha Stull, married Charles Swearington. They had a son, Abijah Swearington.
8. Margaret Stull, daughter of John and Martha Stull.
9. Susannah Stull, daughter of John and Martha Stull.

John Stull of Clarksville, was born in Maryland in 1752, and died in Washington County, Pennsylvania, January 18, 1824. He is the John Stull of the adjoiner deeds, and at one time owned "Orleans," which was warranted to him February 23, 1786. He served as a private in Captain Andrew Fairley's Militia Company, and was on the Morgan Township tax lists for 1784-85. The 1790 Census shows him at the head of a family consisting of one adult male, two males under 16 years, and four females. His will is in Washington County Will Book 4, pp. 41, and shows it was made January 16, 1824, two days before he died. It was probated February 13, 1824. His wife was Elizabeth ...., who died August 3, 1842, at the age of 80 years and 16 days. Both are buried in the Lutheran Cemetery near Marianna. From his will it is learned that he was living at the mouth of Hupp's Run at the time of his death, and Elizabeth was permitted to live at this place during her lifetime.

Children of John and Elizabeth Stull
(Courtesy of Mrs. W. A. H. McIlvaine)

1. John Stull, Jr., sold land with wife, Elizabeth, to Samuel Clark on September 13, 1830. (Greene County Deed Book 6, pp. 703-04).
2. George Stull, with wife, Elizabeth, went to Knox County, Ohio.
3. Andrew Stull.
4. Phillip Stull, got $100 more than the others because he was partially blind. His wife was Frances .... He died before June, 1853, leaving six minor children.

Children of Phillip Stull
(O. C. Docket 3, pp. 337)

   1. Lavina Stull.
   2. Maria Stull.
   3. Lewis Stull.
   4. Louisa Stull.
   5. Eliza Jane Stull.
   6. James Stull.
5. Abraham Stull.
6. Martin Stull, died October 20, 1836, aged 32 years and 19 days. Buried with his parents.
7. Isaac Stull, born September 4, 1807, died December 26, 1888. Married Matilda Hawkins, who was born May 5, 1809 and died April 15, 1885. She was a daughter of Richard and Cynthia (Crawford) Hawkins.

Children of Isaac and Matilda (Hawkins) Stull

   1. Joseph Stull. Married Amy Cox.
   2. John Stull. Married Mary Newsom.
   3. Elizabeth Stull. Married Jacob Overholt.
   4. Jackson Stull. Married Mary Gass.
   5. Richard Stull. Married Margaret Lewis.
   6. Absolom Stull. Died in infancy.
   7. William Stull.
   8. James Stull. Died in infancy.
   9. Thomas Stull, twin of James, married Lou Smiley.
   10. Melissa Stull. Married .... Franks.
8. Barbara Stull. Married John Hupp.
9. Elizabeth Stull.
10. Mary Stull. Married Bennet Horner. They had Maryann, Abraham and Martin Horner under age in 1828. Benedict Horner and Adam Bottomfield served as guardians for these children. (O. C. Docket 1, pp. 277, Greene County).

THE ROFELTY FAMILY

Historians have left the story of the Rofelty (or O'Felty) massacre a bit confusing. They have also failed to say just what year it took place, but it is to be assumed that it happened during the Revolutionary period. At the time of the massacre the Rofeltys were living on their tract of land across the Tenmile from Benjamin Stites' Mill, later Pollock's Mill, on land later owned by DeGuids, adjoining Edward Burson. Mathias Rofelty was away from home, leaving his wife and two grown daughters on the plantation. The Indians killed the wife and one grown daughter and scalped the other, who miraculously recovered from her wounds. She was taken to the home of Edward Burson, the same place the Indians had stopped after perpetrating their foul deed, and here she lived for some time before marrying and raising a large family. Local court records show that there were a number of other children in this family, including one son, who brought about a partitioning of the estate of the father on January 30, 1815. (O. C. Docket 1, pp. 56). The other children of the Rofeltys were:

1. Catherine Rofelty, who married Harman Moore.
2. Sarah Rofelty, who married Silas Estill. She is probably the one who was scalped and lived, for her descendants were connected with the Haines family, as stated by Waychoff. Her husband, Silas Estill, was a son of Daniel Estill, and he died about 1833. Their children were:
   1. Mathias Estill (or Estle), who married Mary Stewart.
   2. Daniel Estle.
   3. Elizabeth Estle, who married (1) Samuel Hathaway and after his death in 1824, she married .... Haines.
   4. Caty (Catherine) Estle, married .... McMasters.
   5. Hannah Estle, who married .... Whitman.
   6. Barbara Estle, who married .... Hixenbaugh.
   7. Delilah Estle, who married .... Daniels.
3. Barbara Rofelty, who married Levi Blackledge, who moved to Ohio. She was the mother of:
   1. Sarah Blackledge, who married Nathan Harris.
   2. Jesse Blackledge.
4. Hannah Rofelty, who married .... Collins.
5. Susannah Rofelty, who married William Teagarden, and moved to Columbiana County, Ohio.
6. Mathias Rofelty, Jr.

THE ESTLE FAMILY

Daniel Estle (Estill, Estel, etc.,) and his son, Silas Estle, both warranted tracts of land on Muddy Creek, adjoining that of Jacob Cline. The tract of Daniel Estle included the present Guy Scott farm, while that of Silas Estle was later owned by Joseph Cowell. Daniel Estle was a member of Captain James Archer's Militia Company, which was mostly recruited within the confines of the present Franklin Township, though a few of the members were from what became Jefferson Township. Daniel Estle died in Greene County in 1821 and his will is in Will Book 1, pp. 214. His wife is not named and there is evidence of a deceased daughter and son, who are not named in the will.

Family of Daniel Estle

1. .... Estle, whose wife was named Mary. Guardians were appointed for his children in the settlement of his father's estate. (O. C. Docket 1, pp. 184, June, 1822). That this son died about 1816 is evidenced by another Orphans' Court entry of January, 1816, when a guardian was appointed for his son, George, and son, Jacob. The other children were Catherine and Isaiah. Barnet Whitlatch was the guardian.
2. Silas Estle, probably the eldest son, died about 1833, and his will, which was proven in Greene County, is in Will Book 2, pp. 21. His wife was Sarah Rofelty, a daughter of Mathias Rofelty. She was the Rofelty daughter who was scalped and left for dead by the Indians when they wiped out a number of Mathias Rofelty's children and wife, and had been raised by Edward Burson.

Children of Silas Estle

1. Mathias Estle, who died May 30, 1880. He married Mary Stewart. He was born February 25, 1793, and his wife was born March 17, 1801. He was the father of the following children:
   1. Hiram Estle, born August 20, 1821.
   2. Eli Estle, born July 20, 1834, died November 20, 1910.
   3. Phoebe Estle, wife of A. J. Smith, was born September 25, 1825.
   4. John Estle, born April 20, 1831.
   5. Jeremiah Estle, born September 27, 1838.
   6. Mary Estle, who married David Waters, was born May 21, 1824.
   7. Zillah Estle, born September 25, 1822.
   8. Sarah Estle, born July 1, 1827.
   9. Mathias Estle, born July 29, 1829.
2. Daniel Estle seems to have died pior to his father, Silas Estle, leaving a daughter, Elizabeth Estle, who is named by her grandfather in his will.
3. Elizabeth Estle. She first married Samuel Hathaway, who died early in 1820, leaving one son, John Hathaway, who was raised by his uncle, Mathias Estle. This son was born May 19, 1820. He married Ary Anderson and was the ancestor of many of the Carmichaels family of the name. Elizabeth (Estle) Hathaway then married .... Haines and raised a large family.
4. Caty Estle, married .... McMasters.
5. Hannah Estle, married Jacob Whitemore.
6. Barbara Estle, married .... Hixenbaugh.
7. Delilah Estle, married .... Daniels.

3. Joseph Estle, son of Daniel Estle.
4. .... Estle, married a man named .... Boner, and had Sarah Boner, who married James Pratt; also a daughter, Sarah, and a daughter, Eleanor, all named in the will of Daniel Estle.
5. Sarah Estle, married .... McCullough.
6. Margaret Estle, daughter of Daniel Estle.
7. Elizabeth Estle, married .... Oliver, and had a son, John Oliver.
8. Delilah Estle, married .... McMasters.
9. William Estle, married Crissy Strawn.

THE RUSH FAMILY

Jacob Rush is said to have settled in the Castile Run section of Morgan Township about 1769. He was born in Fairfax County, Virginia, about 1738, and family tradition claims he was a descendant of John Rush, an officer in Cromwell's Army. Relationship is also claimed to Benjamin Rush, early Revolutionary Patriot. While Jacob Rush is not listed in the 1772 tax list for Springhill Township, tradition says he was here at that time. Veach had several errors in his copy of the original tax list.

The patent map for Morgan and Jefferson Townships in Greene County, show that Jacob Rush received a warrant for a tract of land at the mouth of Castile Run, under the title of "Mathilda," dated July 24, 1784. It was patented to him on May 30, 1793. By purchase he obtained other tracts which were in his neighborhood. One of these of particular note is the tract he bought of Benjamin Stites in 1787, described as "Stites' Old Mill Site," and located "across the Creek from Rofelty." This tract has long since been operated for mill purposes and is familiar to many as "Pollack's Mill." (Washington County Deed Book 1, B. 198). Jacob Rush served in Captain Benjamin Stites' Company, First Battalion, Washington County, Pennsylvania, Militia, in the War of the Revolution. In the company roster for 1782, are the names of his brothers-in-law, Sergeant James Bell, Abel Bell, and Nathaniel Bell. (Pennsylvania Archives, Series VI, Vol. 2, pp. 11, 15, 20). Another brother-in-law, Thomas Woolverton, served a tour of duty with the same company under Sergeant Gray, (pp. 242) and it would appear that Jesse Rush, a son of Jacob, went out for his father on a tour of duty under Lieutenant Elijah Mills. (pp. 247). This latter list seems to be those who were out on the ill-fated Colonel Crawford's Expedition to Sandusky, on which expedition the three Bells and Thomas Woolverton served in Captain Ezekiel Rose's Company. Pension applications disclose that an alarm at Wheeling diverted several parties due to go on this expedition, after they had rendezvoused at Mingo Bottoms.

Jacob Rush and his wife, Lydia, were members of Goshen Baptist Church, Lydia having joined on July 6, 1788, when the Church met at Bennet (Barnet) Rineharts, while Jacob was received into the congregation on October 5, of the same year. There are reasons for believing that Jacob Rush was married twice, and his first wife may have been Elizabeth Leonard. Some of his children may have been of this first marriage, namely: Elizabeth, Jesse, and Leonard. Jesse Leonard lived nearby and some of the Leonards were of Benjamin Stites' Company.

Lydia is the wife named in Jacob Rush's will and she is buried with him in the Cox Cemetery on Castile Run. She was Lydia Bell, daughter of Nathaniel and Hannah Bell. (Will Book 1, pp. 20, probated in 1800, witnessed by William Heaton, Isaac Heaton and Benjamin Lyon). The tombstone of Jacob Rush says he died October 5, 1820, aged 82 years, while his wife's tombstone says she died January 3, 1828, aged 80 years. The will of Jacob Rush was probated March 7, 1825, and had been made in 1809. His wife and children are named in the order listed rather than by ages. (Greene County Will Book 1, pp. 263).

Children of Jacob Rush

1. Moses Rush.
2. Isaac Rush. Died January 9, 1827, aged 49 years.
3. Nathaniel Rush, born 1786, died December 22, 1867, married Elizabeth ...., who died August, 1861, aged 52 years, 2

months. Buried in the Cox Cemetery.
4. Mathias Rush, born, 1789, died April 15, 1863, married Sarah Iams, who died in 1874.

Children of Mathias Rush

1. Jacob Rush, born January 27, 1823, died October 10, 1895, married Elizabeth Cox, born May 13, 1824.
2. William Rush, born October 20, 1825, died April 21, 1897, married March 21, 1861, Martha Josephine Hughes.

5. Mary Rush, born 1797, died April 17, 1870, married David Hayes.
6. Jesse Rush, died 1827.
7. Leonard Rush, born January 10, 1769, died in Hamilton County, Ohio. His wife was Jemima Hormell.
8. James Rush, born 1770, died August 4, 1842, married Priscilla Case, who is buried in the Cox Cemetery. She was a daughter of Samuel and Mary (Heaton) Case.

Children of James Rush

1. Abigail Rush, born February 14, 1801, died September 11, 1879; married William Cox, born December 13, 1796, died November 2, 1835.
2. Mary Rush, born January 7, 1803, died August 31, 1857; married Christopher Cox.
3. Elizabeth Rush, married Dr. Crawford.
4. Samuel Rush, born December 29, 1807, died September 24, 1858; married Minnie Heise, born March 11, 1814, died December 4, 1891.
5. Charlotte Rush, born May 31, 1812, died May 1, 1846; married William Litzenberg.
6. Nancy Rush, born September 5, 1814, died April 28, 1866; married Moses Cox.
7. Sarah Rush, born 1817, died 1904; married Fletcher Allman, born 1812, died 1877.
8. Rachel Rush, born September 21, 1820, died October 16, 1880, never married.
9. Priscilla Rush, born May 20, 1822, died May 22, 1912.

9. Jacob Rush, born 1761, died August 4, 1842.
10. Nancy Rush.
11. Elizabeth Rush.
12. Hannah Rush.

THE COX FAMILY

Several members of the Cox family were among the first to settle on Castile Run, where Andrew, Michael, and Christopher Cox are listed in Captain Andrew Ferley's Militia Company. It may be that they came with the Enoch family, as there were come intermarriages with Enoch and Cox families in Virginia.

Christopher Cox, buried in the Cox Cemetery on Castile Run, was not the man in Andrew Ferley's Company, for that soldier is buried in the Old Lutheran Cemetery at Marianna, along with his wife, Margaret, and son, Christopher. They were the ancestors of our good friend, Dr. Wayne E. Booher. Christopher Cox of Castile Run, was born January 10, 1767, and died October 3, 1815. His wife, Anna ...., was born April 10, 1768, and died April 25, 1847. Mrs. Stephen Hill has the Bible records of this family.

AND ITS PIONEER FAMILIES 63

Children of Christopher and Anne Cox
1. Jacob Cox, born March 16, 1792.
2. John Cox, born June 4, 1793, married Anne ...., and went to Knox County, Ohio.
3. Jesse Cox, born June 4, 1794, died 1826, married Dorcas Bell, born October 27, 1806, died in 1876.
    1. John B. Cox, born August 17, 1824, married, April 17, 1845, Maria Crayne, born April 29, 1825, died at the age of 100 years and 11 months.
4. Phillip Cox, born October 12, 1795, died June 24, 1804.
5. William Cox, born December 13, 1796, died November 2, 1835; married Abigail Rush, born February 14, 1801, died September 11, 1879.

Children of William and Abigail (Rush) Cox
1. James Cox, born January 28, 1818.
2. Samuel Cox, born September 22, 1819, died June 23, 1874.
3. Enoch Harvey Cox, born August 20, 1820, died February 17, 1894.
4. Mary Cox, born April 28, 1822, died January 9, 182......
5. Aaron Cox, born April 28, 1823, died April 2, 1899.
6. Elizabeth Cox, born May 13, 1824, died December 17, 1887; married Jacob Rush.
7. Priscilla Cox, born March 7, 1826.
8. Anna R. Cox, born March 23, 1827.
9. Charlotte Cox, born January 29, 1829.
10. Sarah Jane Cox, born November 25, 1830.
11. Marinda Cox, born December 21, 1831.
12. William Cox, born October 4, 1833, died October 10, 1839.
13. Maria Abigail Cox, born March 22, 1835, died October 9, 1840.

6. Indiana Cox, born March 8, 1797, married, 1818, David Bricker, born 1799, died September 14, 1878. Went to Utica, Ohio.
7. Anna Cox, born October 29, 1799, died November 11, 1871; married John Bell, who died June 14, 1880, aged 79 years, 10 months, 26 days.

Children of John and Ann (Cox) Bell
1. Hiram Bell, born 1826, died in Iowa, married Hannah J. Shelby.
2. Lucinda Bell, born January 18, 1821, married May 14, 1840, Miller Crayne, born April 22, 1817.
3. Martha Bell, married Michael Franks.
4. Matilda Bell, married .... Clark.
5. Emeline Bell, born May 22, 1834, died November 18, 1897.
6. John Bell, killed in the Civil War November 8, 1863, aged 25 years, 4 months, 4 days.
7. Emily Bell, born 1828, died February 29, 1884, married John Dowlin, who died May 19, 1904.

8. Christopher Cox, born March 16, 1801, died June 29, 1861, married Mary Rush, born January 6th, 1803, died August 31, 1857.
9. Hiram Cox, born October 25, 1802, died May 28, 1851, went to Knox County, Ohio.
10. Mary Cox, born July 4, 1804, married Abraham Wise.
11. Moses Cox, born December 1, 1805, died December 15, 1855, married Nancy ...., who died April 28, 1866.
12. Matilda Cox, born September 25, 1807, died June 26, 1869, married Daniel Turner, born 1800, died January 2, 1890, aged 89 years, 8 months, 15 days.
13. Aaron Cox, born October 28, 1809, died August 26, 1874, married Malinda Hupp.

THE ROSE FAMILY

Tichicus Rose was an early settler in the Clarksville area, where he served in Captain Andrew Ferley's Company of Washington County, Pennsylvania, Militia, in the War of the Revolution. He does not appear to have patented any land in the section, but is listed in the 1784 tax list for Morgan Township. He died about 1793, leaving a will that was probated in Washington County on October 10, 1793. (Will Book 1, pp. 202). His wife's name was Catherine ...., and the children named in the will were:

    John Rose, of whom later.   Jeremiah Rose.
    Robert Rose.   Sarah Rose.
    James Rose.   Anna Rose.
    Elizabeth Rose.

John Rose, son of Tichicus and Catherine Rose, owned a lot in Clarksville when he died on November 28, 1825, at the age of 61 years, 4 months and 28 days. Three children are named in his will filed in Greene County, November 29, 1825, and his wife, Hannah ...., shared in the estate. She and Abraham Young were the administrators. She died April 4, 1847, at the age of 77 years. Both are buried on the Rose farm near Clarksville. The children named (in Will Book 1, Greene County, pp. 276) were:

    John Rose, Jr.
    David Rose, whose wife was Mary Hewitt, of whom later.
    Hannah Rose, who married Abraham Young.

David Rose, son of John and Hannah Rose, died May 14, 1879, aged 71 years, 3 months and 9 days. His first wife was Mary M. Hewitt, who died December 12, 1875, aged 69 years, 7 months. She is buried with her husband on the Rose farm. David Rose married a second time, his wife being the former Eliza Greenlee. The following were the children of David and Mary (Hewitt) Rose:

    Adam Rose.
    Levi Rose.
    Demas Rose.
    Sarah Rose, who married .... Gardner.
    Susannah Rose, who married .... Leighley.
    Rebecca Rose, who married William Burson.
    Malinda Rose, who married David Porter.
    Mary Rose, who married .... Deguid.
    Abijah Rose, who married Rebecca Williard.
    Hannah Rose, who married Demas Horn.
    John Rose, who married Priscilla Litzenberg.

THE WALTON FAMILY

Mr. John Walton of Manchester, Ohio, sent in the record of some of the first Waltons to settle on the Tenmile. He, like numerous other Walton Genealogists, has failed to identify the immediate ancestors of the three Waltons, who made this settlement prior to 1782. He is of the opinion that these three, James Walton, Job Walton, and Amos Walton were brothers, and that they may have come from Northern New Jersey. This may be true and they may have been among the many families from Morris County, New Jersey, who settled in what is now Amwell Township, Washington County, in 1778, as reported in Crumrine. Efforts to connect them with the Quaker family of that name who settled first in Bucks County, Pennsyvania, have been unsuccessful, nor does any connection appear positive with the Moses Walton family of the Shenandoah Valley.

AND ITS PIONEER FAMILIES 65

After serving in Captain Abner Howell's Mitilia Company from Amwell Township, Washington County, in whose muster roll for 1782 all three pioneers are listed, Job Walton got a warrant for a tract of land on Ruffs Creek in what is now Washington Township, Greene County. The date of the warrant is September 30, 1786, but the tract was patented later in 1806 to Dennis Smith. Job Walton also served in Captain Benjamin Stites' Morgan Township Militia Company, before joining the migration to Kentucky, where he died in Flemming County in 1815. His wife was Margaret ...., who was from Scotch Plains, New Jersey, as shown by her Kentucky Church record. James Walton disappears from the records after his militia service.

Amos Walton was born about 1751, family tradition says, in Bucks County, Pennsylvania, and died in Washington County, Pennsylvania, in 1827. His will was made October 31, 1815, but was never probated; however, there was a settlement of his estate on February 21, 1827, by which his land, lying in both Washington and Greene Counties, was distributed among his five heirs. He and his wife are buried in the old cemetery at the North Tenmile Baptist Church Cemetery, where his tombstone, still partly legible, says he was 76 years of age when he died. His wife was Marcy Lacock, who died June 14, 1838, at the age of 79 years, 9 months and 14 days. They were married before 1776. After coming to the Tenmile Amos Walton served frequent tours of duty with the Frontier Rangers and also, as before noted, had regular service with Captain Abner Howell. (Pennsylvania Archives, Series III, Vol. 23, pp. 310, and Pennsylvania Archives, Series VI, Vol. 2, pp. 120). Two tracts of land were patented to Amos Walton, one of which had been warranted to Rees Gaddis, and adjoined the tract warranted to Amos Walton, February 28, 1785. The land was situated in what is now West Bethlehem Township, Washington County.

Children of Amos and Marcy (Lacock) Walton

1. Sarah Walton, born 1776, died 1857; married, in 1795, William Gordon, born in 1773, and died in 1874.

   ### Children of William and Sarah (Walton) Gordon

   1. Marcy Gordon, born 1796, died 1857; married, 1816, Samuel Renner, born 1785, died 1843.
   2. Abel M. S. Gordon, born 1809, died January 9, 1833, aged 25 years, 9 months and 1 day; buried in North Tenmile Baptist Cemetery.
   3. Ruth Gordon, born 1811, died 1887; married, 1829, Samuel Wright, born 1808, died 1882. A number of their children are buried in Tenmile Baptist Cemetery.
   4. Jane Gordon, born 1815, died November 27, 1815, aged 6 months. Buried in North Tenmile Baptist Cemetery.
   5. Jonathan Gordon, born 1820, died 1887; married Catherine Overtorf, born 1820, died 186......
   (NOTE: There were probably other children not named in the record).

2. Jonathan Walton, died September 10, 1855, aged 78 years, 2 months and 24 days. His wife was Keziah ...., who died January 1, 1857, aged 78 years. They are buried in the North Tenmile Baptist Cemetery.

   ### Children of Jonathan Walton

   1. Betty Walton, who married Daniel Paul.
   2. Mary Walton, who married William Paul.
   3. Ann Walton, died May 7, 1842, aged 32 years and 1 month;

buried in North Tenmile Baptist Cemetery. She married Andrew S. Paul.
4. Amos Walton, who married Lydia Myers.
5. Phoebe Walton, died April 1, 1827, in her 22nd year. She, and her infant child, are buried in North Tenmile Baptist Cemetery. She married Jonathan Egy, who died October 12, 1847.
6. Marcy Walton, who married James Hughes.
7. .... Walton, who married Amos Swart.
8. Caroline Walton.

3. Phoebe Walton, daughter of Amos and Marcy (Lacock) Walton, married .... Ball.
4. James Walton, son of Amos and Marcy (Lacock) Walton. No information.
5. John Walton, son of Amos and Marcy (Lacock) Walton, was born in 1785, and died October 6, 1834. He married, about 1805, Sarah Paul, born July 26, 1786, died September 7, 1874. Both are buried in the Walton Cemetery at Clarksville. Sarah Paul married, for her second husband, Levi Burson, who died in 1863.

Children of John and Sarah (Paul) Walton

1. James Paul Walton, born 1806, died ....; married Eliza Hickman, born 1810, died 1842.
2. Amos Paul Walton, born 1807, died 1890; married, 1830, Sarah A. Stephenson, born 1813, died 1875.
3. Sophrona Walton, who married Daniel Spindler.
4. Jonathan Walton.
5. William Walton, twin of Jonathan.
6. David Walton.
7. Daniel McFarland Walton, born August 4, 1815, died 1904. He was married three times: first to Mary Drake, who died in 1859; second to Sarah Emery, who died in 1869, and third to Harriet Alexander Cook.
8. Sarah Walton, married Barnet Hughes, son of Thomas and Elizabeth (Swan) Hughes.
9. Margaret Ann Walton, born 1823, married Isaac Hayes.
10. John Walton.
11. Massy Walton, born March 19, 1819, married Edward Burson, son of Judge Isaac Burson.
12. Martha Walton.

THE NYSWANER FAMILY

When Christian Newswanger arrived in this Country from the Palatinate on the British ship "Mortonhouse," in August 1728, the official records started doing tricks with the family name, with the result that any way it may be found spelled today is bound to be correct. To be safe in our title we take the spelling as found in the local directory, and will wager it is not the right way to spell the name. In order to follow this family in local records, it is almost a requisite that a few of the odd ways the name appears should be listed. In the 1790 Census the name is Nosenger; in Revolutionary service it is Nofsinger, Knuffsinger, Nostringer; in patent records it is Nostringer and Nassinger, and in subsequent deeds, almost any manner in which the letters can be arranged, is used.

Three men of the name seem to have been the pioneers of the family in the Tenmile Country. They are Samuel, John and Christian, the latter an early settler on Wheeling Creek, who died in Ohio

County, West Virginia. Samuel Nyswaner (spelled Nostringer) and his wife, Susannah, in a deed of January 26, 1808, sold the tract of land which had been patented to them March 21, 1796. This land was the tract of land on Castile Run which became the home property of Isaac Weaver, and had originally been warranted to William Groom, in 1787. (Deed Book 2, pp. 308).

John Nyswaner (spelled here, Nassinger) first settled on Plumb Run branch of North Tenmile, where he served in the Revolution, under Captain Ezekiel Rose, in the Militia Company of the section. (Pennsylvania Archives, Series VI, Vol. 2, pp. 206, etc. Nuffsinger, Noftsinger, etc). He bought the warrant right of Isaac Mellon to a tract of land known as "Maple Bottom," and had it patented to him on May 14, 1790, under the title, "Jace." Later John Nyswaner bought a tract, near Clarksville, on July 3, 1798, from John and Sarah Heaton. (Deed Book 1, pp. 270). John Nyswaner died in Morgan Township about 1827, leaving a wife, Anne ...., and a number of married children. Names of these children and their spouses are given in Orphans' Court Docket 1, pp. 242, March Court, 1827.

Children of John and Anne (......................) Nyswaner

(Dates given may be correct; source material not reliable).

1. Susannah Nyswaner, born May 19, 1781; married Michael Crumrine.
2. Elizabeth Nyswaner, born July 12, 1782; married Balzer Lohr.
3. Mary Nyswaner, born October 2, 1783; married Peter Landers.
4. Nancy Nyswaner, twin of Mary, born October 2, 1783; married Joseph Sommers.
5. John Nyswaner, born April 4, 1785.
6. Sarah Nyswaner, born December 25, 1788.
7. Jonathan Nyswaner, born July 9, 1790; married Elizabeth Clark.
8. Juliana Nyswaner, born December 25, 1793; married Jacob Booze. She died before 1826, leaving Sarah Ann, Eliza, and Morgan Booze.
9. Samuel Nyswaner, born August 6, 1797.
10. Daniel Nyswaner, born December 27, 1802.
11. Catherine Nyswaner, born May 29, 1804; married Daniel Sommers.
12. Lydia Nyswaner, who married Absolom Hawkins, was born May 4, 1805, died July 1, 1871. She was married September 22, 1826, and died in childbirth in 1827, leaving a daughter, Lydia, who was born June 16, 1827, and died June 16, 1850.

CHRISTIAN NYCESWANGER FAMILY

Christian Nyceswanger made his will in Ohio County, (West) Virginia, on February 20, 1828. It is filed in Ohio County Will Book 3, pp. 76. It is most likely that he went to the Wheeling Creek section with the Enoch, Teagarden, Stull, Fairley, and other families, who were located at the forks of North and South Tenmile during the Revolutionary days.

Children of Christian Nyceswanger

1. Abraham Nyceswanger.
2. John Nyceswanger.
3. Ann Nyceswanger.
4. Susan Nyceswanger, who married, 1814, John Scott.
5. Sally Nyceswanger, who married William Gray in 1815.
6. Rebecca Nyceswanger, who married Solomon White.
7. Mary Nyceswanger, who married Henry Harsh in 1815.

THE ARNOLD FAMILY

It is difficult, if not impossible, to identify the numerous men of this name who were among the early settlers of the Tenmile Country, both on the North and South branches, and on the Fayette County side of the Monongahela River opposite the Mouth of Tenmile. It has been noted that Jeremiah Arnold was one of the men of Captain Michael Cresap's Company, which suggests that some of the family came from Hampshire County, Virginia. The name is found there, and on both sides of the Potomac River in both Virginia and Maryland. Since the family is quite frequently found neighbors of the Enochs and Teagardens in the older settlements, it is not surprising to find the same situation on the Tenmile. One can follow the movements of this Jeremiah Arnold during the Revolution, for, after his service with Cresap, he returned to the Tenmile Country where he took the Oath of Allegiance in Ohio County, Virginia, in 1777, before Thomas Waller. Joseph Arnold took the oath at the same time. Later, in 1781-2, they are both found, along with Josiah Arnold, in Captain Robert Sweeney's Militia Company, which was recruited in the vicinity of Sandy Plains, on the Washington County side of Tenmile. None of these men took up land here, so it may be assumed that they moved farther west. Some of their Militia Company was on the Crawford Expedition, but these men are not in the lists.

There was a Jonathan Arnold, Sr., who settled in Fayette County, Pennsylvania. His son, Jonathan, Jr., warranted a tract of land next to Rezin Virgin, in Luzerne Township, just across the river from the Mouth of Tenmile Creek. Since there are a number of his descendants living in the Tenmile County at this late date, Jonathan Arnold, Sr., must be included in any history of this family. Fayette County records show that he died in Luzerne Township about 1798, and that his will was probated there January 24, 1799. His wife was Sarah .... (Fayette County Will Book 1, pp. 47). He patented land in Luzerne Township under the title of "The Squirrell," on October 27, 1785.

Children of Jonathan and Sarah Arnold

1. Jonathan Arnold, Jr., who warranted a tract called "Eden," on October 27, 1785, and had it patented to him August 8, 1787.
2. Benjamin Arnold.
3. Jemima Arnold, married Rezin Virgin, from whom the Clarksville family of that name are descended.
4. Rachel Arnold, married .... Hammond. A James Hammond had land close to her father.
5. Hannah Arnold.
6. Levi Arnold.
7. William Arnold, whose wife was Francy .... Some of their children are buried in the cemetery between East Millsboro and Rices Landing.
8. James Arnold.

Daniel Arnold, Sr., Frederick Arnold, and Daniel Arnold, the latter not designated "Junior," were members of Captain Andrew Ferley's Militia Company, which was recruited in the Castile Run section. Daniel Arnold, Sr., seems to have answered but one tour of duty, and that in October, 1781. On March 7, 1793, a Daniel Arnold and wife, Agnes, sold land in Washington County to Ludwick Bricker. The name then disappears from the records. (Washington County Deed Book 1-I, pp. 536). Daniel Arnold, Sr., may have been the father of Frederick, Daniel, Abraham, and John Arnold, all of whom lived near the site of the present town of Clarksville.

Family of Abraham Arnold

On October 3, 1787, Abraham Arnold warranted a tract of land on the hill north of the town of Clarksville, and this was patented to him November 14, 1788. The Pennsylvania Archives give service for an Abraham Arnold, but it is evident that this service is for another Abraham Arnold and not the Morgan Township man. Greene County records show that he died before June 1830, and left a wife, Elizabeth .... (Orphans' Court Docket, June, 1830, Term).

Children of Abraham and Elizabeth Arnold

1. Hannah Arnold, born 1793-4, died January 19, 1868, aged 74 years. Her husband was John Lewis, who died June 11, 1868, aged 87 years. They are buried in the old Lutheran Cemetery near Marianna.

   ### Children of John and Hannah (Arnold) Lewis
   1. Sarah Lewis, born March 11, 1809, died August 28, 1892.
   2. Daniel Lewis.
   3. Isaac Lewis, died before his father.
   4. Andrew Lewis.
   5. John Lewis, born June 9, 1814, died March 9, 1893.
   6. Betty Lewis, married Jesse Regester.
   7. Mariah Lewis, born May 15, 1819, died February 6, 1893.
   8. George Lewis.
   9. Mary Ann Lewis, died November 15, 1904, aged 87 years; married Abel Hoover, who died December 5, 1880, aged 65 years.
   10. Samuel Lewis, born 1823, died March 19, 1890; married, 1854, Martha Blackledge, born October 24, 1830, died 1863.
2. Catherine Arnold, married Thomas Petterson. They were divorced.
3. Andrew Arnold, died before 1839. His wife was Mary ....

   ### Children of Andrew and Mary Arnold
   1. Abraham Arnold, minor child in 1858.
   2. John Arnold, minor child in 1858.
4. Rachel Arnold, married John Briant.
5. Sarah Arnold.
6. Samuel Arnold.
7. Elizabeth Arnold, married David West.

   ### Children of David and Elizabeth (Arnold) West
   1. Jane West.
   2. Ann West.
   3. John West.
   4. Rachel West.

John Arnold Family

When John Arnold died, about 1798, he left a will in which he made his wife, Elizabeth Arnold, and young son, Daniel Arnold, Jr., his administrators. (Greene County Will Book 1, pp. 10, probated June 21, 1798). One can consider this rather strong evidence that John Arnold was one of the sons of Daniel Arnold, Sr., mentioned as a member of Captain Andrew Ferley's Militia Company. Orphans' Court Docket 1, pp. 4, shows that this Daniel Arnold, Jr., was a minor, over 14 years of age, in December, 1799, when William Heaton was appointed guardian for him. However, Daniel Arnold, Jr., had married Elizabeth ...., prior to December 17, 1799, for they joined with the widow of John Arnold to make a deed. (Deed Book

1, pp. 315). Prior to his death John Arnold had purchased the warrant of Robert Benham for a tract of land on North Tenmile, just north of Clarksville, and had patented it on July 6, 1797. On December 30, 1799, Elizabeth Arnold, widow of John, had gone into court and asked that guardians be appointed for seven minor children, two named being above 14 years of age. When the estate of Elizabeth Arnold was settled, in 1851, another child is mentioned. (Orphans' Court Docket 3, pp. 243). No military service can be shown for this John Arnold, although it would appear he was of military age during the Revolution.

Children of John and Elizabeth Arnold

1. Daniel Arnold, Jr., whose wife was Elizabeth ....
2. David Arnold, over 14 years of age in 1799.
3. Margaret Arnold, who married John Palmer; under 14 years of age in 1799.
4. John Arnold, Jr., under 14 years of age when father died.
5. Jacob Arnold, under 14 years of age in 1799; went to Elkhart, Indiana.
6. Abraham Arnold; died before his mother.
7. George Arnold.
8. Susannah Arnold, wife of Nathaniel Gass; mentioned in mother's estate.

THE PRONG FAMILY

There is an interesting story found in the traditions of the Christopher (Stophel is the German spelling usually found) Prong family. While on the voyage to America the ship on which Christopher Prong was a passenger sighted a little girl floating in mid-ocean and ressued her. She was placed in Mr. Prong's care, and he raised her and later married her, she probably being his second wife. The girl's name was Elizabeth, whom he mentions in his will, and she remarried after the death of Mr. Prong on March 4, 1809, at the age of 53 years, 10 months. (Washington County Will Book 2, pp. 201). Christopher Prong is buried in the Lutheran Cemetery near Marianna.

As Stophel Prong, he enlisted on January 13, 1776, in Captain Thomas Craig's Company of the Second Pennsylvania Battalion, under Colonel Arthur St. Clair, and was in the Ticonderoga Campaign. (Pennsylvania Archives, Series V, Vol. 2, pp. 93-96). After serving his enlistment he removed to the Tenmile Country and settled on a tract of land called "Prong's Quarry," situated in Morgan Township, near Mt. Zion Church. With Peter Heckt he served until his death as one of the executors of the estate of John Lewis (signed Loos in German script in his will). Christopher Prong was living in Washington County when he died, where in the settlement of his estate, quit claim deeds show it was divided into eleven parts, and proves the marriages of several of his daughters. (DB. 3-D—54, etc).

Children of Christopher Prong

1. Margaret Prong. She was the first wife of Peter Bricker, son of Ludwig Bricker of Greene County.
2. Susannah Prong, died January 28, 1856, aged 71 years, 3 months and 20 days. She married Adam Hewitt, who died January 25, 1872, aged 88 years, 5 months and 19 days. Both are buried in Hewitt's Cemetery at Rices Landing.

Children of Adam and Susannah (Prong) Hewitt

1. Mary Hewitt, died December 12, 1875, aged 69 years, 7 months; married David Rose, who died May 14, 1879, aged 73 years, 3 months, 9 days. Buried in the Rose Cemetery. He was a son of John and Hannah (Addelman) Rose.
2. Elizabeth Hewitt. No record.
3. Isaac Hewitt, born January 12, 1809, died September 29, 1881; married Amy ...., born August 1, 1819, died March 2, 1876. Buried in Hewitt's Cemetery.
4. Peter Hewitt, born April 12, 1811, died March 27, 1886; married (1) Ruth Taylor, who died July 22, 1846, aged 31 years, 11 months, 25 days. He married (2) Rose Ann Ainsley who died January 12, 1899, aged 65 years. All are buried in Hewitt's Cemetery.
5. John Hewitt, died July 16, 1879, aged 66 years, 6 months, 16 days. His wife was Mary ...., who died December 2, 1895, aged 71 years. Buried at Hewitt's Cemetery.
6. Levi Hewitt.
7. Solomon Hewitt, died February 28, 1843, aged 25 years, 4 months, 1 day. He married (1) Mary R. ....; (2) Hannah Swan. Buried at Hewitt's Cemetery.
8. Margaret Hewitt, died November 5, 1891, aged 71 years. Buried at Hewitt's Cemetery.
9. George Hewitt, born December 1, 1822, died March 3, 1880; married Margaret A. Swan, born September 3, 1837, died January 30, 1882. Buried at Hewitt's Cemetery.
10. Jacob Hewitt, died April 18, 1887, aged 61 years, 1 month, 3 days; married Rachel ...., who died February 12, 1855, aged 33 years. Buried at Hewitt's Cemetery.

3. Ann Prong, born November 7, 1786, died December 22, 1826; married, March 14, 1808, John Litzenberg, born June 13, 1786, died March 7, 1841, in Milford Township, Knox County, Ohio. His second wife was Eleanor, widow of Jester Hedges, whom he married July 17, 1828. An excellent genealogy of the Litzenberg family has been published in late years by Mr. J. E. Litzenberg of Centerberg, Ohio, and gives a full record of the children of John and Ann (Prong) Litzenberg. The author recalls with pleasure the many visits of Mr. Litzenberg while compiling this excellent genealogy.
4. Catherine Prong, married Frederick Shyette.
5. Sarah Prong.
6. Christina Prong.
7. Mary Prong; married John Conkey.
8. Elizabeth Prong; married Samuel Braden.
9. Rachel Prong; married Daniel Baxter.
10. Ulian (Julian or Juliann?) Prong.

THE BRICKER FAMILY

A history of Knox County, Ohio, published in 1881, says that Ludwick Bricker was one of three immigrant brothers who came to America and settled for a time in Maryland. In 1790 he was living in Washington County, Maryland, but a short time later removed to the Tenmile Country, where, on March 7, 1793, he purchased land from Daniel Arnold and wife, Agnes. (Deed Book 1-I, pp. 536, Washington County, Pa.) This same Knox County History states that Ludwick Bricker served in the Revolution. In Deed Book 7, pp. 31, Greene County, Pennsylvania, there is a list of his heirs.

Children of Ludwick Bricker
1. Rachel Bricker, wife of John Holpruner.
2. Solomon Bricker, whose wife was Mary ....
3. Elizabeth Bricker, wife of Christian Booze.
4. Lewis Bricker, whose wife was Catherine ....
5. Juliana Bricker, who married James Barnet.
6. Elizabeth Bricker of Knox County, Ohio.
7. George Bricker, whose wife was Catherine Thomas.
8. Catherine Bricker, wife of John Conkle.
9. Peter Bricker, who married Margaret Prong.
10. Susan Bricker, wife of George Lewis.

THE LEWIS FAMILY

There should be no question as to the nationality of John Lewis, who settled on the farm adjoining Christopher Prong in Morgan Township, Greene County, about one mile due north from the old Castile School House, because his signature to his will is written in the German script and spelled "Loos." His method of naming his children is distinctly in the German manner of using the prefix "John" before several children. By naming Peter Heckt and Christopher Prong his executors, in his will probated at Waynesburg, August 27, 1805, one is led to believe that he lived in the vicinity of Hagerstown, Maryland, prior to his arrival on the Tenmile. Peter Heckt, Ludwick Bricker, and some Lewis names are in the Census of Washington County, Maryland, for the year 1790. There was also a Henry Huffman ("Hogman") listed in the same vicinity, and John Lewis mentions his brother-in-law, Henry Huffman, which suggests that the wife, Elizabeth, mentioned in his will, was Elizabeth Huffman. Members of the Lewis family are of the opinion that John and Elizabeth Lewis are buried in the unmarked graves next to his sons, John and Daniel Lewis, and say that there were sandstone markers which were very old and undecipherable on these graves at an earlier date, but in late years another burial had been made at the site. If John Lewis was in this section at the time of the Revolution, he may have been the man of that name who served in Captain John Walls' Militia Company.

Children of John and Elizabeth Lewis
1. John Lewis, apparently the Tilghman John Henry Lewis mentioned in the will of John Lewis, Sr., although it may be possible that a comma is missing in the copy of the will of the latter. It was not uncommon for the German families to use a plurality of given names, with the name John repeated several times. It was a term of endearment customarily applied, with the recipient using whichever name he chose for business. John Lewis died in Greene County, June 11, 1868, aged 87 years. His wife was Hannah Arnold, who died on January 19, 1868, at the age of 74 years. Both are buried in the Lutheran Cemetery. Hannah Arnold was the daughter of Abraham and Elizabeth Arnold.

Children of John and Hannah (Arnold) Lewis
1. Sarah Lewis, born March 11, 1809, died August 28, 1892.
2. Daniel Lewis.
3. Isaac Lewis.
4. John Lewis, born June 9, 1814, died March 9, 1893.
5. Andrew Lewis.
6. George Lewis.
7. Mariah Lewis, born May 15, 1819, died February 6, 1895.

8. Betty Lewis, married Jesse Regester.
   9. Samuel Lewis, born 1823, died March 19, 1890; married, 1854, Martha Blackledge, born October 24, 1830, died 1863.
2. John George Lewis, removed with the Brickers to Knox County, Ohio. His wife was Susan, daughter of Ludwick Bricker.
3. Elizabeth Lewis.
4. Sarah Lewis.
5. Daniel Lewis, died March 3, 1819, aged 26 years, 10 months, 11 days. He is buried in the Lutheran Cemetery near his brother, John Lewis. His wife was Esther Woodruff, who applied, in Greene County Court in June, 1822, for guardians for her three minor children. Nehemiah Woodruff was appointed to serve. She was born January 24, 1792, died August 12, 1868; buried at Franklin Cemetery.

Children of Daniel and Esther Lewis
   1. John Lewis.
   2. Elizabeth Lewis.
   3. Mary Lewis, died November 15, 1904, aged 87 years; married Abel Hoover, who died December 5, 1880, aged 65 years.
6. Anna Mary Lewis, died February 19, 1872, aged 61 years, 11 months, 19 days. She married Isaac Keys, who died April 25, 1833, aged 46 years. They are buried in the Lutheran Cemetery. (Keys also spelled Kees).

Children of Isaac and Anna Mary (Lewis) Keys
(Orphans' Court, Washington County, Pa., August, 1853)
   1. Daniel Keys.
   2. John Keys, born August 1, 1813, died April 19, 1887; married, March 29, 1837, Hannah McClelland, born May 20, 1814, died April 19, 1887; daughter of John and Nancy (Montgomery) McClelland.
   3. Isaac Keys, unmarried.
   4. Elizabeth Keys, married Otho West. Two of their children are buried in the Lutheran Cemetery with the Keys and Lewis families.
   5. Maria Keys, married (H)Eaton Huss.
   6. Sarah Keys, never married.
   7. Mary Keys, never married.
   8. Delilah Keys, never married.
   9. Hester Keys, never married.
   10. Nancy Keys, married George Wise.

THE GAYMAN FAMILY

It seems certain that the Gayman family of Morgan Township, are descended from the family of that name who settled early in Berks County, Pennsylvania, where the widow of one Christian Gayman took out letters of administration on the estate of her husband July 19, 1772. This family lived in Hereford Township at that time. Another Christian Gayman died in Brecknock Township, Berks County, Pennsylvania, in 1789, leaving sons Christian, Daniel and Benedict. In an address at the Gayman Family Reunion, in 1920, Jacob Gayman of Scenery Hill, Washington County, gave a history of his family in which he stated that their Christian Gayman came from the Rhine Canton of Switzerland, to Berks County, Pennsylvania, about 1750. He was naturalized there September 24, 1762, and his son, Daniel Gayman, was born there about 1753-57. They were

Amishmen. Christian Gayman had married a widow Clymer, whose daughter, Sarah Clymer, married John Kees. The family removed to Washington County about 1781 and, in April, 1782, Christian (written Christopher in the record) and his son, Daniel Gayman, served in Captain Andrew Ferley's Washington County Militia Company. On June 20, 1786, Christian Gayman warranted a tract of 390 acres of land under the title of "White Oak Level," on the south bank of North Tenmile Creek adjoining the land of Miles Haiden and John Arnold. The family history says he bought his grant of land from the Enochs and it was probably a part of the original land granted, in 1769, to George Bumgarner. On November 5, 1813, Christian Gayman deeded this land to his only son, Daniel Gayman, in preparation for the death that soon was to follow, in 1816. Christian Gayman, his wife, his son, Daniel, with his third wife, are all buried on the Isaac Gayman farm near Marianna, where tombstones indicate that Christian Gayman was 103 years of age at the time of his death.

Daniel Gayman, only son of Christian, and the widow, Clymer Gayman, died in 1849, at the age of either 92 years (or 96 years. The inscription is almost obliterated). He was married three times: first to Olivia Kees, sister of John Kees, by whom he had at least three children. The second wife of Daniel Gayman was a Miss Pieksler, who lived but a short time and died without issue. His third wife, whom he married in 1802, was Olivia Baughman. The 1790 Census record shows two Daniel Gaymans in the same location in Washington County, one of whom is listed as "Junior." The other may have been an uncle living near the subject of this sketch; or, since no Christian Gayman is listed, there may have been an error in the Census.

Children of Daniel and Olivia (Kees) Gayman

1. Jacob Gayman, born January 3, 1790-91, died, 1872, in Indiana. His wife was Mary VanBuskirk, born October 30, 1801, died in Indiana, April 8, 1894. They lived in Pickaway County, Ohio, for a time before settling in the State of Indiana. A son, Samuel Gayman, was born January 22. 1840, in Ohio.
2. Mary Gayman, moved to Pickaway County, Ohio, with her husband, ... Jones, a soldier of the Revolution.
3. Elizabeth Gayman, married Henry Harsh and moved to Pickaway County, Ohio, and later to Moultrie County, Illinois.
4. Isaac Gayman, son of Daniel and Olivia (Baughman) Gayman, born 1804, died 1880; buried in the Lutheran Cemetery near Marianna. He was twice married: (1), Elizabeth Greenlee, who died February 2, 1839, aged 28 years; (2), Amanda Nyswanger, born 1817, died 1905. There were six children by the first marriage and three by the second.

Children of Isaac Gayman

1. George Gayman, married Elizabeth Barnard.
2. Daniel Gayman.
3. Olivia Gayman, married Brewer Gary.
4. Caroline Gayman, married John Gary.
5. Maryann Gayman, married Benjamin Bigler.
6. Samuel Gayman, married Rebecca Grable.
7. Isaac Gayman.
8. Emeline Gayman.
9. Barbara Gayman.

5. Catherine Gayman, daughter of Daniel and Olivia (Bauman) Gayman, born 1805, died 1870; married George Zollars, who died in 1859.

Children of George and Catherine (Gayman) Zollars
1. Neal Zollars.
2. Solomon Zollars.
3. Daniel Zollars.
4. Irving Zollars.
5. Mahala Zollars.
6. Sarah Zollars.
7. Elmina Zollars.

6. John Gayman, son of Daniel and Olivia (Baughman) Gayman, born December 25, 1806, died November 22, 1884; married Barbara Wise, who died November 8, 1858, born July 11, 1810.

Children of John and Barbara (Wise) Gayman
1. David Gayman.
2. Morgan Gayman.
3. Isaac Gayman.
4. Esther Gayman.
5. Lydia Gayman.
6. Nancy Gayman.

7. Sarah Gayman, daughter of Daniel and Olivia (Baughman) Gayman, born 1809, died 1897; married Samuel Barr, Jr.

Children of Samuel and Sarah (Gayman) Barr
1. Elizabeth Barr, married John I. Martin.
2. Andrew J. Barr, married Emma Vankirk.
3. John G. Barr, married (1), Eunice Craig; (2), Hannah Craig.
4. Hannah Barr, never married.
5. Emeline Barr, married David Craig.
6. Isabel Barr, married (1), Henry Montgomery; (2), John Martin.
7. Samuel Barr, married Rebecca Zollars.

8. Joseph Gayman, son of Daniel and Olivia (Baughman) Gayman, born July 9, 1811, died March 26, 1884; married Susan Greenlee.

Children of Joseph and Susan (Greenlee) Gayman
1. Jacob Gayman, married Eveline Crumrine.
2. Thaddeus Gayman.
3. James Gayman, married Elizabeth Addleman.
4. Eliza Gayman, married John Horn.
5. Daniel Gayman, married Ida Leatherman.
6. Emma Gayman, married John Bigler.
7. Margaret Gayman.
8. Sarah Ann Gayman.
9. Samuel Gayman.

9. Solomon Gayman, son of Daniel and Olivia (Baughman) Gayman, died young.
10. Nancy Gayman, daughter of Daniel and Olivia (Baughman) Gayman, died young.

THE KOUTZ FAMILY

Michael Koutz (Kouz, Kauz, Kautz, etc.) was one of the German settlers on the dividing ridge between what is now Washington and Greene County, he living on the Greene County side. His will, made January 18, 1823, was probated at Waynesburg, January 27, 1823. He died January 21, 1823, and is buried in the Lutheran Cemetery near Marianna. He was 57 years, 6 months and 7 days old. No marker exists for his wife, Mary ...., who is mentioned in his will. Ludwick Bricker and Adam Bottomfield witnessed his will, which was administered by John Horn, Sr.

Children of Michael and Mary Koutz
1. John Koutz.
2. Peter Koutz, a blind man.
3. Daniel Koutz, never married.
4. Elizabeth Koutz.
5. Barbara Koutz, married Daniel Smith.
6. Mary Koutz, never married.
7. Jacob Koutz.
8. George Koutz.
9. Michael Koutz, Jr., died November 4, 1819, aged 19 years, 2 months; buried with his father.

THE WISE FAMILY

When Frederick Bumgarner, one of the heirs of George Bumgarner, sold his interest in the land, at the forks of the Tenmile, to Henry Enoch, Sr., he described it as adjoining the lands of Zacheus (Tichnicus) Rose, John Miller, John Shidler and Andrew Wise, the last being the son of Adam Wise, and brother of Frederick Wise, founder of Fredericktown.

Adam Wise was born in Hesse Darmstadt about 1718, and came to America about 1748. He is probably the John Adam Weiss who came over on the British ship Hampshire, Thomas Cheesman, master, that sailed from Rotterdam. After a brief stop at Falmouth, England, the ship arrived at the Port of Philadelphia where, on September 7, 1748, John Adam Weiss took the Oath of Allegiance to the British. He soon removed to Carroll County, Maryland, where, for the next 22 years, he lived as a farmer, distiller and miller, until 1770, when he removed to the Tenmile and took up land to the extent of some 400 acres, some four miles from the mouth of the stream. He is buried in the Wise Cemetery on his original land. His first wife died in Maryland, leaving five sons. Adam Wise then married Catherine ...., by whom eight more children were born. In the year 1775, Adam Wise built a grist mill on his land and raised his large family.

Children of Adam Wise
1. Andrew Wise, born in Germany May 7, 1748, is the man spoken of in the Bumgarner deed. He served in Captain Ezekiel Rose's Company, Fifth Battalion, Washington County Militia. His wife was Zeruah Hartman. He died March 4, 1840, in Washington County.
2. Peter Wise, also a member of Captain Ezekiel Rose's Company. He patented land across the Tenmile from the land of John Arnold. His wife was Mary Miller. They removed to Ohio.

Children of Peter Wise
1. Andrew Wise.
2. Hannah Wise, wife of Jacob Zollars.

3. Frederick Wise, founder of Fredericktown, served in Captain James Craven's Company in the Fifth Battalion, Washington County Militia. Patented land next George Bumgarner.

Children of Frederick Wise

1. Henry Wise, mentioned in deed 1-Z, 407, November 22, 1815, Washington County.
2. Catherine Wise, wife of Jesse Bumgarner; mentioned in above deed as only daughter of Frederick Wise.
3. Jacob Wise.
4. Henry Wise, born in Maryland; served in Captain Ezekiel Rose's Company, Fifth Battalion, Washington County Militia. Removed to (West (?) Virginia).
5. Adam Wise, Jr., born in Maryland, April 5, 1763, died in Washington County, Pennsylvania, July 15, 1842; served in Captain Ezekiel Rose's Company, Fifth Battalion, Washington County Militia. He married Barbara Zollars, born 1759, died September 29, 1852. Both are buried in the Wise Cemetery.

Children of Adam and Barbara (Zollars) Wise

1. Elizabeth Wise, born May 8, 1785; married Jacob Shidler.
2. David Wise, born March 8, 1787; married (1), Esther Shidler; when she died he married Rachel Garrett. He was the father of 18 children.
3. Samuel Wise, born August 10, 1789; married .... Shidler.
4. George Wise, born November 13, 1791; married Margaret Uhlery.
5. Frederick Wise, born September 2, 1793, died February 14, 1846; married Elizabeth Burson, born January 28, 1799, died December 23, 1879; both buried in the Wise Cemetery.
6. Rebecca Wise, born November 20, 1795; married Peter Crumrine.
7. Joseph Wise, born May 22, 1797, died April 20, 1863; married (1), Permelia Barnard; (2), Julia Welch.
8. Solomon Wise, born May 16, 1799; married (1), Permelia Alexander; (2), Jane Alexander.

6. Jacob Wise, son of Adam and Catherine Wise, Sr.
7. Daniel Wise, settled in West (?) Virginia; second son of Adam and Catherine Wise, Sr.
8. Abraham Wise, son of Adam and Catherine Wise, Sr.
9. Tobias Wise, son of Adam and Catherine Wise, Sr.
10. Mary Wise, daughter of Adam and Catherine Wise, Sr.
11. Mary Ann Wise, daughter of Adam and Catherine Wise, Sr.
12. Ulian Wise, son of Adam and Catherine Wise, Sr.
13. Judith Wise, daughter of Adam and Catherine Wise, Sr.; married Rev. John Spohn.

THE HAWKINS FAMILY

Historians for the Hawkins family state that their ancestor was Robert Hawkins, born in Lancastershire, England, in 1695, who came to America about 1716 and settled in Harford County, Maryland, about eight miles from Havre de Grace. One Robert Hawkins died in Harford County, November 5, 1801, and his will was probated at Bel Air, November 11, 1801. It may well be that the Robert Hawkins, immigrant, and the one who died in 1801, were different persons, for one is usually skeptical of such great age as claimed in this case. The Robert Hawkins, of the will record, married, about 1739, Lydia Crutchet of Anne Arundel County, Maryland, who died in 1808, at the age of 85 years.

Children of Robert and Lydia (Crutchet) Hawkins

1. Thomas Hawkins, born 1741, died May 15, 1826; removed to the Tenmile Country before the end of the Revolution, in which he served as a sergeant of the Maryland Line. His wife was Sarah Hargrove, born 1747, died April 15, 1827. The will of Thomas Hawkins, made on October 14, 1825, was probated at Washington, June 9, 1826. Thomas Hawkins and wife are buried in the Hawkins Cemetery near Bealsville.

Children of Thomas and Sarah (Hargrove) Hawkins

1. Absolom Hawkins, born July 21, 1765, died July 6, 1827; married Elizabeth Crawford, born in Fayette County, Pennsylvania, 1779, died March 19, 1824.

Children of Absolom and Elizabeth (Crawford) Hawkins

1. John Hawkins.
2. Cynthia Hawkins.
3. Matilda Hawkins. Married (1), John Cooper; (2), Thomas Howden.

2. Richard Hawkins, born in Maryland, August 25, 1770, died in Greene County, Pennsylvania, February 6, 1856. His will, made September 3, 1841, was probated at Waynesburg, February 18, 1856. (W. B. 3, pp. 209). His wife was Cynthia Crawford, daughter of James and Sarah (Jones) Crawford. She was born February 8, 1786, died July 16, 1845. They were married May 12, 1803.

Children of Richard and Cynthia (Crawford) Hawkins

1. Absolom Hawkins, born March 4, 1805, died July 1, 1871; married (1), September 22, 1826, Lydia Nyswanger, who died in 1827. He married (2), Sarah Hawkins, who died 1893.
2. Elizabeth Hawkins, born April 8, 1807, died January 27, 1859; married Nelson Greenfield, born February 15, 1802, died August 4, 1865.
3. James C. Hawkins, born October 8, 1808, died January 15, 1891; married, March 24, 1836, Margaret Wise, born October 2, 1818, died January 15, 1892.
4. Matilda Hawkins, born May 5, 1810, died April 15, 1886; married Isaac Stull, born 1807, died December 26, 1889.
5. Sarah Hawkins, born November 1, 1811, died September 1, 1883; married James Crawford, born April 3, 18........, died 1869.
6. Richard C. Hawkins, born November 11, 1814, died October 22, 1900; married, November 25, 1841, Emeline Wise, born November 28, 1820, died August 10, 1897. She and Margaret Wise were children of Frederick and Elizabeth (Burson) Wise.
7. Mary A. Hawkins, born March 17, 1817, died August 9, 1884.
8. Cassandra Hawkins, born January 17, 1819, died May 17, 1841; married Henry Uhlery.
9. Thomas H. Hawkins, born January 11, 1821, died January 25, 1892; married, December 5, Emily Parshall, born July 13, 1842, died April 19, 1921.
10. William Hawkins, born August 10, 1823, died October 27, 1885.
11. John C. Hawkins, born December 5, 1825, died May 20,

1903; married, June 8, 1882, Elizabeth McMurray, born December 5, 1846, died March 19, 1920.
3. Lydia Hawkins, married Joseph Fowler.
4. Mary Hawkins, born November 25, 1776, died April 28, 1791.
5. Elizabeth Hawkins, born February 23, 1775; married Alexander McCoy.

Children of Alexander and Elizabeth (Hawkins) McCoy

1. Thomas McCoy.
2. Absalom McCoy.
3. Ruth McCoy.
4. Sarah McCoy.
5. Matilda McCoy.
6. Eliza McCoy.
7. Mary McCoy.

6. Sarah Hawkins, born February 26, 1779, died March 9, 1779.
7. William Hawkins, born November 23, 1780, died February 8, 1853; married Ann Mosier, born 1784, died December 31, 1876.

Children of William and Ann (Mosier) Hawkins

1. John Hawkins.
2. Sarah Hawkins.
3. Susan Hawkins.
4. Mary Hawkins.
5. Catherine Hawkins.
6. Rebecca J. Hawkins.
7. Eliza Hawkins.

8. Thomas Hawkins, born October 14, 1784, died February 5, 1868; married Mary Mosier, born 1794, died September 26, 1885.

Children of Thomas and Mary (Mosier) Hawkins

1. William Hawkins.
2. Noah Hawkins.
3. John Hawkins.
4. Richard Hawkins.
5. Jonathan Hawkins.
6. Thomas Hawkins.
7. Samuel Hawkins.
8. James Hawkins.
9. Mary Ann Hawkins.
10. George Hawkins.

9. Ruth Hawkins, born July 6, 1789, died May 26, 1851; married Rev. Robert Hawkins, who died April 15, 1853.

Children of Rev. Robert and Ruth (Hawkins) Hawkins

1. Thomas Hawkins.
2. Elijah Hawkins.
3. Gideon Hawkins.
4. Louisa Hawkins.
5. Mary Hawkins.
6. Richard Hawkins.
7. Avarilla Hawkins.
8. Elizabeth Hawkins.
9. Robert Hawkins.

2. Robert Hawkins, Jr., born in Maryland, 1745. He died at Valley Forge while serving in the Maryland Line during the War of the Revolution. His wife was Elizabeth ....

Children of Robert and Elizabeth Hawkins

1. Robert Hawkins, born December 14, 1773, died March 7, 1847; married Ann ...., born in 1777, died November 28, 1862.

Children of Robert and Ann Hawkins

1. Elizabeth Hawkins, died 1853; married David Silvers.
2. Mary Hawkins, married John W. Hawkins of Columbiana, Ohio.
3. John Hawkins, died 1880.
4. William Hawkins, born September 11, 1799, died September 25, 1889.
5. George Hawkins, born March 11, 1809.

3. Richard Hawkins was born in Maryland in 1748. He served in the Maryland Line during the Revolution. It is probable that he came to the Tenmile Country with his brother, Thomas Hawkins, and is the Richard Hawkins who served as clerk in Captain Robert Sweeney's Company, Fifth Battalion, Washington County Militia, and was on the Crawford Expedition to Sandusky. He was twice married, first to Elizabeth Cox, daughter of William and Mary (Goldhawk) Cox, by whom he had one child. His second wife was Avarilla Durbin, by whom he had a large family.

Child of Richard and Elizabeth (Cox) Hawkins

1. Elizabeth Hawkins, born 1775, died 1859; married Gregory Barnes.

THE BOTTOMFIELD FAMILY

There is evidence that this Greene County family is descended from ancestors who were natives of the Palatinate or Rhine Valley, three of whom came to America on the British ship "Two Brothers," Thomas Arnott, master. This ship left Rotterdam and, after touching at Cowes, England, arrived at the Port of Philadelphia, where, on August 28, 1750, Johannes Battenfeld, Phillip Battenfeld, and Hans Adam Battenfeld, took the Oath of Allegiance to the British. Two years later, on September 15, 1752, an ancestor of this writer arrived on this same ship and, with the same sailing master, and took the oath at Philadelphia. We have the signed pledge of Johannes Peter Puterbach, our great-great-great grandfather, secured from the Library of Congress.

No doubt this Hans Adam Battenfeld was the immediate ancestor of the family who settled on "Essex," the tract of land outside Clarksville, originally patented to Samuel Bell. John Bottomfield, probable son of Adam Battenfeld, was born in Virginia, September 28, 1756, and died in Morgan Township, Greene County, February 21, 1798. His will, signed in German script, was filed for probate on March 17, 1804, and is in Will Book 1, pp. 42. His wife was Barbara, who some descendants claim was a Hill, while others say she was Barbara Hammond. There is some reason for believing she was related to Michael Koutz. Barbara was born June 26, 1758, and died October 10, 1851. Both are buried in the Bottomfield Cemetery in Morgan Township. The late Edward Bottomfield, formerly in the shoe business in Waynesburg, and Mr. J. E. Litzenberg of Centerberg, Ohio, are authority for much of the record of the family.

Children of John and Barbara Bottomfield

1. Susannah Bottomfield, married Peter Miller.

AND ITS PIONEER FAMILIES

2. Adam Bottomfield, born May 18, 1786, died in Greene County, January 27, 1862; married Mary Litzenberg, daughter of George and Grace (Coats) Litzenberg, born May 17, 1788, died in Columbus Junction, Iowa, March 29, 1876. Adam Bottomfield was accidentally killed when a log rolled on him while cutting timber. His widow then moved to Iowa to be with a number of her children.

Children of Adam and Mary (Litzenberg) Bottomfield

1. Mary Ann Bottomfield, born March 20, 1810, died on June 27, 1836; married Joseph Masters, who later married Hannah Woodward.
2. Rachel Bottomfield, born January 14, 1812, died October 30, 1865; married John Mitchenor, born February 16, 1804, died January 12, 1879.
3. Maria Bottomfield, born December 30, 1813, died November 21, 1848. She was the first wife of George Greenlee, Jr.
4. Lucinda Bottomfield, born September 13, 1816, died May 4, 1901, in Iowa. She married, January 7, 1841, Greer MacIlvaine Greenlee, born November 18, 1816, died October 10, 1901. They went by covered wagon to Iowa in 1855.
5. Isaac Bottomfield, born October 7, 1818, died 1904, at South English, Iowa; married Mary Jane Heaton, born August 19, 1827, died November 23, 1868.
6. Margaret Bottomfield, born May 12, 1821, died in 1826.
7. John Bottomfield, born October 1, 1823, died December 31, 1894, in Louisa County, Iowa. He married (1), Rachel Heaton, born May 28, 1828, died August 21, 1864; (2), Lucy (Jenkins) Robertson.
8. George Bottomfield, born about 1825; killed while threshing, in 1847.
9. William C. Bottomfield, born August 22, 1829, died at Anderson, Iowa, January 17, 1888. He married, August 8, 1852, Jane Drake, born November 8, 1833, died March 3, 1917.
10. Adam Bottomfield, Jr., born April 3, 1832, died in Iowa, August 14, 1865. His wife was Ruth Burson, born 1839, died 1906; married (2), Daniel Smith.

3. John Bottomfield, born April 27, 1788, died August 7, 1866, in Knox County, Ohio; married Mary Woodruff, born in New Jersey, April 13, 1794, died December 6, 1871.

Children of John and Mary (Woodruff) Bottomfield

1. Sarah Bottomfield, born December 10, 1812, died January 16, 1889; married (1), November 10, 1833, William Ferguson; (2), ... Wolfe.
2. Joseph Bottomfield, born September 20, 1814, died August 6, 1895; buried near Oblong, Illinois. He married (1), March 20, 1845, Sarah Jane Williams. His second wife was Eliza Ann Myers, and third wife was Jane Tracy.
3. Barbara Bottomfield, born August 17, 1816, died December 1898; married Job Sutton, on February 14, 1836.
4. Meeker Bottomfield, born August 17, 1816, twin of Barbara, died February 15, 1897; married, March 16, 1843, Bethia Hubble.
5. Esther Bottomfield, born January 30, 1821, died December 24, 1895; married, June 15, 1843, William Bishop, born June 12, 1822, died June 21, 1810.
6. Phoebe Bottomfield, born February 16, 1823; married, September 12, 1844, James McClelland.

7. Jane Bottomfield, born July 19, 1825; married, April 20, 1845, William Williams.
   8. Elizabeth Bottomfield, born July 24, 1827, died June 7, 1885; married, January 14, 1855, David Martin.
   9. Nehemiah Bottomfield, born April 11, 1833, died May 17, 1904; married (1), February 21, 1856, Cordelia Redman, born May 10, 1835, died June 20, 1874; married (2), September 17, 1876, Salina Mouser, born January 30, 1848.
   10. William L. Bottomfield, born May 2, 1839, died February 6, 1920, at Cushing, Oklahoma. He married Lumercia Stephens.
4. Magdelina Bottomfield, married George Zollars.
5. Christina Bottomfield, born October 29, 1791, died November 25, 1862; married William Litzenberg, born May 7, 1790, died February 16, 1868. On April 1, 1843, they left Millsboro, Pennsylvania, and traveled all the way by water to Stewartsville, Missouri, where they arrived exactly one month later.

Children of William and Christina (Bottomfield) Litzenberg
   1. John Litzenberg, born October 29, 1812, died January 13, 1869; married (1), June 20, 1840, Catherine Jenkins, who died May 2, 1855. John Litzenberg was married twice later.
   2. James Litzenberg, born October 2, 1814, died February 8, 1815.
   3. George Litzenberg, born November 1, 1815, died December 21, 1817.
   4. Cynthia Litzenberg, born May 13, 1818, died August 16, 1868; married, July 29, 1840, John Shearer.
   5. Mary Litzenberg, born January 10, 1821; married, March 10, 1842, William Addleman.
   6. Hiram Litzenberg, born March 23, 1823, died October 29, 1861; married, February 6, 1846, Elizabeth Snoderly.
   7. Rebecca Litzenberg, born June 24, 1825, died August 6, 1912; married, September 24, 1845, Ezekiel Downing, who died April 24, 1870.
   8. Harriet Litzenberg, born November 19, 1827, died June 22, 1848; married, August 28, 1846, Strother Wilson, who died June 17, 1851.
   9. Simon Litzenberg, born September 6, 1830, died April 23, 1859; married, November 29, 1855, Amanda Burnett, born May 18, 1838. His widow remarried.
   10. William Litzenberg, born September 6, 1830, twin of Simon; married, August 28, 1858, Elizabeth Mobley. They went to California.
   11. Lucinda Litzenberg, born May 19, 1835, died October 29, 1922; married January 31, 1856, Thomas L. King, born September 26, 1828, died June 27, 1907. He was a judge in DeKalb County, Missouri.
6. Samuel Bottomfield, married Margaret Mitchell.
7. Catherine Bottomfield, married John Gass.
8. Barbara Bottomfield, died at Lincoln, Illinois; married Aaron Heaton, born at Coshocton, Ohio, died about 1839.

Children of Aaron and Barbara (Bottomfield) Heaton
   1. Lemuel Heaton, born February 3, 1830, died August 23, 1904; married, March 20, 1853, Charlotte Bell, born February 1, 1833, at Jefferson, Pennsylvania, died November 1, 1904.
   2. Rachel Heaton, married John Bottomfield.
   3. Jane Heaton, married Isaac Bottomfield.

4. Amanda Heaton, married Mr. McGlumphey, a professor of Lincoln College and later of Marshall College, Missouri.
5. Catherine Heaton, married William Hartsock.

THE QUAKERS

A short distance to the west of Clarksville, on the south bank of South Tenmile, a number of Quaker families bought land prior to the end of the Revolutionary War. Most of these families were from Bucks County, Pennsylvania, or had lived there before migrating to the Shenandoah Valley. A good history of the background of these families is to be found in "Early Friends Families of Upper Bucks County," by Clarence V. Roberts. Further information regarding the migrations of these families is to be found in "Old Hopewell," by Griffith. The excellent records kept by the Friends, are so complete, that vital statistics in these families are readily obtainable. Henshaw's several books, copied from the original Friends Meeting House records, even trace many of the descendants of the Greene County Quakers. The rules of the Friends demanded a permit to move from place to place, and the certificates issued by the Monthly Meetings, to its members, makes their migrations easy to follow. From Richland, Buckingham, Springfield, and other Monthly Meetings in Bucks County, to Hopewell, Crooked Creek, Gunpowder, and other Monthly Meetings in Virginia and Maryland, to Westlands Monthly Meeting in Washington County, the movements of the members of this faith were accurately recorded. The families of this group that settled in this area on Tenmile above Clarksville, included the Blackledges, Hoges, Strawns, Bursons, Van Buskirks, Garwoods, and Adamsons.

These people had no cause to fortify, and through the worst times, lived at peace with the Indians. Even the section in which they settled there was little molestation of their neighbors, the Rofelty Massacre being the only one recorded. They were non martial, but one does find where some of them took up arms and the church dismissed them. At other times when their neighbors were victims of the Redmen, these people would hasten to the relief of the unfortunates, though it meant risking their own lives. Probably the distance from the meeting houses, and the real independence of these people, account for the movement of the second generation of these settlers from the tenets of their faith, so that by 1855 it was deemed advisable to move the church to a more fertile field.

The Friends did not believe in any show, which extended to the erection of tombstones after death, so that many records of this sort are missing, but the locations of their several family cemeteries are known, and Bible records supply some of the missing information.

BLACKLEDGE FAMILY

William Blackledge, first American ancestor of the Blackledge Family, came from England about 1682, and a short time later purchased a tract of land on the west bank of the Neshaminy, in Southampton Township, Bucks County, Pennsylvania. Mr. Roberts states that William Blackledge married a daughter of Benjamin Duffield, and sometime prior to his death in 1718, transferred his real estate to his father-in-law, who in turn conveyed the joint holdings in entail to Benjamin Blackledge and his male heirs forever. This Benjamin Blackledge, eldest son of William, tanner in Lower Dublin Township, Bucks County, removed to Johnson County, North Carolina in 1758 and almost immediately, was joined by his son, Richard Blackledge of Craven County, in a deed to Samuel Swift for the purpose of docking the entail, in which they were successful, and Richard made a conveyance in fee.

The Known Children of William Blackledge

1. Benjamin Blackledge, married December 26th, 1728, Christ's Church, Philadelphia, Sarah Philpot.
2. Thomas Blackledge, born 1707 in Bucks County, Pa. Died there in lower Milford Township on December 7, 1790. He married by New Jersey license April 15, 1730, Elizabeth Randell.
3. Robert Blackledge, married June 19, 1732, in Christ's Church, Elizabeth Howard.
4. John Blackledge, married in First Presbyterian Church in Philadelphia July 7, 1736, Briget Grimes.

Family of Thomas Blackledge, Sr.

Thomas Blackledge, Sr., son of William Blackledge, was born in Bucks County about 1707. At the time of his marriage he settled in Lower Milford Township, taking up a tract of land by warrant, and adding to it by purchase of a tract from Thomas Banks. He took an active part in Bucks County politics, and was elected sheriff of the county. In 1757 he was elected to the Colonial Assembly. (Penna. Arch Series VI, Vol. 11, pp 90-92.) During that year he was one of a group of persons that appealed to the Assembly for relief from Indian depredations. He took no part in the Revolution, paying very heavily for non service. He was a tanner and distiller by trade as shown by tax lists. The Blackledge Family were not originally Quakers, but Thomas and his family became affiliated with Richland Monthly Meeting and continued in that faith. Having outlived most of his children, Thomas Blackledge by a will made February 18, 1790, disposed of his large estate, mostly among his grand-children. He died in Lower Milford Township on December 7, 1790. His wife was Elizabeth Randell, whom he married by New Jersey License on April 15, 1730. Their children were:

1. William Blackledge, born January 16, 1731, died December 8, 1761, married June 15, 1757, Ann Lewis, born August 11, 1738.
2. Robert Blackledge, born about 1735, a shoemaker by trade, and later a store keeper. He appears to have come into Greene County, where he remained a short time and later removed to Columbiana County, Ohio. He married February 18, 1763, Joanna Van Lude. They were ancestors of the Denny Family of Waynesburg.
3. Elizabeth Blackledge, born in Bucks County about 1737. She married December 9, 1756, at Richland Monthly Meeting, George Hoge, son of William and Ann Hoge, originally of Opequan Monthly Meeting in Virginia. He was born February 6, 1733, and died in Greene County, Pennsylvania in 1805. His wife died in 1804. Their family record will be given under the Hoge Family.
4. Mary Blackledge, died without issue. Married on September 16, 1765, John Clymer.
5. Thomas Blackledge, Jr., was born in Bucks County about 1738, and died in Washington County, Pennsylvania (now Greene) in 1787. (Will Book 1., pp. 77.) His wife was Margaret Wright.

Family of Thomas and Margaret (Wright) Brackledge

Thomas Blackledge, Jr., born in Bucks County about 1738 was married at Richland Monthly Meeting, April 11, 1756, to Margaret Wright. About 1778 he removed to the Tenmile Country and settled on the farm near Jefferson, which he had patented to him under the title of "Farmer's Tract" and which remains to this day in the hands of his descendants. It is obvious from the will of James Burson, that Thomas Blackledge came into the section some time before he brought his family, and when he returned to Bucks County, sold a part of his selected lands to the father of his son-in-law. Hopewell Monthly Meeting of Frederick County, Virginia, shows that on August 4, 1782, Thomas Blackledge and wife Margaret, with eight of their children, brought a certificate from Richland Monthly Meeting to Hopewell. Later they transferred to Westlands Monthly Meeting. The will of Thomas Blackledge, made June 23rd, 1786, and filed in Washington County, names his wife, Margaret, who survived him, and the children. Thomas and Margaret Blackledge are buried in the Burson Cemetery, but their graves are unmarked.

1. Elizabeth Blackledge, born on October 26, 1758, died in Greene County July 26, 1853. She married Edward Burson, son of James and Sarah (Price) Burson, also a Tenmile pioneer. (of whom, later)
2. Enoch Blackledge, born March 1, 1759 (a Bible record probably correct, in which case Elizabeth's birth must be in error). His wife was Sarah Adamson, born in Bucks County, January 14, 1763. He and his brother, William Blackledge, patented land in their own right, and on the death of his father, he inherited the home plantation. Enoch died about 1842. (Greene County Will Book 2, pp. 161.) Most of their children settled in Ohio, but his son, Levi, remained on the home place, and with his wife Margaret Sharpnack, were the ancestors of the present family of the name, living in the county.
3. Mary Blackledge, remained in Bucks County with her husband, Jeremiah Williams, whom she married April 25, 1779, at Richland Monthly Meeting. He was born May 9, 1749.
4. William Blackledge, died in Greene County about 1847, leaving a wife, Mary .... but no children. (Will Book 3, pp. 17-18.)
5. Thomas Blackledge, removed to Jefferson County, Ohio. His wife was Margaret ....
6. Levi Blackledge, removed to Columbiana County, Ohio. His wife was Barbara Rofelty.
7. Isaac Blackledge, born in Bucks County, November 3, 1770, died in Greene County June 22, 1826, buried in the Burson Cemetery. His wife was Allee Evans, born July 4, 1777, a daughter of John and Margaret Evans. She died September 28, 1866. No children of their own, but raised Noah Teal.
8. Martha Blackledge, removed with her husband Uriah White, to Columbiana County, Ohio. They appear to have been among the early settlers in Whiteley Township, Greene County, but certainly not the people for whom the Whiteley Creek was named, as stated in some histories. The Creek was so named long before they settled on it.
9. Abraham Blackledge, died in Columbiana County, Ohio, in 1823. He owned several lots in Rices Landing, as well

as a tract of 400 acres in the county. Died unmarried.
10. James Blackledge, also died unmarried in Ohio. Was owner of lots in Rices Landing.
11. Margaret Blackledge, also died unmarried in August 1819, her brothers and sisters sharing her estate. (Greene County Will Book 1, pp. 193.)

FAITHFUL RICHARDSON'S LETTER

Middleton Township
March the 11th 1825

Friend Teagarden: I received a letter in company with a valentine there is more contained in the letter than I am capible of answering at this time thee must not not look for as well composed a letter from as young a person as I am not being in practice of writing letters. in the first place I must acknowledge the kindness of my relations interducing us to you as strangers and the kind reception we got in your family I would suppose thee would not have any fears of coldness received by me nor my parents for they have never been in the practice of misusing any Decent person and I beleive from the acquaintance and the recomindation we gave them of the reception we got at your house thee need not be afeared to come and see for thyself if I should by way of my pen tel thee too many flatring tails of my good abilities and the different sensations of my mind these lines might fall in the hands of a stranger or be abuse made of them some other way and as it is five miles from the mill to Lisbon and fifteen hear so as the Queen of the North did by King Solomon she had heard a grait deal of his excellancy and she went and saw for hirself and I shant undertake to rite much at this time for if thee should come this way thee will find I have a better use of my tung than I have of my pen   I remain your well wisher

Faithful Richardson

To Uriah Teagarden

Mr. Floyd E. Neikirk of Clyde, Ohio, has sent in the photostat copy of the above quaint letter of a Quaker Maid to her future husband. In spite of poor spelling and grammer, Faithful Richardson won her man and they were married December 24, 1826.   (H. L. L.)

ENOCH BLACKLEDGE FAMILY

Enoch Blackledge, son of Thomas and Margaret (Wright) Blackledge, was born in Bucks County, Pennsylvania on March 1, 1759, and died in Greene County on July 23, 1842. He joined his father in the migration to the Tenmile Country, but being an adult his name is not included in the certificate taken from Richland Monthly meeting to Hopewell Monthly Meeting by Thomas and Margaret Blackledge on August 4, 1782. He married Sarah Adamson, daughter of Thomas and Mary Adamson, and Hopewell Monthly Meeting disowned her for breach of the Society rules on June 3, 1784, so it is probable that Enoch Blackledge had withdrawn from the Friends before that date. He is found among the names of those who petitioned for the formation of a new State, but no military record is available. Enoch Blackledge and his brother, William, patented in trust for his mother and the minor children of Thomas Blackledge on July 16, 1792, the land known as "Farmers Tract," which had been warranted to his father on June 17, 1786. Later he inherited this land, which remains in the hands of his descendents. He also added land by purchase. His wife,

Sarah Adamson, was born January 14, 1763, in Bucks County. Enoch Blackledge left a will in Greene County, which was made July 26, 1836, and probated August 1, 1842. (Will Book 2. pp. 161.)

Family of Enoch and Sarah (Adamson) Blackledge
(From Bible owned by Mrs. Roxy Blackledge)

1. Mary Blackledge, born April 6, 1782, died near Little Berea, Ohio, September 28, 1862, married in Greene County, Pennsylvania, Samuel Richardson, son of John and Lydia (Baker) Richardson. A letter written by Samuel Richardson in 1848 says he was 70 years of age and had 28 grandchildren and one great grandchild at that time. He was born February 27, 1779, and died July 22, 1861.

Children of Samuel and Mary (Blackledge) Richardson
(Bible dates from Floyd E. Neikirk, Clyde, Ohio)

1. Alfred Richardson, born November 11, 1805.
2. Faithful Richardson, born June 12, 1807, married December 14, 1826, Uriah Teagarden, born June 10, 1798. He died January 4, 1882. His wife had died October 10, 1833.
3. Sarah Richardson, born August 10, 1809, married .... Campbell.
4. Lydia Richardson, born October 28, 1811, married .... Dixon.
5. Enoch Richardson, born October 10, 1813.
6. Margaret Richardson, born January 5, 1816, married .... Smith.
7. Mary Richardson, born January 5, 1816, twin of Margaret. She married .... Fisher.
8. Samuel Richardson, born August 19, 1821, married 1844, Elizabeth Fisher, daughter of Michael and Eliza Fisher.
8. Phoebe Richardson, twin of Samuel, born August 19, 1821.
10. Stillborn child, born August 16, 1826.

2. Thomas Blackledge, born July 21, 1784. An old letter says he removed to Iowa and names a living daughter.

Children
1. Maryann Blackledge married .... Bearer.

3. John Blackledge, born July 21, 1786, went to California during the Gold Rush.

Children
1. Isaac Blackledge, lived at Oneida, Ohio, in 1859.

4. Margaret Blackledge, born June 11, 1789 married (1) Nehemiah Richardson, and after his death married Dr. Eli Vale of Jefferson, Pennsylvania.
5. William Blackledge, born October 16, 1793, died in Carroll County, Ohio, December 19, 1853, married Sophrona Sturgeon, born October 8, 1797, died April 1870.

Children
1. Hiram Blackledge, born August 21, 1816, died in Delaware County, Ohio, December 1885, married November 1, 1838 Eleanor Mills.
2. Maria Blackledge, born December 18, 1817, died December 26, 1855, married January 15, 1846, John Rollison.
3. Enoch Blackledge, born October 14, 1819, died June 1857, never married.
4. Isaac Blackledge, born October 10, 1823, died May 27, 1829.
5. Margaret Blackledge, born October 14, 1825, died in 1904,

married September 3, 1854, William Wiley. They went to Vinton County, Iowa.
6. Mary Blackledge, born September 15, 1827, married January 4, 1848, Samuel Groves. They went to Ricland County, Michigan.
7. William Blackledge, born September 14, 1830, died about 1910. Married November 27, 1857, Phoebe Jones. Went to Rockville, Indiana, and then to Kansas City.
8. Phoebe Blackledge, born September 26, 1832, married John Hartgrove. They went to Isabelle County, Michigan.
9. Martha Blackledge, born January 15, 1835, died October 1895, married George W. King of Carroll County, Ohio.
10. Levi Blackledge, born November 17, 1836, died January 20, 1930, in Carroll County, Ohio. He married December 1865, Matilda Permar.
11. Elizabeth Blackledge, born February 2, 1839, died November 6, 1926, in Carroll County, Ohio, married December 1892, Thomas Hales.
12. Franklin Blackledge, born June 9, 1843, died in Carroll County, Ohio, July 4, 1930. He never married.

6. Martha Blackledge, born August 21, 1795, married Joseph Baker.
7. Levi Blackledge, born October 15, 1797, died in Greene County, November 15, 1870. He married Margaret Sharpnack, daughter of Henry and Elizabeth Sharpnack. She was born on February 14, 1801, and died April 11, 1876. Both are buried in the Cemetery on Stockton Lane. Levi Blackledge received the home farm from his father.

Children

1. Mary Blackledge, born 1822, died 1858, married June 23, 1852 James Rhodes, born 1806.
2. Sarah Blackledge, born 1825, died March 29, 1859, married December 25, 1855, Samuel Stewart.
3. Martha Blackledge, born October 24, 1830, died 1863, married March 16, 1854, Samuel Lewis, born 1825, died ....
4. Stiers Blackledge, born 1833, died 1911. Married Alena Crouch, who died September 29, 1837. He got the home from his father.
5. Enoch Blackledge, died in infancy.

8. James Blackledge, born April 24, 1803, lived at Oneida, Ohio.

LEVI BLACKLEDGE FAMILY

Levi Blackledge, son of Thomas and Margaret (Wright) Blackledge, was born in Bucks County, Pennsylvania. He married Barbara Rofelty, daughter of Mathias Rofelty, and for this marriage was disowned by Westland Monthly Meeting on February 25, 1804. The same year he removed to land he had bought in Salem Township, Columbiana County, Ohio, a year earlier. With him was Uriah White, who had married his sister, Martha Blackledge, and William Teagarden, who had married his wife's sister, Susannah Rofelty. He was also accompanied by Robert Blackledge, his cousin, a son of Robert and Joana (Van Lude) Blackledge. Levi Blackledge built a grist mill on the middle fork of Beaver Creek in the summer of 1804 and the following year added a saw mill. Mack's "History of Columbiana County" says Levi Blackledge died about 1812. This same history says that Barbara (Rofelty) Blackledge's mother went to the same locality with her daughter who married William Teagarden, but this does not agree with the story of the Rofelty Massacre told in Greene County History, which says the mother and several children were killed by the Indians Perhaps Mathias Rofilty married after the death of his first wife and the lady mentioned was a step mother. When Levi Blackledge died he left his property to his brothers Abraham and James Blackledge, after giving the mill and 165 acres to his daughter, Sarah. In will on file in Greene County, William Blackledge, a brother of Levi, mentions another child of Levi and Barbara (Rofelty) Blackledge, and a deed of record in Columbiana County includes this same son Jesse Blackledge in the sale by Barbara Blackledge after she became a widow. No others are known.

Children of Levi and Barbara (Rofelty) Blackledge

1. Sarah Blackledge, married Nathan Harris. They bought land from the widow of Levi and her son Jesse Blackledge. In 1860 Sarah (Blackledge) Harris, evidently a widow, was living in Springfield, Logan County, Illinois, as shown by quit claim deeds.
2. Jesse Blackledge, mentioned in several records as a son of Levi and Barbara (Rofelty) Blackledge.

JEREMIAH WILLIAMS FAMILY

Mary Blackledge, daughter of Thomas and Margaret (Wright) Blackledge, was born in Bucks County, Pennsylvania. She married at Richland Monthly Meeting on April 25, 1779, Jeremiah Williams, son of Benjamin and Mary (Newbury) Williams, of Noximixon Township. He was born on May 9, 1740, and died in Bucks County in 1834. They did not accompany the Blackledges to the Tenmile.

Children of Jeremiah and Mary (Blackledge) Williams

1. John Williams, born January 27, 1780; died June 6, 1858. Married Christina Kimball.
2. Thomas Blackledge Williams, born April 11, 1781. Married Rebecca Arndt.
3. Benjamin Williams, born December 18, 1782. Married (1) Mary (Meredith) Burson, widow of John W. Burson of Springfield, Bucks County. His second wife was Rachel Williams, daughter of Benjamin and Dorothy (Lieper) Williams.
4. Susan Williams, born June 10, 1785. Never married.
5. William Williams, born June 12, 1789. Married Hannah Whiting.
6. Samuel Williams, born June 18, 1792. Died 1812.
7. Isaac Burson Williams, born April 23, 1794. Married Martha Shelton White.
8. Margaret Williams, born April 28, 1796; died March 1, 1867. Married Abel Lester, son of Shipley and Margaret (Nixon) Lester, born October 11, 1792; died in Delaware County, Ohio, in April 1868.
9. Jeremiah Williams, born December 28, 1799. Married Margaret Lake.

FAMILY OF URIAH WHITE

Martha Blackledge, daughter of Thomas and Margaret (Wright) Blackledge, was born in Bucks County, Pennsylvania. On August 4, 1782, her father took a certificate from Richland Monthly Meeting to Hopewell Monthly Meeting in Virginia for himself, wife Margaret, and children, among whom was Martha. Martha Blackledge married Uriah White between 1793 and 1796, for we find his parents, Jesse and Mary White, affiliated with Goose Creek Monthly Meeting in Virginia, from which Mary White took a certificate to Hopewell Monthly Meeting on June 3, 1793. At that time she named her children as Uriah, Elizabeth, James, Rachel, and Jesse. When she took a letter from Hopewell to Westlands Monthly Meeting on February 1, 1796, Uriah and Elizabeth were of an age that they took separate certificates. It is probable that Uriah White and Martha Blackledge were married on the Tenmile, and there is indication that they lived for a time in present Whiteley Township before moving to Columbiana County, Ohio.

Children of Uriah and Martha (Blackledge) White

1. William White. Removed to California.
2. Thomas White. Married Catherine ....
3. James White. Lived at Salem, Ohio, in 1860. His wife was Margaret ....
4. Isaac White. Married Hannah ....
5. Jesse White. Died before 1860.
6. Margaret White. Married David Goucher. They lived at Findlay, Ohio, in 1860.

FAMILY OF ROBERT BLACKLEDGE

Robert Blackledge, brother of Thomas Blackledge, and son of Thomas and Elizabeth (Randall) Blackledge, also left records in Greene County. He was born in Bucks County about 1735, where he lived until shortly before 1800, when he joined the migration to the Tenmile. He married, in Philadelphia on February 18, 1763, Joanna Van Lude, and they became the parents of ten children. After the death of his father, Robert Blackledge, and his son of the same name, he opened a store in Buckingham Township, Bucks County, but soon sold it and joined his brother, Thomas Blackledge, near Jefferson. Then in 1804 he bought land in Columbiana County, Ohio, where Robert and wife, Joanna, joined in a number of deeds. Several of his children accompanied him during the several migrations, while some are known to have remained in Bucks County.

Children of Robert and Joanna (Van Lude) Blackledge

1. Elizabeth Blackledge, born 1765. Married, June 8, 1786, Eli Kennard.
2. Thomas Blackledge, born about 1767. Married Sarah .... Sold land in Bucks County in 1795 and came west.
3. Robert Blackledge, Jr., born in Bucks County about 1768. Married, March 6, 1787, Ruth Edwards, daughter of John and Elizabeth (Saunders) Edwards. He inherited from his grandfather, Thomas Blackledge, but sold out with his father and came first to the Tenmile, and then, in 1804, moved to Columbiana County, Ohio, where he died about 1812 leaving a will, which is on record at Lisbon, and which he had made June 2, 1812.

Children Named in His Will

1. Thomas Blackledge
2. Hannah Blackledge
3. Robert Blackledge
4. William Blackledge
5. Rebecca Blackledge
6. Joseph Blackledge
7. Mary Blackledge
8. Rachel Blackledge
9. Benjamin Blackledge
10. Isaac Blackledge
11. Margaret Blackledge
12. David Blackledge

4. Rebecca Blackledge, born about 1770. Married, about 1790, John Wheeler. Came to the Tenmile, and then went to Mason County, (W.) Virginia.

Children of John and Rebecca (Blackledge) Wheeler
1. Elizabeth Wheeler. Died in Ohio.
2. John Wheeler. Died in the Mexican War.
3. Wilhelm Wheeler. Died at Willow Tree, West Virginia. Buried at Jackson Chapel Cemetery. Married Ann Saylor.
5. Joseph Blackledge. Taxed in Greene County. Was granted a certificate from Westlands Monthly Meeting to Middleton Monthly Meeting on September 22, 1804.
6. Hannah Blackledge. Born December 19, 1769; died July 12, 1850. Married, in 1787, John Denny, who was born in England on February 8, 1762, and died March 29, 1847.

Children of John and Hannah (Blackledge) Denny
1. Thomas Denny. Born August 3, 1788; died May 28, 1864. Married Sarah Richardson.
2. Mary Denny. Born August 8, 1789.
3. Rebecca Denny. Born February 16, 1791.
4. Ann Denny. Born March 16, 1792.
5. William Denny. Born October 27, 1793; died July 12, 1845 (or August 15). Married, October, 1815, Rachel Woodruff, who died January 25, 1817, leaving a son, Meeker Woodruff Denny. William Denny married (2) Rebecca Litzenberg, who died February 10, 1844.
6. James Denny. Born April 16, 1795; died August 15, 1883.
7. John Denny. Born June 2, 1797; died young.
8. Hannah Denny. Born April 3, 1799. Married Thomas Ross who died about 1832.
9. George Denny. Born February 23, 1801.
10. Rachel Denny. Born February 2, 1803. Married Harvey Woodruff.
11. Robert Denny. Born November 12, 1804. Married Pera Hixenbaugh.
12. Joseph Denny. Born December 6, 1806; died February 13, 1893. Married Elizabeth Myers.
13. Joel Denny. Born August 24, 1810; died young.

7. William Blackledge. Granted certificate by Westlands Monthly Meeting to Short Creek Monthly Meeting, June 24, 1809, having come to Westlands June 22, 1799. Wife's name was Elizabeth .... Children were Robert, Sarah, Elizabeth, Samuel and John Blackledge, as listed on certificate.
8. .... Blackledge.
9. .... Blackledge.
10. .... Blackledge.

THE BURSON FAMILY

George Burson, ancestor of the American Family of that name, came from Scarborough, Yorkshire, England about the year 1684, and settled in the vicinity of Abington, Montgomery County, Pennsylvania, where he became a member of Abington Monthly Meeting of Friends. His wife, whom he probably married in England was Hannah (Goode ?). Late in life he located on a tract of land in Gilbert's Manor, a few miles from Valley Forge, where he died in 1715. His will is on file in the City Hall at Philadelphia, and was made November 26, 1715, and probated February 11, 1716. In it he names his wife, Hannah, and six children, namely: James Burson, Joseph Burson, Mary Burson, Ann Burson, William Burson, George Burson. Mr. Clarence V. Roberts in "Upper Bucks County" gives some records of these children, and Thomas Potts in his "History of the Potts Family" names them frequently as attendants at marriage ceremonies of the Friends. (D. pp. 16, Philadelphia Co.)

Two branches of the Burson Family came into Greene County, they being descendants of George Burson, through his sons, Joseph and George Burson. George Burson, Jr.'s family did not remain here long, but some of his descendants settled in Columbiana County, Ohio. There is an excellent genealogy of this branch.

The Greene County pioneer family of this name, whose descendants still live in the County, are descended from Joseph Burson, son of George and Hannah (Gooda ?) Burson. He was born in Philadelphia County, Pennsylvania, December 25, 1689, and died in Loudon County, Virginia, after 1776. He inherited the tract of land on which his father settled, which he still owned on June 13, 1754. (Penna. Gazette advertisement). However in 1739, he moved to Bucks County, and then about 1751, he went to Virginia as shown by certificate for wife and children and Joseph Burson to Fairfax Monthly Meeting on July 2, 1751. There are a number of references to him in Friends records for Virginia, some as late as 1762. He died in Loudon County sometime after 1776, for in that year he got into some mixup over his son, Benjamin's Estate. Benjamin had died in 1769, and left money to take care of his aged father. Joseph Burson married before some 52 witnesses on August 15, 1719, Rachel Potts, daughter of Jonas and Mary Potts. The names of seven of the children of Joseph and Rachel (Potts) Burson have been taken from Friends records, they are; Ann Burson, James Burson, Joseph Burson, Benjamin Burson, Absolom Burson, Rachel Burson, Debora Burson, the latter three being minor children when the family moved to Virginia.

James Burson, son of Joseph and Rachel (Potts) Burson, was born at Gilbert's Manor on November 21, 1722. He removed with his parents to Bucks County, Pennsylvania in 1739. After his marriage, he settled in Springfield Township, where he attached himself to Richland Monthly Meeting. He did not go to Virginia with his father, but took a grant of land from the Colonial Authorities, and purchased other lands at various times. He either made a trip west with Thomas Blackledge, when the Tenmile Country was being opened up, or when Thomas Blackledge made the trip, he returned and sold a tract of land on Tenmile to James Burson. James Burson mentions this tract in his will which he made January 30, 1785, and on file in Bucks County. One item states, "I give and bequeath unto my son Edward Burson, all that piece or parcell of land at the Monongohale, which I bought of Thomas Blackledge . . . which my son Edward Burson now lives on." etc. This land remained in the posession of his descendants until 1935. James Burson was twice married, first to Sarah Price in 1748. She was the mother of all his children, and died about 1780. Two years later, on February 6, 1782, he married Sarah (Worth) Twinning, a widow, born 1740, who died August 20. 1833.

Children of James and Sarah (Price) Burson

1. David Burson, born 1749, died October 8, 1824, in Bucks County. He married 1774, Lydia Williams, born August 18, 1752. She died February 2, 1836.
2. Mary Burson, born December 4, 1752. She was twice married, first to Lewis Lewis, and secondly to Edward Roberts.
3. Isaac Burson, born in 1754, in Springfield Township, Bucks County, Pennsylvania. He died there November 24, 1811. He was a big land owner and the town of Bursonville was laid out on his property. He also got a warrant for land in Greene County. On February 29, 1776, he married Elizabeth Blackledge, daughter of William and Ann (Lewis) Blackledge.

4. Edward Burson, born in Springfield Township, Bucks County, Pennsylvania, September 20, 1756. He was the Tenmile pioneer, of whom later.
5. Sarah Burson, born ...., married November 2, 1786, Jonathan Griffith, born September 21, 1754, died March 18, 1809, in lower Richland.
6. Ann Burson, born ...., married Jacob Poston.
7. James Burson, Jr.
8. Joseph Burson, died March 16, 1842. He married Mary Twinning, daughter of his stepmother by her first marriage.

FAMILY OF EDWARD BURSON

Edward Burson, son of James and Sarah (Price) Burson was born in Springfield Township, Bucks County, Pennsylvania, on September 20, 1756, and died in Jefferson Township, Greene County, on February 9, 1841. With his father-in-law, Thomas Blackledge, he came to the Tenmile about 1778, and settled on land purchased for him by his father. The first cabin of the pioneer Burson was built at the head of a hollow that runs from Tenmile Creek toward the house later built by Abraham Burson. This hollow carried the significant name of "Wolf's Den." This was not the protecting cabin of so many settlers, and had only a blanket for a door. It was but a few hundred yards from the site of the Rofelty massacre, but the only inconvenience the Bursons suffered from that disaster, was the loss of a pot of beans Mrs. Burson fed to the Indians when they left the scene of the murder. Edward Burson was a very good business man, and during his life he accumulated enough farms to settle all but one of his ten living children on comfortably. In addition he sought and sold other farms in Greene County and various places in Ohio. We find him borrowing large sums of money in the disastrous years of 1817-18, when frost hit the county every month of the year and no crops except buckwheat could be raised. His wife was Elizabeth Blackledge, daughter of Thomas and Margaret (Wright) Blackledge. There seems to be an error in the date of her birth, which is given as October 25, 1758, in Friends records. They were married out of unity in the Tohicken Reformed Church, but by the acknowledgement of her error on August 16, 1781, she was granted a certificate to the Friends Monthly Meeting at Frederick, Maryland. We have been told that she was a frail and at times sickly woman, but she lived to be over 94 years of age. She died July 26, 1853, at her home near Jefferson, where her last years were spent with her son, Abraham Burson. She and her husband are buried in the Burson Cemetery on the Luse Farm adjoining the original Edward Burson Tract. In custom with Friends belief, neither the graves of Edward or his wife are marked. The names of the children of Edward and Elizabeth (Blackledge) Burson are to be found in Edward Burson's will, while an old Quaker Tract, the property of the writer's wife, (herself a descendant of this couple) contains the birth dates of each child.

Children of Edward and Elizabeth (Blackledge) Burson

1. James Burson, born February 14, 1780, probably in Bucks County. He died in Columbiana County, Ohio, in 1843. McCrod's "History of Upper Ohio Valley" states that in 1802, while living in Greene County, Pennsylvania, James Burson floated a flat boat down the Monongahela, Ohio, and Mississippi, with a load of flour, selling it at New Orleans and realizing a profit of $800. He returned by boat to Philadelphia, and came overland to his home on Tenmile. Then taking the $800 received on his venture, he and his brother, David Burson, walked from Waynesburg to Steubenville, Ohio,

where he bought 640 acres of land at $1.25 per acre, then followed the blazed trail of the surveyors to the vicinity of his new land near Lisbon, Ohio. He married out of unity in 1804, Elizabeth, daughter of Isaiah Myers.

Children of James and Elizabeth (Myers) Burson

1. Nelson Burson, died in Hanover Township, Columbiana County, Ohio, where his will, made June 22, 1898, was probated March 12, 1900. His wife was Lennie Ann Harris.
2. Margaret Burson, married Isaac Malsberry of Damascus, Columbiana County, Ohio. She died in Iowa.
3. Abraham Burson, blacksmith, born November 20, 1813, died in Columbiana County, Ohio, where his will, made December 17, 1870, was filed at Lisbon on October 8, 1889. He married Nancy Bosserman, whose parents removed to Stark County, Ohio, from Gettysburg, Pennsylvania. They lived on the Myers Farm northwest of Hanover in 1841.
4. William Burson, born in Columbiana County, died there in Hanover Township in 1864. His wife was Rebecca Bennet of Butler Township.
5. Sinah Burson, married Allen Hinchman. They removed to Vernon, Jennings County, Indiana.
6. David Burson, married Elizabeth Bennet. He served as a lieutenant in the Civil War, and then removed to Iowa, where he died.

2. Thomas Burson, born in Greene County, Pennsylvania, November 16, 1781, died there January 11, 1864. Thomas Burson was a well educated man, who took a wide interest in public affairs. As a young man he was a candidate for sheriff, but was defeated. Later he was elected Associate Judge for two terms, and served two terms in the State Legislature. He was one of the first members of Lodge 153 F. and A. M. Thomas Burson studied law and his name is frequetnly found as executor of his neighbors estates. Interested in the education of others, he gave the land on which the old Burson School was built, on his farm, which adjoined that of his father. He married out of unity December 13, 1810, Ann Swan, daughter of Richard and Martha (Vanmeter) Swan. She was born July 21, 1787, and died on November 2, 1840. Both are buried in the Burson Cemetery.

Children of Thomas and Ann (Swan) Burson

1. Richard Burson, died unmarried in Iowa about 1860.
2. James Burson, left Greene County with a group of men for the Gold Fields of California in 1849, and returned home in 1857. On January 2, 1861, he again started for California but on May 20, 1865, was killed by the Indians. He never married.
3. Thomas Burson, Jr., died in Iowa in 1896, a well to do bachelor.
4. Samuel Burson, died in youth.
5. Edward Burson, died in infancy.
6. Martha Burson, died in Henry County, Iowa, October 5, 1865. married Hugh Swan, born in Greene County, August 22, 1809, died in Henry County, Iowa, June 8, 1851. He was a son of Henry and Elizabeth (Bowen) Swan.
7. Elizabeth Burson, died un-married.
8. Sarah Ann Burson, married Reuben Beers and removed to Mt. Pleasant, Iowa. No issue.
9. Mary Burson, lived in Ottawa, Illinois in 1898. She wrote the story of the Swans and Vanmeters that appears in the L. K. Evans Papers, published by the Waynesburg Republican. Her husband was Bowen Hill, son of Isaac and Nancy (Virgin)

Hill, and grandson of Rees and Nancy (Heaton) Hill.
3. David Burson, born December 15, 1783, went to Ohio with his brother, James Burson, but returned to Greene County for a time before he finally settled at Salem, Ohio, in 1818. He married out of unity in 1809, at New Garden, Ohio, Jane Whiney.
4. Sarah Burson, born May 28, 1786, married in 1811, John Johnson of Greene County. An old letter shows she was living at Salem, Ohio, in 1860.

Children of John and Sarah (Burson) Johnson

1. Edward Johnson, signed for his mother's share of her father's estate. Deeds in Columbiana County, Ohio, show his wife's name was Susannah ....
2. William Johnson.
3. Mary Johnson.
4. Robert J. Johnson.
5. James P. Johnson.

5. Levi Burson, born July 23, 1788, died at Clarksville about 1863. Levi Burson was one Burson who believed in letting "Nature take its course." His father bought him several farms, including the one later owned by Jackson Waychoff near Carmichaels, but when the weather was hot he preferred to sit on the porch and let things grow, when wet or cold, one just couldn't work out. He lived in Ohio for a time with his brothers, James and David, and while here his son, Edward Burson, was born in 1815. Levi Burson married (1) Ruth Carter, daughter of James and Ann (Bowen) Carter. After her death Levi Burson married Sarah Paul, widow of John Walton of Clarksville.

Children of Levi and Ruth (Carter) Burson

1. Sinah Burson, married Thaddeus Horn and went to Cass County, Illinois.
2. Mary Ann Burson, died in Greene County, Pennsylvania, March 5, 1844, married Benjamin Hartley, buried together in the Burson Cemetery.
3. Edward Burson, (Neddy), born April 20, 1815, died at Clarksville, January 19, 1880. He married June 7, 1836, Maria Stewart, born April 3, 1815, died July 23, 1874. She was a daughter of Alexander Stewart.

6. Joseph Burson, born October 12, 1790, died on June 18, 1855, from wounds given him by a boy he had raised. The boy fled to Kentucky, where his boasting about killing a Quaker brought about his arrest and punishment. Joseph Burson married at the Rex homestead in Jefferson in 1814, Catherine Rex, daughter of George and Margaret (Kepler) Rex. She was born at Jefferson December 25, 1793, and died at Richmond, Ohio, October 11, 1873.
7. Isaac Burson, born in Greene County, October 20, 1792, died near Millsboro in 1881. He went to Ohio after reaching his majority, but later returned to Greene County, where he settled on a portion of his father's farm. While living here he became an Associate Judge of Greene County, and was an early member of the Waynesburg Masonic Lodge. Late in life he married Mary Swan, widow of William Collins. She was born December 6, 1785, a daughter of Charles and Sarah (Vanmeter) Swan.

Children of Isaac Burson

1. Hiram Burson, who remained in Columbiana County, Ohio.
2. Daughter that married Dr. Whinnery, of Columbiana County, Ohio.
3. Edward Burson, born December 12, 1814, in Columbia

County. Died at Millsboro, August 24, 1898. He married Massy Walton, daughter of John and Sarah (Paul) Walton. She was born March 19, 1819, and died June 28, 1886.

8. Abraham Burson, born November 9, 1794, died on the original Burson Farm on December 11, 1885, married out of unity Mary Carter in 1817. She was born near Amity November 25, 1790, died July 17, 1839, a daughter of James and Ann (Bowen) Carter. He married (2) Hannah Crawford, born 1806, and died August 12, 1866. She was a daughter of Joseph and Hannah (Hufford) Crawford.

Children of Abraham Burson

1. Elizabeth Burson, born October 22, 1821, died November 22, 1901, married David McClain, born March 27, 1823, died December 9, 1894. Both are buried in Hewitts Cemetery.
2. Ann Burson, born October 6, 1823, died August 24, 1912, married 1845, Dr. Alexander Patton, born 1819, died December 5, 1884. He was a son of Joseph and Esther (Paxton) Patton, and prominent in politics during the Civil War period. Served in both Houses of Legislature, and was State Senator at the time of his death. Both are buried at Jefferson, Pennsylvania.
3. James Carter Burson, born December 27, 1825, died September 5, 1897, married December 30, 1849, Rebecca J. Reynolds, born December 24, 1827, died December 11, 1891, both are buried at Clarksville. Rebecca Reynolds was a daughter of John and Jane (Kincaid) Reynolds.
4. Ruth Burson, died un-married.
5. Mary Margaret Burson, child by the second marriage, born June 11, 1849, died October 19, 1925, married Alexander Flenniken, born December 29, 1840, died January 12, 1912.

9. Margaret Burson, born November 5, 1796, married out of unity Joseph Burson, son of James and Jane (Orlton) Burson. He was born in Loudon County, Virginia, and with his wife, removed to Guernsey County, Ohio. His father was a captain of Virginia troops in the Revolution.

Children of Joseph and Margaret (Burson) Burson

1. Jane Burson, born June 15, 1822, died before 1869, married William Ward.
2. Edward Burson, born September 20, 1824, died in 1900, married 1848, Patience McBurney, born 1823, died 1860.
3. James Burson, born September 20, 1824. Twin of Edward.
4. Elizabeth Blackledge Burson, born March 28, 1827, married S. S. Emerson.
5. Thomas Burson, born August 25, 1829.
6. Minerva Burson, born November 8, 1831, married Stephen Williams.
7. Margaret Ann Burson, born April 22, 1839, married Adam Millhon.

10. Elizabeth Burson, born January 26, 1799, died December 23, 1879, married out of unity September 4, 1817, Frederick Wise, born September 2, 1793, died February 14, 1876. He was a son of Adam and Barbara (Zollars) Wise. Both are buried in the Wise Cemetery.

Children of Frederick and Elizabeth (Burson) Wise

1. Margaret Wise, born October 2, 1818, died January 15, 1892, married March 24, 1836, James C. Hawkins, born October 8, 1808, died January 15, 1891. Buried in Hawkins Cemetery.
2. Emeline Wise, born November 28, 1820, died August 10, 1897,

married November 25, 1841, Richard Hawkins, born March 11, 1814, died October 22, 1900. He was a son of Richard and Cynthia (Crawford) Hawkins and brother of James C. Hawkins.
3. Adam Wise, born March 8, 1823, died October 28, 1825.
4. Joseph Burson Wise, born May 29, 1833, died May 24, 1910, married November 30, 1859, Sarah Stockdale, who died March 4, 1910. She was a daughter of William and Hannah (McQuaide) Stockdale.
11. Sinah Burson, born Bebraury 1801, died in infancy.

THE STRAWN FAMILY

Thomas, John, and Jacob Strawn were among the first settlers in the Friends colony on Tenmile Creek. They were descendants of Lancelot Strawn, who spelled his name "Straughan," a native of Wales, who settled in Upper Bucks County, where he died about 1720. Lancelot's wife's name was Mary Buckman. They were parents of one son, Jacob Strawn, who spelled his name "Strawhen." Jacob Strawhen was born in Middletown Township in 1717 but moved to Hunterdon County, New Jersey, where he lived until 1749, when he returned to Haycock Township, Bucks County, where he died in 1801. Jacob Strawhen married about 1741 Christiana Pursell, and Richland Monthly Meeting reports the births of nine of his twelve children, including the three sons who came to Tenmile. His wife died in Haycock in 1807. Jacob Strawhen served on the Committee of Safety, but in respect to his faith, he resigned when War with Great Britain became inevitable.

Thomas Strawhen was born in New Jersey in 1742, and returned to Haycock with his parents where he bought land in 1772. Roberts says he remained on this farm until 1797, when he went to settle on the east bank of the Monongahela, but local records indicate that he came to the Tenmile before 1786, for in that year he signed the will of Thomas Blackledge, while on October 26, 1785, he warranted the tract of land adjoining Blackledge. This was tne land on the road to Clarksville from Jefferson, where the high bridge crosses Laurel Run. He must have been living here when he witnessed his neighbor's will. He was twice married, first on June 8, 1769, to Mary Heacock, who was born in Bucks County on May 11, 1752. She died on March 27, 1770, and he took a second wife, whose first name was either Sophia or Hannah. In 1799, he removed to Richmond, Kentucky. Known children of Thomas Strawhen were Thomas, John, Benjamin, Jacob, James, Sallie, and Mary. The land which he warranted was patented to Obediah Garwood on May 30, 1788.

Jacob Strawn was born in New Jersey in 1747, and died in Greene County in 1809. (WB. 1 pp. 78 filed 8-28-1809). He married Susannah Van Buskirk, daughter of George Van Buskirk, born 1754, who died in 1829. Enoch Rush of Jefferson, Pennsylvana, gives the information regarding the children, and states he was a grandson of Jacob Strawn. In 1802, Jacob Strawn got a patent for land in Wayne Township, close to where it joins with Franklin Township, in Greene County, Pennsylvania. The following list of children with birth dates, is a Bible Record. Several are buried in the Smith Cemetery and records have been taken from the tombstones.
1. Sarah Strawn, born July 19, 1774, married Benjamin Morris.
2. Mary Strawn, born November 2, 1776, married .... Nicholas.
3. Isaiah Strawn, born November 22, 1778, died February 1840, married Susannah Rinehart.

4. George Strawn, born April 2, 1781, died November 22, 1851, married Anne Van Buskirk.
5. Moses Strawn, born April 3, 1783.
6. Enoch Strawn, born September 10, 1785, died 1787.
7. Abel Strawn, twin of Enoch. (One informant says his name was Solon.)
8. Susannah Strawn, born November 11, 1787, died December 26, 1856, married John T. Rinehart.
9. Elizabeth Strawn, born June 17, 1788, died July 1847, married .... Duvall.
10. Hannah Strawn, born February 14, 1790, died October 12, 1852, married .... Rush.
11. Jacob Strawn, born February 2, 1794, died March 25, 1865, married Martha Erwin.
12. Christiana, born May 1, 1795, died August 1858, married .... Strawn, a cousin.
13. Elenor Strawn, born February 4, 1798.

John Strawn, son of Jacob and Christiana (Pursell) Strawn was born in Hunterdon County, New Jersey in 1744. He died in Greene County, Pennsylvania, in 1808. (WB. 1. pp. 71 filed August 29, 1808.) He married in April 1770, Kezia Dennis, born February 22, 1753. John Strawn of Wolfs Run, West Virginia, a grandson of John, supplied the following information regarding the children of John and Kezia, stating there were nineteen of them.

Benjamin Strawn, born 1774, lived to be 97 years of age.
Jacob Strawn, born 1778, lived to be 92 years of age.
Job Strawn, lived to be 80 years old.
Joseph Strawn, lived to be 79 years old.
Mahlon Strawn, lived to be 90 years old.
Enos Strawn, lived to be 75 years old.
John Strawn, lived to be 70 years old.
Abel Strawn, lived to be 5" years old.
Israel Strawn, no information.
Grael Strawn, no information.
Amelia Strawn, lived to be 90 years old.
Joel Strawn, lived to be 87 years old.
Christiana Strawn, married William Estill ?
Rachel Strawn, no information.

We are of the opinion that the following three names found in Bates History are also children of John Strawn.

Levi Strawn, who married Elizabeth Inghram.
Abner Strawn, who married Juda Grant.
Charlotte Strawn, married James Scott.

The information on the Strawn Family is taken from Court, Cemetery, and Bible records, and much of it was collected by Lily Strawn Painter, of Denver, Colorado, a descendant of George and Van Buskirk Strawn.

THE VAN BUSKIRK FAMILY

The Van Buskirks were from Northampton County, Pennsylvania, although the family records go back to the Dutch Settlement in New York before 1660. George Van Buskirk, fourth in line from the imigrant, died in Chestnut Hill Township, Northampton County, Pennsylvania, leaving the following children:

John Van Buskirk, his wife was Mary ....
Lawrence Van Buskirk, born 1747, died December 21, 1841, married Catherine Johnson.

Joseph Van Buskirk, married Mary Strawn, daughter of Jacob Strawn.
Susannah Van Buskirk, married Jacob Strawn, brother of Mary.
Sarah Van Buskirk, married Nicholas Johnson, who warranted land patented to Jacob Strawn in Wayne Township, Greene County.
Andrew Van Buskirk, married Hester Adamson.
Daniel Van Buskirk, married Sarah Cluldren.

LAWRENCE VAN BUSKIRK FAMILY

There appears to have been two Van Buskirks who settled in Greene County, Pennsylvania, but one of these, George Van Buskirk, has left no records other than the appearance of his name in an old ledger. Lawrence Van Buskirk, however, still has descendants living in the County. He is buried in the Smith Cemetery near the Children's Home, where his marker says he died December 21, 1841, at the age of ninety four years eight months and four days. His wife was Catherine Johnson of Hamilton, Northampton County, Pennsylvania, who is buried with him and whose marker says she died October 1, 1842, aged eighty nine years one month and eight days. Lawrence Van Buskirk settled early near Fort Swan as shown by land records, but later moved to the vicinity of the mouth of Ruff's Creek. He left an estate which was probated in Greene County on February 15, 1842. (WB. 2. pp. 150).

Children of Lawrence and Catherine (Johnson) Van Buskirk

Lawrence Van Buskirk, Jr., married Sarah Richardson, went to Carroll County, Ohio.
Enoch Van Buskirk, born May 16, 1790, died July 4, 1858, married Maria Adams, born December 21, 1803, died July 8, 1878.
Susannah Van Buskirk, married Jacob Brown.
Anne Van Buskirk, married George Strawn, she was born August 22, 1784, died February 18, 1842.
Catherine Van Buskirk, married Jacob Harry.
Mary Van Buskirk, married .... Probst (or Brobst).
George Van Buskirk.
Nicholas Van Buskirk, married Elizabeth Cree.
Sarah Van Buskirk, married .... Overpack.

OBEDIAH GARWOOD

There were several men of this name, but the one who joined the Friends trek to Tenmile, removed from Warrington Monthly Meeting to Hopewell Monthly Meeting by a certificate of November 7, 1785. His wife, whose name is not given, and his children, Joseph, Obediah, Mary, Elizabeth, Samuel and Tacy, were listed with him. Obediah Garwood had patented to him, the land on Laurel Run, next to Thomas Blackledge, which had been warranted to Thomas Strawhen. It is not definite whether he settled there, but he removed to Fayette County, where he died in 1798. His estate was probated in Fayette County, Pennsylvania, on July 3, 1798, and he mentions his son, Joseph Garwood, as living on land next to Blackledge in Greene County. He also mentions his children as follows: Rebecca, Rachel, Elizabeth, Mary, Obediah, Jr., Samuel, who was deceased at the time, (he married Sarah Crawford), and Tacy.

THE HOGE FAMILY

There are a number of excellent genealogies on branches of the Hoge Family, two branches of which came to Greene County. We think it unnecessary to give more than an outline of the beginnings of this family in America. Frederick County, Virginia, abounds in records of the original ancestor, William Hoge. Also there are excellent records of his illustrious sons.

William Hoge, Sr., the first American ancestor, was born in Scotland in the year 1660. He came to America and settled first at Perth Amboy, New Jersey, from which place he went to Chester County, Pennsylvania. With the migration into the Shenandoah Valley, William Hoge was among the first. Several places are named for him, such as Hoge's Creek, Hoge's Bridge, etc. He settled on the Opequan, where he died about 1745. His will 's on file at Winchester, Virginia, in Will Book 1. pp. 338. In it he names his wife, Barbara, and eight children. His wife was Barbara Hume, born 1670, who died in 1745. His children were John Hoge, William Hoge, Jr., a daughter that married Neal Thompson, another daughter that married Robert White, Alexander Hoge, James Hoge, wife's name Agnes, George Hoge, and Jureter Hoge.

William Hoge, II, was born about 1700. On April 16, 1748, he and his wife, Ann ...., whom he married on February 9, 1723, removed from Virginia to Bucks County, Pennsylvania, bringing a certificate from Opequan Monthly Meeting to Richland Monthly Meeting. Friends records certify to these births of William and Ann Hoge's children.

James Hoge, born December 6, 1724-5.
William Hoge, 3rd, born January 4, 1726, married Esther Ewing.
Solomon Hoge, born March 21, 1729, married Esther ....
George Hoge, born February 6, 1733, died 1805, married Elizabeth Blackledge.
Joseph Hoge, born December 1, 1735-36.
Jebulon Hoge, born April 13, 1738.
Ann Hoge, born December 26, 1740-41, married Everhard Roberts.

These records are from Richland Monthly Meeting in Bucks County, Pennsylvania, and are as reported by Clarence V. Roberts in "Early Friends Families of Upper Bucks County." Ann Hoge died in Bucks County March 21, 1759, and William Hoge, 2nd, returned to Virginia in 1760. His sons, James, William, Solomon, George, Joseph, and Zebulon Hoge, either went with him or had preceded him in the migration back to Virginia. Before the end of the Revolution at least two of these sons came to the Tenmile, while a third seems to have removed to Fayette County. William and George Hoge, sons of William and Ann Hoge, after a short time in the vicinity of Rices Landing, took up land near Fort Bell on a branch of Ruffs Creek, where George Hoge had warranted to him on February 9, 1785, a tract of land he named "Deer Park." William Hoge on September 22, 1787, received a warrant for the adjoining tract under the title of "Smithfield" which later was patented to Thomas Hoge. Zebulon Hoge seems to have stopped for a time in Fayette County.

FAMILY OF WILLIAM HOGE, III

Through Bible and Hopewell Monthly Meeting records it is learned that William Hoge, 3rd, born January 4, 1726, married Esther Ewing. Their children were:
1. John Hoge, who on May 14, 1778, married Mary Jenkins, daughter of Jacob and Elizabeth Jenkins of Frederick County and later Hampshire County, Virginia, where Jacob Jenkins died about

1795, leaving a will, found in Will File No. 36.
2. Asa Hoge, who married December 11, 1799, Mary Griffith.
3. Jesse Hoge.
4. William Hoge, 4th.
5. Solomon Hoge, born in Virginia March 4, 1767, died in Greene County, Pennsylvania, July 7, 1813. He married March 5, 1794, at Hopewell Monthly Meeting, Mary Fisher, daughter of Barak and Mary (Butler) Fisher. Mary (Fisher) Hoge, was born March 19, 1761, and died in Greene County, September 12, 1847. Solomon and his wife are buried in the Smith Cemetery near the Childrens Home.

Children of Solomon and Mary (Fisher) Hoge

1. Barak Hoge, who died before 1850. His wife was Experience Doty, daughter of Anthony and Mary Doty. They are probably both buried in the old cemetery at Grimes School House, where a marker shows that Experience died October 13, 1859, at the age of 55 years.

Children named in O. C. Docket 3. pp. 154

1. William Hoge.
2. Experience Hoge.
3. Sarah Ellen Hoge.
4. Elizabeth Hoge.
5. Samuel Hoge.

2. Esther Hoge, born June 3, 1796, died January 9, 1894, married March 17, 1816, John Hoge, son of Thomas and Ann (Clark) Hoge, born February 23, 1794, died May 28, 1873. Both are buried in the Adamson Cemetery. (See George Hoge Family Record.)
3. Sarah Hoge, born December 4, 1797, died March 7, 1862, married James Call, born on September 24, 1796, died June 13, 1886. They were the parents of eight children.

Children

1. Solomon Call, removed to Pickway County, Ohio.
2.
3. Elizabeth Call.
4. Sarah Ann Call, born August 13, 1840, died September 20, 1894, married March 4, 1865, Samuel Thompson, born January 1, 1839, died November 29, 1925.
5. Thomas J. Call.
6. James Call, born September 17, 1825, married October 22, 1849, Martha Vanwey, born in Perry County, Ohio, December 31, 1833, daughter of John and Anna (Mains) Vanwey.
7. John Call, born September 21, 1833, married 1855, Elizabeth Fry.
8.

4. William Hoge.
5. John Hoge, born May 20, 1801, died March 17, 1863, married October 13, 1831, Rebecca Oaks, born December 7, 1804, died February 23, 1888. Both buried in the Smith Cemetery.

Children

1.
2. Norval Hoge, born March 8, 1835, married 1856, Catherine Huffman.
3.
4. Mary Hoge, born 1839, died 1889.

5.
6. Esther Hoge, born 1843, died 1852.
6. Solomon Hoge, born March 13, 1803, died May 17, 1877, married 1828, Rachel Huss, daughter of John and Elizabeth (Heaton) Huss, born January 6, 1811, died January 20, 1890.

Children

1. Martha A. Hoge, born 1830, died 1886, married William Inghram, born 1825, died 1889.
2. Mary M. Hoge, born April 9, 1832, died April 27, 1923, married November 7, 1851, Benjamin A. Rinehart, born May 27, 1826, died December 7, 1907.
3. John Huss Hoge, born 1834, died 1917, married Irene Penney, born 1841, died 1872.
4. Jacob Hoge, married (1) Rachel Bell, married (2) Elizabeth Johns.
5. Asa B. Hoge, born September 23, 1841, married 1877, Mary Phelan.
6. Elizabeth Hoge, born October 27, 1844, died June 26, 1938, married James K. Scott.
7. Solomon F. Hoge, born April 1, 1848, married (1) October 15, 1874, Marietta Bell, married (2) May 25, Emma J. Downey, who died 1881, married (3) Lydia L. Evans.
8. William H. R. Hoge, married Emily Stewart.

7. Asa Hoge, born June 8, 1805, died April 27, 1889.
8. Joseph Hoge, born November 16, 1806, married (1) December 4, 1828, Mary Coen, who died 1842. (Ten children) Married (2) 1843, Jane Blair, who died August 22, 1852, (seven children) married (3) June 22, 1857, Mrs. Jane (Wood) Watson, born November 16, 1812, died September 1, 1897. He died November 9, 1893. Buried at Pursley.
9. Mary Hoge.
10. Elizabeth Hoge.
11. Israel Hoge.

FAMILY OF SOLOMON HOGE

Solomon Hoge, son of William and Ann Hoge, was born May 2, 1729. He married (1) Ann Rollings, and after her death he married Mary (Esther ?) Nichols.

Children

1. Sarah Hoge, born November 11, 1752, married Joshua Gore.
2. Joseph Hoge, born April 1, 1754, died young.
3. David Hoge, born November 3, 1755, died in infancy.
4. Solomon Hoge, born October 30, 1757, died in Belmont County, Ohio, August 12, 1835. Married (1) Mary Iden (1757-90), married (2) Hannah Brown, born 1763.
5. David Hoge, born March 21, 1759, died November 23, 1840, married Ruth Gregg, born November 15, 1765, died February 24, 1845.
6. Nancy Hoge, born February 20, 1761, died May 31, 1839, married George Nichols, born December 25, 1756, died June 10, 1817.
7. Isaac Hoge, born January 30, 1763, died September 20, 1838, married Elizabeth Nichols, born October 16, 1767, died July 9, 1836.
8. Mary Hoge, born March 7, 1865, married Isaac Nichols, went to Kentucky.
9. Hannah Hoge, born March 7, 1767, died 1769.
10. Tamer Hoge, born April 12, 1768, died February 22, 1770.

11. Rebecca Hoge, born December 11, 1770, died July 26, 1837, married William Kenworthy.
12. Lydia Hoge, born September 26, 1774, died February 2, 1853, married Joshua Gregg, born May 25, 1774, died July 25, 1854.
13. William Hoge, born November 23, 1775, died January 11, 1842, married Sarah Nixon.
14. Joshua Hoge, born February 8, 1779, died December 25, 1854, married Mary Pool.
15. George Hoge, born January 23, 1781, died 1782.
16. Margery Hoge, born December 20, 1783, died March 18, 1823.
17. Jesse Hoge, born April 2, 1785, died September 20, 1826, married Elizabeth Gregg who died July 24, 1842.
18. Amy Hoge, born May 25, 1788, died July 10, 1794.

FAMILY OF GEORGE HOGE

George Hoge, son of William and Ann Hoge, was born February 6, 1733, and died in Greene County, Pennsylvania, about 1805. While living in Bucks County, Pennsylvania, he married on December 9, 1756, Elizabeth Blackledge, born in 1727, who died in 1804. She was a daughter of Thomas and Elizabeth (Randall) Blackledge. On January 11, 1773, George Hoge was disowned by Hopewell Monthly Meeting for bearing arms. This does not seem to have weighed heavily upon him for he served in the Revolution that followed in Captain Benjamin Stiles' Militia Company from Morgan Township. On March 20, 1798, he and wife Elizabeth joined in a deed of a part of "Deer Park" to Thomas Adamson, and then shortly before his death he and wife Elizabeth made a deed on December 2, 1803, for the balance of "Deer Park" to his son, Thomas Hoge. (See Deed Book 2. pp. 415.) He and his wife are probably buried in the Adamson Cemetery but no markers are shown. A Bible record copied by Norval Hoge and sent to this author by Miss Tillie Hoge gives the birth dates of each of the children of George and Elizabeth (Blackledge) Hoge.

Children of George and Elizabeth (Blackledge) Hoge

1. Elizabeth Hoge, born July 8, 1757, died near Homeville on November 7, 1816. She married, about 1779, Lot Leonard, born in New Jersey October 5, 1754, and died near Homeville November 7, 1847. (See Lot Leonard Records).
2. Anne Hoge, born April 19, 1759, married Noah Smith, son of Anthony and Lydia (Willis) Smith. He was born March 20, 1756, in New Jersey, where he served in the Revolution in Gloucester County Militia. He died in Greene County in 1835. (Stryker pp. 759). (Greene County Will Book 2, pp. 60).

Children named in will

1. Jacob Smith.
2. Richard Smith.
3. Mary Smith; married .... Funk.
4. Lavina Smith; married Henry Funk.
5. George Smith.
6. Lydia Smith; married .... McGlumphey.
7. Noah Smith.
8. John Smith.
9. David Smith.

3. Isaiah Hoge, born March 9, 1761, served in Captain Benjamin Stites' Company. He married Sally Daines.
4. Mary Hoge, born May 14, 1763, died June 19, 1817, married .... Depreast.

5. Thomas Hoge, born September 25, 1765, died January 4, 1837; married Ann Clark, died July 1, 1832. Both buried in the Adamson Cemetery. Ann Clark was born September 7, 1771.

Children

1. George Hoge, born October 4, 1792, died October 7, 1872; married, January 14, 1814, Sarah Moore, born May 24, 1797, died August 9, 1886. They settled on Purseley Creek.

   ### Children
   1. Rachel Hoge, born January 8, 1815, died February 12, 1848.
   2. Thomas Hoge, born July 8, 1816, died July 17, 1889; married Catherine Grim.
   3. Mary Hoge, born April 2, 1818, died September 26, 1897.
   4. Morgan Hoge, born July 18, 1820, died May 10, 1893.
   5. Anna Hoge, born September 30, 1822, died October 30, 1829.
   6. John Hoge, born September 19, 1825, died March 31, 1899; married Margaret ...., born 1825, died 1905.
   7. William Hoge, born January 8, 1828, died November 7, 1829.
   8. David Hoge, born March 21, 1830, died June 8, 1890.
   9. George Hoge, born September 31, 1832, died March 12, 1884; married, January 28, 1858, Abigail Wood, born August 9, 1835, died March 20, 1932.
   10. Levi Hoge, born September 22, 1834, died July 24, 1845.
   11. James Hoge, born September 23, 1834; married, December 23, 1855, Margaret Kent, born September 2, 1835.
   12. Sarah Hoge, born January 2, 1837, died April 13, 1911.
   13. Abner Hoge, born January 15, 1839, died April 19, 1928.
   14. Robert Hoge, born May 21, 1842, died January 4, 1919.

2. John Hoge, born February 23, 1794, died May 28, 1873; married, March 17, 1816, Esther Hoge, daughter of Solomon and Mary (Fisher) Hoge, born June 3, 1796, died January 9, 1894. Buried in the Adamson Cemetery.

   ### Children
   1. Anne Hoge, born December 16, 1816, died March 2, 1836; married James Crockard.
   2. Mary Hoge, born September 9, 1818; married Thomas Adamson, born October 5, 1816, died February 14, 1856.
   3. Eliza Hoge, born December 1, 1820, married Dr. John Smith. She died March 2, 1886.
   4. Sarah Hoge, born November 2, 1822, died February 28, 1874; married Thomas Adamson, born November 9, 1819, died July 11, 1904.
   5. Levi Hoge, born February 23, 1829, died in infancy.
   6. Esther Hoge, born December 7, 1830, died January 18, 1905; married Cyrus Adamson, born April 19, 1826, died November 23, 1913.
   7. Thomas Hoge, born March 4, 1834, died April 22, 1899; married Nancy Rinehart.
   8. Elizabeth Hoge, born September 1, 1838, died December 10, 1888; never married.
   9. Mariah Hoge, born September 19, 1840, died November 13, 1867; married James Mendenhall.
   10. John Fisher Hoge, born October 27, 1842, died April 12, 1870; married Emily Adamson, who died November 15, 1905, aged 57 years, 5 months and 28 days.

11. Infant born November 11, 1849.
3. James Hoge, born January 15, 1796, died October 29, 1844; married Phoebe F. Randolph who died May 19, 1864, aged 70 years and 10 months.
4. Mary Hoge, born October 15, 1797, died June 19, 1817.
5. Morgan Hoge, born December 21, 1799, died October 9, 1875; married Elizabeth Lippencott, born May 19, 1804, died May 19, 1886.

Children
1. Mary Ann Hoge, born July 2, 1824, died January 1, 1899; married, March 11, 1844, James Wood, born October 14, 1819.
2. Jane Hoge, born September 19, 1828.
3. William Hoge, born December 31, 1830; married (1) October 20, 1867, Eliza McQuay, who died August 17, 1875. He married (2) Esther M. Carter, born 1859.
4. Levi Hoge, born June 24, 1833; married, October 12, 1868, Susannah Orndorff, born April 22, 1840.
5. Sarah Hoge, born February 15, 1836, died October 4, 1918; married .... Caseman.
6. Uriah Hoge, born August 30, 1838.
7. Elizabeth Hoge, born July 23, 1841.
8. Harriet Hoge, born July 2, 1845.

6. Thomas Hoge, born September 3, 1801, died July 30, 1834; married Anical Flinch.
7. Elizabeth Hoge, born April 6, 1805, died August 23, 1851; married Henry Lantz.
8. Levi Hoge, born December 26, 1804, died May 15, 1862; married Mary Ann Overturf.
9. William Hoge, born January 2, 1807, died April 20, 1840; married Phoebe Huss.
10. Priscilla Hoge, born September 28, 1808, died May 7, 1889; married Hugh Montgomery, born 1804, died June 14, 1882.

Children
1. Levi Montgomery.
2. Ellen Montgomery, married Samuel Clayton.
3. Elizabeth Montgomery, born October 14, 1833, died January 1913; married, January 20, 1853, John Clayton, born June 27, 1826.
4. Samuel Montgomery, born July 17, 1835, died March 21, 1906; married (1) Mary Stentz, who died September 28, 1869; he married (2) Cyrene (Dale) Davis, born January 16, 1837.
5. Priscilla Montgomery, married James Mendenhall.
6. Henry L. Montgomery.
7. Marinda Montgomery, married Silas Cowan.
8. Hugh Montgomery, born November 22, 1843, died June 5, 1906; married (1) Anna J. Vankirk; married (2) Mrs. Dorcas (Cox) Horn.
9. Mary Ann Montgomery, married Martin Shirk.
10. Lou M. Montgomery, married John Tarbell.
11. Nancy M. Montgomery, married, December 28, 1875, J. K. Polke.
12. Thomas Montgomery, born January 24, 1847, died August 19, 1922; married, October 17, 1878, Virginia Gordon, born April 14, 1853, died March 18, 1895.

11. Anne Hoge, born May 10, 1810, married Isaac Leonard.

12. Abner Hoge, born November 1, 1812, died February 26, 1890; married, February 16, 1839, Maria Wise, born February 16, 1816, died August 8, 1897.

Child
1. George Hoge, born April 1, 1843, died April 16, 1900; married Tabitha E. McBride, born August 1847, died April 19, 1888.

13. Solomon Hoge, born June 27, 1815, died December 6, 1874; married Sarah Overturf.

Children
1. Thomas Hoge.
2. John Hoge.
3. James Hoge, born June 16, 1853, married, 1878, Martha M. McNeeley.
4. Cassandra Hoge, married .... Titus.
5. Martha Ellen Hoge, married Daniel King.
6. William Hoge.
7. Alice Hoge.
8. Leroy Hoge.
9. Priscilla Hoge.
10. .... Hoge.
11. .... Hoge.
12. .... Hoge.

6. Leah Hoge, daughter of George and Elizabeth (Blackledge) Hoge, born October 23, 1767. She married Abraham Luzader, born in New Jersey in 1757, and served in the Revolution from Greene County. He died in Guernsey County, Ohio, in 1826. His will was made December 13, 1825, and filed in Guernsey County on February 14, 1826.

Children of Abraham and Leah (Hoge) Luzader
1. Elizabeth Luzader, married .... Goves.
2. Mary Luzader, married .... Smith.
3. Patty Luzader, married .... Warne.
4. Rachel Luzader, married .... Bonnell.
5. Sally Luzader, married .... Daugherty.
6. Leah Luzader, married .... Smith.
7. John Luzader.
8. Isaac Luzader.

7. George Hoge, born August 13, 1769, son of George and Elizabeth (Blackledge) Hoge. He died, unmarried, about 1800, in Greene County, Pennsylvania.
8. Rachel Hoge, daughter of George and Elizabeth (Blackledge) Hoge, born September 23, 1772.
9. William Hoge, born June 23, 1776.
10. James Hoge, born August 25, 1778.

LOT LEONARD

With the migration of New Jersey Families to the Tenmile, William Leonard and several of his sons, including Lot, Amos, and Benjamin Leonard, made the journey about 1779, with Lot Leonard tarrying in Frederick County, Virginia, long enough to marry Elizabeth Hoge, daughter of George and Elizabeth (Blackledge) Hoge. For this breach of the Quaker rules, Elizabeth Hoge was disowned by Hopewell Monthly Meeting on August 2, 1779, Lot Leonard being a Presbyterian. Lot Leonard and his wife settled near her father, where he patented a tract of land on the Tenmile at the site of Homeville. He also bought the tract of land which Ezekiel Morris had patented to him. Amos and Benjamin Leonard settled on Pigeon Creek, in what became Washington County. While living near Homeville in 1782, Lot Leonard served in Captain James Archer's Militia Company, while Amos and Ziba Leonard were in the company of Benjamin Stites of Morgan Township. About 1799, William Leonard and a number of his neighbors, William then being near 85 years old, decided to seek new homes in Ohio and five years later settled in Knox County, with some ten or more other Tenmile Families, including that of Abner Brown, Ebeneezer Brown, John Mills, Henry Haines, Amos, Benjamin, and Ziba Leonard, Peter Baxter Families and others. Here in 1805, William Leonard died at the age of 87 or 88 years.

Lot Leonard was born in New Jersey on October 5, 1754, and died near Homeville on November 7, 1847. He married about 1779, Elizabeth Hoge, who was born in Bucks County on July 8, 1757, and died near Homeville on November 7, 1816. Lot Leonard then married Francis Willis, and had a daughter, who married David Bowser.

FAMILY OF LOT LEONARD

1. William Leonard, died about 1814, under mysterious circumstances. His wife was Elizabeth Whitlatch, daughter of William and Nancy (Veatch) Whitlatch. She then married Henry Jacobs.

Children

   1. Nancy Leonard, born March 2, 1809, died October 22, 1855, married March 11, 1827, Archibald Fordyce, born December 4, 1807, son of Jacob and Elizabeth (Guthrie) Fordyce.
   2. John Leonard, a Methodist Preacher.
   3. William C. Leonard.
   4. Lot Leonard, died young.

2. John Leonard.
3. George Leonard.
4. Leah Leonard, born 1787, died December 1, 1861, aged 93 years, 6 months, and 26 days, she married Jonah Fitz Randolph, who died in 1843. They are buried in the cemetery on Stockton Lane.

Children

   1. Lucinda Fitz Randolph.
   2. Elizabeth Fitz Randolph, got land in Randolph County Indiana.
   3. ....Fitz Randolph, also got land in Indiana.

5. Nancy Leonard, married her cousin, Joseph Leonard, who was born July 10, 1779.
6. Lot Leonard, Jr., died December 26, 1865, aged 71 years, 11 months, and 26 days. Married Elizabeth Mosier, who died June 27, 1850, aged 53 years, 3 months and 24 days.

Children

   1. Merritt Leonard, died in Michigan, January 18, 1871, aged 52 years, 4 months, and 27 days.
   2. Jonathan Leonard.
   3. Melinda Leonard, married John S. Bayard.
   4. William Leonard, married Cynthia Dickenson.
   5. Levi Leonard.
   6. Lot Leonard.
   7. Aaron Leonard, married Elizabeth Church.

7. Isaac Leonard.

THE ADAMSON FAMILY

This family is descended from John Adamson, of Haddonfield, New Jersey, who on March 31, 1726, brought a certificate to Gwynnedd Monthly Meeting, and settled in Springfield Township, Bucks County. With him were his wife and several children including his son Thomas Adamson. Thomas Adamson succeeded to his father's property in 1753. He sold this land in 1775 in a deed in which he is joined by wife, Mary .... Shortly thereafter he left Bucks County, and appears on the Tenmile during the period of the Revolutionary War. Here he bought a tract of land adjoining Fort Swan. His will, probated in Washington County, Pennsylvania, on February 2, 1790, shows John Swan, Abraham Scott, and William Shepherd as witnesses, indicating he died near Fort Swan. His wife, Mary, was granted a certificate from Richland Monthly Meeting to Hopewell Monthly Meeting on August 4, 1783, for herself and three children, Thomas, James, and Sarah, while Thomas Adamson, Sr., and son, John, had a similar certificate granted them from Richland to Westland Monthly Meeting in 1784. Thomas Adamson, Sr., was born in New Jersey, December 23, 1717.

FAMILY OF THOMAS AND MARY ADAMSON
Richland Monthly Meeting records

1. Rachel Adamson, died before her father, her husband was .... Burson, and she left a son, Aaron Burson.
2. Ann Adamson, born September 12, 1742, married Abraham Ball.
3. Joseph Adamson, born January 17, 1745, wife's name was Mary ....
4. Mary Adamson, born December 7, 1747.
5. Hannah Adamson, born May 15, 1749, married .... Stroude.
6. Esther Adamson, (Hester), born April 2, 1751.
7. John Adamson, born November 1, 1753.
8. Deborra Adamson, born December 8, 1755, married Caspar Johnson.
9. James Adamson, born January 4, 1757.
10. Thomas Adamson, Jr., born May 15, 1758, died July 27, 1816, married Sarah Eagon, who died December 24, 1831.
11. Martha Adamson, born November 2, 1760, married Thomas Hatfield.
12. Sarah Adamson, born January 14, 1763, married Enoch Blackledge.

FAMILY OF THOMAS AND SARAH (EAGON) ADAMSON

Thomas Adamson, Jr., son of Thomas and Mary Adamson, was born in Bucks County, Pennsylvania, on May 15, 1758. He accompanied his parents to the Tenmile Country about 1780, and settled on land bought by his father from George Hoge, situated near Lippencott, on the road from the Children's Home in Greene County. He died there on July 27, 1816. (WB. 1. pp. 170.) His wife, whom he married in Greene County, was Sarah Eagon, daughter of James and Mary Eagon, near neighbors to his farm. She died December 24, 1831, aged sixty six years, ten months and fifteen days. Both are buried in the Adamson Cemetery.

Children
1. John Adamson, who married .... Smith.
2. James Adamson, born 1784, died June 27, 1851, married Margaret Smith, born January 6, 1789, died May 6, 1866.
3. Barnet Adamson, no record.

4. Joseph Adamson, born May 1, 1791, died April 23, 1853, married Hannah Smith, who died August 5, 1871, aged 78 years and 11 months.
5. Charles Adamson, born 1787, died September 1867. He married Sarah Hatfield, born 1798, died May 2, 1879.
6. Josiah Adamson, born ...., married Elizabeth Hatfield.
7. Mary Adamson, born 1792, died January 7, 1870, married .... Cary.
8. Cassandra Adamson, born 1804, died 1846, married Uriah Eagon.
9. Sarah Adamson, born ...., married Jesse Rice.
10. Debba Adamson, born 1807, died March 13, 1837, married Samuel Mickle.

These children are listed according to will record and not order of birth.

NICHOLAS JOHNSON

A series of court actions extending over a period of more than thirty five years, supplies an accurate genealogy of the family of Nicholas Johnson. It is probable that he came to the vicinity of Fort Jackson at the time of the migration of a number of Quaker families from Bucks County, Pennsylvania, about 1780. He is first noted in the Census for 1790, when he was living in the same neighborhood with the Van Buskirks, Strawns, Adamsons, Ball, and Burson families, early Friends pioneers, with whom his family was closely intermarried. It does not appear that the Johnsons belonged to that faith. Nicholas Johnson was probably a descendant of one Claus Johnson, who located in Germantown about 1708, through an apparent son John Jansen or Johnson of Upper Dublin Township, Philadelphia County. This John Johnson had sons Casper, Nicholas, Benjamin, Joseph, and William, all of whom joined in a deed for Germantown Property on June 13, 1769. (Robert's "Early Friends Families of Upper Bucks County.")

Nicholas Johnson married probably after he settled on the Tenmile, Sarah Van Buskirk, a daughter of George Van Buskirk, originally of Chestnut Hill Township, Northampton County, Pennsylvania. A number of her brothers and sisters were in the migration to the Tenmile Country, including Lawrence Van Buskirk, who had married a sister of Nicholas Johnson. Lawrence and his wife, Catherine, are buried in the Smith Cemetery near the Children's Home. Sarah (Van Buskirk) Johnson's sister, Susannah, wife of Jacob Strawn, also was of the party and it would appear that her brother, John and brother, George, also came here, as their names are found in local records. Nicholas Johnson died early in 1809, and his will was filed on March 6, 1809, with the widow Sarah and John Van Buskirk as administrators of his estate. His widow soon remarried, her second husband being John Adam Gordon, who was born in Maryland, November 3, 1762. This marriage is said to have been a stormy one, but Sarah outlived her second husband, who died in 1816, by many years. She is reported as "living but very old" in February 1849. There is no record to show the date of her death nor the burial place of either Nicholas or Sarah Johnson. A number of men named Nicholas Johnson served in the Revolution, but it would require other search to identify each one specifically.

In the settlement of the estate of Nicholas Johnson, he is described as "late of Waynesburg." It is here that the family came in contact with the Thomas Kent Family, which resulted in the many marriages between the two.

FAMILY OF NICHOLAS AND SARAH (VAN BUSKIRK) JOHNSON

1. Joseph B. Johnson, son of Nicholas and Sarah (Van Buskirk) Johnson, was of legal age in January 1812, as shown by Orphans Court Docket 1. pp 46. His wife was Sarah Kent, daughter of Thomas and Ann (Rolston) Kent. She was born November 22, 1790, and was living when her husband died November 16, 1861, then died about 1867. The will of Joseph B. Johnson was made November 11, 1861, and mentions his wife Sarah, and names three of their children, two of whom were already dead. Children of the deceased are also named in the will. (Greene County Will Book 4. pp. 6 and pp. 178.) Jesse Kent served also as administrator. Tombstone records in Bethany Church Cemetery do not check with courthouse records. They say Joseph B. Johnson died March 5, 1862, aged 75 years, 3 months, and 16 days, and his wife died January 24, 1867, aged 73 years, 9 months, and 7 days.

Children of Joseph B. and Sarah (Kent) Johnson

1. David Johnson, living at the death of his father. Had a son, Francis Marion Johnson. He died September 12, 1880, and with wife, Catherine, who died August 29, 1872, in 62nd year, is buried in Bethany Cemetery. He was 67 years old at the time of his death.
2. Nicholas Johnson, deceased in 1861, had a son Joseph B. Johnson.
3. Sarah Johnson, deceased in 1861.

2. John Johnson, son of Nicholas and Sarah (Van Buskirk) Johnson, was of legal age in 1812. His wife was Elizabeth Kent, daughter of Thomas and Ann (Rolston) Kent. She was born November 17, 1789. They were married February 3, 1811.

Child of John and Elizabeth (Kent) Johnson

1. Anna Johnson, married Daniel T. Ullom, son of George and Margaret (Bowen) Ullom. They were the parents of George, Jesse, Elizabeth, Margaret, Catherine, John T., Sarah, Jennie, and Martha.

3. Jacob Johnson, son of Nicholas and Sarah (Van Buskirk) Johnson, was a minor over 14 years of age in 1812, when Robert Whitehill was made his guardian. (O. C. Docket 1. pp. 36.) His wife was Sarah Gordon, daughter of William and Mary (Carroll) Gordon. She was born on January 10, 1795, and died April 1, 1872. Jacob Johnson died on May 31, 1831, his estate in O. C. Docket 2. pp. 6 names five children, with Jesse Kent and Joseph B. Johnson serving as administrators.

Children of Jacob and Sarah (Gordon) Johnson

1. Mary Johnson.
2. Nicholas Johnson.
3. William Johnson.
4. Jackson Johnson.
5. Sarah Johnson.

4. Catherine Johnson, daughter of Nicholas and Sarah (Van Buskirk) Johnson, was above the age of 14 years in 1812. She married Thomas Smith, Jr., son of Thomas and Mary (Williams) Smith. He died about 1848, and Jesse Kent acted as guardian for their children. (O. C. Docket 3. pp. 39, March 1848.) The children named included three over 14 years of age and four under that age.

Children of Thomas and Catherine (Johnson) Smith

1. Hannah Smith.

AND ITS PIONEER FAMILIES 111

    2. Caroline Smith.
    3. George Morris Smith.
    4. Olive Smith.
    5. Minerva Smith.
    6. Harriet Amanda Smith.
    7. Hugh Smith.
5. Nicholas Johnson, Jr., born April 4, 1802, died April 14, 1843; married, September 21, 1824, Sarah Smalley, born July 8, 1801, died 1853, daughter of Jonas and Rebecca (Dwire) Smalley.

Children of Nicholas and Sarah (Smalley) Johnson

1. Mathew Johnson, born April 28, 1825, died in infancy.
2. Jacob S. Johnson, born February 16, 1826, died March 13, 1884; married, October 18, 1855, Mary Ann Robbins, born July 7, 1830.
3. Rebecca Johnson, born March 11, 1827, died November 13, 1897; married James H. Ganier, born August 22, 1824, died February 14, 1864.
4. Sarah Johnson, born May 8, 1830, married Frank Tuttle.
5. Mary Johnson, born December 23, 1832, died December 12, 1912; married, October 9, 1850, Eli F. Morris, born July 12, 1828, died January 14, 1899.
6. Catherine Johnson, born August 19, 1836, died August 15, 1879, married .... Waples.
7. Abigail Johnson, born September 15, 1838.
8. Susannah Johnson, born February 18, 1842, married Jasper Dickison.

6. William Johnson, son of Nicholas and Sarah (Van Buskirk) Johnson, a minor under 14 years of age in 1814, died May 3, 1847. He was a tanner. Joseph B. Johnson served as administrator of his estate, which was filed for probate November 1, 1847. (Will Book Book 3. pp. 25.) His wife was Hester Haines, and they had six children.

Children of William and Hester (Haines) Johnson

1. .... Johnson.
2. Nicholas H. Johnson, born February 1, 1829, died August 26, 1902, buried in the Higgins Cemetery in Jackson Township. He married (1) Charlotte Coen, (2) Elvira Burge, (3) Susannah Wagoner, born July 22, 1830, died January 22, 1890.
3. .... Johnson.
4. .... Johnson.
5. .... Johnson.
6. .... Johnson.

7. Susannah Johnson, daughter of Nicholas and Sarah (Van Buskirk) Johnson, was born in 1802, and died April 26, 1822. She was the first wife of Jesse Kent, and is buried at Morrisville Cemetery.
8. Sarah Johnson, daughter of Nicholas and Sarah (Van Buskirk) Johnson, was the second wife of Jesse Kent, son of Thomas and Ann (Rolston) Kent. He was born November 17, 1798, and married three times, first to Susannah Johnson on February 24, 1821 and on the death of his wife in 1822, married her sister, Sarah Johnson. His last wife was Hannah Tyler, who was living at the time of her husband's death in 1873. The first four children are named in O. C. Docket 3. pp. 114 and were minors in 1847. The others are named in the Kent Book.

Children of Jesse Kent

1. Nicholas Kent.
2. Maria Kent.

3. Nancy Kent.
4. Thomas Kent.
5. Minerva Kent.
6. Mellissa Kent.

THE JOHNSON FAMILY OF BLACKSVILLE

A History of Monongalia County, West Virginia, published in 1895, states that the ancestor of the Johnson Family who settled in Wayne Township and around Blacksville, West Virginia, was John Johnson, who came to Muddy Creek from Philadelphia. This John Johnson had served in the Revolution for seven years, and since his name follows that of Nicholas Johnson in the Census for 1790, it is likely that they were brothers. The Census shows six males under 16 years of age, one of whom is identified in the above history. We believe another son was John Johnson, Jr., who married Sarah Burson, and whose record is given in the record of the Bursons.

Nicholas Johnson, son of the above John Johnson was a soldier in the War of 1812, settled near Blasksville, where in 1834 and 1837, he gave land to his son, William, and in 1837, a tract of 238 acres to son Nicholas Johnson, Jr. Nicholas Johnson, Sr., is said to have died about 1863. It is to be noted that the census record for these men is written "Johnston," which one authority on the family states is a separate name from "Johnson" but all the local records use the latter spelling.

Family of Nicholas Johnson, Sr.

1. William Johnson, born December 1, 1803, died November 3, 1857. He married Nancy Lantz, born August 21, 1807, and died May 8, 1901. They were married on April 10, 1828. His wife was a daughter of John and Elizabeth (Bonnett) Lantz. Both are buried in the Lantz Cemetery near Blacksville. Record of family in O. C. Docket 4. pp. 256, Greene County.

Children of William and Nancy (Lantz) Johnson

1. Mary Johnson, married Remembrance S. Thomas.
2. Sarah Johnson, married Caleb Spragg.
3. Delilah Johnson, born June 22, 1837, died 1915, married Enoch Maple, born December 16, 1838, died July 10, 1898.
4. William H. Johnson, born November 4, 1840, died October 8, 1911, married January 30, 1862, Sarah Ann McDougal, born October 24, 1843, died October 26, 1925.
5. John Nicholas Johnson, born ...., married Zelma Thomas.

2. Nicholas B. Johnson, born November 17, 1809, died 1890, married Margaret Minor, daughter of Samuel and Susannah (Clegg) Minor, born 1823, died 1923.
3. Perry Johnson.
4. John L. Johnson.

JONATHAN HOGE, ESQ.

Another Hoge Family was indentified with the Tenmile Country, but as far as can be discovered, was not related to the Quaker family of the same name. Jonathan Hoge, Esq., was a brother of David Hoge, founder of Washington, Pennsylvania. This family came from Cumberland County, Pennsylvania, where David Hoge was sheriff from 1768 to 1770. It is not certain that Jonathan Hoge came to the Tenmile, but on March 10, 1786, he had warranted to him a tract of land on Robinson's Run under the title of "Rich Bottom." He died intestate about 1801-02, and his land described as being in Cumberland Township, was divided among his heirs. (Deed Book 2, pp. 32.) He is mentioned in Crumrine's History of Washington County, in connection with his son-in-law David Redick, prominent in civil history of that County. (pp. 479.) Jonathan Hoge was a member of the Committee of Observation for Cumberland County. (Penna. Arch. Series V., Vol. 6, pp. 4.)

Children of Jonathan Hoge

1. John Hoge.
2. James Hoge.
3. Ann Hoge, wife of David Redick.
4. Rachel Hoge, wife of Robert Bell.
5. Elizabeth Hoge, wife of John Armstrong.
6. Sarah Hoge, wife of John Carothers.
7. Isabella Hoge, wife of David Bell.
8. Mary Hoge, wife of Jonathan Wallace.

ANTHONY DOTY FAMILY

Anthony Doty died intestate in Greene County, in 1815, his widow, Mary ...., taking out letters in his estate on March 14, 1815. (WB. 1. pp. 143.) She later secured a patent to land next to Stephen Harris and one farm removed from that of William Hoge. In 1821, when five of his children were yet minors, guardians were appointed for them. (O. C. Docket 1. pp. 167.) A complete list of children of Anthony and Mary Doty is found in the Orphans Court settlement of his estate.

Children

1. Sarah Doty, married George Fix, son of Henry and Anna Louisa Fix.
2. Elizabeth Doty, married Valentine Mills.
3. Leah Doty, married Samuel House.
4. Jacob Doty.
5. Experience Doty, born 1804, married Barak Hoge. She died October 13, 1859.
6. Phoebe Doty.
7. Hannah Doty.
8. Anthony Doty, married Catherine Virgin.
9. William Doty, married Susan Shroyer.
10. John Doty.

THE ANTHONY SMITH FAMILY

According to Bates, this family came from New Jersey in 1793, and belonged to the Friends Society. The Smith Bible owned by S. M. Smith, Esq., of Waynesburg, notes that Anthony Smith, Sr., was born on July 26, 1723, the son of Thomas and Mary Smith of Monmouth County. He settled near Jefferson, Greene County, and later bought land from Captain James Hook in the vicinity of the present Children's Home. Anthony Smith died here in 1809-10 and his will was probated January 29, 1810. (Will Book 1. pp. 83). His wife was Lydia Willis according to Mrs. Harvey Pratt, and she was born January 16, 1726. Since she is not named in the will, it is probable that she died before her husband.

Family of Anthony and Lydia (Willis) Smith (Bible Record)

1. Timothy Smith, born January 25, 1747.
2. Thomas Smith, son of Anthony and Lydia (Willis) Smith, born in New Jersey December 2, 1748. Hopewell Monthly Meeting of Friends at Frederick County Virginia, shows that Thomas Smith and wife, Deborra, brought a certificate from Crooked Run Monthly Meeting, and then on March 7, 1796, took a certificate from Hopewell to Westlan..s Monthly Meeting. Their children are included in the certificate.

Children of Thomas and Deborra Smith

1. David Smith.
2. Anne Smith.
3. Lydia Smith.
4. Copperthwaite Smith, who married Lydia Morris.
5. John Smith.
6. Margaret Smith.
7. Elizabeth Smith.
8. Judith Smith.

3. Judith Smith, daughter of Anthony and Lydia (Willis) Smith, born May 9, 1751, married (1) Jacob Burge. She married (2) John Hank. (Record under John Hank Family.)
4. Anthony Smith, Jr., son of Anthony and Lydia (Willis) Smith, born February 10, 1753. Deed book 2. pp. 226 Greene County, shows his wife's name was Hannah ....
5. Noah Smith, son of Anthony and Lydia (Willis) Smith, born in New Jersey, March 20, 1756, died in Greene County, Pennsylvania, 1835, his will being proven December 30, 1835. His wife was Anne Hoge, born April 19, 1759, daughter of George and Elizabeth (Blackledge) Hoge. Noah Smith patented a tract of land between Jefferson a: i Muddy Creek, adjoining Jacob Cline in August 1801, and then in 1810, warranted and patented a tract near the mouth of Coal Lick on the Tenmile.

Children of Noah and Ann (Hoge) Smith

1. Jacob Smith.
2. Richard Smith.
3. Mary Smith, married .... Funk.
4. Lavina Smith, married Henry Funk.
5. George Smith.
6. Lydia Smith, married .... McGlumphey.
7. Noah Smith, Jr.
8. John Smith.
9. David Smith.

6. James Smith, son of Anthony and Lydia (Willis) Smith, was born May 9, 1758.
7. Marjory Smith, daughter of Anthony and Lydia (Willis) Smith, was born May 12, 1760.
8. Job Smith, son of Anthony and Lydia (Willis) Smith, born in New Jersey March 27, 1762. His estate is in Greene County Will Book 4. pp. 172. (See Deed Book 3. pp. 57). His wife was Sarah ....

Children of Job and Sarah Smith

1. Elizabeth Smith, who married .... Heaton.
2. Lydia Smith, who married .... Johnson.
3. Mary Ann Smith, who married .... Bell.
4. James C. Smith.

5. Edmund Smith, who died in 1838, married Hannah Porter, daughter of James and Nancy (Inghram) Porter. She died November 15, 1818.
6. John Smith.
7. Thomas Smith.
8. Jacob B. Smith.
9. Sylvanus Smith, son of Anthony and Lydia (Willis) Smith, was born in New Jersey, January 20, 1764, and died in Greene County, August 16, 1854. He married (1) February 13, 1792, Lydia Hullett, daughter of .... Hullett and .... (Inghram) Hullett. She was born September 20, 1770, and died December 13, 1815, buried with her husband in the Smith Cemetery. He married (2) Rebecca Rachel Pew, daughter of William and Alice Pew, born in 1782, died April 9, 1836.

Children of Sylvanus Smith

1. William Smith, born December 16, 1792, married Sarah Jane Bodkin. He died May 18, 1874, his wife, born 1823, died July 13, 1873, aged 50 years, 4 months, 15 days.
2. Joseph Smith, born February 5, 1794.
3. Samuel Smith, born April 4, 1796, died September 7, 1879, married November 17, 1825, Elizabeth Huss, born March 19, 1807, died September 3, 1874. (Tombstone says 72 years).
4. Abigail Smith, born November 22, 1798.
5. Stockton Smith, born December 2, 1800, died March 2, 1833.
6. Elizabeth Smith, born January 25, 1803.
7. Catherine Smith, born May 9, 1805.
8. Thomas Smith, born August 15, 1807, died May 5, 1809.
9. Judith Smith, born May 26, 1810.
10. Lydia Smith, born July 16, 1812, married Thomas Freeman.
11. Sylvanus Smith, Jr., born July 31, 1818, died 1863, married Sarah Simonton.
12. Rebecca J. Smith, born September 29, 1819.
13. Alice A. Smith, born August 17, 1823.
14. Jonathan J. Smith, born November 24, 1826.

10. Elihu Smith, son of Anthony and Lydia (Willis) Smith, born March 25, 1767.
11. John Willeth Smith, born July 30, 1769, son of Anthony and Lydia (Willis) Smith.

WILLIAM PEW FAMILY

The application for a pension, made September 20, 1825, by William Pew of Greene County, Pennsylvania, states that he enlisted as a private in the Fall of 1776, for a period of one year in Captain Smock's Company of Colonel Samuel Foreman's Regiment of New Jersey. He was in the Battle of Germantown, after which he was taken prisoner by the British and held for nine months. He was then exchanged and returned to New Jersey, where he continued in the service until the Fall of 1778, when he was discharged at Morristown. His wife made application after her husband's death and added the information that William Pew had served after 1778, in a number of skirmishes under Captain Jonathan Pears and performed coast guard duty. William Pew stated that he had thirty acres of land in Greene County, Pennsylvania, having moved there before 1792. (Pension Application National Archives W. 2847 Continental N. J.)

With the application of his widow for pension after the death of her husband went a very complete Bible record of the family of

William Pew. William Pew was born April 28, 1755, and died at James Wood's house in Greene County, March 11, 1841. He married December 21, 1780, in New Jersey, Alice Peairs, who was born August 17, 1755. She died after 1844, when she was living in James Wood's house in Waynesburg. William Pew left a will, probated in Greene County on March 15,.1841. (Will Book 1. pp. 137.)

Children of William and Alice (Peairs) Pew

1. Rachel Pew, born January 13, 1782, died April 9, 1836. She was the second wife of Sylvanus Smith, Sr., son of Anthony and Lydia (Willis) Smith, born January 20, 1764, died August 16, 1854. She is buried at Lippencott, he in the Smith Cemetery.

Children of Sylvanus and Rachel (Pew) Smith

1. Sylvanus Smith, Jr., born July 31, 1818, died 1863, married Sarah Simonton.
2. Rebecca J. Smith, born September 29, 1819.
3. Alice A. Smith, born August 17, 1823.
4. Jonathan J. Smith, born November 24, 1826.

2. James Pew, son of William and Alice (Peairs) Smith, born April 13, 1784, died April 21, 1784, aged 8 days.
3. Deborra Pew, daughter of William and Alice (Peairs) Pew, born April 9, 1786, died March 19, 1829. She married .... Smith.
4. Mary Pew, daughter of William and Alice (Peairs) Pew, born November 20, 1787, died on October 9, 1838. She married .... Leonard. Had a son Benoni Leonard, born December 28, 1817.
5. Elizabeth Pew, daughter of William and Alice (Peairs) Pew, born September 12, 1790, died March 3, 1839. She married .... Whitlatch.
6. Anna Pew, daughter of William and Alice (Peairs) Pew, born April 28, 1793, married .... Watkins.
7. Sarah Pew, daughter of William and Alice (Peairs) Pew, born April 15, 1795, died April 20, 1833.
8. Alice Pew, daughter of William and Alice (Peairs) Pew, born January 25, 1798, married James Wood.

NATHANIEL TEMPLE

Another prominent Quaker, but of the Muddy Creek Group of this denomination, was Nathaniel Temple, who was born in Ewing, New Jersey, in 1747, and died in Greene County in 1842. The ridge above Fordyce known as Temple's Ridge was named for him. Nathaniel Temple served as Second Lieutenant in Captain John Mott's Company, First Regiment, commanded by Colonel Joseph Phillips. His service was with the Hunterdon County Militia beginning May 10, 1777. His wife was Sarah Blaker, whom he married about 1785. An excellent History of the Temple Family has been prepared.

Children of Nathaniel and Sarah (Blaker) Temple

1. Return Temple, born September 13, 1787, died about 1866. His wife was Sarah Darr, born January 18, 1793, died in 1867.

Children

1. Benjamin Temple, born August 12, 1812, died in Iowa, February 25, 1885, married on August 7, 1832, Matilda Reeves, born July 25, 1810, died April 5, 1891.
2. Mary Temple, born 1814, married John Starkey.

3. Rebecca Temple, born 1816, married John Wise of Wadestown, West Virginia.
4. Nancy Temple, born 1817, died young.
5. Hannah Temple, born 1819, died young.
6. Sarah Temple, born 1821, died 1872, married Robert Anderson.
7. Nathaniel Temple, born 1823, married Henrietta Rice.
8. William Temple, born 1825, married Eliza Wade.
9. Eliza Temple, born 1827, married Theodore Wade.
10. Elizabeth Temple, born 1829, married .... Haines.
11. Charlotte Temple, born 1831, married (1) Noah Fox, (2) Jesse Eddy.

2. Benjamin Temple, married Jane Douglass.
3. John Temple, married Elizabeth Douglass.

Children

1. Justus Fordyce Temple, born February 13, 1834.
2. Alpheus Temple.
3. Jane Temple.
4. John Temple.

4. Sarah Temple, married Benjamin Gillett.
5. Hannah Temple, married James Murdock. Hannah Temple was born August 7, 1807, and died April 25, 1883. James Murdock was born May 9, 1807 and died March 11, 1864. He was a son of John and Margaret (Hufty) Murdock.

JOHN HANKS FAMILY

First mention of John Hanks (or Hank) is on October 15, 1806, when he served with Lacy Hibbs as executor in the estate of Jacob Hibbs. From the will of John Hank probated November 20, 1823, and recorded in Greene County Will Book 1. pp. 243, it is evident that he was married twice, his second wife being Judith (Smith) Burge, daughter of Anthony and Lydia (Willis) Smith and widow of Jacob Burge. She also had been mother of a family prior to her marriage with John Hank. The various connections suggest that the family came from New Jersey and were at one time members of the Friends Society. The estate of John Hank was divided among the heirs named below:

1. Rebecca Hank, who appears to have been married (1) to Jesse Bowell, son of Bazil and Margaret (Bowen) Bowell of Fayette County. Her husband at the time of her fathers death was .... Cherry. She was probably the mother of the two grand children named by John Hank.
    1. John Bowell.
    2. Catherine Bowell, wife of .... Barnes.
    3. Hannah Bowell, wife of Warren Luse, not named but of record.
2. John Hank.
3. Daniel Hank.
4. Lydia Burge, named a step child by John Hank. She was born August 23, 1770, a date found in the John Morris Bible. She married Richard Morris, born in New Jersey December 25, 1774, died July 10, 1821, in Belmont County, Ohio. He was a son of Richard and Mary (Throckmorton) Morris of Middletown, New Jersey.

Children

1. Elihu Morris, born May 29, 1797, married (2) Mary Hartley.

2. Jacob Morris, born October 22, 1799.
3. Job Smith Morris, born August 29, 1802, married Harriet Jones.
4. William Morris, born April 16, 1805, married Rebecca Thomas.
5. Joseph Morris, born May 31, 1808, died August 25, 1832.
6. Lydia Morris, born August 9, 1810, died November 17, 1893, married Thomas Ball.

5. Joseph Burge, stepchild of John Hank named in will.
6. Anthony Burge, stepchild of John Hank named in will.
7. Jacob Burge, born 1783, as shown by John Morris Bible, named in will of John Hank.
8. Marian Burge, named in will of John Hank, had married .... Negus.

THE CARTER FAMILY

Perhaps this family should be taken up in an article on the north branch of Tenmile, as it settled first on a branch of North Tenmile to which it gave the name of Carter's Fork. But so many of the descendants removed to the south branch of Tenmile, where many still live, it may justly be included with the Tenmile Country. The family goes back to John Chenowith, Gentleman, born at St. Martins in Menage, Cornwall, Wales, about 1682. He married about 1705, Mary Calvert, erroneously said to have been a daughter of Charles Calvert, 3rd Lord Baltimore. They came to America about the time of her father's death in 1715, and settled on Gunpowder River, near Joppa, Maryland, on an estate of the Calverts called "Gunpowder Manor," later to be known as "Chenowith Manor." Here John Chenowith became an early iron master. His will is on file in Frederick County, Virginia, and was made April 11, 1746, filed May 6, 1746, as he died there while on a visit with some of his children. His children included John Chenowith, Jr., born 1706, whose wife was Mary Smith; Mary Chenowith, who married a man named Watson; Richard Chenowith, born 1710, whose wife was Keziah; Hannah Chenowith, born 1713, who married James Carter, of whom later; Arthur Chenowith, whose wife was Sapphira; William Chenowith, whose wife was Anne; Thomas Chenowith, whose wife was Mary Prickett; and Ruth Chenowith, born 1722, who married John Pettit.

James Carter and wife Hannah Chenowith, removed to Frederick County, Virginia, where they bought land described as being on the road from Winchester to Bellhaven. Here James Carter died about November 18, 1758, the date his will was made at Winchester, in which he names his wife Hannah, a married daughter Jane, probably the wife of John McMahan, who got 50 acres of property mentioned above, and who acted as guardian for the other Carter children, who were yet minors. Besides Jane, the other children named were Ann, Ruth, Hannah, James, William, and John, each of whom got bequests. James, the eldest son, was to get the home property when he became of age. (Frederick County Will Book 2. pp. 328.) The will was filed on December 6, 1758.

When James Carter, Jr., became of age, he and his brother, William Carter, removed to the north branch of Tenmile, where both of them are found serving in Captain Abner Howell's Militia Company in the Third Battalion, Washington County, Pennsylvania Militia from Amwell Township. James Carter also received payment for being on the Sandusky Expedition. (Penna Arch. Series VI Vol. 2. pp. 119 and 400.) Before leaving Frederick County, Virginia, James Carter had married Ann Bowen in 1771. She was a daughter of Henry and Anna

(Moon) Bowen, and sister to Isaac Heaton's wife and Rees Hill's mother, Priscilla (Bowen) Hill. She was a native of Apple Pie Ridge, Frederick County, Virginia. William Carter, brother of James, had married Eleanor ....

FAMILY OF JAMES CARTER

James Carter, son of James and Hannah (Chenowith) Carter, was born on October 14, 1750. He received a warrant for a tract of land in Amwell Township, Washington County, called "Potato Patch" on January 28, 1785. This was at the site of the familarly known "Hart's Mills" of a later date. He died here August 15, 1817, and is buried in the cemetery at Amity. His will was made August 9, 1817, and filed at Washington, September 20, 1817. (Will Book 3. pp. 169.) His wife, Anna (Bowen) Carter, was born in Virginia, February 1, 1752, and died on March 18, 1828. She is buried with her husband at Amity and both graves are marked, but of late years have become illegible. She also left a will. (Will Book 4. pp. 234.) Numerous transactions in Winchester indicate she received considerable wealth from her father's and brother's estates in Frederick County, Virginia. Her heirs shared also after her death.

Children of James and Ann (Bowen) Carter

1. Henry Carter, died at the age of 23 years. He married Bethany Cook, born January 13, 1787, daughter of Stephen and Sarah (McFarland) Cook.
2. William Carter, died young. (Washington County Estate C-61-1830.)

Children of William Carter

1. James Carter, married Nancy Lytle.
2. Isaac Carter, married Nancy Sowers.
3. Mary Carter, married Edward Wier.
4. Nancy Carter, born 1810, died 1839, married Caleb Evans, born 1807, died 1875.

3. John Carter, born June 5, 1778, died July 11, 1844, married in 1802, Rebecca McFarland, born August 8, 1780, died March 14, 1850. Both are buried with James Carter in Amity. She was a daughter of William and Hannah (Kelsey) McFarland, who were married by Rev. Thaddeus Dodd on October 20, 1799, and Rebecca was baptized by this same minister on January 1, 1783. John Carter was a sheriff of Washington County.

Family of John and Rebecca (McFarland) Carter

1. Cynthia Carter, born September 2, 1804, died February 21, 1899, married October 23, 1823, Thomas Patterson Pollock, born September 2, 1798, died January 3, 1876. Both are buried in the C. P. Cemetery at Jefferson.

Children

1. John C. Pollock, born September 5, 1824, died October 25, 1897, married November 8, 1854, Melissa Ailes, born June 27, 1833, died February 15, 1924. Buried in C. P. Cemetery at Jefferson.
2. Rebecca Pollock, born August 12, 1825, died September 23, 1907.
3. Thomas Patterson Pollock, born September 6, 1826, married Mary Ailes, who died on November 29, 1849.
4. David Pollock, born January 4, 1828, died November 7, 1905, married Jane Birch, who died November 5, 1884, aged 51 years, 4 months and 13 days.

5. Hannah Pollock, born 1830, died August 24, 1905, married October 25, 1849, James Murdock.
6. William Pollock, born August 30, 1832, married October 6, 1853, Rachel Luse, born 1834, died October 23, 1861, aged 26 years, 11 months, 12 days. William Pollock married (2) Mary Davis.
7. James Carter Pollock, born December 15, 1835, died May 4, 1913. Married Minerva Cloud.
8. Cynthia Pollock, born July 23, 1839, married John Montgomery.
9. Harvey C. Pollock, born October 14, 1843, died October 1886, married Florinda Bayard, daughter of John S. and Melinda (Leonard) Bayard.
10. Nancy Pollock, born March 31, 1847, died February 13, 1934, married David Kennedy.
11. Charles Pollock, born October 13, 1850, died 1934, married Louella Love.

2. Martha Carter, born October 15, 1805, died August 27, 1881, married John B. Montgomery, born May 26, 1814, died February 11, 1893. Buried at Amity. Among their children were:
   1. David Montgomery, born September 1835, died September 28, 1845.
   2. Rebecca Montgomery, born 1840, died December 23, 1844.
   3. James Montgomery, born 1842, died of wounds received at the Battle of Spotsylvania Court House, June 26, 1864.
   4. William Montgomery, born 1846, died 1895.

3. Jesse Carter, born October 17, 1806, died November 9, 1875, married 1830, Susan Hughes, born June 23, 1806, died August 23, 1877. Lived at Nineveh.

   Children of Jesse and Susan (Hughes) Carter
   1. Sarah Ann Carter, married Francis Day.
   2. James Carter.
   3. Rebecca Carter, married J. W. Swart.
   4. George Carter.
   5. Margaret Carter.
   6. Samuel A. Carter, married Julia Parkinson.
   7. Henry Carter.
   8. John B. Carter, born August 19, 1842, died January 21, 1908, married October 12, 1876, Caroline Loughman, born December 22, 1852, died August 31, 1932.
   9. Mary Carter, died in infancy.

4. Hannah Carter, born August 12, 1809, died July 20, 1893, married Nathan Bane, born August 24, 1803, died June 5, 1854. Both are buried in the Lantz Cemetery near Brave.
   Children of Nathan and Hannah (Carter) Bane

   (Partial List)
   1. Louisa Bane, born 1834, died 1921, married Harvey Day, born 1831, died 1914.
   2. Emeline Bane, married Columbus Johnson.
   3. Rebecca Bane, died October 10, 1857, aged 22 years, 7 months and 22 days.

5. Nancy Carter, born August 12, 1809, twin of Hannah, died June 10, 1900, married John McFarland, born October 13, 1809, died February 18, 1878. Buried at Amity.

6. Rachel Carter, born February 12, 1812, died August 22, 1885, married John McClenathan, born February 13, 1807, died November 10, 1878. Both buried at Amity.

7. Harvey Carter, killed by fallen tree in 1840. His wife was Charlotte ...., who is buried with him at Tenmile Cemetery.
8. Rebecca Carter, born April 3, 1816, died December 14, 1907, married George Shrontz, born August 9, 1815, died April 17, 1885. Both are buried at Lone Pine.
9. James Carter, married Jane Taylor. Both are buried at Waynesburg.
10. Mary Carter, born December 27, 1821, died January 9, 1907, married Thomas McClenathan, born October 17, 1816, died June 29, 1894. Both are buried at Jefferson.
   Children of Thomas and Mary (Carter) McClenathan
   1. Sarah McClenathan, born November 10, 1843, died April 22, 1930.
   2. Jennie McClenathan, born ...., married Rex Moredock.
11. John Carter, born June 26, 1826, died April 28, 1884, married Emeline Birch. Both are buried at Jefferson.
4. Hannah Carter, daughter of James and Ann (Bowen) Carter, married (1) .... Coleman, married (2) David Montgomery. They went to Knox County, Ohio.
5. Ruth Carter, born about 1788, died about 1840, married Levi Burson, born July 23, 1788, died 1863. Buried at Clarksville. He signed for wife's share in estate of her mother. (See Burson Records.)
6. Rachel Carter, daughter of James and Ann (Bowen) Carter, born 1781, died February 8, 1812. She married .... Hanks, by whom she had two sons. She is buried beside her father in Amity, but in late years the marker has been removed.
7. Mary Carter, born November 25, 1790, died July 17, 1839, married about 1817, Abraham Burson, born November 7, 1794, died December 11, 1885. Signed for his wife's share in her father's estate. They are buried together in the Burson Cemetery near Clarksville. (See Burson Records.)
8. Nancy Carter, daughter of James and Ann (Bowen) Carter, no record.
9. Permelia Carter, daughter of James and Ann (Bowen) Carter, married Samuel Wier. He was a bondsman in James Carter's Estate, and executor in the estate of Ann (Bowen) Carter.

THE QUAKER FAMILY OF CRAWFORD

When Commissioner John Steel met with the settlers on the Monongahela in 1768, among those he met at Redstone were James and Josias Crawford, whose names are listed in his report. There can be little doubt that these men had been here for some time prior to that date. Certainly this Josias (or Josiah) Crawford was the same man who made an improvement on upper Muddy Creek in the year 1766, which improvement he later sold to William McCleary, and which was located in the vicinity of Jacob Cline's Fort. (Washington County Deed Book 1-A-195.) In his "History of Washington County" Crumrine, who knew and lived among many of the descendants of these two men, reported that they opened ferries over the Monongahela as early as 1770, but he erroneously included Oliver Crawford as a brother of these two men. Oliver Crawford did open a ferry on Muddy Creek about this time as will be shown, but he was not a brother of James and Josias Crawford.

The ancestor of this Quaker family of Crawfords was James

Crawford, probably of that part of Baltimore County, Maryland, which later went to form Harford County. He lived on a tract of land known as "Double Purchase Plantation," when he made his will which was filed in Baltimore County in 1755. There are a number of references to James Crawford in the Black Books of Maryland, and one mentioning his son James distinctly shows that they were members of the Society of Friends. The will of James Crawford shows he left a wife, Sarah. (Baltimore County Will Book 2. pp.......) Mr. Ellis B. Hawkins of New Wilmington, Pennsylvania, has supplied an abstract of this will, and traced a number of the descendants.

Children of James and Sarah Crawford

1. James Crawford, Jr., born in Maryland, died near Chillicothe, Ohio, one of the ferrymen.
2. Josiah Crawford, born in Maryland, died in Luzerne Township, Fayette, County, Pennsylvania, about 1822. Also operated a ferry on the Monongahela.
3. Mordecai Crawford, settled in Fayette County.
4. Elias Crawford, was in Greene County. Name found in the Muddy Creek Ledger.
5. John Crawford.
6. Jennet Crawford.
7. Ruth Crawford.
8. Sarah Crawford.
9. Hannah Crawford.
10. Rebecca Crawford.

FAMILY OF JAMES CRAWFORD, JR.

James Crawford, Jr., was born in Maryland, probably the James Crawford, Quaker, who contributed to the sufferers of the Boston Fire, while living in Baltimore County, September 6, 1760. He is definitely the James Crawford who settled on the Monongahela before 1768, and named by Commissioner Steel. He is the James Crawford who opened a ferry on the Fayette County side of the river, opposite the mouth of Fish Pot Run, near the present LaBelle Coal Works. He then bought land on the Washington County side of the river for a landing for his ferry. On January 1, 1781, he is shown to have moved his membership from Deer Creek Monthly Meeting to Hopewell Monthly Meeting in Frederick County, Virginia, and later his family is shown to be members of Westlands Monthly Meeting in Washington County, Pennsylvania. His wife is not given in the removal from Deer Creek to Hopewell, but the certificate names most of his children. Mr. Hawkins says he died near Chillicothe, Ohio. At his death his son, John Crawford, inherited the Fayette County land, along with the ferry property, while his son, Joseph, inherited the salt works in Washington County.

Children of James Crawford

1. James Crawford.
2. William Crawford, born in Maryland, December 1765, died in Fayette County, Pennsylvania, October 27, 1860. His wife was Margaret Wilson, born in Maryland in December 1775, died April 4, 1839. They were buried first in the Crawford Cemetery opposite Millsboro, but at a later date the remains were moved to the cemetery at Millsboro, where markers were erected. Named in certificate to Hopewell Monthly Meeting.

Children of William and Margaret (Wilson) Crawford

1. Benjamin Crawford, married Mariah Anderson.

2. Margaret Crawford, born December 20, 1803, died October 21, 1859, never married.
3. Hannah Crawford, born April 5, 1805, died October 1, 1887, married Ephriam Crawford, son of Joseph and Hannah (Hufford) Crawford. He was born April 13, 1803, and died September 9, 1893. Both are buried in the old Redstone Cemetery.
4. Ann Crawford, married Zepheniah Crawford, son of Joseph and Hannah (Hufford) Crawford.

3. Ephriam Crawford, named in certificate. Apparently the Ephriam Crawford granted permission from Redstone Monthly Meeting July 22, 1797, to marry Susannah Nichols.
4. John Crawford, not named in certificate to Hopewell, but got the ferry tract of land.
5. Joseph Crawford, named in the certificate to Hopewell Monthly Meeting. Inherited the salt works property in Washington County. He was born in 1770, and died in Fayette County, April 27, 1837, married Hannah Hufford, who was born in 1772, died April 22, 1837.

Children of Joseph and Hannah (Hufford) Crawford

1. James A. Crawford, married Polly Cope.
2. William G. Crawford, married Margaret Hargrove.
3. Ephriam Crawford, married Hannah Crawford, daughter of William and Margaret (Wilson) Crawford. Has Greene County descendants.
4. Zepheniah Crawford, married Ann Crawford, sister of Hannah.
5. Dr. George Crawford.
6. Dr. John W. Crawford.
7. Josiah W. Crawford.
8. Burgess W. Crawford.
9. Samuel B. Crawford.
10. Hannah B. Crawford, born 1806, died August 12, 1866. She was the second wife of Abraham Burson, son of Edward and Elizabeth (Blackledge) Burson. They had a daughter, Mary Margaret Burson, who married Alexander Flenniken.
11. Joseph W. Crawford, his wife was Cyrene ....

6. Sarah Crawford, mentioned in the certificate from Deer Creek Monthly Meeting.
7. Rachel Crawford, also named in the certificate.
8. Margaret Crawford, last named in the certificate, was disowned by Westlands Monthly Meeting May 25, 1793, for marrying out of unity, when she became the first wife of Zepheniah Beall, founder of Beallsville, Pennsylvania. They had twelve children. When she died Zepheniah Beall married again and had twelve more children by the second union.
9. Ruth Crawford, born March 26, 1764, named in the certificate to Hopewell. She married January 12, 1791, at Westlands Monthly Meeting, William Campbell, born July 11, 1761.

Children of William and Ruth (Crawford) Campbell

1. Mary Campbell, born October 22, 1791.
2. James C. Campbell, born February 17, 1793.
3. Ephriam Campbell, born June 10, 1795.
4. William Campbell, born August 13, 1796, married December 19, 1875, Mary Antrim.
5. Margaret Campbell, born June 22, 1798.
6. Elizabeth Campbell, born February 16, 1800.

7. Ruth Campbell, born July 19, 1801.
8. Regal Campbell, born June 15, 1803.
9. Rachel Campbell, born May 5, 1805.
10. Abel Campbell, born October 26, 1807.
11. Benjamin Campbell, born August 14, 1809.

10. Mary Crawford, named in the certificate, married William Hargrove. Lived near Beallsville.

FAMILY OF JOSIAH CRAWFORD

Josiah (or Josias) Crawford, son of James and Sarah Crawford, was on Muddy Creek in the Summer of 1766, where he made an improvement that he later sold to William McCreary. He met with the commissioners at Fort Redstone in 1768 in an endeavor to convince them that the settlers were wanted by the Indians and considered them friends. With his brother, James Crawford, he accumulated much land on the Monongahela River between Brownsville and LaBelle, and was in 1770, owner of a ferry near Brownsville. Probably gave his name to Crawford's Riffles, a shallow place in the Monongahela River about where the Brownsville Dam now is located. Hopewell Monthly Meeting reports that Josiah Crawford and wife, Cassandra, with eight of their ten children, were joined to that Society on November 5, 1781. The will of Josiah Crawford was made January 24, 1822, and probated on April 24, 1823 at Uniontown. (Will Book 1. pp. 232.)

Children of Josiah and Cassandra Crawford

1. James Crawford, born about 1759, in Maryland, died in Island Creek Township, Jefferson County, Ohio, where he had settled in 1796. His will was made December 4, 1844, and filed August 26, 1844. James Crawford married Sarah Jones, daughter of John Jones of the Fort Jackson vicinity. They are buried in the Mt. Tabor Cemetery.

Children of James and Sarah (Jones) Crawford

1. Cynthia Crawford, born February 8, 1786, died at Beallsville, July 16, 1845, married May 12, 1803, Richard Hawkins, born August 25, 1770, died February 6, 1856. (Ancestors of Colonel Alexander Hawkins, 10th Penna. Regt. N. G. P.)
2. Benedict Crawford, married Sarah ....
3. Cassandra Crawford, born 1790, married William Growdy.
4. Elijah Crawford, born 1794, died 1868, married Elizabeth Cooper.
5. Ruth Crawford, born 1796, married Robert Phillips.
6. Elizabeth Crawford, married .... Harrison.
7. John Crawford, a Methodist minister, born 1799.
8. James Crawford, born October 10, 1801, married Ann Taylor.
9. Greenberry Crawford, born September 16, 1803, married (1) Rhoda Winters, (2) Margaret Ecky.
10. Abel Crawford, born April 18, 1806, married Mary Winters.
11. Josiah Crawford, died 1875, married Nancy Cooper.

2. Benedict Crawford, is named in the certificate of membership at Hopewell, but is reported to have been killed by the Indians.
3. Josiah Crawford, listed as Joseph by Hopewell Monthly Meeting. He was disowned on December 22, 1792, by Westlands Monthly Meeting for his marriage out of unity. He went to Jefferson County, Ohio.
4. Elijah Crawford, named as a son of Josiah by Hopewell and also named in the will of his father. He married Christina Oase, and was the ancestor of some of the Clarksville family. Died in Luzerne Township, Fayette County.

Children of Elijah and Christina (Oase) Crawford
1. Lee Crawford
2. Levi Crawford.
3. Cassandra Crawford.
4. Josiah Crawford.
5. Elizabeth Crawford, married Johnson Craft.
6. James Crawford, born July 25, 1809, married April 14, 1836, Sarah Hawkins, born November 1, 1811, died September 1, 1882.
7. Jacob Crawford, married Susan Hertzog.

5. Levi Crawford, called Eli in the Hopewell record, died in Luzerne Township, Fayette County.
6. Abel Crawford, died in Jefferson County, Ohio.
7. Ephriam Crawford, died in Luzerne Township, Fayette County.
8. Sarah Crawford, not named in Hopewell list, but was probably married then to Samuel Garwood, who was a member originally of Worthington Monthly Meeting.
9. Ruth Crawford, married Joshua (?) Shaw.
10. Cassandra Crawford, married William Davis.

ASSESSMENT ROLLS

FREQUENT references will be made in these articles to first tax lists. The Springhill Township, Bedford County, Pennsylvania, Tax List has been published in Veach, but has an important place in this history. We have seen the original Springhill Tax List in the Court House at Bedford, showing the assessment roll for 1773, and taken for tax purposes in 1772. At that time Springhill Township, Bedford County, included all the territory that went to make up Washington and Greene Counties. It also included the part of Fayette County lying south of Redstone to the mouth of Jacob's Creek. Bedford County was formed from Cumberland County on March 9, 1771, so this is the first list of taxables taken by that county.

The tax lists for Washington County, Pennsylvania, were taken from the assessment rolls after the settlement of the Virginia-Pennsylvania controversy over the boundary line. When Washington County was set up on March 28, 1781, it included all of Greene County and parts of Allegheny County. It had been a part of Westmoreland County, which had been taken from Bedford County on February 26, 1773, but no lists of Westmoreland taxables have been found. Thus from the period between 1772 until 1784, there exists a lapse in which one can only refer to the militia lists for a knowledge of the inhabitants of this section.

When Washington County was formed, in 1781, and the line finally agreed upon, the number of original townships set up for administration purposes included Morgan, Cumberland and Greene, which, on February 9, 1796, were included in the new Greene County. The northern tier of present townships were included in Amwell and Donegal Townships. Morgan Township, in the first arrangement of Washington County, included roughly all the section north of Tenmile, and south of the Dividing Ridge, extending from the Monongahela River, at the mouth of Tenmile, to Bates Fork of Tenmile, west of Fort Jackson. It also took in the few settlers opposite the mouth of Purseley Creek. Cumberland Township was roughly that portion of present Greene County located between the Tenmile and Big Whiteley Creeks, extending from the Monongahela River to Purseley Creek. Greene Township included the territory between Big Whiteley Creek and the present West Virginia line. By keeping these boundaries in mind, it is possible to locate the early settlers with a great degree of accuracy. Franklin Township was set up in 1788, and its boundaries were about the same as at present.

ASSESSMENT ROLL
Springhill Township, Bedford County, Pennsylvania for the year 1773
(Copied from Veach's "Monongahela of Old")

John Allen	George Boydstone	Manus Brown
William Allen	Peter Bachus	Thomas Brown
Edward Askins	Bazil Brown	John Brown
John Armstrong	James Brown	Walter Brisco
John Artman	Dunlap's Creek	Peter Baker
Ichabod Ashcraft	Thomas Brown	James Burdin
John Alley	Tenmile Creek	John Burris
John Allison	Joseph Brown	Robert Brownfield
Samuel Adams	Samuel Brown	Edward Brownfield
Robert Adams	Adam Brown	Empson Brownfield

Jeremiah Beek
Charles Burkham
Henry Beeson
Jacob Beeson
Alexander Buchanan
James Black
John Barkley
Nicholas Bauk
  (Blake)
Thomas Banfield
Thomas Batton
William Brashears
Joseph Barker
Lewis Brimet
  (Bonnet)
James Branton
  (Brinton)
Henry Branton
  (Brinton)
John Braddock
Michael Carn
George Craft
William Case
Adam Cumbert
John Craig
Joseph Caldwell
James Crooks
William Campbell
John Carr
John Carr, Jr.
Moses Carr
William Cochran
George Conn
Nicholas Croshoe
Anthony Coshaw
Wm. Crawford, Capt.
Wm. Crawford, Quak.
William Crawford
Josiah Crawford
Oliver Crawford
Richard Chinner
Peter Cleam
Jacob Cleam
John Castile
George Church
Michael Cox
Joseph Cox
Michael Catt
Abraham Cills
Anthony Cills
William Conwell
Jehu Conwell
Michael Cresap
William Colvin
George Colvin
Peter Drago
John Drago
Samuel Douglass
Jeremiah Downs

Augustus Dilliner
Edward Death
John Death
Owen David
Jesse Dument
William Downard
Henry Debolt
George Debolt
Henry Dever
Lewis Davison
Andrew Davison
William Dawson
Jacob Dicks
Lewis Deem
Henry Enoch 3
John Evans
Richard Evans
Hugh Evans
Edward Elliot
Michael Franks
Jacob Franks
James Fleeharty
John Fisher
James Frame
Nathan Friggs
  (Frakes)
Henry Friggs
  (Frakes)
Hugh Ferry
James Flannegan
  (Flenniken)
David Flowers
Thomas Flowers
Thomas Gaddis
Samuel Glaspy
  (Gillespie)
William Garrat
John Garrard
John Garrard, Jr.
William Goodwin
Joseph Goodwin
Thomas Gooden
John Glasgo
Frederick Garrison
Leonard Garrison
Jacob Grow
  (Crow)
Zachariah Gobean
  (Gapen)
John Griffith
Hugh Gilmore
Robert Gilmore
Thomas Gregg
Charles Gause
Daniel Goble
Nicholas Gilbert
Andrew Gudgel
Henry Hart
David Hatfield, Jr.

John Hendricks
Henry Hall
John Hall
Adam Henthorn
James Henthorn
James Henthorn
  (the less)
John Henthorn
Charles Hickman
Aaron Hackney
Martin Hardin
Benjamin Hardin
John Hardin, Jr.
John Harman
George Huckleberry
John Huffman
John Harrison
David Hawkins
James Herrod
William Herrod
Levi Herrod
Henson Hobbs
Samuel Howard
William House
Philomen (Felix)
  Hughes
Thomas Hughes
  Muddy Creek
Thomas Hughes
Owen Hughes
John Huston
Hugh Jackson
David Jennings
Aaron Jenkins
Jonathan Jones
John Jones
Thomas Lane
Absolom Little
Samuel Lucas
Thomas Lucas
Richard Lucas
Hugh Laughlin
David Long
John Long
John Long, Jr.
Jacob Link
Aaron Moore
John Moore
John Moore
  (Over the River)
Simon Moore
Hans Moore
David Morgan
Charles Morgan
William Masters
John Masterson
Henry Myers
George Myers
Ulrick Myers

Martin Mason
John Mason
Alexander Miller
John Messmore
John Mene (Minor)
Daniel Moredock
James Moredock
Adam Mannon
John Mannon
John Marr
William McDowell
John McFarland
Francis McGinnis
Nathaniel McCarty
Samuel McCray
James McCoy
Hugh McCleary
Tunis Newkirk
Barnet Newkirk
James Neal
George Newell
James Notts
  (Knotts)
James Notts, Jr.
Charles Nelson
Adam Newlon
  (Newland)
Barnet O'Neal
Jacob Poundstone
Frederick Parker
Philip Pearce
Theophius Phillips
Thomas Phillips
Adam Penter
Richard Parr
Henry Peters
John Peters
Christian Pitser
Ahimon Pollock

Samuel Paine
John Wm. Provance
John Pollock
Ieronemus Rimley
  (Remley)
Casper Rather
Telah Rood (Rude)
Jesse Rood (Rude)
Daniel Robbins
John Robbins
Roger Roberts
Jacob Riffle
Ralph Riffle
William Rail
David Rogers
Thomas Roch
  (Roach)
Edward Roland
  (Rollins)
William Rees
Jonathan Rees
Jacob Rich
Thomas Scott
Edward Scott
Andrew Scott
James Scott
John Smith
  (Dunlap's Creek)
John Smith
Robert Smith
James Smith
Philip Smith
William Smith
Conrad Seix
  (Sykes)
Isaac Sutton
Isaac Sutton, Jr.
Jacob Sutton
Samuel Stillwell

Lewis Saltser
  (Selsor)
William Spangler
John Swearingen
William Shepherd
John Swan
John Swan, Jr.
Thomas Swan
Robert Sayre
Stephen Styles
Samuel Sampson
Joseph Starkey
David Shelby
Elias Stone
Obediah Truax
John Thompson
Michael Tuck
Abraham Teagarden
George Teagarden
Edward Taylor
Michael Thomas
Henry Vanmeter
Abraham Vanmeter
Jacob Vanmeter
John Vantrees
John Varvill
David White
James White
George Williams
David Walters
Ephraim Walters
David Wright
George Wilson, Esq.
James Wilson
John Waits
John Watson
George Watson
Joseph Youger
Telah Yourk

INMATES—(Boarders—not Heads of Families)

Richard Ashcraft
Ephraim Ashcraft
Samuel Adams
John Bachus
William Burt
James Beeson
Samuel Bridgewater
Coleman Brown
Bazil Brown
Benjamin Brashears
Richard Brownfield
Benjamin Brooks
Alexander Bryan
William Bells
Gabriel Cox
Israel Cox
Robert Cavines

Samuel Colson
  (Coulson)
Joseph Coon
  (Kughn)
John Cross
Edward Carn
Christian Coffman
John Curley
Nathaniel Case
John Crossley
Christopher Capley
  (Caplaid)
George Catt
John Chadwick
Jonathan Chambers
John Cline
  (Jacob Cline?)

Benajah Dunn
Zepheniah Dunn
Timothy Downing
Jeremiah Davis
  (Davison)
James Davis
Thomas Edwards
Bernard Eckley
  (Eckerlein?)
James Fugate
John Guthery
William Groom
Capt. John Hardin
William Henthorn
William Hogland
Edward Hatfield
John Hawkins

AND ITS PIONEER FAMILIES

Samuel Herrod
John Hargess
  (Hargus)
Thomas Hargess
  (Hargus)
Joseph Jackson
Jacob Jacobs
John Kinneson
Thomas Kendle
  (Kendall)
William Lee
Elijah Mickle
William Murphy
John Morgan
Morgan Morgan
Andrew Link

Samuel Merrifield
John Main, Jr.
William Martin
John Morris
George McCoy
John McFall
Alexander McDonald
William McClaman
John Pettyjohn
Baltzer Peters
Richard Powell
Thomas Pyburn
  (Pribble?)
John Phillips
Thomas Provance
Thomas Rail

Noah Rood
  (Rude)
William Spencer
Alexander Smith
John Smith
Francis Stannater
John Taylor
William Thompson
Jonah Webb
John Williamson
Alexander White
Benjamin Wells
Michael Whitelock
  (Whitlatch)
Jeremiah Yourk
Ezekiel Yourk

SINGLE FREEMEN

John Brown
Joseph Batton
  (Patton?)
Isher Budd
David Blackston
Hugh Crawford
John Crawford
Francis Chain
William Cheney
Daniel Christy
James Chamberlain
James Carmichael
James Campbell
John Catch
John Dicker
  (Decker)
John Douglass
Edward Dublin
Elias Eaton
Alexander Ellener
Samuel Eckerly
  (Echerlein)

Thomas Foster
Jacob Funk
Martin Funk
Barnet Griffith
Joseph Gwin
  (Gwynne)
John Holton
Abraham Holt
John Holt
Joshua Hudson
John Hupp
Cornelius Johnson
Joshua Little
William Marshall
James Morgan
Hugh Murphy
George Morris
Joseph Morris
David McDonald
Abraham McFarland
John McGilty
Philip Nicholas

John Notts (Knotts)
James Peters
Isaac Prichard
  (Prickett)
Jonathan Paddox
Ebenezer Paddox
Noble Rail
Nathan Rinehart
Samuel Robb
James Robertson
Philip Rogers
John Shively
Christopher Swoop
  (Swope)
Ralph Smith
John Sultzer
  (Selsor)
William Teagarden
John Taylor
John Verville, Jr.
John Williams

ASSESSMENT ROLL

Morgan Township, Washington County, Pennsylvania
for the year 1784

BENJAMIN JENNINGS
Collector

DEMAS LINDLEY AND GEORGE McCORMICK
Commissioners

Arnold, Frederick
Arnold, Daniel
Benham, Robert
Baily, Groombride
Burge, Jacob
Bell, Nathaniel
Benham, Peter

Bell, Nathaniel, Jr.
Bell, Abel
Brown, Paul
Brown, Abner
Bell, James
Brown, Ebenezer
Brown, Mary

Beedle, Francis
Beedle, Joseph, Jr.
Beedle, Joseph
Bristo, James
Cox, Andrew
Call, Samuel
Case, Joseph

Chidester, Holdridge
Cox, Michael
Crain, Silas
Crain, Daniel
Dunham, Nathaniel
Daniels, John
Dunn, Sarah
Daniels, Benjamin
Enoch, Henry
Fix, Henry
Fox, Philip
Gayman, Christian
Gragson, Philip
Grooms, William
Goodman, John
Gatrail, John
Gray, Archibald
Griffin, Rachel
Gray, Mathew
Gray, Archibald
Groom, Solomon
Galloway, Patrick
Hill, Thomas
Hays, William
Haiden, Myles
Hartly, William
Herrod, Levi
Hardesty, Richard
House, Samuel
Hogue, George
Huffman, Henry
Heaton, John
Hathaway, Samuel
House, Felty
Hook, James
Hardesty, Hezekiah
Hathaway, Nathan
Hurley, Zachariah

Hardesty, Francis
Johnson, Zepheniah
Jennings, Benjamin
Jennings, David
Jackson, Richard
Johnston, Isaac
Kelly, Nathan
Kelsey, Thomas
Kelly, Elias
Lines, Samuel
Leonard, Jesse
Lee, William
Leonard, William
Lowrie, John
Lindsecomb, Joseph
Leonard, Ziba
McKinney, John
McCray, Samuel
Mills, Joseph
Messemer, John
Miligan, James
Mills, Jacob
Minor, Josiah
Mills, John
Morris, Richard
Miligan, William
Miranda, James
Meeks, Nathan
Matheny, James
McCray, Phineas
McVau (gh) Benj.
Martin, John
Miller, Cornelius
Morris, Archibald
Minor, Thomas
Moore, Tobias
Moore, John
Mills, Elijah
SINGLE FREEMEN

Morris, James
Need, Jacob
Owens, Judith
Parker, James
Perkins, Elisha
Perkins, Reuben, Sr.
Perkins, Richard
Ross, John, Jr.
Rush, Jacob
Rush, William
Rose, Tichicus
Ross, Henry
Ross, John, Sr.
Slater, Thomas
Stites, Benjamin
Stewart, Joseph
Seals, Samuel
Stites, Elisha
Smith, Ralph
Seals, James, Sr.
Sellers, Jacob
Stull, Henry
Stull, John
Sellars, Leonard
Stump, Booth
Swart, Philip
Timmons, Lazarus
Taylor, John
Veatch, John
Wright, William
Wiley, Joseph
Wilson, Thomas
Wiley, John
Wright, James
Wright, Lewis
Walton, Joab
Woolverton, Thomas
Yeats, John

ASSESSMENT ROLL

**Morgan Township, Washington County, Pennsylvania
for the year 1785**

Arnold, Daniel
Brown, Paul
Brown, Abner
Bell, James
Bell, Abel
Bell, Nathaniel, Jr.
Arnold, Abraham
Arnold, Daniel
Baily, James
Linsecum, Cobbus
Perkins, Reuben
Leonard, David

Bell, Nathaniel, Sr.
Benham, Robert
Benham, Peter
Bristoe, James
Beedle, Joseph, Sr.
Beedle, Joseph, Jr.
Leonard, Amos
Young, Andrew
Kenny, John
Ross, Robert
Ross, William
Ross, Reuben

Beedle, Daniel
Beedle, Francis
Baily, Groombride
Burge, Jacob
Brown, Ebenezer
Brown, Mary
Ross, Ignatius
Seals, James
Seals, Joseph
Teater, Francis
Gaskins, John
Hogue, Isaiah

AND ITS PIONEER FAMILIES 131

Bashiers, Thomas
Cawl, Samuel
Crosley, John
Cox, Michael
Cox, Andrew
Crane, Daniel
Crane, Silas
Case, Joseph
Dunham, Nathaniel
Daniels, John
Daniels, Benjamin
Davis, Robert
Daniel, Griffith
  (Griffin) a minor
Enoch, Henry
Enoch, Hannah
Fulton, John
Ferley, Andrew
Fee, George
Fix, Henry
Forward, William
Grooms, Solomon
Grooms, William
Gaitrael, John
Gayman, Christian
Gregston, Philip
Gray, Archibald
Gray, Archibald, Jr.
Gray, John
Gray, Mathew
Goodwin, John
George, Samuel
Galloway, Mary
Glass, John
Gladen, Elizabeth
Heaton, John
Heaton, Ephraim
Hathaway, Samuel
House, John
Hill, Thomas
Hartly, William
Hurley, Cornelius
  Estate
Harrod, Levi
Hook, James
Hurley, Zachariah

Hogue, George
House, Samuel
Chidester, Holdridge
Haidan, Myles
Hardesty, Obediah
Hardesty, Hezekiah
Hays, William
Hays, John
Hook, John
Jennings, David
Jennings, Benjamin
Johnston, Zepheniah
Jackson, Richard
Johnston, Isaac
Kelly, Elias
Kelsey, Thomas
Kelly, Thomas
Leonard, William
Kelly, Nathan
  Estate
Leonard, Ziba
Lee, William
Lines, Samuel
Lowry, John
Linsecum, Joseph
Leonard, Joseph
Leonard, Jesse
Leonard, Lydia
Minor, Thomas
Martin, John
Milekin, James
Milekin, William
Meek, Nathan
Mceown, James
McGill, Robert
McCray, Phenhas
Moore, Tobias
McCray, Samuel
McKenny, John
McIntyre, Daniel
Mills, Jacob
Mills, John
Mills, Elijah
Mills, Joseph
Morris, Richard
Meranda, James

Meranda, Samuel
Morris, Archibald
Morris, James
Need, Jacob
Owens, Judith
Perkins, Reuben
Perkins, Richard
Pitcock, Benjamin
Perkins, Elisha
Parker, James
————, Jesse
Rush, Jacob
Reed, James
Rose, Tychicus
Reed, Joseph
Rush, William
  Estate
Ross, John
Ross, William
Ross, Henry
Ross, John, Sr.
Stewart, Joseph
Slater, Thomas
Stites, Benjamin
Stites, Elijah
Stull, John
Stull, Henry
Swart, Philip
Stump, Booth Robert
Smith, Ralph
Seals, Samuel
Seals, James
Seals, James, Sr.
Timmons, Lazarus
Thomas, Samuel
Veech, John
Whyly, John
Woolverton, Thomas
Walton, Jobe
Wright, William
Wright, Lewis
Whyly, Joseph
Woolverton, John
Yate, John
Young, Andrew
Dunn, Sarah

SINGLE FREEMEN

Arnold, Daniel
Arnold, Abraham
Beaves, George
Gray, Andrew
Gayman, Daniel

Linsecum, Cobbus
Leonard, Amos
Line, John
Leonard, David
McKown, John

Martin, Lewis
Perkins, Reuben, Jr.
Ross, Robert
Ross, Ignatius
Teeter, Francis

ASSESSMENT ROLL
Cumberland Township, Washington County, Pennsylvania for the year 1784

Arthur Inghram
Andrew McClelland
Alexander Coughran
  (Cockran)
Abraham Armstrong
Amos Miller
Adam Kirke
Aaron Linadah
  (Luzada)
Andrew Lewis
Andrew Lewis
  Estate
Alexander Finley
Anthony Mayher
Abraham Scott
Arthur Inghrum
Abraham Summorren
  (Zimmerman)
Aaron Bollings
Aaron Bollings, Sr.
Aaron Bolling
  Estate
Billy Seaton
Betty Hughston
Benjamin Hughes
Benjamin Lemon
  (Liming)
Bernet Rinehart
Barnes Vandevender
Charles Swan
Charles McDowell
Charles Anderson
Daniel Anderson
Demas Durhan
Daniel Clark
Daniel Estle
David Duncan
Daniel Stewart
Daniel Stewart
David Kennedy
Daniel Murdock
Daniel Duvall
Daniel Duvall
  Estate
Elias Garrard
Ezekiel Morris
John Coin
James Moralty
James Clerke
John Willson
John Tumblestone
John Davis
John McElroy
Joseph Eastwood
John Gates

James Winns
John Hul
John Purdoin
Isaac Wood
John Gernon
  (Vernon?)
James Henderson
Ichabod Smith
John McCurry
James Murdock
John Jones
  Muddy Creek
John Simonton
Elisha Stewart
Enoch Blackledge
Edward Dunn
Edward McLaughlin
Edward Burson
Francis Veatch
Felty Cooper
Francis Seaton
George Gilguce
  (Gilkesie)
George Gregg
George Moore
George Church
George Carrol
George Santee
George Coones
George Teagarden
Hugh Stephenson
Hezekiah Stewart
Henry McQuade
Hugh Johnstone
James Carmichaels
  Do for land in
  Greene Township
James Seaton
John Crawford
John Holton
Joseph Rankins
  Do Estate
John Huston
Joseph McKenny
James Porter
James Blan(e)
John Bloir (Blair)
John Doughan
John Doughan
  Estate
James Flenniken
Jacob Bloney
James Hazlett
John Burns
John McKey

John Armstrong
Nathaniel Hughes
Michael Jones
Oliver Crawford
Priscilla Israel
Philip Clark
Peter Livengood
Peter Livengood, Jr.
Peter Myers
Patrick Cone
Patrick Archer
Patrick Cree
Robert McKinny
Richard Gregg
Robert Reed
Robert Gorrell
Robert Bradford
Roland Hughes
Richard Stewart
Jeremiah Veach
Joseph Rinehart
John Flenniken
Jacob Smith
John Jones
John Bryant
John Smith
Jeremiah Prail
John Lee
Israel White
James Archer
John Hook
James Hogan
  (Eagon)
Joseph Ball
Joseph Adams
John Adams
Isaac (H)Eaton
Jacob Rush
Joseph Archer
Joseph Dunn
Isaac Miller
John Wright
James Dailey
James Wilson
Isaac Miller
Joseph Frakes
Isaac Israel
Keener Seaton
Michael Coon
Moses Crago
Mary Crawford
Mary Newton
William Crawford
William Woods
William Shepherd

AND ITS PIONEER FAMILIES   133

William Cree   Samuel Thomas   Thomas Wilson
William Cathers   Simon Archer   Thomas Blackledge
William Inghrum   Thomas Eaton   Thomas Fares
Robert McClellan   Thomas Thorowman   (Ferris)
Richard McMullen   Thomas Sedgewick   Thomas Roach
Robert Warton   Thomas Sedgewick   Thomas Strahon
Stephen Pribble   Estate   (Strawn)
Samuel Dullon   Thomas Rinehart   Thomas Brown
Samuel Barnhill, Jr.   Thomas Rinehart, Sr. Vallon (Volentine)
Samuel Polk   Thomas Lee   Nichols
Stephen Stiles   Thomas Wells   William Gray
Samuel Shannon   Thomas Weakly   William McCleary
Sarah Rinehart   Thomas Adams   William McDowell
Samuel Jackson   Thomas McDowell   William Herrod
Samuel Strong   Thomas Adams, Jr.   William Davis

SINGLE FREEMEN

Alexander Crawford   James McClellan   Richard Seaton
Abraham Luzadah   John McCon   Samuel Foster
Barns Vandedor   Joseph Gun   Thomas Pribble
Bernard Hogan   John Bradford   Gabriel Aken
   (Eagon)   Joseph Garratt   William Jacob, Sr.
Cornelius Johns   Michael Dougherty   William McClean
David White   Levy Gregg   William Whitlatch
Daniel Duvall   Paul Huston   Robert Cree
George Seaton   Robert Vandredods
George Rankins   Robert McClellan

The following refused to give in their property but must pay taxes

Acquilla Martin   John Villiers   Nathan Frakes
Azariah Davis   John Swan   Frakes Estate
George Nott   Samuel Veach   Richard Swan
Henry Vanmeter   Thomas Hughes   Thomas Cragoe
James Hughes   Jesse Vanmater   Widow Foster
James Hughes   James Pribble   (Thomas)
   Estate   Joseph Vanmeter   Lott Leonard
John Thatcher   Jesse Pigman   George Newland
John Ankrom   John Rice

ASSESSMENT ROLL

Cumberland Township, Washington County, Pennsylvania
for the year 1788

Anderson, Charles, Sr.   Brown, Thomas   Barnhill, Samuel
Anderson, Charles, Jr.   Brown, John   Bonner, William
Anderson, Daniel   Brown Estate   Crawford, William
Armstrong, John   Bloney, Jacob   Crawford, John
Armstrong, Abraham   Bloir, James   Crawford, Oliver
Adamson, John   (Blair)   Crawford, Alexander
Adamson, Joseph   Booz, Henry   Croughan, Alexander
Blatchley, Margaret   Bell, James   Carmichaels, James
   (Blackledge)   (James Bell)   Cree, Robert
Blackledge, Enoch   Barnes, Job   Cree, Robert
Boreman, John   Bailey, Electious   Cree, James
   Estate   Burson, Edward   Cree, William
Boreman, John   Ball, Joseph   Cree, Patrick

Clark, James
Cain, Patrick
Cain, John
Curtain, Robert
Carter, Thomas
Holton, John
Huslin, Elizabeth
Hughes, James
Hughes, James, Sr.
Hughes, Thomas
Hughes, Thomas
Hughes, Richard
Hillman, Daniel
Hannah, James
Herrod, William
Heaton, John
Hill, John
Rinehart, Joseph
Seaton, James
Seaton, Francis
Seaton, George
Seaton, Betty
Sedgewick, Thomas
Clarke, Michael
Clyne, Jacob
Cunce, Michael
Crosley, Robert
Daugherty, John
Daugherty Est.
Dunham, Demas
Duncan, David
Davis, John
Davis, Ezeriah
Davis, Stephen
Dunn, Joseph
Dunn, Isaac
Dunn, Edmund
Dickeson, Jesse
Dailey, James
Eagon, James
Eagon, Barnet
Eastwood, Joseph
Eastel, Daniel
Flenniken, James
Flenniken, John
Finley, Alex
Fee, John
Greggs, George
Greggs, Richard
Gerrard, Elias
Gerrard, Joseph
Gerrard, Jesse
Gerrard, William
Gallespie, Henry
Gallespie, James
Gwyne, Joseph
Greene, John
Garwood, Midian
Hannah, Francis

Hartman, Adam
Hoge, Solomon
Hally, Samuel
Hartfield, Thomas
Hager, William
Huff, Peter
Holdon, John
Huston, John
Hale, William
Henderson, James
Hibbs, William
Harbor, Thomas
Johnson, Bailey
Stewart, Daniel
Stewart, Elisha
Stewart, Ezra
Stewart, Daniel, Jr.
Swan, John
Swan, William
Johnson, Hugh
Jameson, Alex
Jackson, Samuel
Jones, John
Israel, Isaac
Korby, Joseph
Jones, Michael
Kella, Robert
  (Kelly)
Linsley, Jacob
Lucas, John
  (Or Luas)
Livengood, Peter, Sr.
Livengood, Peter, Jr.
Leonard, Lott
Limming, Benjamin
Lucas, Andrew
  (Or Luas)
Luzader, Aaron
McElroy, William
McClelland, James
McClelland, Andrew
McMillen, Rich
McDowell, Charles
McCleary, William
Morris, Ezekiel
McClellan, Robert, Jr.
McCally, John
Moor, John
Moore, Samuel
Moore, William
Murdock, James
Murdock, Daniel
Marrato, James
Marrato, Daniel
Munroe, Alexander
Myers, Peter
McClelland, Robert, Sr.
McDowell, William
McDowell, Thomas

Miller, Nicholas
Newland, George
Newland, Herrod
Nicholas, Holmes
Nicholas Estate
Pigman, Jesse
Powers, Michael
Pribble, Thomas
Pribble, Job
Pribble, Ruben
Pribble, Stephen
Prior, John
Purtee, John
Purtee Estate
Purkins, William
Purkins Estate
Roach, Thomas
Rice, John
Swan, Charles
Swan, Richard
Sedgewick Estate
Strawn, Jacob
Strode, Samuel
Stiles, Stephen
Shephard, William
Simonton, John
Saxton, Joseph
Stump, Booth
Stull, Benjamin
Stephenson, Hugh
Shelby, Evan
Scott, Abraham
Smith, Jacob
Thuramon, William
Thuramon, Thomas
Teagarden, George
Thomas, Samuel
Vanmeter, Henry
  Esquire
Vanmeter, Joseph
Vanmeter, Jesse
Villiars, John
Veach, Jeremiah
Veach, Nathan
Whitlatch, William
Willson, Thomas
Willson, Thomas
Willson, John
Willson Estate
Wilson, Abraham
Wims, James
Wood, Isaac
Wright, John
Wright, Benjamin
Wood, Thomas
Wiggar, Philip
Wiggar Estate

SINGLE FREEMEN

Akins, Gabriel
Anderson, Rich
Askins, Thomas
Brown, Ebenezer
Blackledge, William
Bowman, Benjamin
Daugherty, Michael
Edward, Timothy
Greggs, Levi
Grimes, James

Huston, Paul
Hull, Nathaniel
Hannah, James
Kenedy, John
Lewis, David
Lewis, Robert
Lewis Estate
McKain, John
McClelland, John
Miller, Matthew

Mitchell, Alexander
Plummer, Elisha
Quinlan, Isaac
Seaton, Hanson
Scott, William
Stonesby, John
Thomas, Ellis
Vanmeter, Absolom

UNSEATED LANDS

Nicholas Blake
David Whitemore
Daniel Whitemore

ASSESSMENT ROLL
Greene Township, Washington County, Pennsylvania
for the year 1784

Alley, John
Burke, John
  Estate
Bruner, Jacob
Burns, Michael
Burns, William
Brown, John
Baldwin, Francis
Balshear, James
Brown, William
Brown, John, Hatter
Baker, Nicholas
Benefield, John
  Estate
Coughian, Thomas
Canon, Richard
Carel, John
Covalt, Abraham
  Estate
Clegg, Alexander
Corbly, John
Clawson, Mary
Chaffins, John
Clark, Joshua
Carby, John
Dillinger, Augustine
Dye, Andrew
Davis, John
Dawson, Allen
Douglas, Timothy
Dewal, John
Evans, John, Sr.
Evans, John, Jr.
Edwards, John
Evans, David
Fast, Christian
Futner, Henry
Frakes, Henry
Flum, James

Fewart, Francis
  (Feurt)
Frazee, Joseph
Frazee, Jacob
Flowers, David
Flowers, Thomas
Ferry, Onner
Fast, Jacob
Garrison, Frederick
Glasgow, John
Garrett, Justus
Gerrett, John
Griffith. Ossie
Greene, John
Garrison, Leonard
Gutherie, John
Gapen, Zachariah
Huzzy, Hamilton
Herrod, Samuel
Huckle, Joseph
Hyde, Samuel
Hobbs, Henson
Hutson, William
Hannon, Matthew
Jackson, Henry
Jackson, Alexander
John, Isaac
Irwin, William
Jenkins, Aaron
Ive(r)s, Richard
Johnson, Baily
Jones, Robert
Irwin, Richard
Knotts, Solomon
Kidd, Nathaniel
Keener, Samuel
Knotts, Benjamin
Knotts, James
Knotts, William

Lewis, Philip
Long, John
Lemley, George
Lance, (Lantz) John
Lambert, Mary
Lance, Andrew
Long, Jeremiah
Long, John, son
Long, James
Long, Eliel
Long, Noah
Long, Gideon
Long, David
Miller, Peter
Morris, George
Morris, Joseph, Sr.
Morris, Joseph, Jr.
Mundle, James
Mundle, Abner
Minor, John
Minor, William
McClure, John
More, John
Masters, William
Night, William
Neelson, Garrard
Pyles, Zachariah
Pickenpaugh, Peter
Province, Sarah
Prickett, Josiah
Prickett, Isaah
Parker, James
Parkins, William
Pain, Richard
Raily, Peter
Reed, Joseph
Robinson, Susanna
Robinson, William
Rutter, John

Rinehart, Daniel
Ritchie, John
Roberts, John
Ross, Joseph
Six, Henry
Six, Margaret
Selzer, Lewis
Selzer, George

Shriver, John
Smith, Henry
Sutton, Ebenezer
Sutton, Nathan
Sutton, Benjamin
Stone, Elias
Shelby, David
Truelock, Thomas

Thomas, William
Williams, Lewis
Winson, James
Williams, Elenor
Wilford, Joseph
Wood, Isaac
Yoho, Peter

SINGLE FREEMEN

Alley, Ross
Anderson, Daniel
Bonner, John
Cook, Ziba
Dye, Benjamin

Douglas, John
Douglas, Thomas
Evans, John
Evans, Zachariah
Evans, George

Fast, Francis
Howard, Zadock
Prickett, John
Sutton, Stephen

LIVE OUTSIDE THE TOWNSHIP

Boils, William
Boydstone, David
Crouse, Widow
Crouse, Everton
Dillison, Henry
Everly, Leonard
Fast, Nicholas
Gapen, Samuel
Hoover, Jacob
Hooper, Robert

Jones, Jacob
Keener, Boston
Ketch, John
Luckey, Rev.
McCracken, John
Henry, Calson
Newman, Isaac
Morris, Jonathan
Shriver, Adam
Shannon, Robert

Shriver, George
Williams, Jeremiah
William, George
   Heirs
Worley, Bryce
Weaver, Henry
Wilson, Samuel
White, Benjamin
Wood, William

ASSESSMENT ROLL

Franklin Township, (Greene County) Washington County, Penna. for the year 1788

Ankrom, John
Ankrom, Richard
Archer, James
Aldridge, John
Brown, Mary
Bonner, John
Bradford, Robert
Brown, Vincent
Brient, John
Cathers, William
Carrell, William
Carrel, George
Cellers, Christian
Cellers, Leonard
Cellers, George
Devall, Daniel
Davis, James
Dailey, Peter
Fee, Thomas, Jr.
Fee, Thomas, Sr.
Fee, George
Fee, John
Gorrell, Robert
Gray, John
Gaskin, John

Hathaway, William
Hathaway, Samuel
Hughes, Nathan
Huffman, Henry
Hook, John
Huffman, George
Jones, John
Jackson, Richard
Inghram, Arthur
Inghram, William
Kent, Thomas
Kirck (Church)
   George
Lakin, Joseph
Lorain, John
Lakin, Samuel
Merrandy, James
Merrandy, Samuel
Moore, George
McMullen, John
Morris, Archer
Nott, George
Parker, Abraham
Porter, James
Parker, John

Pratt, John
Peckenpough, George
Parkinson, William
Rinehart, Barnet
Rinehart, Thomas, Jr.
Rinehart, Sarah
   (Widow of Simon)
Rinehart, Thomas, Sr.
Smittle, Jacob
Slatter, Thomas
Seals, James
Sears (Sayers) William
Smith, John
Zimmerman, Abraham
Smith, Thomas
Schroffe, Sebastian
Thresher, John, Jr.
Thresher, John, Sr.
Wells, Thomas
White, David
Whiley, John
Whiley, Elisha
Gillespie, John

SINGLE FREEMEN

Wheby, Elis
  (Eli Wiley) (?)
Hathaway, Silas
Hathaway, Simon
Linsecum, Cobus
Sears, Joseph

ASSESSMENT ROLL

Amwell Township, Washington County
for the year 1784

THOMAS LACKEY
Collector

Axtell, Thomas
Allison, Patrick
Atkinson, Thomas
Atkinson, George
Axtell, Daniel
Baldwin, Caleb
Bilby, Richard
Bryson, William
Baldwin, Jabez
Bane, Joseph, Jr.
Bates, Ephriam
Bane, Ellis
Bane, Jesse
Bane, Joseph
Bane, Nathan
Brownlee, John
Brownlee, James
Barnett, Robert
Bane, Isaac
Carter, Stephen
Camp, Aaron
  (Van Camp?)
Chamberlain, Arthur
Coulson, Samuel
Creacraft, Charles
Carson, John
Carter, George
Carmichael, John
Coe, Joseph
Craft, Lawrence
Craft, John
Cahill, Dennis
Clemmens, Nicholas
Craig, Samuel
Carter, James
Carter, William
Camp, Isaac
  (Van Camp?)
Covalt, Cheniniah
Camp, Lawrence
  (Van Camp?)
Cook, Stephen
Carmichael, John, Jr.
Cook, Jacob
Cary, Calvin
Corwin, William

Cooper, Moses
Cooper, Zebulon
Craig, John
Dickerson, John Green
Dustman, Daniel
Davis, John
Dorman, George
Dickerson, John
Dickerson, Henry
Dodd, Thadeus
Dodd, Daniel
Mrs. Draper, a widow.
Dille, Price
Dille, John
Dille, David
Dille, Samuel
Dille, Isaac
Dille, Caleb
Eddy, John
Elliott, William
Evans, Abraham
Evans, Caleb
Enoch, David
Evans, David
Fordyce, Abraham
Frazee, David
Frazee, Jonathan
Frazee, Benjamin
French, George
Fairley, Andrew
Gregg, Amos
Grandon, Edward
Gregg, John
Goble, John
Golden, Mathew
Goble, Ebenezer
Goble, Daniel
Gardner, John
Goble, Benjamin
Horn, John
Horn, Hardman
Horn, Hardman, estate.
Hill, John
Hewitt, Philip
Hewitt, Peter
Howell, Abner

Heaton, Ebenezer
Hazlet, Samuel
Hughes, John
Hill, Thomas
Hathaway, Richard
Hathaway, Abraham
Hathaway, Nathan
Ingel, John
Johnson, Abraham
Jennings, Joseph
Kitten, Thomas
  (Caton?)
Ketch, Christian
Kimble, John
Leacock, William
Leacock, Joseph
Leacock, Elisha
Lindley, Demas
Lindley, Zenas
Lee, Richard
Lindley, Joseph
Lindley, John
Lindley, Caleb
Love, Leonard
Lucas, Thomas
Larrison, John
Minton, Joseph
McCracken, David
McCullough, Samuel
McCormick, William
McFarland, William
McConkey, William
McVeigh, John, Sr.
McVeigh, John, Jr.
McVeigh, James
McVeigh, Isaac
McVeigh, Edward
  (Edmund)
Miller, John
  (Dutchman)
McGiffing, Nathnaiel
Morris, Robert
Morris, Isaac
Miller, John
  (English)
Miranda, Samuel

McVeigh, John, Jr.
Morris, Jacob
Newell, John
Phillips, John
Parker, Peter
Peacock, John
Peck, Jacob
Pettit, Isaac
Paul, James
Parkhurst, Samuel
Ross, Nathaniel
Rush, John
Reynolds, Thomas
Rickey, Benjamin

Royce, Benjamin
Rude, John
Ryan, Timothy
Rees, John
Rees, Morris
Sutton, Abraham
Swinehart, Gabriel
Simmon, Michael
Sedegar, Christopher
Shuster, Daniel
Sargent, Thomas
Tucker, James
Sanders, Elihu
Thomas, David

Teagarden, William
Valaly, Daniel
Vineyard, Francis
  (Venard)
Vineyard, William
Vineyard, Thomas
Virgin, Jeremiah
Venom, George
Whitten, John
Whosong, Jacob
Whosong, Jacob, Jr.
Williams, Moses
Wright, Alexander
Swart, Philip

SINGLE FREEMAN

Atkinson, William
Atkinson, Thomas
Bryson, Andrew
Bryce, John
Caterling, Abraham
  (Keterling)
Craig, Thomas
Cook, Abel
Dickerson, Gideon
Dunlevy, Francis
Davis, Nathan

Evans, Nathan
Eddy, Joseph
French, John
Goble, Caleb
Howell, Daniel
Lacock, Isaac
Lindley, Daniel
Lucas, Abraham
Marshall, Robert
Miller, Michael
MacIntosh, Laughlin
Morris, William

O'Daniel, John
Pool, John
Parkhurst, Daniel
Rude, Jacob
Riddle, John
Stanley, John
Vineyard, John
Vineyard, Francis
Vineyard, James
Virgin, Thomas
Young, John

List of Soldiers who took the Oath of Allegiance to the Commonwealth of Virginia in Ohio County in 1777

(National Genealogical Society Quarterly)

(April 1914 to October 1915)

DANIEL McCLAIN LIST

September 25, 1777
James Ogle
Jacob Ogle
Charles Stephenson
James Moore
Ezekiel Hedges
Robert Pyatt
Jacob Newland
James Andrews
John Rigdon
William Wilson
Benjamin Rogers
John Biggs
James McConnell
Joseph McClain

October 1, 1777
Zepheniah Blackford
Hugh McConnell
John Saunders
Adam House
Uttelendin Stell
October 4, 1777
John Mitchell
William Cochran
Joseph Wilson
James Dement
James Thomas
Henry Taylor
William McWilliams
Minty Northern

John William
John Pyatt
George Phillieburn
Jacob Fisher
Abraham Rice
Jacob Drinnon
Adam Rowe
James Patten
Wiliam Buchanan
Hercules Roney
John Handley
William Hawkins
Refused:
James Fugate
Jeremiah Williamson

ALFRED CALDWELL LIST
September 4, 1777

David Shepherd
David McClure
Ebenezer Zane
Jonathan Zane
Samuel Teter
James Smythe
Jacob Reager
Reason Virgin
John Virgin
Samuel McCullock
Robert Harkness
Thomas Mills
Edward Robinson
John Ward
William Flahavan
John Caldwell

Hugh Brison
William Swan
Conrad Wheat
Edward Richardson
William Alexander
Hugh Sidwell
Mark Iler
Conrad Iler
Moses Conger
Samuel Harris
James Harris
Stephen Harris
Mathew Kerr
Martin Whetsell
John Boggs
Ezekiel Dewitt

Yates Conwell
Windle Counts
Conrad Stroup
John Moore, Jr.
James Caldwell
James McMechen
James Graves
Thomas Mills, Jr.
Edward Mills
Walter Cain
John McCulloch, Jr.
Isaac Phillips
James Roney
Samuel Mason
Samuel Harris, Sr.

Note: Ohio County, Virginia at this time included the western third of what is now Washington and Greene County, Pennsylvania.

SILAS HEDGES LIST

September 4, 1777
Samuel Mason
Samuel Harris, Sr.
September 24, 1777
Conrad Wheat, Jr.
Zachariah Sprigg, Jr.
Aaron Delong
Aaron Delong, Jr.
October 9, 1777
Phillip Lutes

James Fugates
Thomas Waller
Edward Gaither
Annaniah David
Jeremiah Dunn
John Best
Francis Delong
October 10, 1777
John Kinser
Henry Fullenwider

Francis Miller
Edward Smyth, Jr.
Edward Smyth, Sr.
Jecob Rason
John More, Sr.
Solomon Delong
John Delong
Petter Keller
Charles Hedges

ZACHARIAH SPRIGG LIST

September 24, 1777
Joseph Van Metre
John Van Metre
Daniel Morgan
James Bous
John Wilson
John Warford
John McCannes
John Hook
Joseph Cassey
Thomas Lackay
Samuel Lemmon
October 29, 1777
William Scott
October 6, 1777
Thomas McGuire
David Cox
Gabriel Cox
Peter Cox
Iscil Cox
Edward Wiggins
John Carpenter
Charles Wells

Luke Scarmerhorn
Luke Scarmerhorn, Jr.
John McCormick
William Spencer
Alexander Young
Francis McGuire
Aaron Marshall
Cornelius McEntire
John Ash
John Botkin
James Newell
Orlano Barber
Edward Perine
John Johnson
John Hill
William Hervey
Henry Hervey
Jacob Forkler
William Clarke
Samuel Bruse
Edward Robbinson
John Tilton
Joseph Hedge

Andrew Ramsey
George McCollech
Robert Mitchell
Derrick Houghland
John Harris
Wiliam Boner
Oliver Gorrill
Patrick Tolbert
John Ramsey
James Harris
Edward Morgan
Solomon Hedges
Christopher Giller
William White
James Park
Isaac Meek
November 9, 1777
Samuel Glass
James Miller
Aaron Robeson
John Bukett
November 10, 1777
John Springum

OHIO COUNTY, WEST VIRGINIA
1777
WILLIAM SCOTT LIST
October 7, 1777

John Walker
Andrew Scott
George Marquis
Richard Wells
Henry Wells
Absolum Wells
George Sparks
Henry Levins
Henry Nelson
George Biggs
John Ferguson
Thomas Cantwell
Thomas Wells
Richard Wells, Sr.
Morris West
John Doddidge
October 8, 1777
Thomas Nichols
Williams McGuines
James Downing
James Henward
Isaac Wells
Robert Morgan
Thomas Bays
Samuel Johnson
Thomas Beaty
Samuel Smyth
Thomas Crawford

October 24, 1777
John Smith
October 29, 1777
Isaac Taylor
November 1, 1777
James Gillespy, Jr.
James Gillespy, Sr.
Thomas Clarke
William Caldwell
James Caldwell
John Chapman
James Kerr
Arthur McConnell
October 17, 1777
William Williams
Patrick McGaughan
Jonathan Byrn
October 18, 1777
William Campble
James Campble
James Richardson
John Nichols
Isaac Myles
David Caldwell
November 5, 1777
Robert Cavin
Ezekiel Boggs
William Boggs

Samuel Taylor
Absolom Sparks
December 18, 1777
Joseph Willis
December 27, 1777
Thomas Shannon
December 30, 1777
John Huff
Thomas Gilleland
Thomas Chapman
Samuel Patterson
William Shearer
RECUSANTS 9
December 1777
Edward Anderson
Francis Riely
Ephriam Johnston
Abell Johnston
Solomon Shepherd
William Sparks
William Ellis
Isaac Ellis
Elijah Huff
Sworn to before
WILLIAM SCOTT
February 2, 1778.

THOMAS WALLER FIRST LIST
1777

David Barr
Nathaniel Redford
William Scott
October 1777
David Hosack
John Hupp
Henry Holmes
Barnet Boner

Charles Boner
James Boner
William Boner
Mathew Boner
Samuel Byers, Sr.
Samuel Byers, Jr.
James Byers
Thomas Byers

Moses Williamson, Jr.
Stephen Bennett
James Martin
Samuel Kennedy
Moses Williamson, Sr.
John Snyth
Francis Starnater

Second List No Date

Samuel Williamson
John Williamson
Jeremiah Williamson
James Williamson
Thomas Williamson
James Cluny
Joseph Arnold
Jeremiah Arnold
October 13, 1777
Jacob Link

George Allhance
Christopher Winemor
Jacob Miller
Mathias Alt
October 15, 1777
George Hupp
October 16, 1777
Michael Stults
October 17, 1777
James Brownlee

October 20, 1777
Jeaniat McCleannon
October 23, 1777
John Waits
October 25, 1777
William Carson
James Carson
William Huston
John McGloan
John Kelly

Robert Taylor	Lawrence Deeds	Murty O'Handly
Jacob Pyatt	Henry Deeds	John Sinclair
Benjamin Pyatt	Andrew Deeds	
Benjamin Hammitt	Jacob Lefler	Balance all accepted
December 3, 1777	James Manly	O a t h of Allegiance
Nicholas Maulson	Jacob Rice	Sworn to before
Charles McRobbin	**REFUSERS**	
December 17, 1777	October 4, 1777	THOMAS WALLER
John Dunnavin	Hercules Roney, Sr.	
Conrad Fillebun	October 23, 1777	March 2, 1778

PETITION FOR A NEW STATE

Waychoff speaks of a petition to the Continental Congress for a new State to be known as "Westsylvania." He says that "between the years 1770 and 1780 great feeling existed between Virginia and Pennsylvania as to whom was rightful owner of land between the Laurel Hills and to the west as far as the Ohio. Open hostilities and bloodshed were narrowly averted at times. To settle this strife and ill-feeling many prominent and influential citizens prepared an elaborate petition and presented it to the Continental Congress, praying that this disputed territory be organized into a new state." Waychoff quotes much from this petition, and had evidently seen the original or a copy of it, which included the scope of the proposed state with the request that it be known as "the Provinse and Government of Westsylvania." It stated that since 1768 at least 25,000 families had settled within the lines prescribed.

There seems to have been a number of these petitions floating through the section at the time mentioned, so many in fact and so persistent that the State of Pennsylvania saw fit to order them discontinued, terming them an act of treason, and setting punishment for those persons who continued the proscribed practice. The final adjustment of the boundary line agreed to in 1779 and temporarily run in November 1782 did not end the agitation and was the reason for the above "act of treason" being passed in December 1782. The permanent line was run in 1784, and since Washington County, which at the time included what is now Greene County, was already organized in 1781, the uncertainty postponed the assessment of those living within the borders until that year, thus the tax lists for what is now Greene County begin in 1784. Pennsylvania Archives, Series III, Vol. 22, contains an assessment list for 1781.

In the Fall of 1945 we learned of an original petition in existence in the Library of Congress, and through the help of friends in Washington, D. C., discovered that the list of names was those of pioneer settlers of what is now Fayette, Washington and Greene Counties and perhaps Ohio and Monongalia Counties in Virginia. The wording of the petition differed somewhat from that reported by Waychoff, but was evidently one which was circulated in this immediate neighborhood. The names in this petition, which is not dated, seem at times to be taken from the militia rolls, and if circulated after 1780 contains names of persons deceased or moved from the district, as witness the names of Simon Rinehart, killed by the Indians in 1780-81, and Jacob Vanmeter, who left for Kentucky in 1780. It is also apparent that some of the names are of boys, as in the case of Henry Swan, born in 1774. There is no attempt to conceal the fact that the signatures were written by the prime agitators of the movement, for it is well known that many of those whose names appear, could only make their mark. The grouping of the names suggests that those in charge of getting signers, went from one neighborhood to another, getting permission to enter the names of those living in the vicinity. One familiar with the settlers can pick out the groups of those living on the Tenmile, or Muddy Creek, or Laurel Run, etc. As usual the spelling of the names differs frequently from the present spelling. There are many duplications, but a five year study of the petition has failed to show up a single faked name of persons who did not exist. The names used are entirely authentic, and add much to our knowledge of the pioneer settlers.

(This Petition is taken from the Papers of the Continental Congress No. 48, and is Folios 251-6. Pages 89-96. Photostatic copies in possession of the author.)

PETITIONERS

John Stinson
Richard Yates
John Gaddis
Thomas Gist
William Goe
Richard Noble
Charles Wheeler
Thomas Freeman
Benjamin Johnston
James Hammon
Hez. McGruder
Philip Shute
Robert Jackman
Thomas Brown
Charles Hickman
John McClelland
John Huston
Thomas Waring, Sr.
Samuel Bradley
Samuel Sacket
John Beeson
John Downer
Lewis Burris
John Ferguson, Jr.
Daniel Culp
Aaron Sackett
Peter Hook
Adam Crum
Samuel Pounds
Levi Springer
Patrick Talbot
Howson Seaton
James Neil
Robert Wharton
Thomas Lazel
Daniel Ward
James White
Jonathan Nixon
Thomas Heady, Sr.
Jacob Prickett, Sr.
Jacob Lowthard
David McFawl

Isaac McDonald
John McDonald
John Bright
James Templing
Conrad Walters
Erasmus Bochan
Jacob Sutton
James Nealey
John Collins
Robert Mainke
Charles Williams
John Patten, Jr.
James McKullick
Thomas Patterson
Andrew Hoover, Jr.
James McDonald
Edward Oleh (?)
John McCoy
Joseph Morris
Thomas Gaddis
Jeremiah Gard
Richard Tenant
William Sheehan
Francis Clark
Elijah Curr
  (Kerr)
David Reed
Hanagay Rumley
John Shepley
Benjamin Brownfield
William McCoy
John Bradford
Arthur McChristy
James Wilkey
William Mininger
James Orr
James Kendall
James Kendall, Jr.
Jeremiah Ross
Elijah Huff
John Huff
Michael Huff, Jr.

William Sparks
William Baylor
Michael Huff, Sr.
Barnet Waller
Charles Brown
Thomas Carr
Philip Smith
Henry Smith
Frederick Pusbaum
Michael Frank
Jacob Rissel
Nicholas Eberle
John Herdorf
Philip Mann
Leonard Eberle
John Jones
Peter Brunner
Adam Brunner
Morris Stern
Elias Thomas
David Shelby
Richard Clark
Francis Simbrel
Obediah Truax
Lambert Flowers
John Chadwick
Azor Reis
James Canday, Jr.
Basil Williams, Jr.
Jonathan Osborn
Jonathan Potts
Samuel Cane
James Finley
George Curvey
John Stevens
Benjamin Rutter
Jeremiah Pearce
Benjamin Carter
Henry Gaddis
Samuel Stevens
John Murphy
John Pearce

Benjamin Stevens
Charles Cade
John Rutter
John Crosley
Peter Naughton
Aaron Rawlins
Jeremiah Fenton
John Veich
  (Veatch)
Thomas Durbin
Frederick Sellars
Francis Castile
Isaac Poak
James Mitchell
Maurice Mitchell
Jacob Husong
Jacob Dicks
John Hartley
Samuel Evans
Joseph Howard
Richard Murry
James Wright
Thomas Wright
John Bain
Thomas Lloyd
Pearson Crain
Benjamin Phillips
Samuel Hand
William Phillips
James Rutter
William Morrison
Alexander Clark
Ezekiel Parkhurst
Charles Dawson
Bernard Isanhoot
Joseph Sillwell
  (Stillwell?)
Baldwin Cleffron
Charles McDonald
William Brownfield
Richard Waller
George Seaton
Isaac Sutton
John Mein
Rowen Frink
George McCoy
Jacob Prickett
Obediah Stillwell
John King
Thomas Kendall
Thomas Keday (?)
William Case
John Parr
William McCoy
Witmen Reinild
Abraham White
John Collins
James Collins
James White

Robert Newell
Moses Bradley
Philip Jones
James Waley
Zachariah Connell
Marius Stephenson
John Massey
Isaac Cell
Benjamin Whaley
Patrick Archpol
Daniel Caton
Joseph Huckett (?)
John Steven
James Mannin
Alexander Chanford
Elijah Johnson
Joseph Crawford
Nathaniel Crawford
Joseph Mannin
James Mantler
Joseph Moore
James Innis
William Holson
Godfree Peters
Aaron Moore
Martinson Clark
William Norris, Sr.
William Norris, Jr.
Phillip Gilleland
John Carr
Zackariah Masterson
David Hathaway
Edmund Purdy
Jonathan Hathaway
James Alexander
William Shaver
William Castleman, Sr.
George Clark, Jr.
Hugh Clark
Henry Casilman
John Casilman
William Alexander
James Poor
John Whittenton
Basil Brown
Thomas Brown, Jr.
William Galagin
John Connor
Elisha Craven
Gideon Walker
Michael Vanluscatch
James Henthorn
John Abboyinnis
Levin Wilcoxon
Benjamin Roebuck, Sr.
Samuel Seals
Joseph Seals
Ichabod Smith
Charles Smith

Charles Anderson, Sr.
Charles Anderson, Jr.
Richard Anderson
James Anderson
William Anderson
Daniel Anderson
William Davis
Azariah Davis
Stephen Davis
John Cowen
Benjamin Wright
James Wilson
Jeremiah Wilson
Michael Jones
Ralph Smith
John Cannon
Christopher Grabble
James McCullough
Otho Brashers
Jonathan Downs
Joseph Grabble
Benjamin Craft
Sisory Craft
David Craft
Samuel Craft
William Law
Samuel Miller
James West
Barnabas Peters
John West
Thomas Macintire
Joseph Wayt
  (Wait)
Augustine Moore
Joseph Brownfield
James Burns
Dennis Springer
John Lemon
John Wilson
Philip Shute, Jr.
Robert Henkins
Richard Henkins
Abraham McDonald
William Ahern
Charles Stephens
Nicholas Dawson
Isaac Pearce
George Pearce
Thomas Rogers
Mathias Shepler
Arthur Inghram
William Cathers
James Eagon
Barnet Eagon
Dennis Smith
Simon Archer
Michael Archer
Joseph Archer
Jacob Archer

John Gunn
John Bradford
James Bradford
Joseph Reinhart
Daniel Estle
Stephen Stlyes
Francis Hannah
James Hannah
John Thrasher
William Shepherd
Thomas Corbra
John Littleton
Moses Davidson
Nathan Garrett
Caleb Pumphery
Richard Ray
William Cummins
Patrick Morgan
James Baxter
Christopher Purkey
Asher Rude
Philip Miller
Reuben Pearson
Peter Colley
Joseph Price
Edmund Price
Andrew Grimes
David Grabill
Samuel Grabill
Benoni Crane
Masson Metcalfe
Asahel Rollings
Hezikiah Stiles
 (Stites)
John McMaster
William Shurkur
Valentine Lanthrop
Thomas Roberts
Thomas Peck
Chester Litman, Sr.
Richard Watts
Joseph Ross
Nathaniel Flemming
John Garrett
William Garrett, Sr.
James Laughlin
Joshua Allen
James Winders
Morgan Hughes
Richard Hall
James Dinna
James Cain
James Morris, Jr.
Rollin Hughes
John Hughes
Nathaniel Hughes
Ezra Hoge
Richard Jackson
Robert Gorrell

Benjamin White
Charles McDole
Robert Carroll
Michael Daugherty
Simon Rinehart
William Smith
Jeremiah Long
Robert Ivers
John Ivers
William Ivers
Baranee Allers
Jonathan Miller
John Moore
George Coolvin
John McDaniel
James Campbell
Abraham Hickman
Jonathan Hickman
Solomon Miller
John Swighard
Robert Booth Stump
Mark Easter
John Greeger
Jacob Easter
Conrad Erdenhouse
Daniel Arnold
George Main
Michael Brunner
John Peckinbach
Jacob Brunner
George Peckinbach
Peter Peckinbach
Nicholas Miller
John Work
Henry Work
Hans Moore
John Root
Jacob Root
Ludwig Miller
Abraham Lesley
John Salliday
George Church
William Carter
William Gartner
Thomas Hill
David Zook
David Miller
Michael Sprenkle
Henry Sprenkle
Jacob Ubb
Jacob Sprenkle
John Moyer
Leonard Garrison
Jacob Garrison
Michael Gaple
Henry Walters
George Walters
Jacob Walters
Peter Walters

Michael Rudisell
Henry Collance
Thomas Collance
Jonathan Tambre
Abraham Miller
Jacob Miller
Peter Leatherman
William Owens
Patrick Daugherty
Benjamin Rowbuck
Dennis Springer
John Patton, Sr.
William Campbell, Sr.
William Campbell, Jr.
Abel Campbell
George McChristy
John Oakerson
John Moor
Messer Beeson
Samuel Sutton
John Hall
Samuel Musgrove
William Marsh
Richard Shore
Joseph Neil
Adolph Eiler
John Collings, Sr.
John Carr, Sr.
Absolom Carr
James McCoyer
Nathan Springer
Henry Hoover
David Wilson
John Stoop
Burdett Clifton
Isreal Dille
Samuel Haslet
Daniel Lindley
Joseph Henthorn
James Draper
John Rude
Edward Hevay
John Goble
Gabriel Balting
Stephen Carter
Joseph Coe
Stephen Saunders
Elihu Saunders
Timothy Ryan
Leonard Lee
Mallis Halberg
John Hatt
Peter Lebegut
John Erdman
George Dillinger
George Balsinger
George Hilligas
Nicholas Russell
Manus Brown

Richard Waits
Isaac Drilling
William Asa
Thomas Reid
James Cochran
John McCarty
Phineas Killiam
Thomas Hardesty
Thomas Whitefoot
Dennis Jones
Henry Hart
Charles Broughton
James Henthorn, Sr.
John Phillips
George Welch
John Conely
Daniel Rawlins
Benjamin Phillips
Richard Stephens
Edward Sherer
David Hill
Samuel Hill
Jacob Easter
William Swan
Thomas Thurraman
John Moore
George Fairleigh
Jesse Pigman, Sr.
William Thoroughman
Joshua Vanmeter
Scarty House
John Tomlinson
Richard Swan
James Mordock
Samuel Swindler
John Knotts
Gilbert Mills
Rodham Seaton
John Gaskins
Hugh Halls
Thomas Johnston
Thomas McRoy
William Halls
Edward Halls
Jacob Smith
John Bich
Joseph Smith
John Moffett
Peter Devanter
Jacob Wolfe
Isaac Phillips
Samuel Fenton
Jeremiah Fenton
Peter Romine
James Blackstone
John Minter
Joseph Stephenson
Edward Doil
John Archbole

Thomas Archbole
Lewis Flemins
Garrett Ragan
James Connel
William Masy
Thomas Stascy
John Smith
Benjamin Wells
Thomas Huie
William Mackee
William Carmichael
John Crawford
Noble Grimes
Samuel Murphey
Henry Hartley
Robert Clifford
Edmund Ewings
John Stephenson
John Dean
Peter Coleman
William Greathouse
Abraham Ritchie
Peter Miller
Robert Ritchie
Jeremiah Ellis
John Warth
Peter Cildin (?)
Timothy Twin
George Faber
Robert Glass
Reuben Steves
George A. Martin
Casper Giger
William Mucelroy
John Murphey
John McGlaughlin
Mathew Wadley
William Sevel
Thomas Dunn
Daniel Springer
William Carson
Thomas Ackvan
James Young
Nicholas Daly
Isaiah Stephens
Robert Namight
David Purcel
Thomas Stephens
Robert McGlaughlin
Joseph Pope
John Tolsin Lindsey
James Carr
Nathaniel Dowden
John Carson
Thomas Davis
Joshua Jenkins
John Ankrom
William Wells
John Jones

Patrick Archer
James Archer
Simon Hobson
James Hook
John Hook
Ezekiel Morris
Richard Morris
John Morris
James Morris
James Seals, Jr.
Robert Stevens
Daniel Smith
William McDonald
George Woling
Harman Greathouse
William Ketch
William Love
James Forman
Ephriam Bilderbach
Jacob Bilderbach
William Norris
Jacob Norris
William Johnson, Sr.
William Johnson, Jr.
William Johnson, 3d
Samuel Orford
Henry Frakes, Sr.
Henry Frakes, Jr.
Nathan Frakes, Jr.
David Frakes
George Rankins
Gabriel Eakins
Reuben Pribble
Thomas Pribble, Sr.
Thomas Pribble, Jr.
Jobe Pribble
James Perry
George Teagarden
George Ennis
Isaac Miller, Sr.
Isaac Miller, Jr.
Amos Miller
Nicholas Miller
Thomas Adams, Sr.
Thomas Adams, Jr.
John Adams
James Adams
Joseph Ball
Abraham Scott
Samuel Polke
James Cummings
Thomas Strawn
Samuel Strode
Daniel Stewart
Elisha Stewart
James Stewart
Daniel Stewart
John Smith
John Rinehart

Thomas Rinehart, Sr.
Barnet Rinehart
Thomas Rinehart, Jr.
William Inghram
James Prichard
Thomas Wells
Joshua Davis
John Vance, Jr.,
Samuel Lyon
Isaac Vance
John Vance, Sr.
Samuel Davis
Alexander White
Richard Yates
David Snowden
Phillip Clark
Daniel Clark
Lawrence Clark
Joseph Snowden
Josuha Hazelbrigg
Henry Holmes
Obediah Holmes
John Shepherd
Samuel Shepherd
James Craven
Richard Sowards
Stephen Pribble
James Pribble
Samuel Jackson
Peter Romine
Isaac Dunn
Edmund Dunn
Samuel Dunn
James Dailey
Joseph Blackburn
Samuel Wharton
John Wright
James Wright
George Fee
John Fee
John Yates
Enoch Blackledge
Thomas Weakley
William Thomas
Ellis Thomas
William Frakes
John Holt
John Villiers, Sr.
John Villers, Jr.
Daniel Clark
Lawrence Clark
James Ferry
James Blair
Elias Garard
John McClelland
John Frakes
Peter Dailey
John Carter
Joseph Lyons

Benjamin Hughes
Peter Leans
  (Zanes ?)
Yates Connor
Jonathan Zeans
  (Zanes ?)
Daniel House
John Allison
George Myers
Thomas Hawood
John Johnson
Edward Davis
James McClean
Patric Pharlin
Robert Gregg
  (Craig ?)
Samuel Goldsmith
John Mills
John Willis
Isaac Chadwick
Mason Davis
Thomas McClean
Daniel Preston
Oliver Crawford
Andrew Burns
John Kenedy
John Hoge
John Six
Morris Morris
James McWade
William Cree
Robert Kelso
Thomas Kelso
James Jones
William Jones
Thomas McDaniel
James Haslet
John Davis
Isaac Wood, Jr.
James Long
Henry Vanmeter
Henry Swan
James Adams
James Gray
Robert Gray
Thomas Gorrell
David Long
John Bryant
Ebenezer White
William Hughes
Richard Morris
Michael Cone
Robert Clark
James Dunn
Charles Whitlatch
John Whitlatch
William Whitlatch
Thomas Whitlatch
Joseph Whitlatch

John Newland
Rezin Virgin
William Nippy
William White
Edward Jackman
Robert Jackman
Josias Stibbs
William Hawkins
Richard Hawkins
Jacob White
Amos White
Benjamin White
Henry Gregg
John Gregg
Lawrence Crow
John Crow
August Wells
George Riggle
Mark Riggle
Mark Deems
Christian Leatherman
John Lyder
Jacob Deem
Demas Lindley
John Dille
Samuel Parker
Caleb Lindley
John Carmichaels, Sr.
John Carmichaels, Jr.
Benjamin Goble
Richard Hathaway
Benjamin Royce
Nathaniel Hathaway
Abraham Fordyce
Zenas Lindley
David Dille, Sr.
David Dille, Jr.
Thomas Atchison
  (Atkinson ?)
John Mevan, Sr.
John Mevan, Jr.
John Lindley
Joseph Lindley
Ebenezer Goble
Daniel Goble, Sr.
Caleb Goble
Daniel Axtell
Thomas Axtell
Stephen Cook
Jacob Cook
Noah Cook
John Miller
Daniel Dodd, Rev'd
Ephriam Bates
Harial Dodd
John Whitten
Benjamin Rickey
Mathew Golding
Richard Davis

Thomas Richardson
William Hill, Sr.
William Hill, Jr.
Thomas Hill
James Barnett
Ignatious Barnard
John Forest Davis
Kinsey Davis
Samuel Reve
Samuel Fry
Thomas Maginniss
Andrew Link
George Hiley
Amos Mills
Lewis Pearce
Benjamin Davis
Lebbeus Dodd
Caleb Dille
John Craft
Lawrence Craft
Thomas Reynolds
Robert Carroll
Edward Carroll
George Seaton
Josiah Springer
Jacob Isreal
Thomas Hughes
Jeremiah Long
Jonas Garard
William Knight
Moses Tyler
John Hopewell
Thomas Edwards
Josiah Prickett, Sr.
John Prickett
Josiah Prickett, Jr.
Isaac Wood
Thomas Truelock
Jonathan Myndal
Charles Swan
John McCann
Joseph Hughes
Richard Connor
Felix Hughes
Phillip Clark
John Brown
James Clark
Macal Connor
James Hughes
Thomas Prichard
Richard Iverson, Jr.
Benjamin Hixon
John Daugherty
William Potts
John Cain
Jesse Pigman, Jr.
Patrick Sheehan
Isaac Guyton
Joseph Rankin

William Tirpen
Robert Frakes
Macal Daugherty
Robert Wilson
Moses Conger
Mathew Cain
John Riley
Henry Vanmeter
Joseph Vanmeter
Jesse Vanmeter
Absolom Vanmeter
George Newland, Jr.
Arthur Inghram
Harrod Newland
George Newland
William Harrod
Samuel Harrod
Benjamin Limming
Felix Hughes
Henry Neal
Barnet Neal
John Hughes
James Merato
Caleb Hardesty
Mathew Murato
James Smith
Thomas Cannon
William McCabe
Edward McGraw
Edward McLaugh
John McLaugh
Charles Pigman
Samuel Pigman
James Prather
John Prather
Dennis Dunan
Thomas Wells, Sr.
Thomas Wells, Jr.
John Tatman
Joseph Tatman, Sr.
James Tatman
Joseph Tatman, Jr.
Jesse Tatman
Thomas Roach
Samuel Thurriman
Charles Thurriman
Samuel Swan
Michael Daugherty
Daniel Mordock, Sr.
John House
Samuel House
Andrew House
James Gunner
Thomas Gillis
Thomas Wilson
James Harrod
William Harrod, Jr.
John Wilson
Abner Wilson

James McKoy
Benjamin Martin
Joshua Martin
Thomas Chapters
Christopher Forts
John Hank
John Work
Henry Huble
John Lane
William Nist
Solomon Spears
John Dousman
Joseph Hill, Jr.
Stephen Hill
Joseph Hill, Sr.
Mathias Russell
Andrew White
Solomon Nighswinger
Peter Reasoner
Jacob Decker
John Burkhame
George Burkhame, Sr.
George Burkhame, Jr.
Joseph Burkhame
Henry Spears
Jacob Spears
David Martin
Andrew Arnold
Robert Curry
George Franklin
Nicholas Murphy
John McCalister
Samuel Rankin
William Rowan
William Scott
William Acklin
James Wood
George Gilmore
Elisha Pearce
John Shirer
Alexander Carson
Hugh Glover
Samuel Johnston
John Pope
John Johnson
William Pope
Nathaniel Dowden
John McClelland
David Cathcart
William Smith
Thomas Woodward
Alexander Moling
William Boling
John Greathouse
Charles Norris
Thomas Swearingin
John Swearingen
Daniel Swearingen
James Ferrell

David Connor
William Connor
Elisha Veasy
John McCoy
James Anderson
William Walls
William Anderson
Thomas Bilderback
Ephriam Bilderback
John Morrison
Francis Morrison
William Morrison
William Murphey
Mordicai Richards
William Lamb
Moslener Richards
Hartley Sappington
John Sappington
George Sappington
Caleb Sappington
Jeptha Sappington
David McLure
James Caldwell
John Caldwell
Moses Chaplain
Samuel Williamson
Moses Williamson
Jeremiah Williamson
Ezekial Dewitt
Jeremiah Dewitt
Peter Drake
Isachar Huntington
Christian Miller
George Mitchell
Walter Briscoe
Edward Truman
William Colvin
Jeremiah Downs
John Laughlin
Henry Dever
Francis Pursel
Hulor Alexander
William Holmes
Obediah Holmes, Jr.
Abraham Holmes
Isaac Holmes
Jacob Holmes
Isaac Felty
John Lawrence
John Dicks
Jacob Barnet
James Fortner
Isaac Newkirk
Abraham Newkirk
Corsla Grabil
John Grabil
Nathaniel Redd
Daniel Watson
Thomas West

John Worff
Isaac Mills
Ephriam Wilson
Josias West
John Duncan
Abraham Lesly
Frederick Wise
Joseph Burt
Ignatious Brashers
Thomas Brashears
Henry Tillion
James Steel
Abraham Lucas
Gideon Walker
Jacob Fowler
Levin Coxan
Richard Watts
James Brinton
Robert Peters
Phillip Font
Ephriam Johnson
Joseph Grabil, Sr.
Joseph Grabil, Jr.
Thomas Moody
Edward Richardson
Thomas Nichols
James Nichols
John Nichols
William Forbes
Robert Forbes
William Jenkins
Samuel Nail
John Collins
John Abergast
William Goe, Jr.
Michael Tygart
Samuel Clark
Edward Chambers
William Parris
Masterson Clark
Nathaniel Clark
Joshua Clark
William Parris, Jr.
Hugh Masterson
John Purdy
Edmund Purdy
James Coombs
Michael Flood
John Coombs
John Blackmore
Milburn Coombs
John Goe
William Picquit
Jacob Brunner
James Henthorn
John Deams
Andrew Zeans
Jacob Riger
James Smith

Henry Smith
Thomas Smith
Adam House
Alexander McDole
Conrad Wheat
Andrew Scott
Robert Scott
Peter Nicewanger
Hamilton Karr
James Prather
George Green
Archibald Karr
James Clark
Henry Clark
John Boggs
William Boggs
Casper Frish
John Tait
Archibald Morris
John Williams
Enoch Williams
Herbert Wallis
Moses Haney
Jacob Springer
Thomas Pussley, Sr.
Henry Moore
Thomas Kitten
George Atkinson
Thomas Sargent
Benjamin Jennings
Job Watson
John Gray
Robert Ross
William Ross
John Ross
Samuel House
Elijah Mills
Joseph Mills
Ignatious Ross
Archibald Gray
Thomas Bond
Jacob Long, Sr.
Jacob Long, Jr.
John Long
Adam Henthorn
William Henthorn
Charles Hickman
James Hammond
Rezin Virgin
Thomas Freeman
George Frankman
Cornelius Cummins
Richard Ward
William Hopkins
John Hopkins
James Hopkins
William Wilson
Patrick McKinley
Jonas McKinley

AND ITS PIONEER FAMILIES 149

Archibald McKinley
Charles Osler
Nathan Parr
John Tucker
Nathan Glass
John Flemming
Nathan Powell
James Powell
Adam Hatfield
William Jollife
Hugh Jackson
Patrick Lynch
Christopher Hausman
Zachariah Stall
William Conwell
Robert Chalfont
Chads Chalfont
Joseph Wells
William Colvin
Robert Walker
William Walker
Jacob Cicily, Sr.
Lewis Cicily
Benjamin Cicily
Jacob Cicily
Michael Springer, Sr.
Michael Springer, Jr
Mathias Springer
Daniel Springer
John Springer
William Garrett
Francis Smith
Samuel Applegate
Peter Laughlin
Benjamin Davis
Nathaniel Biggs
Moses Cussenberry
Edward Mills
Joseph Tomlinson
Thomas Mills
William Freeman
Henry Prestor, Sr.
Henry Prestor, Jr.
Isaac Zeans
Isaac Williams
John Shaver
Robert Thornton
Reuben Moreland
Joseph Syphers
Jacob Syphers
James Lynn
George Mercer
Joseph Clemmons
Lawrence Green
John Clemmons
Lawrence Craft
Joseph Warman
Samuel Hoskins
John Warman
Henry Inghram
Robert Iverson
Thomas Brown
James Crago
William Iverson
Thomas Crago
Bildad Derter
Nathan Frakes
John Iverson
John Swan
Quebri Morton
John Rice
Daniel Mordock
James Henderson
William Marchant
Samuel Foster
Thomas Reed
Charles Macmanama
William McManama
Neil Gillespie
Isaac Powell
Jonathan Down, Jr.
David Norris
Adam Hatton
Joseph Jones, Sr.
Joseph Jones, Jr.
William Jones
Gilbert Simpson
Samuel Simpson
William Tyler
Thomas Simpson
Samuel Simpson
Anthony Styles
Thomas Bartlet
Robert Watson
Samuel Shreve
James Morlan
Henry Taylor
Moses Thompson
Joseph Frakes
Richard Stuart
John Veatch
William Veach
Samuel Veach
Nathan Veach
Jacob Veach
Jacob Clyne
Peter Clyne
Cornelous Johnston
John Simonton
John Garvin
John Hill, Sr.
John Hill, Jr.
Benjamin Wood
Acquila Wood
Thomas Foster
Joseph Main
Phillip Main
James Seals
William Sutton
Lawrence Crow, Jr.
Robert Taylor
James McCormick
Hugh Murphy
John Crow
John McCartney
Thomas Finch
James Cullings
William Scotten
John Williams
Samuel Hill
John Everett
John Brooks
John Cunningham
Thomas Cox
Jesse Martin
Enich Williams
Thomas German
James Gilmore
Isaac Newman
Abraham Henricks
Benjamin Goodwin
Henry Newman
Joseph Newman
Richard Yates, Jr.
Edward Grandon
Joseph Snoden
James Templeton
Adam Alexander
William Metkirke
Isaac Leet, Sr.
Reason Pumphry
George Selbriner
Edward Carroll
George McCormick
Garard Warfield
Charles Bilderback
Andrew Swearingen
Lewis Duvall
Aaron Forman
William Hays
Alexander Montgomery
James Cochran
William Eagon
Joshua Dickerson
Thomas Dickerson
Thomas Davis, Sr.
Thomas Davis, Jr.
Lamach Davis
John Dawson
William Stewart
John Ward
James Stewart
Robert Stewart
John Rogers, Jr.
John Davis
George Brickel
Arthur McNeil

James Whitcraft
Patric Logan
James Thompson
Benjamin Power
Esly Power
John Niwel
Nicholas Harrison
Thomas Downs
William Cheney
Zachariah Brashears
James Mustard
Atlee Rea
Hugh Murray
Benjamin Brashears
John Hollis
John Miller
William Colvin, 3d
John Matson
Basil Brown, Jr.
Basil Brown, Sr.
Thomas Brown, 2d
Thomas Brown, 3d
Otho Brashears
Basil Brashears
Barruch Brashears
William Wood
Mannoah Long
James Long
David Long
Thomas Choaron
James Flowers
David Flowers
Elias Garrard
John Garrard
Joseph Garrard
Joseph Guin
  (Gwynne ?)
Elias Stone
Richard Gregg
Levi Gregg
Francis Seaton
Samuel Hill
Phillip Smith
James Mundle
Abner Mundle
Jonathan Mundle
Hugh Stevenson
William Gray
William Lee
Daniel Hollis
William Forbes, Jr.
Phillip Clark, Jr.
William Alexander
John Alexander
James Roney
William Snowden
Joseph Snowden
James Buchanan
George Knox

Peter Starnator
Nicholas Pumphery
William Pumphery
Rezin Pumphery
John Dickerson
Conrad Stroup
John McGee
Mathew Karr
John Gill
John Clark
Ebenezar Zane
Cornelious Cummins Jr.
Peter Wise
James McCullom
Nathaniel Wallace
Michael Spencer
Richard Eglin
Samuel Fortner
Jacob Frederick
Phillip Smith
Richard Hoagland
Thomas Braddock
John McCullom
John McVay
Malcolm McCullom
John Heron
Robert Wier
James Wier
John Blair
John Wier
Edward Manning
Henry Cossill
George Nailor
Alexander Nailor
William McDaniel
William Atkinson
William Long
John Tannehill
Francis Kinder
Robert Ulery
Samuel Buchanan
James Buchanan
James Roney
Hercules Roney, Sr.
Hercules Roney, Jr.
Robert MacKay
Christopher Grabil
Thomas Wells
Andrew Baker
Edward Elliott
Abraham Elliott
Amos Mills
Thomas Shane
Peter Colly
Hezikiah Ellis
James Crawford
Isaac Pennington
John Rutan
William Shearer

Gias Ritchie
Jacob Shearer
Peter Keller
Lot Masters
James Harsh
Nathan Masters
Jeremiah Ellis
William Harris
Nathan Ellis
John Riggs
Robert Wilkes
William Riggs
Jeremiah Riggs
Donond Riggs
Gideon Forman
James Ellis, Sr.
Hezekiah Ellis
John Milford
Francis Keller
Joseph Dorsey
Benjamin Powell
Samuel Miller
John Cray
John Hatfield
William Bryson
Richard Hopkins
Alexander Hopkins
Thomas Hopkins
Jonathan Glaze
Basil Glaze
Nathan Glaze
William Hopkins, Jr.
John Hopkins, Jr.
James Wallace
William Wallace
Nathan Wallace
  of William
William Wallace
  of William
Nathan Offord
Isaac Darnall, Sr.
Levi Darnall
Nathan Darnall
George Featherhill
George House
John Yates
Caleb House
Azariah Davis
John House
George House
Thomas Truelock
John Gaskins
Samuel House
Thomas Weakley
John Gattral
Thomas Wells
Henry Huffman
Gorsufax Chy
Arthur Inghram

John Forks
John Chaney
Elihu Horton
John Quin
Peter Vandoler, Sr.
Thomas Harris
Peter Vandoler, Jr.
Joseph Vandoler
John Vandoler
Benoni Burcham
Benjamin Clark
David Mitchell
William Macintire
Thomas Brownlee
James Brownlee
Samuel Fulton
Daniel Cameron
William Ketchum
Andrew McKune
Peden Cook
William Cummins
William Williams
James Kelly, Sr.
James Kelly, Jr.
William Kibby
Samuel Clemmens
John Castleman
David Wolfe
Nicholas Carpenter
John Lindsey
Baldwin Parsons
John Warson
Samuel Seal
Francis Hardesty
John Enloe
Enoch Nox
John Purtee
William Johnson
Barnet Rinehart
Theophilus Dodd
Samuel Coapstick
Daniel Teagarden
Moses Teagarden
Richard Morton
William Quissinberry
John Goram
Thomas Goram, Sr.
Thomas Goram, Jr.
Niles Goram Burdin
Thomas Gorby
James Mullen
James Robb
Edward Powey
John Johnson
Peter Harcum
Edward Gibson
Joseph Hall
Anthony Lindsey
Nicholas Lindsey

Benjamin Cock
Benjamin Piersol
William Clark
Patrick Burnes
Richard Shore
John Tetrack
Samuel Martin
Zachariah Martin
Thomas Jones, Sr.
  of John
Joseph McLane
John Vinics
Ignatius Oden
John Kreps
Cristian Kreps
Benjamin Stevens
Samuel Arrowsmith
Elverton Calwell
Henry Stevens
William Gilmore
Hugh Gilmore
Mathew Gilmore
James Shacar
John McConnel
William Downard, Sr.
William Downard, Jr.
Jacob Downard, Sr.
James Downard
Jacob Downard, Jr.
William Briscoe, Jr.
Christopher Speck
Francis Shain
James Howe
James Magill
William Rose
Leonard Roberts
John Burrington
Listin Glass
Abraham Osborn
Benjamin Dye
Mathew Neily
Thomas Dawson
John Murphy
Benoni Dawson
Robert Craig
Jabez Emery
James Bryson
Conrad Buckler
Robert Shannon
Reuben Kemp
Edward Kemp
Samuel Stevens
Benjamin Jackson
John Sherard
Ralph Newell
James Harling
George Harling
John Knox
George Knox

Robert Ross
Joseph Mooney
William Schooler
Charles Harrison
William Reddick
Adam Dunlap
Michael Sullivan
James Paul
Thomas Reddick
William Cracraft
Edward Hatfield
Robert Doyne Dawson
Aaron Longstreet
Thomas Waller
Jacob Knap
Peter Knap
Adam Brown
Conrad Long
Thomas McEntyre
Joseph Wayton
Augustine Morton
Joseph Brownfield
Samuel Poak
James Cummins
William Sinclair
Christopher Waggoner
Josias Linsecum
Sash Bentley
John Petitt
Thomas Hughes
Edward Right
James Mathews
John Altman
Thomas Allison
George Hoskinson
John Armstrong
David Thomas
Absolom Hawkins
Thomas Hawkins
Nicholas Crist
Abraham Lucas, Sr.
Abraham Lucas, Jr.
Thomas Lucas
William Chain
Edward Augur
John Alder
Henry Tillon
Nathan Chaffin
Abner Chaffin
David Chaffin
Thomas Chaffin
Mathias Hook
Wiliam Albin
John Riggs, Jr.
Conrad Weaver
James Mathews, Sr.
Frederick Leatherman
Abraham Inlow, Sr.
Abraham Inlow, Jr.

Basil Clark
Christopher Cox
Andrew Cox
Michael Cox
Benjamin Nailor
Alexander Wilson
Niny Selvy
William Forred
Luther Cary
John Burch
Isaac Bane
Daniel Crane
Lewis Wright
Thomas Lucas
William Allman
Thomas Pennick
Thomas Alman
Thomas West
Joseph West
Samuel Pettit
Nehemiah Pettit
Josiah Pettit
Thomas Carson
James Carson
Edward Jackman
Richard Jackman
Richard Jackman, Jr.
Richard Pendry
Patrick McArdle
John Almon
Naser Alman
Daniel Watson
Daniel Whitacre
John Jackman
John Young
Silas Young
John McCall
William Fribby
James Young
Edward West
Samuel Wilkes
George Mifford
Nathan Mathews
Ellis Paremore
Isaac Williams, Jr.
James Henderson, Jr.
Archibald Henderson, Junior
William McMahan
John Bartley
Obediah Stout
Jesse Ellis
George Mifford, Sr.
Henry Spiers
Daniel Whitacre
James Davis
James McCormick
Jacob Drinnon
William Call

Alexander Patterson
Henry Gregg, Sr.
Henry Gregg, Jr.
John Perry
Moses Haney
John Nicholas
Thomas Nicholas
William Nicholas
William Howe
Ebenezer Scott
Fergus McArdle
Phillip Chansler
David French
Hugh McMullen
Anthony Asher
Jacob Pindal
Pierce Burns
Frederick Bollinger
Henry Clubrick
Ebenezer Hican
James McMund
James Sherley
Phillip James
John Wilson
Charles Wells
John McAtee
Francis Wells
James Perry
Henry Walker
John Connell
Samuel McDole
Dennis Delaney
John James Ward
John Cross
John Scott
William Morrison
George Read
Benjamin Allison
John Broughton
Nathan Griffith
Jacob Vanmeter
George Underwood
Robert Sturgeon
William Surgeon
Hezekiah Sutton
Isaiah Hoskinson
Jeremiah Hoskinson
John Buckle
James Davis
Alexander McDaniel
John Stradlers
Adam House
Bladen Ashby
Abner Reve
Thomas Maginniss, Jr.
John Maginniss
John Riggle
Frederick Leatherman
William Jackman

George Meffit
William Mechen
William Edwards
Alexander Scott
William Teel
Daniel Whitacre
Daniel Watson
Edward Jackman
Edmund Riggs
James Scott
Abraham Tea
John Means
Fergus McArdle
Joseph Pearce
Henry Wilson
Thomas Swearingen
Adam Stull
William McKay
James Trimbly
Joseph Reddick
John Lyon
Christopher Price
Richard Osborne
Benjamin Randel
John Huggins
William Huggins, Jr.
James Finley
William Mooney
Isaac R. Mooney
John Hamilton
James Burns
Edward Crawford
William Huggins, Sr.
James Huggins
Jacob Huggins
David Morland
George Brickle
Daniel Kenny
Charles Young
Richard Morris
Jesse Vanmeter
James Prichard
Robert Reed
James Dunn
Robert Jones
Henry Stevens
Aaron Jenkins
Thomas Atkinson
William Atkinson
Charles Cracraft
William Crawford
John Blair
James Blair
John Burns
Andrew Burns
Alexander Crawford
Thomas Sargent
Richard Sargent
Jeremiah Sargent

Abraham Luzader
Isaac Luzader
John Long, Sr.
John Long, Jr.
Gideon Long
Henry Coffman
Michael Moor
James Right
Michael Thomas, Sr.
Michael Thomas, Jr.
Nathan Griffin
Thomas Guin
Silas Hopkins
James Wallace
John Davidson
John Hinch
Caleb Leonard
Silas Leonard
Abner Leonard
Stephen Barker
Peter Grub
Jacob Speck
John Campbell
Edward West
Thomas West
John Darnall
William Darnall
Rudolf Wildman
Friendly Webb
William Wallace
Nathaniel Reid
Miachael Taylor
James Henderson
Archibald Henderson
John Barklay
Isaac Newkirk
Henry Hull

George Hull
Andrew Haize
John House
John Worth
Samuel Fry
Elijah Whitacre
Peter Whitacre
Joseph Wilson
Ephriam Wilson
John Allen
James Nelson
John Williams
William Williams
Abraham Newkirk
Henry Newkirk
Henry Fortner
John Wallis
Ignatius Jones
Abraham Rickey
Alexander Robinson
Thomas Calsy
Abraham Lucas
John Gooden
James Gunner
John Hughes
Roland Hughes
Jacob Cline
Daniel Wright
John Hoff
James Seals
Joseph Seals
Michael Jones
Thomas Pribble
Michael Archer
Charles Anderson
Thomas McDaniel
Jeremiah Wilson

Benjamin Jennings
Ezekiel Mirandy
Levi House
James Pribble
John Hook
James Hook
Jacob Smith
John Carroll
George French
Gabriel Eakins
Azariah Hoskinson
Joseph Rogers
John Rogers
Samuel Linch
John Jones, Sr.
James Craig
Zachariah Connell
Thomas Fossett
John Fossett
William Moffett
John Butler
James Peoples
John Craven
Francis Vineyard
Joseph Taylor
James McClelland
John McClelland
James Richardson
John Wickwire
Alpheus Wickwire
James Walker
Thomas Stanton
Thomas Stewart
John McCally
Richard Burgess
Abraham Miranda

The First Census of the United States

By an Act of Congress, approved March the First 1790, the marshals of the several districts of the United States, were authorized and required to cause the number of the inhabitants of their districts to be taken, omitting the Indians, who were not taxed, distinguishing between free persons and all others, and naming the sex and color of the persons enumerated. The enumeration was to be based upon residence as of the First Monday of August 1790. This Census included the seventeen organized States, and was filed with the State Department. They are complete except for the records of Delaware, Georgia, Kentucky, New Jersey, Tennessee, and Virginia, which were destroyed when the British burned the Capitol at Washington during the War of 1812.

Unfortunately the systems used were not uniform, some lists being taken by towns or townships, others being for whole counties. Some alphabetically arranged, while others are in order of the calls of the census men. Washington County, Pennsylvania, while apparently taken by townships, was not so arranged, so that the published version lists the county as a unit. Thus the Census of Greene County, which was a part of Washington at that time, is intermixed with the various lists of the mother county. By careful comparison with the land grants, first tax lists, and knowledge of the first settlers, it is possible to separate the names of the Greene County inhabitants with a fair degree of accuracy, fully 95 per cent correct, except for those living on the dividing line of the northern border of the County, and perhaps the western portion of the County.

It is to be noted that the western tier of townships of the present Greene County, except for the Forks of Wheeling Creek was practically devoid of individual land owners as late as 1790, so that persons living there would have been squatters, who would not have preferred enumeration. At that date six or seven persons owned all of what is now Aleppo Township, with Robert Morris and Daniel McFarland holding title to more than 15,000 acres. The same two men held title to a similar amount of land in what is now Springhill Township, where not more than eight persons owned the entire township. The present Richhill Township had more individual holders of land, but Thomas Lieper and Robert Morris held patents for more than 18,000 acres. Morris had almost 10,000 acres in present Jackson Township, and Lieper had half that amount in Morris Township, and both held scattered tracts in Center and Gilmore Townships. In addition to these holdings in this section, there were numerous 400 acre tracts owned by John Hughes and Timothy Ryan, Joseph Ball, Thomas Shields, Charles Shoemaker, Thomas Stokely, and other alien land speculators. From these known facts it will be evident that only a few families that may have lived in this section were counted in this first census. It may account for a few names of persons known to be living in the County, but not found in any list.

In a study of the Census of Washington County, it is evident that the enumeration which took place in the portion now recognized as Greene County, was done by the townships then in existence, namely Morgan, Cumberland, Greene, and Franklin Townships. Of these Cumberland and Greene Townships were taken alphabetically. Morgan and Franklin were listed in order of proximity. The Greene Township list was divided into three sections, but can be accurately selected from the whole. Both Greene and Cumberland lists show evidence of a re-check, where missing names were added, contributing to the accuracy of this census. As usual the spelling of names, either in the original or the printed version, contains errors, which can frequently be corrected, and which we have done in the lists copied for this history.

Crumrine in his History of Washington County says just when the original thirteen townships were divided is not shown, nor can any report of their boundaries be found, but enough can be found to indicate that the boundaries followed the courses of the larger streams and dividing ridges. (pp. 228). In his discussion of the boundaries of Donegal Township he also says that it originally extended southward to include one half of western Greene County, and from Donegal Township was erected Finley Township in 1788, so that any census of what is now Richhill Townsship, Greene County would be found among the names of those counted in Finley Township . . . As explained, these would be very few, and the greatest margin of error occurs in this list. A map of these townships is found in Crumrine opposite page 222 with the approximate positions as they existed two years prior to the Census of 1790.

To those persons not familiar with the use of the Census of 1790, it may be explained that the names of the persons are those considered the heads of the families. The numerals which follow the names refer to adult males over 16 years of age in the first column. The second column refers to the males under 16 years, while the third column includes all the female members of the family. In most cases the listing will be a complete family unit, with the father as one of the adult males, and the mother one of the females, but occasionally further knowledge will disclose that the household had in it hired hands, orphan children, homeless mothers, fathers, brothers, or sisters. It would also appear that where more than one cabin was situated on a tract of land, each cabin was considered a separate family unit, and so enumerated, thus one is safe in saying that each house or cabin was chosen as the place of enumeration. This is borne out in the wording of the Fifth section of the Act of Enumeration.

It is also evident that not all persons were counted in this Census. Some persons did object to being counted because of religious scruples, others had more sinister reasons, like indentured servants who had run away, debtors who had fled debtors prison, and certain criminal elements found on the frontiers. Still others like trappers and woodsman were out of reach of the enumerators or had no fixed abode.

Some authority has figured that the average for all the Census of 1790 showed on the average, households of six persons. If this figure holds good for the Greene County list of known families, then the confines of the county must have held some 5000 to 6000 persons at the time of the Census. When one considers the number of persons who had already been here and had migrated to the West, a better understanding of the progress of the Tenmile Country can be arrived at. It must be remembered that all of Washington and Greene County held approximately 24,000 persons at the time of the Census of 1790, so that between one fifth and one fourth of this population lived then in the Tenmile Country of Greene County.

CUMBERLAND TOWNSHIP 1790

Name				Name			
Allen, Moses	1	0	2	Blaney, Jacob	1	4	4
Anderson, Chandler	3	1	1	Blair, James	1	4	1
Anderson, Charles	1	2	1	Bailey, Elexius	2	1	1
Anderson, Daniel	1	1	2	Burson, Edward	1	5	2
Anderson, James	1	1	1	Booze, Henry	1	0	1
Anderson, Richard	1	0	2	Buskirk, Samuel	1	0	3
Armstrong, John	2	5	2	(Vanbuskirk ?)			
Armstrong, Abraham	1	4	6	Buskirk, George	1	1	1
Adamson, Joseph	3	1	3	Brookover, John	1	2	1
Adamson, James	1	1	1	Brooks, Joseph	1	0	1
Allison, James	1	6	3	Brant, Joseph	1	0	2
Argo, William	1	0	0	Clark, Elizabeth	0	3	1
Adamson, John	3	1	4	Carter, Richard	1	1	4
Boardman, Robert	1	0	1	Cline, Jacob	4	2	3
Reesen, Aaron	1	0	1	Cree, William	1	0	5
(Burson ?)				Crossley, Robert	1	1	1
Ball, Joseph	1	3	4	Cox, George	1	1	2
Biddle, Everhard	1	0	1	Crawford, William	2	1	6
Boner, William	1	3	3	Crawford, John	2	7	3
Brown, John	1	4	3	Crawford, Oliver	2	1	5
Barnes, Job	1	1	3	Coone, Michael	2	6	7
Blackledge, Margaret	5	1	2	Cockran, Alexander	1	1	3
Boreman, John	2	1	2	Carmichael, James	2	1	3
Blackledge, Enoch	1	2	3	Cree, Robert	1	1	3
Bowman, John	1	1	2	Cree, Robert, Jr.	1	0	4
Brown, Thomas	1	0	1	Crée, James	1	1	2

Name				Name			
Cain, John	1	1	3	Hughes, James	4	2	5
Carter, Joseph	2	1	2	Hughes, Thomas	2	2	5
Crago, Thomas	1	3	4	(Three slaves)			
Curtis, Robert	1	2	4	Holton, John	2	3	4
Carter, Thomas	1	3	3	Hale, William	3	1	3
Ketchum, Phillip	1	1	2	Henderson, James	1	1	5
Crago, James	1	1	1	Harrod, William	2	1	4
Crago, Robert	1	2	2	Heaton, Isaac	2	4	3
Clawson, John	1	1	1	Hill, John	1	1	3
Simmons, James	1	0	2	Hartman, George	1	1	5
(Cummins ?)				Hannah, James	2	0	1
Connor, John	1	0	0	Hiller, William	1	1	4
Eaton, William	1	1	4	Ingledue, Thomas	1	2	3
Carns, James (Kerns?)	1	0	1	Inghram, Elijah	1	2	2
Davis, John	1	2	4	Israel, Isaac	1	4	5
Davis, Azariah	1	3	4	Johnston, Cornelius	1	2	2
Davis, Stephen	3	0	2	Johnson, Nicholas	1	2	1
Dunn, Isaac	1	2	4	Johnson, John	1	6	1
Dickison, Jesse	1	1	2	Jamison, Alexander	3	0	6
Dalrimple, Joseph	1	2	5	Jackson, Samuel	1	1	3
Davidson, William	1	2	2	Jones, John	1	2	3
Davis, William	1	9	2	Jones, Michael	1	2	3
Dollison, William	1	0	3	Johnston, Hugh	1	3	3
Eagon, James	1	1	1	Knight, John	1	0	1
Eagon, Barnet	1	2	2	Kelly, Robert	1	0	5
Estle, Daniel	1	2	7	Kirby, Joseph	1	3	3
Estle, Silas	1	1	1	Kirby, Richard	1	1	2
Eastwood, Joseph	1	0	0	Leonard, Lot	1	1	7
Fordyce, Samuel	2	2	2	Livengood, Peter	1	1	1
Fox, Peter	1	0	4	Lewis, Andrew	3	0	2
Flenniken, James	3	2	6	Lewis, Robert	1	0	1
Flenniken, John	2	2	4	Lindsey, Jacob	1	0	5
Flenniken, Elias	1	3	5	Lewis, John	1	0	2
Fordyce, James	1	1	2	Limming, Benjamin	1	3	4
Finley, Alexander	1	1	2	Lowery, Josiah	2	2	1
Gwynne, Joseph	1	2	1	Longenacker, Daniel	1	1	1
Green, John	1	0	1	Luzader, Abraham	1	0	3
Gately, Thomas	1	0	0	Little, Michael	1	5	2
Gregg, George	1	2	2	Lockey, Hugh	1	1	2
Gregg, Richard	1	3	4	Morrow, Charles	2	1	3
Gillespy, Henry	1	0	1	McClelland, Andrew	3	1	2
Garwood, Midean	2	1	7	McClelland, Andrew, Jr.	1	0	2
Grary, Joel (Creary?)	1	3	4	McClelland, Robert	1	1	3
Gardner, James	1	1	3	McClelland, Robert, Jr.	1	1	3
Kentner, William	1	3	5	Morris, Ezekiel	2	3	7
Holden, John	1	3	2	Morris, Robert	3	1	2
Hibbs, Aaron	1	3	2	Marratta, James	1	2	3
Hibbs, Lacy	1	1	1	Myers, Peter	2	3	2
Harden, Savil	1	2	2	Martin, Thomas	1	1	2
Harbough, Thomas	1	3	4	Masters, Moses	1	2	2
Hickman, Robert	1	1	3	McElroy, William	1	1	4
Haines, Aaron	1	1	2	McCartney, Michael	1	1	2
Heaton, John	1	0	0	McElroy, John	1	2	2
Hannah, Francis	1	2	3	Moore, John	1	3	4
Hartman, Adam	1	6	3	Moore, Samuel	1	1	5
Hoge, Solomon	1	2	6	Moore, William	1	1	2
Holley, Samuel	1	1	2	Mustards, William	1	4	2
Hughes, James	2	0	7	McDowell, William	2	1	3
(blacksmith)				Murdock, James	3	5	4

Name				Name			
Murdock, Daniel	1	0	6	Stewart, Daniel	2	1	2
McClelland, James	1	1	2	Smith, Noah	1	5	3
Myers, George	2	1	4	Sayers, Josiah	1	2	2
Martin, Patrick	1	2	3	Seaton, James	1	1	4
Murdock, Daniel, Jr.	1	1	1	(One slave)			
Manning, John	1	2	2	Seaton, Francis	1	4	2
Maxon, Wm. (Maxer?)	1	2	2	Seaton, Elizabeth	0	0	2
McClean, Abraham	1	1	4	(Five slaves)			
Miller, Mathew	1	1	3	Swan, John	1	1	1
Moore, Ezekiel	1	1	2	(Six slaves)			
McKean, Robert	1	1	2	Swan, Charles	1	4	5
McCoy, George	1	2	1	Swan, Richard	1	1	5
Moore, John	1	5	11	Swan, William	1	2	2
McGlaughlin, Ann	1	1	3	Sedgewick, Thomas	2	4	2
Montgomery, William	1	1	1	Strawn, Jacob	1	5	6
Mills, Amos	2	0	3	Strode, Samuel	1	3	3
Morrison, Jane	1	2	3	Critchfield, William	1	1	1
Nevitt, Philip (Nevill?)	1	2	2	Critchfield, Absolom	2	3	3
Newland, George	2	2	4	Critchfield, Arthur	1	2	1
Newland, Richard	1	2	4	Shephard, William	1	6	4
Newland, John	1	1	2	Stephenson, William	1	2	4
Nichols, John	1	1	4	Stephenson, Hugh	3	2	3
Nichols, Richard	1	2	2	Scott, Abraham	1	4	1
Prior, Timothy	1	2	3	Smith, Jacob	1	5	4
Prior, John	1	2	3	Smith, Benjamin	1	3	5
Porter, Robert	2	4	2	Stewart, John	1	3	1
Pugh, William	1	0	5	Santee, George	1	3	4
Pigman, Jesse	1	1	2	Shelby, Evan	1	1	1
Pribble, Thomas	1	1	1	Spencer, John	1	1	4
Pribble, Thomas, Jr.	1	1	2	Strawn, John	3	8	7
Pribble, Job	1	1	1	Stiles, William	1	0	1
Pribble, Reuben	1	3	4	Thomas, Edward	1	3	4
Prior, Isaac	1	2	1	Thoroughman, William	1	3	3
Purtee, John	1	2	2	(Thurman)			
Perone, Obediah	1	5	3	Thoroughman, Samuel	1	1	2
Perkins, William	1	3	2	(Thurman)			
Parker, James	2	1	3	Throughman, Thomas	1	1	3
Prior, Nathan	1	2	3	(Thurman)			
Pipengas, John	1	0	2	Teagarden, George	1	8	3
Riley, James	2	1	4	Aikens, Gabriel	1	0	1
Rude, Andrew	1	1	3	Barnes, Zachariah	1	2	1
Reese, John	1	1	2	Blackstaff, William	1	1	0
Reese, John	1	0	1	Bowman, Benjamin	1	0	1
Roberts, Edward	2	1	3	Cleavenger, Isaiah	1	0	2
Randall, David	3	4	4	Driver, John	1	1	1
Roach, Thomas	1	3	0	Dunn, Samuel	1	0	1
(One slave)				Evans, David	1	1	2
Rose, Ezekiel	1	2	2	Foster, John	3	1	1
Johnston, John	4	1	4	Gregg, Levi	1	0	1
Rinehart, Joseph	1	2	2	Heerdman, Abel	1	0	1
Ramsey, Charles	1	3	5	Hull, Nathaniel	1	1	1
Roseberry, John	1	1	1	Hill, Samuel	1	2	1
Rockhold, Charles	1	0	2	Thomas, Samuel	1	3	3
Reed, Joseph	1	0	2	Thomas, Ellis	2	2	2
Rush, Jesse	1	1	2	Tomlinson, John	1	2	5
Ruggles, James	1	1	3	Tater, John	1	1	2
Styles, Stephen	1	2	3	Lewis, David	1	1	2
Simonton, John	2	1	2	Leeman, James	1	1	0
Stewart, James	1	1	3	McClelland, John	1	1	1

Name				Name			
Masters, Henry	1	1	2	Wright, Thomas	1	1	3
Fort, Francis	1	2	6	Ullom, Peter	2	6	2
Veal, David (Vale?)	1	2	2	(Woolham ?)			
Veach, Nathan	1	2	4	McIntosh, John	1	1	1
Villiers, John	1	2	7	Miller, James	1	0	1
Vanmeter, Henry, Esq.	2	3	6	McCann, John	1	2	1
Vanmeter, Joseph	1	4	4	Moore, Patrick	1	1	2
Vanmeter, Jesse	1	0	3	Morris, John	1	2	3
Vanmeter, Absolom	1	0	1	Wright, Lucy	0	0	3
Vandeeren, Hezekiah	1	1	4	White, Rachel	1	1	1
Valentine, Amos	1	1	1	Whitlatch, Thomas	1	1	2
Vansicle, Zachariah	1	1	4	Whitlatch, Charles	2	0	1
Wise, Thomas	1	1	2	Wood, Daniel	2	1	2
Whitlatch, William	1	1	3	Newland, John	1	1	1
Wood, Benjamin	2	3	5	Vansickle, Samuel	1	1	3
Wright, Benjamin	1	3	2	Rose, John	1	2	1
Ullom, Shem	1	1	3	Plummer, Elisha	1	2	2
(Woolham ?)				Quinlan, Isaac	1	1	2
Williams, George	3	2	1	Roseberry, Mathias	2	0	1
Wells, William	1	4	2	Anderson, Daniel	1	2	1

GREENE TOWNSHIP 1790

Name				Name			
Alley, John	1	2	2	Campbell, Dougal	1	3	4
Asher, Anthony	1	2	5	Clegg, Alexander	1	0	1
Anders, John	1	2	3	Clevenger, Zachariah	1	3	3
Badcock, Andrew	2	2	4	Davis, Johnathan	1	1	6
Belshas, James	1	3	3	Drake, Joseph	1	1	4
Burtnett, Adam	2	2	4	Douglas, Thomas	1	1	3
Baker, Roger	1	2	4	Douglass, Timothy	1	2	3
Brown, Andrew	2	1	6	Daugherty, James	1	3	3
Blake, Nicholas	1	3	2	Davis, Ignatius	1	1	2
Baker, Nicholas	2	3	5	Daugherty, Elizabeth	0	1	1
Brown, Thomas	1	2	3	David, Henry	1	1	2
Burns, Michael	1	4	5	Davie, Benjamin	1	2	4
Burt, William	1	2	3	Diamond, Daniel	1	1	2
Bowers, John	1	3	2	Dye, James	1	1	3
Bowers, Jacob	1	1	2	Dye, Andrew	1	4	4
Bradford, John	1	3	2	Dye, Elizabeth	1	1	2
Bradford, James	1	3	3	Dawson, Alexander	1	1	6
Boydstone, George	1	1	3	Dobbins, John	1	1	2
Boydstone, David	1	2	4	Dillinger, Augustine	1	2	2
Boyles, William	1	1	1	Dixon, Stophel	1	3	2
Britton, Jane	0	0	2	Darraugh, Henry	1	2	2
Brekin, William	2	4	3	Davis, John	1	1	5
Bushill, Barbara	0	2	3	Eddy, John	1	2	2
Baldwin, John	1	0	1	Eddy, Isaac	1	1	2
Compston, John	1	1	1	Rogers, William	1	2	6
Cannon, Richard	1	5	2	Irvine, William	1	2	3
Caldwell, William	1	2	4	Evans, John	1	1	4
Kimble, Leonard	1	3	2	Evans, Jesse	1	1	0
Kirby, Elizabeth	0	1	2	Enoch, Catherine	0	0	2
Cain, Edmund	1	1	4	Enoch, John, Sr.	1	2	2
Caldwell, Elverton	1	2	6	Flowers, David	1	5	6
Campbell, Obediah	1	1	5	Flowers, Thomas	1	2	5
Corbley, The Rev. John	1	1	6	Flowers, Aaron	1	2	4
Crawford, Alexander	1	2	2	Fee, John	2	2	4
Colvin, George	1	2	4	Freeland, Robert	1	4	4
Chaffin, William	1	1	1	Freeland, Benjamin	1	5	5
Chaffin, John	1	0	1	Frick, Henry (Frakes ?)	1	3	2

Name				Name			
Frick, Henry, Jr.	1	8	2	Morgan, James	1	4	5
(Frakes ?)				Jones, Amos	1	4	2
Frakes, David (Frekels)	1	1	1	Ivers, Richard	1	1	1
Frakes, Nathan (Frekels)	1	0	2	Johnson, Baily	1	2	2
Frazer, Joseph (Frazee)	1	2	2	Jones, Mary	0	3	4
Frazer, Joseph	1	2	4	Jenkins, Aaron	1	5	3
Feurt, Francis	1	3	3	Jamison, William	2	1	2
Feurt, Benjamin	1	4	2	Johnson, Thomas	1	1	1
Fulner, Henry	1	3	2	Jackson, Jesse	1	2	1
Fast, Joseph	1	4	4	Jackson, Henry	3	3	5
Fast, Christian	1	4	3	Johnston, Henry	1	3	4
Garwood, William	1	3	5	Knox, James	2	2	4
Gilmore, Mathew	1	4	2	Gilkesee, Hans	1	1	3
Strain, Gilbert ?	1	1	3	Knox, Samuel	1	4	4
Garwood, Jonathan	1	1	2	Knotts, Solomon	1	1	2
Gerrard, Isaac	1	2	5	Kidd, Nathaniel	1	4	3
Gerrard, Jonathan	1	2	3	Kitch, John	1	5	5
Garrard, Justus	1	3	4	Moore, Daniel	1	2	1
Gustin, Benjamin	1	1	1	Miller, John	1	0	2
Jameson, William	1	1	1	Mundle, Abner	1	2	4
Gustin, Jeremiah	2	1	4	Mundle, James	1	4	2
Garrison, Leonard	2	1	2	Moore, John	2	2	6
Glasgow, John	2	4	3	McCracken, Alexander	1	1	4
Garrison, Frederick	1	1	3	McCoy, William	1	3	4
Garner, Adam	1	2	2	McKinnon, Joseph	1	1	2
Grimes, William	1	5	2	McClurg, John	1	1	3
Grimes, Richard	1	1	1	McDowell, Charles	1	0	1
Gapen, Zachariah	2	2	3	Moore, Philip	1	1	2
Huston, Paul	1	1	4	McKibbens, Richard	1	2	2
Huston, John	1	1	2	McCready, Alexander	1	2	3
Hazlett, John	1	1	2	McDonnough, Hugh	1	3	5
Hart, John	1	3	3	Marks, Samuel	1	2	2
Huston, William	1	4	6	McMullen, Alexander	1	1	1
Hyde, Samuel	2	2	6	Morrison, Robert	1	4	4
Hobbs, Henson	1	2	2	Mills, Samuel	2	2	2
Hobbs, Solomon	1	2	3	McMullen, Richard	1	1	5
Hardy, Thomas	1	1	4	McKee, John	1	2	5
Huggins, William	1	1	1	Morris, Jonathan	3	6	9
Hannah, Mathew	1	1	2	McDowell, Thomas	1	1	1
Hannah, James	1	2	4	Mills, John	1	2	2
Holmes, Thomas	1	2	1	Martin, Thomas	1	1	3
Howard, Samuel	1	1	7	Masters, William	1	4	6
Howard, John	1	2	3	McKelvy, John	1	3	6
Hallman, Thomas	1	3	3	McMullen, James	1	2	3
Herrod, John	1	2	1	Morris, Joseph	1	3	3
Howard, Cornelius	1	1	3	Morris, Levi	1	2	2
Gallup, Jesse	1	0	1	Mawfell, Daniel	1	2	1
Woodman, Samuel	1	1	0	Long, Eliel	1	3	2
Miller, Benjamin	1	0	1	Lemley, John	1	2	1
Miller, James	1	1	2	Miller, James	1	1	2
Drake, Charles	1	1	1	Maple, Benjamin	1	1	3
Flowers, Samuel	1	2	2	Mannon, Samuel	1	2	1
Hickson, Benjamin	2	1	2	Alley, John	1	1	2
Smith, John	1	0	0	Gustin, Samuel	1	0	2
Gapen, William	1	1	1	Livengood, Benjamin	1	2	1
Gapen, Stephen	1	2	2	Eddy, William	1	1	1
Gapen, John	1	0	0	Eddy, Alexander	1	2	2
Jones, Robert	1	1	4	Martin, Levi	1	1	2
Jordon, Jacob	1	2	2	Sykes, Jacob	1	2	3

Name				Name			
Sykes, Lewis	1	0	2	McFarland, Jesse	1	1	4
Glasgow, Stephen	1	1	2	Minor, William	3	2	5
Chaffin, John	1	2	1	Three slaves			
Pollock, Oliver	1	0	1	Noble, William	1	1	1
Thomas, John	1	2	2	Knap, John	1	4	5
Davis, John	1	2	1	Nevill, John (Nevitt)	1	1	2
Roberts, William	1	1	2	Nowland, John	1	1	1
Lemon, James	1	2	1	(or Newland)			
Jackson, William	1	2	3	Preston, Jonathan	1	4	1
Prickett, John	1	1	1	Parker, Samuel	1	1	5
Evans, Zachariah	1	2	2	Patterson, James	1	2	1
Evans, John	1	3	4	Passover, George	1	2	3
Shelby, Jonathan	1	0	0	(or Passmore)			
Bellman, Christian	1	2	1	Pollock, John	1	3	3
Ross, Robert	1	0	1	Peckinpaugh, Peter	1	1	1
Ross, John	1	1	0	Robinson, Susannah	1	1	3
Bartholomew, John	1	0	2	Roberts, John	1	4	1
Stewart, John	1	2	1	Rutter, John	3	3	4
Rankin, George	1	0	1	Rutter, George	1	1	2
Everly, Nicholas	1	2	2	Ross, John	1	1	4
Garrison, Jacob	1	2	1	Rhinehart, Daniel	1	3	2
Alley, Thomas	1	0	2	Robbins, William	1	2	5
Knotts, William	1	1	5	Williams, William	1	3	4
Keener, Sebastian	1	3	3	Worley, Bryce	1	2	3
Knotts, Benjamin	2	2	4	Wolf, George	1	1	2
Leaton, Samuel	1	1	1	Westbrook, Samuel	1	1	1
Long, Noah	1	3	2	Watters, John	1	2	3
Leaton, William	1	5	3	Woodmaney, James	1	3	2
Long, David	2	3	6	White, Israel	1	3	5
Long, Thomas	1	3	1	White, Isaac	1	0	0
Lantz, John	1	7	3	White, Thomas	1	1	1
Long, Gideon	1	4	3	Baldwin, Benjamin	1	3	4
Lattimore, John	1	2	5	Chaffin, Thomas	1	1	3
Lewis, Philip	1	3	1	Belcher, Elijah	1	1	2
Lantz, Andrew	1	1	1	Hawkins, Peter	1	0	1
Long, Jeremiah	1	3	5	Hawkins, Samuel	1	3	3
Long, John	1	4	4	Williams, Paul	1	1	1
Livengood, Jacob	1	2	4	Drake, Lewis	1	2	2
Lemley, George	1	4	5	Debolt, George (Teaboe)	1	1	3
Lemley, Jacob	1	1	1	Stone, Elias	1	5	6
Drake, Mannon	1	3	1	Sutton, Ebenezer	1	2	2
Mundle, Andrew	1	1	1	Savary, John	2	1	2
Allison, Abner	1	2	2	Stone, James	1	1	1
Gilkesee, George	1	2	0	Shroyer, John	1	3	4
Lewis, William	1	1	1	Shoemaker, Adam	1	1	2
Knotts, John	1	0	0	Soonover, Henry	1	1	4
Daniel, Michael	1	2	2	Shriver, Jacob	1	3	4
Christ, George	1	1	2	Shriver, John	1	2	2
Donald, John	1	2	3	Stewart, Elijah	1	4	2
McKnight, William	1	3	4	Shelby, David	3	2	3
McKnight, Ezekiel	1	0	1	Statton, Joseph	1	4	2
Montgomery, Robert	1	2	2	Selsor, Lewis (Subzar)	1	0	1
Mayfield, Samuel	1	3	4	Selsor, George (Subzar)	1	3	3
Morgan, Temperance	2	1	4	Selsor, Frederick	1	0	1
Morris, George	1	5	4	(Subzar)			
Myers, Andrew	1	2	3	Sutton, Stephen	1	1	1
Marshall, Samuel	1	1	2	Sutton, Benjamin	1	1	3
Minor, John, Esq.	1	3	7	Sykes, Margaret (Six)	0	0	1
Two slaves				Sykes, Henry (Six)	1	1	3

AND ITS PIONEER FAMILIES

Name				Name			
Terrance, William	1	2	6	Terrance, Samuel	1	1	4
Thompson, John	1	1	2	Villery, David	2	1	4
Truelock, Thomas	1	2	3	Vernes, John	3	5	4

MORGAN TOWNSHIP 1790

Name				Name			
Heaton, Miles (Haiden)	1	3	3	Biggs, Abigail	3	1	1
Clayton, Elizabeth	0	1	1	Brown, Abner, Sr.	1	1	1
Hook, James	3	4	2	Bell, Benjamin	1	1	1
Reese, John	1	0	2	Timmons, Nichols	1	0	1
Prong, Stophel	1	0	5	Mills, John	1	2	3
Grooms, Solomon	1	3	4	Jail, Samuel (Jewell ?)	1	2	2
Beeman, Peter (Benham)	1	4	1	Bell, James	1	5	4
Smith, Andrew	1	1	1	Jennings, Cyrenus	1	1	2
Smith, James	1	0	1	House, Samuel	1	3	3
Martin, Zepheniah	1	2	3	Lee, William	2	3	3
Martin, John	1	2	1	Lee, John	1	0	1
Bell, Nathan	1	3	3	Ross, Henry	1	0	1
Arnold, John	1	0	1	Ross, Robert	1	0	3
Lolle, James (Lalley)	1	1	4	Bell, Abel	2	0	7
Young, Phillip	1	1	4	Wolverton, John	1	1	1
Ball, William	1	3	3	Crayne, Caleb	1	4	4
Moore, Christian	1	2	3	Clark, Isreal	1	2	2
Stogdon, James	1	0	3	Bell, Nathaniel	1	0	1
Hill, Thomas	2	1	2	Wright, William	1	1	4
Wise, Adam	1	2	2	Wolverton, Thomas	1	3	2
Wilson, Samuel	1	3	2	Eaton, Jonah	1	5	2
Arnold, Abraham	1	0	2	Davis, James	2	2	2
McDowell, Andrew	1	1	2	Davis, James, Sr.	1	1	2
Johnston, Zepheniah	1	0	2	Parker, David	2	3	1
Coleman, Joel	1	3	5	Smith, Ralph	1	6	3
Harrod, Levi	1	3	2	Fletcher, Thomas	1	1	2
Johnston, David	1	1	2	Ball, Grace	0	1	2
Polson, George	2	3	3	Luse, Samuel (Lucey)	1	1	3
Burge, Jacob	1	4	5	Heaton, John	1	2	4
Bell, William (Bills)	1	2	1	One slave			
Bell, John (Bills)	2	1	3	Heaton, Isaac	4	2	5
Enoch, Henry	1	1	4	One slave			
Hull, Zachariah	1	3	3	Heaton, Henry	1	0	3
Stull, John	1	2	4	One slave			
Heaton, Daniel	1	0	1	Luse, Eleazer	3	2	2
Pettit, Nathaniel (Pitnid)	1	1	4	Moore, Thomas	3	5	3
Doty, Anthony	1	0	1	Allen, Thomas	2	1	4
Ball, Davis	1	3	1	Case, Samuel	1	0	2
Woodruff, Stephen (Woodrough)	1	0	4	Heaton, William	1	1	1
				Heaton, David	1	2	1
Stites, Rachel (Stiles)	0	0	1	Hays, George	1	1	1
Huttenfield, Phoebe	1	2	2	Smith, Jacob	1	0	1
Mills, Joseph	1	3	5	Hays, William	2	2	4
Cowplane, Caleb (Copeland ?)	1	1	1	King, Joseph	1	1	2
				Parson, Daniel	1	0	2
Trumph, John	1	1	3	Chidester, Holdridge	1	2	3
Rush, Jacob	2	6	5	James, William	1	1	2
Headlee, Samuel	1	1	1	Shorter, George	1	1	4
Dunn, Benajah	0	0	1	Reese, John	1	4	1
Dunn, Sarah	0	0	1	Meeks, Nathan	1	6	3
McEwen, James	1	3	2	Gray, Andrew	1	0	2
Batten, Margaret	1	1	1	Miller, John	1	3	3
Brown, Abner	1	3	1	Swart, Philip	2	2	2
Casto, David	1	2	1	Crain, Daniel	1	0	2

Wright, Lewis	1	0	3	Morris, Richard	1	5	3
Crain, Silas	2	3	4	Wead, Nathan	1	0	2
Brown, Paul	1	4	4	Chambers, Smith	1	0	2
Ross, William	1	0	4	Pounds, Samuel	2	2	4
Lyons, Benjamin	1	3	3	Bell, Nathaniel	1	1	4
Jewell, Seth	1	2	2	Howard, Jordan	1	1	2
Lyons, Solomon	1	5	3	Ross, Timothy	1	1	2
Murford, Benjamin	1	3	4	Lutes, George	1	4	2
Weakley, Thomas	1	4	1	Smith, Dennis	1	3	6
Lunback, Nicholas	1	1	2	Julien, Isaac	3	4	4
Bradburry, Andrew	1	1	2	Stewart, Joseph	1	2	4
(Browbury)				Cox, Michael	1	3	3
Cary, Abel	1	6	2	Case, Joseph	1	5	3
Fulton, Isreal	1	2	2	Holloway, Samuel	1	0	1
Martin, John	2	3	4	Johnston, Isaac	1	5	5
Timmons, Jean	2	2	5	Briston, James	1	2	3
Timmons, Eleven	1	0	2	(Brinton ?)			
Mintor, Daniel	1	2	5	Ross, John	1	2	6
Milliken, William	1	2	5	Four slaves			
Robinson, John	1	1	4	Parker, Stephen	1	0	2
McGiffin, Nathaniel	2	1	2	Parker, Jesse	1	1	4
Milliken, James	2	5	2	Dunham, Nathaniel	2	6	2
Fix, Henry	1	6	3	(Denham)			
Adamson, Thomas	1	3	1	Shelby, David	2	2	2
Burson, Aaron	1	0	1	Leonard, Ziba	1	1	4
Hoge, George	3	2	3	Leonard, William	1	1	1
Darnal, Peter	2	2	5	Cooper, Nathan	1	2	3
Seals, James	1	0	1	McGill, Robert	1	0	6
Seals, Joseph	1	1	2	Lowrey, John	4	3	5

FRANKLIN TOWNSHIP 1790

Sellars, Christian	1	3	5	Leakins, Joseph	1	0	1
Slater, Thomas	2	2	5	Leakins, Samuel	1	4	4
Stewart, Hezekiah	1	2	3	Aldridge, John	1	2	2
Scott, John	1	2	2	Haines, Daniel	1	3	3
White, David	2	3	4	Cummins, Andrew	1	1	1
Bowers, Rachel	0	2	3	Wood, John	1	2	3
Hickman, William	1	1	1	Kent, Thomas	1	4	3
Adkins, Charles	2	2	2	White, Solomon	1	2	2
Stein, Alexander	1	4	4	Peckenpaugh, George	2	2	2
Mirandy, Samuel	1	3	4	Ross, Reuben	1	1	1
Sellars, Leonard	1	2	2	Cowan, William	2	4	4
Gooden, Thomas	1	0	1	Raper, Leonard	1	3	2
Morris, Caleb	1	2	2	Vanasdale, Cornelius	1	3	2
Huffman, George	1	2	2	Craig, John	1	1	1
Markins, Samuel	1	0	2	Morris, Archibald	1	3	2
Love, Leonard	1	2	3	Wells, Thomas	1	3	3
Sellars, John	1	2	1	Potter, John (Porter ?)	2	6	5
Devall, Daniel	1	3	4	Fee, Thomas	1	4	5
Pratt, John	2	2	4	Fee, Thomas, Jr.	1	2	1
Lewis, Robert	1	4	1	Fee, William	1	1	1
Freeland, James	1	2	3	Inghram, Arthur	1	4	4
Sayers, William	2	3	4	Inghram, William	1	3	4
Church, George (Kerkle	1	2	1	Bryan, John (Bryant ?)	2	2	4
Dillon, Peter	2	2	2	Carroll, George	1	2	4
Eaton, Thomas	1	0	1	Carrall, William	1	4	2
Maple, William	1	2	1	Zimmerman, Abraham	1	1	1
Davis, James	2	2	3	Archer, Elizabeth	1	1	1
Archer, Jacob	1	2	2	Grogan, Lawrence	1	2	3

Barker, Abraham	1	2	1	Hathaway, Samuel	2	2	3
Parker, John	1	3	3	Hathaway, William	2	6	3
Ankrom, Mathew	1	3	4	Rinehart, Thomas	1	5	3
Gordon, John	1	1	1	Rinehart, Thomas, Sr.	1	1	1
Hughes, Nathaniel	1	4	4	Delaney, William	1	0	2
Knight, David	2	4	5	Rinehart, Barnet	1	4	3
Ankrom, Richard	2	2	2	Rinehart, Sarah	0	2	2
McCoy, William	1	1	4	Smith, Thomas	2	6	3
Brown, Mary	0	3	3	Smith, John	1	4	3
Devall, John	1	3	4	Smetley, Jacob	1	4	2
Devall, Leonard	1	1	1	Seals, James	1	0	5
Devall, Daniel	1	0	2	Gorrell, Robert	1	4	5
Bradford, Robert	1	2	3	Gray, David	1	6	4
Knotts, Ann	0	3	4	Gray, John	1	2	1
Dollison, Alexander	1	2	2	Archer, James	2	4	5
Devall, Conrad	1	2	3	Archer, Joseph	1	3	3
Livengood, Peter	1	3	2	Wiley, John (Whealy)	2	4	2
Sellars, George	1	2	1	Wiley, John, Jr.	3	6	5
Dailey, Peter	1	3	4	Wiley, Elijah	1	2	2

PETITION OPPOSING FORMATION OF "TRANSYLVANIA"

Collins, Lewis and Richard, HISTORY OF KENTUCKY, Vol II, Covington, Ky., 1878. Pp. 510-511. "The Petition of the inhabitants, and some of the intended settlers, of that part of North America now denominated TRANSYLVANIA, humbly sheweth:

"Whereas some of your petitioners became adventurers in that country from the advantageous reports of their friends who first explored it; and others since, allured by the specious show of the easy terms on which the land was to be purchased from those who style themselves proprietors, have, at a great expense and many hardships, settled there. But your petitioners have been greatly alarmed at the late conduct of those gentlemen, in advancing the price of the purchase money. At the same time they have increased the fees of entry and surveying to a most exorbitant rate. And your petitioners have been more justly alarmed at such unaccountable and arbitrary proceedings, as they have lately learned that the said lands were included in the cession or grant of all that tract which lies on the south side of the river Ohio. We humbly expect and implore to be taken under the protection of the honorable Convention of the Colony of Virginia, of which we cannot help thinking ourselves a part, and request your kind interposition in our behalf."

December, 1775, Harrodsburg.

Ranck, George W., BOONSBOROUGH Louisville, 1901, Filson Club Publ., No. 16. Appendix U. From Va. Journal of Convention. Petition of Transylvanias, received in May 1776. (Drawn up in December 1775.)

This is followed by the signatures of 84 men, many from the Tenmile Country.

James Harrod	Barnerd Walter	John Moore
Abm. Hite, Jun.	Hugh M'Million	John Corbie
Patrick Dorane	John Kilpatrick	Abm. Vanmetre
Ralph Nailor	Robt. Dook	Saml Moore
Robt. Atkinson	Edward Brownfield	Issaac Pritcherd
Robt. Nailor	John Beesor	Joseph Gwyne
John Maxfield	(Beeson ?)	Geo. Uland
Sam Pottinger	Conrod Woolter	Michl Thomas

Adam Smith
Saml. Thomas
Henry Thomas
Wm. Myars
Peter Paul
Henry Simons
Wm. Gaffata
James Hughes
Thos. Bathugh
Jonh Connway
Wm. Crow
Wm. Feals (Seals ?)
Benja. Davis
Beniah Dun
Adam Neelson
Wm. Shepard
Wm. House
Jno. Dun
Jno. Sim, Sen.
John House
Sime. House
Chas. Creeraft.

James Willie
John Cameron
Thos. Kenady
Jesse Pigman
Simon Moore
John Moore
Thos. Moore
Herman Consoley
Silas Harland
Wm. Harrod
Levi Harrod
John Mills
Elijah Mills
Jehu Harland
Leonard Cooper
Wm. Rice
Arthur Ingram
Thos. Wilson
William Wood
Joseph Lyons
Andrew House
Wm. Hartly

Thos. Dean
Richard Owan
Barnet Neal
John Severn
James Hughes
James Calley
Joseph Parkison
Jediah Ashraft
John Hardin
Archd. Reves
Moses Thomas
J. Zebulon Collins
Thos. Parkinson
Wm. Muckleroy
Meridith Helm, Jun.
Andw. House
David Brooks
John Helm
Benja. Parkison
Wm. Parkison
Wm. Crow

THE SWAN - HUGHES BIBLE

Much of the data used in the history of the families of Charles Lucas, John Swan, and Thomas Hughes, is taken from an old Family Bible, pages of which are here reproduced. It was first reported to us by M. Marie Perrin Lemley, a professional genealogist of Los Angeles, California, who copied the records from it, at the home of Thomas Hughes in Palms, California, in the Fall of 1916. At that time Mrs. Lemley described the Bible as being bound in deer skin, laced with the same material, with the hole left in the skin, showing the mark made by the bullet, with the pages worn at the edges, blotting out some of the dates. Then in 1940, Mr. Henry Swan of Denver, Colorado, visited Mr. Hughes, who permitted the Bible to be photographed, after which Mr. Swan sent copies of these photographs to the author.

Mr. Thomas Hughes, owner of the Swan-Hughes Bible, was born at Rices Landing, Pennsylvania, on August 25, 1859, a son of James and Mary Francis (Kline) Hughes, grandson of Thomas and Sarah (Swan) Hughes, a great-grandson of Thomas and Elizabeth (Swan) Hughes, great-great grandson of John and Elizabeth (Lucas) Swan, (two lines) and great-great-great-grandson of Charles and Elizabeth (Evans) Hughes. Mrs. Lemley and Mr. Swan are direct descendants of John and Elizabeth (Lucas) Swan.

This Bible, which we have designated the "Swan-Hughes Bible," as shown in the photograph was printed by T. Wood and E. Palmer for the Company of Stationers, in London, England, in the year 1732. It was probably first the property of Charles and Elizabeth (Evans) Lucas of Prince George's County, Maryland, passing from them to their eldest daughter, Elizabeth (Lucas) Swan, who brought it to the Tenmile Country. At her death or more probably, at the time of marriage, the Bible passed to the eldest daughter, Elizabeth, wife of Thomas Hughes. One can but stop and ponder over the romantic wanderings of this precious volume of authentic records. One error alone may be recognized, and that does not surprise since it is carried out on a tombstone record. This record says John Swan was born in 1721, and died in 1799, whereas the will of John Swan as filed in Greene County shows that it was signed by John Swan on November 3, 1800. As this will was probated on January 6, 1801, it is evident that John Swan must have died about December 1800, rather than in 1799, the dates of the Swan-Hughes Bible and his tombstone.

The above is a reproduction of the Swan-Hughes Bible which was printed by T. Wood and E. Palmer for the Company of Stationers in England in 1732. It was translated from the Original Greek. The New Testament portion was printed by Baskett in 1735, and contained the Books of the Aprocrapha. Much of the data used in the history of the families of Charles Lucas, John Swan and Thomas Hughes were taken from the record pages of it.

The Bible is bound in deerskin and laced with the same. There are bullet holes left in the skin and the pages are badly worn at the edges, blotting out some of the dates.

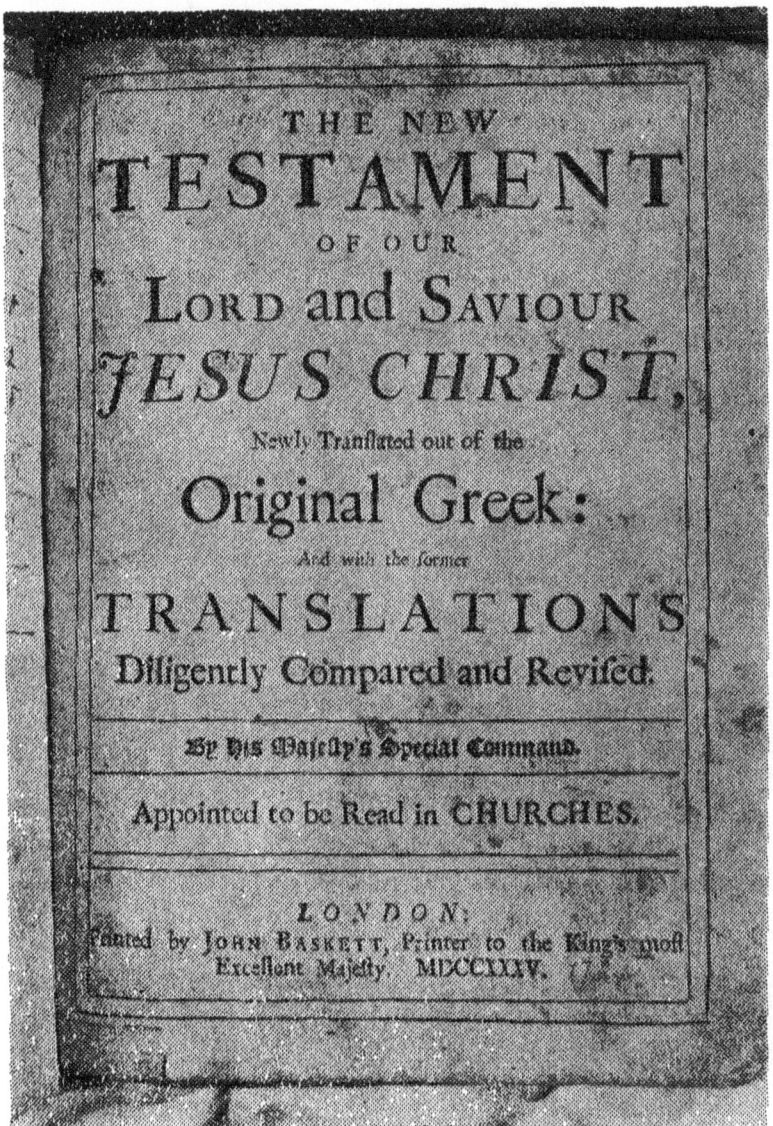

Thomas Hughes, owner of the Bible, was born at Rices Landing, Pennsylvania, in 1859, a son of James and Mary Frances (Kline) Hughes.

Copy of Records of Family Bible of
SWAN—HUGHES
(Printed by T. Wood and E. Palmer, for the Company of Stationers, London, England, MDCCXXXII)
(In the hands of Thomas Hughes of Los Angeles, California)

Swan, Elizabeth—departed this life October 24, 1805.
Swan, John—departed this life 1799. (Note: this is an error. Will made 1800).
Swan, John, (son) born 5-7-1744.
Swan, Hannah, born 12-7-1778?
Swan, Thomas, born May 1779.
Swan, Mary, born 12-17-1782.
Swan, Elizabeth, born 6-20-178—illegible.
Swan, Thomas—(just names written in Bible).
Swan, Richard.
Swan, John
Swan, Thomas.
Swan, Charles.
Swan, Richard.
Swan, Elizabeth.
Swan, Sarah.
Swan, Mary.
Swan, John, 1721-1799 (should be 1800).
Williams, Bazle, born 5-20-1759.
Foster, Samuel, born 2-1-1763.
Kendall, Thomas, born 10-14-1749.
Kendall, Elizabeth, born 2-3-1751.
Kendall, Mary, born 12-17-1752.
Kendall, Sarah, born 8-1-1755.
Evans, Mary, born 10-30-1718.
Evans, Samuel, born 5-22-1723.
Evans, Sarah, born 4-5-1725.
Evans, Persiler, born 12-26-1726.
Evans, John, born 11-2-1728.
Evans, Hugh, born 10-7-1730.
Evans, Elener, born 6-25-1732.
Evans, David, born 3-26-1734.
Evans, Richard, born 5-26-1736.
Evans, Thomas, born 9-27-1740.
Evans, Rachel, born 7-6-1742.
Lucas, Charles, born 7-1-1720.
Lucas, Thomas, born 4-12-1722.
Lucas, Elizabeth, born 3-1-1723.
Lucas, Mary, born 6-13-1725.
Lucas, Ann, born 4-27-1728.
Lucas, William, born 7-7-1730.
Lucas, Richard, born 7-19-1732.
Lucas, Sarah, born 10-12-1734.
Lucas, Samuel, born 11-25-1736.
Lucas, Elizabeth, born 1-12-1757.
Lucas, Thomas, born 1-—-1759.
Lucas, John, born 9-7-1760.
Lucas, Elizabeth, born 10-22-1762.
Lucas, Samuel, born 5-28-1764.
(NOTE: Two first named as children of Richard Lucas. Others likely his).
Lucas, Charles, born 2-16-1747.
Lucas, Elizabeth, born 3-22-1749.

Lucas, Thomas, born 2-24-1751.
Lucas, Josiah, born 5-28-1764.
   (NOTE: Children of Thomas Lucas).
Hughes, Elizabeth, born 3-15-1776; daughter of Joseph and Sarah.
Hughes, Samuel, born 8-28-1782.
Hughes, Thomas, born 5-5-1749.
Hughes, Elizabeth, born 2-28-1751; married 2-20-1770.

Children of Thomas and Elizabeth (Swan) Hughes

Hughes, Elizabeth, born 11-2-1771.
Hughes, John, born 5-7-1774.
Hughes, Mary, born 12-10-1776.
Hughes, Sarah, born 1-27-1779.
Hughes, Martha, born 5-11-1781.
Hughes, Thomas, born 2-18-1783.
Hughes, Ann, born 9-2-1785.
Hughes, James, born 1-19-1788.
Hughes, Luca, born 12-19-1790.
Hughes, Remembrance, born 4-23-1793.
Hughes, Catherine, born 11-18-179—.
   (Pages badly worn on edge, blotting dates).
Curl, Elizabeth, daughter of James and Ann Curl, born July 6, 1805.
Lindsey, James, son of James and Judith Lindsey, born 5-31-1772.
   James and Mary (Hughes) Lindsey married 6-2-1796.
O'Neel, Barnet; married Martha Hughes 6-6-1799.
John Hughes and Mary Rex married 8-27-1795.

JOHN SWAN, PIONEER

The best known, but by no means the first permanent settler of the Tenmile Country, is John Swan, who for the sake of clarity we shall call John Swan, pioneer, to distinguish him from his father and son of the same name. John Swan, pioneer, was a son of John Swan, who in 1722, bought a tract of land in Anne Arundel County, Maryland, known as "Evans' Range." The elder John Swan had married about 1720, the widow, Elizabeth (Green) Foster. Her first husband, John Foster had died, leaving four sons, John, Richard, Thomas, and Hugh Foster. She then had two children by the elder John Swan, namely a daughter, Comfort Swan, and a son, John Swan, the pioneer, who was born in 1721. The elder John Swan died about 1727.

John Swan, pioneer, married about 1744, Elizabeth Lucas, daughter of Charles and Elizabeth (Evans) Lucas. The names of her brothers and sisters and the dates of their births are to be found in the "Swan-Hughes Bible," which is still in existence, and photostatic copies are, through the courtesy of Henry Swan of Denver, Colo., in our possession. Charles Lucas was a son of Thomas Lucas and wife, Dorothy (?) Maryland pioneers. Charles Lucas was born April 20, 1693, and married Elizabeth Evans on November 20, 1718. Elizabeth Lucas, wife of John Swan, pioneer, was born March 11, 1723.

About 1767, Thomas Gist led a party of Maryland and Virginia people to the Tenmile Country to settle on land which had been sold December 12, 1757, by John Owens, Indian Trader at Fort Pitt, to Abraham Teagarden of Frederick County, Maryland. The subsequent transfers of this land have not been found to show how John Swan, pioneer, obtained the land, which he later patented. The party led by Gist included in addition to Swan, the Henry Vanmeter family, the James Hughes family, the Hillers, the O'Neals, and probably the family of Thomas Foster, half brother of John Swan, pioneer, all of whom settled close together, between the Tenmile and Muddy Creek.

When John Swan, whom we now call John Swan, Sr., and the

party of immigrants settled in the Tenmile Country, the Indians were at peace with the whitemen, but this condition was broken by Lord Dunmore's War in 1774, and forting became necessary, and continued until a few years after the end of the Revolutionary War. Strong cabins were erected at strategic points to repel the roving bands of savages, while in other places, stockaded forts were built. One such stockade was built around John Swan's cabin on Swan's Run (later Pumkin Run and in some records, Enoch's Run) and another was built around Henry Vanmeter's cabin on another branch of Swan's Run. There is no evidence that John Swan, Sr., served in any capacity as a soldier in either Dunmore's War or the Revolution which followed, but he did maintain at all times, a stronghold which was used almost continuously from 1774, until 1782, as a place of refuge, and for recruiting soldiers, many of whom were quartered at his fort for periods of enlistment. John Swan, Sr., also loaned money and supplies to Lord Dunmore, as well as advancing supplies to the militia of the Revolution.

Though not a native Virginian, John Swan, Sr., maintained an allegiance to that State long after the border had been settled, but his acts never reached the violence stage as did that of his neighbor, Henry Vanmeter. After the need for forting was over, John Swan, Sr., set about improving his land and buying other tracts, on which to settle his sons and work his slaves. He was quite a wealthy man for his times, when he made his will on November 3, 1800. It was probated on January 6, 1801, which gives the approximate date of his death. There is an error in his tombstone record which gives his death as December 29, 1799. His wife died on October 17, 1805, and is buried with her husband in the Swan Cemetery. She was probably the second owner of the Swan-Hughes Bible.

Children

1. John Swan, Jr., was born in Maryland May 7, 1744, (Bible Record) died while on the way to Kentucky, about 1782-3. With members of his own and his wife's families, John Swan, Jr., with his wife and small children were floating down the Ohio River to take up land, and when a short distance below Fort Pitt, while John Swan, Jr., was fast asleep on the flat boat with his young daughter in his arms, he was shot through the breast by an Indian on the shore. So fatal was the shot that those aboard were unaware of the incident until the child cried out: "Oh! Papa has been shot and warm blood is running over me." The party on board made ready to repel an attack and began a vigorous fire at the enemy on the shore, the newly-made widow of John Swan, Jr., loading guns for Joseph Hughes, brother-in-law of the dead man, until they drove off the raiders. The party then sadly proceeded to their destination. The date of this unfortunate happening may be judged from the filing of the will of John Swan, Jr., in Will Book A, pp. 11, in Harden County, Kentucky. The will was made September 12, 1780, and probated February 18, 1783. In his will he mentions his wife, Elizabeth, and children, John, Joel, Elizabeth, and Letitia. A son, Thomas, was born posthumously. The widow, her father, and Richard Swan, are named executors. The witnesses were Mary Hinton, Rebecca Rollins, and Margaret Haycroft, all sisters of the widow, and who were of the party on the way to the Severn Valley in Kentucky. John Swan, Jr., had married in the Tenmile Country, Elizabeth Vanmeter, daughter of Jacob and Letitia (Strode) Vanmeter. Jacob Vanmeter was in charge of the party, which Colonel Thomas Jones, in an interview with Draper relating to his settlement at Louisville in 1780, said "consisted of 27 family boats in

charge of Vanmeter who had a fort on Muddy Creek on the Monongahela." (Draper Mss CC-11-pp. 232.) After the death of her husband, Elizabeth (Vanmeter) Swan married (1) on August 20, 1793, Thomas McNeil, and after his death, she married John Ventrees, a widower with a large family. They were then settled on Rollin Fork of Salt River, near Elizabethtown, Kentucky. In the Journal of the Western Commissioners 1782-1783, in the Virginia Historical Library (pp. 84) it is shown that Elizabeth Swan, widow of John Swan, received the sum of 12 pounds, 5 shillings and 4 pence for flour and pork purchased by her husband for the Clark Expedition, in which he served as second in Command to Captain William Harrod. The George Rogers Clark Papers of the Illinois Historical Society, note that an entry in Clark's Diary of March 1778, showing that Clark "appointed a rendezvous of Captain Harrod's Company at John Swans on the 30th." (pp. 28) Then in Clark's Papers of 1781-1783 Volume 4 of the Virginia Series (pp. 388) there is the entry "Received and settled Captain John Swan's payroll of the Jefferson Militia, etc." John Swan, Jr., was a lieutenant in the Foreman Party that was ambushed near Wheeling.

Children
1. John Swan, married Margaret Coburn.
2. Elizabeth Swan, married (1) Solomon Brandenburg, (2) Thomas McNeil, (3) John Ventrees.
3. Letitia Swan, her tombstone in the old cemetery near Elizabethtown, Kentucky, shows she died October 10, 1845, aged 67 years. She married in Hardin County, December 10, 1795, Andrew Fairleigh, who had been married previously to her cousin, Letitia Hart.
4. Joel Swan.
5. Thomas Swan, born posthumously, married Ruth Rollins.

Draper Mss 61-J says "At a meeting of the Commissioners at Louisville, the 31st of August, 1789: to John Swan's heirs for his four surveys, 500 acres to each, and one other deed for the balance of 156 acres."

2. Thomas Swan, son of John and Elizabeth (Lucas) Swan was born in Maryland about 1747. (See Brumbaugh Maryland Records pp. 47.) He took up claims to three tracts of land, which is not entered in official records, but when he made his will January 6, 1779, filed for probate in Monongalia County, December 6, 1779, he passed the land over to his son, Samuel Swan, then a minor child. When Samuel Swan became of age he secured a warrant by virtue of a Virginia Certificate to the tract called "Difficulty" on April 21, 1786, and had it patented to him on June 24, 1794. He sold the other tracts given him by his father. Thomas Swan's wife was a Vanmeter, probably a daughter of Jacob and Letitia (Strode) Vanmeter. Four children of Thomas Swan are named in his will.

Children of Thomas Swan
1. Samuel Swan, mentioned above, born September 18, 1773. (Swan-Hughes Bible). He owned the farm later the property of Ellis Baily near Carmichaels. Records also show that he bought land from James and Mary Murdock. Both tracts he deeded to his wife, Mary Swan, on February 10, 1806. She was Mary Hiller, who became the mother of a daughter, Elizabeth Swan, wife of James Bell of Carmichaels.
2. Elizabeth Swan.
3. Letitia Swan.
4. Sarah Swan.

The Thomas Swan Will

This will record is a copy of the will that was filed in Monongalia County, West Virginia, prior to the fire in the court house at Morgantown, in 1796, which destroyed all the records filed up to that time. We have seen a few records that were transferred to Washington County, Pennsylvania, following the running of the permanent line, but this is the only will that has come out of the lost records, so far as we have been able to learn.

SWAN, THOMAS:
      Monongahelia County, Virginia, January 6, 1779
      Wm. McCleery, Clerk, filed December 6, 1779
      Recorded in the same County.

IN THE NAME OF GOD AMEN:

I, Thomas Swan, of Monongalia Co. and Colony of Virginia, being weak and low in sickness, but being perfect sound of memory, blessed be God, do this Sixth Day of January in the year of our Lord one Thousand Seven Hundred and Seventy Nine make and publish this my last Will and Testament in the manner following: that is to say—leaving

First: To my son Samuel Swan, that place that I now live on it lying on the south side of Muddy Creek. He is not to debar his mother of her Third her lifetime and likewise I give to the said boy a Horse and Saddle and I leave to his mother to her own generosity to give him as much more as she pleases; and likewise:—

I give and bequeath to my Three Daughters, Elizabeth Swan, Litta Swan, and Sarah Swan each of the said girls and my Dear Wife to have an equal share of the moveables and the Two places on Ten Mile to be sold and to have an equal share of it, And if the boy should died before he comes of age the surviving heirs to have an equal share . . . .

And I make John Swan, Abraham Van Meter, Jacob Cline and James Hughes Excrs. of this my Will in Trust for the intents and purposes in this my will contained, and . . . . I make my friend James Hughes overseer of this my Will to take care and see the same performed according to my true intent and in meaning.

And in witness whereof, I the said Thomas Swan have to this my Last Will and Testament, set my hand and seal the day and year above mentioned.

      THOMAS SWAN

Signed, Sealed and Delivered, by the said .... and testament in the presence of us who were present at the signing and sealing hereof.
 James Hughes,
  John Vincent Prov'd
  Isaac Pritchard Prov'd

MONONGALIA CO. SS:

I do hereby Certify that the Original Will of which this is a true copy, was brought into the Court of said County and after being proved, according to the law, was ordered to record.

Given under my hand (No publick sale being in my office) this 6th day of December, 1779.

      WM. McCLEERY, Clerk.

3. Charles Swan, son of John and Elizabeth (Lucas) Swan, born 1749, died February 25, 1839, aged 83 years and 14 days. He married Sarah Vanmeter, born 1758, died July 4, 1825, aged 67 years, 10 days. She was a daughter of Henry and Martha Vanmeter, who as a child had accompanied the Swan-Hughes-Van-

meter Party to settle in the Tenmile Country, and history romantically records that during the dangerous journey, she had ridden the same horse with her future husband. Charles Swan took an early and active part in the Revolution, going out first as Ensign in Captain Jesse Pigman's Company in the Spring of 1777. (James Pribble Pension application, Nat. Arch. W. 3595). On May 1, 1783, he was commissioned a Captain in the Pennsylvania Militia, serving under Lieut.-Colonel Henry Enoch in the Second Battalion from Washington County. (Penna. Archives, Series VI, Vol. 2, pp. 75). (Name is mis-spelled or error in copy makes it "Sevan"). Serving after the Revolution Charles Swan rose to the rank of Colonel. Much has been written of the life of Charles Swan, a man largely interested in the affairs of his community. He is especially noted for being one of the founders of Greene Academy. His first settlement was made on the south side of Muddy Creek, including a portion of the land on which Carmichaels was laid out, a tract of 356 acres of land warranted to him under the title of "Delay", on December 23, 1785. Here he is said to have erected the first slab sided house, where too the first Episcopal Church services were held. Charles Swan and his wife are buried in the Swan Cemetery near Rices Landing.

Children of Charles and Sarah (Vanmeter) Swan
1. Henry B. Swan, born March 12, 1774, died at Grave Creek, (West) Virginia, March 26, 1823. He married Elizabeth Bowen, who after the death of her husband, married William Burge.

Children of Henry B. and Elizabeth (Bowen) Swan
1. Sarah Swan, born January 19, 1797, married John Ward. They went to Des Moines, Iowa, in 1844.
2. Charles Swan, born November 10, 1798; drowned while young.
3. Thomas Swan, born November 21, 1800; died young.
4. Henry V. Swan, born September 16, 1804, died February 18, 1865. Served as Lieutenant-Colonel of 37th Iowa Volunteer Infantry. He married (1) January 1, 1829, Esther Ward, who died January 6, 1862. He married (2) January 21, 1864, Mrs. Sarah De Long.
5. Elizabeth Swan, born September 10, 1802, married Minor Burge, son of her step-father, William and Frances (Long) Burge.
6. John Swan, born April 30, 1807, died April 1852, at Danville, Iowa. He married, October 23, 1827, Margaret Brock.
7. Hugh Swan, born August 27, 1809, died June 8, 1851, in Henry County, Iowa. He married Martha Burson, daughter of Judge Thomas and Anne (Swan) Burson. She died October 5, 1865.
8. Simeon Swan, born January 15, 1812, died in Iowa; married, 1833, Elizabeth Hughes, daughter of Thomas and Elizabeth (Swan) Hughes, Jr. After the death of Simeon Swan, his widow married John Lucas, son of Thomas and Martha (Swan) Lucas.
9. Remembrance Swan, born May 18, 1814, died in West Virginia in 1877. His wife was Mary Long.
10. William Swan, born March 13, 1816, died August 12, 1885; married Lucinda Shroyer, who died March 30, 1907, aged 88 years, 5 months and 12 days. Both are buried in Hewitts Cemetery at Rices Landing.
11. Phoebe Swan, born February 23, 1820, married Ned

Garrison.
12. Martha Swan, born March 14, 1821, married George Rice.
2. John Swan, born November 15, 1776, drowned in a spring on his father's homestead.
3. Martha Swan, born July 11, 1778, married, December 17, 1795, Thomas Higgins Lucas, son of William and Sarah Lucas.

Children of Thomas Higgins and Martha (Swan) Lucas
1. Cassandra Lucas, born April 4, 1797, married James Hufty, son of Jacob and Sarah (Barclay) Hufty.
2. Sarah Lucas, born January 17, 1798, died April 27, 1890; married James Deeming.
3. Elizabeth Lucas, born October 11, 1799; married John Neff, born 1799, died March 29, 1865.
4. Nancy Lucas, born June 24, 1801, died October 17, 1804.
5. William Lucas, born March 20, 1803, died August 21, 1889; married, December 9, 1828, Sarah Lucas.
6. Swan Lucas, born April 27, 1805, died 1881; married (1) Permelia Emery, (2) Catherine (Emery) Litzenberg, (3) ....
7. Mary Lucas, born September 28, 1806, married Warren Foster.
8. Solomon Lucas, born September 25, 1808, died July 25, 1820.
9. John Lucas, born September 21, 1809, married Elizabeth Hughes, widow of Simeon Swan.
10. Thomas Lucas, born October 19, 1811; married Rebecca Emery, born 1813.
11. Charles Lucas, born November 30, 1813, died December 26, 1817.
12. Jesse Lucas, born May 2, 1816, died December 29, 1847; married Rachel Garret.
13. Charles Alexander Lucas, born April 4, 1818, died January 28, 1894; married Catherine Barnhart.
14. Richard Lucas, married Susan Neel.
15. Isaac B. Lucas, born March 1, 1823, died April 10, 1852; married Lydia Hughes, born November 16, 1831, died at Marysville, California, 1899.

4. Elizabeth Swan, born December 28, 1779, died January 30, 1860; married, October 17, 1779, James Seaton, born October 26, 1780, son of Francis and Rebecca (Gregg) Seaton.

Children of James and Elizabeth (Swan) Seaton
1. Hiram Seaton, born October 1, 1801; married, December 4, 1823, Sarah Vorhees.
2. Francis Seaton, born May 6, 1803, died September 15, 1826.
3. Susannah Seaton, born December 10, 1805, died January 11, 1879; married, August 17, 1826, Daniel Collier.
4. Sarah Seaton, born December 16, 1807, died October 23, 1858; married William Crawford.
5. Mary Seaton, born June 23, 1810; married, June 2, 1831, William Inghram, son of William and Agnes (Fee?) Inghram, born February 24, 1794, died September 3, 1843. His first wife was Sarah Adams, who died May 3, 1830.
6. Rebecca Seaton, born July 18, 1812; married, May 1835, George Martin.

7. Marchant Seaton, born September 21, 1814, died October 22, 1831.
8. Juliet Seaton, born March 31, 1817; married, November 20, 1834, Robert L. Barry.
9. James C. Seaton, born August 3, 1819, died September 9, 1851.
10. John S. Seaton, born September 12, 1823; married, November 26, 1846, Emma Rawls.

5. Thomas Swan, born November 13, 1781, died April 11, 1845, in Fayette County, Pennsylvania. He married, (1) March 3, 1809, Eleanor Anderson, born 1788, died 1837; married, (2) November 16, 1837, Harriet Barclay, daughter of Hugh and Ann (Darrah) Barclay, born January 1805.

Children of Thomas and Eleanor (Anderson) Swan
1. Sarah Swan, died young.
2. Charles Swan, died young.
3. Eliza Swan, married February 11, 1828, Felix Hempsted.
4. Mary Swan, born 1814, died July 1, 1836; married Reuben Hague.
5. Charlotte Swan, born December 20, 1812; married, July 3, 1832, Samuel Houlsworth.
6. Martha Swan, born February 14, 1819, died May 8, 1845; married George Darragh Rex, born November 10, 1816, died 1890 in Jefferson County, Ohio.
7. James Swan, born 1824, died August 4, 1850; married Sophia Wiltner, born 1828.
8. William Swan, died July 3, 1860; married, May 20, 1855, Martha McGilkin.
9. Thomas Swan, born 1828, died October 10, 1857; married Sarah E. Cannon, Uniontown, Pa.
10. Colonel Simeon Swan, born March 20, 1832, died at Creston, Iowa, January 22, 1900. He married, (1) October 22, 1851, Dorcas Ayers of Uniontown, Pa., born April 22, 1834. He went out as Captain in the First Iowa Cavalry, and later served through the rank of Major to Colonel in the Fourth Iowa Cavalry. Was the first mayor of Creston, Iowa.

6. John Swan, (two of same name in family) born December 10, 1783; married Mary Barclay, daughter of Hugh and Ann (Darrah) Barclay. She was born January 29, 1789. John Swan left with a flatboat of merchandise on his wedding day. He suffered losses through bad luck and poor sales and never returned. Both he and his wife remarried and raised families.

7. Mary Swan, born December 6, 1785; married, (1) William Collins, who died soon afterwards. She married (2) Judge Isaac Burson, son of Edward and Elizabeth (Blackledge) Burson.

Child of William and Mary (Swan) Collins
1. Ann Collins, born July 30, 1811, died July 18, 1885; married, October 17, 1826, John Lindsey, born March 11, 1803, died May 28, 1865, son of James and Mary (Hughes) Lindsey.

8. Charles Swan, born December 9, 1787, died 1873, in Knox County, Ohio. Married, January 24, 1811, Margaret Barclay, born January 14, 1792, and died in 1863.

Children of Charles and Margaret (Barclay) Swan

1. Mary Swan, born November 26, 1811; married, (1) Hiram Litzenberg; (2) Hiram Brown.
2. Ann Swan, born February 26, 1813; married, November 20, 1832, Russell Armstrong.
3. Charles Swan, born December 8, 1815, died in Knox County, Ohio, January 13, 1873; married Ann Curry. He was a prisoner in the War Between the States.
4. Hugh B. Swan, born December 17, 1816; married, April 13, 1837, Helen Stephenson.
5. Henry Swan, born November 8, 1818; married, November 25, 1840, Clara Fuller. Their sons formed the famous Swan Brothers, cattle kings of Cheyenne, Wyo. Were the ancestors of Henry Swan of Denver, Colorado, banker and historian of the Swan family.
6. Solomon B. Swan, born October 29, 1820, died February 4, 1901; married Anne Davidson, born April 24, 1824, died January 28, 1901.
7. Sarah Swan, born September 7, 1822; married, (1) John Patterson, (2) .... Giles.
8. Helen Swan, born May 17, 1824; married Solomon Hewitt, born 1818, died February 28, 1843.
9. William Swan, born March 22, 1826, died in infancy.
10. Thomas Swan, born September 29, 1827; married, (1) Belle Bomar, (2) Mary Gordon.
11. B. Franklin Swan, born August 25, 1829; killed by runaway ox team when two years old.
12. Alexander Swan, born November 24, 1831; was in the cattle business in Cheyenne. He married, (1) Anne McCullough, (2) Elizabeth Richey.
13. Margaret Swan, born October 30, 1833; died in infancy.

9. Sarah Swan, born January 5, 1790, died at Findlay, Ohio. Married, (1) Elias Flenniken, who died March 14, 1836; (2) Rev. George Vaneman.
10. Phoebe Swan, born March 17, 1791, died March 16, 1856; married, September 4, 1812, John F. McClain, born October 18, 1791, died in Knox County, Ohio, April 17, 1848. He was a son of Abijah and Permelia (Doughty) McClain.

Children of John F. and Phoebe (Swan) McClain

1. Charles S. McClain, married Ruth Berryhill.
2. Abijah McClain, married Catherine Hook.
3. Henry McClain, married Sarah Smith.
4. Samuel McClain.
5. William McClain, married Sarah Marquis.
6. Sarah McClain, married Edward Welsh.
7. Permelia McClain, married James Hufty.
8. Mary Ann McClain, married Morgan Booze.
9. Cassandra McClain, married Levi Sellars.

11. William Swan, born April 4, 1794, died March 5, 1847; married Mary Murdock, who died in Wisconsin, October 14, 1863.

Children of William and Mary (Murdock) Swan

1. Thomas Swan, born October 10, 1820, died November 20, 1875; married Miranda Clawson.
2. Daniel Swan, born March 10, 1822, died March 2, 1844; married Emily Gabes.
3. Elizabeth Swan, born 1824, died October 1864; married John Armstrong.

4. Charles Swan, died in infancy.
5. Samuel S. Swan, born June 18, 1832, married Rebecca Denny.
6. John B. Swan, born September 1, 1834, married Priscilla Dumwoodie.
7. Milton B. Swan, born February 19, 1836, died December 19, 1846.
8. Richard Swan, born March 1, 1838; killed in action while serving with Company K, 22nd Wisconsin Regiment in War Between the States.
9. Isaac W. Swan, born 1840; served in Company K, 13th Wisconsin Regiment. Married, January 15, 1880, Belle Merlotte.
10. Sarah B. Swan, born 1842, married N. W. Hartman.

12. Richard Swan, born September 14, 1796, died in Uniontown, December 29, 1873; married, 1818, Susan Gregg, born May 22, 1795, died June 22, 1866.

Children of Richard and Susan (Gregg) Swan
1. Presley Swan, born 1820, died 1891; married, (1) January 25, 1843, Miranda Hibbs. He married, (2) September 1855, Clarissa Carter.
2. Sarah Ann Swan, born February 26, 1822; married, March 25, 1845, William Barton.
3. Charles H. Swan, born February 20, 1824; married, March 16, 1854, Ruth Phillips.
4. Alford Swan, born February 12, 1827; married, March 25, 1858, Elma Phillips, born February 21, 1837.
5. Ruth Swan, born December 30, 1829, died December 2, 1869; married, March 16, 1854, William Phillips.
6. William B. Swan, born 1833; married, May 21, 1857, Jane E. McMullen, born February 11, 1834.
7. Emily Swan, born November 8, 1835; married, July 27, 1878, Joseph Boyd.

13. Jesse Swan, born July 1, 1798, died February 8, 1852; married Phoebe Jennings. They went to Ohio and later to Peoria, Illinois.

Children of Jesse and Phoebe (Jennings) Swan
1. Charles Swan.
2. Thomas Swan.
3. Henry Swan.
4. Obediah Swan.
5. Lewis Swan.
6. Sarah Swan.
7. Phoebe Swan.
8. Mary Swan.

4. Elizabeth Swan, daughter of John and Elizabeth (Lucas) Swan, born February 28, 1751, died at Jefferson, Pennsylvania, in 1825; married, February 20, 1770, Major Thomas Hughes, born May 5, 1749, died at Jefferson February 4, 1823. (See Thomas Hughes Records).

5. Richard Swan, son of John and Elizabeth (Lucas) Swan, born January 31, 1752, died February 11, 1822. Waychoff says Richard Swan served in the Revolution. Proof of this service is to be found in the pension application of Thomas Wells, who says that when he enlisted on April 1, 1776, for service under Captain Jesse Pigman, Charles Swan was the Lieutenant and Richard Swan was the Ensign in Colonel McFarland's Regiment. (Nat. Arch. R-11, 318). Richard Swan married Martha Vanmeter, born December 24, 1754, died October 24, 1836, daughter of Henry and

Martha Vanmeter. He patented several tracts of land, including "Delight" and "Point Lookout," the latter a tract of 36 acres at Rices Landing. A similar title was used for a tract of land near Carmichaels, originally warranted to Charles Swan, under the title of "Delay," but patented June 12, 1787, to Richard Swan. His wife, Martha (Vanmeter) Swan, left a will in which she named her children, some of whom are listed in the Swan-Hughes Bible. (Will Book 2, pp. 72). Both Richard and Martha (Vanmeter) Swan are buried in the John Swan Cemetery. Their homestead is said to have been on the Alfree Farm.

Children of Richard and Martha (Vanmeter) Swan

1. Hannah Swan, born December 7, 1777.
2. Thomas Swan, born May 1779, married Susannah Seaton. No issue.
3. Mary Swan, born December 17, 1782, married John Prickett. They went to Kentucky and later to Iowa.
4. Elizabeth Swan, born June 20, 1784, married George Alfree. He died and Thomas Burson acted as guardian for the children of this marriage. She then married Isaac Soefel, who died in February 1830.

Children of George and Elizabeth (Swan) Alfree

1. Thomas Alfree, married Louisa Stephenson.
2. Jacob Alfree, went to Kentucky.
3. Mary Alfree, died 1867; married Peter Sharpnack, who died in 1845.
4. James Alfree.

5. John Swan died at the age of 19 years.
6. Richard Swan, moved to Mason County, West Virginia. He married Sarah McCullough, who was born in 1798.

Children of Richard and Sarah (McCullough) Swan

1. Samuel Swan.
2. James Swan.
3. John Swan.
4. Alexander Swan.
5. Olivia Swan.
6. Sarah Swan.
7. Louisa Swan.

7. Sarah Swan, born June 26, 1786, died at Rices Landing July 11, 1852; married Thomas Hughes, born February 18, 1784, died May 8, 1867. He was a son of Thomas and Elizabeth (Swan) Hughes.

Children of Thomas and Sarah (Swan) Hughes

1. Barnet Hughes, married (1) Sarah Walton, (2) Catherine Woodcock.
2. Elizabeth Hughes, married (1) Simeon B. Swan, born January 15, 1812; married (2) John Lucas, born September 21, 1809, died January 31, 1859.
3. Lindsey Hughes, born 1813, died December 10, 1869; married Clementine Crago.
4. Samuel Hughes, married Maria Clark.
5. Maria Hughes, born December 31, 1818, died April 10, 1873; married William Kincaid, born 1819, died July 10, 1885.
6. John Hughes, born November 7, 1820, died December 24, 1887, married Cassandra Hufty, born June 25, 1825, died August 15, 1906. Both buried at Rices Landing.
7. James Hughes, died at Rices Landing May 1, 1889,

married Mary Frances Kline, born 1834, died March 25, 1875. They were married January 1, 1857.
8. Ann Swan, born July 21, 1787, died November 2, 1840, married about 1811, Judge Thomas Burson, born November 16, 1781, died January 11, 1864, son of Edward and Elizabeth (Blackledge) Burson.

Children of Thomas and Ann (Swan) Burson
1. Edward Burson, died at age of 2 years.
2. Richard Burson, died in Iowa about 1860. Never married.
3. James Burson, made one trip to California in the Gold Rush, but on the second trip he was killed by Indians May 20, 1865. Never married.
4. Thomas Burson, died after 1896 in Iowa. Never married.
5. Samuel Burson, died in childhood.
6. Martha Burson, died October 5, 1865, in Henry County, Iowa. Married Hugh Swan, born August 22, 1809, died June 8, 1851, son of Henry and Elizabeth (Bowen) Swan.
7. Elizabeth Burson, died unmarried.
8. Sarah A. Burson, married Reuben Beers. No children.
9. Mary Burson, married Bowen Hill, son of Isaac and Nancy (Virgin) Hill. They went to Ottawa, Illinois. Mary (Burson) Hill sent the letters to L. K. Evans, which he used in his articles on the Swans and Vanmeters.

9. Martha Swan, married David McClain. (See O. C. Docket March 18, 1822.)

Children of David and Martha (Swan) McClain
1. Thomas McClain, went to Knox County, Ohio.
2. Sarah McClain, married Mathias Roseberry, born February 28, 1811, died in Harvard, Nebraska in 1878. He was a son of Mathias and Sarah (Hughes) Roseberry.
3. Martha McClain, married John Hughes, born at Jefferson, March 31, 1816.

10. Rebecca Swan, born 1795, married George Litzenberg, Jr., born 1796, went first to Knox County, Ohio and then to Iowa.

Children of George and Rebecca (Swan) Litzenberg
1. John Litzenberg, born December 9, 1816, married December 6, 1838, Eliza Williams, born March 24, 1814. He died July 2, 1886, in Holt County, Nebraska.
2. Martha Ann Litzenberg, born February 15, 1822, died July 15, 1829, buried in the Swan Cemetery.
3. Andrew Litzenberg, born in 1830, married November 4, 1853, Elizabeth Smith. They went to Iowa in 1855.

11. Rachel Swan, married Samuel Vansickles, son of Captain Anthony Vansickles and Patsy (Vanmeter) Vansickles. They went to Mason County, West Virginia.
12. Samuel Swan, born May 29, 1799, died July 1861, in Marion County, Kentucky. He married Susannah Vaun. They had no children.

Sarah Swan, daughter of John and Elizabeth (Lucas) Swan, born in Maryland September 24, 1755, died in Howard County, Missouri, February 9, 1838. Married at Fort Pitt about 1775, Joseph Hughes, born in Maryland September 23, 1753, died at Estill, Missouri, February 7, 1837. He was a soldier with Captain William Harrod on the Clark Expedition. Received a pension for his war services. Was a member of the party that included

John Swan, Jr., on the fatal flat boat journey to Kentucky. He is buried in the Mt. Pleasant Cemetery near Glasgow, Missouri.

Children

1. Elizabeth Hughes, born March 15, 1776, (Swan-Hughes Bible) married (1) Leland Asbury.
2. John Hughes, born November 26, 1777, married Berry on July 3, 1801. She was born 1776.
3. Samuel Hughes, born August 28, 1782, married Nancy Price, daughter of Colonel William Price.
4. Thomas Hughes, married Nancy Veatch.
5. Charles Hughes, married Elizabeth Lawless.
6. James Hughes, married Nancy Craig.
7. Merritt Hughes, Married Polly Craig.
8. Richard Hughes.
9. Joseph Hughes, married Susan Singleton.
10. Jemima Hughes, married .... Scott.
11. Sally Hughes, married .... Neal.
12. William Hughes, married Polly Neal.

7. Mary Swan, daughter of John and Elizabeth (Lucas) Swan, was born in Maryland. She married (1) in Greene County, Samuel Moore, who died leaving one son. She then married John Isaacs, and settled in Kentucky.

Children

1. Samuel Moore.
2. Elisha Isaacs, married Sarah Lawless of Bradfordville, Kentucky.
3. David Isaacs, born in Danville, Kentucky, October 8, 1796, died January 17, 1891, in Howard County, Missouri. Married (1) Tacy Hourighan.
4. Nancy Isaacs, married February 14, 1837, Joseph M. Gray.
5. Louisa Isaacs, married William Scott.
6. Artemesia Isaacs, married (1) Price, (2) McCarty.
7. Martha Isaacs, married .... Cunningham.
8. Elizabeth Isaacs, married .... Haydon.
9. Elvira Isaacs.
10. Robert Isaacs, married Lucy Ann McClenahan.
11. Mary Ann Isaacs.
12. John Marshall Isaacs.
13. William H. Isaacs.
14. Jemima Isaacs.

8. Martha Swan, daughter of John and Elizabeth (Lucas) Swan, born about 1760, died in Howard County, Missouri. Married at Fort Pitt 1783, William Hughes, brother of Joseph. He was born September 23, 1760, and died in Howard County, Missouri, on January 10, 1828. We have a photostat of a letter from him to Charles Swan written in 1817 in which he inquires of the health of his older brother Nate. It was written from Missouri.

Children

1. Joseph Swan Hughes, born October 28, 1787, died March 6, 1863, married May 14, 1807, Cassandra G. Price.
2. Elizabeth Hughes, died young.
3. John Hughes, married Sallie Williams.
4. Roland Hughes, married (1) Jane Shanklin (2) Mary Ann Hughes.
5. William Hughes, married Nancy Morrison.
6. Samuel Hughes.
7. Annie Hughes.

8. Mary Hughes, married John Morris.
9. Louisiana Hughes, married John Cleveland, uncle of Grover Cleveland.
10. George Hughes, married Elizabeth Agnes Belt.

9. William Swan, youngest son of John and Elizabeth (Lucas) Swan, born in 1762, died December 25, 1835, aged 73 years, 5 months, 29 days, married about 1782, Sarah Harrod, born August 3, 1766, died November 16, 1822, daughter of Captain William and Amelia (Stephens) Harrod. Both are buried in the Swan Cemetery. When he was not much more than 12 years of age he went out with Captain William Harrod on the George Rogers Clark Expedition, his brother, John Swan, Jr., being the lieutenant under Captain Harrod. He did much service under Captain Harrod, and then came back to marry the captain's daughter. William Harrod also served as an ensign in Captain Jesse Pigman's Company. His estate was probated December 29, 1835.

Family of Ensign William Swan and Sarah (Harrod) Swan

1. John Swan, disappeared without a trace, according to the wording of his father's will.
2. Thomas Swan.
3. Elizabeth Swan, died before 1836, married Elijah Roseberry, who died intestate about 1851. Both are said to have been buried in the Swan Cemetery, but no markers are found.

   Children of Elijah and Elizabeth (Swan) Roseberry
   1. John Roseberry.
   2. Sarah Roseberry.
   3. Permelia Roseberry, (or Amelia) married Joseph Yoders.
   4. Elizabeth Roseberry, married Thomas Ammons.
   5. William Roseberry.
   6. Elijah Roseberry, married Elizabeth ....

4. Amelia Swan, married William Thomas, born December 17, 1788. He was a son of William and Elizabeth (Vanmeter) Thomas. The elder William Thomas after serving in the Revolution, removed to Miracle Run, near where it empties into Dunkard Creek. While clearing his land an Indian wounded him, from which wound he died on April 21, 1789.

THE ALFREE LOG CABIN
(Located on land originally occupied by Richard Swan)

Children of William and Amelia (Swan) Thomas

1. Sarah Thomas, married William Lantz.
2. William Thomas, born January 6, 1812, died September 19, 1882, married Amelia Minor, born March 6, 1817, died July 28, 1879.
3. Jesse Thomas, never married.
4. Thomas Hughes Thomas, never married.
5. Atinacea Thomas, married Jacob Lantz.
6. Amelia Thomas.
7. Ellis Thomas, married Mary Francis.
8. Saul Thomas, married Mary Cooper.
9. Nimry Thomas, never married.
10. Cyrus Thomas, never married.
11. Remembrance Thomas, born March 13, 1828, married Mary Johnson.

5. William Swan, born 1791, died April 21, 1852, married Hannah Kelly. His tombstone says he was 61 years, 1 month, 26 days old.
6. Samuel Swan, died in Greene County in 1843. He married Priscilla Crago, born 1796, died February 10, 1876. She was a daughter of Thomas and Priscilla (Thurman) Crago.

Children of Samuel and Priscilla (Crago) Swan

1. Rachel Swan, born March 31, 1824, died November 15, 1910. She was the third wife of James Luse, born February 5, 1816, died July 25, 1889.
2. Sarah Swan, married James McElroy.
3. Elizabeth Swan, married Robert Reynolds.
4. William Swan.

AND ITS PIONEER FAMILIES 183

  5. Thomas Swan, married .... Sharpnack.
  6. Samuel Swan, Jr., married Martha Mashie.
  7. Amelia Swan, born April 4, 1832, died June 14, 1904, married John McClain, born January 6, 1825, died October 15, 1891.
  8. Jesse Swan.
  9. Priscilla Swan, born 1836, died June 11, 1861, aged 25 years, 2 months, 17 days. She married John Cotterall, Jr., born November 29, 1832.
  10. Margaret Swan, born September 3, 1837, died January 30, 1882, married George Hewitt, born December 1, 1822, died March 3, 1880.
 7. Jesse Swan, born August 3, 1800, died February 8, 1851, buried in the Swan Cemetery. He married April 5, 1828, Elizabeth O'Neil, born November 19, 1806, died in Appamoose County, Iowa, December 6, 1884.

Children of Jesse and Elizabeth (O'Neil) Swan
  1. Neel Swan, lived at Neel, Kansas.
  2. William Swan, Plano, Iowa.
  3. Henry Swan, died June 12, 1844, aged 1 year.
  4. John Swan.
  5. James Neel Swan, born August 13, 1837, died January 1927, at Concord, Iowa. He married Mary Maulding.
  6. Jesse Swan, Jr., died young.
  7. George W. Swan, Plano, Iowa, married Ann Willis.
  8. Emeline Swan, never married.
  9. Sarah Swan.
  10. Martha Swan, married George Staley, Plano, Iowa.
  11. Remembrance Swan.
 8. Rachel Swan, died April 24, 1853, buried in the Swan Cemetery.
 9. Sarah Swan, born 1799, died October 9, 1842, aged 50 years, 19 days, married Joseph Ailes, who died in 1849. She is buried in the Swan Cemetery.

Children of Joseph and Sarah (Swan) Ailes
  1. Nancy Ailes, married .... Crago.
  2. Mary Ailes, married .... Kelly.
  3. Rachel Ailes, born November 23, 1832, died November 13, 1913, married A. J. Young, born February 7, 1831, died July 13, 1903.
  4. Elizabeth Ailes, born April 3, 1835, died December 8, 1892.
  5. Eliza Ailes, married .... Deum.
 10. Mary Swan, born June 4, 1806, died February 15, 1876, married Richard Willis, who died September 1, 1870, aged 85 years. Buried in Hewitt's Cemetery.

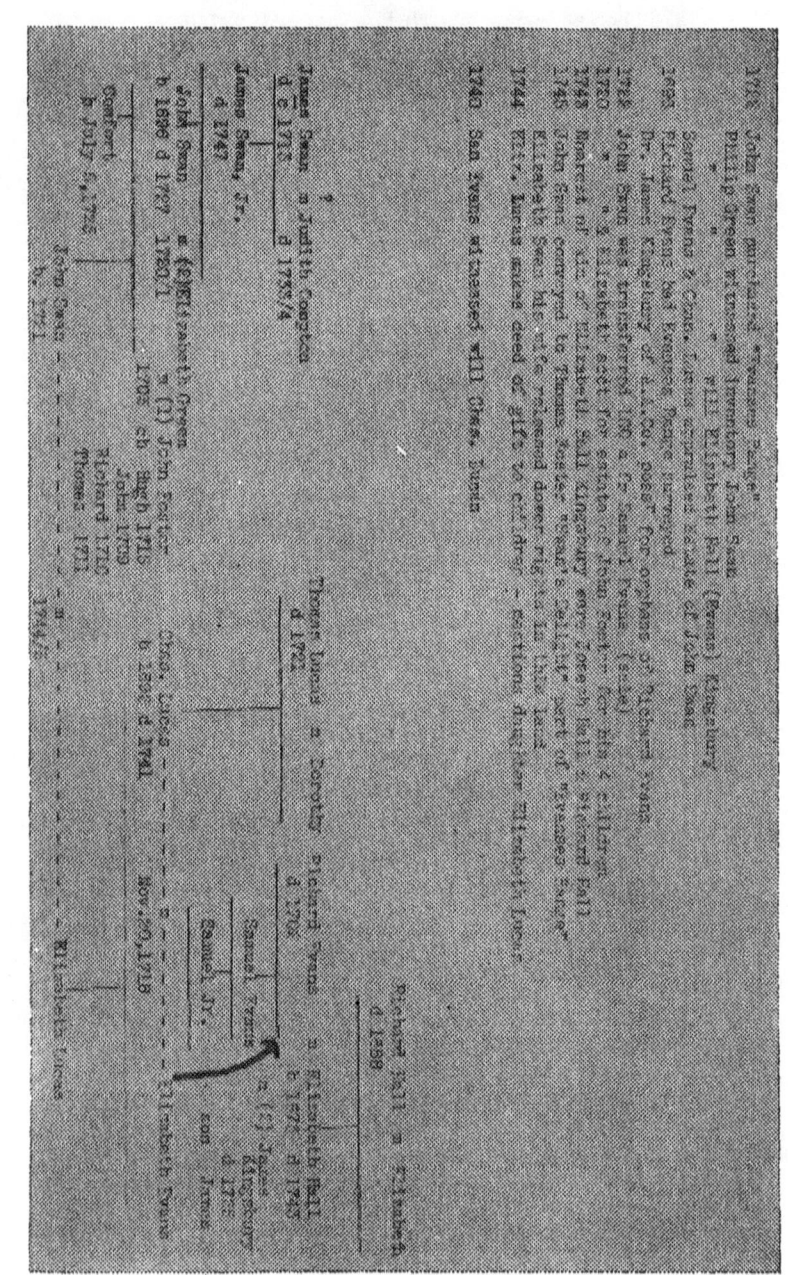

Children of Richard and Mary (Swan) Willis

1. Sarah Willis, born April 5, 1832, died May 30, 1874, married William Nutt, born April 27, 1829, died August 8, 1888. Buried in Hewitt's Cemetery.
2. William Willis, born 1833, died 1904, married Priscilla Reynolds.
3. Richard Willis, born 1834, died 1905, never married.
4. Joseph Willis, went west at age of 19 years.
5. Rachel Willis, born 1838, married Arthur M. Hill, born 1831.
6. Mary Willis, married Andrew Rice.
7. Grace Willis, married George W. Swan.
8. Isaac Newton Willis, married .... Mt. Joy.

THOMAS FOSTER FAMILY

Thomas Foster, Sr., probably the half brother of John Swan, Sr., bought a tract of land on Cole Run branch of Muddy Creek, where he died about 1790. (Washington County DB. 1-G-176.) His children were:

1. Sarah Foster, who married James Henderson.
2. Priscilla Foster, wife of Thomas Gilbert.
3. Samuel Foster, born February 1, 1763, member of Captain William Harrod's Company on the George Rogers Clark Expedition. His name and birth are found in the Swan-Hughes Bible.
4. Else Foster.
5. John Foster.
6. Thomas Foster, whose wife was Rachel ....
7. Evan Foster.
8. Richard Foster, whose wife's name was Eleanor.

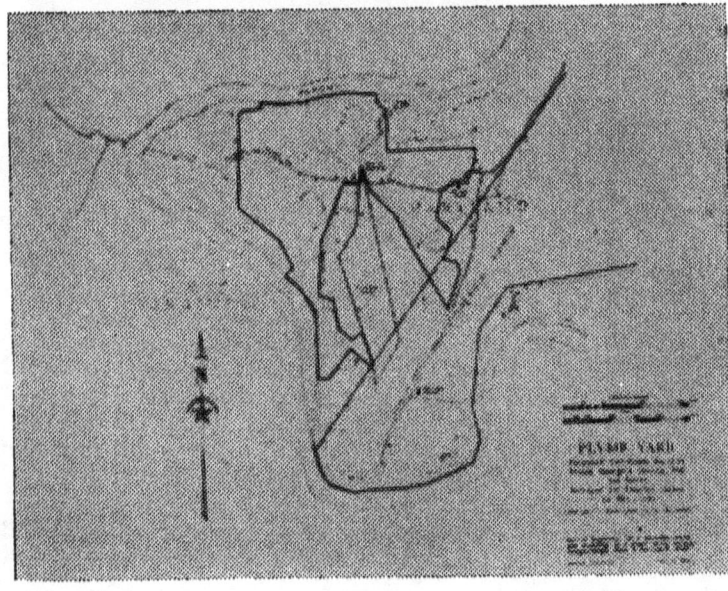

THE LUCAS FAMILY

Three groups of Lucas names are found in the Swan-Hughes Bible, giving dates of birth. The first of these was the children of Charles and Elizabeth (Evans) Lucas, and included the name of John Swan's wife, Elizabeth Lucas. Charles Lucas was born April 20, 1693, in Prince George's County, Maryland, the son of Thomas Lucas. He married in 1718, Elizabeth Evans, a daughter of Richard and Elizabeth (Hall) Lucas. The Swan-Hughes Bible gives this information regarding their children:

1. Charles Lucas, born July 1, 1720 (his wife was Elizabeth ....)
2. Thomas Lucas, born April 12, 1722 (he married Anne Keene)
3. Elizabeth Lucas, born March 11, 1723 (wife of John Swan, Sr.)
4. Mary Lucas, born June 13, 1725
5. Ann Lucas, born April 27, 1728 (married James Kendall ?)
6. William Lucas, born July 7, 1730 (wife's name was Sarah)
7. Richard Lucas, born July 19, 1732 (twice married, first to Elsie ...., secondly to Rachel Duvall ?)
8. Sarah Lucas, born October 12, 1734 (married Jesse Pigman, Sr.)
9. Samuel Lucas, born November 25, 1736 (married Elizabeth Beall)

Of the above names, Elizabeth and Sarah, wives of John Swan, Sr., and Jesse Pigman, Sr., respectively, came to the Tenmile. Thomas, Ann, Richard, and Samuel came to Fayette County, Pennsylvania, and William also came to Fayette where he tarried for a time and then bought land in Greene County, in the vicinity of Garard's Fort.

The second list of Lucas names in the Swan-Hughes Bible is designated the children of Richard Lucas and includes these names and dates:

1. Elizabeth Lucas, born January 12, 1757
2. Thomas Lucas, born January 1759
3. John Lucas, born September 7, 1760
4. Elizabeth Lucas, born October 22, 1762 (2)
5. Samuel Lucas, born May 28, 1764

The third group of names and dates give no parents name, but we are certain they were children of Thomas and Anne Keene Lucas. They are:

Charles Lucas, born February 16, 1747.
Elizabeth Lucas, born March 22, 1749 (she married .... Tyler).
Thomas Lucas, born February 24, 1751.
Josias Lucas, born May 28, 1764.
Basil Lucas (he married Elizabeth Brashears).
Gabriel Lucas.
Barton Lucas.
Cassandra Lucas.
Ellender Lucas.

From another source we get the names of the family of William Lucas, who with wife Sarah ...., settled for a time in Fayette County, and then bought "Swansburg" in Greene County from John Swan, Sr. His sons, William, Jr., and Richard, purchasing portions of the same tract, which in 1807 was conveyed to Joseph Hammer. This land was one farm removed from land of Jacob Livengood. William Lucas, Sr., and wife, Sarah, were parents of:

Jesse Lucas, wife's name was Mehitable ....
William Lucas, Jr., wife's name was Sarah ....
Richard Lucas, married Ann Kendall, daughter of James Kendall of Fayette County.
James Lucas, wife was Catherine Livengood, probably a daughter of Jacob.
Basil Lucas.
Charles Lucas.
Thomas H. Lucas, wife was Martha Swan, daughter of Charles Swan.

The first six of these went to Highland County, Ohio. Jesse and Thomas Lucas bought out the heirs of Thomas Foster, and then sold to Hugh Barclay in Greene County. (DB. 1 pp 607) Thomas Higgins

Lucas took out a patent on land near John Swan, Sr., and married Martha Swan, daughter of Charles and Sarah (Vanmeter) Swan. Thomas was the father of:

 Cassandra Lucas, who maried James Hufty.
 Sarah Lucas, who married James Deming.
 Elizabeth Lucas, who maried John Neff.
 Nancy Lucas, never married.
 William Lucas, married Sarah Lucas, a cousin.
 Swan Lucas, married three times, first wife was Permelia Emery, second was her sister, Catherine Emery. Third wife was ....
 Mary Lucas, married Warren Foster.
 Solomon Lucas, never married.
 John Lucas, married Elizabeth Hughes, daughter of Thomas Hughes.
 Thomas Lucas, married Rebecca Emery.
 Charles Lucas, never married.
 Jesse Lucas, married Rachel Garrett.
 Charles Alexander Lucas, married Catherine Barnhart.
 Richard Lucas, married Susan Neal.
 Isaac Lucas, married Lydia Hughes, granddaughter of Thomas Hughes, Sr.

The dates of birth of all the above children are included in the Swan Genealogy, which states that Martha Swan was born July 11, 1778, and married Thomas Lucas on December 17, 1795. Many descendants of this family are still living around Carmichaels and Rices Landing.

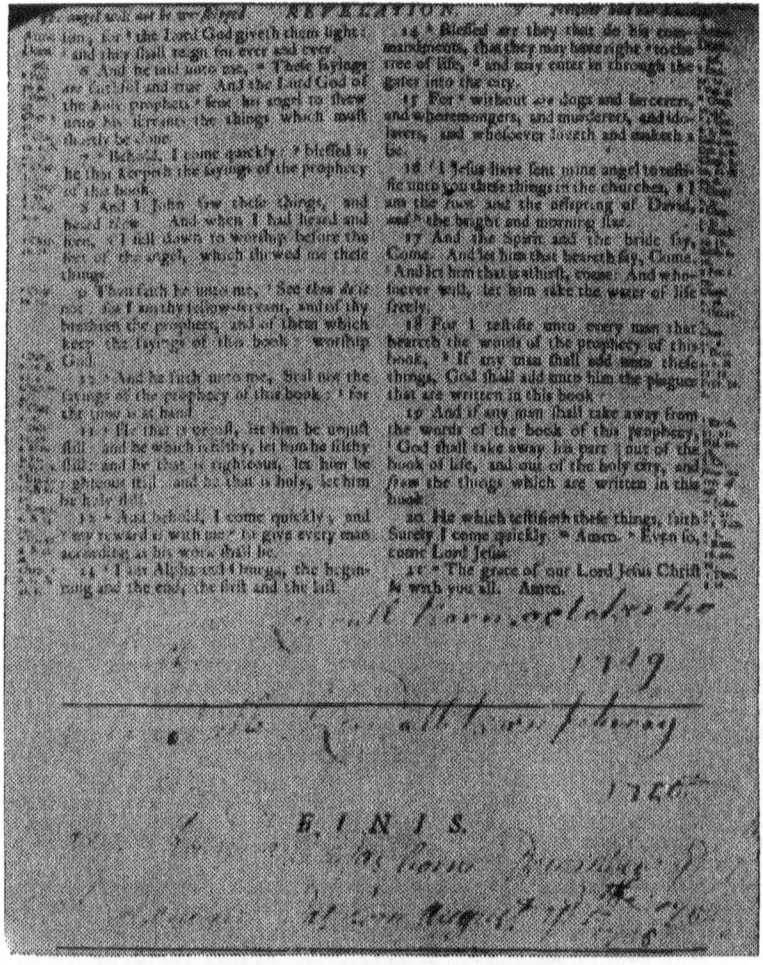

THE KENDALL FAMILY

Ann Lucas, daughter of Charles and Elizabeth (Evans) Lucas, was born in Maryland April 27, 1728. She married James Kendall, a fact explaining the Kendall entries in the Swan-Hughes Bible, and born out by the will of James Kendall, filed in Fayette County Will Book 1. pp. 129. This will was made June 13, 1797 and mentions the wife Ann (Lucas) Kendall. The children are named in the order found below and indicates their order of birth.

Children of James and Ann (Lucas) Kendall

1. Thomas Kendall, named eldest son, Swan-Hughes Bible shows he was born October 14, 1749.
2. Elizabeth Kendall, deceased, Bible record shows she was born February 3, 1751.

3. Mary Kendall, born December 17, 1752.
4. Sarah Kendall, born August 1, 1755.
5. Rena Kendall, not in the Bible record.
6. Jemima Kendall.
7. James Kendall.
8. John Kendall.
9. Samuel Kendall.
10. Anne Kendall, named as the wife of Richard Lucas. Richard Lucas is named executor of the will.

CAPTAIN JESSE PIGMAN

The search for the Family of Captain Jesse Pigman has met with the same ill success, which has accompanied the search for the names of his militia Company. There seems little doubt that he was a native of Maryland before he came to the Tenmile Country. Nor are there any deeds to show just where he settled after coming here about 1772-73, but it is fairly evident that he lived in the vicinity of Fort Swan, and very probably at the site of the present town of Jefferson. His wife was Sarah Lucas, born in Maryland October 12, 1734, a daughter of Charles and Elizabeth (Evans) Lucas, and through this marriage he was a brother-in-law of John Swan, Sr. Draper notes that "Captain Jesse Pigman commanded a company in 1774 (Dunmore's War) at Wappatonika and was an old Indian fighter. That he lived in the Muddy Creek Settlement." (Draper Mss 37-J-174.) Numerous pension applications tell of service under Captain Jesse Pigman, and show that he was one of the first captains to serve from this neighborhood in the Revolution, continuing in the service throughout the most of the War.

Captain Pigman and Captain Henry Enoch were ordered by General Edward Hand, commander at Fort Pitt, to raise two companies and go under Colonel Shepherd against Pluggy's Town in April, 1777. A letter from Colonel Zachquill Morgan to General Hand dated August 25, 1777, reports that Captain Pigman "marches this day with his company to take up the flour at Wheeling." (Draper Mss. NN-3 128-154.) A letter from Colonel Gibson at Fort Pitt dated October 22, 1777, regarding the drowning of Higginson, the noted Tory, later handcuffed and tumbled into the mouth of the Cheat River by Colonel Zach Morgan and others, with Colonel Morgan being ordered to Williamsburg for trial, says that "Captain Pigman and several other captains have resigned and will not go on the Expedition (being planned) without Colonel Morgan." (Draper Mss. NN-3-pp. 183.) The John Crawford Narrative (Draper Mss. NN-6-90 pp. 77-102.) says that in the Spring of 1777 that "on this day there were 30 men to meet at the house of Captain Pigman to march to Wheeling, for as that fort was expected to be attacked by the Indians as related by the honored old Dutch Tory W.............. William Crawford thought it wiser to warn Pigman and his company of their enemies nearer home and went with four of his neighbors to Pigman's home. Pigman was an active man in the defense of his Country, and on hearing what was going on, went to John Swan's Fort taking every man as he went along. He addressed them in this manner. There is at this time a large portion of our fellow citizens in arms against the Country, and there must be no skulking between parties. We will take you as friends or enemies and the choice lies with yourselves. On this representation no man hesitated but all turned out from Swan's Fort. They marched to meet the Tories not knowing as yet what had been the fate of Colonel Thomas) Gaddis and his party (of 40 Whigs), but when they met with him, the Tories, poor fellows, were scattered to the four winds and crying to the rocks and mountains to cover them from the vengeance of the Whigs." (pp.91.)

Captain Jesse Pigman appears to have gone on a trip to Kentucky sometime in 1780 for on October 6, 1780, he entered claim for 1000 acres of land in Jefferson County, Kentucky, to be situated on Clear Creek. (Book A-177). Later on June 12,1784, he claimed another tract of 4000 acres. (Book A. pp. 363.) But there is nothing to show that he ever went to this land. He was back in Pennsylvania on February 4, 1782, at the head of a militia company of 7 officers and 70 enlisted men, whose names he refused to the Pennsylvania authorities. Nothing has been found to show when he left here, nor to what place he removed. An important clue is found by the presence of an Adam Pigman with the Harrods of a later generation in the State of Indiana. It may be that Jesse Pigman followed the Herrods and Newlands to Kentucky and then to Clark County, Indiana. Another clue is the presence of Joshua Pigman, Sr., in Lower Clermont, County, Ohio, at an early date.

Because of the dearth of records which might locate the final settlement of Jesse Pigman, no certain record of his family is encountered. The petition for the State of "Westsylvania" contains the name of Jesse Pigman, Sr., with a number of his sons and may be reliable.

Children of Captain Jesse and Sarah (Lucas) Pigman

1. Jesse Pigman, Jr., listed in the petition to the Continental Congress for the setting up of a new State to be known as Westsylvania. A deed in Washington County shows that he married Lurene Newland, daughter of Adam and Mary (Harrod) Newland. Her mother was a sister of Captain William Harrod, and after the death of Adam Newland, married (2) Evan Shelby. (Deed Book 1-F-pp. 64 dated August 29, 1789.)
2. Charles Pigman, in the Petition to the Continental Congress.
3. Samuel Pigman, in the same petition.
4. Anna Pigman. The History of Ross and Highland Counties in Ohio (Williams Brothers 1880) says she was the wife of Alexander Crawford, who in 1796, with his wife and four children, floated down the Ohio from Greene County, Pennsylvania, until he came to the mouth of the Scioto River, thence up that river with his flat boat until he landed near Chillicothe. He was a millwright and helped to build the famous "Floating Mill." Alexander Crawford lived at the mouth of Waugh's Run on Deer Creek until 1779 at which time he removed to Fairfield Township and lived for another six years. In 1805, they removed to Paint Township, Ross County, Ohio, and set up a mill on Main Paint at Hewitts Crossing, where in 1823, Alexander Crawford was drowned attempting to cross the creek in a canoe. They were the parents of:
    1. Jesse Crawford, a soldier in the War of 1812.
    2. Alexander Crawford.
    3. Mary Crawford, married Nathan Thomas.
    4. Sarah Crawford, married James Greenfield.
    5. Elizabeth Crawford, married William Greenfield.
    6. Susan Crawford, married John McElvaine, lived in Illinois.
    7. Elsie Crawford, married Joseph Esthe.

THE HENRY VANMETER FAMILY

Who was Henry Vanmeter, Sr., and wife, Martha, and from whom did he purchase the land on which he settled in 1769, when he brought his family to the Tenmile Country with the Swans, Hughes, Hillers, and O'Neils? This was the party led by Thomas Gist, which settled on land sold by Indian Trader, John Owens, of Fort Pitt, in 1757 to Abraham Teagarden of Frederick County, Maryland. It was the land on which John Swan and Henry Vanmeter each built a fort, on separate branches of a run, variously known as Enoch's Run, Swan's Run, and now Pumpkin Run.

Virgil A. Lewis, former State Historian of Point Pleasant, West Virginia, in his "Pioneer Families of Mason County, West Virginia"

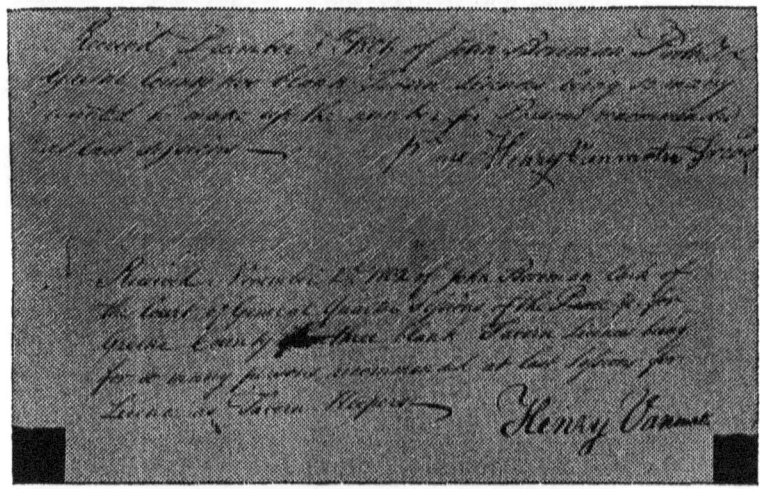

SIGNATURE OF HENRY VANMETER

published in the Weekly Register on April 17, 1886, says he was a son of Isaac Vanmeter, the later a son of John Vanmeter, the Indian Trader, and that he was born on the South Branch of the Shenandoah River in Hardy County, Virginia, in 1740. Smyth's "Duke-Shepherd-Vanmeter Family" suggests that he was a son of Henry Vanmeter, another son of John, the Indian Trader, and that he was born in Virginia in 1742. It looks as though both of these are wrong, because the evidence clearly shows that Henry Vanmeter and his wife Martha had children before 1750, probably as early as 1744-46. Their sons, Joseph and Jesse were grown men at the time of the Revolution, when both served as officers of the Frontier Rangers, and Joseph was old enough when the family settled on the Frontier in 1769 to take up land in his own right, adjoining the land of his father. Sarah Vanmeter, daughter of Henry and Martha, was twelve years old at the time of the migration, and born in 1758, according to her tombstone, appears to have been about the middle child of the thirteen, indicating that a brother or sister was probably born about 1745-6. The birth of Martha Vanmeter, the eldest daughter of which we have a record, on December 24, 1754, would just about disprove either of the historians above named, as they would leave Henry Vanmeter but 12 to 14 years of age at her birth. Comparing the ages of the other heads of families in the Swan-Hughes-Vanmeter Party, we find that John Swan was born in 1721, and Felix Hughes in 1723, we are inclined to believe that Henry Vanmeter was of a similar age and place his birth at about 1720, and his wife, Martha, a few years his junior. Unfortunately the Vanmeter Cemetery, which stood on the hill above their home, has been destroyed and no certain date can be given.

Mr. Lewis said in his history that Henry Vanmeter, Sr., was a son of Isaac Vanmeter, and grandson of John Vanmeter, the hunter and Indian Trader, while Smythe thought he was a son of Henry Vanmeter and grandson of John by his second wife, Margaret. Enough records are available to discount either claim. Henry Vanmeter of Greene County was too near the same age of either Isaac Vanmeter, who was born in Somerset County, New Jersey, in 1713, and Henry Vanmeter of Smythe's history, listed as born about 1717. Local historians may have furnished the clue, when they claimed that Henry and Jacob Vanmeter, the pioneer Greene County settlers were brothers. There is much to justify this assertion, which if true, would make Henry Vanmeter, Sr., of Greene County, the son of John Vanmeter and wife Margaret, rather than the grandson, and it would only substitute his record for the Henry of Smythe. Jacob Vanmeter, son of John and Margaret, is known to have been a brother of Elizabeth Vanmeter, wife of Thomas Shepherd, for in 1778, Captain Abraham Shepherd wrote to his brother, Colonel David Shepherd of the (West) Virginia Panhandle: "I have just had a visit with Uncle Jake on Muddy Creek." The families were close together before they left the Shenandoah Valley to settle in Greene County, Henry on Swan's Run and Jacob on Muddy Creek, and not more than a couple of miles apart. This is proven by the intermarriage of John Swan's Family with both branches of the Vanmeter Family. Henry Vanmeter's Family were members of Goshen Baptist Church, which had been established at Garards Fort by Jacob's Family. Another act one would expect from brothers is the record that shows Henry Vanmeter and Jacob Vanmeter with his older sons were arrested together for riot, when they made a show of force to hold this territory for Virginia in the border dispute, as shown by Pennsylvania records of 1772. A John Vanmeter, who was not the son of Henry Vanmeter, Sr., nor the brother of Jacob, was also with this party and is not identified. But there are weaknesses in this identification of Henry Vanmeter, Sr., and the answer remains unsolved.

The Vanmeters were all of the adventuresome stock, with a preference for lands "out beyond." They had preceeded Jost Hite into the Shenandoah and then followed him with their families to select choice sites there while it was still a wilderness, and certainly they were in the forefront of the migration to the Tenmile County. Henry Vanmeter was a loyal Virginian as long as there was any hope of having this section become a part of that state. He is even cited for having led a band of armed men to prevent the survey party from running the line. This band appears to have been the militia company of Captain Jesse Pigman, in which two sons of Henry Vanmeter, Joseph and Jesse, served as officers, the company that as late as 1782, refused to furnish the State of Pennsylvania a copy of their muster roll. However, after the line had been run and it was no longer a question of ownership of the territory, Henry Vanmeter, Sr., became resigned to it and took an active part in the affairs of his community. He became one of the first Commissioners of the new Washington County, served a term as an Associate Judge, and then when Greene County was formed was serving as County Treasurer when he died in 1803. During the Revolution he maintained a fort at his residence on Swan's Run. Early historians have joined his name with the name of John Swan, Sr., and mention but one fort, but

William Harrod, Jr., in his interview with Draper states there were two forts, Fort John Swan and Fort Henry Vanmeter, both on Swan's Run. Harrod would be well informed about it as he was raised on the adjoining farm and had to go to the forts with his parents in times of danger.

The old stone house that stood near Henry Vanmeters first settlement, and which was destroyed by a flash hurricane a few years ago, has been falsely pointed to as the original Henry Vanmeter Fort, but was in reality the house built by his son Jesse Vanmeter. The home of Henry Vanmeter was across the road from this site, about where the spring-house of the Price home now stands. There is no indication that Henry Vanmeter, Sr., lived in any other. He is buried on the hill above the house as is his wife and probably his son, Jesse, but no markers remain. A copy of the will of Henry Vanmeter, which was filed for probate in Greene County on February 10, 1803, is in Will Book 1. pp. 35, but the file on the Estate is missing from the box. Martha Vanmeter out-lived her husband by some 22 years and is named in the will along with 13 children. A number of grandchildren are named in the will, and there is a mistake in the will that names a son Abraham, which should have been copied as "Absolom."

Children of Henry and Martha (...................) Vanmeter

1. Joseph Vanmeter, named in the will as the eldest son, was lieutenant in Captain Jesse Pigman's Company of Frontier Rangers in 1777, according to the pension application of James Pribble. Later he served as captain of the same company. He patented the tract of land adjoining his father and which is now owned by Mr. Randolph. Cyrus Vanmeter of New Castle, wrote that Joseph had removed to Indiana and came back to Pennsylvania on a trip. The horse which he was riding came back to Indiana without its rider, and backtracking they found the body of Joseph on the Kentucky side of the Ohio. He had either been thrown and killed or had struck a low overhanging branch, as there were no signs of any struggle. The wife of Joseph Vanmeter was Elizabeth Aiken.

    ### Children of Joseph and Elizabeth (Aiken) Vanmeter
    1. Joab Vanmeter, mentioned in grandfather's will.
    2. Henry Vanmeter, mentioned in grandfather's will.
    3. Absolom Vanmeter, mentioned in grandfather's will. Married April 13, 1803, Tabitha Harris, lived in Athens County, Ohio.

2. Jesse Vanmeter, served as a lieutenant in his brother's company in 1779. His wife was Nancy Seals, a sister of Captain Seals, daughter of James Seals, Sr., and wife, Sarah. After the death of Jesse Vanmeter, his widow married Richard Morris, whose first wife had been her sister, Mary Seals. Jesse Vanmeter died about 1814, with his wife administering his estate. His father and mother had deeded to him before death of the father, a portion of the home plantation, on which tract he erected the stone house spoken of as Fort Vanmeter.

    ### Children of Jesse and Nancy (Seals) Vanmeter
    1. Sarah Vanmeter, married (1) Richard Morris, son of Ezekiel and Mary (Linvil) Morris. He died leaving a son Henry Morris, and his widow then married (2) William Kinkaid, son of Robert and Susannah (Powell) Kinkaid.
    2. Rachel Vanmeter, who married Jacob Ketcham.
    3. Jesse Vanmeter, Jr.
    4. Martha Vanmeter, married (1) Samuel Crago, son of Thomas and Priscilla (Thurman) Crago. Samuel Crago died leaving

Sarah Crago, who married William Bradford; Nancy Crago, wife of Jacob Ramer; Jesse and Henry Crago. Martha (Vanmeter) Crago then married William Kinkaid, and was his wife when he died April 9, 1843.
3. Rachel Vanmeter, daughter of Henry and Martha Vanmeter.
4. Absolom Vanmeter, son of Henry and Martha Vanmeter, was with his father on a trip to purchase land on the Kanawha River from Isaac Robertson. Settled in Mason County, (West) Virginia, about 1800. Mason County records say he was married in Greene County to his cousin Priscilla (Vanmeter). He died in Mason County, 1803. The marriage of Absolom and Priscilla (Vanmeter) is recorded in Berkley County, Virginia.

Children of Absolom and Priscilla Vanmeter

1. Rezin Vanmeter, born in Greene County in 1792, mentioned in his grandfather's will. He married Mary Peck and settled on his father's land in Mason County.
2. Absolom Vanmeter, Jr., born in Greene County in 1794, married in Mason County to Sarah Peck.
3. Patsie Vanmeter, born in Greene County in 1794, married John M. Swallow of Fayette County, Pennsylvania.

5. Rebecca Vanmeter, daughter of Henry and Martha Vanmeter.
6. Martha Vanmeter, daughter of Henry and Martha Vanmeter, was born December 24, 1754, and died in Greene County, Pennsylvania, October 24, 1836. (Tombstone says she was aged 81 years and 10 months.) She married about 1775-6, Richard Swan, son of John and Elizabeth (Lucas) Swan. He was born January 31, 1752, and died February 11, 1822. (Tombstone says he was 69 years, one month and 11 days old.) He died intestate, but his wife left a will to be found in Greene County Will Book 2. pp. 72.

Children of Richard and Martha (Vanmeter) Swan

1. Hannah Swan, born December 7, 1777. (Swan-Hughes Bible Record).
2. Thomas Swan, born May 1779. (Swan-Hughes Bible Record). He married Susannah Seaton. No children.
3. Mary Swan, born December 7, 1782. (Swan-Hughes Bible Record). She married John Prickett and they moved first to Kentucky and later to Iowa.
4. Elizabeth Swan, born June 20, 1784. (Swan-Hughes Bible Record). She married (1) George Alfree, after whose death she married (2) Isaac Soeffel, who died February 1830. Isaac Soeffel is mentioned in Martha (Vanmeter) Swan's will.
5. John Swan, died at the age of nineteen years.
6. Richard Swan. He married Sarah McCullough, daughter of John and Olivia (Morgan) McCullough. They went to Mason County, Virginia. She was born in 1798.
7. Martha Swan married David McClain.
8. Sarah Swan, born June 26, 1786, died July 11, 1852; married Thomas Hughes, born February 18, 1784, died May 8, 1867. Both are buried at Rices Landing, Pa. Thomas Hughes was a son of Thomas and Elizabeth (Swan) Hughes.
9. Ann Swan, born July 21, 1787, died November 2, 1840; married, about 1811, Judge Thomas Burson, born November 16, 1781, died January 11, 1864. He was a son of Edward and Elizabeth (Blackledge) Burson.
10. Rachel Swan married Samuel Vansickle.
11. Rebecca Swan married George Litzenberg and went to Knox County, Ohio.

12. Samuel Swan, born May 28, 1799, died July 1861, in Marion County, Kentucky. He married Susannah Vaun. Had no children.
7. Alice (Elsie) Vanmeter, daughter of Henry and Martha Vanmeter, was born about 1756, and died before 1800, in Greene County, Pennsylvania. She married, about 1780, Azariah Davis who was born February 12, 1756, and died in Knox County, Ohio, in 1839. His second wife was Mrs. Mary Harrington Smith, who died September 1, 1839.

Children of Azariah and Alice (Vanmeter) Davis

1. Henry Davis, born about 1781.
2. William Davis, born 1783, died 1859; married, 1806, Lydia Fields.
3. Azariah Davis, Jr.
4. Martha Davis, born December 7, 1784, died 1828; married James Harrington Smith.
5. Rebecca Davis, married, about 1796, Jacob Hanger; settled in Knox County, Ohio, in 1809.
6. Sarah Davis, married George Miller and went to Licking County, Ohio.
7. Elizabeth Davis.
8. Rachel Davis, married Uzzel Stephens of Knox County, Ohio.

8. Sarah Vanmeter, daughter of Henry and Martha Vanmeter, was born June 24, 1758, and died July 4, 1825 (tombstone record). She married, about 1772, Captain Charles Swan, son of John and Elizabeth (Lucas) Swan. He was born February 11, 1756, and died February 25, 1839 (tombstone record). Charles Swan was Ensign in Captain Jesse Pigman's Company in 1777, and later served as Captain in the militia company of his district in the War of the Revolution. (See Swan Records). Both are buried in the Swan Cemetery near Rices Landing.

Children of Charles and Sarah (Vanmeter) Swan

1. Henry B. Swan, born March 12, 1774, died at Grave Creek, West Virginia, March 26, 1823. He married, in 1796, Elizabeth Bowen, who later became the wife of William Burge.
2. John Swan, born November 15, 1776, drowned as a child in a spring on the homestead.
3. Martha Swan, born July 11, 1778; married, December 17, 1785, Thomas Higgins Lucas.
4. Elizabeth Swan, born December 28, 1779; married James Seaton, born October 26, 1780.
5. Thomas Swan, born November 13, 1781, died in Fayette County, Pennsylvania, April 11, 1845; married (1), March 3, 1809, Eleanor Anderson, born in 1788, died 1834. He married (2), November 16, 1837, Harriet Barclay.
6. John Swan, born December 10, 1783; married Mary Barclay and left on his wedding day. It is said he was unfortunate on a business deal and never returned to his wife.
7. Mary Swan, born December 6, 1785; married (1) William Collins, by whom she had one daughter, Ann Collins. Her second husband was Isaac Burson, son of Edward and Elizabeth (Blackledge) Burson.
8. Charles Swan, born December 9, 1787, died 1873 in Knox County, Ohio. He married, on January 24, 1811, Margaret Barclay, daughter of Hugh and Anne (Darragh) Barclay, who died in 1863.
9. Sarah Swan, born January 5, 1790, died in Findlay, Ohio. She married (1) Elias Flenniken, who died March 14, 1836,

aged 49 years. Her second husband was Rev. George Venneman. They lived at Findlay, Ohio.
10. Phoebe Swan, born March 17, 1791, died March 16, 1856; married, September 4, 1812, John F. McClain, son of Abijah and Permelia (Doty) McClain, born October 18, 1791, died in Knox County, Ohio, April 17, 1848.
11. William Swan, born April 4, 1794, died March 5, 1847; married Mary Moredock, daughter of James and Mary Moredock, who died in Wisconsin, October 14, 1863. He is buried at Garards Fort.
12. Richard Swan, born September 14, 1796, died in Uniontown, December 29, 1873; married, in 1818, Susan Gregg, born May 22, 1795, died June 22, 1866.
13. Jesse Swan, born July 1, 1798, died February 8, 1852. He married Phoebe Jennings. Went first to Ohio and then to Peoria, Illinois.

9. Phoebe Vanmeter, daughter of Henry and Martha Vanmeter. She married Ellis Thomas and settled on Grave Creek in Tyler County, West Virginia.
10. Elizabeth Vanmeter, daughter of Henry and Martha Vanmeter, married William Thomas, who died from wounds received from an Indian attack on his new home on Miracle Run, near Blacksville, West Virginia, on April 21, 1789.

Child of William and Elizabeth (Vanmeter) Thomas
1. William Thomas, born December 17, 1788; married Amelia Swan, daughter of William and Sarah (Harrod) Swan.

Children of William and Amelia (Swan) Thomas
1. Sarah Thomas, married William Lantz.
2. William Thomas, born January 6, 1812, died September 19, 1882; married Amelia Minor, born March 6, 1817, died July 28, 1879.
3. Jesse Thomas, never married.
4. Thomas Hughes Thomas, never married.
5. Artinacea Thomas, married Jacob Lantz.
6. Ellis Thomas, married Mary Francis.
7. Saul Thomas, married Mary Cooper.
8. Nimry Thomas, never married.
9. Cyrus Thomas, never married.
10. Remembrance Thomas, born March 13, 1828, married Mary Johnson.
11. Amelia Thomas.

11. Mary Vanmeter, daughter of Henry and Martha Vanmeter.
12. Henry Vanmeter, Jr., son of Henry and Martha Vanmeter, born in 1767, and went to Mason County, (West) Virginia, about 1800, and settled on land granted him in his father's will. His wife was Christena Vansickle, sister of Captain Anthony Vansickle.

Children of Henry Vanmeter, Jr., and Christena (Vansickle) Vanmeter
1. Rebecca Vanmeter, married Peter Peck and removed to Illinois.
2. John Vanmeter, married Litha Peck.
3. Jesse Vanmeter, married Catherine Peck.
4. Maria Vanmeter, married Zebulon Gibbs.
5. Rezin Vanmeter, married Catherine Oliver.

13. John Vanmeter, son of Henry and Martha Vanmeter, born in 1769. His wife was Millicent Kelly, daughter of Robert and Margaret Kelly, neighbors of the Vanmeters in Greene County, Pennsylvania. John Vanmeter went to Mason County, (West) Virginia, about 1800, with his brothers Henry and Absolom Vanmeter.

Children of John Vanmeter and Millicent (Kelly) Vanmeter

1. Mark Vanmeter, married Delilah Cooper.
2. Patsie Vanmeter, married Rev. Gideon Hinkle.
3. Polly Vanmeter, married Henry Devault.
4. Margaret Vanmeter, married James Johnson.
5. Elisha Vanmeter, married .... Stephenson, daughter of Captain James Stephenson.
6. Elizabeth Vanmeter, married Jacob Fisher.
7. Zilpha Vanmeter, married John Husher.
8. Nancy Vanmeter, married Dryden Watkins.
9. Permelia Vanmeter, married Samuel Edwards, Jr.

THE JACOB VANMETER FAMILY

Jacob Vanmeter, son of John and Margaret (Bodine(?)) Vanmeter, was born in Somerset County, New Jersey, March 17, 1723, and died in what is now Hardin County, Kentucky, on November 16, 1798. He married, in Virginia, Letitia Strode, daughter of James Strode of Frederick County. She was born August 3, 1725, and died December 25, 1799. In April 1769, he was granted land on the west side of the Monongahela River but may not have settled there immediately for, in 1770, Jacob and Letitia Vanmeter were among those who instituted the Great Bethel Baptist Church at, what is now, Uniontown, Pennsylvania. Then in December 1773, Jacob and Letitia Vanmeter, with their married children and a few others, organized Goshen Baptist Church in what is now Greene County, Pennsylvania. At that time they were living near Carmichaels close to what is known as Baily's School House. Here probably the following year they erected the Jacob Vanmeter Fort on the high ground just to the south of Bailey's School House, where at one time there was in existence one branch of Goshen Baptist Church, about which there was a cemetery, which has since disappeared. On September 18, 1779, Jacob Vanmeter, with his wife and most of their children—three sons and seven daughters with their husbands and wives—were granted certificates of dismission by Goshen Baptist Church, preparatory to leaving for Kentucky. They left soon after, in what was to prove an ill-fated journey to some, in a party reported to have consisted of 27 flat-boats, and ended their eventful journey in the Severn Valley, near the present Elizabethtown. Here, with several others of their party, they erected three forts, each about one mile from the other, at a time when they were they only inhabitants between the Ohio and the Green River.

Jacob Vanmeter served in the French and Indian Wars and was one of those chosen at Pittsburg, on May 16, 1775, to act as a Committee of Observation for that part of Augusta County, Virginia, lying west of Laurel Ridge. (Penna. Archives, Series VI, Volume 2, pp. 3). Other service in the Revolution is confusing because of a similarity of names, with another Jacob Vanmeter, son of Abraham, of Berkeley County, Virginia, also being a settler in the Severn Valley. (Berkeley County Will Book 1, pp. 348).

Family of Jacob and Letitia (Strode) Vanmeter

1. Eleanor Vanmeter, born October 1742—probably the eldest child of Jacob and Letitia (Strode) Vanmeter, and the only one of their children known to have remained in Greene County—married Jacob Cline, one of the first Virginia Justices of the Tenmile Country. On August 30, 1785, Jacob Cline received, by virtue of Virginia Certificates, two tracts of land totaling about 750 acres, which he had patented to him on March 4, 1786, under the titles of "Clinesburg" and "Jacob's Addition." It was on "Clinesburg" that Jacob Cline maintained the fort mentioned as Fort Cline

by William Harrod, Jr., in his interview with Draper. This fort as pointed out to the writer by the late Professor Waychoff, was situated on the knoll to the east of the marker erected to commemorate the site of the first Court of Greene County. This first Court was held in the home of Jacob Cline, and Professor Waychoff identified the spot by a row of shrubbery that grew along the ravine just back from the present marker, and visible twenty-five years ago. Waychoff remembered seeing the remains of the log cabin during his boyhood days spent in this vicinity. On a ramble at this site with this writer and Joseph Patton, Esquire, then owner of the tract, Waychoff also pointed out the location of the Cline cemetery in the old orchard at this place, which he said was destroyed when the new cemetery at the Church was established. The cabin, in which the first Court was held, was of hewed logs and built after the need of forting was past. It was the stopping place also of a bi-weekly mail route from Cumberland, Maryland, to Wheeling, West Virginia. It was here that Jacob Cline died, about 1802, leaving a will recorded in Greene County Will Book 1, pp. 29.

Children of Jacob and Eleanor (Vanmeter) Cline

1. Peter Cline, married Nancy Inghram, daughter of Arthur and Olive (Smith) Inghram.
2. Jacob Cline, Jr.
3. Isaac Cline, born 1777, died October 3, 1838, in Elizabeth Township, Miami County, Ohio. He married Olive Inghram, daughter of Arthur and Olive (Smith) Inghram, who died in Miami County, Ohio, in 1851.

Children of Isaac and Olive (Inghram) Cline

1. John Cline, born October 3, 1804, died August 20, 1873.
2. Hannah Cline, married Levi DeWeese.
3. Minerva Cline, married Levi Hart.
4. Mary Cline, married Joseph Martin.
5. Jacob Cline, died 1833.
6. Elizabeth Cline, married, September 5, 1834, Isaac Dye, Miami County, Ohio.
7. Letitia Cline, married Patterson Crayne.
8. Isaac Cline, Jr., born March 8, 1818; married Elizabeth Knight, born January 10, 1818.
9. Inghram Cline
10. William Cline.

4. Letitia Cline, daughter of Jacob and Eleanor (Vanmeter) Cline.
5. Eleanor Cline
6. Elizabeth Cline, daughter of Jacob and Eleanor (Vanmeter) Cline, born 1776, died in Miami County, Ohio, January 6, 1853; married John Minor Dye, born August 24, 1773, died in Elizabeth Township, Miami County, Ohio, on April 1, 1842.
7. Ruth Cline, married Nathan Veach; went to Knox County, Ohio.

2. Abraham Vanmeter, born June 13, 1744; was killed a short distance from his father's fort in Kentucky, in 1781. His wife was Elizabeth Cline. Abraham Vanmeter served with Captain William Harrod's Company in 1780. His estate was appraised in Hardin County, December 4, 1781. There were four sons and four daughters to the union.

Children of Abraham and Elizabeth (Cline) Vanmeter
1. .... Vanmeter.
2. .... Vanmeter.
3. .... Vanmeter.
4. .... Vanmeter.
5. Catherine Vanmeter; married Bladen Ashby.
6. Sarah Vanmeter; married .... Edelin.
7. Elizabeth Vanmeter; married Jacob Swank.
8. Letitia Vanmeter; married Thompson Ashby.

3. Rebecca Vanmeter, born in September 1746, married Edward Rollins, and, with her husband, was one of the founders of Goshen Baptist Church. They went to Kentucky with her father and settled in the Severn Valley, where Edward Rollins died. His widow then married Enoch McKenzie. Will of Edward Rollins (Rawlings) Hardin County, Kentucky, filed July 26, 1796. (W. B. A., pp. 28). Enoch McKenzie died about 1805. (W. B. A., pp. 238).

Children of Edward and Rebecca (Vanmeter) Rollins
1. Stephen Rollins, one of the executors.
2. Elizabeth Rollins, married .... Hart.
3. Ann Rollins, married Josiah Hart.
4. Letitia Rollins, married (1) Silas Hart; (2) Andrew Fairleigh. (see later).
   ### Children of Andrew and Letitia (Rollins) Fairleigh
   1. Rebecca Fairleigh, born May 24, 1794, married Miles Chenowith.
   2. Sarah Fairleigh, married Isaac Chenowith.
5. Rebecca Rollins.

4. Elizabeth Vanmeter, born about 1748, married John Swan, Jr., son of John and Elizabeth (Lucas) Swan. He was born May 7, 1744, according to the Swan-Hughes Bible. The pathetic death of John Swan, Jr., while floating down the Ohio with the Jacob Vanmeter party, is told in both Evans and Waychoff. His record is also given under the family of John and Elizabeth (Lucas) Swan. In that article we used a record taken from McAdams' "Kentucky Pioneers," (pp. 58) in which the will of John Swan was reported filed in Hardin County, Kentucky, Will Book A. pp. 11, where the will was reported probated on February 18, 1783. After writing that history of John Swan, Jr., a copy of the will of John Swan, Jr., has been placed in our hands, which shows it was filed in Will Book A. pp. 11, in Lincoln County, Kentucky. There are several points of difference to be noted in the comparison of this record and the previous record printed under the heading of John Swan Family. First the date of the will is shown to have been July 17, 1780, probably at the time he was preparing for the journey to Kentucky. And the wording of the will plainly discovers that the son Thomas Swan was living at the time John Swan made the will, and not born posthumously as reported. Here is a copy of the will of John Swan, Jr., as shown in Lincoln County, Kentucky, records.

> "In the name of God, Amen, I, John Swan of Kentucky County, being sound in body and perfect memory, Blessed be God, do this day, it being the 17th day of July in the year of our Lord, one thousand seven hundred and Eighty, make this my last Will and Testament in manner following, that is to say—first, I give and bequeath to my son John the choice of three hundred acres out of mine laying on the North fork of Elkhorn with Mill seat, Mill stones, and Mill Irons; also I give and bequeath to my son Joel the next choice of three hundred acres of land across; also I give to my son Thomas three hundred acres—this makes up the nine

hundred acres of land.

I give and bequeath to my son or daughter that my wife is Big with if-born and if not born the two hundred acres to be equal divided amongst the three boys; also I give to my daughter Elizabeth two hundred and fifty acres of land that John may clear out, laying on Salt River waters, and one Negro girl Hanner; also I give to my daughter Lettie two hundred and fifty acres of land that John may clear out to the halves laying on the waters of Salt River, and also one Negro girl Judy; also I give to my wife one Negro woman, Beck, and her rising generation to my boys shall be equally divided and all my..........................
I give to my wife to raise my children and my money I give all to my wife but three thousand Pounds to my three sons above mentioned I do make and ordain my wife Richard Swan, Jacob Vanmeter Executrix and executor of this my will in trust for the intent and purpose in this my will contains and make my living funds of this my last will take care and on the same performed according to my intent and meaning to-wit: In witness I the said John Swan as witness I set my hand, sign, sealed, and delivered in the presents of you all by me."

                                    JOHN SWAN   (SEAL)

MARY M. HENTON (X)   Her Mark.
REBEKAH RAWLINGS (X)   Her Mark.
MARGARET HAYCROFT.

According to the Kentucky "Domesday Book" SHS. 21:271:

"1776 Certificate issued for 1000 acres—John Swan, Jr., this day claimed a preempt of 1000 acres of land at the State price in the District of Kentucky on account of marking and improving the same in the year 1776, lying on the South Fork of Rolling Fork of Salt River about two or three miles from the mouth of the said Fork about two miles from where a large Buffaloe Road crosses the Rolling Fork to include his improvement satisfactory proof being made to the Court, they are of the opinion that the said Swan has a right to a preempt of 1000 acres of land to include the above location and that a certificate be issued accordingly."

NOTE: At the time of filing of the will of John Swan, Lincoln County covered almost a half of southern and western Kentucky. While it would seem that John Swan, Jr., did live in what was then Nelson County, and later became Hardin County, it is likely that copies of the will were filed in both places.—H. L. L.

After the death of John Swan, Jr., his widow married (2) Thomas McNeil. He died leaving two children born of this union. Elizabeth then married, July 7, 1783, John Ventrees, a widower with six children. He had been a member of Goshen Baptist Church before going to Kentucky. A son was born by this last marriage. John Ventrees died about 1802-03, leaving a will showing that Elizabeth survived him.

Children of Elizabeth (Vanmeter) Swan-McNeil-Ventrees

1. John Swan, married Margaret Coburn.
2. Joel Swan.
3. Elizabeth Swan, married Colonel Solomon Bleandenburg, proprietor of the present town of that name on the Ohio River. In early days the place was a noted crossing point for persons moving West.
4. Thomas Swan, married Ruth Rollins.
5. Letitia Swan, born about 1778, died in Hardin County, Kentucky, October 10, 1845. She married (1) December 10, 1795, Andrew Fairleigh, who died March 1, 1829. His widow married (2) April 7, 1831, James Williams. She is buried with her first husband at Elizabethtown, Kentucky.

Children of Andrew and Letitia (Swan) Fairleigh

1. William Fairleigh, born April 16, 1797, died September 16, 1865, in Meade County, Kentucky; married, November 4, 1819, Elizabeth Enlow, born November 3, 1803, died June 17, 1867. She was a daughter of Isom and Mary (Brookes) Larue-Enlow.
2. Thomas Fairleigh, married, March 24, 1824, Elizabeth Nall.
3. Elizabeth Fairleigh, born February 6, 1804, died February 3, 1875; married (1) on October 6, 1820, Leonard B. Parker, born May 23, 1786, died May 1841. She then married (2) October 22, 1844, Miles Hart Thomas, born August 28, 1802, died April 1, 1878.
4. George Fairleigh, born March 23, 1806; married, August 19, 1833, Elizabeth Qu nn, born July 21, 1816.
5. Andrew Fairleigh, Jr., married Jane Talbott; went to St. Joseph, Missouri.
6. Mary Fairleigh, born September 16, 1811, died April 15, 1855; married Robert Kennedy, born December 18, 1800, died May 6, 1861.
7. John Fairleigh, lived near Jacksonsport, Arkansas.

6. Daniel McNeil, married Eleanor Hackley. (See Will Book A, pp. 161. John Ventrees, Hardin County, Kentucky).
7. Susan McNeil. (See Will Book A, pp. 161, John Ventrees, Hardin County, Kentucky).
8. Charles Ventrees.

5. Susan Vanmeter, born July 2, 1750; married Rev. John Garard (Gerrard) one of the Jacob Vanmeter party, and a former member of Goshen Baptist Church. After he arrived in Kentucky he was installed as first minister of the Second Baptist Church, organized on June 17, 1781, near Hynes Station. In May 1782, he was captured by the India s and he was never heard from again.

Children of Rev. John and Susan (Vanmeter) Garard

1. Hetty Garard, born 1769, died October 17, 1839; married, February 24, 1789, Hardin Thomas.
2. Sarah Garard; married, December 1, 1789, Adam Miller.
3. Margaret Garard, born July 27, 1774, died August 13, 1822; married, March 28, 1793, Samuel Gooden, born 1764, died September 26, 1816.
4. Letitia Garard, born January 2, 1776, died September 21, 1856; married, April 21, 1796, Thomas Miller, born February 11, 1773, died July 11, 1842.

6. Ailsey Vanmeter, born October 25, 1752, married (1) James Rhodes. After his death she married (2) .... McIntyre. She died in Grayson County, Kentucky.

Children of Ailsey Vanmeter

1. Samuel V. Rhodes.
2. Henry Rhodes.
3. Jacob Vanmeter Rhodes.
4. John Rhodes.
5. Isaiah Rhodes.
6. Josiah Rhodes.
7. Jesse Rhodes.
8. Letitia Rhodes.
9. Susan Rhodes.

7. Rachel Vanmeter, born in Virginia about 1754, married Isaac Prickett (or Pritchard).

8. Mary Vanmeter, born February 11, 1757, died June 29, 1832, married (1) David Henton, one of the organizers of Goshen Baptist Church at Garards Fort. He was drowned on the way to Kentucky with the Jacob Vanmeter Party. His widow then married (2) Major William Chenowith, born 1760, died 1828.

Children of Mary Vanmeter

1. Hetty Henton, married .. .. Briscoe.
2. John C. Henton.
3. William Chenowith, Jr.
4. Abraham Chenowith, born 1782, died 1861, married Rachel Chenowith.
5. Jacob Vanmeter Chenowith.
6. Isaac Calvert Chenowith, born July 6, 1789, died July 23, 1858, married Sarah Elizabeth Fairleigh, daughter of Andrew and Letitia (Rollins) (Hart) Fairleigh.
7. Miles Hart Chenowith, born July 7, 1791, died 1846 near St. Joseph, Missouri. He married May 23, 1811, Rebecca Fairleigh, born May 24, 1794, died September 22, 1857. She was a sister of Sarah Elizabeth Fairleigh.
8. Hardin T. Chenowith.
9. Letitia Vanmeter Chenowith, married .... Hawkins.
10. Ruth Chenowith, married .... Farman.
11. James Hackley Chenowith.

9. Isaac Vanmeter, born February 2, 1759, died in Grayson County, Kentucky, November 4, 1840. He married (1) Mrs. Martha Hoagland, widow of Captain Henry Hoagland, and they had five children. The Office of Pensions shows that on October 22, 1832, Isaac Vanmeter appeared at Court in Hardin County and asked for a pension, saying he was 73 years of age on February 1. He gave his service as having enlisted in January 1778, under Captain William Harrod, in the western part of what is now Pennsylvania but was then claimed by Virginia. They shortly entered the service of George Rogers Clark of Virginia, at Redstone, on the Monongahela. William Lynn was his Major and John Swan his Lieutenant. From Redstone they went down the Monongahela and Ohio. He was discharged at Kaskaskia with the rest of Harrod's men after eight months' service during which several Indian towns were taken. He returned to the place of his enlistment by way of the Falls of the Ohio. In the Spring of 1780 he removed to the State of Kentucky, and in the Fall of the same year, in August, he volunteered under John Swan for three weeks against the Indians. He was discharged and again in the Fall of 1782 he volunteered. Witnesses were John Helms, Sr., of Hardin County, and Jacob Vanmeter, and the statement was signed by John Morris, a Justice of Peace.

Isaac Vanmeter was married twice and his second wife made application for a pension, supplying her marriage bond as evidence. This stated that "a marriage about to be solemnized between Isaac Vanmeter and Jane Carson, for which a license is given this day, dated April 4, 1825," and was signed by Isaac Vanmeter and Aaron Hart. She lived in Elizabeth Town, Hardin County, at the time—May 6, 1853—saying that Isaac Vanmeter had died in Grayson County, November 4, 1840. On April 12, 1853, she had stated she was 67 years of age.

Children of Isaac and Martha Vanmeter

1. Mary Vanmeter (Polly), married .... Hicks.
2. Letitia Vanmeter, married .... Hubbard.
3. Matilda Vanmeter, married .... Porter.

4. .... Vanmeter.
5. .... Vanmeter.
10. Margaret Vanmeter, born in Virginia December 27, 1759, died April 12, 1843; married, September 9, 1778, Samuel Haycroft, born in Virginia September 11, 1752, died in Kentucky October 15, 1823. Samuel Haycroft was prominent in Kentucky politics, built a Station, was sheriff of Hardin County in 1802, Judge in 1804, and served in the Legislature in 1804. He had served in the Revolution.

Children of Samuel and Margaret (Vanmeter) Haycroft

1. Nancy Haycroft, married .... Ventrees.
2. John Haycroft.
3. Letitia Haycroft.
4. Amelia Haycroft, married Jonathan Shepherd on April 18, 1807.
5. Mary Haycroft, married Jacob Chenowith on January 7, 1808.
6. Elizabeth Haycroft, married .... Morrison.
7. Rebecca Haycroft, married Atkinson Shepherd on January 14, 1811.
8. Margaret Haycroft, married .... Williams.
9. Samuel Haycroft, Jr.
10. Presley Neville Haycroft, Presbyterian Minister.

11. John Vanmeter, born about 1761; he married Rebecca Strode, daughter of Samuel Strode, who patented a tract of land next to Henry Vanmeter. He and Rebecca were among the organizers of Goshen Baptist Church. He accompanied his father's party on the voyage to Kentucky. A Kentucky source says he married Diana Holtzclaw, but this may have been a second marriage.

Children of John Vanmeter

1. Moses Vanmeter.
2. Strode Vanmeter.
3. Cyrus Vanmeter.
4. John Vanmeter, Jr.
5. Nathan Vanmeter.
6. Zillah Vanmeter, married .... Kellar.
7. Cynthia Vanmeter, married .... Kellar.
8. Etersa Vanmeter, married .... Ross.
9. Letitia Vanmeter, married .... Swank.

12. Jacob Vanmeter, Jr., known as "Valley Jake," was born in Virginia October 4, 1762, died in Meade County, Kentucky, February 27, 1852; married, November 11 (or 16), 1786, Elizabeth Rhoads, born October 6, 1770, died in 1852. The Bible record of their children came through their daughter, Mary Jane Lewis, and is now owned by Mr. Charles B. Lewis of 436 West 90th Street, Los Angeles, California.

Children of Jacob and Elizabeth (Rhoads) Vanmeter

1. Sarah Vanmeter, born February 2, 1788; married, November 7, 1807, ...
2. Abraham W. Vanmeter, born April 1, 1789; married, May 19, 1814, Sally ....
3. John Vanmeter, born January 20, 1791.
4. Joseph H. Vanmeter, born September 29, 1792, died in infancy.
5. Thomas R. Vanmeter, born May 8, 1794; married, November 12, 1818, Harriet ....
6. Susan B. Vanmeter, born April 9, 1796.
7. Jacob V. Vanmeter, born January 15, 1798; married, June

21, 1821, Susan ....
8. Henry R. Vanmeter, born June 3, 1800; married Hopey B. .... on September 3, 1823.
9. Daniel B. Vanmeter, born May 6, 1802.
10. Nathaniel W. Vanmeter, born March 8, 1804.
11. Miles C. Vanmeter, born November 15, 1806.
12. Elizabeth Vanmeter, born December 23, 1808; married, January 15, 1826, John Calvin.
13. Mary Jane Vanmeter, born October 11, 1811; married, January 15, 1828, William Lewis, born in Culpepper County, Virginia, April 1, 1797, son of William Lewis, Sr.
14. David R. Vanmeter, born November 17, 1813; married, August 13, 1840, Ann Mariah ....

13. William Vanmeter; married, 1795, Phoebe Hart.

CAPTAIN ANTHONY VANSICKLES

When Henry Vanmeter went to purchase land in Mason County, (West) Virginia, he was, as he states in his will, accompanied by his son Absolom, and Zachariah Vansickles, and probably the latter's son, Anthony Vansickles. Captain Anthony Vansickles was born in 1771, and married on April 29, 1799, to Patsie Vanmeter. He bought land on Old Town Creek in Mason County, where he removed in 1800, and became prominent as a Captain of Militia in the War of 1812. His wife Patsie Vanmeter was one of the daughters of Henry and Martha Vanmeter, probably Mary Vanmeter in the list of Henry and Martha Vanmeter's children. The indentification is strengthened by a report that she was also known as Polly Vanmeter, a nickname for Mary, while Patsie usually is a nickname for Martha, and we know that their daughter, Martha Vanmeter, married Richard Swan.

Children of Anthony and Patsie (Vanmeter) Vansickles

1. Henry Vansickles, did not go to Mason County.
2. Samuel Vansickles, married Betsy Swan, daughter of Richard and Martha (Vanmeter) Swan.
3. Jesse Vansickles, member of militia in 1823.
4. Abraham Vansickles.
5. John Vansickles.
6. Eli Vansickles.
7. Patsie Vansickles.
8. Joseph Vansickles.

THOMAS HUGHES

Because Thomas Hughes was identified chiefly with the Tenmile Country located about Jefferson, and because he is better known than his father, it is perhaps best to place his family in that section and under a separate heading. This is also justified because of the many direct descendants still living in Greene County, Pennsylvania.

Thomas Hughes was born May 5, 1749, in Loudon County, Virginia, a son of Felix and Cynthia (Kaighn) Hughes, natives of Donegal, Ireland, who had settled in Virginia about 1739. He was a grandson of Thomas and Briget (O'Neil) Hughes. Tradition says that Thomas Hughes took to the Wilderness at an early age and became a roving hunter. This may be true, or he may be confused with his uncle, Thomas Hughes, who was indeed a famous hunter. But it is evident that Thomas Hughes acquired an early education in woodcraft, for his later experiences on the frontier, and his seeming disregard of danger from raiding Indians, could only have been the result of his early training. He had the advantage of a good education, which was later to aid him in business and politics. After settling at Jefferson, which he helped lay out on a part of his land, he entered a variety of interests, such as milling, distilling, farming, and tanning. He was one of the first to recognize the importance of the coal outcroppings in his locality, and put his slaves to work at mining this product. From them he demanded a certain amount of production, which when attained, was rewarded with freedom.

During the Revolution Thomas Hughes served as a Major of the Frontier Rangers, holding a strict allegiance to Virginia. His service in this capacity is attested in the pension application of James Pribble, who served under his command in 1777. (Nat. Arch. W. 3, 595.) His loyalty to the cause of Liberty is shown by his willingness to accept a reduction to the rank of Captain, when it placed the Country in a better position for defense in 1782. This was done at a time when many other officers became disgruntled and resigned their commissions, rather than accept a reduction in rank. This action came when his company was ordered to rendezvous at Fort Jackson for service in Colonel William Crawford's proposed Sandusky Expedition. However, an alarm at Wheeling sent the company of Thomas Hughes to that place, instead of the disaster on Sandusky Plains.

When Thomas Hughes first came to the Tenmile Country, he settled at what is known as the "Old Town" at Carmichaels, but on July 24, 1780, he deeded this tract of land to James Carmichaels, who is reported to have lived at the site of Jefferson at the time. Sale of this land is reported in Washington County Deed Books, but no sale from Carmichaels to Hughes is on the record to confirm the tradition that Hughes and Carmichaels traded land, however on April 17, 1785, he obtained a warrant for 175 acres under the title of "Partridge Harbour," where on he was later to lay out a portion of a town which he called Jefferson. Then on September 4, 1790, he bought another tract across the Tenmile from his patented land, from Isaac and Hannah (Bowen) Heaton. The Heatons and Thomas Hughes were of different political beliefs, with Colonel John Heaton a strong supporter of Alexander Hamilton. Colonel Heaton became the owner of a tract of land next west of Thomas Hughes and he proceeded also to lay out a number of lots, calling his own town Hamilton. A bitter controversy raged between the two men which was not shared by the people, who had settled in the village which sprang up between the two plans, and they gave the name of Harmony to their section. This feud must have only extended to the political lives of the two men for the family intermarried in private life.

On February 20, 1770, Thomas Hughes married Elizabeth Swan, daughter of John and Elizabeth (Lucas) Swan, with whom the Hughes Family had made their journey to the Tenmile. She was born in Maryland on February 28, 1751, and died at Jefferson in 1825. Thomas Hughes died there February 4, 1823. They are buried in the old Presbyterian Cemetery, west of the stone house built by Thomas Hughes, and their markers are readable. A section of this old cemetery in a corner next to the present church, was set aside by Thomas Hughes for the burial of his slaves, whose huts stood a little to the north of the cemetery.

Much of the family history of Thomas Hughes is found in the well-preserved Swan-Hughes Bible, which passed down to his wife. We are indebted to M. Marie Perrin Lemley of Los Angeles, for locating the Swan-Hughes Bible at the home of Thomas Hughes of Palms, California. Mrs. Lemley, a direct descendant of Thomas Hughes, began a genealogy of the Hughes Family many years ago, and much of the record of the family is taken from her files. She has graciously shared it with the writer. Mrs. Lemley now lives at Long Beach, California.

The Thomas Hughes Family

1. Elizabeth Hughes, born November 2, 1771. When she was 17 years of age she married John Manning, who had served as ensign in Captain Joseph Vanmeter's Company of Rangers in 1779. He moved with his family to the Benjamin Stites Settlement on the Ohio and later to Kentucky, where he left a large family. No record of this family has been given.
2. John Hughes, born May 7, 1774, died July 23, 1844, married Mary Rex, born 1773, died 1849. She was a daughter of George and Margaret (Kepler) Rex, and with her husband, is buried at Jefferson. They were married August 27, 1795.

Family of John and Mary (Rex) Hughes

1. Elizabeth Hughes, born July 26, 1796, died at Yam Hill, Oregon, August 29, 1865, married about 1816, John Buckingham, born July 13, 1793, son of John and Mary (Bell) Buckingham. They went to Missouri in 1848, and from there went overland to Oregon.

Children of John and Elizabeth (Hughes) Buckingham

1. George Buckingham, born November 17, 1817, died at Mt. Vernon, Ohio, in 1844, married 1838, Elizabeth Campbell, born 1820, died 1885.
2. Mary Buckingham, born January 3, 1820, married Thomas Hines, born May 1, 1819. They went to Oregon with her parents, and lived at Forest Grove.
3. Hiram Heaton Buckingham, born July 13, 1821, married February 4, 1844, Margaret Kincaid, born May 8, 1822, died 1847. They are buried at Yam Hill, Oregon.
4. John Buckingham, born January 1824, married and went to Texas.
5. Nancy Buckingham, born October 1827, married Lewis Kimes, who was drowned enroute to Oregon, while crossing the Missouri River in 1853.
6. Elizabeth Buckingham, born January 1829, married .... Riley. Stayed in Missouri.
7. Mariah Buckingham, born April 1831, married Robert Pittock, publisher of the "Oregonian."
8. Hannah Buckingham, born March 1833, died 1845.
9. Charles Buckingham, born May 7, 1835, married October 2, 1862, Adeline Landers. She died and he married (2) Effie Trowbridge. He died June 1, 1895.
10. Melissa Buckingham, born November 1837, married Vincent Roberts.

2. Margaret Hughes, born January 12, 1798, died in Menard County, Illinois, December 8, 1863, married December 8, 1818, John Hyatt Virgin, born April 9, 1798, died October 14, 1828, son of Eli and Nancy (Hyatt) Virgin.

Children of John and Margaret (Hughes) Virgin

1. Eli Virgin, born January 25, 1821, died in an accident July 1856.
2. Mary Virgin, died young.
3. George Virgin, born May 10, 1827, married February 16, 1852, Eliza Ann Enlow, born December 18, 1837, died at Pekin, Illinois, November 18, 1898.
4. John Virgin, born September 16, 1830, married (1) in

1856, Emily Gibbs, who died December 21, 1891. He married (2) Mattie Conway. He died in Illinois November 18, 1898.
  5. Margaret Ruth Virgin, born 1832, married Egbert Davis. They went to Des Moines, Iowa.
  6. Maria Virgin, born February 10, 1834, died at Charitan, Iowa, married December 12, 1859, Lewis Bonnett.
3. Thomas Hughes, born April 8, 1800, died June 3, 1872, married December 13, 1821, Elizabeth Hickman, born May 1, 1803, died July 3, 1872, daughter of Solomon and Elizabeth (McCombs) Hickman.

Children of Thomas and Elizabeth (Hickman) Hughes
  1. Mary Ann Hughes, born October 7, 1822, died July 5, 1904, married February 10, 1839, Uriah Zollars, born January 5, 1818, died August 16, 1889, son of Jacob and Hannah (Wise) Zollars. They removed to Oscaloosa, Iowa. They were the grandparents of Marie Perrin Lemley.
  2. Elizabeth Hughes, born at Clarksville in 1804, died February 27, 1910, in Knox County, Ohio, married March 5, 1845, Thomas Odbert, born at Beallsville, died in Knox County, Ohio, June 12, 1908.
  3. Margaret Hughes, born January 27, 1827, died May 18, 1903, married January 7, 1851, William Buckingham, born February 21, 1828, died February 8, 1886, son of William and Mary (Barnard) Buckingham. They lived near Zollarsville, Pennsylvania.
  4. Alexander Hughes, born 1831, died in Marion County, Iowa, January 2, 1898, married (1) Martha West, married (2) at Bussey, Iowa, Barbara Hupp.
  5. William Hughes, born March 20, 1834, died December 28, 1896, married November 25, 1857, Margaret (Rex) Hickman, born June 27, 1832, died June 18, 1904.
  6. John Hughes, born January 19, 1836, died at Mt. Pleasant, Iowa, 1913 married January 31, 1864, Jane Mitchenor, born August 21, 1843, daughter of William and Mary (Way) Mitchenor.
  7. Henrietta Hughes, born January 25, 1849, died at Canton, Ohio, May 1923, married December 4, 1870, Montgomery D. Alexander, born September 15, 1840, died December 21, 1922.
4. Nancy Hughes, born March 3, 1802, married Benjamin Montrees.
5. John Hughes, born February 1805, died in Knox County, Ohio, married Mary Ann Haver.

Children of John and Mary Ann (Haver) Hughes
  1. George Hughes, married Amanda Bell, daughter of William and Nancy (Hanger) Bell.
  2. Mary Hughes, born January 1, 1826, died March 4, 1925, married December 17, 1856, Hiram Bell, born October 6, 1833, died at Centerburg, Ohio, July 6, 1900.
  3. Elizabeth Hughes, married Virgil Mitchell, Utica, Ohio.
  4. Priscilla Hughes, married G. W. Porterfield, Blandenburg, Ohio.
6. George Hughes, born December 9, 1807, died March 24, 1881, married (1) 1829, Sarah Elston, who died September 7, 1850, married (2) Margaret Weaver, born July 23, 1827, died 1926 in Knox County, Ohio.

Children of George and Sarah (Elston) Hughes

1. Mary Hughes, born 1831, died 1908, married March 10, 1854, Cary Bell, born November 11, 1830, son of Jacob and Rachel (Letts) Bell.
2. Catherine Hughes, born 1835, died March 1908, married Scott Vance, Newark, Ohio.
3. John O. Hughes, born 1837, died 1867, Clifton, Iowa.
4. Thomas Hughes, born July 20, 1838, died 1923, Lacona, Iowa, married August 1, 1887, Elizabeth Davis, who died February 6, 1891.
5. Hughes Hughes, died young.
6. Amelia Hughes, died young.
7. Sarah Hughes, born 1850, died 1926, Eagle Lake, Texas, married Joseph Ulery.

7. Mary Hughes, born September 25, 1809.
8. Catherine Hughes, born December 27, 1811, married Amos Gordon.
9. Lindsey Hughes, born February 26, 1814, died September 30, 1844, Harpster, Ohio.
10. Charles Hughes, born August 22, 1816, died November 9, 1892, married (1) September 21, 1843, Catherine McQuen, who died June 13, 1856, at Jefferson. He married (2) May 26, 1858, Elizabeth Hill, who died November 26, 1887, aged 56 years, 4 months, 14 days.

Children of Charles Hughes

1. John Swan Hughes, born July 4, 1844, died November 29, 1909, married April 22, 1869, Lizzie Babbitt, daughter of William and Augusta (Higginbotham) Babbitt.
2. George Hughes, born July 22, 1846, died young.
3. Mary Elizabeth Hughes, born February 19, 1848, died January 31, 1916, married on October 4, 1868, Hamilton Riggle, who died March 11, 1882, at Bedford, Iowa, married (2) September 1883, Noah Emerick of Webb, Idaho.
4. Anna Hughes, born July 23, 1850, died aged 4 years.
5. Millie Hughes, born September 6, 1854, died February 16, 1909, at Delaware, Oklahoma, married December 25, 1879, David A. Bumgarner.
6. Maria Hughes, born February 23, 1856, married March 29, 1882, B. Frank Kendall of Jefferson, Pennsylvania.
7. Hannah Hughes, born May 31, 1863.
8. Anna May Hughes, born January 9, 1866.

11. Barnet Hughes, born October 12, 1819, died at Jefferson, March 30, 1884, married Permelia Young, born March 25, 1825, died September 12, 1890, daughter of Christopher and Rachel Young.

Children of Barnet and Permelia (Young) Hughes

1. John H. Hughes, married Mary Bell, daughter of David and Lettie (Huss) Bell, who died in 1906.
2. George Hughes, married Anna Crayne, daughter of Stephen and Mary (Bell) Crayne.
3. Rachel Hughes, died September 7, 1860, aged 17 years, 4 days.

12. Mariah Hughes, born February 12, 1822, died January 11, 1900, married December 13, 1840, Joseph McNeely, born December 26, 1814, died October 7, 1860, at Jefferson.

Children of Joseph and Mariah (Hughes) McNeely
1. Infant son, born October 13, 1841, died same day.
2. Mary Ann McNeely, born December 26, 1842, died August 3, 1843.
3. Nancy McNeely, born April 30, 1845, died May 6, 1866.
4. John Hughes McNeely, born April 30, 1845, died September 19, 1850. (twin)
5. George A. McNeely, born June 10, 1848, died April 18, 1875, married Sarah Dean.
6. Harriet Zelma McNeely, born February 11, 1851, died 1888, married Isaac Dean.
7. Henrietta McNeely, born November 24, 1853, died February 27, 1854.
8. Charles N. McNeely, born December 19, 1855, died February 27, 1932, married Martha Lancaster, born June 1, 1862.
9. Joseph M. McNeely, born February 19, 1859, died March 1898.

3. Mary Hughes, born December 10, 1776, died at Jefferson, May 31, 1855, married June 2, 1796, James Lindsey, born May 31, 1772, died February 21, 1816, son of James and Judith (Moore) Lindsey.

Children of James and Mary (Hughes) Lindsey
1. Thomas Hughes Lindsey, born February 4, 1797, died July 17, 1810.
2. James Lindsey, born December 6, 1798, died May 28, 1830, married May 14, 1818, Mary Shroyer, whose second husband was Edward Parkinson. He died July 18, 1878 and is buried in the C. P. Cemetery at Jefferson.

Children of James and Mary (Shroyer) Lindsey
1. Hiram Lindsey, born October 27, 1823, Prothonotary of Greene County in 1869, married in 1847, Sarah Minor, daughter of Phillip Minor.
2. Maria Lindsey, born 1823, died 1916, never married.
3. Elizabeth Lindsey, married Lorenzo Dow Inghram.

3. Elizabeth Lindsey, born February 6, 1801, died in Ohio, married (1) July 6, 1820, Hiram Heaton, born March 19, 1797, died August 15, 1832. She then married John M. Swallow and went to Ohio.
4. John Lindsey, born March 11, 1803, died May 28, 1865, married October 17, 1826, Anna Collins, born July 30, 1811, died July 18, 1885, daughter of William and Mary (Swan) Collins.

Children of John and Anna (Collins) Lindsey
1. Judge James Lindsey, born November 21, 1827, died September 1864, married in 1855, Sarah Inghram, daughter of Arthur and Elizabeth (Cathers) Inghram.
2. Mary Lindsey, born February 25, 1832, died February 21, 1875, married Lawrence L. Minor, born July 11, 1823, died January 11, 1897.
3. William C. Lindsey, born December 7, 1834, killed while leading a charge at Hagerstown, Maryland, July 6, 1863, as captain of Co. A. 4th Penna. Cavalry.
4. Minerva Lindsey, married (1) Rev. Freeman, (2) Dr. A. J. McGlumphey.
5. Maria Lindsey, never married.
6. Elizabeth Lindsey, born June 30, 1839, died November

AND ITS PIONEER FAMILIES 211

  24, 1862, married .... Gillespie.
7. Rachel Lindsey, married Rev. J. B. Hale.
8. Judge Remembrance Lindsey, Fayette County, Pennsylvania, married .... Wilson.
9. John Lindsey, twin of Remembrance.
10. Emma Lindsey, born February 11, 1846, died June 24, 1876.
11. George Lindsey, born March 26, 1852, died September 11, 1853.

5. Alexander Lindsey, born April 30, 1805, died June 5, 1845, married May 30, 1829, Susan Kincaid, born February 12, 1812, died at New Castle, Indiana in 1870. She married (2) John Shroyer.

Children of Alexander and Susan (Kincaid) Lindsey

1. James M. Lindsey, born June 15, 1830, married Sophia Winters.
2. Mary Lindsey, born December 20, 1831, married Thomas F. Teagarden.
3. William M. Lindsey, born January 3, 1834, buried in Indiana.
4. Barnet Neel Lindsey, born November 12, 1837, died January 21, 1914, married July 8, 1866, Isabella Houldsworth.
5. Hiram Lindsey, born September 4, 1835, killed at the Battle of Charles City Cross Roads, June 30, 1862. Thomas Markle, Steubenville, Ohio.
6. Martha Ann Lindsey, born August 12, 1839, married

6. Remembrance Lindsey, born April 5, 1807, died June 4, 1849, married Mary Luse, born September 12, 1818, died February 19, 1907, daughter of Eleazer and Hannah (Buckingham) Luse. Both are buried in Green Mount Cemetery.

Children of Remembrance and Mary (Luse) Lindsey

1. Elizabeth Lindsey, born June 18, 1831, died June 3, 1898, married February 5, 1857, David Crawford, born June 18, 1825, died March 28, 1886, son of David and Nancy Crawford.
2. Hannah Lindsey, married .... Sweeney.
3. George Lindsey, born September 3, 1835, died November 13, 1861.

4. Frank Lindsey, went to Ohio.
5. James Lindsey, born April 11, 1840, died April 29, 1899, married (1) Mary Woods. He married (2) Mary C. Sayers, born December 18, 1849, died April 13, 1870.
6. Martha Lindsey, born September 20, 1843, died November 15, 1861.
7. Fanny Lindsey, married Captain Benjamin Ross, went to Silver Mines, Colorado.

8. Remembrance Lindsey.
7. Rachel Lindsey, born March 8, 1809, died un-married.
8. Mary Lindsey, born February 13, 1811, died March 18, 1837, married July 30, 1833, James Workman Hailman, born November 8, 1809, died July 3, 1860.

Child of James W. and Mary (Lindsey) Hailman
1. George W. Hailman, married Mary Dickey.

9. Sarah Lindsey, born December 7, 1812, died September 10, 1813.
10. Forsythe Lindsey, born August 16, 1814, died September 4, 1814.

4. Sarah Hughes, born January 27, 1779, died at Holbrook, October 29, 1858, married October 8, 1795, Mathias Roseberry, born January 11, 1772, died December 2, 1851, son of Michael and Mary (Maple) Roseberry.

Family of Mathias and Sarah (Hughes) Roseberry
1. Mary Roseberry, born April 10, 1797, died July 19, 1892, married (1) Robert Scott. She married (2) Archibald Guthery, born March 3, 1779, died Auguest 23, 1845, son of Archibald and Rebecca (Phillips) Guthery. His first wife was Elizabeth Lemley.

Children of Mary (Roseberry) Scott-Guthery
1. John Roseberry Scott, born May 23, 1819, died March 6, 1844, married February 28, 1841, Mary McClain.
2. Mathias Scott, born February 1, 1821, married Loretta Phillips.
3. Sarah Scott, born February 24, 1824, died October 7, 1864, married Cephas Guthery, born September 10, 1818, died January 18, 1898.
4. Catherine Scott, born September 27, 1826, married Thomas Odenbaugh.
5. Thomas Hughes Scott, born March 1, 1830, died July 8, 1911, married July 28, 1860, Eliza McGlumphey, born April 27, 1840, died October 2, 1901.
6. Mary Jane Guthery, born September 23, 1836, died April 28, 1927, married December 9, 1854, George Remley, born September 20, 1828, died February 23, 1917.
7. Martha Guthery, married Henry Church.

2. Elizabeth Roseberry, born June 24, 1799, married Shadrack Mitchell, son of S h a d r a c k and Margaret (Rinehart) Mitchell (?).
3. Martha Roseberry, born October 7, 1801, died December 14, 1866, married February 24, 1820, Ephriam Morris, born November 18, 1797, died June 21, 1868, son of James and Phoebe (Sayers) Morris.

Children of Ephriam and Martha (Roseberry) Morris
1. Ignatius Morris, born May 12, 1821, died October 29, 1821.
2. Thomas Morris, born February 16, 1823, died July 18, 1864, while in Civil War. He married Elizabeth Glenn.
3. Asa Morris, born April 11, 1826, married (1) Elizabeth Zimmerman, who died December 22, 1864. He married (2) June 6, 1874, Mary Alice Campbell, born January 1, 1853.
4. Sarah Roseberry Morris, born July 9, 1829, died Feb-

ruary 20, 1918, married (1) September 12, 1849, Alexander Black, born 1822, died April 9, 1856. She married (2) November 16, 1856, George Hoskinson, born October 22, 1811, died July 24, 1884, son of Thomas and Nancy (Watson) Hoskinson.
5. Captain John Morris, born March 28, 1832, died January 5, 1922, married (1) November 11, 1854, Sarah Church, who died March 10, 1878. He married (2) November 30, 1879, Elizabeth Phillips, and married (3) October 28, 1905, Mrs. Mary V. Bresock.
6. Mathias Lot Morris, born November 12, 1834, died June 24, 1913, married November 24, 1860, Sarah Ullom, born February 22, 1840, died November 12, 1910, daughter of Daniel and Anna (Johnson) Ullom.
7. Martha Morris, born August 19, 1837, died July 17, 1865, married October 6, 1859, George Bayard, born April 11, 1832, son of Samuel and Hannah (Mitchell) Bayard.
8. James F. Morris, born January 29, 1840, died May 18, 1928, married November 9, 1864, Maria Bayard, born January 26, 1843, died January 26, 1926.
9. Phoebe Morris, born November 11, 1842, died November 17, 1912, married March 29, 1861, Jesse Ullom, born June 20, 1836, died March 2, 1901, brother of Sarah Ullom.
10. Catherine Mary Morris, born July 7, 1848, married January 28, 1864, Henry A. Scott, born April 11, 1842, died April 9, 1894, son of James and Charlotte (Strawn) Scott.

4. Sarah Roseberry, born January 27, 1804, died July 31, 1882, married December 16, 1834, Frank Gray, born September 23, 1802, died February 26, 1844, son of David W. Gray.

Children of Frank and Sarah (Roseberry) Gray
1. Lindsey Gray, born November 6, 1825, married March 21, 1847, Letta Glenn, married (2) in 1860, Susan McClain, who died in 1901.
2. Dr. David Gray, born February 22, 1827, died at Muscatine, Iowa, November 6, 1877. He married September 21, 1851, Mary Palmer, born February 18, 1821.
3. Elizabeth Gray, born March 25, 1829, died March 30, 1916, married December 10, 1846, Garrett Garrison, born 1824, died 1895.
4. Frank A. J. Gray, born February 11, 1831, died March 3, 1905, married May 31, 1854, Addie Palmer, born December 17, 1832, died December 28, 1908.
5. Sarah Gray, born November 12, 1833, died at Oak Park, Illinois. She married Sumner Root.
6. Lucinda Gray, born November 11, 1835, died July 3, 1869, married October 13, 1857, C. H. Wilson, born April 25, 1834. Merchant at Washington, Iowa.
7. Abasha Gray, born November 21, 1837, married July 4, 1856, Dr. James Burroughs.
8. Catherine Gray, born November 28, 1840, married Dr. Benoni Parkinson.
9. Caroline Gray, born March 8, 1843, died January 7, 1908, married 1859, James M. McClelland. She married (2) Francis L. Pierce of Lakins, Kansas.

5. Thomas Hughes Roseberry, born May 13, 1806, died in Ver-

non County, Missouri, March 29, 1891, married March 19, 1829, Mary Hill, born February 3, 1810, died January 3, 1895, a daughter of Colonel Rees and Nancy (Heaton) Hill.

Children of Thomas and Mary (Hill) Roseberry
1. Barnet H. Roseberry, born April 6, 1831, died August 3, 1905, at Woodland, California. His wife was Mary High.
2. Amanda Roseberry, born October 25, 1833, died May 20, 1911, married November 6, 1858, Dr. Abraham S. Tinsman, born September 18, 1831, died December 16, 1911, Clark County, Missouri.
3. James Roseberry, born March 20, 1836, died in California in 1906, married in 1871 Emma Jane Adamson, born 1845.
4. Sarah Roseberry, born March 12, 1838, married September 30, 1857, William Hiller, son of William and Charlotte (Milliken) Hiller, Clark County, Missouri.
5. Mathias Roseberry, born December 14, 1840, killed at Fort Blake, Oklahoma, in the Civil War.
6. Thomas Roseberry, born July 17, 1842, died in California in 1905, married Viola Lowery. Land Registrar in California for 25 years.
7. Rees Heaton Roseberry, born April 21, 1844, died at Leavenworth, Kansas, July 23, 1924, married Sue Wayland.

6. Nancy Roseberry, born November 1, 1808, died March 15, 1875, married December 13, 1827, Thomas Hill, born October 5, 1805, died May 24, 1875, son of Samuel and Elizabeth (Cathers) Hill.

Children of Thomas and Nancy (Roseberry) Hill
1. Sarah Hill, born October 18, 1830, died October 8, 1896, at Bloomington, Illinois. She married (1) Dr. Alexander Reed, (2) Michael J. White.
2. Elizabeth Hill, born January 5, 1833, died April 17, 1919, married James Steele, who died at Waynesburg in 1896.

7. Mathias Roseberry, born February 28, 1811, died at Harvard Nebraska, in 1878, married at Jefferson, Pennsylvania, Sarah McClain, who died in 1850.

Children of Mathias and Sarah (McClain) Roseberry
1. Thomas Roseberry, married Julia Ann Stewart.
2. Minerva Roseberry, born March 4, 1840, married November 2, 1867, John Orndorff, of Harvey's, born April 9, 1839, died August 9, 1914, son of William and Salome (Wisecarver) Orndorff.
3. Mary Roseberry, born 1842, married William Galentine, son of John and Sarah (Ritenhouse) Galentine.
4. John Roseberry, born 1844, married Mary Ann Robinson, daughter of James and Sarah (Anderson) Robinson.
5. Sarah Roseberry, born 1846, married 1871, Benjamin F. Phillips, son of Levi and Sarah (McCracken) Phillips, born July 10, 1833.
6. Lucinda Roseberry, born February 26, 1849, married December 23, 1865, Clifford Burleigh, born December 26, 1845, died January 22, 1871, at Cameron, West Virginia.

8. Catherine Roseberry, born June 14, 1814, died in Marshall County, West Virginia, 1852. She married Joshua Burleigh, son of Jacob and Mary (Hughes) Burleigh.

   Children of Joshua and Catherine (Roseberry) Burleigh
   1. Sarah Burleigh.
   2. James Burleigh, married Lucy Price.
   3. Frank Burleigh.
   4. Elizabeth Burleigh, married Jerry Clemmons.

9. John Hughes Roseberry, born March 31, 1816, married Mary McClain, daughter of David and Martha (Swan) McClain.

   Children of John Hughes and Mary (McClain) Roseberry
   1. Hughes Roseberry, married Hettie Miles.
   2. James Roseberry, married .... Johnson.
   3. Martha Roseberry, married Frank Miles.
   4. David Roseberry, married .... Caldwell.
   5. Sarah Roseberry, married .... Johnson.
   6. John Roseberry.
   7. Hiram Roseberry.
   8. Ellsworth Roseberry.

10. Lucinda Roseberry, born April 16, 1819, died March 22, 1901, at Tonica, Illinois. She married about 1839, John Vannatta, born June 1817, died May 1858.

    Children of John and Lucinda (Roseberry) Vannatta
    1. Sarah Vannatta, born May 17, 1840, died February 16, 1918, married Jonathan Gregory who died in Libby Prison.
    2. Samuel Vannatta, born September 14, 1841, died November 15, 1912, married April 2, 1864, Elizabeth Strawn, born April 11, 1841, died at Winterset, Iowa, November 15, 1917.
    3. James Lindsey Vannatta, born May 29, 1843, died June 17, 1868, married Samantha B. Paul, born April 29, 1844, died May 1919.
    4. Mathias Roseberry Vannatta, born July 31, 1845, died in the service June 5, 1864.
    5. John C. Vannatta, born December 25, 1847, died March 17, 1903, married Nora Courtright.
    6. Thomas Vannatta, died at the age of 8 months.
    7. Katherine Vannatta, born September 15, 1851, died June 9, 1878, married Dewitt Snow.
    8. Benjamin Vannatta, born October 10, 1853, married (1) Rachel York, (2) Libbie Caverly, (3) Clara Beckwith.
    9. William Vannatta, born November 28, 1855, married Mary Morehead, who died at Geneva, Illinois, January 26, 1921.

11. James Roseberry, born October 10, 1823, died un-married, when kicked by a mule on an overland trip to the Gold Fields in California.

5. Martha Hughes, born May 11, 1781, died October 31, 1857, married June 6, 1799, Barnet O'Neil, born April 23, 1776, died September 15, 1860. He was a son of Barnet O'Neil, Sr., who died about 1779, leaving sons Barnet and Henry and a daughter Sarah O'Neil.

Family of Barnet and Martha (Hughes) O'Neil
1. Thomas O'Neil, born January 3, 1800; married, January 7, 1821, Mary McCall.
2. Henry O'Neil, born March 30, 1802, died February 26, 1856; married, July 28, 1825, Rhoda Hiller, born March 30, 1799,

died 1868 at Red Bluffs, California. She was a daughter of William and Margaret (Myers) Hiller.

Children of Henry and Rhoda (Hiller) O'Neil

1. Barnet O'Neil, born October 20, 1827, died in 1870 at Red Bluffs. He married, March 31, 1858, Caliphunia Johnson, born in Missouri.
2. Martha O'Neil, born May 17, 1830; married, August 15, 1847, John Minor. They went to Peoria, Illinois.
3. William O'Neil, born November 11, 1832, died August 1, 1872, at Red Bluffs.
4. Margaret O'Neil, born January 5, 1835; married, March 21, 1863, James D. Potts.
5. Elizabeth O'Neil, born October 12, 1838; married, April 30, 1863, Remembrance Hughes Campbell, born December 3, 1839. Lived at Santa Cruz, California.
6. Mary O'Neil, born November 14, 1841, died May 6, 1915; married, December 3, 1868, William Sample Wilcox, born March 24, 1832, died June 5, 1892, at Red Bluffs.

3. Lucretia O'Neil, born October 11, 1805, died December 9, 1807.
4. Elizabeth O'Neil, born November 19, 1806, died December 6, 1884, in Appamoose County, Iowa. She married, April 3, 1828, Jesse Swan, born August 31, 1800, died February 8, 1851; son of William and Sarah (Harrod) Swan. They lived at Carmichaels, Pennsylvania.

Children of Jesse and Elizabeth (O'Neil) Swan

1. Neil Swan.
2. William Swan, married Ellen ....
3. Mary Swan.
4. Henry Swan.
5. John Swan.
6. James Neil Swan, born August 12, 1837; married (1) Mary Maulding, who died February 4, 1877; married (2) 1879, Mary F. Andrews.
7. Jesse Swan, Jr., died in Des Moines, Iowa, 1913.
8. George Swan, married Ann Willis.
9. Emeline Swan.
10. Sarah Swan.
11. Martha Swan.
12. Remembrance Swan.

5. Mary O'Neil, born May 4, 1806, died December 6, 1876; married, May 21, 1829, James Wiley, born April 8, 1809, died March 4, 1889, son of Joseph and Elizabeth Wiley.

Children of James and Mary (O'Neil) Wiley

1. Barnet Wiley, born September 11, 1843, died March 12, 1922; married Margaret Ullom, born April 24, 1845, died August 20, 1917, at Cameron, West Virginia.
2. Elizabeth Wiley, born June 14, 1830, died March 30, 1871; married, October 27, 1860, Henry Church, who died in 1911.
3. Martha Ann Wiley, born September 6, 1834, died April 1, 1912; married, March 23, 1854, Eli Orndorff, born February 25, 1828, son of William and Salome (Wisecarver) Orndorff.
4. Remembrance Wiley, born November 2, 1838, married Abigail Heaton.
5. Katherine Wiley, born August 19, 1841, died October 20, 1868.

6. Barnet O'Neil, born September 5, 1810, died April 12, 1899, at Appamoose County, Iowa. He married, September 25, 1831, Margaret, daughter of William Kincaid.

   Children of Barnet and Margaret (Kincaid) O'Neil
   1. Martha O'Neil, died October 26, 1860; married, December 27, 1855, George Teagarden.
   2. William Kincaid O'Neil, born December 19, 1833, died December 13, 1883; married, September 19, 1872, Sarah Haver.
   3. Mary O'Neil, born August 27, 1836, died April 12, 1913; married, April 2, 1864, George Lloyd, born March 25, 1837, died February 20, 1929.
   4. Sarah O'Neil, born February 21, 1839, died July 31, 1913; married, January 1, 1856, George Haver, born May 10, 1833, died August 2, 1914.
   5. Jane O'Neil, born February 14, 1842, died May 27, 1863.
   6. Elizabeth O'Neil, born November 11, 1843; married, March 11, 1891, Wells Peppers.
   7. Catherine O'Neil, born December 20, 1846; married, February 7, 1866, George Teagarden.
   8. Emma O'Neil, born January 1850; married, February 25, 1869, Eldred Glover.

7. Sarah O'Neil, born March 22, 1813, died June 15, 1893; married, December 7, 1837, William Sharpnack, born July 9, 1810, died January 18, 1892, son of Samuel and Nancy (Crago) Sharpnack. Both are buried at Hewitt's Church.

   Children of William and Sarah (O'Neil) Sharpnack
   1. Martha Sharpnack, born April 20, 1838, died March 2, 1885; married Napoleon Wishart, born December 2, 1838, died January 1, 1893, son of James and Mary Ann (Hawthorn) Wishart.
   2. Samuel Sharpnack, born November 30, 1839, died January 20, 1919; married Elizabeth Moredock, born February 17, 1840, died May 9, 1911, daughter of George and Priscilla (Anderson) Moredock.
   3. Barnet Sharpnack, born 1841, died 1913; married Priscilla Moredock, born 1850, died 1908, daughter of Simon and Jane (Reynolds) Moredock.
   4. Dr. Thomas Hughes Sharpnack, born November 20, 1843, died April 11, 1902; married, June 23, 1870, Cynthia Moredock, born June 7, 1852, died August 16, 1887, daughter of James and Hannah Moredock.
   5. Nancy Sharpnack, born October 11, 1845; married, July 31, 1870, G. M. Church, born February 13, 1845, son of Elijah and Ann (Moore) Church.
   6. Elizabeth Sharpnack, born June 24, 1849, died February 18, 1886; married June 30, 1872, J. D. Flenniken, born June 14, 1847, died February 1, 1929, son of Elias and Mary Ann (Kerr) Flenniken.
   7. Margaret Sharpnack; married Calvin House, son of Samuel and Martha (Leonard) House.
   8. Sarah Sharpnack, born September 27, 1853, died June 18, 1919; married T. N. Swan, born August 20, 1858, died June 4, 1936, son of William and Lucinda (Shroyer) Swan.
   9. William F. Sharpnack, born 1853, died 1903; married Anna B. Walton, daughter of Samuel and Sarah Ann (Hildebrand) Walton.

8. John O'Neil, born November 24, 1815, died September 2, 1868; married, July 6, 1835, Sarah Moredock, daughter of George and Priscilla (Anderson) Moredock.

Children of John and Priscilla (Moredock) O'Neil
1. Priscilla O'Neil, born April 25, 1838, died March 26, 1929; married, December 8, 1866, Israel Shultz, born January 30, 1843, died December 2, 1918, son of Henry and Delilah (Shriver) Shultz. They went to La Harpe, Illinois.
2. Minerva O'Neil, born June 29, 1842; married, December 13, 1865, Andrew Jackson Young, son of Christopher and Rachel (Boyd) Young. He was born December 28, 1837, died January 27, 1910.
3. Mary Ellen O'Neil, born August 8, 1853; married John Lawson Bane, born March 13, 1858, son of Nathan and Mary (McClenathan) Bane.

9. James O'Neil, born January 29, 1818, died March 21, 1867; married, July 17, 1840, Eliza Ann McElvaney, who died November 12, 1896, at Carmichaels, Pennsylvania.

Children of James and Eliza Ann (McElvaney) O'Neil
1. Barnet O'Neil, born October 11, 1841, died same day.
2. Martha O'Neil, born September 29, 1842, died March 11, 1898.
3. Susan O'Neil, born July 29, 1845, died July 11, 1909; married March 21, 1871, David Kerr, born 1843, died 1920.
4. Aliff Shepherd O'Neil, born September 10, 1848, died 1916.
5. Elizabeth O'Neil, born January 26, 1851, died June 6, 1883; married, March 21, 1879, Hiram Kerr, born 1847.
6. Margaret O'Neil, born January 12, 1854; married, March 17, 1885, J. S. Burwell.
7. Virtue O'Neil, born April 8, 1857, died July 4, 1899.
8. Ella O'Neil, born April 8, 1859, died in 1919.

10. Nancy O'Neil, born March 6, 1820; married September 15, 1842, John Veon.
11. Remembrance O'Neil, born June 9, 1822; married (1), March 21, 1844, Eleanor Thomas, born August 4, 1824. After her death he married, July 29, 1866, Mary Neff, born March 10, 1832.

Children of Remembrance O'Neil
1. Catherine O'Neil, born June 8, 1845; married J. S. Courtier.
2. Joshua O'Neil, born December 20, 1846; wife's name was Mary ....
3. Barnet O'Neil, born December 20, 1846 (twin), died September 15, 1896; married, November 15, 1871, Mary Catherine McCall, who died at Greenbush, Illinois, September 9, 1883.
4. Martha O'Neil, born February 10, 1849; married, August 4, 1872, Albert E. Jacobs, born April 12, 1846.
5. Aliff S. O'Neil, born March 2, 1851; wife's name was Anne ....
6. Ellen O'Neil, born March 21, 1853; married, May 11, 1872, Spencer Huffman, born September 26, 1847, died February 5, 1899, son of Joseph and Sarah (Hunt) Huffman.

7. John O'Neil, born April 29, 1867; married Linda ....
   8. Elizabeth O'Neil, born January 4, 1871; married, May 28, 1892, Benjamin F. Myers, born April 12, 1869.
   9. Louemma O'Neil, born September 5, 1874; married John Corcoran, Windom, Kansas.
12. Aliff Shepherd O'Neil, born September 4, 1824, died November 21, 1863; married, March 13, 1851, Lucy Thomas, born 1830, died February 20, 1885, daughter of Joshua and Catherine (Livengood) Thomas.

Children of Aliff Shepherd and Lucy (Thomas) O'Neil

   1. Emma O'Neil, born February 3, 1852.
   2. Elizabeth O'Neil, born March 23, 1854, died July 2, 1873.
   3. Rev. J. Thomas O'Neil, born January 17, 1857, died November 17, 1926; married Rhoda Gregg, born November 12, 1855, daughter of Aaron and Phoebe Gregg.
   4. Remembrance O'Neil, born April 13, 1859; married Martha May Garwood, daughter of Obediah and Ellen Garwood.
   5. Ella O'Neil, born February 9, 1872; married John Shape, son of Samuel and Patience (Adelman) Shape.

NOTE: Because there are many living persons of the fourth generation of the Thomas and Elizabeth (Swan) Hughes, whose privacy might be imposed upon by publication of personal data we deem it proper to omit that generation, beginning with the family of Thomas Hughes, Jr. It will be quite easy for the descendants of the balance of Thomas Hughes Sr's., family to connect up with the information given in these pages.

   6. Thomas Hughes, Jr., born February 18, 1784, died at Rices Landing May 8, 1867; married Sarah Swan, born June 26, 1786, died May 11, 1852; daughter of Richard and Martha (Vanmeter) Swan. They are buried in the old cemetery, overlooking the Locks at Rices Landing.

Children of Thomas and Sarah (Swan) Hughes

   1. Barnet Hughes, married (1) Sarah Walton, daughter of John and Sarah (Paul) Walton. He married (2) Catherine Woodcock.
   2. Elizabeth Hughes, married (1) Simeon Swan, born January 15, 1812, son of Henry and Elizabeth (Bowen) Swan. She married (2) John Lucas, born September 12, 1809, died January 31, 1859; son of Thomas H. and Martha (Swan) Lucas. They went to Iowa.
   3. Lindsey Hughes, born 1812, died December 10, 1869, married Clementine Crago.
   4. Samuel Hughes, married Maria Clark.
   5. Maria Hughes, born December 31, 1818, died April 10, 1873; married William Kincaid, born in 1819, died July 10, 1885.
   6. John Hughes, born November 7, 1820, died December 24, 1887; married Cassandra Hufty, born June 25, 1825, died August 15, 1906; daughter of John and Cassandra (Lucas) Hufty.
   7. James Hughes, died May 1, 1889, married Mary Kline, on January 1, 1857. She was born in 1834, and died March 25, 1875.
 7. Nancy Ann Hughes, born September 2, 1785, died near Carmichaels August 2, 1836; married about 1804, James Curl, who died at Carmichaels September 15, 1851; son of John and Susan Curl.

Children of James and Nancy Ann (Hughes) Curl

1. Mary Curl, died May 7, 1832; married George Wiley.
2. Elizabeth Curl, born July 6, 1805, died August 29, 1874; married January 1824, William Kerr, born August 12, 1803, died October 21, 1891; son of James and Elizabeth (Boke) Kerr. Buried at Laurel Point Cemetery.
3. John Curl, born 1808, died February 1892; married Sarah

McMinn, born 1815, died 1844; a daughter of Robert and Rachel (Rice) McMinn.
4. Thomas Curl, married Mary Ann Flenniken.
5. Remembrance Curl, married Emeline Anderson, born 1820, died 1916.
6. Susan Curl, born October 18, 1818, died November 12, 1882; married William Armstrong, born February 19, 1816, died April 13, 1889. Buried at Glades.
7. James Curl, born in 1820, drowned in 1860; married Levina Smith, born 1825, died 1906.
8. Hiram Curl, born March 1, 1826, died January 25, 1892; married 1849, Sarah Ann Rice, born February 25, 1830, died February 23, 1902. Buried at Laurel Point.
9. Alexander Curl, born April 24, 1828, died September 13, 1908; married November 8, 1847, Sarah O'Neil, who died at Browning, Missouri in 1888.

8. James Hughes, born January 19, 1788, died July 11, 1861; married Margaret Hiller, born 1794, died January 26, 1833; daughter of William and Margaret (Myers) Hiller.

Children of James and Margaret (Hiller) Hughes

1. Mary Hughes, born 1813, died May 21, 1855; married November 29, 1838, Joseph Milliken, born 1812, died September 14, 1854, son of John and Mary (Campbell) Milliken.
2. Charlotte Hughes, born 1815; married Ambrose Stout.
3. Lucy Hughes, born 1817; married William Gordon, removed to Ohio.
4. Thomas Hughes, born March 28, 1819, died February 16, 1899; married in 1866, Susannah Loar, born August 31, 1840, died July 8, 1925; daughter of George and Mary (Gump) Loar. They are buried at Rogersville.
5. William H. Hughes, born June 6, 1821, died in Missouri, December 12, 1897; married (1) June 12, 1844, Margaret Hill, who died March 3, 1850; daughter of Caton Hill. He married (2) Eliza Jane Dye, born February 20, 1834, died March 11, 1888.
6. Elizabeth Hughes, died January 9, 1897; married 1844, Jonas R. Milliken, born December 18, 1817, died April 7, 1900; son of John and Mary (Campbell) Milliken. They went from Delphine, Greene County, to Limestone, West Virginia.
7. Catherine Hughes, died in infancy.
8. H. T. Hughes, died in infancy.
9. John Hughes, died in the Civil War, buried at Garards Fort.
10. James Hughes, born February 12, 1829, died at Bristoria, October 18, 1907; married October 29, 1854, Hester Nichols, born January 25, 1834, died October 1907; daughter of Volentine and Nancy (Cooper) Nichols.

9. Remembrance Hughes, born May 13, 1793, died May 31, 1856 at Montezuma, California. He married (1) Margaret McClain, born January 17, 1799, at Rices Landing; died May 17, 1832; daughter of Abijah and Permelia (Doughty) McClain. He married (2) Mrs. Ophelia Shered. After his second marriage Remembrance Hughes sold his saw mill at the mouth of Tenmile and went to Oregon. He joined the Gold Rush to California, where he staked a claim on Pitt River. For a time he prospered, then found a large nugget, which made him a wealthy man. He sold the nugget and bought a ferry, but a flood wiped out his ferry and with it his fortune. He died in California at the home of one of his daughters.

Children of Remembrance Hughes

1. Elizabeth Hughes, born March 1, 1816, died at Yolo, California in 1902; married in 1838, William Campbell, born 1815, died at Yolo in 1887.
2. Sarah Hughes, born May 26, 1819, died at Bentleyville, July 25, 1894; married February 6, 1839, Abram Herrington, born 1814, died March 31, 1904.
3. Permelia Hughes, born in Pennsylvania; married George Porter.
4. Catherine Hughes, born May 6, 1828, died at Rices Landing, February 4, 1898; married Peter Sharpnack, born September 22, 1822, died September 29, 1907.
5. Thomas Hughes, joined the Gold Rush to California in 1849, returned to Iowa and in 1851 married at Brighton, Sarah Heaton. Went back to Red Bluffs, California.
6. Abijah Hughes, joined his brother in the Gold Rush, came back to Missouri and married Mary Alice Darling. Returned to California in 1870, and died at Red Bluffs.
7. Mary Hughes, married (1) Henry Martin in California. He died and she married (2) Henry Liggett, who died in 1859. Settled at Lompas, California.
8. Lydia Hughes, born November 16, 1831, died in 1899; married (1) 1847, Isaac Lucas, born March 1, 1825, died April 10, 1852; son of Thomas and Martha (Swan) Lucas. She married (2), in California, ... Pender.
9. Nancy Hughes, born 1832; married Joseph Wiley, son of George and Nancy (Curl) Wiley. They went to Elmwood, Illinois.
10. Remembrance Hughes, died at age of 8 years.
11. Martha Hughes, married March 21, 1861, William Rush, born born October 20, 182' died April 21, 1897; son of Mathias and Sarah (Iams) Rush.
12. Sophia Hughes, died in infancy.

10. Luca Hughes, born December 19, 1790, died at age of two years.
11. Catherine Hughes, born November 18, 1795; married June 29, 1816, John Hiller, son of William and Margaret (Myers) Hiller. They lived at Carmichaels.

Children of John and Catherine (Hughes) Hiller

1. Artinace Hiller, born September 29, 1817; married November 10, 1836, Joseph McGee.
2. Elizabeth Hiller, born November 23, 1819; married June 27, 1847, Thomas Milligan, born September 4, 1823, died November 21, 1858; son of William and Isabella (Brown) Milligan.
3. William Washington Hiller, born March 28, 1822; married January 1, 1851, Mary Luse, born March 27, 1832; daughter of Henry K and Mary (Buckingham) Luse.
4. Margaret Hiller, born January 12, 1825, died April 13, 1897; married July 31, 1845, William R. Milligan, born August 4, 1821; died October 30, 1892 at Ottawa, Illinois.
5. Thomas Hughes Hiller, born March 18, 1827; married Alice Johnson. Went to Kansas, 1855.
6. John Teagarden Hiller, born October 29, 1829, died in Kansas October 3, 1882; married April 7, 1867, Maria Benson Cock, born November 1, 1831.
7. Samuel Hiller, born April 29, 1832, died at Waynesburg,

July 5, 1896; married December 24, 1857, Harriet Kent, who died April 20, 1925.
8. Leroy Hiller, married Mary E. Morris; daughter of Captain Benjamin and Sarah (Miller) Morris.
9. George W. Hiller, born February 23, 1838; married Emma Luse.

THE O'NEAL FAMILY

When Felix Hughes brought his family to the Tenmile Country about 1767, two of his cousins, Henry and Barnet (Barnabas or Barney, etc.) boys about the age of Felix Hughes' own sons, were in the party. Tradition says that one of these boys was bitten by a poisonous snake in the journey over the mountains and almost lost his life. As Felix Hughes was a son of Thomas and Briget (O'Neal) Hughes, the relationship with the two boys may easily be seen. The same tradition says they were orphans, though this fact is not proven. A frayed page in the Swan-Hughes Bible indicates that Barnet O'Neal was born in 1751. He appears to have married before 1772 when he is found at the head of a household in the Springhill Township, Bedford County tax list. It is almost certain that both Barnet and Henry O'Neal served in the Revolution, but the evidence for Barnet O'Neal is not as conclusive as for his brother Henry O'Neal, whose name is found among the Frontier Rangers from Washington County for 1778-1783. But when David Owens was relieved of the command of his company at Fort Jackson, and replaced by Captain William Harrod, a group of men who had served under Owens, requested on October 22, 1776, that Captain Owens be restored to command them on a coming expedition. They stated that Barney O'Neal and Harrod were competent to judge the ability of their former captain, indicating that Barnet O'Neal had been in the service. (Draper Mss 4 NN 30-31)

Barnet O'Neal did not survive the Revolution, for Washington County court records show that he died about 1779, his estate being filed in Monongalia County, (West) Virginia, where on March 6, 1779, William Crawford, William Shepherd, and Charles Swan made an appraisal. The estate was administered by Thomas Hughes, who filed an account on March 5, 1780. A will is mentioned but it was probably destroyed by the fire at Morgantown in 1796. As Barnet O'Neal left three minor children, the care of these minors devolved upon Washington County after the boundary controversy had been settled, thus guardians were appointed there and a recital of the estate is found in the Orphan Court Docket. The land on which the elder Barnet O'Neal had settled was near the old Shepherd Church and was warranted to his heirs April 18, 1785, under the title of "Turkey Flat," and then patented to them when they reached legal age, under the title of "Union." These court actions show the names of the children of Barnet O'Neal, but no wife's name is found.

Family of Barnet O'Neal (O'Neil, O'Neel, Neal, Neel, etc.)

1. Sarah O'Neal, married Samuel Harrod, son of William and Amelia (Stephens) Harrod. He was born January 8, 1769, and died in 1832. While living in Bracken County, Kentucky, on September 19, 1797, Samuel and Sarah (O'Neal) Harrod made a deed for their share of "Union." (Greene County Deed Book 1. pp. 198.)

Children of Samuel and Sarah (O'Neal) Harrod

1. William Harrod, married Nancy Bottorf.
2. Henry Harrod, married Elinor Bowman.
3. Catherine Harrod, married George Taffe.

4. Sarah Harrod, married Lewis Bottorf.
5. Mary Harrod, married David Reed.

2. Barnet O'Neal, born April 23, 1776; died September 15, 1860; married, June 6, 1799, Martha Hughes, born May 11, 1761; died October 31, 1857. She was a daughter of Thomas and Elizabeth (Swan) Hughes. The Bible record of the family is found in the Swan-Hughes Bible. (Some of the family were known as O'Neals, other as Neals, etc.)

Children of Barnet and Martha (Hughes) O'Neal

1. Thomas O'Neal, born January 3, 1800; married, January 7, 1821, Mary McCall. They went to Ohio and then to Indiana.
2. Henry O'Neal, born March 30, 1802, died February 26, 1856; married July 28, 1825, Rhoda Hiller, born March 30, 1799. She was a daughter of William and Margaret (Myers) Hiller. After the death of her husband she removed to Illinois and then in 1859 by water to California, where she died at Red Bluffs about 1868.
3. Lucretia O'Neal, born October 11, 1804, died December 9, 1804.
4. Elizabeth O'Neal, born November 19, 1806, died December 6, 1884; married, April 3, 1828, Jesse Swan, born August 3, 1800, died February 8, 1851, son of William and Sarah (Harrod) Swan.
5. Mary O'Neal, born May 4, 1808, died December 6, 1876; married May 21, 1829, James Wiley, born April 8, 1809, died March 14, 1889, son of Joseph and Elizabeth Wiley.
6. Barnet O'Neal, born September 15, 1810, died April 12, 1899; married September 25, 1831, Margaret Kincaid. Went to Appamoose County, Iowa.
7. Sarah O'Neal, born March 22, 1813, died June 15, 1893; married December 7, 1837, William Sharpnack, born July 9, 1810, died January 18, 1892, son of Samuel and Nancy (Crago) Sharpnack. Had a hotel at Rices Landing.
8. John H. O'Neal, born November 24, 1815, died September 2, 1868; married, July 6, 1835, Sarah Moredock, daughter of George and Priscilla (Anderson) Moredock.
9. James C. O'Neal, born January 29, 1818, died March 21, 1867; married, July 17, 1840, Eliza Ann MacElvaney, who died November 12, 1896. Lived at Carmichaels.
10. Nancy O'Neal, born March 6, 1820; married, September 15, 1842, John Veon. Went to West Virginia.
11. Remembrance O'Neal, born June 9, 1822; married (1) March 21, 1844, Eleanor Thomas, born August 4, 1824. After her death he married (2) July 29, 1866, Mary Neff, born March 10, 1832.
12. Aliff Shepherd O'Neal, born September 4, 1824, died November 21, 1863; married, March 13, 1851, Lucy Thomas, born 1830, died February 20, 1885. Eleanor and Lucy Thomas were daughters of Joshua and Catherine (Livengood) Thomas.

3. Henry O'Neal, no record.

THE REX FAMILY

The story that George Rex was a son of George III, King of England, by a morganatic marriage, with the beautiful Quakeress, Hannah Lightfoot, is a lot of balderdash, just as the statement that he wrote with his own hand in his family Bible, that he was born in England. The truth of the matter is that he did not write—he made his mark. This also sets aside the suggestion that he came over as an officer in the British Army, officers had to write out reports. The truth is that the Rex Family settled around Philadelphia, and that there were quite a few of them in Montgomery County in an early date. It is evident that George Rex was of that Montgomery County group which moved from the vicinity of Philadelphia to Lancaster County, and then to Mifflin County, Pennsylvania. Quite a number of Jefferson families were in this migration, which came to the Tenmile after the Revolution. It is true of the Staggers, Honnells, Eisenmingers, Johns, Tustin, Styles, and other familiar names.

There can be little doubt that the George Rex, who served in Captain David Boal's Second Company of the Seventh Battalion of Cumberland County, Pennsylvania Militia, was the ancestor of the Jefferson family. (Penna. Arch Series V. Vol. 6, pp. 476) The name appears elsewhere as George Rexworthy, but someone dropped a comma, i. e. George Rex, worthy, when he took the Oath of Allegiance and Fidelity at Lancaster on December 8, 1777.

George Rex was born in 1750, probably in Montgomery County. He married in 1772, in Pennsylvania, Margaret Kepler, said to have been a native of Holland, newly arrived, who could speak very little English. Their first child was born in Lancaster County in 1773, but before the next child was born in 1775, he had moved to Mifflin County (a part of Cumberland County, Pennsylvania, until 1789) and then about 1791 he removed to the Tenmile, where he bought the tract of land of Captain Willia.. Harrod and spent the remainder of his life. He died here on May 1, 1821, and his will was filed for probate in Greene County, on November 15, 1822. His wife, Margaret (Kepler) Rex, was born in 1752, and died September 5, 1828. Both were buried in the old cemetery on their farm, but in late years the remains were moved to the new cemetery at Jefferson, and the markers set up anew. During his life, George Rex erected an Episcopal Church upon his land but this too has long since disappeared.

The following is the family record of George and Margaret (Kepler) Rex:

1. Mary Rex, born in Lancaster County, Pennsylvania in 1773, died in Greene County in 1849. She married, August 27, 1795, John Hughes, son of Thomas and Elizabeth (Swan) Hughes, born May 7, 1774, died July 23, 1844.
2. Elizabeth Rex, born in Mifflin County, Pennsylvania, April 20, 1775, died at Fredericktown, Washington County, Pennsylvania, September 20, 1852; married, July 15, 1794, John Bower, born at Lancaster, April 23, 1772, died at Fredericktown, July 29, 1836.
3. George Rex, Jr., born in Mifflin County, October 14, 1778, died at Jefferson October 18, 1856. He married, 1806, Jane Black, born August 18, 1785, died December 27, 1850. She was probably born in Adams County, and a sister of Judge Samuel Black, and Mrs. Marcena Michenor.
4. Edward Rex, born in Mifflin County, November 24, 1782, died at Bolivar, Ohio, February 28, 1845; married, December 21, 1821, in Muskingum County, Ohio, Hatty Huffsdale, born October 20, 1796. After the death of Edward Rex, his widow married

Abraham Milliken. They lived near Zanesville, Ohio, where their eight children were born.

5. Martha Rex, born in Mifflin County, January 15, 1783, died in Jefferson County, Ohio, January 31, 1853. She married William Winters, born in Lancaster County, in 1777, died September 19, 1849.

6. Jonas Rex, born in Mifflin County, February 4, 1785, died in Jefferson County, Ohio, where he had moved in 1811. His wife was Rhoda Milliken, daughter of John and Permelia (Styles) Milliken, whom he married February 16, 1808. She was born December 8, 1788, and died March 22, 1870.

7. Hannah Rex, born in Mifflin County, July 16, 1787, died December 25, 1866; married, October 6, 1805, at Jefferson, Isaac Shane, son of James Shane. They settled near Richmond, Ohio.

8. Margaret Rex, born in Mifflin County, November 9, 1789, died May 1, 1808, about one year after she married William McCullough.

9. Benjamin Rex, born in Greene County, January 9, 1792, died in Jefferson County, Ohio, September 17, 1854. He married January 23, 1816, Anna Barclay, daughter of Hugh and Ann (Darragh) Barclay, born April 20, 1795, died June 7, 1838. Benjamin then married Martha Thompson, born October 6, 1806, who died August 17, 18......, and after her death, Martha Jane Winters.

10. Catherine Rex, born in Greene County, December 25, 1793, died October 11, 1873; married in 1814, Joseph Burson, son of Edward and Elizabeth (Blackledge) Burson, born in Greene County, October 12, 1790. He was killed by Samuel Goff, a boy he had raised, dying June 18, 1855.

11. Sarah Rex, born in Greene County in 179.... She married (1) John Day, and (2) Samuel Cloakly (or Cloakey).

12. Charles Rex, born in Greene County, June 1, 1801, died there September 13, 1854; married, October 2, 1831, Mary Hickman, daughter of Solomon and Elizabeth (McCombs) Hickman, who was born in Fayette County, Pennsylvania, January 1, 1801. She died the same day as her husband, he at 7 P. M., and she at 9:30 P. M.

Because of the number of descendants of Charles Rex still living in the County, we shall give the record of his children.

1. Margaret Kepler Rex, daughter of Charles and Mary (Hickman) Rex, born June 27, 1832, died June 18, 1904, at Mt. Pleasant, Iowa. She married (1) Richard Watkins, who died October 1, 1854. She married (2) William F. Hughes, son of Thomas and Elizabeth (Hickman) Hughes.

2. Elizabeth Rex, born August 23, 1834, died April 11, 1877; married November 25, 1849, Daniel Moredock, born March 19, 1820, died October 16, 1906. His second wife was Rosa Stephens. Daniel Moredock was a son of George and Priscilla (Anderson) Moredock.

3. Experience Rex, born October 12, 1836, died June 18, 1856, while on her wedding trip. She married May 1, 1856, David Moffitt Hart.

4. George Rex, born November 30, 1836, died May 29, 1897; married December 8, 1861, Mary E. Strickler, born January 5, 1843, died April 11, 1891, daughter of Isaac and Catherine (Heath) Strickler.

5. Mary Rex, born December 12, 1842, died in infancy.
6. John B. Rex, born May 6, 1844, died at Shannon City, Iowa, January 21, 1917. He married, December 31, 1865, Mary A. McMinn.

FAMILY OF SOLOMON HICKMAN

Solomon Hickman removed from Fayette County, Pennsylvania, about 1800 and settled near Jefferson, Pennsylvania, on the Waynesburg Road near Laurel Point, where his home is still standing. He was born November 10, 1770, probably in Maryland, and died in Greene County, Pennsylvania, on June 9, 1845. He is buried with his wife in Green Mount Cemetery at Waynesburg. He married, June 4, 1795, Elizabeth McCombs, who was born August 11, 1775, and died December 22, 1870. Their children were:

1. Joseph Hickman, born 1796, died young.
2. Archibald Hickman, married Barbara Cyphers.
3. Mary Hickman, born January 1, 1801, died September 13, 1854; married October 2, 1831, Charles Rex, born June 1, 1801, died September 13, 1854. (See Rex Records.)
4. Elizabeth Hickman, born May 1, 1803, died July 3, 1872; married Thomas Hughes, born April 8, 1801, died June 3, 1872. (See Hughes Records.)
5. Sarah Hickman, married (1) .... Hixenbaugh, (2) .... Bradley.
6. Solomon Hickman, Jr., married Eliza Cary.
7. Eliza Hickman, born 1810, died 1842; married James Paul Walton, born 1806, died ....
8. Ann Hickman, married Elias McClelland.
9. Experience Hickman, born May 23, 1815, died September 9, 1899, married (1) Mathias Hunn'll, born 1806, died September 28, 1846, she married (2) .... Sharp. (See Hunnell Records.)

THE ROSEBERRY FAMILY

There are two versions of the ancestry of the Roseberry Family of Greene County, both of which are the result of much study and on the spot investigation and backed by existing records. Backed by proof furnished by deeds of record in Sussex County, New Jersey, and by much documentary proof, Mr. J. B. Orndorff of Graysville, bases his claim that the common ancestor of the family was Joseph Roseberry, who at one time owned 228 acres of land where the town of Phillipsburg, New Jersey, now stands. This Joseph Roseberry had at least two sons, John Roseberry and Michael Roseberry, the latter being the ancestor of the local branch of the family. Tradition further supports this claim as Mr. Orndorff, who is a careful investigator, says the Roseberrys were of English origin and this seems correct.

The other version of ancestry are from notes compiled by Mr. J. M. Roseberry, claiming the family is of German ancestry, descended from Michael Roseberry, who lived on the Susquehanna River during the Revolution, having moved there from the Tuscarora Valley on the Juniata River. It is true there was a Michael "Rausberry" in the Frontier Rangers from Northampton County, Pennsylvania, and that a Michael Roseberry from this section was on the Wyoming Expedition July 29, 1779, but this man doesn't seem a possible ancestor of the Greene County family. (Penna. Arch. Series III Vol. 23. pp. 300 and Series VI Vol. 14 pp. 32-33.) The similarity of names may have brought about this selection of an ancestor.

It is possible however that Michael Roseberry, immediate ancestor of the local family, did live for a time on the Juniata River. A "Michle Roseberry" was living there at the time of the 1790 Census, being the head of a family of 2 males over 16 years of age, three males under 16 years, and 2 female persons. No such person is found in the Census of Washington County for that year, nor in any other available records. His sons, John Roseberry and Mathias Roseberry (the latter but 18 years of age) are in the list of those living near Jefferson in 1790. Known records of Mathias Roseberry show that he was married October 8, 1795, so that the Census record of 1790 showing him head of a family of 2 adult males and one female may be taken as further proof that Michael Roseberry may have come west with his sons in 1784, and been living with his wife at a home provided by Mathias. In such event it would further substantiate the claims of Mr. J. B. Orndorff, that Michael accompanied his son Mathias to Center Township, where he died and is buried.

All claims say that Michael Roseberry married Mary Mapel for his first wife, and this points again to New Jersey ancestry. It may have been the only marriage made by Michael Roseberry, though Mr. J. M. Roseberry claims a marriage with a wealthy Ruth Chambers. Here again the Tuscarora Valley would be considered, but there is no evidence to support the claim that Ruth Chambers was the mother of the children of Michael Roseberry. All evidence would indicate that Mary Mapel was the mother of the children. The death of Michael Roseberry and his wife (or wives) is not given in any records.

Family of Michael and Mary (Mapel) Roseberry

1. John Roseberry, born April 28, 1761, died June 20, 1853 (or August 20, 1855), buried with his wife in the old Point Pleasant Cemetery, Mason County, West Virginia. He had removed from Greene County to Mason County, (West) Virginia in 1812, and was living there in 1832 when he applied for a pension for services in the Revolution. His application said he enlisted in Hunterdon County, New Jersey, on September 1, 1776, serving until 1781, during which time he took part in the Battles of Princeton and Trenton. He wintered with Washington's Army at Valley Forge and was with the Army when Cornwallis surrendered at Yorktown. John Roseberry married Florence Cree, daughter of Robert and Janet Cree. It is not known where they were married nor is the date shown. Robert and Janet Cree were living in Cumberland County, Pennsylvania at the time of the Revolution, but settled on land near John Swan's Fort soon afterwards. If John Roseberry married before the end of the Revolution it would confirm residence of the Roseberrys on the Juniata, prior to their settlement in the Tenmile Country.

Children of John and Florence (Cree) Roseberry

1. Mary Roseberry.
2. James Roseberry.
3. Margaret Roseberry.
4. Jane Roseberry.
5. Robert Roseberry, married Sarah Owens, born 1796, died 1880.
6. Michael Roseberry.
7. Ann Roseberry.
8. Elijah Roseberry.

2. Mary Roseberry, daughter of Michael and Mary (Mapel) Roseberry, married Andrew Brown.

3. Elizabeth Roseberry, daughter of Michael and Mary (Mapel) Roseberry, married James Crouse.
4. Elijah Roseberry, son of Michael and Mary (Mapel) Roseberry, died intestate in Greene County in 1851. His wife was Elizabeth Swan, daughter of William and Sarah (Harrod) Swan. She died before her father and with her husband is buried in un-marked graves in the Swan Cemetery.

Children of Elijah and Elizabeth (Swan) Roseberry
1. John Roseberry.
2. Sarah Roseberry.
3. Amelia Roseberry, married Joseph Yoders.
4. William Roseberry.
5. Elizabeth Roseberry, wife of Thomas Ammons.
6. Elijah Roseberry, whose wife was Elizabeth ....

5. James Roseberry, son of Michael and Mary (Mapel) Roseberry, no record.
6. Mathias Roseberry, son of Michael and Mary (Mapel) Roseberry, born January 11, 1772, died December 2, 1851, married October 8, 1795, Sarah Hughes, daughter of Thomas and Elizabeth (Swan) Hughes. She was born January 27, 1779, died October 29, 1858.

Children of Mathias and Sarah (Hughes) Roseberry
1. Mary Roseberry, born April 10, 1797, died July 19, 1892; married (1) Robert Scott, born 1799, died 1833. She was the second wife of Archibald Guthrie, born March 3, 1779, died August 23, 1845. He was a son of Archibald and Rebecca (Phillips) Guthrie.
2. Elizabeth Roseberry, born June 24, 1799, married Shadrack Mitchell.
3. Martha Roseberry, born October 7, 1801, died December 14, 1866; married February 24, 1820, Ephriam Morris, born November 18, 1797, died June 21, 1868. He was a son of James and Phoebe (Sayers) Morris.
4. Sarah Roseberry, born January 27, 1804, died July 31, 1882; married December 16, 1824, Frank Gray, born September 23, 1802, died February 26, 1844. He was a son of David W. Gray, and grandson of the pioneer David Gray.
5. Thomas Hughes Roseberry, born May 13, 1806, died in Vernon County, Missouri, March 29, 1891; married March 19, 1829, Mary Hill, born February 3, 1810, died January 3, 1895. She was a daughter of Rees and Nancy (Heaton) Hill.
6. Nancy Roseberry, born November 1, 1808, died March 15, 1875; married December 13, 1827, Thomas Hill, born October 5, 1805, died May 24, 1875. He was a son of Samuel and Elizabeth (Cathers) Hill.
7. Mathias Roseberry, born February 28, 1811, died at Harvard, Nebraska, in 1878; married Sarah McClain, who died in 1850.
8. Catherine Roseberry, born June 14, 1814, died in Marshall County, (West) Virginia, in 1852. Married Joshua Burley, son of Jacob and Mary (Hughes) Burley.
9. John Hughes Roseberry, born March 31, 1816; married Mary McClain. Went to Missouri.
10. Lucinda Roseberry, born April 16, 1819, died March 22, 1901, at Tonica, Illinois; married about 1839, John Vanatta, born June 1817, died May 1858.
11. James Roseberry, born October 10, 1823, was killed by a

mule, while making an overland journey to California during the Gold Rush. He never married.

7. Michael Roseberry, son of Michael and Mary (Mapel) Roseberry, born July 7, 1777, died in Jennings County, Indiania, January 3, 1852; married (1) Elizabeth Murdock, daughter of Daniel and Ruth (Williams) Murdock. His second wife was Nancy Buckingham. In 1812 Michael Roseberry removed to Clermont County, Ohio, where his first wife died near Batavia. After his second marriage he removed his family by flat boat, arriving in Jennings County, Indiana April 3, 1839. Both he and his second wife are buried in the Graham Cemetery.

Children of Michael Roseberry, Jr.

1. Elijah Roseberry, born May 15, 1798.
2. Elmoth (Ella) Roseberry, born May 21, 1805.
3. James Roseberry.
4. Elmer Roseberry.
5. Nancy Roseberry, born May 2, 1817, married (1) Benjamin Butler (2) U. S. Ulery.
6. George Roseberry.
7. Marion Roseberry, born March 15, 1828; married November 27, 1849, Zerelda Miller, born March 31, 1828.
8.
9.

THE MILLIKEN FAMILIES

At least three separate Milliken (Milligan) Families are represented in Greene County. Rev. G. T. Ridlon in an excellent genealogy of the families, published at Lewiston, Maine, in 1907, gives some information on the three branches. One of these families was descended from Thomas Milliken, born in Northern Ireland as early as 1730, who with his brother, James Milliken, came to America about 1750-54 and settled first in Chester County, Pennsylvania. Between 1760 and 1770 he secured a grant of several hundred acres of land on the Juniata River, in what is now Sprucehill Township, in the Tuscarora Valley. At the outbreak of the Revolution, he with several of his neighbors walked to Lancaster, where they enlisted in a company of expert riflemen, which became a part of the Second Regiment of the Continental Line. The company arrived at Boston August 4, 1775, and participated in several engagements about Cambridge under General Lee. Thomas Milliken afterward joined Arnold in his march to Quebec, rendering valuable service as a spy. In 1778 he was sent home, broken in health by the long marches and exposure from cold and hunger, dying soon after his arrival at home. He is buried in the so-called McKee Graveyard. Records say his wife was Jane McConnell.

Family of Thomas and Jane (McConnell) Milliken

1. John Milliken, born about 1765. We think there is an error in this date, and that he was probably born a few years earlier. He died at Jefferson, Pennsylvania, January 17, 1843. (Will Book 2 pp. 169.) He is probably the John Milliken, who served in Captain Noah Abraham's Company, First Battalion, Cumberland County Militia in 1778. Later his name is found in the rolls of Captain John Carothers Company, Third Battalion, Cumberland County Militia in 1780, and Captain John Flemming's Company in 1781-82-83. (Penna. Arch. Series V Vol. 6 pp. 53-227-646.) John Milliken was twice married, his first wife being Parmelia Stiles,

who died in the Summer of 1794. His second wife was Mary Campbell, born in Ireland in 1771, who came to America in 1787. She died near Jefferson at the age of 95 years, 5 months. There were four children by the first marriage.

Children of John Milliken

1. Abraham Milliken, born 1785, died Auguest 4, 1860, married Jane Hufty, born 1786, died March 2, 1844.

    #### Children of Abraham and Jane (Hufty) Milliken
    1. Benoni Milliken, born 1813, married Cassie Craft.
    2. Mary Milliken, married John Hewitt. She was born in 1816.
    3. Abraham Milliken, born 1811, married Jane Gwynne.
    4. Joseph Milliken.
    5. Jacob Milliken, born 1821, married Rachel Hopkins.
    6. Permelia Milliken, born 1823, married John Hartman.
    7. Mary Jane Milliken, born 1829, married Tillman Clark.
    8. Martha Milliken.

2. Rhoda Milliken, born December 8, 1788, died March 22, 1870; married February 16, 1808, Jonas Rex, born February 4, 1785, died December 6, 1841. Buried in Two Ridge Cemetery, Richmond, Ohio.

    #### Children of Jonas and Rhoda (Milliken) Rex
    1. George W. Rex, born May 18, 1809, died April 7, 1871; married April 3, 1838, Rachel Coe, who died June 7, 1884, aged 75 years.
    2. Permelia Rex, born February 14, 1811, died March 26, 1844; married January 20, 1834, Rosalis Castmer.
    3. William Rex, born July 11, 1813, died April 8, 1886; married March 20, 1846, Harriet Johnson, who died December 21, 1880.
    4. Mary Rex, born September 17, 1815; married December 24, 1840, Aaron Gladden.
    5. Margaret Jane Rex, born May 14, 1818, died May 12, 1889; married February 10, 1841, David Johnson.
    6. John Stiles Rex, born May 7, 1821, died November 20, 1898; married March 3, 1848, Rachel Scott, born November 7, 1826, died October 31, 1919, daughter of John and Elizabeth Scott. They lived at Steubenville, Ohio.
    7. Eliza Rex, born September 6, 1824, died March 4, 1856; married March 3, 1840, James Snowden, born March 23, 1818, died at Cornwall, Missouri, January 5, 1896.
    8. Martha W. Rex, born May 1, 1827, died March 8, 1833.
    9. Joseph Burson Rex, born October 10, 1829, died March 10, 1833.
    10. James Rex, born April 5, 1832, died April 1, 1895.

3. Thomas Milliken, died in infancy.
4. Patience Milliken, married John Prior. They had 14 children.

Family of John and Mary (Campbell) Milliken

5. Thomas Milliken, born about 1796, died at Mt. Pleasant, Iowa October 12, 1870; married Elizabeth Cain, born 1803, died September 12, 1877.

Children of Thomas and Elizabeth (Cain) Milliken

1. John Milliken, born November 12, 1822, died at Majorsville, West Virginia; married Mary Ketchum, born August 30, 1827.
2. Samuel Milliken; married Elizabeth Williams. Both died in Henry County, Iowa.
3. James Milliken; married Catherine Cree.
4. Joseph Milliken; died in Illinois.
5. Mary A. Milliken, born February 11, 1831; married, March 31, 1853, John Smith. Both are buried in the Smith Cemetery.
6. Edward Milliken, born August 31, 1832, died December 25, 1898; married Ruth Ann Shelby, born December 10, 1833, died August 13, 1897. Buried at Melissa, Texas.
7. Katherine Milliken, born August 28, 1834, died October 1918; married Stockton Smith, born 1826, died 1876. They were married November 20, 1854.
8. Millie Milliken; married Hamilton Scott.
9. Jonas Milliken, died in Polk County, Iowa, November 20, 1909; married Matilda Rinehart, daughter of Hiram and Mariah (Porter) Rinehart.
10. Thomas Milliken, born July 8, 1844. His second wife was Jane Robinson.
11. William Milliken; killed by runaway horse in Des Moines, Iowa.
12. Elizabeth Milliken.

6. Samuel Milliken, born January 11, 1800, died in Tuscarora County, Ohio, in 1874. His wife was Clementine Hiller. They had ten children.
7. James Milliken, born January 26, 1802, died in Shawnee County, Kansas, in 1895. His wife was Elizabeth Haver, born 1805, died 1889.
8. John Milliken, died February 1, 1893, aged 88 years, 3 months, 27 days. Never married.
9. Edward Milliken, born 1806, died May 30, 1882; married Lydia Sharpnack, who died April 8, 1886, aged 78 years, probably a daughter of John and Sarah (Antrim) Sharpnack.
10. Permelia Milliken, born 1806, died June 5, 1869; married, 1826, John Cotterall, born 1802, died 1865, son of William and Isabell (Livingstone) Cotterall.

Children of John and Permelia (Milliken) Cotterall

1. Isabel Cotterall; married William Anderson.
2. Mary Ann Cotterall; married Dr. James W. Haucher.
3. William Cotterall; married Olive Gordon.
4. Jonas Cotterall; married Anna Short.
5. Elizabeth Cotterall; married Joseph A. Bell.
6. Martha Cotterall; married Jacob Haver.
7. George Cotterall.
8. John Cotterall; married Priscilla Swan.

11. Mary Milliken; married Peter Hiller, Jr.

Children of Peter and Mary (Milliken) Hiller

1. Elizabeth Hiller.
2. Permelia Hiller.
3. John Hiller.
4. Mary Ann Hiller.
5. Peter Hiller.
6. David Hiller.

12. Joseph Milliken, born 1810, died September 14, 1854; married (1) Miss Emory; (2), November 29, 1836, Mary Hughes, born 1813, died May 21, 1855. (See Hughes Records).
13. Frances Milliken; married John Moredock; removed to Berwick, Illinois.
14. Elizabeth Milliken. Never married.
15. Isabella Milliken; married Thomas Scott, born May 18, 1817, died January 1, 1879, son of James and Margaret (Kincaid) Scott.

Children of Thomas and Isabella (Milliken) Scott
1. James K. Scott, born July 7, 1841; married Elizabeth Hoge.
2. John M. Scott, born January 31, 1843, died October 10, 1929; married, October 9, 1866, Elizabeth Rinehart, born February 13, 1843, died January 25, 1905.
3. Margaret Scott, born January 6, 1845; married Arthur Rinehart.
4. Chinsworth Scott, born April 1, 1848; lived 3 days.
5. Catherine Scott, born December 31, 1848, died in infancy.
6. Mary Scott, born December 31, 1851; never married.
7. Catherine Scott (2), born May 21, 1854; married (1) Solomon Shriver; (2) Jack Rush.

16. Jonas Milliken, born December 18, 1817, died in 1900 at Limestone, West Virginia; married, in 1846, Elizabeth Hughes, born 1813, died January 9, 1855. (See Hughes Records).
17. Anna Milliken, born 1821, died in Calhoun County, Virginia, May 27, 1898; married Levi Morris, son of Henry and Ede (Hickman) Morris.

THOMAS MILLIKEN

Another branch of the Milligan (Milliken) Family represented in Greene County, is descended from Thomas Milligan, born in the County Tyrone, Ireland, where he married a Miss Mitchell. With six sons and one daughter, they came to Canada during the building of the Welland Canal. They settled near Floydstown in Ontario, where they took up the pursuit of agriculture—with the exception of one son. The children of Thomas Milligan were William, James, John, Thomas, Joseph, Robert, and Jane.

William Milligan, son of Thomas, did not stay long in Canada, but came to the United States, and located in Fayette County. He acquired much land in Washington, Canonsburg, and Millsboro. Born in Ireland about 1797, he married, in Fayette County, October 20, 1820, Isabella Brown, a daughter of Kennedy Brown. She died August 29, 1833, and her husband died on August 27, 1862. They were the parents of five children.

Children of William and Isabella (Brown) Milligan
1. William R. Milligan, born August 4, 1821, died October 30, 1892; married, July 31, 1845, Margaret Hiller, born January 12, 1825, died April 13, 1897; daughter of John and Catherine (Hughes) Hiller.
2. Kennedy Brown Milligan, born September 1, 1822, died April 12, 1845.
3. Mary Jane Milligan, born March 26, 1824, died October 29, 1836.
4. Thomas Milligan, born July 4, 1825, died November 21, 1858; married Elizabeth Hiller, born November 23, 1819; daughter of John and Catherine (Hughes) Hiller.
5. Samuel Milligan, born January 22, 1833, died December 3, 1847.

DR. JOHN MILLIKEN

Dr. John Milliken was the fourth child of James Milliken. James Milliken was born in Castle Dawson, Ireland, in 1744, and came to America, arriving in Boston on November 4, 1765. With him was his first wife, Elizabeth McCine, and their child, born in Ireland. He served in the Revolution in Captain Joseph Parker's Company, which was raised out of Colonel Enoch Hale's Regiment. He was mustered out on July 18, 1776. The second wife of James Milliken was Elizabeth McCoy. James Milliken died in South Charleston, New Hampshire, April 4, 1830.

Dr. John Milliken married Harriet Roberts, daughter of Sarah (Morgan) Roberts by her first marriage. By her second marriage, Sarah (Morgan) Roberts became the wife of Colonel John Heaton of Jefferson, Pennsylvania, and Harriet Roberts was raised in the Heaton home. Dr. John and Harriet (Roberts) Milliken were the parents of eight children, two of whom were:
1. Hiram Milliken.
2. Charlotte Milliken, born August 31, 1803, died March 3, 1851; married, August 15, 1822, William Hiller, son of William and Margaret (Myers) Hiller.

Children of William and Charlotte (Milliken) Hiller
1. Harriet Hiller, born 1823; married, 1842, Samuel Spruance.
2. John M. Hiller, born 1825.
3. James M. Hiller, born 1827; married, 1858, Rebecca Reynolds.
4. Margaret Hiller, born 1829; married Dr. Nehemiah Richardson.
5. William Hiller, born 1832; married, 1857, Sarah Roseberry.
6. Hiram M. Hiller, born 1834; married, 1857, Sarah F. Bell.
7. George M. Hiller, born 1836; married, 1868; Mary A. Miller.
8. Amelia Hiller, born 1838; married, 1863, John E. Stafford.
9. Royal M. Hiller, born 1842; married, 1868, Edie Baker.
10. Alonzo Hiller, born 1845, died 1845.

THE HILLER FAMILY

Peter Hiller was a member of the Swan-Hughes-Vanmeter Party that came to the Tenmile Country about 1767-68. The Hiller (sometimes spelled Heller, etc.) Family seems to have come from Prince George's County, Maryland, where the name is found as early as 1739. No military record is found for Peter Hiller, but he could have served in Captain Jesse Pigman's Company of which there is no record.

Peter Hiller died in Greene County, February 8, 1833, when he was 80 years of age. His wife was Agnes ...., who died December 8, 1835, at the age of 79 years. Both are buried in the old cemetery at Shephard's Church. Peter Hiller left a will in which he named a son, Peter Hiller, and a daughter, Elizabeth Hiller. (Will Book 2. pp. 17.) A John Hiller, either a son or grandson, was named executor. Orphan Court records disclose that William Hiller was another son, who shared in the estate. (O. C. Docket 2. pp. 17.)

Family of Peter and Agnes Hiller
1. Elizabeth Hiller.
2. Peter Hiller, married Mary Milliken, daughter of John and Mary (Campbell) Milliken. In the settlement of his father's estate, he requested that guardians be appointed for his minor children. He later settled in Ohio. (O. C. Docket 2. pp. 45.)

Children of Peter and Mary (Milliken) Hiller

1. David Hiller.
2. Elizabeth Hiller, married .... Davis.
3. Permelia Hiller.
4. John Hiller.
5. Mary Ann Hiller.
6. Peter Hiller.

3. William Hiller, died intestate about 1837, his sons John and Samuel Hiller administered on his estate, taking out letters on May 22, 1837. John Hiller, dying on January 8, 1839, Samuel Hiller closed the estate. (O. C. record of September 18, 1837, Docket 2. pp. 113.) William Hiller married Margaret Myers, daughter of Captain George Myers.

Family of William and Margaret (Myers) Hiller

1. John Hiller, died January 8, 1839. He married in 1816, Catherine Hughes, born November 18, 1795; daughter of Thomas and Elizabeth (Swan) Hughes. (See Thomas Hughes Family.)
2. William Hiller, married August 15, 1822, Charlotte Milliken, born August 31, 1803, died March 3, 1851. She was a daughter of Dr. John and Harriet (Roberts) Milliken.

Children of William and Charlotte (Milliken) Hiller

1. Harriet Hiller, born 1823, married 1842, Samuel Spruance.
2. John M. Hiller, born 1825.
3. James W. Hiller, born 1827, married 1858, Rebecca Reynolds.
4. Margaret Hiller, born 1829, married 1852, Dr. Neihemiah Richardson.
5. William Hiller, born 1832, married 1857, Sarah Roseberry.
6. Hiram M. Hiller, born 1834, married 1857, Sarah Bell.
7. George M. Hiller, born 1836, married 1868, Mary A. Miller.
8. Amelia Hiller, born 1838, married 1863, John E. Stafford.
9. Royal M. Hiller, born 1842, married 1868, Edie S. Baker.
10. Alonzo Hiller, born 1845, died 1845.

3. Samuel Hiller.
4. Mary Hiller, married Samuel Swan, son of Thomas and .. . . Swan. He was born September 18, 1783.

Child of Samuel and Mary (Hiller) Swan

1. Elizabeth Swan, born May 8, 1816, died May 30, 1904; married in 1842, James Bell, son of Isaac and Elizabeth (Harrod) Bell.

5. Sarah Hiller, married Thomas Teagarden, son of George and Rachel (Pribble) Teagarden.
6. Margaret Hiller, born 1794, died January 26, 1833; married James Hughes, born January 19, 1788, died July 11, 1871, son of Thomas and Elizabeth (Swan) Hughes. (See Hughes Records.)
7. Rhoda Hiller, born March 30, 1799, died about 1868, at Red Bluffs, California. She married, July 28, 1825, Henry O'Neil, born March 30, 1802, died February 26, 1856; son of Barnet

and Martha (Hughes) O'Neal. (See Thomas Hughes Records.)
8. Susan Hiller, married William Galbreath.
9. Amelia Hiller, married Samuel Morgan Heaton, son of John and Sarah (Morgan) Heaton, born July 23, 1803, died 1862 at Mt. Pleasant, Iowa.

Children of Samuel and Amelia (Hiller) Heaton
1. Margaret Heaton.
2. Sarah Heaton.
3. Charlotte Heaton.
4. William Heaton.

THE THOMAS FAMILY

One branch of the Thomas Family of the Tenmile Country is descended from Ellis Thomas, a native of Frederick County, Virginia, who made his will August 4, 1760, which was probated at Winchester, on October 4, 1763. His wife was Elizabeth ...., who survived him. He could be the Ellis Thomas, mentioned in Kerchaval's "History of the Valley" as having been killed by the Indians, and his wife miraculously saved. (pp. 100.)

Children named in his will
1. Evan Thomas, a minor child.
2. John Thomas, from information furnished by the late Florin Thomas of Smith Creek, and family traditions of his family, it seems certain that this was the John Thomas that on December 10, 1811, received a warrant for "Aberdeen," a tract of 264 acres of land near White's Church. His wife was Cassandra ....

Children (Greene County Deed Book 9. pp. 50)
1. Eli Thomas, married Sarah Knight.
2. Eleanor Thomas, married Hiram Hughes.
3. Isaac Thomas, married Mary ....
4. Joshua Thomas, married (1) Catherine Livengood, (2) Margaret ....
5. Cassandra Thomas, married James Knight.
6. George Thomas, married Catherine Sellars.

3. William Thomas, his wife was Elizabeth Vanmeter. He was a Frontier Ranger in the Revolution. (Penna. Arch. Series III Vol 23 pp. 219.) Was killed by the Indians on Miracle Run on April 21, 1789.

Child
1. William Thomas, Jr., born December 17, 1788, married Amelia Swan. (See Vanmeter Records.)

4. Ellis Thomas, married Phobe Vanmeter, daughter of Henry and Martha Vanmeter. Went to Ohio County, (West) Virginia, and then to Tyler County, where he and wife made a deed. His home for a time was on Grave Creek. An Ellis and William Thomas are listed together in the Militia Company of Charles Gobin in Berks County, Penna. (Penna Arch Series V. Vol. 5.-237.)

Children ?
1. Ellis Thomas, Jr., married in Tyler County, July 6, 1826, Evilla A. Jones.

2. Martha Thomas, married in Tyler County, April 8, 1822, Samuel Nicklin.
   3. Elizabeth Thomas, married in Tyler County, February 2, 1820, John Booth.
   4. Saul Thomas, married in Tyler County, August 20, 1820, Isabella Love.
   5. Evan A. Thomas, married in Tyler County, September 2, 1822, Harriet Jones.
5. Elizabeth Thomas.
6. Isaac Thomas, a minor child.
7. Rachel Thomas.
8. Mary Thomas, a minor child in 1760.

THE HARRODS

No one locality can lay exclusive claim to the Harrods. They are as much a part of the Tenmile Country as they are of Kentucky. James Harrod alone lived a longer period of time in Kentucky than he lived in Pennsylvania. The Tenmile was the home of William, Levi and for his brief life, Samuel Harrod. Thomas and John Harrod, half brothers of James, William, Samuel and Levi, were not of the Tenmile nor of Kentucky except for brief periods of time. It is unfortunate that so much confusion has grown up concerning the history of these men. The errors that have crept into the history of these men is perhaps due to the fact, that like Daniel Boone, their contemporary and at times their companion, they were trail blazers, and were continually skirting the frontiers. Always on the trails, seldom at home, their feats made possible the security of the border settlements. It is not surprising that their deeds have become a national folklore.

Mrs. Otis W. Swainson, now of Piedmont, California, with whom the writer has collaborated during the past ten years, is probably the best living authority on the Harrod Family geneology. A descendant of Levi Harrod, she has sifted every source of material in her search to clear up the many errors previously printed. Her coming book on the Harrods should go a long way in correcting the errors. It is obvious that certain writers, who do not have the facts, have frequently tried to create them. Mrs. Swainson produces the data she has uncovered, and lets it go at that.

Mrs. John B. Mason is also printing a book on the Harrods, which will be the most readable and entertaining yet printed. Mrs. Mason has collected a trunkful of material, which she recently brought to Waynesburg, for the purpose of getting the local angle on the Harrods. She is more concerned with the story than the geneology of the family, but her geneology will be correct so far as she uses it.

A three way correspondence between Mrs. Swainson, Mrs. Mason and the writer of these articles, has uncovered early Harrods in New England, New Jersey, and at the head of the Chesapeake Bay, where almost invariably the name is spelled Harrod or Herrod. The name Hayward, or Harwood seldom appears in these records to connect the family with the early family of that name, which settled in Virginia and Maryland. It has been the contention of this writer that the Sergeant John Harrod, who was serving in Colonel Pfarmer's New Jersey Militia Regiment under Captain Leonard in 1715, and the man with whom we start this sketch, were the same man. (Old East New York Vol. 5. pp. 670.) This has not been proven.

From Rachel Henton's Notebook, frequently mentioned in Harrod histories, we learn that John Harrod was the father of two sons by his first marriage. They were John and Thomas Harrod, the later named settled in North Carolina. The note book states that while John Harrod was away from home, the Indians came and burned his house, and killed his wife. The note book states this John Harrod came from England and settled in one of the New England States, and that John Harrod married again and had children by the second wife.

From here we shall quote the interview of Draper with William Harrod, Jr., born on January 10, 1773, on South Fork of Tenmile, Greene County, Pennsylvania. Draper had this interview with William Harrod, Jr., in November 1845, when visiting him near Germantown, Bracken County, Kentucky. It is remarkable for the correctness of the report of the local events, which should qualify it for the other points of the interview.

Copy of Draper Mss 37J168

"The father of the Harrods (Thomas or Samuel, probably) came from England when a young man—married Sarah Moore, on the Shenandoah; oldest son, Samuel, born there, and then removed to the Big Cove in then Cumberland County, Penna., and there William was born on the 9th day of December 1737—then Nellie (married to Voluntine House)— then James, born in 1742—then Rachel (married to George Newland) then Mary (married to Adam Newland)— Levi, Sallie (never married)— then Elizabeth (married to Benjamin Davis, cousin of Anthony Wayne)—and Jemima (never married.)

"William Harrod served as a sergeant on Fobers (Forbes') campaign in 1758, greatly pressed for provisions and had to kill some of the pack horses, and Harrod went out one day and killed three deer, Forbes having given permission—this was on the return to Fort Cumberland.

"Before the close of the French War, Captain Harrod was stationed at Juniata and Captain James Piper commanded at a neighboring fort. A party of Indians came and killed some men near Juniata Fort. Others with them fled and reported about fifty Indians. Harrod raised at his own and Piper's Fort, 35 men; took the trail, and overtook them in the evening, camped at the head of a hollow. Harrod's men surrounded the Indian camp, and as the day was dawning and the Indians just getting up, fired on them and killed several; the others fled without firing a gun, leaving several guns and other plunder in camp. Harrod's party returned victorious, and no depredations were committed in that region for some time.

"On the first of October 1765, Captain Harrod married Amelia Stephens, moved from the Big Cove to the Little Cove, and in 1772, removed to the Monongahela country, and settled on the south fork of Tenmile Creek.

"It was Samuel Harrod who in 1767 was with Michael Stoner hunting in Illinois *** Samuel was a great hunter, remained in the French country, killed buffalo meat and took it to New Orleans to supply the garrison, and thus remained until the spring of 1780, when he was killed at the mouth of the Tennessee by an Indian hired to do so from some pique by a French trader at Kaskaskia, whom William Harrod had apprehended and put in irons, took his store of goods and divided them among his soldiers.

"War of 1774. In the summer of 1774 Captain Harrod commanded at Ross's fort on Rough Fork of Tenmile. (Ruff's Creek) Captain Harrod aided in getting supplies for Dunmore's Army and went out with a company in the Fall of 1774. Dunmore's Treaty was made on Kinnekenic Creek, a branch of the Sciota.

"Early in 1776 and perhaps late 1775 Captain William Harrod visited Kentucky.

"Late in 1776 he was placed in command at Grave Creek and there remained the most of 1777. He was of Foreman's party, took to the hillside with Samuel Thomas and others. Foreman's men were fired on. Harrod and others hollowed and ran down the hill firing on the Indians. The latter fled and several swam the Ohio. One Thomas shot swimming and both the Indian and his gun sank.

"Thinks he commanded at Wheeling in 1776 and 1777.

"Aided in taking Kaskaskia—went down the Monongahela with his company in a keel boat. John Swan (Jr.) was his lieutenant.

"At the taking of Vincennes, Harrod was ordered by Clark to march and remarch around the Sugar Loaf Hill in sight of the British garrison. (Here Draper says that Harrod was not there.)

"Bowman's Campaign. William Harrod commanded a company. John Moredock was killed either here or at Pickaway in 1780, and his brother Edward killed two Indians.

"Clark's Campaign 1780—William Harrod was out—James Harrod commanded the right wing, and Col. William Harrod the left—and at the battle, Col. William killed two Indians. His cousin, Samuel Moore was killed in this battle. He had dreamed before leaving Harrodsburg that he would either be killed or wounded, but rather than remain and be considered a coward, he went along, taking bandages with him.

"Captain Harrod commanded at the Falls of the Ohio—had a town laid off there.

"During the hard winter of 1780 (3 feet of snow on the Monongahela country and the river froze over in November and continued till the last of March—snow 4½ feet deep on the mountains between Redstone and Cumberland) G. R. Clark spent a part of his time at Jacob Vanmeter's Fort on Swan's Run. (note—This was Henry Vanmeter's Fort.)

"Swan's Fort and at Captain Harrods—Adam Rowe's family, wife and several children killed, two sons not killed; hid some pot metal, plowing irons; going down the Ohio with Captain Harrod, and Rowe would go and get his hidden articles against Harrod's advice, who saw fresh Indian signs; Rowe and Isaac Perry, a young man, went to Rowe's cabin, under the floor of which the articles were hidden, and as they recovered it, they discovered several Indians sitting down in front of the cabin eating. Several fired and shot Perry, who ran a few steps and fell. Rowe escaped and joined Harrod, abandoned their canoe where it was tied and had to go around back water, and thus were so long in getting to Wheeling.

"Harrod, Rowe, and Perry had left a large keel boat, in a large keel boat to Rowe's plunder, and then rejoin the keel boat. Accompanying the keel boat were other boats—a day or so after Perry was killed, this keel boat was fired upon and Mrs. Richard Swan was wounded in the shoulder.

"William Swan was Colonel of the militia of Washington County, Pennsylvania. (This should be Charles Swan). This was before Greene County was laid off. In some way William Harrod gave his vote against slavery.

"In April 1793, William Harrod lost his wife, about that time he commanded a block house high up on Wheeling Creek, some 22 miles. Commanded at Fish Creek a while.

"While Harrod was at the Block House up Wheeling Creek in the Spring of 1793, perhaps in May, Captain William Enochs, with a party of men, pursued Indians that had killed two of widow Crow's daughters. About seven miles up Captina, they fell in with the enemy and a battle ensued. Captain Enoch killed an Indian, Abraham McCoun killed another. The whites were defeated with the loss of Abraham and Isaac McCoun, Abraham Enochs and John ...... ines, and perhaps more. Duncan MacArthur was in this defeat. When the party returned subsequently, the body of Abraham Enochs, (the first who was killed in the fight, he being in advance) was found, cut up and mangled. The body of one of the McCouns was not found. Harrod had advised Captain Enochs not to follow much over the river.

"Jackson's Fort on south fork of Tenmile, was principal station in that region. Ross's, and John Antrim's (Ankrom's) on the south fork. Jacob Vanmeter's on Muddy Creek, Legg's (Clegg's) on Dunkard Creek, William Minors on Big Whitley Creek, Guthrie's on Big Whitley, John Swan's on Swan's Run, Henry Vanmeter's also on Swan's Run, Henry Enoch's at the forks of the Tenmile, (he was the father of Captain Enochs) Bell's Fort on Rough Creek and others.

"The Harrods forted at Ross's Fort in 1774, subsequently they forted at Swan's Fort, while Captain William Harrod was in Kentucky in 1780 or before.

"In the Spring of 1782 Simon Rinehart, William Brown, and one English (William) some two miles down from Jackson's Fort, while moving some merchandise on sleds were fired upon and all three killed. Vincent Brown and Michael Archer escaped to the fort, chased there.

"In July 1787 Colonel William Harrod and several others went out hunting on Fish Creek. Michael Archer, while on the way to join the hunting party, nearly a dozen miles above Jacksons Fort on Tenmile, was killed by the Indians. His body was found with his fists clenched, and full of hair, evidently had fought till the last. His dog was found lying, three days after, beside his master and very active.

"About 1782 or 1783 Caleb Linsecum and Michael Archer, when on Laurel Run, a mile from Jackson's Fort, were surprised by the Indians. Archer beckoned Linsecum to mount their only horse, but Linsecum was so overcome with fear that he was easily killed, Archer escaping.

"About 1783 Indians fell upon the families of Robert McClennan (McClelland) and James Archer, whose families lived in the same cabin, about three fourths of a mile from Fort Jackson. They came on a foggy morning. Eight or nine of the two families were killed, a few escaped. Jane Archer, a small girl was tomahawked and scalped, and left for dead but recovered.

"Col. William Harrod was a little short of six feet, (not more than an eighth of an inch wanting) raw-boned, about 180 pounds, dark hair and complexion. He was fond of hunting, in one day he killed eleven deer, a wolf, and a wild cat on Fishing Creek. One Fall in Kentucky, he killed 110 deer and sent the skins up the river. This was somewhere in the 1780s. He killed 28 bear and 75 deer on a six weeks fall hunt up on Fish Creek.

"Col. Harrod came to Kentucky in the Spring of 1795 and lived with his son William in Bracken County at the head of Locust Creek, and died October 9th 1801 after a few days illness with fever. He was buried near the present Sharon Meeting House.

"Col. James Harrod may have been out on the Forbes Campaign, dont recollect. In 1773 he explored Kentucky with several in a party. Went to Greenbriar. Next Spring, went again and settled Harrodsburg, etc.

"The elder Harrod (John) had two sons, John and Thomas, by a first wife, then married Sarah Moore. Thomas Harrod (Col. James Harrod's half brother) settled in North Carolina, and James used to go and visit him, and there very likely met Boone and others and learned of Kentucky. He was six feet, could read and write, spare, dark black hair and eyes. He (James) probably met foul play out trapping. Made his will at Washington, Kentucky, and then went out on his last trapping on the Sandy.

"Col. David Williamson boarded at William Harrod's at Big Cove. Levi Harrod was one of the pilots on the White Woman's Campaign, this about 1790 or 1791. Williamson and someone else commanded, quite a body of men. Captain William Crawford was a captain, no fighting, all horsemen. Found the Indians too strong. Thomas Stokely was along.

"Captain Ezekiel Rose was wounded thru the body, a very bad one, had a silk handkerchief pulled thru the wound several times, got well and lived on Shirtee or Pigeon Creek.

"General James Ray, when a man was out plowing at Harrodsburg, and an Indian was stealing up behind him, got in the rear and shot the Indian. The man escaped to the fort and reported.

"Ben Eulèn, perhaps a man killed with him, ran and jumped down from the eastern bank of the Kanawa, some 60 or 70 feet. Would have been killed but for grape vines, as it was he had his thigh broken and perhaps an arm. Was taken to the fort at Pt. Pleasant. Had a halt in his walk when my informant saw him at Pt. Pleasant. A heavy set small man.

"James Harrod, once out hunting on horse back, fired, horse jumped and threw him and broke his thigh. At a subsequent period he had the other broken the same way.

"Captain Jesse Pigman commanded a company at Wappatomika in 1774, an old Indian fighter, who lived in Muddy Creek Section.

"Col. William Harrod—early in the French War, prior to Forbes Expedition. Harrod was stationed at, and this was probably his first service, and very likely in 1755, at Fort Littleton, (so his son thinks) and rather than receive the contumelious insults, he engaged in a fisticuff fight, and came out first best amid the shouts of 'hurrah for the widow's son.' Hence his father had deceased prior to this date." November 1845

Any person familiar with Greene County history will recognize how close this son of William Harrod was to the actual facts of our local history. He must therefore have been equally well versed in the make up of his father's family for he had full opportunity of seeing most of them during his lifetime. No other statements have appeared from any source which should be or could be more acquainted with the facts, than the record given by William Harrod, Jr. Born on Tenmile in 1773, and living there until close to 1800, where his parents, Uncle Levi, and Aunts Rachel and Mary, lived in close neighborliness to him, his information certainly was first hand. If his age did not dim his recollection of events that took place in this part of the country, then why would not his family information be equally reliable. In the face of official records, it is.

JOHN HARROD, SENIOR

The first official record we have of John Harrod, Senior, is found in Pennsylvania Colonial Records in a letter of May 1750, from Secretary Richard Peters to the Colonial governor. Secretary Peters had been sent into what is now Cumberland and adjoining counties in Pennsylvania to warn the people off the land which had not yet been purchased from the Indians. It was on this trip that the story of the "Burnt Cabins" occurred. Trader George Croghan was with Peters in the Augwick Valley where he had a home.

near the close of his life, that he removed to Bracken County, Kentucky, where he died a few years later and is buried in the old Sharon Cemetery.

Children of William and Amelia (Stephens) Harrod
1. John Harrod, of whom little is known.
2. Sarah Harrod, born August 1, 1766, died in Greene County, November 16, 1822; married William Swan, son of John and Elizabeth (Lucas) Swan. Her husband, a lad of but 16 years, served under her father on the Clark Campaign. He was born in 1762, and died December 25, 1835. Both are buried in the Swan Cemetery near Rices Landing.
3. Samuel Harrod, born January 19, 1769, died in Bracken County, Kentucky, where he was living on September 19, 1798, when he and wife Sarah made a deed for a tract of land called "Union," originally warranted to Sarah, Henry, and Barnabas O'Neal. (Deed Book 1. pp. 198.) When the patent for this tract was granted, Samuel Harrod was included with his wife Sarah, which indicates he had married Sarah O'Neal, daughter of Barnet O'Neal, Sr. Guardians had been appointed for these O'Neal children in Washington County Courts.
4. Elizabeth Harrod, born April 16, 1770.
5. William Harrod, Jr., born January 10, 1773, died in 1847. He is best known for his interview with L. C. Draper in which he gave the most authentic genealogy of the Harrod Family yet found. William Harrod, Jr., married Nancy Rice, daughter of John and Sarah (Roach) Rice. They moved to Bracken County, Kentucky, with William Harrod, Sr., about 1796. William Harrod, Jr., signed deeds in his father's estate in Clarke County, Indiana. Known children were:
   1. John Harrod.
   2. Ann Harrod, who married John Poe.
   3. Elizabeth Harrod, who married Daniel Kiger.
   4. James Harrod, whose wife was Mary ....
6. James Harrod, who died before 1814.
7. Rachel Harrod, who married February 13, 1796, Isaac Miranda.

6 Colonel James Harrod, the founder of Harrodsburg, Kentucky. Books have been written about this member of the family and there is little room here for his biography. One fact not given much notice, is that he dwelt on the Tenmile for some time before leaving to settle the town that bears his name. He is in the Bedford Tax lists for 1772, for Springhill Township, as the head of a household, perhaps that of his mother and any unmarried children of Sarah (Moore) Harrod. Indications are that he spent four or five years in the Tenmile Country, or used it as his base, before making Kentucky his permanent home. A late record not used in previous biographies, shows he enlisted at the age of 16 years in Captain Gavin Cochrane's Company in Colonel Boquet's Campaign, and was on that muster roll on June 7, 1760. At that age he was 5 feet 2½ inches tall and later references in the Henry Boquet Papers indicate that he was not cut out for an officer's servant but satisfactory as a soldier. (Boquet Papers Series 21645 pp. 2.)

7. Rachel Harrod was one of the older Harrod girls, possibly older than her brother, James. Her husband was George Newland, who went out on Boquet's Campaign under Captain Evan

Rachel Henton Notebook. Rachel Henton was a descendant of this couple.

Children

1. Sarah Harrod, born April 29, 1757.
2. Thomas Harrod, born January 15, 1761. He removed to Western Pennsylvania and his name is in the Muddy Creek Ledger, after which he removed to Kentucky. He was killed by the Indians on Harrod's Creek, Ross County, Ohio in 1803. During the Revolution he served as a Frontier Ranger in the Bedford County, Pennsylvania, Militia, where he attained the rank of Ensign.
3. Mary Harrod, born December 15, 1763.
4. William Harrod, born October 1, 1765. He received a pension for his services in the Revolution while living in Scott County, Indiana in 1836. Died at Madison at the age of 82 years.
5. Catherine Harrod, born January 14, 1767, no records.
6. Elizabeth Harrod, born July 14, 1769, married Robert Stinson, parents of Rachel Henton.
7. Rachel Harrod, born August 5, 1771.
8. John Harrod, born April 3, 1773. He and his brother, Levi, went to Kentucky before 1796, and later moved to Scott County, Indiana.
9. Levi Harrod, born August 21, 1776.

3. Samuel Harrod, eldest son of John and Sarah (Moore) Harrod, born in the Shenandoah Valley about 1735-6. Was in the Big Cove with his father in 1750. Listed in Springhill Township Tax lists for Bedford County, Pennsylvania in 1772. Was with Stoner on several exploration trips to the Mississippi before 1767. Never married. Killed by an Indian about 1780.
4. Nellie Harrod, married Valentine House. Probably parents of Andrew, Levi, and Samuel House, who came to Tenmile Country. Not yet proven.
5. William Harrod, son of John and Sarah (Moore) Harrod, was born in the Shenandoah Valley on December 9, 1737, and died in Bracken County, Kentucky, April 1, 1801. A book could easily be written about him. His son, William Harrod, Jr., in an interview with Draper, has given the highlights of the career of this soldier frontiersman. Draper is full of references to him. From boyhood to old age he served the calling of arms, and while the major part of his adult life was spent in the field, one thing to be remembered is the fact that the Tenmile Country was his home from youth to old age. He came to the Tenmile just after his marriage in Bedford County, Pennsylvania, on October 1, 1765, to Amelia Stephens. Here the most of his children were born and here his wife died in September 1793. She is probably buried on the tract "Drawl" warranted to William Harrod, December 23, 1785, but later patented to George Rex. A part of this tract now lies in the town of Jefferson. It was here that he recruited for his many campaigns, using Fort Jackson, Fort John Swan, and the fort at Redstone as a rendezvous. His children married here and at least one of them is buried here. Many of his neighbors were among those who served under him on his campaign under George Rogers Clark, perhaps the highlight of his military career. Many Greene County familes can feel justly proud that their teen-age ancestors served under this experienced commander on that campaign. It was not until after 1796,

When the commission went to the Little Cove and Big Cove, they report that they ordered a number of persons off their improvements, including John Harrod. This was at a time when William Harrod, Jr., reports his grandfather as living in the Big Cove. It was the same locality that saw James and William Harrod begin their military service under Forbes, and where William Harrod got his first commission a few years later. John Harrod is the only one that is reported of that name and he had been there at least three years. It is in the same vicinity that John Harrod, Jr., half brother of James, William, etc., spent the last years of his life. There can be little doubt that this was the father of the famous sons. From William Harrod, Jr., we must assume that John Harrod, Sr., did not stay out long, and like many of his compeers, he returned at once where he died before 1755, as William was called the "widow's son" at that time. It was in this location that John Harrod, Sr., a hardy Frontiersman himself, fitted his sons for the future lives they were to lead. He had been a pioneers in the Shenandoah after the death of his first wife, for it was here that he met and married Sarah Moore, his second wife. He could have been following the fortunes of Jost Hite, who was making the moves from New Jersey to Germantown, Pennsylvania and then into the Shenandoah about the time John Harrod, Sr., is reported in these places. We do not choose to go into the various records compiled by Mrs. Swainson and Mrs. Mason, since we are in this case concerned more in the genealogy of the Tenmile Pioneers. It would also appear that at one time or other members of each family of sons and daughters of John Harrod, Sr., came to the Tenmile Country, and there are quite a few descendants still living there.

Children of John Harrod, Sr.

1. Thomas Harrod, son by the first marriage, settled in North Carolina, where he died in Rutherford County in 1798. He made several trips to Kentucky, and there is evidence he visited the Tenmile Country. He owned land in Kentucky, and a dispute over this land discloses his children. They were:
   James Harrod, who married Elizabeth Stewart.
   Mary Harrod, who married Stephen Montgomery.
   Jane Harrod, who married William Grooms. It is to be noted that a William Grooms warranted a tract of land one farm removed from Levi Harrod in Morgan Township, Greene County, which was patented to Samuel Nyswanger.
   Elizabeth Harrod, married John Fauch.
   Leah Harrod, who married William McCallister.
   Lucinda Harrod.
   Rachel Harrod.
   Susannah Harrod.
   Hannah Harrod.
   John Harrod.
   Samuel Harrod, who married Polly Paullin.
2. John Harrod, Jr., born in Chester County, Pennsylvania about 1734, died in Bedford County, Pennsylvania, December 26, 1781. He was known as John Harwood, and as a major in the Revolution was captured when serving in Colonel Parker's Regiment under Baron DeKalb. He was taken to Canada but after returning, his injuries made him unable to do further service, and he retired to Bedford County, Pennsylvania. He married August 5, 1758, Rachel Shepherd, who died November 10, 1806. This information and the dates of the children are from the

Shelby, (Boquet Papers 21644 Vol. 2. pp. 182) and is listed in the muster roll of that company July 1759. While serving under Captain Clapham in that campaign he was taken prisoner, but on December 26, 1760, was released by the Indians and brought into Fort Pitt. He had been a member of the Pennsylvania Light Horse Regiment. (Boquet Papers 21655 pp. 103.) After Boquet's Campaign the family of George Newland removed to Berkeley County, Virginia, and then a few years later settled on the Tenmile near the present town of Jefferson, where he patented a tract of 400 acres of land on March 23, 1785, under the title of "Yellow Banks," now the Riggle Farm on Stokton's Lane. This tract he arranged to sell in 1796, when he left for Bracken County, Kentucky, but he died before the completion of the transfer and his widow, through her brother, Levi Harrod, completed the deal in 1798. (Gr. Co. Deed Book 1. pp. 185.) When Benjamin Stites sold the mill site where Pollack's Mill was later built, to Jacob Rush, and removed to the site near Fort Jackson, George Newland took an assignment of the tract from Jacob Rush, in 1787. (Washington County Deed Book 1-B-pp. 198.) Rachel Newland died in Bracken County, Kentucky, about 1811, where her will, made on August 17. 1810, was probated on October 13, 1811. Mrs. C. A. Delzell of Cheyenne, Wyoming, sent record.

Children (Bible Record)

1. Harrod Newland, born May 17, 1766 in Berkeley County, Virginia. His pension application states that in August 1833, at the age of 67 years, he was living in Indianapolis, but that when he was forty-nine years old he had left the Tenmile Country, where he had served in Captain Jesse Pigman's Company in the Revolution, and gone to Franklin County, Indiana. In 1829, he had settled in Marion County, later moving to Indianapolis. He patented a triangular tract of land adjoining the Yellow Banks tract of his father.
2. George Newland, Jr., born December 28, 1768, married, April 26, 1796, Ann Day, born November 20, 1776, a daughter of Isaac and Anna (Ambrose) Day. The Newland record is copied from their Bible.
3. John Newland, born April 28, 1772.
4. Jacob Newland, born August 8, 1775.
5. Elizabeth Newland, born January 1, 1779.
6. Joel Newland, born April 11, 1782.
7. Sarah Newland, born April 6, 1785, married, 1803, in Greene County, Ohio, Jonathan Donnell, born 1772, son of John and Mary (Fleming) Donnell.
8. Rachel Newland, born April 16, 1789.

8. Mary Harrod, daughter of John and Sarah (Moore) Harrod, married Adam Newland, who is listed as a tax payer in the Bedford County, Pennsylvania tax lists for 1772, as head of a household. As a widow on March 4, 1785, Mary Newland got a warrant for a tract of land where a part of Jefferson, Pennsylvania, now stands, but this tract was later patented by Colonel John Heaton. She had remarried before August 20, 1789, for on that date she made a deed in which she is joined by her husband, Evan Shelby, and is described as "formerly the widow of Adam Newland." Two of her children by the former marriage are represented by guardians, one of whom is married. (Washington Co. D. B. 1-F-64.)

Children

1. Lurene Newland, wife of Jesse Pigman, Jr., as shown by deed.
2. Sarah Newland, Joseph Mills was her guardian.
3. John Newland? Mentioned in Muddy Creek Ledger.
4. Richard Newland? Mentioned in Muddy Creek Ledger.

9. Sarah Harrod, daughter of John and Sarah (Moore) Harrod, never married.
10. Levi Harrod, youngest son of John and Sarah (Moore) Harrod, was born in Bedford County, Pennsylvania, on January 22, 1750, and died in Knox County, Ohio, on October 2, 1825. He married about the time his family settled on the Tenmile and is listed in the 1772 tax list as the head of a family. As a military man his services did not attain the prominence of his older brothers, but he performed his regular tours of duty in the militia, where he advanced to the rank of lieutenant, serving much of the time in the company of Captain Benjamin Stites. This service extended beyond 1790, for he is listed as a guide on the "White Woman's Campaign." (Draper Mss. 37J174.) In civil life his activities played an important part in the refinement of the frontier community. As Justice of Peace at a time when that office was more important than the present, Levi Harrod acted as wise judge and counselor. His office at his home near the present Harold Bell Poultry Farm, was the scene of many early weddings in which he performed the ceremony. For many years he served as Moderator in Goshen Baptist Church, where he and his wife both belonged, and where he was frequently called upon to settle differences among members, or recall some erring member to his or her duty. It may be said that his influence was a factor in all walks of life in the Tenmile Country. Shortly before 1800, his sons began pioneering in Knox County, Ohio, and in the twilight of his years, Levi Harrod sold his plantation on Tenmile to join his children at that place. Goshen Baptist Church records disclose that on July 28, 1811, he and his wife asked for letters of dismissal and in 1813, they moved to Ohio. His wife was Rachel Mills, who was born October 22, 1752, and died September 28, 1834. She is buried with her husband in the Union Graveyard in Harrison Township. Levi Harrod's will was made on September 24, 1825, and names nine of his twelve children.

Children of Levi and Rachel (Mills) Harrod

1. John Harrod, born 1770-72, died in Knox County, Ohio, March 17, 1814; he married in Greene County, Pennsylvania, Mary Stocton, who joined him in a deed of July 1, 1806, in the sale of their land to William Buckingham. His burial was the first made in Owl Creek Cemetery in Knox County.
2. Michael Harrod, born 1774, died April 11, 1853; married Agnes Ulery. He and his wife sold their land in Greene County in 1811 to Allan Topping and Stephen Crayne, and moved to Knox County, Ohio, where at one time he owned 1700 acres of land. They were parents of fifteen children.
3. Sarah Harrod is mentioned in her father's will, though an estrangement is indicated, as her father is uncertain as to whether she was living at that time, and makes certain that any of her children may not inherit from his estate if she be dead. It has been ascertained that she had re-

moved to Kentucky about 1800, and settled in Harrison County where the heirs of her husband, Benajah Dunn, are found in Deed Book 15 pp. 421. Her husband, Benajah Dunn, probably the son of Benajah Dunn, Sr., who in 1774, sold cattle to Captain William Harrod for the Dunmore War, had died in Kentucky about 1835, his estate being settled there in January Term of Court in 1835. Sarah is not named among the heirs and it may be presumed she had died before her husband, but the names of the heirs clearly indicate the relationship. A Bible record has been sent by Mrs. Price Doyle of Murray, Kentucky.

Children of Benajah and Sarah (Harrod) Dunn
1. Elizabeth Dunn, who married, February 2, 1815, John Swinford. A Bible record of this family shows that she was born October 18, 1793, and died in Nodaway County, Missouri, April 26, 1880. Her husband was born April 14, 1796, and died September 18, 1847.
2. Rachel Dunn, married, February 19, 1818, William Price.
3. Benajah Dunn, Jr., executor in his father's estate, married, February 19, 1818, to Susannah Harris.
4. Zepheniah Dunn, married, November 3, 1823, Lavina Brownfield.
5. Abijah Dunn, wife's name was Nancy ....
6. Massy Dunn, married, September 2, 1823, George Wolf.
7. Levi Dunn, married, October 31, 1804, Sarah Hinton.
8. Sarah Dunn, married, March 8, 1828, Samuel Smith.
9. John Dunn, whose wife was Patsy ....
10. James Dunn, who died prior to his father and left children.

4. Levi Harrod, Jr., born in Greene County, Pennsylvania, January 30, 1777, died in Knox County, Ohio, December 14, 1862. He married, February 14, 1800, Rebecca Burge, daughter of Elijah and Mary (Minor) Burge, born in Greene County in 1780, and died in Knox County on July 7, 1866. Removed to Ohio in 1804.

Children
1. Levi Harrod, 3d, born June 10, 1801, married, September 27, 1821, Martha Henry. He died January 20, 1883. His wife, who was born June 5, 1800, died August 14, 1879.
2. Jacob Harrod, born November 7, 1803.
3. Mary Harrod, born March 28, 1806, married .... Holt.
4. James Harrod, born September 3, 1808.
5. Jemima Harrod, born October 1, 1810.
6. John Harrod, born February 3, 1813.
7. Elijah Harrod, born January 18, 1815.
8. Elizabeth Harrod, born June 13, 1817.
9. William Harrod, born October 4, 1819.
10. Rachel Harrod, born April 16, 1822.
11. Martha Harrod, born October 3, 1824.
12. Minor Harrod, born March 27, 1827.

5. William Harrod, son of Levi and Rachel (Mills) Harrod, married Rhoda Pipes.
6. Mary Harrod, daughter of Levi and Rachel (Mills) Harrod, married Daniel Johnson.
7. Samuel Harrod, son of Levi and Rachel (Mills) Harrod, born 1788, died in Clay Township, Knox County, Ohio, August 12, 1863. He married Eleanor Mills, daughter of John and Eleanor Mills. She died April 10, 1875.

Children

1. Rachel Harrod, born April 6, 1811.
2. Levi Harrod, born May 18, 1813.
3. Sarah Harrod, born July 28, 1815.
4. Charity Harrod, born September 9, 1817.
5. Mary Harrod, born September 24, 1819.
6. Joseph Harrod, born September 27, 1823.
7. Jemima Harrod, born January 14, 1825.
8. Elizabeth Harrod, born July 6, 1827.
9. Martha Harrod, born August 15, 1830.
10. Samuel Harrod, his wife was Hannah Mellick, born November 11, 1833.

8. Thomas Harrod, died young.
9. Jemimah Harrod, married Jeremiah Biggs, son of Jeremiah and Abigail Biggs.
10. James Harrod, married Rhoda Mills.
11. Rachel Harrod, married William Biggs.
12. Elizabeth Harrod, daughter of Levi and Rachel (Mills) Harrod, born 1785, died in Greene County, Pennsylvania, December 1861. She married Isaac Bell, son of James and Mary (Knox) Bell, born in 1784, died January 1824. Both are buried in the old cemetery on the Stephen Hill Farm near Jefferson.

Children

1. Levi Harrod Bell, born March 12, 1807, married Sarah Fulton, born July 2, 1807.
2. James Bell, born 1809, died 1897, married Elizabeth Swan, daughter of Samuel and Mary (Hiller) Swan. She was born May 8, 1816, and died May 30, 1904.
3. David Bell, born 1814, died July 18, 1871, married Lettice Adamson.
4. Isaac Bell.
5. Rachel Bell, born 1812, died July 12, 1863, never married.
6. Mary Bell, born May 26, 1816, died September 16, 1899; married Stephen Crayne, born January 4, 1813; buried in Baptist Cemetery, Jefferson.
7. John Bell, born 1825, died October 15, 1866, married Sarah Whitlatch.
8. Catherine Bell, died in infancy.

11. Elizabeth Harrod, daughter of John and Sarah (Moore) Harrod, married Benjamin Davis, a cousin of General Anthony Wayne. (Draper Mss 27J. 169.)
12. Jemimah Harrod, daughter of John and Sarah (Moore) Harrod, never married.

Philadelphia, Wednesday, September 26, 1787

The following draft of a Proclamation, was laid before Council, read and adopted:

PENNSYLVANIA, ss:

By the Supreme Executive Council of the Commonweath of Pennsylvania.

A PROCLAMATION

WHEREAS, A certain agreement was entered into between this Commonwealth and the Commonwealth of Virginia, on the thirty-first day of August, 1779, which Agreement was afterwards, to wit: on the twenty-third of June, 1780, confirmed by the State of Virginia, subject to several conditions, one of which was: "That the private property and rights of all persons, acquired under, founded on, or recognized by the laws of either State, previous to the twenty-third of June, 1780, aforesaid, be secured and confirmed to them, although they should be found to fall within the other; and that in the decisions of disputes therein, preference shall be given to the elder or prior right, whichever of the said States, the same shall have been acquired under; such persons paying to the State within whose boundary their lands shall be included, the same purchase money which would have been due from them to the State, under which they claimed the right, etc."

AND WHEREAS, It hath been made manifest to Council, that divers persons have applied to the State of Virginia, and have procured patents after the said twenty-third of June, 1780, whereby this Commonwealth is deprived of part of one of the branches of the revenue, and many well disposed persons may be led by such examples to procure patents in the same manner, to the future loss and damage of themselves, and of such may come into their place by purchase or otherwise:

WE DO THEREFORE, Warn all such persons who have procured patents from Virginia, since the said twenty-third day of June, 1780, not to rely on them as good titles to their lands, as also all such as are entitled to a confirmation of their titles to unpatented lands, whether originating in Virginia or Pennsylvania, that the Act of Assembly in being respecting the patenting all such lands, will expire on the tenth day of April, 1788, of which all persons concerned, are to take notice, and govern themselves accordingly.

GIVEN IN COUNCIL, Under the hand of the Honorable Charles Biddle, Esquire, Vice President, and the seal of the State, at Philadelphia, this twenty-sixth day of September, in the year of our Lord one thousand seven hundred and eighty-seven.

CHARLES BIDDLE, V. P.

ATTEST: JOHN ARMSTRONG, Junior Secretary.

GOD SAVE THE COMMONWEALTH

(From the "Minutes of the Supreme Executive Council of Pennsylvania" published by the State, Harrisburg, 1853. Volume XV, PP. 281.)

LAND TITLES

The above Proclamation answers a number of questions that are frequently asked. It also refutes the statements frequently found in Family Histories, that land in the Tenmile Country was granted for military service. Virginia promised and gave land for services in the French and Indian War, Dunmore's War, and the Revolution, and Pennsylvania set aside land which it granted for service in the Revolution. But none of these grants lay within the present borders of Washington, Greene, or Fayette Counties. The military land granted by Pennsylvania lay in the north western counties of the State, while Virginia set aside a large acreage for that purpose on the western bank of the Scioto River, north of the Ohio. It explains the rush to secure legal titles in the period from 1779 to 1788. For all practical purposes it disposed of the mythical tomahawk rights, corn grants, and squatters rights, though these were sometimes later settled by purchase rather than taking the matters through the Courts. In a way too, it accounts for some of the migration westward during these years. Persons without legal titles obtained through either Pennsylvania or Virginia, found it more profitable to buy up unimproved land in Kentucky, Virginia, and Ohio, than to pay the fees demanded by Pennsylvania. It is true that much land was patented at a later date than 1788, some even in the late years. Much of this land was probably considered valueless, while much of it was also abandoned by the first purchasers and reverted to the State again. Some of it was overlooked in the earlier surveys, and only taken up when it became valuable for the coal that was found underneath the surface. The late patents are noted to have been secured during the coal, gas, and oil leasing, and are for small overlooked triangles or worthless stream beds, rocky hillsides, or swamp lands. The Proclamation also explains the legend "by virtue of a Virginia Certificate" which is found so often in the patent specifications.

CAPTAIN WILLIAM HARROD'S COMPANY
AT THE FALLS OF THE OHIO, 1779

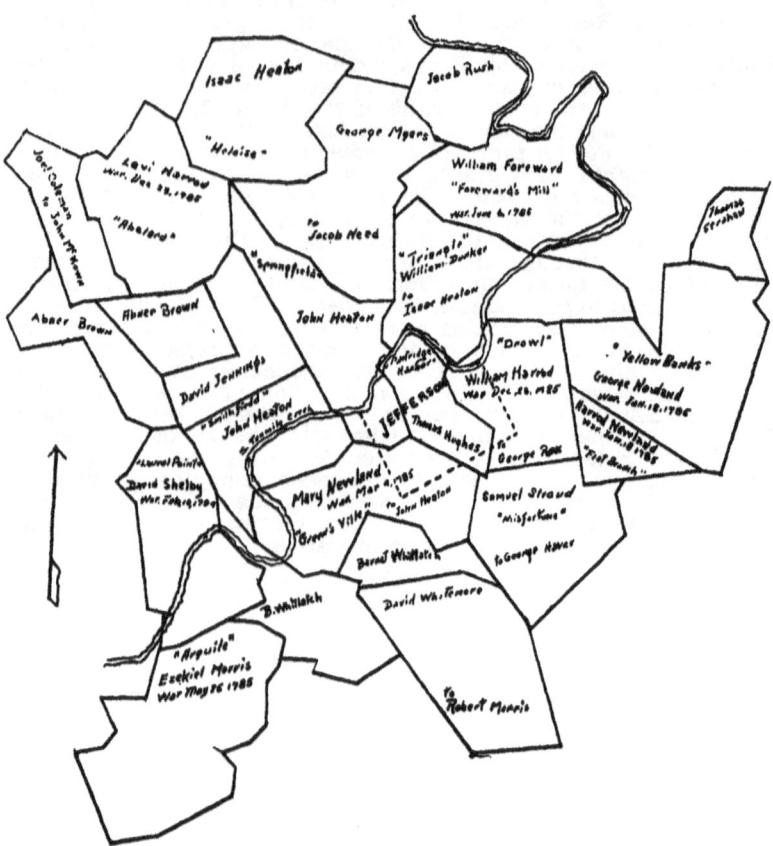

After the Illinois Campaign with Clark, William Harrod spent the winter building a town at the Falls of the Ohio, present day Louisville. The following is the list of his company sent in by Mrs. John B. Mason, presumably taken from the rolls in the Draper Collection. The second list is William Harrod's Company at Chillicothe in June 1779, and from the same source.

WILLIAM HARROD, Captain

James Patton, Lieutenant
Edward Bulger, Ensign

James Harris, Sergeant
Henry Honacker, Sergeant
Levi Teal, Sergeant

PRIVATES

George Smyth
William Smyth
Samuel Harris
  (killed)
Stephen Harris
Mahu Harris
John McManus, Sr.
John McManus, Jr.
George McManus
Abraham James
William Swan
Peter Parel
John Paul
Frederick Honaker
John Williams
Richard Chenowith
John Saunders
Joseph Line
John Shinn
Thomas Simpson
John Tuel
Henry Prather

Thomas Cochran
Levi Young
George Pugh
Francis Gimlet
Andrew Gimlet
Samuel Frazee
Daniel Hall
William Hannah
Isaac McBride
William Ray
John Swan
Isaac Vanmeter
Jacob Vanmeter
Van Swearington
Thomas Batten
Edward Richardson
Charles Bilderback
Alex McIntyre
William Greathouse
John Hughes
John Handley
Nathan Randolph

Leaton White
Handel Vance
Jacob Spears
Herman Canolspice
Richard Clark
Arisabum Goodman
Aaron Forman
Henry French
Francis Hannah
John Crable
John Backus
Thomas Bull
Alexander Wilson
Jeremiah Slater
John Griffith
Gabriel Griffith
Richard Morris
Morris Morris
Joseph Frakes
Henry Hall
William Hall

Chillicothe List, June 1779

WILLIAM HARROD, Captain

James Patton, Lieutenant
Edward Bulger, Ensign

William Oldham, Sergeant
Daniel Stull, Sergeant
Beverley Trent, Sergeant

PRIVATES

James Guthery
Cap. Sullivan
Solomon Carpenter
Samuel Hinch
Peter Sturgis
Michael Humble
Samuel Pottinger
James Stewart
Jonas Potts
Thomas Simpson
Angus Cameron
William Smilley
John Hunt
Thomas Pribble

Hardy Hill
John Crable
Henry Hall
John Paul
Daniel Driscoll
John Honacker
Samuel Frazee
Joseph Frazee
Thomas Suttles
Reuben Pribble
Edward Murdock
Patrick McGee
John Stapleton
James Welch

Moses Kuykendall
Abraham Vanmeter
John Lewis
Samuel Foster
Isaac Dye
Adam Wickerham
Michael Vitits
Jacob Speck
Peter Bellos
John Wickerham
Samuel Moore
  (killed)

ABNER BROWN

Abner and Ebeneezer Brown, said to have been brothers, and Paul Brown, were members of Captain Benjamin Stites' Militia Company from Morgan Township. Abner Brown received patents for two tracts of land between the land of Levi Harrod and Tenmile Creek, one on February 20, 1786, and the other on March 22, 1796, for a total of about 265 acres. His wife was Abigail Luse, daughter of Eleazer and Jemima Luse. In the Spring of 1805, Abner Brown, Sr., with his brother, Ebeneezer, and Abner Brown, Jr., removed to Knox County, Ohio, where they erected the first grist-mill, an entirely wooden structure on Delano's Run above the Martinsburg Road. The building was about ten feet square and made of rough logs, and when the stream was full of water, had no difficulty in supplying the neighborhood with its corn meal, ground in a sort of sugar trough. Abner Brown, Sr., died in Knox County, Ohio, where his will was proven on October 29, 1827. The will had been made on August 28, of the same year. The children below are named in the will.

Children of Abner and Abigail (Luse) Brown

1. Abner Brown, Jr.
2. Ebeneezer Brown.
3. Mary Brown.
4. Jeremiah Brown, who, on April 16, 1816, married in Ohio, Margaret Merritt.
5. Aaron Brown.

THE BIGGS FAMILY

The Census for Washington County, Pennsylvania, shows a widow, Abigail Biggs, living on the land between Abner Brown, Sr., and Abner Brown, Jr., in what is now Morgan Township, Greene County. She was the widow of Captain John Biggs, who was captured and burned at stake on the Crawford Expedition. It is thought that she was a daughter of Abner Brown, Sr., whose wife was Abigail Luse.

Benjamin Biggs, father of Captain John Biggs, was born in Marbletown, Ulster County, New York, April 28, 1723, and died in West Liberty, Ohio County, West Virginia, November 1782. His wife was Henrietta Prudence Margaretta Munday, whom he married September 26, 1745, in All Saints Church, Frederick, Maryland. She died May 16, 1807, at West Liberty at the age of 79 years. Benjamin Biggs sold his land in Maryland in 1769 to his brother William Biggs and moved first to Fort Cumberland and then to Beesons Fort (Uniontown) where he was taxed in 1772, then in 1774, he removed to Black's Cabin in Ohio County, (West) Virginia, where he died. Six of his sons were famous Indian fighters.

Children of Benjamin and Henrietta (Munday) Biggs

1. Prudence Biggs, born 1748, died 1777.
2. Catherine Biggs, born February 1, 1750, married James Moore.
3. John Biggs, born December 27, 1751, married Abigail Brown (?)
4. Henry Biggs, born January 31, 1753, died November 26, 1774.
5. Benjamin Biggs, twin of Henry Biggs.
6. William Biggs, born June 3, 1755.
7. George Biggs, born January 31, 1758, took Oath of Allegiance in Ohio County in 1777.
8. Thomas Biggs, born May 19, 1760.
9. Joseph Biggs, born May 2, 1762.
10. Zacheus Biggs, born June 1, 1764.
11. Mary Biggs, born June 3, 1767, married James Moore after the death of her sister. They lived on Buffalo Creek, Ohio County.

FAMILY OF JOHN BIGGS

Captain John Biggs, born December 27, 1751, son of Benjamin Biggs, was appointed a lieutenant of militia at the first session of the Virginia Court at Blacks Cabin on Short Creek, Ohio County, in January 1777, and took an active part in the defense of the frontiers. He was a frequent visitor to the Tenmile Country where his wife's people had settled. He was chosen one of the captains at Mingo Bottoms on the Sandusky Expedition and was captured and burned at the stake. He had performed with outstanding bravery on the Expedition, saving the life of a wounded brother officer who had been badly injured. He was in possession of an Indian Scalp when captured, a fact that may have hastened the death of Captain Biggs, for both he and the officer whom he had saved were murdered before the Colonel. The story of his death was told by Dr. Knight. At the time of his death in June 1782, it is not likely that Captain John Biggs was father of more than five or six children, and certainly not nine as given by one of the Ohio historians. After the death of Captain John Biggs, his wife, Abigail, returned to her people on the Tenmile, living on land of Abner Brown, Sr., adjoining the land of Levi Harrod. As her children went to Knox County, Ohio, about 1804, it is most likely that she went with them to that place.

Children of John and Abigail Biggs

1. Rachel Biggs, wife of David Casto, lived next to her mother on Tenmile.
2. William Biggs, married Rachel Harrod, daughter of Levi and Rachel (Mills) Harrod.
3. Jeremiah Biggs, married Jemima Harrod, daughter of Levi and Rachel (Mills) Harrod.
4. Andrew Biggs, married Esther Howell.
5. Joseph Biggs, went to New York.
6. Daughter? Said to have married .... Clagget.

THE RICE FAMILY

The town of Rices Landing, at the Mouth of Swan's Run (Enoch's or Pumpkin Run) was an important shipping point on the Monongahela River for many year, and because of this it is not surprising that one of the first boat yards was situated at this place. Until comparatively recent years it was the shipping point for the bulk of freight from Waynesburg and other parts of Greene County. Before the advent of railroads to this section, passengers took the boats here for Pittsburgh. Tanneries, saw mills, and at one time a pottery were located in this vicinity. The town which grew up here was laid out on land originally owned by John Rice, from whom it took its name. Abijah McClain laid out another portion of the town on his own land.

John Rice was an early settler, obtaining by virtue of a Virginia Certificate, issued to him April 13, 1780, a tract of 389 acres, which he patented under the title of "Prospect." This was a fitting title since the site had a fine view of the Monongahela River in both directions. On the same day Acquilla Martin obtained his patent to the tract adjoining. A law suit in Hardin County, Kentucky, indicates that Acquilla Martin was a half brother of John Rice's wife. There is evidence to indicate that John Rice and his brother-in-law, Thomas Roach, came from the upper Shenandoah Valley, after living for a time on Patterson's Creek in Hampshire County, (West) Virginia. A will on file in Frederick County, Virginia, shows that a John Rice made his will there November 2, 1782, which was probated May 3, 1785, naming his wife, Hannah, and children, Mary, Sarah, George, Edmund, John and James Rice. (Will Book 5. pp. 73.) Mention is made of brothers, George and Edmund Rice, the latter of whom is listed in the Bedford County tax list of 1772, as living in what is now Fayette County, Pennsylvania (Tyrone Township).

Another item that connects John Rice of Rices Landing with the Hampshire family is a sale by Rev. John Corbly on April 16, 1773, for the small sum of 5 shillings, 52 acres of land which Rev. Corbly had obtained by a grant from Lord Fairfax and situated on the Great Cacapon, to John Rice of Hampshire County. There is a tradition in the Corbly family that after the death of Rev. John Corbly's first wife, he left his children by that marriage with John Rice of Hampshire County, Va., until his second marriage to Elizabeth Tyler. The small sum paid in this transaction seems to confirm this tradition, and the presence of Thomas Roach, brother-in-law of John Rice, among the members of Rev. Corbly's Church at Garards Fort, seems to confirm the belief that John Rice of Rices Landing, was the son mentioned in the will of John Rice of Frederick County, Virginia. (Deed Book 3. pp. 137 Hampshire County, Virginia.)

John Rice died intestate in Greene County in 1802, his estate being administered by his son, Nathan Rice, who filed papers February 8, 1802. But it is from the will of Thomas Roach, who made the children of his sister, Sarah Rice, wife of John Rice, heirs of his estate after the death of his wife, Rachel Roach, that we learn the names of all the children of John Rice. The will of Thomas Roach was probated December 18, 1828. (Will Book 1. pp. 350.)

Children of John and Sarah (Roach) Rice

1. William Rice, died in Cumberland Township about 1851. For many years he operated the Brick Tavern House at Rices

Landing, where he also maintained the ferry across the Monongahela River. His estate also mentions the ownership of a coal bank at that place. (O. C. Docket 4. pp. 7. December 1854.) His wife's name was Rebecca ....

Children of William and Rebecca Rice

1. Lucinda Rice, married Thomas Crago.
2. Margaret Rice, married Hiram Horner.
3. William Rice, Jr.
4. Isabella Rice, married George Kline.
5. Sarah Ann Rice, born February 15, 1830, died February 23, 1902, married 1849, Hiram Curl, born March 1, 1826, died January 25, 1892.
6. James Rice.
7. Samuel Rice.
8. Elizabeth Rice.
9. Henry Rice.

2. John Rice, Jr.
3. Thomas Rice, born April 5, 1774, married Susannah Myers, born July 2, 1776, daughter of George Myers, Sr., and wife,

Child of Thomas and Susannah (Myers) Rice

1. Rachel Rice, born 1798, died April 16, 1866, married Noah Teal, born August 22, 1800, died September 17, 1876.

4. Nancy Rice married William Harrod, Jr., born January 10, 1773, died in Clark County, Indiana, in 1847, son of Captain William and Amelia (Stephens) Harrod. William Harrod, Jr., was the man who gave the interview to L. C. Draper, which has been quoted so frequently in this record. He moved first to Bracken County, Kentucky, and then to Indiana.

Children of William and Nancy (Rice) Harrod

1. John Harrod.
2. Ann Harrod, married John Poe.
3. Elizabeth Harrod, married Daniel Kiger.
4. James Harrod, married Mary ....

5. Mary Rice, married Henry Sharpnack. (See separate record to follow.)
6. Rachel Rice, married Robert McMinn. Bates "History of Greene County" says he was born in Ireland, and was a school teacher for many years before taking up farming. There are no dates available for Robert McMinn or his wife. The family reports that they died near Carmichaels and were buried in an old cemetery in "the Old Town," but that their bodies were later removed to Laurel Point Cemetery. It may be well to note that a William McMinn was naturalized at Waynesburg on January 26, 1818, while a John McMinn was also naturalized here in August 1808. William McMinn stated he had come from Ireland to America, arriving here on June 18, 1812. John McMinn stated he had lived in the United States at least five years prior to the date of his application for naturalization. No such application is found for Robert McMinn. Because of this circumstance, it may be well to mention that one Robert McMinn was a soldier in Captain James Denny's Company, Chester County, Pennsylvania

Militia, under Colonel John Gardner in August 1780, and apparently the same man served in Captain Thomas Laird's Cumberland County Militia Company from September 10, 1780, until October 21, 1780. The relationship of these men is not shown, but these records indicate this Irish Family was migrating to America before the end of the Revolution.

Children of Robert and Rachel (Rice) McMinn

1. Elizabeth McMinn, married James Mahana.
2. Mary McMinn, married James Pogue.
3. Sarah McMinn, born 1815, died 1844, married John Curl, born 1808, died February 4, 1894.
4. Thomas R. McMinn, born April 22, 1820, married Elizabeth Pollock.
7. Jesse Rice.
8. Nathan Rice, administrator of his father's estate. He died intestate about 1821.
9. Hannah Rice, married .... Miller.
10. Sarah Rice, married .... Harling.
11. Benjamin Rice, named youngest son in the will of Thomas Roach. The will of Benjamin Rice was made March 30, 1852, and probated February 24, 1854. His wife was Sarah Crago, a daughter of Thomas and Priscilla (Thurman) Crago. Charles Rice and Clark Rice were the administrators for the estate of Benjamin Rice. (Will Book 3. pp. 153.)

Children of Benjamin and Sarah (Crago) Rice

1. John Rice.
2. Thomas Rice, married Priscilla Crago, daughter of John and Ann (Hiller) Crago.
3. Samuel Rice.
4. Charles Rice.
5. David Rice, born 1822, died March 10, 1892.
6. Clark Rice, born 1828, died 1899; married Susan ...., born 1841, died 1914.
7. Andrew Rice.
8. Priscilla Rice, died before her father leaving children. Her husband was Joseph Sedgewick, born October 5, 1811, died March 3, 1882.

THE HENRY SHARPNACK FAMILY

There can be little doubt that there are certain inaccuracies in the traditions of the Sharpnack Family, but just where tradition leaves off and facts take hold, that portion must be left to the family historians. One story is published in the "History of Ritchie County, West Virginia." It states that the ancestor of the Sharpnack Family, first name not given, left Prussia in 1759, with wife and one child, but died enroute to America and was buried at sea. The widow and son Peter Sharpnack, landed at Philadelphia, where soon afterwards the son, Henry Sharpnack, was born. The tradition goes on to say that the sons, Henry and Peter, grew up and became silk merchants in Philadelphia. In due time they disposed of their business, with Peter Sharpnack returning to Prussia at Eberfield Half Camp, and Henry Sharpnack coming to Rices Landing, where he married in 1783, Mary Rice, daughter of John and Sarah (Roach) Rice.

A portion of this story may be true, but it is evident from known facts that a part of it must be revised or explained. In the year 1790, Henry Sharpnack was still living in Germantown, Philadelphia County, at the head of a family that consisted of one adult male, two males under 16 years of age, and three females. At the same time Peter Sharpnack was living in Mifflin County Pennsylvania, the head of a family of three adult males, three males under 16 years of age, and three females. We shall hazard an explanation that Peter Sharpnack may have gone back to Prussia long enough to settle his father's estate, and then returned to Pennsylvania to live for a time at least, in that portion of Mifflin County, where in 1790, lived the families of George Rex, Robert Pennington, Archibald Hamilton, Benjamin Smalley, and other names later identified with the Tenmile Country. As for Henry Sharpnack marrying Mary Rice at Rices Landing in 1783, if that is a true statement, then he must have returned to Philadelphia to be living there in 1790. From what we know of the family of Henry Sharpnack, it is true that he must have married about 1783, and the will of Thomas Roach shows that Mary Rice married Henry Sharpnack. Could it be that she was a second wife, married after settlement of Henry Sharpnack at Rices Landing?

Burials in Hewitts Cemetery at Rices Landing disclose another interesting fact not mentioned in the family traditions. At least two Henry Sharpnacks, whose ages cannot differ more than 12 years, must have come to that place about the same time, and descendants of both men are buried there. The explanation seems to be that Henry Sharpnack, who died May 14, 1860, at the age of 88 years, and is buried in Hewitts Cemetery with wife, Elizabeth, who died March 22, 1851, aged 80 years, was a son of Peter Sharpnack, orphaned immigrant, and thus a nephew of Henry Sharpnack, posthumously born son of the man buried at sea. The latter Henry Sharpnack is reported to have died in 1848, but no cemetery record is found for either he or his wife. It may be presumed that they died at the home of one of their children, then living away from the Tenmile Country.

Known children of Henry Sharpnack

1. Daniel Sharpnack, died about 1821 in Greene County. (O. C. Docket 1. pp. 175 March 1822.) His wife was Mary Shroyer, born November 26, 1782, died August 25, 1870. She has a marker in Hewitts Cemetery.

Children of Daniel and Mary (Stroyer) Sharpnack

1. Anthony Sharpnack, over 14 years of age in 1822.
2. John Sharpnack, over 14 years of age in 1822.
3. Samuel Sharpnack.
4. Daniel Sharpnack.
5. Elizabeth Sharpnack.
6. Mary Sharpnack.
7. Thomas Sharpnack, born June 9, 1805, died October 2, 1876; married Catherine Haver, born November 27, 1813, died November 3, 1887.
8. Rachel Sharpnack.

2. William Sharpnack, born 1785, died 1840 in Wetzell County, West Virginia. His wife was Sarah Anderson, whom he married about 1808. (Tyler County D. B. 9. pp. 546.)

Children of William and Sarah (Anderson) Sharpnack

1. Richard Sharpnack.
2. Daniel Sharpnack.
3. Samuel Sharpnack, married in Tyler County, December 23, 1838, Lucretia Long.
4. William Sharpnack, born 1810, died July 8, 1890; married in Tyler County, November 12, 1835, Sarah Harris. His second wife was Margaret Cokely, and third wife was Eleanor Pipes of Tyler County.
5. John Sharpnack, married in Tyler County, September 19, 1827, Margaret Hunter.
6. Peter Sharpnack.
7. Jacob Sharpnack.
8. Hiram Sharpnack, born April 11, 1818, married 1843, Lydia Harris.
9. Jane Sharpnack.
10. Hester Sharpnack.
11. Mary Sharpnack, married in Tyler County, April 2, 1829, Josiah Twibble.
12. Rachel Sharpnack, married January 1, 1834, John Hays.

3. Peter Sharpnack, died in Greene County in 1845, married Mary Alfree, who died in 1867.

Children of Peter and Mary (Alfree) Sharpnack

1. Thomas Sharpnack, born June 30, 1827, married, June 27, 1852, Elizabeth Craft, born November 6, 1826.
2. Dr. George Sharpnack went to California.
3. Lettie Sharpnack, married Joseph Alfree, born August 28, 1823, died December 21, 1916, son of Thomas Alfree.
4. Elizabeth Sharpnack, married (1) John Neel, married (2) Joseph Crago.
5. Mary Sharpnack, never married.

4. Samuel Sharpnack, born August 13, 1788, died February 13, 1852, married Nancy Crago, born February 26, 1791, died August 26, 1870. She was a daughter of Priscilla (Thurman) Crago. Both are buried at Hewitts.

Children of Samuel and Nancy (Crago) Sharpnack

1. William Sharpnack, born June 9, 1810, died September 29, 1907, married Sarah Neel, born March 22, 1813, died June 15, 1893. Buried at Hewitts.

2. Thomas Sharpnack, born 1811, died February 9, 1844, aged 32 years, 5 months, 11 days. He married Lucinda ...., born 1820, died March 26, 1895.
3. Priscilla Sharpnack, born 1815, died July 6, 1847, married Josias Anderson.
4. Mary Sharpnack, married Jeremiah Reynolds, born 1811, died January 4, 1869.
5. Elizabeth Sharpnack, married James Thompson.
6. Clementine Sharpnack, married John Ridge.
7. Peter Sharpnack, born September 22, 1822, died September 29, 1907, married Catherine Hughes, born May 6, 1828, died February 4 1898.
5. Jacob Sharpnack (?) no record.
6. John Sharpnack, died about 1858. His wife was Sarah Antrim. There were 10 daughters and one son in this family.

Children of John and Sarah (Antrim) Sharpnack

1.   6.
2.   7.
3.   8.
4.   9.
5.   10.
11. Levi Sharpnack, born December 24, 1850, married Elizabeth Curl.
7. Henry Sharpnack, born February 18, 1799, died January 27, 1879, married Elizabeth Rice, born August 24, 1804, died March 5, 1896. Both are buried at Hewitts.

Children of Henry and Elizabeth (Rice) Sharpnack

1. Mary Ann Sharpnack, never married.
2. Margaret Sharpnack, died March 13, 1871, aged 42 years. She married Hiram Estle.
3. Elizabeth Sharpnack, born 1836, died 1913; married, February 8, 1869, John Kerr, born December 28, 1832, died 1912.
4. William Henry Sharpnack born 1839, died December 13, 1890; married, July 3, 1862, Elizabeth Kerr, born September 12, 1841, died April 21, 1931.
5. Sarah Priscilla Sharpnack, married George Hewitt.
6. Abel J. Sharpnack, born August 25, 1847, married (1) Caroline Rinehart, born 1847, died March 6, 1873, married (2) Martha Bowser.
8. Margaret Sharpnack, born February 14, 1801, died April 11, 1876; married Levi Blackledge, born October 15, 1797, died November 15, 1870; son of Enoch and Sarah (Adamson) Blackledge. They are buried in the cemetery on Stockton's Lane.

Children of Levi and Margaret (Sharpnack) Blackledge

1. Mary Blackledge, born 1822, died 1858; married, June 23, 1852, James Rhodes.
2. Sarah Blackledge, born 1825, died March 29, 1859; married, December 25, 1855, Alexander Stewart.
3. Martha Blackledge, born October 24, 1830, died 1863; married March 16, 1853, Samuel Lewis, born 1825. Buried in Stockton's Lane Cemetery.
4. Stiers Blackledge, born 1833, died 1911; married Allena Crouch, who died September 29, 1937. Buried at Jefferson.
5. Enoch Blackledge, died in infancy.

DAVID DUNCAN

David Duncan was a native of Cumberland County, Pennsylvania before removing to Westmoreland County, where he was an important Indian Trader during the early days of the Revolution. He had been taken prisoner during Dunmore's War and escaped the danger of death through the intercession of Chief White Eyes. For three months beginning May 1, 1778, he was a Captain of 52 officers and men under General Hand, his junior officers being John Bradley and Robert McKinley. (Draper Mss 3NN-8.) While living in Westmoreland County, he was appointed Assistant Commissary General, probably through the influence of his Cumberland County neighbor, Ephraim Blaine, who served as Commissary General for Pennsylvania. In 1781, we find him listed as Commissioner of Purchases for Westmoreland County. (Penna. Arch. Series VI Vol. 2. pp. 261.) When General Brodhead was called up for court-martial and forced to give up his post at Fort Pitt, David Duncan also came under censure for his part in the dealings in the supply department, being accused and apparently not unjustly, of furthering his own financial position.

During his stay in the district he had plenty of opportunity to become acquainted with the land in the Muddy Creek Section, and he became the patentee of a number of tracts including "Plenty," "Felicity," and "Content," tracts that were at the present village of Khedive, for which he obtained a warrant in 1786, having obtained them through a Virginia Certificate. These tracts which he probably owned at a much earlier date than his warrant shows, were close to the land mentioned as having been improved in the Summer of 1766, by Josias Crawford. General Brodhead reports sending him down here for gathering of supplies for the garrison at Fort Pitt and not always with success. He also helped gather recruits in the district for the Eighth Pennsylvania Regiment, which fought at Saratoga, Brandywine, and Germantown, in which regiment his son-in-law, John Finley, served as a Captain.

David Duncan was born in Pennsylvania about 1730-35 and died in Allegheny County, Pennsylvania, in 1792. His wife, Margaret Hamilton, survived him more than thirty-two years, dying in Fleming County, Kentucky, in 1824. They were parents of Samuel Duncan, who married Ann Smith; David Duncan, Jr.; Hanah Duncan, who married Major John Finley; Mary Duncan, wife of David Clark; and Margaret Duncan, who married Isaac Holvey.

THE MOREDOCK FAMILY

I refuse to enter into the controversy as to how the name should be spelled, other than to say I have seen it written Moredock, Mordoc, Murdock, Murdick, Mordock, etc., in records that all refer to the same family. Following usage by the branches of the family we will use the Moredock spelling for the Rices Landing settlers and Murdock for the Muddy Creek group. The two groups are descended from brothers, Daniel Moredock at Rices Landing, and James Murdock on Muddy Creek, and they were among the first settlers in their respective locations. Both men are listed in the tax list for Springhill Township, Bedford County, in 1772. They appear to have come from Maryland, though the name is found in the lower Shenandoah Valley and in eastern Pennsylvania at an early date.

On May 20, 1772, Daniel Moredock bought two tracts of land from Adam Smith of Virginia, one of which was bounded by Rushy Run and the other by Enoch's or Swan's Run. The two tracts joined and included the fine land about the Dry Tavern at Rices Landing. This sale was recorded on February 24, 1782, in Washington County, Pennsylvania, (Deed Book 1-A-pp. 214) and is pretty good refutation of the value of tomahawk claims.

Daniel Moredock does not appear on local military rolls, but this is not strange since he lived in the district from which the Captain Jesse Pigman Company was recruited. But we do find the names of Edward Moredock and John Moredock in Captain William Harrod's Company which was on the George Rogers Clark Expedition. They were also out under Harrod in 1780, on Bowman's Campaign, when John Moredock was killed probably at Pickaway. Edward Moredock was also reported killed in Ohio. These deaths are reported by William Harrod, Jr., in his interview with Draper, and the familiar way in which he speaks of them indicates they were well known to him. As the Harrods were near neighbors of the Moredocks, and since Captain William Harrod's Company was made up mostly of young men and boys from his Tenmile neighborhood, we are of the opinion they were sons of Daniel Moredock. A Robert Murdock got a pension from Greene County in 1818, but the recital of his application says he enlisted in Philadelphia in 1775, and was on the Expedition to Quebec. It does not say when he and wife Ann, settled in Greene County.

Daniel Moredock, Sr., died in Greene County about 1797, his will being probated on July 5, 1797. He mentions his wife Ruth. There seems little doubt that she was a daughter of George Williams of Fayette County, Pennsylvania, who made a will June 7, 1784, which was probated at Uniontown on July 17, 1784, in which he mentions his daughter, Ruth Moredock. (Will Book 1. pp. 18.) Ruth (Williams) Moredock died in 1813. She joined the other heirs of Daniel Moredock in the sale of land as shown by a deed in Greene County Deed Book 2. pp. 629½. It is from this deed we learn the names of the husbands of the daughters of Daniel and Ruth (Williams) Moredock. Daniel Moredock and his wife are probably buried in the old cemetery on Stockton's Lane, where a number of the family are buried.

Family of Daniel and Ruth (Williams) Moredock

1. Daniel Moredock, Jr., was an executor in his father's estate. It was he who secured a patent to the land bought by his father from Adam Smith. He secured a warrant for this land on June 7, 1786, and it was patented to him under the title 'The Park" on July 12, 1790. He died a short time after the death of his father. Daniel Moredock, Jr., married in March, 1789, Sarah Fitz Randolph, born November 8, 1763, died November 1840, daughter of Samuel and Margaret Fitz Randolph. Records show that before 1808, she had re-married to .... Rice, but she is buried in the cemetery on Stockton's Lane as Sarah Moredock. (O. C. Docket 1. pp. 20 November 3, 1808.)

Children of Daniel and Sarah (Fitz Randolph) Moredock

1. Margaret Moredock, born 1791-92.
2. George Moredock, born February 2, 1795, died November 15, 1881, married (1) August 24, 1816, Priscilla Anderson, born January 10, 1798, died May 16, 1841 daughter of James and Priscilla (Israel) Anderson. George Moredock married (2) Mary Worthington on May 5, 1843. She died June 22, 1864. George and Priscilla are buried in the cemetery on Stockton's Lane.

   #### Children of George Moredock

   1. Sarah Moredock, born July 28, 1817; married, June 6, 1837, John O'Neil, born November 4, 1815, died September 2, 1868.
   2. Daniel Moredock, born March 29, 1820, died October 16, 1906; married (1) November 25, 1849, Elizabeth Rex, born August 23, 1834, died April 11, 1877, daughter of Charles and Mary (Hickman) Rex. He married (2), 1885, Rosa Stephens.
   3. Minerva Moredock, born July 20, 1822, died February 11, 1854; married, December 18, 1845, George M. Teagarden.
   4. Simon Moredock, born June 25, 1824, died September 25, 1904; married, December 20, 1849, Mary Jane Reynolds, born February 11, 1830, died August 15, 1904.
   5. James Moredock, born December 2, 1826, died February 18, 1904; married, October 25, 1849, Hannah Pollock, born 1830, died July 8, 1917.
   6. Margaret Moredock, born June 5, 1829, died April 6, 1914; married, March 24, 1850, William Kincaid Reynolds, born April 24, 1826, died July 17, 1915, son of John and Jane (Kincaid) Reynolds, and brother of Mary Jane Reynolds.
   7. George H. Moredock, born June 20, 1832; married, August 26, 1857, Matilda Ailes, born July 1, 1836, daughter of Stephen and Mary (Nixon) Ailes.
   8. Samuel Moredock, born January 3, 1835, married January 31, 1861, Mary Jane Riggle.
   9. Eliza Ellen Moredock, born February 17, 1840; married, March 10, 1852, A. J. Martin.
   10. Elizabeth Moredock, born February 22, 1844; married August 4, 1861, Samuel Sharpnack.

3. Samuel Moredock, born 1797.
4. Tabitha Moredock, born 1799, married Abner Butler.

2. Susannah Moredock, daughter of Daniel and Ruth (Williams) Moredock, married John Rees.
3. Martha Moredock, daughter of Daniel and Ruth (Williams) Moredock, married Morgan Dickenson.
4. Ann Moredock, daughter of Daniel and Ruth (Williams) Moredock, married William McCollister.
5. Elizabeth Moredock, daughter of Daniel and Ruth (Williams) Moredock, married Michael Roseberry. (See Roseberry Records.)

THOMAS CRAGO

The first of the Crago Family to settle in the Tenmile Country was the unfortunate Thomas Crago, who about 1770 chose land on a bend in the Monongahela River close to the present town of Crucible. This tract was near that of Oliver Crawford, who operated the first ferry at the Mouth of Muddy Creek. Thomas Crago and Oliver Crawford were natives of the Conochacheague where both of them along with Alexander Crawford and other early Tenmile settlers had served in Captain Evan Shelby's Company in Colonel Henry Boquet's Army, from July 15, to November 1, 1759. (Boquet Papers Vol. 2.-21644-pp. 182.) Evans, quoting from John Crawford's Journal, definitely states that Thomas Crago and his two small sons were living near the home of William Shepherd in a leanto shelter, when Crago was killed by the Indians, when he resisted their attempt to steal his horse. He further states that the elder of the two sons, Thomas Crago, Jr., was a lad of eleven when this tragedy struck. Since we have the Bible record showing that Thomas Crago, Jr., was born December 28, 1759, we can be certain that this event took place in 1770. The two small sons were returned over the mountains where Robert Crago served in Captain McKinney's Company of Cumberland County Militia. Thomas Crago, Jr., now Thomas Crago, Sr., soon returned to his father's land, which he in due time had patented to him. With him came James and Moses Crago, neither of whom became permanent settlers. Thomas Crago must have come back to the Tenmile Country during the War of the Revolution, since his name is not listed in the rolls of Cumberland County Militia, and since he was in the section from which the company of Captain Jesse Pigman was recruited, it is most likely that he was a member of that company, for which no muster roll exists. (James Crago was bound out to Robert Crawford of Peters Township, Cumberland County, Pennsylvania, and is named in the will of Robert Crawford on August 28, 1778.)

After his return to the frontier, Thomas Crago married Priscilla Thurman, (also spelled Thoroughman, Thiramin, Thurriman, etc.) and raised a large family of children, fifteen of whom reached maturity. Greene County Orphans Court Docket for June 1844, partitions his estate, from which can be learned the names of Thomas Crago's children. Thomas Crago died in 1843. His wife died September 14, 1828, as shown by the Bible record owned by Mrs. L. B. Donham of Greensboro, Greene County, Pennsylvania.

Children of Thomas Crago

1. Elizabeth Crago, died April 14, 1861, married James Kelley, born 1783, died April 21, 1848. Both are buried in Hewitts Cemetery at Rices Landing, Pennsylvania.

    #### Children of James and Elizabeth (Crago) Kelley
    (O. C. Docket 3. pp. 73)
    1. John Kelley.
    2. Elizabeth Kelley.
    3. Priscilla Kelley, intermarried with William Kelley, he living in Ohio.

2. John Crago, born 1782, died 1852, married Ann Hiller, born 1782, died 1854. Both are buried in the Shepherd Church Cemetery. Their children were:
    1. Thomas Crago, born 1801, died 1884, married Cassandra Hughes.

2. Elizabeth Crago, married .... Barnett.
3. Nancy Crago, married John Hughes.
4. Peter Crago.
5. Priscilla Crago, married Thomas Rice.
6. David Crago, born June 17, 1818, died September 26, 1900, married Martha Neff.
7. Hannah Crago.
8. Smith Crago married Elizabeth Rex.
9. John Crago, born February 15, 1814, married Eleanor Flennekin.
(O. C. Docket June 19, 1852)
3. Sarah Crago, married Benjamin Rice, son of John and Sarah (Roach) Rice.
4. Samuel Crago, born 1787, died 1827, married Martha Vanmeter, daughter of Jesse and Nancy (Seals) Vanmeter. She married (2) William Kincaid.

Children
1. Sarah Crago, married William Bradford.
2. Nancy, married Jacob Ramer.
3. Jesse Crago.
4. Henry Crago.

5. Thomas Crago, Jr., born July 13, 1790; married, April 28, 1814, Anna Fordyce, born July 13, 1793, daughter of Isaac and Susanna (Jennings) Fordyce.

Children
1. Samuel Crago, born November 26, 1814.
2. Mary Crago, born .... 28, 1816.
3. Priscilla Crago, born September 27, 1817, married Rees Thomas.
4. Susannah Crago, born August 29, 1820.
5. Isaac Fordyce Crago, born October 22, 1822.
6. Clemma Crago, born April 9, 1826.
7. Thomas Thurman Crago, born September 7, 1829.

6. Nancy Crago, born February 1791, died August 26, 1870, married Samuel Sharpnack, born 1790, died February 13, 1852. Both are buried at Hewitts Church. (O. C. Docket 3. pp. 270.)

Children
1. William Sharpnack.
2. Thomas Sharpnack died before 1852, leaving Sarah Ann, Mary, Nancy and Thomas.
3. Mary Sharpnack, married Jeremiah Reynolds.
4. Peter Sharpnack.
5. Priscilla Sharpnack, married Josias Anderson.
6. Elizabeth Sharpnack, married James Thompson.
7. Clemmentine Sharpnack, married John Ridge.

7. Mary Crago, died 1833, married Joseph Ridge, son of Jonathan and Sarah (Jennings) Ridge.

Children
1. Priscilla Ridge.
2. John Ridge.
3. Elizabeth Ridge.
4. Josephus Ridge.
5. Mary Ann Ridge.
6. Rachel Ridge.
7. Thomas Ridge.

8. William Crago. Wife Caroline ....
9. Priscilla Crago, born 1796, died 1876, married Samuel Swan, who died 1843.
10. James Crago, born December 25, 1798, married Sarah Fordyce, daughter of Isaac and Susannah (Jennings) Fordyce. She was born March 19, 1799.

Children
1. Elizabeth Crago, born November 29, 1822.
2. Joseph Crago, born February 22, 1825.
3. Priscilla Crago, born March 6, 1827.
4. Thomas Crago, born March 6, 1827.
5. Susannah Crago, born May 11, 1831.
6. Sarah Margaret Crago, born May 5, 1835.
7. Rhoda Ann Crago, born May 27, 1840.
8. Nancy Jane Crago, born September 26, 1841.

11. Charles Crago, married Sarah ...., who died October 21, 1840, aged 40 years.
12. Rachel Crago, died March 14, 1838, married .... Inghram.
13. Clemmentine Crago, born 1805, died June 19, 1888, married James Davidson, born 1807, died March 10, 1871.
14. David Crago.
15. Joseph Crago, born August 7, 1811, died August 29, 1889, married Maria Thomas, born August 9, 1824, died January 6, 1899.

GEORGE HAVER FAMILY

George Haver (or Heaver) was a native of New Jersey, where according to Bates' History of Greene County, his son George Haver, Jr., was born. When he came to the Tenmile, George Haver bought the tract of land called "Misfortune," which had been warranted to Samuel Stroud. This tract which George Haver patented on April 30, 1801, remains in the hands of his descendants to this date. The will of George Haver was probated on December 26, 1812 and names his wife Elizabeth .... (Will Book 1. pp. 105.)

Children of George and Elizabeth Haver
1. George Haver, Jr., born 1779, died March 30, 1862, aged 82 years and 3 months. His wife was Priscilla Villiers, daughter of John and Mary Villiers. She died June 15, 1852 at the age of 69 years, 8 months, and 3 days.

Children of George and Priscilla (Villiers) Haver
(Bible Record)
1. John Haver, born October 12, 1802, died April 17, 1894; married, March 8, 1832, Jane Rex, daughter of George and Jane (Black) Rex. She was born March 13, 1813, and died January 9, 1879. Both are buried in the C. P. Cemetery at Jefferson.

Children of John and Jane (Rex) Haver
1. George Rex Haver, born May 19, 1833, married, January 1, 1856, Anna Sarah Neil, born February 1, 1839, died July 31, 1913, daughter of Barnet and Margaret (Kincaid) Neil.

2. John Haver, born October 18, 1837, disappeared from home.
3. Sarah Jane Haver, born September 25, 1835, died May 25, 1870; married, February 21, 1856, John Davis, born May 15, 1834, died December 22, 1919. His second wife was Helen Brooks.
4. Priscilla Haver, born 1840, died 1913.
5. Mary Elizabeth Haver, born 1842, died 1924. Never married.
6. Hiram Haver, born March 20, 1844, died June 4, 1912. Served in Co. D. 85th Regt. P. V. I. He married Hannah Rush, born March 29, 1846, died March 3, 1923. Lived at Centerville, Iowa.
7. Jacob Haver, born September 13, 1846, died August 15, 1905; married, January 30, 1871, Martha N. Cotterall, born January 17, 1847, died 1910.
8. Charles Haver, born January 22, 1849, died January 4, 1929; married, January 22, 1880, Isabella McClure, born September 21, 1851, died October 5, 1903.
9. Hannah M. Haver, born April 12, 1851, died September 25, 1880; married, July 1, 1874, David A. Cosgray. He married (2) Martha Meighen.
10. Emma Haver, born January 23, 1853, died May 23, 1860.
11. James H. Haver, born March 11, 1856; married, August 14, 1879, Elizabeth Vernon. They lived at Hiawatha, Kansas.

2. George Haver, born October 1, 1803, married Rebecca Smith, daughter of Daniel and Anne (Woodmancy) Smith.
3. James Haver, born January 25, 1806.
4. Mary Ann Haver, born December 6, 1809, married John Hughes, born February 1805, son of John and Mary (Rex) Hughes. They went to Knox County, Ohio.

Children of John and Mary Ann (Haver) Hughes

1. George Hughes, married Amanda Bell.
2. Mary Ann Hughes, born January 1, 1836, died March 4, 1925; married, December 17, 1856, Hiram Bell, born October 6, 1833, died July 6, 1900.
3. Elizabeth Hughes, married Virgil Mitchell.
4. Priscilla Hughes, married G. W. Porterfield.

5. Elizabeth Haver, born January 6, 1812.
6. Catherine Haver, born November 27, 1813.
7. Jacob Haver.
8. Hiram Haver, born June 3, 1816.
9. Priscilla Haver, born August 10, 1819.

2. Isaac Haver. His wife was …………. Cree.
3. Elizabeth Haver.
4. Ann Haver.
5. Catherine Haver.
6. Jacob Haver, went to Ohio. Wife Mary …………. (Greene County, Pa. DB. 3. pp. 388. March 1, 1809.)
7. William Haver, went to Mississippi. His wife was …………. Bonham.

JOHN VILLIERS

In the old cemetery on "Manfield," a tract of land warranted on May 7, 1789, and patented June 13, 1794, to John Villis, there has been erected in late years a modern tombstone marking the resting place of the original warrantee of the land. Beside it is an old stone partly legible which was the original marker. Unfortunately the persons who erected the new stone did not examine the records, which show that the will of John Villiers was probated May 25, 1826 as the new stone bears the inscription placing the death date as 1836. The old stone must then have read that he died in 1826 at the age of 92 years. Thus John Villiers was born in 1734 and died in 1826, and is buried on the tract of land near Jefferson, which had been warranted to him. The new stone says that he served at Fort Pitt in Lieutenant William Wither's Rangers in the Revolutionary War in the years 1776-1779. He must have been on the Tenmile prior to 1780 as his name is among those who signed the petition for the new State of "Westsylvania" in 1779. In the tax list for 1784, he refused to turn in a list of his property to Washington County, still claiming Virginia Allegiance. John Villiers was twice married, his first wife being Mary ...., who died October 22, 1807, at the age of 64 years. His second wife was Elizabeth ...., who died July 26, 1834, at the age of 59 years, who remarried after the death of her husband, her second marriage being to Archibald Ewart. (O. C. Docket 1. pp. 281.) Both wives are buried with John Villiers. The marriages of his children suggest he lived in Cumberland County, Pennsylvania, before he came west.

Children of John Villiers named in his will

1. John Villiers, whose wife was .... Cree.
2. Elizabeth Villiers, born October 12, 1763, married Robert Cree, Jr., and went to Harrison County, Ohio. (See Robert Cree records.)
3. Victoria Villiers, married John Barclay.
4. Nancy Villiers, married John Adams.
5. Millicent Villers, married Jacob Ullom.
6. Mathew Villiers, no record.
7. James Villiers, born 1774, married Rebecca Davidson.
8. Eleanor Villiers, married George Gregg, and died before her father leaving sons, George and John Gregg.
9. Cassandra Villiers, married Aaron Masterson.
10. Rebecca Villiers, married Joseph Vanbuskirk.
11. Priscilla Villiers, born October 12, 1782, died June 15, 1852; married George Haver, who was born December 31, 1789, and died March 30, 1862. (See Haver Records.)
12. Mary Villiers, daughter of John Villiers by his second marriage, born 1809, died September 30, 1844; married Michael McGovern. Buried in the Villiers Cemetery.
13. Jane Villiers, born February 24, 1811, died April 24, 1829, buried in Villiers Cemetery.
14. Ralph Villiers, born 1813, died July 26, 1843, buried in Villiers Cemetery.

THE KELLY FAMILY

Apparently two and probably three families of this name settled near Henry Vanmeter's Fort about the close of the Revolution. Robert Kelly obtained a warrant for 187 acres of land situated at the head of the Vanmeter Branch of Swan's Run, and secured a warrant April 12, 1785. His patent was issued to him on March 17, 1786, under the title of "Buffalo Flats". He was probably the Robert Kelly who served in the Eighth Pennsylvania Regiment of the Continental Line with Joseph Gwynne, Gideon and Jeremiah Long, and a number of others who joined this regiment when it was recruited at Fort Pitt. He was probably a brother of William Kelly who, with Thomas Lucas and Henry Snively, served in Captain James Poe's Company of Cumberland County Militia in the arrangement of the year 1782. (Penna. Arch. Series V, Vol. 3, pp. 369 Robert Kelly; Penna. Arch. Series V, Vol 6, pp. 576, William Kelly.)

Robert Kelly died in Greene County, where his will was probated November 9, 1808. (Will Book 1, pp. 73.) His wife, Margaret, was mentioned in his will. On September 29, 1816, she married Daniel Moore. Record of this is found in Jay Thompson's Journal. It is also noted in Orphans' Court Docket 1, pp. 160. In both the will of Robert Kelly and the Orphans' Court Docket, the names of Robert Kelly's children are given. The widow and Thomas Lucas were executors of the will.

Family of Robert and Margaret Kelly

1. Millicent Kelly, married John Vanmeter, born 1769, son of Henry and Martha Vanmeter. They removed about 1800 to Mason County, West Virginia.

   #### Children of John and Millicent (Kelly) Vanmeter
   1. Mark Vanmeter, married Delilah Cooper.
   2. Patsie Vanmeter, married Rev. Gideon Hinkle.
   3. Polly Vanmeter, married Henry Devault.
   4. Margaret Vanmeter, married James Johnson.
   5. Elisha Vanmeter, married .... Stephenson.
   6. Elizabeth Vanmeter, married Jacob Fisher.
   7. Silpha Vanmeter, married John Husher.
   8. Nancy Vanmeter, married Dryden Watkins.
   9. Permelia Vanmeter, married Samuel Edwards.
2. Elizabeth Kelly, married Richard Williams.
3. Mary Kelly, married Wilson Prior.
4. Anne Kelly, married Nathan Prior.
5. Ruth Kelly, married Jacob Snively.
6. Rachel Kelly, married Thomas Lawyer.
7. Margaret Kelly, a minor child in 1821.
8. Robert Kelly, only son mentioned in either record.

William Kelly saw much service in the Revolution while living in Cumberland County, Pennsylvania. He served in James Poe's Company and also in Thomas Askey's Company. He died at Rices Landing July 14, 1841, at the age of 82 years. His wife, Elizabeth, died there on October 18, 1856, at the age of 79 years 6 months and 21 days. Both have markers in the cemetery at Hewitts Church. The will of William Kelly is in Will Book 2, pp. 141 and was probated July 24, 1841. It was witnessed by Samuel Sharpnack and James Kelly. But two children are mentioned in this will.

Children of William and Elizabeth Kelly
1. Elizabeth Kelly, married James Weel.
2. Morris Kelly.

THE PRIOR FAMILY

Nathan, Timothy, and John Prior served in the Cumberland County, Pennsylvania Militia in 1780-81, Nathan and Timothy in Captain John Taylor's Company, Third Division, Seventh Battalion, commanded by Colonel James Purdy, while John Prior served in Captain Phillip Mathews' Company of the same Division and Battalion. Soon after this service they removed to the Tenmile Country, where Timothy Prior took title to 75 acres of land near the head of Coal Run on the Jefferson-Cumberland Township line, and had this land warranted to him September 6, 1796. His brother, Nathan Prior, died before this date leaving an estate which was placed in the hands of his brothers Timothy and John Prior as guardians for his minor children. (Washington County O. C. Docket 1. pp. 107.) His wife was Abigail (Ross?)

Children of Nathan Prior

1. Margaret Prior, when she came of age, she joined her husband, Samuel Williams, in a deed dated April 16, 1810, to sell her share to Edward Burson.
2. John Prior also sold his share (Deed Book 2. pp. 457.)
3. Sarah Prior, joined her husband, Adam Miller, with her sister, Margaret, in the sale to Edward Burson.
4. Nathan Prior, Jr., sold by deed in Deed Book 3. pp. 23.
6. Luther Prior, named in the O. C. Docket.

ABIJAH McCLAIN

It would seem that Abijah McClain lived in the vicinity of Elizabeth, Pennsylvania, when he served as a Frontier Ranger in Captain Richard Johnson's Company of Westmoreland County Militia. Prior to that time he had served in the Eighth Pennsylvania Regiment of the Continental Line, when that Regiment took part in the Battles of Brandywine, Germantown, and Saratoga. He drew a pension for his service as shown by the list of pensioners in the 1840 Census.

Abijah McClain was born in 1754 and died at Rices Landing July 11, 1848. He married Pamelia Doughty, one of the six daughters of Edward Doughty, who warranted the tract of land between Thomas Blackledge and the Monongahela River, under the name of "Pigeon's Resort." She was born March 17, 1759, and died January 5, 1833. Both are buried in the cemetery on the hill above Rices Landing, overlooking the Monongahela River.

About 1792, Abijah McClain began buying out the heirs of Edward Doughty in order to obtain a full title to "Pigeon's Resort." The six daughters, including Pamelia, wife of Abijah McClain; Mary, wife of James McCreary of Brownsville; Martha, wife of James Blackburn; Eleanor, wife of Samuel West; Ruth and Rebecca Doughty, sold their claims, while Enoch Enochs, John Wright, and Jesse Bumgarner, gave quit claim deeds for some interests they had in the property. Abijah McClain then proceeded to lay out a number of lots on this land it later becoming a part of Rices Landing.

When Abijah McClain died at the age of 94 years, a number of his children had died before him. His will notes this circumstance. (Will Book 3. pp. 36.) It was proven July 24, 1848.

Children of Abijah and Pamelia (Doughty) McClain

1. James McClain.
2. John McClain, born October 18, 1791, died April 17, 1848; married, September 4, 1812, Phoebe Swan, daughter of Charles and Sarah (Vanmeter) Swan. Phoebe was born March 17, 1791, and died March 16, 1856. They removed to Knox County, Ohio, in 1828.

Children of John and Phoebe (Swan) McClain

1. Charles McClain, married Ruth Berryhill.
2. Abijah McClain, married Catherine Hook.
3. William McClain, married Sarah Marquis.
4. Sarah McClain, married Edward Welsh.
5. Pamelia McClain, married James Hufty.
6. Mary McClain, married Morgan Booze.
7. Cassandra McClain, married Levi Sellers.
8. Henry McClain, married Sarah Smith.

3. David McClain, married Martha Swan, daughter of Richard and Martha (Vanmeter) Swan. She died and he married Rebecca .... (O. C. Docket March 18, 1822.)

Children of David and Martha (Swan) McClain

1. Thomas McClain, went to Knox County, Ohio.
2. Sarah McClain, married Mathias Roseberry, born February 28, 1811, died at Harvard, Nebraska, in 1878, son of Mathias and Sarah (Hughes) Roseberry.
3. Martha McClain, married John Hughes Roseberry, born March 21, 1816.

4. Charles McClain, whose wife was Margaret ....
5. Abijah McClain, Jr.
6. Lydia McClain, married .... Evans.
7. Mary McClain, married Henry Fitz Randolph.
8. Margaret McClain, born January 17, 1799, died May 17, 1832, married Remembrance Hughes, born May 13, 1795, died May 31, 1856, son of Thomas and Elizabeth (Swan) Hughes. (See Hughes Records.)

THE KINCAID FAMILY

The first mention of the Kincaid Family refers to Samuel Kincaid, a lieutenant under Captain McClure in Lord Dunmore's War. Samuel Kincaid was wounded by four members of a party of Indians under Chief Logan, who ambushed Captain McClure's party on the Tenmile in 1774. He was an early settler at the mouth of the Cheat River, where he operated a ferry, devised to him by Colonel George Wilson, whose daughter, Elizabeth Wilson, was the wife of Samuel Kincaid. He came to the Monongahela from the Marsh Creek Settlement of York County, Pennsylvania, and patented land obtained by virtue of a Virginia Certificate, indicating ownership prior to 1769.

Robert Kincaid, ancestor of the Tenmile family of the name, seems to have served in the Revolution in Eastern Pennsylvania, and is probably the Robert Kincaid found in the York County Census of 1790. There are numerous references to his service in the Pennsylvania Archives. It is not certain that Robert Kincaid came to the Tenmile Country, nor are there any records to suggest that he lived in this area, but his family settled in the vicinity of Jefferson about 1800, where several of them became prominent citizens. The Family Bible of Robert Kincaid came with them and was owned by the late J. N. Scott of Muddy Creek and Waynesburg. This Bible shows that Robert Kincaid was born in 1727, and died April 19, (or 29), 1806. His wife, who was Susannah Powell, is shown, but no dates are given. They were probably married about 1771-72.

Family of Robert and Susannah (Powell) Kincaid

1. Samuel Kincaid, born April 4, 1773, no further record.
2. Eleanor Kincaid, born September 12, 1775, no further record.
3. Robert Kincaid, born March 29, 1777, died in Greene County, 1815. His wife was Polly ...., who died May 24, 1806, and is buried in the old Presbyterian Cemetery at Jefferson. Her marker states she was 18 years, 10 months and 12 days old at her death. The will of Robert Kincaid notes that a deed is to be made to his only child and heir by Colonel John Heaton.

Child of Robert and Polly Kincaid

1. Elizabeth Kincaid.

4. William Kincaid, born January 21, 1779, died at Jefferson, April 9, 1843. He was a prominent attorney, and one of the earliest members of the Masonic Lodge at Waynesburg. The first wife of William Kincaid was Mary, probably Mary Cree, though this is not clear as William Cree in his will, dated 1835, mentions his daughter Mary, intermarried with William Kincaid, and does not say she is deceased, while the marker in the Old Presbyterian Cemetery at Jefferson shows this Mary, wife of William Kincaid, died February 5, 1815, at the age of 34 years and eleven months. If Mary Cree was not the first wife of William Kincaid, then she was wife number three, for he married (2) Sarah (Vanmeter) Morris, widow of Richard Morris, and daughter of Jesse and Nancy (Seals) Vanmeter, with whom he was married from 1825-29. The last wife of William Kincaid, who claimed a dower in his estate, was Martha (Vanmeter) Crago, sister of Sarah, and widow of Samuel Crago. William Kincaid was a soldier in the War of 1812. His will is in Will Book 2, pp. 176, naming his brother, James Kincaid, administrator.

Children of William Kincaid

1. Jane Kincaid, born 1801, died October 19, 1832, buried in the Old Presbyterian Cemetery at Jefferson. She married John Reynolds, who died February 20, 1882. His second wife was Mrs. Priscilla (Long) Gwynne.
    ### Children of John Reynolds
    1. William Reynolds, born April 24, 1826, died June 17, 1915, married Margaret Moredock, born June 5, 1829, died April 6, 1914.
    2. Rebecca J. Reynolds, born December 24, 1827, died December 11, 1891; married, December 30, 1849, James C. Burson, born December 27, 1825, died September 5, 1897.
    3. Mary Jane Reynolds, born February 11, 1830, died August 15, 1904, married Simon Moredock, born June 24, 1824, died September 25, 1904.
    4. Sarah Reynolds, married Dr. Enochs.
    5. George Reynolds, veteran of the Civil War.
    6. Patricia Reynolds, married (1) .... Davy (2) Worthington.
    7. Miriam Reynolds.
2. Mary Kincaid, married John Dance, son of Daniel and Phoebe (Hufty) Dance.
3. Esther Kincaid, married .... Hill (?).
4. Susan Kincaid, born February 12, 1812, died at New Castle, Indiana in 1870. Married (1) Alexander Lindsey, born April 30, 1805, died June 5, 1845. She married (2) John Shroyer. Alexander Lindsey was a son of James and Mary (Hughes) Lindsey.
    ### Children of Alexander and Susan (Kincaid) Lindsey
    1. James M. Lindsey, born June 15, 1830, married Sophia Winters.
    2. Mary Lindsey, born December 20, 1831, married Thomas F. Teagarden.
    3. William K. Lindsey, born January 3, 1834.
    4. Barnet Neal Lindsey, born November 12, 1837, married Isabella Houlsworth born April 5, 1845.
    5. Hiram Lindsey, born September 4, 1835, killed in the Battle of Charles City Cross Roads.
    6. Martha Ann Lindsey, born August 12, 1839, married Thomas Markle.
5. Margaret Kincaid, married, September 25, 1831, Barnet O'Neal, son of Barnet and Martha (Hughes) O'Neal, born September 15 1810, died April 12, 1899, at Appamoose, Iowa.
    ### Children of Barnet and Margaret (Kincaid) O'Neal
    1. William K. O'Neal.
    2. Martha O'Neal, married George Teagarden.
    3. Mary O'Neal.
    4. Anna Sarah O'Neal, married 1855, George Haver, born 1833.
    5. Jane O'Neal.
    6. Elizabeth O'Neal.
    7. Catherine O'Neal.
    8. Emma O'Neal, married E. S. Glover.
6. William Kincaid, Jr., born 1819, died July 10, 1885, married Mariah Hughes, daughter of Thomas and Sarah (Swan)

Hughes. She was born in 1819 and died April 10, 1873. He is buried at Hewitts Church, while his wife is buried in the family plot at Rices Landing. William Kincaid was also a prominent attorney.

Children of William and Mariah (Hughes) Kincaid
1. Sarah Kincaid, married James Bell.
2. Rachel Kincaid, married William Rinehart, son of Arthur and Rebecca (Roberts) Rinehart.
3. James O. Kincaid, crippled in infancy.
4. Samuel S. Kincaid.
5. Thomas Kincaid.

7. James Kincaid, died February 18, 1851, will was probated in Greene County on April 22, 1851. His wife was Jane McCaslin, whose brother, Maxwell McCaslin, served as administrator of James Kincaid's estate. Children are listed in O. C. Docket 4. pp. 212.

Children of James and Jane (McCaslin) Kincaid
1. William M. Kincaid, married Emma Nichols.
2. Sally Kincaid, married, Augst 1862, W. W. Clendenning, born October 28, 1838.
3. Robert Kincaid.
4. Elizabeth Kincaid.

5. James Kincaid, born February 1, 1781, no further record.
6. John Kincaid, born February 30, 178..
7. Margaret Kincaid, born April 22, 1790, died April 1, 1888, married James Scott, who died April 12, 1866, aged 77 years, 2 months, 5 days. He was a son of Mordecai and Kizzie (Poteet) Scott of Maryland.

Family of James and Margaret (Kincaid) Scott
1. Susannah Scott, born February 4, 1816.
2. Thomas Scott, born May 18, 1817, died January 1, 1879, married Isabella Milliken. She was a daughter of John and Mary (Campbell) Milliken.

Children of Thomas and Isabella (Milliken) Scott
1. James K. Scott, born July 7, 1841, married Elizabeth Hoge, born October 27, 1844.
2. John M. Scott, born January 31, 1843, married Elizabeth Rinehart, born February 13, 1843, died January 28, 1905.
3. Margaret Scott, born January 6, 1845, married Arthur Rinehart.
4. Mary Scott, born December 31, 1851. Never married.
5. Chinsworthy Scott, born April 1, 1848, lived 3 days.
6. Catherine Scott, born December 31, 1848, died young.
7. Catherine Scott, born May 21, 1854, married (1) Solomon Shriver, (2) Zach Rush.

3. William Powell Scott born May 1,, 1820, died February 12, 1908, married, March 21, 1844, Sarah Long, born .. ..

Children of William Powell and Sarah (Long) Scott
1. James Madison Scott born December 10, 1844, died November 29, 1930, married on September 7, 1872, Mary Ann Rinehart, daughter of Hiram and Mariah (Porter) Rinehart.
2. Richard Long Scott, born October 1, 1846, married November 11, 1875, Mary Amanda Baily, born February 19, 1852, died 1950.

3. Mary Elizabeth Scott, born October 30, 1849, died December 20, 1928, married, September 12, 1872, William J. Bayard, son of Thomas and Sarah (Bradford) Bayard.
4. Margaret Helen Scott, born August 9, 1855, died July 12, 1928, married, February 1, 1879, George W. Gordon, son of John B. and Delilah (Inghram) Gordon.
5. Columbus M. Scott, born June 28, 1858, died June 19, 1937, married, September 13, 1883, Phoebe C. Rich, daughter of Daniel and Lany (Stephens) Rich.
6. Chinsworth Kincaid Scott, born June 28, 1858, died August 7, 1929, married (1) on September 8, 1887, Margaret Bell. He married (2) Nan Lemon.
7. Ruth Ann Scott, born June 20, 1860, married (1) September 5, 1878, Albert G. Kent. She married (2) September 13, 1910, Benjamin F. Collins.

4. James Scott, born October 6, 1822, died September 30, 1878, married Mary (Margaret on tombstone) A. Spencer, born July 18, 1833, died June 20, 1913.

Children of James and Mary A. (Spencer) Scott

1. Elizabeth E. Scott, married Isaac N. McNay.
2. Anna S. Scott, married Dr. J. L. Milliken.
3. William S. Scott.
4. Emma K. Scott, married Ellsworth Minor.
5. J. Newton Scott, married Elizabeth Baily.

5. Chinsworth Scott, born January 3, 1826, died August 9, 1847. Never married.

MIFFLIN COUNTY PIONEERS

It is interesting to examine the 1790 Census Record for that portion of Mifflin County, Pennsylvania, situated South of the Juniata River. (pp. 151 of the published version). Living there at the time in close proximity, were a number of families that were shortly to move to the Tenmile Country. Most of these families had previously lived near Philadelphia in Chester and Montgomery Counties, where a number had served in the Revolution prior to their migration to Mifflin County. A few of them appear to have made survey trips to the Tenmile, to select their land, but Indian troubles had sent them back over the mountains until the frontier was safe for removal of their families. When conditions became more settled, they immigrated in a group and found their new home between Jefferson and the upper reaches of Whiteley Creek. Among the names we recognize as heads of families are: Jacob Tustin, Michael Roseberry, Jacob Hunnil (or Honnell), Jacob and John Staggers, Abraham Stiles, George John, John Milligan, Andrew Isenminger, Hamilton Grim, Archibald Hamilton, Peter Dailey, James Jacobs, and others, while on the Northern side of the Juniata we find the names of George Rex and several of the Smalley Families. It is curious to note how they intermarried before and after coming here. It is the same story of clannishness shown in all these westward migrations. We shall take up these families in the sections where they settled or with families with which they are closely allied, rather than as a separate group.

THE JOHN HONNELL FAMILY

John Honnell (or as his name is sometimes spelled and is now in general usage, Hunnell) was of Scottish descent, and came to the Tenmile with John and Jacob Staggers and John Isenminger, to settle in Cumberland Township, not far from Jefferson, where John Staggers bought land that had been patented to Robert Crosley. On November 11, 1797, near the close of his life, John Staggers made a deed for his personal chattels to his son, Jacob Staggers, and to John Isenminger and John Honnell, the latter two, apparently his sons-in-law. Then on September 10, 1798, John Staggers and wife, Eve, deeded the Crosley tract to James Henderson and James McCalley (McCullough ?).

John Honnell, or Hunnell, settled in the same vicinity, and several of his children were married here. His will, which was made on May 9, 1813, was probated nine days later and mentions his brother, Jacob, whom we find listed in the 1790 Census of Mifflin County. He also mentions a tract of land in Mercer County, Pennsylvania, which he had bought from his brother, Jacob Honnell. Records in Mercer County indicate that this land, called "unseated land," was sold for taxes. Land in that part of Pennsylvania was in many cases obtained for services in the Revolution and since Census records for 1800 and 1810 indicate that John Honnell was born between 1756 and 1760, it may well be that he and his brother, Jacob, both served. One reference in the Pennsylvania Archives does give service for John and Jacob Honnal, both of whom were paid for service in Washington County Militia. (Penna. Archives, Series V, Volume 4, page 712). I am a bit skeptical of this record, however, and believe it refers to Hormells who lived near Beallsville, Washington County, and are known to have served. (Penna. Archives, Series VI, Volume 2, pages 207, 208, 235, 265).

John Hunnell, or Honnell, died in Franklin Township, Greene County, between May 9 and May 19, 1813, leaving a will in which he mentions his wife, Catherine (Staggers) Honnell, and his living children. Catherine lived until 1837, apparently with her son, Jacob. She left a will which was probated December 26, 1837, and is found in Will Book 2, page 91. She is shown by the census records to have been younger than her husband. The burial place of John and Catherine is not certain, but they may be buried near Grimes' Hill in Jackson Township, Greene County.

Children

1. Margaret Hunnell, married Henry Thomas, who died about 1822 in Greene County. His wife and her brother, Jacob Hunnell, administered his estate which was probated September 14, 1822. Orphans' Court records disclose that they had seven children.

Children

(DB. 11, pp. 293, and DB. 9, pp. 269½)

1. John Thomas, married Ola... ... .
2. George Thomas.
3. Rosanna Thomas, witnessed John Hunnell's will.
4. Michael Thomas, witnessed grandfather's will.
5. Elizabeth Thomas.
6. Mary Thomas, married Peter Rush.
7. Margaret Thomas, lived in Monroe County, Ohio.

AND ITS PIONEER FAMILIES 281

2. Jacob Hunnell, died March 18, 1835. (Est. No. 778). He lived in Jackson Township, near White Cottage. Does not seem to have married, as his estate went to his brothers and sisters.
3. Elizabeth Hunnell, married John Tuttle, son of Amos Tuttle.
4. David Hunnell, married Perie Hart.
5. Frederick Hunnell, born August 5, 1795, died June 22, 1842; married Rebecca Stewart, daughter of Isaac and Elizabeth (Parrish) Stewart, born September 19, 1797, died November 30, 1877. Both are buried in Green Mount Cemetery. They lived in Franklin Township.

Children

1. John Hunnell, married Mary Seals.
2. Catherine Hunnell, married, in 1860, Jacob Shoup, born May 24, 1825, in Fayette County, Pennsylvania.
3. Jesse Hunnell, born January 1, 1825, died October 5, 1894; married Catherine Smalley, born July 1, 1825, died December 5, 1869.
4. Elizabeth Hunnell, married Samuel Garner.
5. David Hunnell, died March 18, 1896; married Margaret Wylie.
6. Morgan Hunnell, married Caroline Donahue.
7. James Hunnell, married Caroline Rush.
8. Delilah Hunnell, born May 28, 1839, died October 5, 1903; married William Thomas Webb, born February 21, 1840, died July 15, 1903, son of W. T. E. and Hannah (Stull) Webb.

6. John Hunnell, born April 14, 1800, died May 25, 1883; married Joanna Sensebaugh, born December 1798, died June 10, 1864. Buried with husband on Huffman Farm in Jackson Township, near White Cottage.

Children

1. Jacob Hunnell, born 1833, married Mary Ellen Duvall.
2. Margaret Hunnell, married Richard Hughes.
3. William Hunnell, born December 7, 1826, died June 3, 1887; married Emeline ... ., born 1837, died March 4, 1860. Buried on the Huffman Farm in Jackson Township.
4. Catherine Hunnell, married Jacob Hughes.
5. Isaac Hunnell, married Elizabeth Knight, who died July 3, 1884.

7. Mathias Hunnell, born in 1806, died September 28, 1846; married Experience Hickman, born May 23, 1815, died September 9, 1899. Buried in Green Mount Cemetery with three unmarried children. She was a daughter of Solomon and Elizabeth (McCoombs) Hickman of Jefferson.

Children

(In addition to those buried with parents)
1. Francis B. Hunnell, a minor in 1846.
2. Joseph Hunnell, minor in 1846.

RACHEL HEATON'S LETTER

Before taking up the Heaton Family, who settled on Tenmile, in and about the present town of Jefferson, I believe it would be of interest to quote a letter written by Rachel (Heaton) Colver on January 25, 1861. Rachel Heaton was a daughter of Isaac and Hannah (Bowen) Heaton. She married Thomas Colver, an early attorney of Greene County. Their son, Samuel Colver, built the old stone house, that in late years, has been the home of Norval Rogers and his widow, Hattie Rogers. Rachel (Heaton) Colver died January 21, 1864, three years after this letter was written. She was in her eightieth year when she died. The letter reads:

"My Grandfather, Samuel Heaton, emigrated from Ireland early in the Seventeenth (she means early 1700s) Century. His name was Samuel H. Eaton. He went into business with a merchant of Connecticut, where they did a good business. In the multitude of the Yankees, he married an English lady by the name of Sarah Handcock by whom he had nine children: Samuel, Sarah, Mary, John, Jabesh, Daniel, Hannah, James and Isaac. The latter was my father, who was born on June 12, 1730. My grandfather moved to New Jersey, Sussex County, when my father was young, with his eldest son, Samuel, Jr., who was married and was a Baptist preacher. He constituted a church in a village, which was afterwards called Morristown. Sarah, Mary and John married and remained in the New England States. My grandfather brought with him five unmarried children: Jabesh, Daniel, Hannah, James and Isaac. My grandfather died before my father arrived at manhood. My father married Mary Booth and moved, with his father-in-law, to new Virginia, Berley County, Mill Creek, on which he built a saw mill which did a good business.

"But in the midst of prosperity there was adversity. His wife and child died and he remained a widower for some years, in which time he married my mother, Hannah Bowen. She was the daughter of Henry and Anna Bowen. Their ancestors were from Wales and Scotland. My grandmother Bowen's father's name was Simeon Moon. He was from Wales, and his wife from Scotland. Grandfather Bowen's father was from Scotland and his wife from Wales. My mother's ancestors were mostly Quakers. My grandfather Bowen and his wife had ten children, four sons and six daughters. Their names were: Rees, Henry, John, Jacob, and the daughters, Mary, Hannah, Margaret, Jane, Nancy and Priscilla. The daughters all married and had twelve children apiece, except one, who had thirteen. The sons all died single men, three in the bloom of youth—Rees, Henry and Jacob—and John died an old bachelor. Not one married to keep their father's name. My mother, the eldest, was born May 3, 1742, and was married to my father March 3, 1760. Since I came here Josiah Robb requested me to give him a record of my family, his mother's family. I did so. I now send you a record to the best of my recollection:

"John Heaton was born December 16, 1760.
"Mary Heaton was born December 2, 1762.
"Sarah Heaton was born December 16, 1764.
"Henry Heaton was born September 16, 1766.
"Isaac Heaton was born October 29, 1768.
"James Heaton was born February 2, 1771.
"Daniel Heaton was born March 22, 1773.
"Nancy Heaton was born June 11, 1775.
"Hannah Heaton was born April 3, 1778.

"Rachel Heaton was born April 3, 1780 (herself)
"Rees Heaton was born February 4, 1783.
"Jacob Bowen Heaton was born May 9, 1786.
"My father left Mill Creek, Virginia, in the fall of 1785, the 19th of November, and arrived at the desired place the fourth of December, where he remained a permanent citizen of Greene County, Pennsylvania. In the commencement it was all Washington County. Since my recollection, it was struck off and called Greene. My father was a man of not much learning, but of good judgment and a strong mind. His mind little abated until the day of his death. He died April 2, 1814. My mother died May 19, 1827. They were gathered home to their fathers.

"JOHN HEATON (married Sarah Morgan Roberts) was the father of Mary, Morgan, Bowen, Elizabeth, Charlotte, Hiram, John, Samuel, Alexander and Isaac.

"MARY LUCE (she married (1) Zepheniah Luce and (2) Samuel Luce) was the mother of Delilah, James, Henry, John, Warren, Charlotte, Susannah and Zepheniah.

"SARAH WATHEN (she married Nicholas Miles Wathen) was the mother of Mary, Henry, Hannah, Nancy, Rachel, Druscilla, Charlotte, Eli, Delilah, Cynthia and Sarah.

"HENRY HEATON (he married Martha Morgan, sister of Sarah) was the father of Rhuana, Cynthia, Samuel, Nancy, Franklin, Henry, Mary, Harriett, Martha, Hannah and Minerva.

"ISAAC HEATON (he married Hannah Wilson (Williams ?) was the father of two children, William and Maria.

"JAMES HEATON (he married Margaret Williams) was the father of Isaac, Enoch, Lewis, Hannah, Warren, Maria, John, Owens and Shevy.

"DANIEL HEATON (he married Amy Hill) was the father of Rees, Eli, Jacob, Bowen, John, Robert, Isaac, Priscilla, Anna, Hannah and Amy.

"NANCY HEATON (she married Rees Hill) was the mother of Bowen, Elizabeth, Isaac, Hannah, Daniel, Priscilla, Mary, Heaton, Amy, Rees and Naomi.

"HANNAH HEATON (she married Isaac Buckingham) was the mother of John, Jane, Rachel, Henry, Charlotte, Bowen, Mary and Hannah.

"RACHEL HEATON (she married Thomas Colver) was the mother of Samuel and Elizabeth.

"REES HEATON (he married Sarah Weaver) was the father of Nancy, William, Isaac, Hannah, Abigail, Daniel, Elizabeth and Cyrus.

"JACOB BOWEN HEATON (he married Rachel Weaver) was the father of Weaver, Abigail, Hannah, Henry, Eliza, Sarah, Nancy, Mary, Rachel and Mariah.

"John Heaton died August 1820.
"Mary Luce died January 1838.
"Sarah Wathen died June 1852.
"Henry Heaton died 1834.
"Isaac Heaton died 1834-5.
"James Heaton died December 9, 1855.
"Daniel Heaton died May 4, 1858.
"Hannah Buckingham died March 1850.
"Bowen Heaton died October 22, 1839.
"Thomas Colver died October 26, 1852.

"These are all gone to their companions. There are remaining our brother, Rees, and wife; our sister, Rachel, and Rachel Colver. Twenty-one dead and four alive. We are as leaves of the Autumn,

dropping off every year. This would be no grief to me if I could find them again in one eternal day.
(Signed)
Dated January 25, 1861.   "RACHEL COLVER."

This letter has been checked by the author through the various courts of Greene and Washington Counties, Pennsylvania; Frederick County, Virginia, and in other sources, and is found to be fairly correct. A similar letter was sent the author from Raymond Luse of Angola, Indiana, and had been written by Rachel Colver to his ancestor. Inspection of some thirty quit claim deeds in Frederick County, Virginia, disclosed much of the correct Bowen records of this letter. There the wills of Henry Bowen and Simeon Moon were found, along with the settlement of Rees Bowen and Henry Bowen's estates. Fayette County, Pennsylvania, uncovered the records of Henry Heaton. In the records of Isaac and Hannah (Bowen) Heaton, which will follow, the discrepancies of Rachel (Heaton) Colver's letter will be corrected.

It is not strange that Rachel Colver did not mention the fact that her uncle, Jabesh or Zabesh, also came to Greene County, for it is but natural that older people can remember the things of an early day that associate them with the subject at hand, and she was in this case concerned only with her immediate family. We regret she did not elaborate on the Ruff's Creek Heatons and those of the Castile Run section, other than her own family. The letter was written with a clear mind peculiar to the Heatons, for in the course of searching the records of this family, the writer received from Austa Heaton Daniels of Princeton, Illinois—a dear old lady past her eightieth year—the complete record of the Rees Heaton family, copied by this lady in long hand and kept up-to-date to the last birth and death.

For a number of years we have sought to unravel the various Heatons who came to the Tenmile Country. Two of these elder Heatons can be definitely established as brothers. They are Zabesh (or Jabesh) and Isaac Heaton, who settled along Tenmile Creek, between Clarksville and Jefferson. Zabesh speaks of lands owned by him, when he made his will on October 24, 1793, but there is no record of possession in his name. The letter of Rachel (Heaton) Colver recalls that her father, Isaac Heaton had a brother Zabesh. The will of Zabesh Heaton is witnessed by this brother and his son, John, as well as Isaac Heaton, mason, son of the testator. It also mentions a legacy coming to him from his brother, James Heaton's Estate.

There is evidence that a third brother came into these parts and was the ancestor of the Ruff's Creek Heatons. This brother was John Heaton, whom Rachel states "remained in the New England States." In this case she was wrong, for John Heaton removed first to "Big Swamp Meadow" in upper New Jersey, where he lived for a time with his wife, the former Abigail Paxton. Then about 1760 he moved to Loudon County, Virginia, where in 1777 he and his sons, John, William, and Benjamin, were taxed in that year. Either the father, John Heaton, or his son, John, removed to the Tenmile and took an active part in the Revolution. Since the father was born in 1716, we are inclined to identify the son as the early Captain John Heaton. The William Heaton, who settled near Grimes School House on Ruff's Creek, was the one of that name. who was taxed in Loudon County. He patented the Henry Ross tract of land in 1812.

Zabesh Heaton died in Greene County about 1798, leaving a wife, Abigail .... His children living at that time were:
1. Phoebe Heaton.
2. Priscilla Heaton, wife of William Bell.
3. Mary Heaton, born April 30, 1756, died March 10, 1836. She married Samuel Case, born 1757, died April 7, 1815. Both are buried in the Cox Cemetery on Castile Run.
4. Isaac Heaton, who was always called "Isaac Heaton, mason," to distinguish him from his Uncle Isaac of Jefferson. His wife was Susannah ...., who died July 6, 1832, aged 79 years. They patented the tract of land near Clarksville under the title of "Ashley" which they sold to Samuel Clark. (D. B. 1. pp. 628). They had a son, Micajah, but other children are not known. Susannah is buried in the Cox Cemetery and a marker still stands. No marker is found for her husband.
5. ....Heaton, this daughter married a man named Courser, leaving a son, Jacob, mention made in the will of Zabesh.

Our information is that Zabesh Heaton came from Bucks County, Pennsylvania, to the Tenmile. He is probably buried in the Cox Cemetery, where a number of graves dating before 1800 are marked by simple field stones.

William Heaton, probably the son of John of Loudon County, Virginia, became owner of the tract of land at Grimes School House, patented to Henry Ross under the name "Phillips." As this land was in the vicinity of Ross's Fort, it is possible that later historians have credited the existence of Heaton's Fort, for there is no confirmation of a Heaton's Fort other than in the Waychoff Papers. Orphan's Court Docket No. 1. pp. 53-54-114 etc. disclose that William Heaton died about 1815 leaving a wife Abigail ...., and the following children:

1. Abijah Heaton, born April 27, 1789, died January 9, 1847. His wife was Rachel Wathen, daughter of Miles and Sarah (Heaton) Wathen, born May 1, 1792, died August 1, 1840.
2. Daniel Heaton, born January 17, 1794, died August 21, 1856. He was twice married, his second wife being Elizabeth Woods, who died January 28, 1877, aged 84 years. He was the father of:
    William Heaton, who married Clementine Miller.
    Mary Heaton, wife of W. H. Fitz Randolph.
    Rachel Heaton.
    Daniel Heaton, who never married.
    Elizabeth Heaton, wife of Morgan Hedge.
3. Samuel Heaton.
4. Phoebe Heaton, who married Colonel John Ross, son of Timothy and Rachel (Wolverton) Ross. John Ross died August 4, 1873, aged 86 years, 4 months, and 16 days.
5. Elizabeth Heaton, who married John Huss, son of Elisha and Rachel Huss. John Huss died April 27, 1854.

All these mentioned are buried in the cemetery at Grimes School House.

ISAAC HEATON FAMILY

Isaac Heaton, youngest son of Samuel and Sarah (Handcock) Heaton, was born in Connecticut on June 12, 1730. He died in Greene County, Pennsylvania, April 2, 1814. While still a minor, his father moved to Sussex County, New Jersey, where he soon sickened and died. When Isaac was old enough, he married in New Jersey, Mary Booth, and removed with his father-in-law to Berkeley County, Virginia, and settled on Mill Creek where he built a mill. His bride and the first born child died there and in due time, Isaac Heaton married again. His second wife was Hannah Bowen, of Apple Pie Ridge, Frederick County, Virginia, a daughter of Henry and Anna (Moon) Bowen, and granddaughter of Henry Bowen, Sr. She was also a granddaughter of Simeon and Laura (Humphries) Moon. Hannah Bowen was born May 3, 1742 (O.S.) and died at Jefferson, Pennsylvania, May 19, 1827. A number of persons who have joined the D. A. R. and S. A. R. have claimed that Isaac Heaton served as a sergeant in the War of the Revolution, stating that he served in Captain Thompson's Company, in the Philadelphia Battalion of the Flying Camp, under the command of Colonel Robert Lewis. This Battalion was in the Battle of Long Island. We have already seen that Zabesh Heaton was living in the Philadelphia area at the time of the Revolution, and that he had a son, Isaac Heaton, who was much closer the military age, than Isaac Heaton of Berkeley County, Virginia, some two hundred miles away. Thus the service credited is open for speculation.

In the Fall of 1785, Isaac Heaton left Berkeley County to take up his residence near Jefferson, Pennsylvania, where he spent the remainder of his days. He took out several patents for land along the Tenmile and in Morgan Township, and bought up other tracts, becoming with his sons, John and Henry, one of the biggest landowners in the district. Being a miller by choice, it is not surprising that he chose lands on the streams best suited for milling, and operated grist mills in the section. Five of his sons went into Ohio to set up iron furnaces, which were the forerunners of the large steel industry of the Mahoning Valley in that State. He and his wife are buried on the old Stephen Hill Farm near Jefferson, Pennsylvania.

Family of Colonel John Heaton

1. Colonel John Heaton, son of Isaac and Hannah (Bowen) Heaton, was born in Frederick County, Virginia, December 16, 1760, died in Greene County, Pennsylvania, July 17, 1820. (Est. 354). At an early age he entered the military service of his state, and became a proficient soldier. There is a tradition in the family that he and his brother, Henry Heaton, disagreed with the higher officers under whom they served and that they removed to Western Pennsylvania, to escape punishment. Here they took up residence in the vicinity of Jefferson, to which place their father followed after the end of hostilities. The proficiency of the Heatons in the military arts soon won them recognition on the Frontier, and while still a very young man, in 1782, we find him serving as a major of the Frontier Rangers. (Pension Application of James Pribble. Nat. Arch. 3,595). The Indian troubles that followed the Revolution made the maintenance of troops imperative for some years following the war and John Heaton attained the rank of Inspector of Militia. (Penna. Arch. Series VI, Vol. 5. 611-623). He served under Major General John Minor of Big Whiteley, in

whose regiment Captain William Crawford and Captain James Seals commanded companies. As soon as John Heaton arrived in the western country, he proceeded to obtain land, by grant and by purchase, until a time when he was one of the largest land owners in what is now Greene County. The diary of his son, Hiram Heaton, also shows he was buying land in the State of Louisiana. John Heaton obtained a patent to land where he laid out a town, which became a part of Jefferson, Pennsylvania. The quarrel between Colonel Heaton and Thomas Hughes over the naming of the town is too well known to bear repetition, and politics entered into the question at that early day. Colonel John Heaton's home was situated at the turn of the road that leads from Jefferson to the mining community of Mather, and was afterward owned by David Bell. A well dug on the place at a very early date was still to be seen from the road a very few years ago. Colonel John Heaton married, on March 3, 1780, Mrs. Sarah Roberts, nee Morgan. By her first marriage with a Mr. Roberts, she had incurred the displeasure of her parents, but they were well pleased with the marriage with Colonel Heaton. A daughter, Harriet Roberts, was born to the first marriage, and raised by Colonel Heaton, later marrying Dr. John Milliken of Jefferson. Sarah Morgan Roberts was born February 20, 1763, and died at Jefferson, March 30, 1835. Both are buried in the old Presbyterian Cemetery at Jefferson.

Children of Colonel John and Sarah (Morgan) Heaton

(Bible Records of Charlotte [Heaton] Black)
1. Mary Heaton, born January 13, 1785, died April 25, 1807.
2. Morgan Heaton, born in Jefferson 1786, died in Sullivan County, Indiana, 1826-27, married Elizabeth Weaver, born September 18, 1785, died Scott County, Illinois, January 13, 1870. She was a daughter of Isaac and Abigal (Price) Weaver.
3. Charlotte Heaton, born August 27, 1788, died at Jefferson, January 9, 1877, married, on December 10, 1810, Judge Samuel Black, born in Adams County, Pennsylvania, April 12, 1787, died while in the Pennsylvania Legislature, September 21, 1846.
4. Henry Bowen Heaton, born January 11, 1791, died about 1842, leaving three children.
5. Elizabeth Heaton, born June 10, 1793, died December 31, 1793.
6. John Heaton, born November 25, 1794, died in Sullivan County, Indiana, March 18, 1842, married, April 19, 1819, Nancy Weaver, sister of Elizabeth. She was born June 17, 1797, died at Indianapolis in 1855. Her second husband was Demas McFarland.
7. Hiram Heaton, born March 19, 1797, died August 15, 1832, married Elizabeth Lindsey, born February 6, 1801. She married (2) J. N. Swallow and moved to Ohio.
8. Samuel Morgan Heaton, born July 23, 1803, died at Mt. Pleasant, Iowa, in 1862, married Amelia Hiller.
9. Alexander Heaton, born April 21, 1807, died September 9, 1831, married Caroline Topping, daughter of Alanson and Elizabeth Topping.
10. Isaac Heaton, born March 7, 1809, died June 17, 1809.

2. Mary Heaton, daughter of Isaac and Hannah (Bowen) Heaton, born December 2, 1762, in Virginia. She died in Greene County,

Pennsylvania, November 7, 1838. Her first husband was Zepheniah Luse, son of Eleazer and Elizabeth Luse, and after his death married Samuel Luse, brother of Zepheniah. Samuel Luse was born in New Jersey in 1762, and died in Greene County, September 5, 1830. Both are buried on the Stephen Hill Farm near Jefferson.

Family of Samuel and Mary (Heaton) Luse
1. Jane Luse.
2. James Luse.
3. Henry K. Luse, born May 13, 1794, died August 19, 1873. He married (1) Mary Buckingham, daughter of John and Mary (Bell) Buckingham, born December 29, 1790, died April 15, 1845. Second wife of Henry K. Luse was Mary Nelson, born October 2, 1803. Record from Bible of Gloria (Minor) Luse.
4. John Luse, born in 1798, died October 20, 1857, never married, buried with parents.
5. Warren Luse, born in 1800, died at Niles, Ohio, October 24, 1859, married Hannah Bowell, daughter of Jesse and Rebecca (Hanks) Bowell, born 1808, died September 27, 1864.
6. Charlotte Luse, married William Russell, son of James and Rachel (Kennedy) Russell. He was born March 28, 1800. Removed to Iowa in 1854.
7. Susannah Luse.
8. Zephaniah Luse.

3. Sarah Heaton, daughter of Isaac and Hannah (Bowen) Heaton, born in Virginia, December 16, 1764, died in Greene County, Pennsylvania, September 5, 1830, married in 1784, Nicholas Miles Wathen, born in Maryland, June 22, 1760, died in Greene County, April 24, 1811. Both are buried with Sarah's father. They lived on the Jim Gladden Farm near Jefferson, Pennsylvania.

Children of Nicholas Miles and Sarah (Heaton) Wathen
1. Mary Wathen, born October 2, 1785, died May 5, 1853, married Cary McClelland.
2. Henry Wathen, born February 10, 1787, died November 1787.
3. Hannah Wathen, born September 10, 1788, died February 12, 1834.
4. Nancy Wathen, born July 1, 1790, died at Indianapolis, September 24, 1851. She married Demas McFarland, who built the first house in Indianapolis.
5. Rachel Wathen, born April 29, 1792, died August 1, 1840, married Abijah Heaton, who died June 9, 1847, aged 57 years, 7 months, and 12 days. Both are buried at the Grimes School House.
6. Druscilla Wathen, born May 1, 1794, died January 8, 1834, at Fort Wayne, Indiana. She married James McFarland, brother of Demas.
7. Charlotte Wathen, born August 24, 1796, died May 16, 1802.
8. Eli Wathen, born October 22, 1798, died February 22, 1854.
9. Delilah Wathen, born June 3, 1801, died May 16, 1802.

10. Cynthia Wathen, born December 20, 1803, died May 5, 1833, married John Hanks.
11. Sarah Wathen, born July 12, 1806, died October 20, 1875, married, February 9, 1826, James Russell, born April 24, 1798, son of James and Rachel (Kennedy) Russell.

Family of Colonel Henry Heaton

4. Colonel Henry Heaton, son of Isaac and Hannah (Bowen) Heaton, was born in Virginia, September 16, 1766. When he attained legal age, he purchased several tracts of land in Greene County, and operated a mill on Castile Run. Deed Book 1. pp. 374 discloses that he and wife Martha sold this land after which he removed to Fayette County, opposite the town of Millsboro, where he built the stone house going up the road from the Ferry toward Brownsville. Here he also operated a mill on an island that formerly existed in the Monongahela at this point. This mill was destroyed by fire at one time and James Heaton, a brother of Henry, helped him build a new one. While working at the mill, Colonel Henry Heaton was bitten by a cat, and developed hydrophobia from which he died on March 27, 1833. This accounts for the nuncupative will on file in Uniontown, Pennsylvania. Henry Heaton first married Martha Morgan, a sister of his brother John's wife. She died on April 19, 1821, after which he married the widow Nancy (Hyatt) Virgin, widow of Eli Virgin. Henry and Martha (Morgan) Heaton are buried in the old cemetery near East Millsboro.

Children

1. Susannah Heaton.
2. Cynthia Heaton, married a John Heaton.
3. Samuel Heaton.
4. Nancy Heaton, married Joseph Heaton.
5. Franklin Heaton.
6. Henry Heaton.
7. Mary Heaton.
8. Harriet Heaton, married Coleman Topping.
9. Martha Heaton, married .... Dillingham.
10. Hannah Heaton.
11. Minerva Heaton.
12. Morgan Heaton.

Family of Isaac Heaton

5. Isaac Heaton, son of Isaac and Hannah (Bowen) Heaton, born in Virginia, October 29, 1768, died in Ohio in 1834. He with four of his brothers were early settlers in the Mahoning Valley, where they operated iron furnaces which were the forerunners of the huge steel mills of the present day. He married Hannah Williams or Wilson, and lived at Howland, Ohio.

Children named by Rachel Colver

1. William Heaton.
2. Maria Heaton.

Family of James Heaton

6. James Heaton, son of Isaac and Hannah (Bowen) Heaton, born in Virginia, February 2, 1771. He removed to Ohio with brothers, where he died at Niles in 1823. His wife was

Margaret Williams, who is buried with him at Niles. When he first settled at Howland, he discovered a valuable deposit of "kidney ore" which he used to manufacture stoves, called Maria Stoves, and named for his first daughter. He is described as being a powerful man and well read. When he first went to Ohio he settled at Athens, but later went with his brothers to the Mahoning Valley.

Children

1. Isaac Heaton, removed from Ohio to Kinmundy, Illinois, where he died March 12, 1872. His wife was Elizabeth Robbins.
2. Enoch Heaton.
3. Lewis Heaton.
4. Hanna Heaton.
5. Warren Heaton, born 1802, died at Niles in 1842, married Elizabeth McConnell.
6. Maria Heaton, born before 1800, died at Niles in 1835, married Josiah Robbins.
7. John Heaton.
8. Owens Heaton.
9. Shelvy Heaton.

Family of Daniel Heaton

7. Daniel Heaton, son of Isaac and Hannah (Bowen) Heaton, born in Virginia, March 24, 1773. Became an ardent prohibitionist at 18 and shortly thereafter left Greene County to settle in the Mahoning Valley of Ohio, where he made quite a success in the iron making business. He entered politics in Ohio and was elected to Legislature, serving from Trumbull County. While in Legislature he had his name changed to "Eaton" because as he said, they never pronounced the "H" anyway. He died May 4, 1858. His wife was Amy Hill, daughter of Robert and Priscilla (Bowen) Hill, his first cousin. They were parents of:
   1. Bowen Heaton.
   2. Rees Heaton.
   3. Priscilla Heaton.
   4. Eli Heaton.
   5. Jacob Heaton.
   6. John Heaton.
   7. Robert Heaton.
   8. Isaac Heaton.
   9. Hannah Heaton.
   10. Amy Heaton.
   11. Anna Heaton.

Family of Rees Hill

8. Nancy Heaton, daughter of Isaac and Hannah (Bowen) Heaton, was born in Virginia on June 1, 1775, died in Greene County June 16, 1828. She married Colonel Rees Hill, son of Robert and Priscilla (Bowen) Hill, and grandson of Johnson and Naomi Hill of Augusta County, Virginia. Robert Hill, father of Rees Hill, served in Captain Abner Howell's Washington County Militia Company in the War of the Revolution, and Rees Hill served as a Colonel in the war of 1812. Rees Hill was one of twelve children and was born April 1776, in Virginia. He was a prominent merchant of Waynesburg, and served the county for twenty years in the Pennsylvania Legis-

lature, seven of which were served as Speaker of the House. After the War of 1812, he was active in securing pensions for widows of men who lost their lives in that war, as well as getting pensions for soldiers of the Revolution, who had become indigent. The old ledgers of his store, conducted in Waynesburg in partnership with John Depui, are in the hands of this writer and show many interesting transactions, as well as the people who lived here at that time. After leaving the Legislature, Rees Hill went to Frederick County, Virginia, where over a period of years, he attempted to collect together the estate of his grandfather, Henry Bowen, and also the estates of his two uncles who had died in the Revolution. His efforts for a time were successful, but eventually he overextended himself and got into financial straits. The litigation was still in the courts when he died near Winchester, but the transactions in the case are excellent for discovering the relationship and heirs of Henry Bowen. Nancy (Heaton) Hill died during this period and Rees Hill married the widow, Louise Abbott. He and his second wife are buried at Winchester. Rees Hill was one of the first members of the Waynesburg Masonic Lodge.

Children

1. Elizabeth Hill, died July 6, 1824, at the age of twenty one years. At the intersection of the Oak Forest and Rogersville Road on the way to Waynesburg, there is a lonely grave, where Elizabeth Hill, wife of William G. Hawkins, is buried. He was a prominent Greene County attorney, who afterwards settled at Pittsburg. They were married August 28, 1820.
2. Isaac Hill, married Nancy Virgin, a daughter of Eli and Nancy (Hyatt) Virgin. She died in Greene County at the age of 79 years.
3. Daniel Hill, born February 5, 1803, died August 5, 1882; married, January 9, 1831, Matilda Penn, born March 26, 1805, died March 8, 1896. Both are buried in South Tenmile Baptist Church Cemetery.
4. Bowen Hill.
5. Hannah Hill, married Samuel Hill, son of Samuel and Elizabeth (Cathers) Hill. He was born August 30, 1803, and died April 1840. Buried in the Hill Cemetery.
6. Priscilla Hill.
7. Mary Hill, born February 23, 1810, died in Missouri, January 3, 1895; married, March 19, 1829, Thomas Hughes Roseberry, born May 13, 1806, died March 29, 1891. He was a son of Mathias and Sarah (Hughes) Roseberry.
8. Heaton Hill, married Jane Stone.
9. Rees Hill, Jr.
10. Amy Hill.
11. Naomi Hill, married Gordon Rowland.
12. Louisa Hill, daughter by second marriage, married (1) .... Showalter, (2) .... Fellows.

Family of Isaac Buckingham

9. Hannah Heaton, daughter of Isaac and Hannah (Bowen) Heaton, born in Virginia, April 3, 1778. She died in Washington County, Pennsylvania, March 30, 1850; married about 1796, Isaac Buckingham, born August 20, 1777, died April 11, 1853. Both are buried in Franklin Cemetery, near Marianna. He

was a son of John and Mary (Bell) Buckingham. John Buckingham was a Soldier in Captain George Myers' Company of Washington County, Pennsylvania Militia.

Children

1. John Buckingham, born July 31, 1797, died January 13, 1882; married, May 4, 1820, Jane Dalrymple, born May 15, 1797, died March 25, 1878.
2. Rachel Buckingham.
3. .... Buckingham.
4. Charlotte Buckingham, died August 14, 1819, aged 11 years, 11 months, and 18 days.
5. Henry Buckingham, born December 19, 1809, died May 11, 1891; married, December 25, 1833, Mary Morton, daughter of Thomas and Mary (Cree) Morton, born October 18, 1814, died July 17, 1895. Buried in C. P. Cemetery at Jefferson.
6. Bowen Buckingham, died intestate in Greene County in 1855, his wife, Jane, waiving the right to administer his estate.
7. Mary Buckingham.
8. Hannah Buckingham, born February 17, 1817, died September 2, 1886; married John A. Greenlee, son of Samuel and Nancy Greenlee.

Family of Thomas Colver

10. Rachel Heaton, daughter of Isaac and Hanna (Bowen) Heaton, born in Virginia, April 3, 1780, died in Brooke County, West Virginia, January 21, 1864. She married Thomas Colver, an early attorney, who died October 26, 1852. Both were members of Goshen Baptist Church. It was Rachel (Heaton) Colver's letter that is quoted to show the Heaton lineage. She is buried near Independence, Washington County, Pennsylvania.

Children

1. Dr. Samuel Colver, died in 1877. He built the stone house across from Jefferson, later occupied by Norval Rogers and now by his widow. Never married.
2. Elizabeth Colver, married Joseph Gist. Both are buried near Independence, Pennsylvania.

Family of Rees Heaton

11. Rees Heaton, son of Isaac and Hannah (Bowen) Heaton, born in Virginia, February 7, 1783. From Mrs. Austa Heaton Daniels of Princeton, Illinois, a fine lady over eighty years of age, we received a long-hand transcription of the entire genealogy of the Rees Heaton Family. She had prepared this without so much as an erasure, or a single error, writing a smooth hand, with pen and ink, that would shame many younger persons. We copied it, in toto, for the Heaton Book. Mrs. Daniels is a granddaughter of Rees Heaton. She states that Rees Heaton spent his youth in Greene County, where he met and married, on September 4, 1811, Sarah Weaver, daughter of Isaac and Abigail (Price) Weaver, who was born in Harrisburg, Pennsylvania, December 29, 1792. In 1814, Rees Heaton joined his brothers, James, Isaac, Daniel, and Jacob, in Trumbull County, Ohio, where he remained until 1835, at which time he removed with his eldest son, William, to Illinois, to build a new home about seven miles from Princeton, on land that had been

entered from the government by William Shirley, who left it about the time of the Black Hawk War and never returned to it. It was then taken up by a Mr. Frankenberger, who sold his rights to Rees Heaton for the sum of ten dollars. In 1836 Rees Heaton prepared his family for the long journey west and in May they set out with three teams, wagons and buggy for the new home. The journey consumed seven weeks. The new home had all the requirements that the pioneers needed, rich fertile prairie land, with a stream running through it, and adjacent to needful timber. This timber which in Illinois, usually followed streams, came to an abrupt end on a few acres on a corner of the farm, where Rees Heaton built his cabin, which soon took the name of "Heaton's Point." All his children settled near by when they reached maturity and married, either buying the land from the government at one dollar per acre, or purchasing it from others who had made improvements. They were all farmers and improved their properties with good durable buildings. In the early days, the pioneers missed the schools, which were few and far between. A neighbor of Rees Heaton, who had several children, and lived about three miles from the Heaton home, had a two room log cabin and offered the use of one room for a school. Isaac Heaton, son of Rees, obtained his certificate and taught there until a new school was built near the Heaton home. Marketing was a big problem in those days, with Chicago still a small village, but with good shipping facilities, it proved the only outlet for surplus grain. For several years the pioneers had to haul their grain 104 miles to Chicago, a custom in vogue until the C. B. & Q. came to Princeton in 1854. Elizabeth Heaton and her husband gave two acres of land for a church and erected upon it the "Heaton's Point" Baptist Church. The Cemetery plotted on the remaining land, took its name from the Church. It is here that Rees Heaton, his wife, and many of his descendants are buried. In 1855, Rees Heaton and his wife sold their farm to their daughter, Abigail, and her husband, but continued living there for a time, finally moving to the home of their son, Isaac, with whom they spent their last days. Rees Heaton died on June 7, 1878. His wife died on December 16, 1876.

Children

1. Nancy Heaton, born July 6, 1812, died November 7, 1865; married, March 6, 1837, in Illinois, Hezekiah Epperson, son of Elijah and Susie (Hickman) Epperson, who was born November 1807, and died June 6, 1880. Both are buried in Heaton Point Cemetery.
2. William Heaton, born November 28, 1813, died at Weir, Kansas, January 17, 1891. He married at Mt. Vernon, Missouri, August 28, 1865, Jane Newman, born September 25, 1845. She died at Weir, Kansas on April 21, 1909.
3. Isaac Heaton, born in Trumbull County, Ohio, on February 21, 1816, died December 17, 1887, and is buried in Heaton Point Cemetery with his second wife. He married (1) January 20, 1848, in McDonough County, Illinois, Ann Sullivan, who was born June 12, 1824, and who died March 27, 1854. On November 7, 1855, Isaac Heaton married at Marion, Iowa, Amanda Kennedy, daughter of Montgomery and Mary Kennedy, born July 8, 1828, and died December 8, 1894.

4. Hannah Heaton, born March 9, 1818, died at Princeton, May 18, 1852; married James Wilson, son of Ambrose and Parthena (Lay) Wilson, born July 25, 1813, at Morgansfield, Kentucky, died October 1, 1886, at Princeton.
5. Abigail Heaton, born January 17, 1820, died December 14, 1886; married, August 28, 1838, Harrison Epperson, born August 1, 1816, died September 16, 1894. Both are buried at Afton, Iowa.
6. Daniel Heaton, born Trumbull County, Ohio, January 5, 1826, died December 11, 1894, at Curtis, Nebraska. Married, November 27, 1854, Rachel Baxter, born at Pittsburg, Pennsylvania, June 11, 1833. She died at Curtis, Nebraska, December 29, 1906.
7. Elizabeth Heaton, born June 1, 1828, died February 28, 1888, at Heaton's Point. She married, December 18, 1854, Samuel Elliott, born September 1, 1824, died June 10, 1899.
8. Cyrus Heaton, born March 12, 1835, died February 18, 1845. He is buried in the Mason Cemetery, near Princeton, Illinois.

Family of Jacob Bowen Heaton

12. Jacob Bowen Heaton, youngest child of Isaac and Hannah (Bowen) Heaton, was born at Jefferson, Pennsylvania, May 9, 1786. He spent his early life on his father's farm near Jefferson, where he married, August 24, 1809, Rachel Weaver, daughter of Isaac and Abigail (Price) Weaver, who was born September 4, 1787. In 1812, they removed to Trumbull County, Ohio. They returned to Pennsylvania in 1826 and in 1834 removed to Fulton County, Illinois, where Jacob died on October 23, 1839. His widow returned to Pennsylvania where she died November 1858.

Children

1. Weaver Heaton, born August 8, 1810, died December 1873, married Rebecca Sharp.
2. Abigail Heaton, born January 8, 1812, married Daniel Hayden.
3. Hannah Heaton, born February 23, 1814, died January 31, 1838.
4. Eliza Heaton, born February 14, 1816, never married, a physician and teacher in Illinois.
5. Henry Heaton, born January 18, 1818, died in Illinois in 1843.
6. Sarah Heaton, born February 22, 1820, married Claudius Cook Sackett.
7. Nancy Heaton, born May 22, 1822, died April 20, 1856 at Deerfield, Illinois.
8. Mary Heaton, born May 27, 1824, died May 17, 1848, married William Allen Secor.
9. Rachel Heaton, born July 20, 1826, died May 20, 1839.
10. Mariah Heaton, born September 21, 1829, died in Illinois in 1851.

DIARY OF HIRAM HEATON

The following is an account of the journey of Hiram Heaton of Jefferson, Pennsylvania, to Baton Rouge, La., in the Spring of 1819. Hiram Heaton was the son of Colonel John Heaton (Virginia John) of Jefferson, Pennsylvania. The Title page of his Journal, the original of which is owned by Howard L. Leckey of Waynesburg, Pennsylvania, is "Memorandam of my Account and Expenses in going to settle the Business of my Father and Stephen Batro, late of Baton Rogue, decs." and is dated April 4, 1819.

Left Jefferson on the 4th of April 1819, detained at Waynesburg until the 8th inst. A. M. Bill $7.62.

Arrive at Washington the same evening. Dist. 22 mi. Detained until the 12th in company with Slater and Jackson, gave Slater as purser for the company $20.00. In addition 13.25.

Arrive at Wheeling the same evening.

Breakfast at St. Clairsville on the 13th.

Passed through Zanesville and crossed the Ohio at Cincinnati.

From thence to Big Bone Lick (saw there some large mammoth bones dry out of the earth, three teeth and part of the jaw supposed to weigh 13 lbs).

Thence to Jack's for breakfast

Thence down the Ohio. Passed through Fredericksburg, Ghent and Port William, there crossed the Kentucky River at its mouth.

Thence to New Castle, thence to Louisville.

Crossed the Ohio at New Albany. Thence to Orleans.

Then to Sholtts Ferry on the East Branch of the White River.

Thence to Washington, Indiana; thence to the West Branch of White River; thence to Morgans, near Carlisle. Arrove on the 29th inst.

Sunday the 2nd of May, went 7 mi. from Carlisle to hear the Society called Shakers and was much surprised to see their mode of worship which was chiefly in singing and dancing. The females wore white caps and danced separate from the males. I understood their doctrine to be, from their discourse, to prevent the propagation of the human species.

May 4th Vinnes (?) Arrove same evening. Horse badly foundered, unable to travel, forced to sell him. Sold him to M. Barnet for $120, sacrificing in his price, $55.

May 6th, started for Shawneetown on Mr. Slaters horse so far as the Ferry. Bill inclusive of the horse Ferry $5.00. There bought a canoe price $5.00. Arrove at Palmyra same evening, tired from very much padling of and much surprised to see Alex. Haslet at Palmyra. Delivered the letter sent by Jack to Jesse Brown, Esq.

May 7th stayed nine Mi. above Harmony, Bill 50 cents.

May 8th Arrove at Harmony for Breakfast. Much pleased indeed with the situation and buildings of the place. The handsomest village I have seen by far in my travels. Arrove in 25 miles of Shawnee Town much alarmed in consequence of a severe storm which dashed the water in my canoe.

Unsafe to go by water on the 9th. Paid for a horse and sadle $5.00.

May 9th, arrove at Shawnee Town. Could not sell my canoe. Bill at Dr. Wilson's in Shawnee $1.25.

May 10th, took passage on the Sarrs and Smith Boat for Natches. Paste board tin cup .50. Put off half past 3 o'clock P. M. landed same evening 2 miles above the mouth of the Salien River.

May 11th, put off 4 o'clock A. M. This day went out in a skiff to see the cave in rock or house of Nature. Wonderful curiosity indeed. Vide Naugato, published by Cr. and Spear, page 120.

Landed same evening above the first of the Cumberland Islands, passed by Galconda, the seat of Justice of Pope County, Ill.

May 12th put of at 5 O'Clock P. M. passed the mouth of the Cumberland River, also passed Fort Massac, passed the Tennessee River, ante Fort Massac. Landed the same evening at the Grand Chains. Detained till the 14th on account of wind. S & S 50 cents.

May 14th put off at 8 O'Clock P. M. entered the Mississippi at 1 O'Clock A. M. Landed the same evening 1 Mi. below the chaulk banks, 5 Mi. above which at the horn banks is the line between Kentucky and Tennessee.

May 15th put off at 4 O'Clock P. M. Landed 10 Mi. above New Madrid at 1 O'Clock consequence of hard winds. Detained till the 17th.

May 17th putt off at 5 O'Clock A. M. Landed at New Madrid at nine O'Clock same day. Detained till the 19th. Went and took a view of the tremendious effects of the earth-quake which happened at this place, Dec. 1816. Ground sunk eight feet below its natural level. M. $1.50.

Put off at 5 O'Clock A. M. Landed same evening at the head of island No. 19.

May 20th Put off at 5 O'Clock A. M. Landed at 8 O'Clock same day in consequence of high winds. Detained till the

May 21st. Put off at 4 O'Clock A. M. passed Bayou River on the left. Landed same evening at the foot of Chickasaw Bluffs (second)

May 22nd Put off at 5 O'Clock P. M. Landed same evening at Wolf River, which puts in immediately above the 4th Chickasaw Bluffs on which Bluff is situated Fort Pickering.

May 23d Sunday. Put off at 3 O'Clock A. M. Landed same evening 2 miles above Council Island.

May 24th. Put off at 5 O'Clock A. M. Landed same evening 5 Mi. below Island No. 60.

May 25th. Put off at 4 O'Clock A. M. Landed same evening at Island No. 68.

May 26th. Put off at 4 O'Clock A. M. Passed White and Arkansas Rivers on our right. Landed same evening at Island No. 76.

May 27th Put off at half past 2 Passed Tennessee line 3 miles below F. P. Landed same evening at Neco Point.

May 28th Put off at 4 O'Clock A. M. Landed same evening at Island No. 85. Detained until

May 30th in consequence of a severe storm. Sunday the 30th Put off at 4 A. M. Landed same evening on Island No. 95.

May 31st Put off at 3:30 O'Clock. Landed same day opposite the Mouth of the Yazoo River.

June 1st Put off at 4 O'Clock. Landed same day at Warren

June 2nd Put off at 4 O'Clock A. M. Landed same evening at Bayou Pierre.

June 3d Put off at half past 3 O'Clock landed same evening at Natchez. Mr. Turner left us at Bayou Pierre went to Port Gibson. All the Boats stopped for some time at Natchez so took passage with three others on Wallons Boat. No loading except one mare and some fowls.

June 5th Put off at 7 O'Clock P. M. run all night.

June 7th Landed at St. Francisville at which place I met C. B. Esquire, our agent. Made the arraingements with him and went on the ninth to see the land 20 Mi. below Baton Rouge. Much pleased wih the land. Offerred 7$ per acre all on credit. After some contention and some difficulty got the land, clear of all incumbrances. Paid the taxes and returned to St. Francisville.

June 13th, walked 12 Mi. and bought an Appulusa horse, price 40 dol.

June 14th. Started for home. Stayed all night at Mr. Browns. Bill $1.50. Breakfast at Woodville $1.00.

June 15th Lodged at Buffalow.

June 16th Arrove at Natchez. Detained till the 18th. in the evening came one mile as far as Nichols.

June 19th, started at 4 O'Clock, passed Washington and took breakfast at William Tavern. Lodged there 31 Mi. from Natchez.

June 20th, lodged at 11 mi. of the Chickasaw Line.

June 21st, Came to old Mr. Hayes, he had nothing to eat or drink, and he refused us lodging. A hard case too. Camped all night in the woods.

June 22nd. Lodged at Wardses

June 23d Arrived at Doaxes, unwell, stayed till the 23d.

Took the Reynoldsville Road at the Chickasaw Old Town and crossed the Tennessee River at Reynoldsburg, from thence to Dover on the Cumberland River.

No particular acct. of the above rout on acct of loosing my inkstand, but suffered much from hunger. Nothing to eat for self or horse. 75 miles, no house.

From thence to Hopkinsville, Kentucky; thence to Reads Forks.

Thence to Evansville, there crossed the Ohio; thence to Princeton; thence to Morgan Again. Arrove on the 11th of July.

Started for home on the first of August, stayed at Mr. Hawks same night.

Aug. 2nd Arrove at Washington for breakfast and stayed at Shrontts same noght.

Aug. 3d. Arrove and lodged at Orlens.

Aug. 4th Lodged 7 Mi. on this side of Salem.

Aug. 5th Lodged at Madison.

Aug. 6th, Arrove at Biers Tavern for breakfast, stayed same evening at Checks Tavern 3 Mi. on this side of Wilmington.

Aug. 7th Arrove at Hamilton, detained till the 9th with James Heaton, a relative.

Aug. 9th Arrove at Job Smiths, six Mi. this side of Lebenon.

Aug. 11th Went to see old Mr. Batro, got my business arrainged with much difficulty. At last he executed deed to my father, by me aggreeing my obligation to give him a horse when called on, also to give him any balance after the debt of my father is deducted out, if the place of Stephen Batro can be sold within two years at a reasonable price, from the 11th of August 1819.

Aug. 12th Stayed at Henry Tavern.
Aug. 13th.———————
Here ends the Diary of Hiram Heaton. An account of expenses is given in the final page and on one of the covers is the name of Joseph L. Turner of Talbot County, Maryland, who was a companion of Heaton on the boat down the Mississippi, from Shawnee Town. It is to be regretted that Mr. Heaton lost his ink stand in his trip through Mississippi, Tennessee, and Kentucky, on his return trip, for he must have had some experiences that impressed him deep enough to note his hunger and the desolate country through which he passed.

THE BUCKINGHAM FAMILY

This early Pennsylvania family was among the earliest settlers on the North Tenmile, and since their arrival have been more or less identified with the Jefferson and Clarksville communities. The family is directly descended from one William Buckingham, who came from England in the 17th Century, and settled in Chester County, where he bought land in Birmingham Township on April 7, 1687. He became a Baptist preacher and was identified with the Cohansey Baptist Church of New Jersey, and later with the Brandywine Church in Birmingham Township, Chester County, Pennsylvania. He died about 1701, leaving a wife, Margaret, and a number of children.

John Buckingham, son of William and Margaret Buckingham, was one of these children. He was born about 1670 and removed to New Castle County, Delaware, where he died at the age of 84. He married, in Delaware, Hannah Brundsen, a daughter of John Brundsen, an immigrant from England, about 1678. He and his wife were members of Brandywine Baptist Church.

Children of John and Hannah (Brundsen) Buckingham

1. John Buckingham, married Sarah Knowles Shallcross, a widow. He bought land on April 27, 1744, and constructed a mill on his property. On February 18, 1750, he sold an interest to Joseph Buckingham, and on January 30, 1751, sold another part to William Buckingham. On the same day, John and William Buckingham, with their wives, sold an interest in the mill to Hannah Heath.
2. Mary Buckingham, married William Kirk of Kennet.
3. Hannah Buckingham, married (1) .... Heath; (2) Rev. Nehemiah Bonham.
4. Sarah Buckingham, married Daniel Nichols.
5. James Buckingham, married, 1755, Jane Chambers, daughter of Robert Chambers.
6. William Buckingham, married, July 20, 1726, Jane James, apparently a granddaughter of Howell James, through a son, William James, who died before his father. Howell James names Jane James in his will, as a daughter of son, William, deceased. William Buckingham died in 1789, aged about 87 years. The names of his children with the birth records, were found among the papers of a grandson, Levi Buckingham, of Hamilton County, Ohio.

Children of William and Jane (James) Buckingham

1. Margaret Buckingham, born December 28, 1798, baptized August 2, 1746, in the Welsh Tract Baptist Church.

2. John Buckingham, I, born November 30, 1731, died September 1735.
3. Enoch Buckingham, born August 31, 1732, died before his father.
4. William Buckingham, born June 2, 1734, died in Washington County, Pennsylvania, June 23, 1827. He married, December 7, 1762, Jane Jones, daughter of James and Susannah (Williams) Jones. She was born June 28, 1744, and died in Washington County, Pennsylvania, March 16, 1826. Both are buried in the Buckingham Cemetery near Fredericktown, Pennsylvania. William Buckingham served in Captain Ezekiel Rose's Militia Company in the Fifth Battalion, Washington County Militia, in the War of the Revolution. (Penna. Arch. Series VI Vol. 2. pp. 206-242). He removed to Ohio about 1779, but returned. Family Bible record was copied in 1827, by Mark Buckingham of Hamilton County, Ohio. The names of his daughter's husbands were obtained from a suit filed by the daughter, Jane Kelly, against her father's estate, for services in caring for her mother eight years before her death.

Children of William and Jane (Jones) Buckingham
1. Enoch Buckingham, born November 3, 1763, died in Hamilton County, Ohio, in 1845. His wife was Mary Jeffries, daughter of Matthew and Mary (Alexander) Jeffries. His son, Mark Buckingham, is named above, and Levi Buckingham, also named, was another son.
2. Levi Buckingham, born May 14, 1765, married Lydia Sears (Sayers?). Lived in Ohio.
3. Catherine Buckingham, born August 22, 1767, married Jonathan Mundel, son of James and Margaret (Garret) Mundel. They went to Ohio before 1827.
4. John Buckingham, born August 20, 1769, not named in suit, so probably died young.
5. James Buckingham, born November 16, 1770, died November 1, 1781.
6. Isaac Buckingham, born May 15, 1772, married Sarah Jones. They lived for a time near Garards Fort, where a child is buried. Later removed to Indiana.
7. Susan Buckingham, born October 20, 1773, married James Sutton. Lived in Ohio.
8. Hannah Buckingham, born November 6, 1775, married Moses Bonnell.
9. Esther Buckingham, born June 17, 1777, married Samuel Betson.
10. Lydia Buckingham, born May 1, 1779, married Adam Wise, moved to Ohio.
11. William Buckingham, born February 19, 1781, died August 30, 1851, married (1) Mary Barnard, who died December 3, 1829. He married (2) Rachel Sibbetts, who died June 14, 1876. Both are buried in the Buckingham Cemetery near Fredericktown, Pennsylvania.
12. Jesse Buckingham, born February 2, 1783.
13. Jane Buckingham, born November 15, 1784. Brought suit in Washington County, Pennsylvania. Her husband was William Kelly as shown in the suit.

5. Hannah Buckingham, born October 31, 1736, baptized May 9, 1754, married .... Thomas.

6. Ruth Buckingham, born November 6, 1738, baptized June 4, 1746, married William Cloud, an executor of the will of his father-in-law.
7. John Buckingham, II, born November 10, 1740, baptized June 4, 1746, died in Washington County, Pennsylvania, December 1, 1794. He married, on September 5, 1776, Mary Bell, daughter of Nathaniel and Hannah Bell of Bell's Fort on Ruffs Creek. Both are buried in the old cemetery at Franklin School House, but the marker for Mary (Bell) Buckingham is no longer legible. John Buckingham served as clerk in Captain George Myers' Company, Fifth Battalion, Washington County Militia in the War of the Revolution. (Penn. Arch. Series VI. Vol. 2 pp. 167-168). He died intestate, but guardians for his minor children were appointed in Washington County. (O. C. Docket 1. pp. 128-171.) Mrs. George B. Drake of Waynesburg, has the Family Bible.

Children of John and Mary (Bell) Buckingham
1. Isaac Buckingham, born August 20, 1777, died April 11, 1833; married Hannah Heaton, born April 3, 1778, died March 30, 1850. Both are buried beside John Buckingham in the Franklin Cemetery. (See Heaton Records.)
2. Jane Buckingham, born 1779, died February 3, 1795, aged 15 years, 6 months, 19 days. She is buried with her parents.
3. William Buckingham, born November 26, 1781, married Nancy McClelland, daughter of Cary and Henrietta (Myers) McClelland.
4. John Buckingham, born 1784, died March 14, 1784, aged 4 weeks, 2 days.
5. Hannah Buckingham, born August 21, 1786, died December 18, 1837; married, February 20, 1806, Eleazer Luse, Jr., son of Eleazer Luse of Jefferson. He was born January 3, 1777, in Sussex County, New Jersey, and died May 11, 1859, aged 82 years, 5 months, 8 days. Both are buried in the old Presbyterian Cemetery at Jefferson. (See Luse Records.)
6. Mary Buckingham, born December 29, 1790, died April 15, 1845, married Henry K. Luse, born May 13, 1794, died August 17, 1873, son of Samuel and Mary (Heaton) Luse.
7. John Buckingham, II, born July 13, 1793, died at Yam Hill, Oregon. He married in 1816, Elizabeth Hughes, born July 26, 1796, daughter of John and Mary (Rex) Hughes. (See Thomas Hughes Records.)

ISAAC WEAVER

Isaac Weaver was born at Providence, Pennsylvania, March 1, 1756. He was educated at Philadelphia, and taught school when a young man. His first wife was one of his pupils. He served in the Revolution in Captain Jonathan Vernon's Company of Chester County Militia, under the command of Lieutenant Colonel Caleb Davis. He was a very large man, six feet four in height, weighing about 240 pounds, handsome and distinguished looking. Originally a Quaker, he was cited in the Chester County Meeting for being married by an outside minister, as of July 28, 1783. He served in both houses of Legislature, being selected for Speaker of the Senate in 1800. He was elected Treasurer of the State in 1802, and succeeded in putting the finances of the new State in order. At the time of his death he was candidate for governor and would probably have been elected. At one time a descendant of Isaac Weaver, living in Greene County, had the trunk in which the entire funds of the state were carried from Philadelphia to the home of Isaac Weaver on Castile Run. He died May 22, 1830, and with his wife, Abigail (Price) Weaver, is buried on his home farm on Castile Run. It is a sad commentary on the people of this State that a man who served so long and so well, is left in a neglected grave in a barn lot. His descendants, still living here should take it into their hands to see that a suitable re-interment be provided in Jefferson of Clarksville, where a proper marker should commemorate his fame. His first wife was Abigail Price, who was born in 1766, and died in 1813. The second wife was Rachel Husband.

Children

1. Ann Weaver, died in infancy.
2. Elizabeth Weaver, born September 18, 1785, married Morgan Heaton.
3. Rachel Weaver, born September 4, 1787, married Jacob Bowen Heaton.
4. Price Weaver, born July 2, 1789, married Hannah Burns.
5. William Weaver, born February 19, 1791, married Mary Cornwell, daughter of Henry and Nancy (Price) Cornwell. She was born May 4, 1797, and died April 19, 1855. He died April 11, 1879. Both are buried in the Weaver Cemetery in Fulton County, Illinois.
6. Sarah Weaver, born December 29, 1792, married Rees Heaton.
7. Joshua Weaver, born July 21, 1795, died at the age of 21 years, buried with parents.
8. Nancy Weaver, born June 17, 1797, married John Heaton.
9. Isaac Weaver, born December 13, 1800, died October 21, 1866; married, July 21, 1823, Eliza Cornwell, born October 6, 1802, died May 25, 1886.

Children

1. Baldwin Weaver, born February 2, 1824, married Elizabeth Roberts.
2. Nancy Weaver, born November 17, 1825, died July 20, 1883; married, October 25, 1844, John Murdock.
3. Amelia Weaver, born September 17, 1827 on Muddy Creek, married James Eaton.
4. Adaline Weaver, born December 10, 1829.
5. Elizabeth Weaver, born March 20, 1832, married Robert McClelland on August 19, 1852.

6. John Weaver, born April 29, 1834; married, February 15, 1859, Mary F. Nurm.
7. Harmon Weaver, born July 2, 1836, died July 17, 1846.
8. William Weaver, born November 23, 1838, died at Antietam, September 16, 1884.
9. Orphia Weaver, born September 28, 1840, married . ... Venard.
10. George Weaver, born August 14, 1842; married, September 9, 1884, Henrietta Fulton.
11. Theodora Weaver, born September 20, 1844, died June 15, 1845.
12. Isaac Weaver, born June 11, 1847, died July 1923; married, September 11, 1879, Mary Wallace.
13. David P. Weaver, born February 21, 1849.

10. David Weaver, born January 23, 1803, married Charlotte Cornwell.
11. Harmon Weaver, born May 24, 1809, married Permelia Day.

ROBERT HILL

Robert Hill, son of Johnson Hill and his wife, Naomi ...., was born in Augusta County, Virginia. He was 16 years old when his father died about 1761, and Robert had Daniel Smith appointed as his guardian. His mother, Naomi, remarried, this time to Adam Thompson, who died in 1769. Robert Hill was the only child by the first marriage. He married Priscilla Bowen, daughter of Henry and Anna (Moon) Bowen of Frederick County, Virginia. During the War of the Revolution, Robert Hill with his wife and several children, removed to Amwell Township, Washington County, Pennsylvania, where he served in Captain Abner Howell's Militia Company. When his son Rees settled at Waynesburg, Robert Hill seems to have come to live with him, and the Ledger of Rees Hill and John Depui indicates that he died at Waynesburg about 1820. Only three of the twelve children of Robert and Priscilla (Bowen) Hill are known, they are:

Rees Hill, who married his first cousin, Nancy Heaton.
Amy Hill, who married Daniel Heaton, her cousin.
Johnson Hill, whose wife's name was Phoebe.
John Hill, who died in 1819, in Greene County, may have been another.

THE SHELBY FAMILY

It is apparent that all the Shelbys of the Tenmile Country were descendants of the immigrant Evan Shelby who came from Cardiganshire, Wales, to settle first in the Cove section of now Franklin County, Pennsylvania. He remained there but a short time and then removed to Maryland about 1739, and settled near the present town of Hagerstown, where he lived the life of a planter, dying there about 1751, without leaving a will. His son, Evan Shelby, was a captain under Colonel Henry Boquet and later served with distinction in the Revolution. History of this branch is well known. Mr. Cass K. Shelby of Hollidaysburg, Pennsylvania, has prepared an extensive genealogy of the Immigrant Evan Shelby, and has permitted us to draw heavily upon his records for the story of the Greene County Shelbys.

Neither Mr. Cass Shelby, nor the author, are certain regarding the parentage of David Shelby, Jr., who settled on a tract of land patented to him under the title "Laurel Point" on July 2, 1795. This was the site of a point in the Jefferson Road still known as Laurel Point, or more familiarly as "Stumpy Point." Inclined at first to consider him a son of David Shelby of the Garards Fort section, though not named in the settlement of David Shelby's estate, later search does not confirm this belief. It seems more likely that he was a son of Evan Shelby, grandson of the immigrant Evan, through his son, Rees Shelby.

Rees Shelby, second son of the immigrant Evan Shelby, was born in Wales about 1721, moved to Maryland with his father and then about 1750, to the Little Cove, near Welsh Run, Pennsylvania. He migrated to the Carolinas about 1760, and finally settled in Chesterfield County, South Carolina, where he died about 1802. His wife, Mary, may have been a Miss Blair.

Evan Shelby, son of Rees Shelby, was born about 1740, and served as an ensign in the French and Indian War. He was a captain in the Bedford County, Pennsylvania Militia in the Revolution, removing after the War to what is now Greene County. He was twice married but the first wife is unknown. His second wife was Mary (Harrod) Newland, widow of Adam Newland, and sister of Captain William Harrod. Mary Newland warranted the tract of land next to "Laurel Point," an item which is not overlooked in the identification of David Shelby, Jr. None of the children of Evan Shelby are known, he probably being the Evan Shelby who helped settle at the present site of Cincinnati, being of the Benjamin Stites Party.

David Shelby, Jr., was born June 5, 1765, in the "Little Cove" where he married Mary Williams, daughter of Enoch and Hannah (.................) Williams, of Air Township, Bedford County. They were married about 1782. Mary Williams was born July 2, 1762, and died in Pickaway County, Ohio, October 3, 1830. Her sisters, Hannah and Margaret, married Isaac and James Heaton, respectively. After a short stay in Fayette County, David Shelby, Jr., came to "Laurel Point," where he lived until he migrated first to Adams County, Ohio, and then to Pickaway County, where he died December 25, 1845. He served as Justice of Peace, member of the Ohio Legislature and captain in the War of 1812 after leaving the Tenmile.

Children of David and Mary (Williams) Shelby

1. John Shelby, born 1783, married in July 1806, Eleanor Morris, daughter of Ezekiel and Mary Morris, former neighbors on the Tenmile. Both were killed in a runaway carriage accident in 1825.
2. Joseph Shelby, born 1785, at Covington, Indiana, died 1846; married, June 17 or 18, 1811, Sarah Steeley.
3. Charity Shelby, born September 15, 1787, died at Circleville, Ohio, December 21, 1876, married Henry O. Morris, son of Ezekiel and Mary Morris.
4. Hannah Shelby, born 1789, died Edgar County, Illinois, 1884; married November 13, 1815, Rev. Joseph Curtis, itinerant Methodist preacher.
5. Rezin Shelby, born December 22, 1781, died in Vermillion County, Indiana, in 1856; married in 1825, Jane Thompson.

6. Rachel Shelby, born 1794, died in Edgar County, Illinois; married (1) November 4, 1817, George Webster. She married (2) March 4, 1835, James M. Blackburn.
7. Benjamin Shelby, born April 8, 1796, died in Pickaway County, Ohio, May 4, 1876. He married about 1824, Nancy Enochs.
8. Isaac Shelby, born 1798, died Tippecanoe County, Indiana; married, December 26, 1826, Jane Boggs.
9. Mary Shelby, born February 24, 1801, died June 27, 1820.

DAVID SHELBY, SENIOR

This son of the immigrant, Evan Shelby, would in our plan be included in the Big Whiteley section of the Tenmile Country, but for the sake of convenience the history of David Shelby, Sr., can be best entered at this place. David Shelby, Sr., was born about 1732, lived for a time in Washington County, Maryland, and then removed to the Tenmile Country about 1771-72. He married, in Bedford County, Pennsylvania, for his first wife, Elizabeth Balla. His second wife was Catherine (Bell) Ferris. He removed in 1795, to New Madrid, Missouri, then in Spanish territory, where he died January 8, to the 16th, 1799. His first wife died in 1778-83 and Catherine died in 1802. At the time of death David Shelby owned land in Greene County and had children still living here. They settled his estate at this place. Three children are known to belong to each marriage, with a possibility that David Shelby, Jr., of "Laurel Point," being another child.

Children of David Shelby, Sr.
1. Jonathan Shelby, born before 1770, died in Greene County about 1798.
2. James Shelby, born November 22, 1772; married, June 23, 1796, Hannah Ross. He died November 11, 1845, and his wife in 1854.
3. Elizabeth Shelby, born 1777-78; married James Burns. Removed to Perry County, Missouri.
4. Rees Shelby, born 1784-85, died prior to 1816.
5. Eli Shelby, born about 1787, lived in Scott County, Missouri, in 1830.
6. Mary Shelby, born about 1792.

ROSTER OF RANGERS
COMMANDED BY CAPTAIN EVAN SHELBY, JR.

The following is a list of soldiers commanded by Captain Evan Shelby, Jr., under Colonel Henry Boquet, as reported by that officer in the period from July 15, to November 1, 1759. (Boquet Mss. 21644 Fol. 476 pp. 182. A. D. S.) Captain Evan Shelby, Jr., son of the immigrant of the same name was born in Tregaron, Wales, where he was baptized October 23, 1719. He settled in Maryland, where he was a planter, store-keeper, and Indian Trader until about 1773, when he removed to Sullivan County, Tennessee, where he died December 4, 1794. He served as a captain in the French and Indian War and in Dunmore's War. During the Revolution he was a major and colonel of the Washington County, Virginia, Militia, and in 1787, he was a brigadier general of North Carolina Militia. His first wife was Letitia Cox, whom he married about

1744. She died in 1777, and he married (2) about 1787, Isabella Elliott. The most of these men in his company were inhabitants of the Conochacheague and nearby counties of Virginia, Maryland, and Pennsylvania, a number of whom were among the first settlers of the Tenmile Country. They served from July 15, 1759, to November 1, 1759.

Samuel Simpson
Thomas Cowper
Robert Plowman
Benjamin Merchant
Philip Smith
James Stephens
Elijah Mason
Charles Swain
Thomas Iams
Thomas Harrow
John Cooke
Charles Russell
John Simpson
William Pagett
Paul Nowland
William Logan
Alexander Crawford
Christopher Rever
John Peters
John Purdee
Philip Price
Richard Devar
 (or Devore)
William Thompson
James Butler

Daniel Smith
Jacob Foardum
John Graves
Thomas Walter
James Green
Samuel Plummer
William Colvin
William Glenn
Henry Smith
Henry Wedge
John Parkinson
William Osman
Daniel Guthery
William Serigis
Edward Rees
William Tilley
Isaac Short
John Levan
George Waldron
Thomas Crago
Daniel Sullivane
John Parks
Edward Disney
John Norris
Jacob Rood

John Harle
Jeremiah Deache
George Steel
James Hamilton
Thomas Slater
Oliver Crawford
Philip Dick
Daniel McCrory
Thomas Canada
 (Kennedy)
James Hazlett
Benjamin Savage
Thomas Dunning
George Newland
Henry Hessey
Anthony Devonen
James Logan
John Stammers
John Shea
Peter Conrad
Charles Hessey
Christopher Haines
John Busby
John Phillips
Samuel Walker

Drafted from other Battalions, August 18, 1759

Joshua Morris
Peter Cutright
William Hood
John Stewart

Dennis Lackey
Thomas Brannon
Michael Coleman
John Cribbs
William Cutter

William English
Charles Lewis
Thomas Camplin
Robert McCuller

Additions November 1, 1759

John Beard
John Murrow
James Right
Josiah Porterfield
John Nichols
William Waters
John Smith
Hugh Cunningham
Josiah Phelps
William Freeman
Robert Flemming

Charles Stafford
John Cramplin
Bedro Phillips
John McCormick
George Boston
John Anderson
Thomas Howper
Benjamin French
Alexander Henry
Sylvester Tipton
John Bell

Benjamin Ogden
Jacob Kitts
Joseph Hagan
Joseph Engoll
Gabriel Hughes
Stephen Gordon
William Able
William Bowen
William Bradford
William Costelo

Returned to Battalion August 18, 1759

John Campbell
John Roach
Edward Stradling
John Groom

John Houp
Ben Lovely
Michael Agnew
John Land
John Ward

Thomas May
Richard Hoy
James Tapper
Michael Lingerfield

Peter Heningshaw, died September 24.
Andrew Demuss, died October 1.
Richard Hall, died October 8.
John Howe, died October 24.

For the first fifty years of the County's history, Jefferson and its surroundings practically ruled Greene County politics. Old timers claimed that any person born or raised beyond the High Rocks, was practically ineligible for office. Of course some deals were made which left outsiders in, but they were, in many cases, former Jefferson families, who had moved to other parts of the county. These vigorous politicians were also vigorous fighters, and I have heard many a story told of a fight in which the losing adherent claimed his rear hit the ground so fast that he couldn't count three. It was of such stuff that many of the men, who left to join the Army of the Potomac, were made of and accounts for the fact that so many of them fell on the battlefield, never to rise again.

It was the same kind of vigor that sent many of the Jefferson youth to the "Gold Rush" in 1849. One such account is given in a little book put out by George W. Reed, one of the "Forty-niners." In 1849, a group of Jefferson men calling themselves "The California Company" was formed and started for the gold fields. They went by boat to St. Louis and then on to Independence, Missouri, by Steamer. At St. Louis they had laid in provisions for the overland trip, which they report, included 1,920 pounds of Sea Bread, 200 pounds of hams, 500 pounds of parched corn meal, 300 pounds of dried beef, 300 pounds of rice, and 300 pounds of middlings, the latter for the animals. Instead of packing through they bought wagons at 98 dollars each, and six mules and one pony per wagon, in all the cost being more than $500 per team. They organized at Independence into 7 teams and were composed as follows:

Team No. 1—6 mules and 1 horse.
    George W. Reed, Captain and Surgeon.
    Charles W. Meighen, secretary.
    George Sharpnack.
    Barney O'Neal.
    Marcellus Strohman, cook.

Team No. 2—6 mules and 1 horse.
    Solomon B. Wise.
    Morgan R. Wise.
    Thomas Weaver.
    Morgan Zollars, cook.

Team No. 3—with one pony that could out pace Greene County.
    James Burson.
    James French.
    S. U. Wise.
    James Dunn, cook.

Team No. 4—5 mules and 1 horse.
    Lewis Shatterly.
    William Shatterly.
    Isaac White.
    Benjamin Conn, cook.

Team No. 5—6 mules and 1 horse.
    Colonel John Ross.
    Thomas Ross.
    Isaac Lewis.
    Uriah Mitchenor, cook.

Wagon No. 6—6 mules and 1 horse.
    Asa Morris.
    James Roseberry.
    Frank Gray.
    William Black, cook.

Wagon No. 7—6 mules and 1 horse.
    John Houlsworth.
    Dr. John Clark.
    Hiram Brown, (was from Virginia.)
    James Riley, cook.

They started from Colonel Grant's, 9 miles south of Independence, on May 1, 1850, where Charles Meighen took sick with cholera. He eventually had to be left behind. They headed for the River Platte, which they reached in 19 days. On May 24, they were 400 miles from the starting place. The next day they were host to a Mr. Van Vorhees of Washington County, Pennsylvania, who was packing through. On May 28, they had antelope for supper and on June 1, the menu was buffalo steak. On June 4, they crossed the Laramie River to Fort of the same name, and here bought more bread and stayed until the 8th, writing letters and resting up. To cross the River on June 12, they had to pay the ferryman $4 per wagon and 50 cents per mule, and report that one to two hundred wagons are passing over every day. They also report 33 companies ahead of them. June 5, they reached the headwaters of the Columbia, and on June 20, one of the wagons gave out and was abandoned by Clark, Hollingsworth, (Houlsworth) Riley, and Brown who decided to pack it out. A week later Roseberry, Black, Morris, and Gray threw their wagon away. They were then crossing the desert, which took them from July 26, to August 10, when they came to a place where they could get flour, but had to pay $1 per pound for it. On August 18, they drove into Hangtown, California, after a twelve mile drive before breakfast. They were five months on the trip, and had covered 2200 miles after leaving the Missouri River. The experiences, illnesses, thrills, etc., are given in a little book published by Little, Brown and Company, and are a daily diary of the journey.

All these men, with the exception of Brown, were from the Jefferson Section and have relatives living here yet today. It is also to be noted that some of them returned the same year and made another such journey in 1851, this time by the southern route. On this second trip, they encountered Indians and James Burson was killed in Arizona.

I also have an interesting diary of Hiram Heaton on which he tells of a trip from Jefferson in 1819, to Baton Rouge, Louisiana, to wind up some business in his father's estate. He traveled by horse, by canoe, and by River boat, on the trip down, then came back by horse, traveling for days at a time, through Kentucky and Tennessee, without seeing a single habitation. Hiram Heaton, in company with a man named Slater, and one named Jackson, left Waynesburg on April 4, 1819, and did not get back until the last part of August. It is an interesting account of Inns and handicaps of travel at that time.

Interesting Events In
FRANKLIN TOWNSHIP
1794-1830

(Copied from the Journal of William Rhodes, loaned to the author by Hallie Rhodes).

November 29, 1783—Joseph Porter born on Laurel Run.
February 11, 1794—Polly Cathers married to Peter Lemley of Tenmile.
Sally Hook married to Freeman.
Smiths come from Jerseys.
April 23, 1795—Thomas Sayers (rest un-readable).
Thomas Gorrell married to S. Stewart.
May 29, 1795—Samuel Hill married to Betsy Cathers.
January 26, 1796—Shadrack Mitchell married to Peggy Rinehart.
September 29, 1796—Waynesburg laid out in lots, bought from Thomas Slater for $3200, sold by lots for $3271 Gappen and Metkirke.
September ......, 1797—Rachel Ankrom married William Duvalls.
Caty Duvall married to Daniel Wilson.
January 23, 1798—Richard Ankrom married Nancy Rinehart.
Planted orchard.
December 27, 1799—David Worley married Peggy Cathers, Laurel Run.
January 1, 1800—First Auditors for Greene County, Boreman, Heaton, and Weaver.
October ......, 1800—Finished and moved into new house.
March ......, 1803—James Porter, Jr., died aged 26 years.
December 20, 1804—Thomas Inghram married Patty Ankrom.
June 24, 1806—James Rodman Rhodes born.
October 15, 1807—Polly Rhodes died.
The Halyconites began to preach with great boldness.
November 27, 1810—Nancy Porter, consort of James Porter, Sr., died.
May 10, 1812—The commissioners survey a state road from Connellsville through Waynesburg to Grave Creek.
...., 1816—Struggle between the Methodist and New Lights is almost hellish.
November 15, 1818—Hannah Porter, consort of Edmund Smith died at Winchester, Virginia.
October ......, 1819—Edmund Smith, remarried.
December 19, 1819—Joseph Rhodes married to Elizabeth Rinehart.
August ......, 1820—Widow Betsy Cathers died at 80 years of age.
January 8, 1821—David Porter, aged 45 years, died on Laurel Run.
The State Road between Jefferson and Waynesburg sold by the quarter mile by the Commissioners to the lowest bidders.
June ......, 1822—Stone Bridge built by the County Commissioners through our lane and saw mill.
August 4, 1822—James Porter died aged 87 years and 7 months.
June 9, 1823—Thomas Rhodes starts for Washington City in pursuit of a patern. (Patent ?)
June .. .., 1824—Thomas Rhodes began peddling in a small wagon.
November ......, 1825—James Rhodes married in Virginia.
March ......, 1826—Joseph Porter died on Laurel Run.
March 24, 1830—William Cather died.

Relationship of Some
FORT JACKSON PIONEERS

Thomas Fee married (1) Miss .... Thrasher; (2) Sarah Leith, settled on Laurel Run.

William Inghram, married Agnes Fee; had tract next to Thomas Fee.

Richard Jackson, founder of Fort Jackson, married Mary Fee, daughter of Thomas by first marriage.

John Fee married Elizabeth Bradford, daughter of Robert Bradford, who had land next to Thomas Fee.

John Fee settled Estate of Richard Jackson in Bracken County, Kentucky.

James Hook married Mary Leith, sister of Sarah (Leith) Fee, her mother was .... Lakin.

John Ankrom, married Martha Wells, lived one farm removed from John Thrasher.

Richard Duckett Wells, brother of Martha (Wells) Ankrom, married Sarah Lakin.

Elizabeth Ankrom, sister of John Ankrom, married .... Thrasher.

Joseph Lakin, married Mary Slater, daughter of Thomas Slater of Fort Jackson. He lived next to William Inghram.

Samuel Lakin, lived next to Joseph Lakin.

Michael Archer, married Elizabeth Wells, sister of Martha Wells.

Joseph Archer, married Margaret Church, daughter of George Church of Laurel Run.

George Church, married Jane .... Lived next to Joseph Archer.

Nancy Church, daughter of George and Jane Church, married Jacob or Simon Archer.

William Wells, brother of Martha Wells, married Elizabeth Archer, sister of Joseph Archer.

George Carroll, married Isabel Church, daughter of George and Jane Church. Lived next to Joseph Lakins, and Robert Cathers.

Elizabeth Fee, married, January 29, 1779, Frederick County, Maryland, William Carroll.

James Porter, married Nancy Inghram, sister of William Inghram. He had land next Thomas Fee.

Arthur Inghram, borther of William Inghram, married Olive Smith.

Thomas Smith, brother of Olive Smith, married Mary Williams.

Robert Gorrell, married Susannah Smith, sister of Thomas Smith. Had land next Thomas Smith.

William Cathers, married Elizabeth Inghram, sister of William Inghram.

Thomas Rinehart, married Hannah Inghram, sister of William Inghram.

Nancy Cathers, daughter of William Cathers, married Thomas Fee, Jr.

William Fee, married Margaret Inghram, sister(?) of William and Arthur Inghram.

George Fee, married Mary or Nancy Archer, sister of Joseph Archer.

From Democrat-Messenger, Waynesburg, Pa., September 1930

In compliance with the request of many Greene County people, we republish the following letter which appeared in the Messenger nearly 47 years ago.

AULD LANG SYNE

Woodfield, Monroe County, Ohio
December 26, 1883

EDITOR MESSENGER:-

I am now an old woman, unable to do much except think of the many changes that have taken place during my long life, and occasionally to write a letter to some of my descendants. My principal occupation is recalling to mind my early associates and school mates. In committing to writing some of these early recollections I may awaken an interest in some of the older people of Greene County, and perhaps some of the younger.

To speak first of myself I will say that I was born in Hillsborough, Washington County, Pennsylvania, May 20, 1795, and should I live to see my next birthday, will be 89 years old. My father's name was James Hill and my mother's maiden name was Elizabeth Mitchell. My parental grandfather was William Hill and his wife was Elizabeth Atkinson. My father was the first of their children born in the United States after leaving Ireland. My maternal grandfather was Kent Mitchell and his wife was Hannah Wood. After the death of my grandfather Mitchell, my grandmother married John Jones. Some of the very old people of Waynesburg and vicinty may remember seeing Grandmother Jones. After the death of my father, mother left Hillsboro and went to her mother's—Grandmother Jones', and after being a widow some two years, married Isaac Wood, who lived out in the "Rich Hills," about four or five miles from Waynesburg. Mother had 11 children, 5 by her first husband, and 6 by her second, two of whom died in infancy. The other Wood children were John, Thomas, Edward and Elizabeth Wood. The children of Edward still occupy the old homestead I believe. Of the 11 children I am the only survivor.

I was married to Joseph Morris March 12, 1816. His father's name was James, and his mother's Phoebe Sayers, a sister of Ephraim Sayers, who was the father of William and Ezra M. Sayers, who I hope are still living. James Morris died before the age of 30 years, leaving three children—Thomas, Joseph and Ephraim. His widow married George Remley, by whom she had one son. James, who was born September 4, 1800, and not long after his birth she also died. Thomas Morris married Martha Hughes, daughter of James Hughes; Ephraim married Martha Roseberry, daughter of Matthias Roseberry, and James Remley married Margaret Penn, daughter of William and Mary Penn. My husband's grandfathers' name was Richard Morris.

But I did not intend, when I began that, to write so much about myself, but to give a sketch of five families, all the children of whom, 31 in number, I well know, and most of them were my school mates, but most of them older than I. I have reference to Arthur, William, Mollie, Elizabeth, and Hannah Inghram.

1. The children of Arthur Inghram and Olive, his wife.
    1. William, married Lizzie Rinehart.
    2. Thomas, died unmarried.
    3. Arthur, married Susan Eagon.

  4. Margaret, married John Rinehart.
  5. Delilah, married William Rinehart.
  6. Cassa, married Thomas Mooney.
  7. Elizabeth, married Ignatius Morris.

  Elizabeth died shortly after the birth of her only child, and the child died about the same time and was buried in the coffin with its mother. Elizabeth was the youngest of all these 31 cousins, and but little older than I was. I can never forget the strong and lasting impression made upon my mind at seeing my dearly loved playmate and her child lying cold in death in the same coffin. My recollection is that all her numerous cousins were at the funeral.

2. The children of William Inghram (I cannot recall to mind name of his wife)
  1. John, married Mrs. Katy Burbridge, whose maiden name was Workman.
  2. Thomas, married a Miss Smith.
  3. William, married Sallie Adams.
  4. James died young with consumption.
  5. Sallie, married Kinnear Boreman.

3. The children of Mollie Inghram who married James Porter.
  1. Joseph, married Elizabeth Rinehart.
  2. David, married a Miss Smith (Hannah).

4. The children of Elizabeth Inghram who married William Cathers.
  1. Robert, married Sallie ....
  2. John, married Sallie Shields.
  3. William, died unmarried.
  4. Margaret, married David Worley.
  5. Elizabeth, married Samuel Hill.
  6. Mary, married George Lemley.

5. The children of Hannah Inghram who married Thomas Rinehart.
  1. John, married Margaret Inghram.
  2. William, married Delilah Inghram.
  3. Thomas, never married.
  4. Joseph, never married.
  5. Jesse, married Lucy Workman.
  6. Levi, married Maria McClelland.
  7. Arthur, married a Miss Roberts.
  8. Margaret, married Shadrach Mitchell, a brother of my mother.
  9. Elizabeth, married Joseph Porter.
  10. Nancy, married Richard Ankrom.
  11. Hannah, married Thomas Rinehart.

  I have no doubt that all these old associates of mine are now numbered among the dead.

  A remarkable circumstance about these families was the fact that they all lived on Laurel Run, or in its close vicinity, and no two of the families lived at a greater distance from each other than two and a half miles. My step-father's residence was at no further distance.

  Having removed from Waynesburg in April 1829, and having since had but little if any opportunity of talking with these families, I may be mistaken in some of the names, but I think not.

  What a great pleasure it would be to me if I could, once more, see and talk to some of my old Greene County friends. But it may not be. I spend a great portion of my time in thinking of other old citizens of Greene: among them the Hooks, the Woods, the Sayers, the McClellands, the Adams, the Bayards, the Randolphs, and many others. I do not know that I could be as exact with these last named families as with the Inghrams, but pretty nearly so.

The Messenger, Mr. Editor, was about the first newspaper that I had the perusal of, and if you think the insertion of the foregoing will be of any interest to your readers, you may publish it.

SARAH MORRIS

THE INGHRAM FAMILY

There has not appeared as yet, any authentic story of the origin of the Inghram Family which settled on Laurel Run. However, there is evidence that seems to connect them with Robert and William Inghram who lived in Potomac Hundred, Prince George's County, Maryland, as early as 1733. These two men were taxed there along with John Jones, John Jackson, John Smith, William Williams, William Brown, John Gray, and other names familiar among the Fort Jackson pioneers. In fact the above named William Inghram could well be the ancestor of the Inghram Family of the Tenmile. It seems quite likely that at least some of the children of the elder William Inghram were married before they came west, and these marriages point to Harford County, Maryland, origin. One Isaac Inghram came from Surry, England, with William Penn on the "Welcome."

Evans claimed that the first ancestor of the family was William Inghram, who came here and built his cabin on land situated on Laurel Run. He tells a story of how this William Inghram sought safety from the Indians by removing to the vicinity of Vanmeter's Fort during the Revolution, and either died there or went back over the mountains. He further states that the mother of the Inghram children later lived on Muddy Creek with two daughters and William Inghram, Jr. The story is further confused by the presence of another Inghram Family that did live on Muddy Creek, which would be expected to use Jacob Vanmeter's Fort. We do know that at least six brothers and sisters of this family did settle on Laurel Run, all of them living within two and a half miles of each other. Their names are furnished in a letter written by Sarah (Hill) Morris, from Woodfield, Monroe County, Ohio, to the Waynesburg "Messenger" on December 26, 1883, at which time Mrs. Morris was in her 89th year, and recalled 31 children of the six branches of the family. (She said five branches, but was confused in one.)

Both Evans and Wychoff tell us that Arthur Inghram, head of one branch, came here with Thomas Smith, Billy Lafferty, and Thomas Kent to plant a field of corn on Smith Creek in 1774, and became permanent settlers in 1776. No mention of a William Inghram being with them is made so it is presumed that he followed soon afterward. Evans says there were two sons and six daughters in the elder Inghram's Family, while Mrs. Morris names the two sons and but three daughters, and an error in her record accounts for another daughter. They were:

1. William Inghram, who died about 1809. His wife was Agnes Fee ?

2. Arthur Inghram, born 1746, died October 28, 1834, married probably in Maryland, about 1775, Olive (or Allive) Smith, born 1754, died June 4, 1839, daughter of Thomas and Hannah Smith.
3. Mollie Inghram, married David (?) Porter. Mis. Morris said she married James Porter, but the Journal of William Rhodes shows James Porter was married to Nancy. However, there is a letter from J. Smith, written from Penn Green, Ohio, in 1835, saying that Aunt Mollie Porter is still alive at that date, and asking about a legacy due him from his Uncle James Porter's estate.
4. Nancy Inghram, died November 27, 1810, married James Porter, born 1735, died August 4, 1822, dates taken from the William Rhodes Journal. Rhodes should know as he was a son-in-law.
5. Hannah Inghram died about 1808, married 1775, Thomas Rinehart, born 1746, died August 2, 1804.
6. Elizabeth Inghram, born about 1740, died August 1820, married William Cathers, who died in 1815.
7. .... Inghram, said to have married a Mr. Kent.
8. Sarah (?) Inghram, there is a possibility that Job Smith's wife was an Inghram. Her first name as shown in deeds, was Sarah, and old letters suggest a close relationship with the Inghrams and Porters.

WILLIAM INGHRAM

The early records do not disclose much information regarding William Inghram, Jr. Evans says that he had land which he sold for "Continental Currency" which soon became worthless, leaving him bankrupt with plenty of money in his pockets. After this disaster he is said to have moved into his father's deserted cabin on Laurel Run. No record of such sale appears to how where his land was located, nor the year that he made his settlement. William Inghram, Jr., is not mentioned as having come with his brother, Arthur Inghram, in 1774, and it is entirely possible he was the William Inghram, who enlisted in the Fifth Maryland Regiment on March 18, 1777, and was discharged July 18, 1780, in Maryland. His name is found in the roster of Captain James Archer's Company of Washington County, Pennsylvania Militia, in the arrangement for 1782, (Penna. Arch. Series VI Vol. 2, pp. 17.) which indicates he was living on Laurel Run at this time. Evans further states that William Inghram, Jr., with his mother and two sisters, were living on Muddy Creek near Vanmeter's Fort during the days of the Revolution, but we are of the opinion that Evans had him confused with the brother of Meredith Inghram of the same name and apparently no relationship. Meredith Inghram and his brother, William Inghram, are said to have come directly from Ireland and did settle on the South Branch of Muddy Creek near Jacob Vanmeter's Fort, where they owned a tract of land jointly as shown by partition proceedings.

William Inghram, Jr., was probably the oldest son of William Inghram, Sr. No dates of his birth or death have been found, though it is probable that he died during the year 1809, as his son Arthur Inghram, took out letters on his estate on February 11, 1809. His wife was Agnes, (probably Fee) who joined him in a deed to sell a lot in Waynesburg to Thomas Wolverton on May 9, 1800. This lot at the corner of Greene and Cumberland streets, had been bought from George Sargeant on November 16, 1797, and was lot No. 197 in the original plan of Waynesburg. Agnes Inghram is also named his widow in the Orphan Court proceedings in the settlement of his estate in November 1810, in which proceedings it is shown that his son, John, was of age, while his sons, William and James, are over 14 years of age but under 21. Sons Arthur and Thomas Inghram, are also over 21 years of age, and daughter, Sarah Inghram, then married to Kenner Boreman. (O. C. Docket 1. pp. 32-48.) The son, Thomas Inghram, was probably named for Thomas Fee, father of Agnes. The burial place of William and Agnes (Fee?) Inghram is not known, but is probably in the Inghram and Fee Burial Ground on the Thomas Montgomery Farm.

Family of William and Agnes (Fee?) Inghram

1. John Inghram, born 1780, died March 4, 1851. He was a soldier in the War of 1812 and an important business man. John Inghram built and operated the "Bulls Head Tavern" on the site of the present Fort Jackson Hotel. This was later moved intact to a location on Franklin street, where it served in late years as a hospital and then the home of Paul D. Inghram, a direct descendant. He married Mrs. Catherine (Workman) Burbridge, widow of Thomas Burbridge, his business partner. Thomas Burbridge died May 1, 1808, leaving three children, J. W. Burbridge, Lucy Burbridge, who married Jesse Hook, and Fanny Burbridge, who married James B. Lazear. Catherine (Workman) Burbridge was born in 1781, and died April 3, 1858. She was a daughter of James and Lucy Workman. Both are buried in Green Mount Cemetery.

Children of John and Catherine (Workman) Inghram

1. John Inghram, born March 27, 1810, died October 6, 1872, never married.
2. William Inghram, born February 9, 1812, died April 6, 1822.
3. Jesse Inghram, born April 4, 1814, died July 24, 1845. His wife was Emeline ...., who died May 2, 1853, aged 42 years.
4. Isaac Slater Inghram, born June 27, 1816, died October 17, 1879, married Melissa B. Inghram, daughter of Arthur and Susan (Eagon) Inghram. She died July 1, 1871. Record of family given under Arthur Inghram Family.
5. Catherine Inghram, born February 1, 1821, died December 3, 1897; married, March 3, 1842, Robinson Webb Downey, who died December 18, 1874.

Children of Robinson and Catherine (Inghram) Downey

1. John Inghram Downey, born December 11, 1842, killed in Battle of Fredericksburg, March 17, 1863.
2. Frances Downey, born March 2, 1844, died 1846.
3. Emma J. Downey, born November 20, 1846, died May 31, 1881.
4. Robinson Downey, born May 18, 1849, died December 19, 1923, married Jean (Wilson) Lindsey.
5. Lucy Downey, died young.
6. Catherine M. Downey, born February 11, 1855, died December 12, 1899.
7. Frank Downey, born December 5, 1857, died March 17, 1920.

6. Benjamin F. Inghram, born November 3, 1825, died of fever in New Orleans, October 2, 1858.

       7. Thomas Inghram, born November 3, 1825, died March 12, 1837.
2. Thomas Inghram, married, December 20, 1804, Martha Ankrom, daughter of John and Martha (Wells) Ankrom. They moved to Tyler County, (West) Virginia, where Thomas Inghram died, leaving a will that was probated November 4, 1850. (Will Book 2. pp. 125.)

Children of Thomas and Martha (Ankrom) Inghram

1. Matilda Inghram, married Duckett Wells.
2. Martha Inghram.
3. Elizabeth Inghram.
4. Mahala Inghram, married John J. Engle.

3. William Inghram, born February 24, 1794, died September 3, 1843; married (1) June 27, 1813, Sarah Adams, born March 10, 1799, died May 3, 1830, daughter of Robert and Rebecca (Blackmore) Adams. He married (2) Mary Seaton, born June 23, 1810. The second marriage was on June 2, 1831, and his wife was a daughter of James and Elizabeth (Swan) Seaton.

Children of William Inghram

1. Eliza Inghram, born July 13, 1817, died May 4, 1901; married, January 14, 1836, John T. Hook, born January 20, 1814, died November 3, 1883, son of Arthur and Catherine (Kent) Hook.

Children of John T. and Eliza (Inghram) Hook

1. Sarah Hook, married Josiah Inghram.
2. William Hook, never married.
3. Thomas Hook, born September 27, 1840, died April 28, 1906; married, (1) August 30, 1863, Sarah Patterson; married, (2) May 16, 1885, Sudie Inghram.
4. Catherine Hook, born November 17, 1842, died September 29, 1922; married, October 18, 1862, William Blair.
5. Rebecca Hook, never married.
6. John P. Hook, born January 25, 1849, died December 30, 1873. Mary Elizabeth Holmes was his wife.
7. Agnes Hook, born July 29, 1851, died April 14, 1885; married, June 22, 1882, George Huggins.
8. Robert Hook, born September 26, 1853, died May 6, 1909; married, September 27, 1877, Grace Stephens.
9. Eliza Hook, born March 19, 1856; married, June 30, 1877, A. F. Silveus.
10. Jane (Jennie) M. Hook, born March 12, 1858; married, May 31, 1886, John D. Sturgis, born December 18, 1849, died September 13, 1910. Jane died January 20, 1946.

2. Agnes Inghram, born April 24, 1819, died September 19, 1851, married Lewis Roberts.
3. Robert Inghram, born September 27, 1821, married Maria Gregg, went to Iowa.
4. Elijah Inghram, born December 10, 1823, died May 19, 1844.
5. Rebecca J. Inghram, born November 26, 1825, died December 12, 1825.
6. Sarah B. Inghram, born February 16, 1827, married Jefferson Morris, born April 9, 1819.

7. William Arthur Inghram, born October 3, 1829, died December 21, 1833.
   8. Juliet Inghram, born April 23, 1832.
   9. James Inghram, born March 20, 1835.
   10. Mary F. Inghram, born September 11, 1838.
   11. John T. Inghram, born November 18, 1842.
4. James Inghram.
5. Sarah Inghram, born 1791, died in Tyler County, (West) Virginia, November 16, 1870, married Kenner Seaton Boreman, son of John and Sarah (Seaton) Boreman.

   Children of Kenner Seaton and Sarah (Inghram) Boreman
   1. William Boreman, a lawyer at Middlebourne.
   2. Kenner Seaton Boreman, born April 19, 1819, married Theresa Alexander.
   3. Arthur Inghram Boreman, born July 24, 1823, died May 19, 1896. He was the First Governor of West Virginia, served in the U. S. Senate, and was Judge of the U. S. Circuit Court. His wife was Laurene Tanner.
   4. James Mason Boreman, Postmaster of Parkersburg, West Virginia, for many years.
   5. Thomas I. Boreman.
   6. Jacob Smith Boreman, onetime Judge of U. S. Circuit Court in Utah.
   7. Agnes Mason Boreman, married James Stephenson.
6. Arthur Inghram.

ARTHUR INGHRAM

Lacking complete records, it would appear that Arthur Inghram was the youngest member of his father's family. His tombstone in the Inghram Cemetery indicates he was born in February 1746, and died October 28, 1834. L. K. Evans says that Arthur Inghram with Billy Lafferty, joined Thomas Smith and Thomas Kent in the Spring of 1776, to make a field of corn on Smith Creek. Arthur Inghram and Thomas Smith moved into a cabin on the Inghram Farm, with Thomas Kent and Billy Lafferty living in "Black" David White's cabin on the farm later owned by the Hooks, about the site of the stone house. It has been shown that both Smiths and Kents were here before 1776, and evidence would indicate that Arthur Inghram had been here at least the year prior to that date. Evans says that "Black" David White had gone to Kentucky leaving his empty cabin, but records show he returned and was here again in 1782, when he served in Captain James Archer's Company. But there is also evidence to show that Arthur Inghram was also in Kentucky in 1776, selecting a tract of 1000 acres of land on Fox Run, near its mouth, on which he made an improvement, which he later assigned to John Hughes. (Register of Kentucky State Historical Society, I, p. 304. Records of Land Commission of Virginia 1780, held in Kentucky to settle first claims under 1779 law.) Shortly after the founding of Harrodsburg, Arthur Inghram joined James Harrod and others in opposing the formation of a new state. As late as May 8, 1789, an Arthur Inghram was taxed as owner of land in Fayette County, Kentucky. Warrants and patent claims of Arthur Inghram do not explain his rights to land on Smith Creek, but he did join his brother, William Inghram, to warrant land at the head of Laurel Run, and seems to have bought the warrant rights of Joseph Larkins (Lakins?) adjoining "Inghram's Choice" on the south. Arthur Inghram served in Captain James Archer's Militia Company and took an active part in the protection of the frontier during the Revolution. (Penna. Arch. Series VI. Vol. 2, pp. 17.) The experiences of the Inghrams have been given in a number of early histories and are too well known for repetition. Sometime before 1777, Arthur Inghram married Allive or Olive Smith, a sister of Thomas Smith, daughter of Thomas and Hannah Smith. Her father calls her Olivia in his will on file in Harford County Maryland, where she was born in 1754. She died in Greene County, on June 4, 1839. Both are buried on the late Thomas Montgomery Farm.

Children of Arthur and Allive (Smith) Inghram

1. William Inghram, born November 24, 1778, died in 1845, married Elizabeth Rinehart, born on September 17, 1783, died March 3, 1864, daughter of Barnet Rinehart. They were married on March 3, 1803.

    ### Children of William and Elizabeth (Rinehart) Inghram

    1. Arthur Inghram, born December 7, 1804, died March 3, 1870, married Elizabeth Cathers, born July 21, 1804, died March 18, 1884. Buried in Green Mount Cemetery.

        ### Children of Arthur and Elizabeth (Cathers) Inghram
        1. George Inghram.
        2. Judge James Inghram, married Mary Black.
        3. Sarah Inghram, married Judge James Lindsey.
        4. Elizabeth Inghram, married Enos Hook.
        5. Lucy Inghram, married H. D. Patton.
    2. Sarah Inghram, born September 22, 1805, died September 23, 1858, married Solomon Gordon, born April 2, 1801.
    3. Thomas Inghram, born February 23, 1807, died July 14, 1894; married, Janu ry 24, 1850, Harriet Crayne, born March 2, 1823, died August 12, 1891.

        ### Children of Thomas and Harriet (Crayne) Inghram
        1. Thomas Inghram, married Belle Rinehart.
        2. William Inghram, married Rachel Lippencott.
        3. Cynthia Inghram, married Samuel B. Wood.
        4. Arthur Inghram.
        5. Laura Inghram.
    4. Olive Inghram, born November 7, 1808, died December 16, 1883; married, June 25, 1829, Armstrong Porter, born August 23, 1808, died December 31, 1890.

        ### Children of Armstrong and Olive (Inghram) Porter
        1. Elizabeth Porter, born April 24, 1830, married William Barnes.
        2. Anna Eliza Porter, married Abijah Huss.
        3. Thomas Porter, born December 5, 1835, died August 9, 1897; married Catherine Gordon, born July 4, 1837, died May 6, 1921.
    5. Elizabeth Inghram, born July 10, 1810, died 1876, married Levi Strawn.
    6. Cassandra Inghram, born November 24, 1811, died December 19, 1900, married Madison Bell.

        ### Children of Madison and Cassandra (Inghram) Bell
        1. Maria Bell, married Adam Gordon.
        2. Eliza Bell, married John Kent.

AND ITS PIONEER FAMILIES 317

    3. William Bell, married Mollie Jacobs.
    4. Alice Bell.
    5. Thomas Bell, married Nancy Kent.
    6. Harriet Bell, married Adam Shriver.
7. Margaret Inghram, born October 23, 1813, died June 2, 1890, married Hiram Porter.

Children of Hiram and Margaret (Inghram) Porter
    1. Thomas Porter.
    2. Agnes Porter.
8. Nancy Inghram, born December 11, 1815, died March 5, 1889, married William Bell.
9. Agnes Inghram, born December 11, 1815, twin of Nancy.
10. Delilah Inghram, born April 23, 1821, died November 5, 1898; married, July 12, 1847, J. B. Gordon, born December 4, 1798, died December 28, 1876.

Children of J. B. and Delilah (Inghram) Gordon
    1. George W. Gordon, married Margaret Helen Scott.
    2. Caroline Gordon, never married.
    3. Elizabeth Gordon, never married.
    4. Lucy E. Gordon, married Dr. R. E. Brock.
    5. John Brice Gordon, married Amanda Cowell.

2. Margaret Inghram, born 1780, died December 20, 1862; married about 1800, John Rinehart, born 1776, died January 29, 1855, son of Thomas and Hannah (Inghram) Rinehart.

Children of John and Margaret (Inghram) Rinehart
1. Nancy Rinehart, married John Griffith.
2. Matilda Rinehart, born 1811, died April 23, 1881, married Uriah Rinehart, born June 17, 1809, died July 25, 1877.
3. Olive Rinehart, married Henry Vandruff.
4. Hannah Rinehart, born April 21, 1813, died December 22, 1880; married, November 10, 1839, John Porter, born 1813, died January 21, 1856.
5. Emeline Rinehart, married Lewis Dowlin.
6. Thomas Rinehart, born February 14, 1802, died February 26, 1888, married Mary ....
7. Hiram Rinehart, born November 21, 1805, died March 31, 1871, married (1) Hannah Inghram, married (2) Mariah Porter, born December 22, 1818, died May 27, 1895.
8. Presley Rinehart.
9. Jesse Rinehart, born 1817, died April 16, 1868.
10. Levi Rinehart, died July 30, 1854, aged 33 years.
11. Margaret Rinehart, married Rea Dowlin.
12. William Rinehart.
13. Arthur Rinehart.
14. Joseph Rinehart, died September 1, 1898.

3. Olive Inghram, died in Miami County, Ohio, in 1851, married Isaac Clyne, son of Jacob and Eleanor (Vanmeter) Clyne, born 1777, died October 3, 1838, in Miami County, Ohio.

Children of Isaac and Olive (Inghram) Clyne (or Cline)
1. John Clyne, born October 3, 1804, died August 20, 1873.
2. Hannah Clyne, married Levi Deweese.
3. Minerva Clyne, married Levi Hart.
4. Mary Clyne, married Joseph Martin.
5. Jacob Clyne, died 1833.
6. Elizabeth Clyne, married Isaac Dye.

      7. Letitia Clyne, married Patterson Crayne.
      8. Isaac Clyne, married Elizabeth Knight.
      9. Inghram Clyne.
    10. William Clyne.
4. Nancy Inghram, married Peter Clyne, brother of Isaac Clyne.
5. Arthur Inghram, born 1793, died August 1875, married Susan Eagon, born 1795, died November 1, 1859, aged 64 years, 9 days.

Children of Arthur and Susan (Eagon) Inghram

1. Melissa Inghram, died July 1, 1871, married Isaac Slater Inghram, born June 27, 1816, died October 17, 1879.

Children of Isaac and Melissa (Inghram) Inghram

  1. William G. H. Inghram, born July 28, 1845, died June 1915.
  2. John F. Inghram, born November 10, 1847, died December 9, 1855.
  3. Isaac Slater Inghram, born March 16, 1850, died May 1919, married Ruth Church.
  4. Thomas Arthur Inghram, born March 26, 1852, died January 2, 1930, married Rebecca Frye.
  5. James Burbridge Inghram, born August 7, 1854, died December 1918, married Henrietta Brewer.
  6. Jesse L. Inghram, born November 15, 1856, died July 20, 1859.
  7. Joseph Inghram, born May 18, 1859.
  8. Norman W. Inghram, born September 11, 1861.
  9. Robert D. Inghram, born April 22, 1864, died November 8, 1866.
10. Uriah G. Inghram, born June 3, 1868, married Flo Rinehart.

2. Mariah Inghram, born January 11, 1828, died September 28, 1894; married, May 20, 1847, Basil Gordon, born December 27, 1822, died March 28, 1899.

Children of Basil and Mariah (Inghram) Gordon

1. John Adam Gordon, married Mariah Bell.
2. Jennie Gordon, married Thomas Montgomery.
3. Sudie Gordon, married James Hatfield.
4. James A. J. Gordon, married Emma Cox.
5. Alice D. Gordon, married William B. Wood.
6. Mark Gordon, died young.

3. Elizabeth Inghram, born 1815, died February 22, 1855, married Jacob Shriver, born August 7, 1807, died February 1, 1887.

Children of Jacob and Elizabeth (Inghram) Shriver

1. Inghram Shriver, married Velinda Gutherie.
2. Sudie Shriver, married Benjamin Baily.
3. Mariah Shriver, married Samuel Bradford.
4. John Shriver, married Margaret Morris.
5. Hicey Shriver, married Eliza Frye.
6. Melissa Shriver, married Allen Berkey.
7. Minerva Shriver, married Isaac Shriver.
8. Elizabeth Shriver, married Jack Stephens.
9. Arthur Shriver, married Ella Hickman.

4. Minerva Inghram, born July 25, 1817, died February 10, 1874; married, December 24, 1837, David A. Worley, born August 11, 1811, died March 13, 1870.

AND ITS PIONEER FAMILIES 319

Children of David A. and Minerva (Inghram) Worley
1. Milton Worley, married Elizabeth Lippencott.
2. Norman Worley, married Nannie Wisecarver.
3. Melissa Worley, married J. M. Kennedy.
4. Margaret Worley, married Hiram Axtell.
5. Mary Worley.
6. Emma Worley.
7. Jesse Worley.
8. Sudie Worley.
9. David Worley.
10. Brice Worley.

5. Uriah Blackburn Inghram, born October 5, 1819, died August 1, 1903, married Alice (Elsie) Gordon, born September 15, 1827.

Children of Uriah and Alice (Elsie) Gordon) Inghram
1. Susan Inghram, married Thomas Hook.
2. Delilah Inghram, married Abner Hoge.
3. Rebecca Inghram, married Frank Inghram.
4. Josiah Inghram, married (1) Laura McNeely (2) Laura Everly.
5. Emma Inghram.
6. Catherine Inghram.
7. William Inghram, married Harriet Bell.
8. Thomas Inghram.
9. Frances Inghram, married C. W. Spragg, M. D.

6. Josiah Smith Inghram, born October 5, 1819, died August 8, 1879; married, October 31, 1861, Sarah Hook, born October 26, 1836, died November 22, 1913.

Children of Josiah and Sarah (Hook) Inghram
1. Eliza Inghram, born August 7, 1862, died October 14, 1876.
2. Lucy Inghram, born May 9, 1864, died November 23, 1925.
3. Louise Inghram, born May 27, 1867, married, October 16, 1890, E. L. Denny.
4. Lizzie Inghram, married John Rinehart.
5. John T. Inghram, married Olive Inghram.

7. Mary Jane Inghram, born 1826, married Tellford Lewis.
8. Thomas Inghram, born 1829, married Salome Coen.
9. Arthur Inghram, married Mary Jane Coen.
10. Susan Inghram, born 1839, married Harrison Babbitt.

Children of Harrison and Susan (Inghram) Babbitt
1. Thomas Babbitt.
2. Arthur Babbitt.
3. Cora Babbitt, married James Reynolds.
4. .... Babbitt.

11. Hicey Inghram, never married.
12. Sarah Ann Inghram, born January 11, 1843, died ....; married, October 12, 1862, Simon Strosnider, born March 9, 1834, died March 16, 1899.

Children of Simon and Sarah (Inghram) Strosnider
1. Dolly died young.
2. Lillie Strosnider, married Frank Eisenminger.
3. Laura Strosnider, married Brazilla Stephens.
4. Lucy Strosnider, married Presley Patterson.

6. Thomas Inghram, son of Arthur and Allive (Smith) Inghram, married (1) Sarah Rinehart. He married (2) .... There were two children by first marriage and one by the second.
    1. Thomas Inghram, married Lucy Cathers.
    2. Elizabeth Inghram, married Rev. Betts.
    3. Johiel Inghram.
7. Cassandra Inghram, born 1787, died March 21, 1882, married Thomas Mooney, born 1783, died August 26, 1855. Their children were:
    1. Hannah Mooney who never married, born April 28, 1813, died March 30, 1892.
    2. Jemima Mooney, married Elijah Patterson.
    3. Olive Mooney, married John Thomas.
    4. William Mooney, never married.
    5. Arthur Mooney, never married.
    6. Eliza Jane Mooney, born November 20, 1820, died May 31, 1864; married, December 16, 1843, Lisbon Staggers, born December 17, 1820, son of John and Catherine (Maple) Staggers.
    7. Isabel Mooney, married Jesse Orndorff.
    8. Eleanor Mooney, never married.
    9. Delilah Mooney, married George Thomas.
    10. Thomas Mooney, married Mary Cosgray.
8. Delilah Inghram, married William Rinehart.
9. Hannah Inghram, married Hiram Rinehart.
10. Elizabeth Inghram, married Ignatius Morris.

JAMES PORTER FAMILY

Nancy Inghram, sister of William and Arthur Inghram, died November 27, 1810. She married James Porter, born 1735, died August 4, 1822. James Porter was a member of Captain James Archer's Company, though the name is mis-spelled "Potter." He settled on the County Home Farm.

Children

1. Eleanor Porter, married, September 18, 1791, William Rhodes, born March 6, 1759.
    1. Ann Rhodes, born July 29, 1792, died September 26, 1807.
    2. Joseph Rhodes, born September 9, 1793, married, December 19, 1819, Elizabeth Rinehart.
    3. Mary Rhodes, born February 20, 1795, died October 15, 1807.
    4. William Rhodes, born August 31, 1796, married Nancy Rinehart.
    5. Sarah Rhodes, born February 23, 1799.
    6. Independence Rhodes, born February 9, 1802.
    7. Thomas Rhodes.
    8. James Rhodes, born June 24, 1806.
2. Hannah Porter, died November 15, 1818, at Winchester, Virginia. She married Edmund Smith, who died in Oxford, Ohio, in 1838.
    1. John Porter Smith born January 28, 1813.
    2. James W. Smith.

3. David Porter, born 1776, died January 8, 1821, married Hannah Smith.
   1. Nancy Porter.
   2. Thomas Porter.
   3. James Porter.
   4. John Porter, born April 8, 1813, married, November 10, 1839, Hannah Rinehart, born April 21, 1813.
   5. Elizabeth Porter.
   6. Zeiza Porter.
   7. Martha Porter.
4. James Porter, Jr., born 1777, died March 1803.
5. Mary Porter, never married.
6. Joseph Porter, born November 29, 1783, died March 1826, married Elizabeth Rinehart, daughter of Thomas and Hannah (Inghram) Rinehart.
   1. Armstrong Porter, born August 23, 1808, died December 31, 1890, married Olive Inghram, born November 7, 1808, died December 16, 1883.
   2. Hiram Porter, married Margaret Inghram, born October 23, 1813, died June 2, 1890.
   3. Nancy Porter.
   4. Eliza Ann Porter, married Jacob Lough.
   5. Hannah Porter, married Corbly Hill, born March 2, 1813.
   6. Emanuel Porter.
   7. Maria Porter, born 1818, died May 27, 1895, married Hiram Rinehart, born 1805, died March 31, 1871.
   8. Rinehart Porter.

WILLIAM CATHERS FAMILY

Elizabeth Inghram, sister of William and Arthur Inghram, was born about 1740, and died August 1820. She married William Cathers who was born about 1737, and died about 1815. Old papers in the hands of the author indicate that William Rhodes administered in the estate of William Cathers, making payments to the heirs of James Porter, brother-in-law of William Cathers. William Cathers was the son of Robert Cathers of Scotland, who came to America and settled first in Frederick County, Virginia, from which place he removed to the Tenmile. In 1814, Robert and Sarah Cathers deeded "Rich Hills" to William Cathers. This tract of land was one of several that bore that title and all were in the Gordon Hill section of Greene County. William Cathers was a member of Captain James Archer's Company of Washington County Militia.

Children
1. Robert Cathers, said to have married Sarah (Strosnider) Thompson, widow of George Thompson, who died on Block House Run.
2. Polly Cathers, married Peter Lemley, born 1770, died 1850. Rhodes Papers say they were married on February 11, 1794. After marriage they removed to Belmont County, Ohio. Their children were:
   1. Robert Lemley, born 1794.
   2. Catherine Lemley, who married Samuel Martin.
   3. Elizabeth Lemley, who married Jesse Carter.

4. Nancy Lemley, who married Isaac Brown.
5. Peter Lemley, born 1802.
6. Sarah Lemley, who married Oath West.
3. Elizabeth Cathers, born January 12, 1777, died August 20, 1850; married, May 29, 1795, Samuel Hill, born November 24, 1767, died February 8, 1827. Their children were:
    1. Margaret Hill, born August 1, 1796, married Morford Throckmorton.
    2. John Hill, born July 4, 1798, died young.
    3. William Hill, born July 4, 1798, married Margaret Milliken.
    4. Elizabeth Hill, born January 1, 1801, married Jotham Jennings.
    5. Samuel Hill, born August 30, 1803, married Hannah Hill, daughter of Rees Hill.
    6. Thomas Hill, born October 10, 1805, married Nancy Roseberry.
    7. Sarah Hill, born March 30, 1809, died October 17, 1811.
    8. Corbly Hill, born March 2, 1813, married Hannah Porter.
    9. Jesse Hill, born November 23, 1814, married Maria Hoskinson.
    10. Nancy Hill, born January 23, 1817, married Jacob Smith.
    11. Mary Hill, born March 21, 1819, married John Moore.
4. Margaret Cathers, born May 20, 1780, died August 5, 1853; married December 30 1799. David Worley, born May 8, 1775, died August 10, 1851. They were parents of ten children.
    1. William Cathers Worley.
    2. Elizabeth Worley, married John Wells.
    3. Robert Worley.
    4. Jesse Worley.
    5. Dr. Ashberry Worley.
    6. David A. Worley, born August 11, 1811, died March 13, 1870, married Minerv' Inghram.
    7. Martha Worley, married Andrew Brown.
    8. .... Worley.
    9. .... Worley.
    10. John I. Worley, born December 1, 1823, married (1) Maria Gordon. Married (2) Mrs. Delilah (Gordon) Higgins.
5. Nancy Cathers, married Thomas Fee.
6. William Cathers, died March 21, 1830, aged 43 years.
7. John Cathers, born 1796, died 1855, married Sarah Shields.

THE RINEHART FAMILY

Johan Thomas Reinhart arrived in America on the British ship "Lydia," Thomas Allen, master, and took the Oath of Allegiance to the British at Philadelphia on December 11, 1739. In due time he migrated to Frederick County, Maryland, where he was living in 1776, when his son, Simon, enlisted in Captain Philip Graybill's Company of the German Regiment under the command of Colonel Ludwick Weltner. A short time later Thomas Reinhart, Sr., with his wife, Anna Maria, and five sons, Simon, Thomas, Joseph, John, and Barnet Reinhart, removed to the Tenmile Country and settled at the head of Coal Lick Branch of South Tenmile. Here they made their improvements and two of the sons were to fall at the hands of the ever present Indians. When Thomas Reinhart, Sr., died in

1793, he mentioned these deceased sons in dividing his estate, giving their proper share to their children. His wife, Anna Maria, survived him as shown by the probate of the will on November 23, 1793. (Washington County Will Book 1. pp. 211.)

Family of Thomas Rinehart, Jr.

Thomas Rinehart, Jr., was born about 1746, and died in Greene County, August 2, 1804. About 1774, he married Hannah Inghram, daughter of William Inghram, Sr. She died in 1808, and with her husband is buried on the Solomon Gordon Farm. Thomas Rinehart, Jr., was a member of James Archer's Company First Battalion, Washington County Militia. He received a tract of land from his father adjoining the land of Stewart and Ball. His will was probated August 6, 1804.

Children of Thomas and Hannah (Inghram) Rinehart

1. John Rinehart, born 1779, died January 29, 1855, married Margaret Inghram, born 1780, died December 20, 1862. She was a daughter of Arthur and Alive (Smith) Inghram. They are buried on the Ross Scott Farm in Franklin Township.

    #### Children

    1. Nancy Rinehart, married John Griffith.
    2. Matilda Rinehart, born 1811, died April 23, 1881, married Uriah Rinehart, born June 17, 1809, died July 25, 1877.
    3. Olive Rinehart, married Henry Vandruff.
    4. Hannah Rinehart, born April 21, 1813, died December 22, 1880; married, November 10, 1839, John Porter, born 1813, died January 21, 1856.
    5. Emeline Rinehart, married Lewis Dowlin.
    6. Thomas Reinhart, born February 14, 1802, died February 26, 1888, married Mary ....
    7. Hiram Rinehart, born November 21, 1805, died March 31, 1871, married Maria Porter, born December 22, 1818, died May 27, 1895, daughter of Joseph and Elizabeth (Rinehart) Porter. His first wife was Hannah Inghram.
    8. Presley Rinehart.
    9. Jesse Rinehart, born 1817, died April 16, 1868.
    10. Levi Rinehart, died July 30, 1854, aged 33 years.
    11. Margaret Rinehart, married Rea Dowlin.
    12. William Rinehart.
    13. Arthur Rinehart.
    14. Joseph Rinehart, died September 1, 1898.
2. Thomas Rinehart, married Jane Gooden, born 1783, died August 3, 1875.
3. William Rinehart, married Delilah Inghram, daughter of Arthur and Alive (Smith) Inghram.
4. Margaret Rinehart, married January 26, 1796, Shadrack Mitchell. He died in 1862.

    #### Children

    1. Thomas Mitchell.
    2. John Mitchell.
    3. Jesse Mitchell.
    4. Asa Mitchell, born October 6, 1811, married January 25, 1835, Rachel Johns, born December 1, 1815.
    5. Elizabeth Mitchell.
    6. Delilah Mitchell.

7. Isaac Mitchell, born September 9, 1816, married, October 4, 1838, Elizabeth Barnes.
8. Hannah Mitchell.
9. Maria Mitchell.

5. Elizabeth Rinehart, born ...., married Joseph Porter, son of James and Nancy (Inghram) Porter, born November 29, 1783, died March 1826. Her second husband was an Inghram.

Children

1. Armstrong Porter, born August 25, 1808, died December 31, 1890, married Olive Inghram, born November 7, 1808, died December 16, 1883, daughter of William and Elizabeth (Rinehart) Inghram.
2. Hiram Porter, married Margaret Inghram, born October 23, 1813, died June 2, 1890, she was a daughter of William and Elizabeth (Rinehart) Inghram.
3. Nancy Porter.
4. Eliza Ann Porter, married Jacob Lough.
5. Hannah Porter, married Corbly Hill.
6. Emanuel Porter.
7. Maria Porter, married Hiram Rinehart. She died May 27, 1895, aged 76 years, 6 months, 5 days; he died March 31, 1871, aged 65 years, 5 months, 10 days.

6. Nancy Rinehart, married, January 29, 1798, Richard Ankrom, son of John and Martha (Wells) Ankrom. They went to Tyler County, West Virginia.
7. Jesse Rinehart, born 1790, died March 31, 1872, aged 81 years, 11 months, 16 days. His first wife was Lucy Workman, and after her death he married Sarah Dill, born September 26, 1815, died March 26, 1893. Jesse Rinehart and Lucy Workman were married June 25, 1817.

Children

1. J. Workman Rinehart.
2. Harriett Rinehart, married Dr. A. G. Cross, born July 23, 1823, son of Robert and Mary (Syphers) Cross.
3. Thomas Rinehart, never married.
4. Hannah Rinehart, married William Minor.
5. Elizabeth Rinehart, married William H. Cooke.
6. Dill Rinehart, never married.
7. Margaret Rinehart, married Philip Bartleson.
8. Henry Rinehart, married Ella Gilmore.
9. George Rinehart, married Letitia Smith.

8. Joseph Rinehart, married Sarah Smith.
9. Arthur Rinehart, died April 6, 1872, aged 78 years, 5 months, 21 days. He married Rebecca Roberts, who died June 5, 1873, aged 72 years, 2 months, and 29 days. She was a daughter of Richard and Jemima Roberts.

Children of Arthur and Rebecca (Roberts) Rinehart

1. Richard Rinehart, married Nancy Gordon.
2. Lucinda Rinehart, born April 16, 1824, died August 25, 1866.
3. Benjamin Rinehart, born May 27, 1826, died December 7, 1907, married, November 7, 1851, Mary Hoge, daughter of Solomon and Rachel (Huss) Hoge. She was born April 9, 1832, died April 27, 1923.
4. Hannah Rinehart, born 1827, died July 23, 1845.
5. Elizabeth Rinehart, born 1831, died 1916, married Joheil

Rinehart, born 1831, died 1905. He was a son of Jacob and Abigail (Huss) Rinehart.
6. Wesley Rinehart, born August 4, 1833, died December 15, 1909; married, December 29, 1864, Sarah Hayes, born February 18, 1841, died May 31, 1931.
7. Thomas Rinehart, born 1834, died July 27, 1845.
8. Harriet Rinehart, born November 26, 1838, died January 28, 1905; married, January 15, 1861, Henry Grimes.
9. William Arthur Rinehart, married Rachel Kincaid.
10. Henry Porter Rinehart, born June 1, 1844, died February 25, 1892; married, June 28, 1866, Mariah Bowers, born February 22, 1844, died December 30, 1932.
10. Levi Rinehart, son of Thomas and Hannah (Inghram) Rinehart, married Maria McClelland, a daughter of Asa and Catherine (Brown) McClelland. He died in 1854.
11. Hannah Rinehart, daughter of Thomas and Hannah (Inghram) Rinehart, married Thomas Rinehart, son of Joseph and Elizabeth (Huffman) Rinehart.

FAMILY OF SIMON RINEHART

Simon Rinehart, son of Thomas and Anna Maria Rinehart, after serving a tour of duty in Captain Philip Graybill's Company of the German Regiment under Colonel Ludwick Weltner in Frederick County, Maryland, in 1776, removed with his father's family to the head of Coal Lick Run. Evans says that he and William Brown agreed to the exchange of their lands, and in the process of moving both men were ambushed and killed by the Indians; Simon Rinehart being shot by an Indian lurking behind a tree on Laurel Run. This tree, frequently pointed out to early inhabitants of the section, was for many years known as the Simon Rinehart Tree. The story told by William Harrod, Jr., and Harrod Newland, both of whom were called up to avenge the slaying, says that the men were making maple sugar and were ambushed at their camp. John Owens and William English were the other unfortunate men in this event. It is possible that both stories are true, and since we know from court records that John Owens was killed in the Spring of 1781, we can place that date as the death of Simon Rinehart. His name is on the petition for the formation of the new state to be called "Westsylvania," which was sent to the Continental Congress about 1779. Simon Rinehart was born about 1750, and married about 1772, to Sarah ...., who survived her husband and remarried. They had four children, all of whom are mentioned by Thomas Rinehart, Sr., in his will of record. (Maryland Archives Vol 18. pp 266 etc.) Sarah's second husband was .... Fuller. (Petition of October 7, 1857.)

Children of Simon and Sarah Rinehart

1. Simon Rinehart, Jr., married Elsie Mulrine, daughter of John and Elsie (Meighen) Mulrine.

Children

1. John Rinehart.
2. Rezin Rinehart.
3. Enos Rinehart.
4. Joseph Rinehart.
5. Samuel Rinehart, married 1841, Mary Zook, born 1823. He died in Libby Prison.
6. Asa Rinehart.

2. Nancy Rinehart, who died in 1820, married John Gordon, born

1775, died 1830. He was a son of John and Mary (Duke) Gordon.

Children

1. Sarah Gordon, born September 1794, died November 1881, married Samuel Seals, who died in 1859.
2. Nancy Gordon, born January 1796, died in Perry County, Ohio, 1869, married Ar+hur McCartney.
3. Mary Gordon, married William Orndorff.
4. Charlotte Gordon, married Peter Strosnider.
5. William Gordon.
6. Patty Gordon, married ... Smith.
7. Bazil Gordon.
8. Elly Gordon, married George Hoy.
9. Samuel Gordon, married Dolly Wells.
10. Barnet Gordon, died October 7, 1820.
11. Zedidiah Gordon.

3. Barnet Rinehart, son of Simon and Sarah Rinehart, born September 8, 1777, died January 2, 1843; married Sarah Hook, who died in 1826. Both are buried in the old cemetery in East Waynesburg. Barnet Rinehart was an early sheriff of Greene County.

Children of Barnet and Sarah (Hook) Rinehart

1. Judge James Rinehart, born August 22, 1802, died March 29, 1879; married Delilah Eagon, daughter of Solomon and Mary (Blackburn) Eagon. They are buried in Oscaloosa, Iowa.
2. Simon Rinehart, born February 22, 1805, died September 1, 1881; married Hannah Morris, born 1809, died 1893. Buried in Green Mount Cemetery.
3. Lucy B. Rinehart, born February 10, 1810; married James Green, born December 6, 1803, died March 20, 1879.
4. Samuel Rinehart, married Mary Eagon.
5. Mary Rinehart, born 1812, died April 17, 1847; married John R. Hughes.

4. Samuel Rinehart, son of Simon and Sarah Rinehart, married Amelia .... She died August 8, 1846, aged 66 years.

Children

1. Samuel Rinehart.
2. Jesse Rinehart.

FAMILY OF JOHN RINEHART

John Rinehart, son of Thomas and Anna Maria Rinehart, was born about 175... and killed by the Indians in 1782. He was a member of Captain James Archer's Militia Company. Waychoff says he lived at the site of the present County Home, from which he was lured away by what seemed to be the bawling of a calf, but was a lurking savage, who killed and scalped him after a terrible fight. His wife was Mary ...., who died about 1805, leaving a will, which mentions her two children. They are also named in the will of Thomas Rinehart, Sr.

Children of John and Mary Rinehart

1. Susannah Rinehart, married Isaiah Strawn, who was born November 22, 1778, and died February 1840.

Children
1. John Rinehart Strawn, married Adeline Dance.
2. Louisa Strawn, married John Hughes.
3. Ellis Strawn, married Lydia Smith.
4. Eleanor Strawn, married Thomas Hughes.
5. Samuel Strawn, married Hannah Roberts.

2. John T. Rinehart, born October 1, 1782, died December 26, 1864; married Susannah Strawn, born November 1787, died December 26, 1856, daughter of Jacob Strawn.

Children
1. Susannah Rinehart.
2. Eleanor Rinehart, born 1812, died August 13, 1861, aged 48 years, 11 months, 2 days.
3. Dorcas Rinehart, born November 8, 1819, married, January 5, 1862, Robert Zimmerman.
4. Morgan Rinehart.
5. Letitia Rinehart, married .... Gwynne.
6. Peter Rinehart.
7. Hannah Rinehart, married .... Adams.
8. Elmira Rinehart, married .... Harvey.
9. Rhoda Ann Rinehart, married .... Russell.
10. Uriah Rinehart, born June 17, 1809, died July 25, 1877; married Matilda Rinehart, born 1811, died April 23, 1881, daughter of John and Margaret (Inghram) Rinehart. Buried at Hewitts Church Cemetery.
11. Ruth Rinehart, married .... Turner.

FAMILY OF BARNET RINEHART

Barnet Rinehart, son of Thomas and Anna Maria Rinehart, was born about 1758, and died in Greene County, about 1822, his will being probated October 26, 1822. He warranted a tract of land on Coal Lick on December 23, 1784, under the title "Lions Bush," located adjoining the land of Thomas Rinehart, Sr. He was living there when he served in Captain James Archer's Militia Company. He is said to have married twice, his first wife being Elizabeth .... His second wife was Ruth Styles, probably the mother of most of his children. She is called Ruth Reinhardt in the will of her father, Stephen Styles, in Monongalia County, West Virginia.

Children of Barnet Rinehart
1. John Rinehart, born 1776, married Elizabeth ....
2. Thomas Rinehart, killed in a hunting accident.
3. Mary Rinehart, married Richard Hughes.
4. Susan Rinehart.
5. Stephen Rinehart, died about 1845 (Estate 1144 Greene County.) His wife was Lydia Britt.
6. Elizabeth Rinehart, born September 17, 1783, died March 3, 1864; married William Inghram, born 1778, son of Arthur and Alive (Smith) Inghram. He died August 6, 1845.

Children
1. Arthur Inghram, born 1803, died March 3, 1870; married Elizabeth Cathers, born July 21, 1804, died March 18, 1884.
2. Sarah Inghram, born 1805, died September 23, 1858; married Solomon Gordon.
3. Thomas Inghram, born February 23, 1807, died July 14, 1894; married, January 24, 1850, Harriet Crayne, born March 2, 1823, died August 12, 1891.

4. Olive Inghram, born November 11, 1808, died December 16, 1883; married Armstrong Porter, born 1808, died December 31, 1890.
5. Elizabeth Inghram, born July 10, 1810, died 1876; married Levi Strawn.
6. Cassandra Inghram, born November 11, 1811, died December 18, 1900; married Madison Bell.
7. Margaret Inghram, born October 23, 1813, died June 2, 1890; married Hiram Porter, son of Joseph and Elizabeth (Rinehart) Porter.
8. Nancy Inghram, born December 11, 1815, died March 5, 1889; married William Bell.
9. Delilah Inghram, born April 23, 1821, died November 5, 1898; married John Brice Gordon, born December 4, 1798, died December 28, 1876.
10. William Inghram, born July 31, 1828, died May 15, 1888; married (1) Martha Hoge, who died in 1885. His second wife was Rebecca Inghram.

7. Sarah Rinehart, daughter of Barnet Rinehart, born December 15, 1786, died June 5, 1872; married, 1817, Henry Church, born January 20, 1779, died August 28, 1851. Her first husband was Thomas Inghram, son of Arthur Inghram.

Children

1. Ruth Church, born January 18, 1818.
2. William Church, born December 5, 1819.
3. Rinehart B. Church, born March 29, 1822, died December 11, 1882; married, December 6, 1842, Charlotte Gutherie, born January 30, 1825, died March 16, 1911.
4. Delilah Church, born July 9, 1824.
5. John Church, born November 21, 1826, married Elizabeth Fordyce.
6. Elizabeth Church, born August 2, 1831.

8. Delilah Rinehart, died December 22, 1871; married David Huss, born 1801, died July 14, 1873, he a son of Elisha and Rachel (Heaton) Huss.

Children

1. Charlotte Huss, died February 1911; married (1) Smith Adamson, (2) Samuel Braden.
2. Simon R. Huss, married Elizabeth Gordon. He was born in 1824, and died 1905.
3. John K. Huss, married Eleanor Lantz,
4. Harvey Huss, married .... Bell.
5. Emily R. Huss, married Richard Lantz,
6. David R. P. Huss, born August 25, 1839, died November 24, 1910; married, September 21, 1860, Mary Jane Lantz, born April 4, 1843, died December 10, 1908.

9. Simon Rinehart, born August 7, 1795, died October 29, 1852; married Sarah Jane Armstrong, who died May 26, 1893.
10. Nancy Rinehart, married William Rhodes, born August 21, 1796, son of William and Elinor (Porter) Rhodes.
11. Jacob Rinehart, son of Barnet and Ruth (Styles) Rinehart, was born February 1803, and died May 1, 1874. He married (1) Abigail Huss, born March 1, 1810, died May 5, 1841. He then married Elizabeth Hoge.

Children

1. Harriet Rinehart, born November 11, 1829, married, November 5, 1857, Martin Love, who died in 1899.
2. Joheil Rinehart, born 1831, died 1905; married Elizabeth Rinehart, daughter of Arthur and Rebecca (Roberts) Rinehart. She was born 1831, and died 1916. Buried in Green Mount.
3. John Rinehart, born 1838, died 1916; married Mira Baily.
4. William Rinehart, died 1874, married, 1852, Ruth Ann Bowen, daughter of Corbly and Joanna (Garrison) Bowen.
5. David Rinehart, born 1836, killed in the Civil War, May 1, 1865.
6. James Benjamin Franklin Rinehart, West Point graduate, never married.
7. Thomas J. Rinehart, never married.
8. George Rinehart.
9. Elsworth Rinehart.
10. Charlotte Rinehart, married Morris Morris.
11. Ruth Rinehart, married .. .. Johnson.
12. Abigail Rinehart, married .... Kincaid.
13. Josephine Rinehart.
14. Louisa Rinehart, died January 12, 1849.
15. Charles Rinehart, died February 18, 1849.

12. Charlotte Rinehart, daughter of Barnet and Ruth (Styles) Rinehart, married Joseph Ankrom, who was born in 1807.

FAMILY OF JOSEPH RINEHART

Joseph Rinehart, youngest son of Thomas and Anna Maria Rinehart, was willed a tract of land by his father. He was also a member of Captain James Archer's Company of Militia. Joseph Rinehart died about 1816, leaving a will that was probated April 23, 1816. His wife was Elizabeth Huffman, sister of Benjamin Huffman.

Children of Joseph and Elizabeth Rinehart

1. Thomas Rinehart, died young leaving two children. His wife was Hannah Rinehart, daughter of Thomas Rinehart, Jr.

Children

1. Delilah Rinehart, married Isaac Nelson.
2. Elizabeth Rinehart, married Joseph Rhodes.

2. Joseph Rinehart, born November 5, 1776; married, November 29, 1807, Sarah Smith, daughter of Ichabod Smith. They went to Ashland County, Ohio.

Children

1. Elizabeth Rinehart, born December 21, 1808.
2. Aaron J. Rinehart, born January 9, 1810.
3. Joseph Rinehart, born January 9, 1813.
4. John H. Rinehart, born January 18, 1815.
5. Mary Rinehart, born October 5, 1817.
6. Rev. Hiram Rinehart, born January 15, 1820.
7. William H. Rinehart, born May 2, 1823.
8. Sarah Rinehart, born June 22, 1825.
9. Benjamin F. Rinehart, born August 29, 1829.

THE HOOK FAMILY

From the beginning of the settlement of the Tenmile Country about Fort Jackson, no one family has played a more important part in the organization and development of this section than the Hook Family. Mr. James W. Hook of New Haven, Connecticut, a careful worker and keen investigator, has compiled an excellent "Hook History," from which the author has been permitted to draw for much of the record of the family. Until he visited Waynesburg some twenty-five years ago, very little of the family history had been preserved. His painstaking research uncovered the records that resulted in the familiary known "Hook Book," a revised edition of which is now in the manuscript form. It was his search that took the story of the Hook Family back to the immigrant ancestor.

Mr. Hook's records show that Thomas Hook, (Hooke) great-grandfather of Captain James Hook, was born near London, England, about 1645, and came to Maryland in April 1668. About 1680, he is known to have moved to what is now Prince George's County, where he lived on leased land not far from the present site of Laurel. Here he made his will on September 23, 1697, leaving his property to his sons, James and Thomas Hook, with provisions that they remain with their mother, whose name is given as Annaple in the administration bond signed May 26, 1698. In the sworn inventory filed July 24, 1699, it would appear that Annaple Hook had married again, and her second husband was John Wright.

James Hook, son of Thomas Hook, the immigrant, was born about 1680. He was one of the organizers of the Rock Creek Parish of the Church of England, and was elected Warden of the Parish on April 10, 1732. He was elected Vestryman on March 26, 1733, when George Murdock was the pastor. (Records of Rock Creek Parish, Maryland Hist. ·ical Society, Baltimore, Maryland). Charles Parry's list of taxables for Rock Creek Hundred, Prince George's County, for the year 1733, includes the name of James Hook. This same list also includes the names of Slater, Thrasher, Hardin, Williams, White, and others soon to be familiar to the Tenmile Country. (Black Books of Maryland pp. 43.) A similar list taken by David Jones in 1719, includes the name of James Hook among some 212 other taxables. (Ibid. pp. 22.) James Hook married Margaret Thrasher in 1706. In 1727, Benjamin Thrasher, probably the father of Margaret, recorded a gift of a dark bay mare to James Hook, son of James Hook, Sr. (DB. Libra M. pp. 174 Upper Marlboro.) The inventory of Benjamin Thrasher's estate was signed May 18, 1741, by John Jackson and Ninian Beale. James Lee and Mary Lee were listed as near relatives. James Hook died in 1738.

John Hook, son of James and Margaret (Thrasher) Hook, was born about 1718, in Prince George County, and died in Lower Frederick County, Maryland, in 1762. He married, probably, Sarah Simpson, though there is a suggestion of doubt about her last name and there are some who think she may have been Sarah Snowden, a family that seems closely connected in some unknown way. After the death of his father, John Hook, with his brother, James Hook, he removed to Lower Frederick County, where they settled on a tract of 150 acres of land conveyed to James Hook by a deed of gift August 26, 1740, by John Magruder. Then James Hook gave, on November 27, 1740, fifty acres of this land to his "loving brother," John Hook. John Hook accumulated other tracts of land, and then on January 16, 1752, John Hook and wife, Sarah, sold a tract of 133 acres to Richard Ankrom (Ankrum) a deed that was repeated a year later with slightly different wording. The will of John Hook was made May 19, 1761, and filed in Frederick County, December 4, 1761. His wife, Sarah, apparently survived him and he mentions two sons, James Hook and John Snowden Hook. (Libra A-1. pp. 170.)

CAPTAIN JAMES HOOK

Captain James Hook, son of John and Sarah Hook, was born in Lower Frederick County, Maryland, about 1749, a date determined from information given in his pension claim. Family traditions say he removed to the Tenmile about 1772, but his name is not found in the Springhill Township, Bedford County, tax lists for that year. He made three deeds of conveyance in Frederick County during the period from 1771 to 1775. One of these was dated August 20, 1771, another on April 10, 1775, and the last on June 17, 1775, which disposed of the property received by the will of his father. He settled on land which by deed of March 1, 1780, he purchased from David Owens, and which was patented to James Hook on May 13, 1789, under the title of "Hook's Delight." This land was on Owens' Run and had been granted to David Owens by virtue of a Virginia Certificate. His wife, Mary, who had joined in the deeds of 1771 and 1775, and at least a son and daughter accompanied him to the Tenmile Country. Mr. James W. Hook has confirmed the fact that Mary, wife of James Hook, was Mary Leith, (also spelled Lyeth, Lieth, etc.) a daughter of Robert and Sarah (Lakin) Leith. Sarah Lakin was a daughter of Abraham Lakin, who married, October 10, 1717, Martha Lee, born June 20, 1699, daughter of William and Ann Lee of Prince George's County, Maryland. Robert Leith was of Ann Arundel County, Maryland. Mary (Leith) Hook died in Greene County, Pennsylvania. In 1902, Mr. Charles Kent of Waynesburg, reported that he had found an old grave some four miles East of Waynesburg, on which was carved, "Here lies the body of Mary Hook, wife of James Hook, who dep. this life Jan. 30, A. D. 1815 aged 71 years, 4 months, and 19 days." Mr. James W. Hook states he saw this stone in 1923, when it was all but obliterated.

Mary (Leith) Hook was a niece of Abraham Lakin to whom James Hook sold a portion of his property in Maryland. Her sister, Sarah Leith, had become the second wife of Thomas Fee, who also settled on the Tenmile. Thomas Fee had first married a Miss Thrasher and one of his daughters, by the first marriage, was Mary, second wife of Richard Jackson, who built the fort that bore his name.

As Captain James Hook stated in his pension deposition of June 1821, it is evident that he married again after the death of his wife. This second wife, whom he married about 1818, is said to have been Mrs. Rebecca Roach, widow of George Roach, and daughter of William and Mary (Smith) Miller. Her husband, George Roach, had died at Monongahela City, Pennsylvania, and she had moved to Waynesburg to be near her sister, Mrs. Henry Shearin. She died May 29, 1823.

The pension application dated October 5, 1818, and amended by Captain James Hook in June 1821, in Greene County, says that he was a captain of a company in 1775—one of the earliest on the Tenmile—but was not commissioned in Colonel William Crawford's 13th Virginia Regiment on the Continental line until the Fall of 1776. He served on the Western Frontier until the Summer of 1777, being stationed for a time at Wheeling, and doing guard on a shipment of powder to Fort Pitt. He was then ordered to the Headquarters of Washington's Army at Trenton, where the regiment was taken over by Colonel Russell, under whom he served in the Battles of Brandywine and Germantown. Joseph Gwynne supported his claim by saying he had seen Captain James Hook at Grimes Park, about 20 miles out from Philadelphia, marching under Colonel Russell to take part in the battle. Captain Hook further stated that he had remained in the service until June 1779, when he left with the consent of Colonel Brodhead. (National Achives B. 39713.)

Additional references to Captain Hook's services in the Virginia Militia prior to the start of the Revolutionary War will be found in his sworn statement in behest of bounty land dated November 21, 1822, and the sworn supporting statement of James Seals, dated November 23, 1822, in which Seals declares "that he was acquainted with Captain James Hook in 1774 at which time said Hook was a Captain in the Virginia Militia." These sworn statements also say that, after returning to the western frontier in the fall of 1778, Captain Hook "continued in command until the close of the war." (These papers are on file at the Virginia State Library, Richmond, Virginia.)

An interesting sidelight on the service of Captain James Hook is shown in the pension claim of Levi House, then living in Jefferson City, Indiana, on October 9, 1834. Levi House said he enlisted in May 1777, in Captain James Hook's "Calico Hunting Shirt Company" of the Virginia Line. The men were assembled at Fort Redstone, from whence they marched down to Maryland to join General Daniel Morgan's Rifle Company, but after marching 80 miles, an express brought an order to go to Wheeling. He was there until November 1778, when he returned to Fort Jackson. Thus it will be seen that all of the men of Captain James Hook's Company did not accompany him on the march to Trenton. For this service Captain Hook was awarded a pension of $320 per year, and further records show he received a grant of 4000 acres of land from Virginia for his part in the service of that State. Deeds recorded shortly after his death disclose that this Bounty Land was disposed of by Captain James Hook, giving a half of it, or 2000 acres, to Colonel Rees Hill for his aid in securing the grant. One-half of the remainder went to his son, Daniel Hook, on the condition that he examine the land and make a division of it. It was probably situated in the Virginia Military Grant, west of the Scioto River in Ohio. Two other sons of Captain James Hook were to get the remainder of this land. They were Stephen and Israel Hook, and there is no reliable evidence to indicate that either or both these sons lived in this part of Ohio for a time. Stephen Hook, however, did move to Carrol County, Ohio, in 1817, and settled on a farm of 81.58 acres patented to him by the Government on June 3, 1816. This county was not a part of the Virginia reserve.

While living on this tract of land on David Owens' Creek, which was just across the Tenmile from John Thrasher land and but one farm removed from John Ankrom's Fort, James Hook began buying up parts of his neighbors' tracts of land. The dealings of Captain James Hook in local land are disclosed in several warrants and patents from Pennsylvania and from deeds of record at Waynesburg, Pennsylvania. His transactions were extensive. "Smithfield," a tract of 112 acres situated near his Owens' Run property was warranted to him April 7, 1798. It was later sold to Sylvanus Smith, who secured the patent. On September 19, 1793, he purchased a part of "Mt. Pleasant," originally patented to Nathaniel

Hughes. This he sold to his son, Stephen Hook, on November 7, 1800. He bought "Sugar Camp" on April 9, 1795, from William Hayes and wife, Ann. This tract, opposite the mouth of Coal Lick, was disposed of by various deeds, including one to his brother, John Snowden Hook. When Waynesburg was laid out by the Commissioners appointed for that purpose, Captain James Hook bought two lots, which he later sold to Thomas Slater, original owner of "Eden" the site of Waynesburg. On August 16, 1799, he bought out Isaac Sharp's interest in a tract of land on Richard Jackson's Run, originally warranted to Mainyard Rockhold. He got the patent for this tract, the original of which is still preserved by the present owner, Mr. Harvey Pratt. James Hook sold parts of this land to Benjamin Smalley and Acquilla Knight. The tract of land west of "Sharp's Rake" and situated on Wiley's Run (now Purman Run) passed into his hands in partnership with Isaac Jenkinson. This tract, known as "Sharp's Delight," purchased April 4, 1790, joined up with land owned by John Jones.

For the purpose of clearing up a genealogical tangle, one other venture in real estate by James Hook should be mentioned. He obtained a portion of a tract of land next to his own tract on Owens' Run, warranted to Richard Morris under the title of "Horse Head," and patented to Job Smith under the title of "Patience." This Richard Morris moved to Circleville, Ohio, and in 1801, James Hook sold this 123 acres to his son, James Hook, Jr., who in 1818, sold it to another Richard Morris, a latecomer from New Jersey, who later passed it along to his daughter, Mary, wife of John Greene. No known relationship existed between these two Richard Morris families.

Numerous other transactions are of record, some of which show that Captain James Hook provided well for his sons before retiring from active business. But real estate was not his entire activity. Old court records in Washington County, Pennsylvania, disclose that in 1789, he secured a license to operate a tavern in Morgan Township, and before 1790, he is shown to have owned a mill on Whiteley Creek. Although much opposed to drunkenness, it is probable that he operated a still as was customary on all well regulated plantations in his day. This would explain his active part in the Whiskey Rebellion. The abrupt failure of this movement sent him into hiding, along with a number of other prominent citizens, during which time, Professor Waychoff reports, a daughter, Sarah Hook, later the wife of Barnet Rinehart, carried food to his hiding place in the woods. It is also reported by Waychoff, that after the Whiskey Rebellion ended, James Hook joined with Albert Gallatin, Colonel William Crawford, Colonel John Minor, John Canon, and other influential men, in allaying the aroused sentiment of the defeated partisans, even though they had at times aided and abetted the insurrection. Through their efforts further bloodshed was avoided. It was about this time the new Greene County was formed and Captain James Hook was confirmed the first sheriff on November 8, 1796.

Waychoff says that on March 2, 1811, some thirty civic minded men met in Waynesburg for the purpose of establishing a subscription school. It was agreed at this meeting to purchase from Snowden Slater a half of a quarter of an acre of ground situated on land adjoining the "Commons" at Washington Street. (Site of the Northside School Building.) This school was to be forever known as the "Franklin School House." (Has Waynesburg forgotten this charge?) A building of brick, with stone foundation, twenty six feet by eighteen feet and eight feet high was to be built.

The specifications called for six windows of nine lights each, three in front and two in the rear, with the other on the east side. James Hook was one of the thirty subscribers. The following year his son, James Hook, Jr., became one of the members replacing his ageing father. John W. Meredith is the first teacher mentioned in the minute book.

James Hook died on January 23, 1824, and it is probable that he was buried with his first wife, but no marker has been found.

FAMILY OF CAPTAIN JAMES AND MARY (LEITH) HOOK

1. John Hook, born in Frederick County, Maryland, July 4, 1766, died near Augusta, Bracken County, Kentucky, January 9, 1850; married, about 1784, Hannah Morris, born January 4, 1767, probably in Ireland, died April 14, 1838. The wedding was objected to by John's parents, so the young couple left after their marriage and settled on a farm near Augusta, Bracken County, Kentucky. (We are of the opinion that John Hook may have joined the migration to this place, which included Richard Jackson, James and Samuel Mirandy, Sebastian Schroffe, John Fee, Leonard Sellars and others from the vicinity of Fort Jackson. This migration took place close to 1789.) In Kentucky, John Hook amassed considerable estate, including 40 slaves, whom John, before his death, distributed among his children, except Rebecca, who refused and took money instead. Old family documents, including the Family Bible, give the vital statistics on 11 children. Mention is also made of certain of John Hook's brothers and sisters. Record secured by James W. Hook in 1931.

   Children of John and Hannah (Morris) Hook
   1. Mary Hook, born March 27, 1785, married Samuel Poe.
   2. Rebecca Hook, born December 21, 1788, died July 27, 1855; married, October 18, 1810, John Marsh, born August 6, 1789, died April 29, 1827. They settled near Laurel, Ohio.
   3. James Hook, born January 16, 1790, died August 1, 1813, leaving a wife andd five children.
   4. Sarah Hook, born March 11, 1792, died January 1, 1860; married, May 5, 1825, John Taylor, born November 18, 1799, died March 30, 1887.
   5. John Hook.
   6. Eleanor Hook.
   7. Hannah Hook, born July 17, 1799, married Solomon Taylor.
   8. Samuel Hook.
   9. Elizabeth Hook, born October 13, 1803, died June 14, 1880; married Daniel Byers.
   10. Stephen Hook, born May 12, 1806, died January 21, 1874; married Nancy Heck.
   11. Martha Hook, died young.
2. Isreal Hook his wife was Mary ...., lived in Waynesburg as late as 1824. He visited his brother, Stephen Hook, in Perry County, Ohio, in 1845. Said to have lived in Kentucky many years.
3. Sarah Hook, born 1770, died 1826; married Barnet Rinehart, born September 8, 1777, died January 2, 1843. He was a son of Simon and Sarah Rinehart, and had been left an orphan, when the Indians killed his father about 1779-80. He is mentioned in the will of his grandfather, Thomas Rinehart. Both Barnet and his wife are buried in the old cemetery in East Waynesburg. Like his father-in-law before him, Barnet

Rinehart served as sheriff of Greene County, being inducted into office in 1808. It is possible that Sarah Hook may have been married twice for William Rhodes noted in his Journal that on February 11, 1794, Sally Hook was married to .... Freeman.

Children of Barnet and Sarah (Hook) Rinehart

1. James Rinehart, born August 22, 1802, died March 29, 1879; married Delilah Eagon, a daughter of Solomon and Mary (Blackburn) Eagon. They are buried in the Forest Cemetery in Lincoln Township, Mahaska County, Iowa. Delilah Eagon was born March 21, 1805, died December 7, 1878.
2. Simon Rinehart, born February 22, 1805, died September 1, 1881; married Hannah Morris, born 1809, died 1893. Both are buried in Green Mount Cemetery, Waynesburg, Pennsylvania.
3. Samuel Rinehart, married Mary Eagon.
4. Lucy B. Rinehart, born February 10, 1810; married James Green, born December 6, 1803, died March 20, 1879.
5. Mary Rinehart, born 1812, died April 17, 1847, aged 35 years and four months.

4.
5. The documents of John Hook of Kentucky, mentions two sisters, one of whom married James Faree, and another who married a Slater, and had a son, Thomas. This latter marriage indicates a marriage with one of Thomas Slater's sons, whose wives have not been identified. Census records suggest they were older children of Captain James Hook, and married prior to 1790.
6. James Hook, Jr., was born in 1776, and died in 1838. He married about 1795, Charlotte Morris, daughter of Richard and Mary (Seals) Morris, who died May 13, 1827, aged 52 years; one month, 19 days. Both are said to have been buried in the old cemetery in East Waynesburg, but markers have disappeared. James Hook, Jr., was equally prominent with his father and quite successful in business. It is apparent that men seeking to leave for the west, found him a ready buyer of their property from which he profited nicely. He was among the list of first owners of lots in the new Town of Waynesburg, and purchased other lots from original owners, among them being the "hotel corner," which he bought from Christian Fair. This lot he sold on May 29, 1814, to John Inghram, who then established the "Bulls Head Tavern" on the site. After the death of his father James Hook, Jr., bought on July 1, 1825, from Greenberry Ridgely Jones, and wife, Rebecca, 226 acres of land described as "being the tract of land on which Jackson's Fort formerly stood, adjacent to the Town of Waynesburg." Here James Hook, Jr., laid out a town which he called Perrysville, but later familiarly known as "Hookstown," the plot of which may be seen in Deed Book 13, page 387. The town extended roughly from the present Woodlawn Avenue to Porter Street, and was on both sides of Main Street. A number of lots were given to his children, including one on which there has been erected a tanyard, which he gave to his son, Benedict Hook. One lot on which a smith shop stood, adjoined lots sold to Barnet Adams. The old Jackson and Hathaway mill site became the property of his son, Jesse Hook. Tradition mentions a saw mill operated by James Hook, from which

timbers were donated to build a bridge at the foot of "town hill," the people of the town donating the labor to build it. Under the heading of James Hook, Sr., we have seen where the son had taken part in the establishment of "The Franklin School House," where it is probable that the children of James Hook, Jr., were educated.

Family of James and Charlotte (Morris) Hook

1. Sarah Hook, born October 28, 1796, died August 2, 1849; married, February 7, 1818, John Ganiear, born November 6, 1795, died September 1, 1852. It seems most certain that John Ganiear was a son of Peter Ganiear, (spelled Ganier) who is buried in the old cemetery in East Waynesburg, and whose marker shows he died September 17, 1859, at the age of 90 years. Records of the family are copied from a Family Bible owned by Mr. Wood Ganiear of Waynesburg, and from O. C. Docket 5. pp. 90.

Children of John and Sarah (Hook) Ganiear

1. Mary Anna Ganiear, born March 5, 1820.
2. Hannah Ganiear, born November 25, 1822, died October 14, 1863.
3. James H. Ganiear, born August 22, 1824, died February 14, 1864; married, July 8, 1846, Rebecca Johnson, born March 11, 1827, daughter of Nicholas and Sarah (Smalley) Johnson, and granddaughter of Jonas and Rebecca (Dwire) Smalley, natives of New Jersey. She died November 13, 1897.
4. Charlotte Ganiear, born February 17, 1825.
5. John Ganiear, born April 29, 1827, died June 9, 1858.
6. Ignatius Ganiear, born April 29, 1827 (twin) died.
7. Enos Ganiear, born April 25, 1829, died May 18, 1858, wife was Sarah ....
8. Sarah Jane Ganiear, born April 25, 1829 (twin).
9. Nancy Ganiear, born October 27, 1832, died July 26, 1854.
10. Israel Ganiear, born August 28, 1834, died December 22, 1862.
11. David M. Ganiear, born November 6, 1836, died April 11, 1861.
12. Leroy Ganiear, born June 1, 1838.

7. Samuel Hook.
8. Stephen Hook, ancestor of Mr. James W. Hook, born August 15, 1780, died in Perry County, Ohio, March 3, 1856; married (1) August 10, 1803, Anne Subah Grant, born in Connecticut, January 31, 1780, died in Greene County, Pennsylvania, October 8, 1816. He married (2) February 5, 1818, Margaret Bodkin, born July 15, 1791, died in 1842. He married (3) on November 17, 1846, Rebecca Glum. Six children were born to the first marriage and four by the second.

Children of Stephen Hook

1. Samuel Hook, born May 5, 1804, died July 27, 1873; married, November 2, 1826, Rebecca Carlisle, born May 5, 1796, died June 6, 1871. Family lived in Perry County, Ohio. Had sons, Israel and Samuel, and five daughters.
2. James Grant Hook, founder of the Hook family in Wapello County, Iowa; born September 7, 1805, died at Agency City, Iowa, September 4, 1884; married, March 6, 1828,

Sarah Lyle, born October 3, 1807, died August 4, 1882. Had sons, Stephen, William, Walter, James, John, Alexander, Thomas and Samuel, and daughters, Maryann, Sarah, Nancy and Martha.
3. Daniel Hook, born 1807, died July 17, 1880; married, 1836, Elizabeth Shuman, born June 4, 1811, died September 9, 1887. Lived in Perry County, Ohio, no issue.
4. Sylvanus Hook, born July 27, 1809, died May 14, 1862; married, 1836, Nancy Redmond. Lived in Vinton County, Ohio. No issue.
5. John Hook, born April 2, 1811, died January 24, 1887; married Lydia Shuman, born February 10, 1814, died October 31, 1906. Lived in Vinto County, Ohio. Had four daughters and one son, Barnett, who never married.
6. Stephen Hook, born February 2, 1813, died April 5, 1814.
7. Anna Subah Hook, born April 8, 1819; married, August 6, 1840, Hugh Lockhart. Lived in Perry County, Ohio.
8. Sarah Hook, born July 12, 1822; married, May 3, 1841, John S. Allwine.
9. Arthur Hook, born January 9, 1826, died September 18, 1827.
10. Enos Hook, born October 10, 1829, died April 8, 1842.

9. Daniel Hook, born June 11, 1781, died July 8, 1867; married September 8, 1808, Nancy Kent, born October 18, 1785, died May 14, 1872. She was a daughter of Thomas and Ann Rolston Kent.

Children of Daniel and Nancy (Kent) Hook

1. Son died in infancy.
2. Mary Hook, born June 22, 1815, died May 30, 1891; married Peter Kent, who died in 1852.

10. Thomas Hook. His wife was Mary Ann ....
11. Arthur Hook, born 1790. died January 20, 1820, married April 12, 1812, Catherine Kent, born February 8, 1787, died May 27, 1866. She was a daughter of Thomas and Ann (Rolston) Kent.

Children of Arthur and Catherine (Kent) Hook

1. Samuel Hook, born December 31, 1812, died November 13, 1897; married, April 18, 1839, Sarah Scott, born October 14, 1817, died October 18, 1903.
2. John T. Hook, born January 20, 1814, died November 3, 1883; married January 14, 1836, Eliza Inghram, born July 13, 1817, died May 4, 1901. She was a daughter of William and Sarah (Adams) Inghram.
3. James Hook, born July 8, 1815, died June 23, 1895, married Vienna Herring, born May 24, 1821, died April 24, 1897.
4. Thomas Hook, born November 20, 1816, died October 11, 1888. Thomas Hook was married twice, his second wife being Anna Conklin Greenfield, who died May 28, 1895.
5. Sarah Hook, born February 13, 1818, died at Jefferson, Pennsylvania, October 15, 1895. Married Job Ridgeway, born April 3, 1814.

With respect to John Snowden Hook, son of John and Sarah (Simpson) Hook, evidence clearly points to his continued residence in Frederick County, Maryland, moving to Cumberland, Maryland, about 1786. He died there in 1825, leaving a will. We are at loss to explain the name of a John Hook with Captain James Hook's Company on the Tenmile in the latter part of 1776. It is certain that John Snowden Hooke was enrolled August 8, 1776, by Lieutenant Clement Hollyday, along with William Carroll, James Weakley, Richard Sarjeant, Jr., and others, names that are associated with the Tenmile. But as enlistment periods were short, it could well be that John Snowden Hook enlisted with his brother's company, either while surveying the Tenmile Country for possible settlement, or at the time "The Calico Hunting Shirt Company" was in Cumberland on the way to join Washington's Army. (Maryland Archives Volume 18, pp. 49.) The appearance of John Hook in the tax list of Morgan Township in 1784, and in Franklin in 1788, is also not explained as no deeds appear to show the ownership or sale of property. At this later date, the taxable could also have been the son of Captain James Hook, though this is complicated with reported movements of the captain's son. Because of the lack of evidence it is unwise to suggest the possible relationship of the Tenmile Country John Hook.

JOHN JONES FAMILY

John Jones, one of the older settlers in the Ten Mile Country, was here as early as 1772. It has been stated that he owned land where Waynesburg is situated but there is no evidence available that any improvements were made prior to those of Thomas Slater in 1771. Since John Jones' date of arrival in Ten Mile Country coincides with the Inghrams and his land was close to theirs, we are inclined to feel that Waynesburg's present location was not the original settlement of John Jones. In view of the fact that he settled near, and at about the same time as the Smiths, Gorrells, Inghrams, Ankroms, Hooks, Cathers, Duvalls, Wells, and the Seals, who are known to have migrated from Maryland, it is more than likely that he also came from the same locality (near Elk Ridge, Md.) He served under Captain James Archer, Washington County, Pennsylvania Militia (Penna. Archives).

After Richard Jackson moved to Kentucky about 1790, the land which he owned, and on which had stood Fort Jackson, soon came into the hands of John Jones. On August 8, 1806, John Jones and his wife, Hannah, sold a part (154 perches) of this tract to Trustees of M. E. Church, James Eagon, Solomon Eagon, Greenbury Jones, Ami Moor, and Christian Fry. Jones was living on tract at the time (DB 2, p. 197, Greene County, Penna.) The Methodists later built a church on this property and at present it is the site of the Old Cemetery in East Waynesburg.

Greenbury Ridgely Jones, son of John, inherited the remainder of the tract of land at the time of his father's death in 1816. In 1825, Greenbury sold this property to James Hook, Jr., (D. B. 5, p. 383, Greene County, Penna.) In 1853, Hook laid out a plan of lots called Perrysville, commonly called Hookstown, bounded roughly by present Porter Street and Woodlawn Avenue.

John Jones was twice married, with no record of his first wife available, although it is certain that she was mother of children named in his will. Second wife was Hannah Wood, widow of Kent Mitchell. In 1776, Kent and Hannah Mitchell were living in Susquehanna Hundred, Anne Arundel County, Maryland, and were each 33 years of age. They had several children (Brumbaugh History). Kent Mitchell died here about 1786, and some time later Hannah married John Jones. Hannah Jones died September 19, 1823, aged

81 years, and was buried at Morrisville (Greene County, Penna., Tombstone still standing). The probabilities are excellent that the first wife of John Jones was a daughter of Greenbury (Greenberry) Ridgely of Maryland.

John Jones' will on file in Greene County, Penn., (W. B. 1, p. 177) was probated May 7, 1816. He named wife Hannah and the following children:
1. Cassandra.
2. Mary.
3. Sarah.
4. Elizabeth.
5. Martha.
6. Susannah.
7. Thomas (son of Thomas, deceased)
8. John, Jr.
9. Samuel.
10. Nancy.
11. Greenbury Ridgely.

The first six girls inherited a tract of 400 acres on Middle Island Creek, (Tyler County, West Virginia). To grandson Thomas, he willed tract "Beach Bottom" in Brooke County, Virginia, while John, Jr., received an adjoining tract in Brooke County, Virginia. Samuel and Nancy inherited land in Morgan Township, Greene County, Pennsylvania. Greenbury inherited remainder of tract originally purchased from Richard Jackson.

It has been reported that Mary became wife of Elijah Fee, but we know only that Sarah married James Crawford and she died in Jefferson County, Ohio.

Greenbury Ridgely Jones married Rebecca Connell, daughter of the founder of Connellsville, Pennsylvania, on May 29, 1804, and they later moved to Ohio.

BENJAMIN LAKIN MANUSCRIPT

Through the courtesy of Mr. James W. Hook, we are privileged to print the text of a paper written in 1847, by Reverend Benjamin Lakin (1767-1849) for his nephew, John Lakin. The original paper has been lost but many copies were made for various members of the family, thus it can be accepted as authentic. Benjamin Lakin was born in what is now Montgomery County, Maryland, August 23, 1767, and died February 5, 1849. He married Elizabeth Ray of Kentucky, but had no children. He was a noted pioneer minister of the Methodist Society, and was out on the frontiers as far as Indiana as early as 1803. He was a son of Benjamin and Rachel (Fee) Lakin, and grandson of Abraham and Martha (Lee) Lakin. It can be seen from this record that he could have been well acquainted with many of the settlers of the Tenmile Country, especially the many members of his own kinfolk that settled about Fort Jackson. This paper "written in my 80th year" attests to the keenness of memory of this man, and the intimate knowledge of his kith and kin. Of those names mentioned in the paper, it is easy to recognize as pioneers of the Tenmile Country, the Lakins, Fees, Aldridges, Ankroms, Wells, Slaters, Archers, Bradfords, Owenses, and James Hook and Richard Jackson. The paper reads as follows:

"I have here given the genealogy of our family and connections, as far as I can attain to the family of the Lakins, they come from England and are perhaps of the Saxon stock, as I find in Mr. Wesley's Journal, he mentions coming to a place called 'Lakin's Heath.' The Fees, I think, are either from England or Wales.

"The Lakins sprang from Abraham and Martha Lakin. Their sons were Abraham, Joseph, and Benjamin. They had some daughters but I know not their names;—one of them was married to a man by the name of Leith, from whom, on the mothers side, the younger family of the Fees sprang.

"Abraham had two sons; Daniel and Abraham. I know not whether he had any other children. They lived in Frederick County, Maryland. What their posterity is I know not.

"Joseph was married to Elizabeth Fee. They lived in Frederick County, Maryland. They had three children—John, Samuel, and Mary. I know not whom John married. He had no children. Samuel married Sarah Musgrove, and Mary married John Aldridge. These with their father moved to Ohio. You know their families and if you see cause you can trace them up.

"Benjamin Lakin, the youngest son of Abraham and Martha, was born March 29, 1739, and was married October 23, 1760, to Rachel Fee, daughter of George and Parnel Fee. Rachel was born April 11, 1739, and died December 30, 1811. Benjamin Lakin died April 6, 1776. They had a son named William, and a daughter, Elizabeth, who died in childhood.

"The following were their other children: Thomas, John, Benjamin, Joseph, James, and Rachel, their sister. Thomas married Priscilla Sullivan, moved from Montgomery County, Maryland, where my father lived and died and settled in Beans Cove, Bedford County, Pennsylvania, where he raised a large family, and afterwards with some of his children, moved and settled in Harrison County, Ohio, where he died some years since.

"John Lakin married Elizabeth, the daughter of John and Martha Ankrom, they had besides Elizabeth:—Deborra, Sarah, and Martha, and two sons, Richard and William. If there were any others I have forgotten them. Martha Ankrom's maiden name was Wells, sister of Thomas and William Wells, who lived on Middle Island. John and Elizabeth's children were:—William, Martha, John, Rachel, Benjamin, and Elizabeth. You can trace your brothers and sisters children.

"Joseph Lakin married Mary Slater, by whom he had children:—Thomas, Eleanor, Benjamin, John, and James. This first wife died, and he married the second time Margaret Simmons, by whom he had Joseph, Leonard, William, Wesley, and daughters, Mary, Rachel, Margaret, and Elizabeth.

"All my brothers and sisters are gone, and I am left alone in my 80th years, and how soon I shall go I know not.

"Our maternal line commences in George and Parnell Fee. As far as I know they had one son and two daughters:—Thomas, Rachel, and Elizabeth. Of the daughters I have already spoken. Thomas was twice married. His first wife was a Thrasher, by whom he had children:—George and John and Mary and Ruth. George married an Archer, John married Elizabeth Bradford, and Mary married Richard Jackson, the proprietor of Jackson's Fort on Tenmile Creek. Ruth married an Owens. Thomas Fee's second wife was Sarah Leith, a niece of my father, by whom the family of Fees on this side of the Ohio came. Mary Leith, a sister of Sarah, was married to James Hook, the father of John Hook. They had a large family.

"I have given you as much as I can recollect of our family."

THE LAKIN FAMILY

Before we start into the Lakin Family, proper credit must be given to Mr. James W. Hook of New Haven, 6, Conn., for a considerable amount of the following material on the Lakin and Fee Families.

As the story goes, two brothers, Joseph and Abraham Lakin, came to this country from "Lakin's Heath" in northern England and landed prior to, or near, 1700, at Baltimore, Maryland. Joseph was granted land in Maryland in 1683, and Abraham was granted land in 1729, in Prince George's County, Maryland. In 1743, Abraham was granted a tract called "Two Brothers" in present Frederick County, Maryland.

Abraham Lakin lived in Prince George's County, Maryland. (Name written Laking or Leakin). He married Martha Lee, October 10, 1717, a daughter of William and Ann Lee of the same County. His will dated November 25, 1744 (Liber No. 1, f. 342, Upper Marlboro, Md.) mentions wife Martha and ten children, but only sons, Abraham, Joseph and Benjamin are named. Abraham Lakin died before August 28, 1745 (Guardian Bonds 1708, p. 142, Upper Marlboro, Md.) Children were named as follows:

Children of Abraham and Martha Lee Lakin

1. Sarah Lakin, married Robert Lyeth (Leith).
    1. Mary Lyeth, born 1743, died January 30, 1815; married James Hook, born 1749, died January 24, 1824, in Waynesburg, Pennsylvania. (See Hook Family for children.)
    2. Sarah Lyeth married widower Thomas Fee, son of George and Parnell Fee. (See Fee Family for children).
2. Abraham Lakin, Jr., born October 16, 1722, married Sarah Hook (tradition) born May 18, 1724. Lived in Frederick County, Maryland, on portion of tract "Two Brothers" which he inherited, along with brother, Joseph, from Abraham, Sr. The tract of land adjoined the tract called the "John and Sarah" owned by John Hook. They had the following children:
    1. Eleanor, born January 29, 1745.
    2. Deborra, born December 5, 1746.
    3. Benjamin, born December 21, 1748.
    4. John, born December 28, 1750.
    5. Sarah, born April 28, 1755, married Richard Duckett Wells.
    6. Abraham, born December 29, 1757, married, July 18, 1788, Mary Ungleby.
    7. Daniel, born January 20, 1759, married Ann Sheckels, January 30, 1787.
    8. Nancy, born September 27, 1762, married Abraham Deaver, June 25, 1778.
3. Martha Lakin, married .... Plummer.
4. Joseph Lakin, married Elizabeth .... (probably a daughter of George and Parnell Fee), lived in Frederick County, Maryland and they later moved to Ohio.
    1. John.
    2. Samuel.
    3. Mary, married John Aldridge.
5. Deborra Lakin.
6. Elizabeth Lakin.
7. Mary Lakin.
8. Rachel Lakin.
9. Ruth Lakin.
10. Benjamin Lakin, born March 29, 1739, died April 6, 1776; married, October 23, 1763, Rachel Fee, who was born April 11,

1739, died December 20, 1811. She was a daughter of George and Parnell Fee. They lived on land willed to Benjamin by his father, and which was situated in what is now Montgomery County, Maryland.

Children of Benjamin and Rachel Fee Lakin

1. William Lakin, died young.
2. Elizabeth Lakin, died young.
3. Thomas Lakin, born March 26, 1763, died February 23, 1835. He married Priscilla Sullivan, January 15, 1782. Priscilla was born April 8, 1757, and died in 1833. She was a daughter of Daniel and Mary (Lovejoy) Sullivan who lived in Montgomery County, Maryland. Thomas and Priscilla Lakin moved from Montgomery County, Maryland, and settled in Bedford County, Pennsylvania, and later moved to Harrison County, Ohio, where both died. Thomas Lakin was an itinerant Methodist preacher.

Children of Thomas and Priscilla Sullivan Lakin

1. Mary Lakin, born October 11, 1782, died 1824; married Archibald Blair.
2. Elizabeth Lakin, born August 4, 1785, died 1854; married William Barthalow. Family lived at New Philadelphia, Ohio.
3. Daniel Lakin, born July 16, 1786, died 1854, married Theodasia Shreve. Family lived at Rushville, Ohio.
4. Thomas Lakin, born November 5, 1790; married (1) Elizabeth Long of Hampshire County, Virginia. Married (2) Margaret Slate.
5. William Lakin, born January 2, 1791, died at Freeport, Ohio, March 7, 1855; married, (1) Sarah Chapman, at Flintstone, Maryland. Married (2) January 11, 1836, Lewessa Packer. There were four children born to the first marriage and eight to the second.
6. Anna Lakin, born August 4, 1792; married, April 4, 1815, Moses Wright, in Bedford County, Pennsylvania. Later lived in Freeport, Ohio.
7. Rebecca Lakin, born November 14, 1794; married Benjamin Robertson of Allegheny County, Maryland. Removed to Tennessee.
8. Benjamin Lakin, born January 16, 1796, died 1821; married Rebecca Blair.
9. John Wesley Lakin, born April 7, 1798, died 1862 in Cumberland, Maryland; married, 1823, Eletha Willison of Flintstone, Maryland.
10. Moses Lakin, born about 1800; married, February 15, 1842, Jane Dryden of Harrison County, Ohio.

4. John Lakin, born February 1765, married Elizabeth daughter of John and Martha Wells Ankrom. Family lived in Greene County, Pennsylvania.
5. Benjamin Lakin, born in Montgomery County, Maryland, August 23, 1767, died February 5, 1849; married Elizabeth Ray of Kentucky. No issue. He was the author of the Benjamin Lakin Manuscript (see same) and was a Methodist minister.
6. Joseph Lakin, born 1769, lived in Greene County, Pennsylvania; married (1) Mary Slater and had Thomas, Eleanor, Benjamin, John and James. He married (2)

Margaret Simmons and had the following children: Joseph, William, Wesley, Mary, Rachel, Margaret, and Elizabeth.
7. James Lakin, born 1771.
8. Rachel Lakin, born 1773.

THE FEE FAMILY

Apparently the Fee family were Scotch people who moved to Ireland (County Fermanaugh) about 1600. George Fee arrived in Baltimore, Maryland, about 1725, and settled for a time in Maryland and later moved to Pennsylvania, near present Brownsville, Pennsylvania. His wife was Parnell ....

Children of George and Parnell Fee

1. Elizabeth Fee, married Joseph Lakin.
2. Rachel Fee, married Benjamin Lakin, October 23, 1763 (See Lakin Family).
3. Thomas Fee, born in Maryland, and died near Moscow, Ohio, in 1816. He moved to Pennsylvania near Old Fort Redstone. In 1793, he moved to Mason County, Kentucky, and in 1795, to Smith's Landing, Clermont County, Ohio. Sons George and John, remained in Kentucky. Thomas Fee was twice married. His first wife was .... Thrasher and his second wife was Sarah Leith, daughter of Robert and Sarah Lakin Leith.

Children of Thomas and .... Thrasher Fee

1. George Fee, married .... Archer (Mary or Nancy). Lived in Greene County, Pennsylvania, for a time and owned land on South Fork of the Ten Mile which he sold to Vincent Brown in 1790, (Washington County, Penna., D. B. 1, p. 399). He later moved to Kentucky, probably Mason County.
2. John Fee, born March 13, 1757, married Elizabeth Bradford, daughter of Robert Bradford of Greene County, Pennsylvania. John was patentee of land in Greene County, but later moved to Bracken County, Kentucky, where he was a neighbor of Thomas, William, and Dinah Bradford. Dinah Brandford married Thomas Hevrin. All are mentioned in the will of Robert Bradford of Greene County, Pennsylvania. The will of John Fee (Bracken County, Kentucky, W. B. B., p. 281, filed November 5, 1822) mentions son James and three daughters, although he was supposed to have had nine children. It is known that he had a son John, born March 18, 1792, who was the fourth of nine children, and who married Sarah Gregg There son, John Gregg Fee, was founder of Berea College in Kentucky, in 1855. (Dict. Am. Biog. Vol. 6, p. 310). The other children of John and Elizabeth Fee are not known.
3. Mary Fee, married Richard Jackson, founder of Fort Jackson within present limits of Waynesburg, Pennsylvania. The Jacksons moved to Bracken County, Kentucky, where Richard died in 1793, and his brother-in-law, John Fee, was administrator to the estate. In his will Richard

left money for the education of his children, but they were not named.
4. Ruth Fee, married .... Owens.

Children of Thomas and Sarah (Leith) Fee

1. Thomas Fee, married Nancy Cathers. He died in Clermont County, Ohio (Will Rcd. D. p. 161-1831, will dated October 1, 1827). Witnesses to will were Samuel Buchannon, Daniel Fee and Robert Fee.
   1. Margaret Fee, married John (?) Buchannon.
   2. Sarah Fee, married .... Gregg.
   3. Elizabeth Fee, married .... Hopkins.
   4. Nancy Ann Fee.
   5. Robert Fee, eldest son.
   6. Enos Fee, youngest son.
   7. Thomas Fee, married Helen .... and lived near Moscow, Clermont County, Ohio. (Will dated May 5, 1861) named wife Helen and his brother Enos as Executor. No children were named.
2. William Fee, born December 13, 1768, married Margaret Inghram, who died February 18, 1827, and who was probably the daughter of William Inghram, Sr., of present Greene County, Pennsylvania. His second wife was Mrs. Mary Sargent Prather (Clermont County, Ohio). He was a member of the Legislature, 1803 and 1804, and was twice a member of state senate. He had at least one daughter, who in 1815, gave the name of Felicity to a town in Ohio. He had one son, Arthur Fee, born 1791, at Felicity, Ohio, who married Sarah Miller.
3. James Fee, married .... Lakin.
4. Samuel Fee, married .... Thrasher.
5. Elias Fee, married .... McCary.
6. Elijah Fee, married .... Jones, probably a daughter of John Jones who was from Greene County, Pennsylvania.
7. Elisha Fee, married .... Brown.
8. Jesse Fee, married Martha Kelly.
9. Rachel Fee.
10. Sarah Fee.

THE ARCHER FAMILY

The Archer Family settled East of Fort Jackson about 1774, taking up land in the vicinity of the old double bridge at Morrisville. William Rhodes, who conducted a trading post in Fort Jackson, made note in his Journal that they were the first Roman Catholic Family to settle in the neighborhood. He says that they were a family of roving hunters and that Captain James Archer was the first to come here. He went back over the mountains and convinced his father to come out with him. Patrick Archer, the father, brought out his whole family, consisting of five sons and three daughters, all of whom are named by Mr. Rhodes, who also says that when game got scarce and forting was no longer necessary, the Archers moved further West. However, during the troublesome days the Archers played an important part in the defense of the Frontier, with at least one son giving his life in the struggle against the Indians. The children of Patrick Archer were: James, Joseph, Michael, Simon, Betsy, Polly, and Nancy.

Captain James Archer

The pension application of David White states that he served in Captain David Owens' Company of Frontier Rangers in 1776, when John Boggs was the lieutenant and James Archer was the ensign. When Owens was dismissed, James Archer succeeded him as the captain, and he proved to be a fearless commander and an implacable foe of the Redskins. This may have brought about the destruction of a part of his family at the time of the massacre of his father-in-law, Robert McClelland's Family near the double bridge. The will of Robert McClelland makes a provision for his grandchildren, Jane and Elizabeth Archer, children of James Archer. (Washington County Will Book 1, pp. 140.) This accounts for the story told by Waychoff of James Archer's desire to follow the perpetrators of the Robert McClelland massacre. William Harrod, Jr., tells of the incident and says that Archer and McClelland lived in the same house when the Indians struck, and that several members of both families were killed. James Archer became possessed of a tract of land near the site of the present Airport, but about 1792, he was joined by his wife, Sophia, in sale of the property to William Rhodes. At this time they are described as being of Ohio County, Virginia. Investigation has shown that this was in the part of Ohio County which later went to form Brooke County.

Joseph Archer, son of Patrick, is described by Waychoff as "quite a character" and relates several tales of his escapades. He warranted the tract of land at the mouth of Laurel Run on February 17, 1780, under the title of "Mamon" but before the patent was issued, traded this site with Henry Huffman for a tract called "Huffman's Mistake" on Pursley Creek. Joseph Archer married Margaret, daughter of George and Jane Church. The History of Knox County, Ohio, tells of the last Indian raid in that County about 1811, in which James Copus, a brother-in-law of Joseph Archer, was killed by the Indians. It further relates that Joseph Archer, who was at that time living in Guernsey County, Ohio, came to Knox County, and got his wife's sister, who had become a widow by this episode, and several of her children and took them back with him until all danger had passed. Investigation at Cambridge, Ohio, indicates that soon after this Joseph Archer departed from Guernsey County for other parts of the country. Joseph Archer was a member of his brother, Captain John Archer's Militia Company. (Penna. Arch. Series VI. Vol. 2. pp. 18.)

MICHAEL ARCHER FAMILY

Michael Archer, son of Patrick Archer, was frequently named as a Frontier Ranger. He was also a member of his brother, James Archer's Militia Company. (Penna. Arch. Series VI. Vol 2. pp 18.) He was also a companion of Captain William Harrod on many of his scouting parties, and was on his way to join this captain, when he was ambushed on Fishing Creek in 1787. Captain Harrod's men later recovered the body of Michael Archer, and reported from the evidence they found, reconstructed the fight which must have taken place. Archer's body was badly scratched and many bones broken, while in his hands he clutched hair taken from the heads of his slayers. His wife was Elizabeth Wells, who went to live with her brothers and later followed them to Tyler County, West Virginia. Her brother, William Wells, died without issue, and a portion of his estate went to Elizabeth Archer and her son, Joseph. (Tyler County Will Book 1-A. pp. 325, probated January 2, 1835.) The Census of 1790, taken shortly after the death of Michael Archer, lists Elizabeth Archer with but one child.

Child of Michael and Elizabeth (Wells) Archer

1. Joseph Archer, died in Tyler County, West Virginia, leaving a will he made on May 23, 1855. It named his wife Sarah ...., and was probated during the August Court of the same year. (Will Book 2. pp. 166.)

Children of Joseph and Sarah Archer

1. Elizabeth Archer, married .... Gorrell.
2. William Archer, married, March 28, 1828, Mary Gorrell.
3. Sarah Archer, maried .... McKay.
4. Matha Archer, married August 18, 1844, Jacob Carroll.
5. Eliza Archer, married, January 8, 1835, Arthur Ankrom.
6. Rachel Archer, married, July 2, 1840, William Kellar.
7. Lucretia Archer, married, June 17, 1851, Milton Tallman.
8. Esther Archer.
9. Neil Archer, married, December 15, 1840, Mary Ann Cookus.
10. Arthur Archer, married, October 29, 1846, Nancy Tallman.

SIMON ARCHER

Simon Archer, son of Patrick, was also a member of his brother, James Archer's Militia Company. It is an error that reports him killed by the Indian, as he was living as late as 1797, when he joined in a deed to Thomas Stokely. His wife was probably Nancy Church, whose mother left a will in which she mentioned her daughter as Nancy Archer.

JACOB ARCHER

There is no military service noted for Jacob Archer, son of Patrick Archer. In the Census for 1790, he is listed as head of a family that had one male over 16 years, two males under 16 years, and two females.

ELIZABETH ARCHER

Elizabeth (Bett or Betsy) Archer, daughter of Patrick Archer, was probably the wife of William Wells, who joined him in a deed in Greene County. This interpretation is arrived at by interpretation of the will of William Wells, who made a bequest to his niece, Mary Thomas, a daughter of J. E. Archer.

POLLY ARCHER and NANCY ARCHER

Polly Archer or her sister Nancy Archer, daughters of Patrick Archer, was the wife of George Fee, son of Thomas Fee and his first wife, ... Thrasher. George Fee also served in Captain James Archer's Company. He went to Bracken County, Kentucky.

THE ANKROM FAMILY

The Ankrom Family (also spelled Ancrum, Ancrom, Ankrim, etc.) of the Tenmile Country, are descended from one Richard Ankrom of Frederick County, Maryland, where at an early date he and George Fee, ancestor of the Tenmile Fee Family, joined in buying land from John Hawkins. (BB 3. pp. 57ᶜ Annapolis Land Office.) While living in Frederick County, Richard Ankrom made his will on November 29, 1790, which was probated February 8, 1794, in which he named his sons, Richard Ankrom, Jacob Ankrom, Aron Ankrom, and John Ankrom. He says his son, John Ankrom, is deceased, and leaves that share in the estate to two sons of John Ankrom, namely: Richard and William Ankrom. He also mentioned granddaughters, Nancy and Sarah Delashmutt. Richard Ankrom's wife was Elizabeth .... (Frederick County, Maryland Will Book 2. pp. 507.)

When Elizabeth Ankrom, widow of Richard, died she also left a will, which she had made on August 24, 1796, and which was probated November 20, of the same year. In addition to naming the same sons as heirs, with John Ankrom deceased leaving children, she mentions the children of Mary Delashmutt, apparently a daughter and mother of the two girls mentioned in the will of Richard Ankrom. She also gave a portion of her estate to Elizabeth Thrasher, another daughter and probably the wife of John Thrasher, warrantee of a tract of land on Tenmile but one farm removed from the deceased John Ankrom. This tract called "Chance," warranted to John Thrasher May 7, 1785, by virtue of a Virginia Certificate, was patented to him on February 26, 1788. (Frederick County Will Book 3. pp. 149.)

It seems probable that another son William Ankrom, not mentioned by these two wills, but named one of the executors of John Ankrom's Will in Washingon County, Pennsylvania, made in 1782, had also died before the parents, probably without issue.

THE ANKROM FAMILY OF TENMILE

This Maryland family of English extration was represented on the Tenmile prior to 1776 at which time John Ankrom maintained a fort, perhaps one of the stronger kind, since it was being used in 1777 as a rendezvous for the Frontier Rangers under Colonel William Crawford. It is described in pension records as being four or five miles from Fort Jackson, and was certainly on the tract of land warranted to John Ankrom under the title "Pocket Money" on February 22, 1788, and was located to the east of the Mouth of Coal Lick on land still owned by the Ankroms. Joseph Archer had an adjoining tract and John Thrasher lived to the west of them. All three men were members of Captain James Archer's Militia Company. James Pribble says he was stationed here in 1777 and several subsequent years under Captain Jess Pigman and frequently met men of Archer's Company on his patrols. Soon after getting the warrant for the land in 1788, John Ankrom died leaving a will with his brother, William Ankrom, and his brother-in-law, William Wells, as executors of his estate and guardian of his children. William Ankrom refused to act, "Letters Testamentary dated May 21, 1789, were duly granted to said William Wells"—(Land Office Grants, Harrisburg, Pennnsylvania.) William Wells then secured the patent for the land as the Adminstrator of the estate and later went to the heirs of John Ankrom. The will states that Thomas

Wells was living on John Ankrom's land at the time of the writing, November 2, 1782.

In addition to John Ankrom, son of Richard and Elizabeth Ankrom of Frederick County, Maryland, a brother, Richard Ankrom, also settled on the Tenmile, but a few miles west of Fort Jackson, taking titles to several tracts of land, including "The Square" on Purseley Creek and "Newburn" and "Emsworth" between Purseley and Smith Creeks. From the sale of this land we know that he and wife, Ruth ...., went to Tyler County, (West) Virginia, where Richard Ankrom died in 1828. (Greene County Deed Book 3, pp. 605.)

After service in the Revolution while living in Maryland, Jacob Duckett Ankrom, another brother of John Ankrom, went to Tyler County about 1784. His tombstone says he was born in 1752, the son of Richard Ankrom, Sr. The presence of the "Duckett" name and the similarity of surnames, along with the many intermarriages with the Wells family, supports this belief of relationship as clearly as it points to the original location of the family in Maryland, where we find the Ducketts, Wells, Duvall, and other close neighbors of the Ankroms on the Tenmile.

Tyler County deeds, Wills, Marriages, etc. show that the family moved to that location early, in some cases before they had sold their Greene County tracts, early enough to give their name to settlements, creeks, etc. From the numerous descendants still living there, we have received much help in uncovering the relationships and descendants of this pioneer family.

Family of John Ankrom

John Ankrom served in Captain John Archer's Washington County Militia Company in 1782. His wife was Martha Wells, and is identified as such since John Ankrom made his brother-in-law, William Wells, one of the Administrators of his estate. She was further identified by William Wells in his will filed in Tyler County, West Virginia, on January 2, 1835, in which he names his sister, Martha Ankrom, as one of his heirs. She remained a widow.

There is considerable confusion about the families of John and Martha Ankrom.

He made his will on November 2, 1782, but it is known that he was in the Cumberland Township, Washington County, Tax List for 1784, when he refused to turn in his property for tax purposes, claiming under Virginia law. He also received land warrant from Pennsylvania in 1788, and in same year was taxed in Franklin Township, Washington County.

His will was probated February 1, 1789, so that he died between the fall of 1788 and the spring of 1789. His will named wife Martha, sons, Richard Duckett, and William, and an unborn child and is on file in Washington County, Pennsylvania. (Will Record 1, p. 97; File A-8-1789) Orphan's Court records show no appointment of guardian for the children.

The Benjamin Lakin Mss. states definitely that children of John and Martha, Ankrom were Elizabeth, who married John Lakin, Debora, Sarah, Martha, Richard, and William. On this basis and fact that nearly seven years expired between date of John Ankrom's will and his death we feel that children as named by Benjamin Lakin are correct.

Children of John and Martha (Wells) Ankrom

1. Richard Duckett (Ducat) Ankrom. The William Rhodes Papers says he married Nancy Rinehart on January 3, 1798.

She was a daughter of Thomas and Hannah (Inghram) Rinehart. She seems to have died before 1822, for on February 10, 1822, Richard D. Ankrom sold land in Greene County to John and Thomas Ankrom and is not joined by his wife in the deed. (DB. 4, pp. 704).

Children
1. John Ankrom, to whom he deeded land.
2. Joseph Ankrom, born 1807, married Charlotte Rinehart, daughter of Barnet and Ruth (Styles) Rinehart.
3. Thomas Ankrom, also received land by deed from Richard Duckett Ankrom. He married a daughter of Barnet Eagon.
4. Agnes Ankrom, married .... Thomas.
5. Sarah Ankrom, married Jacob Thomas.
6. Amanda Ankrom, married .... Wells.

2. William Ankrom, son of John and Martha (Wells) Ankrom, married Mary Eagon, eldest daughter of Solomon and Mary (Blackburn) Eagon. A number of letters in the papers of Daniel Bonar's estate, show that this family removed to Pickaway County, Ohio, soon after they had sold their land in Greene County, Pennsylvania, to Samuel Luse. (Greene County Deed Book 5. pp. 551.) These old letters show some of the grandchildren of William and Mary Ankrom, living in Allensville and Circleville, Ohio, in 1860, and are addressed to Uncle Dan and Aunt Sally, and give interesting accounts of their families, naming many of the descendants.

Children
1. William Ankrom, a letter from him in Ohio, dated March 18, 1847.
2. Sally Ankrom, born June 10, 1807, died December 23, 1891; married Daniel Bona, born August 1, 1797, died November 6, 1869, at Waynesburg, Pennsylvania.
3. John Ankrom, a blind man living in Ohio in 1860.
4. Solomon Ankrom, in Ohio in 1860.
5. Richard Ankrom, a letter from him shows he lived at Allensville, Ohio, on February 6, 1860. His wife was Elizabeth ...., and he names the following children:
   1. Sampson Ankrom.
   2. Mary Jane Ankrom, married, June 6, 1859, James Scott.
   3. Thomas Ankrom.
   4. John Ankrom.
   5. Joseph Ankrom.
   6. Elizabeth Ankrom.
   7. Daniel Ankrom.
   8. Solomon Ankrom.
   9. Angeline Ankrom.
   10. Ivy Hulda Ankrom.
6. Thomas Ankrom.
7. Elizabeth Ankrom.
8. Sampson Ankrom.
9. Martha Ankrom.
10. Clementine Ankrom.
11. Uriah Ankrom.

3. Martha Ankrom, born between 1782-1789, married, December 20, 1804, according to the Rhodes Papers, Thomas Inghram, son of William and Agnes (Fee) Inghram. She is named as one of the heirs of her uncle, William Wells, in his will of

January 2, 1835, in Tyler County. They sold land in Greene County on April 3, 1820, to Thomas Kent. (Deed Book 5. pp. 72.) She died November 4, 1857. Thomas Inghram's will was made in Tyler County, West Virginia, April 4, 1842, and is filed in Will Book 2. pp. 125, where it was probated on November 4, 1850.

Children of Thomas and Martha (Ankrom) Inghram
1. Matilda Inghram, married Duckett Wells.
2. Mahala Inghram, married John J. Ingle
3. Martha Inghram, married, April 7, 1821, Van B. Delashmunt?
4. Elizabeth Inghram, married, October 4, 1821, James Steeley.

4. Elizabeth Ankrom, married John Lakin.
5. Sarah Ankrom, married Arthur Inghram.
6. Deborra Ankrom.

FAMILY OF RICHARD AND RUTH ANKROM

Richard Ankrom owned several tracts of land on Pursley and Smith Creeks, including "The Square," "Emsworth," and "Newburn," which he had patented to him. In the deed for the sale of "The Square" on Pursley Creek in 1816, he and wife, Ruth, are described as of Ohio County, Virginia, or what later became Tyler County, West Virginia. (DB. 3-605.) They sold to John Burkhamer. On March 3, 1802, they sold "Emsworth" to Elizabeth Cree. When he died in Tyler County, he mentions only his son, John, by name, giving him the home place, stating he had already taken care of the other children, whose names are not listed.
1. Rachel Ankrom, who, on September ......, 1797, married William Duvall, was probably one of his daughters.
2. John Ankrom.
3. Joseph Ankrom?

FAMILY OF JACOB DUCKETT ANKROM

Jacob Duckett Ankrom, son of Richard Ankrom, Sr., was born in 1752, according to his tombstone, and died in Tyler County, West Virginia, where his will was probated in March 1824. His wife's name was Nancy .... He served in the Revolution, going to Tyler County, then a part of Ohio County, Virginia, in 1784.

Children Named in Will
1. William Ankrom.
2. Richard Ankrom.
3. Jacob Ankrom, Jr.
4. Mary Ankrom.
5. Elizabeth Ankrom.
6. Delilah Ankrom.
7. Margaret Ankrom, married, October 2, 1821, William Wells.
8. Rachel Ankrom.
9. Julian Ankrom.
10. Cassa Ankrom, married, February 11, 1819, John Bowman.

THE WELLS FAMILY

There is a wealth of evidence to show that one branch of the Wells Family was on the Tenmile as early as 1776. Pension records, muster rolls, estates, wills, deeds, account books, etc., mention various members of an integrated family of brothers and sisters of this name. Only a single clue 'ɔ found to indicate the head of this family, and this clue is not conclusive nor altogether acceptable evidence. It is the petition for the new State of "Westsylvania" which names a Thomas Wells, Sr., followed by a Thomas Wells, Jr., and a number of the neighbors correctly found on the Tenmile, where the Wells Family is known to have resided. As this petition was made to the Continental Congress in the period of 1779-1781, if the genuineness of the signers ɪ ames is accepted, then Thomas Wells, Sr., would have been the head of this family, which for clearness we have designated the "Tenmile" Wells Family to distinguish it from the Cross Creek and other families of the same name.

There can be no doubt, however, about the origin of the family, which is shown by pension applications to have been the Valley of the Conochacheague in Frederick County, Maryland. It is also clear that the family was closely connected with the important Duckett Family of Prince George's County, Maryland, probably through Jacob Duckett, who removed to Frederick County, Maryland, where he died in the Summer of 1764. Jacob Duckett's will, made June 3, 1764, was probated at Frederick, Maryland, on August 24, 1764, and names his wife Sarah ...., with children as follows: Ann Duckett, wife of William Boteler (or Butler); Thomas Duckett, Jacob Duckett, Joseph Duckett, Richard Duckett, Josiah Duckett, Margaret Duckett, Mary Duckett, Elizabeth Duckett, and Charity Duckett. (Frederick C ɪnty, Maryland Will Book 2. pp 221.) This name has been carried down through both the Wells and Ankrom Family, proving a connection as yet not disclosed.

Finally it can be clearly shown that these members of the Wells Family all lived on the Tenmile near the mouth of Coal Lick for some time during the Revolution. Their migration from this section took place about 1800, with most or all of them settling in Tyler County, (West) Virginia. Except for William Wells, none of them seem to have owned land here, and his transactions seem to have been limited to his capacity as executor for his brother-in-law, John Ankrom.

THE WELLS FAMILY OF TENMILE

1. Thomas Wells, his pension application from Tyler County, (West) Virginia, dated January 8, 1834, says he was born in the Conochacheague Valley in Maryland, in October 1751. He also said that while living in Pennsylvania, he enlisted at Fort Jackson on Tenmile Creek on April 1, 1776, and served as an orderly Sergeant in Captain Jesse Pigman's Company of Indian Spies under Colonel McFarland. His service included tours of duty in the Spring, Summer, and Fall until October 1783. His pension was not granted. (Nat. Arch. R.-11,318.)
2. William Wells, executor for John Ankrom's estate, with wife Elizabeth (Archer ?) Ankrom he made a deed in Greene County on April 16, 1811. (Deed Book 2. pp. 601.) William Wells served in Captain James Archer's Militia Company. He went to Tyler County, (West) Virginia, where he died about

1835, apparently without heirs. His will was probated at Middlebourne, January 2, 1835. (Tyler County Will Book 1-A.pp. 325.) In his will he gave his estate to his sisters, Martha Ankrom and Elizabeth Archer, and a number of nieces and nephews, naming Rachel Wells, Martha Inghram, Joseph Archer, Martha McKay, Mary Thomas, and Elizabeth Rice. Niece Mary Thomas is listed as a daughter of J. E. Archer.
3. Martha Wells, wife of John Ankrom, see Ankrom Family record.
4. Elizabeth Wells, widow of Michael Archer. Her husband had been killed on Fishing Creek in a fight with the Indians, which was described by William Harrod, Jr., in his interview with L. C. Draper.

Child

1. Joseph Archer, born 1781, made a will in Tyler County, May 23, 1855, which was probated in August of that year. (Will Book 2. pp. 166.) His wife, Sarah ...., was born in Maryland in 1784.

Children (See Michael Archer Record)

1. Elizabeth Archer, wife of John Gorrell.
2. William Archer, married Mary Gorrell.
3. Sarah Archer, married .... McKay.
4. Martha Archer, married Jacob Carroll.
5. Eliza Archer, married Arthur Ankrom.
6. Rachel Archer, wife of William Kellar.
7. Lucretia Archer, born 1827, married Milton Tallman.
8. Esther Archer.
9. Neil Archer, married Mary A. Cookus.
10. Arthur Archer, married Nancy Tallman.

5. Richard Duckett Wells. The pension application of this man (Nat. Arch. Md. W. 4380) as it is reported in the "West Virginia Quarterly Magazine" Vol. 3. No. 1. of October 1946, says he was born in Frederick County, Maryland, March 22, 1752, where he still resided at the beginning of the Revolution. He enlisted in 1776, under Captain Frazure White in the Regiment commanded by Colonel Johnson. After this service he removed to Greene County in Pennsylvania, in 1778-89 (another record says 1798-99) and then moved to Tyler County in 1800. His service record was supported by affidavits by Thomas Jones, William Wells, and Thomas Weekley. Richard Duckett Wells married, on January 20, 1774, Sarah Lakin, born April 28, 1755, who died in Tyler County on February 17, 1843.

Children

1. Nancy Wells, born July 15, 1776.
2. William Wells, born July 15, 1776.
3. Abraham Wells, born July 20, 1778.
4. David Wells, born March 8, 1780.
5. Thomas Duckett Wells, born April 11, 1782.
6. Sarah Wells, born April 22, 1784.
7. Deborra Wells, born July 23, 1786.
8. Richard Duckett Wells, born October 16, 1788, died 1816.
9. Otha Wells, born July 18, 1790, married, October 21, 1817, Julyann ....
10. Mary Wells, born September 22, 1792.
11. Elizabeth Wells, born May 29, 1797, died 1826.
12. Eli Wells, born December 8, 1799, died 1853, in Pleasants County, married, 1819, Hannah Gorrell.

PENSION CLAIMS OF THOMAS WELLS

Mrs. Henry Montgomery of Hilton Village, Virginia, has examined the file on Thomas Wells, and calls it an amazingly complete account of his services in the Revolution. She is of the opinion that Thomas Wells had a very methodical memory or kept a diary, from which the ten large pages of factual material was supplied. The number of this file is R-11318 indicating that in spite of the amount of record, his claim was denied.

In abstract the claim of Thomas Wells says he volunteered on April 1, 1776, at Fort Jackson, as an Indian spy, at a time when Colonel McFarland was commanding the fort. He served under Captain Jesse Pigman, with the other officers being Lieutenant Charles Swan and Ensign Richard Swan. (These men were brothers, and nephews of Captain Pigman, and this is the first authentic record for service of Ensign Richard Swan.) A short time later he received from Captain Pigman, and signed by Colonel McFarland, a warrant or commission for the privilege of being orderly sergeant of Pigman's Indian spies.

In orders given he was detailed with 8 or 10 fellow spies engaged during the summer of 1776, in spying and defending by regular tours of duty, to wit: from Fort Jackson they marched and spied to Swan's Fort and Muddy Creek, thence to Strickler's Fort on the Monongahela River, thence to Redstone Old Fort and down the Monongahela to Muddy Creek. From here they went to (Jacob) Vanmeters Fort on Muddy Creek, and from here to Jenkin's Fort, (near Glades) from which place they returned to Fort Jackson, where they would take up another tour of duty, going by wilderness route to Fort Wheeling. From Wheeling they would go to Fort Pitt, thence up the Monongahela to the mouth of Tenmile, and then back to Fort Jackson.

Thomas Wells says they packed their provisions on their backs, and frequently suffered from hunger and fatigue.

They followed this route throughout the summer of 1776, until December, when Pigman's Company took up winter quarters at Fort Jackson. In March 1777, they again took up regular excursions, in which he acted in his former capacity under the same officers. During the same month they marched to Fort Pitt, and then down the Ohio to Wheeling. They spied and assisted in protecting the frontiers to the Great (Kanawa?), going down the Ohio as far as the mouth of Fishing Creek, returning to Wheeling in July 1777. From here they went up Wheeling Creek and across the country to Fort Jackson on the Tenmile. The year 1777, he says, should be long remembered, when the Indians over ran the country. In explaining this he describes the siege at Fort Wheeling. He was discharged December 1, 1777.

THE SEALS FAMILY

The Seals Family was of Maryland origin, probably from Collin Hundred, Prince George's County, where the name is found as early as 1733. Before the revolution, probably about 1773, the elder James Seals migrated with his family to settle in the vicinity of Fort Ankrom, near the mouth of Coal Lick, on land warranted to his sons, Samuel and Joseph Seals. This tract of 309 acres, located near the confluence of Ruffs Creek and the Tenmile, and fronting on both streams, was warranted under the title "Seals Chance," and was devised by will to Samuel Seals and Joseph Seals, who secured the warrant for it on December 23, 1785. Joseph Seals secured a patent to it January 22, 1799, after the death of his father. The elder James Seals may have been the James Seals who was a private in Captain Benjamin Stites' Militia Company in 1782 as his son, James Seals, was a captain in his own right prior to this date. (Penna. Arch. Series VI Vol. 2. pp. 21.) His family had all left him by the time of the 1790 Census. James Seals made a will, which was probated May 13, 1797, in which he mentions his wife Sarah ...., and other children besides the two sons who got the home property. (Will Book 1. pp. 4.) He apparently died in 1797.

Family of James and Sarah Seals

1. Captain James Seals, states in his pension application that he was born in 1755. In addition to serving as a captain of the Frontier Rangers, he served in Captain David Owens' Company in the Summer of 1777, as a volunteer. He was employed as a scout and spy in the McIntosh Campaign, and served four months under Colonel Evans and Captain Baunton in 1778. He served in the Spring of 1778, under Captain Enoch, and at times was a scout under Captain James Archer. He does not speak of service under Captain Benjamin Stites, which strengthens the theory that his father, James Seals, may reasonably be credited with that service. Records show that Captain James Seals served long after the Revolution as a captain of a Ranger Company. (National Archives W. 3117.) In July 1784, James Seals was married by Rev. John Corbly to Sarah Brown, daughter of Willian and Mary Brown. She was a girl of fifteen years of age when she married Captain James Seals, but had been left an orphan when her father was killed by the Indians while out making maple sugar in 1781. Her father had settled on the land where West Waynesburg now stands, and it was from him that "Bloody Run" now "Toll Gate Run," but on early maps "Brown's Run" got its name. Matthew and Vincent Brown, who as boys were with their father at the time of his death, joined their mother, Mary Brown, to sell their father's improvement to Captain James Seals, blacksmith, on March 29, 1785. (Washington County Deed Book 1-B-61 and 62). Then on February 12, 1791, Thomas Kent and wife, Ann, sold a part of "Fogeronian" to the mother of Sarah (Brown) Seals, and on May 30, 1791, James Seals purchased the remainder of "Fogeronian." It was here that in 1782, Captain James Seals erected the fine stone house which stood in the bottom land along the W. & W. Railroad until a few years ago. Here Captain James Seals died November 6, 1832. His widow lived until 1847, when her estate was settled on March 1, 1847. Rev. Hanna's "History of Greene County," gives the names of the children of Captain James and Sarah (Brown) Seals. James

AND ITS PIONEER FAMILIES 355

Seals was one of the five men chosen to lay out the county seat when the new Greene County was formed from Washington County.

Family of Captain James and Sarah (Brown) Seals

1. William Seals, born October 26, 1785, died 1846; will probated May 21, 1846. His wife was Eleanor Hood.

    #### Children of William and Eleanor (Hood) Seals
    1. James Seals, died about 1854 (O. C. Docket 3. pp. 392). Children named were Archibald, Elizabeth, John, James, George, Maria, and Arthur.
    2. Margaret Seals, married (1) Ephraim McClelland; (2) William Baltzell.
    3. Eliza Ann Seals, married William Zimmerman. They had James, Caroline, Enos, Ann, Eliza, and Vanamburg.
    4. Eleanor Seals, married Henry Zimmerman.
    5. Sarah Seals, married Abraham Baltzell.
2. John Seals, died in 1856. His wife was Mary ...., who died March 19, 1866, aged 63 years, 8 months, and 21 days. She is buried in East Waynesburg Cemetery.
3. Vincent Seals, died about 1848. His wife was Susan .... Estate shows minor children.

    #### Children of Vincent and Susan Seals
    1. William Seals.
    2. Sarah Jane Seals.
    3. Vincent Seals.
    4. James Seals.
4. Samuel Seals, died in January 1859. His wife was Sarah Gordon, daughter of John and Nancy (Rinehart) Gordon, she was born September 1794, and died November 1881. They had a son, John Seals.
5. Sarah Seals, married .... Bloomfield.
6. Charlotte Seals, married Robert Hicks.
8. Matilda Seals, born August 10, 1804, died April 19, 1887; married, about 1824, Cornelius Ogden, born 1792, died April 6, 1853.
9. Mary Seals, married .... Black.
10. Catherine Seals, married Bradley Mahannah, went to Iowa.

2. Samuel Seals, son of James Seals, Sr., and wife, Sarah, served in Captain Benjamin Stites' Militia Company from Morgan Township, in the War of the Revolution. He was one of the warrantees of his father's land east of Fort Jackson. (Penna. Arch Series VI Vol. 2, pp. 20). He married Mary McCormich, a native of Maryland. Kentucky records say that some of their children were born in Maryland, but this seems to be in error. Samuel and Mary Seals joined the migration of a number of Fort Jackson families and went to Mason County, Kentucky, where he was listed as a taxable in 1797. Shortly afterward he died there and his widow married John Wiley, Sr., who had moved to Mason County from Wiley's Run near Fort Jackson on the Tenmile.

    #### Children of Samuel and Mary (McCormick) Seals
    1. Elizabeth Seals, born February 4, 1780, married, June 12, 1797, Eli Wiley, born November 7, 1773.
    2. Mary Seals, married, December 27, 1803, Nicholas Strouby.

3. Nancy Seals, married, February 22, 1804, George Owens.
3. Joseph Seals, patentee of his father's land on the Tenmile, died in Greene County about 1814, leaving a wife, Elizabeth .... Probate record is dated January 6, 1814. His widow and James Seals administered his estate. (Also Appearance Docket 1. pp. 50.)

Children named in Records
1. James Seals, marked "gone" in the tax lists for 1822.
2. Elizabeth Seals, called Elizabeth, Jr., when she and Conrad Duvall went bond for her mother in the estate of Joseph Seals.

4. Mary Seals, married Richard Morris, neighbor of the Seals Family on the Tenmile. She is mentioned in ejectment proceedings in the estate of James Seals, in October 1797. Mary Seals died in Pickaway County, Ohio, about 1811, after which her husband married her sister, Nancy Seals, widow of Jesse Vanmeter. (See Richard Morris Record.)

Children of Richard and Mary (Seals) Morris
1. Ignatius Morris.
2. Jesse Morris.
3. Benedict Morris, married Lydia Morris.
4. Joseph Morris.
5. Charlotte Morris, married James Hook, Jr.
6. Hannah Morris, married Lucas (Lewis) Nebeker.
7. James Morris, married Phoebe Sayers.

5. Nancy Seals, married Jesse Vanmeter, son of Henry and Martha Vanmeter. He died about 1814, at the old stone house near the Dry Tavern. The widow then married Richard Morris, husband of her deceased sister, Mary (Seals) Morris. She is also named in the ejectment proceedings in the Appearance Docket 1. pp. 47 in the estate of James Seals, Sr.

Children of Jesse and Nancy (Seals) Vanmeter
1. Jesse Vanmeter, Jr.
2. Sarah Vanmeter, married (1) Richard Morris, son of Ezekiel and Mary (Linvill) Morris. After his death she married (2) William Kinkaid of Jefferson. A son, Henry Morris, was born to the first union, and there were children of the second marriage.
3. Rachel Vanmeter, married Jacob Ketchum.
4. Martha Vanmeter, married (1) Samuel Crago, who died in 1827. She then married William Kinkaid and was living with him at the time of his death.

6. Elizabeth Seals, whom the ejectment proceedings indicate, married Eli Wiley. (Appearance Docket 1. pp. 47.) They went to Mason County, Kentucky.
7. Martha Seals, whom the ejectment proceedings show married Elijah Wiley. They went to Kentucky.

BRADLEY MAHANA FAMILY

The History of Johnson County, Iowa, printed in 1883 (pp. 869-870) has this to say of Captain Bradley Mahana:

"Captain Bradley Mahana, was born March 1, 1806, in Hopwood, Fayette County, Pennsylvania; died September 11, 1874, in Iowa City. He was married September 1, 1827, to Miss Catherine Seals of Waynesburg, Pennsylvania. This union was blessed with the following children:

1. Amanda M. Mahana, born April 18, 1828, died December 9, 1896; married, May 23, 1848, John D. Patterson, born January 16, 1825, died April 25, 1909, in Greene County, Pennsylvania.
2. John O. Mahana, Drygoods Merchant and President of Western Mutual Aid Association of Des Moines, Iowa, born in Waynesburg, July 15, 1829, married in 1865 to Sarah Shaw.
3. James S. Mahana, a merchant in Iowa City.
4. Harriet Mahana, died at Waynesburg.
5. Sada V. Mahana, married M. R. Luse of Iowa City.
6. Richard Mahana, lived at Beatrice, Nebraska.
7. William D. Mahana, lived at Davenport, Iowa.
8. Bradley B. Mahana, merchant in Iowa City.
9. Frank Mahana, a painter in Iowa City.
10. Kittie Mahana, who died at the age of 15 years in Iowa City.

"Captain Mahana resided at Waynesburg from 1827 to 1855, and settled at Iowa City in April 1855. He was a democrat in politics, and a member of the Methodist Episcopal Church of Iowa City. Fond of military life, he was commissioned a captain of the Washington Blues and attached to the Highland Brigade of Pennsylvania by Governor D. R. Porter in 1842. He was again commissioned in 1849, by Governor W. F. Johnson, and again by Governor Bigelow in 1854. He was Brigade Inspector of the State of Pennsylvania for fourteen years. His long military record under the militia organization, qualified him with tact, skill, and military experience needed in his duties in the late Civil War. When the War between the States came upon the scene, he was among the first to offer his sword and service for the preservation of the Union. He was Captain of a Volunteer Company in Iowa City. His company was accepted by the Governor of Iowa under the 75,000 call and marched to the front as Company B of the First Iowa Volunteer Regiment. At the expiration of the enlistment he came back to Iowa City and raised another company and was elected its captain, and was assigned as Company B., Fourteenth Iowa Volunteer Infantry Regiment, later Company B. of the Forty First Regiment, and still later became Company L., Seventh Regiment, Iowa Volunteer Cavalry, on May 14, 1863. He was mustered out of the service on November 30, 1864. He enjoyed the confidence of his men and was highly respected by his fellow officers. He was a Mason for 35 years (having joined Waynesburg Lodge No. 153, F. & A. M. on February 16, 1842) and held many offices of honor and trust in that Order. When his funeral was held the services were conducted by that benevolent body, with the usual ceremony characteristic of the Brotherhood."

Greene County historians have added other items to the history of Bradley Mahana, and give a possible clue to his ancestry. In his article on Garard's Fort he tells of a scouting party consisting of Amos Morris, Dick Hall, and a man named Mahana, being sent out by Colonel John Minor. The party was ambushed about the site of the Lantz meadow, not far from the present brick house, and Mahana was killed on the spot. Next morning a search was made and the body of Mahana was found stripped of its clothing and badly mutilated. He was buried under the roots of a big tree. Too bad no one recalled the first name of this unfortunate man, as he may well have been the ancestor of Captain Bradley Mahana.

Major James B. Morris in his Centennial Address, reviewing the military history of Greene County, stated that the "Waynesburg Blues" was one of the best drilled companies that was ever in the County, and that Captain Bradley Mahana was a splendid officer.

Another item of interest is told by Professor Waychoff, who states that the statue of General Greene, which stood atop the Court House at Waynesburg, until the Big Fire of 1925, was carved by Bradley Mahana from a locust log.

ROBERT MORRIS

There has lately appeared a biography of Robert Morris, the financier of the Revolution, the first book honoring this great man to be written in the last 50 years. The title is "Forgotten Patriot," certainly a fitting one, and the author, Eleanor Young, now of Denver, Colorado, has indeed produced an excellent and informative history, dealing with the rise and fall of one of our greatest benefactors. Without his services all the battles fought by the armies of George Washington, all the historic documents of Thomas Jefferson, and the labors of John Adams, Benjamin Franklin, Patrick Henry and the others, would have come to nothing. When the credit of the new nation had fallen into such evil repute, so that carrying on the Revolution was an impossibility, to repeat the word of no less a person than Washington himself, the name and credit of Robert Morris saved the situation and made it possible to carry on. We shall with the gracious permission of Miss Young, draw upon her fine book for numerous references and material for this article.

Few persons realize the tremendous effect the private speculations of Robert Morris had upon the settlement of Greene County, Pennsylvania. And except for the attorneys practicing at the Greene County bar, it is doubtful that anyone would expect to find the will of Robert Morries on file at Waynesburg. But it is there and can be read in Will Book 8, pp. 373. Miss Young recalls that the original of this will was lost until 1939, when workers found it "yellowed with age and cracked by heat" near the furnaces beneath the Philadelphia City Hall. The Greene County record is a copy of the Philadelphia record. It was dated June 13, 1804, and registered in Waynesburg on February 26, 1900, during the mad rush of coal speculation. The will reads:

"In the name of God, Amen, I, Robert Morris of the City of Philadelphia, formerly a merchant etc., do now make and declare this present writing to contain and be my Last Will and Testament, hereby revoking all wills by me made and declared of precedent dates.

"Imprimis: I give my Gold Watch to my son Robert, it was my fathers and left to me at his death, and hath been carefully kept and valued by me ever since.

"Item: I give my Gold headed cane to my son Thomas, the head was given to me by the late John Hancock, Esqr, when President of Congress, and the cane was a gift of John Wilson, Esqr. while a member of Congress.

"Item: I give to my son Henry my copying press and the paper which was sent to me a present from Sir Robert Harris of London.

"Item: I give to my daughter Hetty (now Mrs. Marshall) my Silver Vase or Punch Cup, which I imported from London many years ago and have since purchased again.

"Item: I give to my daughter Maria (now Mrs. Nixon) my Silver Boiler which I also imported from London many years ago and which I have lately repurchased.

"Item: I give to my friend Gouverneur Morris Esqr. my telescope Espying Glass, being the same I bought of a French refugee from Cape Francois then at Trenton, and which I since purchased again of Mr. Hall, officer of the Bankrupt Office.

"Item: I give and bequeath all the other property which I now posses or may hereafter acquire wether real or personal or any that shall or may belong to me at the time of my death to my dearly beloved wife Mary Morris for her use and comfort during her life and to be disposed of as she pleases at or before her decease when no doubt she will make such distribution of the same amongst our children as she may then think proper.

"Here I have to express my regret at having lost a very large fortune acquired by honest industry, which I had long hoped and expected to enjoy with my family during my own life and then to distribute it amongst those of them that should outlive me. Fate has determined otherwise and we must submit to the decree, which I have done with patience and fortitude. Lastly I do hereby nominate and appoint my said dearly beloved wife Mary Morris the sole Executrix of this my Last Will and Testament made and declared as such on this thirteenth day of June 1804.

"Robert Morris" (Seal)

His Executrix was sworn May 29, 1806.

This will is a sad commentary on the gratitude of the American people, not only of his day even to this age, in the manner they honor and then tear down the efforts of our greatest benefactors. Miss Young quotes Samuel Breck, who visited Robert Morris while he languished in debtors prison and who reported "I visited this great man in his ugly whitewashed vault in the Prune Street (Philadelphia) debtors apartment. In Rome or Greece a thousand statues would have honored his mighty services, yet in America, Republican America, not even a single voice was raised in Congress or elsewhere in aid of him or his family." Even George Washington, wealthy and influential, who visited him in his cell, and who with his family had shared on numerous occasions the hospitality of Robert Morris, does not seem to have raised his hand to alleviate the prison sentence meted out to this great man.

It is true that speculation and risk were a part of the cause of Robert Morris' ill fortune. He gambled in buying up some 8,000,000 acres of land in America with partly borrowed money, and when sent to prison he was in debt to the extent of a fabulous sum of money for that period—proven to have been almost $3,000,000—but it was his boundless faith in the future of America, which he foresaw long before others began to realize the potential greatness, that brought about his downfall. The values of the surface and the mineral wealth beneath his holdings in Greene County alone would far exceed the total debt which sent him to debtors prison for three years, six months, and ten days.

Robert Morris was an immigrant boy of twelve years of age when he first came to America. He had been born in Liverpool,

England, on January 20, 1735 (January 31, O. S.) the son of Robert and Elizabeth (Murphet) Morris. His grandparents were Andrew and Magdeline (Simpson) Morris. His father had preceeded him to America and settled near Oxford, Maryland, where he had prospered. From the will of Robert Morris, Sr., it appears that he had taken up with a certain Sarah Wise, by whom he had three children, one of whom called Thomas Morris Wise, was to later prove an embarrassment to the financier. From his father, Robert Morris inherited, at his accidental death, a sum of $7000 and the gold watch mentioned in the financier's will. This may have been a large sum for that day, and been but token money in the flush years of the son's life, but it laid the foundation for the wealth that was to pass through his hands.

Robert Morris married in Christ's Church, Philadelphia, on March 2, 1769, Mary, daughter of Colonel Thomas White by his second marriage with Esther Hewlings Newman White. She was born April 13, 1749. It was a happy marriage in which Mary shared faithfully the good and bad of his hectic life. She outlived him by many years, dying on January 16, 1827. Robert Morris died on May 8, 1806. To Robert and Mary (White) Morris were born seven children, only five of whom were living at the death of the father. The children were:

1. Robert Morris, born in 1770, married Ann Shoemaker.
2. Thomas Morris, born 1772, married, May 28, 1799, Sally Kane.
3. Hetty Morris, married in 1795, James Marshall.
4. William Morris, died young on October 9, 1798.
5. Charles Morris, presumably lost at sea. He was born July 11, 1777.
6. Maria Morris, born 1780, married Henry Nixon.
7. Henry Morris, born July 24, 1784, died December 1, 1842, married Eliza Jane ....

Americans should read "Forgotten Patriot." Robert Morris had in his day, the same sort of citizens so often met with today, demanding much from our democratic form of government, yet refusing to pay or complaining bitterly of the cost of their own demands. Legislators might well learn a lesson from this one man then in charge of finances, who followed his own religion, "System, Economy, and Vigor."

There is a trend in genealogy which always seeks to tie the family history to the family of great men of the same name. From the foregoing record it will be seen that relationship with Robert Morris can only come through un-named children of his grandfather, Andrew Morris, or undisclosed children of Robert Morris, Sr. Direct descent can come through the three sons and two daughters of the financier, and these must be well known to interested genealogists.

One needs only to examine the patent maps to learn the extent to which Robert Morris controlled the settlement of the Tenmile Country. Professor Waychoff has stated that he owned 40,940 acres and 8 perches, the land being in Aleppo, Richhill, and Jackson Townships. He should have included Springhill Township, where Morris owned almost one-half of the entire township. He had small holdings in Gilmore, Jefferson, and Center Townships. Broken down, his holdings show roughly 7800 acres in Aleppo, 8400 acres in Springhill, 9200 acres in Jackson, and 10,000 acres in Richhill. Nearly all of these holdings were taken up on patents from the State in the Fall of 1784, with some of his Richhill land acquired in 1788.

Crumrine in his "History of Washington County" tells of the

sale of this land on March 30, 1795, to Edward Tilghman for a sum of 10,200 Pounds. (pp. 983-984.) In this he is correct as the deed is also on record at Waynesburg. (DB. 36-pp. 145.) But Crumrine says next, "at that time this entire body of land was within the limits of Washington County but now lies partly in West Finley Township and Greene County." He then gives a complete list of the titles under which the various tracts were patented, there were 75 of them. In one respect Crumrine was not correct. All these tracts named lay within the present limits of Greene County, with a few of them extending into Ohio County, West Virginia, as it existed at the time of sale. Robert Morris did not patent any land in what is now Washington County. Waychoff carried the abstract of this land a step further to show that Edward Tilghman deeded his new purchase in trust to William Cooke on May 26, 1798, after which Cooke willed it to his heirs. However his statement that William Cooke was a son-in-law of Robert Morris, is not borne out by the genealogy of the family of Robert Morris and is refuted in his will. Nor were these the "Lieper Lands" for they were separate lands entirely, 35 tracts amounting to more than 16,000 acres, situated in Richhill, Morris, Jackson, and Center Townships. Thomas Lieper had patented them and by deed of September 5, 1835, they passed through Samuel McLean Lieper and others named executors of Thomas Lieper, to John Bell, Jr., Thomas Patterson, and Benjamin Ross. (DB. 7. pp. 647 and DB. 8. pp. 185, Greene County.)

Daniel McFarland, John Hughes and Timothy Ryan, Thomas Shields, and Joseph Ball, with Thomas Lieper and Robert Morris had hodlings in this western tier of townships of Greene County, more than 80,000 acres of land from 1784, until 1795, and after. This is the reason no early settlements of any size were made by individuals in the western third of Greene County as it is now measured. The few hardy settlers known to have been in these parts before 1795 were there by virtue of Virginia grants, which a few saw fit to patent under Pennsylvania law. The others were by nature of their possession either squatters with no legal title, or tenants by agreement with rightful owners. In Aleppo and Springhill alone not more than eight alien owners possessed the entire acreage of the townships. From this recital of ownership it can be seen how Robert Morris effected the early settlement of Greene County. He knew fully well the value of his possessions and their speculation possibilities, but he went beyond his cedit before the buyers appeared and in doing so he opened the door of the Prune Street Gaol. Even the sale to Edward Tilghman could effect but little the eventual tragedy which struck him on February 15, 1798.

Some tracts of land not included in the deed to Tilghman were claimed by the sheriff of Greene County and by him sold to Thomas Ryerson on October 1, 1798. They included the site where Christopher Gist had viewed the county and reported it in his journal on March 7, 1752. With these nine tracts Thomas Ryerson perpetrated the hoax reported by L. K. Evans, and which bears repetition. Evans called Ryerson a shrewd and unscupulous land speculator, who after he had posseessed himself of these lands, conceived the idea of drafting on paper, his dream of a sylvan paradise, complete with its dwellings and towns. This drawing he took east with him and succeeded in palming it off on an unsuspecting sea captain, said by Evans to have been named Connell. When the sea captain came to inspect his supposedly earthly heaven, all he found was "a few rude huts at the confluence of two wild streams, amid a dense tangle of thickets, and surrounded by rugged hills covered by unbroken forests." The site may easily be recognized as the place now called Ryerson's Station, and must not be confused with Ryerson's Fort, which was on Ryerson's original "Vallodolid" tract and now known as Wind Ridge.

A separate individual tract of land owned by Robert Morris, was "Walnut Bottom" situated on Muddy Creek, adjoining the site of Jacob Cline's Fort. This was patented to Robert Morris in 1792, and was included in a collateral note of $2749 to David Briggs on March 11, 1795. Briggs, evidently a lenient man, did not strike while Robert Morris was at a disadvantage. He awaited his time, and on May 21, 1800, received a deed from Robert Morris, merchant of Philadelphia, joined by his wife, Mary, conveying this more than 400 acre tract, before Morris had been released. Thus when Robert Morris was released on August 26, 1801, by virtue of a Bankruptcy Act passed by Congress, none of his fine Greene County land was his to convey. In addition he had lost everything he possessed, even the personal items he treasured so highly, and which he set about to reclaim by honest means, and which he was able to do in the cases noted in his will.

The benevolent State which he served so well before he joined the patriots' cause in the fight for freedom, has in late years set up a game preserve on some of the lands once owned by Robert Morris. Should it see fit to expand this preserve to a natural park at the Forks of Wheeling Creek, what more fitting tribute could be paid to this man than to name it for Robert Morris, whose faith in the future of America was greater than all his wealth.

RICHARD MORRIS

The first Richard Morris to settle on the Tenmile selected a site bordering upon that stream and close to David Owen's Run. He may have accompanied Captain James Hook about 1772, as there is evidence of a Richard Morris living in Baltimore County, Maryland, in 1739, his name being found in a list containing the Hooke name also, as well as a number of other familiar Tenmile Country Families. Richard Morris and Captain James Hook became neighbors on Owen's Run and the family intermarried. It was this Richard Morris, who served in Captain William Harrod's Company on the George Rogers Clark Expedition and was later a member of Captain James Archer's Militia Company recruited in his neighborhood. This pioneer Richard Morris, on February 10, 1794, had warranted to him a tract of 300 acres of land under the title of "Horsehead," and was taxed on it in Benjamin Stites' Morgan Township assessment roll of 1784, indicating a late registration of his claim. Richard Morris never took a patent out on this tract, but sold his claim to Job Smith, who obtained the patent on March 9, 1805, under the title of "Patience." In order to clarify certain family records, it may be well to extend the title to this piece of land to the next owner, for on March 20, 1806, Job Smith and wife, Sarah, sold a portion of this tract to another Richard Morris, who had lately come to the Tenmile from New Jersey. (Greene County, Penna., D. B. 4. pp. 100 and 101.) This Richard Morris and wife, Lydia (Burge) Morris, in turn conveyed it to a third Richard Morris, "late of New Jersey," and father of the second owner so named. It is the tract of land now being improved by Mr. and Mrs. Russell Milliken.

The pioneer Richard Morris married Mary Seals, daughter of James and Sarah Seals, who lived on the tract of land East of "Horsehead." She was a sister of Captain James Seals and of

Nancy Seals, wife of Lieutenant Jesse Vanmeter. In 1798, Richard Morris and wife, Mary, brought suit against Joseph Seals, along with the other heirs of James Seals, Sr. (Greene County Appearance Docket 1. pp. 50.) About 1800, Richard Morris and wife, Mary (Seals) Morris, removed with a number of their family to Pickaway County, Ohio, and settled near Circleville, where Mary (Seals) Morris died about 1811. Then about 1814, Nancy (Seals) Vanmeter became a widow through the death of Lieutenant Jesse Vanmeter, and in due time she became the second wife of Richard Morris. From the estates of Richard Morris and his wife, Mary (Seals) Morris, in Circleville, the following children can be identified:

1. Ignatius Morris, mentioned in the estates of both, married .... Wood.
2. Jesse Morris, named in both estates.
3. Benedict Morris, mentioned in the estate of Mary (Seals) Morris. His wife was Lydia Morris, daughter of Ezekiel and Mary (O'Neal ?) Morris. Ezekiel Morris' estate calls him Benjamin Morris.
4. Joseph Morris, named in the estate of Richard Morris.
5. Charlotte Morris, born 1775, died May 13, 1827, married James Hook, Jr., born 1776, died 1838. They are mentioned in the estate of Richard Morris.
6. Hannah Morris, mentioned in both estates, married Lucas (or Lewis) Nebeker.
7. James Morris, not mentioned in either estate, but he had died in 1798, at the age of 28 years. (O. C. Docket 1. pp. 7.) Richard Morris petitioned for the heirs of James Morris and named three sons. A granddaughter wrote that her father was Joseph Morris, son of James Morris, and grandson of Richard Morris of Pickaway County, Ohio. The wife of James Morris was Phoebe Sayers, daughter of William and Mary (Fithian) Sayers. Phoebe (Sayers) Morris married (2) .... Remley.

Children of James and Phoebe (Sayers) Morris
1. Thomas Morris, born 1794.
2. Joseph Morris, born 1796.
3. Ephraim Morris, born November 18, 1797, died June 21, 1868; married, February 24, 1820, Martha Roseberry, born October 7, 1801, died December 14, 1866. She was a daughter of Mathias and Sarah (Hughes) Roseberry. (See Hughes Records.)

EZEKIEL MORRIS

There is no reference to the origin of Ezekiel Morris, who warranted a tract of land in the vicinity of Homeville, just south of the "Laurel Point" tract of David Shelby, Jr. This tract consisting of 405 acres was warranted May 25, 1785, under the title of "Argyle," and he secured his patent to it on December 15, 1789. He was probably living here when he was taxed in the assessment rolls for Cumberland Township, Washington County, in 1784. It also seems certain that he was living here when he served as a member of Captain James Archer's Company of Militia in 1782. An informant denies he is the Ezekiel Morris who married Mary Turmond of Botetourt County, Virginia, on August 18, 1770, though his wife's name is shown to be Mary. It has also been proven that her name was not Mary Linvill as had been believed by several of the descendants. A better clue seems to indicate she was Mary O'Neal, and probably a sister of Henry and Barnet O'Neal, orphan children related to Felix Hughes, who accompanied the Swan-Vanmeter-Hughes Party to settle here about 1767. Felix Hughes' mother was Bridget O'Neal, and the brothers, Henry and Barnet O'Neal, settled near Shepherd's Church, and not far from Fort Henry Vanmeter. The marriages of the children of Ezekiel Morris with descendants of Vanmeters strengthens this theory. If this is the case and Ezekiel did marry Mary O'Neal, we are inclined to believe him to be be a brother of Richard Morris, who settled near him on Tenmile, and therefore a native of Maryland or possibly Loudon County, Virginia.

Ezekiel Morris was born in 1744 and died in Pickaway County Ohio, September 24, 1822. His wife Mary (O'Neal?) Morris was born in 1747 and died in Pickaway County, on November 15, 1836. They are buried in the Morris Evans Cemetery. They had settled in Pickaway County about the time that the "Congress Lands" were opened up for settlement, having secured patents for two tracts, one in 1804 and another in 1809. Will of Ezekiel Morris in Will Book 1, pp. 40.

Children of Ezekiel and Mary Morris

1. John Morris, born in 1770, died in Pickaway County, Ohio, in 1842; married Elizabeth Wells, born August 20, 1775.
2. Samuel Morris.
3. Richard Morris, died before his father. His wife was Sarah Vanmeter, daughter of Lieutenant Jesse and Nancy (Seals) Vanmeter. There were heirs among whom was a son, Henry Morris. Sarah (Vanmeter) Morris married (2) William Kincaid of Jefferson, Pennsylvania.
4. Elizabeth Morris, married Jacob Cline, son of Jacob and Eleanor (Vanmeter) Cline.
5. Henry O'Neal Morris, born September 6, 1788, died December 30, 1840; married, March 28, 1811, Charity Shelby, daughter of David and Mary (Williams) Shelby, born April 15, 1787, died December 21, 1876. They lived in Pickaway County, Ohio.
6. Rebecca Morris, married Benjamin Bowman.
7. Sarah Morris, married George Lemley, son of Jacob and Sarah Lemley.
8. Ann Morris, married .... Thomas.
9. Eleanor Morris, married, July 1806, John Shelby, born 1783. He was an associate judge of Logan County, Ohio. Both husband and wife were killed in a runaway carriage accident in 1825.
10. Lydia Morris, married Benjamin Morris, (called Benedict in the will of his parents). He was a son of Richard and Mary (Seals) Morris.

RICHARD MORRIS OF NEW JERSEY

A second Richard Morris who has confused the records, moved into the Tenmile Country at a time too late to have served in Captain James Archer's Company during the Revolution. There is evidence to indicate that the Richard and Ezekiel Morris of Archer's Company came from Virginia, while this second Richard Morris came from New Jersey. A deed dated January 10, 1803, from James Hook and wife, Charlotte, and Robert Whitehill the younger, describes this Richard Morris as "Late of New Jersey." The Anthony Smith family came to the same part of the Tenmile about 1796, and while the term "late of New Jersey" may be broadly interpreted, it seems likely that Richard Morris came with them. It is significant that some of the Smith Family records are found in the Bible of "Jersey" John Morris. Mrs. Sitherwood in her Throckmorton Genealogy, and Dr. Dodds, have both given an account of the Richard Morris Family. A deed in Deed Book 4. pp. 700, helps identify the children.

Richard Morris was born in Monmouth County, New Jersey, in 1744, and died in Greene County, Pennsylvania, March 16, 1825, aged 81 years, 1 month, and 16 days. His wife was Mary Throckmorton, who was born in New Jersey May 25, 1751, died in Greene County, January 19, 1817. Both are buried in the Church Cemetery at Morrisville, ground for which was given by Richard Morris, setting aside one portion for the Morris Family.

Children of Richard and Mary (Throckmorton) Morris

1. Richard Morris, born December 15, 1774, died in Belmont County, Ohio, July 10, 1821. His wife was Lydia Burge, born August 23, 1770, daughter of Jacob and Judith (Smith) Burge, and granddaughter of Anthony Smith.
2. Mary Morris, born 1776, married John Green, son of Major General James Green of Freehold, New Jersey. She died May 24, 1829. Buried in the Morrisville Cemetery.
3. Joseph Morris.
4. Lydia Morris, married Copperthwaite Smith, son of Thomas and Deborra Smith.
5. John Morris, born 1783, died January 27, 1872, married (1) Margaret Eagon, who died October 17, 1833, aged 34 years. He then married Jemimah Pipes, who died May 3, 1875 or 1876. Buried in the Morrisville Cemetery.

THE EAGON FAMILY

The Eagon Family is of Maryland origin, where as on the Tenmile and in Guernsey County, Ohio, the name is frequently spelled "Hagen" etc. At least two branches of this family settled near each other on the Tenmile, where James Eagon was an original patentee of a tract of land. This tract of 300 acres was warranted to him on September 11, 1784, under the title of "Stone Cole" and then on February 19, 1787, a patent was secured for the tract under the title of "Eagons Farm." It was located at the mouth of Coal Lick, next to John Ankrom's fort. James Eagon served in Captain James Archer's Militia Company in the arrangement of 1782, and was a signer of the Petition for the new state to be known as Westsylvania. He was an early purchaser of a lot in Waynesburg, which at the time of his death was rented to William Crawford, Esq. James Eagon died about 1821, leaving a will that was probated November 23, 1821. In his will he named a wife, Mary ...., who collected the rent on his Waynesburg house and lot for a number of years after his death. Only four children are named in his will.

Children of James and Mary Eagon

1. Barnet Eagon, designated "Jr" in his will, for reasons not disclosed. Barnet Eagon was also a member of Captain James Archer's Militia Company. He married Hannah Wood, daugh-

ter of William and Margaret (Mitchell) Wood. They removed to Monroe County, Ohio, and then to Guernsey County, Ohio, where Barnet Eagon died in 1833-34. His will is on file at Cambridge, showing that it was made September 21, 1833, and filed for probate March 24, 1834. He refers to his wife Hannah. They were living in Beaver Township at the time of the will.

Children of Barnet and Hannah (Wood) Eagon

1. A daughter, who had married Thomas Ankrom, son of Richard and Nancy (Rinehart) Ankrom. Her husband was living at the time of Barnet Eagon's will, and her children, Barnet, Maria, and Nancy Ankrom, got bequests.
2. Polly (Mary) Eagon, wife of Michael Donahue.
3. A daughter, who married John Morris, son of John and Rebecca Morris of Jefferson Township, Greene County, Pennsylvania.
4. Barnet Eagon, Jr., who married Mary Morris, sister of John Morris. (Greene Co. WB 2. pp. 190.)
5. Jesse Eagon, whose wife was Elizabeth Morris, sister of Mary and John Morris.
6. James Eagon, with his brother, Jesse Eagon, served as executors of their father's will. He owned a mill in Guernsey County, Ohio, the proceeds of which were to keep his widow during her life. Her name is not given. His will is in Will Book B. pp. 147 and was probated June 8, 1846.

Children of James Eagon

1. James Eagon, Jr.
2. Isaac Eagon.
3. Barnet Eagon.
4. Polly Eagon.
5. Elizabeth Eagon.
6. John Eagon.
7. Hannah Eagon.
8. Margaret Eagon.
9. Charlotte Eagon.
10. Nancy Eagon.

2. Cassandra Eagon, daughter of James and Mary Eagon, married Samuel House, who died in Greene County, Pennsylvania. His will was probated June 12, 1828. Samuel House served in Captain Benjamin Stites' Morgan Township Militia Company. He patented the tract of land called "Pine Grove" on January 22, 1799, which had been warranted to him on October 17, 1785. It was but one farm removed from the James Eagon land. An old cemetery back of the John Harry stone house is the House Cemetery, wherein Samuel and his wife are buried.

Children of Samuel and Cassandra (Eagon) House

1. Samuel House, Jr., married Leah Doty, daughter of Anthony and Mary Doty.

Children (Estate 2216)

1. Rachel House, married William Braden.
2. Mary House.
3. Samuel House.

2. John House, wife's name was Lucinda ...., went to Guernsey County, Ohio.

AND ITS PIONEER FAMILIES 367

    3. James House.
    4. Sarah House, married Peter Martin.
    5. Polly House, married .... Ball.
    6. Rachel House, married .... Day.
    7. Elizabeth House, married .... Lynch, went to Coshocton, Ohio.
    8. Hannah House, married John Montgomery, went to Greene County, Ohio.
    9. Margaret House, married Charles McQuaide.
3. Sarah Eagon, born February 9, 1765, married Thomas Adamson, Jr., son of Thomas and Mary Adamson. He was born May 15, 1758, according to Quaker Records, and died July 27, 1816. His wife died December 24, 1831. Both are buried in the Adamson Cemetery. Their children were:
    1. John Adamson.
    2. James Adamson, born 1784, died June 27, 1851; married Margaret Smith, born January 6, 1789, died May 6, 1866.
    3. Barnet Adamson.
    4. Charles Adamson, born 1787, died September 1857; married Sarah Hatfield, born April 1798, died May 2, 1879.
    5. Josiah Adamson, married Elizabeth Hatfield.
    6. Joseph Adamson, born April 1, 1791, died April 23, 1853; married Hannah Smith, who died August 5, 1871, aged 78 years.
    7. Sarah Adamson, married Jesse Rice.
    8. Mary Adamson, born 1792, died January 7, 1870; married .... Cary.
    9. Cassandra Adamson, born 1804, died 1846; married Uriah Eagon.
    10. Debba Adamson, born 1807, died March 13, 1837; married Samuel Mickle.
4. Margaret Eagon, married .... Anderson.

SOLOMON EAGON

    Solomon Eagon was born in Maryland, March 2, 1766, and married, in Cecil County November 12, 1788, Mary Blackburn, born February 7, 1776. They removed to the Tenmile soon after their marriage, and in 1795, bought a tract of land from Nathaniel and Leah Hughes, situated at the head of Laurel Run. Later Solomon Eagon got the Abraham Zimmerman tract adjoining. He served in several minor offices in the early history of the county, being tax collector in 1829. He was running a store at Waynesburg with his son, William, at that time, but a short time later removed with his family to Guernsey County, Ohio, and then to Mahaska County, Iowa, where he settled near Oskaloosa. He died there August 29, 1853, and his wife died there on October 25, 1857. Both are buried in the old cemetery in Lincoln Township.
    1. Mary Eagon, married William Ankrom, son of John and Martha (Wells) Ankrom.

Children

    1. John Ankrom, a blind man, living in Ohio in 1860.
    2. Solomon Ankrom, lived at Circleville, Ohio, in 1860.
    3. William Ankrom, letter from him to Daniel and Sally Bonar on March 18, 1847, addressed to "Dear Brother and Sister."
    4. Richard Ankrom, his wife was Elizabeth ...., lived at Allensville, Ohio in 1860.

5. Thomas Ankrom.
6. Uriah Ankrom.
7. Sampson Ankrom.
8. Martha Ankrom.
9. Clementine Ankrom.
10. Sarah Ankrom, born June 10, 1807, died December 25, 1891, married Daniel Bonar, born August 1, 1797, died November 6, 1869. A letter from Solomon Eagon from Guernsey County, Ohio, April 12, 18......, addresses them as "Dear Grandson and Daughter." Sarah was probably the eldest child of William and Mary (Eagon) Ankrom.

2. William Eagon, kept store with his father in Waynesburg, where he remained when his father went west. Was still doing business in 1839, then removed to Center Township. His wife was Mary ....

3. Margaret Eagon, born March 9, 1792, died March 25, 1878, married, January 14, 1815, James Kent, born August 5, 1792, died February 12, 1878. He was a son of Thomas and Ann (Rolston) Kent. (See Kent Records.)

4. Sarah Eagon, born January 26, 1794, married, December 7, 1809, William Taygart, son of John and Rebecca (Blackburn) Taygart.

Children

1. Julia Ann Taygart, born December 31, 1810, married Elijah Chalfont.
2. Eagon B. Taygart, born January 2, 1813, married Sally Lantz.
3. Perrigan Taygart, born July 15, 1815, married Mrs. Wells.
4. Mary Taygart, born November 17, 1818, married (1) William Minor; (2) James Wallace.
5. Clementine Taygart, born August 4, 1822, married G. W. Bell.
6. Rebecca Taygart, born June 13, 1820, married Elijah Coleman.
7. William Taygart, born June 19, 1825, died young.
8. Sarah Ann Taygart, born February 6, 1828, married Hiram Lester.
9. Susan Taygart, born March 7, 1830, married Enoch Hennan.
10. John Rinehart Taygart, born October 25, 1832, died 1907; married (1) Sarah Gordon, (2) Mary Jane Murray.
11. Elizabeth Taygart, born February 13, 1835, married William Longstreth.

5. Thomas Eagon, living in Princeton, Illinois, on February 25, 1849. Mentions a sister, Mary, living in Cincinnati, and in Uncle George Kent, whose boys were living in Missouri. Could have meant his wife's uncle? His wife was Eliza ....

6. Lucy Eagon, married .... Ankrom.

Children

1. Uriah Ankrom.
2. Elizabeth Ankrom.
3. Francis Ankrom.
4. Rebecca Ankrom.
5. Jane Ankrom.

7. Delilah Eagon, married Judge James Rinehart, born August 22, 1802, died at Oskaloosa, Iowa, March 29, 1879, buried in Forest Cemetery.

Children
1. Dr. Solomon Eagon Rinehart, born October 19, 1827, died January 18, 1875, at Denver, Colorado. He married, October 19, 1852, Mary J. Davis.
2. Jane Rinehart, married .... Johnson.
3. Minerva Rinehart, married .... McKinley.
4. Letitia Rinehart, married .... Smith.

8. Uriah Eagon, born August 21, 1804, married Cassandra Adamson, born March 21, 1804, died in 1846. She was a daughter of Thomas and Sarah (Eagon) Adamson.

Children
1. Thomas Eagon, married Elizabeth Wise.
2. Lafayette Eagon, married Jane Fordyce.
3. Sarah Ann Eagon, married James Thomas.
4. Solomon Eagon, married Sarah Ann Thomas.
5. Deborra Eagon, born 1835, died March 21, 1864; married George Kent.
6. Barnet Eagon, married Nancy Thomas.
7. Julia Ann Eagon, married Cary Tharp.
8. Mary Eagon, married David Fry.
9. Emily Ann Eagon, married Milton Huffman.

9. Susan Eagon, born October 22, 1795, died November 1, 1859; married Arthur Inghram, born 1786, died August 1875. (See Inghram Records.)
10. Clementine Eagon, married Dr. Greenfield.
11. Elizabeth Eagon, died October 12, 1832, aged 40 years, 9 months, and 16 days; married George Heisse, who died November 1, 1856, aged 89 years. Buried at Shepherds Church Cemetery.
    1. Solomon Heisse.
    2. Minnie Heisse, married Samuel Rush.
    3. Marianne Heisse, died September 26, 1837, aged 26 years, 4 months, and 4 days.
    4. Sinah Heisse, died March 27, 1846, aged 32 years, 1 month, and 6 days.

GEORGE CHURCH FAMILY

On March 16, 1770, George Teagarden sold a tract of land to Philomen (Felix) Askin, which he described as "James Brenton's improvement on Tenmile Creek." Two years later, on October 28, 1772, Askin made an assignment of the land to George Church. (Washington County D. B. 1-C-163.) It was probably the site of Fort Askin, mentioned in several dispatches, and apparently located between Fort Jackson and John Ankrom's Fort. Later George Church patented land between Coal Lick and Laurel Run, including the site of the present Colonial Place, having sold his original tract to James Daily on November 29, 1775. As the name appears in early tax lists as George Kirke, Kirk, etc., it is probable that he came from the German settlement of Upper Frederick County, Maryland. He died intestate in Greene County about 1815, but his wife, Jane Church, left a will in which she named her children (Greene County WB. 1. pp 190, probated February 29, 1819.)
1. Margaret Church, wife of Joseph Archer, removed to Guernsey County, Ohio.

2. Isabel Church, married George Carroll, also went to Guernsey County, Ohio.
3. Ann Church, married James Copus. They removed to Knox County, Ohio, in 1809, where James was killed by Indians in 1812. His widow then joined the families of Joseph Archer and George Carroll in Guernsey County, where she lived for three years, until her children were large enough to help, then she returned to Knox County.
   1. Henry Copus.
   2. James Copus.
   3. Wesley Copus.
   4. Sarah Copus.
4. Elizabeth Church, married Alexander Dollison, who died in Greene County, about 1805.
   1. Jesse Dollison.
   2. Denton Dollison.
5. Nancy Church, married .... Archer. (Simon ?).
6. Jane Church, married .... Gooden.
7. Henry Church was born January 20, 1779, died August 28, 1851. He is buried at Rogersville. He married (1) Jane Archer, born February 20, 1778, and died about 1816. She was one of the Archer family who had been attacked by the Indians, and had been scalped and left for dead herself, but hid beneath some covers and was nursed back to health. After her death Henry Church married Sarah Rinehart, daughter of Barnet and Ruth (Stiles) Rinehart. She was born December 15, 1786, and died June 5, 1872. Ten children were born to the first marriage and six more to the second. Bible record reported by Rev. Hanna.
   1. Jane Church, born March 22, 1797.
   2. Elizabeth Church, born August 17, 1799.
   3. George Church, born October 5, 1801.
   4. Jane (2) Church, born October 8, 1803.
   5. Henry Church, born January 5, 1805, married Martha Guthrie.
   6. Sarah Church, born May 22, 1807.
   7. Elijah Church, born August 20, 1809, married Anna Moore.
   8. Elisha Church, twin of Elijah.
   9. Jesse Church, born August 15, 1812.
   10. Nancy Church, born March 11, 1816.
   11. Ruth Church, born January 18, 1818.
   12. William Church, born December 5, 1819.
   13. Rinehart Church, born March 29, 1822, died December 11, 1882; married, December 6, 1842, Charlotte Guthrie, born January 30, 1825, died March 16, 1911.
   14. Delilah Church, born July 9, 1824.
   15. John Church, born November 21, 1826, married Elizabeth Fordyce.
   16. Elizabeth Church, born August 2, 1831.

THE ULLOM FAMILY

While browsing through some old records in the Berkeley County, West Virginia, Court House at Martinsburg, the author noticed a name that sounded familiar. The name was spelled "Woolam" and the record was the will of one Jacob Woolam, who made the paper on April 13, 1778, which was filed for probate on November 17, 1778. He named his wife Magdelina and the names of his children. (Will Book 1. pp. 150.)

Children of Jacob and Magdelina Woolam

1. Balser Woolam.
2. Mathias Woolam.
3. Peter Woolam, of whom later.
4. Wendle Woolam.
5. Shem Woolam, who was living in the Tenmile Country in 1790. He was in Captain William Crawford's Company in 1793.
6. Daniel Woolam.
7. John Woolam.
8. Jacob Woolam, youngest son.
9. Juliana Woolam, wife of Jacob Shillengood.
10. Magdelina Woolam, wife of John Morrisey.
11. Hannah Woolam.

PETER WOOLAM FAMILY

Two of the sons of Jacob Woolam and his wife, Magdelina, were living on the Tenmile in the 1790 Census, when the name is spelled Woolham. Other records spell the name Whoolam, Woollom, etc., but it eventually became Ullom by the spelling adopted in the family of Peter Ullom. On September 19, 1793, Peter Ullom (spelled then Woollom) bought 98 acres of land from Captain James Hook's purchase of "Hook's Delight." (Washington County Deed Book 1-I. pp. 765.) Here he resided until his death. His will was made January 29, 1816, and probated August 24, 1824. He gave his home farm to his widow, Margaret, after which it was to go to his six named sons. The indications are that Margaret died soon after her husband and on May 18, 1829, these sons sold out to Isaac Ullom. (Greene County Will Book 1. pp. 257.)

Family of Peter and Margaret Ullom

1. Peter Ullom, Jr., died about the same time as his father. His wife was Mary .... He left a number of minor children. (O. C. Docket 1. pp. 214 and O. C. Docket 2. pp. 36.)

Children

 1. Harrison Ullom.
 2. Elisha Ullom.
 3. Shem Ullom.
 4. Rachel Ullom.
 5. Nancy Ullom.
2. Joseph Ullom, son of Peter and Margaret Ullom.
3. Jacob Ullom, son of Peter and Margaret Ullom, married Millicent Villiers.

4. Elijah Ullom son, of Peter and Margaret Ullom.
5. Stephen Ullom, son of Peter and Margaret Ullom.
6. George Ullom, son of Peter and Margaret Ullom, born presumably in Berkeley County, Virginia, on October 31, 1779, died in Franklin Township, Greene County, September 24, 1830; married Margaret Bowen, born April 18, 1779, died February 19, 1853, both are buried in the Morrisville Cemetery.

Children

1. Maryann Ullom, married .... Edgar.
2. Peter Ullom, married Matilda Kinney.
3. Isaac Ullom.
4. Elijah Ullom.
5. Thompson Ullom.
6. William Ullom.
7. Jacob Ullom.
8. John Ullom.
9. Jesse Ullom.
10. Stephen Ullom.
11. Rachel Ullom, died in 1848, married William Lippencott.

Children

1. Uriah Lippencott.
2. Margaret Lippencott.
3. Melissa Lippencott.
4. Martha Lippencott.
5. Maria Lippencott.

12. Daniel T. Ullom, born December 23, 1809, died October 14, 1881; married Anna Johnson, born July 4, 1812, died October 29, 1894, daughter of John and Elizabeth (Kent) Johnson.

Children of Daniel and Anna (Johnson) Ullom

1. George Ullom.
2. Jesse Ullom, born June 20, 1836, married March 29, 1861, Phoebe Morris, born November 11, 1843.
3. Elizabeth Ullom, married John Clutter.
4. Margaret Ullom, married (1) .... Loar, (2) Barnet Wiley.
5. Catherine Ullom.
6. John T. Ullom, born April 11, 1847, married Mary Ann Sellars, born January 8, 1875.
7. Sarah Ullom.
8. Maria Ullom, married Lindsey Orndorff.
9. Martha Ullom, married William Orndorff.
10.
11.

NATHANIEL HUGHES FAMILY

Nathaniel Hughes is thought to have been a descendant of John Hughes, born in Wales, who came to America and settled in Maryland. Before the end of the Revolution, Nathaniel Hughes, with his brothers, Joseph, William, and Roland Hughes, removed to the Tenmile Country, where they performed service in the ranks of the Frontiersmen. Joseph Hughes, while in the Army at Fort Pitt, married Sarah, daughter of John and Elizabeth (Lucas) Swan. William Hughes married her sister, Martha Swan. Both families removed first to Kentucky and then to Howard County, Missouri, where they were living in 1817, when William wrote an informative letter to Colonel Charles Swan, whom he called "Brother." He inquired about his "old Brother Nate," and tells of his brother, Joseph, also living in Missouri. In April 1834, Joseph Hughes obtained a pension in Howard County. The letter also asks about his Brother Tom Hughes, meaning Thomas Hughes of Jefferson, in which case he means his brother-in-law. Photostat of this letter is in our possession. Joseph and Roland (also spelled Rollin) both served under Captain William Harrod on the Clark Expedition. Records also disclose that Rollin Hughes and wife, Susannah, were baptized at Muddy Creek, when Goshen Baptist Church met at that place on October 27, 1787. He had warranted a tract of land called "Richmond" on October 17, 1785, located near the mouth of Coal Lick, next to the land of James Eagon. He and wife, Susannah, sold their warrant to Nathaniel Dunham and on February 14, 1789, took letters of dismission from Goshen. Rollin Hughes and wife settled in Indiana or Illinois.

Nathaniel Hughes was living across the Tenmile from his brother Rollin's land, when he served in Captain James Archer's Militia Company. He had this tract of land warranted to him, under the name of "Mount Pleasant" on February 6, 1788. He appears to have been married twice as a deed made in 1795 shows a wife, Leah, then in his will made in Greene County, where it was probated June 19, 1817, he refers to his wife, Rebecca. The land referred to in the deed of March 5, 1795, was sold to Solomon Eagon. The Census of 1790 suggests that he had four sons and three daughters born before 1790, and since guardians were appointed for some of his children in 1817, there is reason to believe he had children by both marriages. (WB. 1. pp. 179.)

The following record has been reconstructed from Orphan Court and will records and lacks absolute confirmation. On the whole we think it is correct in most cases. Without a record of the family of Rollin Hughes, there may be a chance for error. We are especially aware of a John Hughes, who died about 1821, leaving a wife, Phoebe Polk, and two sons, John Hughes, who married Catherine Hunnell, and Richard Hughes, who married Margaret Hunnell. His widow then married Isaac Higgins. (WB. 1. pp. 213.) This family may fit in the family of Nathaniel Hughes, through one of the elder sons.

Children of Nathaniel Hughes

1. Richard Hughes, married Mary, daughter of Barnet Rinehart, Sr. The name of Richard Hughes is found in the Franklin Township tax lists from 1809 until 1826. No certain record is found for his family, but it seems most likely he was the father of Barnet Hughes, born about 1795, as this man is

sometimes taxed for the same piece of property as is taxed to to Richard Hughes.

Children of Richard and Mary (Rinehart) Hughes ?

1. Barnet Hughes, born 1795-97, died in Knox County, Ohio, in 1841, married Sarah Gettys, born June 27, 1798, also died in Knox County. Barnet Hughes married a second time.

   #### Children of Barnet and Sarah (Gettys) Hughes
   1. John Hughes.
   2. James Hughes.
   3. Mary Hughes.
   4. Sarah Hughes.
   5. Elizabeth Hughes.

2. Nathan Hughes, died in Knox County in 1839, married Isabella Grimes. Nathan Hughes was but 27 years of age when he died. His widow died in October 1869, aged 61 years.

   #### Children of Nathan and Isabella (Grimes) Hughes
   1. William G. Hughes.
   2. David H. Hughes.
   3. William N. Hughes.

3. Thomas Hughes, married Eleanor Strawn, an executor of Barnet Hughes.
4. Hiram Hughes, wife's name was Emily, died in Knox County before 1841. Wife was a Thomas.
5. John Hughes.

2. Joseph Hughes.
3. Nathan (iel) Hughes, Jr., born 1785, died November 28, 1854, married Nancy Shearin, daughter of Henry and Sarah (Miller) Shearin, born 1791, died April 17, 1843. Both are buried in the old cemetery in East Waynesburg. Nathaniel Hughes, Jr., estate in O. C. Docket 4. pp. 2 December 1854.

   #### Children of Nathan and Nancy (Shearin) Hughes
   1. Andrew Hughes, born November 1, 1810, married Hannah Crayne, born April 4, 1815.
   2. Nathan Hughes, married Margaret Rinehart, daughter of Samuel S. and Mary (Zook) Rinehart. She was born October 12, 1842. (O. C. Docket 3. pp. 317.)

   #### Children of Nathan and Margaret (Rinehart) Hughes
   1. H. H. Hughes.
   2. Frank Hughes.
   3. Bessie Hughes, married .... Hoge.
   4. Mary Hughes, married .... Maxwell.

   3. Sarah Hughes, married Dawson McClelland, son of Asa and Catherine (Brown) McClelland.
   4. William Hughes, married Jane ...., died before his father. (O. C. Docket 4. pp. 1 December 1854.)

   #### Minor children of William and Jane Hughes
   #### (John Young, Guardian)
   1. John Hughes.
   2. Thomas J. Hughes.
   3. William Porter Hughes.
   4. Elizabeth Hughes.
   5. Rebecca Hughes.

5. Caleb Hughes.
6. Hiram Hughes, married Sarah Ann Burke. (O. C. Docket 3. pp. 428.)

Minor children of Hiram and Sarah Ann (Burke) Hughes
(Charles Black, Guardian)

1. James M. Hughes.
2. Mary C. Hughes.
3. William S. Hughes.
4. Nancy Hughes.

7. Lucy Hughes, married James Connely.
8. John Hughes, married Bessima ...., (O. C. Docket 3. pp. 285 September 1852.)

Children of John and Bessima Hughes

1. Rebecca Jane Hughes, married .... Filby.
2. Sarah Elizabeth Hughes, married James Piatt.
3. John Thomas Hughes.
4. William Spencer Hughes.
5. Arabella Hughes.
6. Nathan Griffith Hughes.
7. Lucy F. Hughes, married .... Babbitt.
8. Nancy Hughes, married George Connely.

4. Sarah Hughes.
5. Elizabeth Hughes, married .... Bell.
6. Jemima Hughes, married .... Harbert. On September 21, 1805, Sarah Harbert and Thomas Hughes took out letters in the estate of Samuel Harbert.
7. James Hughes.
8. John Hughes, a minor child over 14 years of age and under 21 years at the time of the death of Nathaniel Hughes. Richard Ankrom was appointed his guardian in 1817 (O. C. Docket 1. pp. 120.) On March 2, 1847, letters were taken out in the estate of John Hughes. (Estate No. 1254 Greene County.) His wife was Louisa Strawn, daughter of Isaiah and Susannah (Rinehart) Strawn. John Ankrom and Armstrong Pater served as guardians for their minor children. (O. C. Docket 3. pp. 27 September 1847.)

Children of John and Louisa (Strawn) Hughes

1. Elizabeth Hughes.
2. John R. Hughes.
3. Mary Hughes.
4. Ellis Hughes.
5. Eleanor Hughes.
6. Isaiah Hughes.
7. Sarah Hughes.
8. Susannah Hughes.

9. William Hughes, minor over 12 years of age in 1817, Richard Morris appointed guardian.
10. Susannah Hughes.

STEPHEN STILES FAMILY

Stephen Stiles (Styles, etc) is said to have been born in New Castle County, Delaware, on September 5, 1744. This has not been proven beyond any question of doubt, but the date must be approximately correct, for in 1772, Stephen Stiles (spelled Styles) was head of a family, and as such, taxed in Springhill Township, Bedford County, which at that time included the Tenmile Country. It is evident that about this time Stephen Stiles had settled on a 429 acre tract of land near the present Harry Murdock Farm, though he did not secure a patent to this tract until November 26, 1804, calling his site "Independence." While living here he served in the Revolution in Captain James Archer's Company, First Battalion, Washington County Militia, along with his neighbors Thomas Rinehart, Francis Feurt, and John Jones. (Penna Arch. Series VI Vol. 2. pp. 17.) The name is mis-spelled "Hyles" in the muster roll of this company, but one who has seen the flourishes of the early writing could easily mistake an "St" for an "H", thus the error must have been made in the copying from the original militia return.

On October 23, 1792, Stephen Stiles bought out the warrant to another tract of land which he had warranted to Stephen Barber, and had it patented to him May 30, 1793, under the title of "New Stile." This tract of about 254 acres was two farms removed from his original settlement of Stephen Stiles, and located near Love's Hill. He did not own this tract for long, for on May 1, 1795, he sold the entire farm to Christian Cowell, by a deed in which he was joined by his wife, Bithena, being described as of Washington County, Pennsylvania. Then on the 18th of February 1805, Stephen Stiles, joined by wife, Deborra, joined in a deed to John Reynard and sold a part of "Independence," being described then as living in Monongalia County, Virginia. On April 16, 1805, Stephen Stiles and wife, Deborra, of Monongalia County, sold the balance of "Independence" to Ezekiel Knight, with William Stiles, a son, as a witness to the transaction. All these deeds were recorded on October 12, 1805, but the evidence is that Stephen Stiles had lost his wife, Bithena, after 1795, and married Deborra before 1805. (Deed Book 2. pp. 130-131.)

When Stephen Stiles removed to (West) Virginia he settled in the vicinity of Wana, where he died about 1818. His will, made October 27, 1815, naming his wife, Deborra, and seven children, was filed for probate in Monongalia County in May 1819. (Will Book 1. pp. 1.)

Children of Stephen Stiles

1. Job Stiles.
2. Aaron Stiles, may have married Polly Ritenbark.
3. William Stiles, witnessed deed for his father in 1805. He married Sarah Ann (Nancy) Morris, daughter of Robert Morris, who owned "Liberty Hall" adjoining Stephen Stiles. In a suit over "Liberty Hall" Nancy Morris is mentioned as wife of William Stiles. They removed to Monongalia County and settled in the vicinity of Wana, where William Stiles was living when he made his will on February 26, 1850. This will was probated May 24, 1852.

Children of William and Sarah Ann (Morris) Stiles

1. Stephen Stiles.
2. Thomas Stiles, married Frances Cross.
3. Benjamin Stiles, born May 28, 1806, died June 20, 1877; buried at Wana.
4. Cassandra Stiles, married .... Randolph.
5. Sarah Stiles, married .... Bland.
6. John Stiles.
7. Elizabeth Stiles, married .... Cross.

4. Jonathan Stiles, born July 18, 1774, died in Guernsey County, Ohio, November 15, 1860. He married in 1797, Mary Lantz, daughter of John Lantz. She died September 4, 1833. They were parents of fourteen children.

Children of Jonathan and Mary (Lantz) Stiles

1. John Stiles, born May 23, 1800, married Betsie Frankbauer.
2. Stephen Stiles, born March 4, 1802, died July 7, 1886; married (1) Eliza Linn, (2) Francena Lanning.
3. William Stiles, born February 14, 1804, married Mary McCulley (McCullough?).
4. Andrew Stiles, born March 18, 1806, died September 25, 1885; married (1) Mary Kirkpatrick, (2) Amy Henderson.
5. Thomas Stiles, born March 6, 1808, died April 19, 1890; married Catherine McCullough.
6. Simon Stiles, born June 16, 1810, married (1) Phoebe Kirkpatrick, (2) Betsy Donely.
7. Mary Stiles, born June 28, 1812, died 18......; married Jesse Gunn.
8. Jacob Stiles, born July 31, 1814, died July 12, 1892; married Mary M. Gunn.
9. George Stiles, born August 6, 1816, died March 6, 1904; married Sarah Corzinne.
10. Margaret Stiles, born December 14, 1818, died 1910; married Joseph Culbertson.
11. Jonathan Stiles, born November 9, 1820, died March 3, 1871; married Rebecca J. Walker.
12. Deborra Stiles, born October 9, 1822, died September 1, 1890; married Stout Patterson.
13. Lewis Stiles, born November 9, 1824, died May 15, 1892; married Rosanna Barnes.
14. Eliza Stiles, born April 3, 1827, died 1909; married Jacob Barnes.

Of the 14 children above, Thomas, George, Jonathan, Jr., and Lewis lived and died in Martin County, Indiana. Jacob and Margaret were buried in Grant County, Indiana. The other eight children lived and died in Guernsey County, Ohio.

5. Thomas Stiles, not named in will. Died young.
6. Elizabeth Stiles, married John Knight.
7. Ruth Stiles, was the second wife of Barnet Rinehart, who names her in his will, which was probated October 26, 1822. (See Rinehart Records).
8. Lydia Stiles, married in Monongalia County, February 21, 1803, Levi Long.

FORT JACKSON

There is no record to show definitely who built the first fort on the Tenmile, at the site where the town of Waynesburg now stands, nor has the name of the fort been handed down to us. The only reference to the earlier fort is in "Trans Allegheny Pioneers," which states a fort was erected on Tenmile at the site of Fort Jackson in 1759. Richard Jackson also indicates that his fort was on the site of an earlier fort, for in a deed for a portion of his land, which he sold to William Hathaway on March 12, 1790, he called the land "Jackson's Old Fort Site." (Washington County Deed Book 1, F-151). It was on this site that Richard Jackson, William Hathaway and Samuel Hathaway had built a mill, which in later years was operated by Rosses, and is still remembered by many present citizens of Waynesburg.

What sort of building was first used as a place of refuge, can only be surmised, as no description is given, but we can be safe in assuming that it was some trader's strongly built station, probably only a single building, with some sheds for storage and animals. A later account of the actual fort, states that Fort Jackson was originally only the house that Jackson had erected. The full description of the fort, which was built in 1774, when forting again became necessary, is given in Evans and other local historians. This description is not needed in this place, suffice to say, that Richard Jackson's strong house became the center, around which a cluster of cabins were built, with the side facing out, having no windows, and all the cabins joined by a picketed stockade. Each nearby settler was alloted a cabin for his place of safety during any alarm. From what we now know of the population at that date, we would consider the one acre, which it was supposed to cover, a rather conservative estimate of the size, though Evans mentions having seen the outlines of the fort in his day. In one thing, however, Evans is wrong. Richard Jackson built the fort in 1774 and not Samuel Jackson. Records of the land ownership, including the patent from the State of Pennsylvania, and sale deeds showing when and how the land was owned back to 1771 are in court records, and show only Richard Jackson in possession from that date, until he sold out and moved to Bracken County, Kentucky, about 1790.

One thing that lends credence to the belief that the fort was larger than is claimed in Evans, is the fact that it was the most important fort during and for a time after the War of the Revolution. It was used as a rendezvous for the Rangers from all the section. It was the recruiting station of such famous frontiersmen as the Enochs, William Harrod, David Owens, James Seals, and of course, James Hook, who took the first company out of this district to fight for the cause of Freedom. Statements from pensioners all state it was the most important fort, outside Fort Pitt and Fort Henry at Wheeling. It would appear that its environs saw more action and more tragic incidents than either of the other two. Those who defended it remembered the occasions long after they had forgotten other strong points, a thing most evident in the pension applications.

Who were the early pioneers of the vicinity of Fort Jackson? Fortunately a large list of these are available through the land grants, and service records. Comparing the list of these names with statements issued by the owners, and with the known families from whence they came, one might almost claim that the environs of Fort Jackson was an isolated colony of Northern Maryland. Practically all the first settlers were from the head of the Chesapeake Bay. A few are known to have lived across the Maryland Line in the Eastern Pennsylvania Counties, but they, too, had Maryland connections, either ancestral or through business operations. A few like Richard Jackson are still to be determined; even now we are seeking information that will connect him with the Jackson Family who lived in Maryland, on the tract of land that later became a part of Washington, D. C., for there is a tradition in one of the Jackson families, who settled in Greene County, that their antecedents came from the marsh land farm on which the White House now stands.

A few of the names that can be positively traced back to Upper Maryland include James Hook, Thomas Kent, Thomas Slater, John Fee, John Biddle (or Beedle), John Wiley, Kent Mitchell, the Duvalls, John and Richard Ankrom, Thomas Wells, Thomas and Ralph Smith, William Inghram and his sons, Arthur and William; Thomas Rinehart, Sr., George Carroll, James and Solomon Eagon, John Hargus, Booth Stump, John Thrasher, John Jones, William Williams, John Calhoun, possibly the Owenses, Richard Morris, the Whites (Red David and Black David), James Seals, and several others. The Mirandys we know were originally from Lancaster County, Pennsylvania, but Samuel Mirandy was for a time in Upper Maryland. One family whom we have not included in this list is the Hathaways, originally a New Jersey family, but possibly a branch that went into Maryland, where the name is found. The same is true of the Pipes Family, certainly one of the first at Fort Jackson. (For confirmation of this list we refer to the Black Books of Maryland and Brumbaugh's Histories of the Upper Counties of Maryland).

While the settlement was being made about Fort Jackson by Marylanders, there is evidence that a number of families from the Lower Shenandoah Valley, some of whom had gone there from Maryland and Pennsylvania, were also making improvements on the Tenmile in the vicinity of the fort. Augusta County, Virginia, records, of which this section was an administrative part, give numerous references to these attempts at settlement. William Robinson, with Levi Shin, attempted an improvement in 1772, said to have been near the mouth of Tenmile. But from the knowledge of the presence of the Teagardens, Hupps, and Bumgarners being there several years prior to that date, we are inclined to place their locations nearer the fort. This is the more likely since we know the names and locations of others from that section who followed Shin and Robinson. Shin later settled at what is now Shinnston, West Virginia, and Robinson on the run which takes his name.

Jacob Rees, Sr., recorded a deed on July 31, 1775, for land he bought on Tenmile from William Williams, who had bought it on January 8, 1774, from John Jones, who had it from the original improver, John Simpson. This Jacob Rees had been here with Isaac Horner in 1773, and with wife, Hannah, may have been the ancestors of the Rees Family of Rees's Mill, for the land at that place has been mentioned frequently in early records. The John Jones mentioned in this recital is credited by some as being the original owner of the land about Fort Jackson, but he would have had to have been here much earlier, since we know when Richard Jackson got his claim to the land. He is the same John Jones that did settle at the head of Coal Lick.

These Augusta County records also state that James Anderson was employed by David Scott to make an improvement on Tenmile in 1773. He is probably the Anderson who settled at Dotysburg, and whose family intermarried with that of James Eagon in the same vicinity. Rev. David Jones, a native of Chester County, but well known in Lower Augusta, also was here before the Revolution, and closely connected with David Owens, said by some to have been a brother-in-law of Rev. Jones. They first made selections of sites on Grave Creek in 1770, but were driven back to the Tenmile when the Indians resented the encroachments on their land. Martin Wetzel, of that famous family of Indian figthers, also got a survey for land in November 1768. Some of the Sellars Family and the Livengoods were mentioned as early as 1747. It is to be noted that most of these families did not stay on Tenmile, but settled on the West Virginia side, or close to the border on Dunkard Creek.

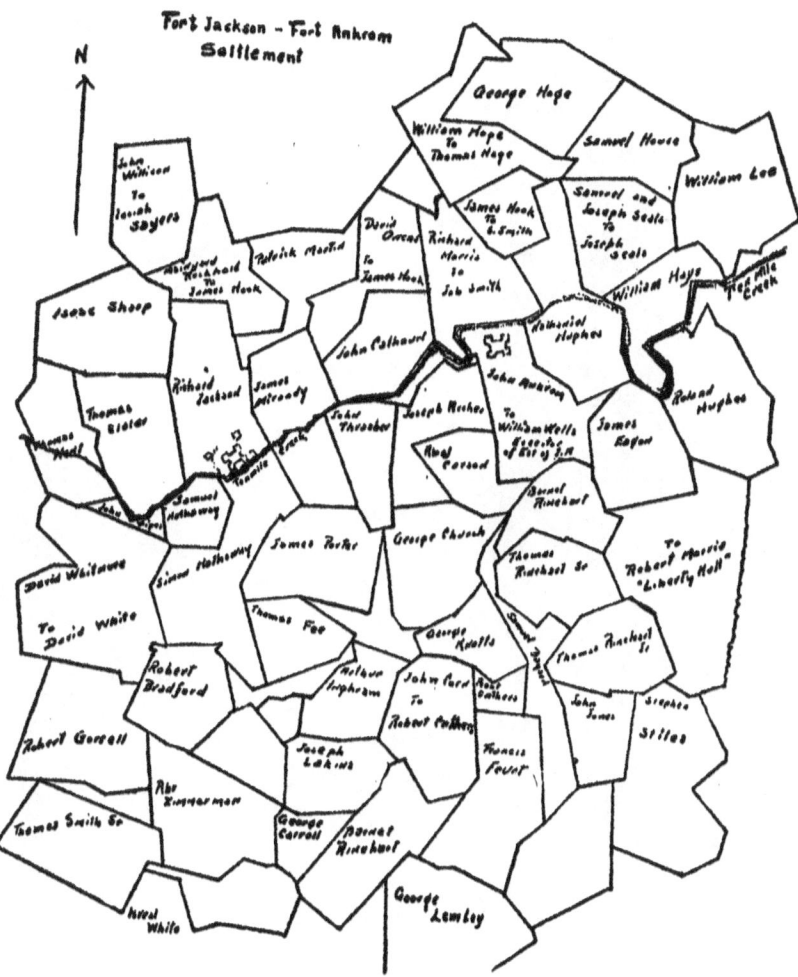

A LETTER OF WILLIAM RHODES TO HIS FATHER
(and the translation)

Boston, March 19, 1782.

HON. FATHER:

I have the pleasure to acquaint you that we are well at present and in hopes you are also. I have been to London since and found everything agreeable but on return was cast away on Cape Cod, lost our vessel but no lives. I expect to go again but to no great advantage. We are all thankful for our health and hope you'll write every opportunity. I remain your dutiful son.

WILLIAM RHODES.

Some time after 1785 William Rhodes, a sea captain from New England, appeared at Fort Jackson, where he opened a trader's post. There is some mystery about this man, who is variously described as a privateer, pirate, etc. His part in the War of the Revolution does not fit into that of a patriot, for we have a letter of his showing he was in London on one of his sea voyages while the War was still on with the mother country. He was a well educated man, his father, Joseph Rhodes, being a school master, first in New England and later at Northampton, Virginia. William Rhodes kept copious papers with business transactions and, along with these, frequent comments on people and happenings of the times at Fort Jackson. A few years ago the papers of William Rhodes were being taken to the city dump for destruction when the author recognized their historical character and rescued them, but not before some had been destroyed. Among them were the accounts of William Rhodes for the years of 1789 to 1794, giving the names of the people who were dealing with him at the fort. These lists, along with many other papers, have been photostated by the Library of Congress, and are now a national reference source. The originals remain in the possession of the author, awaiting a safe depository. We believe it a part of our historical papers to publish the list of creditors as shown for August 27, 1789. We have endeavored to fill in the first names, where authentic proof can be found, since most of the list has only initials or last names. This is the list of names. The sums after the names are in pounds, shillings, and pence:

Name	£	s	d	Name	£	s	d
Simeon Archer	0	1	4	James Thrasher	1	3	4
Joseph Archer	1	5	3	John Thrasher	0	5	4
James Archer	2	16	6	.... Tribble	0	2	0
Michael Bowen	0	17	3	Elisha Wiley	1	6	1
William Bradford	0	12	3	Solomon White	0	8	3
John Bryant	1	2	10	William White	0	15	4
.... Bills (Bell)		13	4	George Church	0	3	9
Andrew Commons (Cummins)	2	4	0	Jacob (?) Crow	0	9	0
				Silas Crayne	0	4	3
John Coyan (Cowan)	1	7	7	William Delany	0	4	0
.... Chanler	0	11	9	.... Die	0	3	3
John Crag (Craig)	0	3	0	Alexander Dollison	1	3	0
.... Camp	0	3	0	John Duvall	0	10	0
William Cathers	0	12	5	Jacob Duvall	2	7	0
P....... Jones	0	4	6	.... Davie (Davis)	1	12	0
John Jones	1	1	0	Conrad Duvall	0	1	6
Thomas Kent	0	18	6	Philip Durbin	0	4	3
.... McGuire		12	2	Jonah Eaton	0	10	0
James Morandy	1	11	10	John Gray	0	2	0
Samuel Morandy	0	19	0	Robert Gorrell	1	12	8
N....... Morandy	0	1	9	Davy Gray	0	5	0
George Morandy	2	7	3	.... Glover	0	4	0
Isaac Meeks	0	4	0	James Galloway	1	6	0
James Morise (Morris)	0	2	6	James Gunner	0	1	6
Basil Morise	0	8	2	Samuel Hathaway	0	18	7
Ezekiel Morrie (Morris)	0	5	0	Nathan (?) Hughes	0	2	3
Richard Morrie (Morris)	0	3	0	William Hathaway	3	0	9
Archibald Morrie	0	3	0	Solomon Hoge	0	11	6
Hezekiah Stewart	0	8	3	William Hickman	0	4	1
John Shriver	0	2	6	Arthur Inghram	0	5	0
Josias Sowers (Sayers)	0	15	5	William Inghram	0	6	3
Isaac Stewart	0	11	6	Elevin Timmons	0	12	6
James Seals	2	4	3	David Jennins (gs)	0	5	0
Elisha Stewart	0	19	10	Samuel Morandy	1	14	11
.... Southerland	0	3	0	Widow Owens	0	5	3
Abraham Simmerman	0	11	3	William McCoy	0	14	6

E....... McCoy	0	18	0	Thomas Wells	0	3	8
Mathias O'Felty	0	12	0	Elijah Wiley	1	8	7
James Parker	3	14	1	David White	0	2	6
Richard Parker	0	11	3	Thomas Watson	0	1	6
James Parker	0	11	3	John Wiley	0	9	0
Thomas Parker	1	1	0	Levi White	0	19	10
Philip Hibbs	0	11	0	Thomas Wolverton	1	13	3
Lacy Hibbs	1	6	10	James Morandy	3	14	6
.... Purdom	3	0	0	John McMillen	1	5	3
A....... Parker	1	15	9	J. McKee	0	4	0
John Pratt	0	19	0	.... Adams	0	13	10
Thomas Slater	0	2	0	Clifton Bowen	0	6	0
Samuel Seals	0	8	6	William Boner	1	4	0
Leonard Sellars	0	15	3	.... Bell	0	9	0
Joseph Seals	1	19	6	John Bowler	2	10	0
Barnet Rinehart	0	8	0	.... Dunham	0	5	0
W. Wright	0	10	6	Francis Feurt	0	19	0
Lewis Wright	0	10	6	Silas Hathaway	0	3	0
Thomas Rinehart	0	15	4	Thomas Smith	0	9	3
Reuben Ross	1	0	2	Simon Hathaway	0	15	0
John Ross	1	3	0	George Hoge	0	16	0
Joseph Ross	0	12	6	Samuel House	0	18	0
Henry Ross	0	5	0	Joseph Seals	0	17	0
J. Ryan	0	2	0	John Scott	1	5	9
Jacob Smittle	0	14	6	James Stewart	2	1	6
B. Steal	1	19	0	Stephen Stiles	0	3	3
John Wiley	2	2	4				
Jonah Wiley	1	0	5	Izrael Wiley	0	9	11
Israel White	0	9	10	Red David White	0	2	9

This list is almost a census for what became Franklin Township, Greene County, for with few exceptions, they all lived within the borders of that township.

RICHARD JACKSON

There can be little doubt that Richard Jackson, founder of Fort Jackson, which bore his name, came to the Tenmile from Lower Frederick County, Maryland. Prince George's County, Maryland, was formed in 1695, and in the list of taxables in Rock Creek Hundred in 1719, as gathered by David Jones, constable, are found the names of Abraham Lakin, James Hook, Thomas Stump, John Bradford, William McCoy, John Williams, John Hardin, and John Jackson. These are names to keep in mind. Rock Creek Hundred took its name from Rock Creek Parish, and both take their name from the stream of that name that runs through the present District of Columbia. In the list of taxables for the same Rock Creek Hundred in 1733, a number of these names are still found, to which can be added the names of Benjamin Thrasher and George Slater. The name of John Jackson is then found in Potomac Hundred with the names of Robert Inghram and William Inghram, William Brown, John Gray, and John Jones. At the same date Abraham Lakin, John Jackson, William Prather, John Pigman, and Thomas Smith are in Eastern Branch Hundred. Frederick County, Maryland, was formed in 1748, and included the present county plus what is now Montgomery and Washington Counties, both of which were a part of Frederick until 1776, and included the site of present Washington, D. C. A petition was sent to the Assemblies of Maryland in 1751, asking for the formation of a new county out of Frederick and Prince George's Counties, and among the names of the petitioners are found John Jones, Alexander Jackson, William Stump, William Fee, Joseph Lakin, James Crawford, and Thomas Fletcher. To the same session of the Assembly went a petition from Nicholas and Greenberry Ridgely to have an entail removed from tracts of land in Prince George's County, known as "Lakins Forest" and "Ridgely's Addition." These facts of history are given in order to show the various family ties of those who settled in the vicinity of Fort Jackson, and to back up traditions in the Jackson Family.

Of these traditions, there is a parallel in the lives of Henry Jackson, Sr., and Richard Jackson of Fort Jackson. A story is told about both these men in which each is supposed to have been the actor. Both families claim their ancestor was caught at one eventful date of their lives, outside the fort by a party of Indians too large to fight single-handed. Coming within sight of the fort in their retreat, and while the Indians still could not see clearly, this Jackson turned and made as though he was leading a sally from the fort. The Indians thinking a body of men were coming to meet them, turned and fled and Jackson got back within the safety zone with his scalp. As this story is told about both Richard and Henry Jackson, a relationship of the families is suggested, and the story may refer to a common ancestor rather than either individual.

As Henry Jackson, Sr., settled on Whiteley Creek, we hope to present a story of his family under that heading, yet a recital of his family record here is necessary to connect the Jackson Family with the Rock Creek section of Maryland. He is said to have lived in that part of Frederick County, Maryland, which went to make up the District of Columbia. Their farm was located in what was known as "The Poison Fields" or where Washington, D. C., was later built. His wife was Elizabeth Stump, daughter of Thomas and Jane (Booth) Stump. When Robert Booth died in Loudon County, Virginia, across the Potomac from Frederick County, Maryland, he mentions Thomas Stump in his will, which was witnessed by Henry Jackson and Alexis (Alexander) Jackson. A Robert Booth Stump was one of the first taxables in the vicinity of Fort Jackson. While the name John Jackson is a very common one, a possible ancestor for the Tenmile pioneers seems to be a John Jackson, whose will was filed in Frederick, Maryland, May 27, 1761, in which he names his wife, Ruth, a son, Alexander, and "other children." As Alexander, Henry, and Richard Jackson all were among the Tenmile Country Pioneers, it is possible that Henry and Richard were in the "other children."

Benjamin Lakin, born August 23, 1767, who died February 5, 1849, son of Benjamin and Rachel (Fee) Lakin, and grandson of Abraham and Martha (Lee) Lakin, wrote a manuscript record of his family. Among other things he pointed out that his Uncle Thomas Fee, had a daughter, Mary, who became the second wife of Richard Jackson. This daughter of Thomas Fee was by a first marriage with a Miss Thrasher. The second wife of Thomas Fee was Sarah Leith, sister of Captain James Hook's wife, Mary Leith, both of them daughters of Robert Leith and his wife Sarah Lakin.

Recital of all these genealogical facts is given here to identify and explain the probable background of Richard Jackson. Later the Benjamin Lakin Manuscript will be given in its entirety, along with the genealogical record of the Lakins and Fees, both of whom were Fort Jackson Pioneer Families. Frequent other references will also be made to it in pointing out relationships in the Tenmile Country.

Richard Jackson first appears officially in local records when he bought in the Fall of 1771, a tract of land from Winser Pipes. On December 10, 1772, he sold a part of this land, described as being "situated on the South side of Williams' Run, joining Hendrick's land," to Ralph Smith of Baltimore, Maryland. At the same time he sold Ralph Smith another piece of land described as being on Richard Jackson's Run. Ralph Smith had purchased this land for his father, Thomas Smith, and on August 17, 1773, made a deed to him. The first of these tracts contained 800 acres and was the place to which Thomas Smith, Jr., came to settle and impart the name of Smith's Creek, to what had been known as Williams's Run. The other tract was near Fort Jackson. (Greene County Deed Book 1. pp. 25.) The recital of these deeds place Richard Jackson in posession of the land on which he built his fort in 1774, Jackson's Run or Jackson Creek, being still marked so on local maps. It is the stream that flows along the Eastern end of Waynesburg, entering the Tenmile back of the Nazarene Church. No wife joined these deeds.

Richard Jackson considered himself still possessed of much land when he applied on November 13, 1779, to the Pennsylvania Land Office for 1400 acres of land by virtue of a Virginia Certificate. In accordance to a ruling limiting the amount of land allowed under the Virginia Certificates, Richard Jackson was granted 404 acres, including the site of the fort.

During the Revolution Richard Jackson was a member of Captain James Archer's Company of Washington County Militia. (Penna. Ach. Series VI. Vol. 2. pp. 17-18.) Then in March 1785, he joined with Samuel Hathaway, who owned the land across the Tenmile, to erect a mill, setting aside to Hathaway 5½ acres. It was before this time that Richard Jackson married Mary Fee, for by a deed dated March 12, 1790, Mary joined him in selling out to Samuel and William Hathaway. (Washington County Deed Book 1-F-147-151.) It was about this date that Richard Jackson went to Mason County, Kentucky, where he took ill suddenly in 1792, and died before he could make a will. But a nun-cupative will was filed in his estate by his widow and James Mirandy, a former neighbor on the Tenmile. They conveyed to the Court the wishes of Richard Jackson as expressed before he died, and Mary (Fee) Jackson, with her brother John Fee, were named to administer the estate for a son, John Jackson, and a number of school age children, who were not named. Two years later Mary Jackson completed the purchase of land from Phillip Buckner and wife, Tabia. It is probable that she went to live on this one-hundred acre tract of land on Locust Creek, for on March 7, 1811, she deeded it, along with her household effects, to her son, Richard Jackson, Jr. At the time of his death, Richard Jackson was possessed of considerable wealth, for Mary Jackson was bonded to the amount of 2000 pounds, compared with the 30 pounds of "Lawful Virginia Money," which Mary Jackson paid for the Locust Creek Property.

Children of Richard Jackson

1. John Jackson, got the Family Bible, and is probably the John Jackson, who died in Mason County, Kentucky, where his will was filed September 1801. This will was made October 10,

1795, and gave his estate to his wife, Margaret, then to go to her brothers and sisters, and his own brothers and sisters, indicating he left no children.
2. Sally Jackson, married, January 9, 1792, John Schroffe, a former neighbor at Fort Jackson. Her father, Richard Jackson, gave his consent.
3. Richard Jackson, Jr., who got his mother's land on Locust Creek, by deed recorded in 1811.

JAMES MIRANDA

James Miranda (Mirandy, Morandy, etc.) was born in Lancaster County, Pennsylvania. He settled on Tenmile Creek before 1774. In an interview with Draper, Mrs. Phoebe Miranda stated that Samuel and James Miranda were boys when they settled at Fort Jackson in 1774. (3S256) They must have been pretty big boys for Samuel Miranda was born January 5, 1751. James Miranda took out a patent to the tract of land adjoining Fort Jackson, roughly a part of the Bonar addition and the Sayers Farm, which he had warranted to him on December 23, 1784. It was not patented to him until 1790, at which time he appears to have left for Kentucky and settled in Mason County, in the part that later went to make up Bracken County. It was here that he died sometime after June 1, 1816, for on that date he made his will in which he named his children.

Children (Book B. 109 Bracken County, Kentucky)

1. James Miranda, Jr.
2. Samuel Miranda.
3. Isaac Miranda.
4. Thomas Miranda.
5. Jonathan Miranda.
6. John Miranda.
7. ...., ..., who married Michael C. Snyder.

SAMUEL MIRANDA

Samuel Miranda was born in Lancaster County, Pennsylvania, January 5, 1751. In June 1774, while living in Lancaster County (?) he went out in Lord Dunmore's Campaign and served under Captain Michael Cresap, when they destroyed a small town across the Muskingum and then returned to Fort Pitt. In the War of the Revolution he entered the service at the Fort on Redstone under Captain David Rogers. He served some time as a spy on the movements of the British Forces of Lieutenant Thomas Nichols. Later he served with Captain David Owens and Captain John Wetzel as a Frontier Ranger, and was also a member of Captain James Archer's Company at Fort Jackson. His pension application made on May 20, 1833, in Bracken County, Kentucky, is as hazy as one would expect from a man in his 82nd year, and we have tried to correct some of his statements with known military movements of the time. In an interview with L. C. Draper, Mrs. Phoebe Miranda said that Samuel and James Miranda were boys on the Tenmile at

Fort Jackson in 1774. From the known age we would hardly call Samuel a boy, but there seems to be truth in the rest of her statement. In the Census of 1790, Samuel Miranda was head of a family, which apparently consisted of himself, wife, three minor aged sons, and three daughters, however he left here very soon afterwards and settled in Bracken County, Kentucky. His wife died about that time and Samuel Miranda married in Kentucky in 1798, Elizabeth Salt. Sometime before February 12, 1834, he died according to records of the pension office, his widow being still alive. His children are not mentioned in the estate records of Bracken County, but we have the birth records of four children by his first marriage, while the marriage records below appear to be those of Samuel's children by his first marriage.

1. George Miranda, married in Kentucky on March 29, 1793, Sarah Wood.
2. Polly Miranda, married on May 5, 1803, in Kentucky, David Owens.
3. Isaac Miranda (?), married, February 13, 1796, Rachel Harrod, daughter of Colonel William and Amelia (Stephens) Harrod.
4. James Miranda, son by second marriage, born in 1800.
5. John Miranda, son by second marriage, born 1802.
6. Amanda Miranda, daughter by second marriage, born 1804.
7. Rebecca Miranda, daughter by second marriage, born 1806, married Robert Lytle.

THE SLATER FAMILY

This family name is found among the list of taxables for Rock Creek Hundred, Prince George's County, Maryland, for the year 1733. Other names of families in this same list include Bradford, Riley, Hoskinson, Williams, White, Parker, and James Hook, all names that are familiar among the settlers about Fort Jackson. The name of Thomas Slater is found in the muster roll of Evan Shelby's Company in General Forbes' Campaign, as is the name of William English, a later neighbor of Slater on the Tenmile. (Boquet Papers 21644 Vol. 2. pp. 182.) A number of other local pioneers are also in this list.

The Pennsylvania Land Office reports that when Thomas Slater applied for his patent to the tract of land known as "Eden," which was granted to him on January 12, 1780, he stated that he had made his original improvement on the Tenmile on May 17, 1771. It is not clear that he stayed on after making his improvement as his name is not in the Springhill Township tax list for 1772, and we find a Thomas Slater among others in a petition to Governor Robert Eden of Maryland, about August 6, 1774. It may well be that he returned the following Spring along with his neighbor, Thomas Kent, the Inghrams and others to make his permanent settlement. A number of reasons have been given to show why he named his tract "Eden," but this item suggests that it was in honor of the governor of Maryland with whom he came in contact. It was on a part of this tract that the county town of Waynesburg was laid out in 1797.

Thomas Slater was born in Maryland on February 4, 1739, and died at Waynesburg on January 24, 1814. His wife was Eleanor .... who died May 10, 1813. She was born January 10, 1746, and is buried with her husband in the old cemetery in East Waynesburg. The name of Thomas Slater is found in the muster roll of Captain James Archer's Company. Due to his advanced age it is probable that this service mostly consisted of guard duty at Fort Jackson, which is related in some of the earlier histories. The will of Thomas Slater is in Will Book 1. pp. 124, and it was probated January 28, 1814.

Children of Thomas and Eleanor Slater

1. Sarah Slater, born 1760, died August 1, 1854; married at Fort Jackson, to Israel White, who was born June 6, 1761, and died January 3, 1816. She then married John Shriver. (See Israel White Records.)
2. Mary Slater, married Joseph Lakin, son of Benjamin and Rachel (Fee) Lakin. After her death Joseph Lakin married Margaret Simmons.

Children of Joseph and Mary (Slater) Lakin

1. Thomas Lakin.
2. Eleanor Lakin.
3. Benjamin Lakin.
4. John Lakin.
5. James Lakin.

3. Jemima Slater, married (1) .... Hathaway, and after his death she married (2) September 20, 1810, in Warren County, Ohio, John Flemming.
4. Thomas Slater, Jr., removed to Knox County, Ohio, where in the third term of Court in that County on April 9, 1812, he sought a divorce from his wife, Lovina .... It was not granted as reported in Hill's "History of Knox County."
5. Henry Slater, married Rebecca Jennings, daughter of Jacob and Phoebe (Ball) Jennings. It is reported they went to Knox County, Ohio, where both died in December 1830. A daughter, Esther, born March 1, 1804, married David Roberts in Knox County.
6. Nancy (?) Slater, wife of John Hawn, Sr., who according to Hill's "History of Knox County," was a soldier of the Revolution, and was a member of the first jury in Knox County. It is evident from the will of Thomas Slater that some disagreement existed between him and his son-in-law, whom he mentions by name but does not give the name of John Hawn's wife. A son, John Hawn, Jr., is named.
7. John Slater, no record.
8. James Slater, no record. One of these two sons may have married a daughter of Captain James Hook. A Slater-Hook marriage is spoken of in the Hook records.
9. Elizabeth Slater, no record.
10. Eleanor Slater, born 1778, married at Fort Jackson, John Pipes, who owned land across the Tenmile from Thomas Slater. This land was sold to the Duvalls by the sheriff in 1814. Examination of the Hill-Dupui Ledger of 1819-22 suggests the following children, there may have been others. Mrs. Jacob Jackson, late of Waynesburg, had a set of silver spoons, engraved with "E. S." said to have been the property of Eleanor (Slater) Pipes, from whom Mrs. Jackson was descended.

Probable Children

1. Abner Pipes.
2. James Pipes.

3. John Pipes, Jr.
4. Thomas Pipes.
5. Jemima Pipes, married John Morris; both are buried in the Morrisville Cemetery.
11. Snowden Slater, died March 16, 1819. A deed of March 20, 1819, shows he left a widow Mary (Fry) Slater. (Deed Book 4. pp. 164.) She was a daughter of Christian Fry. (Deed Book 3. pp. 130.)
12. Isaac Slater, born October 21, 1787, died December 17, 1831; married Mary Workman, who died February 11, 1869, aged 82 years. She was a daughter of James and Lucy Workman. Isaac Slater was a very prominent man and large owner of land about Waynesburg, and died without living issue. His only son, Isaac Slater, Jr., is buried with the parents in the old cemetery in East Waynesburg.

WILLIAM BROWN FAMILY

Brown's Run, now known as "Toll Gate Run" or "Bloody Run" was named for William Brown, who settled at this location next to the land of Thomas Slater about 1771. Evans and Waychoff tell an interesting story of the tragic ending of William Brown, when he and Simon Rinehart had planned to exchange their lands, but both were killed in the process of moving to their new sites. A witness of this event tells a slightly different story, while a third narrator expands on both stories. Harrod Newland, a Frontier Ranger living near Jefferson, was one of the men called out to follow the band of marauding Indians that committed the act, and in his pension application from Indianapolis, July 17, 1833, says that the time of the incident was April of 1781, and that William Brown, William English, John Owens, and another man were killed at their sugar camp as they were removing their kettles to go home. William Harrod, Jr., tells almost the same story, adding the name of Simon Rinehart, saying they were removing goods on sleds when the Indians killed them, but sets the date as April 1782. Since we know that John Owens' estate was probated April 6, 1781, we must accept the Newland record as the more accurate. This transfer of land by William Brown and Simon Rinehart being so tragically ended, it was not revived by the heirs of William Brown. Then on March 29, 1785, William Brown and Vincent Brown, sons of the dead man, conveyed a part of the tract to James Seals, who on May 30, 1791, added to his tract by purchase from Thomas Kent and wife, Ann, a part of the tract warranted to Thomas Kent under the title "Fogaronian" December 17, 1784. Prior to that on February 12, 1791, Thomas Kent and wife, Ann, had conveyed a part of their tract to Mary Brown, widow of the slain William Brown, though she was in the tax lists for 1784 through 1788. It was on this land that Captain James Seals built his stone house in the year 1792, after buying out Vincent and William Brown, sons of the deceased William Brown. (Washington County Deed Book 1-B pp. 61-62 and Deed Book 1-I-533.) The widow, Mary Brown, with some of her children, sold out a part of "Fogaronian" to Thomas Mitchell on September 11, 1805. (Greene County Deed Book 2. pp. 124.)

Children of William and Mary Brown

1. Mathew Brown, a lad of 17 years of age when his father was

killed. He escaped being killed by a remarkable leap over an embankment as told by Waychoff. He joined his mother in the deed September 11, 1805.

2. Vincent Brown, who escaped to Fort Jackson and gave the alarm when his father was killed. He made a deed to James Seals, March 27, 1785, for his share of the property. He is listed in the tax list of Franklin Township in 1788, but is missing in the 1790 Census. George Fee released land to him January 20, 1790.

3. William Brown, Jr., sold out his interest to James Seals on March 29, 1785, and disappeared from the record.

4. Sarah Brown, had married Captain James Seals in July 1784, while still a very young girl. Her eldest son, William Seals, stated that she was the mother of three children before she reached her 20th birthday. He was born in 1785.
(See Captain James Seals Records)

5. John Brown, he and wife, Jane ...., joined the deed of September 11, 1805.

6. Catherine Brown, married Asa McClelland, who died about 1854. Asa McClelland and wife, Catherine, sold a lot in Waynesburg, in 1810, but his wife named in his will is listed as Elizabeth .... His first wife seems to have died before 1843 when he made deeds in which no wife joined. His will is in Greene County Will Book 3 pp. 171, and was probated October 19, 1854.

Children of Asa McClelland

1. Nancy McClelland, wife of .... McFann.
2. Elizabeth McClelland, wife of .... Porter.
3. Mary McClelland.
4. Mariah, wife of Levi Rinehart.
5. Dawson McClelland, died before his father. His wife was Sarah Hughes.
6. Asa McClelland, Jr.

THE JOHN WILEY FAMILY

John Wiley was born in Maryland, and settled on a branch of the Tenmile, which is identified in early maps as Wiley's Run, and flowed into the Tenmile a short distance west of Fort Jackson. It originally divided Waynesburg from East Waynesburg, and is now known as Purman Run. John Wiley did not patent any land, but it is probable his tract was the one which was patented to Josiah Sayers under the title of "Old Wiley's Camp" at the head of the Run. John Willison (John Wiley's son?) got the first warrant for this tract on an application describing it as "on or near the Road running from Washington to Hathaway's Mill," showing this road from Waynesburg to Washington was in use August 28, 1792. (Warrant No. 220 Penna. Land Office.) Traditions in the Wiley Family say that John Wiley stopped for a time at Old Fort Redstone, where his son, Eli Wiley, was born in 1773. His wife was a Miss Vernon, though late in life, after the death of his first wife, he married Mrs. Mary (McCormick) Seals, widow of Samuel Seals. In the Revolution, John Wiley served in Captain James Archer's Militia Company. (Penna Arch. Series VI Vol. 2. pp. 18.) He joined the migration to Mason County, Kentucky, and settled on

Locust Creek near the present town of Augusta. History says he was a man of large frame, raw-boned, more than six feet tall, dark complexioned with heavy eyebrows, high cheek bones, and strong chin. He was born about 1732, and lived to be a few days less than 100 years old. He was father of ten children, all by the first marriage.

Family of John Wiley

1. Elijah Wiley, died in Bracken County, Kentucky. Ejectment proceedings in the estate of James Seals show his wife was Martha Seals. (Appearance Docket 1. pp. 47, October 1798.) His children were:
    1. Betsy Wiley, married .... Hickman.
    2. Sarah Ann Wiley, married .... Carter.
    3. Phoebe Wiley, married .... Heck.
    4. John Wiley.
    5. Jesse Wiley.
    6. Hiram Wiley.
    7. Nelson Wiley.
2. Elisha Wiley, served in Captain James Archer's Militia Company. Ran a mill on Locust Creek in Mason County, Kentucky.
3. Susan Wiley, married Rev. Joseph Carter. They went to Rush County, Indiana.
4. Elizabeth Wiley, married .... Wooster, settled in Kentucky.
5. Eli Wiley, ejectment proceedings mentioned in the James Seals estate, indicate he married Elizabeth Seals, daughter of James and Sarah Seals.
6. John Wiley, Jr.
7. Jesse Wiley.
8. Hiram Wiley, lived to a great age in Bracken County, Kentucky.
9. Joseph Wiley, born April 17, 1779, married Susan Worthington, and went to Madison, Indiana, where he died October 16, 1841. He was the ancestor of Dr. Harvey Wiley, famous government chemist, who was the author of the Pure Food and Drug Act.
10. Daniel Wiley.

WILLIAM WOOD

The American ancestor of this family seems to have been Isaac Wood, who came from England, and after his marriage, on Long Island, New York, removed to Harford County, Maryland, and settled near Havre de Grace. His wife was Elizabeth Willborn. At least two and probably three of their children came to the Tenmile Country with the Eagons, Inghrams, and other Upper Maryland families, they being William Wood, Hannah, who married Kent Mitchell, and possibly Martha, wife of James Mitchell.

William Wood was born in Maryland in 1734, and came to Greene County, about the same time William and Arthur Inghram in 1774, for the next year we find him a member of Captain James Hook's Calico Shirt Company that marched to Boston to join the Continental Army. He settled on land near the Inghrams in the Richhills, where he died December 28, 1806, and is buried in the Mt. Pleasant Church Cemetery. His wife was Margaret Mitchell, daughter of Thomas (?) and Hannah (Osborne) Mitchell, born in

1745, and died March 4, 1846, aged 101 years and 6 months. She is buried with her husband. William Wood's Estate was filed for probate January 5, 1807, with James and Solomon Eagon acting as administrators. The children were:
1. Elizabeth Wood, born 1764 (?) died May 26, 1820; married Samuel Bayard, who died in 1814.

Children

1. Sarah Bayard, born March 3, 1799, died February 20, 1855; married, January 20, 1842, Enos Gillette, born April 29, 1796, died June 29, 1834. She then married John Murdock, born September 15, 1773 (or September 14, 1775) who died July 31, 1867.
2. William Bayard, married Nancy Scott, who died in 1840.
3. Samuel Bayard, married Mary Mitchell.
4. James Bayard, married Joanna Scott.
5. Perry Bayard, married Nancy Sayers, born 1803, died January 25, 1891.
6. Nancy Bayard, married .... McBeth.
7.
8.

2. Sarah Wood, married William Donahue.
3. Hannah Wood, married Barnet Eagon. (See James Eagon Records.)
4. Isaac Wood, born October 22, 1774, died April 3, 1852, married Elizabeth (Mitchell) Hill, born June 19, 1769, died April 11, 1852.

Children

1. John Wood.
2. Edward Wood, married Rachel Black.
3.
4. Thomas Wood, never married.
5. Elizabeth Wood.

5. Micajah Wood, born 1776, was in the War of 1812, died August 1858; married Jane Mason, born February 6, 1780, died December 1858; buried with husband in Woodruff Cemetery at Holbrook.

Children

1. Sarah Wood, married George Lightner.
2. Mary Wood, married John Coudy.
3. Thomas Wood, born October 15, 1806, died June 6, 1903; married Mary Ann Strosnider.
4. William Wood, born January 4, 1809, married Hannah Hartley.
5. Isaac Wood, born April 30, 1811, married Catherine Scott.
6. Margaret Wood, born September 9, 1813, married Nicholas Johnson.
7. Martha Wood, born February 8, 1816, married Brad Tukesbury.
8. James Wood, born October 14, 1819; married, March 11, 1844, Mary A. Hoge.
9. Nancy Wood, married Thomas Knight.

6. Mary Wood, born 1776, (June 8), died September 1, 1858, married Ephraim Sayers, born November 6, 1773, died November 1, 1857.

Children

1. Elizabeth Sayers, born 1804, married George Adams.
2. William W. Sayers, born August 12, 1805, died May 22, 1886; married, March 11, 1835, Rebecca Adams, born April 4, 1813, died July 31, 1873.
3. Thomas Sayers, died 1807.
4. Mary Sayers.
5. Margaret Sayers, born 1811, died 1811.
6. Ezra Mitchell Sayers, born May 30, 1812, died March 3, 1909; married (1) December 25, 1839, Jane Adams, born June 26, 1822, died April 3, 1847; married (2) Harriet Tanner, who died February 16, 1892.
7. Ephraim M. Sayers, born May 5, 1817, married Elizabeth Horley.

7. Martha Wood, married John Anderson.
8. Nancy Wood, married Hiram Conwell.
9. Edward Wood, born November 21, 1784, died April 30, 1835; married, October 13, 1808, Margaret Fitz Randolph, born May 14, 1792, died September 21, 1875.

Children

1. John D. Wood, born August 8, 1811, died September 26, 1876; married (1) Nancy Critchfield, born 1816, died October 12, 1849. He married (2) Sybil Barnes, born September 9, 1807, died September 10, 1888. They were married June 11, 1850.
2. Jonah R. Wood, born 1813, died October 5, 1888; married Jane Dunlap, born 1813, died on April 17, 1897.
3. Joel Jackson Wood, born October 3, 1814, died October 10, 1895; married (1) April 21, 1846, Mary Shinn, born March 12, 1817, died September 14, 1852; married (2) Margaret Boyd, born October 26, 1833, died November 5, 1895.
4. Isaac Wood, born July 11, 1820, died June 3, 1902; married August 26, 1852, Rebecca Braden, born January 21, 1831, died July 4, 1912.
5. Hiram Wood, born May 22, 1816, died August 10, 1855.
6. Phoebe Wood, born August 4, 1830, died April 5, 1907.

10. Thomas Wood, born ...., died 1846 in Missouri. Married Anne Fitz Randolph, who died in 1851.

Children

1. James Wood, never married.
2. William W. Wood, born August 20, 1812, died July 31, 1897; married Sarah Wright Gregg, born October 31, 1815, died March 23, 1884. Woodford, Illinois.
3. Israel Wood, born 1814, died December 24, 1893, married Minerva Sargent, born 1815, died June 10, 1896.
4. Nancy Wood.
5. Osborne M. Wood, married Permelia Lanham.
6. Lucinda Wood, died 1853, married Franklin Townsend.
7. Margaret Wood, never married.
8. Clarkson Wood, never married.
9. Elizabeth Wood, married Asa Haverly.

11. William Wood, born May 25, 1792, died November 25, 1841; married about 1814, Anne Chesney, born in Maryland, June 7, 1798, died December 22, 1868.

Children

1. William Wood, born 1815 on January 15. He married .... Frost, Johnson County, Illinois.
2. Elizabeth Wood, born September 20, 1817, married Mordecai Barnes, Monroe County, Virginia.
3. Thomas Wood, born 1820 (February 9).
4. Ephraim Sayers Wood, born May 3, 1822, died June 22, 1895; married, June 7, 1846, Martha A. Moffitt, born March 31, 1821, died January 7, 1903.
5. Mary Wood, born March 11, 1832; married, November 5, 18......, John Thomas.
6. Jesse Wood, born July 31, 1835, died March 29, 1897; married, April 8, 1854, Mariah Fordyce, who died February 4, 1922.

Family of Kent and Hannah (Wood) Mitchell

Hannah Wood, daughter of Isaac and Elizabeth (Willborn) Wood, was born in 1742, and died in Greene County, September 19, 1823. She is buried in the cemetery at Morrisville, near Waynesburg. Hannah Wood first married, about 1764, Kent Mitchell, who according to Brumbaugh, was living in Harford County, Maryland, in 1776, and aged 33 years. He died about 1786, leaving a number of minor children for whom guardians were appointed. (Washington County O. C. Docket 1. pp. 22-28 February 1786.) After the death of Kent Mitchell, Hannah married John Jones and settled near Fort Jackson.

Children of Kent and Hannah (Wood) Mitchell

1. Shadrack Mitchell, born about 1766, (Brumbaugh record), died before 1862. (W. B. 4. pp. 28.) He married January 26, 1796, Margaret Rinehart, daughter of Thomas and Hannan (Inghram) Rinehart. A guardian was appointed for him.

Children of Shadrack and Margaret (Rinehart) Mitchell

1. Thomas Mitchell.
2. John Mitchell.
3. Jesse Mitchell.
4. Elizabeth Mitchell.
5. Asa Mitchell, born October 6, 1811; married, January 25, 1835, Rachel Johns, born on December 1, 1815.
6. Delilah Mitchell.
7. Isaac Mitchell, born September 9, 1816; married, October 4, 1838, Elizabeth Barnes.
8. Hannah Mitchell.
9. Maria Mitchell.

2. Elizabeth Mitchell, born June 19, 1769, died April 11, 1852; married (1) James Hill, son of William and Elizabeth (Atkinson) Hill. He died and his widow then married Isaac Wood, born October 22, 1774, died April 3, 1852.

Children of Elizabeth (Mitchell) Hill-Wood

1. Sarah Hill, born May 20, 1795, married Joseph Morris, son of James and Phoebe (Sayers) Morris.

2. William Hill, for whom Thomas Mitchell served as guardian in 1808.
3.
4.
5.
6. John Wood.
7. Thomas Wood, died April 17, 1877, aged 74 years, 3 months 3 days.
8. Edward Wood, married Rachel Black. He died October 22, 1878, aged 72 years, 6 months, 6 days.
9. Elizabeth Wood, died March 18, 1867, aged 59 years, 10 months.
10.
11.
3. Mary Mitchell, born about 1771. (Brumbaugh record.)
4. Thomas Mitchell born about 1773.
5. Sarah Mitchell, born about 1775.
6. Asel Mitchell, born about 1776.
7. William Mitchell, guardian appointed in 1786.
8. Isaac Mitchell, guardian appointed in 1786.

THE WHITE FAMILIES

There were three men of this name, who were among the pioneers at Fort Jackson, where they had settled prior to 1774. They were "Black" David White, "Red" David White, so named from the color of their hair to distinguish them, and Israel White. "Black" David White served as ensign in Captain James Archer's Militia Company, and later joined the migration to Kentucky.

"Red" David White applied for a pension May 13, 1833, while living in Franklin Township, Greene County, saying he was born in Goshen Township, Chester County, Pennsylvania, in April 1758. He was living in Franklin Township, Greene County (then Washington County) when he was drafted into the company of Captain David Owens in 1776, serving for three months at the mouth of Fishing Creek. John Boggs was his lieutenant and James Archer his ensign. He then served at Jackson's Fort and at Ankrom's Fort under Sebastian Schroffe. Later he and Leonard Sellars went out as spies for three months, patrolling the section between the head of the Tenmile and Dunkard Creeks, giving weekly intelligence to Jackson's Fort and Jannitt's (Jenkins'?) Fort. In 1780, he served under Captain James Archer at the mouth of a run which empties into Dunkard Creek on the Virginia side. He claimed service on Expeditions to the Shawnee Towns and at Wheeling and Mingo Bottom. He also served with Captain James Seals. (Nat. Arch. S-22586.)

He built his cabin on Smith Creek at the site of the Wood "Stone House," and on May 22, 1793, had patented to him some 400 acres of land, beginning near the mouth of Smith Creek and extending south on both sides of that stream. This land had been warranted the year before to David Whitemore, under the title of "Welcome." David White died in Greene County about 1841-42, his will being probated January 4, 1842. (Will Book 2. pp. 146.) The wording of the will indicates that he was twice married with two sons by the first marriage and six daughters by the second. No wife's name is given, though the second wife was surnamed Sarah.

Children of David White

1. Samuel White.
2. James White. In the Orphans Court proceedings in the estate of Thomas Kent (O. C. Docket 2. pp. 200) September 1841, it is shown that James White married Mary Kent, daughter of Thomas and Ann (Rolston) Kent. She was born August 5, 1779, and married (1) about 1800. Her second husband was .... Borden. The court proceedings name the children.

Children of James and Mary (Kent) White

1. David White.
2. Jesse White.
3. John White.
4. William White.
5. Rachel White.
6. Mary Ann White.
7. Thomas White, deceased in 1841.

Children of Thomas White

1. Mary White.
2. James White.
3. Jane White.
4. Rachel White.
5. Samuel White.
6. William White.
7. Nathan White.
8. Thomas White.
9. Uriah White.

8. Uriah White, also deceased in 1841.

Children of Uriah White

1. Thomas White.
2. Mary White.
3. Anna White.

Children of David and Sarah White

3. Rebecca White.
4. Nancy White.
5. Phoebe White.
6. Eleanor White.
7. Mary White.
8. Sarah White, married Robert Lapping, who came from Ireland, about 1800.

Children of Robert and Sarah (White) Lapping

1. David W. Lapping, born 1807, died ...., married Louisa Smith, daughter of John and Mary (Dollison) Smith.

Children of David and Louisa (Smith) Lapping

1. John Lapping, born March 25, 1834, died March 21, 1902; married Margaret Kent, born July 24, 1835, died February 26, 1911.
2. Sarah Lapping.
3. Catherine Lapping.
4. Jane Lapping, married J. S. Lemley, born March 22, 1845, son of Israel and Mazy (White) Lemley.
5. Adeline Lapping.
6. Leah Lapping.

7. Jesse Lapping, born May 17, 1844, married Emeline Goodwin.
8. Eleanor Lapping.
2. Elisha Lapping, born 1817, died 1903; married Jane Mapel, born 1819, died 1903.
3.
4.
5.
6.

ISRAEL WHITE FAMILY

Israel White, brother of "Red" David White, was born in Chester County, Pennsylvania, on June 6, 1761. He probably accompanied his elder brother to the Tenmile Country as early as 1774, and settled on Smith Creek, where on February 10, 1794, he warranted a tract of land under the title of "Rich Hill." This land joined that of Zebulon and Thomas Smith, and was at the head waters of Whiteley Creek, Laurel Run and a branch of Smith Creek, and in the later "Gordon Settlement." Israel White served in Captain James Archer's Company of Washington County Militia in the War of the Revolution. During an alarm caused by the Indians in the year 1784, many of the settlers had fled to Fort Jackson for safety, including Israel White, whose task it was, to blow the large conch shell as an alarm to the ones near enough to hear it, warning them to come to the Fort. Thomas Slater's Family, who lived close by the Fort was among those who sought safety on this occasion, and his daughter, Sarah, decided there could be no more fitting time for a wedding, so she and Israel White were married on this auspicious occasion. Israel White died on January 3, 1816, and his widow, then fifty-six years of age, soon remarried, her second husband being John Shriver. She died August 1, 1854. Israel White's will was probated in Greene County on February 12, 1816, and mentions these children:

Children of Israel and Sarah (Slater) White

1. Elizabeth White, born in 1785, married M. J. Kinney.
2. Eleanor White, died on September 3, 1854. Her husband was George Gordon, who died September 24, 1831. Eleanor (White) Gordon married (2) Timothy Terryl.

Childen of George and Eleanor (White) Gordon
(O. C. Docket 1 pp. 376)

1. Mary Gordon, wife John Munyon.
2. Rachel Gordon, wife of Felix Bell.
3. Sarah Gordon, wife of Thomas Munyon.
4. William Gordon.
5. John Gordon.
6. James Gordon.
7. Israel Gordon.
8. Basil Gordon.
9. Eleanor Gordon.
10. George Gordon.
11. Mazy Gordon.
12. Brice Gordon.

3. Rachel White, born March 17, 1790, died March 3, 1883; married Henry Shriver, born March 1787, died November 19, 1858. He was a son of John and Alice (Richards) Shriver.

Children of Henry and Rachel (White) Shriver
1. John Shriver, married Eleanor Maple.
    ### Children of John and Eleanor (Mapel) Shriver
    1. Minerva Shriver.
    2. Sarah Shriver, married John Stratton.
    3. Cassandra Shriver, married Ehud Steele.
    4. John Shriver.
2. Jennie Shriver, married William Huffman.
3. Sarah Shriver, born July 2, 1811, died September 15, 1897; married Jeremiah Spragg who died March 10, 1878, aged 68 years, 3 months, and 4 days.
4. Mazy Shriver, never married.
5. Christina Shriver, married Henry Shultz.
6. Rachel Shriver, born March 11, 1818, died April 23, 1852; married Joseph Knisely, born October 2, 1817.
7. David Shriver, married Jane Knisely.
8. Henry Shriver, married Elsie Cosgray.
9. Jackson Shriver, born September 10, 1821, died May 20, 1911; married Olive Kent.
10. Elsie Shriver, married Jacob Shields.
11. Presley Shriver, married Sarah Longstreth.
12. Benjamin Shriver, married Margaret Rice.
13. Slater Shriver, born April 10, 1827, died November 2, 1883; married, December 11, 1851, Elizabeth Kent, born April 29, 1826, died January 1, 1914.
14. Lucy Shriver, married Elias Nichols.
15. Ellen Shriver, married Joseph Bowers.
16. Mordica Shriver, born July 28, 1832, died aged 1 month 2 days.
4. Sarah White, married Jacob (?) Lemley.
5. Samuel White.
6. Rev. David White, born 1796, died February 3, 1890; married (1) Leah Strosnider, who died in 1867; married (2) Mrs. Mary (Bradford) Bayard. They are buried at White's Church. (David White Will in Will Book 6. pp. 343.)

Children of Rev. David White
1. Israel White, born 1821, died 1902; married (1) .... Bradford; married (2) Sarah Hoge.
2. Elizabeth White, married John (?) Fry.
3. Sarah White, married John Barnes.
4. Liza Jane White, married .... Bradford.
5. Christina White, married Abner Hoge.
6. Mary Ann White, married Eagon Kent.
7. Rezin White, born January 13, 1833, married Elizabeth Rogers.
8. Mariah White, married John Loar.
9. Martha White, married William Ely.
7. Ann White.
8. Mazy White.
9. Cassandra White, born 1804, died January 1, 1824; married Samuel Lemley.
10. Isaac White, son of Israel and Sarah (Slater) White was born

October 29, 1802, and died July 7, 1890. It is related that he and six of his sons went to West Virginia during the Civil War, and enlisted in a body. Isaac White married (1) Jane Shriver, born March 3, 1802, died January 7, 1831, after which he married Lydia Tustin, who died July 4, 1883. Four children were born by the first marriage and eleven by the second.

Children of Isaac White

1. Alice White, born July 20, 1822.
2. Mazy White, born July 12, 1824, married (1) Israel Lemley, (2) .... Gutherie.
3. Sarah White, born August 6, 1826, married Peter Fox, Jr.
4. Basil White, born January 5, 1829.
5. Abraham White, born December 18, 1832, married Rachel Stewart.
6. Jane White, born May 1, 1835; married (1) John Tustin, married (2) Abraham Cosgray.
7. John M. White, born December 5, 1836, married Helena Pettit.
8. William White, born October 4, 1838, married Elizabeth Cole.
9. Hiram White, born May 1, 1840, married Mary Ann Cole.
10. Elizabeth White, born April 16, 1843, married Basil Wells.
11. Henry White, born March 22, 1845, married Nancy McPherrin.
12. Rebecca White, born April 1, 1847, married Basil Wise.
13. Rachel White, born December 5, 1848.
14. Slater I. White, born June 18, 1851, married Nancy McPherrin.
15. Snowden K. White, born August 2, 1855, married Zella Smith.

THE SHRIVER FAMILY

The Shriver Family of Greene County may all have descended from Adam Shriver, who went from Frederick County, Maryland, to settle in Frederick County, Virginia, where he was living in 1782, at the head of a family of eleven white persons. While living in Frederick County, Virginia, he is known to have supplied 418 pounds of fine flour at 60 Pounds per hundredweight to Richard Eastin for the use of the Colonial Army. (Public Claim No. 86 Frederick County, Virginia.) After the Revolution Adam Shriver moved to Dunkard Creek, and was taxed in Greene Township, Washington County, in 1784, as a foreign resident. On March 10, 1803, he sold 180 acres of land on Dunkard Creek to his son, Abraham, in a deed in which he is joined by wife, Christina. (Monongalia County DB. 30 pp. 4.) His wife may have been a Strosnider.

Adam Shriver is thought to have been born about 1736. He died and is buried near Pentress (West) Virginia, where markers now are un-readable. A family record supplies the names of five children, to which we have added a sixth because of certain evidence that seems to confirm this and warrant the inclusion. A seventh child may have been a Henry Shriver of early record, but certainly George Shriver, who is taxed as living outside Greene Township in 1784, along with Adam Shriver, was a close connection. Several interesting legends are told of the first winter that the Shrivers lived in the Tenmile Country. One legend says they came here in an immigrant wagon in which they lived while preparing their first cabin on the William Orndorff Farm. Another says they found a large hollow sycamore tree on the stream that runs through the Brazilla Stephens Farm, which being cleaned out, furnished a snug haven until the cabin was erected. Old timers used to point out this tree in which the Shrivers were supposed to have spent the first rough winter.

Family of Adam and Christina Shriver

1. Jacob Shriver, born 1759, died May 29, 1815, buried with his wife Jane, on the Isenminger Farm. Markers still legible. His will was probated in Greene County June 17, 1815. (WB. 1. pp. 150.) He married (1) December 2, 1783, Elizabeth Shull, born in 1761, died in 1803. He married (2) Jane Mooney, born 1772, who died December 21, 1836. Ten children were born by the first marriage and three by the second. Jacob Shriver warranted the tract of land on which he spent his first winter, on March 9, 1786, under the title of "Jacob's Inheritance," now the William Orndorff Farm. It was on the same fork of Big Whiteley on which Henry Jackson lived and accounts for the numerous intermarriages with that family.

Family of Jacob Shriver

1. Elijah Shriver, born September 12, 1784, died in Guernsey County, Ohio, in March 1828. His will was made March 11, 1828, and probated March 27, 1828. (Will Book A-183.) Elijah Shriver married Nancy (probably Jackson) daughter of Henry and Elizabeth (Stump) Jackson, neighbors of the Shrivers in Greene County, and later in Guernsey County, Ohio.

Children of Elijah and Nancy Snriver

1. Jacob Shriver.
2. Henry Shriver.
3. Adam Shriver.
4. Elijah Israel Shriver.
5. John Jackson Shriver.
6. Nancy Shriver.
7. Sally Shriver.
8. Cassandra Shriver.
9. Jane Shriver.
10. Mahala Shriver.
11. Ruth Shriver.
12. Elinor Shriver.

2. Christina Shriver, born May 12, 1786, married .... Jackson.
3. Adam Shriver, born February 22, 1788, died in Guernsey County, Ohio, in 1861. His will was made December 9, 1857, and probated October 21, 1861. (Will Book 1. pp. 366.) Adam Shriver married Delilah Gordon, daughter of John Adam Gordon and first wife Cassandra Holland. She was born June 20, 1790.

Children of Adam and Delilah (Gordon) Shriver

1. Eliza Shriver, never married.
2. Elijah Shriver, born 1810, died 1896; married

Margaret Witten.
3. Michael Shriver, born March 18, 1812, died August 4, 1896; married Martha Woodrow.
4. Cassandra Shriver, married Otho Wilson.
5. Margaret Shriver, married John Deets.
6. Mary Shriver, married Henry Piper.
7. Mark Gordon Shriver, born February 11, 1832, died February 26, 1905; married (1) Rachel Kirkpatrick, (2) Caroline Camp.
8. Solomon Shriver.
9. Jane Shriver, married Thomas White.

4. Margaret Shriver, born September 9, 1789, married .... Jackson, son of Henry and Elizabeth (Stump) Jackson.
5. Jacob Shriver, born May 15, 1793, died in Guernsey County, Ohio, in 1844. His will was made September 30, 1843, and probated April 15, 1844. (Will Book B pp. 59.) His wife was Sarah Patterson, daughter of James and Nancy (Doran) Patterson. She was born on September 17, 1793, and died in 1877.

Children of Jacob and Sarah (Patterson) Shriver

1. Elizabeth Shriver, married .... Johnson.
2. Mary Ann Shriver, married John Johnson.
3. James Shriver.
4. Joseph Shriver.
5. Jacob Shriver.
6. Noah Shriver.

6. Elizabeth Shriver, born March 23, 1795, died December 17, 1883; married John Patterson, son of James and Nancy (Doran) Patterson, born February 20, 1791, died July 7, 1851. Both are buried in Hopewell M. E. Cemetery in Greene County, Pennsylvania.

Children of John and Elizabeth (Shriver) Patterson

1. Nancy A. Patterson, born December 17, 1817, died February 12, 1850, married James L. Turner, a Baptist Minister.
2. Jacob Patterson, born January 31, 1819, died July 10, 1864; married Elizabeth Patton, born May 4, 1820, died December 1899. He was a Methodist Minister.
3. Sarah Patterson, died young.
4. John D. Patterson, born January 16, 1825, died April 25, 1909; married, May 23, 1848, Amanda Mahanah, born April 18, 1828, died December 9, 1896.
5. Mahala Patterson, born January 15, 1828, died January 12, 1908; married John Patterson of Washington County, Pennsylvania.
6. Elizabeth Patterson, born May 21, 1830, died November 6, 1923; married Jesse Patterson, brother of John.
7. James Patterson, born February 5, 1832, died January 24, 1918; married Elizabeth Spragg, born December 2, 1833, died April 25, 1925, buried in Hopewell Cemetery.

7. Michael Shriver, born June 30, 1797, died in 1841; went to Ohio.
8. Sarah Shriver, born March 22, 1799, died 1824; married .... Jackson. After her death Mr. Jackson then married her sister, Margaret Jackson. They went to Ohio,

living for a time near Mt. Pleasant, where Sarah is buried.
9. Mary Shriver, born June 25, 1801, died in 1845. She is also said to have married .... Jackson. An old letter says four Shriver girls married two men named Jackson. These two men were Jacob and Samuel Jackson, sons (?) of Henry and Elizabeth (Stump) Jackson.
10. John Shriver, born June 14, 1803, died 1866; went to Iowa.
11. William Shriver, eldest son by the second marriage, born April 13, 1805, died in 1880. He married Elizabeth Shull, who died February 16, 1880, aged about 73 years. Her husband's death was on November 14, the same year. Buried on the Isenminger Farm.

Children of William and Elizabeth (Shull) Shriver

1. Jane Shriver, married William Rhodes, born July 12, 1818.
2. Adam Shriver.
3. Abraham Shriver.
4. Hannah Shriver.
5. Dr. Jacob L. Shriver, born January 11, 1828, died May 5, 1906; married, December 4, 1851, Sarah Goodwin, born January 29, 1833, died June 27, 1917, daughter of John and Sarah (Gardner) Goodwin.
6.
7.
8.
9. Isaac R. Shriver born July 3, 1839, died January 1, 1896; married Susannah John, born November 29, 1839, died September 7, 1918.

12. Isaac Shriver, born April 22, 1807, died December 28, 1861; married Elizabeth Tustin, born October 8, 1808, died February 14, 1897; buried on the Isenminger Farm.

Children of Isaac and Elizabeth (Tustin) Shriver

1. Rachel Shriver, born February 7, 1835, died February 3, 1931; married Harman McNeely.
2. Abraham Shriver, born January 30, 1839, died April 17, 1865, married Sarah Jane Stephens.
3. Mary Jane Shriver, married Frank Higgins.
4. Jacob Shriver, born May 13, 1840, died December 2, 1853.
5. Elenor Shriver, born September 8, 1847, died February 9, 1896; married William Orndorff.
6. Frances Shriver, born June 28, 1848, died September 24, 1919; married Noah Patterson, born March 10, 1847, died December 18, 1921.
7. Isaac Shriver, born 1850, died October 1903.
8. Elizabeth Shriver, born 1853, died September 14, 1891.

13. Elinor Shriver, born February 23, 1814, died 1884; married Adam Gordon, born August 27, 1810, died October 1, 1833, son of William and Mary (Carroll) Gordon.

Child

1. Jacob James Gordon, born 1834.

2. George Shriver (?) There is room here for a possible son of Adam and Christina Shriver, who was taxed with Adam Shriver as living outside the township in the Greene Township tax list for 1784. This is the same George Shriver, who on

August 23, 1806, was deeded a part of "Emsworth," a tract of land on Dunkard Creek, warranted on April 19, 1794, to John Shriver. John Shriver and wife, Sarah, on the same date had deeded a part of the same tract to Cornelius Howard. (Deed Book 2 pp. 200 and 201.) This John Shriver, possibly the John Shriver of the 1784 tax list of Greene Township, has not been identified, but may have been a brother of Adam Shriver. Between the date of these deeds and the date of his will in 1825, he seems to have lost wife Sarah, and married Ann (possibly Cowell) named in his will. (Will Book 1. pp. 261.) He also seems to have bought the land south of his tract from Joseph Wilford, which he deeded to Mathias Cowell before his death. (Deed Book 4. pp. 297.) He left no heirs of his name, but gave his property to Ann Cowell, spinster, and to James Cowell, Christopher Cowell, and Robert Cage, the latter getting a tract of land in Crawford County, described as being donation land to Samuel Sampson. On March 14, 1815, George Shriver and wife, Martha, sold their purchase of "Emsworth" to John Poundstone, and are not found in further local records. (Deed Book. 3. pp. 200.) Mr. J. W. Donley at Bald Hill, wrote Waychoff, "within a few feet of where my house stands, the Indians in 1793-94 killed George Shriver, a gunsmith, and captured John and Sarah Shriver, and took them to Ohio, where they were held prisoners for seven years." Obviously George Shriver was not killed, but may have been a prisoner, then returned to make the above deeds.

3. John Shriver, born 1763, died May 3, 1831; married (1) February 21, 1786, Alice Richards, born in 1766, died about 1816; married (2) Mrs. Sarah (Slater) White, born 1760, died August 1, 1854. Both are buried in the Shriver Cemetery on the William Orndorff Farm, the original tract of John Shriver.

Children of John and Alice (Richards) Shriver

1. Henry Shriver, born March 1787, died November 19, 1858; married Rachel White, born March 17, 1790, died March 9, 1883. She was a daughter of Israel and Sarah (Slater) White.

Children of Henry and Rachel (White) Shriver

1. John Shriver, married Eleanor Mapel, daughter of John and Mary Ann (Grove) Mapel.
2. Jennie Shriver, married William Huffman.
3. Sarah Shriver, born July 2, 1811, died September 15, 1897; married Jeremiah Spragg, who died March 10, 1878, aged 68 years, 3 months, 4 days.
4. Mazy Shriver, never married.
5. Christina Shriver, married Henry Shultz.
6. Rachel Shriver, born March 11, 1818, died April 23, 1852; married Joseph Knisely, born October 2, 1817.
7. David Shriver, married Jane Knisely.
8. Henry Shriver, married Elsie Cosgray.
9. Jackson Shriver, born September 10, 1821, died May 20, 1911; married Olive Kent.
10. Elsie Shriver, married Jacob Shields.
11. Presley Shriver, married Sarah Longstreth.
12. Benjamin Shriver, married Margaret Rice.

13. Slater Shriver, born April 10, 1827, died November 2, 1883; married, December 11, 1851, Elizabeth Kent, born April 29, 1826, died January 1, 1914.
14. Lucy Shriver, married Elias Nichols.
15. Ellen Shriver, married Joseph Bowers.
16. Mordecai Shriver, born July 28, 1832, died in infancy.

2. Christina Shriver, daughter of John and Alice (Richards) Shriver, died December 19, 1877; married, February 27, 1806, George Lemley, born May 17, 1786, died in Wood County, West Virginia, June 10, 1862. After leaving Greene County, he resided for a time in Monongalia County, prior to removing to Wood County, where he is buried.

Children of George and Christina (Shriver) Lemley

(Bible record supplied by Mr. Frederick Lemley)

1. Alva (or Alza) Lemley, born June 15, 1807, died in infancy.
2. Henry Lemley, born May 26, 1808, died un-married at about 40 years of age.
3. Rachel Lemley, born May 30, 1811, married James Bradford.
4. Sarah Lemley, born April 7, 1815, died June 29, 1880; married John Bradford.
5. John S. Lemley, born November 27, 1817, died November 25, 1902; married, December 1, 1839, Elizabeth Hinegardner. Buried in Dawson Cemetery near Burton, West Virginia.
6. Jane Lemley, born June 4, 1820, died December 16, 1890; married Isaac Clark.
7. Abraham Lemley, born November 27, 1822.
8. Elizabeth Lemley, born May 13, 1825, married Levi Wise.
9. Jacob Lemley, born October 4, 1831, died October 5, 1882.

3. Adam Shriver, born April 1794, died July 22, 1845; married Martha Stephens, born 1796, died November 2, 1874.

Children of Adam and Martha (Stephens) Shriver

1. Issac Shriver.
2. John Shriver, born May 23, 1817, died August 17, 1866; married Clementine Kent, born March 14, 1831, died October 11, 1907.
3. Andrew Jackson Shriver, married Elizabeth Adamson.
4. Adam Shriver, married Melinda Dawson.
5. Apollo Shriver, married Elizabeth Haines.
6. Nancy Shriver.
7. Mary Shriver, married David John.
8. Hetty Shriver, married William Staggers.
9. Martha Shriver, second wife of Harvey Staggers.
10. Elsie Shriver, first wife of Harvey Staggers.
11. Elizabeth Shriver.

4. Susannah Shriver, born November 28, 1796, died April 25, 1857; married Mark Gordon, born January 22, 1794, died January 22, 1886.

Children of Mark and Susannah (Shriver) Gordon

1. John A. Gordon, married (1) Rebecca Crawford, (2) Margaret Crawford.
2. Godfrey Gordon, married Elizabeth Crayne.
3. Basil Gordon, born December 27, 1822, married Mariah Inghram.
4. Alice Gordon, married Uriah Inghram.
5. Delilah Gordon, married (1) Harvey Higgins, (2) John I. Worley.
6. William Gordon, married Margaret Whitlatch.
7. Elizabeth Gordon, never married.
8. Catherine Gordon, married Thomas Porter.
9. John B. Gordon, married .... Shull.
10. Cassandra Gordon, married Hamilton Mapel.

5. Sarah Shriver, married Basil Gordon, born January 12, 1797. After his death she married Herman Lester.

Child of Basil and Sarah (Shriver) Gordon

1. Mariah Gordon, born January 6, 1824, died February 7, 1877; married John I. Worley.

6. Jane Shriver, born March 2, 1802, died January 7, 1831; married Isaac White, born on October 29, 1802, died July 7, 1890. Son of Israel and Sarah (Slater) White.

Children of Isaac and Jane (Shriver) White

1. Alice White, born July 20, 1822.
2. Mazy White, born July 12, 1824, married (1) Israel Lemley; (2) .... Gutherie.
3. Sarah White, born August 6, 1826, married Peter Fox, Jr.
4. Basil White, born January 5, 1829.

7. John Shriver, born ....; married Elizabeth Gordon, born December 10, 1803.
8. Jacob Shriver, born August 7, 1807, died February 1, 1887; married Elizabeth Inghram, born 1815, died February 22, 1855.

Children of Jacob and Elizabeth (Inghram) Shriver

1. Inghram Shriver, married Velinda Gutherie.
2. Sudie Shriver, married Benjamin Baily.
3. Mariah Shriver, married Samuel Bradford.
4. John Shiver, married Margaret Morris.
5. Hicey Shriver, married Eliza Frye.
6. Melissa Shriver, married Allen Berkey.
7. Minerva Shriver, married Isaac Shriver.
8. Elizabeth Shriver, married Jack Stephens.
9. Arthur Shriver, married Ella Hickman.

9. Abraham Shriver, son of John and Alice (Richards) Shriver.
10. Isaac Shriver.
11. Frank Shriver.

4. Abraham Shriver, son of Adam and Christina Shriver, born in Frederick County, Virginia, September 6, 1768, died in Monongalia County, West Virginia, November 11, 1837. He married, March 3, 1791, Mary Keckley, born April 19, 1770.

Children of Abraham and Mary (Keckley) Shriver

1. Catherine Shriver born April 16, 1792, married Jacob Horner.
2. Adam Shriver, born September 7, 1793.
3. Elias Shriver, born August 9, 1795.
4. Jacob Shriver, born July 1797.
5. Christina Shriver, born April 12, 1799, married Michael Core.
6. Elizabeth Shriver, born April 5, 1800, married Ezekiel Morris.
7. John Shriver, born April 30, 1801, died 1885; married Sarah Morris.
8. Benjamin Shriver, born May 27, 1805.
9. Isaac Shriver, born May 27, 1807, died March 30, 1880; married Minerva Sine, born 1820, died October 1, 1899.
10. Abraham Shriver.

5. Catherine Shriver, born 1770, died August 24, 1842; married March 3, 1789, Peter Henkins, born 1769, died September 4, 1849.

Children of Peter and Catherine (Shriver) Henkins

1. Margaret Henkins, married Robert Chaffin.
2. Elijah Henkins, married Elizabeth Brown.
3. Elizabeth Henkins, married Emanuel Brown.
4. Mary Henkins, married .... Goodwin.
5. Rebecca Henkins, married .... Long.
6. Allie Henkins, married .... Fletcher.
7. Sarah Henkins, married .... Morris.
8. Abraham Henkins, married .... Dawson.

6. Elizabeth Shriver, born 1772.

THE PATTERSON FAMILY

James Patterson wrote in his family Bible that he was born in Ireland of Scotch-Irish parents in 1757. This Bible was bought in 1774, and is now owned by Mrs. Adam Phillips, nee Brightie Patterson. James Patterson said he came to America in 1774, on the ship "Alexandria," and married Nancy Ann Doran, born in 1767, in Ireland, of English parentage. They were married in 1788. Almost as soon as he arrived in America he joined the Continental Army and served in a Virginia Regiment. Hanna, in his interview with the family, reports in his "History of Greene County," this same service in the Revolution. After the Revolution, probably about 1789, he removed to Greene County, where he died about 1809. His will is in Will Book 1. pp. 79 and was probated September 4, 1809. His widow warranted the tract of land on which they had settled on Big Whiteley Creek, on December 2, 1816, under the title of "Delay." There was patented to her on July 18, 1817, a little more than 356 acres of land. Prior to that date she had bought a farm of 400 acres of land in 1810 for her son, John Patterson, in Morris Township. Nancy Ann (Doran) Patterson died in 1825.

Children of James and Nancy Ann (Doran) Patterson

1. John Patterson, born February 20, 1791, died July 7, 1851; married Elizabeth Shriver, born March 23, 1795, died Decem-

ber 17, 1883. She was a daughter of Jacob and Elizabeth (Shull) Shriver. (See Shriver Records.)
2. Sarah Patterson, born September 17, 1793, died in 1877; married Jacob Shriver, born May 15, 1793, son of Jacob and Elizabeth (Shull) Shriver. They removed to Guernsey County, Ohio, where he died in 1844. (See Shriver Records.)
3. James Patterson, born December 20, 1795, died in 1853.
4. Jane Patterson, born June 3, 1797; married .... White. They went to Noble County, Ohio.
5. George Patterson, born September 13, 1798, died 1801.
6. Mary Patterson, born August 20, 1800; died un-married in 1884.
7. Alexander Patterson, born July 5, 1806, died 1813.
8. William Patterson, born February 16, 1808, died May 13, 1887; married, about 1824, Rhoda Whitlatch, born about 1806, died June 3, 1852. William Patterson next married, on November 6, 1856, Sophia Kuhn, daughter of Abraham and Eleanor (Mooney) Kuhn. She was born October 29, 1815, died .... There were fourteen children by the first marriage and two by the second.

Children of William and Rhoda (Whitlatch) Patterson

1. Joseph Patterson, born March 27, 1829, died 1909; married, 1850, Elizabeth Mooney, daughter of Thomas.
2. James Patterson, born December 5, 1830, died January 2, 1912; married Susan Grove, born April 19, 1830, died July 24, 1905.
3. Elijah Patterson, born March 17, 1832; married (1) Jemimah Mooney; (2) Elizabeth Shultz.
4. John Patterson, born November 4, 1833, died 1917; married Eva Hohman.
5. Nancy Patterson, born November 20, 1836; married Henry Spragg.
6. Elizabeth Patterson, born April 27, 1837; married Caleb Ely.
7. David Patterson, born April 27, 1839; married Mary McCollum, born December 10, 1846, died 1926.
8. Sarah Patterson, born December 31, 1840, died December 9, 1877; married Thomas Hook, born September 27, 1840.
9. William Patterson, born December 4, 1842; married Ruth Baily.
10. Louisa Patterson, born February 11, 1844, died in infancy.
11. Mary Patterson, twin of Louisa, died January 30, 1881; married Edward Wood, born October 28, 1837, died November 30, 1923.
12. Noah Patterson, born March 10, 1847, died December 18, 1921; married Frances Shriver, born June 28, 1848, died October 28, 1919.
13. Cephas Patterson, born February 11, 1849, died young.
14. Jacob S. Patterson, born February 27, 1851; married Melissa Rose, born 1853, died 1932.

Children of William and Sophia (Kuhn) Patterson

15. Ruth Patterson, born February 4, 1860; married Otho Orndorff.
16. Rufus Patterson, born August 11, 1861, died April 7, 1944; married, March 2, 1887, Emma Connor, born February 12, 1861.

THE TUSTIN FAMILY

After serving in the Sixth Battalion, Chester County, Pennsylvania Militia in the War of the Revolution, first in Captain Curtis Lownes' Company, and then under Captain William Kirk, Jacob Tustin, ancestor of the Tenmile Tustins, removed to Mifflin, County, Pennsylvania, and settled for a time in that portion south of the Juniata River. (Penna. Arch. Series V. Vol. 5. pp. 679-759-748.) Then about 1816, he removed with his family to settle on a Branch of Big Whiteley Creek, adjoining the land of a former neighbor, from Mifflin County, George John. Here he had patented to him a tract of land containing 87 acres under the title of "Stevens." The date of his warrant was September 24, 1817, and the patent was secured September 26, 1818. The name of his wife is not given in his will which was probated in Greene County, February 7, 1825, (Will Book 1. pp. 262) so it is probable that she preceded him in death.

Children of Abraham Tustin

1. Abraham Tustin, Jr., a soldier in the War of 1812. He married Mary Hamilton.

    #### Children of Abraham and Mary (Hamilton) Tustin

    1. John Tustin, married Jane White.
    2. William Tustin, married .... Cole.
    3. Joseph Tustin, married Nancy Wells.
    4. Isaac Tustin.
    5. Abraham Tustin.
    6. Elizabeth Tustin, married Isaac Shriver. She was born October 8, 1808, and died February 14, 1897. Isaac Shriver was born April 22, 1807, and died December 28, 1861.
    7. Lydia Tustin, died July 4, 1883; married, January 10, 1832, Isaac White, born October 29, 1802, died July 17, 1890.
    8. Rachel Tustin, married Henry Shultz.
    9. Frances Tustin, married Jacob Cole.
    10. Rebecca Tustin, married William Estle.
    11. Mary Tustin, married Abijah Cole.

2. Mary Tustin, married Peter Dillon. On August 19, 1820, Peter Dillon and wife, Mary, sold land to Abraham Tustin, (D. B. 74- pp. 437.) and then on December 21, 1890, they sold another piece of land to Kendall Goodwin. They removed to Ohio shortly afterward.
3. Andrew Tustin, married Nancy Dulaney, daughter of Dennis and Nancy Dulaney. They first removed to Indiana, but later returned to Tyler County, (West) Virginia, where a number of their children were married.

    #### Children of Andrew and Nancy (Dulaney) Tustin

    1. Jacob Tustin, married in Tyler County, December 22, 1840, Elizabeth John.
    2. Jonathan Tustin, married .... Hennen.
    3. Andrew Tustin, married in Tyler County, West Virginia, September 29, 1859, Margaret Weakley.
    4. Nancy Tustin, married in Tyler County, West Virginia, October 7, 1858, Peyton Baily.
    5. Barbara Tustin, married in Tyler County, West Virginia, March 11, 1852, George H. Kester.
    6. Fanny Tustin, married John Cox.

7. Mary Tustin, married Daniel King.
8. Eliza Jane Tustin, married in Tyler County, West Virginia, August 18, 1853, Absolom George, Jr.
4. Rachel Tustin, born 1789, died 1871; married Henry Jackson, born 1770, died in Guernsey County, Ohio, in 1838. Buried in the Byesville Cemetery. She was the second wife of Henry Jackson, a son of Henry and Elizabeth (Stump) Jackson.

Children of Henry and Rachel (Tustin) Jackson

1. Henry Jackson, born 1819, married Lucretia ....
2. Jacob Jackson, married .... Fox.
3. Eleanor Jackson, born 1827, died 1895.
4. Samuel Jackson, born 1829, died 1912.
5. Jane Jackson, married .... Huff, moved to Indiana.
6. Abraham Jackson, died in Missouri.
7. Lydia Jackson.
8. Charles Jackson.

THE MAPEL FAMILY

The Adjutant General's Office of the State of New Jersey says that William Maple, (the name is so spelled in the War and Census Records) served as a private in Captain Aaron Longstreet's Company, Third Regiment, Middlesex County, New Jersey Militia, enlisting at Philadelphia in the Spring of 1779, after the Battle of Monmouth. He served under Captain Mills and Colonel Seeley, and went to Elizabeth, Newark, and Shrewsberry, and had skirmishes at Middletown with refugees. He served nine months at Philadelphia in 1779. He again enlisted at Cranberry for six months under Captain True Hoagland and was discharged at Monmouth by Colonel Seeley. Went to Princeton, Middletown, and Elizabeth in 1780 under Captain Hoagland, with Colonel Nixon in command. He enlisted again as a teamster in August 1781, and served until the end of the War. William Mapel stated that he was born near Princeton, June 22, 1755. The application of William Mapel for a federal pension gives precisely the same service, and shows that it was filed at Waynesburg, Pennsylvania, on September 16, 1833. In the application he said he had lived in New Jersey until about 42 years ago, when he removed to Greene County, where he had since resided. He was granted a certificate for his service for $50 per year. (Nat. Arch. No. 22,380).

William Mapel was the head of a family of one adult male, two male children under 16 years, and one female in Franklin Township, Greene County (then Washington County) in the Census of 1790, where a deed of record shows his wife's name was Eleanor. He died in Greene County in 1842 as shown by a government marker at his grave on the Mooney Farm now owned by Mrs. Floyd Miller. We are told that his wife is buried there with him, but no marker exists. William Mapel's will is in Will Book 2. pp. 155, naming but two sons by name, but Mrs. Helen (Wood) Scott has added the names of five others from her D. A. R. application record.

Children of William Mapel

1. John Mapel, born 1786, died February 24, 1864; married Mary Ann Grove. They are buried on the Mooney Farm with his

father. He was a soldier in the War of 1812. (Penna. Arch. Series V. Vol. 8, pp. 412-430.)

Children of John and Mary Ann (Grove) Mapel

1. Benjamin Mapel, died September 20, 1812, buried on the Lemley Farm near Brock.
2. Nancy Mapel, married William Spragg, born February 28, 1808, died 1872; son of Caleb and Deborra (McClure) Spragg.

Children of William and Nancy (Mapel) Spragg

1. John Spragg, killed at Mine Run in the Civil War, November 29, 1863.
2. Mary Ann Spragg, married Harrison Pettit.
3. Eleanor Spragg, married Armstrong Phillips. She was born May 5, 1840, and died December 25, 1873.
4. Jeanette Spragg, married Valentine Nichols.

3. Sarah Mapel, married Keener Strosnider.

Children of Keener and Sarah (Mapel) Strosnider

1. Minerva Strosnider, married Albert Spragg.
2. Mahlia Strosnider.
3. Benson Strosnider.
4. Michael Strosnider.
5. John Strosnider.
6. William Strosnider.

4. Margaret Mapel, died October 29, 1869; married William Hamilton, died April 3, 1879.

Children of William ar { Margaret (Mapel) Hamilton

1.
2.
3.
4.
5.
6.
7.
8.
9.
10.
11. Harvey Hamilton, born 1840.
12.
13. Enoch Hamilton, born September 20, 1844; married, 1871, Elizabeth Tustin.
14.
15. Lewis Hamilton, born September 19, 1848; married Harriet Burdine.

5. Eleanor Mapel, daughter of John and Mary Ann (Grove) Mapel, married John Shriver, son of Henry and Rachel (White) Shriver.

Children of John and Eleanor (Mapel) Shriver

1. Minerva Shriver.
2. Sarah Shriver, married John Stratton.
3. Cassandra Shriver, married Ehud Steele.
4. John Shriver.

6. John Mapel, born November 25, 1817, died in Bureau County, Illinois; married August 13, 1834, Margaret Franks, daughter of George and Elizabeth Franks.

   Children of John and Margaret (Mapel) Franks
   1.
   2.
   3.
   4.
   5.
   6.
   7.

7.
8. Hamilton Mapel, born March 31, 1821, died October 21, 1898; married, September 27, 1843, Cassandra Gordon, born May 4, 1825, died February 23, 1891; daughter of Mark and Susannah (Shriver) Gordon.

   Children of Hamilton and Cassandra (Gordon) Mapel
   1. John Adam Mapel, born 1844, married Sarah Ellen Day.
   2. Basil Mapel, married Emma Stewart.
   3. Mark Mapel.
   4. Sydney Mapel, never married.
   5. Sadie Mapel, second wife of Melvin Nichols.
   6. Ida Mapel, married Melvin Nichols.
   7. Lafayette Mapel, never married.
   8. Susan Mapel, married Newton Duvall.
   9. Elijah Mapel, born 1861, died 1937; married (1) Lyda Clark, who died August 7, 1907. He married (2) Mrs. Mary (Orndorff) Kent.

2. William Mapel, son of William and Eleanor Mapel, born about 1788, married Lyda Triston. They went to Indiana. A descendant has established a D. A. R. line.
3. Mary Mapel, daughter of William and Eleanor Mapel, no record.
4. Jacob Mapel, son of William and Eleanor Mapel.
5. Catherine Mapel, daughter of William and Eleanor Mapel, born April 10, 1794, died September 1, 1851; married John Staggers, son of Jacob and Elizabeth (Isenminger) Staggers. He was born September 12, 1792, and died December 16, 1882. Both are buried at the White Barn on Smith Creek. They had fifteen children.

   Children of John and Catherine (Mapel) Staggers
   1. William Staggers, married Hester Shriver, went to Potomac, Illinois.
   2. Susannah Staggers, married Thomas Hoge.
   3. Harvey Staggers, married (1) Elsie Shriver, (2) Martha Shriver, (3) Pernissa ....
   4. Culver Staggers, died at Fort Madison, Iowa.
   5. Jacob Staggers, married a Miss Westfall. Went to Kansas, where he disappeared on a steamboat trip.
   6. Lisbon Staggers, born December 17, 1820; married, (1) Jane Mooney, (2) Sarah (Hoge) Thompson.
   7. Eleanor Staggers, married Christopher Scott of Rutan.
   8. Julia Staggers, married William Gordon.

9. Louisa Staggers, died in youth, was 20 years old in the 1850 Census.
10. Catherine Staggers, born 1834.
11. Margaret J. Staggers, born 1836; married John Kline.
12.
13.
14.
15.
6. Rebecca Mapel, daughter of William and Eleanor Mapel.
7. Benjamin Mapel, son of William and Eleanor Mapel, born 1796, died June 20, 1852; married Nancy ...., who died November 11, 1854. Both buried on the Lemley Farm near Brock.

Children of Benjamin and Nancy Mapel

1. John Mapel, went to Bureau County, Illinois.
2. Thomas Mapel, went to Livingston, Illinois.
3. Jane Mapel, born 1819, died 1903; married Elisha Lapping, born 1817, died 1903.
4. Elijah Mapel, went to Stark County, Illinois.
5. Susan Mapel, married George Hoy.
6. Ellen Mapel, married Louis Hamilton.
7. Nancy Mapel, married .... Vandruff.
8. William Mapel, born 1827, died March 10, 1902, married .... Strosnider.
9. Rachel Mapel, born 1832.
10. David Mapel, born 1835; married Margaret Owens, who died June 25, 1865. He married (2) Sarah Owens.
11. Enoch Mapel, born December 16, 1838, died July 10, 1898; married Delilah Johnson, born June 22, 1837.

THE STAGGERS FAMILY

Evidence indicates that the Staggers Family (also spelled Steger, Stiger, Stayger, etc.) of Greene County, were originally of Chester County, Pennsylvania, where a number of men of the name served in the Revolution, enlisting shortly after the Declaration of Independence. Before the end of the Revolution, a number of the family removed to the Juniata River in Cumberland County, Pennsylvania, and settled on the south bank of that stream, in the portion of the County which became Mifflin County on September 19, 1789. Here in 1781, a John Staggers and a Jacob Staggers served in the Cumberland County Militia. Into the same neighborhood moved the Isenminger, Grim, Styles, Hunnell, Tustin, John, Milliken and Jacobs Families, names which became familiar a little later in the Tenmile Country, and among whom numerous marriages took place before and after the migration to the Tenmile. Here in Mifflin County at the time of the 1790 census, lived John and Jacob Staggers, apparently on adjoining farms. From the evidence it would appear that they were father and son, who then moved before 1797, to settle in Cumberland Township, where John Staggers bought land that had been patented to Robert Crosley. Here, on November 11, 1797, John Staggers made a gift of his personal chattels, for "love and affection" to Jacob Staggers and wife, Elizabeth, (Isenminger), John Hunnell and wife, Catherine, (Staggers), and John Isenminger and wife, not named. (Deed Book 1. pp. 209). Then on September 10, 1798, he sold his farm to James Henderson and James McCalley, by a deed in which he was joined by wife, Eve. This manner of distributing property usually suggests the donor is placing his future care in the hands of his children. As no will is recorded for John Staggers near that date, this theory seems borne out. Thus any other children of John Staggers are not of record, but another son is suggested in the will of Jacob Staggers, who mentions a nephew Jacob Staggers in his will. (WB. 2. pp. 55). Other children of John Staggers may have preceded him in death and one of these could be the John Staggers who served in Cumberland County Militia with Jacob Staggers. John Staggers served in the Seventh Battalion. (Penna. Arch. Series V Vol. 6. pp. 491).

Family of Jacob Staggers

Jacob Staggers (Stigers, Stegers, Staygers, etc.) was born in 1758 and died May 11, 1835, according to his tombstone in the cemetery at the White Barn on Smith Creek. (A family record, which must be wrong, says he was born in 1761 and died May 11, 1830). Jacob Staggers made his will on August 19, 1831, and it was probated June 9, 1835. (Will Book 2. pp. 55). He was probably the Jacob Staggers (Stager, Stegers, etc.) who served in Captain James Horrell's Company, Seventh Battalion, Cumberland County Militia, commanded by Colonel James Purdy, as shown by the roster of May 1, 1781. He was living in Mifflin County, below the Juniata River at the time of the 1790 Census, when he is shown at the head of a family of one adult male and three females. (Military Service, Penna. Arch. Series V. Vol. 6. pp. 496). Other possible service can be found as early as August 5, 1776, in Captain Edward Parker's Company, Second Battalion, Chester County, Pennsylvania Militia, in whose company a Jacob Staggers served as a sergeant. (Penna. Arch. Series V. Vol. 5. pp. 508). Jacob Staggers married, probably in Mifflin County, a part of Cumberland County until September 19, 1789, Elizabeth Isenminger, who died in 1839, at the age of 80 years.

Children of Jacob and Elizabeth (Isenminger) Staggers

1. John Staggers, born September 12, 1792, died December 16, 1882, at the age of 90 years, 3 months, and 4 days. He married Catherine Mapel, daughter of William and Eleanor (White?) Mapel. She was born April 10, 1794, and died September 1, 1851. Buried in the cemetery at the White Barn. Census of 1850 would put her birth in 1796, family says 1804.

Children of John and Catherine (Mapel) Staggers

1. William Staggers, went to Potomac, Illinois. His wife was Hester Shriver.
2. Susannah Staggers, married Thomas Hoge.

Children

1. Catherine Hoge, married (1) Marion Kent; (2) Isaac Grim.
2. Sarah Hoge.
3.
4.

3. Harvey Staggers, married (1) Elsie Shriver; (2) Martha Shriver. By the first marriage they had Adam, John, Martha, and Harvey H. Children of the second marriage were Thomas H. and Virginia Staggers. Harvey Staggers

married (3) Pernissa .... There were no children by this marriage.
4. Culver Staggers, died at Fort Madison, Iowa. He was married and had Michael, Calvin, and Charles Staggers.
5. Jacob Staggers, married Miss Westfall of Kansas. He went on a steamboat trip, and did not return. His fate is not known.
6. Eleanor Staggers, married Christopher Scott of Rutan.

Children of Christopher and Eleanor (Staggers) Scott

    1. Harvey Scott, married Susannah Church.
    2. Lisbon Scott, married Delilah Church.
    3. Margaret Scott, married George Oliver.
    4. Elizabeth Scott, married Samuel Mansfield.

7. Julia Staggers, married William Gordon, and had Brice, H. F., Jesse, and Lizzie Gordon.
8. Catherine Staggers, born 1834; married Harvey Frye; they had, Sudie Frye and Laura Frye.
9. Margaret Jane Staggers, married John Kline, and had a daughter, Alice Kline.
10. Louisa Staggers, born 1830, died after 1850, in youth.
11. Lisbon Staggers, born December 17, 1820, sixth child in a family of 15; married (1) Jane Mooney, by whom he had, John, William, Thomas, Martha, Harvey, Arthur, Cassie, Catherine, and Marion Staggers. His second wife was Sarah (Hoge) Thompson by whom he had, Haman, Alice, Ida, Charles, Selah, and Elva Staggers, the last named is still living and supplied this record.
12.
13.
14.
15.

2. Catherine Staggers, daughter of Jacob and Elizabeth (Isenminger) Staggers, married Basil Smith.
3. Elizabeth Staggers, daughter of Jacob and Elizabeth (Isenminger) Staggers, married David Grove.
4. Jane Staggers, daughter of Jacob and Elizabeth (Isenminger) Staggers, married Abner Clark.
5. Margaret Staggers, daughter of Jacob and Elizabeth (Isenminger) Staggers, married Ellis Strosnider.
6. Mary Staggers, daughter of Jacob and Elizabeth (Isenminger) Staggers, married John Grove.
7. Nancy Staggers, daughter of Jacob and Elizabeth (Isenminger) Staggers, married Isaac Cross.

THE BRADFORD FAMILY

Robert Bradford was the pioneer ancestor of the family of that name, who settled in what is now Franklin Township, at the head of Sugar Run, where in 1785, he patented a tract of land under the name "Pleasure". It is probable that Robert Bradford was a native of Rock Creek Hundred, Prince Georges County, Maryland, where the family is found with the Hooks, Slaters, Thrashers, and other Tenmile settlers, in the early part of the 18th Century. He was born in 1730, and died about 1802, his will being probated in Greene County on October 11, 1802. His wife was Margaret ....

Children named in Will

1. Elizabeth Bradford. She married John Fee, who died in Bracken County, Kentucky. His will in WB. B. pp. 281, dated November 5, 1822, mentions his wife, Elizabeth, son, James, and three daughters, not named; also indicates they owned property in Ohio. John Fee was lieutenant under Captain James Archer.
2. Dinah Bradford. Married Thomas Heavrin and lived in Bracken County, Kentucky. His will on file there mentions the following children and sons-in-law, but not names of daughters.
    1. Thomas Heavrin, married ....
    2. John Heavrin, married Lucy T. Field, November 29, 1834, by Rev. James Savage.
    3. Jane Heavrin, married M. Larkin, February 8, 1837.
    4. .... Heavrin, married .... Thoman Toleman.
    5. .... Heavrin, married .... Beauchanan Dora.
    6. Elizabeth Heavrin, married, April 12, 1821, Joseph Taylor, by James Cortes.
    7. .... Heavrin, married, ..., Joseph Wood.
3. James Bradford, born in 1754, called eldest son, died April 18, 1822, aged 68 years, 3 months, 18 days, buried with first wife on the old James Bradford Farm. He served in Captain James Archer's Militia Company. He married (1) Barbara ...., who died March 10, 1816, aged 51 years, and 15 days. James Bradford then married Catherine ...., born 1779, died September 7, 1844. She is buried in the old cemetery in East Waynesburg.

Children

1. John Bradford, lived in Jackson Township, Greene County. His wife was Cassandra (Dye?).
2. Robert Bradford, born 1791, died November 12, 1857, aged 66 years, 10 months, 24 days. His wife was Nancy Wells, who died September 14, 1856, aged 62 years, 6 months.
3. James Bradford, married Mary (Dye?) (or Bowers?)
4. Jacob Bradford, died September 6, 1861, aged 60 years, 2 months, and 29 days. Lived in Greene County, Penna.
5. David Bradford.
6. Mary Bradford, married Henry Pethel.
7. Margaret Bradford, married Solomon Bowers.
8. Barbara Bradford, married, April 3, 1827, John Lemley.
9. Henry Bradford, born 1805, died 1843; married Hannah Morris.
10. William Bradford, died February 13, 1825, aged 18 years.

4. John Bradford, living in Whiteley Township in 1790.
5. Thomas Bradford, removed to Bracken County, Kentucky, as shown by papers in the estate of Robert Bradford. His wife was Lydia ....
6. William Bradford, named youngest son in the will. Lived in Bracken County, Kentucky.

SMITH FAMILY

L. K. Evans

L. K. Evans says of the Smith Family, "Thomas Smith, the grandfather of my clever old bachelor friend, Hugh Smith, lived in Harford County, Maryland, on the bank of the Susquehanna River. There he kept a tavern and a ferry, and reared a family of thirteen children—eight boys and five girls. In the year 1772, he sent Ralph, his eldest son, then 21 years old, west of the mountains to buy land for a future home for himself and younger brothers. He crossed the mountains with a number of others on a like errand, some of whom stopped in Fayette County, but he pushed on west of the Monongahela, and following up Ten Mile to the present site of Jefferson, purchased a body of six hundred acres of land, some little improved, and situated on both sides of the creek above the Clarksville bridge. He then continued up the creek to Richard Jackson's where Jackson's Fort was afterwards built, and bought him two tracts of land of 440 acres each on Smith Creek—now owned by Uriah and Josiah Inghram, Godfrey Gordon, Hugh Smith and others. No improvement had been made on these lands but that done by the inevitable tomahawk. Ralph next did a very sensible thing—went back home and married him a wife.

"In March, 1774, Ralph Smith and his brother, Thomas, then but eighteen years old, set out with a party of eight or ten others from the same neighborhood, to seek their fortunes in the West, to improve lands and cultivate a summer's crop—those that were married intending to bring on their families in the fall. Ralph went to work on his Jefferson land, whilst Thomas Smith and Thomas Kent, then nineteen years old, repaired to the Smith Creek purchase, and built them a cabin about where Josiah Inghram's brick mansion now stands. They cleared a piece of ground, fenced it, and planted corn and potatoes. About the first of June a man by the name of Morris came to their cabin and informed them that the Indians had been exasperated by reason of the Captina and Yellow Creek murders, and were on the war path, committing indiscriminate slaughter—that the settlers on both the north and south branch of the Ten Mile had met at the Forks, where Clarksville now occupies, to consider the situation—that some favored building a fort and defending themselves, whilst others determined to abandon the country for a season—among the latter were Ralph Smith and Morris."

THOMAS SMITH

In the Name of God Amen: I, Thomas Smith of Harford County, State of Maryland; Farmer being weak in body but of perfect mind and memory, thanks be to God, do constitute make and ordain this my last Will and Testament in manner following:

Principally and First of all, I recommend my Soul to the hands of Almighty God who gave it and my body to the Earth to be buried in decent Christian Burial at the discretion of my Executors and such wordly goods as I am now possessed of I leave in manner following: I will and positively order my lawful debts and funeral charges to be paid.

First, I Will and Bequeath to my dearly beloved wife, Hannah

Smith, all that part of a tract of land bought of John Stumps and Richard Dullam, laying on the South East Side of the Elbow branch now in the possession of James Smith, together with the fourth part of the produce of the Orchard growing on Neighbours Good Will during her natural life, then the land above mentioned to devolve to and become the property of my three sons, James, William, and Nathaniel, their Heirs and Assigns forever share and share equal; also, three Negroes, Jacob, Jean, and Rachal during her natural life then Jacob to become the property of my son Nathaniel, his paying one third part of his value to my Son, James, and on other third part to my son, William, said Negro to be valued at my wife's Decease; and Rachel, at my wife's Decease, to become the property of my Daughter, Mary McCrackin, her Heirs and Assigns forever; and Jean, at my wife's decease, to become the property of my Daughter, Hannah, her Heirs and Assigns forever.

I likewise give and bequeath to my wife, aforesaid, one bed and furniture together with one third of all my moveable property, except such as are herein after mentioned, to her heirs and assigns forever.

Likewise I will and Bequeath to my son, Ralph Smith, the sum of Ten Shillings and no more.

Likewise I will and Bequeth to my son, Hugh Smith, the sum of Ten Shillings and no more.

Likewise I will and Bequeath to my son, Thomas Smith, the sum of Ten Shillings and no more.

Likewise I will and Bequeath to my son, John Smith, the sum of Ten Shillings and no more.

Likewise I will and Bequeath to my sons, James Smith, William Smith, and Nathaniel Smith, all the remaining part of the aforesaid Tract of Land on which my wife was left her part as before mentioned, together with a Tract of Land by the name of Smith's Mistake, also on other Tract of Land known by the name of Neighbours Good Will, to them, their Heirs and Assigns, forever share and share equal.

Likewise I Will and Bequeath to my daughter, Susannan Gorrell, the sum of Ten Shillings and no more.

Likewise I Will and Bequeath to my daughter, Olivia Ingram, the sum of Ten Shillings and no more.

Likewise I give and Bequeath to my daughter, Elizabeth Garrett, the sum of Ten Shillings and no more.

Likewise I give and Bequeath to my daughter, Mary McCrackin, one Negro wench named Rachel, at her Mother's decease, her heirs and assigns forever.

Likewise I will and Bequeath to my daughter, Hanna Smith, one Negro Wench named Jean, at her Mother's decease, also a horse and saddle and bed and furniture to her, heirs and assigns forever; I also leave my aforesaid daughter, Hanna, one half acre of Land together with the House and fishing ground purchase of Benjamin Johnson during her mother's life, then to devolve to and become the property of my three sons, James, William, and Nathaniel, to them, their heirs and assigns, forever.

Likewise my Will is that my Executors dispose of my Title in and to a tract of land purchased in Partnership with John Love of Micaiah Mitchell, for the purpose of discharging my debts and the remainder, if any, to be equally divided amongst my five youngest children, Mary McCrackin, Hanna Smith, William Smith, Nathaniel Smith, and James Smith.

Likewise my Will that my Executors dispose of the remaining

two thirds of my moveable property for the purpose of discharging my debts, the remainder, if any, to be divided equally amongst my five youngest children before mentioned.

I likewise Will and Bequeath to my son, Nathaniel, one Sorrel Mare which he now claims.

And lastly I constitute and appoint John Creswell and James Smith to be sole Executors of this, my Last Will and Testament, revoking and disannulling all former wills heretofore by me made and confirming this and none other to be my Last Will and Testament in Testimony whereof I have hereunto set my hand and affixed my Seal, this Eleventh Day of April in the year of our Lord One Thousand Seven Hundred and Ninety-One.

   (SEAL)   THOMAS SMITH

Signed, Sealed, Published and Declared, by Thomas Smith, the above named Testator, as and for his Last Will and Testament, in the presence of us, who in his presence, subscribed our names as witnesses thereto.

     JOHN HALL HUGHES
     ANDREW COCHRAN
     ROBERT BONER

HARFORD COUNTY SS:

December 19th, 1791, then came John Hall Hughes, Andrew Cochran, and Robert Boner, and made oath that they did see Thomas Smith, the Testator herein named, sign and seal the aforegoing Instrument of writing and that they heard him publish, pronounce and declare the same to be his Last Will and Testament, and that he was at the time of his so doing to be, the best of their apprehension, of sound and disposing mind, memory and understanding, and that they subscribed their names as witnesses to this Will in the presence and at the request, of the Testator and in the presence of each other.

May the 11th, 1803, the Defects in probate and want of signature of the Late Register to probate of the Will of Thomas Smith, was this day cured in Court, Agreeably to an Act of Assembly passed on November Session, 1800.

           ABRAM JARRETT
           R. W. H. Co.

HANNAH SMITH

IN THE NAME OF GOD AMEN: I, Hannah Smith of Harford County, do make and publish this, my last Will and Testament, in the manner following, that is to say, I do hereby manumit and set free my Negro boy Emanuel, in fifteen years from the present date, also my Negro boy, Webster, in seventeen years from the present date, also my Negro boy, Hampton, in nineteen years from the present date, also my Negro girl, Iada, in eighteen years from the present date, also my Negro boy, Winston, in twenty-five years from the present date, also my Negro boy, Hampton, son of Rachel, in twenty-seven years from the present date.

I give and bequeath to my daughter, Mary McCrackin, my Negroes, Hampton and Winston, sons of Rachel, to serve for and during the terms specified above, but in case the said Mary McCrackin should decease before the said Winston and Hampton shall have served out the term specified above as it is my will, they should then be free and released from bondage. ITEM: I give and bequeath to my son, Nathaniel Smith, my Negro boy, Emanuel Western of Hampton, also my Negro girl, Iada, to him, his Executors, Administrators, and assigns, to serve for and during terms specified above. ITEM: All residue of my Estate not herein before given to be sold and the money equally divided amongst my surviving children after paying my just debts. Lastly, I hereby nominate, constitute, and appoint, my son, Nathaniel Smith, Executor of the Last Will and Testament hereby made, and I do revoke all former Wills and confirm this and no other, to be my Last Will and Testament, given under my hand and seal this eighth day of May, Eighteen Hundred and Seven.

    (SEAL)   HANNAH SMITH

Signed, Sealed and Published, pronounce and declared, by the Testatrix to be her last Will and Testament in the presence of us, the subscribers, who in her presence at her request, and in the presence of each other, have subscribed our names as witnesses thereto.

WM. STEPHENSON
JAMES STEPHENSON
WILLIAM X AKONS (His Mark)
STATE OF MARYLAND, HARFORD COUNTY, SS:

          Register's Office, January 7, 1947

I, Robert L. Wheeler, Register of Wills and Ex-officio Clerk of the Orphans' Court of the County of Harford, in the State of Maryland, do hereby certify the foregoing to be a true and accurate copy of the Last Will and Testament of Hannah Smith, late of Harford County, deceased, together with the probate thereof, as the same as recorded among the Will Records of Harford County in Liber A. J. No. C. Folio 227.

IN WITNESS WHEREOF, I have hereunto set my hand and affixed the seal of the Orphan's Court of the said County, the above date.

        Register of Wills and Ex-Officio
        Clerk of Orphan's Court

Nataniel Smith Executor of Hannah Smith
Late of Harford County, Deceased

To the balance of your final account passed on the 24th day of October 1815, and recorded in the office of the Register of Wills for Harford County .... $ 612.60

BY DISTRIBUTION AS FOLLOWS TO WIT:

To Mary McCrackin, one of the children of the deceased, one Negro named Hampton appraised at $80.00, one Negro named Winston appraised at $90.00, and her residuary part of the deceased personal estate .26, as directed by the deceased Will.. 170.26

To Nataniel Smith, one of the children of the deceased, one Negro named Emanuel appraised at $120.00, one Negro named Webster appraised at $120.00, one Negro named Hampton appraised at $100.00, one Negro named Ida appraised at $100.00, and his residuary part of the de-

ceased personal estate .26, as directed by the deceased Will 440.26
To Olive Ingram, one of the children of the deceased, her residuary part of the deceased personal estate, as directed in deceased Will............... .26
To Susannah Gorrell, one of the children of the deceased, her residuary part of the deceased personal estate as directed by deceased Will............... .26
To Ralph Smith, one of the children of the deceased, his residuary part of the deceased personal estate, as directed by the deceased Will............... .26
To John Smith, one of the children of the deceased, his residuary part of the deceased personal estate, as directed by the deceased Will............... .26
To Hugh Smith, one of the children of the deceased, his residuary part of the deceased personal estate, as directed by the deceased Will............... .26
To Elizabeth Garrett, one of the children of the Deceased, her residuary part of the deceased personal estate, as directed by the deceased Will............... .26

Amount Carried Over ....$ 612.08

Amount Brought Over ....$ 612.08

To William Smith, one of the children of the deceased, his residuary part of the deceased personal estate, as directed by the deceased Will............... .26
To Thomas Smith, one of the children of the deceased, his residuary part of the deceased personal estate, as directed by the deceased Will............... .26

$ 612.60

A true distribution of the personal Estate of Hannah Smith, deceased, made under the directions of the deceased Will, agreeably to the heirs, given in to me by the Executor this 24th day of October 1815.

Test: SAM RICHARDSON, R. W. H. Co.

HARFORD COUNTY, SS:

The 29th day of September, 1810, then came William Stephenson who produced the within last Will and Testament of Hannah Smith, late of Harford County, deceased, and made oath on the Holy Evangels of Almighty God, that he wrote the within will and had it in his keeping at the request of the Testatrix, and that it is the true and whole will and Testament of the said deceased that came to his hands and possession, and that he doth not know of any other.

Certified: ABRAM JARRETT, R. W. H. Co.

HARFORD COUNTY, SS:

The 29th day of September 1810, then came William Stephenson and William Akens, two of the subscribing Witnesses to the within last Will and Testament of Hannah Smith, late of Harford County, deceased, and made oath on the Holy Evangels of Almighty God, that they did see the Testatrix therein named, sign and seal this Will, that they heard her publish, pronounce and declare the same to be her last Will and Testament, that at the time of her so doing she was, to best of their apprehension, of sound and disposing mind, memory and understanding, and that they respectively subscribed their names as witnesses to this Will in the presence and at the request of the Testatrix, and in the presence of James Stephenson, who subscribed his name as a witness at the same time.

Certified: ABRAM JARRETT, R. W. H. Co.

STATE OF MARYLAND, HARFORD COUNTY SS:

Register's Office, January 7, 1946

I, Robert L. Wheeler, Register of Wills and Ex-Officio Clerk of the Orphans' Court of the County of Harford, in the State of Maryland, do hereby certify the foregoing to be a true and accurate copy of the Distribution Account of Hannah Smith, Late of Harford County, deceased, and the same is recorded among the Distribution Records of Harford County, in Liber T. S. B. No. 1, folio 132.

IN WITNESS WHEREOF, I have hereto set my hand and affixed the seal of the Orphans' Court of said County, the above date.

Register of Wills and Ex-Officio
Clerk of Orphans' Court

THOMAS SMITH OF SMITH CREEK

The story of the settlement of Thomas Smith on the stream that bears his name, could have included other interesting facts found in official records, which historians have failed to note. It is strange that none of these historians noted the manner by which the Smiths obtained the large acreage on which they settled. These historians missed entirely the deed in Greene County Deed Book 1. pp. 25, showing that Winser Pipes had owned the land as early as 1771, and sold it to Richard Jackson of Jackson's Run, describing it as being on the south side of William's Run, and adjoining Hendricks land. Richard Jackson had sold 800 acres of the tract to Ralph Smith, acting as agent for his father, Thomas Smith, Sr., of Harford County, Maryland, in 1773. Ralph Smith had also bought another tract of some 600 acres on Tenmile from Richard Jackson, and was probably living on this land when he was listed in the tax lists of Springhill Township, Bedford County, in 1772. He did not leave this section immediately as has been stated, but was still living here in what is now Morgan Township in 1782, when he served in Captain Benjamin Stites' Militia Company.

Thus when Thomas Smith, Jr., with William and Arthur Inghram, Billy Lafferty, and Thomas Kent came to the Tenmile Country in 1774, and made a field of corn, they were coming to land already parcelled out, and fairly well inhabited. Robert Gorrell, a brother-in-law of Ralph and Thomas Smith, Jr., while not mentioned by the historians, was probably with this party, as indicated by the fact that he warranted the "Shades of Death" tract of land that adjoined the Smith land. By a deed of November 27, 1787, Thomas Smith, Sr., transferred this land bought for him by his son, Ralph Smith, to Thomas Smith, Jr., Hugh Smith, and John Smith, as their share in his estate, then in his will of 1791, gave them each ten shillings as a token bequest. Hugh Smith and wife, Mary, later sold their interest, as did John Smith and wife, Letitia. (Deed Book 3. pp. 30-47.)

In his pension application dated May 8, 1833, Thomas Smith

said he was born in Baltimore County, Maryland, in 1757. He said he was drafted into Captain David Owens' Militia Company in the Fall of 1776, and was stationed on Fishing Creek for about three months. John Boggs, (Biggs?) was his Lieutenant, and James Archer the Ensign. Later he served under Captain William Harrod on Fishing Creek. In 1780, he was in Captain James Archer's Company, scouting between Fishing Creek and Wheeling Creek. From 1777 until 1781 he was on duty about ten months, scouting from Fort Jackson. David White and James Seals testified as to his veracity.

About 1777, Thomas Smith married Mary Williams, probably a daughter of the man of that name for whom William's Run was named. He died in his 88th year in May 1844. His wife died at the age of 86 years.

Children of Thomas and Mary (Williams) Smith

1. Martha Smith, never married.
2. Hannah Smith, died at the age of 98 years. She married David Porter, son of James and Nancy (Inghram) Porter. He was born in 1776, and died January 8, 1821.

Children of David and Hannah (Smith) Porter

1. Nancy Porter.
2. Thomas Porter.
3. James Porter, never married.
4. John Porter, born April 8, 1813; married, November 10, 1839, Hannah Rinehart.
5. Elizabeth Porter.
6. Zeiza Porter.
7. Martha Porter.
    List printed in notice in "Messenger" May 8, 1849
3. Olive Smith, born 1785, died 1864; married, December 12, 1805, Thomas Kent, Jr., born November 15, 1783, died in 1863. (See Kent Records.)
4. John Smith, married Jane Hamilton.
5. Thomas Smith, Jr., son of Thomas and Mary (Williams) Smith, died about 1848, at the age of 56 years. His wife was Catherine Johnson, daughter of Nicholas and Sarah (Vanbuskirk) Johnson.

Children of Thomas and Catherine (Johnson) Smith

1. Hannah Smith.
2. Caroline Smith.
3. George Morris Smith.
4. Olive Smith.
5. Minerva Smith.
6. Harriet Amanda Smith.
7. Hugh Smith.
6. Basil Smith, son of Thomas and Mary (Williams) Smith, married Elizabeth Staggers.
7. Mary Smith, daughter of Thomas and Mary (Williams) Smith, born 1789, never married.
8. Vincent Smith, son of Thomas and Mary (Williams) Smith, married Elizabeth Bell.

Children of Vincent and Elizabeth (Bell) Smith

1. John Smith.
2. Hiram Smith.

3. Jason Smith.
4. Hugh Smith.
5. Josiah Smith.
6. Thomas B. Smith, married Mary Fordyce.
7. Eliza Smith.
8. Sarah Smith.
9. Margaret Smith, married William Kent.
10. Mary Smith.
9. Nathaniel Smith, son of Thomas and Mary (Williams) Smith, married Lydia Smith, daughter of Thomas and Deborra Smith.
10. Sarah Smith, daughter of Thomas and Mary (Williams) Smith, born 1795, died 1883; married James Smith, son of Job and Sarah Smith, born 1794, died 1845.
11. Hugh Smith, son of Thomas and Mary (Williams) Smith, never married.

THE GORRELL FAMILY

This family is identified with the earliest white soldiers and traders in the Monongahela Country. A lieutenant of that name was in the Army of Colonel Henry Boquet and sat at a court martial in Fort Cumberland, on February 5, 1759. At the same time John Kennedy, the Indian Trader, was acting as interpreter for Boquet, and Michael Cresap was taking up land about Fort Burd (Redstone). Abraham Teagarden was then acting as a suttler from Fort Cumberland to Fort Bedford and Fort Pitt. (Boquet Papers Series 21644 part 1 Fol. 5 A Df. pp. 31-35.)

The local histories do not mention the name of Robert Gorrell in speaking of the first settlement on Smith Creek, but he could well be one of the party who made the field of corn in the Summer of 1774. He was a brother-in-law of Thomas, Ralph, Hugh, and John Smith, and of Arthur Inghram. Robert Gorrell warranted, on December 23, 1785, a tract of more than 395 acres of land under the title "Shadow of Death," which land adjoined that purchased by Ralph Smith from Richard Jackson for his father, Thomas Smith, Sr. He was living on this land when serving in Captain James Archer's Militia Company. (Penna Arch. Series VI Vol 2. pp. 17.)

Robert Gorrell was born in 1747, and was living in Harford County, Maryland, when he married Susanna Smith, daughter of Thomas Smith, Sr., and wife, Hannah. She is mentioned as the wife of Gorrell in her father's will of 1791. He died in Tyler County, West Virginia, on March 24, 1821; his wife, Susannah, died there April 9, 1827, at the age of 85 years. Both are buried at Middlebourne. The 1790 Census record indicates that all of their children were born before 1790. Much of the data on this family is supplied by Mr. Harland P. Gorrell of Charleston, West Virginia, an historian of the family. We are of the opinion that a second marraige to Susannah Wells, is an error, as there is no support for this tradition. The will of Robert Gorrell is in Tyler County Will Book 1-A-pp. 35, in which he names seven of his nine indicated children.

Children of Robert and Susannah (Smith) Gorrell

1. Thomas Gorrell, born December 1774, died August 22, 1829; buried at Middlebourne. His father says in his will that Thomas has already been cared for.

2. Ralph Gorrell, son of Robert and Susannah (Smith) Gorrell, born July 10, 1778, died on October 30, 1834. He too had been taken care of prior to the death of the father. He married Catherine Cooper, who died in Tyler County, in 1859. He was a soldier in the War of 1812.

Children of Ralph and Catherine (Cooper) Gorrell

1. Polly Gorrell, married, March 28, 1828, William Archer.
2. Oliver Gorrell, married Mary Cordell.
3. Elias Gorrell, born March 13, 1808, died January 14, 1881; married, January 15, 1833, Berthiah Galloway.
4. Delilah Gorrell, born ....; married Andrew Deleshmut.
5. George C. Gorrell, born 1816, died February 4, 1880; married, February 14, 1837, Margaret Galloway.
6. Ralph Gorrell, born January 4, 1819, died March 26, 1862; married, September 17, 1840, Rachel Wagoner, born August 20, 1820.
7. Thomas D. Gorrell, born 1822; married, December 23, 1841, Catherine Williamson.
8. Priscilla Gorrell, born ....; married, February 16, 1841, Jacob Hugus.
9. John Gorrell, born December 18, 1823, died March 12, 1852; married, September 4, 1845, Lucinda Flesher.

3. Robert Gorrell, Jr.
4. Susannah Gorrell.
5. William Gorrell.
6. Elizabeth Gorrell.
7. Hannah Gorrell.

THE THOMAS KENT FAMILY

Thomas Kent was born in County Derry, Ireland, on March 1, 1748, and immigrated to Cecil County, Maryland, at the head of the Chesapeake Bay. He is reported to have come to the Tenmile County in 1774, with Thomas Smith, Billy Laferty and Arthur Inghram, at which time they are said to have planted a field of corn on what is now Smith Creek. Thomas Kent certainly returned to Maryland, where on July 1, 1776, he enlisted in Captain James Maxwell's Company of the Flying Camp, and served until April 1, 1777. It was for this service that he received a pension on his application, executed in Franklin Township, Greene County, on September 10, 1832. (Nat. Archives Aw. S. 23741.) About the time of his discharge, he married Ann Ralston, (or Rolston) who was born April 7, 1759, and soon after returned to the Tenmile. It seems probable that he did not return to the Smith Creek land at once, for on December 17, 1784, he got a warrant for the tract of land adjoining Thomas Slater, which he patented under the name of "Fogaronian," separated from Slater by Brown's Run, and situated where West Waynesburg now stands. He may have lived on this tract until he sold a portion of it on February 12, 1791, to Mary Brown, widow of William Brown, by a deed in which he was joined by wife, Ann. On May 30, of the same year, Thomas Kent and Ann joined in a deed for the balance of the tract, which they sold to James Seals. (Washington County Deed Book 1-I-92 and 533.) It was probably about this time he removed to the site on Smith Creek, where he erected a large log cabin, said to have been three stories high and still standing as late as 1930. The stories of his owning large acreage of land on Smith Creek are refuted by the deeds dating back to 1771.

Thomas Kent died in Franklin Township on January 8, 1835, and his wife soon followed him, dying on April 27 of the same year. They were originally buried in the old cemetery in East Waynesburg, but in late years removal was made to the Greene County Memorial Cemetery. The Kent Family Bible, with many entries, is still in existence, and was owned in late years by John K. Lapping. A will of Thomas Kent is on file at Waynesburg. (WB. 2. pp. 48.)

Family of Thomas and Ann (Ralston) Kent

1. William Kent, born December 19, 1778, died January 12, 1856; married in 1807, Ann Niswanger, born March 25, 1781, died August 2, 1846. He then married Susan Shriver, born 1778, died June 24, 1849. Buried at Summerfield, Ohio.

Children of William Kent

1. Sarah Kent, born May 12, 1808, died July 27, 1887; married, August 23, 1826-27, James Porter Reed, born April 1, 1802, died February 7, 1886, at Bailey's Mills, Ohio.
2. Mary Kent, born 1810, never married.
3. Rebecca Kent, born May 2, 1811, died December 25, 1885.
4. Josiah Kent, born January 6, 1813, died April 5, 1866; married Louanna Bates in 1834.
5. James Kent, born December 6, 1814, died April 14, 1865; married (1) September 18, 1838, Elizabeth Adair, who died August 28, 1847. He then married Emily Ann (Porter) Barshears, Oscaloosa, Iowa.
6. John Kent, born December 4, 1816, died January 15, 1888; married, March 27, 1838, Elizabeth Danford, born September 24, 1812, died August 18, 1890.
7. Mariah Kent, born October 29, 1822, died January 4, 1881; married, January 6, 1839, George W. Brown, Summerfield, Ohio.
8. Elizabeth Kent, born December 21, 1823, died June 30, 1883; married, December 11, 1838, Ephraim Rucker.
9. William Thomas Kent, born 1823; married Margaret Lummax, went to Tennessee.

2. Mary Kent, born August 5, 1779; married, about 1800, James White. Her second husband was .... Borden.

Children of James and Mary (Kent) White

1. David White.
2. Jesse White.
3. John White.
4. William White.
5. Rachel White, married George Williams.
6. Mary Ann White.
7. Thomas White.
8. Uriah White.

3. George Kent, born February 11, 1781, died March 26, 1862; his will was made April 16, 1858, and probated April 8, 1862. (W. B. 4. pp. 8.) George Kent married, on February 10, 1802, Susannah Eagon, who died February 16, 1857, aged 75 years, 11 months, 13 days. She was probably a sister of Solomon Eagon. Both are buried in the old cemetery in East Waynesburg.

Children of George and Susannah (Eagon) Kent

1. Ann Kent, born March 15, 1804, died March 23, 1830; married, 1823, James Pipes, born January 14, 1800, died September 5, 1881.
2. Thomas Kent.
3. William Kent, born 1810, died 1882; married Mary Hoge, born 1818.
4. Uriah Kent, born December 19, 1812; married Margaret Cole, born November 1818.
5. Susannah Kent, married .... Engle.
6. Solomon Kent, married Martha Rogers.
7. Sarah Kent, married John Syphers.
8. Layton Kent, married .... Bradford.
9. Ephraim Kent, married Ellen Hunt.

4. Thomas Kent, Jr., born November 15, 1783, died 1863; married, December 12, 1805, Olive Smith, daughter of Thomas and Mary (Williams) Smith. She was born in 1785, and died 1864.

Children of Thomas and Olive (Smith) Kent

1. William Kent, born September 19, 1806, died October 1, 1888; married (1) February 10, 1829, Elizabeth Odenbaugh, born January 8, 1810, died May 4, 1868. He married (2) Jane White, widow of Rev. Michael White.
2. John Kent, born July 27, 1809, died January 28, 1891; married Keziah Shields, born June 5, 1810, died February 25, 1900.
3. Thomas Kent, married Rachel Hoge.
4. George Kent.
5. Harriet Kent, died June 14, 1884; married Elias Scott, who died August 20, 1884.
6. Marion Kent.
7. Hiram Kent, born 1817, died April 26, 1863; buried at Lippencott. Married Nancy Whitlatch.

5. Ann Kent, born October 18, 1785, died May 14, 1872; married, September 8, 1808, Daniel Hook, son of James and Mary (Leith) Hook, born June 11, 1781, died July 8, 1867.

Children of Daniel and Ann (Kent) Hook

1. Son that died in infancy.
2. Mary Hook, born June 22, 1815, died May 30, 1881; married Peter Kent, who died in 1852.

6. Catherine Kent, born February 8, 1787, died May 27, 1866; married, April 12, 1812, Arthur Hook, born 1790, died January 20, 1820.

Children of Arthur and Catherine (Kent) Hook

1. Samuel Hook, born December 31, 1812, died November 13, 1897; married, April 18, 1839, Sarah Scott, born October 14, 1817, died October 8, 1903.
2. John T. Hook, born January 20, 1814, died November 3, 1883; married, January 14, 1836, Eliza Inghram, born July 13, 1817, died May 4, 1901.
3. James Hook, born July 8, 1815, died June 23, 1895; married Vienna Herring, born May 24, 1821, died April 24, 1897.
4. Thomas Hook, born November 20, 1816, died October 11, 1888; married (1) ....; married (2) Anna (Conklin) Greenfield, who died May 28, 1895.

    5. Sarah Hook, born February 13, 1818, died at Jefferson, Pennsylvania, October 15, 1895; married Job Ridgeway, born April 3, 1814.
7. Elizabeth Kent, born November 17, 1789; married, February 3, 1811, John, son of Nicholas and Sarah (VanBuskirk) Johnson.

Children of John and Elizabeth (Kent) Johnson

    1. Anna Johnson, born July 4, 1812, died October 29, 1894; married Daniel Thompson Ullom, born December 23, 1809, died October 14, 1881.
    2.
8. Sarah Kent, born November 22, 1790, died January 24, 1867; married Joseph B. Johnson, brother of John Johnson. He died November 16, 1861; his tombstone record says he died March 5, 1862, aged 75 years, 3 months, 16 days. Both are buried in the Bethany Church Cemetery.

Children of Joseph B. and Sarah (Kent) Johnson

    1. David Johnson, died September 12, 1880, aged 67 years. His wife was Catherine .... who died August 29, 1872, aged 61 years.
    2. Nicholas Johnson, died before 1861, leaving a son, Joseph B. Johnson.
    3. Sarah Johnson, died before her father.
9. James Kent, born August 5, 1792, died February 12, 1878; married January 18, 1815, Margaret Eagon, born March 9, 1792, died March 25, 1878. Buried in Green Mount Cemetery.

Children of James and Margaret (Eagon) Kent

    1. Mary Ann Kent, born July 24, 1817; married (1) .... Eisenminger; married (2) .... Odenbaugh.
    2. Solomon Kent, born May 9, 1819, died October 27, 1852; married Margaret Bradford.
    3. Thomas Kent, born September 11, 1821, died January 7, 1822.
    4. John Kent, born April 27, 1823, died May 27, 1827.
    5. Elizabeth Kent, born September 29, 1826, died January 1, 1914; married, December 11, 1851, Slater Shriver, born April 10, 1827, died November 2, 1883.
    6. Sarah Kent, born January 4, 1828, died March 26, 1894; married, February 4, 1846, Jacob Shriver, born May 1, 1826, died June 20, 1910.
    7. Clementine Kent, born March 14, 1831, died October 7, 1907; married John R. Shriver, born May 23, 1817, died August 17, 1866.
    8. Susannah Kent, born April 2, 1833; married Elihu Brant.
    9. Margaret Kent, born June 24, 1835, died February 26, 1911; married John Lapping, son of David and Louisa (Smith) Lapping, born 1834, died 1902.
    10. Asa M. Kent, born February 12, 1837, died June 1, 1841.
    11. James F. Kent, born June 25, 1839, died January 23, 1886.
10. Rebecca Kent, born April 19, 1795, died young.
11. John Kent, born October 13, 1796, died before 1822.
12. Jesse Kent, born November 17, 1798, died in 1873. He married (1) February 24, 1821, Susannah Johnson, who died April 16, 1822, aged 20 years. She is buried in Morrisville Cemetery. Jesse Kent married (2) Sarah Johnson, sister of his first wife

and daughter of Nicholas and Sarah (VanBuskirk) Johnson. After her death Jesse Kent married (3) Hannah (Morris) Bradford.

Children of Jesse Kent

1. Nicholas Kent, married Phoebe Clutter.
2. Mariah Kent.
3. Nancy Kent, married Eli Phillips.
4. Thomas Kent, married Jane Miller.
5. Minerva Kent, married John C. Riley.
6. Melissa Kent.
7. Jane Kent, married John Wood.

13. David Kent, born July 10, 1801, died April 28, 1855; married, August 5, 1827, Elizabeth Barnes, born July 11, 1807, died May 19, 1883; daughter of William and Eleanor (Ingersol) Barnes.

Children of David and Elizabeth (Barnes) Kent

1. Cecelia Kent, born September 9, 1829, died September 3, 1918; married, March 27, 1849, Weedon J. Bryan, born November 23, 1825, died November 27, 1907.
2. Melinda Kent, born March 2, 1828; married David Thompson.
3. Eleanor Kent, born April 18, 1832, died October 5, 1902; married, July 25, 1854, Henry M. Jacobs, born July 23, 1832, died July 10, 1908.
4. Sarah Kent, born October 11, 1834, died April 20, 1857; married Robert Bradford, born July 20, 1829, died July 10, 1908, son of Robert and Nancy (Wells) Bradford.
5. Maria Kent, married Lindsey Thomas.
6. Marion Kent, born 1836, died ....; married, January 28, 1863, Catherine Hoge.
7. Nancy Kent, married Thomas Bell.
8. John Kent, born September 16, 1840, died February 3, 1895; married, September 8, 1877, Lydia Bell, born May 3, 1841.
9. Spencer Kent, born 1842, died June 14, 1919; married, 1873, Elizabeth Jacobs, who died May 19, 1885.
10. William T. Kent, married Jane Simington.
11. Elizabeth Kent, died October 3, 1883-84; married Levi Porter, born June 5, 1845.

THE ODENBAUGH FAMILY

Charles Odenbaugh came to Franklin Township from Baltimore, Maryland. He was a son of a nobleman, Jonas Schlohter von Adenbaugh. Charles Odenbaugh married (1) June 28, 1785, Martha Dean, who died and he married (2) 1795, Catherine, daughter of Christian Fry. She was born May 30, 1776, and died September 7, 1841. After the death of Charles Odenbaugh, she married (2) James Bradford, born January 31, 1754, died April 18, 1822. Other possible date for Catherine (Fry) Odenbaugh-Bradford, as taken from tombstone in East Waynesburg Cemetery, is "died on September 7, 1844, aged 65 years, 3 months, 8 days." Orphans Court Docket 1, pp. 126, lists the children of Charles and Catherine (Fry) Odenbaugh as of January 1818, after she had married James Bradford. All named were minors for whom William T. Hays served as guardian.

Children of Charles and Catherine (Fry) Odenbaugh

1. George Odenbaugh, took out letters in his mother's estate in March 1847. Probably married Mary Ann (Kent) Eisenminger, born July 24, 1817, daughter of James and Margaret (Eagon) Kent.

Children

   1. Catherine Odenbaugh, married Jesse McCormick.
   2. Ella Rebecca Odenbaugh.
   3. George Odenbaugh.
   4. Charles Odenbaugh.
   5. William Odenbaugh.
2. Christian Odenbaugh.
3. Daniel Odenbaugh.
4. Elizabeth Odenbaugh, born 1806, died May 4, 1858; married William Kent, born 1808, died 1888. (See Kent Records.)
5. Jacob Odenbaugh.
6. Samuel Odenbaugh.
7. Thomas Odenbaugh.

FAMILY OF CHRISTIAN FRY

Christian (or Christopher) Fry died about 1809, when his widow, Eve Fry, took out letters on his estate on June 6. A deed of December 11, 1814, gives a list of his children. (D. B. 3 pp. 130.)

Children named in the Deed

1. Charles Fry.
2. Michael Fry.
3. Catherine Fry, who married Charles Odenbaugh.
4. Mary M. Fry, who married Snowden Slater. He died about 1818.
5. John Fry.
6. George Fry, born in Germany December 6, 1785, died March 27, 1831; married Elizabeth Peckinpaugh, born November 24, 1787, died March 9, 1833, aged 45 years, 3 months, 16 days.

Children of George and Elizabeth (Peckinpaugh) Fry

   1. Tamzen Fry, born May 17, 1806, married .... Crouse.
   2. William Fry, born June 9, 1808, married Susannah Strosnider.
   3. Susannah Fry, born September 19, 1810, married Christian Sellars, Jr.
   4. George Fry, born May 7, 1813.
   5. Sarah Fry, born February 13, 1816, married Job Throckmorton.
   6. Elizabeth Fry, born November 20, 1818, married Solomon Guthrie.
   7. John Fry, born January 8, 1822.
   8. Catherine Fry, born May 9, 1826, died young.
7. William Fry.
8. Elizabeth Fry.

GEORGE LEMLEY

The most complete record of the Lemley Family has been sent us by Mr. Fred Lemley, an attorney at Fairmont, W. Va. There are some questions still unanswered as to the origin of the pioneer George Lemley. One tradition states he served as a soldier at Fort Pitt, leaving the Army prior to the close of the Revolution, to settle in the vicinity of Fort Jackson. There he is said to have traded a great coat for a tract of land. Family tradition also says he was born in Germany about 1741, though it is possible he belonged to the family of that name that were early settlers in the Shenandoah Valley, Virginia, and may have been at Fort Pitt with the troops from that section. He or his family may have settled for a time in Salsford Township, Philadelphia County. It is definite that he served a tour of duty with Captain James Archer's Company of Washington County, Pennsylvania Militia in 1782, and a few years later got warrants for two tracts of land in what is now Whiteley Township, Greene County, and settled on a branch of Whiteley Creek, near the Franklin Township line. It appears that he was twice married, the second wife being Catherine Yoho. He died in Greene County on June 1, 1813, and his estate was probated June 29, 1813. His children were:

1. John Lemley, born 1764 (?) died 1840. His wife was Barbara Livengood, daughter of Peter Livengood, Sr.

Children

1. George Lemley, born 1786, died 1862; married Christena Shriver, removed to Monongalia County, West Virginia.
2. John Lemley, who married Barbara Bradford, daughter of James Bradford. They were married on April 3, 1827.
3. Jacob Lemley, married Sarah White, daughter of Israel and Sarah (Slater) White.
4. Sarah Lemley, born 1789, died 1873, married William Miller, and resided in Wetzel County, West Virginia.
5. .... Lemley, married Jesse Haifhill.
6. .... Lemley, married John Flowers, son of Benjamin and Elizabeth Flowers.
7. Rachel Lemley, married Isaac Rawley.
8. Margaret Lemley.

2. Jacob Lemley, born 1767, died 1833, lived near Newtown, buried on the Fred Gordon Farm. He married Sarah ....

Children

1. Jacob Lemley. His children were William, Jacob, Ruth, Mary, Asa, Jesse, Joseph, and Blanche.
2. Richard Lemley.
3. George Lemley, married Sarah Morris, resided on Whiteley Creek. They had Jacob, Eleanor, Margaret, Charlotte, and George.
4. Ezekiel Lemley, born 1799, married Sarah Bowers. They had Susannah, Jacob, Ezekiel, Solomon, Nancy, Sarah, and Rebecca.
5. Samuel Lemley, born 1802, died 1880. His wife was Margaret Lemley, a daughter of David. They had David S., Jacob, Morris, Sarah, Samuel, Jeremiah, Josephus, and Katherine.

      6. Henry Lemley, born 1812, married Dorothy John, daughter of David. Removed to Tyler County, West Virginia. Their children were William, Jacob, Davis, Jackson, Samuel, Sarah, and Elizabeth.
      7. Elizabeth Lemley, married Archibald Gutherie for his first wife. She died March 5, 1829, was born September 29, 1791. Their children were Jacob, Solomon, Cephus, Samuel, Charlotte, Archibald, Sarah, and Ezekiel.
      8. Rebecca Lemley, married .... Bradford.
      9. Susannah Lemley, married Abraham Dulaney.
    10. Charlotte Lemley, married Ezekiel Bradford.
    11. Sarah Lemley, married Peter Pethtel.

3. George Lemley, born 1768, died 1820; his wife was Catherine .... They removed to Belmont County, Ohio.

Children

1. John Lemley.
2. .... Lemley, who married Job Smith.
3. Catherine Lemley, who married Woodman Okey.
4. Mary Lemley, who married Edward Reed.

4. Peter Lemley, born 1770, died 1850. He married, on February 11, 1794, Mary Ann Cathers, daughter of William and Elizabeth (Inghram) Cathers. They went to Belmont County, Ohio.

Children

1. Robert Lemley, born 1794, died 1865.
2. Peter Lemley, born 1802.
3. Catherine Lemley, who married Samuel Martin.
4. Elizabeth Lemley, who married Jesse Carter.
5. Nancy Lemley, who married Isaac Brown.
6. Sarah Lemley, who married Oath West.

5. Isaac Lemley, born 1781, died 1825; he married Margaret Snider on March 5, 1805. Buried in the Lemley Cemetery near Mt. Morris.

Children

1. Asa Lemley, married Fanny Long. He was born in 1806, and died 1884. Lived on Doll's Run, Monongalia County, West Virginia.
2. George Lemley, born 1809, died 1825; never married.
3. Catherine Lemley, born 1811, died 1888; married Alexander Henderson.
4. John Lemley, born 1812, died 1889; married Priscilla Long, went to Licking County, Ohio.
5. David Lemley, born 1813; his wife was Rebecca ....
6. Isaac Lemley, born 1817, died 1891; married Mary Ann Myers for his first wife. His second wife was Jane Stewart.
7. Jacob Lemley, born 1815, married Margaret ....
8. Clark Lemley, born 1820, removed to Iowa.
9. Rudolph Lemley, born 1825.

6. Samuel Lemley, born 1784, died 1869; married Rebecca Snider, and when she died married (2) Isabel Core. First marriage took place on September 17, 1804. Lived in Monongalia County, West Virginia.

Children

1. John Lemley, born 1806, died 1872 in Iowa.
2. Jacob Lemley, born 1810.
3. Asa Lemley, born 1814, died 1898.
4. Sarah Lemley, married Rezin Liming.
5. Mary Lemley, married Reuben Hague.
6. Samuel Lemley, born 1826, died 1908.
7. Barbara Lemley, born 1837.
8. Elizabeth Lemley.

7. David Lemley, born 1787, died 1843; married Ruhama Snider, lived near Mt. Morris, buried in the Lemley Cemetery.

Children

1. Margaret Lemley, born 1807, married Samuel Lemley.
2. George Lemley, born 1810, married Louisa Morris, born 1812.
3. David Lemley.
4. Jeremiah Lemley, born 1822, died 1855.
5. Asberry Lemley, born June 20, 1823; married Rachel Headley on October 12, 1849.
6. Elizabeth Lemley, born ....; married .... Evans.
7. Sarah Lemley, who married J. R. Donley.
8. Catherine Lemley, married Daniel Donley.

8. Mary Lemley, daughter of George Lemley, Sr. She married .... Bowen.
9. Susannah Lemley, married John Liming, and removed to Licking County, Ohio.
10. Rachel Lemley, married Absolom Wiley, and in 1817, moved to Licking County, Ohio.
11. Catherine Lemley, married Lewis Six.

THE LIVENGOOD FAMILY

There is a very old field stone marker in the Livengood section of the Garards Fort Cemetery on which is carved in very plain letters, July 19, 1785—May 1766. There are no initials nor other marks to identify this burial, the earliest dated marker we have seen in this county. It might well be the first local ancestor of the Livengood Family, as there are traditions which indicate the family was represented in Fayette County as early as 1753. No definite records are uncovered to show the relationship of the three early settlers of the Tenmile Country. They may have been brothers as claimed by some descendants, or they may have been separate individuals.

Jacob Livengood and his wife, Catherine, were warrantees of "Greene Bush" on February 13, 1789. They sold out in 1806 and disappear from local records. It appears they had a daughter, Catherine Livengood, among their children and she married James Lucas, a neighbor on a branch of Big Whiteley Creek. That they had other children is indicated by the Census record of 1790 when Jacob Livengood was head of a family of 1-2-4. Benjamin Livengood, living in the same neighborhood, had 1-2-1 and could have been a son of Jacob and Catherine. The Nicholas Livengood Family say that this Jacob was a brother of their ancestor.

NICHOLAS LIVENGOOD FAMILY

Nicholas Livengood died in Greene County on August 30, 1828, at the age of 65 years and 9 months. His will, made February 17, 1821, was probated September 16, 1828. (Will Book 1. pp. 346). His wife, who was Elizabeth Kughn, died March 31, 1838, at the age of 70 years. Both are buried in the Garards Fort Cemetery.

Children of Nicholas and Elizabeth (Kughn) Livengood

1. Jacob Livengood, who died in 1866, married Hester Henderson, who died in 1856.
2. Nicholas Livengood, Jr., who died November 6, 1874, married Rachel Morrison.
3. Ann Livengood, never married.
4. Catherine Livengood, married .... South.
5. Polly Livengood.
6. Barbara Livengood, married Henry Burge.

PETER LIVENGOOD FAMILY

One gets the impression that Peter Livengood, who had warranted to him on June 5, 1786, a tract of land as "Peters Purchase," was a very old man when he settled on this side of the Monongahela. His land was situated on an upper branch of Muddy Creek, near the ridge where Jack Morris lives. Most of his children had married in Fayette County and were living there at the time of Peter Livengood's death in 1814. His son-in-law, John Smith, served as his executor, and as such sold the land on August 4, 1826, to William Kincaid. His will was probated January 14, 1814, and no wife is named. John Lemley, named as executor, did not serve.

Children of Peter Livengood named in his Will

1. Elizabeth Livengood, who married .... Halfhill, and remained in Fayette County.
2. Magdeline Livengood, who married Robert Hickman and came to Greene County.
3. Catherine Livengood, married John Smith of Fayette County, he serving as executor of the will of Peter Livengood.
4. Mary Livengood, wife of John (?) Waits of Fayette County.
5. Barbara Livengood, married John Lemley of Greene County.
6. Sarah Livengood, wife of .... Franks of Fayette County.
7. Peter Livengood, who married Mary (Povator) Sellars, widow of Jacob Sellars. He settled on Pursley Creek, where he died about 1839. His will, made January 29, 1833, was probated December 25, 1839, with George Hoge and John Hoge as executors. He and his wife, Mary, made a deed for land on June 29, 1833, and another deed that was dated as the date of the probate. The will mentions his step-daughter, Elizabeth Sellars, wife of Joseph Sellars.

Children of Peter and Mary (Provator-Sellars) Livengood

1. Sarah Livengood, wife of John Staggers.
2. David Livengood.
3. Peter Livengood.
4. Jacob Livengood, who died before his father.

5. Catherine Livengood, born March 1, 1790, died August 3, 1848; married Joshua Thomas, born March 11, 1787, died October 12, 1873. He was a son of John and Cassandra Thomas.

Children

1. Anna Thomas, married William McFann.
2. Cassandra Thomas, married James Dye.
3. Harriet Thomas, married William Pratt.
4. Mariah (Lucy ?) Thomas, married Aliff Neal.
5. Susannah Thomas, married Abraham Eisenminger.
6. Inda Thomas, married Isaac Eisenminger.
7. Eleanor Thomas, married Remembrance Neal.
8. Rees Thomas, married Priscilla Crago.

6. Anna Livengood, married Michael Rush.
7. Barbara Livengood, married James Dye.
8. Mary Livengood, married John Fry.

Translation of Article of Agreement between Sarah Inkins and John Gordon of the one part and William Mony of the other part:

Condition of An Article Between Sarah Inkins and John Gordon of the one part and William Money of the other part viz ...

Said Money for a place in the Richhills now in possession of the other partys agrees to lease it for a certain term of time not longer than four or five years but not to leave .... plan before that term of time excepting Giving six months warning for the Clear Ground excepting a Garden spot and acre of flax, Ground each year and potato spot and for wheat, Rye and corn and Oats to deliver the share of each in the shock the same to be divided after twenty four hours warning and to be taken off in a reasonable time the Indian Corn to divided in the heap. Said Mony to have all the use of all the ground he clears for four years free of rent and a sugar Camp lying next Abraham Summermans twenty five shillings is to be allowed for Mony for three hundred feet of Oak Boards for a loft to be paid for out of the first years rents. In testimony whereof we have hereunto set our names this fourteenth of December one thousand seven hundred and Ninety three.

Test)
WM. RHODES
JAMES PORTER

SARAH INKINS
JOHN GORDON
WM. MONEY

THE GORDONS

On the ridge that divides the waters of Whiteley Creek, Smith Creek, Laurel Run, Coal Lick, and Sugar Run, there are several tracts of land that were patented under the name of "Rich Hills." Situated at the head of these waters, which in early days were the highways, it is not surprising to learn this was a site of one of the Ranger Stations, which was sometimes referred to as Fort Enkins, (Ankins, Inkins, eventually becoming Henkins) mentioned frequently in early dispatches. One of these "Rich Hills" sites was warranted to Demas Lindley, a native of New Jersey, that settled at Fort Lindley (Prosperity). But in 1793, Sarah Inkins and William Mooney, made an agreement, by which Mooney was to clear a portion of the land in payment for rent. In this agreement, Sarah Inkins is joined by John Gordon, a part owner, who in due course became sole owner and had the land patented to him. William Mooney, who moved over into Whiteley Township, had come from Ireland at an early date, bringing with him a set of wooden looms, which he set up to weave flax for his neighbors. He died in 1839 leaving three children: Jane, wife of Jacob Shriver; Nellie, and Thomas Mooney, who married Cassandra Inghram.

An excellent genealogy has been written about the Gordon Family. It states that John Gordon was born near Baltimore in 1739. There is some controversy as to his nationality, some of the family claiming to be of German stock, others stating he was Scottish. It is reported that he spoke with an accent, scarcely understood by his listeners, and used to support the theory that John Gordon was of German descent. It is also pointed out that he lived amid a German settlement in Frederick County, Maryland, and Frederick County, Virginia, before coming to the Tenmile, and that his children married into families of that nationality. The strongest argument supporting the theory has been overlooked. That is the custom of using the name "John" several times in the naming of sons. It is used by the Germans as a term of endearment, as a prefix to given names. This happens in the family of John Gordon, though it must be admitted that the name is distinctly Scottish.

It is not easy to pick out which John Gordon served in the Maryland Troops in the War of the Revolution since there are 18 men of that name listed in the Maryland Archives. We note, however, that one John Gordon and a Thomas Holland enlisted in Captain Thomas Ewing's Company on the same day, January 29, 1776. (Md. Arch. Volume XVIII, pp. 12.) In view of the several Gordon-Holland marriages, this reference seems the most likely one. I note also that the name is sometimes written "Jurdin" in these archives. There are several references to "Jurdin" in the William Rhodes Papers for 1790. If these references are of "Gordon" they indicate that John Gordon was on the Tenmile earlier than hitherto suspected.

In 1760, John Gordon married Mary Duke, and in 1780, moved to the vicinity of what is now Fairmont, West Virginia. He definitely was on "Rich Hills" in 1793, and perhaps earlier. Here he died on March 9, 1816. Mary (Duke) Gordon had died in 1789.

Family of John Gordon

1. Elizabeth Gordon, born in 1761, married (1) Christopher Guseman (or Grossman). She died in 1834, aged 73. Married (2) Lewis Snell.

Children

1. Godfrey Guseman.
2. Elizabeth Guseman, who married James Wells.

Children

1. Joseph Wells, married Amy Spragg.
2. James Wells, married .... King.
3. Godfrey Wells, married Rhoda Phillips.
4. Benjamin Wells.
5. Sarah Wells, married Isaiah Steele.
6. Nancy Wells, married Thomas Owens.
7. Susan Wells, married Peter Owens.
8. Mary Wells, married David Kughn.

2. John Adam Gordon, born November 3, 1762; married, 1781, Cassandra Holland, who died 1805, and he married (2) Sarah Johnson. He died January 29, 1816.

Children

1. Delilah Gordon, born June 20, 1790, married Adam Shriver.
2. Lucy Gordon, born February 9, 1792, married Henry Shriver.
3. Mark Gordon, born January 22, 1794, married (1) Susan Shriver; (2) Elizabeth Shultz.
4. Airy Gordon, born July 1, 1796, married (1) Solomon Kaine; (2) Rev. Barnet Whitlatch.
5. John Brice Gordon, born December 4, 1798, married Delilah Inghram.
6. Solomon Gordon, born April 2, 1801, married (1) Sarah Inghram; (2) Sally Willison.
7. Elizabeth Gordon, born December 10, 1803, married John Shriver.

3. Mary Gordon, born 1764, died September 13, 1845; married Jacob Holland.
4. Eleanor Gordon, born October 22, 1765, died 1853-4 in Ohio. Married Louis Karns.
5. Phillip Duke Gordon, born 1767, died about 1845. Married Judith Crull.

Children

1. Mary Gordon, married James Austin.
2. Cassandra Gordon, married James Steele.

6. Bazil Gordon, born July 13, 1770, died April 16, 1853; married, 1794, Elizabeth Dillinger, who died March 4, 1851.

Children

1. David Gordon, born July 22, 1795, died April 1851; married Christiana Washburn.
2. Sarah Gordon, born October 16, 1796, married Joseph Sanlee.
3. Barbara Gordon, born August 4, 1798, died 1871; married George Jameson.
4. Nancy Gordon, born June 29, 1800, died 1872, married Abraham Middleswort.
5. Elizabeth Gordon, born February 14, 1802, married James Jameson.
6. John Duke Gordon, born August 12, 1806, died 1895; married Anna Maria Riffle.
7. Mary Gordon, born March 23, 1807, married Jacob Washburn.
8. Rebecca Gordon, born November 23, 1809, married Zachariah Washburn.

7. William Gordon, born November 5, 1772, married (1) 1793, Mary Carroll, born August 29, 1773, died in 1814; married (2) Mary Cain, who died August 13, 1868. He died November 5, 1849.

Children

1. James Gordon, born March 20, 1794, died November 4, 1844; married Sarah Rinehart.
2. Sarah Gordon, born October 10, 1795, died April 1, 1872; married Jacob Johnson.
3. Bazil Gordon, born January 12, 1797, married Sarah Shriver.
4. Elizabeth Gordon, born November 9, 1801, married John Wiseman.

5. Margaret Gordon, born October 19, 1799, died November 10, 1875; married John S. Hoy.
6. Mary Gordon, born August 31, 1803, married James Clark.
7. Eleanor Gordon, born February 26, 1805.
8. Nancy Gordon, born November 3, 1806, died March 29, 1886; married David Spragg.
9. Anthony Gordon, born August 27, 1807, died young, as did John Gordon, born 1798.
10. Adam Gordon, born August 27, 1810, died October 1, 1833; married Elizabeth Shriver.
11. William Gordon, born January 20, 1817, married Liddy Miller. He died January 6, 1840.
12. Jane Gordon, born October 16, 1818, died December 1, 1859; married William Guyton.
13. Catherine Gordon, born March 15, 1820, died young.
14. Susannah Gordon, born March 6, 1823, married David Hewitt. She died March 8, 1901.
15. Cassandra Gordon, born January 7, 1825, married Peter Cockran.
16. Lucy Gordon, born February 6, 1827, married George Heffley.
17. Mark Gordon, born April 6, 1829, died 1906; married Mary Ann Ryan.
18. George Gordon, born April 1, 1828, married Sarah Ryan.

8. George Gordon, born 1774, married Eleanor White, who died September 3, 1854; she was a daughter of Israel and Sarah (Slater) White. George Gordon died September 24, 1831.

Children

1. Mary Gordon, born 1808, married John Munyon.
2. Rachel Gordon, born 1810, married Felix Bell.
3. William D. Gordon, born December 3, 1812, died December 22, 1874, in Lancaster County, Ohio. He married, April 1832, Catherine Keener, who died March 27, 1877.
4. Sarah Gordon, born 1814, married Thomas Munyon.
5. John Gordon, born 1816, married Eliza Ann Cease.
6. James Gordon, born 1818, died 1879; married Jane Saffel.
7. Israel Gordon, born September 10, 1820, married, February 13, 1843, Susan Irwin.
8. Bazel Gordon, born 1822, married Ellen Wells.
9. Ellen Gordon, born April 7, 1824, married Alexander Evans.
10. George Gordon, born 1826, married Sarah Drumm.
11. Maria Gordon, born 1828, died 1832.
12. Isaac Brice Gordon, born 1832, married Elizabeth Evans.

9. John Gordon, born 1775, married Nancy Rinehart, daughter of Simon and Sarah Rinehart. Her father was killed by the Indians when she was quite small. John Gordon died in 1830-1 and his wife in 1820.

Children

1. Sarah Gordon, born September 1794, died November 1881; married Samuel Seals, who died January 1859. He was a son of Captain James and Sarah (Brown) Seals.
2. Nancy Gordon, born 1796, died December 1869; married, 1821, Arthur McCartney, born March 8, 1792.
3. Mary Gordon, married William Orndorff, who died 1880.
4. Charlotte Gordon, married Peter Strosnider.
5. William Gordon.

6. Patty Gordon, twin of William; married .... Smith.
7. Bazel Gordon, died March 1862.
8. Elly Gordon, died April 1841; married George Hoy.
9. Samuel Gordon, married Dolly Wells.
10. Barnard Gordon, died October 7, 1820.
11. Zebediah Gordon.

THE MEIGHEN FAMILY

The Meighen Family were late comers to the Tenmile Country, not having arrived in America from Ireland until the year 1792, but the imprint they made in the early history, and the numerous descendants left by the common ancestor, demands recognition in any type of history. The Meighen-Fitzer battle is local folklore, and has been told so often that it is not necessary to repeat it, other than to remark that the fighting qualities of the patriarch have diminished little in his descendants. I am indebted to Jimmy Meighen, son of Frank Meighen of Waynesburg, for the record of the immigrant and his children.

James Meighen and his wife, formerly Susan McClaskey, came to America in 1792, bringing with him his three sons and three daughters, all of whom seem to have been born in Ireland.

Children

1. Peter Meighen, died without issue.
2. John Meighen, no records.
3. William Meighen, born in 1774, died in 1829 (O. C. Dockett 1. pp. 340, June 1831). He married, before 1800, Elizabeth Hughes, daughter of James and Cassandra (Dunn) Hughes in Greene County, Pennsylvania. He was the hero of the Meighen-Fitzer fight and ancestor of the family here.

   ### Children
   1. Susanna Meighen, born December 22, 1800, married Christopher Brant.
   2. John Meighen, born September 2, 1802, died July 16, 1848; married, 1823, Elsie Shultz, born July 16, 1805, died December 19, 1893.
   3. James Meighen, born October 14, 1804, died young.
   4. Mary Meighen, born August 5, 1806, married William Terry.
   5. Peter Meighen, born September 25, 1809, died 1867; married Priscilla Dye.
   6. Felix Meighen, born January 16, 1812, died ....; married Eliza J. Foster.
   7. Dennis Meighen, born March 15, 1814.
   8. William Meighen, born December 15, 1816, married .... Foster.
   9. Cassandra Meighen, born February 15, 1819.
   10. Thomas Meighen, born March 5, 1821, married Louisa Morris.
   11. Catherine Meighen, married Samuel W. Felton.
4. Susan Meighen, died without issue.
5. Elsie Meighen, married Dennis Tommony.
6. Margaret Meighen, married John Mulrine. The Mulrines also came to Greene County, and lived at the head of Jackson's Run.

Children
1. Edward Mulrine, married .... Chaffin (Chalfont).
2. Peter Mulrine, married Nancy Pollack.
3. Elsie Mulrine, married Simon Rinehart.
4. Margaret Mulrine, married James Keenan.

THE STEWART FAMILY OF FORT JACKSON

There are so many Stewart Families that settled in the Tenmile Country, that it is almost impossible to identify the different families with any degree of certainty. Mrs. Elizabeth Prickett, a granddaughter of one of the pioneers, gave an interview sometime before her death in 1931, in which she stated that there were four brothers in her grandfather's family, and named them as Hezekiah, James, Isaac, and Samuel Stewart. It can be safely stated that she was wrong in naming Samuel Stewart to this group, as he seems of an age one generation removed, and possibly a brother of her father rather than her grandfather. It is more likely that the fourth brother was Daniel Stewart, who with Hezekiah and James Stewart, served in Captain James Archer's Washington County Militia Company acting out of Fort Jackson. A Richard Stewart, who served in the same company, cannot be identified.

There is also no record to show who was the father of these four brothers, nor where they came from, yet with so many descendants of the early Indian Traders settling at Fort Jackson, it is not unlikely that they were descendants of one Indian Trader, Daniel Stewart, who held a traders license from Pennsylvania in 1742. That being the case, hey probably came from Lancaster County, Pennsylvania, or Upper Maryland where the name appears frequently in early records.

THE ISAAC STEWART FAMILY

The W. P. A. survey of soldiers graves reported Isaac Stewart as being a soldier in the Revolution, but it would appear he was too young to have been in that War. In the list of debtors to the trading post conducted at Fort Jackson by William Rhodes, we find the names of Isaac Stewart, James Stewart, and Hezekiah Stewart. On August 17, 1789, Isaac Stewart owed Rhodes 11 shillings and six pence, indicating he was of mature age at that time. By comparing this age with the census records for 1800, 1810, and 1820, it is indicated that he was born between 1765 and 1768. He was not listed in the 1790 Census for Pennsylvania. He died after 1825, for on April 30 of that year, he deeded his property on Smith Creek, which he had bought January 6, 1811, from Thomas Smith, to his son Isaac Stewart, Jr., and son-in-law, Frederick Honnell. His wife, who was Elizabeth Parrish, joined in the deed. He and his wife are buried in the old cemetery on the Inghram Sisters Farm on Smith Creek. A family tradition speaks of Isaac Stewart trading a rifle for 400 acres of land when he arrived on the frontier, but no record of ownership of such land appears of record, in Greene or Washington County.

Children of Isaac Stewart

1. Samuel Stewart, born about 1790. Probably settled in Monroe County, Ohio. His wife appears to have been Martha Hickman, daughter of William and Margaret.
2. Louis Stewart, born before 1800. An old Justice of Peace Docket presented to the Greene County Historical Society by the writer, shows an entry, where Louis Stewart was sued for debt by Daniel Stewart, before Thomas Kent. Tradition in family says he went west.
3. Delilah Stewart, never married.
4. Isaac Stewart, born before 1800, married (1) Sarah Grove; married (2) Sarah Shaw. He was a soldier in the War of 1812, and is said to have been buried in Green Mount Cemetery.

Children

1. Andrew Stewart, married Elizabeth Shaw.
2. Hiram Stewart, born March 9, 1847, died February 9, 1916; married Francis Ferguson.
3. Isaac Stewart, born July 29, 1849, died December 15, 1913; married Eliza Shaw.
4. Rachel Stewart.
5. Lee Stewart, married Jane Anderson.
6. Emma Stewart, married Frank Yard.
7. Frank Stewart, married Lucy Henderson.

5. Peter Stewart, died about 1860; married Catherine Edgar.

Children

1. Inghram Stewart, married Emma Jones.
2. Jesse Stewart, married Belle Miller.

6. Rebecca Stewart, born September 19, 1797, died November 30, 1877; married, before 1818, Frederick Hunnell (Honnell) born August 5, 1795, died June 22, 1842; both are buried in Green Mount Cemetery.

Children

1. John Hunnell, married Mary Seals.
2. Catherine Hunnell, married Jacob Shoup, born May 24, 1825.
3. Jesse Hunnell, born January 1, 1825, died October 5, 1894; married Catherine Smalley, born July 1, 1825, died December 5, 1869.
4. Elizabeth Hunnell, married Samuel Garner.
5. David Hunnell, married Maude Wiley.
6. James Hunnell, died July 5, 1903, married Callie Rush.
7. Morgan Hunnell, married Caroline Donahue.
8. Delilah Hunnell, born May 28, 1839, died October 5, 1894; married William Thomas Webb, born February 21, 1840, died July 15, 1903.

7. James Stewart, born November 30, 1802, died August 10, 1863; married, about 1820, Mary Blair, daughter of William and Jane (Mason) Blair. She was born June 10, 1800, and died July 8, 1876. Buried in the Stewart Cemetery on the Norman Stewart Farm near Kughntown.

Children

1. Houston Stewart.
2. Israel Stewart, born May 17, 1830, died October 29, 1887; married, March 24, 1853, Rebecca Phillips, born December 18, 1827, died November 21, 1900.

3. Layton Stewart, born March 22, 1825, died January 15, 1902; married Louisa Granlee, born May 5, 1822, died April 21, 1906.
4. Isaac Stewart, married (1) Allie Cole; (2) Eliza Cole.
5. John Stewart, born May 22, 1828, died May 3, 1905; married Sarah Spragg.
6. Spencer Stewart, born December 28, 1835, died March 12, 1915; married Catherine Henkins, born December 6, 1835.
7. Elizabeth Stewart, born ...., died January 11, 1931; married Oliver Prickett.
8. Rebecca Stewart, died in infancy.

THE JAMES STEWART FAMILY

James Stewart was living in the vicinity of Fort Jackson during the Revolution and served in Captain James Archer's Company, Washington County Militia. His name is found in the Rhodes Papers as early as 1789. The name is found in other military rolls for the period of the Revolution, but because of numerous persons of the same name it is only possible to definitely connect him with Archer's Company. He removed to Wayne Township where he died intestate in 1823. Mrs. Prickett says he was killed in an accident. His estate, No. 455, was filed for probate September 13, 1823, with his wife, Eleanor ...., and Henry Shriver, taking out letters to administer. Orphans Court records of November 1826, disclose the members of his family, the last four named being minors at that date.

Children
1. Elizabeth, wife of Nathan Clark.
2. Eleanor Stewart, died January 24, 1843; married George King, who died in 1863.
3. James Stewart, Jr.
4. Daniel Stewart.
5. Rebecca Stewart, married .... Lewis.
6. Letitia Stewart, married Phillip Huffman.
7. Sarah Stewart, married Solomon Huffman.
8. John Stewart.
9. Richard Stewart.
10. Hannah Stewart.
11. Rachel Stewart.

HEZEKIAH STEWART FAMILY

Hezekiah Stewart was an early settler on Pursley Creek, where he was living when he served in Captain James Archer's Militia Company. There is evidence to indicate that he may have lived on Dunkard Creek for a time, since his wife was Susannah Bonnett. Her sister, Catherine Bonnett, married Conrad Sykes, while her sister, Mary Bonnett, married Captain John Wetzel, father of Lewis Wetzel, the famous Indian fighter. It is known that these people were originally from Pennsylvania, then moved to the Shenandoah, from whence they came to Dunkard Creek. Hezekiah Stewart left no will of record, nor any estate settlement to be found in Greene County, but land which he possessed on Pursley Creek has been passed down through generations of his descendants, and there is mention of a purchase of a part of his land by Christian Sellars. Waychoff says that he once operated a powder mill on Pursley Creek, one of the few such mills to be found in the County. His name is found among those who were customers of William Rhodes at the Trading Post at Fort Jackson in 1789. Three sons are known and there may have been two daughters as indicated by the 1790 Census.

Children of Hezekiah and Susannah (Bonnett) Stewart

1. Jacob Stewart, his wife was .... Mason.
2. Jesse Stewart, born October 1, 1794, died December 3, 1885; married Rachel Smith Huffman, born February 1, 1797, died September 14, 1873. Both are buried at White's Church. He secured a patent for the land on Pursley Creek on February 23, 1837.

Children of Jesse and Rachel (Huffman) Stewart

1. Peter Stewart, died March 25, 1892, aged 59 years, 11 months, 20 days; married Catherine M. Fry, daughter of Peter Fry, and his second wife, Elizabeth (Taylor) Fry. She died on December 8, 1922, aged 88 years.
2. Jesse Stewart, married Rachel Babbitt.
3. Catherine Stewart, married (1) William Crouse; (2) Daniel Stewart.
4. Sarah Stewart, married (1) .... Thomas; (2) Chis Bilby.
5. Ezekiel Stewart, married Nancy Fry.
6. Rachel Stewart, married Abraham White.
7. Julia Stewart, married William Thomas.
8. Eliza Stewart, married Jesse Thomas.
9. Rebecca Stewart, whose second husband was Elijah Montgomery.
10. Margaret Stewart, married John Caldwell.
11. Mary Stewart, married (1) .... Sappington; (2) James Shaw.

3. David Stewart, wife was Elizabeth .... Went to Tyler County, Virginia.

DANIEL STEWART FAMILY

Daniel Stewart owned land in Franklin Township, adjoining John Smith, Thomas Hoge, and Hiram Heaton, when he died about 1816. His will was probated March 18, 1816, with his son, Samuel Stewart, and brother-in-law, Willam Hickman, administrators. Hickman, dying in 1817, Samuel Stewart became sole administrator in 1819. (O. C. Docket 1. pp. 138.) Daniel Stewart was a member of Captain James Archer's Company of Washington County Militia in the War of the Revolution.

Children

1. Daniel Stewart. Deed Book 3. pp. 535, shows him an heir of Daniel. With wife, Eleanor, Daniel deeded his interest in his father's estate to brother, Samuel Stewart, on April 1, 1817.
2. Samuel Stewart, died in Greene County in 1871. Buried at White's Church.

Children

1. Daniel Stewart, born May 25, 1813, died July 17, 1887; married (1) Cynthia ....; married (2) Catherine (Stewart) Crouse. (Cynthia .... Stewart died June 28, 1865, aged 47 years.)
2. James Stewart, born 1818, died September 8, 1893, married Lucinda Rush, born December 16, 1833, died September 10, 1893.
3. Mary Margaret Stewart, married Henry Lightner.
4. Jane Stewart, married Isaac Lemley, born 1817, died 1891.
5. Samuel Stewart, born 1821, died February 17, 1902; married Rebecca Lewis, born October 26, 1825.
6. Levi Stewart, born 1824, married (1) Margaret M. ...., born 1821, died February 22, 1861. He married (2) Elizabeth Bell.
7. Jesse Stewart, married .... Hinerman. He was born October 10, 1826, died October 19, 1896.
8. Catherine Stewart, married Craven Gregg.

3. William Stewart.
4. Elisha Stewart.
5. James Stewart, a minor child in 1817.
6. Rebecca Stewart, never married.
7. Nancy Stewart, married Nathaniel Cummings.
8. Rachel Stewart, married .... Staggers.
9. Druscilla Stewart, married Benjamin Bellford.
10. Dorcas Stewart, minor child.
11. Polly Stewart.

THE STEPHEN HATFIELD FAMILY

Stephen Hatfield, the only identified Revolutionary soldier buried in Green Mount Cemetery, was born in New Jersey in 1759, and died at Waynesburg May 19, 1824. He enlisted January 7, 1777, in Captain Abraham Lyons' Company in the Fourth New Jersey Regiment, and saw action in the Battles of Germantown, and Short Hills. He was transferred to Captain Bateman Lloyd's Company of the Third Regiment, on February 1, 1779, and then on March 20, 1780, was chosen for the Commander-in-Chief's Guard. He was wounded in the battles fought in New Jersey, but returned to take part in the surrender at Yorktown. On July 23, 1798, he married Elizabeth Freeborn, born in New Jersey, in 1781, died at Waynesbug, July 19, 1861.

Children of Stephen and Elizabeth (Freeborn) Hatfield

1. Sarah Hatfield, born April 3, 1798, died May 2, 1879; married Charles Adamson, born 1787, died September 1867. He was a son of Thomas and Sarah (Eagon) Adamson.
2. Mary Hatfield, born in 1802, died January 15, 1834; married John Clark.
3. Elizabeth Hatfield, born 1805, died in Iowa; married Josiah Adamson, who died in Greene County, before 1838, leaving minor sons, William and James.
4. Charlotte Hatfield, born May 3, 1809, married Richard Areford.
5. Anthony Smith Hatfield, born 1810, died in Kentucky; married .... Black.
6. Letitia Hatfield, born 1814, married Cyrus Frakes.
7. Jacob Hatfield, born in 1815, died in Indiana in 1838.

8. Maria Hatfield, born June 24, 1818, died in Missouri, May 4, 1902; married R. C. Clark.
9. Andrew Hatfield, born 1819, went to Dayton, Ohio. Died in Ohio in 1896.
10. Sceney Hatfield, born February 11, 1824, died December 30, 1897; married, about 1840, Simon Rinehart, born March 3, 1821, died October 24, 1885.

PETER DAILEY FAMILY

Peter Dailey was a member of Captain James Archer's Militia Company of the First Battalion in Washington County, during the Revolution. He did not patent any land, but lived close to Fort Jackson until he bought land shortly before removing to Ohio County, (West) Virginia. When living in Ohio County, he and wife, Mary, sold their land. He died in Ohio County, West Virginia, where he made a will on February 7, 1804, naming wife, Mary ...., and the following children. (Ohio County Will Book 1. pp. 67.) Jeremiah Williams and Ellis Thomas, former Greene County natives, were his executors.

Children

1. John Dailey.
2. Peter Dailey, Jr.
3. Esau Dailey.
4. Jacob Dailey.
5. Jesse Dailey.
6. Mary Dailey.
7. Nancy Dailey.

THE HATHAWAY FAMILY

The Hathaway Family who settled on the south side of Tenmile Creek opposite Fort Jackson, may have been a Maryland branch of the family, which is found in St. Michael's Parish, Talbot County, in 1760, when we find a William Hathaway listed. At least three members of the family, apparently brothers, settled at the mouth of Sugar Run and Smith Creek, prior to the end of the Revolution. They were William Hathaway, Samuel Hathaway, and Simon Hathaway.

The record of William Hathaway shows that he bought land on the north bank of Tenmile from Richard Jackson and wife, Mary, by deed of record March 12, 1790. (Washington County D. B. 1-F. pp. 151.) The land was known as "Jackson's Old Fort Site" and deed included a tract called "Bengal," and joined John Smith, and Thomas Slater. Census record for the same year shows William Hathaway head of a family which included two adult males, six males under 16 years of age, and three females. We have no record of his family though a Silas Hathaway appears to have been a son. His wife was Rebecca ....

Samuel Hathaway patented a tract of land west of his brother, Simon, that extended to the mouth of Smith Creek. Deeds show also that in March 1785, he bought five and a half acres of land on the north bank of Tenmile from Richard Jackson and wife, Mary, and together with Mr. Jackson, operated a mill or mills, at the mouth of Jackson's Run. On March 12, 1790, Samuel Hathaway bought Richard Jackson's interest and the land where the mill stood, and it became known thereafter as Hathaway's Mill. (Washington County Deed Book 1-F-pp. 147.) On February 2, 1798, sold a tract of his land on the south side of Tenmile to Thomas Stokely, and a short time later was joined by his wife, Sarah, in a deed to Jacob Erhart. (Greene County Deed Book 1. pp. 220-308-506.) In the Census of 1790, his household consisted of two adult males, two males under 16 years of age, and three females.

Family of Simon Hathaway

Simon Hathaway patented the large tract of 423 acres of land on both sides of Sugar Run opposite Fort Jackson, under the name of "Fellowship." With his wife, Mary ...., he made agreements with Samuel Hathaway and with Silas Hathaway in 1823, and on March 26, 1823, he sold land to Sylvanus Smith. (Greene County Deed Book 5. pp. 321-436-45.) His children are named in the estate of his son, Samuel Hathaway, who died about 1824 (Est. No. 449) except a son, John, who died in 1819. Those named were:
1. John Hathaway, not named but whose estate named his brother, Samuel Hathaway, Jr., as executor. He was a member of Captain James Archer's Militia Company from Washington County, Pennsylvania.
2. Samuel Hathaway, Estate No. 449, probated in 1824, April 12; also a member of James Archer's Company, Washington County Militia.
3. Uriah Hathaway.
4. Elijah Hathaway.
5. Martha Hathaway, who married .... Shellet.
6. Sarah Hathaway.
7. Mary Hathaway, who married .... Crayne.
8. Ruth Hathaway.

SAMUEL HATHAWAY

One Samuel Hathaway, possibly a son of William or Samuel Hathaway, died in Greene County before June 22, 1820. He married Elizabeth Estle, daughter of Silas and Sarah (Rofelty) Estle, and granddaughter of Daniel Estle, a member of Captain James Archer's Company. This Samuel Hathaway had apparently been married a short time before his death, and left a son, John Hathaway, who was born May 19, 1820, and is mentioned in the will of his father as well as in the will of Silas Estle. The widow Hathaway remained single for a time and then married .... Haines. Her mother, Sarah Rofelty, was one of the children of Mathias Rofelty that was scalped by the Indians, but she lived to a good old age. Many of the Haines Family are her descendants.

Child of Samuel and Elizabeth (Estle) Hathaway

1. John Hathaway, born May 19, 1820, or 21. Bates History of Greene County is in error as to the date of his birth and also in calling Mathias Estle the grandfather of John Hathaway. This is shown in the will of Silas Estle. But Mathias Estle was the uncle of John Hathaway and did raise him. On January 1, 1846, John Hathaway married Ary Anderson, daughter of William and Kezia (Wiley) Anderson, and they had the fol-

lowing children, who survived him: (This is the Carmichaels Group of the name.)
1. Charles Hathaway.
2. Samuel Hathaway.
3. William Hathaway.
4. Jacob Hathaway.
5. Lawrence Hathaway.
6. Mary Hathaway, who married .... McGinnis.

PATRICK MARTIN

Patrick Martin patented the tract of land on Owens Run to the west of David Owens (later James Hook's land) in 1801, under the name of "Paddy." His pension application of April 14, 1818, while living in Greene County, Pennsylvania, notes that he enlisted as a private in the Spring of 1776, under Captain P. Frazier, joining the command of Colonel Anthony Wayne at Chester. From thence he marched to Long Island, where he was engaged in building fortifications. He next marched to Ticonderoga, where he became sick and was sent to Albany to recuperate, after which he was discharged, but immediately re-enlisted under Captain J. Moore and became a part of the Fifth Pennsylvania Regiment under Colonel F. Johnson. Patrick Martin was in that service until the Battle of Brandywine, when he was severly wounded and taken prisoner, and remained such until the Battle of Monmouth, when he escaped and returned home. He was born in 1750, and died in Greene County about 1825. (Est. 479 WB. 1. pp. 262. prob. January 26, 1825.) Before applying for his pension he distributed his property to his two daughters, except for "Paddy" which he sold in 1808 to William Mason. His wife's name was Mary ....

Children
1. Nancy Martin, who married Job Cornwell.
2. Catherine Martin.

THE SELLARS FAMILY

The late Mrs. Emma Wood worked for many years trying to discover the origin of the Sellars Family who settled on Pursley Creek about the time of the Revolution. We are indebted to her for a number of these records. Mrs. Wood was of the opinion that this branch of the family was connected with the founder of Frankfort, Mineral County, West Virginia, and Fort Sellars that stood on the site of this place. The land on which the town was laid out was granted to Charles Keller (so the name was spelled) by Lord Fairfax in November 1748, but he was killed by the Indians in 1756. Upon legal application his son and heir, John Keller, this plot of 300 acres, designed in a survey made by James Genn and George Washington as "Lot No. 16." was regranted to John Keller of Lancaster, Pennsylvania, on the first day of June 1779. Subsequent records spell the name John Sellars and named the Fort on his land as Fort Sellars. When Washington reviewed his troops at Cumberland, Maryland, during the days of the Whiskey Rebellion, he mentions 500 men stationed at Frankfort, and ordered that two forts be constructed, one of which was Fort Sellars at the Mouth of Patterson's Creek, the other was Fort Ashby, five miles further south. Myers "History of Virginia" says George Washington surveyed land here for Elias Sellars on April 1, 1748.

Chalkley, in his History of Augusta County, Virginia, mentions a George Sellars of Frederick County in September 1747, and a John Sellars, who was naturalized on October 16, 1765. He is probably the man named as a soldier of the French and Indian War as having a balance due him from the State. This may well be the correct identification of the Pursley Creek Family. However, Mrs. Wood and myself were agreed that both Evans and Waychoff, who told a very interesting story of the Sellars participation in events of this frontier, had relied too much on family tradition, which official records prove were somewhat mixed up if not completely wrong.

Both these historians say that an old man named Sellars settled at the mouth of Pursley Creek at an early date. With him were four sons, while a fifth stayed there with him for a time, but later returned to Fayette County for the safety of his family and did not return until all danger was past. They tell also of a young man named Henry Huffman, whom they say was a member of this household, and of a neighbor named Gasper Povator, who lived close by. Thus far Evans and Waychoff are no doubt correct, except that Henry Huffman appears to have been a mature man if not in his middle age. A deed in Washington County, Pennsylvania, recorded May 16, 1791 (DB 1-E. pp. ***) indicates that he was of Berkeley County, Virginia, and had gone to that place where he had a brother, John Huffman, Sr., and nephew, John Huffman, Jr. Evans further states that this Henry Huffman married the widow of Gaspar Povator, which, if true, also suggests that he was a man of mature years.

The rest of the story as told by Evans does not hold up in the light of official record. He states that one of the sons of "old man Sellars" whom he identifies as Leonard Sellars, married Mary Povator, by whom he had two children, one of whom was killed by the Indians, in an episode both tragic and humorous. While out picking grapes in company of the hired girl and her two children, Mary (Povator) Sellars was surprised by the Indians. Snatching up one of the children she fled to the house of "old man Sellars" which she reached in safety. She then thought of the other child and hired girl and went back to search for them, only to find her other child killed and the hired girl missing. Evans concludes this episode with the tale that the tragedy so affected the young husband that he soon "sickened and died," and his young widow, after a period of mourning, married Peter Livengood. The event may have happened as related, but Leonard Sellars could not have been the disconsolate husband, as he lived many years after it occurred. A clue to the real identity is given in Fayette County records. On January 6, 1784, letters of administration were taken out at Uniontown in the estate of Jacob Sellars by Christian Sellars. Then, on May 4, of the same year, Peter Livengood presented a bill in the estate of Jacob Sellars for board and clothing of said Sellars child. In the will of Peter Livengood, Jr., in the year 1839, Peter Livengood provides for his step-daughter, Elizabeth Ankrom, formerly Elizabeth Sellars. From this record it can be seen that Peter Livengood, Jr., had married the widow of Jacob Sellars instead of Leonard Sellars, and the babe that had been saved was Elizabeth, who had married since to Joseph Ankrom, probably a son of Richard and Ruth Ankrom, neighbors of the Sellars on Pursley Creek. The will of Peter Livengood shows he had a wife,

Mary, whom we identify as Mary Povator. Waychoff says that Jacob Sellars was killed on an occasion when he was fleeing to Fort Jackson, being overtaken near the present home of Don Hampson as he sought to cross the Tenmile to the fort.

Neither author identifies "old man Sellars," who maintained the strong house or fort on Pursley Creek, later known as the Walton Farm. It could well be the Christian Sellars with a wife, Elizabeth, both of whom patented tracts of land in that section on February 21, 1785. They may subsequently have returned to Fayette County, for we are at loss to explain why the estate of Jacob Sellars was settled in that county after Washington County was set up in 1781, and Greene County included within its borders. It is known that Christian Sellars, Jr., lived in Fayette County until dangers from the Indians was passed.

Family of Christian and Elizabeth Sellars (?)

1. Christian Sellars is said to have come to Greene County with his father, but left it for the safety of Fayette County. It is not shown if it were he or an older Christian Sellars that settled the estate of Jacob Sellars in 1784. He returned to Greene County where he died about 1839. His wife was Susannah, whom tradition says was Susannah Hill, who died between 1820 and 1834. Orphan Court Docket 3. pp. 82 February 1849, discloses the heirs of Christian and Susannah Sellars.

Children of Christian and Susannah Sellars

1. Elizabeth Sellars, married Abraham Roberts. They went to Ohio.

   ##### Children
   1. David Roberts.
   2. Rebecca Roberts, wife of .... Cooper.
   3. Elizabeth Roberts, wife of .... Selby.
   4. Mary Ann Roberts, wife of .... Hill.
   5. Christian Roberts.
   6. Abraham Roberts.
   7. Susannah Roberts, wife of Burgoon.
   8. John Roberts.
   9. Isaac Roberts.

2. David Sellars, married Elizabeth Mitchell. He was born 1790 and died 1837.

   ##### Children
   1. George Sellars.
   2. Roseberry Sellars.
   3. Atkinson Sellars.
   4. Asa Sellars, born July 8, 1828, married Jane Orndorff.
   5. Shadrack Sellars.
   6. Susannah Sellars, married .... Church.
   7. Margaret Sellars, married .... White.

3. Mary Sellars, married James Scott, born 1774. She was born in 1777.

   ##### Children
   1. Christian Scott.
   2. Joshua Scott, born December 20, 1824, married Nancy Jane Rinehart.
   3. James Scott.

4. George Sellars, married Mary Sherman.

Children

1. Sarah Sellars, married .... Cotterall.
2. Mary Sellars, married .... Iams.

5. Jacob Sellars, born 1785, married Mary Beam; moved to Knox County, Ohio in 1808, where he died in 1846. His wife, born December 18, 1790, died August 6, 1878.

Children

1. John Sellars, born March 2, 1816, married Cynthia Carman.
2. George Sellars, born May 8, 1824, married Adaline Hughes.

6. Catherine Sellars, married George Thomas; she was born about 1797.
7. Sarah Sellars, married Atkinson Hill.
8. Susannah Sellars, born October 15, 1783, married Joshua Braddock, born March 19, 1781; went to Knox County, Ohio, in 1814.

Children

1. Elizabeth Braddock.
2. Sarah Braddock.
3. Margaret Braddock.
4. David Braddock.
5. Susannah Braddock.
6. Joshua Braddock.
7. Mary Braddock.
8. Mary Braddock.
9. Arena Braddock.
10. Anna Braddock.
11. Robert Braddock.

9. John Sellars, born 1793, went to Ohio; married (1) Nancy Mitchell; (2) Susan Honey; (3) Charlotte Taylor.
10. Christian Sellars, born about 1800, went to Ohio in 1850; married (1) Susannah Fry. He married (2) Sarah Braddock.

2. Jacob Sellars, son of Christian and Elizabeth Sellars (?), was a member of Captain James Archer's Militia Company in the First Battalion, Washington County Militia, in 1782. Waychoff says he was killed on the Tenmile, opposite Fort Jackson as he was fleeing from a party of hostile Indians. This tragedy occurred prior to January 6, 1784, at which time letters of administration on his estate were filed in Uniontown. No record of his ownership of land is shown, but since his daughter, Elizabeth (Sellars) Ankrom, sold in a deed joined by her husband, Joseph Ankrom, on April 10, 1816, land which she had inherited, but which had been warranted to Christian and Elizabeth Sellars, it would stand reasonably proven that Jacob Sellars was a son of Christian and Elizabeth Sellars. Jacob Sellars married Mary Povator. Data regarding the wives of the other Sellars brothers excludes any other possibility. Then after the death of her husband Mary (Povator) Sellars married (2) Peter Livengood, Jr., by whom she had eight more children. Waychoff says that the girl who shared in her affair with the Indians and disappeared at the time was a sister-in-law of Mary (Povator) Sellars, but the name is not given, she may have been a sister of her husband.

Children of Jacob and Mary (Povator) Sellars

1. Child killed by the Indians.
2. Elizabeth Sellars, wife of Joseph Ankrom. They seem to have gone to Tyler County, (West) Virginia.
3. Leonard Sellars, a member of Captain James Archer's Company in 1782. Head of a household consisting of himself and wife, two males under 16 years, and another female in the Census of 1790. He left here shortly afterward and settled in Bracken County, Kentucky, where he died in May 1823. His will was made there on May 4, 1823, and filed for probate on May 26, 1823. He mentions his wife, whom he gave one third of his estate, but does not give her name. The balance of his estate was to be divided among his four daughters, only one of whom is named. His executors were John Boysen and William Buckner. (Bracken Co. Will Book B. pp. 306.)

Children of Leonard Sellars

1. Sarah Sellars, only one of four daughters named; married a man named Waters.
2.
3.
4.
4. George Sellars, son of Christian and Elizabeth Sellars (?) was also a member of Captain James Archer's Militia Company. Died in Greene County about 1832. His wife was Elizabeth ...., who survived him. Deed Book 9 pp. 100 shows his heirs appointing David Sellars to serve for them in the Estate of George Sellars.

Children of George and Elizabeth Sellars

1. Christian Sellars, died about 1828.
2. Mary Sellars, wife of William Crouse.
3. George Sellars, with wife Phoebe .... lived in Monroe County, Ohio.
4. Jacob Sellars, who married Cynthia Carpenter.
5. John Sellars, and wife Sarah .... lived in Monroe County, Ohio.
6. Levi Sellars, died single in 1860.
7. Susannah Sellars, wife of Solomon Ankrom.
5. John Sellars, son of Christian and Elizabeth Sellars (?) named as a demented person, yet head of a household in 1790.

THE REES FAMILY

The Rees name is found among the earliest settlers of the Tenmile. Chalkley in his "History of Augusta County, Virginia," says that Jacob Rees, Sr., bought of William Williams, on July 31, 1775, land on the Tenmile which Williams had purchased from John Jones, who had bought it from John Simpson, the original improver, on January 8, 1774. Jacob Rees divided this land with William Robinson. Chalkley says that Jacob Rees had been accompanied to the Tenmile by Isaac Horner. Jacob left a widow, Hannah Rees.

Hanna's "History of Greene County," says that William Rees, known ancestor of the present family of that name, came to Greene County about 1790, but does not give any clue to his ancestry. Since William Rees and Samuel Hill served as administrators of an estate of one Joseph Rees, second owner of the tract of land known as the "Heritage" situated near the site of the well known Rees's Mill, and where William Rees himself lived, it would not be far wrong to suppose that he was a son of this Joseph Rees, who died in 1818. (Will Book 1. pp. 130 and O. C. Docket 1. pp. 138.)

William Rees was born in 1769 and died in Greene County, July 6, 1829, at the age of 60 years, 10 months, and 20 days. His wife was Cassandra ...., who died January 23, 1860, at the age of 88 years. Both are buried in the Hill Cemetery near the site of Joseph Rees's land. William Rees died intestate but a list of his children is found in the settlement of his estate. (O. C. Docket 1. pp. 324-358-367.)

Children of William and Cassandra Rees

1. Joseph Rees, he joined his brothers, Abraham and James, and sister, Elizabeth, with her husband, Michaels Thomas, to sell their interest in their father's estate to William Baltzell.
2. Mary Rees, died May 17, 1848, in the 60th year of her age. Her husband was Peter Brown, Sr., whom she married June 8, 1809. He died at the home of G. H. Huffman in Greene Township, Monroe County, Ohio, September 1, 1872, at the age of 95 years. There are two stories told of the origin of Peter Brown, Sr. One in his obituary says he was born in the Baltic in 1777. The other story tells that he was a Greek child who was taken prisoner in the Mediterranean by the Tripoli Pirates. An American vessel captured the pirate ship and rescued the captive boy and taking a liking to him, brought him to America, and gave him the name of Peter Brown. In due time he arrived in the Tenmile Country, where he married Mary Rees. The family Bible and a number of obitual notices are now owned by Mrs. Lucy (Elms) Dille of Waynesburg, and from it the record of Peter Brown, Sr's., family is taken.

Children of Peter and Mary (Rees) Brown, Sr.

1. Cassandra Brown, born May 27, 1810, died August 13, 1884; married Josiah Conklin, who died in Perry Township, September 1856. Both are buried at Fairall Chapel.
2. William Brown, born May 14, 1812, removed to Wilkinsburg, Pennsylvania.
3. Hannah Brown, born May 10, 1814, died in August 1882. She married James Parker. Their daughter, Martha H. Parker, married P. A. Knox, and became the mother of Judge John Clark Knox of the United States District Court at New York. Another son was the late Dr. James Knox of Waynesburg. P. A. Knox was a son of William and Rosanna (Clark) Knox. James Parker was born 1812, and died 1891; buried in Green Mount.
4. Peter Brown, Jr., born January 5, 1817, died in 1896, at Waynesburg. His wife was Mary Jane Day, born in 1820, died 1887. Both are buried at Green Mount Cemetery. He was Greene County Recorder of Wills in 1863-69.
5. Elizabeth Brown, born March 30, 1819.
6. Charity Brown, born November 22, 1820, died August 16, 1893, unmarried.
7. Catherine Brown, born September 7, 1823, died 1885; married Robert Morris, born 1816, died August 7, 1891.
8. John Rees Brown, born July 1, 1828, died November 1893.

3. James Rees, son of William and Cassandra Rees, joined deed with Joseph Rees.
4. John Rees, born January 1793, died June 20, 1862, aged 69 years, 4 months and 28 days. His wife was Elizabeth ...., as shown in Orphan Court records.

Children of John and Elizabeth Rees
1. John D. Rees, born March 15, 1819, died August 2, 1866; married Catherine ...., born September 25, 1820, died August 13, 1863. Both buried in Hill Cemetery.
2. Nancy Rees, born January 31, 1825, died July 15, 1891; married Samuel Throckmorton, born May 21, 1818, died July 28, 1881, buried at Green Mount.
3. William Rees, born 1829, died June 6, 1891, aged 62 years, 5 months, and 12 days; married Lucy Zollars, born January 9, 1838, died February 20, 1918.

5. William Rees, son of William and Cassandra Rees.
6. Abraham Rees, son of William and Cassandra Rees.
7. Elizabeth Rees, married Michael Thomas.
8. Cassandra Rees, daughter of William and Cassandra Rees.
9. Charity Rees, daughter of William and Cassandra Rees, born 1801, died February 14, 1874, aged 72 years, 5 months, and 22 days; married Obediah Vancleve, born January 30, 1798, died February 22, 1873. They were married May 7, 1821.

Children of Obediah and Charity (Rees) Vancleve
1. John Vancleve, born October 25, 1824, died 1907; married Ursula ...., born August 15, 1825, died 1909.
2. Rebecca Vancleve, died February 24, 1830, aged 3 years, 10 months, and 10 days.

10. Catherine Rees, daughter of William and Cassandra Rees.
11. Sarah Rees, daughter of William and Cassandra Rees.

THE JENNINGS FAMILY

Haddon's History of Fayette and Greene Counties says that the American ancestry of this Jennings Family goes back to a Benjamin Jennings and his seven sons, who came from Suffolk, England, to New Jersey, on the ship "Caledonia." The seven sons being Joseph, Zebulon, Jacob, Benjamin, John, Jonathan, and David. A different story is told by one of the Jennings Family Genealogists, which, though still steeped in tradition, seems more authentic in that it places the family in America before 1685, the date of a will of a John Jennings of Connecticut. This John Jennings of Connecticut, as the story goes, also had seven sons, whose names are the same as Haddon mentions. The sons are supposed to have left Eastern Connecticut in 1726 on the ship "Old Caledonia," which was wrecked off the coast of New Jersey. The party became scattered with Zebulon, Jacob, and Benjamin Jennings, reaching New Jersey, while Joseph, Jonathan, and John Jennings, reached Long Island. David Jennings was reported missing. Our own search of the background for the local settlers seems to end with the sons Benjamin and Zebulon Jennings, located in the vicinity of Scotch Plains, New Jersey. Descendants of both these men were among the early Tenmile Country families.

It is still not clear who the Benjamin Jennings, who met with the Commissioners at Redstone in 1768, might have been, nor does it appear that he remained long in this section. The ancestry of the Morgan Township family is also as yet undiscovered. However, Haddon was probably correctly informed regarding Jacob Jennings who settled near Carmichaels, and whom he says is buried in Glades Cemetery. This Jacob Jennings married Phoebe Ball, daughter of Nathaniel Ball and his wife, a widow of .... Bonnell. Records do not disclose the tombstone of this Jacob Jennings, but his wife, Phoebe, is remembered on the tombstone of Benjamin Jennings in Green Mount Cemetery at Waynesburg. Jacob Jennings and his wife, Phoebe, were the parents of at least nine children, whose names are found in Haddon.

Children of Jacob and Phoebe Jennings

1. Nathaniel Jennings, born June 2, 1770. He first married, on September 30, 1793, Sally Scudder, daughter of Thomas Scudder. After her death he married (2) Mary Jane Flenniken, born March 20, 1786, daughter of Judge John Flenniken. She died at Centerville, Indiana, July 22, 1870.

Family of Nathaniel and Sally (Scudder) Jennings

1. Salome Jennings, born May 13, 1797, died February 22, 1862; married, June 26, 1817, Joseph Baremore, born April 7, 1792, in New Jersey, died May 21, 1874, Monroe, Wisconsin.
2. Jotham Jennings, born April 9, 1800, died January 3, 1870, Knox County, Ohio; married (1) December 3, 1822, Elizabeth Hill, daughter of Samuel and Elizabeth (Cathers) Hill. She was born January 1, 1801, and died about 1834. He married (2) March 10, 1836, Mary Seymore.
3. Ann Jennings, married Carl Moore.
4. Ruth Jennings, born February 12, 1807, died November 13, 1869, in Athens, Ohio; married April 21, 1836, Ira A. Lindley, born September 18, 1803, died August 14, 1858.

Child of Nathaniel and Mary (Flenniken) Jennings

1. Sarah Jennings, born January 19, 1821; married David Wood.

2. Salome Jennings, daughter of Jacob, born 1773, died September 21, 1851; married John Crawford, born 1771, died November 8, 1831, son of Colonel William and Alice (Kennedy) Crawford. Both are buried in Glades Cemetery. See Crawford Records.
3. Rebecca Jennings, daughter of Jacob, married Henry Slater.
4. Benjamin Jennings, son of Jacob, born February 26, 1779, died July 8, 1861; married (1) Dorcas Flenniken, born March 17, 1777, died May 17, 1819. She was a daughter of Judge John Flenniken. Benjamin Jennings married (2) Elizabeth Stockdale, who died March 11, 1850. All are buried in Green Mount Cemetery. Benjamin Jennings was a carpenter by trade, served a term in 1826, as County Commissioner, was Justice of Peace and County Auditor for several terms.

Children of Benjamin Jennings

1. John Flenniken Jennings, born October 28, 1807, married Elizabeth Fitzgerald.
2. Perry Jennings, born January 15, 1814, married Lydia Cary.
3. Jane Jennings, born July 30, 1806, died August 24, 1806.
4. Mary Jennings, born July 15, 1809, died September 4, 1810.

5. Samuel Jennings, born December 18, 1812, died June 12, 1852, married Sarah Garrison.
6. Hannah Jennings, born July 13, 1816, died May 1, 1816.
7. Esther Jennings, married James Cree, son of Hamilton and Agnes (Hughes) Cree.
8. James S. Jennings, born August 22, 1829, married Laura E. Weathee.
9. Mary Jennings (2) married W. T. H. Pauley.
10. Benjamin Jennings, was in the Army when father died. Settled in Iowa, born July 22, 1831; married Eliza Hawley.

5. Phoebe Jennings, daughter of Jacob and Phoebe Jennings, married David Harris.
6. Hezekiah Jennings, son of Jacob Jennings, never married.
7. Jeremiah Jennings, born February 2, 1783, married Jane Ewart, daughter of Ralph Ewart. Jane Ewart was born October 15, 1786. He died about 1834, leaving minor children named in O. C. Docket as Melinda, Lewis, and Henry Jennings.

Family of Jeremiah and Jane (Ewart) Jennings

1. Phoebe Jennings, born January 3, 1810, married Jesse Swan.
2. Ewart Jennings, born April 13, 1812, died young.
3. Jacob Jennings, born July 17, 1814, died young.
4. Jane Jennings, born July 5, 1816.
5. Melinda Jennings, born April 4, 1820, married Stout Prior.
6. Lewis Jennings, born May 20, 1824, married Mary Biddle.
7. Henry Jennings, born November 23, 1827, married Caroline Hart, born September 30, 1830.

8. Keziah Jennings, daughter of Jacob and Phoebe Jennings, married Caleb Lindley.
9. Esther Jennings, daughter of Jacob Jennings, married David Burnett. He died May 21, 1848, aged 51 years, 7 months, and 22 days. Settlement of his estate in May 1850, shows a wife named Sarah, who is buried with him at Laurel Point Cemetery at Carmichaels. She died May 22, 1865, aged 64 years, 10 months, and 10 days.

Children of David Burnett

1. Hiram Burnett, born 1823, died 1894, his wife was Margaret ...., 1819-1852.
2. Jennings Burnett, born November 6, 1852, died December 7, 1870; his wife was Malinda ...., who died March 27, 1871, aged 43 years, 2 months and 19 days.
3. Margaret Burnett, married William Jerome.
4. Harriett Burnett.
5. Sarah Burnett.

THE SAYERS FAMILY

William Sayers, ancestor of the Greene County Family of that name, was a son of David and Ruth Sayers of Cohansey, Salem County, New Jersey. His father, David Sayers, was born in New Jersey and in 1715, was a member of the Militia of that State. His will of 1742, names his wife, Ruth, and children: David, Daniel, William, Thomas, James, Hannah Dayton, Eleanor, Ruth, Mary and Prudence. His widow, Ruth, married (2) Rev. Nathaniel Jenkins of Cohansey Baptist Church, in April 1743.

William Sayers was born in New Jersey, in 1729, and died in Greene County, Pennsylvania, on September 16, 1796. He was buried in the old cemetery outside Fort Jackson, which has since been destroyed. His marker was found at this site by Honorable A. H. Sayers, and is in possession of the family. William Sayers married, at Cohansey, May 25, 1762, Mary Fithian, who died at Waynesburg in 1809. During the Revolution William Sayers served as a lieutenant in the Twelfth Battalion of Foot from Philadelphia, William Cook, Colonel in Command. He was engaged in the Battles of Bonnell Brook, Brandywine and Germantown. (Penna. Arch. Series II Vol. 10, pp. 757-58.) The will of William Sayers is on file in Greene County Will Book 1. pp. 2 and was probated on October 14, 1796.

Children of William and Mary (Fithian) Sayers

1. Josiah Sayers, named as eldest son. His wife was Rhoda Drake.
2. Ruth Sayers, born August 11, 1765, died March 26, 1836; married (1) .... Watson, by whom she had a son, George Watson, mentioned in his grandfather's will. Ruth Sayers married (2) Joseph Evans, a widower with one son. Joseph Evans was born April 24, 1757, and died in Ohio, July 18, 1824. He and Ruth are buried in the Salt Creek Baptist Cemetery near Zanesville, Ohio.

Children of Joseph and Ruth (Sayers) Evans

1. John Evans.
2. Phoebe Evans.
3. Joseph Evans, died near Duncan Falls, Ohio, November 18, 1856, aged 62 years, 3 months, 13 days.
4. Caleb Evans.
5. Mary Evans.
6. William Evans.
7. Reuben Evans.
8. James Evans, married Sarah Comstock.
9. Elizabeth Evans.
10. Anna Evans.

3. Reuben Sayers, son of William and Mary (Fithian) Sayers, born 1768, died unmarried on August 20, 1832. (O. C. Docket 2. pp. 33 March 1834.) Buried at Morrisville Cemetery.
4. Thomas Sayers, son of William and Mary (Fithian) Sayers, born December 26, 1770; married, April 3, 1795, Frances Dye, daughter of Andrew and Sarah (Minor) Dye. She was born January 7, 1777. They were parents of 17 children.
5. Phoebe Sayers, daughter of William and Mary (Fithian) Sayers. She married (1) about 1792, James Morris, a son of Richard and Mary (Seals) Morris. He died in 1798, aged 28 years, and Phoebe Sayers married (2) .... Remley. (See O. C. Docket 1. pp. 5.)

Children of James and Phoebe (Sayers) Morris

1. Thomas Morris, born 1794.
2. Joseph Morris, born 1796.
3. Ephraim Morris, born November 18, 1797, died June 21, 1868; married, February 24, 1820, Martha Roseberry, born October 7, 1801, died December 14, 1866; she a daughter of Mathias and Sarah (Hughes) Roseberry.

6. Ephraim Sayers, son of William and Mary (Fithian) Sayers, born November 6, 1773, died April 1, 1857; married Mary

Wood, daughter of William and Margaret (Mitchell) Wood, born June 8, 1776, died September 1, 1858.

Children of Ephraim and Mary (Wood) Sayers
1. Elizabeth Sayers, born 1804, married 1820, George Adams.
2. William W. Sayers, born August 12, 1805, died May 22, 1886; married, March 11, 1835, Rebecca Adams, daughter of Robert and Rebecca (Blackmore) Adams, born April 30, 1813, died July 31, 1873.
3. Thomas Sayers, died 1807.
4. Mary Sayers, died in infancy.
5. Margaret Sayers, died in infancy.
6. Ezra Mitchell Sayers, born May 30, 1812, died March 3, 1909; married, December 25, 1839, Jane Adams, born June 26, 1822, died April 3, 1847. He then married (2) September 2, 1852, Harriet Tanner, born ...., who died February 16, 1892.
7. Ephraim Sayers, born May 5, 1817, died young.

ISAAC SHARP

Isaac Sharp settled on the tract of land to the north of Thomas Slater, and which was originally occupied by the Parker Family. Like his brother-in-law, Timothy Ross, with whom he went into the surveying business, he was a native of New Jersey, where he married, in 1777, Mary Wolverton, daughter of John and Abigail Wolverton. She was born April 22, 1761, and a Bible record shows her family to have been:
1. John Sharp, born 1779, his wife was Elizabeth .... They went to Ohio.
2. Thomas Sharp, born 1781, his wife was Unity ...., also went to Ohio.
3. Abigail Sharp, born 1783, married John Knight.
4. Mary Sharp, born 1786, married William Sharon.
5. Rachel Sharp, born 1788, married David Conger.
6. William Sharp, his wife was Ruth .... He was born 1790.
7. Isaac Sharp, Jr., married Eliza Nailor. He was born 1792.
8. Rebecca Sharp, born 1794, married Ephraim Corwin.
9. Margaret Sharp, born 1796, married Thomas Largley.
10. Darby Sharp, born 1798, died 1807.
11. Zachariah Sharp, born 1800, married Elizabeth Yoder.
12. Bittia Sharp, born 1802, married Samuel Smith.

THE MOORE FAMILY

It is almost impossible to distinguish which John Moore was the original ancestor of the Moore Family in Greene County. Bedford County Tax Lists for Springhill Township for 1772, list two John Moores and one Hans Moore, with a notation after one John Moore, which states, "living over the river," meaning of course on what is now the Greene County side of the Monongahela. The best that we can do is to give what records are found, hoping that time will discover which man may have been the common ancestor. It is our opinion that the John Moore, "living over the river," was the same man, whose estate is recorded in Westmoreland Orphans Court

Docket Number 3, whose will was probated October 13, 1779, this section being at that time a part of Westmoreland County, Pennsylvania. His wife's name was Ann ...., and he left the following children: Samuel, mentioned as the eldest son; Robert, William, Sarah, John, Archibald, Thomas, and Andrew.

Hans Moore may also have lived over the river, this Germanized name for John being born out in the estate of a John Moore, whose will is in Washington County Will Book 1. pp. 36, probated on June 20, 1784. The heirs of this John Moore were Andrew, John and Stoefel Moore, Stoefel or Stoefell being the German for Christopher. As Peter Hiller, a known Greene County settler, was witness of his will, we can be certain this was a Greene County John Moore.

A third John Moore is found in Greene County Estate Number 35, probated December 13, 1800, he apparently being a young man, since he left but one heir besides his widow, that being a son, John, then under fourteen years of age, for whom Elias Flenniken was appointed guardian. This elder John Moore mentions a brother, William Moore, in his will, suggesting that he was a son of John Moore, above, whose estate was settled in Westmoreland County. His wife, whose name was Elizabeth, did not remain a widow very long until she became the wife of William Armstrong, and from the Armstrong records we note she must have been Elizabeth Russell, prior to her marriage to John Moore. The minor son appears to have come of age about 1808, when the estate of his father was settled by the step-father, William Armstrong.

Still another John Moore is spoken of in Hanna's History of Greene County. This John Moore is said to have come to America in 1770, whether brought by parents or as a young man on his own is not explained. Hanna quoted family traditions, which were sometimes incorrect, and it is possible that this John Moore may have been a son of one of the above listed men. Some things are definitely known about this man. He was a doctor of medicine, and is the John Moore, listed as "schoolmaster on Big Whitely Creek" in the Muddy Creek Ledger. His wife was Hannah Armstrong. He had two tracts of land surveyed to him, one under the title "Station," which was patented to him on April 25, 1793, and the other, which adjoined it, patented under the title "Moorefields" was secured by a warrant dated February 19, 1793. Numerous deeds, including the one for "Moorefields", in which he is joined by wife, Hannah, on January 29, 1810, in a sale to James Bradford, disclose that there were at least three sons born to Doctor John Moore. There may have been daughters, but no mention other than census record indicates the presence of female descendants. Dr. John Moore is buried in the Armstrong Cemetery, where his tombstone says he died December 2, 1816 (1818?) aged 71 years.

Armstrong Moore, who with wife, Christina, made a deed for a part of Moorefields on July 1, 1831, after having sold a portion of the land conveyed to him by John Moore, to Abraham Tustin.

John Moore appears to have been the John Moore, who with wife, Susannah, conveyed land to his son, Thomas, on June 8, 1846. At other times he conveyed land by deeds joined with Susannah, to John Hatfield in 1797, and to John Moore, son of Anthony, on November 28, 1823. It would appear that Hanna had erred in attributing his family to Doctor John and Hannah (Armstrong) Moore, an error uncovered by the late Attorney A. M. Nichols. The names of the children are given in these two records:

    Thomas Moore, born 1809, married Rachel Maple.
    Abraham Moore.

Armstrong Moore, wife Elizabeth ...., Monongalia County, Virginia, in 1818.
John W. Moore.
Elsie Moore.
Jane Moore.
Sarah Moore.
James Moore, born 1806, married (1) Matilda Franks; married (2) Elizabeth (Brown) Provins.

Anthony Moore, died in Wayne Township about 1832. Greene County Will Book 2. pp. 14. His wife was ....

Children

John Moore.
Isaac Moore.
Margaret Moore.
Catherine Moore.
Crawford Moore.
Elizabeth Moore.
Hannah Moore.
Mary Moore.

Where such similarity of names exists there is always room for errors, and the above record could have its share. It may be added that another John Moore was here at the time of the Revolution, when he and his brother, Thomas, joined Captain Harrod's Company for the George Rogers Clark Expedition. They were sons of Simeon Moore, who is in the Bedford County Tax list of 1772. No records are shown for service of John Moore of Whiteley Creek, probably because Captain John Huston's muster roll is not available.

RUFFS CREEK

Crumrine says there was a migration of some twenty or thirty families, who left their homes in Morris County, New Jersey, in 1777, to come to North Tenmile, but that being the "Bloody Year" were compelled to return over the mountains until the following season, when they came back to make permanent settlement. When the County of Washington was formed they gave the name of their New Jersey home to the newly formed Amwell Township, and later to the two Morris Townships in Washington and Greene Counties. These pioneer families included the Gobles, Lindleys, Hathaways, Condits, McVays, some of the Rosses, Pettitts, Wolvertons, etc., who settled about Fort Lindley, now the village of Prosperity. They were soon followed by the Craynes, Leonards, Woodruffs, Martins, Carys, Coopers and others who crossed the "dividing ridge" to settle on Ruffs Creek, where already some of the Bells and Rosses had taken up land, and had built forts.

The earliest grant on record is the warrant issued to William Miller on May 29, 1772, for a tract of land known as "Ruffs Camp," confirming the tradition that an Indian named Ruff lived on the land when the settlers first moved in. But the site of this camp was further down the stream than reported by Professor Waychoff, being near the present Greene County Country Club rather than at Shirk's Store. In some of the early records the creek is merely called the Rough Fork of Tenmile. Waychoff's claim that the land was first owned by a man named Cowan is partially supported by a deed showing that a Mrs. Cowan came here from Philadelphia, to sell some land, but the size of the Cowan holdings did not include the whole valley.

The Bells and Rosses had settled on the land prior to 1774, since William Harrod, Jr., mentions their forts as being the place of refuge of his family in 1774. This was the year in which James Harrod, his uncle, with John Cowen, second in command, went to Kentucky to establish Harrodsburg, the first permanent settlement in that state. It was Bell's Fort on Ruffs Creek rather than Heaton's Fort as mistakenly reported by Waychoff as being on the Hugh Montgomery land. The Heatons did settle at the site of Rosses Fort close to Grimes School House, but as late as 1793, John Ross and Mr. Phillips gave land for the Baptist Church at Lippencott, and in 1797, John Ross still had his mill near Lippencott. This grist mill was then sold to the Lippencotts, from whom the village got its name.

CAPTAIN BENJAMIN STITES

Benjamin Stites was among the first of the New Jersey immigrants to settle in what is now Morgan Township. He was a descendant of a New England Family that removed first to Hempstead, Long Island, and then to Cape May, New Jersey. He first settled at the site of the old Pollock's Mill, where he was living at the time of the Revolution, and where he served as a captain in the First Battalion, Washington County, Pennsylvania, Militia. Later he sold this land to Jacob Rush, who made an assignment to George Newland of the mill site. Then Benjamin Stites bought land on Bates Fork of Tenmile, where he was living when he served as tax collector for Morgan Township in 1784. He later went back to New Jersey and interested Judge Symmes in a land proposition and together they got many thousands of acres of land on the Miami River in Ohio. He was to become the founder of the city of Cincinnati. A hint of his marital trouble is in the Church Book of Goshen Baptist Church, of which he and his wife, Rachel, were members, for on December 29, 1792, it notes that he was cut off from the fellowship of the church for "having married another wife, while the former wife is yet alive". His former wife, Rachel, was living alone on the Tenmile when the Census for 1790 was taken, he having already gone to Limestone, Kentucky, where he made up his Miami Party. From Ohio comes more information about his family troubles and much other information. We learn that he was born at Scotch Plains, New Jersey, about 1740, and married Rachel .... on September 22, 1768. Within a year he removed to the Tenmile, where at least four children were born, and possibly five, before he and Rachel parted in 1786. Ten years later Rachel went to Cincinnati and began suing for a divorce, with Benjamin counter suing in his answer. She accused him of ill treatment, and spending the money that came to her from her family. She also stated that he had bigamously married Mary (Mills?) and after tiring of her had again married, illegally, Hannah Waring with whom he was then living. The testimony in this case reminds one of a Hollywood Trial, and continues after the death of Benjamin Stites in 1804, when Greene County land, patented to John Stites, came up for distribution. From it we learn the line of descent from Benjamin and Rachel Stites.

Children

John Stites, born 1770, on Tenmile Creek, died in Ohio in 1794.
Benjamin Stites, Jr., born February 1772, question of his legitimacy in Ohio Court records, but established by competent witnesses.
Phoebe Stites, born 1774, married James Miranda.
Richard Stites, born 1776.
Rachel Stites, born 1783, married .... Kibby.

THE BELL FAMILY

Nathaniel Bell was the ancestor of the Morgan Township Family of this name. He came from Mill Creek, Berkeley County, Virginia, before 1776. He bought a tract of land containing 202 acres from Lord Halifax, and situated on Mill Creek, on June 25, 1766. This land was near the place that Isaac Heaton, Sr., had built a mill in 1760. As they were neighbors in Virginia, and became neighbors and intermarried after reaching the Tenmile, we are inclined to believe the Bells and Heatons had also been neighbors in New Jersey, before going to Virginia. When Nathaniel Bell and his wife, Hannah, sold this tract, or rather 79½ acres of it, to Rev. William Gerrard on January 31, 1766, they are described as "living on the Western waters of the Ohio" at that time, which places the family among the first settlers of the Tenmile Country. They located on the Ruffs Creek branch of Tenmile close to where Grimes Run and Acklins Run join Ruffs Creek and here they were maintaining a fort when the Revolution came on. There is some evidence that they first settled near Glades Church, on the waters of Whiteley Creek, where a James Bell or Bellshe (Bells, he?) sold the land on which Joshua Hudson built a fort, and where some of Nathaniel Bell's children lived for a time. This seems the more likely for it was to this place the Gerrards (or Garards) also came to settle. But the William Harrod, Jr., interview with Draper, definitely places the family during the forting days. This land he had warranted and patented to him, under the title "Belemoney" in 1785-86. Here Nathaniel Bell, Sr., died in the Spring of 1800, for his will was made on February 19, 1800, and probated in Greene County, on May 2 of that year. His wife is not named and probably died before her husband, both probably being buried on their Ruffs Creek land. (Greene County, Pennsylvania WB 1. pp. 20). The will of Nathaniel Bell, Sr., was witnessed by William Heaton, Benjamin Line, and Isaac Heaton, and names Benjamin Bell, the youngest son, executor. These children are also named, as are the names of the husbands of Nathaniel's daughters:

1. Abel Bell, wife's name, Elizabeth ....; served in Captain Benjamin Stites' Company, Washington County, Pennsylvania, Militia, from Morgan Township. Was on the Crawford Expedition with Captain Ezekiel Rose.
2. Nathaniel Bell, Jr., his wife may have been Mary ...., who, on February 10, 1812, administered an estate of Nathaniel Bell in Greene County. He was also a member of Captain Benjamin Stites' Company and served under Captain Ezekiel Rose on the Colonel Crawford Expedition.
3. James Bell, who died before his father, ancestor of most of the Greene County Bells. Record of his family will be given separately.
4. Lydia Bell, born in 1748, died 1828; married Jacob Rush, who also served in Captain Benjamin Stites' Company. Record given under Jacob Rush Family.
5. Benjamin Bell, died in Iowa, February 10, 1853; married Elizabeth Enoch, daughter of Colonel Henry Enoch. Record of family of Benjamin Bell is given under Enoch Family Record.
6. Jane Bell, married Thomas Wolverton, also a member of Captain Benjamin Stites' Company, and on the Crawford Expedition under Captain Ezekiel Rose.
7. Elizabeth Bell, married Joseph Frazer, who settled at Garards Fort.
8. Mary Bell, not specifically named in the will of her father, but a sum of money was put in the hands of her son, Isaac Buckingham, to pay the interest to his mother as long as she lived, and then to go to her children. She married John Buckingham, whose record is given in another article. The family Bible of this family is owned by Mrs. George Drake, of Waynesburg, Pennsylvania.

Family of James and Mary Bell

James Bell, son of Nathaniel Bell, Sr., and his wife, Hannah, died before his father, while Morgan Township was still a part of Washington County, Pennsylvania. He was a man of considerable prominence in the early history of the Tenmile Country, serving as a Justice of Peace, and being elected to Associate Judge of Washington County a year before his death. He was a sergeant in Captain Benjamin Stites' Company and served under Captain Ezekiel Rose on the Crawford Expedition to Sandusky. (Penna. Arch Series VI Vol. 2. pp. 20 and 399). He appears to have first settled on a tract of land adjoining Provins, which later became the property of Joshua Hudson, and at times known as Jenkins Fort and Hudson's Fort. Later he bought up land in the vicinity of the present Greene County Memorial Cemetery, and at the time of his death was said to have accumulated over one thousand acres, which passed to his sons. His commission for the office of Associate Judge is dated January 11, 1790, but his death the following year cut short his term of service. His estate was probated on April 27. 1791, in Washington County, his brother-in-laws, John Buckingham and Jacob Rush, serving as his executors. From Mrs. Hugh Montgomery, born in 1856, and still living, we learn that James Bell was married to Mary Knox, the marriage having taken place about 1774. Eight children are named in the will of James Bell.

1. Mary Bell, born in Greene County, 1776, died at Jefferson on July 9, 1831, aged 54 years, 9 months, and 8 days; married Meeker Woodruff, born in New Jersey, November 10, 1773, died at Jefferson, August 10, 1819. Both are buried in the Old Presbyterian Cemetery at Jefferson. They were parents of:
    1. Rachel Woodruff, born November 23, 1798, died January 25, 1817; married, January 10, 1815, William Denny, son of John and Hannah (Blackledge) Denny. He was born October 27, 1793, died August 15, 1845.
    2. Eunice Woodruff, died January 19, 1821, aged 21 years, 5 months, and 22 days.
    3. Mary Woodruff, died May 25, 1840, aged 28 years and 10 months.
    4. Phoebe Woodruff, born December 24, 1813, died September 25, 1857; married, September 5, 1833, Samuel Seaton.
    5. Benjamin Woodruff, married Sarah Tuttle.
2. John Bell, Sr., born April 1, 1779, died in Greene County, November 2, 1853; married Mary Phillips, born 1779, died March 30, 1859, aged 80 years, 3 months, and 5 days. Bible of John Bell, Sr., is owned by Howard Porter of East Millsboro. They are buried at Lippencott, Penn., were parents of:
    1. John Bell, Jr., (Old Jackie), died June 4, 1880, aged 79 years, 10 months, and 26 days; married Anna Cox, born October 29, 1798, died November 11, 1871, daughter of Christopher and Anna Cox. Both are buried at Jefferson, Pennsylvania.
    2. James Bell, son of John and Mary (Phillips) Bell, died August 1, 1868, aged 69 years, 7 months and 17 days; married Hulda Headlee, who died January 29, 1879, aged 78 years. Buried in the Lazear Cemetery.
    3. Benjamin Bell, son of John and Mary (Phillips) Bell, died in Knox County, to which place he had moved about 1844. He married Mary Woodruff, daughter of Joshua and Priscilla (Davis) Woodruff.
    4. Dorcas Bell, daughter of John and Mary (Phillips) Bell, died in 1876. She married (1) Jesse Cox, born June 4, 1794, died November 25, 1825. She married (2) Thomas Patterson, born May 10, 1794, died June 16, 1877. Dorcas Bell was born October 27, 1806.
    5. Morgan Bell, son of John and Mary (Phillips) Bell, born December 24, 1808, died February 5, 1880; married Mary Richards, who died April 8, 1878. Buried in Baptist Cemetery at Jefferson, Pennsylvania.
    6. Jesse Bell, son of John and Mary (Phillips) Bell, born in Greene County, died there on June 23, 1874, aged 64 years, 9 months, and 11 days. Married (1) Elizabeth Bricker, who died May 11, 1855, aged 34 years, 5 months, and 2 days. She was a daughter of David and Indiana (Cox) Bricker. Jesse Bell then married Louisa Nichols. who died November 6, 1868. He married (3) ....
    7. Henry Bell, son of John and Mary (Phillips) Bell, married (1) Deborra Adamson, who died April 15, 1886, aged 73 years. He then married Marinda (Keys) Spriggs.
3. James Bell, Jr., son of James and Mary (Knox) Bell, born September 19, 1780, died in Knox County, Ohio, June 4, 1867.

He married (1) Elizabeth Hays, born November 25, 1779, who died December 8, 1820. He married (2) September 13, 1821, Christiana Marriott, born in Virginia, in 1793, died in Ohio, October 1870. They were parents of six children, and by his first wife, James Bell had nine others.
1. Mary Bell, born 1799, never married.
2. Samuel Bell, born December 10, 1800, died October 23, 1895; married (1) Elizabeth Hanger, who died April 12, 1854. He married (2) Nancy Simmons, who died November 10, 1891.
3. Isaac Bell, born in Greene County September 16, 1802, died November 11, 1882; married, in 1820, Catherine Hanger, who died February 12, 1878. Lived in Knox County, Ohio.
4. John Bell, born December 9, 1804, died October 15, 1865; married Mary Harrison, born at Clarksville, January 29, 1808, died December 27, 1897. Her second husband was William Bell, brother of her first.
5. Meeker Bell, born February 3, 1807, died November 15, 1886. He returned to Greene County, Pennsylvania, and married Rachel Crayne, who died January 4, 1898. She was a daughter of Stephen and Phoebe Crayne.
6. William Bell, born June 9, 1809, died July 31, 1888. Married (1) Nancy Hanger, who died December 4, 1881. He then married Mary (Harrison) Bell, widow of his brother, John Bell.
7. Benjamin Bell, born 1812, died March 18, 1884; married (1) Mary Moore, who died November 18, 1860. He was married twice again.
8. Nancy Bell, born 1816, died August 15, 1860; married (1) Jay McNurland; (2) Thomas Clark.
9. Elizabeth Bell, born 1818, died February 4, 1892; married Rev. David G. Mitchell, born September 20, 1811, died February 13, 1895.
10. James Bell, married Nancy Larson.
11. Albert Bell, married Rebecca Crumrine.
12. Charles Martin Bell, married Amy Cooper.
13. Mitchell Bell, died accidentally in a fall from a horse at age of 12 years.
14. David Bell, met death in the same accident.
15. Maria Bell, married .... Beam.

4. Benjamin Bell, son of James and Mary (Knox) Bell, born in Greene County, February 17, 1782, died in Knox County, Ohio, October 19, 1851. He married, about 1804, Elizabeth McClelland, who died near Emporia, Kansas. She was a daughter of Cary and Henrietta (Myers) McClelland. They had:
1. Cary Bell, born August 22, 1805, died March 11, 1826.
2. Jacob Bell, born 1807, died October 15, 1874; married, 1828, Rachel Letts, born 1811, died February 6, 1876.
3. Mary Bell, married S. W. Hanger, and removed to Emporia, Kansas.
4. Henrietta Bell, married Daniel Paul.
5. Nancy Bell, married David M. Elliott.
6. Amy Bell, married Dr. D. M. McCann.
7. Eunice Bell, married Harrison Elliott, removed to Kansas.
8. James Bell, born April 15, 1818, died April 9, 1879; married (1) Rowena Robinson, who died March 12, 1856. He married (2) Phoebe J. Wright, who died October 13, 1908.
9. Belinda Bell, born in 1819, died July 17, 1875; married Rev.

Isaiah Jones, born June 15, 1816, died August 2, 1901. Buried in the Bell Cemetery in Knox County, Ohio.
    10. Benjamin A. Bell, married Elizabeth Gearhart (?). Lived at Sunbury, Ohio.
5. Sarah Bell, daughter of James and Mary (Knox) Bell, born in Greene County, Penna., on October 17, 1783, died in Knox County, Ohio, August 31, 1829; buried in Owle Creek Cemetery. She married, September 20, 1798, James Hays, born September 23, 1772.
    1. Nancy Hayes, born September 5, 1799, died June 23, 1876; married Azariah Davis, son of Azariah and Alice (Vanmeter) Davis, born March 20, 1790, died May 12, 1868.
    2. James Bell Hays, born September 10, 1801, died April 3, 1891; married (1) Jemima Biggs, born December 31, 1802, daughter of Jeremiah and Jemima (Harrod) Biggs. She died in January 13, 1857.
    3. Mary Hays, born June 15, 1804, died June 17, 1843; married Phillip Smith, born June 15, 1793.
    4. John Hays, born October 22, 1806, died December 25, 1890; married Anna Kiser, born March 7, 1812, died June 15, 1874.
    5. William Hayes, born November 7, 1808, died July 3, 1890; married (1) Martha Hood, born August 10, 1808, died September 22, 1844. He married (2) ....
    6. Harlan Hays, born September 1, 1811, died November 4, 1889; married Rebecca Boggs.
    7. Benjamin Hays, born July 2, 1813, died July 9, 1877; married (1) Mary Biggs, who died and he married (2) Nancy Bell, who died and he married (3) Susannah Dixon. Had two children by first marriage, two by the second, and eight by the third.
    8. Elizabeth Hays, born May 28, 1816, died at Fairfield, Illinois; married (1) Elijah Boggs, (2) Samuel Fawcett.
    9. Isaac Hays, born July 27, 1818, died May 1, 1905; married Ann Fawcett, who died April 10, 1903.
    10. Morgan Hays, born May 21, 1820, died April 22, 1900; married Deborra Ann Breece, born May 28, 1828, died May 1, 1911.
    11. David Hays, born July 22, 1823, died August 7, 1829.
6. Isaac Bell, son of James and Mary (Knox) Bell, born in 1784, died in Greene County, January 1824; married, in 1803, Elizabeth Harrod, born 1785, daughter of Levi and Rachel (Mills) Harrod. She died December 30, 1861. Buried in the Heaton Plot near Jefferson, Penna.
    1. Levi Harrod Bell, born March 12, 1807, died December 16, 1862; married, 1827, Sarah Fulton, born July 2, 1807, died June 27, 1871. Removed to Kentucky. His wife was a daughter of John and Isabella (Barr) Fulton.
    2. James Bell, born 1809, died at Carmichaels, Pennsylvania, in 1897; married in 1842, Elizabeth Swan, born May 8, 1816, died May 30, 1904. She was a daughter of Samuel and Mary (Hiller) Swan.
    3. David Bell (Prunty Dave) born 1814, died July 18, 1871; married 1833, Lettice Adamson, who was born 1815, and died 1855.
    4. Isaac Bell.
    5. Rachel Bell, born April 6, 1812, died July 12, 1863; buried at Jefferson.
    6. John Harrod Bell, born 1815, died October 15, 1866; married Sarah Whitlatch, daughter of Rev. Barnet and Sarah

(Morris) Whitlatch.
7. Mary Bell, born May 26, 1816, died September 16, 1899; married Stephen Crayne, born January 4, 1813, died March 12, 1909. He was a son of Samuel and Mary (Huss) Crayne. They are buried in the Baptist Cemetery at Jefferson.
8. Catherine Bell, born 1820, died March 16, 1833.

7. David Bell, son of James and Mary (Knox) Bell, born May 18, 1785, died October 22, 1856. He married Katy Kennedy, born 1790, died April 8, 1864, aged 74 years, 4 months, and 18 days. She was a daughter of David and Rachel (Frazier) Kennedy. David Bell and wife are buried in the old Presbyterian Cemetery at Jefferson. Their chldren were:
   1. John Kennedy Bell, born January 22, 1810, died April 19, 1886; married, May 3, 1832, Mary Black, born August 17, 1813, died January 27, 1900, daughter of Judge Samuel and Charlotte (Heaton) Black. They are buried in the C. P. Cemetery at Jefferson.
   2. Rachel Bell, born ....
   3. Mary Ann Bell, married J. L. Shaw.
   4. Catherine Bell, died 1840, at the age of 18 years.

8. Hannah Bell, daughter of James and Mary (Knox) Bell; married Samuel Woodruff, who died in Greene County, Pennsylvania, about 1835. He went to Knox County, Ohio, with his brothers-in-law, but returned to Greene County. (WB. 2. pp. 46, probated March 10, 1835.)

Children
1. Mary Woodruff, married James Baxter, record of this family in Greene County O. C. Docket.
2. Joanna Woodruff, married David Briant.
3. James H. Woodruff.
4. .... Woodruff, married .... Heaton.
5. Eunice Woodruff, died in 1833; married (1) Abel Cary, who died January 19, 1821. She married (2) John McGinnis.

THE CRAYNE FAMILY

Daniel, Caleb, and Silas Crayne came from New Jersey to settle on Crayne's Run branch of Ruff's Creek. Daniel Crayne served in Captain John Miller's Company of Washington County Militia recruited at Fort Lindley. Caleb Crayne and wife, Catherine, left here after selling out the land they had patented to them on Crayne's Run. Silas Crayne served in Captain Benjamin Stites' Company of Morgan Township Militia.

Silas Crayne (Crane, Crain, etc.) was born in New Jersey in 1737, and died in Greene County, Pennsylvania, on July 30, 1835. His wife was Jane ...., born in 1743, and died January 25, 1845. Both are buried in the Church Cemetery at Lippencott, with markers that attest to their great age.

Family of Silas and Jane Crayne
1. Jane Crayne, married Stephen Ulery, who died in Knox County, Ohio. His will was filed in Greene County, Pennsylvania, on December 18, 1850.

Children
1. Stephen Ulery.
2. Joseph Ulery.
3. Orpha Ulery.
4. Samuel Ulery.
5. Levi Ulery.
6. Rachel Ulery, born February 24, 1819, died July 21, 1853; married, March 6, 1837, Zepheniah Johnson, born

December 21, 1812.
7. Lucinda Ulery.
8. Rhoda Ulery.
9. Elmer Ulery.

2. Stephen Crayne, born 1774, died January 22, 1833, in Greene County. His wife was Phoebe .... She died November 22, 1848, aged 73 years. Both are buried at Lippencott.

Children
1. Elihu Crayne.
2. Silas Crayne, died April 16, 1868, aged 66 years, 9 days.
3. Rachel Crayne, born January 27, 1810, died January 4, 1898; married Meeker Bell, born February 3, 1807, died November 15, 1886.
4. Jane Crayne, born October 30, 1812, died January 14, 1897, married James Acklin, born October 8, 1808, died September 8, 1894.

3. Daniel Crayne, died February 24, 1854, aged 75 years, 11 months, and 6 days. His wife was Hannah Clawson, who died August 20, 1841, aged 50 years. Both are buried at Lippencott.

Children
1. Samuel Crayne, born 1805, died October 11, 1866.
2. Jane Crayne, married William Taylor.
3. Hannah Crayne, born April 4, 1815, died August 26, 1892, married, September 25, 1834, Andrew Hughes, born November 1, 1810, died June 8, 1893.
4. Elizabeth Crayne, married Abijah Clayton.
5.

4. John Crayne, died December 1, 1839, aged 60 years. Buried at Edwards School House. His wife was Elizabeth ....

Children
1. Daniel Crayne, married Thermandes ....
2. John Crayne.
3. Hannah Crayne, married James Kelley.
4. Maria Crayne, married Samuel Rinehart.
5. Rachel Crayne, married Jesse Kelley.
6. James B. Crayne, married Kesiah Walton.

5. Samuel Crayne, died October 27, 1853, aged 69 years and 27 days. He married Mary Huss, who died June 14, 1865, aged 72 years and 29 days. Both are buried at Lippencott.

Children
1. Stephen Crayne, born January 4, 1813; died March 12, 1909; married, March 18, 1834, Mary Bell, born May 26, 1816, died September 16, 1899. Buried in Baptist Cemetery at Jefferson, Pennsylvania.
2. Mary Crayne, married Carey Headley.
3. Miller Crayne, born April 22, 1817, died September 26, 1907; married, May 14, 1840, Lucinda Bell, born January 18, 1821, died February 10, 1901.
4. David Crayne, born February 2, 1818, died December 1, 1902; married Caroline Harry, born March 8, 1825, died November 20, 1888.
5. Phoebe Crayne, born 1821, died 1885; married Frank Moudy, who died 1870; buried in the C. P. Cemetery at Jefferson, Pennsylvania.
6. Harriet Crayne, born March 2, 1823, died August 12, 1891; married, 1850, Thomas Inghram, born February 23, 1807, died July 14, 1894.
7. Silas Crayne, died 1899, married Cassie Bell, born April 20, 1836, died September 26, 1881.
8. Maria Crayne, born April 29, 1827, died February 1926;

married, April 17, 1845, John Cox, born August 17, 1824, died October 18, 1897.
  9. Caroline Crayne, died August 17, 1890.
  10. Martha Crayne, married Jonathan Whitlatch.
6. Phoebe Crayne, died December ...., 18......., aged 59 years, 10 months, and 23 days; married Jacob Barnes, who died April 13, 1852, aged 72 years. Buried at Lippencott.

Children

1.
2. Silas Barnes, born August 22, 1810; married, 1832, Catherine Johns, born 1816, died November 1886, daughter of Jacob and Elizabeth (Smith) Johns.
3. Elizabeth Barnes, married, October 4, 1838, Isaac Mitchell, born September 9, 1816, son of Shadrack and Margaret (Rinehart) Mitchell.
4. Elisha Barnes.
5. John Barnes.
6. Sara Barnes, married .... Rinehart.
7. Jane Barnes, married .... Rinehart.
8. Priscilla Barnes, married George W. Wisecarver.
9. Lucinda Barnes, married .... Johns.

7. Sarah Crayne, died November 15, 1861, aged 74 years; married (1) Ebeneezer Blatchley. Married (2) Zenas Johnson, who died February 17, 1865, aged 85 years. Buried at Lippencott.

Children

1. Zenas Johnson, born April 12, 1827; married October 28, 1862, Sarah J. Watson, born October 28, 1839.

8. Mary Crayne, married Charles Hedge.

Children

1. Charlotte Hedge, married Alexander C. Dallison.
2. Silas Hedge.

9. Rebecca Crayne, married Thomas Young

CARY McCLELLAND FAMILY

During the Revolution Thomas Wolverton, son-in-law of Nathaniel Bell, through his marriage with Jane Bell, lived on the land adjoining Fort Bell, which was warranted to him on January 27, 1785. He sold his warrant to Caleb Crayne, who patented the land under the title "Craynes Fancy" on June 26, 1794. Then Caleb Crayne and wife, Catherine, sold the land to Cary McClelland in deed entered in Deed Book 1. pp. 339. This tract included a part of the farm now owned by my good friend Clarence W. Grimes. It was here that Cary McClelland raised his large family, said by some to have been nineteen children, prior to leaving for Knox County, Ohio.

Cary McClelland was born in Ireland, March 13, 1750 (1753 ?) and came to America, where in 1776, he enlisted in the Regiment of Colonel Walter Stewart, serving in the Battles of Brandywine, Germantown, and Princeton. His pension application from Knox County, Ohio, July 12, 1834, claimed service in the Pennsylvania Lines. He died in Ross County, Ohio, on March 8, 1846, and is buried in the Bell Cemetery at Utica. Cary McClelland was twice married, his first wife being a Miss McVay, the second Henrietta Myers, who died in 1829. The second wife was a widow when she married Cary McClelland.

Children of Cary McClelland
1. Margaret McClelland, born 1781.
2. Cary McClelland,, Jr., born October 6, 1783. His wife was Mary Wathen, born October 2, 1785, who died May 5, 1853. They bought land from Henry Fix, which they sold on May 13, 1830. Another deed of record shows them living in Baltimore, Maryland.
3. Elizabeth McClelland, born 1784, died in Emporia, Kansas, but is buried in the Bell Cemetery, Knox County, Ohio. She married, about 1804, Benjamin Bell, son of James and Mary (Knox) Bell. He was born on Ruff's Creek, February 17, 1782, and died in Knox County, October 19, 1851.

Children of Benjamin and Elizabeth (McClelland) Bell
1. Cary Bell, born August 22, 1805, died March 11, 1826.
2. Jacob Bell, born in 1807, died October 15, 1874; married, 1828, Rachel Letts, born 1811, died February 6, 1876.
3. Mary Bell, married S. W. Hanger, removed to Emporia, Kansas.
4. Henrietta Bell, married Daniel Paul, Jr.
5. Nancy Bell, married David M. Elliott.
6. Amy Bell, married Dr. D. W. McCann.
7. Eunice Bell, married Harrison Elliott.
8. James Bell, born April 15, 1818, died April 9, 1879; married (1) Rowena Robinson, who died March 12, 1856. He married (2) Phoebe J. Wright, who died October 13, 1908.
9. Belinda Bell, born 1819, died July 17, 1875; married Rev. Isaiah Jones, born June 15, 1816, died August 2, 1901.
10. Benjamin Bell, married Eliza Gearhart.

4. John McClelland, born 1786, died 1840, son of Cary McClelland. He married Nancy Montgomery, who died May 5, 1862. She was a daughter of Michael and Nancy (Evans) Montgomery.

Children of John and Nancy (Montgomery) McClelland
1. Ellen McClelland, born in 1818; married in 1838, Samuel Fulton, born January 10, 1818.
2. Marinda McClelland, married Abner Ross, who died about 1855-6, leaving four minor children: Elizabeth, Samuel, John, and Timothy Ross.
3. Nancy McClelland, born February 1, 1823, died September 18, 1873; married Henry Grimes, born September 4, 1820. They were married March 27, 1846.
4. Cary McClelland, wife's name was Mary ....
5. Michael M. McClelland, born December 22, 1824, married Elizabeth Mettler, born May 6, 1826.
6. Hannah McClelland, born ....; married John Keys.

5. William McClelland, son of Cary McClelland.
6.
7. Jane McClelland, daughter of Cary McClelland.
8. Nancy McClelland, daughter of Cary McClelland, married William Buckingham, son of John and Mary (Bell) Buckingham. He was born November 26, 1781.
9. Asa McClelland, son of Cary McClelland, married (1) Catherine Brown. His second wife was Eliza ... .

Children
1. Nancy McClelland, married .... McFann.
2. Elizabeth McClelland, married .... Porter.
3. Mary McClelland.
4. Mariah McClelland, married Levi Rinehart.

AND ITS PIONEER FAMILIES 469

5. Dawson McClelland, married Sarah Hughes.
6. Asa McClelland, Jr.

ELISHA HUSS FAMILY

The ancestor of the Huss Family of Greene County was Elisha Huss, born about 1760, in Chester County (?), Pennsylvania. He died July 12, 1832, and is buried in the cemetery at Grimes School House. His wife was Rachel Heaton, who was born in New Jersey in 1764, and died February 18, 1838. She is buried with her husband. Their children were:

1. Mary Huss, born May 16, 1793, died June 14, 1865; married Samuel Crayne, born September 30, 1784, died October 27, 1853. (See Crayne Records.)
2. John Huss, died April 27, 1854; married Elizabeth Heaton, daughter of William and Abigail Heaton.
3. David Huss, born 1801, died July 14, 1873: His wife was Delilah Rinehart, daughter of Barnet and Ruth (Stiles) Rinehart. She died November 22, 1871.

Children

1. Charlotte Huss, died February 1911; married (1) Smith Adamson, (2) Samuel Braden.
2. Simon R. Huss, born 1824, died 1905; married Elizabeth Gordon.
3. David R. P. Huss, born May 25, 1839, died November 24, 1910; married, 1859, Mary Jane Lantz born 1841, died December 9, 1908.
4. Harvey Huss, married .... Bell.
5. John K. Huss, married Eleanor Lantz.
6. Emily R. Huss, married Richard Lantz.

4. Benjamin Huss, married Sarah ...., who died February 28, 1864. She was born 1808.
5. Elizabeth Huss, born March 28, 1802, died September 13, 1874; married Samuel Smith, born 1796, died September 7, 1879.
6. Abigail Huss, born March 11, 1810, died May 15, 1841; married Jacob Rinehart, born 1803, died May 1, 1874, aged 71 years, 2 months and 21 days.

Children

1. Harriet Rinehart, born November 11, 1829; married, November 5, 1857, Martin Love, who died in 1899.
2. Joheil Rinehart, born 1831, died 1905; married Elizabeth Rinehart, born 1831, died 1916.
3. William H. Rinehart, died 1874; married, 1852, Ruth Ann Bowen.
4. David Rinehart, born 1836; killed in Civil War May 1, 1865.
5. Ruth Rinehart.
6. Abigail Rinehart, married .... Kincaid.
7. John Rinehart, married Mira Bailey.

7. Rachel Huss, born January 6, 1811, died January 20, 1890; married Solomon Hoge, born March 13, 1803, died May 17, 1877.

Children

1. Martha Hoge, born 1830, died 1886; married William Inghram, born 1823.
2. Mary Hoge, born April 9, 1832, died April 27, 1923; married Benjamin Rinehart, born May 27, 1826, died December 7, 1907.
3. John Hoge, born 1834, died 1917; married Irene Penney.
4. Jacob Hoge, married (1) Rachel Bell, (2) Elizabeth Jones.
5. Asa B. Hoge, born September 23, 1841, died 192...; married

Mary Phelan.
6. Elizabeth Hoge, born October 27, 1844, died 1938; married James Kincaid Scott.
7. Solomon F. Hoge, born April 1, 1848, died 1936; married, (1) Marietta Bell, (2) Emma Downey.
8. William H. Hoge, married Emily Stewart.

THE ROSS FAMILY OF RUFFS CREEK

There seems little doubt that the Ross Family was among the first settlers on Ruffs Creek, and the waters of the North Fork of Tenmile Creek, with John Ross and Henry Ross among the first of the family to settle. They took up land next to each other near the present site of Lippencott, with Henry at that place, and John at Grimes School House. Several others of the name were in what is now Morgan Township, including Ignatius, who went to Cincinnati with Benjamin Stites, and Reuben Ross, Robert Ross, William Ross, who with John Ross, served in Captain Stites Militia Company in 1782. John Ross appears to have been the eldest of these and the only head of a family in the early tax lists. William Harrod, Jr., in his interview with Draper, states that his father, Captain William Harrod, was in command of the fort at John Ross's on Ruffs Creek in the Summer of 1774, where he collected supplies for Lord Dunmore's Army. This is the earliest record of settlement on the creek, and the younger Harrod further stated that his family forted there in the same year. As the site was some distance from the Harrod home at Jefferson, it is evident that this was one of the earliest forts in the Tenmile Country, since the Harrods subsequently forted at John Swan's Fort, nearer their home. The date places the erection of the fort at John Ross's the same date as the erection of Richard Jackson's stockade at Waynesburg. This fort, and that one further up Ruffs Creek at Nathaniel Bell's land, later the Hugh Montgomery Farm, were the main refuges of the settlers of the section during the Revolution. Waychoff has mistakenly called this fort at John Ross's "Heaton's Fort," but this is understandable, since the land later passed into the hands of Daniel Heaton. It was here, too, that John Ross built a grist mill that he sold on March 18, 1797, to John Phillips.

William Heaton bought the Henry Ross tract, where, on March 26, 1793, a deed was made to the Baptist Church for land on which the present church and cemetery stands. Henry Ross moved to Bourbon County, Kentucky, where he died about November 1798, leaving a number of children for whom guardians were appointed. These were: John Ross, who reached his majority in 1800; Phoebe Ross, Nancy Ross, Mary Ross, and Elizabeth Ross.

John Ross died intestate in Greene County about 1815, but partition proceedings in the Orphans Court (Docket 1. pp. 67) and a number of deeds, show that he was married to Mary ...., who joined with her sons, John and Jacob Ross, on March 22, 1825, in selling the tract patented by John Ross, Sr., to Daniel Heaton. John and Mary Ross were parents of:

1. John Ross, Jr., who with his wife, Christina ...., moved to Butler County, Ohio.
2. Jacob Ross, who married Abigail Ross, daughter of Timothy and Rachel (Wolverton) Ross. He removed to Jackson Township, where his wife owned a large tract of land, and died there in 1856. His wife died there July 2, 1881. They were the parents of:
   1. John Ross, who removed to Kansas.
   2. Abner Ross, who married Pruda Harvey.

3. Timothy Ross, who married Mary Zimmerman.
   4. Benjamin Ross, who married Rhoda Cathers.
   5. Catherine Ross, who married William Conklin.
   6. Thomas M. Ross, born March 10, 1831, died ....; married, March 13, 1856, Sarah E. Rickey, born April 24, 1837.
   7. Mary Ross, married James Orr.
   8. Rachel Ross, married John Mason.
   9. Phoebe Ross, never married.
3. William Ross, who with wife, Martha ...., removed to Knox County, Ohio.
4. Sarah Ross, married Isaac Parker, and settled in Butler County, Ohio.
5. Elizabeth Ross, married James Haines and went to Butler County, Ohio.
6. Catherine Ross, married Henry Green and also settled in Butler County, Ohio.
7. Martha Ross, married James McNutt.

TIMOTHY ROSS FAMILY

Timothy Ross was born in Westfield, New Jersey, 1765, died at Shinnston, West Virginia, in 1851. Buried with his wife at Bates Fork Baptist Church Cemetery, in Greene County, Pennsylvania. His first wife was Mary Briant, daughter of John Briant of Greene County. After her death he married Rachel Wolverton, who was born in 1767, and died October 20, 1836. She was a daughter of John and Abigail (..................) Wolverton. Timothy Ross and his brother-in-law, Isaac Sharp, were surveyors in partnership, and both patentees of land near Waynesburg.

1. Captain John Ross, born March 19, 1792, died August 4, 1878; buried in Grimes School House Cemetery. He married Phoebe Heaton, daughter of William and Abigail Heaton. She was born in 1793, died 1866. He was one of the "Forty-niners."

   #### Children
   1. John Ross.
   2. Rachel Ross, born December 24, 1832, died January 23, 1903; married, June 22, 1849, Isaac Lewis, born June 7, 1830, died June 5, 1893.
   3. Elizabeth Ross, married Jacob Johns, Jr. (See Jacob Johns Family.)
   4. Charlotte Ross, married .... Wise.
   5. Abigail Ross, married .... Jewell.
   6. Dorcas Ross, married James Dunn.

2. Samuel Ross, no record.
3. Nathaniel Ross, born February 19, 1794, went to Knox County, Ohio in 1817. Married Sally Hair.

   #### Children
   1. Polly Ross, married Adam Crumrine, Hancock, Ohio.
   2. Cynthia Ross, drowned.
   3. John Ross, died young.
   4. Timothy Ross, born December 25, 1820, married Esther Ann Crouse, born 1826.
   5. Delilah Ross, married Robert Mellick.
   6. Rachel Ann Ross, killed in the Burlington Storm May 1825.
   7. Samuel Ross.
   8. Benjamin Ross, died young.

4. Thomas Ross, married Hannah Denny. He died about 1832, and his wife in 1847, both leaving estates recorded in Greene County.

Children

1. John Ross.
2. Rachel Ross.
3. Hannah Ross, died in 1890; married Samuel Braden.
4. Lydia Ross, married .... Crumrine.
5. Thomas Ross.
6. Ann Ross.
7. Timothy Ross.

5. Abigail Ross, married Jacob Ross. (See John Ross Record.)
6. Benjamin Ross, born March 11, 1802, died January 15, 1863; married, November 13, 1827, Hannah Johns, born June 9, 1811, died March 1, 1868.

Children

1. Catherine Ross, born September 20, 1829, died July 20, 1855; married Jesse Cox.
2. Rachel Ross, born July 7, 1831, married James Dunn.
3. Thomas Ross, born October 8, 1833, married Helen Lindley.
4. Elizabeth Ross, born December 2, 1835, died 1858.
5. Abner Ross, born March 30, 1838, married Margaret Mitchell.
6. Jacob Ross, born July 17, 1840, married Frances Lindsey.
7. Lydia Ross, born January 6, 1843, married B. F. Bell.
8. Benjamin Ross, born November 1, 1846, died February 15, 1912.
9. Nathaniel Ross, born August 1, 1849, died 1852.
10. Hannah Ross, born June 6, 1853, died 1856.
11. Heath Ross, born July 12, 1858, died October 21, 1923; married, June 18, 1902, Martha Call, born October 10, 1871.

7. Mary Ross, married Thomas Johns. (See Jacob Johns Record.)
8. Lydia Ross, married .... Huffman.

DENNIS SMITH FAMILY

Dennis Smith is said to have served seven years in the War of the Revolution. Local records show he was a sergeant in Captain George Myers' Company, Washington County Militia as shown in the company return of November 2, 1781. (Penna. Arch Series VI. Vol 2. pp. 167). This company was recruited from the northern part of Morgan Township, and parts of the North Tenmile adjacent to the present Greene County line. Dennis Smith first settled on land warranted to Job Walton, which he patented March 26, 1806, under the title "Patience," and situated near the North Tenmile Baptist Church. He was born in Germany in 1748, and died in Greene County about 1824. His estate was probated on August 31, 1829. His wife was Elizabeth Zook, who was born May 13, 1756, and died in 1845. Both are buried in the cemetery at Lippencott.

Children of Dennis and Elizabeth (Zook) Smith

1. Peter Smith, born 1775, died May 6, 1848; married about 1804, Priscilla Cooper, born 1787, died July 4, 1841. They are buried in North Tenmile Cemetery. She was a daughter of Moses Cooper.

Children

1. Dennis Smith.

2. Moses Smith.
3. Mary Smith, married .... Garber.
4. Peter Smith.
5. Bettsy Smith, married .... Riggle.
6. Sallie Smith, married .... Potts.
7. James Smith.
8. David Smith.
9. Eunice Smith, married .... Johnson.
10. Hannah Smith, married .... Hufford.
11. Priscilla Smith, married .... Beeler.

2. Elizabeth Smith, born 1776, died June 11, 1853; married, October 9, 1794, Jacob Johns, who was born in Delaware, October 1, 1762, and died August 22, 1845, in Greene County. (See Jacob Johns Records.)
3. Abraham Smith, son of Dennis and Elizabeth (Zook) Smith.
4. Joseph Smith, died before 1829.
5. Catherine Smith, married William Seals.
6. Mary Smith, married Thomas Iams, who died about 1843.

Children

1. Dennis Iams, married Priscilla Hopkins.
2. Thomas Iams.
3. Elizabeth Iams, married George Smith.
4. Catherine Iams.
5. Hannah Iams.
6. Mary Iams.
7. Rachel Iams.
8. Charity Iams.

7. Susan Smith, married (1) .... Milliken; (2) .... Clark.
8. Dennis Smith, went to Missouri. His wife was Sarah ....
9. David Smith.
10. Christopher Smith.
11. Hannah Smith, married James Huffman, son of George and Ann Huffman. He died in Greene County on April 25, 1828, leaving a number of minor children for whom Peter Smith served as guardian. He had land adjoining his brother's George Huffman and Jacob Johns.

Children

1. David Huffman.
2. Catherine Huffman, married Lochard Stewart.
3. Susan Huffman, married Charles Pettit. He died June 3, 1861; she died in 1895.
4. Elizabeth Huffman.
5. Benjamin Huffman.
6. Abraham Huffman.
7. Jacob Huffman.
8. James Huffman.

12. Sarah Smith, married Jacob Meeks, who was born September 3, 1777.
13. Rachel Smith, married .... Foster.

JACOB JOHNS FAMILY

Jacob Johns was born in New Castle City, Delaware, on Ooctober 1, 1762. He enlisted on October 1780, in Philadelphia on Frigate

"Confederacy" commanded by Captain Hardy, alias Harding. Other officers were Lieutenant Gore, Lieutenant Gross, Lieutenant Land, Sergeant Land of the Marines, Doctors mate Davis. Around Christmas time of 1780, they sailed for the French Port Hispaniola, during which voyage they captured an English transport vessel. After their return to Philadelphia, they sailed in the Spring of 1781, and met up with a British gunman with four or five hundred Negroes aboard. This they captured and sold and divided the booty among the crew, it amounting to about twenty dollars per man. Then their ship was captured and Johns was made a prisoner of war, not being released until after the end of the Revolution. He then returned home and a short while later removed to the Tenmile and settled on Ruffs Creek, where he died August 22, 1845. (Nat. Arch. Pension Record W. 1192.)

Jacob Johns settled on land which had been warranted to John Wolverton in Washington Township, and acquired other tracts during the course of his life. He was married by Rev. David Sutton on October 9, 1794, to Elizabeth Smith, daughter of Dennis and Elizabeth (Zook) Smith. She died on June 11, 1853, at the age of 77 years. Both are buried in the Lippencott Cemetery. Their children were named in the pension application of the widow and dates of birth of each is given, along with some marriage records.

1. Thomas Johns, born August 31, 1795; married, February 24, 1826, Mary Ross, daughter of Timothy and Rachel (Wolverton) Ross. They removed to LaSalle County, Illinois, where he died about 1809.

Children
1. Heath Johns.
2. Timothy Johns.
3. Thomas Johns.
4. Nancy Johns, married .... Braden.

2. Nancy Johns (Susannah) born June 5, 1797; married, September 2, 1824, John Huffman, son of Benjamin and Sarah Huffman. He was born in 1802, and died July 7, 1883.

Children
1. Elizabeth Huffman, married .... Shoup.
2. Benjamin Huffman.
3. Thomas Huffman.
4. James Huffman.
5. Rachel Huffman, born March 20, 1842.
6. Emeline Huffman.
7. Sarah Huffman, married .... Garner.
8. Jacob Huffman.
9. Joseph Huffman, born July 7, 1838; married in 1869, Nancy Reese.

3. Elizabeth Johns, married (1) June 13, 1825, Samuel Finley. Her second husband was .... Whiting. Elizabeth Johns was born September 14, 1799.
4. Mary Johns, born September 26, 1801.
5. Jacob Johns, Jr., born December 3, 1806, died December 24, 1896; married, March 27, 1834, Elizabeth Ross, daughter of John and Phoebe (Heaton) Ross. She was born March 29, 1816.

Children
1. J. R. Johns, married Mary Jane Huffman.
2. D. W. Johns, married Rachel Meek.
3. Abner Johns, married Elizabeth Meek.
4. Jacob Johns, Jr., married (1) Lourena McClelland; (2) Josephine Hickman.

AND ITS PIONEER FAMILIES

    5. Phoebe Johns, died August 11, 1845, aged 3 years.
    6. Timothy Johns, died June 14, 1853, aged 5 years.
    7. Elizabeth Johns, died March 11, 1840, aged 40 years, 1 month and 13 days. She married Jacob Hoge.
6. Rebecca Johns, born May 5, 1809; married, September 14, 1830, ... Barnes.
7. Hannah Johns, born June 9, 1811, died March 1, 1868; married, November 1, 1827, Benjamin Ross, son of Timothy and Rachel (Wolverton) Ross. (See Ross Records). He was born March 11, 1802, and died January 15, 1863.
8. Catherine Johns, born July 1, 1813, married Silas Barnes.
9. Rachel Johns, born December 1, 1815, married Asa Mitchell, on January 25, 1835. He was born October 6, 1811, and died September 28, 1889, and was a son of Shadrack and Margaret (Rinehart) Mitchell.

Children
    1. Jacob Mitchell.
    2. Maria Mitchell, married Michael Montgomery.
    3. John Mitchell.
    4. Catherine Mitchell, married George V. Shirk.
    5. Shadrack Mitchell.
    6. Thomas Mitchell.
    7. Delilah Mitchell.
    8. Mary J. Mitchell.

THE HUFFMAN FAMILY OF RUFFS CREEK

On September 30, 1754, there arrived in the Port of Philadelphia, the British ship, Neptune, Captain Ware, master, and several hundred passengers from Darmstadt and Zweibruken. Among the passengers were George Hoffman, Daniel Stegner, and Phillipus Frey, who with some one hundred and thirty eight other males, took the Oath of Allegiance to the British at that port. No doubt these men were related or at least from the same locality in the Palatinate, which suggests that they settled in the same neighborhood here, since there are several intermarriages in the next two generations. It is probable from the evidence, that they settled after their arrival, in the German settlement in Frederick County, Maryland, from which they moved into the Upper Shenandoah Valley and later to the Tenmile Country. It is not clear when they arrived on the Tenmile, but in the Census for 1790, a George and Henry Huffman are listed among the names of those living near Fort Jackson. A few years later George Huffman, Sr., bought the land on one fork of Ruffs Creek from Nehemiah Scott, which land has remained in the family to this date. On June 2, 1804, George Huffman and wife, Anne, sold a portion of the tract patented to Nehemiah Scott under the name "South Valley" to William Fonner, in a deed that describes it as joining the land of George Huffman, Jr. The following year on May 1, 1805, they made another deed to George Huffman, Jr., and James Huffman, their sons, for a lot in Waynesburg, either No. 167 or 137, which was used to complete a deal with Robert Whitehill. (Greene County Deed Book 2. pp 65 and 241½.) Benjamin Huffman who had the land adjoining George Huffman, Jr., on Ruffs Creek was another son, and Henry Huffman, whose will was probated in Greene County on January 11, 1812, was probably another. This Henry Huffman had married or lived with Catrouche Frey, mother of his children, who are not named in the will, the wording of which allows different interpretations. It appears that George Huffman, Sr., moved to Hanover Township, Washington County, where he died about 1814, leaving a will naming his wife, Ann, and sons, George and Henry Huffman.

The Benjamin Huffman Family

Benjamin Huffman, son of George and Ann Huffman, lived on land adjoining that of his brothers, James and George Huffman, Jr., and witnessed the will of his brother, George Huffman. He was a soldier in the War of 1812. His wife's name was Sarah .... Benjamin Huffman died in Greene County in 1844, and his wife in 1847.

Children (O. C. Docket 4. pp. 217, etc.)

1. John Huffman, born 1802, died 1883; married Anna Johns, who died at the age of 83.

   #### Children (Haddon's History Fayette and Greene Counties)
   1. Elizabeth Huffman.
   2. Benjamin Huffman.
   3. Sarah Huffman.
   4. Jacob Huffman.
   5. James Huffman.
   6. Thomas Huffman.
   7. Joseph Huffman, born July 7, 1838; married, 1869, Nancy Reese.
   8. Rachel Huffman, born March 20, 1842.
2. James Huffman.
3. George Huffman.
4. Matilda Huffman, married Dennis Iams.
5. Nancy Huffman, married John Swart.
6. Rebecca Huffman, married John Iams.
7. Delilah Huffman, married Thomas Iams.

   #### Children
   Benjamin Iams, killed in the Civil War.
   F. P. Iams.
   James Iams, born January 2, 1857, married Belle Swart.
   Otho Iams, born September 4, 1846, married Sarah Bane.
8. Elizabeth Huffman, married John McGinnis.
9. Joseph Huffman, born 1807, removed to Knox County, Ohio, then to Indiana, and died in Kansas, 1885. He married Hannah McClelland, daughter of Cary and Polly (Wathen) McClelland.

   #### Children
   1. Cary Huffman.
   2. Sarah Huffman.
   3. Rachel Huffman.
   4. Mary S. Huffman.
   5. Henrietta Huffman.
   6. James M. Huffman.
   7. Benjamin Huffman.
   8. Joseph E. Huffman.
10. Benjamin Huffman.

Family of George Huffman, Jr.

George Huffman, Jr., son of George and Ann Huffman, died in Greene County, about 1839. His will, made on February 18, 1839, was probated March 12, 1839, and is in Will Book 2. pp. 102. Benjamin Huffman and Mary Ann Smith witnessed the will. His wife was Julia Frey, who survived him. Beers "History of Washington County" gives a record of his family.

Children of George and Julia (Frey) Huffman

1. Peter Huffman. born in 1802. died in 1885; married Elizabeth

AND ITS PIONEER FAMILIES

Stegner. They were parents of nine children.

Children

1.
2.
3.
4.
5. Julia Ann Huffman, born June 10, 1847; married, 1867, L. H. Mitchell, born June 10, 1846.
6
7. William Huffman, born December 27, 1850; married, November 27, 1870, Jennie Fordyce.
8.
9.

2. Abraham Huffman.
3. Rachel Huffman, married Jesse Stewart.
4. Catherine Huffman.
5. Sarah Huffman, married .... Cameron.
6. Nancy Huffman, married (1) Ira Smith.
7. Margaret Huffman.
8. Eliza Huffman, married (1) Silas Barnes; married (2) John Headley.
9. Mahala Huffman, married .... McCarl.
10. George Huffman, born April 2, 1817, died October 1897; married, November 11, 1838, Susannah Stegner, born March 13, 1818, died March 1902.

Children (Bible Record)

1. Mary Jane Huffman, born January 26, 1839, married J. R. Johns.
2. George W. Huffman, born January 17, 1844, died November 24, 1903; married Phoebe J. Baldwin, September 20, 1865. She was born March 27, 1846, died March 9, 1896.
3. Thomas J. Huffman, born December 17, 1849; married Eliza Mattox, born October 12, 1852.
4. John Huffman, born January 24, 1856; married Alice Swart on November 16, 1876. She was born April 20, 1857, and died September 21, 1913.

THE PETTIT FAMILY

There can be little doubt that the Pettit Family of Greene County is descended from Thomas Pettit of Roxbury, Massachusetts, who sought the more equable climate of New Jersey. His grandson, Nathaniel Pettit, through his son, Nathaniel, married in Bethlehem Township, Hunterdon County, New Jersey, Elizabeth, daughter of Andrew and Hannah (Lambert) Heath. Nathaniel Pettit and wife, Elizabeth (Heath) Pettit, were parents of the following children:

1. Elizabeth Pettit, married Dennis Wolverton, who was born 1711, died 1774.
2. Abigail Pettit.
3. Andrew Pettit, of Amwell Township, Hunterdon County, whose wife was Dinah ....
4. Jonathan Pettit, born 1721, died 1769, married Deborah Robins, who died 1791.
5. Amos Pettit, his wife was Esther ....
6. Nathaniel Pettit, born June 12, 1724, died March 9, 1803; married Margaret McFarlane (?).
7. John Pettit, whose wife was a daughter of Richard Fisher.
8. Isaac Pettit.
9. Charles Pettit, whose wife was Mary ....

10. Thomas Pettit.
11. George Pettit.

Nathaniel Pettit of Greene County, Pennsylvania

Nathaniel Pettit, one of the above sons of Nathaniel and Elizabeth (Heath) Pettit. (Evidence suggests he may have been a son of Isaac Pettit, since an Isaac Pettit with adult sons was living in Amwell Township, Washington County, in 1790.) He was born in New Jersey on January 6, 1762, and died in Washington Township, Greene County, July 26, 1833. His family removed to the Tenmile before 1781, when we find Isaac Pettit serving a tour of duty in the company of Ezekiel Rose under Ensign David Ruble; John Pettit serving tours of duty under Sergeants Thomas Wolverton and Mathew Gray in Captain Benjamin Stites Militia Company, and Nathaniel Pettit in the regular muster roll of Captain Abner Howell's Company of the Third Battalion, Washington County Militia. (Penna. Arch. Series VI Vol. 2. pp. 120-242-244-255.) Bert Pettit, popular mail carrier, and descendant of Nathaniel Pettit, has a Bible Record of the Family of Nathaniel Pettit, which says that he married Sarah ...., who was born April 17, 1768. There is a Sarah, wife of Nathaniel Pettit, buried with him in the Bates Fork Baptist Cemetery, who died May 25, 1839. Records suggest that he may have been married twice, with his first wife dying between 1809, and 1815. Unless our reading of the tombstone of the Sarah Pettit buried with him is in error due to its poor legibility, she was but 42 years of age, plus 5 months and 10 days.

Family tradition tells that Nathaniel Pettit settled on the land on Bates Fork of Tenmile when he came from New Jersey, the section then being a part of Amwell Township, Washington County. This seems correct for on August 9, 1804, he warranted the land under the title of "Buck" and patented the more than 422 acres, February 4, 1805. This land plus some purchases of adjoining land, in all over one thousand acres, was passed along to several of his sons, and extended from the present village of Sycamore to beyond Swarts Station. His will is in WB. 2 pp. 38 and was probated August 22, 1834.

Bible Record of Children of Nathaniel Pettit

1. John Pettit, born February 2, 1788, died March 2, 1848. His first wife was a Miss Warford who became the mother of eight children. His second wife was Helena Stegner, born February 12, 1801, died September 30, 1884. She became the mother of three children. My good neighbor, Adam Phillips, a great grandson of John Pettit, by his second wife, says he inherited the farm at Sycamore and was in good circumstances, but went on paper for his brother, Jesse Pettit, and was compelled to sell out when Jesse failed. He then moved to Wayne Township, where he ended his days. O. C. Docket 3. pp. 96 lists his children, and his wife, Helena.

Children of John Pettit

1. William Pettit, married Mariah Roach.
2. Jesse Pettit.
3. Rachel Pettit, married John Roach and moved to Illinois.
4. Delilah Pettit, married .... Roach.
5.
6. Nancy Pettit, never married.
7. Martha Pettit, married Joseph Hartley.
8. Mary Pettit, married James Kughn.
9. Silas Pettit, married Elmira Driver.
10. Lydia Pettit, born October 14, 1838, died January 12, 1912;

married Adam Spragg.
11. Helena Pettit, married John M. White.
2. Rebecca Pettit, born May 11, 1790.
3. Sarah Pettit, born September 11, 1792, died May 5, 1875; married Francis Barger, born January 1, 1786, died April 12, 1854; both are buried on the David Barger Farm near Ned in Springhill Township. The will of Francis Barger is in Will Book 3 pp. 164.

Children of Francis and Sarah (Pettit) Barger
1. Jane Barger.
2. Mary Barger, married Christian Little.
3. Anna Barger.
4. John Barger, born May 25, 1827; married, November 2, 1854, Emily Lyon, daughter of Noah and Elizabeth (Pettit) Lyon.
5. Francis Barger, Jr.
6. Andrew J. Barger.
7. Susannah Barger.

4. Elizabeth Pettit, born December 10, 1794; married Noah Lyon, son of Benjamin Lyon, and his wife, Joanna Wilcox Lyon. Among their children were:
   1. James Lyon, an old school teacher.
   2. Emily Lyon, who married her cousin, John Barger.
5. Nathaniel Pettit, born December 9, 1796, died 1839; married Rachel Wilson. Nathaniel Pettit, Jr., was constable in 1839, when called upon to dispossess Samuel Vannatta from land on the Thomas Branch of Wheeling Creek at the suit of his brother, Jesse Pettit. At the head of a posse, Nathaniel Pettit, Jr., sought to expel Vannatta by force, and after the door of Vannatta's cabin was broken in, entered to serve his warrant. He was met by the old man and stabbed through the heart, dying almost immediately. Vannatta was then arrested and brought to Waynesburg for trial. Nathaniel Pettit was the father of eight minor children at the time of his death. (O. C. Docket 2. pp. 166.)

Children
1. Bathsheba Pettit, over 14 years of age in 1839.
2. Caroline Pettit, over 14 years of age in 1839.
3. Harrison Pettit.
4. Jemima Pettit.
5. Magdelin Pettit.
6. Noah Pettit.
7. Charlotte Pettit.
8. Rachel Pettit.

6. Isaac Pettit, born March 24, 1799, died February 13, 1881; married Cynthia Hathaway, born 1805, died August 15, 1875. He too became involved through his endorsement of his brother Jesse Pettit's notes but saved his farm near Swarts, through the aid of a kind neighbor. Isaac and Cynthia were married December 27, 1823.

Children of Isaac and Cynthia (Hathaway) Pettit
1. Alexander Pettit, born February 20, 1826. He was married twice.
2. Perry Pettit, born August 6, 1827, died January 26, 1828.
3. Mahala Pettit, born September 13, 1829, died March 24, 1830.
4. John Pettit, born January 23, 1831, married Rachel Pettit, daughter of Charles and Kezia (Coe) Pettit.

     5. Levi Pettit, born November 19, 1832, married Catherine Taylor.
     6. Eliza Pettit, born August 22, 1835, married .... Keys.
     7. Joseph Pettit, born May 6, 1837, married Elizabeth Hedge, daughter of John Hedge.
     8. Betty Pettit, born December 2, 1838, never married.
7. Silas Pettit, born September 5, 1801; got the land next to Dennis Smith. His wife was Sarah ....
8. James Pettit, born December 15, 1803; married Elizabeth, daughter of Joseph Delancy. They went to West Virginia.
9. Jemimah Pettit, born November 27, 1804; married Daniel Rogers.
10. Jesse Pettit, born November 30, 1805; married Charlotte Wilson. He had the farm now owned by Mr. and Mrs. Paul D. Inghram; got into financial difficulties and lost it.
11. Charles Pettit, born November 11, 1809, died June 3, 1861; married Susannah Huffman, daughter of James and Hannah (Smith) Huffman. Susannah Huffman had first married George W. Ferrell and had two sons which she names in her will. She died in 1895. She owned a hotel at Jacktown.

Children

     1. Elizabeth Pettit, married Asberry Antill. (May have been Elizabeth Ferrell).
     2. Marion Pettit.
     3. Hannah Pettit.
     4. Jane Pettit, married .... Carter. (May have been Jane Ferrell).
     5. James Pettit.
     6. Clara Belle, married to .... Smith. (May have been Clara Belle Ferrell).

Susannah's two sons by Ferrell were:
     1. James M. Ferrell, born April 13, 1851.
     2. W. S. Ferrell.
12. Levi Pettit, born April 22, 1815, probably by the second marriage of Nathaniel Pettit.
13. Andrew J. Pettit, born January 4, 1821.
14. William Pettit, born June 6, 1822.

THE IAMS FAMILY

One seldom associates youth with genealogical research, but occasionally young people make it a hobby with surprising results. Such is the case with my good friend Jimmy Meighen, formerly of Lincoln Street, Waynesburg. He has come up with some excellent records of the Iams family, originally of Maryland, and variously spelled "Ijams," "Iiams," "Imes", "Ijames," etc.

The record begins with Thomas Iams (we shall use the modern spelling) born August 7, 1708, son of William and Elizabeth (Plummer) Iams, of South River Hundred, Anne Arundel County, Maryland. On April 17, 1730, Thomas Iams bought from Charles Carrol of Annapolis, for 25 Pounds, 18 Shillings and six Pence, a portion of "Duval's Delight" in Anne Arundel County, and then ten years later bought another portion from Charles Hogan and Mary, his wife. Thomas Iams made his will on October 27, 1766, in which he divided his estate among his four sons, later adding a codicil making his daughter, Susannah Pumphreys, an heir. He died in 1768, and his will was proved at Annapolis on November 28 of that year. A final settlement in 1770 shows he had seven heirs that shared in his estate. His wife's name is not known.

Children of Thomas Iams

1. John Iams, born 1751, died July 4, 1823, buried in Franklin Cemetery near Zollarsville. John Iams served in Colonel John Stone's Regiment in the Revolution, enlisting June 2, 1779, being discharged November 1, 1780. (Maryland Archives Vol. XVIII pp. 126). Near the end of the Revolution he removed about 1784, to the Tenmile and made his home. His wife was Elizabeth Hampton, who died September 1, 1836, aged 72 years, a daughter of Thomas Gill Hampton of Maryland.

   #### Children of John and Elizabeth (Hampton) Iams
   1. Nancy Iams, born January 10, 1787, died January 21, 1871, she was the second wife of Joseph Martin, whom she married December 27, 1821. Joseph Martin was born March 15, 1790, and died December 25, 1850; son of James and Anna (McIntyre) Martin. The first wife of Joseph Martin was Elizabeth Haiden, daughter of Miles Haiden. (Heaton?)
   2. William Iams, born 1792, died April 4, 1869; married Delilah Meeks, daughter of Elisha Meeks, who died September 6, 1876, aged 93 years.
   3. Elizabeth Iams, died at the age of 21 years.
   4. Anna Iams, died at the age of six years.
   5. Sabina Iams, died at the age of four years.
   6. John Iams, born 1798, died March 30, 1846.
   7. Charity Iams, born 1799, died January 19, 1876; married John D. Smith, born 1795, died March 12, 1876.
   8. Mary Iams, born 1800, died September 5, 1859; married Moses Smith.
   9. Sarah Iams, born 1804, died April 15, 1838; married William H. Hathaway.

2. Thomas Iams, born in Maryland, December 26, 1754, died in 1836. He served as a sergeant in Captain Richard Stringer's Company of the Second Regiment in the Maryland Line, enlisting on January 10, 1777, and being discharged on January 1, 1780. (Maryland Archives Vol. XVIII, pp. 126). After his service in the Revolution he removed to what is now Bethlehem Township, Washington County, in 1793. On November 29, 1785, Thomas Iams married Catherine Hampton, sister of Elizabeth Hampton.

   #### Children of Thomas and Catherine (Hampton) Iams
   1. John Iams, died young.
   2. Elizabeth Iams, died un-married.
   3. Samuel Iams, born 1795, died August 21, 1860; married Elizabeth Meek of Belmont County, Ohio.
   4. Thomas Iams, married Mary Hardesty of Richland County, Ohio.
   5. Charity Iams, born 1805; married, 1832, Jacob Myers.
   6. Richard Iams, married Fanny Meek.
   7. Polly Iams, married Jacob Egy.
   8. William Iams, married Susannah Sharp.
   9. Rezin Iams, married Mary Iams of Belmont County, Ohio.
   10. Rebecca Iams, married Jacob Wilson.
   11. Catherine Iams, married Michael Ault.

3. Richard Iams, born 17......, died 1800, will proven in Frederick County, Maryland, November 7, 1800. His wife was Eleanor, probably Jones. He may have been one of the elder children as his son, Richard, is said to have been a soldier in the Revo-

lution, traditions relating his drilling of militiamen and holding Muster at his mill each Saturday night, have been passed to his descendants.

Children of Richard and Eleanor Iams

1. Richard Iams, settled in Frederick, Maryland, with his father, and while there married Elizabeth Pottenger. Then about 1790, he removed to Bates Fork of the Tenmile, where he died about 1825, and is buried in the Bates Fork Baptist Cemetery. He was a millwright, and is said to have been a soldier of the Revolution, holding weekly muster at his mill each Saturday night.

Children of Richard and Elizabeth (Pottenger) Iams

1. Thomas Iams, who married Mary Smith, daughter of Dennis and Elizabeth (Zook) Smith. He died in Greene County about 1843.
2. Richard Iams, married Mary Shidler. He died about 1829 in Greene County.
3. Otha Iams, married Nancy Cole.
4. Rezin Iams, born 1791, died February 19, 1860; married Phoebe Clark, daughter of Isaac and Deborra (French) Clark. She died June 2, 1845, aged 58 years, 4 months, 2 days. Buried in Bates Fork Cemetery.
5. John Iams, married Ruth Barker, removed to Athens County, Ohio.
6. William Iams, married Charity ....
7. Bazil Iams, never married.
8. Eli Iams, married Phoebe Heckathorn.

2. Thomas M. Iams, son of Richard and Eleanor Iams.
3. Nancy Iams, daughter of Richard and Eleanor Iams.
4. William Iams, son of Thomas Iams, married Mary Hampton, daughter of Thomas Gill Hampton, and sister of Elizabeth and Catherine Hampton. He died 1795.

Children of William and Mary (Hampton) Iams

1. Elizabeth Iams, married Daniel Smith.
2. Mary Iams.
3. Thomas Iams, married Mercia Walton.
4. John Iams, born January 25, 1792, died December 12, 1866; married Ann Coulson, daughter of Samuel and Charity (Dearth) Coulson.

5. Susannah Iams, daughter of Thomas Iams; her father, by a codicil to his will, calls her Susannah Pumphreys.
6. Mary Iams. Jimmy Meighen places this Mary Iams as a daughter of Thomas Iams, who had seven heirs who shared in his estate. If the census of 1850 gives her correct age which he notes was 81 years, then it is evident that she was a posthumous daughter. It is also evident that she had an elder sister already married. Neither circumstance is impossible, and Mr. Meighen is too careful in his investigation to merely come up with any wild statements. Mary Iams was married in St. Paul's Church in Baltimore, on April 8, 1788, to William Penn, son of John Penn of Baltimore. His age at the 1850 census is given as 88 years. This age, placing his birth at 1762, suggests that his wife's age was incorrectly given to the enumerator of the 1850 census, and that she was probably more near her husband's age. William Penn was on the Tenmile before his marriage, serving in Captain Ezekiel Rose's Company of the Fifth Battalion, Washington County Militia, and

going out under his captain on the Sandusky Expedition. (Penna. Arch Series VI. Vol. 2. pp. 399, also pp. 205). His company had been recruited in the Pigeon Creek section of Washington County. How. long William Penn remained here after 1782, is not shown, but after marrying in Baltimore in 1788, he seems to have remained there until as late as 1799, when he signed quit claim deeds with his brothers and sisters. Some of his children are said to have been born in Maryland. On May 2, 1825, William Penn got a warrant for land on McClelland's Fork of Tenmile in Morris Township, Greene County. In taking up this land at so late a date he was joined by several former comrades from the Pigeon Creek and Amwell Township section of Washington County, who no doubt waited some time before entering land they had previously chosen. There is no record of the birth or death of either William Penn or his wife, Mary (Iams) Penn. (Note by the author: The census for 1850 roughly estimates the ages of persons listed and in this case they are listed as being from 70 to 80 years of age. We have seen numerous such records that were very unreliable, when checked with true records.)

Children of William and Mary (Iams) Penn

1. Richard Penn, soldier in the War of 1812, married Mary McCullough, sister of Eynon McCullough. (Greene County Will Book 2. pp. 31).

Children
   1. George Penn.
   2. William Penn.
   3. Mary Penn.
   4. Sarah Penn.
   5. Hannah Penn.

2. Nancy Penn, married Jacob Bigler.

Children
   1. Israel Bigler.
   2. Hannah Bigler.

3. Mary Penn, born 1794, died 1870; married Thomas Shidler.

Children
   1. David Shidler.
   2. Nancy Shidler, married James Pence.
   3. John Shidler, married Susannah ....
   4. Sarah Shidler.
   5. Susannah Shidler, married John Pence.

4. William Penn, born March 1, 1799, died February 25, 1891; married Phoebe Bane.

Children
   1. Jacob Penn, born August 3, 1825.
   2. John N. Penn, born May 18, 1829.
   3. Mary Penn, born August 24, 1830; married .... Post.
   4. Clarissa Penn, born March 10, 1832.
   5. Hamilton Penn, born January 10, 1834.
   6. Hiram Penn, born February 23, 1836.
   7. Thomas Penn, born October 27, 1837.
   8. William H. Penn, born September 3, 1841.

5. Nathan Penn, born 1801, married Rachel McCullough, sister of Mary.

Children

1. Rachel Penn.
2. Nancy Penn.
3. Jennie Penn.
4. Mary Penn.
5. Ruth Penn, married Mathias Pettit.
6. Samuel Penn, born December 30, 1831, died September 18, 1903; married Minerva Miller, born 1833, died 1907.

6. John Penn, born June 9, 1808, died September 5, 1892; married (1) Deborah Iams. His second wife was Rebecca Condit, whom he married October 3, 1866.

Children

1. Phoebe Penn, born April 24, 1833; married, December 5, 1850, Thomas Iams. She died November 27, 1890.
2. Mary Penn, born July 28, 1834-35, died December 28, 1884; married Benjamin Huffman.
3. Ellinor Penn, born March 29, 1837, married Fred Fonner.
4. Margaret Penn, born April 10, 1839, died May 2, 1885; married A. J. Barker.
5. John H. Penn, born June 5, 1845, died April 27, 1864.
6. Emma Penn, born by the second marriage, April 13, 1873; living in Ridgeway, Ohio. She is the source of much of the Penn Record which Mr. Meighen duly credits.

7. Margaret Penn, married James Remley. He died and she married (2) William Milliken.

Children

1. Martha.
2. Sarah.
3. Mary.
4. John.
5. George.

8. Sarah Penn, married James Pierson.

Children

1. Vincent Pierson.
2. William Pierson.

9. Susannah Penn, born July 26, 1797, died February 26, 1872; married John Rogers, born March 26, 1800, died March 14, 1879. He was the man for whom Rogersville was named. He and Susannah are buried in the old cemetery at that place. He was a son of William Rogers, who patented land next to William Penn.

Children

1. Levi Munce Rogers, Captain in 58th Penn. Regt. Killed in Civil War.
2. Thomas Rogers, corporal in 58th P. V. I. Killed in action.
3. William Rogers, married Catherine Meegan.
4. James A. Rogers, born October 2, 1826, died March 1903; married, November 1, 1849, Luvina Sellars, born October 24, 1830, died October 2, 1915.
5. Timothy Ross Rogers, married Emma Frantz.
6. Mary Rogers, died young.
7. Nancy Rogers, born December 18, 1822, died November 11, 1903; married George Sellars.
8. Captain John Rogers, married Carrie McCormick.

10. Matilda Penn, born March 26, 1805, died March 8, 1896; married Daniel Hill, born February 5, 1803, died August 5, 1882; son of Rees and Nancy (Heaton) Hill.

Children

1. Mary Hill, born March 16, 1832, died September 6, 1914; married, April 4, 1854, Seth Goodwin.
2. Rees Hill, born December 12, 1833, died July 15, 1910; married Sarah Price.
3. William Hill, born June 5, 1836, died April 27, 1924; married Mariah Tinsman.
4. Thomas Hill, born November 22, 1839, died July 11, 1928; married Adelaide Peake.
5. John Hill, born May 24, 1850, died May 2, 1856.

11. Thomas Penn, died May 24, 1838; married Sarah Moore.

Children

1. Carle Penn.
2. William Penn.

HENRY FIX

Henry Fix lived on the former Johns Farm on Ruffs Creek, which he secured from the State of Pennsylvania by a warrant dated February 10, 1794, giving him title to 362 acres under the title of "Rachel's Camp". He applied for a pension while living in Franklin County, Ohio, on April 10, 1833. In his application, Henry Fix said he was born January 12, 1748, and had served several tours of duty under Colonel Thomas Gaddis, Captain Thomas Wolverton, and Captain B. Bell. The muster roll of Captain Myers' Company, Fifth Battalion, Washington County Militia, includes his name. (Penna. Arch Series VI. Vol 2. pp. 167.) He also served in Captain Andrew Fairley's Company. He was married twice and had four children by his first wife, two sons, twins, were born while he was away on a four month campaign on December 12, 1778, probably by his first marriage. His second wife was Anna Louisa French, who was also granted a pension from Franklin County, Ohio, on April 24, 1846, when she was 83 years of age. Later records show she removed to Delaware County, Ohio, from where she drew her pension September 5, 1848. (Nat. Arch. W. 8087.) Henry Fix died in Franklin County, Ohio, May 14, 1837.

Children

1. Henry Fix, Jr.
2. Jacob Fix.
3. Mary Fix.
4. Dolly Fix.
5. Samuel Fix, oldest son of Henry and Louisa Fix.
6. David Fix, one of the oldest children of Henry and Louisa Fix.
7. George Fix, also a son by the second marriage. He married Sarah Doty, daughter of Anthony and Mary Doty.

PHILLIP SWART

Phillip Swart was an immigrant who came from Germany prior to the Revolution and in due time arrived in Amwell Township, Washington County. Prior to 1782, he was located in the vicinity of Scenery Hill where he served in Captain James Ramsey's Company, Fifth Battalion, Washington County Militia. He then bought the warrant of David Enoch, Jr., for a tract of land south of Amity, where he died about 1811. His will in Washington County Will Book 2. pp. 324, was probated April 13, 1811, and names his daughter, Susan, who seems to have been married twice, first to a man named Evans, by whom she had a son, David Evans, named in the will of Phillip Swart. Beers' Washington County History says she married a man named Phillips. The only other child named by Phillip Swart was his son, Jacob Swart.

Jacob Swart was also a soldier of the Revolution and received payment for being on the Crawford Expedition to Sandusky. (Penna. Arch. Series VI. Vol. 2. pp. 402.) He survived his father by only four years and died in Washington County, where his will was filed March 28, 1815. (Will Book 3. pp. 25.) His wife was Sarah Evans, who died June 11, 1846.

Children of Jacob and Sarah (Evans) Swart

1. Dorothy Swart, married .... Mustard.
2. Phillip Swart, married A... nah Walton; their son, Jacob Swart, born December 25, 1820, married, May 5, 1842, Paulina, daughter of Charles and Jemima (Barnhart) Allum.
3. David Swart.
4. John Swart, married Sarah Huffman, daughter of Benjamin Huffman.
5. Polly Swart, married 1848, Cyrus Huston, born 1797.
6. Henry Swart.
7. Abraham Swart.
8. Charlotte Swart.
9. George Swart, born April 23, 1810, died March 22, 1877; married, January 14, 1830, Elizabeth Smith, born October 9, 1814, died March 4, 1866.

Children

1. Jacob Swart, born July 13, 1831, died March 3, 1833.
2. Harvey Swart, born March 30, 1833; married February 22, 1877, Jane Arnold.
3. Dennis Swart, born January 31, 1836; married, April 30, 1857, Lydia Huffman.
4. Simon Swart, born January 29, 1838, died May 3, 1848.
5. Sarah Swart, born June 19, 1840; married, September 2, 1859, Harrison Sowers.
6. Lucinda Swart, born October 29, 1842; married, March 11, 1864, John Hopkins.
7. Hiram Swart, born October 10, 1844, died September 29, 1851.
8. Elizabeth Swart, born August 27, 1847, died January 1, 1853.
9. Emmeline Swart, born November 5, 1849; married, October 30, 1873, David Baker.
10. George Swart, born January 20, 1853, died August 15, 1865.
11. Deborra Swart, born February 7, 1855; married, February 10, 1875, James Hughes.
12. Alice Swart, born April 20, 1857, died September 21, 1813; married, November 16, 1876, John Huffman, born January 24, 1856.

10. Hiram Swart, born February 12, 1812; married (1) Mary Hastings, (2) Margaret Keys, (3) Charlotte McGinnis.

JOHN STEGNER

John Stegner lived in Maryland until after 1812, when he removed to Greene County with his wife, formerly Mary Redd.

Children of John and Mary (Redd) Stegner

1. Elizabeth Stegner, married Peter Huffman, son of George and Julia (Frey) Huffman.
2. Helena Stegner, born in Maryland, February 12, 1801, died in Greene County September 30, 1884; married, about 1820, John Pettit, born February 2, 1788, died March 7, 1848. He was married twice.

Children

(O. C. Docket 3, pp. 96. First seven by previous marriage.)
William Pettit
Jesse Pettit
Rachel Pettit.
Delilah Pettit.
Nancy Pettit.
Martha Pettit.
Mary Pettit.
Anne Pettit.
Silas Pettit.
Lydia Pettit, born October 14, 1838, died January 12, 1912; married Adam Spragg.
Lany Pettit.

3. Rachel Stegner, born in Maryland in 1812; married, January 15, 1833, Daniel Loughman, born in Maryland, June 15, 1813.

Children

Thaddeus Loughman.
Frederick Loughman.
Mary Loughman, married Oliver McVay.
Susan Loughman, married Warren Conklin.
Adeline Loughman, married S. B. Clutter.
John Loughman.

4. Susannah Stegner, born 1818; married George Huffman, son of George and Julia (Frey) Huffman. See Huffman Records.
5. Mary Stegner, born in Greene County, 1819, died May 27, 1866; married, 1845, Enoch Durbin, born July 24, 1820.

Children

Peter H. Durbin.
George W. Durbin.
Eliza J. Durbin, married Thomas Iams.
John Durbin.

LAZARUS TIMMONS

This name has disappeared locally, but Lazarus Timmons was an early settler in Morgan Township, where two of his sons did frequent service in Benjamin Stites' Militia Company. Lazarus Timmons was not one of the original patentees of land, so there is nothing to show where he settled, but indications are that he lived close to the junction point of the present Morgan, Jefferson, and Franklin Townships. He died here about 1801, and his estate was settled in O. C. Dockett 1. pp. 8 in the March Term of 1801. His wife's name was Jean .... Some of the family settled in Tyler County, West Virginia.

Children of Lazarus and Jean Timmons

1. Catherine Timmons, wife of Ephraim Davidson.
2. Robert Timmons, a member of Captain Benjamin Stites' Morgan Township Militia.
3. Elevin or "Levin" Timmons, also a member of Stites' Company. His wife was .... Heaton.
4. Mary Timmons.
5. Elizabeth Timmons.
6. Nicholas Timmons.
7. Lazarus Timmons, Jr., married Elizabeth Archer.
8. Ann Timmons.
9. Samuel Timmons.
10. Samuel Timmons.
11. Ruth Timmons.
12. Sarah Timmons.

MICHAEL MONTGOMERY

One branch of the Montgomery Family that settled on Ruffs Creek is descended from Michael Montgomery, a native of Harford County, Maryland, where he was living when he enlisted in Captain Samuel Evans' Company, Second Battalion, Chester County, Pennsylvania Militia in the War of the Revolution. After coming to the Tenmile Country, he bought a tract of land on Ruffs Creek from Elihu Woodruff and wife, Mary, of Butler County, Ohio. This land had been patented to Nathaniel Bell in 1786, and had been the site of Fort Bell as early as 1774, as shown by William Harrod, Jr., in his interview with Draper. This fort, the site of which was known to late members of the family, has sometimes been called Fort Heaton, but this is an error. Michael Montgomery was born in 1755, and died February 5, 1835. About 1789, he married Nancy Evans, who was born in 1769, and died July 30, 1836. Both are buried in the old cemetery at Lippencott Baptist Church. Before death, Michael Montgomery conveyed his land to his son Hugh Montgomery. He left a will which is in Greene County Will Book 2. pp. 64, in which he names his wife, Nancy, and these children:

Children of Michael and Nancy (Evans) Montgomery

1. Robert Montgomery, deceased before his father.
    #### Children Named in Grandfather's Will
    1. John Montgomery.
    2. Myers Montgomery.
    3. Charity Montgomery.
2. Charity Montgomery.
3. Eleanor Montgomery.
4. Lurenzer Montgomery.
5. Hugh Montgomery, born 1804, died June 14, 1882; married Priscilla, daughter of George and Elizabeth (Blackledge) Hoge, born September 28, 1808, died May 7, 1889.

Children of Hugh and Priscilla (Hoge) Montgomery

1. Ellen Montgomery, married Samuel Clayton.
2. Priscilla Montgomery, married James Mendenhall.
3. Henry L. Montgomery, father of Elizabeth, Alice, Franklin and Henry.
4. Maryanne Montgomery, married Martin Shirk.
5. Marinda Montgomery, married Silas Cowan.
6. Elizabeth Montgomery, born October 14, 1833; married John Clayton.

    7. Samuel Montgomery, born July 17, 1835; married (1) Mary Stentz. Married (2) Cirene (Dales) Davis.
    8. Nancy M. Montgomery, married John Polke.
    9. Hugh Montgomery, born November 22, 1843; married (1) Anna J. Vankirk; (2) Docas (Cox) Horn.
    10. Lou M. Montgomery, married .... Tarbell.
    11. Thomas Montgomery, born January 24, 1847; married Virginia Gordon.
6. John Montgomery.
7. Sarah Montgomery, married John Huss (?).
8. Nancy Montgomery, died May 5. 1862; married John McClelland, who died in 1840.
9. Samuel Montgomery, born 1812, died April 17, 1833.
10. Levi Montgomery, born July 30, 1814, died August 1, 1882; married Emily Ferguson, born February 16, 1816, died October 18, 1889.

   Children of Levi and Emily (Ferguson) Montgomery
   1. Albert Montgomery.
   2. Andrew Montgomery.
   3. Michael Montgomery, born August 27, 1852, died .... He married (1) Hannah McClelland, born 1851, died August 1, 1882; married (2) Catherine ....; married (3) Maria Mitchell.
   4. Levi Montgomery.
   5. Samuel Montgomery, born January 12, 1835; married Katherine Lantz.
   6. Lemuel Montgomery.

THE CARY FAMILY

The Cary Family of Washington Township is descended from John Cary, one of the proprietors of the town of Bridewater, Massachusetts. He was born near Bristol, Somersetshire, England, about 1610, and joined the Plymouth Colony about 1634. In 1644, he married Elizabeth, daughter of Francis and Elizabeth Godfrey, whose father, in 1643, was a member of the Duxbury Company, commanded by Captain Miles Standish. They had a family of twelve children, all of whom grew to maturity. A fine record of this family has been prepared by Rev. Seth Cary under the title of "Plymouth Pilgrim", published at Worcester Center, Mass.

Francis Cary, second son of John and Elizabeth (Godfrey) Cary, was born at Duxbury on January 19, 1647-48, and married Hannah, daughter of William Bret, in 1676. He lived in Bridgewater, where he died in 1718. Among their children was Ephraim Cary, born 1679, who died at Bridgewater, July 18, 1765. He married Hannah Waldo, born July 17, 1687, died October 18, 1777. They were married February 3, 1709.

Among their children was Daniel Cary, born at Bridgewater in 1716, who removed to New Jersey and bought land on the Black River, on the slopes of Sucksanna Plains, Morris County. He married on June 28, 1741, Martha Cary, daughter of John Cary.

They had a son, Abel Cary, born in 1744, who served in the Revolution in Captain Silas Howell's Company of Morris County, New Jersey Militia. His wife was Elizabeth .... After the Revolution they removed to Washington Township, Greene County, Pennsylvania, where Abel Cary died in December 1815. Orphan's Court Dockett 1. pp. 252, gives a list of their children in the settlement of Abel Cary's Estate in 1827-28. Ezra Cary, Luther Cary, and

Calvin Cary also came to the Tenmile Country, where they served in Captain James Craven's Militia Company in the Revolution. Abel Cary had warranted to him, February 10, 1794, a tract of more than 400 acres of land under the title of "Baltimore," and situated on Ruffs Creek.

Children of Abel and Elizabeth Cary
1. Daniel Cary, born August 13, 1779, died June 7, 1854; married Mary Cooper, daughter of Zebulon and Mary Cooper of Amwell Township, Washington County.

Children of Abel and Mary (Cooper) Cary
1. Abel Cary.
2. Sylvester Cary, born May 6, 1819, died January 3, 1886; married (1) Hannah Cooper; (2) Sarah Jane Cooper, widow of Nathaniel Cooper.
3. Daniel Cary.
4. Jerusha Cary, born 1808, died March 16, 1871; married Elisha Meeks, born June 17, 1802, died June 24, 1884. Don Hampson of Waynesburg is a descendant.

2. John Cary, died before his father. His wife was Harriet

3. Abel Cary, born September 24, 1783, died August 16, 1820; lived and died on the old Cary homestead in Washington County. He married Eunice Woodruff, daughter of Samuel and Hannah (Bell) Woodruff, born March 4, 1787, died May 8, 1833.

Children of Abel and Eunice (Woodruff) Cary
1. Cephas Cary, born August 6, 1812, died December 8, 1896; married Mary Mitchenor, a daughter of Marcena and Mary (Black) Mitchenor. She was born October 8, 1820, and died September 10, 1897; married January 11, 1844.

Children of Cephas and Mary (Mitchenor) Cary
1. Sarah Jane Cary, born February 11, 1849, died November 22, 1876; married, March 1870, Hiram Baker.
2. Mary Elizabeth Cary, born December 26, 1851, died October 26, 1940.
3. Sophrona Craig Cary, born April 7, 1854, died October 5, 1907; married Daniel Hoover, son of Abel and Mary Ann (Lewis) Hoover, born June 4, 1851, died March 11, 1926. Daniel L. Hoover was a grandson of Daniel and Esther (Woodruff) Lewis, and on the maternal grandparent line, a great-grandson of Abiel and Jane Woodruff.
4. Marcena M. Cary, born September 14, 1857, died November 1937; married Elizabeth A. Baker.
5. Jesse W. Cary, born February 1, 1861; married, April 19, 1888, Anna Gogley.

2. Sophrona Cary, born March 5, 1815; married Jesse Craig, born October 20, 1799, died April 26, 1882. They were married April 22, 1832, after the death of his first wife, Hannah (Evans) Craig.

Children of Jesse and Sophrona (Cary) Craig
1. Cephas Craig, married Eunice Bigler.
2. Daniel Craig, married Melinda Bane.
3. Sarah Craig, married Abel Turner.
4. Abel Craig, married Sarah J. Regester.
5. Eunice Craig, married John G. Barr.

6. Mary Craig.
   7. Hannah Craig.
   8. Ellenor Craig, married Silas Horner.
   9. Margaret Craig, married George Stilwell.
   10. Elizabeth Craig.
   11. Sophrona Craig, married William Taylor.
   12. Jesse Craig.
   13. Thomas Craig, married Leah Horn.
   3. Lena Cary, married John Muckle.
4. David Cary, son of Abel and Elizabeth Cary; no record.
5. Lewis Cary, son of Abel and Elizabeth Cary; no record.
6. Jerusha Cary, married Stephen Fulton; she died in 1847, and her husband in 1858.
7. Phoebe Cary, married James Daugherty.

THE CLAYTON FAMILY

Noah Clayton, founder of the Greene County branch of the Clayton Family, was one of five brothers who fought in the War of the Revolution, the others being Elisha and Elijah, (twins), Job Clayton, and an older brother. Noah Clayton, in his pension application, made on September 10, 1832, from Morgan Township, Greene County, Pennsylvania, states that both he and his brother, Elijah Clayton, were in the Battle of Monmouth, and that he was taken prisoner there and remained in the Sugar House Prison in New York, for two years before making his escape. This was on June 28, 1778, the record being found in Pension File No. R 2030, Washington, D. C.

Noah Clayton states that he was born January 21, 1762, in Freehold Township, Monmouth County, New Jersey, but that about 1781, he went to Hampshire County, Virginia, where, on March 21, 1789, he married at Romney, in the same county, Elizabeth Fisher, a native of Hampshire County. He further states that he removed to Morgan Township, Greene County, Pennsylvania, about 1808, and resided there since that date. Records show that he died there on June 14, 1835. His wife, whose birth date is not known, died there on October 23, 1838, according to an affidavit filed by her daughter, Mary Rogers, March 22, 1854, for the purpose of getting pension due her mother at the time of her death. From this affidavit of Mary (Clayton) Rogers, we learn the names and ages of "the now living and surviving children of Elizabeth and Noah Clayton," they being, Mary, aged 64 years and one month; Euphena, aged 62; Delia, (Delilah), aged 59; Martha, aged 57; Charlotte, aged 55, and Susannah, who died in 1802. Cemetery records at Lippencott, Pennsylvania, disclose that a brother, William Clayton, died February 1, 1850, aged 53 years, one month, and one day.

On October 11, 1852, Phillip Rogers went into Greene County, Pennsylvania, Court with a petition to act as administrator of the estate of Elizabeth Clayton (spelled Claton) and presented a renunciation of their rights by the living heirs of Noah and Elizabeth (Fisher) Clayton. This is to be found in File number 1485, and is signed by Delilah Clayton, Charlotte Evans, Uphany Clayton, Susannah Clayton, Martha Richardson, Elizabeth West, and Mary Rogers.

The son, William Clayton, had died prior to this date, and it would appear that the daughter, Elizabeth West, must have died between this date and the date of Mary Rogers' affidavit to the pension board. There is no estate record for Noah Clayton on file in Greene County, Pennsylvania, and no evidence that there were more than these eight children in the family.

Family of William and Sarah (Mickens) Clayton

William Clayton, son of Noah and Elizabeth (Fisher) Clayton, was born December 30, 1796, probably in Hampshire County, Virginia. He died in Greene County, Pennsylvania, on February 1, 1850 (1851). His tombstone record as shown in the church cemetery at Lippencott, gives 1850 as date of death, while Bates' History of Greene County, gives the 1851 date. Both agree on the date of his wife's death. William Clayton was married about 1825, to Sarah Mickens, who was born January 15, 1798, and died October 12, 1869. They were the parents and seven sons and three daughters.

Children

1. John Clayton, born June 27, 1826, in Morgan Township, Greene County, Pennsylvania. He died there June 23, 1888. He married, January 20, 1853, Elizabeth Montgomery, born October 14, 1833; daughter of Hugh and Priscillia (Hoge) Montgomery.
2. Noah Clayton, born in Morgan Township, Greene County, Pennsylvnia. He married Ruth Rigger.
3. Samuel Clayton, born in Morgan Township, Greene County, Pennsylvania. He married Ellen Montgomery, daughter of Hugh and Priscilla (Hoge) Montgomery.
4. David Clayton, born in Morgan Township, Greene County, Pennsylvania, on October 29, 1829, died March 13, 1907. He married, March 7, 1855, Permelia Tapton, born March 14, 1838, died on October 13, 1882. David Clayton married (2) Anna Acklin, who died April 24, 1924. Their son, Samuel Clayton of Waynesburg, Penna., had Bible and supplied records.
5. Abijah Clayton, born in Morgan Township, Greene County, Pennsylvania. He married Betty Crayne, daughter of Daniel and Hannah (Clawson) Crayne, born .... They had no children.
6. Isaac Clayton, born in Morgan Township, Greene County, Pennsylvania. He never married.
7. Joab Clayton, born in Morgan Township, Greene County, Pennsylvania. He married Jane Golden.
8. Nancy Clayton, born in Morgan Township, Greene County, Pennsylvania. Never married.
9. Charlotte Clayton, born in Greene County, Pennsylvania. Never married.
10. Martha Clayton, born in Morgan Township, Greene County, Pennsylvania. Never married.

LEWIS MARTIN

Lewis Martin was a Revolutionary pensioner living in Center Township, Greene County, in 1840, when his age is given as 79 years. He too was from Middlesex County, New Jersey, where he served in the militia before coming to Morgan Township, Washington County, where he served under Captain Benjamin Stites. He is listed in the 1785 tax lists as a single freeman. O. C. Docket 3. pp. 292 of September 1852, indicates he died in Center Township, leaving a wife, whose name was Elizabeth .... His old age had been spent with his son, William L. Martin. Lewis Martin was in John Miller's Company on the Crawford Expedition. (Penna. Arch. Series VI. Vol. 2, pp. 395.)

Children of Lewis and Elizabeth Martin

1. Daniel Martin.

AND ITS PIONEER FAMILIES

2. Hannah Martin, wife of Jeptha Cummins.

Children

1. John Cummins.
2. William Cummins.
3. Andrew Cummins.
4. Catherine Cummins.
5. Sarah Cummins.
6. Mariah Cummins.
7. Nancy Cummins.

Thomas Martin m. Ellen Moore sister of Martha Moor and went to Kansas. David Martin m. _____ Bottomfield and went to Missouri.

Howard W. Martin

3. James Martin.
4. Bonham Martin.
5. John Martin.
6. Rachel Martin, wife of Martin Cornwell.
7. Elizabeth Martin, wife of Pruden Wilson.
8. Mary Martin, wife of Ebeneezer Hartley.
9. William L. Martin.

JAMES MARTIN FAMILY

Zepheniah Martin brought his family, including several grown sons, from Middlesex County, New Jersey, to settle, about 1784 on the Dividing Ridge between what is now Washington and Greene Counties. Among these sons was James Martin, who had served in the New Jersey Militia, and who was already married to Anna McMyrtre. One James Martin seems to have bought out the warrant rights of Phineas McCray, and secured a patent to the land on February 22, 1791. The land joined that of John Fulton, and was one farm removed from Thomas Moore. When James Martin's first wife died about 1800, he married Katherine Moore, daughter of Thomas and Eunice Moore. She was much his junior and outlived him by many years, dying on December 27, 1856, at the age of 77 years and 21 days. She is buried at Mt. Zion Cemetery. James Martin died on September 18, 1827.

Children of James and Anna (McMyrtre) Martin

1. Zepheniah Martin, who married Belle Hood.
2. Thomas Martin, born 1796, died September 1851; married, about 1821, Mary Bradbury. Ancestors of Senator Edward Martin.

Children of Thomas and Mary (Bradbury) Martin

1. John M. Martin, born August 12, 1823, died August 1, 1903; married, January 18, 1848, Martha Moor, born October 21, 1819, died September 18, 1880. They were the grandparents of Senator Martin and are buried in the Martin Vault in Green Mount Cemetery at Waynesburg. Martha Moor was the daughter of Joseph Moor, born March 23, 1775, died March 13, 1855, and his wife, Mary (Shackleton) Moor, born March 20, 1789, died January 18, 1854. They too are buried in the Martin Vault. He married (2) Isabella (Barr) Montgomery.
2. Thomas Martin, Jr., went to Missouri.
3. David Martin, went to Kansas.

3. Joseph Martin, born March 15, 1790, died December 25, 1850; married (1) Elizabeth Haiden (or Heaton) daughter of Miles and Margaret Haiden. She died October 15, 1819, aged 27 years, and is buried in the Lutheran Cemetery at Marianna. Joseph Martin then married Nancy Iams, daughter of John and Elizabeth (Hampson) Iams. Nancy (Iams) Martin died January 21, 1871, aged 84 years and 11 days. They were married on December 27, 1821.

Children of Joseph and Nancy (Iams) Martin
1. Morgan Martin, born October 19, 1823; married Anna Rees.
2. Elizabeth Martin, born November 24, 1825.
3. John Martin, born February 8, 1828.
4. Joseph Martin, born April 2, 1831.
5. Anna Martin, born July 23, 1833.
6. Sarah Martin, born February 1, 1836.

4. Elizabeth Martin, daughter of James and Anna (McMyrtre) Martin, died 1844. She was married in 1822 to Stephen Jewell.
5. Sarah Martin, married David Bowman.
6. Jane Martin, born 1791, died June 13, 1863, daughter of James and Anna (McMyrtre) Martin; married, about 1817, Joseph Dunn, son of Isaac and Elizabeth (Haines) Dunn. He was born in 1789, and died December 15, 1865.

Children of Joseph and Jane (Martin) Dunn
1. Washington Dunn, died March 6, 1888, aged 69 years, 11 months, 12 days; married Sarah Craig, who died March 7, 1882, in her 66th year. Buried at Mt. Zion.
2. James M. Dunn, married Dorcas Ross.
3. Morgan L. Dunn, married three times.
4. William Dunn, married Florence Swartz.
5. Joseph Dunn, married Elizabeth Montgomery.
6. John Dunn, never married.
7. Anna Dunn, never married.

THOMAS MOORE FAMILY

Thomas Moore settled at the dividing ridge in Morgan Township at the headwaters of Castile Run, where on February 10, 1794, he had warranted to him a tract of land under the title of "Dartmouth." He was living there in 1790, at the head of an adult household. He died in Morgan Township about 1813, and his will was

probated December 11, 1813. His wife was Eunice .... It is quite possible that Eunice was the second wife of Thomas Moore.

Children of Thomas and Eunice Moore
1. John Moore, may have been the John Moore of Captain Andrew Ferley's Company, and from Orphan Court records appears to have been a soldier of the War of 1812, dying while in that service, as his widow, Mary Moore, asked for guardians for two minor daughters, Betsy and Mary Moore, noting that her husband was killed in the late war. That was in 1816, and in 1820, George Hoge gave a receipt in the Estate of Thomas Moore, showing he was inter-married with Sarah Moore, a granddaughter of Thomas Moore through his son, John. John Moore is also shown to have left sons Daniel and Thomas Moore.
2. Mehitable Moore, daughter of Thomas and Eunice Moore, married Benjamin Berry.
3. Jonathan Moore, son of Thomas and Eunice Moore.
4. Hannah Moore, daughter of Thomas and Eunice Moore, married William Berry.
5. Jonas Moore, son of Thomas and Eunice Moore.
6. Catherine Moore, second wife of James Martin; see Martin Records.
7. Patience Moore, daughter of Thomas and Eunice Moore, born 1782, died July 17, 1873, aged 91 years, 4 months, 19 days; buried at Mt. Zion. She was the wife of Moses Jewell.

8. Daniel Moore, son of Thomas and Eunice Moore.
9. Thomas Moore, Jr., son of Thomas and Eunice Moore.
10. Josiah Moore, son of Thomas and Eunice Moore. (May have been the Joseph Moore that married Mary Shackleton.)
11. William Moore, son of Thomas and Eunice Moore.

THOMAS WEAKLEY FAMILY

Thomas Weakley was a member of Captain Benjamin Stites' Company, First Battalion, Washington County, Pennsylvania, Militia, which was recruited in Morgan Township, in the arraignment for 1782. He had patented a tract of land on June 26, 1794, in the vicinity of Zion Church at the headwaters of a branch of Ruffs Creek. This tract had been warranted to Jacob Doty two years previously. The Census for 1790, shows Thomas Weakley at the head of a family of one adult male, four males under 16, and one female. Thomas Weakley left Greene County with the Archers, Wells, and Ankrom Families, and removed to Tyler County, West Virginia, where he died leaving a will, which is recorded in Will Book 1-A. pp. 272. This will, made December 17, 1833, mentions his wife, Mary ...., and the following children:

1. Thomas Weakley, Jr.
2. Otto Weakley.
3. Levi Weakley.
4. James Weakley.
5. Mary Weakley.
6. Charlotte Weakley.
7. Michal Weakley.

There may have been others buried in the Weakley Cemetery near Zion Church.

MUDDY CREEK

Nothing is quite so definite as deeds to establish prior ownership to land, and it is unfortunate that so far no deeds have been uncovered to show who the first owners of the land at the Mouth of Muddy Creek were. We have already seen that a deed of 1757, referred to the land immediately to the North of Muddy Creek and extended to "near the Mouth" of that stream. Perhaps future discoveries will show the owners of the land adjoining John Owen's tract, which he sold to Abraham Teagarden. Journals and family accounts are another source that sometimes definitely recite personal ownership, but these too are lacking about Muddy Creek. It remains then to look into possible first ownership by the placement of certain settlers at a given place at a certain date, and the acceptance of certain family traditions, which from the evidence available, seem to be true.

The first official mention of persons that could have been on the ground, and that later definitely settled at this place, is the muster roll of Captain Evan Shelby to be found in the Colonel Henry Boquet Papers. (Mss. 21644 Fol. 476, A. D. S., dated July 15, to November 1, 1759, pp. 183). In this reference are found the names of Oliver Crawford, Alexander Crawford, and Thomas Crago, all of whom settled at the Mouth of Muddy Creek, where according to Crumrine, Oliver Crawford was running a ferry in 1770, the same time that Thomas Crago was living in a lean-to hut with his small sons, Thomas and James, and shortly before Crago was killed by the Indians. As Evan Shelby's Company was in this section, and members of his family later settled here, it is to be supposed that they learned of this land at the Monongahela at that time, and may have selected sites during that period.

It is further possible that if positive identification of the John Kennedy, land jobber from the Conochacheague, could be developed, wherein it would be shown he was the John Kennedy taken prisoner at Gist's in 1752, then we would know that it was he that sold much of the land to the South of Muddy Creek and bounded by Little Whiteley on the South, to his neighbors of Cumberland County, Pennsylvania.

One deed of record from Josias Crawford to Willam McCreary, shows that Crawford had made an improvement on the upper part of South Muddy Creek in the Summer of 1766, which of itself suggests that the lower parts were taken up before that date. (Washington County Deed Book 1-A-pp. 195.) If there were other deeds of earlier date, they may have been lost in the burning of the Monongalia Court House at Morgantown.

It is necessary therefore, to turn to family traditions which seem to have a basis of fact, for possible information on the first owners of land at the Mouth of Muddy Creek, and none seem to be better authenticated than the one handed down from generation to generation by the Flenniken Family, and reported by Mr. Samuel Patterson Flenniken as he got it from the elder men of the family. After telling how the Flenniken brothers, James and John, (with possibly another brother) left their home on the Conochacheague, then in Cumberland County, Pennsylvania, and journeyed South to North Carolina in the early 1750s, with the migration of that period, the tradition states that, "John and James Flenniken rode horseback from their new home in the South, to the Monongahela River, where they arrived in the Spring of 1760, and made a crossing at what was later designated or called 'Wallace's Riffles'. They made a temporary camp at the Mouth of Muddy Creek. They began a day's scouting along the River, and at the mouth of a small run began putting their marks on trees and making 'turkey's nests', which consisted of large piles of stones with lengthy limbs of trees decorating the center of the stone piles. Here they went up the northwest side of Muddy Creek to the South Fork, then across to present Piercville, thence down Little Whiteley Creek to its mouth. This tract, about four miles square, contained approximately 10,000 acres, of which they later patented about 2000, giving the rest of it to any who would settle near them."

Another letter from Samuel Patterson Flenniken of Uniontown, Pennsylvania, carried the tradition further by stating that, "John Flenniken did not return to North Carolina, but went back to Conochacheague, where his son, Elias, purchased a farm on Kinnykinnick Creek. The Flenniken Brothers filed their claim with the Pennsylvania Authorities, who required that claimants must occupy a part of their claims for certain periods each year, as a result of which some members of the family returned to Muddy Creek each year until legal title was granted for the vast estate in 1768. (?) On the first trip in 1761, Elias Flenniken, his cousin, James, John Armstrong, and Zebulon Hollingsworth, made the journey over the mountains, and in 1763, James Flenniken came to make it a permanent home."

This tradition, retold again after almost two hundred years have passed since it first happened, may have a few detectable errors, but it smacks of the truth in all its points. A law suit fought out in local courts with James Hughes over the original site bears it out to some extent, and the location of the Flenniken patents is in the land chosen by the first members of the family that made the original preliminary survey. The location of the John Armstrong and Zebulon Hollingsworth tracts were within the boundaries of the Flenniken claim of 1760. It further bears out our contention that the land at the mouth of Muddy Creek was well taken up prior to the improvement of Josias Crawford in 1766, while the land sold by John Kennedy, the land jobber of the Conochacheague lay outside the limits of the Flenniken claim, or at least outside the land actually granted by the Commonwealth to them. As a side light to this tradition, the Flennikens tell that there was a group of Indians, who had their camp at the mouth of Muddy Creek, visible for many years afterwards, and where numerous artifacts have been taken up. These Indians had among them some white traders, who with the Indians, bargained and bartered this land, and with whom the Flennikens no doubt had to deal. This seems in keeping with the known facts of that period and further strengthens the Flenniken story. It is known that Bald Eagle, the Indian Chief murdered by the whites, had his camp somewhere in the vicinity, and that White Eagle, who raised a brother of Captain William Crawford, made trips to this part of the Monongahela River. Later we shall take up the claiming of land at the Mouth of the Whiteley Creeks about 1757, and have already shown how the Mouth of Enoch's Run and Tenmile were claimed by that date, thus it seems this tradition of the Flennikens at the Mouth of Muddy Creek fills in a portion of the previously unwritten history of the Tenmile Country.

The Muddy Creek Section was well known and well filled up before the Revolution, and the fact that it was a hot bed of Tories during the Revolution, indicates that the early settlers had by that period, reached a comfortable stage of development, and did not seek a change. On the other hand it was also a source of patriotism that furnished many of the troops for both the local militia and the armies in the East. Reports of the commanding officers at Fort Pitt, show it was one of the major sources of supplies for the troops at that post, and before the end of the war, was building boats for military and private expeditions moving to the Western country. Mills had sprung up along its banks and were making flour, sawing timbers, and doing much of the mechanical work for the pioneers. It became a religious center for the Methodist, Presbyterian, and Episcopal Churches, with Reverend Robert Ayers, first a Methodist and later an Episcopalian minister, mentioning it in his journal as having preached there in 1786, and the Reverend John McMillan ten years' previously having taken the Presbyterian faith to the people. It was, and still is, a most favored spot in the whole Tenmile Country.

THE MUDDY CREEK LEDGER

Go to the Library of Congress at Washington, D. C., or to the Pennsylvania Historical Museum at Harrisburg sometime, and ask if they have anything of historical interest on Greene County. Chances are they will bring out photostatic copies of the Muddy Creek Ledger. Unfortunately it is the second book of a series of ledgers, beginning with page 449, with the first entry on May 25, 1793. The first volume has been lost, and this now important reference book would also have been destroyed had not the writer uncovered it when it was being taken to the city dump for destruction.

The Muddy Creek Ledger was kept by a store keeper at or near Carmichaels, in the year 1793 to 1796. It is not just clear who this storekeeper may have been, though the entries point to its having been kept by the Seaton Family, and definitely at one time by William Seaton. The writing is remarkable for the period and each entry is clear and legible. Entries are in Pounds, Shillings, and Pence, with an occasional reference to the newly issued dollars. The exchange rate at the time was three of the new dollars for one Pound, two Shillings, and six Pence. The list of names read like a census of the section for those years, and furnishes a day to day picture of the life they lived. Trade appears to have been mostly by barter, with periodical settlements made by giving a personal note or supplying the store with farm goods. A favorite medium in exchange seems to have been whiskey at the prevailing price of three shillings per gallon.

Merchandise in trade was of a wide variety and must have required a large warehouse in which to store it. Brought over the mountains from Philadelphia with a freight rate of thirty five shillings per hundred weight, it is not surprising that shipments were infrequent. One such shipment is entered in the ledger on October 2, 1793, showing the payment of 51 Pounds, six Shillings and five Pence, to John Washabaugh, per order of Charles Anderson, for the carriage of 2,932 pounds of such goods. Of this shipment, Evans and Hunt had supplied the greater portion to the extent of more than four hundred Pounds value. William Poyntell had supplied stationery to the extent of more than 18 Pounds value. Charles and David Evans had furnished groceries to the extent of 65 Pounds value. Phillip Somerkamp, a Philadelphia Druggist, had supplied medicines and drugs to the extent of another 65 Pounds more. The whole value of the shipment amounted to 564 Pounds, 12 Shillings, and 10 Pence.

On November 5 of the same year, Turnbull and Marmie sent a shipment of Dry Goods, stationery, gunpowder, spices, drugs, and Indigo, amounting to 236 pounds of weight and valued at more than a hundred Pounds of currency. A shipment of 912 pounds of goods brought from Philadelphia, first to Shippensburg, and then to Muddy Creek on July 2, 1795, shows that Isaac Jenkinson was the driver, who got a part of his pay at Shippensburg.

The money to pay for these goods appears to have been made by the shipment of flour to New Orleans, and two such shipments, called "Adventures" are mentioned in the ledger. Colonel Ephraim Blaine seems to have been a partner in these "Adventures". The flour was ground at both John Antill's Mill and Francis Seaton's Mill on Muddy Creek. It was floated down to Pittsburgh, where it was inspected and then to New Orleans, where it had to run the gauntlet of the Spanish Customs officers. The first of these "Adventures" took place in 1791, before this Muddy Creek Ledger was started, but it is noted in the entries. The second "Adventure" is given in full and will be the subject of another article. It took place in the Summer of 1793.

One can almost imagine themselves sitting about the fire on a typical day, when Melchoir Baker brings in one of his 'neat rifle guns" for sale to William Seaton. Samuel Hyde has been loitering outside, or fixing a counter for his brother-in-law Seaton, and just needs such a gun. A deal is made and Samuel Hyde gets the gun for five Pounds, a bit under the usual price. This is on March 12, 1794, and Samuel Hyde is now well armed, for on November 5, of the previous year, he bought a pair of pocket pistols for three Guineas. Seaton does quite a business with Melchoir Baker, whose rifles are becoming famous and which is going to lead to a contract with the United States Government for 12,000 stands of arms in the War of 1812. Just a few weeks ago he had delivered, on February 5, eight new rifles and a smooth gun, along with some guns he had restocked.

While this deal had been going on Squire Thomas Sedgewick had found a pair of glasses that suited his failing eyes, and seeing two rifles he needed, had made a purchase. Samuel Moore, who had married one of John Swan's daughters, comes in for the money due him for a five day trip to Pittsburgh by boat, but he seems to have forgotten the three dollars and a half he borrowed in Pittsburgh, so he owes a Shilling and three Pence to Seaton. Not much else is doing this day, so it is spent auditing the account of Colonel Ephraim Blaine. This item of October 2, 1793, recalls the busy day of that date. First off that day in comes the wife of Stephen Davis with 76 pounds of cheese and a stomach ache: In exchange we gave her a bottle of Essinie for her stomach, some yards of calico and lawn for a dress, and yards of ribbon for trimmings, a neat profit for the store. But along comes Thomas Sedgewick with the money Mr. Ryerson subscribed for the Church, and buys some soap and a gimlet. Abraham Armstrong comes in looking rather shabby and it don't take long to sell him a stick of Mohair, some black velvet and 15 coat buttons. The rest of this day was spent checking up on that last "Adventure" to New Orleans. Seeing Negro Patrick passing outside, recalls that on last November 11, we subscribed seven Shillings and six Pence toward his liberation, maybe it had better be paid now. Better also pay that subscription for Rev. Robert Ayers, promised by George Seaton and me, on the 16th of last November. Can do it if Colonel Blaine brings in the money for the two boats of corn and oats left at Pittsburgh with Messrs. Wilkins the 18th of that month. Could also use that rent from Captain Lang for storage of 17 barrells of flour.

Folks were not too healthy the December of 1793, for James Carmichaels bought some asafoeteda, perhaps for that little bag he wears around his throat. We used some Jesuit's bark. Daniel Anderson wore his clothes too long and bought a box of blue ointment for his fleas. Phillip Ketchum bought a box of sugar plums for worms. Ellis Thomas sent his wife, the former Phoebe Vanmeter, to the store for a pound of copperas and another pound of alum, and while she was there she got her coffee, chocolate, and six darning needles. James Hughes was sick in bed and sent Debby Danley for an Indian Blanket. Thomas Crago traded a coon skin and added his note for a bill of goods that included Terwilligers Balsam and British oil.

The store was closed on Christmas Day, but the owner needed two boxes of Blue ointment and a cake of camphor on the next day after. Nathaniel Irwin was in on the the 28th for a bottle of Godfrey's Cordial, and took with him six grains of Tarter metic. Charles Andersons must have had an addition in his family for his son, James, came in for four yards of diaper cloth. A few days after the new year: Abraham McDowell got a spelling book and three yards of nonsopretty, and a quarter yard of swanskin, and John Brookover brought in some feathers which he traded for six yards of linen. Amos Anderson's note paid for a pair of garters, a pair of stockings, a penknife, some indigo and gun powder. The stockings were described as women's black worsted. They may have looked well with the silver shoe buckles that went along with the sale. At the same time Robert Cree traded six and a half bushels of corn for more than a yard of half thicks. Rev. Robert Davis came in on January 20, 1794, and bought all the makings for a black velvet suit. There is no record to show he ever paid for it, and no note was given.

Rev. Robert Davis was an Episcopalian Minister. He was an

Irishman by birth and originally a Methodist by profession. An Episcopal Church had been established at Brownsville in 1785, and Rev. Davis, who had been ordained by Bishop White, had become its pastor in 1795. Ellis says his life and conduct were so inconsistent with his words and teachings that religion fell into reproach and the principles of the church into abandonment. His ministry was far from being useful to his people and it fell into disrepute. He was followed at Brownsville, and also at Muddy Creek, as shown by the Ledger, by Rev. Robert Ayers, also ordained by Bishop White. Ellis says this next one was more unworthy than his predecessor, and that his principles were so blameworthy that people would not attend on his ministry. This was the beginning of the Episcopal Church mentioned by Evans in his records of Charles Swan, one of the prime movers to secure a church at Carmichaels.

The other minister mentioned in the Muddy Creek Ledger is the Rev. John Corbly, who on alternate Sundays, preached at the Goshen Baptist Church erected at Jacob Vanmeter's place near Baily's School House.

We note that Samuel Hathaway, who was originally in partnership with Richard Jackson in their mill at Fort Jackson, frequently sent to the Muddy Creek store for merchandise. James Hook or Barnet Rinehart acted as errand boys and sometimes brought notes that had been accepted at Hathaway's mill. The Samuel Jackson mentioned in the Ledger, lived near Carmichaels, and as far as we have been able to discover, was in no way connected with Richard Jackson, the owner of the fort which bore his name.

John Clark must have looked pretty well outfitted in his blue persian coating and ribbons, for which he exchanged 253 pounds of beef. Someone died about January 23, 1794, when the store paid James McClelland one Pound for making a coffin. On the 27th of the same month, Colonel William Crawford donated two Pounds for the building of the new church. This may have been the first New Providence or Glades Church, where the colonel is buried. On the same date Charity Noland was outfitted with a scarlet cloke, black silk handkerchief, and a pair of white mitts per the order of Henry O'Niel. She must have made a pretty bride, for Henry's 30 gallons of Cyder paid for it.

On February 7, 1794, the store keeper made a further investment which he charged to Lotts and Buildings, this time purchasing from John Derumple a house and lot for 45 Pounds. The next day he paid Daniel Anderson 35 Pounds for work done by Daniel and his father on the new Church. On the 20th of February, Samuel Hathaway came down from Fort Jackson and bought a wool hat for John Piatt. Colonel William Crawford went fishing on February 26, and he had to have a pike line and a quart of whiskey to be sure it was a successful trip. The whiskey stock was soon replaced for by trading 100 bushels of corn and 81 bushels of rye on January 1, the storekeeper got 181 gallons of whiskey. This must have been a busy day for the distillers for James Hannah brought in 15½ gallons that was under proof, and Thomas Sedgewick traded out 33 gallons of good stuff the same day. William Hiller helped in the unloading, and during the rest of the day by the aid of Phillip Ketchum, got a load of wood and built a hog pen. In his spare time he spent part of it in weaving a fleece.

It took lots of liquor to build boats, and it was hardly used for christening, for on March 17, John Armstrong got 20 quarts of Whiskey and David Armstrong got a like amount for the job on hand. Perhaps it helped out on St. Patrick's Day. Abner Mundle was charged for a bottle of wine, and the bottle was charged extra.

Edward Thomas brought in 25 pounds of sugar to pay for a barrell of flour lent him. Captain William Harrod having lost his wife the Fall before, came in for a pair of spectacles, but records show that they did him little good. Even preachers got fleas in those days, for Preacher Ephraim Chambers had to have blue ointment the day he came in for double milled drab cloth for a new suit. Captain Samuel Swindler was not a hard man to please for there is an entry for a large rose blanket with a hole in it.

Doctors were slow in collecting their bills in those days, or patients were slow in paying, for Dr. Jacob Jennings came in on April 12, 1794, to buy a few items, two sticks of mohair, a skaine of black silk, a quart of brandy, some spotted calico, a keg of nails, and some writing paper, which balanced an account with the notation "the above has lain on a memo until this time, in expectation of the doctor bringing in his bill for settlement". The doctor must have met David Armstrong with a dose of itch and prescribed sulphur and lard, for that is what was bought in the next entry, and Thomas Crawford got through with two boxes of Anderson's Pills. Captain John Holton got a pound of saltpeter and two ounces of asafetida, while Jeremiah Davidson took his hartshorn and turpentine home to make his own linement.

Springtime brought on building, for on April 25, Azaraiah Davis bought two latches with brass knobs, two thumb latches, and a nail apron. Jeremiah Davidson settled for a dozen wood screws. Thomas Sedgewick got 24 panes of glass. Benjamin Hixon delivered an "Orleans" boat, which D. and J. Morford loaded on May 3. The boat was loaded with 470 bushels of oats, and 345 bushels of corn and delivered to Major James Craig at Pittsburgh. From the cash received the store keeper bought himself an eight day clock from James Henry, and still had a note with which to pay Turnbull and Marmie. A copy of Aesop's Fables came home with the boat, perhaps a gift to the family. It is shown that it took Samuel Swindler from March 15 until May 8 to build just such a boat, and that it took 52 quarts of whiskey to make it waterproof (?), but the whiskey was not hard to get since Judge Jacob Cline had just delivered a barrell of 33 gallons. Swindler liked his with sugar in it and had charged to him a pound of it.

Samuel Hitt, another preacher, came around on May 9 and bought on credit some black velvet, for which William Seaton went bail. In the same charge is one for licorice ball, which caught the preacher's fancy. Benjamin Liming got 17 Shillings and four Pence for taking the mare to Pittsburgh on May 10, This included expenses on the road. But Thomas Kent came down from Fort Jackson on May 16, and bought a big order that more than paid the bill. Samuel Swindler's heavy drinking after building the boat, brought on an attack of sickness and on May 22, he needed a dose of rhubarb and eight grains of tarter emetic. We hope he did not take it all at once as the dose of this drug is one-twentieth of a grain.

The only newspaper printed at that time was the Pittsburgh Gazette, and we note that on May 28, 1794, a payment was made to Isaac Pearce for postage for one year's delivery of the newspaper. Again on July 21, 1795, a payment for the same purpose was made to David Jacobs, at which time two dollars was sent to Mr. Scull, the printer.

George James and William Heller must have been some kind

of tailors for there is an entry that shows the former was paid for making a jacket and a pair of overalls, while the latter received pay for making a coat. John Wilson was paid for a clock case. James was also to make a jacket as part payment for a rifle sold him. William Mustard repaired shoes, and was a cabinet maker, being paid for making a bedstead. Mathew Miller and Nathaniel made and repaired shoes.

Someone died at Andrew McClellands about August 8, 1794, when there is an entry for eight pairs of mens black gloves, six pairs of the same for women, some yards of dark cloth, more of crape, seven black gauze kerchiefs, two black silk kerchiefs, numerous black coat and jacket buttons, some black lace and ribbon. The purchase was made by Polly and Frank McClelland. The next day James Cummings came in for 11¼ yards of bleached linen, plus seven yards of the same but of an inferior quality, plus another three yards of the same, all of which was delivered to Abraham Armstrong. The families of James, William, and Andrew McClelland, Jr., went in mourning on the 26th of the same month.

It was possible in those days to throw a man into jail for debt, but the creditor had to pay the debtors board while there. This store seems to have learned that a poor compromise was better than a good law suit, for when John Alley was hauled before Samuel Hyde by Constable James Hughes, Alley was permitted to settle for a portion paid in cash. Another entry shows that Colonel John Heaton made collections from Syrenus Jennings, Jacob Rush, John Baker, Caleb Baldwin, and Henry Kauffman.

The store made errors too, just as they do today, as witness an entry of September 30, 1794. Isaac Israel was billed for goods (four yards of diaper cloth) delivered to James Anderson, and charged by mistake to his father, Charles Anderson, instead of his father-in-law. In other words, Priscilla Israel had married James Anderson, destined to be the ancestors of our good friend, Austin L. Moredock.

When Doctor Charles Wheeler came up from Brownsville, he must have found most of the Seaton Family ailing as he purged James Carmichaels, husband of Betty Seaton, he left a bottle of Stomach Mixture for William Seaton, and gave a number of Cephalic Pills to James Seaton. For these medicines, and the cost of the trip, he charged over seven Pounds. But the wily store keeper took the good doctor aside and talked him into swapping saddles, whereby he ended up by settling for a little more than a Pound. Doctors haven't changed much since then.

William Seaton definitely became sole owner of the establishment by a bill of sale at selling prices on November 12, 1794. The price was five Pence over 908 Pounds. We believe he continued in business until his death and that his son, James Seaton, followed afterward in the same business, being classified as a retail merchant as late as 1839. William Seaton immediately jumped on his brother-in-law, James Carmichaels, from whom he collected money for an old saddle and a silver watch. Then made Carmichaels fork over for a note he had assumed of Samuel Barnhill, Sr., now of Kentucky. The note had been given in 1787, and had been in the hands of Carmichaels since that time. Perhaps Barnhill objected paying because the debt had been made as a favor to Joseph Rankin. Three rifle guns settled the debt. Daniel

Moredock had to pay up too for a debt entered on Page 15 of book one. Jehu Conwell was compelled to pay a debt made for John Stokeley. Phillip Ketchum had to make good for two barrells of flour lent him in 1791, and another in 1792, as well as for a barrell lent Solomon Hoge, for which Ketchum stood security. Alexious Bailey paid for 10 bushells of corn lent him in 1792, and Samuel Jackson became securety for a bill of his son-in-law, Hamilton Cree. Zachary Vansickles settled his debt of two barrells of flour by part cash and a rifle gun. James Seaton was called on for what he owed for a number of hinges and bolts and 104 panes of glass, he had gotten in 1792, and he settled by delivering seasoned pine boards. In fact a general housecleaning took place.

With the proceeds of these collections, William Seaton leased two lots from Oliver Crawford, probably at the ferry at the mouth of Muddy Creek, for which he agreed to pay a fixed quit rent. There was cash on hand no v as men like Captain Anthony Vansickles, James Hughes and others had paid up in coin. Business was running along smoothly with John Moore, the school master from Big Whiteley, and others making purchases. Abraham McDowell was sent out to mow and grub the new lots, and a quart of bounce was added to the pay. A spinning wheel was made for the family by Abner Mundle. And John Antill, with Francis Seaton, continued to turn the grain into flour at their mills. Business had not been too good for John Antill, so when his rent of 50 Pounds came due on April 1, 1795, for the flour mill on Muddy Creek, it was cut to 40 Pounds.

In March 1795, the new owner was called to Philadelphia to serve on the Federal Jury that was trying the case of John Corbly and Thomas Sedgewick for their participation in the Whiskey Rebellion, and it proved more expensive than he had expected. He had to borrow money from Richard Stevens, but on June 1, he received a payment of 46 dollars from the United States Marshall of Philadelphia. This just about covered half of the expense of the journey.

When he got back from Philadelphia he began his plantation house on Muddy Creek, supplying Mr. Williams with two and one-half gallons of whiskey for the log rolling. Anthony Vansickles was engaged to build the stone foundation and Alexander Miller to tend him. Feeling that he was about to become a country gentleman, William Seaton bought himself a horseman's sword on April 17, 1795.

The majority of the final entries in the Muddy Creek Ledger are for purchases of wine, whiskey, and bounce, and one is led to believe that the business had turned to those staples. The final entry, made on February 8, 1796, is the payment of cash by James Blaine for his subscription toward the liberation of the slave Negro, Moses.

ADVENTURES TO NEW ORLEANS

This is a fitting title to a series of accounts in the Muddy Creek Ledger, and it refers to two flat boat trips down the rivers to New Orleans with flour from the mills of John Antill and Francis Seaton on Muddy Creek. The first of these had been undertaken in 1792, and only the results are given in this Ledger. The Second Adventure is covered in full, the entries being made in 1793 and 1794. The stories of these adventures is not told in so many words, but from the entries a good understanding of the hardships, risks, profits and costs can be learned. William Seaton was in charge of both ventures, which were undertaken in partnership with Colonel Ephraim Blaine.

The first of these Adventures took place during the four months of Summer of 1792, and William Seaton reports his personal expenses on the journey, during his stay in New Orleans and Philadelphia, and finally his trip home, as amounting to 33 Pounds and 15 Shillings. The net proceeds from the sale of 284 barrells of flour, which he delivered to William Stephens, was $1,065.70, or 399 Pounds, 14 Shillings, one Penny, which he received in due bills of exchange. The net amount received for the flour, some of which had been damaged by rats when the barrells were broken during the journey, had been $1,064.50, or at a rate of $6 per barrell for the good flour with a discount for the broken barrells. Expenses had included a commission paid to Thomas Speers, storage costs to Mr. Jacobs, labor in getting the flour on the boat, and Negro hire to unload it.

The boat for the first venture had been built on Muddy Creek by John Armstrong and his son David, at a cost of 25 Pounds and 10 Shillings, and was 51 feet long and 10 feet wide. Forty-two quarts of whiskey had also been used in the building of the boat. Perhaps it made it more bouyant. The money gained by the voyage was used to purchase merchandise in Philadelphia, as the return trip to Muddy Creek was made by boat to that place, rather than the long overland journey back home. It took four months to complete the round trip.

The second Adventure was made in a boat built by Daniel Anderson at a cost of 21 Pounds, and was only 42 feet long with a 10 foot beam. This trip was destined to meet with a number of misfortunes. The boat was grounded on an island near Wheeling. James Miller, one of the men of the crew, was paid extra for his exertions in helping get the boat off the sand bar. Henry Haines, Simeon Barnes, Gilbert Seaman, Andrew Crawford, and Samuel McClelland, were the other members of the crew. Some of the men developed "River Fever" before the Muskingum River was reached, and Dr. Dow was called at that place to attend the men. His medicine and a $10 fee failed to save the life of Samuel McClelland, who died at that place. It is ironic that in these days of free welfare for employes, that the estate of Samuel McClelland was charged with the doctor bill, for washing the body, and for the coffin in which he was buried. Four ells of linen used to wrap the body were included in the expense account. A Dr. Paulis was called in at another stage of the journey.

At the Falls of the Ohio (Louisville) a pilot was hired at the cost of one dollar, and with his directions, the boat safely made the descent. When the boat arrived at New Madrid on the Mississippi, the Spanish sentry there had to be given a tip, and when the trip came to its destination at New Orleans a whole series of charges had to met. The owner paid for a petition to discharge cargo, paid the custom officers for a trip on board, then to the custom office to pay duty. Here passports were secured, and arrangements made for Gilbert Seaman and Simeon Barnes to go on the Scow "Mr De del Carmen," which was leaving for Philadelphia. Twenty dollars paid for the passage of each man, while the others remained a bit longer in the city, getting an allowance for part of their board, and supplied with provisions. The owner stayed with Mr. Elliott, who supplied him with board and club, until time came for departure, when the owner and Andrew Crawford got passage on the Schooner

"Dairy Maid." In due time they made their way over the mountains to their Muddy Creek home, which they had left on April 18, 1793. They were gone four and a half months. Samuel McClelland's estate was credited with wages from April 28, until his death on June 23, so it is possible to see that the delay at the Muskingum added much time to the trip.

On the journey down, the men were fed on board, consuming two-fifths of a barrel of beef and five pounds of fish. A barrel of flour was used, part of which was taken ashore enroute so that it could be made into biscuits. But the venture, in spite of hardships, proved to be a profitable one. Two hundred and fifty-three barrels of flour had started down the Monongahela, one had been used for the men, and another had been lost when the boat had gone aground. The balance had sold for $1,878.50. After expenses and commissions had been deducted, there still remained $1,747.50, to be distributed among the partners. It is not surprising to note that a bit of the proceeds was spent for three cases of "liquers" and muscat to celebrate the safe arrival.

THE JAMES MURDOCK FAMILY

When James Murdock (Mordock, Moredock, Mordoc, etc.) came with his brother, Daniel, to settle in the Tenmile Country, he and his wife, Mary, chose two tracts that joined, altogether about six hundred acres lying on Muddy Creek to the west, and on one branch of Coal Run close to the site of the present high school at Carmichaels. They had settled here before 1772, as the tax list for Springhill Township of that year lists James Moredock and his brother, Daniel. After patenting her land in 1785, Mary Murdock sold her land, which she probably obtained from a man named Lyons, (called "Lyon's Bush") to the heirs of Thomas Foster, a half brother of John Swan, and uncle of Charles and Thomas Swan, who took up land opposite the Murdocks on the South side of Muddy Creek. (Washington Co., Pa. DB. 1-G-176.) James Murdock became a member of Goshen Baptist Church, which had a place of worship near the forks of Muddy Creek, and was an active communicant in that congregation. This makes it hard to understand why his name is not found on any military rolls during the Revolution, but as he lived in the section from which Captain Jesse Pigman's Militia Company was recruited, and since that muster roll is not available, it is very probable James Murdock was a member of that company. There is a slight possibility that he had been a Quaker prior to affiliating with the Goshen Baptist Church, for we find his children marrying into Quaker Families. The Muddy Creek Ledger discloses that James Murdock died about 1794, his wife, Mary, surviving him a few years and dying about 1801. Neither left wills, but from Orphans Court Docket 1. pp 6, we learn the names of their children, when the son, Daniel Murdock, settled his mother's estate. One source of record says that Mary was a relative of Jeremiah Glasgow, an early settler on Dunkard Creek.

Children of James and Mary Murdock

1. Ruth Murdock, married George Bowen.
2. Daniel Murdock, died about 1839. His will was made December 17, 1834, and probated on March 16, 1840. He married Elizabeth ....

    #### Children
    1. Samuel Murdock.
    2. Daniel Murdock. He married Prudence ....
    3. Mary Murdock, died in Wisconsin, October 14, 1863; married, 1818, William Swan, born April 4, 1794, died March

5, 1847. He is buried at Garards Fort.

Children
1. Thomas Swan, born October 10, 1820, died November 20, 1875; married Miranda Clawson.
2. Daniel Swan, born March 10, 1822, died March 2, 1844; married Emily Gabes.
3. Elizabeth Swan, born 1824, died October 1864; married John Armstrong.
4. Charles Swan, died in infancy.
5. Samuel Swan, born June 18, 1832, married Rebecca Denny.
6. John Swan, born September 1, 1834; married Priscilla Dunwoodie.
7. Milton B. Swan, born February 19, 1836, died December 19, 1846.
8. Richard Swan, born March 1, 1838, killed in action on January 2, 1863.
9. Isaac Swan, born 1840, died January 15, 1880/90, married Belle Merlotte.
10. Sarah Swan, born 1842; married N. W. Hartman.

4. Sarah Murdock, married .... Ross.
5. James Murdock, born April 2, 1794, died October 18, 1878; married Mary ...., born July 12, 1803, died .... Both are buried in the Pursley Baptist Church Cemetery.

Copy of James Moredock Bible on file as of 10-20-64. This branch spelled name Moredock until about 1880. There is another daughter of Daniel [2] married Wm. Anderson

6. Elizabeth Murdock, died before her father. Married .... McClain.

Children
1. Lydia McClain.
2. Daniel McClain.

7. Joanna Murdock, married .... Haver.

3. James Murdock. On February 28, 1805, he sold out his interest in the Murdock Estate to his brother, Daniel Murdock of Cumberland Township. He joined in the deed by his wife, Rachel, and they are described as being of Cincinnati, Ohio. (Greene County, Pa., Deed Book 2. pp. 162.)

4. John Murdock, born September 14, 1775, died July 31, 1867; married Margaret Hufty, born November 21, 1779, died April 13, 1842; daughter of Jacob and Sarah (Barclay) Hufty. John Murdock married (2) Sarah Bayard Gillett, a daughter of Samuel and Elizabeth (Wood) Bayard. She died February 20, 1855.

Children
1. Sarah Murdock, born January 11, 1801, died May 27, 1866; married (1) .... Worthington, who died March 29, 1855. She married (2) Thomas Hoskinson.
2. Mary Murdock, born February 17, 1803; married Abner Fordyce, born May 5, 1810.
3. Jane Murdock, born March 8, 1805, married Joseph Kirby. Went to Berwick, Illinois.
4. James B. Murdock, born August 7, 1807, died March 11, 1864; married, 1828, Hannah Temple, born May 9, 1807, died April 25, 1883.
5. Jacob Hufty Murdock, born December 7, 1809; married (1) Mary Gillett, who died January 27, 1852. He married (2) Elizabeth Moffett.

AND ITS PIONEER FAMILIES 507

    6. Eliza Murdock, born March 1, 1812.
    7. John Murdock, born February 10, 1814, married Sarah Gillett, born ....
    8. Daniel Murdock, born November 27, 1818, married Rhoda Clawson.
    9. William Hopkins Murdock, born December 20, 1820, died February 26, 1909; married Nancy Gillett, born June 16, 1822, died December 5, 1906.
5. Edward Murdock, died without issue.
6. William Murdock, no record.
7. Thomas Murdock, no record.
8. Charles Murdock, born 1789, died about 1866. (Greene County, Pa., WB. 4. pp. 150, probated March 21, 1866). He married Ann Campbell.

Children
    1. James Murdock, born August 3, 1811, died May 16, 1889; married, 1838, Amanda Baily, born February 17, 1816, died April 25, 1399; daughter of William and Zillah (Johnson) Baily.
    2. Alexander Murdock.
    3. Samuel Murdock.
    4. Elizabeth Murdock, married .... Hufty.
    5. Leggitt Murdock.
    6. John Murdock.
9. Mary Murdock.
10. Martha Murdock, married Benedict Horner, son of William Horner of Fayette County, Penna. Benedict Horner started for Ohio in 1844, and while in Pittsburgh got sick (cholera) and died. The estate of Benedict Mitchell Horner is in Greene County Will Book 2, pp. 197. His wife is said to have been buried in the Horner Cemetery near East Millsboro.

Children of Benedict Mitchell and Martha (Murdock) Horner
    1. Benedict Horner, born March 22, 1815, died August 22, 1869.
    2. Ruth Horner, born February 24, 1817, died April 22, 1905.
    3. William Horner.
    4.
    5.
    6.
    7. Mary Ann Horner, born May 12, 1828, died February 4, 1906; married, April 12, 1846, I. R. Jackson, born April 19, 1824, died October 16, 1899; son of Stephen and Hannah (Miller) Jackson.

JOSEPH GWYNNE

Family tradition says that Joseph Gwynne was born in London and came to America, soon making his way to the Tenmile Country, where he selected land. Deciding to return to London, he went town, and the campaigns of the next few years. It is not known if Joseph Gwynne was detached and sent with the part of the regiment that served at Saratoga under General Morgan, but as that contingent was officered and composed of the riflemen from the frontier, it is probable that he was along with them. The regiment returned to Fort Pitt in 1778, and did duty at that place for sometime. In all Joseph Gwynne served about three years before returning to his Muddy Creek farms. (Penna. Arch. Series V. Vol. 3. pp. 368.) Here he became a member of Captain William Crawford's Company of the Washington County, Pennsylvania Militia, and served many tours of duty. (Ibid Series VI. Vol. 2. pp. 172.) He died in Greene County on April 5, 1831, in his eighty-fourth year, having been born on February 3, 1748. (Greene County Est. No. 677, WB. 1. pp. 385, probated April 30, 1831.) His wife was Esther ...., who was born August 12, 1762, and died November 18, 1834. Both are buried in the family burial plot on his original land. as far as Cuba where he engaged in a sugar plantation, then returned to settle on the tract of land near Khedive, on Muddy Creek. Some of his land had been taken by squatters while he was away, but he warranted two tracts of land on which he lived the part of his life that was not spent in serving his newly adopted country. Records show he was in the Springhill Township Tax Lists for Bedford County in 1772, as a single freeman. On June 7, 1776, he enlisted in the Eighth Pennsylvania Regiment of the Continental Line, and in November of that year, he made the march with that Regiment to join Washington's Army in New Jersey. The march was a terrible one in the mid winter and many men died on the way because of the lack of everything an army needs. The Regiment took part in the Battle of Bound Brook, Brandywine, German-

Children

1. James Gwynne, born 1789.
2. Joseph Gwynne, Jr., born January 26, 1793, died June 5, 1864; married Martha Dowlin, born January 22, 1791, died March 22, 1875. He served in the War of 1812.

Children

1. Margaret Gwynne.
2. Martha Gwynne.
3. Jane Gwynne, married Abraham S. Milliken.
4. Josiah Gwynne, born October 20, 1812; married, March 28, 1841, Lydia Phillips, daughter of George W. and Susannah (Myers) Phillips, who was born in 1824.
5. Elizabeth Gwynne, born 1816, died May 26, 1845. She was the wife of Nicholas Gore. Buried at Glades.
6. John Gwynne, born December 25, 1818, died May 2, 1907; married November 19, 1840, Elizabeth Rea, born October 7, 1820, died May 27, 1899.

3. Alfred Gwynne, born 1799, died 1835; married Priscilla Long.

Children

1. Joseph Gwynne.
2. Vincent Gwynne.
3. Mary Jane Gwynne.
4. Richard Gwynne.
5. Charlotte Gwynne.

4. Elizabeth Gwynne, born November 27, 1786, died September 30, 1878; married John Dowlin, born September 1, 1793, died November 26, 1874. Both are buried at Glades Church. His will in Greene County Will Book 4. pp. 503, probated December 31, 1874.

Children

1. Lewis Dowlin.
2. Martha Dowlin, married .... Driver.
3. Paul Dowlin, married Mary Jane Stephenson, who died May 3, 1875, aged 43 years, seven months and four days.
4. John Dowlin.
5. Crawford Dowlin.
6. Josiah Dowlin.

7. Jesse Dowlin, born March 21, 1830; married, February 22, 1855, Eliza A. Huston.
8. David Dowlin.
9. Mary Jane Dowlin, married .... Baker.

5. Susannah Gwynne, born 1801, married John Long, born ...., died August 6, 1882, son of Jeremiah and Mary (Ivers) Long.

Children

1. Richard Long.
2. William Long.
3. Joseph Long.
4. Emmeline Long.
5. Maryann Long.
6. Lucinda Long.
7. Louisa Long.
8. Hester Long.
9. Martha Long.
10. Mariah Long.
11. Jeremiah Long.

6. Martha Gwynne, born 1795, married James Seaton.
7. Cyrene Gwynne, born September 2, 1783, died August 4, 1874; married Jeremiah Long, born October 5, 1780, died October 10, 1858, son of Jeremiah and Mary (Ivers) Long. Will Book 4. pp. 477, probated August 10, 1874.

Children

1. James Long, born August 22, 1823, died April 20, 1880; married Mary McClelland.
2. Mary Long.
3. Emma Jane Long.
4. Margaret Ellen Long.
5. Ann Eliza Long.

8. Anna Gwynne, born 1805, married Newton Richey.
9. Esther Gwynne, born 1806, married Thomas Kinsey.
10. Jesse Gwynne, born 1803, died young.

FELIX HUGHES

There are several interesting genealogies of the Hughes Family, one of which carries the record of the family back to Ireland in the year 1542, and carries down to where we find Felix Hughes and his two sons, Thomas Hughes and Phelime (Felix) Hughes, in Loudon County, Virginia, in 1739.

Thomas Hughes, one of the sons, had married, in Donegal, Ireland, Briget O'Neill, and had at least three sons when he came to America. They were Felix, who married Cynthia Kaighn; John, who married Mary Hunter, and Thomas Hughes.

Felix Hughes, the subject of this sketch, son of Thomas and Briget (O'Neill) Hughes, was born in County Donegal, Ireland, about 1723, and died in Greene County, Pennsylvania, in 1805. He married, in Loudon County, Virginia, about 1748, Cynthia Kaighn, said to have been an only daughter. Felix Hughes and his family, with some cousins, the O'Neills, joined the party of immigrants,

said to have amounted to some sixty-five persons, who left Virginia in 1769, to settle in what is now Greene County, Pennsylvania. Most local histories tell of this migration, which while early, was not the first settlement made in this section. Felix Hughes, his son, James, and son, Thomas, settled on adjoining tracts of land near the present town of Carmichaels on Muddy Creek, where they erected a large and strong cabin, often used as a fort. Felix and his son, James, warranted the tracts of land on which they settled, but Thomas Hughes sold out on July 24, 1780, to James Carmichaels, and removed to the Tenmile where in later years he laid out the town of Jefferson. (Washington County Deed Book 1-A-207). There is a description of "Bear Harbor", the tract of land warranted to Felix Hughes and over which there was to be considerable litigation, in the several Hughes histories already written. There are also descriptions of the fort erected on this land. While numerous descendants have joined the D. A. R. and S. A. R. on service of one Felix Hughes in the eastern part of the State, we have our own doubts that Felix Hughes left his fort in these trying times. His age and the activities of his sons would have been a retarding feature. As with John Swan, Sr., no service for Felix Hughes can be definitely claimed. Felix and Cynthia (Kaighn) Hughes were parents of at least six children; Thomas Hughes, of whom we have written; James Hughes, whom we shall take up in this article; John Hughes, killed by the Indians, and for whom James Hughes was sued because of revenging his brother's death; Barnet Hughes, who died in Kentucky; Elizabeth Hughes, whose husband, William Hunter, was killed by the Indians on the way to Kentucky, and Martha Hughes, of whom there is no record.

JAMES HUGHES FAMILY

James Hughes, son of Felix and Cynthia (Kaighn) Hughes, was born in Loudon County, about 1750. He came west with his father and took up the land to the east of Felix Hughes on Muddy Creek. During the Revolution he enlisted in the Third Regiment, Pennsylvania, in the Continental Line, transferring to the Commander in Chief's Guard on December 17, 1781. His brother-in-law, William Hunter, had been transferred the month previously. After the war James Hughes returned to his home where he took an active part in the organization of Greene County and became one of the commissioners in 1798. He died intestate in 1836, at the home of his daughter, Mary Burley, with whom the late years of his life had been spent. His wife was Cassandra Dunn, whom he married about 1772, in this county.

Children of James and Cassandra (Dunn) Hughes
1. Thomas Hughes, died young.
2. Felix Hughes, born in 1774, died in 1828. His wife was Mary Donnely.

Children

1. James Hughes.
2. Thomas Hughes, settled in Ohio.
3. Mary Hughes, married William Horner.
4. Francis Hughes, born March 20, 1808, died April 2, 1882, at Parkersburg, West Virginia. He married Elizabeth Hemstead, born November 20, 1804, died July 1873.
5. Ibby Hughes.
6. Cassandra Hughes, born 1800, died 1891; married Thomas Crago, born 1801, died 1884, son of John Crago, and Ann Hiller.
7. John Hughes, married Elizabeth Crago, sister of Thomas above.

8. Jennie Hughes.
3. Mary Hughes, born March 2, 1778, died at Grave Creek, West Virginia, in 1852. Married Jacob Burley.

Children

1. Cassandra Burley, married R............ Howard, Cameron, West Virginia.
2. James Burley, married (1) Mary Alexander; married (2) .... Alexander.
3. Cynthia Burley, married Jefferson T. Martin, Moundsville, West Virginia.
4. John Burley, married (1) .... Clark; married (2) .... Oble, Cameron, West Virginia.
5. Tamor Burley, married Joseph Hix, Cameron, West Virginia.
6. .... Burley, married .... Howard.
7. Elizabeth Burley, died young.
8. Mary Burley, married Bernard Connelly.
9. Joshua Burley, born October 4, 1814, married Catherine Roseberry.
10. Thomas Burley, married Maria Ashbrook.
11. Martha Burley, married Michael Pyles.
12. Catherine Burley, married John Parker, Cameron, West Virginia.

4. Elizabeth Hughes, born 1779, died February 24, 1864; married William Meighen, born 1774, died 1829, son of James and Susan (McCloskey) Meighen.

Children

1. Susannah Meighen, born December 22, 1800; married Christopher Brant.
2. John Meighen, born September 2, 1802, died July 16, 1848; married, 1823, Elsie Shultz, born July 16, 1805, died December 19, 1893.
3. James Meighen, born October 14, 1804, died young.
4. Mary Meighen, born August 5, 1806; married William Terry.
5. Peter Meighen, born May 8, 1809; married Priscilla Dye, daughter of James and Anna Dye.
6. Felix Meighen, born January 16, 1812; married Eliza J. Foster.
7. Dennis Meighen, born March 15, 1814.
8. William Meighen, born December 15, 1816; married .... Foster.
9. Cassandra Meighen, born February 15, 1819.
10. Thomas H. Meighen, born March 5, 1821; married Louisa Morris.
11. Catherine Meighen, married Samuel W. Felton.

5. Catherine Hughes, born 1782, died 1850; married James Clark.

Children

1. Daniel Clark, married Jane Mendenhall.
2. Elizabeth Clark, married Thomas Mitchell.
3. Mary Clark, married .... Heaton.
4. John Clark, born ....; married (1) May Hatfield; (2) .... Rinehart.
5. Cassandra Clark, married John Hanks; to Trumbull County, Ohio.

6. Sarah Clark, married (1) Thomas Mendenhall; (2) Isaac Stewart.
7. Cynthia Clark.
8. Lawrence Clark.
9. Isaac Clark, married .... Edgar.
10. Felix Clark, married .... Price.

6. James Hughes, born 1784; married Rachel Gray; removed to Fulton County, Pennsylvania.

Children

1. Cassandra Hughes, married John Krine.
2. Mary Hughes, married Thomas O. Cooper.
3. Hugh Hughes, died March 1872.
4. Frances Hughes, married Gettys Hidding.
5. James Hughes, married Elizabeth Stewart Burdge.
6. Martha Hughes, married Judge Lemuel Gordon.
7. Rachel Hughes, married Thomas M. Hidding.
8. Thomas Hughes.
9. Julia Hughes.
10. Dr. John G. Hughes, married Ada Kirk.

7. Sarah Hughes, born 1786, died 1833; married Thomas Mendenhall.
8. Thomas Hughes, born January 21, 1789, died June 20, 1849, Wheeling, West Virginia. He married, on March 12, 1815, Mary Odenbaugh, daughter of Charles and Catherine (Fry) Odenbaugh.

Children

1. James Hughes, born January 15, 1816, died August 28, 1816.
2. Eliza Clark Hughes.
3. John Hughes, born November 6, 1818, died March 20 1870; married, on December 9, 1847, Eliza Sterrit McClane.
4. Mary Ann Hughes, married Wolfe Heyman.
5. Thomas Hughes, born November 22, 1822, died March 10, 1886; married (1) March 24, 1864, Bessie McEldowney. Married (2) Fanny Jordon Ballard.
6. Alfred Hughes, born September 16, 1824; married, November 1, 1849, Mary Kirby Adrian.

9. Martha Hughes, born 1790, died in Ohio, 1857; married Thomas Morris, son of James and Phoebe (Sayers) Morris.

Children

1. Eliza Morris, married David Johnson.
2. Phoebe Morris.
3. Charlotte Morris.
4. James Morris.
5. .... Morris, married H. .... Black.
6. Sarah Morris.

CHARLES ANDERSON

Charles Anderson, Sr., patented a tract of land situated on the North Bank of Muddy Creek at Carmichaels, which he had obtained by a warrant dated September 11, 1784, then acquired the adjoining tract of land that had belonged to Major Edmund Polke, making his holdings at this place total more than 700 acres. Deeds of record disclose that he and his wife, Mary ...., disposed of much of this land during his lifetime, Hugh Barclay being one of the early purchasers. No military service for Charles Anderson, Sr., nor his sons is recorded, but that is not strange as he was in the section from which Captain Pigman's Company was recruited. Charles Anderson, Sr.'s will was filed for probate July 22, 1822, but names only two sons. Other records show additional sons, but no daughters.

Children of Charles and Mary Anderson

1. Charles Anderson, Jr., whose wife was Margaret .... DB. 2. pp. 578.
2. William Anderson.
3. James Anderson, who married Priscilla Israel.
4. Richard Anderson.
5. Daniel Anderson.
6. Amos Anderson (?)

THE SEATON FAMILY

The town of Carmichaels, Pennsylvania, might well claim that it was laid out by kin of George Washington, so that the kinfolk of Abraham Lincoln could settle there. If many of the pioneer settlers of this frontier were poor, illiterate, and underprivileged individuals of the Eastern seaboard, there are striking examples of the reverse condition. This is particularly true in the case of the Seatons. The family was closely related and descendants of the land barons of the "Northern Neck" of Virginia. They were direct descendants of George and Hannah (Ashton) Eskridge, and thereby related to the Washingtons, Lees, Allertons, Balls, etc. In fact Mary Ball, mother of George Washington, was raised in the home of George and Hannah (Ashton) Eskridge, after the death of her father when she was but three years of age, and it is generally admitted that George Washington was named for his mother's benefactor. (See Douglass Freeman's "George Washington" Vol. 1, pp. 47n.)

The Seatons of Muddy Creek were descended on the maternal side from Richard and Elizabeth (Rodham) Kenner, who settled in Virginia prior to 1700. Elizabeth Rodham was the daughter of Mathew Rodham, a prominent military figure of the 17th century. Francis Kenner, son of Richard and Elizabeth Rodham Kenner, was born December 27, 1677, and died about 1728, his will being probated April 18, 1728. He left three children among whom was the Rev. Rodham Kenner, first rector of the Parish at Fredericksburg, in 1729, whom Freeman calls "a connection of Mary (Ball) Washington's Family." Another son of Francis Kenner was Howson Kenner, whose will was probated in Fauquier County, Virginia, in 1778, and this Howson Kenner married Margaret Eskridge, daughter of George and Hannah (Ashton) Eskridge. (William and Mary Quarterly Vol. 14. pp. 173.) The family of Howson and Margaret (Eskridge) Kenner is found in Virginia Magazine of History Vol. IX pp. 202, and varies slightly from the record of the Quarterly above mentioned. Both records are further borne out by the Gregg Bible as copied by Miss Lillian Davidson of Uniontown, Penna.

Children of Howson and Margaret (Eskridge) Kenner

1. Francis Kenner, who married Elizabeth Howard.

2. Betty Kenner, who married James Seaton, whose record follows.
3. Rebecca Kenner, who married Burdette Clifton.
4. George Turberville Kenner.
5. Peggy Kenner, who married Rev. Stephen Prichard.
6. Rodham Kenner.
7. Kate Kenner, who married .... Markham.
8. Susannah Kenner, who married Spencer Morgan.
9. Mary Ann Kenner, who married .... Seaton.

The Gregg Bible says that James Seaton, a native of Winchester, Virginia, was twice married and had two sons by the first marriage, then eight sons and four daughters by the second. Thus it would appear that he married Mary Ann Kenner for his first wife and on her death, married her sister, Betty Kenner, who survived him by many years, being frequently mentioned in the Muddy Creek Ledger 1793-96. Before the end of the Revolution James Seaton, with his wife Betty, moved to Middy Creek in Greene County, Pennsylvania, where he died about 1781. He left a will which was filed in Washington County (File 1-L-234) wherein his wife, Betty, was named the executrix. Search for this will discloses that someone has removed it from the files, but the list of his children is found in the Gregg Bible, owned by Mrs. Elizabeth Robinson of Garards Fort, Greene County, and copied by Miss Lillian Davidson of Uniontown, Penna.

Children of James Seaton

1. George Seaton, who went to Kentucky, and is probably the Revolutionary soldier who was reported as living in Brackenridge, Kentucky, in 1840, when his age is given as 86 years. This is an obvious error if he was by the first marriage, but fully understandable in his advanced years. He was probably named for George Eskridge.
2. John Seaton, also went to Kentucky.
3. James Seaton, son of James and Betty (Kenner) Seaton, born July 19, 1751, died March 2, 1830; married, September 5, 1780,

Mary Clark, who was born September 19, 1758, and died December 15, 1826. His will is in Greene County Will Book 1. pp. 371. James Seaton served as clerk in Captain William Crawford's Company, Washington County, Pennsylvania, Militia. (Penna. Arch. Series VI. Vol. 2. pp. 171.) He and his wife are buried in the old Seaton Cemetery at Carmichaels.

Children of James and Mary (Clark) Seaton

1. George Clark Seaton, born June 2, 1783, died September 13, 1849; married (1) Isabella McClelland, who died February 27, 1820. He married (2) Esther Shotwell Smith.
2. Margaret Seaton, born May 14, 1790, died July 13, 1793.
3. James Seaton, born March 17, 1793, died April 18, 1876. His wife was Mary ...., born 1806, died January 2, 1871.
4. Janet Seaton, born ....; married .... Hewitt.
5. Thomas Prather Seaton, born May 24, 1797.
6. Betty Seaton, married .... Cunningham.

4. Kenner Seaton, son of James and Betty (Kenner) Seaton, went to Kentucky.
5. Richard Seaton, son of James and Betty (Kenner) Seaton, served as lieutenant in Captain William Crawford's Militia Company.

6. Rodham Seaton, son of James and Betty (Kenner) Seaton, died in Jefferson County, Kentucky, about 1805. His will, made January 4, 1804, was filed December 2, 1805. In it he named his wife, Mary ...., and four children, mentioning others not yet of age.

Children of Rodham and Mary Seaton

1. Thomas Curry Seaton, eldest son.
2. Sarah Seaton, eldest daughter.
3. Betty Kenner Seaton.
4. Kenner Seaton, youngest son.

7. Howson Seaton, (also Hanson, Harrison, etc.) son of James and Betty (Kenner) Seaton, died in Kentucky in 1803. His will was made February 19, 1803, and filed for probate in Jefferson County on May 2, 1803. In it he mentions his wife Sarah ...., and children who are not named. He also speaks of a lot of ground in "Wainsburg", Pennsylvania. From a deed in Greene County Deed Book 5. pp. 565 we learn the names of four of his children.

Children of Howson and Sarah Seaton

1. Sarah Seaton, who married William Zenor.
2. James Seaton, whose wife was Nancy ....
3. William Seaton, whose wife was Rebecca ....
4. Betty Seaton, who married James Rose.

8. Francis Seaton, son of James and Betty (Kenner) Seaton, was born in Virginia about 1756. He died in Knox County, Indiana, in the Autumn of 1820, and is buried with his wife in the Upper Indiana Cemetery, two and a half miles northeast of Vincennes. His wife was Rebecca Gregg, born August 12, 1758, in New Castle County, Delaware, and died in Indiana, in August 1822. Francis Seaton had warranted to him on May 26, 1785, a tract of land on Muddy Creek, where the town of New Lisbon, later Carmichaels, was laid out. This warrant, under the title of "Elizabeth", was later transferred to the children of his sister, Betty Carmichaels, and they patented the tract. It was on this site that Francis Seaton had his grist mill as noted in the Muddy Creek Ledger. Francis Seaton served in the Eighth Pennsylvania Regiment of the Continental Line, and was an ensign in Captain William Crawford's Militia Company. He was chosen one of the ensigns at the election of officers at the Mingo Bottoms on the Crawford Sandusky Expedition. Francis Seaton's will, made on June 8, 1820, was filed for probate in Knox County, Indiana, on November 8 of that year. Most of this family went to Kentucky and then moved on to Indiana.

Children of Francis and Rebecca (Gragg) Seaton

1. James C. Seaton, born October 26, 1780; married Elizabeth Swan, born December 26, 1779. She died February 20, 1830, and is buried in the old Baptist Cemetery at Uniontown.

Children of James C. and Elizabeth (Swan) Seaton

1. Hiram Seaton, born October 1, 1801; married, December 4, 1823, Sarah Vorhees.
2. Francis Seaton, born May 6, 1803, died September 15, 1826.
3. Susannah Seaton, born December 10, 1805, died Janu-

ary 11, 1879; married, August 17, 1826, Daniel Collier.
4. Sarah Seaton, born December 16, 1807, died October 23, 1858; married, October 4, 1824, William Crawford.
5. Mary Seaton, born June 23, 1810; married, June 2, 1831, William Inghram, son of William and Agnes (Fee) Inghram, born February 24, 1794, died September 3, 1843. His first wife was Sarah Adams, who died May 3, 1830.
6. Rebecca Seaton, born July 18, 1812; married, May 1835, George Martin.
7. Marchant Seaton, born September 21, 1814, died October 22, 1831.
8. Juliet Seaton, born March 31, 1817; married, November 20, 1834, Robert L. Barry.
9. James C. Seaton, Jr., born August 3, 1819, died September 9, 1851.
10. John S. Seaton, born September 12, 1823; married, November 26, 1846, Emma Rawls.

2. Susan Seaton, daughter of Francis and Rebecca (Gregg) Seaton, married John Vaun. Her first husband was Thomas Swan, son of Richard and Martha (Vanmeter) Swan, who was born in May 1779.

Children of Thomas and Susan (Seaton) Swan

1. Thomas Swan, Jr.
2. Mary Swan.

3. John Seaton, son of Francis and Rebecca (Gregg) Seaton, was born in 1785, and died in 1838.
4. Elizabeth Seaton, daughter of Francis and Rebecca (Gregg) Seaton, married, November 25, 1819, John Cochran.
5. Rebecca Seaton, daughter of Francis and Rebecca (Gregg) Seaton, born 1799, died 1837; married, February 7, 1818, in Knox County, Indiana, John McClure, born 1789, died 1837.
6. Hanson (Howson) Seaton, a soldier in the Battle of Tippecanoe, whose estate was settled by Francis Seaton on November 11, 1811; may have been another son.

9. Samuel Seaton, son of James and Betty (Kenner) Seaton, died in Pennsylvania. No record.
10. William Seaton, son of James and Betty (Kenner) Seaton, born in Virginia, 1770, died in Greene County, Pennsylvania, about 1814. (Greene County Will Book 1. pp. 131.) He married in 1792, Sarah Myers. William Seaton ran a store at Muddy Creek in 1793-1796, perhaps for a time employed by his brother, Francis, but later sole owner, and his old ledger, now the property of Howard L. Leckey, Sr., of Waynesburg, has been photostated by the Library of Congress, where it may be used for references to much of the early history of the section. A record of his children is given in the Gregg Bible.

Children of William and Sarah (Myers) Seaton

1. Rhoda Seaton, born February 15, 1793; married William Watt.
2. Maria Seaton, born February 1, 1795; married Aaron Gregg.

AND ITS PIONEER FAMILIES 517

    3. Sarah Seaton, born December 27, 1797; married Nathan Crouch.
    4. Betty Seaton, born May 1, 1801; married, January 1 (or 2) 1823, Joseph Gilbert.
    5. Margaret Seaton, married .... Eckert.
    6. Myers Seaton, born March 2, 1804; married Elizabeth C. Dill on July 2, 1828.
    7. Samuel Clark Seaton, born November 28, 1807, died at age of 39 years.

11. Rebecca Seaton, daughter of James and Betty (Kenner) Seaton; married Samuel Hyde, who served as one of the administrators of the James Carmichaels Estate.

12. Betty Seaton, daughter of James and Betty (Kenner) Seaton, was probably along with her sisters, Sarah and Rebecca, among the older children of this family. She first married James Carmichaels, who served as major of militia under Colonel Henry Enochs in the Second Battalion, Washington County, Pennsylvania, Militia. (Penna. Arch. Series VI. Vol. 2. pp. 75.) There is an unconfirmed record that James Carmichaels first settled on the Tenmile at the site of the present Jefferson, and then traded land with Thomas Hughes, with Hughes moving to the Jefferson site and Carmichaels moving to Muddy Creek. It is certain that James Carmichaels did buy out Thomas Hughes' Muddy Creek land as there is a deed of July 24, 1780, to prove it. (Washington County Deed Book 1-A-207.) Hughes lived in what is now known as the "Old Town," but the present town of Carmichaels was laid out on land warranted to Francis Seaton and was first known as New Lisbon. The two children of James and Betty (Seaton) Carmichaels got the patent for the Francis Seaton land. Major James Carmichaels died about 1796, when his widow and Samuel Hyde settled his estate, taking out letters of administration on August 13, 1796. Betty (Seaton) Carmichaels then married Jay Thompson, an early Justice of Peace.

Children of James and Betty (Seaton) Carmichaels

    1. William Seaton Carmichaels, who with his sister, patented the Francis Seaton tract on October 27, 1801. He married Nancy Harper, daughter of Samuel and Hannah (Swearington) Harper. It is probable that he was married twice as a William Carmichaels also married, on November 14, 1819, Mary Morely as shown in the Jay Thompson Journal.
    2. Margaret Eskridge Carmichaels, her name is so written in a deed as heir of James Carmichaels. (Greene County Deed Book 1. pp. 384.)

13. Margaret Seaton, daughter of James and Betty (Kenner) Seaton, died young.

14. Sarah Seaton, daughter of James and Betty (Kenner) Seaton, married John Boreman, first Prothonotary, Register of Wills, and Recorder of Deeds in Greene County. "History of West Virginia, Old and New", says he was born in England and ran away from his home in Manchester to Havre de Grace, Maryland, from whence he removed to Philadelphia and became a merchant at that place. At the outbreak of the Revolution he joined the Continental Army, where his business acumen and ability advanced him to the rank of Assistant Paymaster General, quartered at Pittsburgh.

Children of John and Sarah (Seaton) Boreman

1. Kenner Seaton Boreman, married Sarah Inghram, daughter of William and Agnes (Fee) Inghram. They removed to Tyler County, West Virginia.

Children of Kenner Seaton and Sarah (Inghram) Boreman

1. William Boreman, an attorney at Middlebourne, West Virginia.
2. Kenner Seaton Boreman, born April 19, 1819, was a merchant at Parkersburg, West Virginia. Married, January 30, 1850, Teressa Alexander, daughter of Robert and Ann (Jennings) Alexander of St. Clairsville, Ohio.
3. Arthur Inghram Boreman, born July 24, 1823, died May 19, 1896. He was the first Governor of West Virginia, later serving as U. S. Senator and Judge. He married, on November 30, 1864, Laurane Tanner.
4. James Mason Boreman, a merchant at Parkersburg, West Virginia.
5. Thomas Inghram Boreman.
6. Jacob Smith Boreman, for a time publisher of the Kansas City Star, later U. S. Judge in Utah.
7. Agnes Mason Boreman, married, February 18, 1830, James Stephenson.

LIST OF MARRIAGES FROM DOCKET BOOK OF JAY THOMPSON, JUSTICE OF PEACE AT CARMICHAELS, PENNSYLVANIA

Sunday, May 21, 1815, Jesse Hopton to Sarah Finch.
Thursday, May 25, 1815, Uria.' Higginbottom to Elizabeth Chance.
Thursday, June 8, 1815, George Cree to Sarah Rice.
Thursday, October 19, 1815, Remembrance Hughes to Margaret McClain.
Saturday, October 28, 1815, Marcena Mitchenor to Mary Stone.
Thursday, November 9, 1815, John Buckingham to Elizabeth Hughes.
Thursday, November 16, 1815, Amos Horner to Nancy Snively.
Friday, November 24, 1815, John McCarter to Sarah Willis.
Monday, November 27, 1815, Benjamin Deguid to Hannah Statler.
Thursday, February 7, 1816, William Dunsmore to .... Groom.
Thursday, June 13, 1816, James Flenniken to Mary McClelland.
Sunday, September 29, 1816, Daniel Moore to Margaret Kelly.
Tuesday, October 22, 1816, George Moody to Lucinda Black.
Thursday, February 27, 1817, Robert Jackson to Ann Blackledge.
Thursday, March 20, 1817, Samuel Swan to Priscilla Crago.
Tuesday, May 27, 1817, Jacob Wiley to Hannah Way
Sunday, August 17, 1817, William Miller to Mary Cann.

Thursday, April 9, 1818, John Dolson to Mary Ewart.
Thur., July 16, 1818, Luke Boldence to Elizabeth Freelove Wooden.
Tuesday, December 1, 1818, David Snively to Mary Anderson.
Thur., Feb. 4, 1819, James Flenniken, Jr., to Mary McClelland.
Saturday, July 31, 1819, George Elliot to Sarah Wilson.
Sunday, November 14, 1819, William Carmichael to Mary Morely.
Thursday, January 6, 1820, James Mundell to Lydia Encey.
Tuesday, June 19, 1821, Samuel McClelland to Mary Pickens.
Sunday, April 7, 1822, Benjamin Maple to Margaret Burriss.
Tuesday, February 4, 1817, John Newsom to Althea Repp.
Thursday, December 26, 1822, William Allison to Martha Londy.
Thursday, January 2, 1823, Joseph W. Gilbert to Betty Seaton.
Sunday, March 23, 1823, Kent Horner to Margaret Anderson.
Thur., Jan. 1, 1824, William Kerr (of James) to Elizabeth Curl.
Wed., July 4, 1827, Thomas Seaton to Elizabeth Brown (Dunkard).

THE LINCOLN FAMILY

The Lincoln Family of Carmichaels and the Yoders Family of Waynesburg, are descended from the same common ancestor as was President Abraham Lincoln. That ancestor was Mordecai Lincoln, grandson of Samuel Lincoln. Samuel Lincoln came to Salem, Mass., in 1637, at the age of 18 from Hingham, England. He moved soon from Salem, Mass., to Hingham, Mass., where his brother, Thomas, had settled 2 years before. Here Samuel became prosperous; he married Martha... They had 10 children. Samuel died May 26, 1690; wife Martha died Apr 10, 1693.

Their 3rd child, Modecai I, was born June 19, 1655; baptised the 24th and died shortly; they then named their 4th child, born June 14, 1657, Mordecai II (a common practice then). This Mordecai II married Sarah Jones (daughter of Abraham Jones). Mordecai II moved south to Scituate, Plymouth Plantation, becoming one of the country's first ironmasters.

Near the turn of the century Mordecai's II wife, Sarah, died and left him with 4 children, the oldest his namesake Mordecai III, born 1686. His second was Abraham, born 1688. Mordecai II married Mary Chapin of Braintree. The home he built for Mary still stands in Scituate. He owned a grist mill, (standing 1947), saw mill, forge and furnace. Mordecai II died 1727.

Soon after the death of Sarah, the sons Mordecai (III) and Abraham, left home and settled in Monmouth County, N.J. This is the Mordecai who became President Lincoln's ancestor. Mordecai (III) like his father, became an ironmaster at Freehold, owning a forge and furnace. He married Hannah Bowne Salter, daughter of Richard Salter. To this union were born 6 children, son John, and 5 daughters, one of whom died in infancy. John became great-great-grandfather of President Lincoln. Hannah, wife of Mordecai III, died 1727 at Freehold, N.J.

While living in New Jersey, Mordecai (III) acquired holdings in Pennsylvania, and was a partner in an iron works at Coventry on the Schuylkill River. In 1730, he moved to Exeter in Berks Co., Pa., with his motherless children and in 1733, built a house (still standing) near the home of Squire Boone, father of Daniel Boone. Mordecai III soon remarried to Mary (?) (probably Robeson), and she bore him 2 sons, one Mordecai (IV) born in 1730, and Thomas born in 1731. 5 months after Mordecai's III death in 1735 (age 49) she had a third son, Abraham, born in 1736.

Mordecai IV was probably born in Berks Co., Pa. & died in Union twp., Fayette Co., Pa., Mar. 1812. Since he was not in the 1790 census, and since he patented land, 186 acre tract, "Union Green", Fayette

County, Penna., on August 23, 1791, it is probable that he was enroute to his new home at the time the census was taken. He served in the Commissary Department in the Army during the Revolution. He married Mary Webb, born 1731, and who died in 1814. She was the daughter of John and Mary (Boone) Webb.

Children of Mordecai and Mary (Webb) Lincoln

(All except Hannah named in will of Mordecai (IV), dated February 22, 1811, Will Book T, page 96, Fayette County, Pennsylvania)

1. Benjamin Lincoln, born October 29, 1756, died October 2, 1821. Married, in 1784, Elizabeth Oaves, born 1766, died December 29, 1846.
2. John Lincoln, born March 28, 1758; married Mary Lafferty. Had thirteen children.
3. Nancy Lincoln, born November 22, 1759; married Jacob Geiger.
4. Hannah Lincoln, born December 31, 1761; died in Berks County, Pennsylvania.
5. Sarah Lincoln, born February 25, 1767, died January 25, 1838. Married John Jones.

NOTE—The numbers following Mordecai were not part of their names, but are used merely to keep the Mordecais straight and separate from each other.

FAMILY OF BENJAMIN LINCOLN

Benjamin Lincoln, son of Mordecai Lincoln, was born in Berks County, Pennsylvania, on October 29, 1756. He served in Captain John Robinson's Company, Berks County Militia, in October 1781, (Penna. Arch. Series V. Vol. 5 pp. 278). He settled in Fayette County, Pennsylvania, with his father about 1791, and died there October 2, 1821. He is buried about four miles North of Uniontown. Benjamin Lincoln married, about 1784, Elizabeth Oaves, born in 1766, who died December 29, 1846, and is buried with her husband.

Children of Benjamin and Elizabeth (Oaves) Lincoln

1. Thomas Lincoln, born August 10, 1785, died October 8, 1864; married, 1812, Mary Evans, born May 9, 1790, died October 10, 1870. Parents of Thomas Lincoln of Carmichaels.

   ### Children of Thomas and Mary (Evans) Lincoln

   1. James Lincoln, born September 13, 1813, died 1878; married Nellie Merrifield.
   2. Elizabeth Lincoln, born November 4, 1815, died April 4, 1911; married William Carson, died December 5, 1871.
   3. Ann Lincoln, born May 1, 1817, died March 1844. Married .... Moore.
   4. Mary Lincoln, single, died December 17, 1899; aged 80 years.
   5. Matilda Lincoln, born November 30, 1820, died May 4, 1910. Graduated from Greene Academy at Carmichaels, Pennsylvania; schooled later in St. Louis, Missouri, and taught several years in Greene County, Pennsylvania. Married (1) James Watson; (2) Captain Watson Grim.
   6. Sarah Lincoln, born January 28, 1823, died November 1906. Married Luther Axtell.
   7. Thomas Benton Lincoln, born March 16, 1825, died February 14, 1901; married Mariah Hart, born November 8, 1825.

2. Nancy Lincoln, born 1787; married (1) Dale Woodmancy; (2) John Henry Zehring, who was the only son of Ludwig (born 1738) who was active in Revolutionary War and was one of

representatives from Colonel Curtis Grubb's Battalion at Lancaster Convention of July 4, 1776. (Penna. Archives.) Nancy had four sons and three daughters. Moved to Fayette County, Pennsylvania, following the Revolution.

Children of John Henry and Nancy (Lincoln) Zehring (Searing)
1. Elizabeth Zehring, born January 10, 1814, died October 28, 1898. Never married.
2. Benjamin Zehring, born May 16, 1816, died October 5, 1897. On March 6, 1842, married Margaret Ann Dunkle (nee Henry). Benjamin had been a wagoner on the National Pike and moved to Lawrence County, Pennsylvania, in 1842.
3. Hannah May Searing (Zehring) born 1821, died September 30, 1896; married Henry Lee Pendleberry, born April 29, 1814, died February 11, 1899. These are the progenitors of the Yoders Family of Waynesburg, Pennsylvania.
4. Sarah, born 1823, died November 9, 1905; married Robinson Layton.
5. William, born April 29, 1832, died July 11, 1901. Never married.
6. Mary, born 1833, died April 21, 1907; married Ashail Snyder.
7. George, born 1819, died November 23, 1898; married Ollie Handlin.

3. Abraham Lincoln, born 1789, died 1864; married Martha Cole.
4. Sarah Lincoln, born 1791, died 1867; married James Russell, January 9, 1820.
5. Mary Lincoln, died 1867; married James Hagan.
6. Hannah Lincoln, born February 19, 1795, died February 10, 1819; married Isaac Hunt.
7. Elizabeth Lincoln, born 1804, died 1887; married James Junk.
8. Phoebe Lincoln, born 1800, died 1884; married Henry Yeagley.
9. Mordecai Lincoln, born 1801, died October 2, 1851; married Jane Gilpin.
10. Henry Lincoln.

THE CRAWFORDS OF MUDDY CREEK

There have been numerous histories written about Colonel William Crawford of Muddy Creek, and most of them mention his brother, John Crawford, because their movements in this section were closely parallel, though John Crawford never attained the military prominence of his brother. It is also possible to confuse Greene County's Colonel William Crawford, with Fayette County's martyr of the same name. In official Pennsylvania records, William Crawford of "the Glades" did not exceed the rank of captain during the Revolution, but under Virginia jurisdiction he was the colonel of Frontier Rangers with headquarters at John Ankrom's Fort on Tenmile. We get this bit of information from various pension applications of these Rangers. (James Pribble, Harrod Newland, etc.). It is regrettable that the life of Colonel William Crawford, as partly finished by his son, John Crawford, was never finished or published, but Crumrine and Evans have both seen and used it in their histories. John Crawford's recollections of the life of his father are in the NN Series of the Draper Papers at Madison, Wisconsin. These recollections give one of the best pictures of pioneer times in this section and are told by a man who grew up with the times, having been born the year his father settled on Muddy Creek.

John Crawford, (or James) father of Colonel William Crawford, was born in Scotland, and came to America, settling at an early date on a tract of land near what is now Chambersburg, Pennsylvania. He died in 1748, leaving three sons and two daughters, namely: George Crawford, Arthur Crawford, who was adopted by the Indian Chief, White Eyes, when in 1756, that chief was head of a party of Indians who destroyed the cabin of John McKinney, the second husband of Colonel William Crawford's mother on Big Kanawha. This story is told in L. K. Evans, along with the future life of our subject, William Crawford; Mary Crawford, and John Crawford.

Colonel William Crawford, after the death of his father, spent some time in Loudon County, Virginia, and then five years in a company of Rangers, returned in 1767, to the Conochacheague, where he married Alice Kennedy, a daughter of David Kennedy. Then in 1770, he removed to The Tenmile County, and settled on a tract of land near Glades Church, where the remainder of his life was spent. His military life included all the period of the Indian massacres from the death of Thomas Crago, until the Crow Massacre, for in 1793, we find him at the head of a company at Fort Ryerson on Wheeling Creek. His round-up of the Tories, while in service under Colonel Thomas Gaddis, and his pursuit of the Indians after the Corbly Massacre, are high lights of his career. Served as captain in the First Battalion, Washington County, Pennsylvania, Militia.

Colonel William Crawford was born in 1744, in Cumberland County, Pennsylvania, and died in Greene County, on August 3, 1826. His wife, Alice Kennedy, is probably buried with him in the Glades Church Cemetery. They had two sons and seven daughters.

1. William Crawford, died before his father.
2. John Crawford, born 1771, died November 8, 1831. He married Salome Jennings, who died on November 21, 1851, at the age of 78 years. They are buried at Glades.

Children

1. John Lynn Crawford, born May 31, 1802, died unmarried in 1860.
2. William Crawford, born December 18, 1803, died 1860; married Elizabeth Rea, born January 16, 1810, died 1858.
3. Jennings Crawford, born September 14, 1805, died September 11, 1881; married Sarah Evans.
4. Jefferson Crawford, born July 1, 1809 (or March 11, 1811) died August 16, 1868. He married, October 19, 1841, Catherine Harper, born August 28, 1816, died February 18, 1886.
5. Alice Crawford, born June 13, 1807, died July 20, 1894; married David Kerr.
6. Lucinda Crawford, born March 11, 1811; married Reverend Joshua Laughran.
7. Rebecca Crawford, born April 12, 1815, died in 1853; married, in 1842, John Adam Gordon. He was born June 16, 1816.
8. Phoebe Crawford, born May 12, 1813, never married.

3. Polly (Mary) Crawford, married William Lynn.
4. Rebecca Crawford, married Henry Slater.
5. Nancy Crawford, born August 6, 1782, died August 3, 1864.

On October 2, 1802, she married Joshua Cobb, born May 27, 1776, died August 27, 1860.

Children of Joshua and Nancy (Crawford) Cobb

1. William Crawford Cobb, born July 10, 1803, died October 5, 1804.
2. Willard Cobb, born June 25, 1805, died July 21, 1832.
3. Dyer Cobb, born August 6, 1807, married Almira Freeman.
4. John Cobb, born December 10, 1809, died June 14, 1895; married Marie Caffyn.
5. Polly Maria Cobb, born June 5, 1812, married Churchel Chrisly
6. Ella Cobb, born October 4, 1814, died February 28, 1883; married John Elder.
7. Oliver Cobb, born April 25, 1817, died March 28, 1891; married Caroline Foulke.
8. Elkhanah Cobb, born October 19, 1819; married (1) Elizabeth Caffyn; (2) Sarah Youtsy; (3) Mrs. Lucy Elliott.

Catherine Crawford, born 1774, died 1852; married Hugh Young.

Children

1. Minerva Young.
2. Robert Young.
3. Alice Young.
4. William Young.

Alice Crawford, born 1776, married Thomas Armstrong, born April 2, 1777, died October 22, 1853. He was a first cousin, son of John and Mary (Kennedy) Armstrong. They removed in 1799, to Athens County, Ohio. Mrs. Armstrong died in 1850. Ruth Crawford, died before her father. Her husband was John Miller. (Greene County O. C. Docket 1. pp. 245.)

Children

1. William Miller.
2. Henry Miller.
3. Rye Miller.
4. Eli Miller.
5. Thomas Miller.
6. James Miller.
7. Haddassah Miller.
8. Angelina Miller.
9. Evalina Miller.
10. John Miller.

9. Lizzie Crawford, married Henry Russell.

JOHN CRAWFORD FAMILY

John Crawford, brother of Colonel William Crawford, was born in Cumberland County, Pennsylvania, November 1, 1748, and died in Venango County, Pennsylvania, February 18, 1812. He came to Muddy Creek with his brother in 1770, and served at times in his brother's Militia Company. His house, built near the Glades was a strong one and frequently used as a place of refuge during the Indian raids, and has been called Fort Crawford, though never so designated in writings of the times. It was at his home Rev. McMillan reports holding services on his first trip into the section. About 1797, John Crawford sold his land on Muddy Creek and removed to Venango County. His wife was Isabell Parker, who was born August 21, 1756, and died December 30, 1839. (Beers "History of Venango County").

Children

1. William Crawford, born August 5, 1774; married Nancy Reed.

2. James Crawford, born March 12, 1776; married Abigail Coulter.
3. John Crawford, born September 27, 1777; married Margaret Reed.
4. George Crawford, born June 10, 1779; married Mary Coulter.
5. David Crawford, born April 5, 1781; married Lucy Applegate.
6. Alexander Crawford, born April 2, 1782; married Mary McMillen.
7. Arthur Crawford.
8. Samuel Crawford, born November 27, 1786; married Fanny Hill.
9. Ebeneezer Crawford, born March 14, 1789; married Janet Grant.
10. Mary Parker Crawford, born ....; married .... Turner.
11. Robert Jennings Crawford, born April 4, 1798; married Margaret Hemphill.

OLIVER CRAWFORD

Extensive investigation has failed to pinpoint the exact origin of Oliver Crawford, who operated the first ferry over the Monongahela River at the mouth of Muddy Creek. What information there is available, is confusing, if not entirely unreliable. Ellis' History of Fayette County, describes an Oliver and Thomas Crawford as eldest sons of a Margaret Crawford, widow of Kenick's Gig, Maryland. Crumrine in his History of Washington County, speaking of the same two men (pp. 724), does not list their origin, but says they were taken prisoners by the Indians and held captive until Oliver Crawford was twenty and Thomas Crawford was eighteen years of age, after which Oliver married and settled on the Monongahela, while Thomas went to Cross Creek, Washington County, where he died in 1783. But Crumrine erred when he stated that Oliver Crawford was a brother of the Quakers, James and Josiah Crawford. It does seem certain that both these authors were speaking of the same two men, who are also alluded to in the mention of another brother, Alexander Crawford, in Williams' Brothers History of Ross and Highland Counties, Ohio.

Our own search for Oliver Crawford first locates him as a member of Evan Shelby's Company of Rangers, under Colonel Henry Boquet in August 1759, at which time his name is found, along with Alexander Crawford, Thomas Crago, and George Newland, neighbors of Oliver on Muddy Creek, and Thomas Slater and William English, settlers on the Tenmile, about the time Oliver Crawford first set up his ferry about 1770, with its western terminal on the north bank of the mouth of Muddy Creek. As Shelby's Company was recruited mostly in the Conachacheague Valley in Pennsylvania and Maryland, it is most likely the Crawfords were living at that location at the time of Boquet's Campaign. It was near this ferry that Thomas Crago was killed by the Indians about 1770. On April 3, 1769, Oliver Crawford received a survey order, Number 623, for his tract of land, containing some 290 acres of land at the mouth of Muddy Creek, which was patented to him February 20, 1789, under the title of "Oliver's Desire". He held the major portion of this tract until shortly before his death in Brown County, Ohio, about 1817-18.

A series of deeds disclose that he had laid out a number of lots with water rights at an early date and that on December 8, 1801, he was joined by his wife, Sarah, in a deed to John Armstrong, who lived on the south side of Muddy Creek, by which they sold about 120 square feet to Armstrong for the purpose of an abutment for a mill dam. Other lots were sold to John Boreman, Daniel Anderson, Joseph Derumple, and John Crawford. (D. B. 1. pp. 568). Then, on April 9, 1817, Oliver Crawford alone, indicating his wife had died, sold 169 acres of land to Jeremiah Davidson, who continued to operate the ferry at that place. Prior to that time, on November 6, 1816, he had made a deed for 101 acres of "Oliver's Desire" to Nasa McCurdy, whom the Muddy Creek Ledger indicates was a freed slave.

It was probably about this time that Oliver Crawford went to Brown County, Ohio, as there is nothing in the record to show the deeds were executed away from Greene County. An account of the family, written by George L. Crawford and entitled "Bits of History" says that the Crawfords settled first in Adams County on Brush Creek, and it seems probable that Oliver Crawford joined his family there. Brown County probate record Number 7382 shows that the estate of Oliver Crawford was opened September 26, 1818, which gives the approximate date of his death. It was kept open until 1835, because of a judgment of Jay Thompson, which necessitated trips to Greene County, Pennsylvania, in 1819, 1820, and 1824. Records of Ruth (Crawford) Clark, a granddaughter, say that Oliver Crawford had two wives named Jane, yet it is certain that in 1801, his wife's name was Sarah. But Bible records make it definite that one wife named Jane was the mother of his children, and show that she died in giving birth to twin children, on November 4, 1781. The same source indicates that Oliver Crawford was born in 1741. No military service other than in the French and Indian War has been found for Oliver Crawford, but this is not surprising since he lived in the area from which the company of Captain Jesse Pigman was recruited and no muster of that company has been found. Living also across the creek from John Armstrong's Boat Yard, where many boats were built for the various expeditions during the Revolution, one would expect that Oliver Crawford spent many days working on these boats, and getting out timber for their construction. A careful investigator might find such service among the George Rogers Clark Papers of the Draper collection. His name is in the 1772 tax list for Springhill Township, Bedford County, Pennsylvania, for the year 1772, and in many local tax lists. He was also a signer of the Petition for a new State, and there are a number of entries in his name in the Muddy Creek Ledger. It is to be noted that the ferry, which he established in 1770, and which no doubt ferried troops to the Fayette County side of the Monongahela on their way to Redstone, is still in operation to this date, it being the shortest route between Waynesburg and Uniontown, on the Old National Road.

Family of Oliver and Jane Crawford
(From Bible Record)

1. Esther Crawford, born October 22, 1766; married Thomas Thoroman (spelled Thurriman, Thurman, Thoroughman, etc.). Thomas Thoroman came to the Scioto River with his brother, Samuel, then moved to Adams County, Ohio, and settled on Brush Creek. A brother, William Thoroman, went to Kentucky about the same time. All three brothers are in the Census of Pennsylvana for 1790, when they were living in the Tenmile Country, probably near the mouth of Muddy Creek. Thomas Thoroman was an executor in Oliver Crawford's estate. He married (2) Charlotte Randle, to whom was born the last three daughters.

Children of Thomas and Esther (Crawford) Thoroman

1. Annie Thoroman, married, July 12, 1821, John Coyle.
2. .... Thoroman, married .... Metz.
3. Thomas Thoroman, born February 4, 1789, died September 15, 1880; married, September 26, 1811, Sallie Smith, born August 10, 1791, died February 19, 1877.
4. Charles Thoroman, married, August 14, 1817, Ruth Florea.
5. Samuel Thoroman, born May 23, 1795, died December 12, 1881; married, October 8, 1818, Annie McDonald Reynolds.
6. Oliver C. Thoroman, married, March 12, 1820, Rebecca Lafferty.
7. William Thoroman, married Maria Kerr.
8. Andrew Thoroman, married .... Brumley.
9. Rachel Thoroman, daughter of Thomas and Charlotte (Randle) Thoroman.
10. Sarah Thoroman, daughter of Thomas and Charlotte (Randle) Thoroman.
11. Rena Thoroman, daughter of Thomas and Charlotte (Randle) Thoroman.

2. Thomas Crawford, born November 9, 1768, died 1811; married Jane McKey. Thomas Crawford is frequently mentioned in the Muddy Creek Ledger. He went to Deerfield Township, Warren County, Ohio, where he bought 106 acres of land from Judge Symmes. His son, Samuel, was the administrator of his estate and guardian for the other children.

Children of Thomas and Jane (McKey) Crawford

1. Oliver Crawford, died young.
2. Samuel Crawford, died 1836; married, January 5, 1815, Charity Scofield, born 1797.
3. Alexander Crawford, married Eliza Scofield. Their grandson, George F. Crawford, wrote the history of the Crawford Family.
4. Ruth Crawford, married, April 1, 1813, Clark Baker.
5. Dr. John Crawford, married Elizabeth Cline.

3. Ann Crawford, born April 4, 1770, died May 13, 1838; married Samuel Thoroman, born 1767, died May 25, 1845. He was in the Census of 1790 for Washington County, Pennsylvania.

Children of Samuel and Ann (Crawford) Thoroman

1. Sarah Thoroman, married, November 15, 1810, Matthew Jones.
2. William Thoroman, born February 21, 1789, died April 7, 1849; married, October 19, 1815, Sarah Tucker, born January 12, 1794, died January 12, 1872.
3. Jane Thoroman, born 1791, died May 1829; married, April 14, 1811, Jacob Treber, born September 18, 1779, died January 4, 1875.
4. Oliver Thoroman, born February 28, 1794, died April 6, 1873; married, February 14, 1822, Ann Treber, born September 17, 1796, died June 24, 1870.
5. Samuel Thoroman, born May 26, 1796, died September 16, 1869; married, January 10, 1822, Rachel Florea, born January 12, 1796, died January 28, 1875.
6. Esther Thoroman, married, July 5, 1821, Joseph Treber, born April 27, 1776.
7. Crawford Thoroman, married, January 29, 1824, Nancy

Porter.
8. Polly Thoroman, married Jesse Williams.
9. Infant, died young.
10. Elizabeth Thoroman, married, December 10, 1829, Simeon Jackman.
11. Charles Thoroman, born October 30, 1812, died March 10, 1890; married, September 23, 1837, Maria Fear.

4. Andrew Crawford, born May 1, 1772; mentioned in the Muddy Creek Ledger.
5. Mary Crawford, born September 4, 1774; married .. .. Alexander.
6. Hugh Crawford, born November 9, 1777.
7. Sarah Crawford, born January 15, 1779.
8. Oliver Crawford, Jr., born November 4, 1781; died about the age of 25 years.
9. Jane Crawford, born November 4, 1781; (twin) died aged 16 years.

ALEXANDER CRAWFORD

It seems quite probable that the Alexander Crawford, whose history is written up in the "History of Ross and Highland Counties, Ohio," published by Williams Brothers in 1880, (pp. 531) was the brother of Oliver Crawford as reported by these and other authors. This history says that Alexander Crawford was born "during the progress of the Revolution," and in 1796, left Greene County, Pennsylvania, with his wife and four children, floating down the Ohio on a flat boat until they came to the mouth of the Scioto River, then continued up the Scioto to make a landing near Chillicothe. We cannot agree with the statement concerning his birth period, for he is known to have been the father of several children prior to 1790. In addition to that status as a father, he was probably the Alexander Crawford, who served in Captain William Crawford's Company during the Revolution. Then there is the record of Even Shelby's Company in Colonel Henry Boquet's Army in 1759, showing Alexander and Oliver Crawford members of that company. Alexander Crawford is also mentioned in the Muddy Creek Ledger, showing him to be an adult before 1796. Finally the article in this Ohio history practically explodes the period of birth given for Alexander Crawford, when it says he was accompanied on his journey by his wife, Anna Pigman, and four children. It would seem therefore, that Alexander Crawford was most likely born before 1745, and married during the Revolutionary period, to Anna, daughter of Captain Jesse Pigman, a neighbor north of Muddy Creek.

The rest of the history says that Alexander Crawford was a millwright and helped build the famous "Floating Mill" of Chillicothe history. He lived at the mouth of Waugh's Run on Deer Creek until 1799, and then removed to the site of Center in Fairfield Township, where he lived for six years. The place was long known as "Crawford's Thicket". (Land warranted to Alice Crawford near Glades Church carried the same title.) In 1805, Alexander Crawford moved to Paint Township, Ross County, Ohio, where he built a mill on Main Paint Creek at Hewitt's Crossing. Here he was drowned while attempting to cross the creek in a canoe in 1823.

Children of Alexander and Anna (Pigman) Crawford

1. Jesse Crawford, died in 1816; was a soldier in the War of 1812.

2. Alexander Crawford, Jr., born 1790, served in the War of 1812, and died in Highland County, Ohio, May 15, 1874. His wife was Elizabeth Brown, daughter of Benoni Brown of Ross County.
3. Mary Crawford, married Nathan Thomas.
4. Elizabeth Crawford, married James Greenfield.
5. Elizabeth Crawford, married William Greenfield.
6. Susan Crawford, married John McElvaine; they went to Illinois.
7. Elsie Crawford, married Joseph Esthe and went to Indiana.

THE DAVIS FAMILY

On May 25, 1785, William Davis got a warrant for a tract of land on Enoch's Run, which was patented to him on June 6. 1787, under the title of "Davis' Delight". He was originally from Chester County, Pennsylvania, and probably a brother of Azariah Davis who went to Kentucky with James Harrod and was one of the founders of Harrodsburg. This is indicated by the fact that the Harrods were near neighbors of William Davis on Enoch's Run, and the naming by William Davis of one of his sons, Azariah. William Davis also mentions a brother, James Davis in his will, probably the James Davis who took up land on Dunkard Creek. The wife of William Davis is not known, nor has the burial place been located. He died about 1789, and his will is on file in Washington County. (Will Book 1. pp. 104, probated December 1, 1789). In it he names three children: Stephen Davis, who patented a tract of land on a branch of Whiteley Creek in Greene Township; Azariah Davis, and Tabitha Davis.

Children

1. Stephen Davis.
2. Azariah Davis was born in Chester County, Pennsylvania, February 12, 1756; came to Western Pennsylvania, where he served in Captain John Guthery's Company of militia in the War of the Revolution. He is listed as "Ess" Davis in the muster roll of Captain Guthery. (Penna. Arch. Series VI Vol. 2. pp. 19.) He married Alice Vanmeter, daughter of Henry and Martha Vanmeter, and in 1811, they removed to Knox County, Ohio, where he died near Utica in 1839. Their children, all born in Greene County, were:
   1. Henry Davis, born 1781; married (1) Rachel ...., who died in 1848. His second wife was .... Ames.
   2. William Davis, born 1783; married Lydia Fields.
   3. Azariah Davis, Jr.; married Nancy Hayes.
   4. Martha Davis, born December 7, 1784, died 1828; married James H. Smith.
   5. Sarah Davis; married George Miller.
   6. Elizabeth Davis.
   7. Rachel Davis; married Uzzel Stevens.
   8. Rebecca Davis, born 1796; married Jacob Hanger.
3. Tabitha Davis, born 1753, died March 15, 1803. She married John Davis, who had served in Captain William Crawford's Company of Militia. He died August 17, 1822 (or 1825). His tombstone in Garards Fort Cemetery being scarcely legible, indicates he was born in 1734, but could be 1754, more nearly the age of his wife. His will in Greene County Will Book 1.

pp. 275, was probated November 23, 1825, and names his children, who were:
1. Mary Davis, who married Eliel (?) Long.
2. Hannah Davis, who married John Lesley.
3. Elizabeth Davis; married James Morrison, who was born June 10, 1773, and died June 18, 1825. He is buried in Garards Fort Cemetery. The children listed in his will (Greene County W. B. 1. pp. 288, probated January 19, 1826), were:
   John Morrison.
   Rebecca Morrison.
   Lydia Morrison.
   Hannah Morrison.
   Mary Morrison.
4. Sarah Davis, born December 25, 1782, died May 7, 1869; married Benjamin Morrison, born July 18, 1776, died June 27, 1853. Both are buried in Garards Fort Cemetery. Their children were:
   Joseph Morris, born 1815.
   Archibald Morrison, born 1817.
   Hester Morrison, who married .... Sicklesmith.
   Rachel Morrison, who married Nicholas Livengood, son of Nicholas and Elizabeth (Kughn) Livengood. He died November 6, 1874.
   Mary Morrison, married .... Eberhart.
   Elizabeth Morrison, married .... Hildebrand.
   ... . Morrison, who married .... Sheets.

MAJOR EDMUND POLKE

Mrs. E. B. Federa of Louisville, Kentucky, writes that Major Edmund Polke of the Fourth Battalion, Washington County, Pennsylvania Militia, in 1781, was a son of Charles Polke, the Indian Trader of Maryland, and that he located in the vicinity of Fort Pitt some time about 1765. Edmund Polke and three of his brothers were soldiers in the Revolution. A John Polke was neighbor to the Harrods in the Little Cove near Chambersburg, Pennsylvania, in 1750, where he signed a petition to the Pennsylvania Authorities asking their lands be held for them pending the running of the dividing line. Draper Mss. 4 NN 11, shows that Captain William Harrod purchased cattle from Edmund, Thomas, and Charles Polke in 1774, for the use of Lord Dunmore's Army in July and August of that year. At that time Edmund Polke may have been living on the tract of land surveyed to him on a Virginia Certificate dated May 16, 1769, and situated where that part of Carmichaels north of Muddy Creek and on Coal Run is now located. This tract, known as "White Licks" was later patented to Charles Anderson. A Samuel Polke obtained a warrant for the tract at the head of Coal Run, known as "Sugar Camp", which was later patented to Edward Thomas. There are no records to indicate these men ever made a permanent settlement in this section. William Polke, brother of Charles, the Indian Trader, was the great grandfather of James K. Polk, President of the United States.

Edmund Polke was born in 1740, probaly in Frederick County, Maryland, and died at Smithfield, Nelson County, Kentucky, in 1825. His wife's name is not known. About the end of the Revolution he moved to Kentucky, where he left many prominent descendants.

Children of Edmund Polke

1. Thomas Polke, born 1768.
2. Rev. Charles Polke, born September 26, 1770; married, July 26,

1790, Willey Dever.
3. Edmund Polke, Jr., born 1772.
4. Hannah Polke, born 1774; married, November 11, 1788, Adam Gutherie.
5. Christina Katherine Polke, born 1776; married, February 22, 1794, Ignatius Able.
6. Sarah Polke, born 1778; married Zachariah Fowler.
7. Polly Polke, born 1780; never married.
8. Nancy Polke, born 1782; never married.
9. James Polke, born 1784; married Nancy Able.

SAMUEL HARPER FAMILY

One of the Revolutionary soldiers buried in Glades Cemetery is Samuel Harper. He came from Eastern Pennsylvania about 1800, and purchased land from John Crawford, and on June 3, 1800, purchased a tract from Isaac Israel. Samuel Harper was born in Eastern Pennsylvania in 1754. At the outbreak of the Revolution in 1776, he joined Captain Francis Murray's Company in Samuel Atlee's Regiment, then in the Spring of 1777, from March until May, he served in Captain Mathew Scott's Company in Colonel John Bull's Regiment. In October 1781, he was a member of Captain Robinson's Chester County Militia Company, stationed at Newton. Benjamin Lincoln was also a member and came west with Harper, and was the ancestor of the Carmichael Lincoln Family. For a time after the Revolution Samuel Harper lived in York County, Pennsylvania, where he was a neighbor of Samuel Houlsworth, who seems to have been some kind of relative, since we find a brother of Samuel Harper named Houlsworth Harper, and Samuel named his youngest son Houlsworth. Samuel Harper was twice married, first to Hannah Swearing(ton), who died April 29, 1809, at the age of forty-eight years, and was buried at Glades. He had ten children by this marriage, and then married Jane (McMillan) Morehead, daughter of Rev. John McMillan, by whom he had four more children. She died February 3, 1857, at the age of 80 years. Samuel Harper died June 8, 1839. His children were:

1. James Harper, died October 6, 1828, aged 28 years, 7 months, and 25 days.
2. William Harper.
3. Jane Harper, who married Stephen Burnett.
4. Nancy Harper, who married William S. Carmichaels.
5. Samuel Harper, Jr., who married Sara ....
6. Hannah Harper, who married Abia Minor.
7. George Harper.
8. Isabell Harper.
9. Sarah Harper, who married John Moore.
10. Henry Harper, who married Matilda Swearington.
11. John Harper, who died July 28, 1869, aged 57 years. He married Isabella Hughes.
12. Moses Allen Harper, married Hester J. Lewis.
13. Catherine A. Harper, married Jefferson Crawford.
14. Houlsworth Harper, born 1817 died 1907; married Rebecca M. Johnson.

ISAAC ISRAEL

According to Burgess' "Virginia Soldiers of 1776", Isaac Israel was originally from Berkeley County, Virginia. (Vol. 3. pp. 1245.) He served for three years as a captain in the Eighth Virginia Regiment of the Continental Line, for which he received Warrant number 5147 for 4,000 acres of land, which he assigned to John Stokely of Wood County, Virginia, on March 7, 1807. Before the end of the Revolution Isaac Israel removed to Washington County, where in 1781, he served in Captain George Sharp's Company, Third Battalion, Washington County, Pennsylvania Militia. On April 18, 1786, he received a warrant for a tract of land near Baily's School House, which he later patented under the title "Alarm Post". He and wife, Eleanor, sold this land about 1800, in two deeds of record and seem to have moved away from here. (Greene County Deed Book 1. pp. 451-696.) The record of his family is to be found in the will of his brother, Jacob Israel, in Will Book 1. pp. 21, probated in Washington County, Pennsylvania, on June 17, 1783. Jacob Israel left his estate to his wife, Priscilla ...., and the children of Isaac Israel, whom he names. Jacob Israel probably preceded his brother, Isaac, to the Muddy Creek section, as he served in Captain William Crawford's Company in 1782.

Children of Isaac and Eleanor Israel

Jacob Israel.
Isaac Israel, Jr.
Sarah Israel.
Priscilla Israel. The Muddy Creek Ledger (pp. 591), discloses that she married James Anderson, son of Charles and Mary Anderson. James and Priscilla (Israel) Anderson were the parents of Priscilla Anderson, who married George Moredock. Through this line, descendants of Isaac and Eleanor Israel still live in Greene County, Pennsylvania.
Druscilla Israel.
Amelia Israel.

THE GREGG FAMILY

At least three distinct lines of the Gregg Family, perhaps all from a common ancestor of Glen Orchy, Argyleshire, Scotland, are represented in the Muddy Creek families of this name. Two lines of the family can be traced back to William Gregg, an immigrant who settled on a tract of land known as "Rockland Manor" in Christiana Hundred, New Castle County, Delaware, in 1682. The other line may be traced back to Captain David Gregg, a native of Glen Orchy, who went to Coleraine County, Ireland, where he was murdered along with his son, John Gregg. Another son, Thomas Gregg, who escaped this murder by the opponents of Cromwell in 1689, had a son, Samuel Gregg, who emigrated to America, and settled in Loudon County, Virginia, where he married Elizabeth Alford for his first wife, and after her death, married (2) Mrs. Esther Dixon.

William Gregg of Delaware, had among others, John Gregg, born 1668, died 1738, who married, in 1694, Elizabeth Cooke; and George Gregg, who died in 1744, leaving a wife, whose maiden name was Sarah Hogg. At one period, John Gregg owned three square miles of land along the Brandywine.

Family of John and Elizabeth (Cooke) Gregg

1. William Gregg, born 1695, died 1747; married, July 29, 1725, Margery Hickey. His second wife was Ann (Dixon) Woodnut.
2. Amy Gregg, who married, August 25, 1721, Joseph Hadley.
3. John Gregg, no record.
4. Thomas Gregg, who died 1748; married, February 10, 1721, Dinah Harlan.

5. Joseph Gregg, born 1710, died 1770; married, August 4, 1735, Hannah Beeson.
6. Samuel Gregg, born 1710, died 1767; married, February 27, 1737, Ann Robinson, born 1717, died 1774, of whom, later.
7. Hannah Gregg, married 1742, George Robinson.
8. Rebecca Gregg, married, 1740, ... Spragg.
9. Stephen Gregg (?).

Family of George and Sarah (Hogg) Gregg

1. John Gregg, born 1716, in Chester County, Pennsylvania, died in Shilbourne Parish, Loudon County, Virginia, June 9, 1788; married, August 13, 1737, Susan Curle, born New Castle County, Delaware; died in Loudon County, Virginia. He was sheriff of Bucks County, Pennsylvania, in 1762-4, and served as a lieutenant in the 13th Pennsylvania Regiment in the Revolution. Record of this family to follow.
2. Richard Gregg, died in New Castle County, Delaware, where his will was filed October 2, 1754. He married, April 12, 1735, Ann, daughter of Simon Hadley.
3. George Gregg, died in Virginia in 1794; married, 1748, Elizabeth Hanby.

Family of John Gregg

John Gregg, son of Captain David Gregg, who was murdered with his father in Ireland, left a family of 12 children, but rigorous laws and high taxes forced a number of his children to leave for America in 1722. There are records of the following:
1. David Gregg, born 1685; married Mary Navin; settled in New Hampshire.
2. John Gregg, went to South Carolina.
3. Samuel Gregg, went to Massachusetts.
4. Rachel Gregg, married Solomon Walker and came to Pennsylvania.
5. Andrew Gregg, born 1710, died in Pennsylvania, May 18, 1789; married (2) Jean Scott.

Family of Thomas Gregg

Thomas Gregg, son of Captain David Gregg, died in Coleraine, Ireland. Three of his sons are known. They are:
1. Thomas Gregg.
2. John Gregg.
3. Samuel Gregg, who died in Loudon County, Virginia, about 1803. Record to follow.

Family of Samuel and Elizabeth (Alford) Gregg

Bible Record from Miss Lilian Davidson

Samuel Gregg was born in Ireland and came to America to settle in Loudon County, Virginia, where he died and his will was filed on April 7, 1803. He married, in Virginia, Elizabeth Alford. His second wife was Mrs. Esther (Tobin) Dixon.

Children

1. Thomas Gregg, born October 26, 1743, died in Fayette County, Pennsylvania, September 29, 1821; married, March 12, 1766, Amy Gregg, born October 28, 1744; daughter of John and Susan (Curle) Gregg.
2. Priscilla Gregg, born September 8, 1745; married Amos Gregg, son of John and Susan (Curle) Gregg. He was born April 13, 1742. They went to Kentucky.
3. John Gregg, born October 14, 1747, died before 1803; married Susan Gregg.
4. Rebecca Gregg, born February 24, 1749; married, November 4, 1767, William Gregg.
5. Ruth Gregg, born April 23, 1753; married, 1769, George Gregg, son of John and Susan (Curle) Gregg.
6. Israel Gregg, born March 2, 1754; married, 1775, Sarah Gregg.
7. Ann Gregg, born May 5, 1756, died July 20, 1817; married, 1775, Richard Gregg, son of John and Susan (Curle) Gregg. He was born March 5, 1752, died November 15, 1812. See later.
8. Samuel Gregg, born April 18, 1758.
9. Aaron Gregg, born January 17, 1761, died in the Army at Fort Adams, Mississippi.
10. Elizabeth Gregg, born April 15, 1763; married Volentine Nichols.

Family of John and Susan (Curle) Gregg

John Gregg, son of George and Sarah (Hogg) Gregg, was born in Chester County, Pennsylvania, in 1716, died in Shilbourne Parish, Loudon County, Virginia, June 9, 1788. He married, August 13, 1737, Susan Curle, daughter of Richard Curle of New Castle County, Delaware. John Gregg was sheriff of Bucks County, Pennsylvania in 1762-4, and served in the 13th Pennsylvania Regiment as a lieutenant in 1778-9.

Children

1. Mary Gregg, born August 8, 1738, married Nixon Gregg. Lived in Virginia.
2. Hannah Gregg, born March 8, 1740; married, 1761, Caleb Dixon; removed to North Carolina.
3. Amos Gregg, born April 13, 1742; married Priscilla Gregg, daughter of Samuel and Elizabeth (Alford) Gregg. Removed to Kentucky. Priscilla was born September 8, 1745, in Virginia.
4. Amy Gregg, born October 28, 1744; married, in 1766, Thomas Gregg, son of Samuel and Elizabeth (Alford) Gregg, born October 26, 1743, died in Fayette County, Pennsylvania, September 29, 1821. They settled in Fayette County prior to 1771.
5. George Gregg, born April 26, 1747; married, in 1769, Ruth Gregg, daughter of Samuel and Elizabeth (Alford) Gregg, born April 23, 1753. They removed to West Virginia. He served in Captain William Crawford's Militia Company.
6. John Gregg, born September 28, 1749, died in Virginia in 1769; married Susannah Underwood.
7. Richard Gregg, born March 5, 1752; died in Greene County Pennsylvania, November 15, 1812. His will is in Greene

County Will Book 1. pp. 108, and was probated April 15, 1813. Richard Gregg served in Captain William Crawford's Company of the Fifth Battalion, Washington County Militia. (Penna. Archives Series VI Vol. 2. pp. 166.) He married, about 1775, Ann Gregg, born May 5, 1756; daughter of Samuel and Elizabeth (Alford) Gregg. She died in 1817, in Greene County.

Children

(Records from the Gregg Bible owned by Miss Davidson)
1. Meylon Gregg, born August 17, 1776, died June 28, 1777.
2. Ruth Gregg, born June 4, 1778, died January 20, 1862; married, 1798, Ellis Baily.
3. Permelia Gregg, born January 17, 1780, died June 3, 1870; married James Hughes.
4. Priscilla Gregg, born October 31, 1781, died July 8, 1836; married Asa Stephenson.
5. Rezin Gregg, born November 30, 1783, died July 25, 1843; married Frances Grove.
6. Craven Gregg, born December 22, 1785, died 1853-5; married Delilah Ball.
7. Presley Gregg, born April 22, 1789, died October 1, 1849; married Sarah Barricklow.
8. Aaron Gregg, born June 19, 1791, died February 23, 1856; married Maria Seaton, born February 1, 1795, daughter of William and Sarah (Myers) Seaton.
9. Pera Gregg, born May 11, 1793, died March 26, 1872; married, January 25, 1815, Eli Baily, born September 27, 1788, died August 17, 1854. He was a son of Eli and Ruth (Taylor) Baily.
10. Susannah Gregg, born May 22, 1795, died June 23, 1866; married, in 1818, Richard Swan, born September 14, 1796, died December 29, 1873; son of Charles and Sarah (Vanmeter) Swan.
11. Alford Gregg, born October 10, 1798, died April 3, 1867; married Mary Kerr.

Family of Samuel and Ann (Robinson) Gregg

Samuel Gregg, son of John and Elizabeth (Cooke) Gregg, born 1710, died 1767, in New Castle County, Delaware. He married, February 27, 1737, Ann Robinson, born 1717, died 1774. Both left wills in New Castle County.

Children

1. Betty Gregg, married (1) Jacob Wilson; (2) Jonathan Woodnut, (3) .... Jones.
2. Sarah Gregg, born 1743, died 1801; married Gideon Gilpin.
3. Samuel Gregg; died 1830; married Dinah Chandler, born 1754, died 1830.
4. Mary Gregg, married John Gibson.
5. John Gregg, born December 7, 1755, died in Greene County Pennsylvania, March 29, 1808. He married, November 25 1781, Orpha Stubbs, daughter of Daniel and Ruth (Gilpin) Stubbs. She was born May 19, 1760, and died March 12, 1830. Family records taken from the Bible of Orpha (Stubbs) Gregg, which was printed in Edinburgh, Scotland, by Mark and Charles Kerr in 1789. John Gregg was a member of Captain William Crawford's Militia Company. He left a will which is in Greene County Will Book 1. pp. 69, and was probated April 5, 1808.

Children of John and Orpha (Stubbs) Gregg

1. Joseph Gregg, born September 1, 1783, died September 27, 1868; married, September 6, 1810, Cassandra Corbly, born June 6, 1791, died December 6, 1869. She was a daughter of Rev. John and Nancy (Lynn) Corbly.

   #### Children

   1. Elizabeth Gregg, born June 15, 1811, died 1821.
   2. Ruth Gregg, born September 19, 1812, died 1834; married, March 1832, Rev. John Fordyce, Jr., born September 5, 1805, died April 18, 1882.
   3. Orpha Gregg, born October 16, 1813, died December 16, 1873; married, March 19, 1843, Thomas Titus, born July 1, 1816, died March 19, 1895.
   4. Sarah Gregg, born October 31, 1815; married William Wood.
   5. John C. Gregg, born July 8, 1818, died 1821.
   6. Nancy Gregg, born August 15, 1820; married Robert J. Evans.
   7. Eliza Gregg, born October 13, 1822; married Thomas Patterson.
   8. Joseph Gregg, born December 1, 1825, died June 8, 1884; married Rebecca Minor.
   9. Cephas Gregg, born March 13, 1827, died December 2, 1866.
   10. Corbly Gregg, born April 6, 1829, died May 1901; married Mary Stephens, born February 14, 1842, died November 18, 1924.
   11. George Gregg, born April 5, 1831.
   12. Matilda Gregg, born October 25, 1834, died 1926; married Napoleon West.

2. Cephas Gregg, born April 3, 1786, died 1849; married Susannah Clymer, born 1786, died 1825.
3. Ruth Gregg, born January 15, 1788; married Enoch South, born July 27, 1787, died 1863.

   #### Children of Enoch and Ruth (Gregg) South

   1. Benjamin South, married Matilda Gapen.
   2. John South, married Velinda Everly.
   3. Delilah South.
   4. Cassandra South, married Jacob Lantz.
   5. Elizabeth South, married Abner Baily.
   6. Rebecca South, married Evan Evans.
   7. Ruth South, married William Knotts.
   8. Sarah South, married Abijah South.
   9. Nancy South, married .... Bowlby.
   10. Malinda South, married William Britton
   11. Mariah South, died young.

4. Orpha Gregg, born November 5, 1790, died 1869; married, 1801, John Myers, born 1789, died 1865.

   #### Children of John and Orpha (Gregg) Myers

   1. Joseph Myers, died young.
   2. Peter Myers.
   3. Oliver Myers.

    4. Josephus Myers.
    5. Sarah Myers, married Abraham Watson.
    6. Orpha Myers, married James Kirby.
    7. Mary Myers, married Henry Stephens.
    8. Pleasants Myers, married Otho Minor.
    9. Emeline Myers, married Phillip Minor.
    10. Louisa Myers, married Jacob Ramer.
    11. Harriet Myers, died young.
    12. Experience Myers, died young.
 5. John Gregg, born December 31, 1792, died November 27, 1820.
 6. George Gregg, born August 10, 1795.
 7. Ann Gregg, born November 18, 1797; married Jonathan Garard, born 1794, died February 26, 1877, aged 82 years, 7 months, 22 days.

Children of Jonathan and Ann (Gregg) Garard

1. Stephen Garard, married Mary Ann Robinson.
2. Joseph Garard, married Emeline Long.
3. Corbly Garard, married Mary Long.
4. Mary Garard, married (1) .... Bell, (2) Albert Myers.
5. Mariah Garards, married Alfred Yeager.

 8. Mary Gregg, born November 11, 1800, died April 4, 1825; married Joseph Myers.
 6. Hannah Gregg, married, in 1795, Thomas Hooper.
 7. Joseph Gregg, married Mary Collins.
 8. Thomas Gregg, married, 1762, Rebecca Janey, Lincoln, Virginia.

VOLENTINE NICHOLS

First mention of Volentine Nichols in the Tenmile Country comes from the pension application of Eliel Long. (Nat. Arch. Pa.-S 2284.) Long states that he served a month in the Spring of 1779 as a volunteer under Captain Volentine Nichols. This service was on Big Whiteley Creek and had followed a tour of duty under Captain John Minor. Volentine Nichols is next found in the tax lists for Cumberland Township, Washington County, Pennsylvania in 1784, when the name is listed as Vallon Nichols. On March 20, 1790, Volentine Nichols bought "Suspense", a tract of land at the head of Sugar Run, from George Knotts, which on September 15, 1796, he sold to Joseph Ball, the latter getting the patent for the land January 7, 1797. (Greene County Deed Book 1. pp. 14.) His wife was Elizabeth Gregg, daughter of Samuel and Elizabeth (Alford) Gregg. She was born April 15, 1763, and must have died prior to the date of the above deed as she does not join in the sale. A deed was made July 16, 1832, from Valentine Nichols to his son, George, and daughter, Vina. (DB. 9. pp. 227.)

Children

1. Valentine Nichols, Jr., married Nancy Cooper.
2. George Nichols.
3. Lavina Nichols.

JACOB CLINE FAMILY

Professor Waychoff sets the date for the building of Fort Cline on Muddy Creek at about 1775, and definitely states that it was in existence at the time of the killing of Simon Rinehart by the Indians, for it was to this fort his family fled after hearing the shot that killed him. This tragic event, however, happened about four years later than the date mentioned by Waychoff. But he is not far from correct in his date, and his knowledge of the land whereon the fort stood as well as the farms of Jacob Cline was gleaned from study of the land during his boyhood days, when he lived on a part of the original land patented to Jacob Cline. It was the privelege of this writer, who has hunted over every inch of the Cline farms, when they were in possession of Mr. Joseph Patton, to go over the historical points in company of Professor Waychoff and have him explain the signs of the earlier dwellings, fort, and cemetery of Jacob Cline. William Harrod, Jr., in his interview with L. C. Draper, also mentions the fort of Jacob Cline on Muddy Creek. The fort stood on a knoll just east of the marker which commemorates the site where the first Court of Greene County was held in 1796. This marker stands but a short distance from the site where Jacob Cline built his second cabin, and when visited with Professor Waychoff, a line of shrubbery clearly marked the original site. The cemetery was cleared to make room for the present orchard.

Jacob Cline was a Virginia Justice during the period this section was in dispute, so it was but natural that the first court of Greene County would be held at his house, people were used to going there, even though Washington County had been set up more than ten years before. He was also a distiller. His wife was Eleanor Vanmeter, daughter of Jacob and Letitia (Strobe) Vanmeter. Jacob Vanmeter had the other fort on Muddy Creek, situated about where Baily's School House later stood. With the loss of the markers that were in the old cemetery, the dates of Jacob Cline and wife, Letitia, have been destroyed. He died about 1802, leaving a will, which was probated on April 28 of that year. (Greene County Will Book 1. pp. 29.) His wife and six children were named in the will.

Children of Jacob and Eleanor (Vanmeter) Cline

1. Peter Cline, married Nancy Inghram, daughter of Arthur and Olive (Smith) Inghram.
2. Jacob Cline, Jr.
3. Isaac Cline, born in Greene County, Pennsylvania, in 1777, died in Elizabeth Township, Miami County, Ohio, October 3, 1838; married Olive Inghram, daughter of Arthur and Olive (Smith) Inghram; she died in Miami County in 1851. They had removed to Ohio about 1809.

Children

1. John Cline, born October 3, 1804, died August 20, 1873.
2. Hannah Cline, married Levi DeWeese.
3. Minerva Cline, married Levi Hart.
4. Mary Cline, married, February 1829, Joseph Martin, son of Levi and Delilah (Corbly) Martin, born in Greene County; both husband and wife died in one night of cholera in 1833, leaving three children, Abijah, William, and Hannah, aged 5, 3, 1 years old respectively.
5. Jacob Cline, died in 1833.
6. Elizabeth Cline, married Isaac Dye.
7. Letitia Cline, married Paterson Crane.
8. Isaac Cline, born March 8, 1818, married Elizabeth Knight, born January 30, 1818.
9. Inghram Cline.
10. William Cline.

4. Letitia Cline.
5. Eleanor Cline.
6. Ruth Cline, married Nathan Veach.
7. Elizabeth Cline, born 1776, died in Miami County, Ohio, January 6, 1852. She married John M. Dye, who died April 1, 1842. He was a son of Andrew and Sarah (Minor) Dye.

AARON LUZADER

On November 28, 1833, in Monongalia County, West Virginia, Aaron Luzader made application for a pension for services in the Revolution, stating that he was 102 years of age and had been born in Somerset County, New Jersey in 1731. That he served in Somerset County Militia for three months in 1776, and then in 1777, moved to what is now Greene County, Pennsylvania. He further stated that in 1778, he was a spy on Whiteley Creek under Captain William Crawford. He said he was discharged in September 1783, with two years and eight months of service. He lived in Greene County until 1793, when he removed to Monongalia County and had been there since.

Aaron Luzader was a member of Goshen Baptist Church, where he was cited on June 28, 1783, for infractions of rules, but on February 24, 1787, he was chosen to represent the church at Laurel Hill. It is probable that Sarah Luzader, who was received into Goshen Church in June 1781, was his wife.

Children of Aaron Luzader

1. Abraham Luzader, who married Leah Hoge, daughter of George and Elizabeth (Blackledge) Hoge. She was born October 23, 1767; he was born in New Jersey in 1757, and died in Guernsey County, Ohio, in 1826. Abraham Luzader was a soldier on the George Rogers Clark Expedition according to the Guernsey County records and is buried on his own farm. His will, made December 13, 1825, was filed February 14, 1826. (WB. A-136. Guernsey County, Ohio.)

Children

1. Betsy Luzader, married .... Goves or Gover.
2. Polly Luzader, married .... Smith; died before her father.

Children

   Morgan Smith.
   Hannah Smith.
   Jane Smith.
   Lot Smith.
   Fanny Smith.
3. Patty Luzader, married .... Warne.
4. Rachel Luzader, married .... Bonnell.
5. Sally Luzader, married .... Dougherty; died before her father.
6. Leah Luzader, married .... Smith.
7. John Luzader.
8. Isaac Luzader.

THE ARMSTRONGS

There can be little doubt that the Armstrongs were among the first to settle at the Mouth of Muddy Creek. There could be truth in the Flenniken traditions that John Armstrong was with John and James Flenniken in a survey trip to the section in 1760.

It seems almost certain that they were there before Josiah Crawford made his improvement at the headwaters of Muddy Creek in the Summer of 1766. It is stated that Abraham Armstrong, son of John and Mary (Kennedy) Armstrong, was born there just after 1767, and was the first white child born on this side of the Monongahela River, a report that may well be correct, though John Armstrong had older children than this son. Guernsey County, Ohio, history says that John and Abraham Armstrong, the pioneer brothers who settled on Muddy Creek, were sons of Adam Armstrong, a native of the Conochacheague, near the present town of Chambersburg, Pennsylvania. Their mother's name is not given.

Land records show that John Armstrong had warranted to him on October 24, 1770, on a Virginia Certificate dated May 27, 1769, a tract of land on the south side of the mouth of Muddy Creek under the title of "Mill Tract." This suggests that he had prior to that date set up some sort of mill, and the record is one of the earliest grants obtained from the Pennsylvania authorities. His brother, Abraham Armstrong, obtained two tracts of land just west of John, one of which was on a warrant dated July 15, 1773, on the north side of Muddy Creek, the other on the south side was warranted to him on December 24, 1785. Abraham Armstrong did not patent either tract. The Muddy Creek Ledger shows that John Armstrong, and his son, David Armstrong, operated boat yards at John Armstrong's site, and that on November 7, 1794, were paid 24 pounds and 10 shillings for a flat boat used in transporting flour from Muddy Creek to New Orleans. It is most likely that this boat yard had by then been in operation for many years, for these boats had been carrying the flow of migration down the rivers since the beginning of the Revolution. Fort Harmar records show that in the year 1788, there had passed the mouth of the Muskingum 967 such boats with 18,379 persons aboard, along with their horses, cattle, sheep, and wagons, most of them headed for Kentucky.

Local history says that John Armstrong built a strong house, which was at times called a fort. We know that it was used as a refuge of the patriots during the dangerous Tory demonstrations. It was at his house also that the first religious services are reported to have been held. Reverend John McMillan reported this in his journal, saying that he had stopped at John Armstrong's House and preached a sermon in 1775. From this meeting began the movement which produced the Church at Glades, where John Armstrong served as one of the original elders.

Events centered about the Armstrongs have been pretty well written up by John Crawford, L. K. Evans, Waychoff, and others, but the records of the families of John and Abraham Armstrong must be gleaned from family and court records. The old Armstrong Graveyard still has a number of legible markers, including the following:

John Armstrong, died July 22, 1822; aged 86 years.
Mary Armstrong, his wife; died April 22, 1812; aged 74 years.
William Russell, died April 23, 1819; aged 93 years.
Elizabeth Russell, his wife; died April 26, 1807.
William Armstrong, died December 20, 1861; aged 81 years.
Elizabeth Armstrong, his wife; died December 15, 1864, aged 88 years. (She was Elizabeth Russell who had married (1) John Moore, who died about 1800.)
Nancy Scott, daughter of Abraham and Mary Ann Scott; died May 25, 1840; aged 24 years.
Mary Scott, died November 24, 1848; aged 71 years. (Widow

of Captain Abraham Scott ?).

Nancy Scott, grave stone obliterated, but has 1786 date cut on it.

Dr. John Moore, died December 2, 1816, aged 71 years (?).

FAMILY OF JOHN ARMSTRONG

John Armstrong, died in Greene County on July 22, 1822, at the age of 86 years, as is shown on his tombstone in the old Armstrong burial ground, indicating he was born in 1736. His wife was Mary Kennedy, sister of Alice Kennedy, wife of Colonel William Crawford, and according to L. K. Evans, a daughter of David Kennedy. The Kennedys were from the vicinity of Chambersburg, Pennsylvania, and probably connected with John Kennedy, the land jobber, who at one time owned much of the land between Muddy Creek and Little Whiteley and from whom most of these pioneer settlers of Muddy Creek may have bought their land. It is quite probable that this John Kennedy may have been the Indian Trader of that name, whom the Indians agreed to recompense for losses incurred in Pontiac's War. David Kennedy, who warranted land next to Abraham Armstrong, and was the ancestor of some of the Bells, was probably a brother of Mary and Alice Kennedy, and from the date of the warrant came out here about the same time they did. Mary (Kennedy) Armstrong is buried with her husband. The will of John Armstrong (Greene County Will Book 1. pp. 222.) mentions his children in the order given. His wife had died on April 22, 1812, at the age of 74 years.

John Armstrong served in Captain William Crawford's Militia Company.

Children of John and Mary (Kennedy) Armstrong

1. Elizabeth Armstrong, married .... McKee.
2. Agnes Armstrong, married Captain Abraham Scott (?).
3. Margaret Armstrong, married James Cummings. He enlisted in 1782, in Captain Alex People's Company, Cumberland County, Pennsylvania Militia. Later served in Captain William Crawford's Company, Washington County Militia. He was born in Virginia in 1755, and died at Janesville, Franklin County, Ohio. Margaret Armstrong and James Cummings were married in 1784.
4. Abraham Armstrong, credited with being the first white child born on Muddy Creek. He was born about 1770, and died in 1848. His wife was Ruth Conwell of Fayette County. She was born June 7, 1774, and died April 22, 1866. They were married January 11, 1795.

Children of Abraham and Ruth (Conwell) Armstrong

1. William Armstrong, born November 11, 1795, died June 5, 1849; married Mary Williams, born May 20, 1808, died October 20, 1894.

Children

1. Margaret Armstrong, born 1844; married Archibald Groomes.
2. George W. Armstrong.
3. Emma Armstrong, married William Murdock.
4. Elizabeth Armstrong, married Josiah L. Minor.
5. Sarah Armstrong, married Oliver Griffith.
6. Alice Armstrong, married James K. Gregg.

7. Cynthia Armstrong, married Richard Gwynne.
   8. James Armstrong.
   9. Lydia Armstrong, married N. H. Biddle.
2. Lydia Armstrong, married Thomas Davidson; removed to Harrison County, Ohio.
3. Ailsie Armstrong, married Isaac Chandler; removed to Belmont County, Ohio.
4. Elizabeth Armstrong, married Liberty Miller, and went to Ohio.
5. Comfort Armstrong, married David Ripley and removed to Guernsey County, Ohio.
6. Mary Armstrong, married David Porter of Fayette County, Pennsylvania.
7. John Armstrong, moved to Fayette County, Pennsylvania.
8. Sarah Jane Armstrong, married Simon Rinehart. She died May 26, 1893.
5. David Armstrong, son of John and Mary (Kennedy) Armstrong, died intestate in 1801. Abraham Scott was the administrator of his estate. He had sons John, James, and Thomas, all named in the will of their grandfather.
6. Samuel Armstrong, son of John and Mary (Kennedy) Armstrong.
7. John Armstrong, son of John and Mary (Kennedy) Armstrong.
8. Thomas Armstrong, son of John and Mary (Kennedy) Armstrong, was born in Greene County on April 2, 1777, died in Athens County, Ohio, October 22, 1853. His wife was Alice Crawford, daughter of Captain William and Alice (Kennedy) Crawford. In March 1799, he with his wife and first children, set out from the Mouth of Muddy Creek in a flat boat loaded with all their possessions, including 40 young apple trees, landing at the mouth of the Hockhocking River in Ohio, a month later. Here the women and children were sent forward by land to their selected home in Alexander Township, Athens County. The history of Athens County, published by Clarke and Company in 1869, tells of the trials and accomplishments of this family, including a story of how Mrs. Crawford once saw a deer chased onto the ice in front of her home. She realizing the helplessness of the deer, procured a big knife and went out on the ice and killed the deer. After dressing the hide she made gloves that she sent back to Greene County to her friends. She was born July 16, 1776, and died October 28, 1850.

Children of Thomas and Alice (Crawford) Armstrong

1. William Armstrong, born January 19, 1799, died August 29, 1837.
2. Samuel Armstrong, born April 3, 1801.
3. Eliphas Armstrong, born December 26, 1803, died July 17, 1895.
4. Eliza Armstrong, born August 15, 1806, died September 11, 1822.
5. John Armstrong, born June 14, 1809.
6. Elmer Armstrong, born January 17, 1812, died April 12, 1895; married, January 7, 1844, Parmetia Booth.

9. William Armstrong, born in 1780, died in Greene County, December 20, 1861. His wife was Elizabeth (Russell) Moore, a widow with a son, John Moore, for whom William Armstrong acted as guardian. She was born in 1776, daughter of William and Elizabeth Russell, who are buried with the Armstrongs in

the family burial ground. She died December 15, 1864.

Children of William and Elizabeth (Russell-Moore) Armstrong

1. Alfred Armstrong, born February 1, 1807, died August 4, 1878; married, February 23, 1837, Helen Davidson, born January 31, 1815, died April 1, 1892.
2. Russell Armstrong, married Anna Swan.
3. Mary Armstrong, born 1813, died June 27, 1864; married John Rea, born 1814, died October 22, 1879. Buried at Glades.
4. Elizabeth Armstrong, married Henry Barclay, born December 6, 1799, went west. Had the following children:
   1. Russell Barclay.
   2. Anne Barclay, married .... Wolfe.
   3. Mary Barclay, married .... Biddle.
   4. Alfred Barclay, married ....
   5. Lizzie Barclay.
   6. Laura Barclay, married .... Kirby.
5. William Armstrong, born February 9, 1816, died April 13, 1889; married Susan Curl, born October 18, 1818, died November 12, 1882.
6. Joseph Armstrong, married Mary Flenniken.

ABRAHAM ARMSTRONG FAMILY

Abraham Armstrong was a younger brother of John Armstrong, having been born, according to Ohio records, on June 27, 1747. He accompanied John Armstrong to the Muddy Creek section before 1770, and on July 15, 1773, had warranted to him, a tract of land on the North bank of the stream. Then on December 23, 1785, he warranted the tract on the South bank, adjoining that of his brother. He did not patent either tract, but at the time of his death in 1813, he directed that after providing for his daughters, all his Greene County land be sold and the proceeds used to purchase a tract of land in Ohio in one piece, to be divided among his seven sons. The history of Guernsey County, Ohio, indicates that this was done, and that the purchased land was located in that County. He served in the Revolution in Captain William Crawford's Militia Company. His wife was Flora McClean, a widow with one daughter by her former marriage, and whom he names in his will which was probated June 8, 1813, in Greene County. (Will Book 1. pp. 111.) They were parents of seven sons and seven daughters, one daughter not living to maturity. These children are listed in the order named in his will.

1. Sarah Armstrong, married .... Stephenson.
2. Barbara Armstrong, married .... Scott.
3. Mary Armstrong, married David Scott, son of Captain Abraham Scott.
4. Hannah Armstrong, married .... Montgomery.
5. Flora Armstrong.
6. Margaret Armstrong.
7. John Armstrong, eldest son, born May 6, 1781, died in Jefferson Township, Guernsey County, Ohio, in 1852. He married, in 1809, Susannah Henderson, who was born in Mifflin County, Penna., on May 20, 1788, died in Guernsey County in 1870.

They had gone to Ohio in 1813, after the death of his father. John Armstrong ran a mill in Guernsey County, which he devised by will to his son, Abraham. (Will Book 1. pp. 26. probated April 12, 1853.)

Children of John and Susannah (Henderson) Armstrong

1. Abraham Armstrong born March 2, 1810; married Elizabeth W. Walker.
2. Amelia Armstrong, married .... Bell.
3. John Armstrong.
4. Thomas Armstrong.
5. McClean Armstrong.
6. Elizabeth Armstrong, married .... Martin.
7. Margaret Armstrong.
8. Alexander McCoy Armstrong.
9. Susannah Jane Armstrong, married .... Theaker.
8. Thomas Armstrong.
9. Abraham Armstrong.
10. Laughlin Armstrong.
11. James Armstrong.
12. Joseph Armstrong, married Elsie Strawn.
13. William Armstrong.

CAPTAIN ABRAHAM SCOTT

In his pension application from Greene County, Pennsylvania, on March 18, 1833, Abraham Scott said he was born in Baltimore County, Maryland, in 1753, and had a Bible record of his birth. He was living in Baltimore County when he entered the service of United States on April 1, 1776, volunteering in Captain John Hobbs' Company in Colonel Lux's Regiment for a period of two months. Again in June 1777, he volunteered under Captain Hobbs and marched to Washington's encampment above Germantown for a like period of service. In August of the same year he joined Captain Whiteside's Company of Pennsylvania Militia under General Potter, and marched to Brandywine on September 1, but does not say he took part in the Battle that took place there on September 11. Then in 1778, he removed from Maryland to what is now Greene County, where the following year he was elected and commissioned a captain of militia. In the year 1781, his company was ordered to their station on Dunkard Creek, where it served for one month protecting the inhabitants from Indian raids. For these services Abraham Scott got a pension of forty dollars per year. (See Pension application).

When Abraham Scott came to Greene County he bought a tract of land near Fort John Swan, which, on March 18, 1785, was warranted to him under the title "Snuff Hill." Later he bought other tracts including one called "Holton's Pleasant" which he and wife, Mary, sold on April 6, 1816, to Samuel Houlsworth.

Captain Abraham Scott died in Greene County about 1845, leaving a will which was made August 1, 1835, and probated February 5, 1845. (Greene County Will Book 2. pp. 204). He names his wife, Mary Ann, indicating that she was his second wife and mother of three children he mentions. There are circumstances that suggest that both wives of Captain Abraham Scott were daughters of John Armstrong, though the names of John Armstrong's daughters do not compare with given names of Captain Scott's wives. Certainly one of these wives was the daughter of John Armstrong, proof of which is in O. C. Docket 2. pp. 60, in the estate of John Armstrong. It is probable that Abraham Scott is buried in the Armstrong Cemetery, where several of his family are buried, and where a Mary Scott, who died November 24, 1848, at the age of 71 years, could be identified as his second wife. She may have died after the will was made, but prior to its probate.

Children of Captain Abraham Scott

1. John Scott.
2. Abraham Scott, Jr.
3. William Scott, died before his father.
4. James Scott.
5. David Scott, patented land adjoining his father. His wife was Mary J. .... (possibly Armstrong, daughter of Abraham and Flora [McClean] Armstrong).
6. Polly Scott, died before 1835, as shown in the will of her father.
7. Jane Scott, married Joseph Wiley. Two of her children, James Boyd Wiley and Rebecca Jane Wiley, are named as grandchildren of John Armstrong. (O. C. Docket 2-60). Jane and her husband, Joseph Wiley, were parties named in a partition proceedings in the estate of Abraham Scott.
8. Rebecca Scott, married John Hartman. They, with John, Abraham, and James Scott, are cited by Joanna Scott and her husband, James W. Bayard, in the partition proceedings above mentioned.
9. Nancy Scott, died May 25, 1840, aged 24 years; buried in the Armstrong Cemetery.
10. Samuel Scott, his wife was Susan ....; he a son by last marriage. See DB. 13. pp. 272.
11. Josiah Scott, wife Alice ....; child of last marriage. Probably the Joseph Scott named in will as having a daughter, Joanna.
12. Jonas Scott, son of last marriage.

THE CREE FAMILY

Sometime before 1781, Robert Cree, Sr., left his home in the Eastern part of Cumberland County, Pennsylvania, and settled in the Tenmile Country near Shepherd's Church, where he was living when serving in Captain William Crawford's Militia Company in the arraingment for October 15, 1781. It is quite evident that he was an elderly man when he migrated to this part of the frontier, for some of his grown up children with their families accompanied him. There is not enough evidence to say that Robert Cree, Sr., was the ancestor of all the Cree Family of this section, but such could be case. If not, then William Cree of Muddy Creek, the Revolutionary soldier buried on the home place, and Patrick Cree, listed in the tax lists for Cumberland Township in 1784, would be the exceptions. A William Cree is mentioned in the will of Robert Cree, Sr., but Patrick Cree disappears from local records. It is evident that all of his children followed his migration and eventually located for a time near him, before moving further west. In his will, which was probated in Greene County on April 6, 1813, he mentions his wife, Janet, whose maiden name was probably Hamilton, as the Hamiltons were near neighbors in Cumberland County, and he perpetuated this name in one of his sons. He is probably buried in Shepherd's Church Cemetery, where at least two of his children are buried.

Children of Robert and Janet Cree

James Cree.
Robert Cree, Jr., who married Elizabeth Villiers.
Margaret Cree, who married Samuel Jackson.
Ann Cree, who married Eli Mundell; she died in 1835, aged 67 years.
Florence Cree, who married John Roseberry.
Jane Cree, who married Robert Rose.
William Cree.
Hamilton Cree, who married Agnes Hughes.

FAMILY OF ROBERT CREE, JR.

Robert Cree, Jr., followed his father to Western Pennsylvania after serving in Captain James Fisher's Cumberland County Militia Company in 1782. (Penna. Arch. Series III Vol. 23. pp. 793). Here he met and married Elizabeth Villiers, daughter of John and Mary Villiers. She was born October 12, 1763, and they were married about 1786. They continued the westward migration by removing from the Tenmile Country to Harrison County, Ohio.

Children

1. Ann Cree, born November 13, 1788.
2. Mary Cree, born December 17, 1789.
3. Janet Cree, born February 5, 1790. (?)
4. Robert Cree, born May 12, 1791.
5. George Cree, born December 28, 1793.
6. Elenor Cree, born April 20, 1795.
7. John Cree, born September 18, 1796.
8. James Cree, born May 12, 1798, died May 16, 1859; married, December 27, 1817, Sarah Woods.

(Taken from Hanna's "Ohio Pioneers")

FAMILY OF SAMUEL AND MARGARET (CREE) JACKSON

According to Haddon, Samuel Jackson came to America with the British Army, changed his allegiance and came to the Tenmile Country, where he served as a frontier Ranger and in June 1782, was a soldier under Captain William Crawford. (Penna. Arch. Series VI Vol. 2. pp. 187). He was born in 1757, and died March 12, 1834. He married Margaret Cree, daughter of Robert and Janet Cree, who was born in 1761, and died January 4, 1843. Both are buried in Shepherd's Church Cemetery. He left a will which was probated May 3, 1835, in which he mentions six children.

Children

1. Stephen Jackson, born 179..., died January 13, 1869; married, about 1818, Hannah Miller, born March 4, 1800, died September 22, 1889. She was his second wife, the first being Ann ...., born 1795, who died .... He and his first wife have headstones in Shepherd's Cemetery.
2. Robert Jackson, got land in Ohio. His wife was Ann Blackledge, whom he married on February 27, 1817. She was a daughter of Thomas Blackledge, Jr., and his wife, Margaret. They had four children. There is evidence that Robert Jackson was married three times.
3. James Jackson, got land in Ohio from his father and probably settled there.
4. Sarah Jackson, married .... Rice.

5. Jane Jackson, married Levi Hart.
6. Elizabeth Jackson, married .... Grooms.

HAMILTON CREE FAMILY

Hamilton Cree was born about 1776, and died in Greene County on December 23, 1848, at the age of 72 years, 11 months, and 12 days. His wife was Agnes Hughes, who died November 27, 1859, at the age of 76 years, 11 months. Both are buried in the Shepherd's Church Cemetery. They were parents of ten children.

Children

1. James Cree. His wife was Esther Jennings, born April 9, 1804, died April 11, 1826.
2. Hamilton Cree.
3. Mary Cree, died January 17, 1852, aged 46 years, 9 months, and 21 days. She married Samuel Horner.
4. John Cree, died March 22, 1829, aged 22 years, 1 month and 16 days.
5. Robert Cree, died August 28, 1820, aged 13 years, 1 month and 21 days.
6. Emily Cree, married .... Horner.
7. Minerva Cree.
8. William Cree.
9. Eliza Cree, born in 1814, died October 26, 1846, aged 32 years, 8 months, and 21 days.
10. Hiram H. Cree, born May 21, 1819, died March 12, 1901; married, 1864, Elizabeth Kerr, born August 6, 1836, died January 1, 1933.

FAMILY OF JOHN AND FLORENCE (CREE) ROSEBERRY

Florence Cree, daughter of Robert and Janet Cree, married John Roseberry, who was born in New Jersey, April 28, 1761. He enlisted in the War of the Revolution in Hunterdon County, New Jersey, on September 1, 1776, and served throughout the war, after which he removed to the vicinity of Jefferson, Pennsylvania. Later he removed with his family to Mason County, Virginia.

Children

1. Mary Roseberry.
2. James Roseberry.
3. Margaret Roseberry.
4. Jane Roseberry.
5. Robert Roseberry.
6. Michel Roseberry.
7. Ann Roseberry.
8. Elijah Roseberry.

FAMILY OF WILLIAM CREE

William Cree served in Captain Edward Grime's Company of Cumberland County, Pennsylvania Militia as shown by the returns of the Seventh Battalion in January 1778. Patrick Cree, John Cree, and Robert Cree were in this same Battalion at various times. (Penna. Arch. Series V. Vol. 6. pp. 459-454-461-587-624 etc.). William Cree was born in 1752 and died in Greene County in 1835. He warranted the farm still in the hands of his descendants, on February 4, 1789, under the title "Ashton," and the old Cree Cemetery, in which he and a number of his family are buried, is situated on this

farm. William Cree married Jane Marshall, who was born in 1752, and died in 1839. Their living children are mentioned in the will of William Cree.
1. Mary Cree, born March 5, 1780, died February 5, 1815. She was the first wife of William Kincaid, born January 21, 1779, who died at Jefferson on April 9, 1843. As William Kincaid was married three or more times, it is not known how many of his children named in his will, were of the first marriage, but the following seem certain:

Children

1. James Kincaid, married Jane McCaslin. He died February 5, 1851.
2. Jane Kincaid, born 1801, died October 19, 1832. She married John Reynolds, who after her death, married Priscilla (Gwynne) Long. He died February 20, 1882.
3. Margaret Kincaid, married, September 25, 1831, Barnet O'Neal, born September 15, 1810, died April 12, 1899. They went to Appanoose County, Iowa.
4. Susan Kincaid, born February 12, 1812, died in New Castle, Indiana, in 1870. Her first husband was Alexander Lindsey, born April 30, 1805, died June 5, 1845. She then married John Shroyer.
5. Mary Kincaid, married John Dance, son of Daniel and Phoebe (Hufty) Dance.
6. Esther Kincaid.

2. Hester Cree, born 1783, died 1858, married James Gwynne, born 1794, died 1866.
3. Elizabeth Cree, married Nicholas Vanbuskirk, son of Lawrence and Catherine (Johnson) Vanbuskirk.
4. Catherine Cree, born in 1788, married Patrick Gregory.
5. Jane Cree, born 1791, died July 26, 1866; married Abraham Holder, born .... He died intestate November 9, 1846. They were parents of seven children, three of whom are known.

Children

1. William Holder, administered his father's estate.
2. Abraham Holder, married Hannah Allman.
3. Thomas Jefferson Holder, born July 27, 1825, died June 30, 1895; married Malinda Cox, born September 25, 1831, died April 2, 1912.

6. John Cree, born 1794, died February 18, 1864; married Ruth Morrison, who was born in 1796, and died January 27, 1861. She was a daughter of Robert and Elizabeth (Cuthbertson) Morrison.
7. William Cree, born May 18, 1796, died November 5, 1871; married Ann DeFrance, born in 1802, died in 1875. Buried in the Cree Cemetery.

Children

1. Allison Cree.
2. John Cree.
3. Catherine Cree, married James Milliken.
4. Eliza Cree, married .... Shroy.
5. Samuel Cree.
6. Joseph Cree.
7. Hugh D. Cree, born September 11, 1840; married, April

26, 1862, Mary Elizabeth Dean.
8. Henry Cree.
9. Alexander Cree.
10. William Cree.
11. Jane Cree, married .... Shroy.

FAMILY OF DAVID KENNEDY

David Kennedy, who warranted "Sugar Camp," the tract of land between John Armstrong and Abraham Scott, on a Virginia Certificate dated May 27, 1769, which was surveyed to him on November 6, 1770, was probably the brother of Mary Armstrong and Alice Crawford. He was probably the man of that name who served in Captain John Orbison's Company, Fourth Battalion of Cumberland County, Pennsylvania Militia in 1782. (Penna Arch. Series V. Vol. VI. pp. 307.). This was the same company in which his neighbors, Elias and James Flenniken, served that year. Shortly after he moved to Muddy Creek, where he married Rachel Frazier, daughter of Joseph and Elizabeth (Bell) Frazier. He died here about 1798, leaving his widow with four minor children. (O. C. Docket 1. pp. 3.). She remarried soon, her second husband being James Russell, by whom she had two more children, and then she died about 1813. (O. C. Docket 1. pp. 49.).

Children of David and Rachel (Frazier) Kennedy

1. John Kennedy, for whom Isaac Weaver was appointed guardian in 1798.
2. Andrew Kennedy, died before 1813, when his brother, Samuel, administered his estate. William Seaton was his guardian in 1798, at which time he was under 14 years of age.
3. Samuel Kennedy, a minor under 14 years in 1798. Hugh Stephenson became his guardian.
4. Katherine Kennedy was born in 1790, and died April 8, 1864, at the age of 74 years, 4 months, and 18 days. Her guardian at the death of her father was Josias Lowrey. She married David Bell, born May 18, 1785, died October 22, 1856, son of James and Mary (Knox) Bell. He and his wife are buried in the Old Presbyterian Cemetery at Jefferson, Pennsylvania. David Bell patented the tract of land which was warranted to David Kennedy.

Children

1. John Kennedy Bell, born January 22, 1810, died April 19, 1866; married, May 3, 1832, Mary Black, born August 17, 1813, died January 27, 1900.
2. Rachel Bell.
3. Mary Ann Bell, married J. L. Shaw, born June 6, 1806
4. Catherine Bell, died in 1840, at the age of 18 years.

THE FLENNIKEN FAMILY

Just when the genealogist thinks he has the history of the Flenniken Family all done up and is ready to write "Finis," along comes an entire new series of information to upset the previous conclusions, carefully gleaned from authentic sources. It all comes about because of the unproven claims of connection with the questionable Mechlenburg Declaration of Independence. No authentic copy of this declaration has been found, and it has been controversial for the last one hundred years. L. C. Draper sought to prove his contention that no such document ever existed, while Colliers Magazine as late as July 1, 1905, published a purported copy, which raised a storm of controversy. One John Flenniken is among the signers of this famous paper, and if the original should be in existence, then there should be no difficulty in deciding if it was signed by Judge John Flenniken of Greene County, Pennsylvania. There are a number of papers on file in the Greene County Court House, bearing his signature, though it is to be noted that he died intestate and no will is filed. From the same records the parentage of Greene County Judge Flenniken could be negatively established. If it is not the same writing as mentioned below, then he was not the son of James and Jane (Glaspy) Flenniken.

In a letter dated December 4, 1873, from S. E. Belk, Charlotte, N. C., to L. C. Draper (Sumter Mss. V. 15, pp. 5 and 11, Draper Collections), Mr. Belk stated, "I find the following names recorded in an old family Bible, once the property of James and Jane Flenniken, the father and mother of David Flenniken. The old Bible is in the hands of the widow of one of his grandsons. James Flenniken, his Bible, bought in the year of our Lord, 1755; Jean Flenniken, her Bible, wrote in the year 1769, wrote by the hand of John Flenniken, her third son, April 4, 1769, on Thursday. (On another leaf is written). On this leaf is continued the age of James Flenniken's children!

"Mary Flenniken, was born May 15, 1731.
"William Flenniken, was born June 12, 1733.
"Elizabeth Flenniken, was born March 12, 1736.
"Esther Flenniken, was born January 12, 1738.
"Sarah Flenniken, was born May 12, 1740.
"James Flenniken, was born March 30, 1742.
"John Flenniken, was born July 19, 1744.
"David Flenniken, was born July 13, 1748.
"I have sent you the foregoing names and dates to show that David Flenniken had a brother whose name was John Flenniken, this being the only family of that name then in Mecklenburg County, North Carolina, it would seem that the said John Flenniken was one of the signers of the Mecklenburg Declaration. He seems to have been the pensman of the family, his name being written in the same old Bible, John Flenniken his hand and pen in the year 1767, which is the same handwriting as the record of names. Martha Flenniken has no recollection of an Ensign Flenniken, or of any one of the family being a signer of the Mecklenburg Declaration."

If the above Bible of James and Jane (her name was Glaspy, or more likely Gillespie) is still in existence, comparison of the writings of Judge John Flenniken with the Bible inscriptions should determine if the same person wrote both, and could settle the controversy for all time. The writer prefers to present the evidence and remain neutral as to which John Flenniken was the Signer and which one was the son of James and Jane (Gillespie) Flenniken. The Southern branch of the family states that their Judge John Flenniken was the son of James and Jean (Glaspy) Flenniken, natives of Edinburg, Scotland, who settled first in Pennsylvania, and then after 1750, removed to Mecklenburg County, North Carolina. They state that Southern Judge John Flenniken was one of the signers of the Mecklenburg Declaration, and made a good record in the Revolution. That he served as magistrate after the Revolution and was on the State Court bench for several terms, was an elder in Old Providence Presbyterian Church, and a successful farmer. He was a lover of fine horses and was thrown from one of them about 1821-2 and killed, leaving but one son, John Flenniken, Jr., born in 1784, who died in 1852. They state that both father and son are buried in Providence Burial Grounds. These and other statements are contained in an excellent booklet prepared by Mr. G. P. Caldwell of R. F. D. 2, Charlotte, N. C., a direct descendant of James and Jane Flenniken.

Against this we have the writings of L. K. Evans, who seems to have taken his information from John Crawford's Journal, or had the story from J. C. Flenniken, whom he calls his "esteemed friend," who was a grandson of Northern Judge John Flenniken. In an article called "Wayside Gleanings" Evans wrote in 1875-6 that, "John Flenniken, who was appointed one of the Associate Judges upon the organization of Greene County. was an early settler. He was at first a resident of North Carolina, and was conspicuous among the first Americans to agitate independent and republican forms of Government. He was the John Hancock among the signers of the Mecklenburg Declaration of Independence in the year 1775. He heard of the death of his brother, James, who had cast his lot in these parts. James Flenniken was reputed to be rich in lands and John came on to pay a last tribute to his deceased kinsman and look after his estate. His land speculations, however, proved to be abortive, through the insufficiency of title and the coveted estate netted but the meager amount of $35.

"It is related that Colonel William Crawford, an old and esteemed friend, induced Mr. Flenniken to stay in this locality by the present of a fine farm of some hundred broad acres, contiguous to the one on which he himself resided. Thenceforward they were lifelong neighbors and inseparable friends. They were ardent patriots and made common cause against the attacks of the British emissaries and their savage allies, and the insurrection of the Tories in their midst.

"Judge Flenniken was a very intelligent and influential man and has bequeathed to the ages a long line of enterprising descendants, having been the father of eleven children, three of whom were born in North Carolina . . .

"Elias and James Flenniken were brothers and among the first settlers, and were cousins of Judge John Flenniken . . . etc."

How much of this is fact one cannot say, but there seems little reason for making such claims unless backed by some proof. Mr. Robert B. Powers of Delaware, Ohio, a descendant of a sister of Elias and James Flenniken, says that his ancestor, Sarah Flenniken, was a cousin of Colonel Crawford, and identifies the relationship to Colonel William Crawford, the Sandusky Martyr, when it should probably have been Greene County's Colonel William Crawford, who is buried with the Flennikens in Glades Cemetery, and who Evans says, gave Judge John Flenniken the land on which he settled. We have not been able to prove this relationship, but the List of Taxables for Peters Township, Bedford County, in 1751, show:

John Flenniken, ancestor of Elias and James, etc.

Adam Armstrong, father of John and Abraham of Greene County, neighbors of the Flennikens.

Robert Crawford.

James Flenniken, who with wife, Jane, went to North Carolina.

A John Crawford is in the 1751 tax list of Lurgan Township,

Bedford County, along with John Kennedy. John Armstrong's wife was Mary Kennedy, and Colonel William Crawford's wife was her sister, Alice Kennedy. Many of the Muddy Creek pioneers were from this section of Pennsylvania. A sequence of dates in the authentic and official records, taken from the Bible record of Greene County Judge Flenniken's children, and from court records in Washington County, Pennsylvania, might indicate that two John Flennikens came to Muddy Creek at the same period, but it seems more likely that it was one and the same John Flenniken following the plan of his life as pointed out in Evans' record. The Bible record of the children of Greene County Judge Flenniken indicates that after the birth of the third child on May 19, 1779, his first wife, a Miss Rankin, died, and after a proper period of mourning, he left his home in North Carolina and came to Muddy Creek. Here he met and married Hannah McClelland and their first child was born on September 9, 1784. It was this period during which the estate of James Flenniken, killed in the Battle of Tenmile, was settled, as witness the following official records:

On June 11, 1782, John and Samuel Flenniken gave bond in Washington County Court, to the amount of 400 Pounds, in order to serve as administrators in the estate of James Flenniken. They were joined in the bond by Elias Flenniken and Robert Wallace, while Samuel Smith signed as a witness. Then, on June 19, 1782, they sold the goods and chattels of James Flenniken, estimated in the inventory as worth 89 Pounds, 2 shillings, and 1 pence. (Office of Register of Wills, Washington County, Pennsylvania, Account 1, Book F, 1784).

Deed of sale of land to Thomas Hughes, dated August 18, 1783, and sworn to before Colonel John Minor on March 10, 1784, starts out with these significant words: "I, John Flenniken, of Mecklenburg, North Carolina, for the estate of James Flenniken, deceased, in behalf of self, Samuel Flenniken, David Flenniken, and James Flenniken, joint heirs in the estate of James Flenniken, Deceased, . . . etc." (Washington County, Pennsylvania, Deed Book 1-C-110).

This deed clearly shows that the John Flenniken who settled the estate of James, was the son of James Flenniken, Sr., and a brother of James, Samuel and David Flenniken, while the appearance of the name of Elias Flenniken as a signatory on the bond, strongly suggests the kinship of these two branches of the family. The Southern Judge John Flenniken is reported to have had a brother, David Flenniken, who lived in Mecklenburg County, North Carolina, where he drew a pension for Revolutionary service. This David Flenniken had a granddaughter, Martha Flenniken, who in an interview with S. E. Belk, quoted by L. C. Draper, said she had no recollection of any of the Flennikens being a signer of the Mecklenburg Declaration but she is reported to have been about 73 years old and her mind somewhat impaired, so that she had forgotten much that she had been told by her grandfather. She did say that the Flennikens were of Irish descent and had come to North Carolina from Pennsylvania.

The genealogist cannot help noting that the records of the North Carolina Flennikens do not mention the tombstone records of their Judge John Flenniken and are uncertain of the date of his death, nor do they quote any settlement of his estate. The tombstone record of Greene County's Judge John Flenniken states he died December 10, 1810, at the age of 65 years. His second wife is buried in New Providence Cemetery at Glades Church, near Carmichaels, beside the grave of her husband. No mention is made of the wife of the Southern Judge. The above age of 65 years compares favorably with the known age of 66 years, 9 months, and 17 days, since many old tombstones give only the approximate age in years.

The letter of Mr. S. E. Belk to Draper states that there was but one family of Flenniken living in North Carolina at the time of the Revolution, that being the family of James and Jane (Glaspy or Gillispie) Flenniken, while the only report of the origin of Greene County's Judge John Flenniken says he came from Mecklenburg, North Carolina. The tax list of Peters Township, Bedford County, Pennsylvania, for 1751, lists only this James Flenniken and a John Flenniken, whose will is on file in Franklin County, where it was probated on November 28, 1793. (Tax list is in Rupp's "History of Dauphin, Franklin, Bedford, and Adams Counties" pp. 460). This John Flenniken, whose will was probated in Franklin County, Pennsylvania, was the father of Elias Flenniken, as shown by law suits over the estate. An account of his family will be given later on in this article. Apparently these two men, James and John, were the immigrant ancestors, and there are traditions that there were three, or possibly five brothers, that came together, including a Robert Flenniken who owned land in New Jersey, Pennsylvania, Maryland, and Delaware. Unless this tradition has some truth in it, it would be hard to reconcile the existence of the two Judge John Flennikens. One would suppose that the parentage of two men, so well known as to be judges in their respective localities, would be well publicized. In this the Southern Judge John Flenniken's family make a claim, the Northern Judge John Flenniken's family, so far as known, made no claim. One item which certainly points to a third ancestor of the Flennikens, other than John and James of the Peters Township, Bedford County tax list of 1751, is the warrant issued on October 10, 1785, to a Thomas Flenniken for a tract of land containing 400 acres, and located on Muddy Creek, adjoining the lands of James Flenniken, Abraham Armstrong, James Hughes, William Crawford and others. Neither the families of James and Jane Flenniken, nor of John Flenniken of Franklin County, have a Thomas listed among their children. Yet there is a suggestion of kinship in this instance, since two years later the land was patented to Elias Flenniken on September 22, 1787.

The most interesting history of the Flennikens, and perhaps the best information yet gathered together is contained in a series of letters from Mr. Samuel Patterson Flenniken, of Uniontown, Pennsylvania, who has made a study of the family all through the more than seventy years of his life, and whose father before him, worked with the Southern branch of the family, to sort out an authentic record. Samuel P. Flenniken is a descendant of Elias Flenniken, through his son, John Wilkins Flenniken, who had a son, Andrew Flenniken, father of the writer of the letters. This would make him a great-great grandson of the John Flenniken who died in Franklin County in 1793. His letters state that since a boy he had questioned members of his own family and those of the Honorable John Flenniken's family, including several grandsons of the Judge and that his memory at this date (1949) retains much of what was told him. He admits that much of what he has written is traditional and not backed by the usual official records. A former newspaper reporter and Fayette County official, he relates stories told him as far back as 1880, when he was but five and a half years of age, and which at this date are more clear to him than things that happened quite recently. He is inclined to believe that the Southern claim to fame is the more authenticated for, as he recalls it, none of the older Flennikens ever mentioned the Mecklenburg Declaration. Like his father before him, he is of the opinion that Greene County Judge Flenniken was a son of Robert Flenniken, but does not have absolute proof for it, unfortunately he does not give any reasons for arriving at this conclusion. That there are errors in some of his statements, he is the first to admit that by checking and rechecking he sometimes finds them and corrects them. If we do not use all that he has written, or make slight changes that are obvious from official records, we are certain that

Mr. Flenniken, like his father before him, is of the opinion there were five brothers who came to America from Ireland, though he states that the older generation claimed but three such immigrant ancestors. His own ancestor was John Flenniken, who was born in 1719 (or 1703) and died in Franklin County, about 1793, whose will was filed there for probate on December 28, 1793. He states that this John Flenniken married Martha Alexander, and his list of children with dates of birth, are the same as those sent by Mr. Robert B. Powers, and as found in the Lizzie Rea and Freemont Flenniken records, with the exception that Mr. Powers supplied the names of their husbands and wives. These are the children of John and Martha (Alexander) Flenniken:

Elias Flenniken, born October 22, 1745; married Mary Dunlap, born October 23, 1752.

James Flenniken, born August 20, 1747; married Jane Dunlap, born 1740.

Hannah Flenniken, born February 17, 1749; married John Gabriel of Maryland.

Elizabeth Flenniken, born November 6, 1750; married John Dunlap.

William Flenniken, born September 1, 1752; married Elizabeth

Sarah Flenniken, born September 30, 1754; married Thomas Sellars; his second wife.

Margaret Flenniken, born December 12, 1758; married Joseph Dunlap.

John Alexander Flenniken, born May 12, 1760; never married.

The family lived in what was then Cumberland County, Pennsylvania, until after 1751, when John, with his wife Martha, and their family, with James and Jane and their family, joined the migration from Pennsylvania to settle in Sharon Township, Mecklenburg County, North Carolina. About 1760, John Flenniken and his family were living in Charlotte, and James and his family still in Sharon Township on McAlpin's Creek, when the two brothers learned of the land on the Monongahela, and rode horseback to what is now Greene County to seek a claim. They arrived at the Mouth of Muddy Creek in the Spring of 1760, after crossing the Monongahela at a place later known as "Wallace's Riffles," and here set up a crude camp. A day's scouting took them a short distance below the Mouth of Muddy Creek to a small run, where they began putting their marks on trees by tomahawk and making turkey nests, which consisted of large piles of stones with lengthy limbs of trees decorating the center of the stone piles. They went up the North side of Muddy Creek to the South Fork and thence across to where Pierceville now stands. Then followed down Little Whiteley to its Mouth, and back to the place of beginning. The acreage amounted to some ten thousand acres, about four miles square, of which some two thousand acres were later patented to the Flennikens. Unlike so many of the later pioneers, they ignored the Virginia authorities, and dealt for their land with Pennsylvania. They seem to have had some agreement by which their land was not molested by nesters or squatters, but were very free with their friends whom they choose to give or sell at a very small cost. Months later they rode back to North Carolina, where James Flenniken chose to remain the rest of his life, but John decided to go back with his family to his old location in Cumberland County, where his last days were spent. (Bedford, Franklin, Westmoreland and as far west as Greene County, were at that time, 1761, a part of Cumberland County, Pennsylvania.) One of the rulings of the authorities regarding new claims, demanded that each year the claimant must be on the claim a part of the year, so each year one or more members of the Flenniken Family made the trip over the mountains and lived on the vast estate until legal claim was established and a title granted about 1769. (Note: This does no agree with the Pennsylvania ruling before the Fort Stanwix Treaty in 1769, by which no claims in this section were recognized by the Colonial Government. The Pennsylvania Authorities even making a death penalty for those caught after being warned off the territory. This was as late as 1768.)

The Flenniken tradition goes on to say that on the first trip back after the survey, Elias and his brother, James, were accompanied by John Armstrong, and Zebulon Hollingsworth, in 1761, but it probabdly errs when its says that James Flenniken, brother of Elias, stayed on after a visit in 1763. It is true we do not find him in the militia lists for Cumberland County with his brothers in Captain John Orbison's Company, in the years 1781-82, but only one James Flenniken is in the Springhill Tax lists for 1772, and this is probably the James Flenniken killed by the Indians in the Battle of Tenmile in 1774.

How much of this tradition is true and what about these dates in the tradition? It is the belief of this writer that the story is true as to the most of the facts given, and that the dates are approximately correct. This belief is based on the deed of Josiah Crawford which tells of his improvement at the head of Muddy Creek in the year 1766, and consider it unlikely that he would have gone so far from the Monongahela had land not been pre-empted at the Mouth of Muddy Creek, possibly years before. We know also that three years prior to 1760, John Owen had sold the land North of Muddy Creek. It is also a matter of record that the Hollingsworths were merchants in Philadelphia and Baltimore, and were trading with the Indians before Pontiac's War of 1763. It is also known that the Indians were granting land to the traders at this time and living peacefully with the first dwellers on this frontier.

This leads to another tradition told by Mr. Flenniken regarding a Stephen Gapen and a Benjamin Maple, said to have been deserters from Braddock's Army in 1755. They eventually made their way to the Mouth of Muddy Creek, where they stopped at an Indian

Camp and chatted with the Indians and made overtures for land. This camp site was well known to the early settlers and from it were taken many artifacts. The men were directed further up the River to the Mouth of Little Whiteley Creek where there were some white traders and some Indians, among whom was an Indian Chief of authority, whom they contacted and made conversation with. The chief asked what they had to offer for land, and was shown a roll of cloth and a few trinkets, for which a deal was made and a walking claim was granted them, Gapen, from the Mouth of Little Whiteley to Big Whiteley, and Maple, from Big Whiteley to near the present site of Greensboro. Such a deal and the refusal to grant the land from Muddy Creek to Little Whiteley may have been brought about by the prior grant to the Flennikens. The Flennikens may have dealt with the Indians rather than with either Commonwealth and thus had their land held for them. It is to be pointed out that this tradition could not apply to the Stephen Gapen of Revolutionary times as he was not born until 1760, but his father, Zachariah Gapen, did eventually about 1765, settle in this general neighborhood, and a Benjamin Maple, and wife, Catherine, sold out land in this vicinity and moved to Kentucky before 1800. Naturally any agreements made with the Indians would not be of record and would only be found in family traditions.

Mr. Samuel Flenniken also states that there are legal papers and traditions to show that James A. Flenniken bought out the interest of his partner, William Henry Jennings, in a ferry at the Mouth of Little Whiteley Creek, in the year 1797, after the partnership had been in existence for thirty years. This is not surprising when we know that the ferries of James, Josiah, and Oliver Crawford were in operation in 1770.

Other items sent by Mr. Flenniken deal with the Flennikens that settled here and will be treated under the names of these settlers.

It is to be noted that the Southern Judge John Flenniken had but one son, who is said to have been born in 1784, at a time when his father, or supposed father, was 40 years of age. It leaves room for the possibility of a wrong identification of this John Flenniken, who married Mary Ried. He could well have been a grandson of James and Jane (Gillespie or Glaspy) Flenniken.

FAMILY OF JUDGE JOHN FLENNIKEN

The tombstone record of Judge John Flenniken of Greene County, Pennsylvania, says he died December 4, 1810, and Court records show he died intestate. The tombstone at his grave in Glades Cemetery says he was 65 years of age, but as in the case of Elias Flenniken, it maye be at variance with the Bible record. The controversy as to his origin has been covered in the history of the Flenniken Family and we believe is still open for argument. There appears to be no arguments against the statements of earlier historians that he was a cousin of Elias and James Flenniken, or the statement that he came here from North Carolina. Sometime between 1779 and 1783, John Flenniken's first wife, a Miss Rankin, died, and he married, in what is now Greene County, Pennsylvania, Hannah McClelland, daughter of Andrew McClelland, Sr., and his wife, Mary (McKnight) McClelland. She was born July 6, 1757, and died April 27, 1838, and is buried at Glades with her husband. The records of their children are taken from Bible records of Miss Lizzie Rea, three children being by the first marriage.

Children of Judge John Flenniken

1. Samuel Flenniken, born April 28, 1774; went to Ohio.
2. Dorcas Flenniken, born March 17, 1777, died May 17, 1819; married Benjamin Jennings, December 15, 1802. He was born February 26, 1779, died July 8, 1861. He married a second time, Eliz Stockdale.

Children

   1. Esther, born March 9, 1804; married James Cree.
   2. Jane, born July 30, 1806, died August 24, 1806.
   3. John F., born October 28, 1807; married Eliz. B. Fitzgerald.
   4. Mary H., born July 14, 1809, died September 4, 1810.
   5. Samuel, born April 18, 1812; married Sarah Garrison.
   6. Jacob P., born January 15, 1814; married Lydia Cary.
   7. Hannah, born May 1, 1816, died July 31, 1816.

3. Audley Flenniken, born May 19, 1779; removed to North Carolina.
4. Andrew Flenniken, born September 9, 1784; removed to Ohio.
5. Mary Flenniken, born March 20, 1786; married Nathaniel Jennings, born February 2, 1770, died 1844. Had Sarah, born January 19, 1821; married David Woods.
6. James Flenniken, born March 12, 1788, died March 10, 1870; married, June 13, 1816, Mary McClelland. She was born May 1, 1791, daughter of James and Sarah (Hannah) McClelland, died April 23, 1866.
7. Sirzah Flenniken, born March 10, 1790; died young.
8. Rebecca Flenniken, born January 31, 1792; died un-married, August 26, 1884.
9. Hannah Flenniken, born January 25, 1794, died in 1884; married Rev. Asa Brooks.
10. John N. Flenniken, born December 24, 1795.
11. Isaac P. Flenniken, born February 28, 1798, settled in Arkansas.
12. Robert Patterson Flenniken, born March 1, 1802; went west where he became a Judge in Utah, and set in on the Comstock Mine Case. He later removed to California where he died in 1879. His wife was Emily Walker, daughter of Zadock Walker.

FAMILY OF ELIAS FLENNIKEN

Elias Flenniken, son of John and Martha (Alexander) Flenniken, was born October 22, 1745, and died in Greene County, Pennsylvania, on March 17, 1834. (Tombstone says he was aged 88 years, one month, and 29 days.) His wife was Mary Dunlap, born October 23, 1752, who died April 23, 1834. She was a daughter of Joseph Dunlap of Franklin County, Pennsylvania, whose will, made April 20, 1783, was attacked in Franklin County Court by Elias Flenniken, and it was declared void. Joseph Dunlap was a son of Andrew and Jane Dunlap of Cumberland County. Andrew died there in the Summer of 1764. Mr. Samuel P. Flenniken says that Elias Flenniken made his first trip to what is now Greene County, Pennsylvania, in 1761, when, with John Armstrong, James Flenniken, and Zebulon Hollingsworth, they visited the site of a tract of land which Flenniken's father had secured the year previous, and that he made other trips to the site in the years which followed before settling here in the years following the Revolution. Elias Flenniken served in the Revolution in Captain John Orbison's Company, Cumberland County Militia in 1781 and 1782. (Penna. Archives Series III Vol. 23 pp. 768-779.) When he finally came to settle he built his log house at the head of Jockey Hollow. Land records show that he took title to the tract of land next north of Oliver Crawford, who had the ferry at the mouth of Muddy Creek. He also got the patent for the land that was warranted to Thomas Flenniken, and later bought out Oliver Crawford's tract at the ferry. He and his wife are buried at Glades Church Cemetery.

Children of Elias and Mary (Dunlap) Flenniken

1. Elizabeth Flenniken, born September 27, 1781, married Thomas Blair. It is said that she was born in Cumberland County, and was brought over the mountain in a burlap sack slung over a horse's back. After her husband's death, she lived with John W. Flenniken, and appears to have been the family historian.
2. Sarah Flenniken, born August 7, 1783, in Greene County; married Thomas Wilson.
3. Margaret Flenniken, born August 7, 1783; married Joseph Flenniken.
4. Mary Flenniken, born August 17, 1785; married James Blair.
5. Elias A. Flenniken, born March 18, 1787, died March 14, 1836; married Sarah Swan, born January 5, 1790; died at Findlay, Ohio. After Mr. Flenniken died his widow married Rev. George Vanneman. A son, John Flenniken, was born to the first marriage.
6. Joseph D. Flenniken, born December 30, 1788.
7. John Wilken Flenniken, born November 2, 1790, died October 16, 1861; married Hettie Wright, born December 29, 1803, died November 22, 1883. She was a daughter of John and Margaret (Darrah) Wright, and granddaughter of Captain Henry and Anne (Jamisen) Darrah. See family of John Wright.
8. Jane M. Flenniken, born December 2, 1792; married Daniel Smith.
9. Ruth Flenniken, born July 12, 1795, died young.

FAMILY OF JAMES FLENNIKEN

James Flenniken, son of John and Martha (Alexander) Flenniken, was born August 20, 1747, and died in Greene County, August 25, 1823, leaving a will that was probated September 3, 1823. Tradition has it that he was the first of the family to settle here and Mr. Samuel P. Flenniken puts that date as the year 1763. We are inclined to believe it was a few years later, though he patented a tract of land called "Delight" on September 25, 1787, on a certificate issued to him May 27, 1769. Mr. Flenniken also says he and William Henry Jennings are shown to have been partners in a ferry at the mouth of Little Whiteley Creek, which James bought out for himself in 1797, after thirty years of partnership. James Flenniken served in Captain William Crawford's Company, Washington County Militia, in the Revolution as shown by the muster roll of 1782, at the time his brothers were still in the Cumberland County Militia. His name is on the tax list for Cumberland Township, Washington County, in 1784. He built the first brick house in Greene County in 1795, at the site of the present Nemacolin and then in 1811, built a stone house on the site of his original log cabin. A very religious man, he would not permit his help to work at any labor on Sunday. His wife was Jane Dunlap, who died April 10, 1829, her tombstone saying she was 89 years of age. She is buried with her husband in Glades Cemetery.

Children of James and Jane (Dunlap) Flenniken

1. John Flenniken, born in 1774, died March 17, 1855; married Mary McClelland, born June 6, 1775, died June 1, 1862. She was a daughter of Andrew and Mary (McKnight) McClelland.
2. Joseph Flenniken, born January 7, 1776.
3. James Flenniken, born December 13, 1778, died March 4, 1858. His first wife was Mary ...., who died September 5, 1809, aged 26 years, seven months and nine days, after which he married, on February 4, 1819, Mary McClelland, born in 1794, who died September 26, 1867. All are buried in Glades.
4. Elizabeth Flenniken, born October 29, 1779; her husband was .... Welsh.
5. Margaret Flenniken, born January 22, 1782; married .... Welsh.
6. Ruth Flenniken, born November 5, 1783, died May 12, 1829 married Josephus Dodd.
7. Jane Flenniken, born February 12, 1786; married John Hughes.
8. Sarah Flenniken, born April 16, 1788; married Andrew Satterfield.
9. Mary Flenniken, born July 23, 1791, died December 22, 1866; married James Irwin.

THE ANDREW M'CLELLAND FAMILY

The Lizzie Rea Records included the dates of birth of the children of Andrew McClelland, Sr., and his wife, Mary (McKnight) McClelland. The McClellands lived at the headwaters of Little Whiteley Creek near Baily's School House, where both James and Andrew patented land. Robert, James, and John McClelland served in Captain William Crawford's Militia Company. A James Hannah patented the land to the south of Andrew McClelland and two of that name served in the same company. They were William and Francis Hannah. This is important since one of the McClellands married Sarah Hannah.

Children

1. Robert McClelland, born October 7, ..., died March 8, 1834. (Greene County O. C. Docket 2, page 33, March 1834.)
    1. Isabella, married John P. Minor.
    2. Cephas.
2. Hannah McClelland, born July 6, 1757, died April 27, 1838. Married Hon. John Flenniken. (See Flenniken Records.)
3. James McClelland, born November 14, 1760, died about 1809; married Sarah Hannah, born 1767, died May 1, 1853. (O. C. Docket 1, page 68, January 1816.)

    #### Children
    1. Ann McClelland, died May 7, 1816, age 14 years. A minor at time of father's death, and George C. Seaton was appointed guardian.
    2. Mary McClelland, born May 1, 1781, died 1866; married James M. Flenniken, born 1788, died 1870.
    3. Isabella McClelland, died February 27, 1820; married George C. Seaton, born June 2, 1783, died September 13, 1849.
    4. Jack McClelland, married Martha Dowlin. (See Bates History of Greene County.) She married (2) Robert Baird.
4. John McClelland, born April 2, 1763, died about 1835. Wife's

name was Mary ...., who died March 2, 1833. Apparently the children were all minors at time of his death and John Rea was appointed their guardian. (Greene County O. C. Docket 2, page 49.)

Children

1. Paul D. McClelland.
2. John R. McClelland.
3. Robert McClelland, died in Illinois in 1860. (Greene County O. C. Docket 4, page 676, December 1860.)
4. Sarah Ann McClelland.
5. Josiah McClelland.
5. Andrew McClelland, born March 28, 1765.
6. William McClelland, born December 9, 1769.
7. Francis McClelland, born July 5, 1771; married Eleanor Hart.
8. Mary McClelland, born June 6, 1775, died June 1, 1862; married John Flenniken, born 1775, died March 17, 1855; he was a son of James and Jane Flenniken.

Children

1. William Flenniken.
2. Hannah.
3. Eleanor.
4. Sarah Flenniken, married Benjamin Cummings.
5. Margaret Flenniken.

FAMILY OF THOMAS SELLARS

Sarah Flenniken, daughter of John and Martha (Alexander) Flenniken, was born September 30, 1754. She died July 18, 1823. Her husband was Thomas Sellars (Cellar, Keller, etc.) born in Maryland, 1741, probably the son of Johannes Keller, who came to America on the Ship "Princess Augustus" September 16, 1736. Thomas Sellars removed to Cumberland County, Pennsylvania, about 1771, where he served with the Flenniken brothers in Captain John Orbison's Militia Company. He was twice married, the first wife being Martha McCoy, who died June 19, 1777. He then married Sarah Flenniken. After the Revolution Thomas Sellars and his family removed to Delaware County, Ohio, about 1800, having sold his land in Franklin County, Pennsylvania, about that date. He died in Delaware County, Ohio, April 16, 1816, aged 75 years.

Children of Thomas Sellars

1. Margaret Sellars, baptized April 7, 1771, married Josiah McKinnie, probably a son of Mrs. John Crawford by her second marriage with John McKinnie, which would explain the tradition of relationship with Colonel William Crawford of Muddy Creek.
2. Jane Sellars, baptized July 11, 1773; married James Gillis.
3. Hannah Sellars, married Nathan Carpenter.
4. Thomas Sellars, Jr.
5. Robert McCoy Sellars.
6. John Flenniken Sellars.
7. George Sellars.
8. James Sellars.
9. Joseph Sellars.

FAMILY OF JOSEPH DUNLAP

Margaret Alexander Flenniken, daughter of John and Martha (Alexander) Flenniken, was born December 12, 1758, and died in 1834, in Delaware County, Ohio. She married Joseph Dunlap, born in Cumberland County, Pennsylvania, in 1754. He died in Delaware County, Ohio, in 1831. He served in Captain Walter McKinnie's Company, Cumberland County Militia, in the War of the Revolution.

Children of Joseph and Margaret (Flenniken) Dunlap

1. John Dunlap.
2. Joseph Dunlap.
3. Alexander Dunlap.
4. Margaret Dunlap.
5. John Flenniken Dunlap.
6. Sarah Dunlap.
7. Mary Dunlap.

CAPTAIN HENRY DARRAH

Captain Henry Darrah, father of Ann (Darrah) Barclay, was the fourth son of Thomas Darrah, an Ulster-Scotsman, who with wife, Mary, came to America about 1725, and soon after settled in the Neshaminy Valley in Bucks County, Pennsylvania. Much is known of the father, Thomas Darrah, including the story of the founding of historic Log College, which later became the College of New Jersey, and then Princeton University. He was also the founder of Neshaminy Presbyterian Church of Warwick and Deep Run Presbyterian Church in Bedminster Township. Thomas Darrah died in March 1750, leaving five sons, all of whom took an active part in the Revolution.

Captain Henry Darrah, probably born in what is now Montgomery County, Pennsylvania, was well educated and a fine horseman. Tradition says that when he went courting the handsome daughter of Henry Jamison, that her father objected very strongly to the match with his daughter, Ann, saying that young Darrah was too fond of fast horses and not fond enough of making a living by tilling the soil. Captain Henry Darrah and the young lady settled the matter by getting on one of the fleet horses and outriding her pursuing father, to be married on August 13, 1760. At the beginning of the Revolution, Henry Darrah was living in New Britain Township, where in 1775, he was appointed one of the Associators, and on the organizing of the "Flying Camp" he was appointed, in 1776, by the Bucks County Committee of Safety, a First Lieutenant in Captain Willian Robert's Company, serving in the New Jersey and Long Island Campaigns. On May 6, 1777, he was commissioned a captain and served at various times under Colonel John Lacey and Colonel William Roberts. He died in Warrington Township in 1782.

Children of Captain Henry and Ann (Jamison) Darrah

Mary Darrah, born September 16, 1762.
James Darrah, born December 12, 1764; married (1) Rachel Henderson, (2) Rebecca McCrea.
William Darrah, born September 23, 1767; married Sara (Walker) Whitten.
Ann Darrah, born January 16, 1770; married Hugh Barclay.
Margaret Darrah, born November 26, 1772; married John Wright.
Joseph Darrah, born September 10, 1775.
George Darrah, born July 12, 1778.

Henry Darrah, Jr., born April 12, 1782.

THE HENRY DARRAH SWORDS

In January 1942, this writer received from Mr. Henry Swan of Denver, Colorado, a photograph of the commission of Henry Darrah, one time the property of Mr. Robert Henderson Darragh of Hartsville, Pennsylvania. With this photograph was a photograph of a Henry Darrah Sword, the most recent view of the Henry Darrah Home, and one of his church, The Neshaminy Church in Bucks County. There can be no doubt that this sword was once the property of Henry Darrah.

Then, on March 4, 1949, a letter from Mr. Samuel P. Flenniken of Nutt Avenue, Uniontown, Pennsylvania, wrote of another Henry Darrah Sword in these words: "This sword was given originally to Margaret Darrah Wright, daughter of Henry and Ann Jamison Darrah, at her home in Bucks County, and in turn she gave it to her daughter, Hester Ann Wright, wife of John Wilkins Flenniken, who brought it to her new home in Cumberland Township, Greene County, after

SAMUEL P. FLENNIKEN

her marriage. The sword was kept in the old homestead originally built by Elias Flenniken, until her new brick house was erected in 1846. The sword remained here until the youngest son of Hester Flenniken was married in 1871, when she gave it to Andrew Stewart Flenniken, who in turn gave it to me. The sword is of solid steel and has the name of Henry Darrah engraved upon it. The handle is enclosed in solid ivory. From what has been told me, I am sure the sword that I now have is the one carried by my ancestor, Henry Darrah, in the Revolution."

Both swords are shown in these pages, and while not a connoisseur of weapons, and being unfamiliar with the use of this weapon, the appearance of the two dis-similar weapons, suggest that one of them may be the sword used on dress occasions, while the other was used in the deadly business of the soldier. We shall leave that to the experts to decide.

NESHAMINY EPISCOPAL CHURCH, BUCKS COUNTY

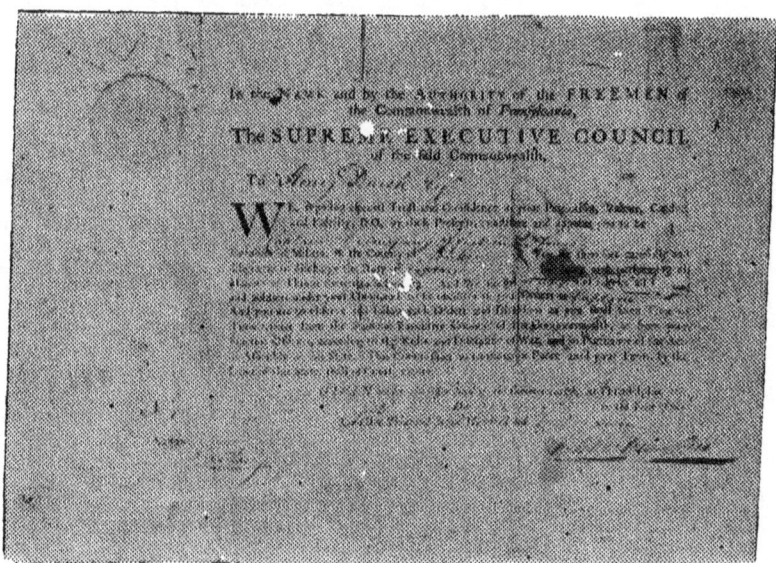

HENRY DARRAH'S COMMISSION

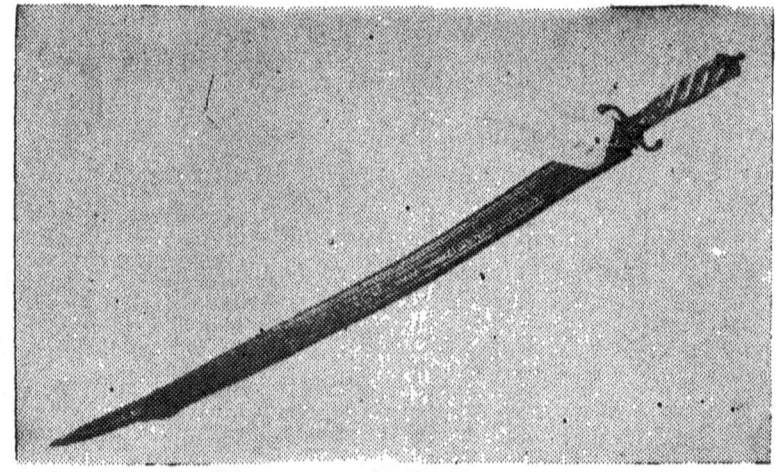

DARRAH SWORD

THE BARCLAY FAMILY

Education and "book learning" were valuable assets to young men in Colonial Days. If accompanied by good common sense and pleasing personality, young men found their talents quickly appreciated in both military and political fields. A number of striking examples of such well equipped youths could be pointed out. These would include Hugh Barclay, subject of this sketch. Possibly in the militia of Pennsylvania before he was fifteen years of age, he was on the frontier but a few years before he was chosen to represent his community in the State Legislature, his reputation well established before he became 40 years of age.

Hugh Barclay was a son of James Barclay of Warrington Township, Bucks County, Pennsylvania. His father was born about 1722, and died in Bucks County, in February 1792, between the dates of his will, February 12, 1792, and the date of its probate, February 24, the same year. James Barclay is listed with his brother, Hugh Barclay, as an associator of the Militia in Warrington Township, April 19, 1775. (Penna. Arch. Series V. Vol. 5. pp. 326). James Barclay married, according to a Bible Record, Margaret Fowland, yet the will of Daniel Craig, probated in Bucks County on April 22, 1777, mentions his daughter, Margaret, wife of James Barclay, suggesting that she was originally Margaret Craig, and had married Fowland for her first husband. The fact that she had but six children by her marriage with James Barclay, further strengthens this theory. She died December 15, 1816. Both James Barclay and his wife left wills in which the six children are named. (Bucks Co. Will Book 5. pp. 291, and Will Book 6. pp. 514).

Children of James and Margaret Barclay

John Barclay of Springfield Township, Bucks County.
James Barclay of Warwick Township, Bucks County.
Mary Barclay, wife of Thomas Barr.
Sarah Barclay, wife of Jacob Hufty.
Richard Barclay, co-executor of his father's will.
Hugh Barclay, first named executor of his father's will.

HUGH BARCLAY FAMILY

Hugh Barclay was born August 27, 1762, (one record says August 24, 1763), and died in Greene County, Pennsylvania, July 25, 1826. A number of his descendants have been accepted for membership in the S. A. R. and D. A. R. by quoting service of Hugh Barclay as a private in the Cumberland County, Pennsylvania Militia. (Penna. Arch. Series V. Vol. 6. pp. 519. Series III. Vol. 23, pp. 617, etc). This Hugh Barclay also served as adjutant of the Cumberland County Frontier Rangers. (Penna. Arch. Series III. Vol. 23 pp. 258). A more substantial service record may be found in the enlistment of Hugh Barclay (spelled Barkley) in Captain Henry Darrah's Company of Bucks County Militia under Lieutenant Colonel John Lacey on November 1, 1777, since it is known that Hugh Barclay married the daughter of Captain Henry Darrah. (Penna. Arch. Series V. Vol. 5. pp. 407). Hugh Barclay and Ann Darrah were married in Bucks County in 1788, and lived there until after the baptism of their first three children. About 1800, he moved to Muddy Creek in Greene County, where he began the purchase of numerous tracts of land, the first of which he bought from David Duncan on December 7, 1801. Later purchases were made from Richard Foster and James Henderson on Coal Run, and in 1811 from Charles Anderson. In 1804, he was sent to the Pennsylvania Legislature as the representative of this district, where he served with distinction. Ann (Darrah) Barclay died at Carmichaels, April 13, 1816, aged 43 years, 3 months, and 16 days, and is buried with her husband in Glades Church Cemetery.

Children of Hugh and Ann (Darrah) Barclay

1. Mary Barclay, born in Bucks County, January 29, 1789; baptized May 9, 1789; married (1) John Swan, son of Charles and Sarah (Vanmeter) Swan, born December 10, 1783. On their wedding day John Swan left his wife to take a load of freight down the river to Tennessee and then to Missouri. He was unfortunate in his venture, losing some by leakage of the boat and the rest by poor markets. Fearing punishment for fraud and the jibes of his friends and new wife, he never returned, and no word was heard from him until later years. Believing him lost, his wife remarried, her second husband being Isaac Johnson, who died in Greene County about 1844. John Swan married again in Missouri.

Children

1. Robert Johnson.
2. Allen Johnson, married Frances Collier.
3. Lewis Johnson, married Mary Patterson.
4. Hannah Johnson, married Abner Forman.
5. Martha Johnson, married Daniel C. Stephenson.

2. Margaret Barclay, born in Bucks County, January 14, 1791, died in Knox County, Ohio, in 1863; married, January 24, 1811, Charles Swan, Jr., born December 9, 1787, died in Knox County, Ohio, in 1873. Records show she was baptized April 3, 1791.

Children

1. Mary Swan, born November 26, 1811; married (1) Hiram Litzenberg, (2) Hiram Brown.
2. Ann Swan, born February 26, 1813; married, November 20, 1832, Russell Armstrong.
3. Charles Swan, born December 8, 1815, died January 13, 1873; married Annie Curry.
4. Hugh B. Swan, born December 17, 1816; married, April 13, 1837, Helen Stephenson.
5. Henry Swan, born November 8, 1818; married, November 25, 1840, Clara Fuller.
6. Solomon Swan, born October 29, 1820, died February 4, 1901; married Anna Davidson, born April 24, 1824, died January 28, 1901.
7. Sarah Swan, born September 7, 1822; married (1) John Patterson, (2) Mr. Giles.
8. Helen Swan, born May 17, 1824, married Solomon Hewitt.
9. William Swan, born March 22, 1826, died in infancy.
10. Thomas Swan, born September 29, 1827; married (1) Belle Bonar, (2) Mary Gordon.
11. B. Franklin Swan, born August 25, 1829, died from accident, 1837.
12. Alexander Swan, born November 24, 1831; married (1)

Ann McCullough, (2) Elizabeth Richey.
13. Margaret B. Swan, born October 30, 1833, died in infancy.
3. Jane Barclay, born April 7, 1793; baptized August 4, 1793.
4. Ann Barclay, born April 20, (or 27) 1795, died in Jefferson County, Ohio, June 7, 1838; she was the first wife of Benjamin Rex, whom she married January 23, 1816. Benjamin Rex, son of George and Margaret (Kepler) Rex, was born January 9, 1792. He was married three times.

Children of Benjamin and Ann (Barclay) Rex

1. George Darrah Rex, born November 10, 1816, died March 12, 1890, in Jefferson County, Ohio. He married, November 12, 1840, Martha Swan, born February 14, 1819, died May 8, 1845. Martha Swan was a daughter of Thomas and Eleanor (Anderson) Swan.
2. Margaret Rex, born February 5, 1818, died April 23, 1912, at Wayne, Pennsylvania; married, May 29, 1842, James Frazier, who died March 28, 1873.
3. Mary Rex, born September 23, 1819, drowned in a spring at her grandfather's home, August 9, 1822.
4. Hugh Barclay Rex, born November 18, 1821, died April 23, 1883; married, June 6, 1855, Mary J. Roberts.
5. Anne Rex, born September 25, 1823, died June 17, 1904, near Bonaparte, Iowa. Married, March 31, 1847, Garretson Vale, born July 7, 1821, died February 17, 1875.
6. Minerva Rex, born June 20, 1825; choked to death October 16, 1826.
7. Charles Rex, born April 18, 1827, died April 12, 1833, of scarlet fever.
8. Benjamin K. Rex, born September 27, 1829, died April 10, 1833, of scarlet fever.
9. James Rex, born August 10, 1831, died April 10, 1833, of scarlet fever.
10. Martha Rex, born July 15, 1833, died May 8, 1866; married, September 25, 1855, John S. McGregor, born March 31, 1825, died September 15, 1897.
11. Sarah Rex, born February 20, 1835, died June 5, 1905; married Hamilton Mitchell.

5. James Barclay, born February 5, 1797 (or June 5, 1797).
6. Henry Barclay, born December 6, 1799, went to Mt. Pleasant, Iowa. His wife was Elizabeth Armstrong, daughter of William and Elizabeth (Russell) (Moore) Armstrong.

Children of Henry and Elizabeth (Armstrong) Barclay

1. Russell Barclay.
2. Anne Barclay, married .... Wolfe.
3. Mary Barclay, married .... Biddle.
4. Alfred Barclay.
5. Lizzie Barclay.
6. Laura Barclay, married .... Kirby.
7. Solon Barclay, born December 23, 1802, died 1824.
8. Harriet Barclay, born January 1, 1805; married (1) ...., married (2), November 16, 1837, Thomas Swan, born November 13, 1781, died in Fayette County, Pennsylvania, April 11, 1845. He had been married before and had 10 children by his first wife.
9. Sarah Barclay, born July 20, 1806, died December 7, 1886;

married, May 5, 1828, Dr. Thomas Laidley, born July 18, 1793, died July 28, 1881. Both are buried in the Laurel Point Cemetery at Carmichaels, Pennsylvania. He was a son of Thomas and Sarah (Osborne) Laidley.

Children

1. Norval Laidley, born May 4, 1829, died April 2, 1902.
2. John B. Laidley, born August 21, 1830, died December 15, 1922; married, June 8, 1859, Mary Galbraith, born October 20, 1829, died 1921.
3. Anna Eliza Laidley, born July 31, 1832, died July 18, 1879; married John Collier, born April 15, 1833, died May 23, 1890.
4. Edmund Laidley, born 1833, died March 3, 1843.
5. Mary Laidley, married, May 28, 1871, Jonah F. Randolph. He was born August 13, 1835.
6. James Laidley, went to Missouri.
7. Thomas Laidley, born May 31, 1837; married, 1861, Sarah Wright Flenniken, born July 24, 1841, died 1883.
8. Leonidas Laidley, went to Missouri.
9. Wilbur Laidley, went to Missouri.
10. Alvin D. Laidley, born October 20, 1842, died March 15, 1892; married Anna McClintock, born November 4, 1847, died July 31, 1913. They were married June 1, 1872.
11. Charley Laidley, born 1846, died August 11, 1867. Went to Iowa.

10. Hugh Barclay, born June 5, 1809, died April 30, 1881; married, February 19, 1833, Phoebe Craft, born June 19, 1810, died January 10, 1891.

Children

1. William H. Barclay, married (1) Sarah Minor, (2) Martha Areford.
2. Isaac J. Barclay, born January 30, 1841, died April 26, 1932; married Caroline Minor, born May 21, 1845, died December 19, 1932.
3. Maramara Barclay, married John Bailey.
4. George A. Barclay, born February 25, 1850, died November 21, 1912; married Rhoda Kendall, born June 25, 1845, died August 30, 1924.
5. Israel C. Barclay married Orpha Gregg.

11. Hannah Barclay, born January 12, 1812; married Morgan Reeves.

FAMILY OF JOHN WRIGHT

Margaret Darrah, fifth child of Henry and Ann (Jamison) Darrah, was born in Bucks County on November 26, 1772, and died in Greene County, Pennsylvania, on April 30, 1838. She married John Wright, who died in Greene County on May 16, 1859, aged 88 years. Both are buried at Glades Cemetery.

Children of John and Margaret (Darrah) Wright

1. James Wright, migrated in early manhood to Ohio.
2. Franklin Wright, lived in Philadelphia.
3. Harriet Wright, was born September 25, 1801, and died October 17, 1883; married, January 4, 1827, David Evans, son of George and Lydia (Brice) Evans. He was born November 11,

1800, and died June 5, 1866.

Children

1. Margaret Ann Evans, born April 20, 1828, died January 22, 1845. Never married.
2. Lydia Sarah Evans, born June 23, 1830, died May 1902. Never married.
3. George William Evans, born April 23, 1832, died February 16, 1901; married Elizabeth Alexander.
4. Martha Jane Evans, born July 14, 1834, died June 7, 1900. Never married.
5. Eliza Helen Evans, born April 3, 1836, died January 26, 1900; married William McGill.
6. Henrietta Evans, born February 4, 1838, died February 21, 1878. Never married.
7. John Wright Evans, born January 15, 1840, died March 10, 1912; married Mary Gilmer.
8. Benjamin B. Evans, born February 17, 1842, died April 1912; married Sarah Clawson.
9. Laura Minor Evans, born March 22, 1845, died May 15, 1911; married Lewis Antram.
10. Abel Evans, born March 20, 1847, died February 10, 1902; un-married.

4. Martha Wright, married John Protsman of Morgantown, West Virginia.
5. Hester Ann Wright, born December 29, 1803, died November 22, 1883; married, 1822, John Wilkins Flenniken, born 1790, died October 16, 1861.

Children

1. Elias Alexander Flenniken, born June 2, 1824, died February 27, 1905; married, February 3, 1847, Mary Ann Kerr, born March 12, 1825, died December 30, 1899.
2. Mary Jane Flenniken, born May 5, 1826, died December 4, 1908; married, 1844, Thomas Curl, born January 13, 1813, died 1878.
3. James Darrah Flenniken, born June 17, 1828, died September 27, 1917; married, September 28, 1854, Martha Ann Curl, born March 18, 1834, died February 1, 1900.
4. Margaret M. Flenniken, born September 23, 1830, died July 23, 1901; married, April 26, 1855, Clemment Krepps, born January 22, 1829, died November 22, 1886.
5. William F. Flenniken, born July 30, 1838, died 1918; married 1863, Eliza Hartman.
6. Sarah Wright Flenniken, born July 24, 1841, died August 17, 1885; married, 1861, Thomas Laidley, born May 31, 1837.
7. Andrew Stewart Flenniken, born August 21, 1848, died February 7, 1932; married, January 4, 1871, Anna Patterson, born March 5, 1849, died June 5, 1932.

JACOB HUFTY FAMILY

Sarah Barclay, daughter of James and Margaret Barclay, married Jacob Hufty, also a native of Bucks County. They removed to the vicinity of Rices Landing, where Jacob Hufty died about 1815, leaving a will which was probated April 3, 1815. (Will Book 1. pp. 146.) Jacob Hufty got a warrant for a tract of land next to

William Cree in Jefferson Township on September 8, 1796, for which a patent was issued to John Hufty on April 8, 1833. Jacob Hufty was a soldier in Captain Dennis Worrell's Company, Second Battalion, Phiadelphia County Militia in the Revolution. (Penna. Arch. Series VI. Vol. 1. pp. 702.)

Children of Jacob and Sarah (Barclay) Hufty

1. Israbel Hufty.
2. John Hufty.
3. James Hufty, executor of father's estate; married Cassandra Lucas, born 1797. (See Lucas.)
4. Hetty Hufty.
5. Margaret Hufty, born July 5, 1779, died April 13, 1842; married John Murdock, born September 15, 1779, died July 31, 1867. He was a son of James and Mary Murdock.

Children

1. Sarah Murdock, born January 11, 1801, died May 27, 1866; married (1) March 29, 1855, ... Worthington. She married (2) Thomas Hoskinson.
2. Mary Murdock, born February 17, 1803; married Abner Fordyce.
3. Jane Murdock, born March 8, 1805; married Joseph Kirby.
4. James B. Murdock, born August 7, 1807, died March 11, 1864; married Hannah Temple, born August 7, 1807, died April 25, 1883.
5. Jacob Hufty Murdock, born December 7, 1809; married (1) Mary Gillett, who died January 27, 1852. He then married Elizabeth Moffett.
6. Eliza Murdock, born March 1, 1812.
7. John Murdock, born March 10, 1814; married, October 7, 1849, Sarah Gillett.
8. Daniel Murdock, born November 27, 1818; married Rhoda Clawson.
9. William H. Murdock, born December 20, 1820, died February 26, 1909; married Nancy Gillett, born June 16, 1822, died December 5, 1906.

6. Sarah Hufty, married .... Brisson.
7. Mary Hufty, married (1) Samuel Dye and went to Miami County, Ohio, where he died in 1814. Mary Hufty then married .... Knight, and after his death she married Stephen Dye, brother of her first husband. Stephen was born December 23, 1770, and died September 14, 1851. Stephen and Mary (Hufty) Dye were married November 1, 1827.
8. Jane Hufty, married Abraham Milliken, born 1785, died 1860.

THE BAILY FAMILY

We have been asked to include a record of the first Bailys to settle in the Carmichaels section, and because of the contributions they have made to the progress of the section, are pleased to comply with the request. Mr. Gilbert Cope of Lancaster, Pennsylvania, has compiled a very complete genealogy of this family, carrying the relationship back to the 1500s, to a Joel Baily who came to America in 1683. Joel Baily's great-grandson, Eli Baily, is the ancestor of the Carmichaels Bailys, and it is evident that he was a late comer to the Tenmile Country. The name is found, however, at an earlier date, for in the tax lists for Morgan Township in 1784-85, Groombride Baily was among those taxed. An Electious Baily was taxed in Cumberland Township in 1788, and his name is frequently found in the Muddy Creek Ledger.

Eli Baily appears to have come to Muddy Creek about 1800. Mr. Ellis Baily Hawkins, now of New Wilmington, Pennsylvania, but a native of Carmichaels, says his ancestor was the Eli Baily who served in Captain George Grist's Company, Eighth Battalion, Chester County Militia, in the War of the Revolution. Eli Baily was born in East Marlboro, Pennsylvania, April 6, 1749, and was married to Ruth Taylor on March 8, 1776, in Swedes Church at Wilmington, Delaware. No record has been found for the deaths of Eli or Ruth (Taylor) Baily. Mr. Hawkins, a careful genealogist of the family, has sent in much of the record of the family of Eli Baily, and credits much of it to Mr. Cope's excellent book. (Penna. Arch. Series V. Vol. 5. pp. 812-819-829.)

Children of Eli and Ruth (Taylor) Baily

1. Jesse Baily, died un-married.
2. Joseph Baily, born February 20, 1778, died in Greene County, February 17, 1851; married, February 13, 1806, Hannah Johnson, daughter of Jonathan and Elizabeth (Richards) Johnson, born August 18, 1780, died August 11, 1820. Joseph Baily married (2) Rebecca Jackson.

Children of Joseph Baily

1. Joanna Baily, died May 30, 1885; married John C. Reppert.
2. Eliza Baily, married (1) Cyrus Shelby, who died 1833. Married (2) Thomas Ross.
3. Ruth Baily, married Jesse Ross.
4. Eli J. Baily, born November 26, 1814, died May 19, 1897; married Mary Cock, born July 30, 1813, died near Brownsville, Pennsylvania, August 11, 1881
5. Johnson Baily, married Amanda Jackson. Removed to Iowa. She died about 1849.
6 Joseph T. Baily, died November 26, 1899; married Martha J. Lee, lived near Carmichaels.

3. William Baily, born October 2, 1779, died March 7, 1862; married, July 1807, Sarah Myers. She died and he married (2), November 16, 1813, Zillah Johnson, daughter of Isaac and Lydia (Miller) Johnson. A daughter was born to the first marriage, later becoming the wife of Miller Haines.

Children of William and Zillah (Johnson) Baily

1. Amanada Baily, married James Murdock.
2. Jesse K. Baily, married Delilah Craft.
3. Eli E. Baily, born August 16, 1818; married Mary Dowlin.
4. Ruth Ann Baily, married Samuel Rea.
5. William Baily.
6. Zillah Baily, married R. Richardson.
7. Lindley M. Baily.

4. Joab Baily, born August 25, 1781, died April 16, 1857; married, February 7, 1804, Jane Mundell, born October 13, 1784, died April 15, 1862

Children of Joab and Jane (Mundell) Baily

1. Ruth Baily, born August 18, 1804, died November 18, 1806.
2. Eli Baily, born October 4, 1805, died October 9, 1868, near Browning, Missouri. Married, January 1, 1837, Elizabeth Patton, born July 13, 1811, died August 1889.

3. Mary Baily, born November 20, 1808, died February 12, 1880, near Carmichaels, Penna. She married, September 23, 1832, Andrew Lantz, born October 4, 1803, died July 13, 1862. After the death of Mr. Lantz, Mary Baily married (2) James Barnes, born 1788, died 1882. Ancestor of of James Barnes Huss of Washington, D. C.
4. Jane Baily, born June 6, 1811, died at Pine Bank, March 17, 1900; married, April 28, 1829, Corbly Fordyce, born June 7, 1807, died November 13, 1862.
5. Abner Baily, born April 30, 1814, died at Newtown, July 22, 1896; married, September 20, 1838, Elizabeth South, born December 3, 1816. Abner Baily married (2), August 16, 1855, Mary Bowen, born June 3, 1830, died August 22, 1874. Married (3) Margaret Taylor. Married (4) Ruth A. Hoover.
6. Eleanor Ann Baily, born April 10, 1817; married, April 6, 1837, Joseph Fordyce, born September 14, 1814. died February 28, 1884, at Cambridge, Ohio.
7. Ruth Ann Baily, born December 28, 1819. died December 18, 1881; married, October 2, 1842, Eli Shultz, born December 3, 1814.
8. Joab Baily, born February 19, 1823, died April 26, 1869; married, April 4, 1848, Pleasant J. Roberts, born November 23, 1826, died April 18, 1876. Lived at Dewitt, Illinois.

5. Hannah Baily, born March 26, 1784; married, in Chester County, Pennsylvania, March 26, 1807, Job Wickersham, born December 17, 1780. They lived at East Fairfield, Ohio.

Children

1. Jonathan Wickersham, born January 15, 1808, died July 23, 1863; married Elizabeth Fitz Randolph.
2. Eli Wickersham, born March 18, 1810, died May 21, 1837.
3. Thomas Wickersham, born July 12, 1812, died July 13, 1878, Watseka, Illinois. He married Elizabeth Fitz Randolph, born December 26, 1816, died August 15, 1870.
4. Joseph Wickersham, born April 16, 1814; married Juliana Warner.
5. Job Wickersham, born June 19, 1816; married Eliza Ballinger.
6. Anna Wickersham, born December 1, 1818; married Joseph Turner.
7. Reuben Wickersham, born February 19, 1821.
8. Lydia B. Wickersham, born January 21, 1824; died in infancy.
9. Hannah Wickersham, born July 31, 1825; married John Rea.
10. Baily Wickersham, born ....; married Mary Milton.

6. Eli Baily, born September 27, 1788, died July 22, 1854; married, January 25, 1815, Pera Gregg, daughter of Richard and Ann (Gregg) Gregg, born May 11, 1793, died March 26, 1872. Eli Baily was born in Chester County, Pennsylvania, and died at Uniontown, Pennsylvania.

Children of Eli and Pera (Gregg) Baily

1. Louisa Baily, born November 8, 1815, died September 16, 1902; married, October 15, 1833, Moses Nixon, born May 12, 1812, died July 22, 1857. They lived near Uniontown, Pennsylvania.

2. Jesse Baily, born May 10, 1817, died at Dyersville, Iowa, August 6, 1893; married, on March 14, 1850, Margaret Moreland, born May 6, 1827, died 1902.
3. Presley Gregg Baily, born February 9, 1819, died in Iowa, October 21, 1878; married, December 27, 1848, Harriet C. Clark, born December 6, 1827, died July 4, 1909.
4. Eliza R. Baily, born October 10, 1820, died at Uniontown, January 15, 1901; married, May 7, 1840, William S. Barnes, born May 8, 1817, died May 5, 1890.
5. Richard Baily, born November 4, 1822, died August 12, 1824.
6. Ellis B. Baily, born November 21, 1824, died January 17, 1897; married, March 7, 1850, Harriet Gaddis, born June 25, 1825, died January 22, 1907.
7. Eli Baily, born December 15, 1826, died August 3, 1842.
8. Ruth Ann Baily, born January 13, 1829; married, March 7, 1850, Andrew Lynn, born September 6, 1822.
9.
10. William H. Baily, born September 11, 1832, died February 11, 1908; married Virginia Patterson, born March 11, 1843, died November 6, 1905.
11. Emily Baily, born August 30, 1834, died March 30, 1900; married William Dixon, born May 8, 1832.

7. Ruth Baily, born May 1, 1791, died May 8, 1876; married October 6, 1808, Jacob Fitz Randolph, born September 30, 1779, died January 27, 1857.

Children

1. Harriet Fitz Randolph, born August 28, 1810, married William Davis.
2. Eli Fitz Randolph, born August 7, 1812, married Letitia Reynolds.
3. Ruth Fitz Randolph, born July 24, 1814, married Peter Hewitt.
4. Elizabeth Fitz Randolph, born December 26, 1816, married Thomas Wickersham.
5. Rebecca Fitz Randolph, born February 24, 1820, married Samuel Bayard.
6. Joseph Fitz Randolph, born October 12, 1824, married Mary Bayard.

8. Mary Baily, born June 3, 1794, died February 11, 1879; married Edward Fitz Randolph. They were married October 15, 1812.

Children

1. Ruth Fitz Randolph, born July 24, 1813; married James Vernon.
2. Elizabeth Fitz Randolph, born February 11, 1816; never married.
3. Amanda Fitz Randolph, born November 11, 1817; married William Hawkins.
4. Anna Fitz Randolph, born June 17, 1819.
5. Eliza Fitz Randolph, born December 7, 1823; never married.
6. Hannah Fitz Randolph, born March 9, 1825.
7. Mary Fitz Randolph, born June 8, 1827.
8. Ellis Fitz Randolph, born April 15, 1830; married Alice Davis.
9. Emily Fitz Randolph, born May 13, 1832; married Lewis Ladd.

10. Harriet Fitz Randolph, born November 30, 1835; married Eli Hudson.
11. Rebecca Fitz Randolph, born March 30, 18......

9. Eliza Baily, born February 15, 1797, died May 24, 1843; married May 15, 1815, Richard Fitz Randolph. who married (2) October 11, 1850, Elizabeth Hartzell.

Children

1. Matilda Fitz Randolph, born February 23, 1816.
2. Hannah Fitz Randolph, born December 26, 1817.
3. Baily Fitz Randolph, born August 27, 1819; married Caroline Ashford.
4. Reuben Fitz Randolph, born January 10, 1821.
5. Kersey Fitz Randolph, born April 10, 1824.
6. Rebecca Fitz Randolph, born September 18, 1825; married Robert McGregor.
7. Jonathan Fitz Randolph, born October 31, 1828; married Rebecca Ashford.
8. Richard Fitz Randolph, born October 5, 1830.
9. Eliza Fitz Randolph, born December 9, 1832; married B. S. Young.
10. Eli Fitz Randolph, born March 26, 1835.
11. Joseph Fitz Randolph, born September 18, 1837; married Susan Ells.
12. Ira Fitz Randolph, born June 5, 1840.

THE MUNDEL FAMILY

The wording of the will of James Mundel (Mundle, etc.) permits the qualified statement, that all of the pioneer settlers in the Tenmile Country bearing this name, were descendants of this man. After making specific bequests to five sons, a bequest is made in this will, which reads "unto my loving children, those who have had no part of my land, all the rest of my movable property to be equally divided among them." (Will Book 1. pp. 50, probated November 12, 1805.) In authentic papers of the descendants of one daughter not mentioned in this will by name, there is a statement that James Mundel came from England to Delaware, where on July 12, 1751, he married, at Wilmington, Newcastle County, Margaret Garret. These same papers show that a son, James Mundel, was born in 1752, and list a son, Jonathan Mundel, not named in the will as another son. The will of James Mundel names his wife, Margaret, and Goshen Baptist Church Book notes that on January 26, 1776, James and Margaret Mundel were received by letter, showing them to have been among the first settlers.

James Mundel chose land near the forks of Little Whiteley Creek, near the present village of Ceylon, including land now owned by Howard Groomes, on which there is the Mundel Cemetery, and which was warranted to him on January 19, 1785, under the title "Mundel's Choice." It is to be noted that in 1871, a five acre plot adjoining this land was not included in any survey and a patent was obtained on March 7, of that year, to this unclaimed land by Abner Mundel, no doubt a grandson of the original patentee of "Mundel's Choice." The location of this land was fortunate as it was within a short distance of Aaron Jenkin's Fort, and the Mundels do not seem to have suffered from the Indians like some of their neighbors.

Family of James and Margaret (Garret) Mundel

1. James Mundel, probably the oldest son of James and Margaret (Garret) Mundel, named by his father in his will. The records of his sister, Margaret (Mundel) Hart, say he was born in 1752. He may have married twice as a deed of record shows him joined by a wife, Elizabeth, yet buried in the Mundel Cemetery with his sister; a marker shows that Sarah, wife of James Mundel, died in 1835, aged 67 years. Sarah Miller, daughter of John and Patience Miller, married one James Mundel. (O. C. Docket 1. pp. 105.)
2. John Mundel, named in the will of his father. He served in Captain William Crawford's Company. (Penna. Arch. Series VI. Vol. 2. pp. 166.) A deed of record lists his wife as Amanda .... (Deed Book 10. pp. 143.)
3. Jonathan Mundel, not named in the will of James Mundel. He was received by baptism into Goshen Baptist Church on October 13, 1786, and is frequently mentioned in their records. His wife was Catherine Buckingham, born August 22, 1767, daughter of William and Jane (Jones) Buckingham.
4. Abner Mundel, not named in the will of James Mundel. Born on April 27, 1758, and baptised at Goshen Baptist Church, October 13, 1786, with John Hart, Jonathan and Andrew Mundel. (See separate record.)
5. Margaret Mundel, born in 1760, died October 15, 1831, aged 71 years. She is not named in the will of her father, but old papers among the records of her descendants give much of the data on James and Margaret (Garret) Mundel, including the date of their marriage at Wilmington, and mention of her brothers, James and Jonathan Mundel. She married John Hart, who was born about 1756. A marker in the Mundel Cemetery is still legible. She was received by baptism at Goshen Baptist Church on August 29, 1789.

Children of John and Margaret (Mundel) Hart

1. Thomas Hart, his wife was Polly ....
2. Eleanor Hart, (Nelly), married Francis McClelland, born July 5, 1771, son of Andrew and Mary (Knight) McClelland.
3. Miles Hart.
4. John Hart.
5. James Hart.
6. Anna Hart.
7. Levi Hart, born January 8, 1798; married Jane Jackson, born 1786, daughter of Samuel and Margaret (Cree) Jackson.

Children of Levi and Jane (Jackson) Hart

1. Samuel Hart, born October 25, 1818.
2. Margaret Hart, born August 3, 1820.
3. Neri Hart, born September 26, 1821, died June 28, 1899; married Margaret Ann Rea, born December 22, 1832, died March 29, 1891, daughter of Paul Rea.
4. Mariah Hart, born November 8, 1825, married Thomas Lincoln.
5. Melinda Hart, born January 8, 1828, died March 27, 1871; married Gennings Burnette, who died December 7, 1870, aged 45 years, 1 month, 1 day.
6. Caroline Hart, born September 30, 1830; married Henry Jennings.
7. Martha Hart, born February 28, 1833, died at the age of 52 years.

8. Asberry Hart, died at Pierceville, at the age of 82 years.
6. Eleanor Mundel, not named in will of James Mundel; received by baptism at Goshen Baptist Church, September 30, 1786.
7. Eli Mundel, executor of James Mundel's will; received by baptism at Goshen Baptist Church, with Margaret Hart on August 29, 1789. He was active in this church, which granted him license to preach on June 25, 1803, but excluded him from the church a short time later because he had joined the Methodist Society and preached their doctrine. His wife was Ann Cree, daughter of Robert and Janet Cree. She died August 22, 1820, aged 54 years, and is buried in the Mundel Cemetery.

Children of Eli and Ann (Cree) Mundel are not known
1.
2.
3.
4
5.
6.
7.
8. Jonathan Mundel, not named in the will of James Mundel, but included in the records of Margaret (Mundel) Hart. He was also a member of Captain William Crawford's Militia Company, and of Goshen Baptist Church, where he was baptised on October 13, 1786.
9. Andrew Mundel, baptised at Goshen Baptist Church on October 13, 1786; not named in the will of James Mundel.
10. Levi Mundel, named in the will of James Mundel.
11. Joseph Mundel, named in the will of James Mundel; died before 1834, when Richard Long was appointed guardian for his minor children. His wife's name was Sarah .... (O. C. Docket 2. pp. 32.)

Children of Joseph and Sarah Mundel
1. Garret Mundel, died March 2, 1881, aged 82 years. Married Hannah ...., born 1804, died 1893.
2. Levi Mundel, married Nancy ....
3. John Mundel.
4. James Mundel.
5. Elizabeth Mundel.
6. Cephas Mundel.

THE ABNER MUNDEL FAMILY

There is little reason to doubt that Abner Mundel was one of the un-named children of James and Margaret (Garret) Mundel. Facts brought out by the pension application of Abner Mundel for services in the Revolution, the naming of his children in a Bible record still in existence, and the records of Goshen Baptist Church, tend to confirm this opinion.

The pension record of Abner Mundel, secured by a descendant, James Barnes Huss, at the Department of Archives in Washington, shows that the application was filed April 3, 1834, from Greene County, Pennsylvania. Abner Mundel stated he was drafted into the company of Captain William Crawford in the Spring of 1781, and sent to a fort on Tenmile Creek, where he served for a period of two months. His duty was to help protect the frontiers against the Indians. In 1779, he had volunteered to go against the Indians on the Allegheny and Ohio Rivers and had gone to Fort McIntosh at the mouth of Beaver Creek on the Ohio. He served two months at this place, but troops destined for this campaign failed to arrive and the expedition was abandoned. This service was under Captain

John Huston in Colonel Brodhead's Regiment. He had also volunteered in 1778, in Captain William Crawford's Company, and gone to Wheeling to bring up some large boats to Pittsburgh for the purpose of transporting troops of General George Rogers Clark's expedition to the Wabash River, this being the most service Abner Mundel had ever performed. In the same year he had been called out by Captain Crawford for the purpose of quieting the Tories in Greene, Fayette, and Washington Counties, at which duty they had arrested upwards of 100 Tories. Abner Mundel said that he had been born in Newcastle County, Delaware, and was 76 years of age. (A slight error as shown by a Bible record.) (Proof of his services in Captain William Crawford's Company is found in Pennsylvania Archives Series VI. Volume 2. pp. 165, etc.)

The Abner Mundel Bible says he was born April 27, 1758, he died in Greene County on May 8, 1845; he married, April 9, 1782, Mary Barnhill. Goshen Church records show that on October 13, 1786, Abner Mundel, Jonathan Mundel, Andrew Mundel, and John Hart, were all baptized on the same day. His wife, Mary Barnhill, was born April 17, 1764, and is mentioned in the will of Abner Mundel. This will, made May 23, 1837, was probated May 13, 1845. (Will Book 2. pp. 213.)

Family of Abner and Mary (Barnhill) Mundel

1. Margaret Mundel, born February 9, 1783, died 1840; married John Morris, born March 17, 1777, son of George and Margaret (Corbly) Morris.

    #### Children of John and Margaret (Mundel) Morris
    1. Abner Morris, married Rachel Bowers.
    2. George Morris.
    3. Mary Morris, married .... Fordyce.
    4. Margaret Morris, married .... Richey.
    5. Rebecca Morris, married .... Jolly.

2. Jane Mundel, born October 14, 1784, died April 15, 1862; married, February 7, 1804, Joab Baily, born August 25, 1781, died April 16, 1857.

    #### Children of Joab and Jane (Mundel) Baily
    1. Ruth Baily, born August 18, 1804, died November 18, 1806.
    2. Eli Baily, born October 4, 1805, died October 9, 1868; married, January 1, 1837, Elizabeth Patton, born July 13, 1811, died August 1889.
    3. Mary Baily, born November 20, 1808, died February 12, 1880; married (1) September 23, 1832, Andrew Lantz, born October 4, 1803, died July 13, 1862; married (2) James Barnes, born 1788, died 1882.
    4. Jane Baily, born June 6, 1811, died March 17, 1900; married, April 28, 1829, Corbly Fordyce, born June 7, 1807, died November 13, 1862.
    5. Abner Baily, born April 30, 1814, died July 22, 1896; married (1) September 20, 1838, Elizabeth South, born December 3, 1816; he married (2) August 16, 1855, Mary Bowen, born June 3, 1830, died August 22, 1874; he married (3) Margaret Taylor; (4) Ruth Hoover.
    6. Eleanor Ann Baily, born April 10, 1817; married, April 6, 1837, Joseph Fordyce, born September 14, 1814, died February 28, 1884.
    7. Ruth Baily, born December 28, 1819, died December 18, 1881; married, October 2, 1842, Eli Shultz, born December 3, 1814.
    8. Joab Baily, born February 19, 1823, died April 26, 1869;

married, April 4, 1848, Pleasants Jane Roberts, born November 23, 1826, died April 18, 1876.
3. Mary Mundel, born July 2, 1786; married Major Lot Lantz.

Children of Lot and Mary (Mundel) Lantz
  1. Malinda Lantz, born April 2, 1808, died February 15, 1890; married John Minor, born June 8, 1802, died March 25, 1891, son of Otho and Rebecca (South) Minor.
  2. Frances Lantz, married Samuel Minor, son of Noah and Sarah (South) Minor.
  3. Mary Lantz, never married.
  4. Jacob Lantz, married Cassandra South, daughter of Enoch and Ruth (Gregg) South.
  5. Margaret Lantz, married John Coleman.

4. John Mundel, born June 24, 1788.
5. James Mundel, born March 23, 1790.
6. Rebecca Mundel, born March 1, 1792, married Jacob Hatfield.
7. Nancy Mundel, born March 18, 1794, married .... Cox.
8. Samuel Mundel, born April 16, 1796.
9. Eleanor Mundel, born May 15, 1798, married .... Dye.
10. Abner Mundel, born June 18, 1800.
11. Priscilla Mundel, born March 31, 1802, married .... Tribby.
12. Hugh Mundel, born February 12, 1804.
13. Joseph Mundel, born May 13, 1807.

THE WHITELEYS

Scull's Map of the Monongahela Region, showing the west side of the River as it was known in 1770, indicates a fair knowledge of the region and its geographical features. There can be no mistake in identifying the stream labeled "Turkey Creek" as being the present Big Whiteley Creek, but the stream labeled "Whitelik" more nearly conforms to the present Muddy Creek. Aside from this error the map is useful in pointing out that the Whiteleys were no doubt named for salt licks found in the section, and were originally called "Whiteliks."

There are neither deeds nor traditions to show the first owner of the land at the mouths of either Big or Little Whiteley, but from facts and family histories known, it seems most certain that the long stretch of land extending from above the mouth of Little Whiteley to below the mouth of Big Whiteley along the Monongahela River was first owned by Thomas Provins. There is evidence to indicate that Thomas Provins was on the Monongahela as early as 1757, and because of indicated Quaker connections, does not seem to have had trouble at that time nor any time thereafter. Perhaps he was one of those persons reported to have secured his land by honest barter with the Indian Chief who claimed ownership. This chief may have been Bald Eagle, a frequent visitor to the Provins home, whose body was recovered by Provins' wife and buried in their yard after it had been set adrift in the Monongahela by the white murderers. Provins was one of those named by the Pennsylvania Commissioners at Redstone in 1768, as being one of the one hundred and fifty persons that were on Indian lands. At this meeting Commissioner Steel reported that the Indians did not wish the whites to move off the lands which they had improved and with whom the Indians lived peacefully. It was in this section that Sarah Provins, second wife of Thomas Provins, patented land astride the mouth of Little Whiteley on a warrant granted December 23, 1785. Back from the River, Thomas Provins had sold the site of Fort Jenkins to Aaron Jenkins by a deed not recorded until May 8, 1782. Describing this land he indicates that James Bell, he, and John Long, Sr., were all early settlers with Joshua Hudson, another neighbor. Long, Provins, Hudson and Jenkins are all in the tax list for 1772. Joshua Hudson died there about 1784, after he had made a deal to buy from James Bellshe, which was completed by William Hudson, his sole heir. (Washington County Deed Book 1-A-200.)

George Morris, the celebrated Scout of Dunmore's War and the Revolution, is said to have visited the section in 1764, during the Spring, when he selected land about eight miles from the mouth of Big Whiteley, and left to return the year following. Written testimony bears out this claim, for in his pension application of March 17, 1834, Jonathan Morris, brother of George Morris, stating that he was born in Virginia, on June 15, 1753, and was brought to what became Greene County by their father, Joseph Morris, when he was about ten or twelve years of age, at which time his brother was already settled there.

The year 1764, is also the date given that John Minor came from Virginia to select land for himself, his brother, William Minor, and for Zachariah Gapen, then returned the following year to make the site his chosen permanent home. It seems most certain that these men would not have chosen land directly on the River had not it been already in the hands of others. The land was not far off the long used Indian Trail mentioned by Christopher Gist and entered in his Journal on March 8, 1752, as following Dunkard Creek to its source near the Forks of Wheeling Creek. This was a route used early by the Wetsells, Bonnetts, Waggoners, and others, to settle near the Ohio on Wheeling, Fishing, and Grave Creeks. And due to the former use by the Indians, it is not surprising to find it a favorite road by which they infiltrated to the settlements to perpetrate the many massacres in the Whiteley Section.

Most of the settlers on the Whiteleys were strong in their allegiance to Virginia, though not native Virginians. Thomas Provins was born in New London Township, Chester County, Pennsylvania, John Long, Sr., was originally from Delaware and later Maryland, the Minors and Gapens were first from New Jersey. They had settled for a time in the Upper Shenandoah, and it is not surprising they were soon followed to the Whiteley by their former neighbors, the Garards, Suttons, Vanmeters, etc., a Baptist group some of whom tarried for a time in Fayette County. Thus we find that in 1773, Goshen Baptist Church was established to supply the civilizing influence needed on this frontier. The Minute Books of this Church afford an interesting picture of the early history of the Whiteley Community and its families.

GOSHEN BAPTIST CHURCH BOOKS

The Reverend John Corbly Chapter, Daughters of the American Revolution, through the generosity of the Garard Family, have copied the records of Goshen Baptist Church from the original Church Books, and are to be commended for having made these available at their National Headquarters. A copy of the first Church Book is also in the Filson Club Library at Louisville, Kentucky. Professor Waychoff quotes L. K. Evans in giving the list of the original members of this Congregation which was organized in 1773. Most of the thirty Charter Members were of the family of Jacob Vanmeter, who lived near Baily's School House on Muddy Creek. It is not surprising that two church buildings were built, the one at Garards Fort, and the other at Jacob Vanmeter's plantation on Muddy Creek, so that people from Fort Jackson and from Ruffs Creek could attend the meetings. Rev. John Corbly preached twice a month at each church. The militant sermons of this minister and the desire for religious service drew additional communicants, so that the organization was able to stand the loss of so many of its members in the migration westward in the years to follow.

An entry in the books dated September 18, 1779, discloses that on that date the following persons ask for letters of dismission: Jacob Vanmeter, Sr., John Garard, John Ventrees, John Eastwood, Joseph Eastwood, John Gates, Isaac Dye, David Henton, Abraham Vanmeter, Jacob Vanmeter, Jr., Rebecca Ventress, Letitia Vanmeter, Hannah Dye, Mary Underwood, Mary Henton, Hannah Eastwood, and the two colored persons, Bambo and Dinah. They were mostly the family of Jacob Vanmeter, Sr., and were preparing-then to go to Kentucky, which journey they effected the following Spring. Letitia Vanmeter was the wife of Jacob Vanmeter, Sr. Rebecca Ventrees was the wife of John Ventrees, she was soon to die and her husband married secondly, Elizabeth (Vanmeter) Swan, whose husband, John Swan, Jr., lost his life to an Indian bullet on the journey down the Ohio. Hannah Dye was the wife of Isaac Dye. Mary Underwood was the widow of Benjamin Underwood, who as shown in the Church Book had died July 21, 1778. Mary Henton was the wife of David Henton, who drowned in the Ohio on the journey to Kentucky. Rebecca Vanmeter, daughter of Jacob, is not listed among the members granted letters of dismission, but with her husband, Edward Rollins, accompanied the migration

Rollins being one of the charter members of the Church. John Garard had married Susan Vanmeter, daughter of Jacob Vanmeter, Sr. Samuel Haycroft, with his wife, Margaret Vanmeter, was also on the boat that made the journey. This migration ended in the Severn Valley near the present town of Elizabethtown, Kentucky. During the last Summer it was the good fortune of this writer to tour this section of Kentucky, to see the grave of John Ventrees, and visit with descendants of Elizabeth Vanmeter-Swan-Ventrees.

The migration of so many members just six years after the organization of this Church was not disastrous because of the additional members who had joined the Church in the years between. A few of these, whose names appear in the records, include Mary Ivers, wife of Richard; Elias Garard, James Moredock, James Crooks, Moses Tyler and wife, Ann; David Evans and wife, Mary; James Mundle and wife, Margaret; Mary Wise, George Morris, Colonel William Crawford, Alexander Bryant and wife, Mary; Henry Hall, Margaret Chenowith, and Hannah Garard.

The losses to the westward migration were made up also by the steady growth of the local community by immigration, so that when a report of the progress of the Church was given on February 1, 1801, it stated that from the original membership of thirty persons in 1773, the rolls had been increased to two hundred and sixty names, out of which number, twenty eight had died, twenty three dismissed by letters, and eighteen excluded from the membership for various reasons. It was a militant Church, whose punishment of the transgressors was thoroughly backed up by public opinion of its members. It righted wrongs and conflicts between its own members, whose every action in daily life was scrutinized and weighed in the customs of the times. The following list of names represents the accruals to the membership before the turn of the century, and is given because many of them are the pioneer ancestors of many local families. The list is probably not complete, but the names noted are the ones received by letter, baptism, and affiliation, as they appear in the minutes of the meetings.

Robert Jones and wife, Jane
Thomas Bowen and wife, Betty
Levi Harrod and wife, Rachel
John Guthery and wife, Lydia
Aaron Luzado and wife, Sarah
Henry Jackson and wife, Elizabeth
Abraham Covalt and wife, Lois
Joseph Dunn and wife, Dinah
William Burk and wife, Jemimah
Justus Garard and wife, Rachel
John Nepp and wife, Druscilla
Mary Gates, wife of John
Hercules Turner and Ann
Joseph Drake from Scotch Plains, N. J.
Joseph Gibbons and Elizabeth
Azariah Davis and Elizabeth Davis
David Price and Susannah
Amos Miller and Ann
Nicholas Shipman and Mary
Samuel Hill and Sarah Hill
Rollin Hughes and wife, Susannah
Jacob and Lydia Rush

Margaret Johnson
Jesse Vanmeter
Alexander Munroe
John Evans
Abner Mundle
Paul Hahn
John Hart
Susan Babcock
Athaliah Minor
David Baily
Joseph Sexton
Sarah Brown
Henry Johnson
Ruth Sayers
Solomon Lyons
Stephen Woodruff
Ross Crosley
Eli Mundle
Daniel Hillman
Hannah Johnson
Elizabeth Hall
Jeremiah Gustin

Elizabeth Morris
William Masters
Ruth Moredock
Robert McKenney
Esther McKenney
Michael Hahn
Joseph Engle
Mary Hartley
Charles Anderson
Benajah Gustin
Ossie Griffith
Phoebe Masters
Andrew Dye
Mary Stewart
William Smalley
Mary Pratt
Charles Shoemaker
Mary Myers
Margaret Hart
Ann Dawson
Jonathan Morris
Catherine Ervin

Benjamin Wood
Daniel Clark
Sarah Crosley
William Knight
Joseph Martin
Sarah Clark
Mary Lynn
Lewis Williams
Moses Lambert
Isaac Wood
Rachel Moore
John Ross
Mary Hudson
Mary Crosley
Nancy Corbly
Rebecca Edwards
Pleasants Johnson
Bailey John
Rhoda Hutchins
Bethania Gustin
Mary Ross
Elsy Davis
Henry Davis
Rachel McDowell
Rebecca Jenkins
Lydia Hinkle
Catherine Miller
Thomas Miller
Eleanor Mundle
Jonathan Mundle
Andrew Mundle
Margaret Shrock
Elijah Moore
Daniel Pursley
Elizabeth Stephens
Sarah Hathaway
Levi Martin
Thomas Roach
Catherine Duvall
John Miller
Leah Hughes
Jemimah Wellington

All of these names are mentioned prior to 1790. Most of them are adult persons, some had already gone westward. Husbands and wives are not always clearly pointed out, often being taken into the Church at different dates. The list represents all sections of the Tenmile Country, that is, from Muddy Creek, Big and Little Whiteley Creeks, Dunkard Creek and the Tenmile Creek itself. One can imagine a typical Sunday Morning at a home twenty miles distant from the Church, with the hurry and bustle of getting ready for the excursion. Then a whole day at the Church, whether it be at Big Whiteley or at Muddy Creek, during which friendships were renewed, matches made, scandals aired, and problems lifted from weary minds. Then with the uplifted spirit from the stirring words of the preacher, the homeward journey with all its dangers, is begun. This was their light in the wilderness, and the blessing is that it still shines.

THE REVEREND JOHN CORBLY

Reverend John Corby, Sr., is probably the best known of all the Greene County pioneers. Evans, Waychoff and other historians have covered most of the events of his life, and Miss Nancy Fordyce has under preparation a genealogy of his family and descendants that certainly warrants publication. For many years, she has been gathering the records of the family, most of whom left here, and has learned many unpublished facts about these people. We are indebted to her for her ready assistance in preparing the record here published.

Several things contribute to his fame at home and abroad. The massacre of a portion of his family, tragic enough to break a strong man, publicized so widely at the time, takes an historic place in the events of the frontier. But the Rev. John Corbly was the type of man, who makes his own history by his vigorous and active life. When he took sides, it was not of the passive type of opposition, and right or wrong, he became a fighting champion for his chosen cause. He was a militant crusader for any cause or controversy he saw worthy of his efforts. His fight for the new religion got him into trouble with the State Church before he came to the western frontier, and he was jailed for his stand at Culpepper, Virginia. (Order Book Orange County, Va., 1763-1769, pp. 514). The charge entered in official records reads: "At a court held in Orange County of Thursday, 28th day of July, 1768."

"This day Allan Wiley, John Corbly, Elijah Craig and Thomas Chambers in Discharge of their Recognizance entered into before Rowland Thomas, Gent, of being charged as Vagrant and Itinerant Persons for Assemblying themselves unlawfully at Sundry times and places under the donominations of Anabaptists and for teaching and preaching Schismatik Doctrines. Whereupon the Court having examined the Witnesses and heard the counsel on both sides are of the opinion that the said Allan Wiley, John Corbly, Elijah Craig, and Thomas Chambers are guilty of a breach of good behaviour and Ordered that they enter into bond each in the sum of 50 pounds and two securities in the Sum of 25 pounds each to be of Good Behaviour until the 25th of October next and in case they fail to enter into such Bond as aforesaid that each of them so failing shall be committed to Gaol until same shall be performed."

Research has not disclosed whether John Corbly gave bond and two securities, or whether he failed to carry out the order of this Court and went to jail. Corbly's confinement in Culpepper jail, near the date of this order, is one of the best known facts of his early ministry.

A family tradition is to the effect Corbly conducted his own defense and made so favorable an impression on the court officials that he was given a license to preach.

Under the Toleration Act of England, Regular Baptists were given licenses to preach in particular places, but this did not keep them from being persecuted and imprisoned.

After the District of West Augusta was divided into three counties, Ohio, Youghiogheny, and Monongalia, October 1776, John Corbly was appointed a judge, or justice-of-the-peace of Monongalia County, by Patrick Henry.

The Virginia court records of Ohio and Youghiogheny counties have been published in Annals of Carnegie Musuem.

A Virginia court was held in Youghiogheny County until August 28, 1780.

Monongalia County Court records were destroyed by fire (Morgantown, W. Va.,) in 1796.

There is at least one record of the Monongalia County Court extant. It is found in the Washington County, Pennsylvania, courthouse. It is a case of bond execution "estate of Lawrence Veech, held in Monongalia County Court, September 15, 1779" heard by Justices, "John Swearingen, John Corbly, Thomas . . . Armstrong Porter, executor, George Myers, bondsman."

The case was not settled in the Monongalia County Court, but was reopened in the court of Washington County, Pennsylvania, after Pennsylvania took over jurisdiction of this district, which accounts for this record being preserved.

He was appointed minister of Goshen Baptist Church at Gararads Fort in 1775, only to leave a short time later, not to return until some of the founders of the church, with whom he had quarreled, left to settle in Kentucky. And then he came back on his own terms. One church was not enough for his boundless energy, so he preached at several which were miles apart. He was in sympathy with the new government, and patriotic to such an extent, that by any measure he would have been termed a rebel by the more conservative element in any community. His pursuit of Tories in his own neighborhood, though apparently without rancor, was so active that it may have played a part in the tragic death of members of his family. He supported his friends and neighbors in the Whiskey Rebellion, and if not an active participant, was arrested and marched to Philadelphia, where he was but lightly imprisoned. He was only one of the few who were penalized for this so called act of treason, and though he suffered much on the march to Philadelphia, he left no word of complaint against his persecutors. To have withstood the disgrace and rigors of punishment on that occasion, then come back to his home and field of endeavor and live another six or seven years, speaks well of the strength of body and soul of this pioneer.

Collin's "History of Kentucky" Volume 1, pp. 12, finds the name of John Corbly in Captain William Harrod's Company in 1780, associated with other members of this early congregation at Goshen Baptist Church. His capacity was that of a private soldier, so we must assume he was a fighting man. As many of the men of this list were with Harrod on the Clark Expedition, it is quite possible that Rev. Corbly went out at that time. It is a period of his life about which little is known.

Reverend John Corbly, Sr., was born in England on February 25, 1733, and died in Greene County, Pennsylvania, June 9, 1803. His first wife was Abigail Bull, born in 1734, and died in Virginia about 1768. His second wife was Elizabeth Tyler, who was killed by the Indians on May 10, 1782. They were married about 1773, though the exact date is not known. His third wife was Nancy

Lynn, daughter of Colonel Andrew and Mary A. (Johnson) Lynn. She was born June 2, 1761, and died August 1, 1826. By these three marriages, Rev. Corbly was father to seventeen children of whom four were by the first marriage, five by the second, and the rest by the third marriage. With the last two wives, Rev. John Corbly is buried in the Garards Fort Cemetery, Garards Fort, Pennsylvania.

A well preserved family tradition holds that John Corbly owned land in Virginia which he gave to the family that kept his children following death of his first wife and until he married again. This is supported by official records noted below.

On June 17, 1765, Corbly was granted 52 acres of land on both sides of Great Cacapon River in Hampshire County, Va., by Lord Fairfax, Proprietor of the Northern Neck. Land adjoined that of John Keith and "yearly and every year on the Feast Day of St. Michael the Archangel fee rent of one shilling money for every 50 acres of land granted" was demanded. On April 16, 1773, John Corbly sold this same land to John Rice for five shillings. (Deed Book 3, pp. 137, Hampshire County, Va.). This amounted to almost an outright gift of the land and included in payment "one ear of Indian corn in and upon the First day of Christmas if the same be demanded."

Children of Rev. John Corbly, Sr.

1. Margaret Corbly, born February 17, 1758, died October 5, 1833; married George Morris, born January 2, 1745, died January 20, 1842; son of Joseph Morris. Both are buried in the Garards Fort Cemetery.
2. Rachel Corbly, born 1760, died May 8, 1842; married Justus Garard, born in Virginia in 1755; the son of Rev. John Garard. Justus Garard died January 10, 1828, and with his wife is buried in the Garards Fort Cemetery.
3. Priscilla Corbly, born 1762, died 1833; married, about 1775, William Knight, born 1751, died 1820. Removed to Miami County, Ohio. They are buried in Staunton Cemetery, near Troy, Ohio.
4. Rev. John Corbly, Jr., born 1768, according to the inscription on his tombstone. He died September 22, 1814; married, about 1791, Elizabeth Fansler, who after the death of her husband, married Mathias Corwin of Ohio.

Children of Second Marriage

5. Delilah Corbly, born July 19, 1774, died in Miami County, Ohio, January 10, 1839; married Levi Martin, born November 18, 1764, died March 22, 1835. Buried in the Staunton Cemetery, near Troy, Ohio.
6. Elizabeth Corbly, scalped by the Indians, but lived to the age of 20 years. Died just before she was to have married Isaiah Morris.
7. Isaiah Corbly, aged about six years at the time he was killed by the Indians.
8. Catherine Corbly, aged about four years when killed by the Indians.
9. Mary Ann (?) Corbly, infant in arms when killed by the Indians.

Children of Third Marriage

10. Mary Corbly, born March 11, 1785, died December 29, 1864; married about 1801, Rev. Jacob Myers, born December 10, 1780, died February 21, 1862.
11. Andrew Lynn Corbly, born 1787, died 1850; married, about 1807, Elizabeth Myers.
12. Pleasant Corbly, born June 8, 1789, died November 18, 1860; married Peter A. Myers, Jr., born July 30, 1787, died November 30 1880. Buried at Garards Fort.
13. Cassandra Corbly, born June 1, 1792, died December 6, 1869; married, September 6, 1810, Joseph Gregg, born 1782, died 1869. Buried at Garards Fort.
14. Sarah Corbly, born October 29, 1793, died December 6, 1814; married, 1813, John Wright, born January 2, 1782, died March 12, 1880; buried at Garards Fort.
15. Amelia Corbly, born June 2, 1796, died July 5, 1855; married, 1814, Amos Wright, born May 1, 1795, died November 17, 1871. Both buried at Garards Fort.
16. Nancy Corbly, born about 1798, killed in childhood in an accident.
17. William Corbly, born 1800, died December 26, 1875, in Athens County, Ohio. His wife was Rebecca Stephens, daughter of Edward and Hannah (Woodward) Stephens.

Family of George and Margaret (Corbly) Morris

Margaret Corbly, eldest daughter of Rev. John Corbly by his first marriage, was born on February 17, 1758, in Virginia, and died October 5, 1833. She married Captain George Morris, born January 2, 1745, died January 20, 1842, son of Joseph Morris, whose wife is said to have been Hannah Lee. Captain George Morris was one of the earliest pioneers to see the advantages of the land about Dunkard Creek, and went back to Virginia where he enlisted a number of his friends to settle on the frontier. Before 1774, he had established himself, his father, and his brothers, Jonathan and Amos Morris, on Big Whiteley Creek, where they speak in pension applications of having helped erect Garards Fort. His captain's rank was earned in the service of Lord Dunmore, but at the outbreak of the Revolution he tore up his British Commission and became one of the best scouts of the frontier, usually in company of his brother, Jonathan Morris. They served during the greater part of the Revolution, with Jonathan being granted a pension, but because his application was almost identical with Jonathan's, George Morris was refused. Amos Morris also got a pension on his claim of having served under his brother George Morris. Many other applications for pensions mention service under George Morris. He and his wife are both buried in the old cemetery at Garards Fort.

Children of George and Margaret (Corbly) Morris

(From Bible record of James B. Morris)

1. Amelia Morris, born November 3, 1775, died near Red Lion, Ohio, July 15, 1857. She married Samuel Gustin, born October 30, 1767, died April 15, 1852. Both are buried in the Todd Cemetery, Warren County, Ohio.

Children of Samuel and Amelia (Morris) Gustin

1. Jeremiah Gustin, born January 22, 1797.
2. Nancy Gustin, born 1799.
3. George Morris Gustin, born November 7, 1800.
4. Margaret Gustin, born 1802.
5. Amelia Gustin, born 1804.
6. Isaiah Gustin, born 1806.
7. John Gustin, born 1807.
8. Mary Gustin, born 1810.
9. Rachel Gustin, born 1813.
10. Hannah Gustin, born 1815.

2. John Morris, born March 17, 1777, died about 1852. (Will Book 3. pp. 215). Married (1) Mary Mundle; married (2) Margaret Mundle.

Children of John Morris

1. Abner Morris, married Rachel Bowers.
2. George Morris.
3. Mary Morris, married .... Fordyce.
4. Margaret Morris, married .... Richey.
5. Rebecca Morris, married .... Jolly.

3. Hannah Morris, born August 8, 1779, died February 13, 1849; married Elkanah Gustin, born, New Jersey, 1769, died Anderson, Indiana, November 1847. Hannah (Morris) Gustin is buried at Red Lion, Warren County, Ohio.

Children of Elkanah and Hannah (Morris) Gustin

1. John Corbly Gustin, born 1796, died 1881.
2. Benajah Gustin, born 1797, died 1886.
3. Jonathan Gustin, born 1798.
4. Eli Gustin, born 1800.
5. Samuel Gustin, born 1802, died 1880.
6. Levi Gustin, born 1805.
7. Thomas Gustin, born 1805.
8. Margaret Gustin.
9. Rachel Gustin.
10. Pernine Gustin.
11. Hannah Gustin.
12. Jane Gustin.
13. Amelia Gustin.
14. Anne Gustin.
15. William Gustin.

4. Jonathan Morris, born December 27, 1781, died July 19, 1848; married Sarah Clymer, born September 20, 1793, died 1824.

Children

1.
2.
3. Dr. Spencer, born October 26, 1820; married Belinda Bowlby.
4.

5. Levi Morris, founder of Mt. Morris. Born April 17, 1783 (or December 15, 1789), died January 20, 1842; married by Reverend Luce, November 2, 1809, Lucretia Stephens, born 1790, died April 15, 1885; daughter of Edward and Hannah (Woodward) Stephens.

Children

1. Margaret Morris, born September 15, 1811, died June 6,

1853. Married, May 2, 1829, Patrick Donley, born February 14, 1805, died October 20, 1891.
2. Louisa Morris, born July 4, 1812, died May 6, 1883; married, November 27, 1832, George Lemley.
3. Hannah Morris, born April 17, 1814; married, April 1, 1832, by Rev. Downey to Abner Garrison.
4. Josephus Morris, born March 14, 1816, died August 9, 1896; married, April 20, 1843, by Reverend A. Poole, Temperance Smith, born January 8, 1823, died December 18, 1904.
5. G. W. Morris, born April 9, 1819, died ....; married August 20, 1846, by Reverend Porter, to Emily Kirby.
6. Jefferson Morris, born April 9, 1819; married, October 28, 1845, by Rev. Porter, to Sarah Inghram.
7. Edward F. Morris, born March 30, 1823; married first by Reverend Cheyney, November 23, 1843, to Elizabeth Smith. Married, second, Rhetta Roberts, nee Bell.
8. Thomas Morris, born November 28, 1825; married Sarah Way.
9. James B. Morris, born November 24, 1827; married September 26, 1848, by Reverend C. McClain, to Keziah Way.
10. Levi A. Morris, born September 15, 1831; married Samantha Brown.
11. Lucretia Morris, born August 8, 1833, died April 15, 1885; married Colonel C. I. Hardin.

6. Isaiah Morris, born January 15, 1785. Engaged to marry Elizabeth Corbly, but she died suddenly from wounds received in the Corbly Massacre. He went to Ohio where he later became a member of Congress. He married in Ohio.
7. George Morris, born March 25, 1788, died October 26, 1839; married Elizabeth .... Kept a hotel at Newtown, Greene County, Pennsylvania.

Children

1. Sarah Morris, born September 12, 1825, died October 21, 1912; married Jack Jolly.
2. John Morris, never married.
3. Marion Morris, killed in Civil War.
4. Harrison Morris.
5. Washington Morris, never married.
6. Perry Morris, never married; had a son Lindsey.
7. Rachel Morris.

8. Rachel Morris, born April 11, 1790, died February 23, 1813.
9. Huston Morris, born December 15, 1792 (?), died in Indiana, December 16, 1879.
10. Priscilla Morris, born December 14, 1794, died November 21, 1811.
11. Margaret Morris, born April 9, 1797; married .... Lemley.

Family of Justus and Rachel (Corbly) Garard

Rachel Corbly, daughter of Reverend and Abigail Bull Corbly, born in 1760, died May 8, 1842. Buried at Garards Fort, Pennsylvania. Married Justus Garard, born 1755, in Virginia, died January 10, 1828, in Greene County, Pennsylvania.

Children
1. Elizabeth Garard, born March 12, 1778, died December 12, 1838. Married, September 16, 1798, Reverend John Fordyce, son of Samuel and Elizabeth Fordyce, born September 17, 1775, died April 30, 1848. Both buried in the Cemetery at Whiteley Chapel, Whiteley Township, Greene County, Pennsylvania.

Bible Record of Children
Bible of James Harvey Fordyce, by Mary Fordyce of Waynesburg, Pennsylvania

1. Rachel Fordyce, born November 9, 1799; married, December 1825, to Thomas Bowen.
2. Justus Garard Fordyce, born September 5, 1801; married, April 1829, Catherine Miller.
3. Samuel Fordyce, born March 15, 1803; never married; died February 4, 1837.
4. James Harvey Fordyce, born July 31, 1804, died 1883; married, November 1827, Nancy Bowers, who was born July 6, 1809, died 1892.
5. Nancy Fordyce, born November 29, 1805; married November 26, 1823, George Rose.
6. Corbly Fordyce, born June 7, 1807, died 1862; married, April 1829, Jane Baily.—
7. John Fordyce, born September 5, 1806, died April 18, 1882; married (1) March 1832, Ruth Gregg, who died. Married, June 1837, Mary Ann Hauser, born November 16, 1817.
8. Abner Fordyce, born May 5, 1810; married (1) Eliza Murdock.
9. Hetty Fordyce, born August 19, 1812, died ....; married, December 1832, James Evans.
10. Joseph Fordyce, born September 30, 1814, died ....; married, April 1837, Eleanor Ann Bailey, removed to Ohio.
11. Benson Fordyce, born December 21, 1816; married, September 1, 1839, Maria Nichols.

2. John Garard, son of Justus and Rachel Corbly Garard, born ....; removed to Ohio.
3. Sarah Garard, daughter of Justus and Rachel Corbly Garard, born August 29, 1782, died July 11, 1868; buried at Pine Bank, Greene County. Married Samuel Morris, born September 7, 1778, died December 1871.

Children
1. Rachel Morris, born March 26, 1803; married John Dye, August 26, 1821.
2. Jonathan Morris, born December 28, 1804, died August 30, 1838; married Barbara Bradford, born 1804.
3. Sarah Morris, born May 8, 1807; married John Hudson.
4. Hannah Morris, born May 8, 1807, died June 3, 1894; married (1) June 2, 1825, Henry Bradford, born 1804, died March 7, 1843. Married (2) Jesse Kent. Married (3) William Orndorff.
5. Justus Morris, born March 25, 1809.
6. Louisa Morris, born May 24, 1811; married Patrick McCullough.
7. Owen Morris, born December 22, 1812.
8. Hetty Morris, born April 12, 1815, died October 6, 1895; married Thomas W. Kent.
9. Abner Morris, born April 23, 1817.
10. Elizabeth Morris, born January 15, 1819; married Atkinson Sellars.
11. John P. Morris, born May 20, 1821, died 1901; married, 1842, Phoebe Eakin, born July 21, 1831, died March 25, 1914.
12. Joseph Morris, born May 15, 1823; married Mary Dye,

born April 2, 1831, died May 16, 1869.
4. Rachel Garard, daughter of Justus and Rachel Corbly Garard. Married .... Long.
5. Justus Garard, son of Justus and Rachel (Corbly) Garard, died about 1872. Estate 2636 Greene County, Probated April 29, 1872. Married (1) ...., married (2) Emeline Mestrezat.

Children

1. George Garrard (Garard).
2. John Garard; married .... Titus.
3. Dan Garard; married .... Cove.
4. Mary Garard; married Morris Roberts.
5. Louisa Garard; married William Cleavenger.
6. Lucinda Garard; married Andrew Walthers (Walters).
7. Charles A. Garard; married Margaret Herrington.
8. J. C. Garard; married A. B. Shroyer.
9. Justus Garard; married Hattie ....
10. William Garard.
11. Oliver Garard.

6. Jonathan Garard, son of Justus and Rachel Corbly Garard; Estate 2951, Will Book V, pp. 89, Greene County, Pennsylvania Born 1794, died February 26, 1877 aged 82 years, 7 months, 22 days. Married Ann Gregg, daughter of John and Orpha Stubbs Gregg, born 1797, died ....

Children

1. Corbly Garard; married Mary Long.
2. Maria Garard; married Alfred Yeager.
3. Mary Garard; married Peter Albert Myers.
4. .... Garard; married .... McClure.
5. Stephenson Garard, born May 18, 1828; married Mary A. Robinson.
6. Joseph Garard; married Emeline Long.

7. Corbly Garard, son of Justus and Rachel (Corbly) Garard, born 1793, died September 24, 1870, aged 77 years, 6 months, 20 days. Married Sarah Hickleberry, died October 1, 1884, aged 86 years, 7 months, 16 days. Will Book No. 4, pp. 309, Estate 2533, Probated May 16, 1868.

Children

1. Lewis Garard, died July 3, 1846, age 29 years, 7 months, 22 days. Never married.
2. Lindsey Leroy Garard, died November 29, 1850, age 27 years, 4 days. Married Susan Emory, died February 27, 1852, age 28 years, 1 month, 21 days.
3. Daughter.

8. Abner Garard, born 1798, died July 25, 1829, age 31 years.

Family of William and Priscilla (Corbly) Knight

Priscilla Corbly, daughter of Rev. John and Abigail (Bull) Corbly, born 1762, died 1833; married, about 1775, William Knight, born about 1751, died 1820; buried in the Staunton Cemetery near Troy, Ohio.

Children

1. Jonathan Knight, born about 1776, died 1822; married Catherine James, who died in 1875. They lived in Hamilton County, Ohio.
2. Elizabeth Knight, married .... Fansler. Hamilton County, Ohio.
3. John Knight, born about 1780.

AND ITS PIONEER FAMILIES   589

4. Abigail Knight, born about 1782.
5. Rachel Knight, born about 1786, married James Frazee.
6. David Knight, born 1786, died 1851; married Patsie Clark, born July 12, 1787.
7. Nancy Knight, married George Green.
8. Mary Knight, married John E. Cory.
9. Priscilla Knight, born 1792, died 1870; married John Webb.
10. Delilah Knight.
11. William C. Knight, born 1797, died 1858; married Matilda Frizell.

REVEREND JOHN CORBLY, JR.

Reverend John Corbly, Jr., was born latter part of 1768. He was by the first marriage of John Corbly, Sr. L. K. Evans says he was a lad of eleven at the time of the Corbly Massacre and shed no light on the maternal parentage. John Corbly, Jr., followed in his father's footsteps, becoming a Baptist Minister and in 1803, became pastor of the Claugh (Cliff) Baptist Church at Mt. Washington on the Claugh Pike near Cincinnati. Previous to this time he had preached at the Miami Island Baptist Church. Of the fifteen delegates who organized the Miami Baptist Association on June 3, 1798, five were originally from the Corbly Baptist Church at Garards Fort. Miami accounts say that John Corbly, Jr., had migrated to that section as early as 1789, but his name is in the Muddy Creek Ledger as late as 1793. He was preaching at the Claugh Church at the time of his death on September 22, 1814. His wife was Elizabeth Fansler, who after the death of her husband, married (2) Mathias Corwin, famous as the father of Thomas Corwin, governor of Ohio and humorous lecturer.

Family of Reverend John Corbly, Jr.
(As taken from a Family Tree prepared in 1859)

1. Stephen Corbly. He was the father of Julian, Nancy, Davis, Jonathan, John, and Rebecca Corbly.
2. Lynn Corbly.
3. Paul Corbly. He was the father of Peggy, Rebecca, John, Samuel, William, Patsy, Harriet, and Elizabeth Corbly.
4. Justus Corbly, born February 28, 1798, died 1888. He was the father of Catherine, Washington, Elizabeth, (who married Joshua Leeds), John, Stephen, William, Mariann, Newton, Rebecca, Paul, Sargent, and Annie Corbly.
5. Nancy Corbly, married in 1815, Orson Clark. They had Corbly, Elizabeth, (who married William Roudebush), James, Julian, Thompson, Susanna, Newton, Shelly, Franklin, Mary, Christopher, Isaiah, and Nancy Clark.
6. Elizabeth Corbly, mother of Nancy, Josiah, Elizabeth, Henry, Davis, Reuben, Sarah, and Priscilla.
7. John Corbly, father of Elizabeth, Philson, Matilda, Jane, Diantha, Sarah, Harriet, and Priscilla Corbly.
8. Priscilla Corbly, mother of Elizabeth, William, Mathias, Stephen, Susannah, Isaiah, Jane, Thomas, Mary, and John
9. William Corbly, father of Araminda, Priscilla, Mary, Julian, Elizabeth, Phoebe, Rebecca, and John Corbly.
10. Newton Corbly, father of Henry, Martly, Milton, Richmond, Sargent, Josiah, Sarah, Keziah, Joseph, and Hamman Corbly.
11. Isaiah Corbly, father of Lou and Mary Corbly.

Family of Levi and Delilah (Corbly) Martin

Delilah Corbly, daughter of Reverend John and Elizabeth (Tyler) Corbly, born July 19, 1774, died in Miami County, Ohio, January 10, 1839. Married, about 1788, Levi Martin, born in Chester County, Pennsylvania, November 18, 1764, died March 22, 1835, in Miami County, Ohio. Both are buried in the old Staunton Cemetery near Troy, Ohio. Levi Martin's will was filed in Miami County, Ohio on April 15, 1835. The story of Levi Martin is best told in his pension application of September 25, 1832, and found in National Archives, File No. S-2751. Levi Martin followed his brother, Joseph Martin, an early Greene County school teacher to Big Whiteley Creek where Joseph had settled about 1781, and married Rachel Garard. It is said that Joseph and Levi Martin were playmates of General Anthony Wayne when they lived in Chester County about 1785,

Children

1. Nancy Martin, married .... Statler.
2. Corbly Martin, married Ansenath Eddy, daughter of Joseph Eddy of Warren County, Ohio.
3. Levi Martin, Jr., born about 1798, died February 11, 1834. Married Sarah ...., born 1795, died 1813.
4. William Martin, no record.
5. Joseph Martin, married, February 1827, Mary Cline, daughter of Isaac and Olive (Ingram) Cline. Both died suddenly of fever leaving three small children.

Children

1. Abijah Martin, born about 1828; married, March 2, 1859, Elizabeth Knoop.

Children

1. ....
2. Daniel Martin.
3. Lucy Martin.

2. William P. Martin, born February 15, 1830.
3. Hannah Martin, born March 20, 1833; married Dr. Kellogg.

6. John Martin.
7. Jesse Martin.
8. Andrew Martin.
9. Asa Martin.
10. Elizabeth Martin.

WILL OF DELILAH MARTIN

I, Delilah Martin relict and widow of Levi Martin deceased, late of the County of Miami and State of Ohio, do make and publish this my last will and testament, in manner and form following, that is to say:

FIRST: It is my will that my funeral expenses and all my just debts be fully paid.

SECOND: It is my will that my daughter, Nancy Statler, and her heirs be allowed and receive out of my money or personal estate in addition to that which she has already received, a sum sufficient to make her share equal with my other children in mine and my late huband's estate at my death.

AND LASTLY: I hereby constitute and appoint my sons, Corbly Martin and William P. Martin, to be the excutors of this my Last

Will and Testament, revoking and annulling all former wills to be made, and ratifying and confirming this and no other to be my Last Will and Testament. In testimony whereof, I have hereunto set my hand and seal this twenty-seventh day of February in the year of our Lord, One Thousand eight hundred and thirty eight. Note: Interlined before signing.

DELILAH (Her Mark) MARTIN

Signed, published and declared by the above named Delilah Martin, as and for her Last Will and Testament, in presence of us, who at her request, who have signed as witnesses to the same.

John ....
John F. Agner
Andrew D. Sayers

WILL OF LEVI MARTIN

IN THE NAME OF GOD AMEN.

I Levi Martin of the County of Miami and State of Ohio, being weak in Body but of sane mind and memory blessed be Almighty God for the same. Do make, ordain, and constitue my Last Will and Testament in Manner and Form as follows:

FIRST: It is my will that my just debts and funeral expenses be paid out of any money on hand or such as may be first collected by my Executors.

SECONDLY: It is my Will that my beloved wife, Delilah, shall remain in the peaceable possession of the farm on which we reside with the appurtenances, during her natural life for her comfortable support.

THIRDLY: It is my will, and I hereby direct that on the decease of my beloved wife, Delilah, my Executors shall make Sale of such personal property as may remain if any and further that they shall have the farm appraised by three disinterested men under oath. After which if any, one, two or more of my children choose to take the place at the appraised value and pay the other heirs their portions within two years, it is my will in such case that they shall take the place. But if none choose to do so, then it is my will that my executors should make sale of the place on the best terms they can and pay out the money arising from such sales as herein after directed.

FOURTHLY: It is my will should my granddaughter, Delilah Statler, live until my estate is sold receive $30.00, but should she decease before that time the same to be considered as a part of my Estate and divided accordingly.

FIFTHLY: It is my will that my Estate be divided equally amongst my children with the exception of Nancy Statler who has already received one hundred and Eighty-two Dollars which is her portion; My son, Corbly has received $70.00; Levi has received $62.00; William P., $56.00; Joseph, $61.00; John C., $56.00; Jesse E., $60.00; Andrew, $64.00; Asa, $50.00; Elizabeth, $129.00, these several sums received are to be accounted for in the Partition of my estate my son, Joseph's children coming in for their Deceased father's full share.

LASTLY: It is my will and I hereby appoint my beloved Wife and beloved Sons, Corbly, Levi, and William B. Martin Executrix and Executors of this my last Will and Testament hereby revoking all former wills by me made. In witness whereof I have hereunto set my hand and Seal as Testator on this the fourteenth day of December in the year of our Lord A. D. Eighteen Hundred and Thirty-three.

LEVI MARTIN (Seal)

Signed, Sealed and Published and declared to be his Last Will and
    Testament by the Testator in presence of us who in his presence
    and in the presence of each other have hereunto subscribed our
    names as witnesses.
Sam Kyle
William Knoop
Thomas G. Knoop (His Mark)

File No. S-2751
Certificate No. 13306

LEVI MARTIN

Levi Martin, of Miami County, Ohio, applied for a pension September 25, 1832, under Act of June 7, 1832. Certificate No. 13306 was issued to Levi Martin, of Troy, State of Ohio, June 22, 1833, for $80. per annum to commence March 4, 1831. The service was two years (2) years as a private under Captain Paxton, Colonel Piper's Regiment.

In his affidavit of September 25, 1832, he states he was drafted in the Spring of 1780. He entered the service as a spy under Captain Paxton, Colonel Piper's Regiment. He says he served about one (1) year under Captain Paxton and six (6) months under Captain McIntyre. The remainder of the war he served under Captain Enslow or Ensley (he is not certain of the name), by whom he was discharged in Bradford County (should be Bedford County), Pennsylvania. He was engaged in guarding the frontier upon which he resided, against the incursions of the Indians in the neighborhood of his place of residence. He was engaged in no battles, but had frequent skirmishes with the Indians.

He was born November 1764, in Chester County, Pennsylvania, about 25 miles from Philadelphia on the Lancaster Road. About two years after the war he removed to the Monongahela near the head of Big Whiteley. He remained there about three years and removed to Ohio about October 1788. In the March following he returned to Pennsylvania and in August 1790, volunteered under Colonel Crawford. He joined the army at Cincinnati. To Fort Wayne. He returned to Pennsylvania in November. In the fall of 1791, he migrated to Ohio on the Ohio River about two miles above the mouth of the Little Miami, and remained there until Wayne's Treaty with the Indians. In the Spring of 1800, he removed to Miami County, where he has since resided.

(See Pennsylvania Archives Series III, pp. 235, Vol. 23, for George Enslow's Company containing name of Levi Martin.)

COMPANY OF FRONTIER RANGERS
1778-1783
Bedford County, Pennsylvania

Captain George Enslow
Ensign George Peek
Cornelius Bourst
Daniel Means
Thomas Arnet
Isaac Seaman
Matheas Sealey
Lawrence Bishop
John Hamashott
Andrew Valentine
Benjamin Martin
Joseph Martin
William Carlister
Henry Sourlay
William Deshong
John Hill
Joseph Commins
Thomas Buck
John Hamilton
John Hamilton, Jr.
Edward Huston
Richard Croy (le)
Ephraim Eakers
John Craven
Benjamin Donald
Alijah Eakers
Jacob Danhouse, Jr.
Jacob Danhouse, Sr.
Christian Enslow
William Eaker
Jonathan Buck
George Enslow, Sr.
Cornelius Seaman
Lott French
Joseph Sparks
Joseph McDonneas
Adam Smythe
Benjamin Davie
Daniel Donalds
William Boyd
John Boyd
Levi Martin

Pennsylvania Archives Series III, Volume 23, pp. 235

Family of Rev. Jacob and Mary (Corbly) Myers

Mary Corbly, daughter of Rev. John and Nancy (Lynn) Corbly, was born March 11, 1785, and died December 29, 1864. She married, about 1801, Rev. Jacob Myers, born December 10, 1780, died February 21, 1862. He was a son of Peter and Mary (Hibbs) Myers.

Bible Record of Children

1. Priscilla Myers, born March 19, 1802, died March 21, 1802.
2. John Myers, born May 11, 1803.
3. Peter Myers, born September 3, 1805.
4. Ayers Myers, born December 14, 1807.
5. Charlotte Myers, born June 14, 1810, died April 29, 1842; married James Clark, born October 1790, died July 8, 1879.
6. Cephas Myers, born October 24, 1817, died February 27, 1902; married Sophia Burkert, born 1820, died 1857.
7. Eliza Myers, born March 30, 1821; married Daniel Taylor.
8. Minerva Myers, born June 27, 1824, died June 17, 1921; married, 1844, James Dunlap, born March 9, 1819, died December 31, 1904.
9. Julian, born April 23, 1828; married .... Gribbs.

Family of Andrew and Elizabeth (Myers) Corbly

Andrew Corbly, son of Rev. John and Nancy (Lynn) Corbly, born 1787, died 1850; married, 1807, Elizabeth Myers, daughter of Peter and Mary (Hibbs) Myers. They removed to Tyler County, (West) Virginia.

Children

1. John Corbly, married Elizabeth McGill.
2. Nancy Corbly, married Alexander Wade.
3. Myers Corbly, married Narcissa Wells.
4. Phoebe Corbly, married September 25, 1839, Abraham Inghram.

5. William Corbly, married Elizabeth Inghram.
6. Mary Corbly, married Abraham Fordyce.
7. Andrew Corbly, married Miranda Moore.
8. Joseph Corbly, married Amanda Joseph.

Family of Peter and Pleasants (Corbly) Myers

Pleasants Corbly, daughter of Reverend John and Nancy (Lynn) Corbly was born June 8, 1789, and died November 18, 1860. She married Peter Myers, Jr., son of Peter and Mary (Hibbs) Myers, born July 30, 1787, died November 30, 1880.

Children

1. Mary Myers, born 1806, died December 16, 1845; married Benjamin Roberts, born March 8, 1808, died December 15, 1837.
2. Nancy Myers, born 1807, died May 14, 1836; married, 1827, Evan Evans, son of Lewis and Rachel (Jones) Evans, born 1805, died 1865.
3. Alfred Myers, born 1809, died 1864; married Jane J. Evans, daughter of Lewis and Rachel (Jones) Evans, born April 12, 1815, died 1895.
4. Sarah Myers, born June 16, 1810, died June 15, 1897; married June 2, 1830, Eli Titus, born May 3, 1808, died April 14, 1896.
5. Melissa Myers, born 1811, died 1840; married Reuben Shelby.
6. Orpha Myers, born 1813, died January 14, 1846; married Vincent Long, who died January 24, 1850, age 23 years, 11 months and 22 days.
7. Amelia Myers, born 1814, died April 9, 1871; married Henry J. Davis, who died November 16, 1862, age 62 years, 1 month, and 9 days.
8. Matilda Myers, born 1816, died 1834.
9. Peter Myers, born 1817, died 1817.
10. Harriett Myers, born 1819, died 1821.
11. Peter Albert Myers, born 1822, died 1867; married Mary Garard, who died July 5, 1884, age 59 years, 3 months, 24 days.
12. Alpheus Myers, born 1824, died 1825.
13. Louisa Myers, born 1825, died 1859; married .... Garard.
14. Ann (?).
15. Liming (?).

Family of Joseph and Cassandra (Corbly) Gregg

Cassandra Corbly, daughter of Reverend John and Nancy (Lynn) Corbly, born June 1, 1791, died December 6, 1869. She married September 6, 1810, Joseph Gregg, born 1782, died 1869, son of John and Orpha (Stubbs) Gregg. They are both buried in Garard's Fort Cemetery.

Children

1. Elizabeth Gregg, born June 15, 1811, died 1821.
2. Ruth Gregg, born September 19, 1812, died 1834; married, March 1832, John Fordyce, Jr., born September 5, 1805, died April 18, 1882.

3. Orpha Gregg, born October 16, 1813, died December 16, 1873; married, March 19, 1843, Thomas Titus, born July 1, 1816, died March 19, 1895.
4. Sarah Gregg, born October 31, 1815, died 1884; married William Wood, born 1813.
5. John C. Gregg, born July 8, 1818, died 1821.
6. Nancy C. Gregg, born August 15, 1820, died 1906; married Robert J. Evans.
7. Eliza Gregg, born October 13, 1822, died 1904; married Daniel Patterson, born December 3, 1821.
8. Joseph Gregg, born December 1, 1825, died June 8, 1884; married Rebecca Minor.
9. Cephas Gregg, born March 13, 1827, died December 2, 1866.
10. Corbly Gregg, born April 6, 1829, died May 1901; married Mary Stephens, born February 14, 1842, died November 18, 1924.
11. George Gregg, born April 5, 1831, died 1895; married Clarissa ....; married (2) Emma Titus.
12. Matilda Gregg, born October 5, 1834, died 1926; married Napoleon West.

Family of Amos and Amelia (Corbly) Wright

Amelia Corbly, daughter of Reverend John and Nancy (Lynn) Corbly, born June 2, 1796, and died July 5, 1855. She married Amos Wright who was born May 1, 1795, died November 17, 1871.

Children

1. Mary Wright, married Henry Sutton.
2. Teresa Wright, married Washington Hilling.
3. Thomas Wright, married Mariah Lantz.
4. Eleven Wright, married Margaret Willett.
5. Melissa Wright, married Joseph South.
6. John Corbly Wright, married Emaline Waychoff.
7. Benjamine F. Wright, married Margaret Chalfont.
8. Elizabeth Wright, married Robert Rish.
9. Elvira Wright, married Richard Hannah.
10. Justus Wright.
11. Emily G. Wright, married Thomas J. Smith.

Family of William and Rebecca (Stephens) Corbly

William Corbly, youngest child of Rev. John and Nancy (Lynn) Corbly, born about 1800, died December 26, 1875. Married Rebecca (or Mary ?) Stephens, daughter of Edward and Hannah (Woodward) Stephens. They went to Athens County, Ohio and then in 1850, he bought a farm near McArthur, Vinton County, Ohio.

Children of William and Rebecca (Stephens) Corbly

1. Edward Corbly.
2. Harrison Corbly.
3. Lynn Corbly, married (1) Sarah Wood; married (2) Mary A. Scholl.
4. John Corbly.
5. Nancy Corbly.
6. Eliza Corbly.
7. Hannah Corbly.
8.

JOSEPH MORRIS FAMILY

Sufficient evidence is found in official papers, which have been recorded, to establish at least a portion of the family of Joseph Morris, and certain salient facts regarding this pioneer settler of Big Whiteley Creek. From the pension application of his son,

George Morris, it is found that Joseph Morris was living in New Jersey when George Morris was born January 2, 1745. From a similar pension application of his son, Amos Morris, we learn that Joseph Morris had removed to Apple Pie Ridge in Berkeley County, Virginia, before August 25, 1758, (or 1760) the date of birth of Amos Morris. (Nat. Arch. S. 7244). Then from the claim of Jonathan Morris that date is extended backward to June 15, 1753, the date of birth of Jonathan Morris in Virginia. And from this last pension statement also comes the information that Joseph Morris had removed to the Monongahela between 1763 and 1765, when Jonathan was 10 or 12 years of age. (Nat. Arch. S. 7247). After his arrival on Big Whiteley it is evident that Joseph Morris obtained a valid claim to his Virginia land from Lord Fairfax on May 31, 1772. Describing the land as 315 acres on Isaac Creek branch of Back Creek, Joseph Morris and wife, Hannah ...., then living in what was considered Monongalia County, Virginia, sold their grant on August 5, 1777, to Robert Rutherford of Berkeley County, for the sum of 30 Pounds. (Deed Book 11. pp. 435). Meantime it would appear that Joseph Morris had borrowed almost a similar sum of money from John Neville on September 16, 1771, which he had partially paid back in goods and two roan mares, before his death which occurred before October 8, 1788. His son, Jonathan, completed the payment May 4, 1789. A note for this indebtedness, showing the payments is on record in Washington, Pennsylvania. Here also is a bill of appraisment in the estate of Joseph Morris, dated December 5, 1788. David Bradford had on October 8, 1788, been paid 15 shillings for advising Jonathan and Joseph Morris, Jr., in the estate of their father. A very old tombstone in Garards Fort Cemetery shows H. Morris, died October 2, 1783, and is probably the marker for Hannah Morris, wife of Joseph while the stone for Joseph Morris in the same plot is not decipherable. One source says that the wife was Hannah Lee.

Family of Joseph and Hannah Morris

1. George Morris, born in New Jersey, January 2, 1745, died in Greene County, January 20, 1842; married Margaret Corbly, born February 17, 1758, died October 5, 1833. Both are buried in the Garards Fort Cemetery. Family record given under the Rev. John Corbly Family.
2. Joseph Morris, Jr., taxed with his father in the Greene Township assessment rolls for 1784. In the Census record of 1790, he was the head of a family consisting of one adult male, three males under 16 years, and three females. His cabin is said to have been on Woods Run branch of Whiteley Creek. His wife was probably Elizabeth .... A child of Joseph and Elizabeth died July 7, 1804, aged 11 years, and was named Joseph Morris.
3. Levi Morris. The Census Record shows him at the head of a family consisting of one male over 16 years of age, two males under 16 years, and two females. On January 6, 1792, he patented a tract of land which had been warranted to Abraham Covalt on October 28, 1785, under the title of "Arabia." It was situated on Frosty Run branch of Big Whiteley Creek and joined with the land of his brother, George Morris, on the south boundary, the land of George Morris being at the mouth of Frosty Run.
4. Jonathan Morris, died March 20, 1841, aged 88 years, 9 months, and 5 days. He was married three times, first to Sarah Davis (?), who died November 11, 1798, at the age of 45 years. The second wife is said to have been Hannah Garard, who died

June 15, 1816, aged 49 years. The third wife was the widow Mary Robbins, who died in 1848, aged 87 years. (The record for Jonathan Morris will be given separately).

5. Amos Morris, born August 25, 1758 (or 1760) at Apple Pie Ridge in Berkeley County, Virginia, died in Wana, (West) Virginia, in 1847. His pension claim S. 7244 says his brother, George Morris, had a Bible record of his birth, and proves service at Garards Fort in May 1778. He lived for twenty years on the farm later owned by Imri Taylor. His wife was Rebecca Tyler.

Children of Amos and Rebecca (Tyler) Morris

1. Isaac Morris, born March 20, 1794, died March 8, 1870, in Ripley County, Indiana. He married (1), August 19, 1826, in Kentucky, Matilda Fitzgerald, born May 2, 1800, died September 19, 1838. He married (2) Anna Alexander, and (3) Sarah Jane Morris, born 1838, died 1886.
2. Amos Morris, Jr., married Joanna Lantz.
3. Hannah Morris, married Lewis Conger.
4. Rebecca Morris, married Zadock Morgan.
5. George Morris, married Nancy Fitzgerald.
6. Mary Morris.
7. Levi Morris.
8. James Morris, born August 29, 1810; married Sarah Hinegardner.

6. Rachel Morris (?). There is no record of any daughters in the family of Joseph Morris, but in the records of Goshen Baptist Church to which they belonged, there is a record of May 29, 1784, showing that a Rachel Morris was received by baptism on that date. Known grandchildren of Joseph Morris would have been too young at that date.
7. Elizabeth Morris (?). On June 2, 1786, an Elizabeth Morris was baptized in the Goshen Baptist Church, and again on July 8, of the same year another Elizabeth Morris was baptized. One of these may also have been a daughter of Joseph Morris.

JONATHAN MORRIS FAMILY

In his pension application from Greene County, dated March 17, 1834, Jonathan Morris said he was born in Virginia, June 15, 1753. When he was 10 or 12 years of age, he accompanied his father, Joseph Morris, to Big Whiteley Creek, then known as the Muddy Creek Settlement, where they joined his brother, George Morris, who was already there. He performed a six month tour of duty in Dunmore's War, and went out later as a spy in pursuit of the Indians, going to the Ohio River. His brother, George Morris, made affidavit that Jonathan Morris served with him, and included several years' service in the Revolution at Garards Fort, which they helped build. Stephen Gapen and Abner Mundle testified to similar service. (Nat. Arch. S. 7247.) On November 9, 1786, he got a warrant for a tract of 407 acres of land on Frosty Run which was patented to him under the title of "Cole Brook." We are informed, however, that he lived at the mouth of Dutch Run on land adjoining that of his brothers, George and Levi Morris, and originally patented to Jacob Frazer. Jonathan Morris was active in Goshen Baptist Church and died in Greene County, where he left a will which was made August 2, 1838, and probated April 1, 1841. He died March 20, 1841. (W. B. 2. pp. 137). The Family Bible was lately owned by Mr. Kenneth Stephens of Waynesburg R. D. 2. Jonathan Morris was married three times, first to Sarah Davis (?), who died November 11, 1798, aged 45 years. His second wife is said to have been Hannah Garard. She died June 15, 1816, aged 49 years, and he married (3) a widow, Mary Robbins, probably the daughter of John Evans of Dunkard Township. (Will Book 1. pp. 9). She died in 1848, aged 87 years, and is said to have been buried near Bobtown. Eight children are listed by the first marriage and three by the second. A step-daughter is named in his will.

Family of Jonathan Morris

1. Samuel Morris, born September 7, 1778, died December 1871; married Sarah Garard, born on August 29, 1782, died July 11, 1868. She was a daughter of Justus and Rachel (Corbly) Garard.

Children of Samuel and Sarah (Garard) Morris

1. Rachel Morris, born March 26, 1803; married, August 26, 1821, John Dye.
2. Jonathan Morris, born December 28, 1804, died August 30, 1838; married, 1825, Barbara Bradford, born 1804, died 1895-96.
3. Sarah Morris, born May 8, 1807, died August 1884 (?); married John Hudson.
4. Hannah Morris, born May 8, 1807, (twin); married, June 2, 1825, Henry Bradford, born 1804, died March 7, 1843. She died June 3, 1894.
5. Justus Morris, born March 25, 1809; went to Lee County, Iowa.
6. Louisa Morris, born May 24, 1811; married Patrick McCullough.
7. Owen Morris, born December 22, 1812; married Abigail ....; went to Miami County, Ohio.
8. Hetty Morris, born April 12, 1815, died October 6, 1895; married Thomas W. Kent.
9. Abner Morris, born April 23, 1817.
10. Elizabeth Morris, born January 15, 1819; married Atkinson Sellars.
11. John P. Morris, born May 20, 1821, died 1901; married, July 1842, Phoebe Eaken, born July 21, 1831, died March 25, 1914.
12. Joseph Morris, born May 15, 1823; married Mary Dye, born April 2, 1831, died May 16, 1869.

2. Joseph Morris, born November 11, 1780. Received land in Luzerne Township, Fayette County, Pennsylvania, in settlement of father's estate.
3. Owen Morris, born October 25, 1783, died May 18, 1860; married Abigail Wilson, born May 19, 1795, died February 9, 1875. They went to Miami County, Ohio, and settled near Casstown.

Children of Owen and Abigail (Wilson) Morris

1. Elizabeth Morris, born September 3, 1814; married, August 14, 1834, Lewis Wilson.
2. Ann Morris, born October 26, 1816; married, June 10, 1833, William Swails.
3. Owen David Morris, born January 3, 1819, died December 10, 1875; married, November 28, 1839, Nancy G. Corey. Buried near Crawfordsville, Indiana.
4. Sarah Morris, born February 18, 1821; married, December 31, 1840, Hanford Kerr.
5. John Morris, born July 31, 1823, died 1914; married

Elizabeth Howell.
6. Letitia Morris, born January 7, 1826, died February 27, 1826.
7. Patty Morris, born March 20, 1827; married, November 29, 1849, Benjamin Pettit.
8. Lucinda Morris, born June 22, 1830; married, December 16, 1852, David Odaffe.
9. Abigail Morris, born May 20, 1833; married (1) John Eyer; (2) Amos Lapham.
10. Elma Morris, born December 31, 1837; married Blakely Gersinger.
11. Harriett Ellen Morris, born July 7, 1842, died 1925; married, December 24, 1864, Moses Robert Frazee.

4. Lucretia Morris, born April 30, 1787, died March 23, 1867; married, May 13, 1807, James Roberts, born July 30, 1785, died June 8, 1864. They lived for a time at the mouth of Dutch Run, then moved to Hancock County, Illinois. Buried near La Harpe, Illinois.

Children of James and Lucretia (Morris) Roberts
1. Richard Roberts, born February 22, 1808.
2. Jonathan Roberts, born May 3, 1809, died July 30, 1809.
3. Sarah Roberts, born June 28, 1810.
4. John Roberts, born November 27, 1811.
5. Morris Roberts, born June 20, 1814, died June 10, 1887; married Mary ...., born December 10, 1818, died July 1, 1890.
.6 Mariah Roberts, born April 3, 1816, died October 9, 1856; married .... Fordyce.
7. Lucretia Roberts, born April 3, 1818, died November 17, 1854; married .... Homer.
8. Elizabeth Roberts, born June 26, 1820, died September 16, 1821.
9. Jemimah Roberts, born October 6, 1823, died July 8, 1870; married .... Smith.
10. Hannah Roberts, born November 9, 1824, died November 28, 1894; married .... Strawn.
11. Pleasant Jane Roberts, born November 23, 1826; married Joab Baily. (See Mundel Record).
12. Louisa Roberts, born September 14, 1829, died February 11, 1911; married .... Anderson.
13. Pera Anne Roberts, born December 10, 1831, died January 26, 1904; married .... Slone.

5. Mary Morris, born March 14, 1790; married .... Knotts.
6. Sarah Morris, born May 7, 1793; married Rev. Barnett Whitlatch, born March 16, 1794, died October 4, 1867. His second wife was Airy Gordon, born July 1, 1796.

Children of Rev. Barnet and Sarah (Morris) Whitlatch
1. William Whitlatch.
2. Jonathan Whitlatch.
3. Sarah Whitlatch, born June 16, 1826, died June 26, 1904; married (1) John Bell, who died October 15, 1866, aged 48 years, 1 month, 20 days. She married (2) .... Smith.
4. Nancy Whitlatch, married Hiram Kent, born 1817, died April 26, 1863.
5. Elizabeth Whitlatch, married (1) .... Wise; (2) Neal Zollars.
6. Margaret Maria Whitlatch, born April 3, 1834, died May 23, 1910; married William H. Gordon, born March 10,

1833, died June 12, 1901.
7. Lucinda Whitlatch, married Dr. John Gordon. They settled at Hancock County, Illinois.
7. Jonathan Morris, born September 16, 1796; married Mary Bice. His will is at Cambridge, Ohio.
8. Elizabeth Morris, born November 11, 1798, when her mother died in childbirth. She married Cephas McClelland, probably a son of Cary and Henrietta (Myers) McClelland. Both are buried in the Fairmont Cemetery, near Newark, Ohio.
9. Levi Morris, born April 10, 1802; first child by second marriage. No record.
10. John Morris, born December 15, 1803, died 1890. He married Charlotte Nichols, born 1812. died 1887.

Children of John and Charlotte (Nichols) Morris
1. Elizabeth Morris, born November 16, 1833; married .... Dowlin.
2. Eleanor Morris, married .... Lindley.
3. Jonathan Morris, born February 21, 1832, died 1915; married Charlotte Rinehart, born 1834, died 1816.

Children of Jonathan and Charlotte (Rinehart) Morris
1. Elizabeth Ellen Morris, born January 26, 1853.
2. Eveleene W. Morris, born March 2, 1856; married, April 20, 1875, A. J. Hedge.
3. John Franklin Morris, born December 23, 1858.
4. David Morris, born October 6, 1860.
5. Ellen Morris, born October 10, 1862, died 1936; married, June 23, 1882, J. Edgar Baily.
6. Clara Belle Morris, born July 25, 1864; married, October 2, 1884, Daniel Fuller.
7. Effie Morris, born December 9, 1866.
8. Lucretia Morris, born January 25, 1870.
9. Albert K. Morris, born August 26, 1873.
10. Jesse Morris, born April 21, 1878.

11. Isaiah Morris, born June 15, 1806; married Eleanor McCormick. They went to Hancock County, Illinois. He died 1887.

Children of Isaiah and Eleanor (McCormick) Morris
1. Hannah Morris, born March 30, 1830; married, May 16, 1852, Daniel Ritzer.
2. Jonathan Morris, born April 14, 1831; married Sarah Jane Cathers.
3. Marion Morris, born June 25, 1832; married, 1858, Alice Blythe at La Harpe, Illinois.

THE GARARD FAMILY

The History of Berkeley County, Virginia, tells of the founding of Gerrardtown on land owned by Rev. John Gerrard. This was the ancestor of the Garard Family of Big Whiteley Creek, the name having changed spelling to the generally accepted form now used by most branches of the family. Rev. John Gerrard was born about 1720, and died in Berkeley County, Virginia, where on August 19, 1787, he made a will, which was proven there on September 18, 1787, so it is evident that he died between the two dates in 1787. Records show that he was twice married, the first wife being Mehitable ....; the second, who with John Gray were executors appointed in his will, was Mary, said to have been a sister of John Gray. The first wife died about 1778-79. At least three children, who were minors at the time of Rev. John Gerrard's death, were of the second marriage. (Berkeley County Will Book 1. pp. 460)

Children of Rev. John Gerrard

1. David Garard, married (1) Margaret ....; (2) Jane ....
2. John Garard, removed to Big Whiteley, where he was one of the earliest members of Goshen Baptist Church. He was chosen Ruling Elder of the church on March 10, 1775, succeeding Elias Garard, who had been elected to that position April 8, 1774. On the same day John Garard was made Moderator, and in July 1776, was licensed to preach. The Vanmeter History says he married Susan Vanmeter, and with her father, Jacob Vanmeter, joined the migration to the Severn Valley in Kentucky, being one of those to whom letters of dismission was given on the 18th of September, 1779. In Kentucky he became the first pastor of the Second Baptist Church organized at Hynes' Station on June 17, 1781. Soon afterward he was captured by the Indians and never heard from again.
3. Jonah Garard, was elected ensign in Captain John Huston's Company in the Washington County Militia in February 1782, and was killed on an expedition while serving in a party commanded by Lieutenant Elijah Mills. His will was filed in Washington County on July 2, 1782, naming a wife, Chloe, and son, Jacob, as heirs. His brother-in-law, Jacob Frazier, was named executor. The tract of land known as "Garards Fort" was warranted in the name of Jonah Garard, on October 28, 1785, but patented later by Peter Myers.
4. Nathaniel Garard, whose wife was Mary ....
5. Jonathan Garard, records of the Garard Family say he married Susan Vanmeter, which may be correct. He may have married her after the loss of her first husband, John Garard.
6. Abner Garard, whose wife was Martha ....
7. William Garard, a minor child at the death of his father.
8. Phoebe Garard, a minor at the time of her father's death.
9. Nancy Garard, also a minor at the time of her father's death.
10. Isaac Garard, given "land on Big Whiteley Creek" by his father's will. Isaac Garard and William Burt warranted the tract of land immediately north of Jonah Garard's "Garards Fort" on November 24, 1786, under the title of "Gath." Isaac Garard was received into Goshen Baptist Church by baptism on July 8, 1785.
11. Sarah Garard, married James Buckles.
12. Mehitable Garard, died before her father; she married a John Garard.
13. Justus Garard, warranted "Shady Banks" immediately west of Jonah Garard's "Garards Fort" on October 28, 1785. His wife was Rachel Corbly. (See Corbly Records).

THE FORDYCE FAMILY

It is recorded in Goshen Baptist Church Book that on January 30, 1791, Samuel Fordyce and Sureman Travis were received by letter from Scholes Mountain and Pittstown. (New Jersey). This may be the approximate time of arrival of Samuel Fordyce on the Western Frontier, yet it is evident that at least one of his sons was on the Tenmile on land later devised to him by his father. The son mentioned was Abraham Fordyce, who was a member of Captain John Miller's Company of Militia recruited in the vicinity of Fort

Lindley. (Penna. Arch. Series VI Vol 2. pp. 11.) A Samuel Fordyce served in the New Jersey Militia from Morris County in the War of the Revolution. It could be either the father or son as indicated by the Bible record of the births of Samuel Fordyce's children. (Strykker pp. 595).

Samuel Fordyce was born near Aberdeen, Scotland, about 1734, and died in Greene County in 1824, his will being filed for probate December 14, 1824. His wife was Elizabeth Huggins, who died July 17, 1814, aged 77 years. Both are buried in Whiteley Chapel Cemetery. There was more than one family of this name that settled in Morris County, New Jersey, where Shooley's Mountain (Scholes) was located. A number of the children of Samuel Fordyce were married in New Jersey, and it is not clear that all of them came to the Tenmile County, but evidence indicates that most of them came along with or preceded their father.

A letter from the Adjutant Generals Office in New Jersey to Miss Ethel Boughner of Uniontown, says that Samuel Fordyce received certificates Number 131 and 1233 on May 3, 1784, signed by Silas Condit for service in the Morris County, New Jersey Militia. They represented depreciation pay.

Family of Samuel Fordyce

1. James Fordyce, born November 18, 1756.
2. Caty (Catherine) Fordyce, born August 23, 1757.
3. Elizabeth Fordyce, born .... 7, 1758.
4. Mary Fordyce, twin of Elizabeth Fordyce, born in 1758; married Ephraim Headlee, son of John Headlee and grandson of Richard Headlee of Morris County, New Jersey. Ephraim Headlee also served in the Morris County, New Jersey Militia in the Revolution. (Ref. Strykker pp. 624). His brothers, John Headlee and Richard Headlee, came with him to the Tenmile Country. A tract of land on Little Shannon Run, warranted in 1786, to David Owl, became the property of Ephraim Headlee, and he secured the patent to it on January 24, 1805. Ephraim Headlee was born in New Jersey on January 21, 1758-59, and died in Greene County late in 1822. His will was made July 12, 1822, and filed for probate December 9, 1822. In it he left his home property to his wife, Mary, for life, and then it was to go to his son, Jesse Headlee.

Family of Ephraim and Mary (Fordyce) Headlee

1. John Headlee, born .... 1784; died .... 1866; married Lydia Headlee.

Children

   1. Eli Headlee, born February 4, 1808.
   2. Lewis Headlee.
   3. Rachel Headlee.
   4. Lucy Headlee.
   5. Phineas Headlee.
   6. Katie Headlee.
   7. Enos Headlee.

2. Isaac Headlee.
3. Silas Headlee, born February 21, 1786, died November 25, 1869; married Elizabeth Headlee, who died May 10, 1860, aged 75 years, 7 months, 14 days.

Children

1. Nancy Headlee, born April 5, 1811, died March 1, 1891.
2. Eunice Headlee, born March 26, 1823, died May 1, 1882.
3. Rachel Headlee, born May 8, 1819, died May 1, 1876.
4. Mary E. Headlee, born 1832, died November 5, 1851; married Cyrenus Haines.
5. John E. Headlee, born 1828, died in the Civil War May 19, 1863. Married Rebecca ...., who died May 24, 1899. She was born December 14, 1831.
6. Elizabeth Headlee.

4. Charles Headlee, married Mary Carney.

Children

1. Harvey Headlee.
2. Leah Headlee.
3. Silas Headlee.
4. Josephus Headlee.
5. Mary Headlee.
6. Jane Headlee.
7. Nancy Headlee.

5. Joshua Headlee, married ....

Children

1. Ephriam Headlee.
2. Stephen Headlee.

6. Samuel Headlee.
7. Isaac Headlee.
8. Elisha Headlee.
9. Jesse Headlee, married Maria Cox.

Children

1. Joseph Headlee.
2. George Headlee.
3. Sarah Headlee.
4. Ephraim Headlee.
5. Elizabeth Headlee.
6. Matilda Headlee.
7. Hester Headlee.
8. Mary Headlee.
9. Rebecca Headlee.

5. Samuel Fordyce, Jr., born December 1, 1760.
6. Abigail Fordyce, born September 7, 1761.
7. Abraham Fordyce, born January 3, 176.... Served in Captain John Miller's Militia Company recruited at Fort Lindley, Washington County, Pennsylvania. His wife's name was Mary
8. Isaac Fordyce, born January 9, 1766; married, August 28, 1792, Susannah Jennings, born at Westfield, New Jersey, April 6, 1772, daughter of Zebulon and Joanna (Little) Jennings. Isaac Fordyce is not mentioned in the will of Samuel Fordyce, but his family came to the Tenmile Country. The Family Bible is owned by Mrs. L. B. Donham of Greensboro, Penna.

Family of Isaac and Susannah (Jennings) Fordyce

1. Joanna Fordyce, born July 13, 1793; married, April 28, 1814, Thomas Crago, born July 13, 1790, died July 13, 1883.
2. Elizabeth Fordyce, born October 8, 1794, married S. Craig.

3. Sarah Fordyce, born March 19, 1799. She married James Crago, born December 25, 1798.
4. Samuel Fordyce, born April 9, 1796; married Gilpah Coney.
5. John Fordyce, born May 23, 1804; married (1) L. Pains; (2) M. Brown.
6. David D. Fordyce, born July 23, 1806, died March 22, 1887; married Margaret Feister.
7. Catherine Fordyce, born September 3, 1812; married P. Myer.
8. Barnet W. Fordyce, born December 15, 1808, died March 30, 1866; married Margaret Shipman, born March 3, 1813, died November 13, 1893.
9. Mary Fordyce, born August 8, 1814; married Rev. Mackey.
10. Rhoda Fordyce, born August 18, 1816; married T. F. Corey.

9. Jacob Fordyce, born October 16, 1772, died November 21, 1859; married, November 29, 1798, Elizabeth Guthrie, born December 20 1774.

Family of Jacob and Elizabeth (Guthrie) Fordyce

1. Solomon Fordyce, born September 16, 1799, died May 1, 1865; married, October 31, 1822, Catherine Crouse, born January 20, 1803, died April 26, 1859; he married (2) Sarah Leonard, born August 26, 1809.
2. Rebecca Fordyce, born January 12, 1802; married, January 1, 1823, Samuel Crouse, who died September 30, 1885.
3. Mary Fordyce born November 22, 1803, died January 13, 1882.
4. Jane Fordyce, born October 16, 1805, died January 8, 1876; married, November 14, 1830, ...
5. Archibald Fordyce born December 4, 1807; married (1) March 11, 1827, Mary Leonard, born March 2, 1809, died October 22, 1855; married (2) October 30, 1856, Elizabeth Simmons, born May 28, 1823, daughter of Spencer and Mary Simmons.
6. Jacob Fordyce, born December 4, 1809; married October 3, 1830, Martha R. ....
7. John Wesley Fordyce, born February 14, 1812.
8. Elizabeth Fordyce, born March 3, 1816, died July 26, 1827.

10. Rev. John Fordyce, born September 17, 1775, died April 30, 1848. (This is the record as shown by his tombstone in Whiteley Chapel Cemetery. Nannie Fordyce informs us that the Bible record gives 1765 as the date of his birth). On September 16, 1798, Rev. John Fordyce married Elizabeth Garard, born March 12, 1778, died December 12, 1838, daughter of Justus and Rachel (Corbly) Garard.

Children of Rev. John and Elizabeth (Garard) Fordyce

1. Rachel Fordyce, born November 9, 1799; married, December 1823, Thomas Bowen.
2. Justus Garard Fordyce, born September 5, 1801; married April 1829, Catherine Miller.
3. Samuel Fordyce, born March 15, 1803, died February 4, 1837. Never married.
4. James Harvey Fordyce, born July 31, 1804, died August 15, 1883; married, November 1827, Nancy Bowers, born July 6, 1809, died October 23, 1862. He had the Family Bible from which these records are copied.
5. Nancy Fordyce, born November 29, 1805; married Novem-

ber 26, 1823, George Rose.
6. Corbly Fordyce, born June 7, 1807, died 1862; married April 1829, Jane Baily.
7. John Fordyce, born September 5, 1808, died April 18, 1882; married, (1) March 1832, Ruth Gregg, who died, and he married (2) June 1837, Mary Ann Hauser, born November 11, 1817, died February 20, 1899.
8. Abner Fordyce, born May 5, 1810; married (1) Eliza Murdock, born March 10, 1812, died March 23, 1860; married (2) Margaret Murdock, who died June 16, 1876.
9. Hetty Fordyce, born August 19, 1812; married, December 1832, James Evans.
10. Joseph Fordyce, born September 30, 1814, died February 28, 1884, at Cambridge, Ohio; married, April 6, 1837, Eleanor Ann Baily, born April 10, 1817, daughter of Joab Baily.
11. Benson Fordyce, born December 21, 1816; married, September 1, 1839, Maria Nichols, born April 23, 1816, died March 25, 1868.

THE RICHARD ROBERTS FAMILY

There were a number of men named Richard Roberts, who served in the Pennsylvania Militia in the Revolution, one of whom may have been the man of this name who removed to Big Whiteley Creek after the war, and settled in the vicinity of Newtown. He died here in March 1844 leaving a will, which was made January 1, 1842, and filed March 11, 1844. His tombstone in Whiteley Chapel Cemetery says he died March 16, (an obvious error) 1844, at the age of 88 years. His will names his wife Jemima ...., and makes a number of bequests to children, whom he names, then divides his remaining property among his children, including his youngest son, Henry. Abner Morris and Henry Roberts were his executors.

Children of Richard Roberts
1. James Roberts, born July 30, 1785, died near La Harpe, Illinois, June 8, 1864; married, May 13, 1807, Lucretia Morris, born April 30, 1787, died March 23, 1867. While James Roberts did not receive a special bequest in the will of Richard Roberts, there seems no doubt but that he was the eldest son of Richard and Jemima Roberts. The pattern of naming his children is excellent evidence. His wife was a daughter of Jonathan Morris.

Children of James and Lucretia (Morris) Roberts
1. Richard Roberts, born February 22, 1808.
2. Jonathan Roberts, born May 3, 1809, died July 30, 1809.
3. Sarah Roberts, born June 28, 1810.
4. John Roberts, born November 27, 1811.
5. Morris Roberts, born June 20, 1814, died June 16, 1887; married Mary A. ...., born December 10, 1818, died July 1, 1890; buried in Whiteley Chapel Cemetery.
6. Maria Roberts, born April 3, 1816, died October 9, 1856; married .... Fordyce.
7. Lucretia Roberts, born May 3, 1818, died November 17, 1854; married .... Homer.
8. Elizabeth Roberts, born June 26, 1820, died September 16, 1821.
9. Jemima Roberts, born October 6, 1823, died July 8, 1870; married .... Smith.
10. Hannah Roberts, born November 9, 1824, died November

28, 1894; married .... Strawn.
11. Pleasant J. Roberts, horn November 23, 1826.
12. Louisa Roberts, born September 14, 1829, died February 11, 1911; married .... Anderson.
13. Pera Ann Roberts, born December 10, 1831, died January 26, 1904; married .... Sloan.

2. Joseph Roberts, born 1786, died November 11, 1851, aged 65 years, 7 months, 14 days. He married Jane Johnson, born October 4, 1793, died February 18, 1851, daughter of John and Alice Johnson. Joseph Roberts is also not specifically named in the will of Richard Roberts, but is buried in Whiteley Chapel Cemetery with his father. Joseph and Jane Roberts were the parents of eleven children, eight of whom are named in Orphans Court Proceedings of September 1858. (O. C. Docket 4 pp. 399).

Children of Joseph and Jane (Johnson) Roberts

1. James Carr Roberts, born November 17, 1816, died March 5, 1869; married Mary Ann McDougal, born September 19, 1827, died December 19, 1875. Both are buried in the Whiteley Chapel Cemetery.
2. Melinda Roberts, born July 14, 1818, died December 30, 1892.
3. Hannah Roberts, born August 24, 1820, died August 24, 1876.
4. Sarah Roberts.
5. Harriet Roberts.
6. Oliver P. Roberts.
7.
8.
9. Joseph Burley Roberts, born March 18, 1832, died 1923; married, December 31, 1879, Elizabeth (Henderson) Lantz.
10.
11.

3. Elizabeth Roberts, mentioned in her father's will.
4. Samuel Roberts, mentioned in the will of Richard Roberts.
5. Benjamin Roberts, mentioned in the will of Richard Roberts.
6. Mary Roberts, mentioned in the will of Richard Roberts; married .... Wilson.
7. Henry Roberts, called youngest son in will of Richard Roberts.
8. Rebecca Roberts, born March 6, 1801, died June 5, 1873; mentioned in the will of Richard Roberts; married in 1819, Arthur Rinehart, born October 17, 1793, died April 6, 1872. He was a son of Thomas and Hannah (Inghram) Roberts.

Children of Arthur and Rebecca (Roberts) Rinehart

1. Richard Roberts Rinehart, married Nancy Gordon.
2. Lucinda Rinehart, born April 16, 1824, died August 25, 1866.
3. Benjamin A. Rinehart, born May 27, 1826, died December 7, 1907; married, November 7, 1851, Mary Hoge, born April 9, 1832, died April 27, 1923.
4. Hannah Rinehart, born 1827, died July 23, 1845.

5. Elizabeth Rinehart, born 1831, died 1916; married Johiel Rinehart, born 1831, died 1905.
6. Wesley Rinehart, born August 4, 1833, died December 15, 1909; married, December 29, 1864, Sarah Hayes, born February 18, 1841, died May 31, 1931.
7. Thomas Rinehart, born 1834, died July 27, 1845.
8. Harriet Rinehart, born November 26, 1838, died January 28, 1905; married, January 15, 1861, Henry Grimes.
9. William Arthur Rinehart, married Rachel Kincaid.
10. Henry Porter Rinehart, born June 1, 1844, died February 25, 1892; married June 28, 1866, Maria Bowers, born February 22, 1844, died December 30, 1932.

PETER MYERS FAMILY

Miss Ethel Boughner of Uniontown, is authority for the information that Peter Myers was born in New Jersey in 1760. Also for the Revolutionary service record, which states he served as wagon master and team clerk in New Jersey, where in 1779, he was stationed at Pittstown. On August 10, 1780, he was serving in Captain John McCalla's Company, Second Regiment of Foot, Philadelphia County Militia, commanded by Colonel Benjamin Eyre. (Penna. Arch. Series VI Vol. 1. pp. 154). Shortly thereafter he removed to the Tenmile Country and settled near Garards Fort, where he became an active member of Goshen Baptist Church, and where he was taxed in Cumberland Township, Washington County, in 1784. From the minutes of the Church it appears that there was quite a migration of Baptists from the vicinity of Pittstown, New Jersey, about that time. Miss Boughner tells that Peter Myers owned thousands of acres of land, in Washington and Sandusky County, Ohio, on which he settled his children, stating that he would never have them living on someone else's land. It was while on a journey to inspect some of his Sandusky land, that he took the fever and returned home to die on September 4, 1820. On September 3, 1782, he married Mary Hibbs, daughter of Jacob and Elizabeth Hibbs. We find in Orphans Court Proceedings of 1806, that Peter Myers and wife, Mary, ask for a partition of Jacob Hibbs' land, in which she is designated as formerly Mary Hibbs. (O. C. Dockett 1. pp. 88). Mary Hibbs was born in 1762, and died March 1, 1826, aged 64 years, 2 months and 21 days. With her husband she is buried in Garards Fort Cemetery. On March 30, 1796, Peter Myers warranted a tract of land at the head of one branch of the South Fork of Muddy Creek, under the title "Germany."

Children

1. Jacob Myers. He became a Baptist minister; married Mary, daughter of Rev. John and Nancy (Lynn) Corbly, and were parents of eight children.
2. Peter Myers, Jr., born July 29, 1787, died November 30, 1830; married, about 1805, Pleasants Corbly, born June 8, 1789, died November 18, 1860. She was a daughter of Rev. John and Nancy (Lynn) Corbly and the record of the family is given in the Corbly Family data.
3. John Myers, born 1789, died 1865; married Orpha Gregg, born 1790, died 1869.
4. Elizabeth Myers, married Andrew Corbly, son of Rev. John and Nancy (Lynn) Corbly. Removed to Tyler County, (West) Virginia.

Children

1. John Corbly, married Elizabeth McGill.
2. Nancy Corbly, married Alexander Wade.
3. Myers Corbly, married Nacissa Wells.
4. Phoebe Corbly, married .... Inghram.
5. Mary Corbly, married Abraham Fordyce.
6. William Corbly, married Elizabeth Inghram.
7. Andrew Corbly, married Miranda Moore.
8. Joseph Corbly, married Amanda Joseph.

5. Joseph Myers. He married (1) Mary Gregg, daughter of John and Orpha (Stubbs) Gregg, who was born in 1800, and died in 1825. He then married (2) Mary Gregg, daughter of Thomas and Amy (Gregg) Gregg.
6. Mary Myers. Married William Baily.
7. Phoebe Myers.

HACKNEY - BALDWIN

It is ironical that at the time this article is being prepared, Mr. Charles Hackney is reported as buying much areage of Greene County coal land, for this article concerns some of the finest and most valuable coal lands in the County. When Thomas Provence (Provins, Provance, etc.) made his first settlement at the Mouth of Little Whiteley Creek is not definitely known, but it is probable that he was on this side of the River as early as 1758, certainly no later than 1768, when he met with the Commissioners at Fort Redstone. There can be little doubt that he owned at that time, the land on the opposite shore in what is now Fayette County at the same period. This land was warranted to his sons, John William Provence and Joseph Yard Provence in 1771. The history of the Provence Family is a separate story, but it has connection with the stretch of land extending South from Little Whiteley Creek to almost the Mouth of Dunkard Creek, for it seems that practically all this land was warranted to members of the same family, and obtained either through relationship to Thomas Provence or by purchase from him.

The warrantees of this land, reading from North to South, finds Sarah Provence at the mouth of Little Whiteley Creek, owning both banks of that stream. There is a break in the bend of the Monongahela River and then the next warrantee is Bathsheba Baldwin, and in order is, Sarah Provence again, Lydia Baldwin, Rebecca Jenkins, and Elizabeth Baldwin. Before the dates of these warrants, Aaron Jenkins had bought a tract in this vicinity from Thomas Provins by deed recorded in Washington on May 8, 1782. Quaker records, aided by information from Haddon's History of Fayette and Greene County, assist in explaining the relationships. Haddon states that Joseph, Aaron, and John Hackney came from London to settle in the vicinity of Jamestown, Virginia, about 1650-75, and that Aaron Hackney had a son, Joseph, who was born September 19, 1700, who died in Fayette County in 1807. Records however, disclose that this second Joseph Hackney settled in New Castle County, Delaware, and that in 1731, he married in Old Swedes Church in Philadelphia, Charity Harlan, daughter of Aaron. Joseph Hackney was a miller, and died in Delaware, March 18, 1744. His widow then married Francis Baldwin, Jr., and removed to Chester County, then later in 1760, to Berkeley County, Virginia, where she and her second husband are buried in the Greene Springs Meeting House Cemetery. Charity (Harlan-Hackney) Baldwin was the mother of at least ten children, six of whom were probably children of her first marriage of thirteen years' duration. The warrantee evidence indicates the last four were by her marriage to Francis Baldwin.

Children of Charity (Harlan-Hackney) Baldwin

1. Sarah Hackney. Records show that her first husband was .... Reese. It is the belief of this writer that her first husband died and that she became the second wife of Thomas Provins, which is suggested by the close settlement with her supposedly half sisters. Thomas Provins had children by his first marriage, and it is definite that he had children by his second wife, Sarah.
2. Mary Hackney. Married .... Lambert.
3. Aaron Hackney, born August 12, 1738, removed to what is now Fayette County, Pennsylvania, in 1758, where he died in 1807. His first wife was Lydia Rees, who died, and then he married Hannah Gregg, daughter of George and Elizabeth Gregg. Hannah Gregg was born April 20, 1744. Eight children were born to the second marriage.
4. Charity Hackney, died unmarried.
5. Joseph Hackney, married, July 20, 1768, at Hopewell Monthly Meeting, Martha McCoole, a daughter of James and Ann McCoole of Back Creek.
6. John Hackney, married Rebecca (Lathland) Lindley.
7. Rebecca Baldwin. She married Aaron Jenkins, and as Rebecca Jenkins had surveyed to her under name "Content" on November 1, 1770, a tract of land situated between her sisters, Lydia and Elizabeth Baldwin's tracts on the Monongahela River. It was later patented to Lewis Williams, but Aaron Jenkins had bought other tracts in the vicinity, including the one at Pierceville, where he maintained a fort during the revolution. Aaron Jenkins was a member of John Guthery's Company of the First Battalion, Washington County, Pennsylvania, Militia. He and his wife, Rebecca, sold out their land in Greene County, after they had removed to Monongahelia County, Virginia. Later he moved to the Cumberland Valley in Tennessee, to settle near Murfreesboro, his wife dying on the way and was buried at Crab Orchard, Kentucky.

8. Elizabeth Baldwin, born March 25, 1747, died in Greene County, Pennslyvania, on April 10, 1830. She and her husband were buried in what is the town of Greensboro but later they were removed to the Cemetery on the hill above the town where their markers were re-erected and are still very legible. As Elizabeth Baldwin she had warranted to her on April 3, 1769, on a Virginia Certificate, a tract of land next south of Rebecca Jenkins. This was surveyed to her on November 1, 1770, and then on September 25, 1787, was patented to Elias and Elizabeth Stone. On this tract was later laid out a part of the Town of Greensboro. Her husband, Elias Stone, also a member of Captain John Guthery's Militia Company, was born July 16, 1740, and died August 27, 1823.
9. Lydia Baldwin, wife of Captain John Guthery, had surveyed to her as Lydia Baldwin on November 1, 1770, a tract of land under the title "Lydia's Bottom." This tract was then patented to John Guthery and Lydia, on April 17, 1792. It was situated between the land of Sarah Province and Rebecca Jenkins, and

was the probable site of John Guthery's Fort. By deeds recorded in Greene County, John and Lydia Guthery disposed of their land and removed to Pike County, Ohio, where John Guthery, at the age of 90, drew a pension on an application dated July 3, 1823, and where he died before March 1, 1824.

10. Bathsheba Baldwin, as such she had warranted to her on a Virginia Certificate dated April 3, 1769, a tract of land north of Sarah Province. This was surveyed to her on November 1, 1770, and then on July 10, 1801, a patent was issued to William McKay and wife, Bathsheba. William McKay served in Captain John Guthery's Company with Aaron Jenkins and Elias Stone.

Family of Elias and Elizabeth (Baldwin) Stone

Elias Stone was born July 16, 1740, probably in Virginia, and died in Greene County on August 27, 1823. He is buried in the Greensboro Cemetery along Route 88 where his tombstone states he was 83 years, one month, and eleven days old, at the time of his death. He and his wife were originally buried in Greensboro, the town which he laid out in lots in 1781, on a tract of land warranted on a Virginia Certificate on April 3, 1769, and surveyed on November 1, 1770, to his wife, Elizabeth Baldwin, but patented September 25, 1787, to Elias and Elizabeth Stone under the title "Delight." Elias Stone was a member of Captain John Guthery's Company, First Battalion, Washington County, Militia in the War of the Revolution. His will, in Will Book 1. page 250, was probated September 3, 1823, names his children, some of whom died before their father. His wife was Elizabeth Baldwin, daughter of Francis and Charity (Harlan-Hackney) Baldwin, and she was born March 25, 1747, and died April 10, 1830, at the age of 83 years and 16 days. Partition Proceedings and deeds, with the above mentioned will, uncover much of the family history.

Children

Elias Stone, Jr. Records in Deed Book 7, show that he and wife, Julia ...., went to Hamilton County, Ohio.
Francis Stone, died before his father.
Rebecca Stone, died before her father. She married Ebeneezer Blackshere, who died in Monongalia County, Virginia, in 1834, where records show he had remarried, his second wife being Elizabeth .... (Will Book 1, pp. 85, probated December 1834.)

Children of Ebeneezer Blackshere

1. Francis Blackshere.
2. Sarah Blackshere.
3. Priscilla Blackshere, married William Richardson.
4. Elias Blackshere.

Bathsheba Stone died September 29, 1858, at the age of 73 years, and is buried at Glades. Her husband was Isaiah Jones.
Elisha Stone, died before his father. He married Mary Black, who after the death of her husband, married Marcena Mitchenor.

Children of Elisha and Mary (Black) Stone

1. Elisha Stone.
2. Elias Stone.
3. Henry Stone, whose wife was Mary .... He died about 1847, leaving Elias, Henry F., Francis F., Harriet,

and George E., minors, whose guardian was Thomas Gabler.
Aaron Stone whose wife was Sarah Peckinpaugh.
Mary Stone.
Lydia Stone.
James Stone, who died in 1825. (Greene County Will Book 1. pp. 267, probated May 9, 1825); married Nancy Sedgewick, who died September 4, 1856, at the age of 70 years and 10 months. She is buried at Glades Church Cemetery, Carmichaels.

Children

1. Mary Stone, married Andrew Dunlap.
2. Elias Stone, born September 22, 1808, died November 22, 1872; married Mary Huston, who died May 4, 1843, at the age of 39 years. Buried in Glades.
3. Thomas Stone, born 1810, died November 12, 1879, at the age of 69 years, one months, and 14 days. He was twice married (1) Mary Ann ...., who died November 15, 1854, at the age of 33 years, and (2) Esther ...., who died April 21, 1869.
4. Elizabeth Stone, born 1811, died November 12, 1885.
5. Pricilla Stone, died at the age of 61 years. She married James Craig.
6. Lydia Stone, born September 25, 1814, died October 8, 1881; married Ellis Campbell, born March 30, 1812, died October 12, 1882.
7. Nancy Stone, born 1816, died August 24, 1868.
8. Rebecca Stone, born 1820, died April 13, 1894.

COLONEL JOHN GUTHERY

John Guthery (Guthrie, Gutherie, etc.,) one of the prominent pioneer settlers on the Monongahela, settled near the mouth of Big Whiteley Creek before 1772, where his name is found as inmate or boarder in the Springhill Township, Bedford County tax lists for that year. According to his pension application from Pike County, Ohio, October 13, 1820, he was living there in May 1776, when he enlisted in Captain Wilson's Company (perhaps Lieutenant Colonel George Wilson) of the 8th Pennsylvania Regiment of the Continental Line under command of Colonel Aeneas McKay, with which he was identified until May 1779. Records of the Regiment show that it was recruited at Fort Pitt and that many of its men came from the Monongahela River country. It assembled at Kittanning in the Fall of 1776, and marched from there in January 1777, to join Washington's Army at Quibbletown, New Jersey. This march, in mid winter, was a terrible ordeal and many men died from exposure. After taking part in the Battles of Brandywine and Germantown, the Regiment went to Bound Brook, New Jersey, where it again saw battle. After this Battle, the Regiment was sent back to Fort Pitt in 1778, though a part of its men were detached and joined Colonel Morgan's Rifle Corps and took part in the Battle of Saratoga. When the Regiment arrived at Fort Pitt a part of the force was sent to Fort MacIntosh, but John Guthery says he was discharged after taking part in Colonel Brodhead's Expedition against the Indians at Coshocton and on the Muskingum River. John Guthery had been made an Ensign on December 21, 1778. (For a complete story of this Regiment see Penna. Archives Series V. Vol. 3. pp. 305-376.)

On his return to the Monongahela John Guthery was elected a captain of the militia company from his district on Big Whiteley Creek, and according to William Harrod, Jr., in his interview with

L. C. Draper, maintained one of the protective forts in his section. He was the captain of this company from 1780, until 1790, and then in 1793, was made a lieutenant colonel of the First Regiment of Washington County Militia in preparation for Wayne's Campaign. From "Revolutionary Soldiers Buried in Ohio" pp. 167, we learn that John Guthery was born in Pennsylvania, April 14, 1744 (although his pension claim of 1820 gives his age as 90 years old), and that he was of Scotch-Irish parentage. After selling his land on the Monongahela by a series of deeds recorded in Greene County Deed Books, he left here about 1797 or 1798, and we have the story of his migration from the pen of his daughter, Lydia (Guthery) Peters. She says that, "my parents with all their children except Francis, who died in infancy, took their flat boat from Greensboro down the Monongahela to Pittsburgh, thence down the Ohio to where Portsmouth now stands. Though not a tree of the primeval forest was cut, we ascended the Scioto River with our goods in a keel boat. Some of the family road on horse back over a blazed trail, while others followed on foot. We passed but one house the whole distance between the mouth of the Scioto and where Piketown now stands. We camped there all night and next morning resumed our journey. Father had to begin felling trees to get room to build a house at our destination, and while building the log cabin depended a great part on the abundance of wild game to feed his large family." From a history of Pike County we learn that his claim was several miles south of Piketown, which he had caused to be laid out and which he was instrumental in making the first county seat. He died here June 1, 1823, and is buried in Mound Cemetery on his own land. This source also says that he married on March 1, 1771, Lydia Baldwin. She was a daughter of Francis and Charity (Hackney-nee Harlan) Baldwin and the mother of twelve children. Greene County records show that Lydia Baldwin had a tract of land facing on the Monongahela, near the present site of Greensboro, warranted to her on November 1, 1770, under the title "Lydia's Bottom." This tract was patented on April 17, 1792, to John and Lydia Guthery. John and Lydia Guthery were members of Goshen Baptist Church.

Children of John and Lydia (Baldwin) Guthery

1. William Guthery, born 1772; married Catherin .... They had six children.
2. Archibald Guthery, married Rachel Hudson, daughter of William and Mary Hudson.
3. John Guthery, Jr.
4. Francis Guthery, died in infancy; born January 11, 1778.
5. George Guthery, born March 26, 1779; married Sarah Howard. Had four children.
6. Elizabeth Guthery, born January 26, 1781; married Jonathan Clark.
7. Priscilla Guthery, born January 1783; married William Collings.
8. Aaron Guthery, born December 1784; married Nancy Howard. Had three children.
9. Rebecca Guthery, born January 21, 1786, died June 16, 1819; married James Daniels. They had two children.
10. Moses Guthery, born February 12, 1787; married Hannah Hastings. He died about 1828. They had three children.
11. Joseph Guthery, born March 29, 1790; married Hannah Dever. They had three children.
12. Lydia Guthery, born October 17, 1794; married William D. Peters. They had ten children.

COLONEL JOHN GUTHERY IN OHIO

Lydia (Guthery) Peters, youngest daughter of Colonel John and Lydia (Baldwin) Guthery, has left an interesting account of the migration of the family to Ohio. In her Memoirs she says that her father left Greene County after living there fifty years. He bought a great tract of land extending a mile South and East toward Beaver Creek. He left for what was then a wilderness just so his children could have good farms or money and a good start in life. His wife became very homesick for her old home on the Mononga hela and the friends she had left, so they started back with their little girl, Lydia (Guthery) Peters, on a visit and got as far as Chillicothe, when the little girl fell sick. The father continued the journey to close up some business back here, but the homesick mother had to return to their home in the wilderness until the child recovered. Later they made the trip back together, but by that time all their friends were gone and so many changes were made that she did not want to stay. The returned to Ohio where the mother was contented to live the rest of her life. This hardy pioneer women trapped wolves for the rewards offered for the scalps, and each morning, accompanied by the older sons, would go out to the traps to see how many they had caught during the night, sometimes finding two or more entangled beasts.

Lydia tells that she was ferried across the Scioto River to school by her big brothers, where one of her brothers, Aaron Guthery, taught school. She is described as being a Guthery absolutely, large blue-gray eyes far apart, close, rather thin lips, and a very straight nose with "wing" nostrils. In telling of her family she says:

"William Guthery, the eldest, took his family and moved to Illinois.

"Archibald Guthery moved to Indiana and died there.

"John Guthery had three daughters, Cynthia, Priscilla, and Eliza.

"George Guthery's children were Samuel, Baldwin, John, and Priscilla. He went to Illinois.

"Elizabeth Guthery had five children, Minerva, Joseph, Aaron, Lovie, and Charlotte.

"Priscilla's children were Maria, Louisa, Lydia, Isaac, James, Minerva, and Rebecca.

"Aaron's children were William, Alfred, and Hannah.

"Rebecca's children were Hiram and Eliza.

"Moses' children were Jane, Silas, and Eliza.

"Joseph's children were William, John, and Isaac."

THE PROVANCE FAMILY

The first will on file in Greene County Will Book I, is the will of Sarah Provance (Provins, Provence, etc.,) and it is remarkable for the extent of the estate, which would be large even at today's figures. Sarah Provance was a widow when she married Thomas Provance, himself a widower, and it is evident that they had children after that marriage. There is reason to believe that she was Sarah Hackney, daughter of Joseph and Charity (Harlan) Hackney, and that her first husband was a man named Rees, though as yet no proof has been found to verify this theory. The situation of her land in the midst of a solid block of holding of her half-sisters supports this theory of Sarah Provance's ancestry. Certainly not all the land she devised in her will could have been owned by her husband, for it was not customary to give such land outright to the widow if there were children living.

Sarah Provance was the woman mentioned in Evans as having rowed out from her home at the mouth of Big Whiteley Creek, to secure the body of the friendly Chief Bald Eagle, when she noticed the canoe with the corpse floating down the Monongahela. This chieftain, who had befriended many of the first settlers, had been murdered by a few treacherous white men near the mouth of the Cheat. They had propped the body in an old canoe and stuffed a piece of Johnny Cake in his mouth, then set the canoe afloat. Sarah Provance towed the boat to shore where the Indian was given a decent burial. Bald Eagle had been a welcome visitor at all the cabins and no doubt very friendly with the Provances.

Thomas Provance, husband of Sarah,, was originally from New London Township, Chester County, Pennsylvania. He was one of the first settlers of Fayette County, probably many years prior to his meeting with the Commissioners at Fort Redstone in 1768. While the Fayette County histories say he came about 1767, it would not be surprising if he had made his settlement at least ten years prior to that date. He may have been one of the men who had permission to settle by the Indians, who at that meeting, begged that the settlers be allowed to stay. If the Flenniken story of securing their land from a friendly Indian Chief at the mouth of Muddy Creek is true, then Thomas Provance is likely the man who already had been granted land on the west bank of the Monongahela before 1760. Certainly he settled on the most favorable sites on both sides of the River, his Greene County land being at the mouth of both Big and Little Whiteley Creeks.

Thomas Provance died some time between 1782, when he served in Captain John Guthery's Militia, and 1784, when his widow is taxed in Greene Township, Washington County, but there is no record of his estate. The following year she was taxed in Fayette County, owner of land in German Township, probably the Provance Bottoms near Masontown. It is probable that Thomas Provance's estate was settled in Monongalia County, and the record burned in the Court House fire of 1796.

Children of Thomas and Sarah Provance

1. John Provance, called step-son by Sarah Provance in her will, and to whom she willed 300 acres of a 1,500 acre tract in Harrison County, (West) Virginia. He is the John William Provance (Provins) who warranted the tract of land in Fayette County at the mouth of Catt's Run, on a warrant dated October 11, 1771. He served in Captain John Whetzell's Ranger Company of 1778. (Penna. Arch. Series VI Vol. 2. pp. 321).
2. Margaret Provance, called step-daughter by Sarah; wife of .... Casto. She got 200 acres of the above 1,500 acre tract in Harrison County.
3. Jane Provance, also called step-daughter by Sarah; wife of .... McClelland. She got 50 acres of the same tract.
4. Rachel ....; she had married .... Hargus, and her children got 500 acres of a tract of land containing 1,000 acres on Mill Creek, Harrison County, situated above land of John McFarland. As Sarah Provance called these children her grandchildren, it is not clear if they were hers by a former marriage or through her marriage to Thomas Provance, nor is it clear if Rachel Hargus had died prior to her mother.
5. Mary ....; wife of .... Brown. Her children, called grandchildren by Sarah Provance, got the balance of this 1,000 acre tract on Mill Creek, Harrison County, Virginia.

AND ITS PIONEER FAMILIES 615

6. Joseph Yard Provance, called son by Sarah Provance; received a tract of 1,000 acres of land on Mill Creek, in Harrison County, Virginia, and land on Dunkard Creek, Greene County. He warranted, in his own name October 11, 1771, in Fayette County, the tract of land south of John William Provance on Catt's Run. He was born March 3, 1764, and died about 1843. His estate was probated October 6, 1843. Joseph Yard Provance was married first to Elizabeth Carter, by whom he had seventeen children. His second wife was Rachel (Jackson) Spencer, and there were seven children born of this marriage. His second wife was born February 12, 1783. He served in the Revolution under Captain John Swearington. (Penna. Arch. Series VI Vol. 2. pp. 252). See Pension record under "Frontier Rangers."

Children of Joseph Yard Provance
1. John William Provance.
2. Benjamin E. Provance; soldier in the War of 1812; married Jean Hartley, born about 1785, died April 19, 1876. Buried near Masontown, Penna.
3. David Provance, married Agnes Hartley.
4. Elijah Provance, married Ann Gallatin.
5. Simeon Provance, married Nancy Howard.
6. Uriah Provance, married Matilda Spencer.
7. Thomas Provance, married (1) Dorcas Williams; (2) Clarissa Bire.
8. Jesse Provance, married Cecelia Spencer.
9. Joseph Provance.
10. Patience Provance, married Thomas Bire.
11. Sarah Provance, married Robert McClain.
12. Lydia Provance.
13. Phoebe Provance.
14. Jane Provance, married George Jught.
15. Mary Ann Provance, married Daniel Brewer.
16. Eliza Provance.
17. Elizabeth Provance.
18. Benjamin F. Provance, born November 27, 1819.
19. Theron Provance, born May 27, 1821.
20. Winnie Provance, died young.
21. Selina Provance, born September 19, 1822; married Washington Rich.
22. Rachel Provance, born June 1, 1826; married David Haight.
23. Joseph Provance, born September 6, 1828.
24. Agnes Provance, married .... Haight.

(Haddon History of Fayette County, Penna.)

7. Sarah Provance, daughter of Thomas and Sarah Provance; called daughter in the will of Sarah Provance. She married (1) Benjamin Wright, who received land in Washington County, Pennsylvania (on Whiteley Creek), and 1,000 acres of land in dispute in Harrison County, Virginia, from his mother-in-law. Benjamin Wright served in Captain John Whetzell's Ranger Company in 1778. After his death his widow married William Robinson.

Children of Benjamin and Sarah (Provance) Wright
1. David Wright, his grandmother willed him 300 acres of land in Harrison County. He died before 1834, and left:
   1. Nancy Wright, who married .... Green.
   2. Samuel Wright.
   3. James Wright.

4. Thomas Wright of Jefferson County, Ohio.
　　　5. David Wright.
　　　6. Eleanor Wright.
　　　7. Minerva Wright.
　2. Samuel Wright, got 400 acres of land in Harrison County.
　3. Sarah Wright, a bequest in the will of Sarah Provance, and mentioned in William Robinson sale.
　4. Elizabeth Wright, mentioned in Sarah Provance will.
　5. Mary Wright, mentioned in Sarah Provance will.

A Permelia Rochold, granddaughter, is named by Sarah Provance, as is her daughter, Sarah. We do not place these heirs.

THE LONG FAMILY

Some time prior to 1771, John Long and wife, Ann, with their seven sons and a daughter, left their home in Maryland to settle on the waters of Whiteley and Dunkard Creeks. One record says that John Long was originally from Williamsville, Baltimore Hundred, Sussex County, Delaware, but it is evident that before 1754, he had removed to Queen Anne's County, Maryland, where some of his children were born. It appears that this family stopped for a time in what is now Fayette County, Pennsylvania, where the daughter, Ann, met and married George Debolt. But such a stop was only an interlude and before 1776, they were on the West side of the Monongahela where John Long died about 1785. His will was probated in Washington, Pennsylvania, on May 12, 1785, and is in Will Book 1. pp. 60. No land was definitely granted to John Long, nor is there any record of military service that can be assigned to him with certainty. His will does mention his wife, Ann, and the sons and daughter.

Children of John and Ann Long

1. David Long, probably the eldest son. Served in John Guthery's Company.
2. John Long, Jr., also in John Guthery's Company.
3. James Long, served in John Guthery's Company.
4. Gideon Long, of whom later.
5. Jeremiah Long, of whom later.
6. Eliel Long, served in John Guthery's Company and had other military service for which he received a pension.
7. Noah Long, served in John Guthery's Company.
8. Ann Long, married George Debolt.

Military record of these sons of John Long, in Pennsylvania Archives Vol. 2. Series VI, pages 18 and 19, except for Jeremiah, which is page 171 of the same volume.

FAMILY OF DAVID LONG

David Long, son of John and Ann Long, served in Captain John Guthery's Company, First Battalion, Washington County, Pennsylvania Militia. On July 4, 1790, he had warranted to him a tract of 127 acres of land on Whiteley Creek, which he and his wife, Sarah ...., sold on April 11, 1804, to James Hartley. (Greene County Deed Book 2. pp. 24).

FAMILY OF JOHN LONG

John Long, son of John and Ann Long (not proven) patented a tract of land on a branch of Dunkard Creek under the title "Mt. Joy," which was on a warrant dated December 14, 1786. Deed Book 2. pp. 322½, Greene County, shows that John Long and wife, Grace ...., sold a portion of "Mount Joy". The tract had been warranted to both John and Jeremiah Long and probably was divided by amicable agreement.

John Long died in Greene County on December 19, 1838, leaving his land in Dunkard Township, which in 1850, was divided among his five living children. He had served in Captain John Guthery's Company of the First Battalion, Washington County Militia. The Census for 1790, shows four males under sixteen years of age, but only one son shared in the distribution of his estate. (O. C. Docket 3. pp. 164).

Children Named in O. C. Docket

1. John Long.
2. Dorcas Long, married Henry H. Goddard; lived in Marshall County, Virginia.
3. Sarah Long, married (1) Thomas Wilkinson; married (2) Jacob Garrison.
4. Rachel Long, married John Phillips.
5. Elizabeth Long, married George Garrison.

GIDEON LONG

Gideon Long, son of John and Ann Long, was born in Queen Anne's County, Maryland, in 1754, and died in Greene County, Pennsylvania, February 16, 1834. Before his death, on April 16, 1833, he applied for a pension for his war services. At that time he was living in Fayette County, Pennsylvania, but a resident of Dunkard Township, Greene County. He says he enlisted in the month of August, 1776, for three years, under Captain (later Lieutenant Colonel) Wilson, and marched to Kittanning, where he joined his regiment, the Eighth Pennsylvania, under Colonel E. McKay. They marched from there over the mountains, experiencing much hardship and exposure, going to Philadelphia, then Bordentown, New Jersey, joining the main army in the Spring of 1777, at Quibbletown. They went to Bound Brook, from whence they made a rapid march across the Delaware and went into winter quarters at Valley Forge until the Spring of 1778. During harvest time in that year, they started westward, stopping at Carlisle, where they were ordered up the Susquehanna to protect the people about Wyoming and Northumberland, then marched back to Pittsburgh. He does not say it, but Draper Manuscripts disclose that he and his brother, Jeremiah, were ordered picked up as deserters about that time, a term without the stigma that it carries today. After he got back to his home on Whiteley Creek he became an Ensign in Captain John Guthery's Company, First Battalion, Washington County, Pennsylvania Militia and later a captain of Frontier Rangers. It is quite evident that he saw much service in the eight years of the war and he got the well deserved pension on May 8, 1833, almost too late to enjoy it. All this service is confirmed in various volumes of the Pennsylvania Archives. His wife was Hannah Phillips, who at the age of 87, while living at Waynesburg, was granted a widows pension on July 5, 1839.

THE JEREMIAH LONG FAMILY

Jeremiah Long, son of John and Ann Long, was born in Queen Anne's County, Maryland, in 1755-6. His services in the Revolution were similar to those of his brother, Gideon Long, except that he served in Captain William Crawford's Company of Washington County Militia after his return from Valley Forge with the Eighth Pennsylvania Regiment of the Continental Line. After the death of his father, Jeremiah and John Long, Jr., got a warrant for the land on Dunkard Creek in December 1786. He died there on July 4, 1820, and with his first wife, is buried in Garards Fort Cemetery. She was Mary Ivers, a daughter of Richard and Mary Ivers, who were also pioneer settlers. She was born in 1758, and died after 1800. After her death, Jeremiah Long married Jane ...., who survived him and who was the mother of six of his children.

Children of Jeremiah and Mary (Ivers) Long

1. Nathan Long.
2. Jeremiah Long, Jr., born October 5, 1780, died October 10, 1858; married Cyrene Gwynne, born September 2, 1793, died August 4, 1874. See Gwynne Records.
3. Frances Long, married William Burge, son of Henry and Mary Burge. She died and he married Elizabeth (Bowen) Swan, widow of Henry B. Swan. William Burge died about 1837.

Children

1. Mary Burge, married .... Long.
2. Jeremiah Burge.
3. James Burge.
4. Priscilla Burge, married .... Stine.
5. Minor Burge.
6. John Burge.
7. Richard Burge.
8. Sarah Burge.

4. Priscilla Long, she was the second wife of Benjamin Dye, born December 27, 1779, son of Andrew and Sarah (Minor) Dye. Her first husband, by whom she had four children, was Vincent Dye, brother of Benjamin. They lived in Miami County, Ohio.
5. Richard Long, son of Jeremiah and Mary (Ivers) Long, born August 31, 1786, died October 19, 1852; married (1) Mary Rankin, born 1781, died July 10, 1829. His second wife was Charlotte Adamson. They are buried in the Muddy Creek Cemetery.

Children of Richard and Mary (Rankin) Long

1. Vincent Long, married Kezia ....

Child

1. Rhoda Long.
2. Mary Long, married Benjamin Worthington.
3. Orpha Long, married .... Clymer.
4. Nancy Long, married .... Minor.
5. Jeremiah Long, born July 18, 1809, died August 1, 1863; married Lucretia Stephens, born 1811, died July 4, 1887. Buried at Muddy Creek.

Children

1. Richard Long, born October 24, 1835, died November 1, 1904; married, December 4, 1861, Phoebe Baily, born May 24, 1840, died June 22, 1915.
2. Milton Long, born January 29, 1838; married Mary McClelland.
3. Winfield Long.
4. Nancy Long, married Wallace Eicher.
5. Elizabeth Long, married Corbly Garard.
6. Sarah A. Long, married James Stephens.

6. Sarah Long, married, March 21, 1844, William P. Scott, born May 1, 1820, died February 12, 1905.

Children

1. James Madison Scott, born December 10, 1844, died November 29, 1930; married, on September 7, 1872, Mary Ann Rinehart, born September 6, 1838, died May 30, 1920.
2. Richard Scott, born October 1, 1846, died ....; married, November 11, 1875, Mary Amanda Baily, born February 19, 1852.
3. Mary E. Scott, born October 30, 1849, died December 20, 1928; married, September 12, 1872, William J. Bayard.
4. Margaret Helen Scott, born August 5, 1855, died July 12, 1928; married, February 1, 1879, George W. Gordon.
5. Columbus M. Scott, born June 28, 1858, died June 18, 1937; married, September 13, 1883, Phoebe C. Rich.
6. Chinsworthy Kincaid Scott, born June 28, 1858, died August 7, 1929; married (1) September 8, 1887, Margaret Bell. His second wife was Nan Leamon.
7. Ruth Ann Scott, born June 20, 1860; married (1) September 5, 1878, Albert Kent. Married (2) September 13, 1910, Benjamin F. Collins.

7. Priscilla Long, married Alfred Gwynne.

Children

1. Joseph Gwynne.
2. Vincent Gwynne.
3. Mary Jane Gwynne.
4. Richard Gwynne.
5.

8. Joseph Long, born January 6, 1813; married, November 11, 1841, Eliza Stephens, born June 17, 1818, died December 26, 1884.

Children

1. Clara Long, married .... Dowlin.
2. James Long, never married.
3. Orpha Long, born July 19, 1845, died July 19, 1919; married, March 7, 1868, John Murdock, born March 18, 1839, died August 6, 1924.
4. Miranda Long, married Dennis Smith.
5. Sarah E. Long, born June 27, 1852, died March 10, 1940; married October 10, 1872, B. F. Murdock, born July 10, 1848, died May 12, 1913.

9. Elizabeth Long, born July 27, 1815; married James Stephens.
10. Eli Long, born April 21, 1821, died October 1, 1881; married, October 25, 1853, Sarah Prior, born July 27, 1831, died August 27, 1886.

Children

1. Elizabeth Long.
2. Albert C. Long.
3. Vincent Long.
4. Della Long.

11. Richard Long, born June 8, 1827, died January 3, 1890; married Emily Porter.

Children of Richard and Charlotte (Adamson) Long

12. Ruth Long.
13. Mariah Long.
14. Jefferson Long.
15. George W. Long.
16. Rebecca Long, born 1843, died July 14, 1851.
6. Sarah Long, daughter of Jeremiah and Mary (Ivers) Long, married James Williamson.
7. David Long, son of Jeremiah and Mary (Ivers) Long.
8. James Long, son of Jeremiah and Mary (Ivers) Long; married Frances Burdge.
9. Elizabeth Long, daughter of Jeremiah and Mary (Ivers) Long; married Perry Johnson.
10. William Long, son of Jeremiah and Mary (Ivers) Long.
11. John Long, son of Jeremiah and Mary (Ivers) Long, died in Greene County, Pennsylvania, August 6, 1882. He married Susannah Gwynne.

Children Named in Will

1. Richard Long.
2. William Long.
3. Joseph Long.
4. Emeline Long.
5. Mary Ann Long.
6. Lucinda Long.
7. Louisa Long.
8. Hester Long.
9. Martha Long.
10. Mariah Long.
11. Jeremiah Long.

Children of Jeremiah and Jane (Jones) Long
Daughter of Morgan Jones

12. Samuel Long.
13. Mary Long.
14. Ruth Long.
15. Hester Long.
16. Sarahann Long
17. Infant.

ELIAL LONG

Elial Long, son of John and Ann Long, was born in Queen Anne's County, Maryland, on August 9, 1756. When he applied for a pension on September 17, 1833, he stated that he was a neighbor of Caleb Spragg, but it appears he was living across the State Line in Monongalia County, Virginia, when he died January 13, 1835, as an attorney, Thomas P. Ray of Morgantown, was handling the application at that time. After his death, his widow, Mary, who was probably the daughter of John and Tabitha (Davis) Davis, made an application for a pension. She is named in the will of her father.

Elial Long says he entered the service in September 1778, under Captain John Guthery and served for two months. In May 1779, he went out again under Captain John Minor, after which he served for a month under Captain Volentine Nichols. In the Spring of 1780, he went out in the militia under Captain Rail. His next service was under Captain Samuel Swingler, and then in the Fall of the same year he served again under the same officer. His service in 1781 was at Darrah's Station under Captain John Holton, with Major James Carmichael as Field Officer. In addition to these regular tours of duty he went out frequently as a spy and minute man, on all occasions when the Indians made incursions into the settlement. His name is listed in John Guthery's Company for the year 1782. (Pennsylvania Archives Series VI Vol. 2. pp. 19).

Children of Elial and Mary (Davis) Davis
1. Elial Long, Jr., served a term as County Commissioner in 1860; died in West Virginia.

NOAH LONG FAMILY

Noah Long, son of John and Ann Long, was a member of John Guthery's Militia Company. He patented a tract of land on Big Whiteley Creek next to that of his brother, David Long. About 1808, he and wife, Sarah ...., sold this land, having removed some time previously to Butler County, Ohio. (Greene County Deed Book 2. pp. 341).

THE DEBOLT FAMILY

George, Henry, and Michael Debolt were early settlers in what is now Fayette County, Pennsylvania, where George and Henry were heads of families in the 1772 Tax Lists for Springhill Township, Bedford County, in 1772, and where Michael Debolt took out a warrant for land on Michael Catt's Run close to the Monongahela River on April 1, 1773. The relationship of these men is not shown, though it may be that Michael Debolt was the father of the first two named. An Elizabeth Debolt died in Fayette County in 1785, leaving a daughter, Mary, wife of .... Walters, and a son, George. (O. C. Docket 1. pp. 13, October 16, 1788. Will is in Will Book 1. pp. 13). A Michael Debolt died in Fayette County in 1784, with Charles Hickman and Jacob Rich serving as his administrators. Guardians were appointed for his minor children, Catherine, Michael, Michlin, and Mary; adult children are not named. Then, on February 4, 1822, a George Debolt made a will in Fayette County which was probated January 16, 1829. In it he named his wife, Elizabeth (Teagarden) and a number of children. The children were:
1. Teagarden Solomon Debolt.
2. William Debolt.
3. David Debolt.
4. Daniel Debolt.
5. Abraham Debolt.
6. Elizabeth Debolt, who was married to .... Lowery.
7. Rezin Debolt.
8. Jacob Debolt.

Deeds of record show that this George Debolt owned land in Masontown Borough, and he may have been the George Debolt that bought land from Michael Debolt (wife Apolonia) on June 24, 1799.

GEORGE DEBOLT OF GREENE COUNTY

No Revolutionary service is shown for this George Debolt, but it is probable that he had considerable service as we find him a lieutenant of the Second Battalion, Washington County, Pennsylvania Militia, in the arrangement of August 1793. In the 1790 Census his name is spelled "George Teaboe" and he was living then on the west side of the Monongahela, on the land patented to him under the title of "White Oak Flats" on October 25, 1787. It was on a part of this land that the present town of Greensboro was laid out. His wife was Ann Long, daughter of John and Ann Long. She is named in the will of her father as Ann Debolt in Washington County Will Book 1. pp. 60, probated May 12, 1785. George Debolt died about 1839, for on August 23, of that year administration of his estate was begun at Waynesburg. (Orphan Court Docket 2.

pp. 110). The list of his children is given in these proceedings.

Children of George and Ann (Long) Debolt
1. Noah Debolt, who died January 24, 1876, leaving a wife, Nancy ....

Children of Noah and Nancy Debolt
1. Morgan Debolt.
2. William Debolt.
3. Mary Debolt.
4. Jeremiah Debolt.
5. Christina Debolt.
6. Isaac Debolt.

2. Jacob Debolt, son of George and Ann (Long) Debolt; no record.
3. Jeremiah Debolt, son of George and Ann (Long) Debolt; died about 1860; his wife was Milky ....
4. George Debolt, Jr., son of George and Ann (Long) Debolt; no record.
5. Elizabeth Debolt, daughter of George and Ann (Long) Debolt; married Amos Herrington.
6. Charity Debolt, daughter of George and Ann (Long) Debolt; married Nathan Thompson.
7. Priscilla Debolt, daughter of George and Ann (Long) Debolt; married Morgan Herrington.
8. Rhoda Debolt, daughter of George and Ann (Long) Debolt; married Ezekiel Calvert.
9. Harriet Debolt, daughter of George and Ann (Long) Debolt; married John Herrington.
10. Mary Debolt, daughter of George and Ann (Long) Debolt; married Teagarden Solomon Debolt of Fayette County.

Children of Teagarden Solomon and Mary (Debolt) Debolt
1. George Debolt.
2. Teagarden Debolt.
3. Eliza Debolt, married John Knotts.
4. Mariah Debolt, married Alexander Mesterzat.
5. Nancy Debolt, married Samuel Bare.
6. William Debolt.
7. Margaret Debolt.
8. Jeremiah Debolt.

11. Catherine Debolt, daughter of George and Ann (Long) Debolt; married Patrick Baily.

Children of Patrick and Catherine (Debolt) Baily
1. Henry Baily.
2. Thornton Baily.
3. Permelia Baily, married Nasa McCurdy.
4. Jane E. Baily, married Samuel Lynn.
5. Anna Baily, married F. P. Bayard.
6. Nelson Baily.
7. Robert Baily.

12. Martha Debolt, daughter of George and Ann (Long) Debolt; married Francis Hupp.

Children of Francis and Martha (Debolt) Hupp
1. George Hupp.
2. Margaret Hupp, married .... Whitlatch.
3. Harriet Hupp, married William Riggle.
4. Clarissa Hupp, died young.
5. Everhart Hupp, married Hannah Sherich.

13. Sarah Debolt, daughter of George and Ann (Long) Debolt; married John McFarland.

THE STEPHENS FAMILY

The Stephens Family of Big Whiteley Creek and Dunkard Creek are of New Jersey origin. They are said to belong to a family which consisted of seven brothers. Two of these brothers, William Stephens and Samuel Stephens, are reported to have stayed in New Jersey, when the other five, Edward, Apollo, James, John, and Stacey Stephens, came west soon after 1800.

THE EDWARD STEPHENS FAMILY

Edward Stephens was born in New Jersey in 1764, and died in Greene County on May 3, 1846. His wife was Hannah Woodward, born in 1770, died February 2, 1854, at the age of 83 years, 9 months, and 21 days. Both are buried in the Whiteley Chapel Cemetery. The estate of Edward Stephens was filed for probate on May 11, 1846. (W. B. 2. pp. 236).

Children of Edward and Hannah (Woodward) Stephens

1. Lucretia Stephens, born December 15, 1789, died August 15, 1885; married, November 2, 1809, by Rev. Luse to Levi Morris, born April 14, 1783, died January 20, 1842. He was a son of George and Margaret (Corbly) Morris.

    #### Children of Levi and Lucretia (Stephens) Morris

    1. Margaret Morris, born September 15, 1811, died June 6, 1853; married, May 2, 1829, Hon. Patrick Donley, born February 14, 1805, died October 20, 1891.
    2. Louisa Morris, born July 4, 1812, died May 6, 1883; married, November 27, 1832, George Lemley, born 1810, son of David and Rhuhama (Snyder) Lemley.
    3. Hannah Morris, born April 17, 1814, died 1863; married, April 1, 1832, Abner Garrison, born 1803, son of George and Elizabeth (Long) Garrison.
    4. Josephus Morris, born March 14, 1816, died August 9, 1896; married, April 20, 1843, Temperance Smith, born January 8, 1823, died December 18, 1904.
    5. George W. Morris, born April 9, 1819, died January 8, 1897; married, August 20, 1846, Emily Kirby, born January 23, 1827, died February 15, 1884.
    6. Jefferson Morris, born April 9, 1819, died February 10, 1857; married, October 28, 1845, Sarah Inghram.
    7. Edward F. Morris, born March 30, 1823; married (1) November 23, 1843, Elizabeth Smith. He married (2) Rhetta Roberts.
    8. Thomas Morris, born November 28, 1825; married Sarah Way.
    9. Major James B. Morris, born November 24, 1827; married, September 26, 1848, Keziah Way.
    10. Levi Morris, born September 15, 1831; married Samantha Brown.
    11. Lucretia Morris, born August 8, 1833, died April 15, 1885; married Colonel C. I. Hardin.
2. William Stephens, born November 22, 1791; married .... Long.
3. James Stephens, born 1793, died December 21, 1848, aged 55 years, 1 month, 26 days; married Elizabeth Long, born July 27, 1815, died March 1, 1901.

Children of James and Elizabeth (Long) Stephens

1. Elizabeth Stephens, died before 1855; married Jesse McFarland.
2. Edward C. Stephens
3. Melissa Stephens; married Henry McCullough.
4. James Stephens; married Sarah Long.
5. Vincent Stephens; married Mary Morris.
6. Richard Stephens.
7. Bowen Stephens, born January 15, 1834, died April 24, 1922; married Adeline Stephens.

4. Nancy Stephens, born December 13, 1795; married James Patterson, born December 20, 1795, died 1853.
5. Samuel Stephens, born March 29, 1798.
6. Rebecca Stephens, born February 14, 1800; married William Corbly, born about 1800, died December 26, 1875. Lived in Vinton County, Ohio. He was a son of Rev. John Corbly.

Children of William and Rebecca (Stephens) Corbly

1. Edward Corbly.
2. Harrison Corbly.
3. Lynn Corbly.
4. John Corbly.
5. Nancy Corbly.
6. Eliza Corbly.
7. Hannah Corbly.
8.

7. Elizabeth Stephens, born November 26, 1801; married John Bowlby.
8. Hannah Stephens, born August 4, 1803; married .... Wells.
9. Edward Stephens, born July 10, 1805.
10. Thomas Stephens, born January 11, 1807.
11. Job Stephens, born September 18, 1809, died July 16, 1848.
12. G. Washington Stephens, born November 2, 1811.

THE STACEY STEPHENS FAMILY

Stacey Stephens was born in New Jersey 1779, died in Greene County October 30, 1861. His wife was Elizabeth Hatfield, who died in 1849, at the age of 68 years.

Family of Stacey and Elizabeth (Hatfield) Stephens

1. Hiram Stephens, born in 1802, died February 6, 1869, aged 66 years, 4 months, 22 days. His wife was Elizabeth Hunt, born 1803, died July 26, 1887, aged 83 years, 8 months, 15 days.

Children of Hiram and Elizabeth (Hunt) Stephens

1. Allan Stephens, born September 4, 1827, died April 5, 1907; married Martha Steele, born December 30, 1828. Both buried at Garards Fort.
2. Oliver Stephens, born January 17, 1830, died August 6, 1851.
3. Druscilla Stephens, born September 4, 1832, died August 5, 1851.
4. Azariah Stephens, born July 24, 1834, died July 28, 1851.
5. Lucretia Stephens, married Thomas Roberts.
6. Lucinda Stephens, born May 20, 1839, died March 1926;

married Otho W. Minor, born January 22, 1830, died January 1912.
   7. Mary Stephens, born February 14, 1842, died November 18, 1924; married Corbly Gregg, born April 6, 1829, died May 1, 1901.
2. Stacey Stephens.
3. John Stephens.
4. Brazilla Stephens, born April 20, 1809, died April 24, 1884; married December 4, 1832, Margaret Lantz, born March 18, 1811.

   Children of Brazilla and Margaret (Lantz) Stephens
   1. Jackson Stephens, married Minerva Minor.
   2. Lindsey Stephens, born June 23, 1836; married Margaret Fordyce.
   3. Adeline Stephens; married B. R. Stephens.
   4. Eliza Stephens; married Samuel Hudson.
   5. Albert Stephens; married Sis Bowlby.
5. Israel Stephens, born 1811, died July 12, 1871; married Rose Ann Steele.
6. Lucretia Stephens, born 1812, died July 4, 1887, aged 75 years, 11 months, 10 days; married Jeremiah Long, who died August 1, 1863, aged 54 years and 13 days.

   Children of Jeremiah and Lucretia (Stephens) Long
   1. Richard Long, born October 24, 1835; married Phoebe Baily.
   2. Milton Long, born January 29, 1838; married Mary McClelland.
   3. Winfield Long.
   4. Nancy Long; married Wallace Eicher.
   5. Elizabeth Long; married Corbly Garard.
   6. Sarah Ann Long; married James Stephens.
   7. Mary Long.
7. Azariah Stephens; married Clarissa Steele.

   Children of Azariah and Clarissa (Steele) Stephens
   1. Ella Stephens.
   2. Unia Stephens.
   3. Stacey Stephens.
   4. Iona Stephens.
   5. Jets Stephens.
8. Eliza Stephens, born June 17, 1818, died December 26, 1884; married, November 11, 1841, Joseph Long, born January 6, 1813.

   Children of Joseph and Eliza (Stephens) Long
   1. Sarah Long; married B. F. Murdock.
   2. Clara Long; married .... Dowlin.
   3. Jane Long.
   4. Orpha Long; married John Murdock.
   5. Miranda Long; married Dennis Smith.
9. Apollo Stephens; married Magdeline ....
10. Washington Stephens; married Joanna Steele.

    Children of Washington and Joanna (Steele) Stephens
    1. Spencer Stephens, born September 15, 1839; married in 1865, Abigail Conner.
    2. Leroy Stephens.
    3. Melissa Stephens; married George Johnson.

4. Ruth Stephens; married Eli Whitlatch.
5. Minor Stephens; married Lillian Minor.
6. Mary Stephens.
7. Grant Stephens.
8. Bowen Stephens; married Ruth Zimmerman.

JAMES WELLS

The Gordon Book does not give the family of James and Elizabeth (Guseman) Wells, nor does it mention the age of Elizabeth Guseman, daughter of Christopher and Elizabeth (Gordon) Guseman. The Gordons had originally lived on Monacocy Creek near Baltimore, but Elizabeth Gordon was probably born in Frederick County, where she married Christopher Guseman on July 3, 1777. A son, Godfrey, was born November 17, 1779, and Elizabeth was the second child and probably born about 1781 in Monongalia County, Virginia. We are told that Elizabeth Guseman was very young when she married James Wells, a very wealthy man and former slave owner before migrating to what is now Greene County, Pennsylvania. Family tradition says he never had to do any work, and never did. It is quite likely that he lived in Monongalia County prior to his migration. He died in Greene County, Pennsylvania, about 1815, his estate being proven on February 28, 1816. Orphan Court Docket 1. pp. 125, shows he had a number of minor children for whom guardians were appointed.

Childdren of James and Elizabeth (Guseman) Wells

1. John Wells, over 14 years of age in 1816, but under 21 years.
2. James Wells, under 14 years of age in 1816; married .... King.
3. Priscilla Wells, over 14 years of age in 1816.
4. Rebecca Wells, under 14.
5. Sally Wells, under 14 years in 1816; married Isaiah Steele.
6. Dolly Wells, under 14 years in 1816; married David Kughn.
7. Eleanor Wells; married Basil Gordon.
8. Joseph Wells; married Amy Spragg.
9. Benjamin Wells; married .... Kughn.
10. Susannah Wells; married Peter Owens.
11. Nancy Wells; married Thomas Owens.
12. Elizabeth Wells; married Joseph Price.
13. Godfrey Guseman Wells; married Rhoda Phillips.

RICHARD IVERS

Richard Ivers was one of the earliest settlers on Little Whiteley Creek, where he and his son, Richard, both warranted tracts of land on December 23, 1785. There is no evidence to show that Richard Ivers was a member of Goshen Baptist Church, but his wife, Mary .... Ivers, was excommunicated from that Church on July 24, 1776. Richard Ivers was probably too old for service in the Revolution, for the names of two sons are in Captain William Crawford's Militia rolls, and the Muddy Creek Ledger shows that his young son, William Ivers was in the distilling business as early as 1793. Richard Ivers died in Greene County, leaving a will that was probated May 19, 1806. (W. B. 1. pp. 53).

Children of Richard and Mary Ivers

1. Robert Ivers, not mentioned in the will, but a member of Captain William Crawford's Company. He was also a signatory to the Westsylvania Petition to the Continental Congress. May

have died prior to the death of his father.
2. John Ivers, also in William Crawford's Company and a signer of the above petition.
3. Richard Ivers, Jr., a signer of the above petition and warrantee of land next his father. His wife was Deborra Leslie, daughter of Patrick Leslie.
4. Jane Ivers; married .... Bosher (Brashears ?)
5. Mary Ivers, born in 1758, died 18..... She was the first wife of Jeremiah Long.
6. Elizabeth Ivers; married Thomas (?) Truelock, a member of Captain William Crawford's Company.
7. Sarah Ivers; married .... Wood.
8. Ann Ivers; married .... Steele.
9. William Ivers; a distiller in Greene County in 1793; signer of the Westsylvania Petition. Removed to Tyler County, West Virginia, where his will, made November 30, 1831, was probated in June 1832. His wife's name was Sarah .... (W. B. 1-A. pp. 208).

Children of William and Sarah Ivers
1. Elizabeth Ivers; married .... Brady.
2. William Ivers, Jr.
3. Robert Ivers.
4. Nancy Ivers, wife of Samuel Love.
5. John Joseph Ivers.
6. Esther Ivers.

COLONEL JOHN MINOR FAMILY

One of the first men to make a permanent settlement in what is now Greene County, was Colonel John Minor. His family says he was on Big Whiteley Creek as early as 1765, and there are no records to dispute this claim. From the first he seems to have been a leader in the settlement and defense of the frontier. Few references are made to him in which he is not honored by some title such as Colonel, Judge, Squire, or Justice John Minor. His industry is shown in the fact that he had scarce raised his cabin when he built a mill on Whiteley, and while he is not credited with constructing a fort, references do indicate that his place was a natural stronghold to which many settlers came in times of danger. With the mill in operation he began the construction of a boat yard, which became the source of equipment for various expeditions making their way down the rivers to the west, including the George Rogers Clark Expedition. With Colonel Thomas Gaddis and Theophylus Phillips, he was most active during the early days of the Revolution, in suppressing the numerous Tories in the section. Because of his attachment for his old home in Virginia, he served that state in various capacities as long as it appeared that this part of Pennsylvania might be included in Virginia's borders, but when the line was run he became just as active in the service of the Commonwealth of Pennsylvania. Because of this allegience to Virginia many of the early records of John Minor's land speculations and business and official transactions do not appear in the written records or if such existed, they were burned when the Court House was destroyed at Morgantown in 1796. For his military records we must look to the pension claims of those who served under him, and refer to written histories, which have covered his record pretty thoroughly. These pension applications bring out a point not covered by the histories, showing that in times of danger Colonel John Minor's plantation was a recruiting station as well as rendezvous for the neighboring inhabitants. When the section became definitely a part of Pennsylvania, Colonel John Minor began the fight for a new county, and almost single handedly pushed through the formation of Greene County, from which he deservedly is called "The Father of Greene County." For the full history of this man, the reader may turn to Evans, Bates, Crumrine and other early historians, who have left little to be told of his activities. This article will confine itself to the family of Colonel John Minor.

We are told that John Minor was born in Loudon County, Virginia, January 5, 1747, the son of Stephen and Athaliah (Updike) Minor. A printed history gives the genealogy of this family, back to Thomas Minor, who came from England on the ship "Arabella" in 1629, and settled first in Massachusetts, and then to Connecticut. There is a possibility of error in the birthplace of John Minor, and it is most likely that he or at least some of his brothers and sisters were born at Hightstown, New Jersey, where Stephen Minor lived when he married Athaliah Updike (Oopdike, etc.) but estate records at Winchester, Virginia, do show that Stephen Minor died in Frederick County, Virginia, about 1751, and that his widow, Athaliah, took out letters to administer his estate. This is as far as the records go, and it would appear that Stephen Minor's estate was of no value, or out of the jurisdiction as no further action was taken by the widow. What became of her is also an unsolved question, unless she is the Athaliah Minor, who was baptized at Goshen Baptist Church on April 28, 1787.

On February 20, 1771, Colonel John Minor married Christina Williams, of a prominent Baltimore Family. She died in childbirth in 1772, and John Minor married, on February 22, 1776, Cassandra Williams, daughter of Joseph and Prudence (Holland) Williams, sister of General Otho Holland Williams, and cousin of his first wife. She became the mother of twelve children, and died March 3, 1799, after which Colonel John Minor married Jane (Wilson) Hawkins, widow of William G. Hawkins of Fayette County, and daughter of General George Wilson. Two children were born by the third marriage. Colonel John Minor died December 5, 1833, and his estate is in File 752 in Greene County, Pennsylvania. Pension file of Colonel John Minor is in National Archives S. 2840, and was for service as a captain under Colonel Zack Morgan in April 1777, along with other services mentioned. It gives his birthplace as Winchester, Virginia.

Children of Colonel John Minor

1. Otho Minor, born December 10, 1776, died October 15, 1831. He married Rebecca South, daughter of Benjamin and Elizabeth (Slack) South. She was born in 1783, and died August 27, 1876. Both are buried near Greensboro, near his father and mother.

Child

1. John Minor, born June 8, 1802, died March 25, 1891; married Malinda Lantz, born April 2, 1808, died February 15, 1890. Both buried at Garards Fort.

Children

1. Francis Minor, born 1828.
2. Otho Williams Minor, born January 22, 1830, died February 12, 1912.
3. Mary Minor, born January 13, 1832, died September 11, 1913. Never married.
4. William Minor, born April 22, 1835, killed by falling tree, January 5, 1875.
5. Rebecca Minor, born September 18, 1837, died August 20, 1877.

2. Stephen Minor, son of John and Cassandra (Williams) Minor, was born December 17, 1778. He was living in Montgomery County, Indiana, in 1841, when he was appointed guardian for two of his minor sons.

Children

1. Ann Eliza Minor.
2. Alfred Minor.
3. Martha Ann Minor.
4. Mailet Minor.
5. Mary S. Minor.
6. Joan Minor; married Clement Fisher.
7. Cassandra Minor; married Hillery Woolery.
8. Matilda Minor; married William Crawford.
9. Edward Minor.
10. Richard Minor.
11. Kitty Minor; married Thomas H. Dodge.
12. James D. Minor, born 1822.
13. Samuel G. Minor, born 1824.

3. Priscilla Minor, daughter of Colonel John and Cassandra (Williams) Minor, born February 24, 1780. Married Samuel Yeamans. Dr. Jesse Paremore was named guardian for their child named below, who was in Butler County, Ohio, in 1841.
    1. William Yeamans.
4. Joanna Minor, daughter of Colonel John and Cassandra (Williams) Minor, born September 22, 1782, lived at Sylvan Retreat, near Oxford, Ohio, in 1841. Her husband was Daniel Milliken, who served as guardian for the following children:
    1. Stephen Milliken.
    2. John Minor Milliken.
    3. Thomas B. Milliken.
    4. Anna Milliken; married Americus Symmes.
    5. Joan Milliken; married Robert Kennedy.
    6. Mary Milliken.
    7. Jane Milliken.
    8. Daniel Milliken.
    9. James Milliken.
    10. Otho Williams Milliken.
5. Eli W. Minor, son of Colonel John and Cassandra (Williams) Minor, born March 22, 1784, died 1849. His wife was Dorcas Brice, whom he married January 7, 1802. She was born July 7, 1785, and died 1855. (Greene County O. C. Docket 2. pp. 159).

Children

1. John B. Minor.
2. Rachel B. Minor, born ....; married Dr. Jesse Paremore.
3. Priscilla Minor; married Flemming Wasson.
4. Cassandra Minor; married James McClelland.
5. Prudence R. Minor; married Andrew McClelland.
6. Phineas Minor, born 1820, died 1868; married Frances Morgan.
7. William H. Minor.

6. Mercy Minor, daughter of Colonel John and Cassandra (Williams) Minor, born November 24, 1785, died at New Paris, Ohio, November 18, 1840. Married Paul Larsh. Nine children:
   1. Newton M. Larsh.
   2. Paul Larsh, Jr.
   3. Benjamin Larsh.
   4.
   5.
   6.
   7.
   8.
   9.
7. Prudence Minor, daughter of Colonel John and Cassandra (Williams) Minor, born September 15, 1787; married John Denny.
8. William Minor, son of Colonel John and Cassandra (Williams) Minor, born June 18, 1789; never married.
9. Frances Minor, daughter of Colonel John and Cassandra (Williams) Minor, born April 8, 1791, died 1823; married George Kramer.

Children

1. Leroy K. Kramer.

10. Mary B. Minor, daughter of Colonel John and Cassandra (Williams) Minor, born February 24, 1793. She married William Shippen.

Children

1. John M. Shippen.
2. Elizabeth F. Shippen.
3. William C. Shippen.
4. Lyda Shippen.

11. John Updike Minor, son of Colonel John and Cassandra (Williams) Minor, born April 9, 1796; married, April 22, 1815, Rebecca Maxwell, born 1795, daughter of Major James and Ann Maxwell. Her birthday was April 27.

Children

1. Ann F. Minor, born January 22, 1816, died November 17, 1859.
2. Otho W. Minor, born May 14, 1817, died November 8, 1867.
3. James Minor, born December 8, 1818, died April 17, 1861.
4. Lawrence L. Minor, born July 11, 1822, died January 11, 1897.
5. John U. Minor, born October 9, 1820, died June 6, 18......

AND ITS PIONEER FAMILIES 631

    6. Maria Minor, born March 20, 1824.
    7. Abia Minor, born June 30, 1825.
    8. George W. K. Minor, born December 20, 1827, died August 25, 1895.
    9. Francis G. Minor, born February 20, 1830, died January 3, 1866.
   10. William H. Minor, born April 5, 1832.
   11. Louise Minor, born October 2, 1835.
   12. Charles A. Minor, born June 9, 1839.
12. Abia Minor, son of Colonel John and Cassandra (Williams) Minor, born October 9, 1798; married Hannah Harper, born March 20, 1797, died April 15, 1856.

Children

1. Sophia Minor, born ....; married John H. Thompson.
2. Sarah Minor; married Samuel Daugherty.
3. Cassandra Minor; married Otho W. Core.
4. Frances Minor; married William Cotteral.
5. John Minor.
6. Hannah Minor, born January 30, 1822, died July 4, 1862; married James W. Hayes, born November 21, 1817, died November 11, 1902.
7. Edwin L. Minor.

13. Lawrence Lewis Minor, son of Colonel John and Jane Wilson (Hawkins) Minor, born August 23, 1801, died March 15, 1883. Married Maria C. Hayes, daughter of William T. and Mary (McKibben) Hayes.

Children

1. Collin Minor.
2. Minerva Minor.
3. Edward Minor.
4. Jane Minor; married William Day.
5. Lawrence Minor.
6. George Minor.
7. Fannie Minor.
8. Joseph Minor; killed at Frederick, Md., in Civil War.
9. Benjamin Minor.

14. Minerva Minor, daughter of Colonel John and Jane Wilson (Hawkins) Minor, born 1803; married John Crawford.

Children

1. John Minor Crawford; married .... Kramer.
2. Lawrence Crawford.
3. Minerva Crawford; married Dr. Phillip Kramer.

CAPTAIN WILLIAM MINOR

Captain William Minor, also called Colonel William Minor, but by what authority we have not been able to discover, (it may have been through command of Virginia Troops from which we find no record) but the authenticity of his captain's status is confirmed in Josiah Prickett's pension application from Clermont County, Ohio, August 1, 1832. (National Archives, Pa.-W-5584). This states that Prickett was hired by Captain William Minor, on the authority of Colonel Williams of Cross Creek, to spy on the Indians who were committing damage on Dunkard Creek. He was a bit less prominent in the settlement of Greene County, than his younger brother, Colonel John Minor. He was born in either New Jersey or Fredcrick County, Virginia, in 1735, son of Stephen and Athaliah (Updike) Minor. After his brother, John, had visited what is now Greene County and selected a site for settlement, he also picked out the adjoining tract of land for William, who followed the following year. William Minor also took up other land on Whiteley before his death in 1804. William Minor was twice married, his first wife being either Ellen or Frances Phillips, sister of Theophylus. She was born in 1737, and died about 1800, and was apparently mother of all his children. His second wife was Hannah ...., who had been a widow before her marriage to William Minor. Eight sons and a daughter are named as children.

Family of Captain William Minor

1. Stephen (Estaban) Minor, who was the last governor of Mississippi under Spanish rule. Draper says he married a sister of David M. Godefroy de Lanctot. He left some slaves to his sister, who had married Andrew Mundell, in Claiborne County, Mississippi.
2. John Minor; also went to Mississippi.
3. Joseph Minor; went to Mississippi.
4. Phillip Minor; went to Mississippi. His wife was Anne Baird.
5. Frances Minor; her first husband was .... Dye, and later she married Andrew Mundell or Mundle.
6. William Minor; drowned in Dunkard Creek. His wife was Ellenor Phillips, his first cousin, by whom he had twin sons.
7. Samuel Minor, born June 26, 1777, died in Monongalia County, West Virginia, August 1, 1851; buried near Wadestown, West Virginia. He married, first, Susannah Clegg, daughter of Lieutenant Alexander and Margaret (Farmer) Clegg. She was one of the Clegg girls taken prisoner by the Indians and kept by them for several years. She was the mother of twelve children, and after her death, Samuel Minor married Permelia Lancaster, by whom he had ten more children.

Children of Samuel Minor

1. William Minor, born June 1797 (tombstone says 1795), died 1884; married Margaret Lantz, born March 9, 1798, died in 1890. They were married January 9, 1818. She was a daughter of John and Elizabeth (Bonnett) Lantz.
2. Noah Minor, born 1798, died 1854; married Lydia Chalfont.
3. Alexander Minor; married Eve Brown, on August 10, 1818.
4. Jacob Minor.
5. Samuel Minor.
6. Massie Minor.
7. Cassandra Minor.
8. Theopylus Minor; married, October 20, 1823, Elizabeth Lantz.
9. Margaret Minor; married Nicholas B. Johnson.
10. Frances Minor.
11. Rebecca Minor.
12. Infant.

Second Marriage

13. Joseph Minor.
14. Lancaster Minor.
15. John Minor.
16. Matilda Minor.
17. Permelia Minor.
18. Sarah Minor.

19. Caroline Minor.
20. Minerva Minor.
21. Elizabeth Minor.
22. Priscilla Minor.
8. Noah Minor, born 1781, son of Captain William Minor, died 1865, (another account says he was born November 2, 1779). His first wife was Sallie Elizabeth South, born November 14, 1779, daughter of Benjamin and Elizabeth (Slack) South. After her death he married Mary Micks (or Menks). There were six children by the first marriage and seven by the second.

Children
1. Otho Minor; who married Pleasant Myers.
2. Samuel Minor; who married Fanny Phillips.
3. Elizabeth Minor; who married .... Thompson.
4. Nancy Minor; who married Ellie Hartley.
5. Sally Minor; who married Josephus Hartley.
6. Rebecca Minor; who married .... Knotts.
7. Jack Minor.
8. Frances Minor.
9. Harriett Minor.
10. Mary Minor.
11. Joseph Minor.
12. Philip Minor; married Emeline Myers.
13. Mariah Minor; married Jacob Reamer.

9. Theophylus Minor, son of Captain William Minor. His wife was his cousin, Ellenor Phillips, widow of his brother, William, and daughter of Colonel Theophylus Phillips of Fayette County, Pennsylvania.

THE GAPEN FAMILY

When Colonel John Minor made his survey trip into what is now Greene County, he selected in addition to sites for himself and brother, William Minor, a tract of favorable land for his good friend, Zachariah Gapen, who came out the next year to settle. This tract, adjoining the land of Colonel John and William Minor, was warranted to Gapen on March 29, 1785. In the Bedford County Tax List for 1772, Zachariah Gapen's name is misspelled in the Veech copy of that list, it being reported as "Gobean." Zachariah Gapen was born in New Jersey on August 10, 1733. He married there, on July 7, 1760, Ruth Tindall, born September 8, 1740, and removed to Monacacy, Virginia, where his son, Stephen Gapen, was born the following year. He died in Greene County, Pennsylvania, in 1812, his will being on file in Will Book 1, pp. 99, was probated on March 15, 1812.

Children
1. Stephen Gapen, born Monocacy, Virginia, May 29, 1761; was one of the most active of the Revolutionary patriots in this section. Various pension applications mention serving under this captain of spies and Frontier Rangers, for it seems that at each alarm in the Dunkard and Whiteley Creek section, Stephen Gapen would be in charge of the scouting parties sent out to intercept the red raiders. With Colonel Minor, he took an active part in the formation of the new Greene County, serving as one of the commissioners to select a site and lay out the County Seat, after which he served a term as county surveyor. He made an application for a pension on November 28, 1832, and was awarded $73 annually. He was then living in Monon-

galia County, Virginia, and it was here that he died, December 26, 1839. Stephen Gapen was twice married, the first wife being Sarah Scott, daughter of David Scott, by whom he had six children. His second wife was Rebecca, daughter of John Snyder and they had twelve children. Rebecca, born April 17, 1788, and died February 17, 1849. She married Stephen, January 13, 1806.

Children of Stephen Gapen

1. Frances Gapen, born 1793, died 1794.
2. Zachariah Gapen, born July 12, 1795. Moved to Indiana, reared family and died there.
3. Stephen Gapen, born July 21, 1797, died September 17, 1858. Married Harriet Eve Mestrazat.
4. Judith Gapen, born August 1, 1799, died March 28, 1876. Married Enoch Dent of near Morgantown, W. Va., about 1817. Enoch was born March 21, 1796, and died November 18, 1872. They removed to Magnolia, Illinois.
5. Matilda Gapen, born October 21, 1801, died October 26, 1804.
6. Nancy Gapen, born June 6, 1804, died August 8, 1875. About 1824, she married Isaac Locke, born March 11, 1795, in New Jersey. He died April 25, 1873. They lived at Belmont, West Virginia.
7. Sarah Gapen, born January 19, 1807, and died about 1885. Married Jesse Garlow.
8. John Gapen, born March 16, 1809, died September 25, 1825, Married Matilda Garlow.
9. Joshua Gapen, born March 16, 1809. Married Matilda Everly, June 28, 1835. Moved to near Stockwell, Indiana.
10. Dorcas Gapen, born March 2, 1812. Married Henry Stoneking, May 3, 1825, and lived at Lima, Tyler County, W. Va.
11. Amos Gapen, born October 3, 1813, died after 1883. Married (1) Minerva Hale, January 1841; (2) Anne Britt. Lived near Morgantown, W. Va.

12. Daniel Marchant Gapen, born March 15, 1815, died February 15, 1882. On September 13, 1847, he married Ann' White, born October 3, 1823, died December 3, 1861. O: March 24, 1868, he married Sarah Evans, born August 5 1829, died January 11, 1912.
13. Ruth Gapen, born September 25, 1816, died after 1880 Married Dr. John J. Stillians, December 28, 1837, and lived at Clarinda, Iowa.
14. Matilda Gapen. Half sister of Matilda Gapen, and born January 3, 1819. Died near 1850. Married Benjamin South and lived near Greensboro, Pennsylvania.
15. Rachel Gapen, born June 24, 1820, died April 7, 1856. Married John Eberhart, October 27, 1842, and lived at New Geneva, Fayette County, Pennsylvania.
16. Eunice Gapen, born February 6, 1822, died after 1872. Married Owen Thomas Swisher, May 25, 1847, and lived near Clarksburg, West Virginia.
17. Elizabeth Gapen, born February 2, 1824. Married William South.
18. Thomas Gapen, born October 12, 1826, died July 15, 1827.

2. William Gapen, born January 20, 1763.
3. John Gapen, son of Zachariah and Ruth (Tindall) Gapen, born September 17, 1764; served as one the executors of Zachariah

Gapen's estate. Although married and father of several children, nothing is known of his wife.
4. Sarah Gapen, daughter of Zachariah and Ruth (Tindall) Gapen, born October 6, 1766; married .... Long.
5. Rachel Gapen, daughter of Zachariah and Ruth (Tindall) Gapen, born September 6, 1767. She died August 17, 1808. About 1790, she married Benjamin Titus, who was born in New Jersey, August 2, 1759, and died in Greene County, Pennsylvania, December 17, 1849. He was a soldier of the Revolution.

Children: See Benjamin Titus Family

6. Zachariah Gapen, Jr., born March 21, 1772, died about 1820 (O. C. Docket 1. pp. 158). His wife was Mary Everette, a cousin from Princeton, New Jersey. Her mother was a sister of Zacariah.

Children: Minors Under 14 in 1820

1. Charles Gapen, moved to Lacom, Illinois.
2. Eleanor Gapen; married .... Keys.
3. Mary Gapen, posthumous child; married .... Belt.
4. Amelia Gapen; married .... Woods.

7. Eleanor Gapen, born May 17, 1774. Married, June 21, 1795. Her husbnd was Charles Clinton.

Children

1. Sally Clinton, born June 18, 1796.
2. Charles Clinton, Jr., born September 2, 1797.
3. William Clinton, born January 28, 1799.

8. Eli Gapen, born January 11, 1777. There is no record of his marriage but he was alive when his father's will was probated.

THE LANTZ FAMILY

There is a well authenticated Genealogy of the Lantz Family, which says that John and Andrew Lantz are descended from one Hans George Lantz, who with his wife, Catherine, and son, Hans George, came from Germany about 1747. Rupp shows a Hans George Lantz that sailed from Rotterdam and arrived in Philadelphia, where, cn October 20, 1747, he took the Oath of Allegiance to the British. A Nicholas Lantz came with the same group. Within a short time Hans George Lantz went to Maryland, where he lived for a time on the Monococy River, then removed to the Shenandoah Valley, where he died about 1778-9. His son, Hans George Lantz, II, went with his father to the Shenandoah and there he received a grant of 470 acres from Lord Fairfax on October 6, 1766. Hans George Lantz, II, died there about 1793, leaving a wife, Maria, and sons, George, who settled in Barbour County, Virginia; John and Andrew Lantz, who came to Greene County, as did son, Jacob. There was a daughter, Margaretha Lantz, mentioned, of whom there is no further record.

JOHN LANTZ

John Lantz, son of Hans George and Maria Lantz, was born on the Monococy on June 5, 1749, and died in Greene County, Pennsylvania, March 27, 1817. He was twice married, one of his wives being Barbara Waggoner, whose family had settled on the South Branch. One record says she was baptized in 1742, at Danzenheim, near Strassbourg, Germany. Before taking up the military record of John Lantz, we believe it well to give a few of the different spellings of his name. In muster rolls, deeds, land grants, etc., we have run into these: Lantz, Launce, Lans, Lanse, Lonce, Lance, Lontz. Lants, and Launtz. A case in mind is the patents of land on Whiteley Creek, where John's name is spelled Launce, while his brother, Andrew, on the adjoining tract, is spelled Lance. Sometime after the Battle of Yorktown, John Lantz joined the migration toward the Western frontier, and like so many of his neighbors, tarried for a time in Bedford County, Pennsylvania, where in 1782, he served a tour of duty in Captain Henry Rush's Company of Bedford County Militia, his name appearing as John Lance. (Penna. Arch. Series V. Vol. 5, pp. 117. He also had other service noted in Penna. Arch. Series VI Vol. 3. pp. 770-562-573).

On January 15, 1785, John Launce was granted a warrant for 250 acres of land, situated on Big Whiteley Creek. About 1796, he began to accumulate land on Dunkard Creek, where he had warranted to him under the name John Lance, 399 acres of land on March 10, of that year. He removed to this section, buying other tracts next to him until at the time of his death he possessed some one thousand acres in one piece, lying partly in Greene County, Pennsylvania, and partly in Monongalia County, Virginia. His home was on the Greene County side of the line so his estate was probated in Greene County on April 5, 1817, his will being recorded in Will Book 1. pp. 175. From his will we also learn he owned land in Ohio, which went to his son, Andrew Lantz. He is buried in the Lantz Cemetery on Miracle Run, near Brave. He died March 27, 1817.

Children of John Lantz

1. John Lantz, Jr., born August 9, 1773, probably in the Shenandoah. He died September 1, 1858, and is buried in the Lantz Cemetery with his wife, who was Elizabeth Bonnett, daughter of Lewis and Elizabeth (Waggoner) Bonnett. She was born September 13, 1773, and died March 11, 1873, just a few months short of her 100th birthday anniversary. They were married March 26, 1795.

   #### Children of John and Elizabeth (Bonnett) Lantz
   1. Mary Lantz, born February 22, 1796; married, November 12, 1816, ... Chandler.
   2. Margaret Lantz, born March 9, 1798, died in 1890; married, January 9, 1818, William Minor, born June 1797, died 1884, a son of Samuel and Susan (Clegg) Minor.
   3. Elizabeth Lantz, born June 5, 1800; married Theophylus Minor.
   4. Lewis Lantz, born August 30, 1802, died July 26, 1818.
   5. John Lantz, born April 3, 1805, died February 27, 1816.
   6. Nancy Lantz, born August 21, 1807, died May 8, 1901; married, April 10, 1828, William Johnson, born December 11, 1803, died November 16, 1807. He was a son of Nicholas and Sarah (Van Buskirk) Johnson.
   7. William Lantz, born March 17, 1810, died January 24, 1881. He married Sarah Thomas, daughter of William and Amelia (Swan) Thomas.
   8. Sarah Lantz, born July 15, 1812; married, March 18, 1836, Eagon Tygart.
   9. Jacob Lantz, born July 22, 1814; married, December 8, 1836, Minerva Minor, daughter of Samuel and Permelia (Lancaster) Minor.
   10. Alexander Lantz, born July 8, 1817; married Nancy Masters, who died July 29, 1876, aged 57 years, 28 days.

AND ITS PIONEER FAMILIES 637

2. Andrew Lantz; got land in Ohio.
3. Catherine Lantz.
4. Mary Lantz, born 1779, died in Guernsey County, Ohio, September 4, 1833; married, about 1797, Jonathan Stiles, son of Stephen Stiles. He was born July 18, 1774, and died in Guernsey County, Ohio, November 15, 1860, aged 86 years, 3 months, 27 days.

Children of Jonathan and Mary (Lantz) Stiles

1. John Stiles, born May 23, 1800; married Betsie Frankbauer.
2. Stephen Stiles, born March 4, 1802, died July 7, 1886; married (1) Eliza Linn, (2) Francena Lanning.
3. William Stiles, born February 14, 1804; married Mary McCulley (McCullough ?).
4. Andrew Stiles, born March 18, 1806, died September 25, 1885; married (1) Mary Kirkpatrick, (2) Amy Henderson.
5. Thomas Stiles, born May 6, 1808, died April 19. 1890; married Catherine McCullough.
6. Simon Stiles, born June 16, 1810; married (1) Phoebe Kirkpatrick, (2) Betsy Doneley.
7. Mary Stiles, born June 28, 1812, died 1828; married Jesse Gunn.
8. Jacob Stiles, born July 31, 1814, died July 12, 1892; married Mary M. Gunn.
9. George Stiles, born August 6, 1816, died March 6, 1904; married Sarah Corzinne.
10. Margaret Stiles, born December 14, 1818, died 1910; married Joseph Culbertson.
11. Jonathan Stiles, born November 9, 1820, died March 3, 1871; married Rebecca J. Walker.
12. Deborra Stiles, born October 9, 1822, died September 1, 1890; married Stout Patterson.
13. Lewis Stiles, born November 9, 1824, died May 15, 1892; married Rosanna Barnes.
14. Eliza Stiles, born April 3, 1827, died 1909; married Jacob Barnes.

5. William Lantz.
6. George Lantz; willed his estate to slaves whom he had freed.
7. Lewis Lantz; married (1) Barbara ....; married (2) October 29, 1854, Elenor McCullough in Tyler County. His age at that time is given as being 65 years, and hers as 44 years. She was a daughter of William and Rebecca McCullough.
8. Jacob Lantz, born October 1, 1791, died April 14, 1858; married Delilah Coen, born 1797, died March 15, 1866; buried in the Lantz Cemetery.

Children of Jacob and Delilah (Coen) Lantz

1. John Lantz, born May 8, 1829; married Sarah Bradford.

Children of John and Sarah (Bradford) Lantz

1. William Lantz.
2. Morris Lantz.
3. John Lantz.
4. Andrew B. Lantz.
5. Simon Lantz.
6. Jacob Lantz.
7. Alexander Lantz.
8. Lewis W. Lantz.
9. Delilah Lantz.

10. Martha Lantz.
11. Sarah Lantz.
2. Alexander Lantz.
3. Simon Lantz; married Lucy Thomas.
4. William Lantz, born August 27, 1835, died May 18, 1905; married Minerva Kent, born November 24, 1837, died September 20, 1904.
9. Alexander Lantz, born 1793, died 1873; married Margaret Minor.
10. Samuel Lantz, born 1797, died May 1, 1809.
11. Elizabeth Lantz, born 1800; married George F. Cumberledge.

ANDREW LANTZ

Andrew Lantz was born on the Monococy River in Maryland, on November 15, 1755, and died at his plantation on Whiteley Creek, Greene County, Pennsylvania, on September 25, 1824. He and his wife are buried in the Garards Fort Cemetery. During the Revolution he served in Captain Henry Kuster's Company, Fifth Battalion, Lancaster County, Pennsylvania Militia, shortly afterwards removing to the Tenmile Country and securing a warrant on November 24, 1786, for 157 acres of land close to his brother, John Lantz's tract. In this warrant the name is spelled "Lance." He married, probably in Frederick County, Virginia, about 1771, Barbara Lemley, who was born in 1760, and died January 11, 1843. When Andrew Lantz made his will he disinherited his son, Andrew Lantz, Jr., and distributed the whole of his estate among the children of Lot Lantz, the latter being neither a Lantz nor relative, but raised by Andrew Lantz.

Andrew Lantz, Jr., was born in the Shenandoah in 1773, coming to Greene County with his parents, where he married Mary Soonover, daughter of Henry and Catherine (Boos) Soonover. He served in the War of 1812, and died in Greene County on March 3, 1859. Mary (Soonover) Lantz was born in 1775, and died December 27, 1851.

Children

1. John Lantz; married Jane Wildman. He died 1876. Honorable Andrew Lantz was their only child.
2. Henry Lantz; married Elizabeth Hoge. She was born April 6, 1803, and died September 23, 1851, a daughter of Thomas and Ann (Clark) Hoge.
3. Andrew Lantz, III, born October 4, 1803, died July 13, 1862; married, September 25, 1832, Mary Baily, born November 20, 1808, died February 12, 1880. Both are buried at Morrisville, Greene County, Penna. She was a daughter of Joah and Jane (Mundle) Baily

Children

1. Baily Lantz, born July 17, 1833, died January 23, 1835.
2. Jacob Lantz, born February 21, 1836, died May 24, 1836.
3. Celia Ann Lantz, born July 4, 1837, died April 24, 1839.
4. Eleanor Ann Lantz, born May 8, 1840; married (1) John K. Huss; (2) John Rinehart; (3) Rev. William Gladden.
5. Mary Jane Lantz, born April 4, 1843, died December 10, 1908; married, September 21, 1860, David R. P. Huss, born August 25, 1839, died November 24, 1910.
6. Ruth Eliza Lantz, born December 7, 1845; married Harrison Schlotterbeck.
7. Katherine Lantz, born December 31, 1848; married (1)

AND ITS PIONEER FAMILIES

       Joseph Adamson; married (2) on December 9, 1872, Samuel Montgomery, born January 12, 1835.
    8. Aleretta Lantz, born November 1, 1854; married Henry Stoy.
4. Catherine Lantz; married Jacob Rose.
5. Margaret Lantz, born March 18, 1811; married December 4, 1832, Brazilla Stephens, born April 20, 1809, died April 24, 1884.

Children

1. Jackson Stephens; married Minerva Minor.
2. Lindsey Stephens, born June 23, 1836; married, September 26, 1861, Margaret Fordyce, born December 30, 1843, died October 27, 1863. He married (2) February 23, 1865, Elizabeth Hatfield, born September 4, 1846.
3. Adeline Stephens; married B. R. Stephens.
4. Elizabeth Stephens; married Samuel Hudson.
5. Albert Stephens; married Sis Bowlby.

HENRY SOONOVER

Henry Soonover, died in Greene County leaving an estate which was probated on January 22, 1812. His will, found in Will Book 1 pp. 95, shows he and wife are estranged and says she was formerly Catherine Boos. He patented a tract of land in Whiteley Township, with his son-in-law patenting the tract next to him. Jacob Livengood was not far away.

Children

1. Mary Soonover, born 1775, died December 27, 1851; married Andrew Lantz, Jr.
2. Catherine Soonover; married John Livengood.
3. Dorothy Soonover; married Peter Miller.

DAVID EVANS FAMILY

Just three years after the organization of the Goshen Baptist Church by the Vanmeter Family, on the last Sunday in July 1776, David Evans and his wife, Mary, were received into the Church and David Evans chosen Deacon the same day. He had been born in Wales and removed to Newcastle County, Delaware, from whence in 1775, he migrated to settle on a tract of land just south of Little Whiteley Creek. This land was warranted to him under the title of "Davids" on October 24, 1788, and lay next to the site of Jenkin's Fort. Miss Blanche Evans of Morgantown, West Virginia, a direct descendant of David and Mary Evans, has a number of old letters that have been handed down to her, and has graciously permitted the following copies to be made:

                                          Newcastle County, Delaware

"Whereas the bearer hereof David Evans of Whiteclay Creek Hundred in the county aforesaid, intends moving with his family to settle on a purchase he hath lately made near the Monongahela River:

"This is to certify who it may concern that I John Evans, Esq. one of his Majestys Justice of Peace in and for said County, unsolicited, from my long and personal acquaintance with the said David Evans and his family, have given him this approbation of his past conduct, and do reccomend him as being strictly honest, and upright in his dealings, of civil deportment, and a good neighbor, nor have I ever heard during my long acquaintance, the least impeachment charged to either his moral or religeous character, but has always been esteemed in his neighborhood as a man justly intitled to respect. And his wife and children have likewise supported a good character. Give under my hand and seal this tenth day of April 1775."

JOHN EVANS (Seal)

Miss Evans says that the children of David and Mary Evans were those named in the will of Zachariah Evans. A son, Abel Evans, never came to America, being an attorney in London, England. She has a number of letters written by Abel Evans to her great-grandfather, George Evans, and to David and Mary Evans, from which it is learned that David Evans was twice married, leaving here with his second wife to join some of his children in the Miami Country of Ohio. In one of these letters Abel Evans speaks on September 29, 1809, of the death of his "Brother Williams" and the removal of his sister, Hannah, to the Ohio Country in 1807. In a letter dated February 24, 1794, Abel Evans wrote his father, "I beg to present my duty to you and to her you have authorized me to call my mother, and to express my wishes that you may both in your connection live as happy as I have known you to live in a former part of your life." In a letter to his brother, George Evans, he wrote, that he lamented the decision that persuaded his father to leave his comfortable home in Pennsylvania to go into the wilderness of the Miami Country, where he was fearful that he would not have the comforts of former years, and because of his age, would probably cost him his life. Finally there is a letter from Abel Evans to his brother, George Evans, in which he asks if the place to which his sister, Hannah, and family, moved is near where his father died.

While living on Little Whiteley Creek David Evans was most active in church affairs, often being chosen to represent his church in matters of policy, there being frequent references to him in the Goshen Church Books. The evidence of these books also indicates that he left this section about 1803.

Children of David and Mary Evans

1. Abel Evans, an attorney in London, England, who inherited a house at that place from his brother, Zachariah Evans. Never came to America.
2. Zachariah Evans, a member of Captain John Guthery's Militia Company. He died in Greene County, while it was still a part of Washington County, apparently without issue as his estate is divided among his brothers and sisters whom he named in a will that was probated at Washington on September 25, 1793. (Will Book 1. pp. 207). It is from this will we learn the children of David and Mary Evans.
3. John Evans, who never married.
4. Hannah Evans, whose husband was .... Williams, and who took a letter of dismission from Goshen Baptist Church, on June 25, 1803.
5. Ann Evans, she married a man named McClung, or probably John McClurg, who lived in the Whiteley Section.
6. Lydia Evans, wife of Captain John Holton. His name and rank is often mentioned in pension applications. His own pension application does not mention this service, but says that he served as a member of the Eighth Pennsylvania Regiment of the Continental Line under Colonel Aeneas Mackey (he says McCloy). He joined the Army of Washington at Morristown. Claims he was 76 years of age when applying for his pension on July 23, 1819, from Franklin County, Ohio. A History of

the Regiment in Pennsylvania Archives Series V. Vol. 3 pp. 312, states that he was in the battles of Ash Swamp and Bound Brook, and was wounded in the thigh at Brandywine, and then at Paoli he was wounded by a bayonet.
7. Phoebe Evans, married Moses Tyler. Goshen Records show that on the Sunday prior to the day on which David Evans and Mary were taken into Goshen Church, Moses Tyler and wife, Ann, were received as members. Then Ann Tyler was excommunicated on February 27, 1779. It is not clear what happened to Ann Tyler, but Moses Tyler and wife, Phoebe, removed to Kentucky, Moses getting a letter of Dismission from Goshen on October 25, 1783. The graves of Moses and Phoebe Tyler are in the old Tyler Burying Ground near Louisville, on the road from Fisherville to Jeffersonville, Kentucky.
8. George Evans, a member of Captain John Guthery's Militia Company, remained on the land of David Evans. He was born May 24, 1762, and died January 22, 1854. His wife was Lydia Brice, born November 15, 1778. died November 5, 1862.

Children of George and Lydia (Brice) Evans

1. Mary Evans, born November 5, 1797; never married.
2. Rachel Evans, born March 2, 1799; married Phillip Minor.
3. William Evans, born November 11, 1800; married Mezza Reynolds.
4. Davis Evans, born November 11, 1800, twin of William; married Harriet Wright.
5. Ann Evans, born July 14, 1803; married George E. Reppert.
6. Sarah Evans, born October 1, 1805; married Jennings Crawford.
7. John Evans, born February 4, 1808.
8. Abel Evans, born February 14, 1810; married Ruhanna Minor.
9. Zachariah Evans, born October 12, 1812.
10. Eliza Evans, born May 1, 1815.
11. Benjamin Evans, born April 15, 1817; married Margaret Minor.
12. Phoebe Evans, born December 18, 1819; married Joseph Hammers.

MOSES LAMBERT

Goshen Baptist Church Book notes that on the last Saturday of 1781, Moses Lambert was received into the church by baptism. He had settled on a tract of land, later patented to his sons, Moses, Jr., and Josias Lambert, situated close to Garards Fort. It is probable that Moses Lambert was a member of Captain John Huston's Company of Washington County Militia, though no record of this company is found. It seems likely that when Moses Lambert was baptized into Goshen Church, that it was at the time he was expecting death as his will was probated in Washington County on April 3, 1782, and is found in Will Book 1. pp. 9. In his will he mentions his brother (in-law ?) Ross Crosley, and disposes of a legacy to John Martin's wife, according to father's will, indicating that John Martin had married his sister, and possibly Ross Crosley another sister. Moses Lambert mentions his wife, Ocie, two sons, Moses, the youngest, and Josias, the eldest, and three un-named daughters

JONAS GARARD OR JONAH GARARD

Jonas (Jonah) Garard was ensign in Captain John Huston's

Company, First Battalion, Washington County, Pennsylvania Militia, in February 1782. He was out on a scouting party, possibly on the Crawford Expedition, or incident to it, when he was killed. He left a will which was filed in Washington County on July 2, 1782, shortly after the Crawford Expedition met its fate. Garards Fort was on the land of Jonah Garard as this land was warranted October 28, 1785, under the title "Garard's Fort," thus it would appear that he had applied for the warrant prior to his death, or was taken out by his estate. It was later patented by Peter Myers. Chloe, widow of Jonah Garard, was a sharp tongued lady for which she was several times cited by the Church. She is mentioned in the will, as is a son, Jacob Garard.

THE MOORE FAMILIES

All efforts to trace the relationship of the several Moore Families, who came to the Tenmile Country, have met with little success, but it is thought that at least some of them are descendants of a common ancestor. Considering this lack of information, it is thought best to treat these families individually, pointing out possible connections if information warrants. Several Moore families were on the west side of the Monongahela River before 1770, with some claiming residence on Muddy Creek as early as 1767.

The Bedford County tax list for 1772, lists five of the name as heads of families, with one John Moore designated as "living over the river." Certainly the Simeon Moore in this list was also on the west side, for his son's pension applications prove that fact. In the Orphans Court Docket No. 3 of Westmoreland County, Pennsylvania, dated October 13, 1779, is the estate of one John Moore, naming his wife, Ann, and a number of children. At that date, what is now Greene County was considered to be in Westmoreland County. It seems most likely that he was the John Moore who settled near John Swan's Fort.

Children of John and Ann Moore

1. Samuel Moore, called the eldest child. There is reason to believe he is the Samuel Moore who married Mary Swan, daughter of John and Elizabeth (Lucas) Swan. His wife, Mary, and James Harrod administered his estate in Lincoln County, Kentucky. (Order Book 1, February 1781). He left a son, Samuel Moore, Jr., who is mentioned in the settlement of John Swan's estate in Greene County. It was probably Samuel Moore, Jr., who patented "Sovereignty" on March 6, 1787. This tract of land on Muddy Creek had been warranted on July 15, 1773, to Abraham Armstrong, and was but two farms removed from John Swan's fort. The Draper Mss. 12-C-24, reports that a Mr. Samuel Moore, present owner of certain land, is the son of the man killed at Pickaway under Colonel Harrod. Another Draper entry, 37-J-171, reports that William Harrod, Jr., said his cousin, Samuel Moore, was killed in Bowman's Battle. (The word "Cousin" may be loosely used in this case, for William Harrod, Jr's., grandmother was a Sarah Moore, and his sister, Sarah Harrod, married William Swan, brother of Mary (Swan) Moore. Exact relationship is not shown). Samuel Moore's widow did go to Kentucky and soon married John Isaacs, one of James Harrod's men, (Draper 12-CC-97) by whom she had 13 more children.
2. Robert Moore, said to have married Nancy Swan, sister of Mary (Swan) Moore. Nancy is not named in her father's will

and it is presumed she died before her father.
3. William Moore, there was a man of this name listed in the Muddy Creek Ledger in 1794.
4. Sarah Moore.
5. John Moore. We believe him to be the John Moore who died in Greene County about 1800. His estate was filed here December 13, 1300, and left a son, John Moore, who in 1807, was still a minor child. He applied for a guardian and had Elias Flenniken appointed. The proceedings of this date, along with Orphans Court proceedings of January 25, 1808, and November 28, 1808, disclose that this John Moore had a brother, William Moore, and that his wife had been Elizabeth Russell. She had remarried before November 1808, her second husband being William Armstrong, son of John and Mary (Kennedy) Armstrong. Haddon says this son of John and Elizabeth (Russell) Moore died in 1861.
6. Archibald Moore.
7. Thomas Moore.
8. Andrew Moore.

Another John Moore seems to have died in what is now Greene County about 1784, for his will was filed at Washington, Pennsylvania June 20, 1784. (Will Book 1. pp. 36). Peter Hiller, one of the pioneer settlers with the Swans, Hughes, Vanmeters, etc., was witness to the will. No wife is named.

Children of John Moore

1. Andrew Moore.
2. John Moore.
3. Stoefell (Christopher) Moore.

A third John Moore is the subject of a sketch in Hanna's History of Greene County. Hanna says he came to this country from Dublin, Ireland, in 1770, and that his wife was Hannah Armstrong. There seems little doubt that this is the Dr. John Moore, who is buried in the Armstrong cemetery. His tombstone says he died December 2, 1816 (or 1818), aged 71 years. This burial place suggests that his wife was closely connected with John and Abraham Armstrong, probably a sister. The estate record in Greene County Will Book 1. pp. 190, lists him as John Moore, M. D., and his son, John Moore, Jr., administrator, filed for probate on February 20, 1819. This John Moore was probably the John Moore, school master, listed in the Muddy Creek Ledger, and described as being of Big Whiteley Creek. This man had warranted to him, on February 26, 1788, a tract of land called "Station" and then on February 19, 1793, warranted the adjoining 400 acres under the title of "Moorefields," both situated on the South Branch of Big Whiteley. On January 29, 1810, John Moore, and wife, Hannah, sold a part of Moorefields to James Bradford. (DB. 2. pp. 443). Following the death of Dr. John Moore a series of deeds from his heirs, disposed of much of the land granted to him by the Commonwealth. The census for 1790 indicates that in addition to the three sons, known heirs of Dr. John Moore, there were probably five daughters whose names are not shown in the settlement of his estate. John Moore is in the Greene Township tax list for 1784, showing his residence at that date.

Children of John and Hannah (Armstrong) Moore

1. Armstrong Moore, with wife, Elizabeth, gave a deed, January 27, 1818, which shows they had removed to Monongalia County,

Virginia.
2. Anthony Moore, removed to Wayne Township, where he died leaving a will which was probated December 1, 1832. Deed Book 2. pp. 544, shows a quit claim from his brother, John Moore, and wife, Susannah ...., to Anthony Moore. No record is found of his wife.

Children of Anthony Moore
1. Isaac Moore.
2. Margaret Moore.
3. Catherine Moore.
4. Crawford Moore.
5. Elizabeth Moore.
6. Mary Moore.
7. Hannah Moore.

3. John Moore, Jr., whose family is given in Hannah, made a number of deeds for land that he received when his father died. His wife was Susannah ....

Children of John and Susannah Moore
1. John Moore.
2. James Moore, born 1806, died 1884; married (1) Matilda Franks; married (2) Elizabeth (Brown) Province.
3. Armstrong Moore, wife was Christina ....
4. Abraham Moore.
5. Thomas Moore.
6. Elsie Moore.
7. Jane Moore.
8. Sarah Moore.

FAMILY OF SIMEON MOORE

From the pension applications of John Moore and Thomas Moore, we learn that their father, Simeon Moore, was a very early settler on Muddy Creek, possibly as early as 1767. Simeon Moore moved to Kentucky in 1779, where he became a Trustee of the City of Louisville. Before his death he removed to Mercer County, where his will was made December 7, 1813, and probated at Harrodsburg in October 1814 (Book 5. pp. 104). His wife's name was Keziah ....

Children

1. John Moore, applied for a pension in Mercer County, Kentucky, December 3, 1832, saying he was born in Frederick County, Maryland, and that he was now 75 years of age. A portion of his pension application has been given in our story of the Frontier Rangers. (National Archives Va. S. 11106).

2. Thomas Moore applied for a pension in Mercer County in September 1832, when in his 78th year. He says when he was 12 years of age his father moved to the Monongahela and settled above old Fort Redstone, where Thomas served under Captain Jesse Pigman. Later under Captain William Harrod he served in the Illinois Campaign. Left Fort Redstone by boat and floated down to the Falls of the Ohio, thence about the first of July to Kaskaskia which they took by surprise. Then in February 1779, marched to Vincennes. He returned to the Monongahela but in 1780, joined Captain Henry Prather and was with

Clarke in the Chillicothe Campaign. Was made a captain and marched aganist a big town on the Miami River. His widow, Elizabeth Harbeson, got a pension on her application of September 1836, saying she was married in March 1783 or 1782, at her father's fort. Said her husband died February 25, 1835. Her father was killed by the Indians in an attack on his fort.
3. Samuel Moore, deceased; his father mentions an heir of this Samuel Moore. There is confusion between this Samuel Moore and the Samuel Moore who married Mary Swan. However, this Samuel Moore's widow married Abraham Chapline.
4. Druscilla Moore, deceased; leaving heirs mentioned by her father.

CHRISTIAN COWELL FAMILY

It is not clear if Christian Cowell was the ancestor of all the Greene County family of that name, indications point that way, further search may confirm it. Christian Cowell was probably a native of Bucks County, Pennsylvania, prior to coming west, and may originally have been in New Jersey. He died in Greene County about 1815, where his will is filed in Will Book 1. pp. 149. It was probated on March 20, 1815. His wife, Mary, probably Hufty, survived her husband. These children are named in the will. They may be according to age:
1. Abraham Cowell.
2. Christiana Cowell; married .. .. Himble.
3. Isaac Cowell.
4. Elizabeth Cowell.
5. Jacob Cowell.
6. Catherine Cowell; married   . .. Abbott.
7. Ann Cowell.
8. Phoebe Cowell; married   , ... Stewart.
9. Joseph Cowell, whose wife, Mary .... , died September 9, 1853, at the age of 80 years, and 25 days.
10. Christopher Cowell, who died in Greene County about 1822, leaving a wife, Phoebe .   ...   . His grown up children were:
    1. John Cowell.
    2. Eli Cowell.
    3. Rezin Cowell; all over 21 years of age.
    4. Christopher Cowell, Jr.
    5. Sarah Cowell.
    6. Agnes Cowell.
    7. Eli Cowell.
    8. Mary Cowell.
    9.
    10.
11. Mary Cowell, who married Stephen Rush (DB. 4. pp. 309).
12. Mathias Cowell.
13. Andrew Cowell, who died about 1829, leaving a wife, Elizabeth .... , and these children:
    1. John Cowell.
    2. Agnes Cowell, wife of Robert McNutt.
    3. William Cowell.
    4. Mary Cowell, wife of William Ogden.
    5. Joseph Cowell.
    6. Elizabeth Cowell, wife of John Webster.

7. Rachel Cowell, wife of Edon Webster.
8. Isaac Cowell.
9. Rebecca Cowell.

ISAAC COWELL FAMILY

Isaac Cowell was a native of New Jersey, who served as a private in Captain Nathan Luse's Company, of the Western Regiment of Morris County, New Jersey Militia during 1776 to 1779. He was in the New Jersey State Troops, enlisting in June 1776. Was in the Battles of Long Island, August 27, 1776; Monmouth on June 28, 1778, and then removed to Bedford County, Pennsylvania, in 1781, where he served in the Pennsylvania Militia. He was born in Hunterdon County, New Jersey, April 22, 1757, and moved to Greene County, Pennsylvania about 1808, dying there about 1841. (Greene County Estate No. 1008, probated November 11, 1841). He drew a New Jersey pension as late as 1840.

Isaac Cowell may well have been the son of Christian Cowell, who died in Greene County in 1815. It is also probable that Isaac Cowell was twice married as he left a widow Sarah ...., named in his will.

Children of Isaac Cowell

1. Christian Cowell, who married Nancy Beall.
2. Dorothy Cowell.
3. Mathias Cowell, born February 15, 1783, died March 22, 1866.

Children of Mathias Cowell

1. Solomon Cowell, born August 22, 1815, died February 21, 1878; married Elizabeth Michael, who died October 15, 1897, aged 76 years.
2. Isaac Cowell.
3. Mary Cowell; married .... Baily.
4. Anna Cowell; married .... Wise.

4. Daniel Cowell, son of Isaac and Sarah Cowell, born April 10, 1799, died May 5, 1876. He married Susannah Bowers, born August 1, 1805, died January 19, 1884. Both are buried in Garards Fort Cemetery.

Children of Daniel and Susannah (Bowers) Cowell
(Bible Record copied by Mrs. Amanda Gordon)

1. John Cowell, born December 11, 1823, died November 3, 1885; married Hannah Rose.
2. Justus Cowell, born October 8, 1825, died July 29, 1851.
3. George Cowell, born July 19, 1827.
4. David Cowell, born November 5, 1829, died April 13, 1915; married September 15, 1864, Harriet Long, born October 15, 1843.
5. Mary Cowell, born June 30, 1833, died June 6, 1863.
6. Sarah Cowell, born September 8, 1835, died October 21, 1884.
7. Isaac Cowell, born June 30, 1837, died July 27, 1907.
8. Elizabeth Cowell, born June 6, 1839, died May 25, 1864; married .... Johnson.
9. Rebecca Cowell, born September 12, 1842, died July 11, 1860.
10. Catherine Cowell, born January 13, 1844, died July 16, 1924; married .... McInturff.
11. Jarrette Cowell, born May 1847, died January 6, 1868.
12. Pleasant Jane Cowell, born October 15, 1849, died May

AND ITS PIONEER FAMILIES 647

29, 1863.
5. Jacob Cowell, son of Isaac and Sarah Cowell, born August 21, 1800, died September 18, 1881; married Sophia ...., who died June 12, 1856, aged 52 years, 3 months, and 12 days. She is buried at Garards Fort and he in the cemetery on the Joseph Stoops Farm. Children as taken from will record of Jacob Cowell.

Children
1. Elizabeth Cowell, wife of David Vance, died June 10, 1867, aged 38 years, 2 months, 1 day.
2. Mariah Cowell, died before her father.
3. Anne Cowell; married .... Keener.
4. Elias Cowell.
6. Elizabeth Cowell; married .... Covalt.
7. Margaret Cowell; married .... Iams.
8. Sarah Cowell; married Abner Wharton; had a son, Amos Wharton, born in 1813.

THE HUDSON FAMILY

Joshua Hudson is listed as a single freeman in the Springhill Township, Bedford County Tax List for 1772. There seems little doubt that he was living at that time on the land that Thomas Provins sold to Aaron Jenkins, where a fort was maintained during the Revolution, that is mentioned in several pension applications as Fort Hudson, and later became known as Fort Jenkins. Washington County Deed Book 1-A-pp 200 shows that Thomas Provins sold land to Aaron Jenkins, which was next to James Bellshe and John Long, and that James Bellshe at the same time, sold land adjoining Thomas Provins to William Hudson, heir to Joshua Hudson, who died in 1784, making William Hudson his beneficiary. There seems to be other deeds that escaped recording at that time, but on January 15, 1785, William Hudson received a warrant for a tract of land containing some 235 acres, situated at the first bend in Big Whiteley Creek, and almost surrounded by the crook in the creek. William Hudson died before 1815, leaving a wife Mary ...., and a number of grown children, as shown by quit claim deed. (Greene County Deed Book 3. pp. 131, dated October 11, 1814. Also O. C. Docket 1. pp. 78.) Letters in his estate were taken out by his widow on April 13, 1813.

Children of William and Mary Hudson
1. Rachel Hudson, who married Archibald Gutherie.
2. Elizabeth Hudson; married Robinson Jones.
3. Mary Hudson; married James Jones.
4. Corbly Hudson.
5. James Hudson.
6. William Hudson.
7. Joshua Hudson.
8. Prudence Hudson.
9. Joanna Hudson; married Ephriam Crawford.

THE KEENER FAMILY

When Betty Spicer was returned from captivity among the Indians, she related the events of June 5, 1774, the day on which her parents and five brothers and sisters were killed by the Indians and she and her brother, William Spicer, were carried off into captivity. She told how the Indian Chief Logan with another Indian called The Snake, left the scene of her family's massacre and went directly west, where they met and killed a man named Keener.

Various family traditions have identified this man as the father of Sebastian Keener or as David Keener, but it is now definitely evident that both these traditions are incorrect. Both these men were living at a period ten or more years after this event.

Ulrich Keener (his name is spelled Ulric, Whoolery, Woly, Ulery, and Kiener, Kyner, Kyhner, Canor, and other ways in official records) was a native of the Palatinate, who came to America on the ship "Goodwill," David Crocket, master, which had set sail from Rotterdam and after a brief stop at Falmouth, had arrived at Philadelphia, where on September 27, 1727, he was one of the passengers who took the Oath of Allegiance to the British. In due time he arrived in the Shenandoah Valley, where on February 19, 1746/7, his petition to "Build a water grist mill on ye Narrow Passage Creek near his house" was rejected. (Chalkley Vol. 1 Augusta Co., Va.; Original Petition and Papers in Court 1745-1748).

Sometime after 1773 he left his home in the Shenandoah and became the owner of a tract of land in German Township, Fayette County, Pennsylvania, near the headwaters of Brown's Run, where his neighbors were the Gillelands, Balsingers, Overturfs, etc. It is certain that some of his sons were with him, probably John, Samuel, and Sebastian Keener. Then, in October of 1782, on the 22nd and 23rd, Ulrich Keener described as being of Monongahela County, Virginia, sold land on the North Branch of the Shenandoah River by the Great Wagon Road to Palser Hoover, he of the county aforesaid. The tract contained 300 acres and in addition to the cash involved, required the yearly payment of one "pepper corn," the usual quit claim, lease and release deed. This deed was witnessed by three of his sons who signed their names Ulrich Caner, David Caner, and Boston Caner. (Shenandoah County, D. B. D--pp 34-35). No wife joined the deed so it is safe to assume his wife was dead.

On April 9, 1784, Keener made his will in what is now Fayette County, Pennsylvania. The will was in German script and has been poorly translated. It was witnessed by John Overturf, Valentine Overturf, and John Gilleland, and was probated September 13, 1784. This item disposes of any possibility that he was the man killed on Whiteley Creek. (Fayette County Will Book 1, pp. 11-12).

Nancy (Jackson) Dennison, a descendant, in an interview of 1861, claimed that her mother's grandmother's name was an Airhart or Ehrehard and this is the only record of the wife of Ulrich Keener, but nothing confirms this nor is any wife named in the will. In the mention of his children Ulrich Keener named a grand-daughter, daughter of his son, John Keener, deceased, which is the clue to the identity of the man killed by the Indians.

FAMILY OF ULRICH KEENER

1. John Keener, deceased prior to the date of his father's will in 1784. There seems little doubt that this was the man killed by the party of Indians under Logan and The Snake, and buried by the settlers on the Lantz Bottoms on Big Whiteley Creek. Deveraux Smith in a letter to the Pennsylvania Assembly, dated June 10, 1774, refers to the Spicer Massacre and says in a postscript that "word has just been received that two men were killed the same day at the site of a fort just lately built on Dunkard Creek." His reference refers to Garards Fort, on Big Whiteley Creek, rather than Dunkard Creek, an error easily understood. John Crawford in his Journal tells the same story, saying that Logan sent his prisoners (the Spicer children) ahead with some of his party, and went over on Big Whiteley

where he killed a man named Keener, whose body was found sometime later and buried in the famous meadow of the John Lantz Farm. This site is just east of where Sebastian Keener patented his land after the death of the father in 1784. Two deeds of record of a later date may identify the site where John Keener was killed while making his improvement. In Washington County Deed Book 1-I-559 there is a deed dated December 29, 1792, from John and Mary Bradford for 98½ acres of land at a price of 20 Pounds, being a part of a tract patented to Bradford under the title of "Deer Park." The purchasers were Joseph Price and Hannah Keener. Then on November 16, 1795, Joseph Price, joined by his wife, Elizabeth, and the same Hannah Keener, sold this same land to Michael McCarty for 53 Pounds. Hannah made her mark. The logical conclusion is that Elizabeth Keener, called eldest daughter of John Keener, deceased in the will of Ulrich Keener and given 15 Pounds by him, with her other sister, Hannah Keener, had made a deal for an indistinct claim of their father in the land patented to Bradford and arrived at a settlement which they turned into a neat profit. The land was located at a point where the murder took place. It is also evident that any delay in making a deal was because these children were of an age that would have reached their majority about this time. It is also possible that prior to coming of age they had been back in Shenandoah County where an Ann Keener, widow, was living

near David and Ulrich Keener as the head of a family of three persons in the Census for 1785, and that after Elizabeth had married Joseph Price, accompanied by her sister, Hannah they had come here to settle their father's affairs.

Children of John Keener

1. Elizabeth Keener, called eldest daughter of John Keener, deceased, in will of Ulrich Keener, from whom she received the sum of 15 Pounds.
2. Hannah Keener, called daughter of the murdered Keener by Nancy (Jackson) Dennison, according to a chart communicated to her son, Henry Jackson Dennison, in 1861. Nancy (Jackson) Dennison stated that the widow of the murdered man was named Hannah, which is another name for Ann. She is also the authority for the rest of the history of Hannah Keener, whom she states married Henry Jackson, Jr., and died when about 30 years of age, after being the mother of eight children. Henry Jackson, Jr., was a son of Henry and Elizabeth (Stump) Jackson, and was born in 1770. In 1808, he went with his daughter, Mary Jackson, then but eleven years of age, to Guernsey County, Ohio, where he settled on a farm a half mile from Pleasant City Railroad Station. A brother, Samuel Jackson, settled next to him on the south. After building a cabin and clearing some land he returned to Greene County, Pa., to move his young family to the new location, but while in Ohio his wife had died, so he returned to his clearing with his orphaned children. Several years later he came back to Pennsylvania where he married Rachel Tustin, who accompanied him back to preside over the new home. Eight more children were born of this second marriage. Henry Jackson, Jr., died in 1838, at the age of 68 years, and is buried with his second wife in the Byesville

Cemetery. (Ohio). Rachel (Tustin) Jackson was born in 1789, and died in 1871.

Children

1. Elizabeth Jackson, born in Greene County; married John Fish and lived near Moundsville.
2. Mary Jackson, born October 18, 1797, died January 7, 1893; married, February 14, 1822, Henry Woodrow; lived near Byesville, Ohio.
3. Ruth Jackson; married, November 7, 1822, David Thompson.
4. Nancy Jackson, born in Greene County; married, in 1817, Elias Dennison; lived in Gernsey County, Ohio. She gave the chart to her son telling of the family record.
5. Andrew Jackson; removed to Indiana; wife was .... Booker.
6. James Jackson; killed by a horse at the age of 18 years.
7. Margaret Jackson; married Samuel Kirkpatrick and lived in Guernsey County.
8. Hannah Jackson; married Vincent Dillon; lived in Lawrence County, Ohio.

2. Samuel Keener, son of Ulrich and .... (Ehrehard) Keener, is mentioned in the will of his father as having already received a place. His name is found in the list of taxables in Greene Township, Washington County, Pennsylvania, in 1784. Only later records of him are found in Monongalia County, West Virginia.

Probable Children of Samuel Keener

1. Nancy Keener, daughter of Samuel Keener; married, November 4, 1802, in Monongalia County, West Virginia, to William Phillips.
2. Samuel Keener; married in Monongalia County, West Virginia, November 30, 1807, to Sarah McCormick.
3. Ulrich Keener; married in Monongalia County, West Virginia, December 22, 1810, to Mary Hill.

3. Sebastian (Boston) Keener, son of Ulrich and .... (Ehrehard) Keener, received a Bill of Sale for his father's home place and served as one of the executors with his brother, Samuel Keener, in the estate of Ulrich Keener. The muster roll of Lieutenant William Cress' Company under Colonel Zackwell Morgan is found among the General Edward Hand papers in the Draper Mss. (3NN6) and proves that Sebastian Keener enlisted in the Militia of Monongalia County on September 2, 1777, and was in the service at Fort Pitt on October 1, 1777. The name of Sebastian Keener is on the Greene Township, Washington County, Pennsylvania, Tax lists for 1784, with the notation "lives out of the Township," which is explainable as he had just received the home farm in Fayette County, Pennsylvania. He was taxed in German Township, Fayette County, in 1785. Sebastian Keener was born September 12, 1755. He was probably pioneering on the west side of the Monongahela River when his brother was killed by the Indians. He secured a warrant for his tract of land on Whiteley Creek, next to John Lantz's land, on February 19, 1793, and the same year added to his holding by a purchase from William Minor.

His wife was Margaret Gilleland, daughter of John Gilleland of Fayette County, Pennsylvania, and she is mentioned in his will of March 21, 1820. Margaret (Gilleland) Keener is also mentioned in the will of her sister, Elizabeth Gilleland, and

Margaret's children are named in the will of her sister, Letty Gilleland, who died in Fayette County about 1838. Margaret Gilleland was born January 4, 1758, and died in Greene County on January 26, 1831. She is buried with her husband, who died April 28, 1826. on the original tract of land granted to Sebastian Keener.

Family of Sebastian and Margaret (Gilleland) Keener
1. David Keener, who died in Greene County in 1843. His wife was Margaret Long.

   #### Children of David and Margaret (Long) Keener
   1. Nancy Keener, married William Vance.
   2. Emeline Keener.
   3. Elizabeth Keener.
   4. Benjamin Keener.
   5. David Keener, married Sarah Owens.
   6. Robert Keener.
   7. John Keener.
2. Margaret Keener, daughter of Sebastian and Margaret (Gilleland) Keener, is named in the will of her Aunt Lettie as Jane Duel, while local records indicate she married .... Jewell. Her name was probably Margaret Jane. They had Margaret, William, and Keener Jewell, and went west.
3. Peter Keener, son of Sebastian and Margaret (Gilleland) Keener, died in Greene County, where his estate is listed in O. C. Docket 2. pp. 81-86. Bates History says he married Susan Stewart. There were nine children in the family but only six are named in O. C. Docket.

Jackson, Samuel (A.G. 50,091) d 2 May 1836 in Wash. Co., Tenn. Children listed 2 Sept. 1845.
1. Henry Jackson
2. Susan W. Watkins
3. Adelaide Lyon
4. Harriett Wall
5. Carolina Aiken
6. Alford C. Jackson
   Bounty Land Warrant #2173 Ohio

   #### Children of Peter and Susan (Stewart) Keener
   1. Joseph Keener, married Malinda ....
   2. Peter Keener, Jr.
   3. Rezin Keener.
   4. Sarah Keener.
   5. Susan Keener.
   6. Lindsey Keener, born April 30, 1836.
   7. Elizabeth Keener.
   8. Oliver Keener.
4. John Keener, son of Sebastian and Margaret (Gilleland) Keener, mentioned in the will of Lettie Gilleland. His wife was Elizabeth Herrod.

Children of John and Elizabeth (Herrod) Keener
1. George Keener.
2. Emeline Keener; married .... Wolf.
3. Joseph Keener.
4. David Keener.
5. .... Keener.
6. Leah Keener, married John Durr.
7.

5. William Keener, son of Sebastian and Margaret (Gilleland) Keener, named with six of his children in the will of Lettie Gilleland; none of the children being of age. His wife was Elizabeth Beddler.

Children of William and Elizabeth (Beddler) Keener
1. John Keener, married Sarah Hilderbrand.
2. David Keener, married Sabina Campbell.
3. Margaret Keener, married Conn Franks.
4. Susannah Keener, married George Franks.
5. William Keener, Jr., married Emma Hostetler.
6. Cathy Ann Keener, married Richard Miller.
7. Jane Keener, married Isaac Coldren.

6. Joseph Keener, son of Sebastian and Margaret (Gilleland) Keener, not named by Aunt Lettie Gilleland. His wife was Rebecca Maple, daughter of Stephen and Mary (Slack) Maple.

Children of Joseph and Rebecca (Maple) Keener
1. Amy Keener, married John Wharton.
2. Margaret Keener, married David Moore.
3. Stephen Keener, married Jane Williamson.
4. John Keener, married Phoebe Cox.
5. Benjamin Keener.
6. Nancy Keener, married Phineas Headley.
7. William Keener.
8. Mary Keener, married .... Cravens.
9. David Keener, married Elizabeth Owens.
10. Elizabeth Keener, married .... Stokes.

7. Elizabeth Keener, who died July 9, 1876, was a daughter of Sebastian and Margaret (Gilleland) Keener. She was 88 years, 7 months, and 27 days old when she died and may have been one of the older children. She is listed under her married name in the will of Lettie Gilleland. Her husband was Thomas Owens, and they had eight children. They lived in Perry Township, Greene County, Pennsylvania.

Children of Thomas and Elizabeth (Keener) Owens
1. Thomas A. Owens, born 1806, died November 27, 1874; married Nancy Wells.
2. Margaret Owens, born November 17, 1809, died August 5, 1890; married Benjamin Kiger, born December 27, 1804, died April 21, 1877.
3. John E. Owens, born 1811; married Margaret Brock, born 1823, died July 22, 1843.
4. Louis Owens, moved to Iowa.
5. Peter Owens, married Susan Wells.
6. David Owens, born April 2, 1817, died February 11, 1905; married Louisa Emery, born January 28, 1823,

died September 14, 1896.
7. Elizabeth Owens, married a cousin, David Keener.
8. Jane Owens, born 1825, married Joseph Whitlatch.
8. Charles Keener, son of Sebastian and Margaret (Gilleland) Keener, married Elizabeth Garrison. He is named in the will of Lettie Gilleland.
9. Robert Keener, son of Sebastian and Margaret (Gilleland) Keener, named in the will of his Aunt Lettie Gilleland. He was born April 12, 1803, died April 12, 1889; married Elizabeth Eberhart, born January 19, 1805, died September 12, 1895. They had a family of seven children.

Children of Robert and Elizabeth (Eberhart) Keener

1. Charles Keener, born October 9, 1828, died September 3, 1895; married, October 16, 1857, Tabitha Stewart, born in 1833, died November 28, 1909.
2. Mary Keener, married Gideon Long.
3. Sarah Keener.
4. Sophia Keener, married Jacob Williamson.
5. Sebastian Keener, married Margaret Vance.
6. Elizabeth Keener.
7.

4. Elizabeth Keener, daughter of Ulrich Keener and wife, ... (Ehrehard) Keener, was the wife of Peter Miller when her father died in 1784. He is probably the Peter Miller living in Shenandoah County, Virginia, near the Keeners in the Census of 1785. A Peter Miller patented a tract of land on Dye's Fork of Big Whiteley Creek on March 11, 1807. The same year, on April 30, Peter Miller and others patented a tract of land in Fayette County. A Peter Miller died in Fayette County about 1838, when his will was probated on June 29, 1838.

Children of Peter Miller of Fayette County
(W. B. 2, pp. 123)

1. Joseph Miller.
2. Tacy Miller.
3. Margaret Miller, wife of .... Sharpless.
4. Ann Miller, wife of .... Hoge; had a daughter, Tacy Hoge.
5. Mary Miller, wife of .... Downs.
6. David Miller.

5. Barbara Keener, daughter of Ulrich and .... (Ehrehard) Keener, married .... Souter (or Souder).
6. Ulrich Keener, one of the elder sons of Ulrich Keener, remained in the Shenandoah where in 1785, he was at the head of a household of nine persons. His father had already provided for him prior to the will. On March 23, 1795, he got a patent for land in Shenandoah from Jonathan Clark and others for acreage which he sold by a deed of April 11, 1797. Another tract patented to him by the same authorities in 1799, he sold September 29, 1801, to John Stover. In both deeds he is joined by his wife, Ann .... (Shenandoah County Deed Book K-477, K-488, L-94, M-546). It is presumed that he moved from there as no record is found of his estate.
7. Peter Keener, also previously provided for by his father. He paid a hemp tax in Shenandoah County, Virginia. Was one of the elder sons of Ulrich Keener.
8. David Keener, also previously taken care of by his father, Ulrich Keener; remained in the Shenandoah, where he was head

of a household of seven persons in 1785. He died there before 1809. Partition of his land shows that his wife was Eva ...., who got 36 acres of his tract in the partition. (Deed Book V-268, Shenandoah County). (WB. K-352, WB. H-45-47-108). His widow, Eva, died before March 1817, as shown by Court Records.

Children of David and Eva Keener

1. Rebecca Keener; married, November 25, 1807, Benjamin Bowman.
2. Eve Keener; married, February 4, 1797, Isaac Bowman.
3. Barbara Keener; married, April 24, 1798, George Spots.
4. Abraham Keener, died prior to 1817.
5. William Keener.
6. Elizabeth Keener; married, March 14, 1807, David Gochenour.
7. Ann Keener, died before her father. Her husband was John Brown, whom she married in 1791.

Each of these children got a strip of land as shown by a map of the partition.

THE DYE FAMILY

John, Benjamin, and Andrew Dye, sons of James and Sarah Dye of Middlesex County, New Jersey, were among the early settlers on Big Whiteley Creek. An Isaac Dye, with wife, Hannah, also was a settler, but went to Hardin County, Kentucky, with the Jacob Vanmeter Family about 1780, as shown by his letter of dismission from Goshen Baptist Church, granted September 18, 1779. Pension records show that John Dye removed to Brown County, Ohio, where on July 22, 1819, he applied for a pension for Pennsylvania service, stating that he was then 79 years of age. His name is among the members of Goshen Baptist Church at Garards Fort. Benjamin Dye, whose wife was a Lemley, died about 1788, and left minor children among whom were a son, James Dye, for whom Stephen Gapen was appointed guardian by Greene County, Pennsylvania, Orphan's Court on September 12, 1799. Daniel Jones was appointed guardian for George Dye and Sarah Dye, children of Benjamin, on November 14, 1806.

Andrew Dye, son of James and Sarah Dye, was born in Middlesex County, New Jersey, in 1744. He removed to Maryland and from there to Whiteley Creek in what is now Greene County, Pennsylvania, where, in May 1785, he had warranted to him a tract of land under the title "Sparrows Nest." He had met and married Sarah Minor, sister of Colonel John Minor, one of the first settlers on Whiteley Creek, a daughter of Stephen and Athaliah (Updyke) Minor. During the Revolution he was a soldier in the Pennsylvania Line (Penna. Arch. Series VI. Vol. 3, pp. 1367) for which service he received a pension. Sometime after 1790, he removed to Kentucky and then in 1803, to Ohio, where he died at Stillwater, Newton Township, Miami County, on July 5, 1835. His second wife was Mrs. Ann (Lamb) Evans, who was born April 11, 1767, and died January 7, 1843. Andrew Dye and second wife are buried in Pleasant Hill, Miami County, Ohio.

Mrs. Ann (Lamb) Evans was the widow of Charles Evans, who died in Mason County, Kentucky. His will, made on November 20, 1812, was probated there on December 14, 1812. They had at least two children who are named in the will, Job Evans and Elizabeth, wife of William Dye.

Children of Andrew and Sarah (Minor) Dye

1. James Dye, son of Andrew and Sarah (Minor) Dye, was born December 1, 1769. He died in Greene County, Pennsylvania, on June 11, 1842, and is buried with his first wife on the Oscar Hunnell Farm, near Brock. His will is in Greene County Will Book 2. pp. 159, and was probated on November 3, 1842. List of his children is also in O. C. Docket 2, pp. 238, dated March 1843. His first wife was Mary ...., who died June 15, 1821, at the age of 53 years. His second wife was Anna ....

Children

1. William Dye, died in Wayne Township, Greene County, about 1853. (Will Book 3. pp. 135, probated August 18, 1853).

    #### Children
    1. Nancy Dye.
    2. Priscilla Dye.
    3. John Dye.
    4. Elizabeth Dye.
    5. James Dye.
2. Andrew Dye.
3. Sarah Dye; married .... Lantz.
4. John Dye.
5. Litel Dye.
6. Rezin Dye.
7. Massy Dye; married .... Lantz.
8. Cassandra Dye; married John Bradford.
9. Mary Dye; married James Bradford.
10. Priscilla Dye.
11. Melinda Dye; minor under 14 years in 1853.
12. Lucretia Dye; minor under 14 years.
13. Elizabeth Dye; minor under 14 years.

2. Stephen Dye, son of Andrew and Sarah (Minor) Dye, born December 23, 1770, died September 14, 1851. He married, (1) in Shelby County, Ohio, Mehitable Garard. After her death he married, (2) on November 1, 1827, Mary (Hufty) Dye-Knight, widow of his brother, Samuel Dye, and of .... Knight. He married, (3) July 27, 1841, Margaret Stillwell, and on her death he married, (4) November 25, 1843, Rachel Moreland. Thirteen children were born to the first marriage, and three to the second. He was father of nineteen children by his four wives.

Children
1. John Dye.
2. Sarah Dye, born March 12, 1794.
3. Andrew Dye, born December 14, 1795.
4. Benjamin Dye, born October 1, 1797.
5. James Dye, born July 7, 1800.
6. Rachel Dye, born December 1, 1801; married, March 21, 1821, John W. Lee.
7. Stephen Dye, born February 9, 1802; married, March 14, 1821, Nancy N. Lee.
8. Susannah Dye, born December 1805; married, August 12, 1823, Aaron French.
9. Fielding Dye, born January 4, 1808; married, April 26, 1845, Catherine Abbott.
10. Nancy Dye, born March 14, 1809.

11. Jacob Dye, born July 19, 1810.
12. Cornelius Dye, born February 9, 1812.
13. Madison Dye, born April 15, 1819.
14. Sarah Dye, born 1844.
15. Samuel A. Dye, born 1846.
16. Margaret Dye, born 1851.

3. John Minor Dye, born August 24, 1773, died in Elizabeth Township, Miami County, Ohio, on April 1, 1842. His wife was Elizabeth Clyne, daughter of Jacob and Eleanor (Vanmeter) Clyne, who was born in 1776, on Muddy Creek, Greene County, Pennsylvania, and died in Miami County, Ohio, January 6, 1852. They were parents of fourteen children. Named in Will Book A. and B. pp. 229, Miami County, Ohio, are ten of them.

Children of John Minor and Elizabeth (Clyne) Dye

1. Clyne Dye (or Clyme); married, January 14, 1851, James Winters.
2. Isaac C. Dye.
3. Andrew C. Dye.
4. John C. Dye.
5. Priscilla Dye; married, March 6, 1834, John S. Armstrong.
6. Simon Dye.
7. Eleanor Dye; married .... Statler.
8. Sarah Dye; married, May 27, 1813, Abraham Statler.
9. Ruth Dye; married, May 30, 1822, Thomas DeWees.
10.
11.
12.
13.
14.

4. Andrew Dye, Jr., born December 25, 1774, died in Miami County, Ohio, April 3, 1838. He may have married twice, one of his wives being Elizabeth Martin, whom he married in 1814. He was the father of ten children.

5. Frances Dye, born January 7, 1777. She married, April 3, 1795, Thomas Sayers, son of William and Mary (Fithian) Sayers. He was born December 26, 1770. They had 17 children.

6. Benjamin Dye, born December 27, 1779, died July 23, 1843; buried in Knoop Cemetery in Elizabeth Township, Miami County, Ohio. He married, (1) in 1798, Elizabeth Jackson, born 1777, died February 5, 1817. He then married, on June 6, 1817, Priscilla (Long) Dye, widow of his brother, Vincent Dye. She was born in 1786 and died December 12, 1848, a daughter of Jeremiah and Mary (Ivers) Long. There were eleven children by first marriage and six by the second. Ten children are named in Will Book 2. pp. 12, Miami County, Ohio.

Children of Benjamin Dye

1. Vincent Dye; married, October 12, 1820, Rebecca Sevaile.
2. James Dye.
3. William Dye; married, April 5, 1826, Nancy Meeks. .
4. Benjamin Dye.
5. Jeremiah Dye.
6. Elizabeth Dye; married John Pettit.
7. Sarah Dye.
8. Maria Dye; married John Karsh.
9. Priscilla Dye.
10. Letty Dye; married, August 24, 1843, Aaron A. Meredith.
11. Horatio Dye.

AND ITS PIONEER FAMILIES 657

12. John Dye.
13.
14.
15.
16.
17.
7. Samuel Dye, died in 1814, and is said to have been first person buried in Bethel Church Cemetery on old Troy Pike in Miami County. His wife was Mary Hufty, born in Bucks County, Pennsylvania, daughter of Jacob and Sarah (Barclay) Hufty. After the death of Samuel Dye, she married .... Knight, and then on November 1, 1827, she married Stephen Dye, a brother of her first husband. No children are recorded.
8. Vincent Dye, died in 1815, leaving a widow, Priscilla, and six children. His widow then married Benjamin Dye, brother of her first husband and had six more children. She was a daughter of Jeremiah and Mary (Ivers) Long.

Children of Vincent and Priscilla (Long) Dye

1. Malen Dye.
2. Francis Dye.
3. Fanny Dye.
4. Mary Dye.
5. Belinda Dye; married, December 19, 1833, Montgomery Smith.
6. Minor Dye; married, October 25, 1840, Maria H. Thomas.

9. Rachel Dye, daughter of Andrew and Sarah (Minor) Dye, died in Miami County, Ohio, in 1823. She married there, on April 25, 1809, Cornelius Westfall. It is probable that they had no children as her estate was divided among her relatives.
10. Jane Dye, daughter of Andrew and Sarah (Minor) Dye; married .... Lewis.
11. William Dye, son of Andrew and Sarah (Minor) Dye, born March 10, 1791, died January 28, 1823; buried in the Knoop Cemetery in Miami County. His wife was Elizabeth Evans, daughter of his stepmother, and she died in 1850.

THE FRANKS FAMILY

The Franks Family of Greene County, is descended from Michael Franks, an immigrant from Franconia, probably the same Michael Franks who arrived at Philadelphia on the ship Priscilla, William Meier, Captain, and took the Oath of Allegiance to the British at Philadelphia on September 11, 1749. From there he proceeded to Baltimore where he probably spent the remainder of his life. He brought with him to America two sons and a daughter, the latter, of whom all records are lost. The sons, Michael and Jacob Franks, born in 1782, removed to what is now Fayette County, Pennsylvania, in 1753, the date being established by the fact that Michael's eldest son was born at one of their camps on the Youghiogheny, during the course of the journey. This son, Henry Franks, was born on June 11, 1753. His mother was a Livengood. The second Michael Franks settled on Brown's Run, Fayette County, as did his brother, Jacob, and both Michael and his son, Henry, were soldiers in the Revolution. (Penn, Arch. Series III, Vol. 23, pp. 228-285-321-335, and Series VI, Vol. 2, pp. 400). The family of Michael and Sarah (?) (Livengood) Franks as given in Haddon were:

Henry Franks, born June 6, 1753.
Charlotte Franks; married Jacob Furst and remained in Fayette County.
Abraham Franks.
John Franks; removed to Wayne County, Ohio.
Mary, married Nicholas Helmic and went to Ohio.
Elizabeth Franks, married Phineas Flaherty and went to Ohio.
Dorothy Franks, married Jacob Miller.
Catherine Franks, married Jacob Hatfield.
George Franks, who married Elizabeth ...., of whom later. Settled in Greene County, Pennsylvania.
Michael Franks, born in 1773; married Amy Furst.
(Haddon's History of Fayette and Greene County, pp. 560.)

FAMILY OF GEORGE FRANKS

There is evidence that one of the Franks crossed the Monongahela before 1771, and had some sort of title to land on Smith Creek, possibly only a squatters claim, but in due time George Franks, son of Michael and .... (Livengood) Franks, removed from Fayette County and made a permanent settlement in the vicinity of Blacksville. His wife was Elizabeth .. . . George Franks died in Whiteley Township, Greene County, before 1857, as shown by O. C. Docket 4, pp. 236, which shows his wife was Elizabeth and that he had these children:
1. Alexander Franks.
2. Jacob Franks.
3. George Franks, living in Wood County, West Virginia.
4. James K. Franks.
5. Matilda Franks; married James Moore, born 1806, died 1884.

Children

1. James F. Moore.
2. Thomas Moore; removed to Wood County, West Virginia.
3. George W. Moore, born January 3, 1834; married, 1859, Louisa Phillips.
4. Susannah Moore.
5. Elsie Moore; married Abraham Cosgray.
6. Nancy Moore.
7. Peter D. Moore.
8. Alexander Moore, born June 27, 1842, died March 20, 1900; married, January 15, 1863, Susan A. Minor, born May 16, 1845, died June 4, 1900. She was a daughter of William and Margaret (Lantz) Minor.

6. Sarah Franks; married Alexander McDougal.
7. Margaret Franks, married John Mapel.

ROBERT JONES FAMILY OF GREENE TOWNSHIP

Some time prior to 1780, Robert Jones settled on a tract of land on a branch of Big Whiteley Creek, near Fort Hudson, for on July 29 of that year he was chosen to represent Goshen Baptist Church "in the affair over the River." Tombstone records at Gararts Fort indicate that he was born in 1743, probably in Chester County, Pennsylvania, or the State of Delaware. His wife was Jane Bolton, who joined the Goshen Church on October 29, 1785. Both husband and wife secured warrants for tracts of land on April 15, 1785, Robert's tract being known under the title "Patriots Grove," while Jane's tract was known as "Lions Head." He could be the Robert Jones who received pay for service in defense of the Frontier in 1782, for a number of his neighbors are found in the same list. (Penna. Arch. Series VI, Vol. 2. pp. 348). Robert Jones died April 15, 1809, and his estate was filed in O. C. Docket 1. pp. 28. His wife, who was born in 1744, died July 22, 1826, at the age of 82 years and two months. Both are buried in Garards Fort Cemetery, and markers are still legible.

Children of Robert and Jane (Bolton) Jones
1. John Jones.
2. Rebecca Jones, wife of George Reynolds.
3. Rachel Jones, born 1785, died March 20, 1867; married, 1803, to Lewis Evans, born 1778, died April 28, 1858. He was a son of Jeremiah and Mary (Evans) Evans of Chester County, Pa.

Children of Lewis and Rachel (Jones) Evans
1. Evan Evans, born December 20, 1805, died June 18, 1865; married, March 22, 1827, Nancy Myers, born October 10, 1806, died May 14, 1836. His second wife was Rebecca South. Nancy Myers was a daughter of Peter A. and Pleasants (Corbly) Myers. Their son, Lewis K. Evans, born October 10, 1831, was the author of the "Evans Papers" and later a newspaper editor in Michigan.
2. Mary Evans, born May 9, 1807; wife of Dr. Joseph Stephenson.
3. Jesse Evans, born June 15, 1810.
4. Jeremiah Evans, born December 10, 1812.
5. Jane Evans, born April 12, 1815; married Alfred Myers.
6. Robert Evans, born June 15, 1817.
7. Eliza Evans, born February 24, 1819.
8. Rebecca Evans, born October 10, 1821; married Isaac Lynn.

4. Mary Jones, deceased at the time of her father's will; had been the wife of Jesse Evans. She left the following children:
   1. Samuel Evans.
   2. Eliza Evans.

DUNKARD CREEK

There is nothing in the History of the Tenmile Country more definite than the settlement of the Eckerlein Brothers on Dunkard Creek in 1745. It is related with this date in the Euphrata Chronicles on pages 158-195-197 and reported by I. D. Rupp in his "Thirty Thousand Names." While it is true they were not permanent in that they went back to the Cheat, where they suffered at the hands of the Indians, they nevertheless were here long enough to give the name of their religion to the stream. This Valley being the old trail followed by the Indian warriors on their raids to the north and south, was naturally the first trail followed by the white man after he struck the Cheat River in Virginia.

The next official notice is of 1757, when the surveyors of the Mason Dixon Line reached Dunkard Creek, where they were stopped by the Indians and the line remained unfinished until 1784. The following year, in 1758, Thomas Decker and others attempted a settlement near the site of Morgantown, and no doubt made survey trips down the Monongahela, where others soon to follow found a place in the River that could be forded at low water, and crossed near the mouth of Dunkard Creek. Within the next two years, Augustine Dillinger, who had come to the Fayette County side, crossed the "Cheat Riffle," as the ford was later called, and erected his cabin in a grove of poplars a short distance south of the mouth of Dunkard Creek. He was followed in a short time by the party from Lancaster County, Pennsylvania, the Sykes, Waggoner, Bonnett, Wetzel, and Selsor Families, who tarried on this creek for a time before moving further westward to what became Wetzel and Marshall Counties in West Virginia. They were followed by the Garrisons of Maryland, the Enochs of Virginia, and the Shelbys, also from Maryland.

Even after the Mason-Dixon Line had been chosen and the boundaries decided, Dunkard Creek almost saw a bloody war between the adherents of Virginia and Pennsylvania, for we read in the Pennsylvania Archives, how a group of men under Henry Vanmeter, and apparently chosen from Jesse Pigman's Company, approached the surveyors on Dunkard Creek and dared them to cross, backing up their defiance with a show of arms. The disturbers of the peace were promptly indicted for riot and peace came to a peaceful stream.

BENJAMIN TITUS FAMILY

Benjamin Titus, son of John Titus of New Jersey, and grandson of John and Rebecca Titus, originally of New England and later of New Jersey, was born in New Jersey on August 2, 1759. Benjamin Titus was a member of Captain John Mott's Militia Company from Hunterdon County, New Jersey, and took part in the Battle of Trenton, when his captain acted as guide to General George Washington in that Battle. He was first married to Rachel ...., in New Jersey, his wife dying there sometime after 1782. On October 15, 1787, Benjamin Titus got a warrant for a 425-acre tract of land lying astride Rudolph's Run, but sold it to George and Jacob Wolf, who secured a patent in 1789. It is not probable that Benjamin Titus ever lived on this land, but settled first in Dunkard Township, where he met and married for his second wife, Rachel Gapen. She was born September 6, 1767, and died August 17, 1808, and was a daughter of Zachariah and Ruth (Tindall) Gapen. The year following the death of Rachel Gapen, Benjamin Titus married his third Rachel, this time the bride being Rachel Mercer, with whom he was living at the time of his death, December 17, 1849. Benjamin Titus was father of two children by his first marriage; seven by the second, and five by the third.

References: Strykker's "New Jersey in the Revolutionary War," pp. 787 and 402; Greene County WB. 3, pp. 120, probated January 26, 1853.

Children of Benjamin Titus

1. Charlotte Titus, born May 9, 1780; married .... Snyder.
2. Sarah Titus, born July 7, 1782.
3. Ruth Titus, born July 17, 1792.
4. Elizabeth Titus, born November 12, 1794.
5. Stephen Titus, born January 1, 1797.
6. Benjamin Titus, Jr., born May 16, 1799.
7. Nathaniel Titus, born September 12, 1801.
8. Rebecca Titus, born May 3, 1804.
9. Eli Titus, born May 3, 1808, died in Greene County, Pennsylvania, April 14, 1896. He married, June 2, 1830, Sarah Myers, born June 16, 1810, daughter of Peter and Pleasants (Corbly) Myers. She died June 15, 1897.
10. Maria Titus, born January 15, 1810; married Lewis Gapen.
11. Matilda Titus, born August 28, 1812; married Levi Prickett.
12. Rachel Titus, born August 15, 1815; married .... Prickett.

13. Thomas Titus, born July 1, 1816, died March 19, 1895; married Orpha Gregg, born October 16, 1813, daughter of Joseph and Cassandra (Corbly) Gregg. They were married March 19, 1843. Orpha (Gregg) Titus died December 16, 1873.
14. Levi Titus, born September 29, 1821. He married .... Stewart.

THE SOUTH FAMILY

Mr. Richard P. South of Ardmore, Pennsylvania, has sent in the will record of Joseph South, the New Jersey ancestor of the South Family of Greene County. Joseph South made his will on May 2, 1811, while a resident of East Windsor Township, Middlesex County, New Jersey. This will was filed for probate in that County on January 18, 1813. Mr. Richard South says that his ancestor's wife was Sarah Mann, whose name was signed as a witness to the will. I believe this is in error as it is not probable that a wife would be the witness of a will in which she must be a beneficiary, and since no wife is mentioned in the will, it seems more likely that the wife of Joseph South had died prior to the making of the will. Charles South and Abiah Danser were the administrators. Suggest that the wife of Joseph South was a Miss Gilpin.

Children Named in the Will of Joseph South

1. Elisha South.
2. Isaac South.
3. Benjamin South.
4. Keziah South, who married .... Barmore; had sons, Samuel and Joseph Barmore.
5. Major South.
6. Charles South; administrator.
7. Mary South; married .... Danser.
8. Sarah South; married .... Danser.
9. Daughter, un-named, who married .... Jewell; leaving a son, Gill Jewell.

FAMILY OF ELIJAH AND RACHEL SOUTH

Elisha South, son of Joseph South, later known as Elijah South was born in New Jersey and served as a Teamster in Captain Cahill's Team Brigade and in the Middlesex County Militia from Middlesex County, New Jersey. (Strykker pp. 762-867). He removed to Greene County, Pennsylvania about 1796 and settled on Dunkard Creek, where he died about 1837, his estate being set up for administration in March Court of that year. (O. C. Docket 2. pp. 99). His wife was Rachel ....

Children

1. Elijah South, died March 1, 1880, aged 82 years, 5 months, and 15 days; married Nancy Johnson, daughter of Joseph Johnson. Nancy died August 20, 1877, aged 77 years, 4 months and 8 days.
2. Charles South.
3. Dissaway South, died about 1843 as shown by partition proceedings of September 8, 1843. His wife was Rhuannah ....

Children of Dissaway and Rhuannah South

1. Justus South.
2. Elijah South.
3. William South.

4. Job South.
   5. Clarissa South.
   6. Ann South.
   7. Dissaway South.
   4. Keziah South; married .... Taylor.
   5. Rachel South; married .... Billingsley.
   6. Joseph South.
   7. Rebecca South, who married .... Kerns.
   8. John South.

BENJAMIN SOUTH FAMILY

The pension claim of Benjamin South, son of Joseph South of Middlesex County, New Jersey, states that he was born in Windsor Township in February 1758. He entered the Militia of Middlesex County in 1776 and did numerous tours of duty including the Battle of Staten Island. His service included: one month under Captain James Barr in Colonel William Scudder's Regiment; one month in Captain Jonathan Coomb's Company; two months in Captain John Schenk's Company in Colonel John Nielson's Regiment; one month in Captain Samuel Stout's Company under General Dickinson; one month in Captain James Debow's Company in Colonel Nixon's Regiment. He also served with his brother, Elijah, in Captain Cahill's Team Brigade.

Benjamin South was allowed a pension for his services on his application from Greene County, August 27, 1832. He stated that he had married, 1778-80, in New Jersey, Elizabeth Slack, daughter of Benjamin and Rebecca (Shooley) Slack, who was born June 4, 1755. (Pension claim No. 9939). Benjamin South died in Greene County on May 2, 1839, and his wife died there on April 3, 1848. Both are buried in the South Cemetery near Garards Fort. His will is in Will Book 2. pp. 106, Greene County.

Children of Benjamin and Elizabeth (Slack) South
1. Sarah Elizabeth South, born November 14, 1779. She married Noah Minor, son of Colonel William and Ellen (Phillips) Minor. He was born November 2, 1779, and died in 1865. After the death of Sarah (South) Minor, Noah Minor married Miss Minks, by whom he also had children.

Children of Noah and Sarah (South) Minor
   1. Otho Minor; married Pleasants Myers.
   2. Samuel Minor; married Fanny Phillips.
   3. Elizabeth Minor; married .... Thompson.
   4. Nancy Minor; married Ellis Hartley.
   5. Sarah Minor; married Josephus Hartley.
   6. Rebecca Minor; married .... Knotts.
2. Rebecca South, born 1783, died August 27, 1876; married Otho Minor, son of Colonel John and Cassandra (Williams) Minor, born December 10, 1776; died October 15, 1831.

Child of Otho and Rebecca (South) Minor
   1. John Minor, born June 8, 1802, died March 25, 1891; married Malinda Lantz, born April 2, 1808, died February 15, 1890. Both buried at Garards Fort.
3. Enoch South, son of Benjamin and Elizabeth (Slack) South, born July 27, 1787, died 1863; married Ruth Gregg, daughter of John and Orpha (Stubbs) Gregg. She was born in 1788.

Children of Enoch and Ruth (Gregg) South
1. Benjamin South; married Matilda Gapen.
2. John South; married Velinda Everly.
3. Delilah South.
4. Cassandra South; married Jacob Lantz.
5. Rebecca South; married Evan Evans.
6. Elizabeth South; married Abner Baily.
7. Ruth South; married William Knotts.
8. Sarah South; married Abijah South.
9. Nancy South; married .... Bowlby.
10. Malinda South; married William Britton.
11. Mariah South; died at age of 14 years.

4. Elizabeth South, daughter of Benjamin and Elizabeth (Slack) South, was born July 1798.

STEPHEN MAPEL FAMILY

The pension record of Stephen Mapel says he was born in Middlesex County, New Jersey on February 17, 1758. He died in Greene County, Pennsylvania, October 23, 1844, but his tombstone in the old cemetery at Mapletown gives the dates 1763-1844. Mr. E. L. Williamson says he was a son of an older Stephen Mapel. He received his pension for services as a drummer in the New Jersey Militia, but his application for a pension says he served in all more than five years with New Jersey Troops. His captains were Jonathan Coombs and James Barr, under Colonels Robert Nixon and Scudder. He was granted his pension on his application from Greene County executed on January 11, 1833, and he is listed as a pensioner aged 81 years of age in the 1840 census. After his death his widow also drew a pension. She was Mary Slack, daughter of Benjamin and Rebecca (Schooley) Slack, and was born in Monmouth County, New Jersey, August 26, 1758. She died April 25, 1845. Stephen Mapel and Mary Slack were married in New Jersey on November 2, 1780. Family tradition says they migrated to the Tenmile Country when the son, Robert, was six years old, about 1788-89.

Children of Stephen and Mary (Slack) Mapel
(Dates from Pension Record of Mary Mapel)

1. Thomas Mapel, born August 5, 1781, died in Dunkard Township, Greene County, September 12, 1849. His wife was Elizabeth Shroyer. Thomas Mapel was a preacher. Elizabeth died May 14, 1846, aged 73 years, 9 months, 24 days. Buried in Bald Hill Cemetery.

Children of Thomas and Elizabeth (Shroyer) Mapel
1. Benjamin Mapel; removed to Zanesville, Ohio.
2. Rebecca Mapel; married Rev. Edward Evans Parrish. They went to Oregon.
3. Stephen Mapel; married Ruth Furman. They lived in Missouri.
4. Nancy Mapel; married Samuel Caldwell of Jefferson, Pennsylvania.
5. Mariah Mapel, born November 11, 1809, died October 28, 1815.
6. John Mapel; married Nancy Smith. Went to Des Moines, Iowa.
7. Sarah Mapel; married Ebenezer McGuire.

8. Simon Mapel; married (1) Joanna McGuire; (2) Rachel Thrapp; (3) Catherine McClure.
9. Thomas Mapel; married Susannah Peckinpaugh.
10. Elizabeth Mapel; married George Ray. Lived at Morgantown, West Virginia.
11. Lydia Mapel; married George Keener of Taylortown.
12. Joseph Mapel; married Margaret Sweeney.
13. Lewis Mapel; married Debora Ritter, Maples, Indiana.
14. Andrew J. Mapel; married Ruhama Taylor.

2. Robert Mapel, born November 3, 1783, died February 16, 1872; buried with his father in the old cemetery at Mapletown. In 1825, he purchased land at the site of present Bobtown. Here he built a mill for grinding flour, also a carding mill, and operated a store. It is said that he also operated an underground station for escaped slaves. He was a member of the Masonic Lodge at Greensboro. Robert Mapel is credited with being the first to discover oil in Greene County. He was married (1) to Jane Hall on December 25, 1802. She was the mother of his children. His second wife was Julia Griffin, (3) Sarah Tucker.

Children of Robert and Jane (Hall) Mapel

1. Alfred Mapel; married Mariah Kinsey.
2. Eliza Mapel; married Bowers Davis.
3. Malinda Mapel; married Thomas H. Higginbottom.
4. Robert Mapel, Jr., died unmarried at the age of 27 years, on March 22, 1850.
5. Elmer Mapel; died young.
6. Mary Mapel; married George Johnson of Brownsville, Pennsylvania.

3. Amy Mapel, born April 22, 1785; married Lewis Donham. She died before her father.

Child of Lewis and Amy (Mapel) Donham

1. John Donham; married Rebecca Engle.

4. Rebecca Mapel, born August 26, 1788; married Joseph Keener, son of Sebastian and Margaret (Gilleland) Keener.

Children of Joseph and Rebecca (Mapel) Keener

1. Amy Keener; married John Wharton.
2. Margaret Keener; married David Moore.
3. David Keener; married Elizabeth Owens.
4. John Keener; married Phoebe Cox.
5. William Keener.
6. Benjamin Keener, went to Michigan.
7. Elizabeth Keener; married (1) .... Stokes; (2) Dr. Hunt; (3) .... Reese.
8. Stephen Keener; married Jane Williamson.
9. Mary Keener; married .... Craven.
10. Nancy Keener; married Phineas Headley.

5. Elizabeth Mapel, born May 3, 1792; married Solomon Altman.
6. Stephen Mapel, born February 9, 1795; died young.
7. Sarah Mapel, born January 25, 1797; married Moses Royce.
8. Benjamin Mapel, born November 7, 1799; married (1) Mary Burris (Burrows ?). His second wife was Mary Ann Phillips. There were nine children by the first wife and six by the second. His third wife was Margaret .. ..

Children of Benjamin Mapel

1. Mariah Mapel; married Dissaway South.

2. Matilda Mapel; married Williamson Hart.
3. Albert F. Mapel; married (1) Rebecca Hensel.
4. Alpheus Mapel; married (1) Martha Shaefer; (2) Maria Long.
5. Clark Mapel, born October 22, 1832, died March 1, 1837.
6. Stephen Mapel; married Belle Pratt.
7. George Mapel; married Frances Neil.
8. Malinda Mapel; married Archibald Sicklesmith.
9. Harry Mapel; married Lizzie Dunlap.
10. Margaret Mapel; married .... Ruff.
11. Mary J. Mapel; married .... Malone.
12. Amanda Mapel; married .... Cannon.
13. Belle Mapel; married .... Core.
14. Robert T. Mapel; married Barbara Linton.
15. Thomas Mapel.
9. Mary Mapel, born May 3, 1802; married Edward Gregg.

THE WILLIAMSON FAMILY

On September 11, 1833, Lieutenant James Williamson, a resident of Dunkard Township, Greene County applied for a pension stating he was 77 years of age. He says that while a resident of Reading, Pennsylvania, he enlisted in June 1775, and served for one year as a sergeant in Captain George Nagel's Company in Colonel William Thompson's Regiment. In the Fall of 1776, he was appointed a second lieutenant and served for several months in Captain Peter Withington's Company and then was made a first lieutenant in Captain Hannaniah Lincoln's Company. He was in the Battles of Brandywine, Princeton, and Monmouth during his more than two years' service. (National Archives S-22597).

James Williamson appears to have removed from Berks County to Northampton County, Pennsylvania, where he was living in 1790, and to which his son, Hugh Williamson, returned after the death of his father in Greene County about 1840. James Williamson's estate was filed for probate March 28, 1840, and an account is in O. C. Docket 2, pp. 205, filed in December 1841. He was twice married, the first wife being Elizabeth Evans, who was the mother of his children. His second wife was Elizabeth, widow of Leonard Garrison, whose maiden name had been Gray.

Children of James and Elizabeth (Evans) Williamson
1. Hugh Williamson, went back to Northampton County, where he was living on May 10, 1845, in Bushkill Township, when he and his wife made a deed to his son, Daniel. His wife was Susannah Higler (or Hicker). Hugh Williamson died in Northampton County.

Children of Hugh and Susannah (Higler) Williamson
1. Jacob Williamson, born 1823, died January 20, 1894; remained in Greene County. Married Sophia Keener, born 1831, died February 2, 1902; daughter of Robert Keener.
2. Daniel Williamson, married Orpha Morrison and had Hugh, Benjamin, and Mary, wife of B. L. South.
3. Joseph Williamson, went East with his father.
4. James Williamson, went East with his father.
5. George Williamson, went East with his father.
6. Mary Williamson.
7. Susan Williamson.
2. James Williamson; married Sarah Long.

Children of James and Sarah (Long) Williamson
1. Jeremiah Williamson.
2. James Williamson.
3. William Williamson.
4. Hugh Williamson.
5. Mary Williamson; married Nathaniel Knotts.
6. Frances Williamson; married Isaac Long.
7. Elizabeth Williamson; married Wesley Sicklesmith.
8. Louisa Williamson.

3. Mary Williamson; married John Able.
4. Jane Williamson; married Henry Forster.

Children of Henry and Jane (Williamson) Forster
1. George Forster.
2. Rachel Forster; married Jack Cumpston.
3. Wilhemine Forster; married Eli Dukate.
4. Mary Forster; married John Johnson.
5. Charity Ann Forster; married .... Phillips.

5. Sarah Williamson; married John Russell.
6. Rachel Williamson; married William Hart.

THE CALEB JOHNSON FAMILY

An interesting account was filed in the September Session of the Orphans Court of Greene County, in the year 1833, interesting because of the number of heirs named in the proceedings which covered the next ten years, and the number of Greene County families that shared in the distribution. Caleb Johnson patented a tract of land on a warrant dated March 20, 1794, situated on a branch of Dunkard Creek, but there is no evidence that he lived here. He died in Chester County, Pennsylvania, where he had served in Captain William Newman's Company of the Eighth Battalion of Chester County Militia in the War of the Revolution. His wife's name was Mary ...., who died in New Castle County, Delaware, before the final settlement of her husband's estate. (O. C. Docket 2, pp. 22, 232, etc.) No attempt has been made to secure dates for this record.

Family of Caleb and Mary Johnson
1. Simon Johnson.

Children and Grandchildren of Simon Johnson
1. Lewis H. Johnson.
2. Esther Johnson; married Samuel Temple.
3. Mary Johnson; married Eli Shankleton.

Children
1. Thomas Shankleton.
2. Anne Shankleton.
3. John Shankleton.
4. George Shankleton.
5. Joanna Shankleton.

4. George Johnson.
5. Simon Johnson, Jr.
6. William Johnson.

2. Robert Johnson.

Children of Robert Johnson
1. Minton Johnson.
2. Jehu Johnson.

3. John Johnson.
4. Robert Johnson.
3. Joseph Johnson.

Children of Joseph Johnson
1. Mary Johnson, born May 12, 1796, died February 22, 1879; married, April 27, 1820, Adam Everly, born January 26, 1795, died June 2, 1869.
2. Rachel Johnson; married David Garrison.
3. Ann Johnson; married Elijah South, Jr.
4. Sarah Johnson; married John Huggins.
5. Lydia Johnson; married .... Phillips.
6. Ruth Johnson; married .... Wharton.
7. Eliza Johnson; married Thomas Stewart.
8. Abigail Johnson; married, November 22, 1842, James Burdine, born March 7, 1820.

4. Joshua Johnson.

Children of Joshua Johnson
1. Ann Johnson; married .... Miller.

Children
1. Sybil Miller.
2. Samuel Miller.
3. Joshua Miller.
4. Adeline Miller.

5. Bennet Johnson.

Children of Bennet Johnson
1. Ruth Johnson; married Stephen Reeves.
2. Delilah Johnson; married Samuel Dougherty.
3. Ann Johnson.
4. Mary Johnson.
5. Bennet Johnson.

6. Jehu Johnson.
7. Caleb Johnson, Jr.
8. Margaret Johnson; married Isaac Sharp, who died before 1842.

Children of Isaac and Margaret (Johnson) Sharp
1. Abigail Sharp; married James Crossen.
2. Elizabeth Sharp; married Eli Sharp.
3. Samuel Sharp.
4. Margaret Sharp; married James Kerns.
5. Hannah Sharp; married William Querl.
6. Isaac Sharp, Jr.
7. Phoebe Sharp.
8. Caleb Sharp.
9. Mary Sharp.
10. Anna Sharp.

9. Deborrah Johnson; married Samuel Burroughs.

Children of Samuel and Deborrah (Johnson) Burroughs
1. John Burroughs.
2. Caleb Burroughs.
3. Bennet Burroughs.
4. Samuel Burroughs.
5. Mary Burroughs; married William Britt.

6. Beulah Burroughs; married James Dunlap.
7. Elizabeth Burroughs; married George Cook.
8. Nancy Burroughs; married Denton Dollison.
9. Lydia Burroughs; married .... Barnet.
10. Mary Johnson; married Joseph Pierce.

Children of Joseph and Mary (Johnson) Pierce
1. Samuel Pierce.
2. Ann Pierce; married Joshua Hudson.
11. Ann Johnson; married Garret Jackson.

THE ISAAC JOHNSON FAMILY

Isaac Johnson, who patented the land adjoining Caleb Johnson on Dunkard Creek, was a native of Delaware, but removed to Chester County, Pennsylvania, near the site of the Battle of Brandywine. He served with Caleb Johnson in Captain William Newman's Company, Eighth Battalion of Chester County Militia before moving to Dunkard Creek. While in Chester County he married Lyda Miller. He died in Greene County, where his will was probated May 4, 1825. His will names a number of his children as heirs, which differs slightly in the O. C. Docket in the final settlement of his estate in September 1834.

Children of Isaac and Lyda (Miller) Johnson
1. Jonathan Johnson; not in the O. C. Docket, but named in the will and in History of Monongalia County.
2. Rewell (Ruel) Johnson; he got the patented land on Dunkard, but is not named in the O. C. Docket.
3. Imry Johnson; named in both accounts but not in West Virginia History.
4. Isaac Johnson, Jr.; named in all accounts.
5. Hadley (Headley) Johnson; born 1780, died 1863; married Rachel Ramsey.
6. William Johnson; named only in O. C. Docket 2. pp. 41.
7. Phoebe Johnson; married Philip Hupp. who was born in 1780.
8. Lyda Johnson; married John Ramsey.
9. Joanna Johnson; married Jacob Garrison.
10. Zillah Johnson; married William Baily.
11. Catherine Johnson; married (1) .... Kirby, and (2) .... Gregg.

AUGUSTINE DILLINER

Augustine Dilliner, or Dillinger, was made the subject of a sketch by L. K. Evans in his series of Historical Papers, and the material of this sketch has generally been accepted by subsequent historians and members of Dilliner's Family. There seems to be little doubt that he was one of the first to settle permanently on the west side of the Monongahela River and the date given as 1760, or before, is not out of line with the known facts. Evans says that Augustine Dilliner came from the Shenandoah Valley. In the history of the Shenandoah Valley by Wayland, there is a clue that bears this statement out. It reports that a George Dillinger was on the Cedar Creek Branch of that river as early as 1747. It also reports that in 1764, a John Dillinger was killed by the Indians, at which time his wife, Rachel, and a child, were taken prisoners, while another child was killed. This George Dillinger of Cedar

Creek may well have been the father of Augustine, and the murdered John, since Augustine named a son George.

Dilliner records say that Augustine Dilliner was born in Switzerland in 1732, and died in Greene County on February 10, 1832, and that he married Margaret Leonard in 1751. She died June 8, 1829. The census record for 1790 suggests that they had two sons under 16 years and a daughter living with them at that time, and it is quite probable that a David Dilliner, who died in 1787, leaving a wife, Barbara and four minor children, David, Elizabeth, Catherine, and Jacob, in Fayette County, Pennsylvania, was an older son of Augustine and his wife, Margaret. (Fayette County, Penna. O. C. Docket 1. pp. 4, December 1787). Family records say that Augustine Dilliner went out frequently on tours of duty as a Frontier Ranger, and officially he was a member of Captain John Guthery's Militia Company. (Penn. Arch. Series VI Vol. 2. pp. 19).

Children of Augustine and Margaret (Leonard) Dilliner

1. George Dilliner, one of the first white children born in Greene County, Pennsylvania, was born January 9, 1769, and spent his entire life on the tract of land first settled by his father, about 1760, and on which he died November 8, 1824. His wife was Sarah Ramsey, born July 2, 1772, who died September 24, 1824.

Children of George and Sarah (Ramsey) Dilliner

1. Margaret Dilliner, born February 12, 1791; married ...... Robbins. Removed to Indiana.
2. Augustine Dilliner, born March 22, 1793; removed to Indiana.
3. Martha Dilliner, born September 24, 1795; married .... Cochran, removed to West Virginia.
4. James Dilliner, born March 22, 1797, died 1798.
5. George Dilliner, born October 6, 1799, died in Missouri, June 30, 1890.
6. Samuel Ramsey Dilliner, born May 5, 1802, died at New Geneva, August 3, 1890.
7. Jacob Dilliner, born June 24, 1804, died at Dilliner, November 6, 1887.
8. Sarah Dilliner born April 10, 1807, died September 15, 1841. She married .. Keiser.
9. Albert Gallitan Dilliner, born September 19, 1807, died in Colorado.
10. Allan Dilliner, born January 1, 1812; married, 1833, Anna Eliza Morris, who died in 1886.
11. Ambrose Dilliner, born September 14, 1815; married, March 23, 1857, Elizabeth Griffen.
12. Elizabeth Dilliner, born February 3, 1817 (or 1819), died July 18, 1904. She married, September 1, 1839, Samuel Frankenberger, born July 3, 1816, died January 18, 1889.

THE GARRISON FAMILY

Frederick Garrison was one of the first settlers on Dunkard Creek, coming here about 1770 from Maryland. He is on the tax list for Springhill Township, Bedford County, Pennsylvania, in 1772, when he and son, Leonard Garrison, are listed as heads of households. There are traditions in the Garrison Family that say they came from Germany to New Jersey, but it is definite that they lived in Maryland at the time Leonard Garrison was born.

When Frederick Garrison died in 1813, he left a wife, Margaret, three sons and three daughters, whom he named in his will. (Greene County Will Book 1. pp. 113, probated June 17, 1813). There are reports of the use of their house as a fort, but this would mean only a temporary refuge at times of danger.

Family of Frederick Garrison

1. George Garrison was born in Maryland about 1759, and died in Greene County, Pennsylvania, about 1843. There are several biographies of this man, one published in Haddon's "History of Fayette and Greene Counties," another by John W. Gordon of the Pennsylvania Historical Society, and another written by his son, Josephus Garrison. All of them contain some errors as are usual in most family traditions. None of them contain definite dates for his family, nor do they prove Revolutionary service for George Garrison, although they claim he served as such for seven years, and that is probably true. The pension application of his brother, Leonard Garrison, does give definite service in that war, as will be shown in the record of Leonard Garrison, which will follow. His wife was Elizabeth Long, who survived him and is mentioned in his will. (Greene County Will Book 2, pp. 176, probated April 20, 1843).

Children

1. James Garrison; married (1) Elizabeth South; married (2) Ruth Everly.
2. Joanna Garrison; married Corbly Bowen, who died about 1853.

Children of Corbly and Joanna (Garrison) Bowen

1. Garrison Bowen; removed to Woodford County, Illinois.
2. Lot Bowen; removed to Harrison County, West Virginia.
3. Thomas H. Bowen.
4. Eliza Bowen; married Bennett Bussey.
5. Delilah Bowen; married Thornton Rumble.
6. Rebecca Bowen; married Wesley McClure.
7. Nancy Bowen; married Jarard Bussey.
8. Ruth Bowen; married William H. Rinehart.
9. Joanna Bowen.
10. Emily Bowen.

3. Jerusha Garrison; married Thomas Steele, and lived in Wetzel County, West Virginia.
4. Rachel Garrison; married Richard Cooke.
5. Frederick Garrison; married Amy Evans. He died December 11, 1855, aged 60 years. His wife died July 12, 1890, aged 87 years.

Children Named in Will

Eleazer Garrison; married Elizabeth Kussart.
George W. Garrison, died March 14, 1878, aged 52 years, 3 months, 20 days.
Daniel Garrison; married ....
Nancy Garrison; married William Ruttencutter.

Harriet Garrison; married William South.
Emily Garrison; married John Lynch.
Mary Garrison; married Philip Lynch.
Martha Garrison; married Jesse Steele.
Rebecca Garrison; married John Davis.
Sarah Garrison; married James Bussey.
Frederick Garrison, died April 1, 1849, aged 2 years, 6 months, 10 days.
6. Irad (Ned) Garrison, born 1805, died 1889; married Phoebe Swan, born 1820.
7. Sarah Garrison; married Peter Wolfe.
8. Rebecca Garrison; married Daniel Miller. She was born in 1810, and died in 1837, leaving a son, George Garrison Miller.
9. Matilda Garrison, born June 27, 1812, died January 18, 1885; married Philip Shough. They had a daughter, Mattie Shough.
10. Josephus Garrison, born September 25, 1817, died January 18, 1905; married Rebecca Bowlby.

Children

Philip Garrison.
Thompson L. Garrison, born 1843.
Columbus C. Garrison, born 1847; married Mary June Hostetler.
Melissa Garrison; married .... Hamilton.
George Garrison, born August 5, 1852; married Mary Smith, born June 6, 1858.

11. Abner Garrison, born 1803, died 1863; married Hannah Morris.

Children

Leroy Garrison.
Morris Garrison.
Marinda Garrison; married George Taylor.
Lucy Garrison; married Solomon Shriver.
Matilda Garrison; married John Hagan.
Eliza Garrison.
Mary Garrison.

2. Leonard Garrison, son of Frederick and Margaret Garrison, applied for a pension for service in the Revolution, from Greene County, Pennsylvania, on September 17, 1833. (National Arch. Pa.-W. 7503). From this application, and that of his wife, we learn the service of his brother, George Garrison, and many of the statistics of his own family. He stated that he was born in Maryland on May 5, 1760. In 1777 he went out as a drafted militiaman and served at Garards Fort under Captain Samuel Swindler and served for two months. After he got back home he was called again to serve under Captain Stephen Gapen for a period of a month. In the Spring of 1778, he was drafted to go to Hannastown, but after getting as far as Uniontown, his command under, Lieutenant Henry Myers, was ordered to join Colonel Alexander McClean on the Virginia Line. In the Fall of the same year he served under his brother, George Garrison, as a minute man, scout and spy, and continued this service for the next five years. The pension application of his wife says that Leonard Garrison died March 10, 1836, which is borne out

in Greene County O. C. Docket 2. pp. 88. His widow stated that she (Rebecca) had been born in April 1774, was 65 years old on June 10, 1839, and was married to Leonard on April 27, 1785, by John Minor, Justice of Peace. (She was eleven years of age at the time). In a sustaining affidavit, John Gapen stated that Rebecca had been raised at his home and he had attended the marriage. In an amended application of June 9, 1840, she gave a list of her children according to age, but had lost the Bible record of their births. This list corresponds with the Orphan Court record with one exception. She was still living in 1849.

Children

1. David Garrison, not listed in O. C. Docket, but a Jeremiah Garrison is listed and not in the pension application.
2. Jacob Garrison.
3. Cassandra Garrison; married William Jackson.
4. Mary Garrison; married Isaac Taylor.
5. John Garrison.
6. Barbara Garrison; married William Trimble.
7. Margaret Garrison; married David Steele, who died prior to 1845.

Children

1. Mary Steele; who married Nathaniel Cumpston.
2. John Steele.
3. Leonard Steele; removed to Highland County, Ohio.
4. William Steele.
5. Jacob Steele.
6. Rebecca Steele.

8. William Garrison.
9. Jemima Garrison; marrier Charles Anderson.
10. Hannah Garrison; married Isaac Bayard.
11. Sarah Garrison; married Joseph Bissett.
12. Elizabeth Garrison; married James Wise.
13. Adam Garrison, born 1803.

3. Jacob Garrison, youngest son of Frederick and Margaret Garrison, died in Greene County about 1846. (Orphans Court Docket lists the following record on pp. 57 Vol. 3). His wife was Sarah Long.

Children

1. David Garrison.
2. George Garrison, removed to Illinois.
3. Isaac Garrison.
4. Alfred Garrison.
5. Joab Garrison.
6. Frederick Garrison.
7. Cynthia Garrison; married Amos Snider, removed to Ohio.
8. Elizabeth Garrison.
9. Sarah Garrison; married James Hart, removed to Illinois.
10. Rhuhanna Garrison; married Morgan Buckingham, removed to Illinois.

4. Barbara Garrison, daughter of Frederick and Margaret Garrison; married James Stone, who died in Greene County about 1837. (Greene County W. B. 2. pp. 80, probated April 29, 1837).

Children

1. George Stone.

2. Stephen Stone, died January 8, 1866, aged 72 years; married Dorothy ...., who died January 16, 1869, aged 77 years. Both are buried in the old cemetery near Mapletown, Pa.
   3. Sarah Stone; married .... McKowan.
   4. Elias Stone.
5. Rebecca Garrison, daughter of Frederick and Margaret Garrison; married .... Foreman.
6. Dolly Garrison, daughter of Frederick and Margaret Garrison; married .... Clawson.

Children
   1. Frederick Clawson.
   2. Margaret Clawson.
   3. Peter Clawson.
7. Elizabeth Garrison, daughter of Frederick and Margaret Garrison; married David Dunham.

Child
   1. Job Dunham.

GARRISON

Another Leonard Garrison, died in Dunkard Township about 1819. History of West Virginia Old and New, by American Historical Society, says he was born in Scotland in 1757 and came to Greene County. It is probable that he was related to the family of Frederick Garrison for we find David Dunham administering his estate. (Greene County No. 369-342, probated April 23, 1819). His wife was Elizabeth Gray and the following children are named:
1. Jonathan Garrison.
2. Barbara Garrison, who married .... Nicely.
3. Elizabeth Garrison, who married .... Hoover.
4. Rezin Garrison.
5. Rebecca Garrison, who married .... Blazer.
6. Lot Garrison.
7. David Garrison, born November 8, 1807, removed to Perry County Ohio, and then to Tyler County, West Virginia, and then to Monongalia County, where he died February 22, 1878. His wife was Catherine Engle and they had five sons and three daughters among whom were: Alpheus Garrison, born February 26, 1833, who married Charlotte Henderson.
8. Daniel Garrison.
9. Leonard Garrison.

THE JOHN EVANS FAMILY

This John Evans is not to be confused with Colonel John Evans, who lived but a short distance away but south of the State Line. This John Evans, whom we take to be the one of the 1772 tax list, had warranted to him a tract of land on the border under the title of "Evans' Pleasant Situation." The warrant was dated January 26, 1785, and contained a little over 306 acres. His wife is not known, but a list of his children are found in his will which was filed for probate May 5, 1798, and is copied in Will Book 1, pp. 9, Greene County.

Children of John Evans
1. John Evans, Jr., who on September 6, 1785, had surveyed to him a tract of land called "Tobacco Hill." which tract had been

granted to John McMahan on a Virginia Certificate dated February 19, 1780. John Evans, Jr., was a member of Captain John Guthery's Militia Company. (Penna. Arch. Series VI Vol. 2, pp. 19). His wife was Elizabeth ...., as shown by his will that is recorded in Greene County Will Book 2, pp. 9, and which was proven July 7, 1832. He mentions his land as being on the border of Virginia, adjoining the land of John Herrod. This land was but one farm removed from the first named John Evans.

Children of John Evans, Jr., and wife, Elizabeth
1. Enoch Evans.
2. Lewis Evans.
3. John Evans.
4. David Evans.
5. Samuel Evans.
6. Elizabeth Evans.
7. Eli Evans.
8. Otho Evans.
9. Rolly Evans.
10. Isaac Evans.
11. Alfred Evans.
12. Hugh Evans.
13. Nancy Evans.
14. Sarah Evans.
15. Arimiah Evans.

2. Dorcas Evans, who married John Snyder.
3. Sarah Evans.
4. Mary Evans, who married .... Robins.
5. Samuel Evans.
6. Elizabeth Evans, who married .... Ashcraft.
7. Jesse Evans.
8. Edward Evans.

9. Rachel Evans, who married Edward Parish. They lived in Monongalia County, where Edward Parish died about 1813, and his will was probated March 22, 1813, naming his wife Rachel, and the following children:
    1. William Parish; named in the will of John Evans. His wife was Elenor ....
    2. Joshua Parish.
    3. Mary Parish.
    4. Richard Parish.
    5. Susannah Parish; wife of .... Perrin.
    6. Enoch Parish.
    7. Rachel, wife of .... Cole.
    8. Nancy; wife of .... Hamilton.
    9. Edward Parish; with wife, Elizabeth ...., made deed on February 14, 1823.
    10. Cynthia Parish.
    11. Dolly Parish.
    12. Elenor Parish.
    13. Dorcas Parish.
    14. Cassy Parish.
    15. Jesse Parish.
    16. Evans Parish.
10. Elender (Eleanor) Evans.
11. William Evans.
12. Nancy Evans: married (1) Daniel Stewart, who with his

brothers, James, John, and Charles Stewart, patented a tract of land adjoining that of John Evans, Jr. Daniel Stewart died about 1802, and Stephen Gapen, with the widow Nancy, settled the estate. Two children are mentioned, along with the evidence that Nancy had married (2) David Taylor. (Will Book 1, pp. 31, Greene County; probated June 8, 1802).

Children of Daniel and Nancy (Evans) Stewart
1. Daniel Stewart, Jr.
2. Mary Stewart.

JOHN CONRAD SYKES

Some time during 1764, a party of hardy pioneers left Berks County, Pennsylvania, to seek out new homes on the frontiers of Virginia and Western Pennsylvania, and for a time found the freedom they sought on Dunkard Creek, in what is now Greene County. The party consisted of the families of John Bonnett, John Wetzel, the Eberlys, Waggoners, Rozencranz and Zanes, most of them intermarried to some extent. With them was John Conrad Sykes, who had married Catherine Bonnett, a daughter of John Bonnett. Other children of John Bonnett were Mary, wife of Captain John Wetzel; Susannah, wife of Hezekiah Stewart; Lewis Bonnett, who married Elizabeth Waggoner; John and Samuel Bonnett. Most of this party soon moved on to settle near the Ohio River at Wheeling, but John Conrad and Catherine (Bonnett) Sykes, and some of the Waggoners stayed on Dunkard Creek, where in July 1778, he and his son, John Sykes, Jr., were soldiers in the Frontier Ranger Company under Captain John Wetzel. (Penn. Arch. Series VI Vol. 2, pp. 321). John Conrad Sykes died a few years later and his estate was probated at Washington, Pennsylvania, in February 1786, with his son, Henry Sykes, administrator. (O. C. Docket 1. pp. 26). He was the father of ten children:
1. Henry Sykes, of whom later.
2. John Sykes, Jr.; in Captain John Wetzel's Company in 1778.
3. Phillip Sykes, removed to Mississippi.
4. David Sykes, who went to Texas.
5. Mary Sykes, who married Jonathan Garrison.
6. Barbara Sykes, who married Robert Knotts.
7. Christina Sykes; taken prisoner by the Indians and kept in captivity for some ten years during which time she married Charles Munger.
8. Lewis Sykes, patented a tract of land on Dunkard Creek on warrant of April 19, 1794.
9. Jacob Sykes, patented a tract of land on Dunkard Creek on warrant of April 15, 1785.
10. Edward Sykes, married Jemima Virgin.

HENRY SYKES

Evans, Waychoff, Bates, and other historians have written sketches of the life of Henry Sykes as passed to them by tradition. This article is based on the pension application made by Henry Sykes from Greene County on November 17, 1834, and discloses the active part played by him during the Revolutionary Days. He says he entered the service as a volunteer in August 1776, and marched to the Ohio a short distance below Yellow Creek under Captain James Neale. He says he was living at that time in Fayette County and was out on this service for about three months. He next served a month at Garards Fort under Captain Samuel Swingler in 1777 or 1778. He was a sergeant at that time, but was promoted to

Ensign and served a longer tour at the same place. He went out as a spy under Colonel William Crawford in 1782, during which time he collected a scalp from the Indian who had killed a man named Hall. (Dick Hall.) He served at Garards Fort nearly every Summer from 1776 to 1782, acting in the capacity of spy on Dunkard Creek at various times. Was with the party that pursued the Indians when Enoch Enoch and a man named Robinson were killed. In his application he says he supposed he was born on the Shenandoah River, the date being February 12, 1757, and that his father died in 1782.

Evans says that Henry Sykes was twice married, his first wife being Barbara Selsor, and that he had ten children by each marriage. His will however mentions but five children; (Greene County Will Book 2, pp. 151).

Children of Henry and Barbara (Selsor) Sykes
1. John Sykes.
2. Daniel Sykes, born December 8, 1788, died July 16, 1888.
3. David Sykes.
4. Druscilla Sykes, married John Wilkinson.
5. Rachel Sykes, born 1796, died 1869; married Mathew Greene, born February 17, 1806, died January 24, 1891.

EVANS FAMILY OF DUNKARD CREEK

There were a number of Evans families who settled on Dunkard Creek, on both sides of the present State Line, and efforts to identify each connection ends in confusion. The following records are submitted because they belong in this collection, with a hope that they may aid someone in their ancestral search. The most prominent of the early settlers of this name to settle on Dunkard, was Colonel John Evans, mentioned in frequent dispatches during the Revolution. He was definitely on the West Virginia side of the line, and his family records are well authenticated in West Virginia.

In the Swan-Hughes Bible there is found a list of names and birth dates of the family of Samuel Evans, who settled in Maryland about 1720. This Samuel Evans was probably the uncle of John Swan's wife. As three of the names of this list are found in the Springhill Township, Bedford County tax list for 1772, it is most likely that they came with the Swans or shortly thereafter. One of these, Hugh Evans, settled for a time in Fayette County and then removed to Kentucky, remaining in Bourbon County for a time and then in 1799, removing to Highland County, Ohio. Richard Evans seems to have stayed in Fayette County, Pennsylvania, while John Evans could be the man who moved across the Monongahela and settled on the State line. Here is the Swan-Hughes Bible record:

Mary Evans, born October 31, 1718.
Samuel Evans, born May 22, 1723.
Sarah Evans, born April 5, 1725.
Priscilla Evans, born December 26, 1726.
John Evans, born November 2, 1728.
Hugh Evans, born October 7, 1730.
Elenor Evans, born June 25. 1732.
David Evans, born March 26, 1734.
Richard Evans, born May 26, 1736.
Thomas Evans, born September 27, 1740.
Rachel Evans, born July 6, 1742.

NICHOLAS FAST

One of the larger land owners in what is now Dunkard and Greene Townships, Greene County, was Nicholas Fast, who secured patents to some one thousand acres on the waters of Dunkard Creek. It is not evident if he ever lived in this county, but his son, Christian Fast, was here in 1790, at the head of a family. Deed Book 1, pp. 209, Fayette County, shows that Nicholas Fast and wife, Catherine ...., made a deed in that county on November 20, 1786, at the same time he was entering his Greene County land. He died in Fayette County, Pennsylvania about 1818, his will, written January 1816, was probated there June 10, 1818. (Fayette WB. 1, pp. 187).

Children of Nicholas and Catherine Fast

1. Mary Fast, deceased; left children, who were living with their father, Frederick Wibel, in Jefferson County, Ohio. Children were Mary, Nicholas and Elizabeth Wibel.
2. Francis Fast, a Frontier Ranger.
3. Jacob Fast.
4. Christian Fast.
5. Adam Fast.
6. Barbara Fast; wife of .... Aultman.
7. Katy Fast; wife of .... Bowman.
8. Catherine Fast; wife of .... Weaver; had a son Henry Weaver.

INDEX

The 1977 reprint edition of this book included an every name index. The following index started out as such, however, the original 96 page index exploded into an additional 25 pages just in the verifying/indexing of the first

The original plan was to type in the old index and then go through each page individually and double check the entries. We did this but picked up so many missed entries (and understandably so) considering the double entry index method used. It just got too confusing, so we started from scratch and converted it to a surname index.

A surname index is more than adequate for a book of this nature. Since the majority of the book is comprised of family genealogies the same surname is repeated over and over again on each page of the genealogy thus making it unnecessary, and often confusing, to enumerate each individual name.

Surnames included in long rosters and lists were indexed by page rather than by a letter key as in the original.

Surnames printed in bold print and followed by an asterisk indicate that there is a family biography on that page or group of pages.

It is our sincere hope that between the original efforts of Hilda Chance and the current efforts of Closson Press you will find easy access to the names you are seeking. As avid family researchers, we know the importance of following up every possible lead. The surname index dictates that this be done. You could be doing yourself a disservice by overlooking even one person with the surname you are seeking.

ABBOTT,291,645,655
ABBOYINNIS,143
ABERGAST,148
ABLE,304,530,666
ABRAHAM,232
ACKLIN,147,466,492
ACKVAN,144
ADAMS,15,99,126,128,132,
133,145,146,174,272,310,
311,314,327,335,337,358,
383,393,456,516
ADAMSON* 108-109
ADAMSON,27,83,85,86,87,
99,103,104,108,109,133,
155,162,215,251,264,328,
367,369,404,443,462,464,
469,618,620
ADDELMAN,71
ADDLEMAN,75,82
ADELMAN,221
ADKINS,162
ADRIAN,512
AGNER,591
AGNEW,304
AHERN,143
AHRSON,15
AIKEN(s),157,194,651
AIKEN SEE AKRON
AILES,119,183,267
AINSLEY,71
AIRHART SEE EHREHARD
AKENS,133,420
AKINS,135
AKONS,419
ALBIN,151
ALDER,151
ALDRIDGE,19,136,162,339,
340,341
ALEXANDER,77,139,143,148,
149,150,208,298,315,511,
518,527,553,556,557,559,
560,568,597
ALFORD,531,532,533,534,536
ALFREE,178,182,195,263
ALLEN,126,144,153,155,161,322
ALLERS,144
ALLERTON,513
ALLEY,126,135,136,158,159,
160,502
ALLHANCE,140
ALLISON,39,126,137,146,
151,152,155,160,519
ALLMAN,62,152
ALLUM,486

ALLWINE,337
ALMAN,152,664
ALMON,152
ALT,140
ALTMAN,151
AMBROSE,248
AMES,528
AMMONS,181,231
ANCROM SEE ANKROM
ANCRUM SEE ANKROM
ANDERS,158
ANDERSON* 512-513
ANDERSON,15,27,60,117,
122,132,133,134,136,140,
143,148,153,155,158,175,
196,215,219,220,223,226,
228,234,263,264,267,269,
304,367,380,393,440,445,
498,499,500,502,504,506,
519,525,529,531,565,566,
580,585,599,606,672
ANDREW(s),28,138,218
ANKRIM SEE ANKROM
ANKROM* 347-350
ANKROM,21,22,37,133,136,
145,163,307,308,310,314,
324,329,441,332,338,339,
340,342,346,351,352,365,
366,367,368,369,375,376,
447,449,450,495,521
ANKRUM SEE ANKROM
ANTILL,12,480,498,503
ANTRAM,568
ANTRIM,123,234,243,164
ANTRIM SEE ANKROM
APPLEGATE,149,524
ARCHBOLE,145
ARCHER* 344-346
ARCHER,3,7,22,24,37,59,
107,132,133,136,143,145,
153,162,163,243,308,312,
315,316,320,321,323,326,
327,329,339,340,343,347,
348,351,352,354,363,363,
364,365,369,370,373,376,
382,385,386,388,390,391,
395,397,415,422,423,424,
430,439,441,442,444,445,
449,450,488,495
ARCHPOL(e),143
AREFORD,443,567
ARGO,155
ARMSTRONG* 538-543
ARMSTRONG,4,12,15,36,113,
126,132,133,151,155,176,

1

223,253,328,457,496,499,
500,501,504,506,523,524,
525,544,548,550,551,552,
554,556,565,566,642,643,
656
ARNDT,89
ARNET,593
ARNOLD* 68-70
ARNOLD,15,17,18,34,35,46,
68,71,72,74,76,129,130,
131,140,144,147,161,232,
486
ARNOTT,80
ARROWSMITH,151
ARTMAN,126
ASA,144
ASBURY,180
ASH,139
ASHBROOK,511
ASHBY,152,200
ASHCRAFT,44,48,52,126,128,674
ASHER,152,158
ASHFORD,573
ASHLEY,32
ASHRAFT,164
ASHTON,513
ASKEY,273
ASKIN(s),3,19,44,126,135,
369
ASSON,596
ATCHISON,146
ATKINS,24,36
ATKINSON,23,39,137,138,
146,148,150,152,163,309,
394
ATLEE,530
AUGER,151
AULT,481
AULTMAN,677
AUSTIN,436
AUTON,54
AXTELL,39,137,146,319,520
AYERS,175,497,499,500
BABBITT,209,319,375,442
BABCOCK,580
BACHUS,126,128
BACKUS,255
BADCOCK,158
BAILEY,3,133,155,198,503,
567,576,587
BAILY* 569-573
BAILY,34,129,130,171,198,
278,279,329,405,407,408,
469,507,534,535,537,576,
579,580,587,599,600,605,

608,618,619,622,625,638,
646,663,668
BAIN,143
BAIRD,558,632
BAKER,15,28,38,87,88,126,
135,150,158,236,237,486,
490,498,502,509,526
BALANCE,25
BALDWIN* 608-611
BALDWIN,39,135,137,158,
160,477,502,612,613
BALL, 66,108,109,118,132,
133,145,154,155,161,323,
361,367,388,453,513,534,
536
BALLA,303
BALLARD,512
BALLINGER,571
BALSHEAR(s),135
BALSINGER,144,648
BALTING,144
BALTZELL,355,451
BANE,27,32,39,53,120,137,
152,220,476,483,490
BANFIELD,127
BANKS,84
BARBER,15,139,376
BARCLAY* 564-567
BARCLAY,9,174,175,187,
196,228,272,506,513,542,
560,568,569,657
BARE,622
BAREMORE,453
BARGER,479
BARKER,127,153,163,482,484
BARKLAY,153
BARKLEY,127,564
BARKLEY SEE BARCLAY
BARMORE,661
BARNARD,74,77,147,208,298
BARNES,15,19,80,117,133,
155,157,316,324,377,393,
394,398,428,467,475,477,
504;571,572,576,637
BARNET(t),72,137,147,148,
269,295,668
BARNHART,174,188,486
BARNHILL,36,133,502,576
BARR,25,75,140,464,490,
493,564,662,663
BARRICKLOW,534
BARRY,175,516
BARSHEARS,425
BARTHALOW,342
BARTHOLOMEW,160

BARTLESON,324
BARTLET(t),149
BARTLEY,152
BARTON,28,177
BASKETT,166
BASHIERS,131
BATES,29,39,113,137,146,
260,270,425,558,628,651,
675
BATHUGH,164
BATRO, 295,296
BATTEN,161,255
BATTENFELD,80
BATTERSHELL,15
BATTON,127,129
BAUGHMAN,74,75
BAUK,127
BAUMAN,74
BAUNTON,354
BAXTER,71,107,144,294,465
BAYARD,107,120,214,279,
311,392,398,507,544,572,
619,622,672
BAYLOR,142
BAYS,140
BEALE,330
BEALL,123,187,646
BEAM,449,463
BEARD,304
BEARER,87
BEATY,140
BEAVES,131
BECKETT,15
BECKWITH,216
BEDDIER,652
BEEDLE,129,130,379
BEEK,127
BEELER,473
BEEMAN,161
BEERS,94,179,523
BEESON,127,128,142,144,
163,257,532
BEESOR,163
BELCHER, 160
BELFORD,15
BELK,549,551
BELL* 460-465
BELL,4,9,35,52,53,61,63,
80,82,102,113,114,129,
130,133,161,162,171,207,
208,209,234,236,237,243,
249,251,271,278,279,285,
287,288,292,299,303,304,
316,319,328,361,368,375,
383,383,397,422,428,437,

443,459,466,467,468,469,
470,472,485,488,490,536,
540,543,548,552,578,586,
599,619
BELLE,480
BELLFORD,443
BELLMAN,160
BELLO(s),26,255
BELLS,128,460
BELLSHE,460,578,647
BELSHAS,158
BELT,181,635
BENEFIELD,135
BENHAM,34,70,129,130,161
BENNET(t),15,18,28,94,140
BENTLEY,151
BERKEY,318,405
BERRY,180,494
BERRYHILL,176,275
BEST,139
BETSON,298
BETTS,320
BICE,600
BICH,145
BIDDLE,155,252,379,454,
541,542,566
BIGELOW,357
BIGGS* 257-258
BIGGS,32,138,140,149,161,
251,257,422,464
BIGLER,54,74,75,483,490
BILBY,27,137,442
BILDERBACH,144
BILDERBACK,148,149,255
BILLINGSLEY,662
BILLS,35,161,382
BIRCH,119,121
BIRE,615
BISHOP,81,593
BISSETT,672
BLACK,127,214,227,257,
258,270,287,306,316,355,
375,392,395,443,465,490,
512 518,548,610
BLACKBURN,15,17,34,35,
146,274,303,326,335,349,
367,368
BLACKFORD,28,138
BLACKLEDGE* 83-89
BLACKLEDGE,27,59,69,73,
83,84,89,90,91,92,93,97,
99,100,103,106,108,114,
123,132,133,135,146,155,
175,179,195,196,228,264,
274,462,488,518,538,545

3

BLACKMORE,148,314,456
BLACKSHERE,610
BLACKSTAFF,157
BLACKSTON,129
BLACKSTONE,144
BLAINE,265,498,499,503,
504
BLAIR,15,18,36,102,132,
133,146,150,152,155,302,
314,342,440,557
BLAKE,127,158
BLAKER,116
BLAND, 377
BLANE,132
BLANEY,36,155
BLATCHLEY,133,467
BLAZER,673
BLEANDENBURG,201
BLOIR,132,133
BLONEY,132,133
BLOOMFIELD,355
BLYTHE,600
BOALS,227
BOARDMAN,155
BOCHAN,142
BODINE,198
BODKIN,115,336
BOGGS,24,139,140,148,303,
345,395,422,464
BOILS,136
BOKE,222
BOLDENCE,519
BOLING,147
BOLLINGER,152
BOLLINGS,132
BOLTON,658,659
BOMAR,176
BONA,349
BONAR,35,349,367,368,565
BOND,148
BONER,60,139,140,155,383,
418
BONHAM,271,297
BONNELL,106,298,453,538
BONNER,133,136
BONNET(t),19,28,112,127,
208,441,442,578,632,636,675
BOOHER,62
BOOHER SEE BOOKER
BOOKER,650
BOONE,240,243,519,520
BOOS,638,639
BOOTH,43,239,282,286,384,
541
BOOZ(e),67,72,133,155,
176,275
BOQET,3,4,6,7,41,42,245,
248,268,524,527
BOQUET,301,303,423,495
BORDEN,396,425
BOREMAN,133,155,307,310,
313,315,517,518,525
BOSHER SEE BRASHEARS
BOSSERMAN,94
BOSTON,304
BOTELER,351
BOTKIN,139
BOTTEMFIELD* 80-83
BOTTEMFIELD,58,76,80,82
BOTTORF,225,226
BOUGHNER,602,607
BOURST,593
BOUS,139
BOWELL(s),50,117,288
BOWEN,34,36,37,94,95,96,
110,117,118,119,121,173,
179,196,206,221,282,284,
286,287,288,289,290,291,
292,294,301,304,329,372,
383,432,469,505,571,576,
580,587,604,618,670
BOWER(s),227,158,162,325,
382,398,404,415,430,576,
585,587,604,607,646
BOWLBY,535,585,624,625,
639,663,671
BOWLER,383
BOWMAN,15,135,155,157,
225,242,266,350,364,494,
654,677
BOWSER,45,107,264
BOYD,177,220,393,593
BOYDSTONE,126,136,158
BOYLES,158
BOYSEN,450
BOZARTH,38
BRACKEN,15
BRADBURY,162,493
BRADDOCK,5,9,127,150,449,
554
BRADEN,71,328,366,393,469,
472,474
BRADFORD* 414-415
BRADFORD,28,34,37,132,
133,136,142,144,158,163,
195,269,279,304,308,318,
339,340,343,382,383,387,
398,404,405,426,427,428,
430,431,457,587,596,598,
637,643,649,655

BRADLEY,142,143,229,265
BRADY,24,627
BRANCH,479
BRAND,25
BRANDENBURG,171
BRANDON,19
BRANDY,15
BRANNON,19,304
BRANT,155,427,438,511
BRANTON,12 7
BRASHEAR(s),15,18,22,127,
128,150,187,425,627
BRASHEAR(s) SEE BOSHER
BRASHERS,143,148
BRECK,359
BREECE,464
BREKIN,158
BRENTON,3,19,369
BRESOCK,214
BRET,489
BREWER,318,615
BRIANT,69,465,471
BRICE,567,629,641
BRICKEL,149
BRICKER* .71-7 2
BRICKER,63,68,70,71,72,
73,76,462
BRICKLE,152
BRIDGEWATER,128
BRIENT,136
BRIGGS,362
BRIGHT,142
BRIMET,127
BRINTON,3,32,127,148,162
BRINTON SEE BRENTON
BRISCO(e),126,148,151,203
BRISON,139
BRISSON, 569
BRISTO(e),129,130
BRISTON,162
BRITT,327,634,667
BRITTON,158,535,663
BROADHEAD,19
BROAKIN, 36
BROBST,99
BROCK,173,317,652
BRODHEAD,31,265,332,576,611
BROOKOVER,155,499
BROOKES,202
BROOKS,128,149,155,164,
271,556
BROUGHTON,145,152
BROWBURY,162
BROWN* 256, 389-390
BROWN,7,15,18,21,28,35,

36,38,99,102,107,126,128,
129,130,133,135,136,142,
143,144,147,149,150,151,
155,158,161,162,163,176,
224,230,235,243,256,257,
258,295,296,306,311,322,
325,344,354,355,374,383,
389,406,424,425,431,437,
451,458,468,519,528,565,
580,586,604,614,623,632,
644,654
BROWNFIELD,126,128,142,
143,151,163,250
BROWNING,570
BROWNLEE,127,140,151
BRUMBAUGH,171,338,379,394,
395
BRUMLEY,526
BRUNDSEN,297
BRUNER,135
BRUNNER,142,144,148
BRUSE,139
BRYAN,37,128,162,428
BRYANT,34,132,146,162,382,
579
BRYCE,138
BRYSON,137,138,150,151
BUCHANAN,15,127,138,150
BUCHANNON,344
BUCK,593
BUCKINGHAM* 297-299
BUCKINGHAM,207,208,211,
224,232,249,283,288,291,
292,297,
461,468,518,574
BUCKLE(s),152,601
BUCKLER,151
BUCKMAN,97
BUCKNER,385,450
BUCKRAS,25
BUDD,129
BUKETT,139
BULGER,25,255
BULL,255,530,582,588
BUMGARNER* 49
BUMGARNER,41,48,49,52,74,
76,77,209,274,379
BURBRIDGE,310,313
BURCH,152
BURCHAM,151
BURDGE,512,620
BURDIN(e),126,151,,410,
667
BURGE,111,114,117,118,
129,130,161,173,196,250,

362,365,433,618
BURGESS,15,153
BURGOON,448
BURK(e),135,375,580
BURKERT,593
BURKHAM(e),127,147
BURKHAMER,350
BURLEIGH,215,216
BURLEY,231,510,511
BURNES,151
BURNETT(e),27,28,82,454,
530,574
BURNS,17,19,27,37,132,
135,143,146,152,158,300,
303
BURRINGTON,151
BURRIS,126,142,664
BURRISS,519
BURROUGHS,214,667,668
BURROWS SEE BURRIS
BURSON* 91-97
BURSON,10,27,59,60,64,66,
77,78,81,83,85,89,91,108,
109,112,121,123,132,133,
155,162,173,175,178,179,
195,196,228,274,277,305,
306
BURT,43,128,148,158,601
BURTNETT,158
BURWELL,220
BUSBY,304
BUSHILL,158
BUSKIRK,155
BUSSEY,670,671
BUTLER,101,153,232,267,
304,351
BUTLER SEE BOTELER
BYERS,140,334
BYRN(e)(s),15,140
CADE,143
CAFFYN,523
CAGE,403
CAHILL,137,661,662
CAIN(e),15,28,134,139,
144,147,156,158,233,234,436
CALDWELL,16,127,139,140,
148,158,216,442,550,663
CALHOUN,379
CALL,28,39,101,129,152,472
CALLEY,164
CALSY,153
CALVERT,118,622
CALVIN,205
CALWELL,151
CAMERON,25,151,164,255,
476
CAMP,137,382,401
CAMPBELL, 15, 87,123,127,
129,144,153,158,207,213,
218,223,224,233,236,278,
304,507,611,652
CAMPBLE,140
CAMPLIN,304
CANADA,304
CANDAY,142
CANE,142
CANER,648
CANN,518
CANNADY,15
CANNON, 31,143,147,158,175,
665
CANOLSPICE,255
CANON,31,135,333
CANOR SEE KEENER
CANTWELL,140
CAPLAID,128
CAPLAYD,28
CAPLEY,128
CARBY,135
CAREL,135
CARHILL,39
CARLISLE,336
CARLISTER,593
CARMAN,449
CARMICHAEL,39,129,137,
145,155,519,620
CARMICHAELS, 20, 24, 30, 34,
60,132,133,146,198,206,
499,502,510,515,517,529,
530
CARN(s),127,128,156
CARNEY,603
CAROTHERS,113,232
CARPENTER, 25, 26,139,151,
255,450,559
CARR, 127,142,143,144,145
CARRALL,162
CARRELL,135
CARROL,37,132,480
CARROLL, 110,144,147,149,
153,162,308,338,346,352,
370,379,402,436
CARSON, 137,140,145,147,
152,203,520
CARTER* 118-121
CARTER,25,27,39,95,96,
105,118,134,137,142,144,
146,155,156,177,321,391,
431,480
CARY* 489-491

CARY,109,137,152,162,229,
367,453,459,465,556
CASE,25,62,127,128,129,
131,143,161,162,285
CASEMAN,105
CASSEY,139
CASTILE,35,36,127,143
CASTLEMAN,143,151
CASTMER,233
CAST0,36,161,258
CATCH,129
CATERLING,138
CATHCART,14 7
CATHER,307
CATHERS* 321-322
CATHERS,37,133,136,143,
210,215,231,291,307,308,
310,312,316,320,321,322,
327,338,344,382,431,453,
471,600
CATON,137,143
CATT,25,28,127,128,621
CAVERLY,216
CAVIN,140
CAVINES,128
CAWL,131
CE IL,143
CEASE,437
CELLAR SEE SELLARS
CELLERS,136,559
CHADWICK,128,142,146
CHAFFIN(s),135,151,158,
160,406,439
CHAIN(e),15,129,151
CHALFONT,149,368,439,595,
632
CHALKLEY,6,447,450
CHAMBER,28
CHAMBERLAIN,129,137
CHAMBERS,128,148,162,230,
297,501,581
CHANCE,518
CHANDLER,534,541,636
CHANEY,151
CHANFORD,143
CHANLER,382
CHANSLER,152

CHAPIN,519
CHAPLAIN,148,645
CHAPMAN,140,342
CHAPTERS,147
CHARLTON, 19
CHASE,43
CHEESMAN,76
CHENEY,129,150
CHENOWETH,51
CHENOWITH,15,118,119,200,
203,204,255,579
CHERRY,117
CHESNEY,393
CHEW,28
CHEYNEY,586
CHIDESTER,35,130,131,161
CHINNER,127
CHOARON,150
CHRISLY,523
CHRIST,160
CHRISTY,129
CHRISTY SEE CRISTY
CHURCH* 369-370
CHURCH,3,107,127,132,136,
144,162,213,214,218,219,
308,318,328,345,346,382,
448
CHY,150
CICILY,149
CILDIN,145
CILLS,127
CISC0,15
CLAGGET,258
CLAPHAM,248
CLARK(e),6,20,22,23,25,
31,43,SS,56,58,63,67,101,
104,132,134,135,139,140,
142, 143,146,147,148,
150,151,152,155,161,171,
178,179,181,185,203,221,
233,242,245,246,254,255,
265,266,285,306,362,404,
411,414,437,441,443,444,
451,458,463,473,482,SOO,
S11,512,514,525,538,541,
572,576,580,582,589,593,
612,627, 638,653

CLATON SEE CLAYTON
CLAWSON,38,135,156,176,
466,492,506,507,568,569,
673
CLAY,15
CLAYTON* 491-492
CLAYTON,9,　105,161,466,488
CLEAM,127
CLEAVENGER,157,588
CLEFFRON,43
CLEGG,38,112,135,158,243,
632,636
CLEMMENS,48,137,151
CLEMMONS,149,216
CLENDENNIN,15
CLENDENNING,278
CLERKE,132
CLEVELAND,181
CLEVENGER,158
CLIFFORD,145
CLIFTON,144,514
CLINE* 536-538
CLINE,27,59,114,121,128,
153,155,172,198,199,200,
317,318,362,364,501,526,
590
CLINTON,635
CLOAKLEY,228
CLOAKLY,228
CLOUD,120,299
CLUBRICK,152
CLULDREN,99
CLUNY,140
CLUTTER,372,428,487
CLYME,656
CLYMER,74,84,535,585,618
CLYNE,134,149,317,318,656
COAPSTICK,151
COATS,81
COBB,522,523
COBURN,171,201
COCHRAN(e),15,25,127,132,
138,144,149,155,245,255,
418,516,669
COCKRAN(e),15,437
COCK,151,224,570
COE,137,144,233,479

COEN,102,111,319,637
COFFMAN,15,128,153
COIN,132
COKELY,263
COL,39
COLBERT,19
COLDREN,652
COLE,399,408,426,441,　479,
482,521,674
COLEMAN,121,145,161,　304,
368,577
 COLL,34
COLLANCE,144
COLLEY,144
COLLIER(s),174,516,565,567
COLLINGS,144,612
COLLINS,25,59,95,142,143,
148,163,164,175,196,210,
279,536,619
COLLY,150
COLLYER,15
COLSON,　128
COLVER,11,282,283,284,
289,292
COLVIN,127,148,149,150,
158,304
COMB,28
 COMMINS,593
COMMONS,382
COMSTOCK,455
COMPSTON,158
CONDIT(s),459,484,602
CONE,132,146
CONELY,145
CONEY,604
CONGER,139,147,456,597
CONKEY,71
CONKLE,72
CONKLIN,337,426,451,471,487
CONN,127,305
CONNEL(l),143,145,152,153,
361
 CONNELLY,511
CONNELY,375
CONNER,19,625
CONNOLLY,15

CONNOR,143,146,147,148,156,407
CONRAD,304
CONSOLEY,164
CONSTANT,50
CONWAY,25,164,208
CONWELL,127,139,149,393,503,540
COOK(e),28,39,66,119,136,137,138,146,151,304,324,361,455,531,534,668,670
COOKUS,346,352
COOLVIN,144
COOMBS,148,662,663
COON,128,132
COONE(s),132,155
COOPER(s),78,124,132,137,162,164,182,197,198,223,273,424,448,459,463,472,490,512,536
COPE,123,569
COPELAND,161
COPUS,345,370
CORBIE,163
CORBLEY,158
CORBLY* 581-595
CORBLY,10,25,50,135,259,354,500,503,522,535,537,576,578,579,580,596,598,601,604,607,608,622,624,659,660,661
CORBRA,144
CORBY SEE CORBLY
CORCORAN,221
CORDELL,424
CORE,406,431,631,665
COREY,598,604
CORNWALLIS,230
CORNWELL,300,301,446,493
CORTES,415
CORWIN,137,456,583,589
CORY,589
CORZINNE,377,637
COSGRAY,271,320,398,399,403,658
COSHAW,127
COSSILL,150

COSTELO,304
COTTERAL(l),183,234,271,449,631
COUDY,392
COUGHIAN,135
COUGHRAN,132
COULSON,128,137,482
COULTER,524
COUNTS,139
COURSER,285
COURTRIGHT,216
COUTIER,220
COVALT,135,137,580,596, 647
COVE,588
COWAN,36,105,162,382,459,488
COWELL* 645-647
COWELL,59,317,376,403
COWEN,143
COWPER,304
COWPLANE,161
COX* 62-63
COX,34,35,46,48,51,55,58,62,63,80,127,128,129,130,131,139,149,152,155,162,303,318,408,462,467,472,489,547,577,603,652,664
COXAN,148
COXON,19
COYAN,382
COYLE,526
CRABLE,25,255
CRACRAFT,23,151,152
CRAFT,39,43,125,127,137,143,147,149,233,263,570
CRAG,382
CRAGO(e)* 268-270
CRAGO(e),27,132,133,149,156,178,182,183,194,195,219,221,226,260,261,263,268,276,304,356,434,495,499,510,518,522,524,603,604
CRAIG,12,39,42,46,70,75,127,137,138,146,151,153,162,180,382,490,491,501,

564,581,603,611
CRAIN SEE CRAYNE
CRAIN,130,143,161,162
CRAMPLIN,304
CRANE,131,144,152,537
CRANE SEE CRAYNE
CRAVEN(s),76,143,146,153,
490,593,652,664
CRAWFORD* 121-125,521-528
CRAWFORD,4,15,18,20,21,
22,24,26,27,30,31,32,33,
36,53,58,61,62,68,78,80,
96,97,99,127,129,132,133,
140,143,145,146,150,152,
155,158,174,190,191,206,
211,225,244,257,265,268,
287,304,331,333,347,365,
371,384,405,453,486,495,
496,497,500,501,503,504,
507,514,515,516,530,531,
533,534,538,539,540,541,
544,545,548,550,551,552,
554,555,557,558,559,574,
575,576,579,592,617,626,
627,629,631,641,642,647,
648,676
CRAY,150
CRAYNE(s)* 465-467
CRAYNE(s),35,39,63,161,
199,209,249,251,316,318,
327,374,382,405,445,459,
463,465,469,492
CRAYNE SEE CRAIN
CREACRAFT,50,137
CREARY,156
CREE* 544-548
CREE,36,99,132,133,146,
155,230,234,271,272,276,
292,350,454,499,503,518,
556,574,575
CREERAFT,164
CRESAP,3,14,15,16,17,18,
26,49,68,127,386,423
CRESS,650
CRESSWELL,3,15
CRESWELL,418
CRIBBS,304

CRIST,151
CRISTY,15
CRITCHFIELD,157,393
CROCKARD,104
CROCKET,648
CROGHAN,3,244
CROMWELL,61,531
CROOKS,127,579
CROSHOE,127
CROSLEY,131,134,143,280,
412,580,641
CROSS,28,128,152,324,377,
414
CROSSEN,667
CROSSLEY,128,155
CROUCH,88,264,517
CROUGHAN,133
CROUSE,37,136,231,429,442,
443,450,471,604
CROW,53,57,127,146,149,164,
242382,522
CROY,593
CROYLE,593
CRULL,436
CRUM,142
CRUMRINE,53,54,55,64,67,
75,77,113,121,154,360,361,
459,463,471,472,495,521,
524,628
CRUTCHET,77
CULBERTSON,44,377,637
CULLINGS,149
CULP,142
CUMBERLEDGE,638
CUMBERT,127
CUMMINGS,36,145,443,502,
540,559
CUMMINS,43,44,144,148,
150,151,156,162,382,493
CUMPSTON,666,672
CUNCE,134
CUNNINGHAM,149,180,304,514
CURL,169,221,222,223,224,
260,261,264,519,542,568
CURLE,532,533
CURLEY,128
CURR,142

CURRY,38,147,176,565
CURTAIN,134
CURTIS,156,302
CURVEY,142
CUSSENBERRY,149
CUTHBERTSON,547
CUTRIGHT,304
CUTTER,304
CYPHERS,229
DAILEY,37,132,134,136,
146,163,279,444
DAILY,369
DAINES,103
DALES,489
DALLISON,467
DALRIMPLE,156
DALRYMPLE,292
DALY,145
DANCE,277,327,547
DANFORD,425
DANHOUSE,593
DANIEL,131,160
DANIELS,34,59,60,130,131,
284,292,612
DANLEY,499
DANSER,661
DARLING,224
DARNALL,150,153,162
DARR,116
DARRAGH,196,228
DARRAH* 560-563
DARRAH,175,557,564,565,567
DARRAUGH,158
DARROH,20
DAUGHERTY,106,134,135,144,147,
158,491,631
DAVID,127,139,158
DAVIDSON,21,144,153,176,
270,272,488,501,514,525,
532,534,541,542,565
DAVIE,158,382,593
DAVIS* 528-529
DAVIS,36,38,49,54,105,
120,125,128,131,132,133,
134,135,136,137,138,143,
145,146,147,149,150,152,
156,158,160,161,162,164,
196,208,209,237,241,251,
271,300,369,382,462,464,
474,489,499,500,501,572,
580,594,596,597,620,621,
664,671
DAVISON,127,128,156
DAVY,277
DAWSON,19,127,135,143,
149,151,158,404,406,580
DAY,120,228,248,301,367,
411,451,631
DAYTON,454
DEACHE,304
DEAVER,341
DEBEL,42
DEBOW,662
DeLANCTOT,632
DEAMS,148
DEAN,15,145,164,210,428,
548
DEARTH,482
DEATH,127
DEBOLT* 621-622
DEBOLT,42,47,127,160,616
DECKER,129,147,659
DEEDS,141
DEEM(s),127,146
DEEMING,174
DEETS,401
DEFOREST,19
DEFRANCE,547
DEGUID,59,64,518
DEKALB,247
DELANCY,480
DELANO,256
DELANEY,152,163,382
DELANNEY,19
DELASHMUNT,350
DELASHMUTT,347
DELESHMUT,424
DELONG,139,173
DELOW,15
DELZELL,248
DEMENT,138
DEMING,188
DEMUSS,305
DENHAM,162

DENNIS,15,98
DENNISON,648,649,650
DENNY,84,91,177,260,319,
462,472,506,630
DENT,634
DEPREAST,103
DEPUI,291,301
DERTER,149
DERUMPLE,500,525
DESHONG,593
DESKIN,15
DEUM,183
DEVALL,136,162,163
DEVANTER,145
DEVAR,304
DEVAULT,198,273
DEVER,127,148,530,612
DEVONEN,304
DEVORE,304
DEWAL,135
DEWEES,656
DEWEESE,199,317,537
DEWITT,15,139,148
DIAMOND,158
DICK,15,304
DICKENSON,267
DICKER,129
DICKERSON,39,137,138,149,
150
DICKESON, 27,134
DICKEY,25, 213
DICKINSON,107,111,662
DICKISON,156
DICKMAN,15
DICKS,127,143,148
DIE,382
DILES,36
DILL,324,517
DILLE,39,49,137,144,146,
147,451
DILLENER,38
DILLINER* 668-669
DILLINER,127
DILLINGER,135,144,158,436,
659
DILLINGER SEE DILLINER
DILLINGHAM,289

DILLISON,136
DILLON,162,408,650
DINNA,144
DISNEY,304
DIXON,87,158,464,531,532,
533,572
DOAX,296
DOBBINS,158
DODD,39,119,137,146,147,
151,558
DODDIDGE,140
DODDS,365
DODGE,629
DOIL,145
DOLLING,15
DOLLISON,38,156,163,370,
382,396,668
DOLSON,519
DONAHUE,281,366,392,440
DONALD(s),160,593
DONELEY,377,637
DONHAM,268,603,664
DONLEY,403,432,586,623
DONNELL,248
DONNELY,510
DOOK,163
DORAN(e),163,401,406
DORMAN,137,415
DORSEY,150
DOTSON,38
DOTY* 113
DOTY,101,113,161,197,366,
485,495
DOUGHAN,132
DOUGHERTY,133,538,667
DOUGHTY,52,53,176,223,
274,275
DOUGLAS(s),11,36,38,117,
127,129,135,136,158
DOUSMAN,147
DOWDEN,145,147,317,323,
508,509,558,570,600,619,
625
DOWLIN,63
DOWN,149
DOWNAND,15
DOWNARD,127,151

DOWNER,142
DOWNEY,102,313,470,586
DOWNING,82,128,140
DOWNS,127,143,148,150,653
DOYLE,250
DRAGO,127
DRAKE,66,81,148,158,159,
160,299,455,461,580
DRAPER,26,27,29,30,39,47,
53,137,144,170,171,190,
194,199,225,241,242,245,
246,249,251,254,260,265,
266,352,386,460,470,488,
525,537,549,551,552,612,
632,650
DRILLING,145
DRINNON,138,152
DRISCOLL,25,255
DRIVER,157,478,508
DRUMM,437
DRUSCILLA,45
DRYDEN,342
DUBLIN,129
DUCAT SEE DUCKETT
DUCKETT,348,350,351,352
DUEL,651
DUFFIELD,83
DUKATE,666
DUKE,192,326,435
DULANEY,408,431
DULLAM,417
DULLON,133
DUMENT,127
DUMWOODIE,177
DUN,164
DUNAN,147
DUNCAN* 265
DUNCAN,19,28,31,132, 34,
148,265
DUNHAM,130,131,134,162,
373,383,673
DUNKARD,441,519
DUNKLE,521
DUNLAP *560
DUNLAP,151,393,553,556,
557,558,593,611,665,668
DUNLEVY,138

DUNMORE,7,11,25,170,190,
241,250,253,265,276,386,
470,529,584
DUNN,128,130,131,132,134,
139,145,146,152,156,157,
161,250,305,438,471,472,
494,510,580
DUNNAVIN,141
DUNNING,304
DUNSMORE,518
DUNWOODIE,506
DURBIN,80,143,382,487
DURHAN,132
DURR,652
DUSTMAN,137
DUTTON,38
DUVALL,98,132,133,149,187,
281,307,338,348,350,356,
382,388,411,580
DUVALLS,307
DWIRE,111,336
DYE* 654-657
DYE,25,135,136,151,158,
199,223,255,317,415,434,
438,455,511,537,538,569,
577,579,580,587,598,618,
632,655
DYE-KNIGHT,655
EAGON* 365-369
EAGON,37,108,109,132,133,
134,143,149,156,309,313,
318,326,335,338,349,365,
373,379,380,391,392,425,
426,427,429,443
EAKEN,598
EAKER(s),593
EAKIN(s),22,26,145,153,587
EAKWOOD,28
EASTEL,134 EASTER,144,145
EASTIN,399
EASTWOOD,25,28,35,36,132,
134,156,579
EATON,22,129,132,133,156,
161,162,282,290,300,382
EBERHART,529,634,653
EBERLE,142

EBERLY,675
ECKERLEIN,2,128,129,659
ECKERLY,129
ECKERT,517
ECKLEY,128
ECKY,124
EDDY,117,137,138,158,159,590
EDELIN,200
EDEN,387
EDGAR,372,440,512
EDWARD(s),90,128,135,147,152,198,273,466,580
EGLIN,150
EGY,66,481
EHREHARD,648,650,653
EICHER,618,625
EILER,144
EISENMINGER,227,319,427,429,434
EISMINGER SEE EISENMINGER
ELDER,523
ELLENER,129
ELLIOT,127,519
ELLIOTT,137,150,294,304,463,468,504,523
ELLIS,140,145,150,152,500,524
ELLS,573
ELMS,451
ELSTON,208,209
ELY,398,407
EMERICK,209
EMERSON,96
EMERY,66,151,174,188,652
EMORY,235,588
ENCEY,519
ENGLE,314,426,580,664,673
ENGLISH,7,19,243,304,325,387,389,524
ENGOLL,304
ENLOE,151
ENLOW,202,207
ENLOW SEE ENLOE
ENNIS,145
ENOCB(s)* 49-56
ENOCH(s),3,24,28,29,34,43,45,48,49,53,56,62,67,68,74,76,127,130,131,137,158,161,173,190,242,243,259,274,277,303,378,461,486,517,660,676
ENIX SEE ENOCH
ENSLEY,592
ENSLOW,592,593
ENSLOW SEE ENSLEY
EPPERSON,292,294
ERDENHOUSE,144
ERDMAN,144
ERHART,445
ERVIN,580
ERWIN,98
ESKRIDGE,513,514,517
ESTHE,191,528
ESTILL,9,37,59,98
ESTLE* 59-60
ESTLE,27,59,132,144,156,264,408,445
ESTLE SEE ESTILL
ETTING,5
EULEN,244
EVAN,245
EVANS* 639-641,673-675,676
EVANS,4,7,27,35,36,38,44,49,85,94,102,119,127,135,136,137,138,143,157,158,160,165,168,169,179,186,189,190,200,268,275,311,312,315,325,354,361,364,378,389,416,432,437,447,455,468,486,488,490,491,498,500,520,521,522,535,539,540,550,568,578,579,580,581,587,589,594,595,598,605,614,628,634,654,657,659,663,665,668,670,675
EVERETT,149
EVERETTE,635
EVERLY,136,160,319,535,634,663,670
EWART,272,454,519
EWING(s),100,145,435

EYER,599
EYRE,607
FABER,145
FAIR,335
FAIRFAX,259,446,583,596
FAIRLEIGH,145,171,200,
201,202,203
FAIRLEY,15,17,18,56,57,
58,67,137,485
FANSLER,583,588,589
FAREE,335
FARES,133
FARMAN,203
FARMER,15,632
FAST* 677
FAST,135,136,159
FAUCH,247
FAWCETT,464
FEALS,164
FEAR,527
FEATHERHILL,150
FEDERA,529
FEE* 343-344,379
FEE,37,131,134,136,146,
158,162.174,308,311,312,
313,322,331,334,339,340,
341,342,346,347,349,384,
385,388,390,415,516,518
FEISTER,604
FELIX,3,44,369
FELLOWS,291
FELTON,438,511
FELTY,148
FENTON,143,145
FERGUSON,81,140,142,440,
489
FERLEY,34,43,62,64,68,69,
74,131,494
FERRELL,147,480
FERRIS,133,303
FERRY,127,135,146
FEURT,37,135,159,376,383
FIELD,415
FIELDS,43,196,528
FILBY,375
FILLEBUN,141
FINCH,149,518

FINLEY,36,132,134,142,
152,156,265,474
FINNIGAN,15
FISH,650
FISHER,87,101,104,127,
138,198,273,477,491,492,
545,629
FITHIAN,363,455,656
FITZ,571,572
FITZER,438
FITZGERALD,453,556,597
FITZPATRICK,15
FITZRANDOLPH,107,266,267,
275,285
FIX* 485
FIX,34,113,130,131,162
FLAHAVEN,139
FLAHERTY,658
FLANNEGAN,127
FLARITY,15
FLEEHARTY,127
FLEMING,248
FLEMINS,145
FLEMMING,144,149,232,304,
388
FLENNIKEN* 548-558
FLENNIKEN,36,96,123,127,
132,134,156,176,196,219,
223,269,453,457,496,497,
518,519,538,542,548,559,
560,561,567,568,614,643
FLESHER,424
FLETCHER,44,161,3884,406
FLINCH,105
FLOOD,148
FLOREA,526
FLOWERS,28,38,127,135,
142,150,158,159,430
FLUM,135
FLYNN,28
FOARDUM,304
FOBERS,241
FONNER,475,484
FONT,148
FORBES,148,150,241,243,
244,247,387
FORD,15

FORDYCE* 601-605
FORDYCE,21,39,107,137,
146,156,269,270,328,369,
370,394,423,477,506,535,
569,571,576,581,585,587,
594,599,608,625,639
FOREMAN,115,171,241,673
FORESTER,25
FORHEE,15
FORKLER,139
FORKS,151
FORMAN,145,149,150,255,565
FORRED,152
FORSTER,666
FORT(s),147,158
FORTNER,148,150,153
FORWARD,131
FOSSETT,153
FOSTER* 185
FOSTER,25,27,129,133,149,
157,168,169,174,187,188,
255,438,473,505,511,565
FOULKE,523
FOWLAND,564
FOWLER,34,79,148,530
FOX,34,117,130,156,399,
405,409
FRAKES,25,27,127,132,133,
135,145,146,147,149,158,
159,255,443
FRAKES SEE FRIGGS
FRAME,127
FRANCIS,182,197
FRANKBAUER,377,637
FRANKENBERGER,293,669
FRANKLIN,147,358
FRANKMAN,148
FRANK(s)* 657-658
FRANK(s),28,36,58,63,127,
142,411,433,458,644,652
FRANTZ,484
FRAZEE,25,36,39,135,137,
159,255,589,599
FRAZER,29,159,461,597
FRAZIER,4,43,446,465,548,
566,601
FREDERICK,150

FREEBORN,443
FREELAND,158,162
FREEMAN,115,142,148,149,
210,304,307,335,513,523
FREKELS,159
FRENCH,137,138,152,153,
255,304,305,482,485,593,
655
FREY,475,476,487
FRIBBY,152
FRICK,158,159
FRIGGS,127
FRINK,143
FRISH,148
FRIZELL,589
FROST,394
FRY(e)* 429
FRY(e),15,101,147,153,318,
338,369,389,398,405,414,
428,429,434,442,449,512
FUGATE(s),128,138,139
FULLENWIDER,139
FULLER,176,325,565,600
FULNER,159
FULTON,131,151,162,251,
301,464,468,491,493
FUNK,103,114,129
FURMAN,663
FURST,658
FUTNER,135
GABES,176,506
GABLER,611
GABRIEL,553
GADDIS,65,127,142,190,485,
522,572,627
GAFFATA,164
GAITREAL,131
GAITHER,139
GALAGIN,143
GALBRAITH,567
GALBREATH,238
GALENTINE,215
GALLESPIE,134
GALLATIN,333,615
GALLOWAY,25,53,130,131,
382,424
GALLUP,159

GANIEAR,336
GANIER,111
GANIER SEE GANIEAR
GAPEN* 633-635
GAPEN,23,24,28,29,36,127,
135,136,159,535,554,555,
578,597,654,660,663,671,
672,675
GAPLE,144
GARARD• 600-601,641-642
GARARD,23,29,35,36,146,
147,202,259,536,580,583,
586,587,588,590,594,596,
598,604,618,625,655
GARBER,473
GARD,142
GARDNER,28,54,64,137,156,
261,402
GARLOW,634
GARNER,159,281,440,474
GARRARD,37,127,132,150,
159,578,579,588
GARRARD SEE GERRARD
GARRAT(t),36,127,133,174,
188,298
GARRET(t),77,135,144,149,
417,420,573,574,575
GARRITT,28
GARRISON* 669-673
GARRISON,23,25,29,127,
135,144,159,160,174,214,
329,454,556,586,617,623,
653,660,665,667,668,670,
671,675
GARTNER,144
GARVIN,149
GARWOOD* 99
GARWOOD,45,83,97,99,125,
134,156,159,221
GARY,74
GASKIN(s),130,136,145,150
GASS,58,70,82
GATELY,156
GATES,132,579,580
GATRAIL,130
GATTRAL,150
GAUSE,127

GAYMAN* 73-75
GAYMAN,34,73,74,130,131
GEARHART,464,468
GEHO,28
GEIGER,520
GENN,446
GEORGE,131,409
GERMAN,149
GERNON,132
GERRARD* 600-601
GERRARD,19,134,159,202,460
GERRARD SEE GARARD
GERSINGER,599
GETTYS,374
GIBBONS,580
GIBBS,197,208
GIBSON,18,23,151,190,534
GIDEON,273
GIG,524
GIGER,145
GILBERT,127,185,517,519
GILES,176,565
GILKESEE,159,160
GILGUCE,132
GILKESIE,132
GILL,150
GILLELAND,648,651,652,653,
664
GILLER,139
GILLESPIE,127,136,149,211,
549,552,555
GILLESPIE SEE GLASPY
GILLESPY,140,156
GILLETT,117,506,507,569
GILLETTE,392
GILLILAND,140,143,648
GILLILAND,15
GILLIS,147,559
GILMER,568
GILMORE,127,147,149,151,
159,324
GILPIN,521,534,661
GIMLET,255
GIRTY,25,31,32
GIST,4,5,49,142,169,192,
292,578
GLADDEN,233,288,638

GLADEN,131
GLASG0,127
GLASGOW,135,159,160,505
GLASPY,127,549,552,555
GLASS,131,139,145,149,151
GLAZE,15,150
GLENN,213,214,304
GLOVER,147,219,277,382
GLUM,336
GOBEAN,127
GOBEAN SEE GAPEN
GOBIN,238
GOBLE,39,127,137,138,144,
146,459
GOCHENOUR,654
GODDARD,617
GODFREY,416,489
GOE,142,148
GOFF,228
GOGLEY,490
GOH0,28
GOINS,25
GOLDEN,39,137,492
GOLDHAWK,80
GOLDING,146
GOLDSMITH,146
GOODE,91
GOODEN,127,153,162,202,
323,370
GOODMAN,130,255
GOODWIN,25,27,34,127,131,
149,397,402,406,408,485
GOOSEY,28
GORAM,151
GORBY,151
GORDON* 434-438
GORDON,9,19,65,109,110,
163,176,209,223,234,279,
304,316,317,318,319,322,
323,324,325,326,327,328,
355,368,397,400,402,404,
405,411,414,416,430,469,
489,512,522,565,599,600,
606,619,626,646,670
GORE,102,474,508
GORREL,37
GORRELL* 423-424

GORRELL,132,136,139,144,
146,163,307,308,338,346,
352,382,417,420,421
GOUCHER,90
GOVES,106,538
GOVER,538
GABIL(1),144,148,150
GRABBLE,143
GRABLE,74
GRAGG,515
GRAGG SEE GREGG
GRAGSON,130
GRAGSTON,7
GRANDON,137,149
GRANLEE,441
GRANT,98,306,336,524
GRARY,156
GRAVES,139,304
GRAY,35,36,37,61,67,130,
131,133,136,146,148,150,
161,163,180,214,231,306,
311,382,383,478,512,600,
665,673
GRAYBILL,322,325
GREATHOUSE,15,57,145,147,
255
GREEGER,144
GREEN,148,149,156,169,304,
326,335,365,471,589,615
GREENE,134,135,333,358,676
GREENE SEE GREEN
GREENFIELD,78,191,337,369,
426,528
GREENLEE,64,74,75,81,292
GREGG(s)* 531-536
GREGG(s),36,102,103,127,
132,133,134,135,137,146,
150,152,156,157,174,177,
197,221,272,314,343,344,
393,443,513,514,515,516,
540,567,571,577,584,587,
588,594,595,605,607,608,
609,625,661,662,663,665,
668
GREGORY,216,547
GREGSTON,131
GRIBBS,593

GRIFFEN,669
GRIFFIN,130,153,664
GRIFFING,39
GRIFFITH,15,83,93,101,
127,129,135,152,255,317,
323,540,580
GRIM,39,104,279,412,413,
520
GRIMES,84,135,144,145,
159,325,374,459,467,468,
469,471,546,607
GRINSTAFF,28
GRIST,570
GROGAN,162
GROOM(e)(e),34,67,128,130,131,
161,247,304,518,540,
546,573
GROSS,474
GROSSMAN,435
GROVE(e),88,403,407,409,
410,414,440,534
GROW,127
GROWDY,124
GRUB(b),153,521
GUDGEL,127
GUFFEY,27,39
GUIN,150,153
GUMP,223
GUN(n),133,144,377,637
GUNNER,19,27,35,147,153,
382
GUSEMAN,435,626
GUSTIN,36,159,580,584,585
GUTHERIE,135,318,328,370,
399,405,431,530,647
GUTHERIE SEE GUTHERY
GUTHERY* 611-613
GUTHERY,24,38,128,213,255,304,
528,580,609,610,614,
616,617,620,621,640,641,
669,674
GUTHREY,38
GUTHRIE,20,25,54,107,231,
243,429,604
GUTHRIE SEE GUTHERY
GUYTON,147,437
GWIN,129

GWYNE,134
GWYNNE* 507-509
GWYNNE,36,39,129,150,156,
163,233,273,277,327,541,
547,618,619,620
HACKLEY,202
HACKNEY* 608-611
HACKNEY,127,612,613
HADDON,452,453,545,608,
615,657,670
HADLEY,531,532
HAGAN,304,521,671
HAGER,134
HAGUE,175,432
HAHN,580
HAIDAN,131,161
HAIDEN,74,130,481,493
HAIGHT,615
HAILMAN,213
HAINES,59,60,107,111,117,
156,162,304,404,445,471,
494,504,570,603
HAIR,471
HAIZE,153
HALBERG,144
HALE,134,156,211,236,634
HALES,88
HALFHILL,430,433
HALIFAX,460
HALL(s),15,18,24,25,26,
28,127,144,145,151,186,
255,305,357,359,579,580,
664,676
HALLMAN,159
HALLY,134
HAMASHOTT,593
HAMILTON,152,206,262,265,
279,304,408,410,412,422,
593,671,674
HAMMER(s),187,641
HAMMITT,141
HAMMON,142
HAMMOND,68,80,148
HAMPSON,448,490,493
HAMPTON,481,482
HANBY,532
HANCOCK,358,550

HAND,18,38,143,190,265,
650
HANDCOCK,282,286
HANDLEY,138,255
HANDLIN,521
HANEY,148,152
HANGER,196,208,463,468,
528
HANK(s)* 117-118
HANK(s),35,39,114,117,
121,147,288,289,511
HANNA,3,4,6,24,370,457,
545
HANNAH,19,36,38,134,135,
144,156,159,255,500,556,
558,595,649
HANNON,135
HANON,38
HARBERT,375
HARBESON,645
HARBOR,134
HARBOUGH,156
HARCUM,151
HARDEN,156
HARDESTY,27,34,130,131,
145,147,151,481
HARDIN,127,128,164,330,
383,586,623
HARDING,474
HARDY,159,474
HARGES,28
HARGESS,129
HARGROVE,78,123,124
HARGUS,15,18,19,28,129,
379,614
HARKNESS,139
HARLAN,531,608,609,610,
612,613
HARLAN SEE HACKNEY
HARLAND,164
HARLE,304
HARLING,151,261
HARMAN,127
HARPER* 530
HARPER,517,522,631
HARRINGTON,196
HARRIS,9,59,89,94,139,
150,151,194,250,255,263,
359,454
HARRISON,17,32,124,127,
150,151,463
HARROD* 240-251
HARROD,7,9,20,21,22,23,
25,26,29,35,47,53,131,
135,147,156,161,163,164,
171,179,181,185,191,194,
197,199,203,218,225,226,
227,231,237,240,254,255,
256,258,260,266,302,315,
325,345,352,362,373,378,
387,389,422,458,459,460,
464,470,488,501,528,529,
537,580,582,611,642,644
HARROD SEE HARWOOD
HARROW,304
HARRY,99,466
HARSH,67,74,150
HART,127,145,159,171,199,
200,203,205,228,281,317,
454,520,537,546,559,574,
575,576,580,665,666,672
HARTFIELD,134
HARTGROVE,88
HARTLEY,35,95,117,143,145,
392,478,493,580,615,616,
633,662
HARTLY,130,131,164
HARTMAN,27,76,134,156,
177,233,506,544,568
HARTSOCK,83
HARTZELL,573
HARVEY,327,470
HARWOOD,240,247
HASLET,144,146,295
HASTINGS,486,612
HAT,28
HATFIELD* 443-444
108,109,127,128,149,150,
151,318,367,457,511,577,
624,639,658
HATHAWAY* 444-446
HATHAWAY,15,19,27,37,39,
59,60,130,131,136,137,
143,146,163,378,379,382,

383,385,388,390,459,479,
481,500,580
HATT,25,144
HATTON,149
HAUCHER,234
HAUGHT,28
HAUSER,587,605
HAUSMAN,149
BAVER* 270-271
HAVER,208,219,234,263,
270,272,277,506
HAVERLY,393
HAWKINS* 77-80
HAWKINS,15,18,58,67,77,
78,96,97,122,124,125,127,
128,138,146,151,160,203,
290,347,570,572,628,631
HAWKS,296
HAWLEY,454
HAWN,388
HAWOOD,146
HAWTHORN,19,219
HAYCRAFT,19
HAYCROFT,170,201,204,579
HAYDEN,294
HAYDON,180
HAYES,62,66,296,325,333,
464,528,607,631
HAYS,35,130,131,149,161,
263,428,463,464
HAYWARD,240
HAZELBRIGG,146
HAZLET(t),36,132,137,159,
304
HEACOCK,97
HEADLEE,161,462,602,603
HEADLEY,432,466,477,652,664
HEADY,142
HEATH,228,297,477,478
HEATON* 282-297
HEATON,11,22,26,34,56,61,
62,67,69,81,82,95,102,
114,119,130,131,132,134,
137,156,161,206,210,215,
218,224,231,236,238,248,
276,282,299,300,301,302,
306,307,328,442,459,460,

461,464,465,469,470,471,
474,481,485,488,493,502,511
HEAVER,270
HEAVRIN,343,415
HECK,334,391
HECKATHORN,482
HECKT,70,72
HEDGE,285,467,480,600
HEDGES,71,138,139
HEFFLEY,437
HEGLE,34
HEISE,62
HEISSE,369
HELLER,236,501
HELM,164
HELMS,203
HELMIC,658
HEMPHILL,524
HEMSTEAD,175,510
HENDERSON,27,132,134,149,
152,153,156,185,280,377,
412,431,433,440,542,543,
560,565,606,637,673
HENDRICKS,4,5,18,127,385,
421
HENINGSHAW,305
HENKINS,143,406,441
HENNAN,368
HENNEN,408
HENNING,50
HENRICKS,149
HENRY,136,250,304,358,501,
521,582
HENSEL,665
HENSHAW,38
HENTHORN,127,128,143,144,
145,148
HENTON,25,201,203,240,246,
579
HENWARD,140
HERDMAN,157
HERDORF,142
HERON,150
HERRING,337,426
HERRINGTON,224,588,622
HERROD,127,129,130,133,
134,159,240,651,652,674

HERTZOG,125
HERVEY,139
HESSEY,304
HEVAY,144
HEVRIN SEE HEAVRIN
HEWITT,70,137,176,183,
233,262,263,264,437,514,
565,572
HEWLINGS,360
HEYMAN,512
HIBBS,36,117,134,156,
177,383,593,594,607
HICAN,152
HICKENBOTTOM,19
HICKER,665
HICKEY,531
HICKLEBERRY,588
HICKMAN* 229
HICKMAN,25,66,127,142,
144,148,156,162,208,228,
229,235,267,281,293,318,
382,391,405,433,440,442,
474,621
HICKS,203,355
HICKSON,36,159
HIDDING,512
HIGGINBOTHAM,209
HIGGINBOTTOM,518,664
HIGGINS,322,373,402,405
HIGGINSON,190
HIGH,215
HIGLER,665
HILDEBRAND,219,529
HILDERBRAND,652
HILEY,147
HILL* 301
HILL,9,25,26,34,36,62,80,
94,119,130,131,134,137,
139,144,145,147,149,150,
156,157,161,179,185,209,
215,223,231,251,255,277,
283,290,291,307,309,310,
311,321,322,324,332,392,
394,395,448,449,451,453,
485,524,580,593,650
HILLEGAS,144
HILLER* 236-238

HILLER,27,45,156,169,171,
192,215,217,218,223,224,
225,226,234,235,236,251,
261,268,287,457,464,500,
510,643
HILLING,595
HILLMAN,134,580
HIMBLE,645
HINCH,15,25,153,255
HINCHMAN,94
HINEGARDNER,404,597
HINERMAN,443
HINES,207
HINKLE,198,273,580
HINTON,170,250
HITE,8,9,163,193,247
HITT,501
HIX,511
HIXENBAUGH,59,60,91,229
HIXON,147,501
HOAGLAND,150,203,409
HOBBS,38,127,135,159,543
HOBSON,145
HOFF,153
HOFFMAN,15,475
HOGAN,132,133,480
HOGE* 100-106
HOGE,9,27,35,83,84,100,
106,107,108,112,113,114,
134,144,146,156,162,235,
278,319,324,328,374,382,
383,392,398,411,413,414,
426,428,433,442,469,470,
475,488,492,494,503,538,
606,638,653
HOGG,531,532,533
HOGLAND,128
HOGUE,9,130,131
HOHMAN,407
HOLDEN,156
HOLDER,547
HOLDON,134
HOLPRUNER,72
HOLLAND,400,435,436,628
HOLLEY,156
HOLLINGSWORTH,306,496,497,
554,556

HOLLIS,150
HOLLOWAY,162
HOLLYDAY,338
HOLMES,43,140,146,148,159,314
HOLSON,143
HOLT,129,146,250
HOLTON,20,24,30,36,129,132,134,156,501,543,620,640
HOLTZCLAW,204
HOLVEY,265
HOMER,46,599,605
HONACKER,25,255
HONEY,449
HONNELL* 280-281
HONNELL,227,279,280,281,439,440
HOOD,304,355,464,493
HOOK* 330-338
HOOK,7,18,19,35,113,130,131,132,136,139,142,145,151,153,161,176,275,307,308,311,314,316,319,326,338,339,340,341,356,362,363,364,371,378,379,383,384,387,388,391,407,414,426,427,446,500
HOOKE,337,362
HOOKE SEE HOOK
HOOPER,136,536
HOOVER,55,69,73,136,142,144,490,571,576,673
HOPEWELL,124,125,147
HOPKINS,148,150,153,233,344,473,486,507
HOPTON,518
HORLEY,392
HORMELL,62,280
HORN,15,64,75,76,95,105,137,489,491
HORNER,5,46,58,260,379,406,450,491,507,510,518,**519,546**
HORRELL,413
HORTON,151
HOSACK,140

HOSKINS,149
HOSKINSON,151,152,153,214,322,387,506,569
HOSTETLER,652,671
HOUGHLAND,139
HOULDSWORTH,211
HOULSWORTH,175,277,306,330,543
HOUP,304
HOURIGHAN,180
HOUSE,18,19,25,26,35,113,127,130,131,138,145,146,147,148,150,152,153,161,164,219,241,246,332,366,367,383
HOWARD,84,127,136,143,159,162,403,511,513,612,615
HOWDEN,78
HOWE,151,152,305
HOWELL,65,118,137,138,258,290,301,478,489,599
HOWPER,304
HOY,304,326,412,437,438
HUBBARD,203
HUBBLE,81
HUBLE,147
HUCKETT,143
HUCKLE,135
HUCKLEBERRY,127
HUDSON* 647
HUDSON,4,129,460,461,573,578,580,587,598,612,625,639,647,668
HUFF,134,140,142,409
HUFFMAN* 475-477
HUFFMAN,19,27,37,72,101,127,130,136,150,162,220,281,325,329,345,369,398,403,441,442,447,451,472,473,474,480,484,486,487
HUFFORD,96,123,473
HUFFSDALE,227
HUFTY* 568-569
HUFTY,117,174,176,178,188,221,233,275,277,506,507,547,564,645,655,657
HUGGINS,152,159,314,602,667

**HUGHES* 205-225,373-375,
         509-512**
HUGHES,15,17,18,21,22,25,
26,27,33,36,37,42,55,62,
66,120,127,132,133,134,
136,137,144,146,147,151,
153,154,156,163,164,165,
166,167,168,169,170,172,
173,174,175,177,178,179,
180,181,186,187,188,189,
192,193,195,200,205,225,
226,227,228,229,231,235,
236,237,238,255,264,268,
269,271,275,277,278,281,
287,291,299,304,309,315,
326,327,333,361,363,364,
367,382,390,418,438,449,
454,455,466,468,486,496,
502,503,517,518,530,545,
545,546,551,552,558,580,
643,676
HUGHSTON,132
HUGUS,424
HUIE,145
HUL,132
HULL,135,153,157,161
HULLETT,115
HUMBLE,26,255
HUME,100
HUMPHREYS,34
HUMPHRIES,286
HUNNELL* 280-281
HUNNELL,229,280,373,412,
440,655
HUNNELL SEE HONNELL
HUNNIL,279
HUNT,26,220,255,426,498,
521,624,664
HUNTER,39,263,509,510
HUNTINGTON,148
HUPP* 45-49
HUPP,27,41,43,44,45,58,
63,129,140,208,379,622,
668
HURLEY,130,131
HUSBAND,300

HUSHER,198,273
HUSLIN,134
HUSONG,27,143
HUSS* 469-470
HUSS,73,102,105,115,209,
285,316,324,325,328,465,
466,489,571,575,638
HUSTEAD,15
HUSTON,24,29,36,37,42,44,
127,132,133,134,135,140,
142,159,458,486,509,576,
593,601,611,641
HUTCHINS,580
HUTSON,135
HUTTONFIELD,161
HUZZY,135
HYATT,207,289,292
HYDE,135,159,498,502,517
HYNES,16
IAMS* 480-485
IAMS,62,224,304,449,473,
476,487,493,494,647
IDEN,102
IIAMS,480
IIAMS SEE IAMS
IJAMES,480
IJAMES SEE IAMS
IJAMS,480
IJAMS SEE IAMS
ILER,139
IMES,480
IMES SEE IAMS
INGEL,137
INGERSOL,428
INGHRAM* 309-320
INGHRAM,27,37,98,102,115,
132,136,143,146,147,149,
150,156,162,174,199,210,
270,279,307,308,320,321,
322,323,324,325,327,328,
335,337,338,344,349,350,
352,369,379,382,383,387,
391,394,405,416,417,420,
421,422,423,424,426,431,
435,436,439j466,469,480,
516,518,537,586,593,594,
606,608,623

INGHRUM,132,133
INGLE,350
INGRAM,164,590
INGLEDUE,156
INKINS,434
INLOW,151
INNIS,143
IRVINE,31,33,158
IRWIN,135,437,499,558
ISAACS,180,642
ISENMINGER,279,280,400,
402,411,412,413,414
ISANHOOT,143
ISHMAEL,34,36
ISRAEL* 530-531
ISRAEL,36,132,134,147,
156,267,502,513,530
IVERS* 626-627
IVERS,36,135,144,159,509,
579,618,620,656,657
IVERSON,147,149
JACKMAN,142,146,152,527
JACKSON* 383-386,545-546
JACKSON,22,27,34,35,37,
127,129,130,131,133,134,
135,136,144,146,149,151,
156,159,160,243,295,306,
308,311,330,331,333,334,
338,339,340,343,378,379,
388,400,401,402,409,416,
421,423,444,445,470,500,
503,507,518,545,570,574,
580,615,648,649,650,651,
656,668,672
JACOB,133
JACOBS,16,107,129,220,279,
317,412,428,501,504
JAIL,161
JAMES,26,37,152,161,255,
297,588
JAMESON,134,159,436
JAMISON,156,159,557,560,
561,567
JANEY,536
JARRETT,418,420,421
JEFFERON,358
JEFFRIES,298

JENKINS,38,81,82,100,127,
135,145,148,152,159,454,
573,578,580,608,609,610,
647
JENKINSON,333,498
JENNINGS* 452-454
JENNINGS,27,35,127,129,
130,131,137,148,153,161,
177,197,269,270,322,382,
388,501,502,518,522,546,
555,556,557,574,603
JENNINS,382
JEROME,454
JEWELL,161,162,471,494,
651,661
JOHN,135,279,295,402,404,
408,412,431,580
JOHNS* 473-475
JOHNS,102,133,227,323,394,
467,471,472,473,476,477,
485
JOHNSON* 109-112,666-668
JOHNSON,6,16,19,27,31,36,
38,39,42,47,57,95,98,99,
108,109,114,120,129,130,
134,135,137,139,140,143,
145,146,148,151,156,159,
182,197,198,214,216,218,
224,233,251,273,274,329,
336,352,357,369,372,392,
**401,412,422,427,428,435,
436,446,465,467,472,473,**
507,512,530,547,565,570,
580,583,606,620,625,632,
636,646,647,661,664,666
JOHNSTON,36,130,131,140,
142,145,147,149,156,157,
159,161,162
JOHNSTONE,132
JOLLIFE,149
JOLLY,57,576,585,586
JONES* 338-339,658-659
JONES,5,6,16,34,35,36,37,
74,78,88,118,124,127,132,
134,135,136,142,143,145,
146,149,151,152,153,156,
159,170,238,239,298,309,

311,330,333,335,344,352,
376,379,380,382,383,384,
394,440,450,464,468,469,
481,519,520,526,534,574,
580,594,610,620,654,
JORDAN,512
JORDON,159
JOSEPH,594,608
JUGHT,615
JULIEN,162
JUNK,521
JURDIN,435
JURDIN SEE GORDON
KAIGHN,205,509,510
KAINE,436
KANE,360
KARNS,436
KARR,148,150
KARSH,656
KAUFFMAN,502
KECKLEY,405,406
KEDAY,143
KEENE,187
KEENER* 647-654
KEENER,28,135,136,160,437,
647,664,665
KEES,34,74
KEISER,669
KEITH,50,51,583
KELLAR,204,346,352
KELLER,139,150,446,559
KELLER SEE SELLARS
KELLER SEE KELLAR
KELLEY,34,268,466
KELLOGG,590
KELLY* 273
KELLY,16,19,27,47,130,
131,134,140,151,156,182,
183,197,198,273,344,518
KELSEY,34,119,130,131
KELSO,36,146
KEMP,151
KENADY,164
KENDALL* 189-190
KENDALL,129,142,143,168,
187,189,209,567
KENDLE,129

KENDRICK,19
KENNARD,90
KENNEDY* 548
KENNEDY,4,120,132,135,
140,146,202,288,289,293,
304,319,423,453,465,496,
497,522,523,539,540,541,
548,551,629,643
KENNER,513,514,515,516,
517
KENNY,26,130,152
KENT* 424-428
KENT,104,109,110,111,136,
162,225,279,311,312,314,
315,316,317,331,337,350,
354,368,369,372,379,382,
387,389,396,398,403,404,
411,413,416,421,422,423,
425,429,440,501,587,598,
599,619,638
KENTNER,156
KENWORTHY,103
KERCHAVAL,238
KEPLER,95,207,227,566
KERKLE,162
KERNS,156,662,667
KERR,139,140,142,219,220,
222,264,519,522,526,534,
546,568,598
KESTER,408
KETCH,136,137,145
KETCHAM,194
KETCHUM,9,151,156,234,356,
499,500,503
KETERLING,138
KEYS,73,462,468,480,486,
635
KIBBY,151,460
KIDD,38,135,159
KIENER SEE KEENER
KIGER,245,260,652
KILLGEES,36
KILLIAM,145
KILPATRICK,163
KIMBALL,89
KIMBLE,137,158
KIMES,207

KINCAID* 276-279
KINCAID,96,178,194,195,
207,211,219,221,226,235,
267,269,270,276,325,329,
364,433,469,547,607
KINKAID,356
KINDER,26,150
KING,82,88,106,143,161,
409,435,441,626
KINNESON,129
KINNEY,372,397
KINSER,139
KINSEY,509,664
KIRBY,19,156,158,506,512,
536,542,566,569,586,623,
668
KIRCK,136
KIRK(e),132,158,369,408,
512
KIRKPATRICK,377,401,637,
650
KISER,464
KITCH,159
KITTEN,137,148
KITTS,304
KLINE,19,165,167,179,221,
260,412,414
KLINE SEE CLINE
KNAP,151,160
KNIGHT,31,32,147,156,163,
199,238,258,281,318,333,
376,377,392,456,537,569,
574,580,583,588,589,657
KNISELY,398,403
KNOOP,590,592,656,657
KNOTT(s),24,37,128,129,
133,135,136,145,159,160,
163,535,536,599,622,633,
662,663,666,675
KNOWLES,297
KNOX,150,151,159,251,
451,462,463,464,465,468,
548
KNUFFSINGER,66
KNUFFSINGER SEE NYSWANER
KORBY,134
KOUTZ* 75-76
KOUTZ,75,76,80
KRAMER,630,631
KREPPS,568
KREPS,151
KRINE,512
KUGHN,128,433,435,478,529,
626
KUHN,407
KUSSART,670
KUSTER,638
KUYKENDALL,16,18,26,225
KYHNER SEE KEENER
KYLE,592
KYNER SEE KEENER
LACEY,560,564
LACKEY,137,139,304
LACOCK,65,138
LADD,572
LAFERTY,424
LAFFERTY,311,315,421,520,
526
LAIDLEY,567
LAIRD,261
LAKE,89
LAKIN* 339-343
LAKIN,136,308,315,331,343,
348,350,352,383,384,385,388
LAKINS,308
LALLEY,161
LAMB,148,654
LAMBERT* 641
LAMBERT,135,477,580,609
LANCASTER,210,632,636
LANCE,135
LANCE SEE LANTZ
LANO,304,474
LANDERS,67,207
LANE,127,147
LANEBAUGH,28
LANG,499
LANHAM,393
LANNING,377,637
LANS SEE LANTZ
LANSE SEE LANTZ
LANTHROP,144
LANTS SEE LANTZ
LANTZ* 635-639

LANTZ,48,105,112,135,160,
182,197,328,357,368,377,
469,489,535,571,575,577,
595,597,606,625,628,632,
639,649,650,655,658,662,
663
LAPMAN,599
LAPPING,396,397,412,425,
427
LARGLEY,456
LARKIN,315,415
LARRISON,137
LARSH,630
LARSON,463
LARUE-ENLOW,202
LATHLAND,609
LATTIMORE,160
LAUGHLIN,127,144,148,149
LAUGHRAN,522
LAUNCE SEE LANTZ
LAUNTZ SEE LANTZ
LAW,143
LAWLESS,180
LAWRENCE,28,148
LAWSON,19
LAWYER,273
LAY,294
LAYTON,521
LAZEAR,313
LAZEL,142
LEACOCK,137
LEAKINS,162
LEAMON,619
LEANS,146
LEATHERMAN,75,144,146,
151,152
LEATON,160
LEBEGUT,144
LECKEY,295,516
LEE,16,35,36,38,39,129,
130,131,132,133,137,144,
150,161,232,330,331,339,
384,513,570,584,655
LEECH,17,42
LEEDS,589
LEEMAN,157
LEET,17,149

LEFLER,141
LEGG,243
LEIGH SEE LEITH
LEIGHLEY,64
LEIPER,154
LEITH,307,308,331,334,
340,341,343,344,384,426
LEMLEY* 430-432
LEMLEY,12,37,135,159,160,
165,206,207,208,213,307,
310,321,322,364,396,398,
399,404,405,410,412,415,
433,443,586,623,638,654
LEMMON,139
LEMON,132,143,160,279
LEONARD* 106-109
LEONARD,9,34,35,37,61,
103,105,116,120,130,131,
133,134,153,156,162,219,
240,459,604,669
LESLEY,144,529
LESLIE,627
LESLY,148
LESTER,89,368,405
LETTS,209,463,468
LEVAN,304
LEVIN(s),140
LEWIS* 72-73
LEWIS,26,36,58,69,70,72,
84,88,92,132,135,156,157,
160,162,163,192,193,204,
205,255,264,286,304,305,
319,441,443,490,530,657
LIEPER,89,361
LIETH SEE LEITH
LIGGETT,224
LIGHTFOOT,227
LIGHTNER,392,443,392,443
LIMING,9,27,132,432,501
LIMMING,134,147,156
LINADAH,132
LINCANT,26
LINCH,153
LINCOLN* 519-421
LINCOLN,26,513,530,574,
665
LINDLEY,27,39,43,129,137,

138,144,146,434,453,454,
459,472,600,609
LINDSECOMB,130
LINDSEY,145,151,156,169,
175,210,211,212,213,277,
287,313,316,472,547
LINE(s),34,130,131,255,
461
LINGERFIELD,304
LINK,127,129,140,147
LINN,377,637
LINSECUM,7,34,35,36,130,
131,137,151,243
LINSLEY,134
LINTON,665
LINVIL,194
LINVILL,356,363
LIPPENCOTT,7,9,105,316,
319,372,426,459
LITMAN,144
LITTLE,127,129,156,306,
479,603
LITTLETON,144
LITZENBERG,62,64,71,80,
81,82,91,174,176,179,195,
565
LIVENGOOD* 432-434
LIVENGOOD,132,134,156,
159,160,163,187,221,226,
238,380,430,447,449,529,
639,657,658
LIVINGSTONE, 234
LLOYD(s),143,219,443
LOAR,223,372,398
LOCK,16
LOCKE,634
LOCKEY,156
LOCKHART,337
LOCKRY,20
LOGAN,150,276,304,647,648
LOHR,67
LOLLE,161
LONCE SEE LANTZ
LONDY,519
LONG* 616-621
LONG,20,29,36,38,47,48,
127,135,144,146,147,148,

150,151,153,159,160,173,
263,273,277,278,342,377,
406,431,508,509,529,536,
547,575,578,588,594,621,
622,623,624,625,627,635,
646,647,651,653,656,657,
665,666,670,672
LONGENACKER,156
LONGSTREET,151,409
LONGSTRETH,368,398,403
LONGSTRETH SEE LONGSTREET
LONTZ SEE LANTZ
LORAIN,136
LOUGH,321,324
LOUGHMAN,120,487
LOUGHRY,31
LOVE,39,120,137,145,162,
239,329,417,469,627
LOVEJOY,342
LOVELY,304
LOWERY,156,215,621
LOWERY SEE LOWRY
LOWNES,408
LOWREY,4,34,54,162,548
LOWRIE,130
LOWRY,55,131
LOWTHARD,142
LUAS,134
LUCAS* 186-188
LUCAS,17,127,134,137,138,
148,151,152,153,165,166,
168,169,171,172,173,174,
177,178,179,180,181,189,
190,191,195,196,200,206,
221,224,245,273,373,432,
569,642
LUCE,283,385
LUCE SEE LUSE
LUCEY,161
LUCKEY,136
LUMMAX,425
LUNBACK,162
LUSE,117,120,161,182,211,
224,225,256,257,284,288,
299,349,357,623,646
LUTES,139,162
LUX,543

LUZADA,36,132
LUZADAH,133
LUZADER* 538
LUZADER,106,134,153,156
LUZADO,580
LYDER,146
LYETH SEE LEITH
LYLE,337
LYNCH,149,367,671
LYNN,149,203,522,535,572,
580,583,593,594,595,607,
622,659
LYON(s),16,17,18,26,44,
61,146,152,162,164,443,
479,505,580,651
LYTLE,119,387
MacARTHUR,242
MacELVANEY,226
MacINTIRE,143,151
MacINTOSH,24,138
MACK,88
MacKAY,150,
MacKEE,145
MACKEY,604,640
MacMANAMA,149
MADISON,28
MAGILL,151
MAGIN,16
MAGINNIS,147,152
MAHANA* 357-358
MAHANA,261
MAHANAH,401
MAIN,129,144,149
MAINS,101
MAINKE,142
MAJOR,26
MAKIN,16
MALONE,665
MALSBERRY,94
MAN,56
MANN,26,53,142,661
MANNIN,143
MANNING,22,26,34,150,157,
207
MANNON,128,159
MANSFIELD,414
MANTLER,143

MANLY,141
MAPEL* 409-412,663-665
MAPEL,230,231,397,398,403,
405,413,658
MAPLE,112,159,162,213,320,
457,519,554,555,652
MARCHANT,149
MARKHAM,514
MARKINS,162
MARKLE,211,277
MARKS,159
MARMIE,498,501
MARQUIS,140,176,275
MARR,128
MARRATO,134
MARRATTA,156
MARRIOTT,463
MARSH,144,334
MARSHALL,129,138,139,160,
359,360
MARTIN* 446,492-494
MARTIN,27,35,75,82,129,
130,131,133,140,145,147,
149,151,156,157,159,161,
162,174,199,224,259,267,
317,321,367,431,459,481,
494,516,537,543,580,583,
590,591,592,593,641,656
MASHIE,183
MASON,16,128,139,240,247,
254,304,392,440,442,446,
471
MASSEY,143
MASTERS,38,81,127,135,
150,156,158,159,580,636
MASTERSON,127,143,148,272
MASY,145
MATHENY,130
MATHEW,16
MATHEWS,151,152,274
MATSON,150
MATTOX,477
MAULDING,183,218
MAULSON,141
MAWFELL,159
MAXER,157
MAXFIELD,163

MAXON,157
MAXWELL,374,424,630
MAY,304
MAYFIELD,160
MAYHER,132
McADAMS,200
McARDLE,152
McATEE,152
McBETH,392
McBRIDE,106,255
McBURNEY,96
McCABE,147
McCALL,152,217,220,226
McCALLA,607
McCALLEY,280
McCALLISTER,147,247
McCALLEY,412
McCALLY,134,153
McCANN,147,158,463,468
McCANNES,139
McCARL,477
McCARTER,518
McCARTNEY,149,156,326,437
McCARTY,128,145,180,649
McCARY,344
McCASLIN,278,546
McCHRISTY,142,144
McCINE,236
McCLAIN* 274-275
McCLAIN,16,42,53,96,138,
176,179,183,195,197,213,
214,215,216,223,231,259,
274,506,518,586,615
McCLAMAN, 129
McCLANE,512
McCLASKEY,438
McCLEAN,6,23,43,133,146,
157,542,544,671
McCLEANNON,140
McCLEARY,25,26,121,128,
133,134
McCLEERY,22,172
McCLELLAN,133,134
McCLELLAND* 467-469,558-559
McCLELLAND,21,31,32,36,
73,81,132,134,135,142,
146,147,153,156,157,214,

229,243,288,299,300,310,
311,325,345,355,374,390,
463,474,476,489,500,502,
504,505,509,514,518,519,
551,555,556,558,574,600,
614,618,625,630
McCLENAHAM,180
McCLENATHAN,120,121,220
McCLENNAN,243
McCLINTOCK,567
McCLOSKEY,511
McCLOY,640
McCLUNG,19,640
McCLURE,135,139,271,276,
410,516,588,664,670
McCLURG,159,640
McCOLLISTER,267
McCOLLUM,407
McCOMBS,208,228,229,281
McCONKEY,137
McCON,133
McCONNEL(1),138,140,151,
232,290
McCOOLE,609
McCORMICH,355
McCORMICK,129,137,139,
149,152,304,355,390,429,
484,600,650
McCOUN,242,243
McCOY,38,49,79,128,129,
142,143,148,157,159,163,
236,382,383,543,559
McCOYER,144
McCRACKEN,15,136,137,159,
215
McCRACKIN,417,418,419
McCRAY,34,128,130,131,493
McCREA,560
McCREADY,159
McCREARY,124,274,496
McCROD,93
McCRORY,304
McCULLER,304
McCULLEY,377,637
McCULLOCH,130
McCULLOCK,139
McCULLOM,150

McCULLOUGH,60,137,143,
176,178,195,228,280,377,
483,566,587,598,624,637
McCURDY,525,622
McCURRY,132
McDANIEL,16,144,146,150,
152,153
McDOLE,144,148,152
McDONALD,7,41,129,142,
143,145
McDONNEAS,593
McDONNOUGH,159
McDOUGAL,112,606,658
McDOWEL,38
McDOWELL,36,128,132,133,
134,156,159,161,499,503,
580
McELDOWNEY,512
McELROY,36,132,134,156,
182
McELVAINE,191,528
McELVANEY,220
McENTIRE,139
McENTYRE,151
McEWEN,161
McFALL,129
McFANN,390,434,468
McFARLAND,27,28,34,119,
120,128,129,137,154,160,
177,287,288,351,353,361,
477,614,622,624
McFAWL,142
McGAUGHAN,140
McGEE,26,150,224,255
McGIFFIN,162
McGIFFING,137
McGILKIN,175
McGILL,131,162,568,593,
608
McGILTY,129
McGINNIS,128,446,465,476,
486
McGLAUGHLIN,145,157
McGLOAN,140
McGLUMPHEY,83,103,114,
210,213
McGOVERN,272

McGRAW,147
McGREGOR,566,573
McGRUDER,142
McGUINES,140
McGUIRE,43,139,382,663,
664
McILVAINE,58
McINTIRE,481
McINTIRE SEE McINTYRE
McINTOSH,158,354
McINTURFF,646
McINTYRE,131,202,255,592
McKAIN,135
McKAY,152,346,352,610,611,
617
McKEAN,157
McKEE,36,159,232,383,540
McKELVY,159
McKENNA,35
McKENNEY,580
McKENNY,16,131,132
McKENZIE,200
McKEY,132,526
McKIBBEN(s),159,631
McKINLEY,148,149,265,369
McKINNEY,130,268,522,559,
560
McKINNY,132
McKINNON,159
McKNIGHT,160,555,558
McKOWAN,673
McKOWN,131
McKOY,147
McKULLICK,142
McKUNE,151
McLANE,151
McLAUGH,147
McLAUGHLIN,132
McLEAN,361
McMAHAN,118,152,674
McMAHON,38
McMANAMA,149
McMANUS,255
McMASTER(s),59,60,144
McMECHEN,139
McMILLAN,497,523,530,539
McMILLEN,134,383,524

McMILLIN,21
McMILLION,163
McMINN,223,229,260,261
McMULLEN,133,136,152,159,177
McMUND,152
McMURRAY,79
McMYRTRE,493,494
McNARY,19
McNAY,279
McNEELEY,106,
McNEELY,209,210,319,402
McNEIL,149,171,201,202
McNURLAND,463
McNUTT,471,645
McPHERRIN,399
McQUADE,36,132
McQUAIDE,97,367
McQUAY,105
McQUEN,209
McROBBIN,141
McROY,145
McSHERRY,14
McVAUGH,27,130
McVAY,35,39,137,138,150,459,467,487
McVEIGH SEE McVAY
McWADE,146
McWILLIAMS,138
MEANS,19,152,593
MECHEN,152
MEEGAN,484
MEEK,34,131,139,474,481
MEEKER,466
MEEKS,130,161,382,473,481,490,656
MEEOWN,131
MEFFIT(t),152
MEICHEN* 438-439
MEIGHEN,271,305,306,325,480,482,484,511
MEIN,143
MELLICK,251,471
MELLON,67
MENDENHALL,104,105,488,511,512
MENE,128

MENKS SEE **MICKS**
MERANDA,131
MERATO,147
MERCER,16,149,660
MERCERLY,16
MERCHANT,214,304
MEREDITH,89,334,656
MERLOTTE,177,506
MERRANDY,136
MERRIFIELD,129,520
MERRITT,256
MESSEMER,130
MESSMORE,34,57,128
MESTERZAT,622
MESTRAZAT,634
MESTREZAT,588
METCALF(e),144
METKIRK(e),149
METTLER,468
METZ,526
MEVAN,146
MICHAEL,646
MICHENOR,227
MICKENS,492
MICKLE,109,129,367
MICKS,633
MIDDLESWORT,436
MIFFORD,152
MILEKIN,131
MILES,34,46,216
MILFORD,150
MILLBURN,55
MILLER,19,27,28,34,39,46,48,76,80,128,130,132,134,135,137,138,139,140,143,144,145,146,148,150,157,158,159,161,196,202,225,232,236,237,261,274,285,331,344,374,409,428,430,437,440,459,465,484,492,502,503,504,507,518,523,528,541,545,570,574,580,587,601,603,604,639,652,653,658,667,668,671
MILLHON,96
MILLIGAN,34,35,130,224,232,235,279

MILLIKEN* 232-236
MILLIKEN,162,215,223,228,
232,236,237,278,279,287,
322,362,412,473,484,508,
547,569,629
MILLS,28,35,61,87,107,
113,130,131,139,145,146,
147,148,149,150,157,159,
161,164,249,251,258,409,
460,464,601
MILTON,571
MININGER,142
MINKS,662
MINOR(s)* 627-633
MINOR,5,11,12,18,20,24,
29,30,38,112,128,130,131,
135,160,182,197,210,218,
243,250,279,286,288,324,
333,357,368,455,530,535,
536,538,540,551,558,567,
577,578,580,595,618,620,
625,626,636,638,639,641,
650,654,655,657,658,662
MINTER,145
MINTON,137
MINTOR,162
MIRANDA* 386-387
MIRANDA,37,130,137,153,
245,460
MIRANDY,3,153,162,334,379,
385,386
MITCHELL,53,82,135,138,
139,143,148,151,208,213,
214,231,235,271,307,309,
310,323,324,338,366,379,
389,391,392,394,395,417,
448,449,456,463,467,472,
475,477,489,511,566
MITCHENER,490
MITCHENOR,81,208,305,518,
610
MOBLEY,82
MOFFETT,145,153,506,569
MOFFITT,394
MOLING,147
MONROE,22,26
MONTGOMERY* 488-489

MONTGOMERY,9,19,73,75,
105,120,121,149,157,160,
247,313,316,318,367,442,
459,462,468,470,475,492,
493,494,542,639
MONTREE(s),208
MONEY,434
MONY,434
MOODY,148,518
MOON,119,282,284,286,301
MOONEY,12,151,152,320,400,
407,409,414,434,435
MOOR,134,144,153,338,493
**MOORE* 456-458,494-495,
642-645**
MOORE,17,22,23,25,26,31,
33,34,37,46,59,104,127,
130,131,132,134,136,138,
139,143,144,145,148,156,
157,158,159,161,163,164,
180,210,219,241,242,243,
245,246,247,248,249,251,
255,257,273,322,446,453,
463,485,493,494,499,503,
518,520,530,539,540,541,
542,566,580,594,608,652,
658,664
MORALTY,132
MORANDY,382,383,386
MORDOC,265
MORDOCK,145,147,149,265
MORE,135,139
MOREDOCK* 265-267
MOREDOCK,27,121,128,197,
219,220,226,228,235,242,
265,277,502,503,531,579,
580
MOREHEAD,216,530
MORELAND,149,152,572,655
MORELY,517,519
MORFORD,9,501
MORGAN,11,16,19,30,48,
127,129,139,140,144,159,
160,190,195,236,238,283,
287,289,332,507,514,597,
611,628,630,650
MORIN,19

MORISE,382
MORLAN,149
MORRIE,382
MORRIS* 358-365,595-600
MORRIS,9,24,26,27,28,34,
35,37,97,107,111,114,117,
118,129,130,131,132,134,
135,136,137,138,142,144,
145,146,148,152,154,156,
158,159,160,162,181,194,
203,213,214,225,231,235,
255,276,302,304,306,309,
310,311,312,314,318,326,
329,333,334,335,336,357,
358,372,375,376,377,379,
382,389,394,405,406,415,
416,422,428,430,432,438,
451,455,465,511,512,529,
576,578,579,580,583,584,
585,586,587,605,623,624,
669,671
MORRISEY,371
MORRISON,143,148,152,157,
159,180,204,433,529,547,
665
MORROW,156
MORTON,16,149,151,292
MOSELEY,16
MOSIER,79,107
MOTT,116,660
MOUDY,466
MT.JOY,185
MOUSER,82
MOYER,144
MUCELROY,145
MUCKLE,491
MUCKLEROY,16,164
MULLEN,151
MULRINE,325,438,439
MUNDAY,257
MUNDEL* 573
MUNDEL,298,599
MUNDELL,519,545,570,632
MUNDELL SEE MUNDLE
MUNDLE,36,135,150,159,160,
500,503,573,579,580,585,
597,632,638
MUNDLE SEE MUNDEL
MUNGER,675
MUNROE,134,580
MUNYON,397,437
MURAT0,27,147
MURDICK,265
MURDOCK* 505-507
MURDOCK,26,117,120,132,
134,156,157,171,176,232,
255,265,300,330,376,392,
540,569,570,587,605,619,
625
MURDOCK SEE MOREDOCK
MURDOCK SEE MORDOC
MORDOC SEE MURDOCK
MURFORD,162
MURPHET,360
MURPHEY,145,148
MURPHY,129,142,147,149,
151
MURRAY,19,46,53,150,368,
530
MURROW,304
MURRY,143
MUSGROVE,144,340
MUSTARD(s),150,156,486,
502
MYARS,164
MYERS* 607-608
MYERS,45,54,66,81,91,94,
127,132,134,146,156,157,
160,218,221,223,224,226,
236,237,260,292,299,431,
447,463,467,472,481,485,
508,516,534,535,536,570,
580,582,583,588,593,594,
600,601,604,633,642,659,
660,662,671
MYLES,140
MYNDAL,147
NAGEL,665
NAIL,148
NAILOR,150,152,163,456
NALL,202
NAMIGHT,145
NASSINGER,66
NAUGHTON,143

NAVIN,532
NEAL,24,128,147,164,180,
188,225,226,434
NEALE,675
NEALEY,142
NEBEKER,356,363
NEED,34,130,131
NEEL,174,225,263
NEELSON,135,164
NEFF,174,188,220,226,269
NEGUS,118
NEIKIRK,86,87
NEIL,142,144,270,665
NEILY,151
NELSON,128,140,153,288,
329
NEPP,580
NEVILL(e),36,157,160,596
NEVITT,157,160
NEWBURY,89
NEWELL,128,138,139,143,
151
NEWKIRK,128,148,153
NEWLAND,15,16,21,27,33,
37,128,133,134,138,146,
147,157,158,160,191,241,
245,248,249,302,304,325,
389,521,524
NEWLON,128
NEWMAN,136,149,293,360,
666,668
NEWSOM,58,519
NEWSWAMGER,66
NEWTON,50,132
NICELY,673
NICEWANGER,148
NICHOLAS,15,28,97,129,
134,152
NICHOLS* 536
NICHOLS,20,29,52,102,123,
133,140,148,157,223,278,
297,304,386,398,404,410,
411,457,462,533,587,600,
605,620
NICKLIN,239
NIELSON,662
NIGHT,135

NIPPY,146
NIST,147
NISWANGER,425
NISWANGER SEE NYSWANER
NIWEL(l),150
NIXON,89,103,142,267,359,
360,409,571,662,663
NOBLE,142,160
NOFSINGER,66
NOFSINGER SEE NYSWANER
NOLAND,500
NOORE,16
NORRIS,143,145,147,149,
304
NORTHERN,138
NOSENGER,66
NOSTRINGER,66
NOTT,37
NOTTS,38,128
NOTTS SEE KNOTTS
NOWLAND,160,340
NOX,151
NURM,301
NUTT,185
NYCESWANGER SEE NYSWANER
NYSWANER* 66-67
NYSWANER,66,67,74,147
NYSWANGER,78,247
NYSWANGER SEE NICEWANGER
O'DANIEL(e),138
O'FELTY* 59
O'FELTY,10,59,60,61,83,
85,88,89,93,383
O'FELTY SEE ROFELTY
O'HANDLY,141
O'NEAL* 225-227
O'NEAL,16,128,169,238,
245,277,305,363,364,547
O'NEEL,169,225
O'NEIL,7,183,192,205,216,
217,218,219,220,221,223,
225,237,267
O'NEILL,509
O'NIEL,27,500
OAKERSON,144
OAKS,101
OASE,124

OAVES,520
OBLE,511
ODAFFE,599
ODBERT,208
ODEN,151
ODENBAUGB* 428-429
ODENBAUGH,213,426,427,429,512
OFFORD,150
OGDEN,304,355,645
OGLE,15,16,138
OKEY,431
OLDHAM,26,255
OLDRIDGE,35
OLEH,142
OLIVER,60,197,414
OOPDIKE SEE UPDIKE
OOPDIKE SEE UPDYKE
ORBISON,548,554,556,559
ORFORD,145
ORITON,96
ORNDORFF,105,215,218,229,230,320,326,372,400,402,403,407,411,437,448,587
ORR,142,471
OSBORN(e),39,142,151,152,391,567
OSBURN,27
OSLER,149
OSMAN,304
OVERHOLT,58
OVERPACK,99
OVERTORF,65
OVERTURF,105,106,648
OWAN,164
OWEN(s),3,6,7,21,24,29,37,41,42,44,50,130,131,144,169,192,225,230,325,331,332,339,340,344,345,354,356,362,378,379,380,382,386,389,395,412,422,435,446,495,554,626,651,652,653,664
OWL,602
PACKER,342
PADDOX,129
PAGETT,304

PAIN(s),38,135,604
PAINE,128
PAINTER,98
PALMER,70,165,166,168,214
PAREL,255
PAREMORE,152,629,630
PARISH,674
PARK,139
PARKER,16,18,35,42,43,50,128,130,131,135,136,138,146,157,160,161,162,163,202,236,247,383,387,413,451,456,471,511,523
PARKHURST,39,138,143
PARKINS,135
PARKINSON,11,19,120,136,164,210,214
PARKISON,164
PARKMAN,3
PARKS,304
PARR,128,143,149
PARRIS,148
PARRISH,281,439,663
PARSHALL,78
PARSONS,151,161
PASSMORE,160
PASSOVER,160
PATER,375
PATTEN,138,142
PATTERSON* 406-407
PATTERSON,140,142,152,160,176,259,314,319,320,361,377,401,402,462,535,565,568,572,595,624,637
PATTON,24,25,96,129,144,199,255,316,401,537,570,576
PAUL,26,65,66,95,96,138,151,164,216,221,255,463,468
PAULEY,454
PAULIS,504
PAULLIN,247
PAXTON, 96,284,592
PEACOCK,138
PEAIRS,116

PEAKE,485
PEARCE,128,142,143,147,
152,501
PEARS,115
PEARSFALL,16
PEARSON,144
PECK,16,53,54,138,144,
195,197
PECKINBACH,144
PECKINPAUGH,160,162,429,
611,664
PECKINPOUGH,136
PEEK,593
PENCE,483
PENDER,224
PENDLEBERRY,521
PENDRY,152
PENN,6,8,291,309,311,482,
483,484,485
PENNEY,102,469
PENNICK,152
PENNINGTON,150,262
PENTECOST,31,32
PENTER,128
PEOPLES,16,153,540
PEPPER{s},219
PERINE,139
PERKINS,35,130,131,157
PERMAR,88
PERONE,157
PERRIN,165,206,208,674
PERRY,145,152,242
PETERS,44,45,52,128,129,
143,148,244,304,612,613
PETHEL,415,431
PETITT,151
PETTERSON,69
PETTIT* 477-480
PETTIT,9,118,138,152,161,
399,410,459,473,484,487,
599,656
PETTYJOHN,38,129
PEW* 115-116
PEW,115
PFARMER,240
PHARLIN,146
PHELAN,102,470

PHELPS,26,304
PHILLIBURN,138
PHILLIPS,16,49,116,124,
128,129,138,139,143,145,
177,213,214,215,231,285,
304,410,428,435,440,459,
462,470,478,486,508,617,
626,627,632,633,650,658,
662,664,666,667
PHILPOT,84
PIATT,375,500
PICKENPAUGH,135
PICKENS,519
PICQUIT,148
PIEKSLER,74
PIERCE,214,668
PIERSOL,151
PIERSON,484
PIGMAN* 190-191
PIGMAN,10,16,17,18,20,21,
22,23,25,26,27,29,33,44,
45,133,134,145,147,157,
164,173,177,181,187,193,
194,196,236,244,248,249,
266,268,347,351,353,383,
SOS,513,525,527,644,660
PINDAL{l},152
PIPER,241,401,592
PIPES,39,251,263,365,379,
388,389,421,426
PIPENGAS,157
PITNID,161
PITTOCK,131,207
PITSER,128
PLOWMAN,304
PLUMMER,135,158,304,341,
480
POAK,143,151
POE,245,260,273,334
POGUE,16,261
POKE,27
POLK,133,373,529
POLKE* 529-530
POLKE,105,145,489,513
POLLACK,248,439
POLLOCK,119,120,128,160,
261,267

POLSON,161
PONTIAC,10
POOL,103,138
POOLE,586
POOR,143
POPE,145,147
PORTER* 320-321
PORTER,64,115,132,136,157,
162,203,224,234,278,307,
308,312,316,317,322,323,
324,328,357,390,405,422,
425,428,434,462,468,527,
541,582,586,619,
PORTERFIELD,208,271,304
POST,483
POSTON,93
POTEET,278
POTTENGER,482
POTTER,37,162,543
POTTINGER,26,163,255
POTTS,26,92,142,147,218,
255,473
POUNDS,142,162
POUNDSTONE,128,403
POVATOR,447,448,449,450
POWELL,129,149,150,194,276
POWER,150
POWERS,45,134,550,552
POWEY,151
POYNTELL,498
PRAIL,132
PRATHER,147,148,255,344,
383,644
PRATT,60,113,136,162,333,
383,434,580,665
PRESTON,146,160
PRESTOR,149
PRIBBLE,21,22,26,42,44,
45,53,129,133,134,145,
146,153,157,173,194,206,
237,255,286,347,521
PRICE,85,92,93,144,152,
180,194,216,250,287,292,
294,300,304,485,512,580,
626,649
PRICHARD,129,146,147,152,
202,514

PRICKETT,5,23,24,29,37,
118,129,135,136,142,143,
147,160,178,195,202,439,
441,660
PRIOR* 274
PRIOR,134,157,233,273,274,
454,619
PRITCHERD,163,172
PROBST,99
PRONG* 70-71
PRONG,70,71,72,161
PROVANCE* 613-616
PROVANCE,128,129
PROVANCE SEE PROVENCE
PROVATOR,433
PROVENCE,36,38,608
PROVINCE,24,25,28,135,609,
610,644
PROVINS SEE PROVENCE
PROVINS,458,577,578,608,
609,647
PUGH,157,255
PUMPHREY,144,149,150
PUMPHREYS,480,482
PURCEL(1),145
PURDEE,304
PURDIE,28
PURDOIN,132
PURDY,143,148,274,413
PURKEY,144
PURKINS,134
PURSEL,37,148
PURSELL,97,98
PURSELY,37
PURSLEY,580
PURTEE,134,151,157
PUSBAUM,142
PUSSLEY,148
PUTERBACH,80
PYATT,138,141
PYBURN,129
PYLES,36,135,511
QUERL,667
QUIN,151
QUINLAN,135,158
QUINN,202
QUISSENBERRY,151

RAGAN,145
RAIL,20,128,129,620
RAILY,135
RALSTON,424,425
RAMER,195,269,536
RAMSEY,139,157,485,668,669
RANDALL,90,103,157
RANCK,163
RANDEL(l),84,152
RANDLE,525,526
RANDOLPH,105,194,255,311,377,393,567,571,572,573
RANKIN,147,160,502,551,555,618
RANKINS,36,132,133,145
RANNER,26
RAPER,162
RASON,139
RATHER,128
RAWLEY,430
RAWLINGS,200,201
RAWLINS,143,145
RAWLS,175,516
RAY,144,244,255,339,342,620,664
REA,150,508,522,542,553,555,558,559,570,571,574
READ,152
READ SEE REED
REAGER,139
REAMER,633
REASONER,147
REDD,148,487
REDDICK,151,152
REDFORD,140
REDICK,113
REDMAN,82
REDMOND,337
REED,31,131,132,135,142,149,152.157,215,226,305,425,431,523,524
REED SEE READ
REED SEE REID
REES* 450-452
REES(e),5,54,128,138,157,161,215,267,304,379,474,
476,494,609,613,664
REESEN,155
REEVES,116,567,667
REGESTER,69,73,490
REID,145,153
REINHARDT,327
REINHART,3,37,144,322,323
REINILD,143
REIS,142
REMLEY,128,213,309,363,455,484
RENNER,65
REPP,519
REPPERT,570,641
REVE,147,152
REVER,304
REVES,164
REX* 227-229
REX,95,169,175,207,208,229,233,246,262,267,269,270,271,279,299,566
REXWORTHY,227
REYNARD,376
REYNOLDS,39,96,138,147,182,185,219,236,237,264,267,269,277,319,526,547,572,641,659
RHINEHART,160
RHOADS,204
RHODES,3,5,13,19,88,202,264,307,312,320,321,328,329,335,344,345,348,349,381,382,402,434,435,439,441,442
RICE* 259-261
RICE,26,27,44,45,109,117,133,134,138,141,149,164,174,185,223,245,259,262,264,266,269,352,367,398,403,518,545,583
RICH,128,279,615,619,621
RICHARD(s),148,163,398,403,404,405,462,570
RICHARDSON,86,87,91,99,139,140,147,148,153,236,237,255,420,491,570
RICHEY,51,52,53,176,509,

566,576,585
RICKEY,39,138,146,153,
471
RIDDLE,138
RIDGE,264,269
RIDGELY,384
RIDGEWAY,337,427
RIDLOW,232
RIED,555
RIELY,140
RIFFLE,28,128,436
RIGDON,138
RIGER,148
RIGGER,492
RIGGLE,47,146,152,209,
248,267,473,622
RIGGS,150,151,152
RIGHT,151,153,304
RILEY,36,147,157,207,306,
387,428
RIMLEY,128
RINEHART* 322-329
RINEHART,38,61,97,98,102,
104,129,132,133,134,136,
141,144,145,146,151,157,
163,213,234,235,243,264,
278,307,308,309,310,312,
316,317,318,319,320,321,
333,334,335,348,349,355,
366,368,369,370,373,374,
375,376,377,383,389,390,
394,422,436,437,439,444,
448,466,467,468,469,475,
500,511,536,541,600,606,
607,619,638,670
RINEHART SEE REINHARDT
RIPLEY,541
RISH,595
RISSEL(1),142
RITCHIE,136,145,150
RITENBARK,376
RITENHOUSE,215
RITTER,664
RITZER,600
ROACH,27,128,133,134,147,
157,245,259,261,262,269,
304,331,478,580

ROBB,129,151,282
ROBBINS,26,111,128,160,
290,597,598,669
ROBERTS* 605-607
ROBERTS,34,38,83,91,92,
97,100,109,128,136,144,
151,157,160,207,236,237,
278,283,287,300,310,314,
324,327,329,388,448,560,
566,571,577,586,588,594,
599,623,624
ROBERTSON,81,129,342
ROBESON,139,519
ROBINS,477,674
ROBINSON,6,16,18,24,38,
135,139,153,160,162,215,
234,379,450,463,468,514,
520,530,532,534,536,588,
615,616,676
ROCH,128
ROCHOLD,616
ROCKHOLD,157
RODHAM,513
ROEBUCK,143
ROFELTY SEE O'FELTY
ROFELTY* 59
ROFELTY,27,45,59,445
ROGERS,48,128,129,138,
143,149,153,158,282,292,
386,398,426,480,484,491
ROLAND,128
ROLLINGS,102,144
ROLLINS,128,170,171,200,
201,203,579
ROLLISON,87
ROLSTON,110,111,337,368,
396,424
ROMINE,145,146
RONEY,138,139,141,150
ROOD,128,129,304
ROOD SEE RUDE
ROOT,144,214
ROSE* 64
ROSE,18,34,48,52,61,64,
67,71,76,77/130,131,151,
157,158,244,298,407,461,
478,482,515,545,587,605,

639,646
ROSEBERRY* 229-232
ROSEBERRY,157,158,179,
181,213,214,215,216,229,
236,237,267,275,279,291,
306,309,322,363,455,511,
545,546
ROSENCRANZ,675
ROSS* 470-472
ROSS,16,18,27,35,91,130,
131,136,138,142,144,148,
151,160,161,162,204,212,
241,243,274,284,285,303,
305,378,383,456,459,468,
474,475,494,506,570,580
ROUDEBUSH,589
ROWAN,147
ROWBUCK,144
ROWE,47,48,138,242
ROWLAND,291
ROYCE,17,27,39,138,146,
664
RUBLE,478
RUCKER,425
RUDE,27,39,128,129,138,
144,157
RUDISILL,144
RUFF,665
RUGGLES,157
RUMBLE,670
RUMLEY,142
RUPP,552,659
RUSH* 61-62
RUSH,35,61,63,97,98,130,
131,132,138,157,161,224,
235,248,271,278,280,281,
369,434,440,443,459,461,
462,502,580,636,645
RUSSELL,19,27,144,147,
288,289,304,327,332,457,
521,523,539,541,542,548,
566,643,666
RUTAN,150
RUTHERFORD,596
RUTTENCUTTER,670
RUTTER,135,142,143,160
RYAN,39,138,144,154,361,

383,437
RYERSON,21,51,361,362,
499
SACKET(t),142,294
SAFFEL,437
SALLIDAY,16,144
SALT,387
SALTER,519
SALTSER,128
SAMPSON,128,403
SANDERS,39,138
SANDUSKY,515
SANLEE,436
SANTEE,132,157
SAPPINGTON,148,442
SARGEANT,312
SARGENT,34,39,51,138,
148,
152,344,393
SARJEANT,338
SARRS,295
SATTERFIELD,558
SAUNDERS,16,90,138,144,255
SAVAGE,304,415
SAXTON,134
SAYER* 454-456
SAYER(s),38,136,157,162,
212,213,231,298,307,309,
311,356,363,382,386,390,
391,392,393,394,512,580,
591,656
SAYLOR,91
SAYRE,128
SCARMERHORN,139
SCHENKS,662
SCHERICH,47
SCHLOHTER,428
SCHLOTTERBECK,638
SCHOLL,595
SCHOOLER,151
SCHOOLEY,663
SCHROFFE,136,334,386,395
SCOBEY,38
SCOFIELD,526
SCOTT* 543-544
SCOTT,9,16,17,30,59,67,
98,102,108,128,132,

134,139,140,145,147,148,
152, 157,162,180,213,
214,231,233,234,235,276,
278,279,317,323,337,349,
380,383,392,409,411,414,
426,448,470,475,530,532,
539,540,541,542,548,618,
619,634
SCOTT-GUTHERY,213
SCOTTEN,49
SCUDDER,453,662,663
SCULL,1,8,501
SEAL,151
SEALEY,593
SEALS* 354-355
SEALS,29,35,130,131,136,
143,145,149,153,162,163,
164,194,269,276,281,287,
326,332,335,338,357,362,
363,364,378,379,382,389,
390,391,395,422,424,437,
440,455,473
SEAMAN,43,504,593
SEARING,52
SEARING SEE ZEHRING
SEARS,135,137,298
SEATON* 513-518
SEATON,28,36,132,133,
134,142,143,145,147,150,
157,174,175,178,195,196,
314,315,462,498,499,501,
502,503,504,509,519,534,
548,558
SECOR,294
SEDEGAR,138
SEDGEWICK,133,134,157,261,
499,500,501,503,611
SEELEY,409
SEIX,128
SELBRINER,149
SELBY,448
SELLARS* 446-450,559
SELLARS,24,27,37,130,143,
162,163,176,238,334,372,
380,383,395,429,433,442,
484,553,587,598
SELLARS SEE SELLERS

SELLERS,130,275
SELLS,16
SELSOR,128,129,160,660,
676
SELVY,152
SELZER,136
SENSEBAUGH,281
SERGE,19
SERIGIS,304
SERYER,38
SETTLE,26
SEVAILE,656
SEVAN,173
SEVEL,145
SEVERN,164
SEXTON,580
SEYMORE,453
SHACAR,151
SHACKLETON,493,495
SHAEFER,665
SHAIN,151
SHALLCROSS,297
SHANE,150,228
SHANKLETON,666
SHANKLIN,180
SHANNON,36,133,136,140,151
SHAPE,221
SHARON,456
SHARP* 456
SHARP,229,294,471,481,531,
667
SHARPLESS,653
SHARPNACK* 262-264
SHARPNACK,46,85,88,178,
183,219,224,226,234,260,
267,269,273,305
SHATTERLY,305
SHAVER,143,149
SHAW,125,357,440,442,465,
548
SHEA,304
SHEARDINE,39
SHEARER,82,140,150
SHEARIN,331,374
SHECKELS,341
SHEEHAN,142,147
SHEETS,529

SHELBY* 301-303
SHELBY,63,128,134,136,
142,157,160,162,191,234,
248,268,304,363,364,387,
495,524,527,570,594,660
SHELLET,445
SHEPARD,164
SHEPHARD,27,157
SHEPHERD,8,9,108,128,132,
134,139,140,144,146,190,
192,193,204,225,247,268,
546
SHEPLER,143
SHEPLEY,142
SHERARD,151
SHERED,223
SHERER,145
SHERICH,622
SHERLEY,152
SHERMAN,448
SHIDLER,48,76,77,482,483
SHEILDS,154,310,322,361,
398,403,426
SHILLENGOOD,371
SHIN,379
SHINN,255,393
SHIPMAN,36,38,580,604
SHIPPEN,630
SHIRER,147
SHIRK,105,459,475,488
SHIRLEY,293
SHIVELY,129
SHOEMAKER,154,160,360,580
SHOOLEY,662
SHORE,144,151
SHORT,234,304
SHORTER,161
SHOTWELL,514
SHOUGH,671
SHOUP,281,440,474
SHOVER,16
SHOWALTER,291
SHREVE,149,342
SHRIVER* 399-406
SHRIVER,136,160,220,235,
278,317,318,382,388,397,
398,399,406,407,408,410,
411,413,425,427,430,435,
436,437,441,671
SHROCK,580
SHROFFE,7,24
SHRONTT,296
SHRONTZ,121
SHROY,547,548
SHROYER,113,160,173,210,
211,219,262,263,277,547,
588,663
SHRYOCK,42
SHULL,400,402,405,407
SHULTZ,220,398,403,407,
408,436,438,511,571,576
SHULZ,220
SHUMAN,337
SHURKUR,144
SHUSTER,138
SHUTE,142,143
SHYETTE,71
SIBBETTS,298
SICKLESMITH,529,665,666
SIDWELL,139
SIKES,18
SILLWELL,143
SILVERS,80
SILVEUS,314
SIM,164
SIMBREL,142
SIMMERMAN,382
SIMMINGTON,428
SIMMON,138
SIMMONS,156,340,343,388,
463,604
SIMONS,164
SIMONTON,115,116,132,134,
149,157
SIMPSON,5,26,149,255,304,
330,337,360,379,450
SINCLAIR,141,151
SINE,406
SINGLETON,180
SITHERWOOD,365
SIX,28,38,136,146,160,432
SLACK,628,633,652,662,663
SLATE,342
SLATER* 387-389

SLATER,37,130,131,162,
255,295,304,307,308,330,
333,335,338,339,340,342,
379,383,389,397,398,403,
405,414,424,429,430,437,
444,453,456,522,524
SLATTER,136
SLOAN,606
SLONE,599
SLOVER,31,32
SMALLEY,111,262,279,281,
333,336,440,580
SMETLEY,163
SMILEY,26,58,255
**SMITH* 113-115,416-423
472-473**
SMITH,4,9,16,24,28,29,35,
36,48,60,76,81,87,103,
104,106,108,109,110,113,
116,117,118,128,129,130,
131,132,134,136,140,142,
143,144,145,147,148,149,
150,153,157,159,161,162,
163,164,176,179,196,199,
223,234,250,265,266,271,
275,295,296,301,304,307,
308,310,311,312,315,316,
320,321,322,323,324,326,
327,329,331,333,338,362,
364,365,367,369,383,385,
396,397,399,423,424,426,
427,431,433,438,439,442,
444,445,456,464,467,469,
473,474,476,477,480,481,
482,486,526,528,537,538,
551,557,586,595,599,605,
619,623,625,648,657,663,
671
SMITLEY,35
SMITTLE,136,383
SMOCK,115
SMYTHE,139,140,192,193,
255,593
SNAKE(THE),647,648
SNELL,435,442
SNIDER,431,432,672
SNIVELY,273,518,519

SNODERLY,82
SNOW,216
SNOWDEN,146,149,150,233,
330,331
SNYDER,386,521,623,634,
660,674
SOEFEL,178
SOEFFEL,195
SOLOMON,16
SOMERKAMP,498
SOMMERS,67
SOONOVER* 639
SOONOVER,160,638
SOUDER SEE SOUTER
SOURLAY,593
SOUTER,653
SOUTH* 661-663
SOUTH,433,535,571,576,577,
595,628,633,634,659,664,
665,667,670,671
SOUTHERLAND,382
SOWARDS,146
SOWERS,54,119,382,486
SPANGLER,28,128
SPARKS,140,142,593
SPEARS(s),147,255,295
SPECK,26,151,153,255
SPEERS,504
SPENCER,129,139,150,157,
279,585,615
SPICER,647,648
SPIERS,152
SPINDLER,66
SPOHN,77
SPOTS,654
SPRAGG,21,112,319,398,401,
403,407,410,435,437,441,
479,487,532,620,626
SPRENKLE,144
SPRIGG,139
SPRIGGS,462
SPRINGER,19,142,143,144,
145,147,148,149
SPRINGUM,139
SPRUANCE,236,237
SROUFE,37
STAFFORD,236,237,304

STAGGERS* 412-414
STAGGERS,227,279,280,320,
404,411,412,422,433,443
STALEY,183
STALL,149
STAMMERS,304
STANDISH,489
STANLEY,138
STANNATOR,129
STANTON,153
STAPLETON,26,255
STARKEY,116,128
STARNATOR,140,150
STASCY,145
STATLER,518,590,591,592,
656
STATTON,160
STAYGERS,412
STAYGERS SEE STAGGERS
ST.CLAIR,70
STEAL,383
STEEL,35,121,122,148,304,
577
STEELE,215,398,410,435,
436,624,625,626,627,670,
671,672
STEELEY,302,350
STEGERS,412
STEGERS SEE STAGGERS
STEGNER* 487
STEGNER,475,477,478
STEIN,162
STELL,138
STENTZ,105,489
STEPHENS* 623-626
STEPHENS,82,143,145,181,196,
246,260,267,279,304,314,
318,387,400,402,404,405,
504,535,536,580,584,585,
595,597,618,619,639
STEPHENSON,16,36,66,132,
134,138,143,145,157,176,
178,198,273,315,419,420,
421,508,518,534,542,548,
565,588,659
STERN,142
STERRIT,512

STEVENS,142,143,145,151,
152,408,503,528
STEVENSON,150
STEVES,145
STEWART* 439-443
STEWART,5,12,16,18,26,35,
37,59,60,88,95,102,130,
131,132,134,145,149,153,
157,160,162,215,247,255,
264,281,304,307,323,382,
383,399,411,431,467,470,
473,477,512,580,645,651,
653,661,667,674,675
STIBBS,146
STIGERS,412
STIGERS SEE STAGGERS
STILES* 376-377
STILES,133,134,144,157,
161,232,279,370,383,469,
637
STILLIANS,634
STILLWELL,128,143,655
STILWELL,491
STINE,618
STINSON,142,246
STITES* 459-460
STITES,35,52,53,59,61,65,
103,107,130,131,144,161,
207,248,249,256,302,354,
355,362,366,421,461,465,
470,478,487,488,492,495
STOCKDALE,97,453
STOCTON,249
STOCKTON,264
STOCKWELL,16
STOGDON,161
STOKELEY,244
STOKELY,154,346,445,531
STOKES,652,664
STONE,38,128,136,150,160,
191,481,518,
609,610,611,672,673
STONEKING,55,634
STONER,241,246
STOOP,144,647
STOUT,152,223,662
STOY,639

STRADLER(s),152
STRADLING,304
STRAIN,159
STRATTON,398,410
STRAUGHAN SEE STRAWN
STRAWHEN SEE STRAWN
STRAWN* 97-98
STRAWN,60,83,97,99,109,
133,134,145,157,214,216,
316,326,327,328,374,375,
543,599,606
STREET,19
STRICKLER,228
STRINGER,481
STROBE,537
STRODE,134,145,157,170,
171,198,204
STROHMAN,305
STROSNIDER,319,321,326,
392,398,399,410,412,414,
429,537
STROUBY,355
STROUD,270
STROUDE,108
STROUP,139,150
STRYKKER,660,661
STUART,149
STUBBS,534,535,588,594,
608,662
STULL* 56-58
STULL,26,34,43,56,57,67,
78,130,131,134,152,161,
255,281
STULTS,140
STUMP,130,131,134,144,379,383,
384,400,401,402,409,
417,649
STURGEON,87,152
STURGIS,26,255,314
STYLES,37,128,144,149,
157,227,228,327,328,329,
349,376,412
SUBZAR,160
SULLIVAN,26,151,255,293,
340,342
SULLIVANE,304
SULTZER,129

SUMMERMANS,434
SUMMORREN,132
SUTTLES,26,255
SUTTON,24,38,81,128,136,
138,142,143,144,149,152,
160,298,474,578,595
SWAILS,598
SWAIN,304
SWAINSON,240,247
SWALLOW,195,210,287
SWAN* 169-185
SWAN,3,17,20,21,22,23,25,
26,27,36,45,66,71,94,95,
108,128,132,133,134,139,
141,145,146,147,149,157,
165,166,168,186,187,188,
189,190,192,194,195,196,
197,200,201,202,203,205,
206,210,216,218,219,221,
224,225,226,227,230,231,
234,236,237,238,242,243,
245,251,255,259,270,275,
277,314,353,364,373,454,
464,470,499,500,505,506,
510,515,516,518,534,542,
543,557,561,565,566,57,
618,636,642,643,645,671,
676
SWAN-HUGHES,676
SWANK,200,204
SWART* 485-486
SWART,54,66,120,130,131,
138,161,476,477,479
SWARTZ,404
SWEARINGTON,530
SWEARINGEN,26,128,147,
149,152,582
SWEARINGTON,23,29,57,255,
517,530,615
SWEENEY,17,46,68,80,211,664
SWIFT,84
SWIGHARD,144
SWINDLER,20,23,24,29,38,
145,501,671
SWINEHART,138
SWINFORD,250
SWINGLER,620,675

SWISHER,634
SWOOP,129
SWOPE,38,129
SYKES* 675-676
SYKES,23,24,29,38,55,128,
159,160,441,660
SYMMES,526,629
SYPHERS,149,324,426
TAFFE,225
TAIT,148
TALBOT,142,202
TALLMAN,346,352
TAMBAUGH,28
TAMBRE,144
TANNEHILL,19,150
TANNER,315,393,456,518
TAPPER,304
TAPTON,492
TARBELL,105,489
TATER,157
TATMAN,147
TAYGART,368
TAYLOR,16,71,121,124,128,
129,130,138,140,141,149,
153,274,334,415,442,449,
466,480,491,534,570,571,
593,597,662,664,671,672,
675
TEA,152
TEABOE,160,621
TEABOE SEE DEBOLT
TEAGARDEN* 42-45
TEAGARDEN,3,16,17,18,27,
41,42,46,47,48,50,52,56,
59,67,68,86,87,88,128,
129,132,134,138,145,151,
157,169,192,211,219,237,
267,277,369,379,423,495,
621
TEAL,85,255,260
TEATER,130
TEEL,152
TEETER,131
TEGARD,44
TEMPLE* 116-117
TEMPLE, 116,506,569,666
TEMPLETON,17,149

TEMPLING,142
TENANT,142
TERRANCE,161
TERRELL,16
TERRY,438,511
TERRYL,397
TETER,139
TETRACK,151
THARP,369
THATCHER,133
THEAKER,543
THOMAS* 238-239
THOMAS,16,19,27,45,46,72,
112,118,128,131,133,134,
136,138,142,146,151,153,
157,160,163,164,181,182,
191,197,202,220,221,226,
238,241,242,269,270,280,
298,320,346,349,352,364,
369,394,428,434,440,442,
444,449,451,452,499,501,
528,529,581,636,638,657
THOMPSON,26,100,101,128,
129,149,150,273,286,301,
302,304,321,411,414,428,
517,518,525,622,631,633,
650,662,665
THORN,26
THORNTON,149
THOROMAN,525,526
THOROMAN SEE THURRIMAN
THOROMAN SEE THURMAN
THOROMAN SEE THOROUGHMAN
THOROUGHMAN SEE THURMAN
THRASHER,37,144,308,330,
331,332,340,343,344,346,
347,379,382,383,384,414
THRESHER,135
THROCKMORTON,9,117,322,
365,429,452
THURAMON,134
THURMAN,27,133,145,147,
157,182,194,261,263,268
THURRAMAN SEE THURMAN
THWAITE,7
TILGHMAN,361
TILLEY,304

TILLION,148
TILLON,151
TILTON,139
TIMMONS* 487-488
TIMMONS,35,130,131,161,
162,382
TINDALL,633,634,635,660
TINSMAN,215,485
TIPTON,304
TIRPEN,147
TITUS* 660-661
TITUS,48,106,535,588,594,
595,635
TOBIN,532
TODD,16
TOLBERT,139
TOLEMAN,415
TOMLINSON,145,149,157
TOMMONY,438
TOMPTON,26
TOPPING,249,287,289
TOWNSHALL,16
TRACY,81
TRAVIS,601
TREBER,526
TRENT,26,255
TRIBBLE,26,382
TRIBBY,577
TRIMBLE,672
TRIMBLY,152
TRISTON,411
TROTTER,16
TROUP,27
TROWBRIDGE,207
TRUAX,128,142
TRUELOCK,36,136,147,150,
161,627
TRUMAN,148
TRUMBULL,511
TRUMPH,161
TRUSSELL,43
TUCK,128
TUCKER,39,44,138,149,526,
664
TUEL,255
TUKESBURY,393
TUMBLESTONE,132

TURNBULL,498,501
TURNER,63,296,297,327,401,
490,524,571,580
TUSTIN* 408-409
TUSTIN,227,279,399,402,
410,412,457,649,650
TUTTLE,111,281,462
TWIBBLE,263
TWIN,145
TWINNING,92
TYGART,148,636
TYLER,26,50,111,147,149,
187,259,579,582,590,597,
641
UBB,144
UHLERY,77,78
ULAND,163
ULERY,150,209,232,249,465,
466
ULLOM* 371
ULLOM,110,158,214,218,272,
371,372,427
ULLOM SEE WOOLAM
UNDERWOOD,152,533,579
UNGLEBY,341
UNTIS,50
UPDIKE,628,632
UPDYKE,654
VALALY,138
VALE,87,158,566
VALENTINE,158,593
VALLETO,26
VAN BUSKIRK* 98-99
VAN BUSKIRK,98,636
VAN CAMP,137
VAN LUDE,84,88,90
VAN METRE,139,172
VAN VORHEES,9
VANASDALE,162
VANATTA,231
VANBUSKIRK* 98-99
VANBUSKIRK,74,83,97,98,
109,110,111,155,272,422,
427,428,547
VANCE,146,209,255,647,651,
653
VANCLEVE,452

VANDEDOR,133
VANDEEREN,158
VANDEVENDER,132
VANDOLER,151
VANDREDODS,133
VANDRUFF,317,323,412
VANEMAN,176
VANKIRK,75,105,489
VANLUSCATCH,143
VANMATER,133
VANMETER* 192-205
VANMETER,8,9,10,21,22,26,
28,94,95,128,133,134,141,
145,146,147,152,158,163,
169,170,171,172,173,177,
178,179,181,188,207,221,
236,238,242,243,255,269,
273,275,276,311,312,317,
353,356,363,364,464,499,
S00,516,528,534,537,565,
578,579,580,601,639,643,
654,656,660
VANNATTA,216,479
VANNEMAN,557
VANSICKLE,158,195,197
VANSICICLES* 205
VANSICKLES,179,205,503
VANTREES,128
VANWEY,101
VARVELL,35
VARVILL,128
VAULT,493
VAUN,179,196,516
VANVORHEES,306
VEACH,19,28,35,61,107,
126,132,133,134,149,158,
199,538
VEAL,158
VEASY,148
VEATCH,130,132,143,149,180
VEECH,131,582,633
VEICH,143
VENARD,138,301
VENNEMAN,197
VENOM,138
VENTREES,171,201,202,204,
579

VENTRESS,579
VEON,39,220,226
VERNES,161
VERNON,132,271,300,390,
572
VERVILLE,129
VEST,16
VILLERY,161
VILLIARS,134
VILLIERS* 272
VILLIERS,133,146,158,270,
272,371,545
VILLIS,272
VINCENT,172
VINEYARD,138,153
VINICS,151
VIRGIN,15,16,17,45,68,94,
113,138,139,146,148,179,
207,208,289,291,675
VITITS,255
VOLWILER,3
VORHEES,174,515
WADE,16,18,117,593,608
WADLEY,145
WAGGONER,151,578,635,636,
660,675
WAGONER,111,424
WAILIONS,296
WAIT(s),128,140,143,145,433
WALDO,489
WALDRON,304
WALDRUG,16
WALEY,143
WALKER,16,19,140,143,148,
149,152,153,304,377,532,
543,556,560,637
WALL,16,651
WALLACE,113,150,153,301,
368,551
WALLER,17,47,68,139,140,
141,142,143,151
WALLIN,57
WALLING,57
WALLIS,148,153
WALLS,72,148
WALTER,304
WALTERS,128,142,144,163,

588,621
WALTERS SEE WALTHERS
WALTHERS,588
WALTHERS SEE WALTERS
WALTON* 64-66
WALTON,35,64,65,95,96,
130,131,178,219,221,229,
448,466,472,482,486
WAPLES,111
WARD,19,96,139,142,148,
149,152,173,296,304
WARE,475
WARFIELD,149
WARFORD,26,139,478
WARING,142,460
WARMAN,149
WARNE,106,538
WARNER,571
WARREN,15
WARSON,151
WARTH,145
WARTON,133
WASHABAUGH,498
WASHBURN,436
WASHINGTON,14,26,46,49,50,
230,358,359,446,447,513,
543,660
WASSON,630
WATERS,60,304,450
WATHEN,283,285,288,289,
468,476
WATKINS,116,198,228,273,
651
WATSON,102,118,128,148,
149,152,214,383,455,467,
520,536
WATT,516
WATTERS,160
WATTS,144,148
WAY,208,518,586,623
WAYCHOFF,9,44,59,95,141,
177,199,200,285,333,345,
358,360,361,389,390,403,
442,447,448,449,459,470,
536,537,539,578,581,595,
675
WAYLAND,215

WAYNE,241,251,446,590,592,
612
WAYT,143
WAYTON,151
WEAD,162
WEAKLEY* 495
WEAKLEY,146,150,162,338,408
WEAKLY,133
WEARING,15
WEATHEE,454
WEAVER* 300-301
WEAVER,67,136,151,208,
283,287,292,294,548,677
WEBB,129,153,281,520,589
WEBSTER,303,645,646
WEDGE,304
WEEKLEY,35,352
WEEL,273
WEGINS,16
WELCH,26,77,145,255,558
WELLINGTON,580
WELLS* 351-353,626
WELLS,26,37,129,133,136,
139,140,145,146,147,149,
150,152,158,162,177,308,
314,322,324,325,338,339,
340,341,342,345,346,347,
348,349,350,363,367,368,
379,383,399,408,415,423,
428,435,437,438,495,593,
608,624,652
WELSH,176,275
WELTNER,322,325
WEST,69,140,143,148,152,
153,208,274,322,431,491,
535,595
WESTBROOK,160
WESTFALL,411,414,657
WETSEL,19,28,51
WETSEL SEE WHETSELL
WETSELL,578
WETZEL,380,386,441,660,
675
WHALEY,143
WHARTON,142,146,647,652,
664,667
WHEALY,163

WHEAT,139,148
WHEBY,137
WHEELER,90,91,142,419,421,
502
WHETSEL(1),3,139
WHETZELL,614,615
WHILEY,136
WHINE,19
WHINEY,95
WHINNERY,95
WHITACER,26
WHITACRE,152,153
WHITCRAFT,150
WHITE* 89-91,395-399
WHITE,19,24,37,67,85,88,
89,100,128,129,132,133,
136,139,142,143,144,146,
147,158,160,162,215,255,
305,315,330,345,352,361,
379,382,383,387,388,401,
403,405,407,408,410,413,
422,425,426,430,437,442,
448,479,500,634
WHITE EYES,265,522
WHITEFOOT,145
WHITEHILL,110,364,475
WHITELEYS* 577-578
WHITELOCK,129
WHITEMORE,60,395
WHITESIDE,543
WHITING,27,89
WHITLATCH,16,27,47,60,
107,116,129,133,134,146,
158,405,407,426,436,464,
465,467,599,622,626,653
WHITLOCK,16
WHITMAN,59
WHITSELL,28
WHITTEN,39,138,146,560
WHITTENTON,143
WHOOLAM SEE WOOLAM
WHOSONG,39,138
WHOSONG SEE HUSONG
WHYLY,131
WIBEL,677
WICKERHAM,255
WICKERSHAM,25,26,571,572

WICKWIRE,153
WIER,19,27,57,119,121,150
WIGGAR,134
WIGGINS,139
WILCOX,218,479
WILCOXON,143
WILDMAN,153,638
WILEY* 390-391
WILEY,37,88,130,137,163,
218,222,224,226,355,356,
372,379,382,383,432,440,
445,518,544,581
WILFORD,136,403
WILKES,150,152
WILKEY,142
WILKINS,499,561
WILKINSON,617,676
WILLBORN,391,394
WILLETT,595
WILLIAM,136,138
WILLIAMS* 89
WILLIAMS,5,16,19,24,38,
39,53,81,82,85,89,92,96,
110,128,129,136,138,140,
142,148,149,151,152,153,
158,160,168,179,180,191,
201,204,232,234,255,266,
267,273,283,289,290,298,
302,308,311,330,364,379,
383,387,422,423,425,426,
444,450,503,524,527,540,
580,609,615,628,629,630,
640,662
WILLIAMSON* 665-666
WILLIAMSON,9,16,20,129,
138,140,148,244,424,620,
652,653,663,664
WILLIARD,64
WILLIE,164
WILLIS,103,107,113,114,
115,116,117,140,146,152,
153,183,185,218,518
WILLISON,10,342,390,436
WILLSON,132,134
WILSON,16,26,82,122,123,
128,130,132,133,134,136,
138,139,143,144,147,148,

152,153,161,164,211,214,
255,276,283,289,294,295,
307,313,359,401,479,480,
481,493,502,519,534,557,
598,606,611,617,628,631
WILTNER,175
WIMS,134
WINDERS,144
WINEMOR,140
WINKFIELD(s),16
WINN(s),36,132
WINSON,136
WINTERS,124,211,228,277,
656
WISE* 76-77
WISE,48,49,63,73,75,76,
77,78,96,106,117,148,150,
158,161,208,298,305,360,
369,399,404,471,579,646,
672
WISECARVER,215,218,319,467
WISEMAN,16,436
WISHART,219
WITHER,4,272
WITHINGTON,665
WITTEN,401
WOLF,160,250,652,660
WOLFE,81,145,151,542,566,
671
WOLING,145
WOLVERTON,161,285,312,383,456,
459,461,467,470,471,
474,475,477,478,485
WOOD* 391-395
WOOD,3,19,105,116,132,
134,136,146,147,149,150,
158,162,164,165,166,168,
309,311,316,318,338,363,
365,366,387,407,409,415,
428,446,447,453,456,506,
535,580,595,627
WOODCOCK,178,221
WOODEN,519
WOODMAN,159
WOODMANCY,271,520
WOODMANEY,160
WOODNUT,531,534

WOODROUGH,161
WOODROW,401,650
WOODRUFF,73,81,91,161,459,
462,465,488,490,580
WOODS,132,212,285,545,556,
635
WOODWARD,81,147,584,585,
595,623
WOOLAM* 371-372
WOOLAM,371
WOOLAM SEE ULLOM
WOOLERY,629
WOOLHAM,158
WOOLHAM SEE WOLLAM
WOOLLOM SEE WOOLAM
WOOLTER,163
WOOLVERTON,35,61,130,131
WOOSTER,391
WORFF,148
WORK,51,144,147
WORKMAN,16,213,310,313,
324,389
WORLEY,4,5,136,160,307,
310,318,319,322,405
WORRELL,569
WORTH,92,153
WORTHINGTON,267,277,391,
506,569,618
WRIGHT* 567-568
WRIGHT,19,28,34,35,36,39,
65,84,85,86,88,89,93,128,
130,131,132,134,138,143,
146,152,153,158,161,162,
274,330,342,383,393,463,
468,557,560,561,567,584,
595,615,616,641
WYCHOFF,311
WYLIE,281
YARD,440,615
YATE(s),131,142,146,149,
150
YEAGER,28,536,588
YEAGLEY,521
YEAMANS,629
YEATS,130
YODER,456
YODERS,181,231,519,521

YOHO,28,38,136
YORK,50,216
YOUGER,128
YOUNG,64,130,131,138,139,
145,152,161,183,209,220,
255,358,359,374,467,523,
573
YOURK,128,129
YOUTSY,523
ZANE,139,150,675
ZANES,146
ZEANS,146,148,149
ZEHRING,520,521
ZEHRING SEE SEARING
ZENOR,515
ZIMMERMAN,132,136,162,213,
327,355,367,471,626
ZOLLARS,74,75,76,77,82,
96,208,305,452,599
ZOOK,144,325,374,472,
473,474,482

www.ingramcontent.com/pod-product-compliance
Lightning Source LLC
Chambersburg PA
CBHW031537300426
44111CB00006BA/86